Early 1900s	• Variety stores are established.
	• Dealer (retailer) brands begin.
	• Wanamaker begins a one-price policy, marking prices on every item.

1908
- Henry Ford designs the Model T.

1911
- Curtis Publishing Co. appoints a manager to conduct marketing research.

1920s
- Alfred Sloan of General Motors (GM) segments the auto market.
- GM introduces target pricing.
- Questionnaire-based research grows.
- Cash-and-carry wholesalers begin.

1927
- Procter & Gamble introduces the product-manager system.

1928
- Southland Ice Co. opens the first convenience store in Texas.

1930
- King Kullen opens the first supermarket in New York.

1937
- Masters opens the first discount store in a New York loft building.

Mid 1940s
- Rack jobbers begin to sell nonfood items to supermarkets.

1948
- The General Agreement on Tariffs and Trade (GATT) is signed.

(Continued on Rear Endpapers)

Robin R. Jaeger
3266 N. 105 Street

MARKETING

MARKETING

SECOND EDITION

Joel R. Evans/**Barry Berman**

HOFSTRA UNIVERSITY / HOFSTRA UNIVERSITY

Macmillan Publishing Company
NEW YORK

Collier Macmillan Publishers
LONDON

Macmillan Publishing Company
866 Third Avenue, New York, New York 10022

Collier Macmillan Canada, Inc.

Library of Congress Cataloging in Publication Data

Evans, Joel R.
    Marketing.

    Includes indexes.
    1. Marketing. I. Berman, Barry. II. Title.
HF5415.E86 1985   658.8   84-7141
ISBN 0-02-334700-7 (Hardcover Edition)
ISBN 0-02-946180-4 (International Edition)

Printing: 2 3 4 5 6 7 8   Year: 5 6 7 8 9 0 1 2

ISBN 0-02-334700-7

TO
Linda,
Jennifer,
and Stacey

Linda,
Glenna,
and Lisa

Preface

We believe that a marketing principles book in the 1980s must incorporate both traditional and contemporary aspects of marketing, carefully consider environmental factors, and present the roles of marketing and marketing managers. These concepts should be described to readers in a comprehensive, interesting, and balanced manner. As we indicate at the beginning of Chapter 1, marketing is truly "an exciting, dynamic, and contemporary field."

While the basic components of marketing (such as consumer behavior, marketing research, and product, distribution, promotion, and price planning) form the foundation of any principles of marketing text, contemporary techniques and topics also need to be covered in depth. Among the contemporary topics that are examined in full chapter length in *Marketing* are strategic planning in marketing, consumer life-styles and decision making, organizational consumers (including manufacturers, wholesalers, retailers, government, and nonprofit institutions), international marketing, service and nonprofit marketing, marketing and society, and marketing in the future. Environmental effects are noted throughout the book.

Marketing explains all major principles, defines key terms, integrates topics, and demonstrates how marketing personnel make everyday and long-run decisions. Illustrations of organizations such as IBM, Texas Instruments, Greyhound, Holiday Inns, Whirlpool, American Express, Arm & Hammer, DuPont, Giant Food, Coleco, U.S. Postal Service, and Kentucky Fried Chicken appear in each chapter. These illustrations build on the textual material, reveal the exciting and dynamic nature of marketing, and involve students in real-life applications of marketing.

In preparing the second edition of *Marketing*, we surveyed a number of professors and students throughout the country. Our objectives were to retain the material and features most desired from the first edition and elicit suggestions for new material and features to be included in the second edition, while maintaining the length of the first edition.

These pedagogical features are retained from the first edition of *Marketing* and are contained in each chapter:

1. Chapter objectives that outline the major areas to be investigated.
2. An opening vignette that introduces the material through a real-life situation. Among the companies featured in these vignettes are Totes, Levi Strauss, Nike, WD-40, Nissan, Coors, J. C. Penney, Stouffer's, Kroger, and Chem Lawn.
3. Descriptive margin notes that highlight major concepts.
4. Boldface key terms that identify important definitions.
5. Many flowcharts and current figures and tables that explain how marketing concepts operate and provide up-to-date information.
6. Numerous footnotes, most from the 1980s (including many from 1983 and 1984), to enable the reader to do further research.
7. A summary of the material covered.
8. Discussion questions (about 15 per chapter) that vary in scope and depth from requiring definitions to requiring complex decisions.
9. Two cases (except Chapter 1, which has an appendix on hints for analyzing cases) that deal with real companies or situations. There are forty-eight end-of-chapter cases in all, involving companies such as Good Humor, Boeing, Mattel, McDonald's, Cuisinart, Gillette, Johnson & Johnson, Apple, and several small firms.

In addition, the second edition retains an appendix on careers in marketing, a 500-item glossary, and separate company, name, and subject indexes.

These features have been added for the second edition:

- Virtually all vignettes and chapter-ending cases are new.
- A complete chapter on strategic planning in marketing (Chapter 3).
- Fuller coverage of marketing information systems (in Chapter 4).
- A combined chapter on channels of distribution and physical distribution (Chapter 12).
- Expanded coverage of integrating and analyzing a marketing strategy (Chapter 24).
- Longer and more detailed opening vignettes in each chapter.
- Comprehensive cases—At the end of each of the text's eight parts there is an in-depth case, featuring AT&T, General Electric, Kodak, Sears, Chrysler, People Express, Procter & Gamble, and General Motors.
- A more open design, including increased use of a second color for figures and tables.
- Many black and white and color photographs keyed to text material.
- A marketing mathematics appendix.
- Information updated as much as possible, based on available data (such as the 1980 census).

Marketing is divided into eight parts. Part One presents an overview of marketing, describes the environment within which it operates, presents strategic planning in marketing, and discusses the marketing research process. Part Two provides an understanding of final and organizational consumers. It examines demographic data, life-style factors, target market strategies, and sales forecasting. Part Three covers product planning, the product life cycle, new products, mature products, branding, and packaging. Part Four deals with distribution planning, channel relations, physical distribution, wholesaling, and retailing. Part Five examines promotion planning, the channel of communication, advertising, publicity, personal selling, and sales promotion. Part Six covers price planning, price strategies, and applications of pricing. Part Seven shows how the scope of marketing is expanding to include international marketing, service and nonprofit marketing, and societal issues. Part Eight integrates marketing planning and looks to the future.

A comprehensive study guide is available to accompany *Marketing*. The study guide contains chapter objectives, chapter overviews, key terms and concepts, more than 1,700 short-answer questions, more than 150 discussion questions, 75 exercises, and 8 review quizzes. All short-answer questions are answered in the study guide. A substantial teaching package is available for instructors.

We are pleased that the first edition of *Marketing* was adopted at over 200 colleges and universities nationwide. We hope the second edition will be satisfying to continuing adopters and meet the needs of new ones. Thanks for your support and encouragement.

J. R. E.
B. B.

Acknowledgments

Throughout our professional lives and during the period that this book was researched and written, a number of people provided us with support, encouragement, and constructive criticism. We would like to publicly acknowledge and thank many of them.

During our years as graduate students, we benefited greatly from the knowledge transmitted from professors Conrad Berenson, Henry Eilbirt, and David Rachman, and colleagues Elaine Bernay, William Dillon, Stanley Garfunkel, Leslie Kanuk, Michael Laric, Kevin McCrohan, Leon Schiffman, and Elmer Waters. We learned a great deal at the American Marketing Association's annual consortium for doctoral students, the capstone of any marketing student's education.

At Hofstra University, colleagues Herman Berliner, Dorothy Cohen, Seth Buatsi, Nejdet Delener, Keno Kono, Russell Moore, James Neelankavil, Suresh Pradhan, Walter Rosenthal, Saul Sands, and Elaine Sherman stimulated us by providing the environment needed for a book of this type.

We would especially like to thank the following colleagues who reviewed all or part of *Marketing* during its first or second edition. These reviewers made many helpful comments and significant contributions to revisions in the manuscript:

Benjamin Cutler (Bronx Community College)
Homer Dalbey (San Francisco State University)
Rebecca Elmore-Yalch (University of Washington)
Harrison Grathwohl (California State University at Chico)
Thomas Greer (University of Maryland)
G. E. Hannem (Mankato State University)
Laurence Jacobs (University of Hawaii at Manoa)

Albert Kagan (University of Northern Iowa)
Bernard Katz (Oakton Community College)
John Kerr (Florida State University)
John Krane (Community College of Denver)
James Littlefield (Virginia Polytechnic Institute and State University)
William Locander (University of Tennessee)
Ken McCleary (Central Michigan University)
James McMillan (University of Tennessee)
John Mentzer (Virginia Polytechnic Institute and State University)
Jim Merrill (Indiana University)
James Meszaros (County College of Morris)
Edward Popper (University of Florida)
William Qualls (University of Michigan)
Edward Riordan (Wayne State University)
Stanley Scott (Ohio State University)
Richard Sielaff (University of Minnesota, Duluth)
Michael Smith (Temple University)
Robert Swerdlow (Lamar University)
John Walton (University of Minnesota)
Gene Wunder (Ball State University)
Richard Yalch (University of Washington)
William Ziegler (Seton Hall University)

We would also like to thank these colleagues for responding to a lengthy questionnaire on the first edition:

Stephen Batory (Bloomsburg University)
Jim Burrow (University of Northern Iowa)
Nancy L. Hansen (University of New Hampshire)
Mary Joyce (University of Central Florida)
Bettie King (Central Piedmont Community College)
Keith Lucas (Ferris State College)
Terry Paul (University of Houston)
Michael Peters (Boston College)
David Roberts (Virginia Polytechnic Institute and State University)
Donald Robin (Mississippi State University)
Stanley Scott (Ohio State University)
Robert Swerdlow (Lamar University)
Donna Tillman (California State Polytechnic University, Pomona)
Charles Treas (University of Mississippi)
J. Donald Weinrauch (Tennessee Technological University)
Anthony Zahorik (Vanderbilt University)

To the many students at Hofstra who reacted to material in *Marketing*, we owe a special thanks, because they represent the true constituency of any textbook authors.

Our appreciation is extended to the fine people at Macmillan, with whom our relationship dates back to 1976. Among the people who worked diligently on this project were Bill Oldsey, Bob Doran, Dave Horvath, Leo Malek, Ed Neve, Bob Pirrung, Chip Price, Gwen Larson, Andy Zutis, and Steve Vana-Paxhia.

Special thanks to Carol Bloom for fast and accurate typing and Linda Berman for comprehensive indexes.

To our wives and children, this book is dedicated—out of respect and love.

Joel R. Evans
Barry Berman
Hofstra University

Contents

5 Consumer Demographics

6 Consumer Life-Styles and Decision Making

7 Organizational Consumers   176

PART THREE
Product Planning
249

13 Wholesaling   376

14 Retailing   398

PART FIVE Promotion Planning 429

20 Applications of Pricing Techniques   581

21 International Marketing   613

PART SEVEN

Expanding the Scope of Marketing

611

22   Service and Nonprofit Marketing   643

23   Marketing and Society   674

24 Integrating and Analyzing the Marketing Plan

25 Marketing in the Future

PART EIGHT
Marketing Management

APPENDIXES

An Introduction to Marketing

Chapter 1, an overview of marketing, shows the dynamics of marketing. The chapter broadly defines marketing, traces its evolution, and explains the marketing concept. The importance and scope of marketing are examined. Marketing functions and performers are described. A successful marketing company, IBM, is contrasted with a company that has not properly applied marketing, Texas Instruments.

Chapter 2 examines the complex environment within which marketing operates. Particularly emphasized are the controllable and uncontrollable factors that are directed and adapted to by an organization and its marketers. Without adequate environmental analysis, a firm is likely to function in a haphazard manner. A short-sighted, narrow-minded view of marketing and its environment needs to be avoided.

Chapter 3 discusses the strategic planning process in marketing, and stresses the need for coordination between top management and marketing. Different types of marketing plans and the relationships between marketing and other functional areas are studied. The seven steps in the strategic planning process are described in detail. The product/market opportunity matrix, Boston Consulting Group matrix, PIMS, and the Porter generic strategy model are detailed.

Chapter 4 explains why marketing decisions should be based on sound information in order to direct and adapt to the marketing environment. Marketing research is defined and the marketing research process is detailed. Marketing research may involve surveys, experiments, observation, and other forms of data collection. The marketing information system coordinates marketing research, continuous monitoring, and data storage. It thus provides the basis for decision making.

Since 1886, Coca-Cola has been the best-selling soda in the world. It is called for over 260 million times each day in more than 80 languages by consumers in more than 155 countries. Today, the Coca-Cola company spends over $120 million per year advertising Coke, diet Coke, Tab, and Sprite. Reprinted by permission.

As a result of a careful and well-executed marketing plan by IBM, the IBM PC has revolutionized the personal computer industry. In 1984 alone, IBM was expected to market 2 to 3 million of its PCs. Courtesy of IBM.

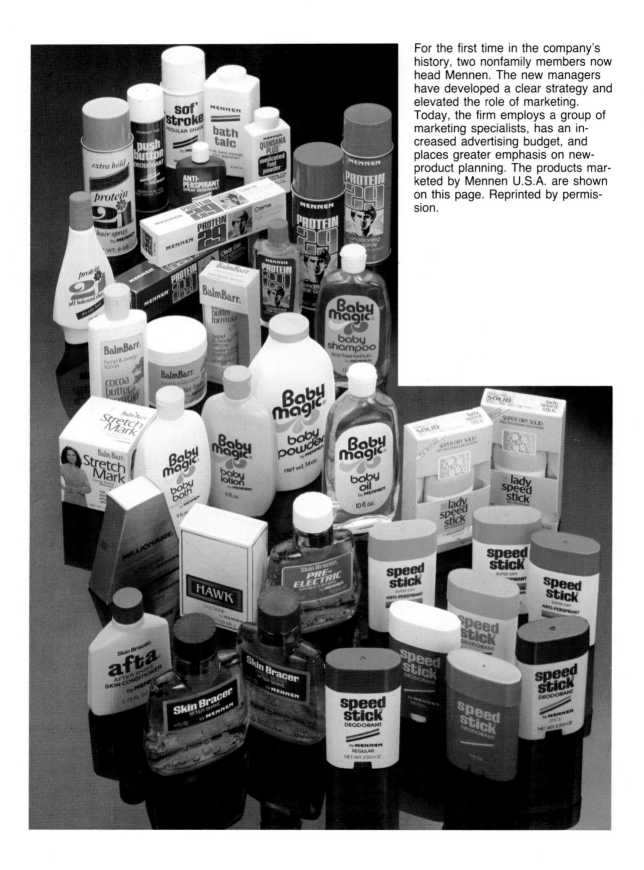

For the first time in the company's history, two nonfamily members now head Mennen. The new managers have developed a clear strategy and elevated the role of marketing. Today, the firm employs a group of marketing specialists, has an increased advertising budget, and places greater emphasis on new-product planning. The products marketed by Mennen U.S.A. are shown on this page. Reprinted by permission.

Campbell Soup Company has broadened its organizational mission, a firm's long-term commitment to a type of business and a place in the market. Campbell's mission encourages it "to be positioned with consumers as somebody who is looking after their well-being." Through its Triangle Manufacturing Corp., Campbell offers a variety of health and fitness products. Reprinted by permission.

A.C. Nielsen monitors the television viewing habits of the American public via audimeters that are attached to television sets in 1,700 households. Nielsen ratings are used by television stations to set advertising rates. Reprinted by permission.

General Foods regularly conducts marketing research on both new and continuing products. For example, although its Maxwell House coffee has been on the market for many years and is an industry leader, it is often evaluated in consumer taste tests. This will help Maxwell House to remain a leading brand. Reprinted by permission.

An Overview of Marketing

1. To illustrate the dynamic, exciting, changing nature of marketing
2. To define marketing and delineate its importance, scope, and functions in a modern society
3. To trace the evolution of marketing from a production to a sales to a marketing department to a marketing company orientation
4. To examine the marketing concept
5. To present and contrast successful and unsuccessful approaches to marketing

In 1961, Bradford Phillips sold his house and automobiles, took out a $20,000 loan from his grandmother, and used his earnings from the stock market to generate enough money to purchase So-Lo Marx Rubber Manufacturing Company. So-Lo Marx made instant gravy, fishing boats, scuba-diving gear, meat tenderizer, and black rubber stretch boots. Phillips quickly dropped all of the company's products except the rubber boots, which were sold under the Totes brand. Today, Totes Inc. is the corporate name of the very successful firm that markets umbrellas, hats, raincoats, and bags, as well as boots. Annual sales are estimated to be $50 million to $100 million.

Totes Inc. has thrived under Bradford Phillips because of his adherence to sound marketing concepts. Totes' products are quite useful and appealing to consumers. As one department-store executive noted, "Totes

3

has made umbrellas into something people want rather than just need."
Most of the products manufactured by Totes are related to one another in
terms of protection against bad weather and convenience of use. Each
new product carries the Totes name and plays upon its reputation for
quality. See Figure 1-1 for a selection of Totes products.

All Totes products are carefully designed and made. Product quality is
given top priority; and a thorough product-testing system is employed.

Figure 1-1
Selected Totes Products

Reprinted by permission.

Retailers have fewer returns of Totes products because of defects or imperfections than of competitors'.

Totes has a large sales force that calls on stores frequently. "Sales merchandisers" (who are Totes employees) help out by setting up and filling store displays and monitoring inventory levels. The company distributes its products almost exclusively through department stores. It has a good relationship with these stores and has been reluctant to alienate them by dealing with discounters. In addition, Totes' reputation for quality has enabled the firm to maintain higher prices than competitors. Only plain, inexpensive boots are sold to discounters.

Phillips is always open to new ideas and applying marketing principles used by others. For example, the advertising approach of Totes is based on a booklet written by a former head of Pepsi-Cola. The product-management organization used by the firm, which assigns a manager to each product, is adapted from Procter & Gamble. Phillips wants to develop one new product every year and avoid fads (this was the reason the women's scarf division was sold). His current philosophy is, "We're not afraid of getting too large now."

Bradford Phillips and Totes have come a long way since 1961, when he "quickly discovered that my industrial sales background wasn't good enough for selling products on the retail market."[1]

The Dynamics of Marketing

Marketing is an exciting, dynamic, and contemporary field. It encompasses a wide range of activities such as environmental analysis and marketing research, consumer analysis, product and service planning, distribution planning, promotion planning, price planning, international marketing, and marketing management.

Marketing is stimulating, quick-paced, and influential.

Marketing affects us as informed citizens and consumers, as well as members of the work force. Some aspect of marketing influences every part of our daily lives, yet the role of marketing changes in each new situation. Through the next several examples, we will glimpse the varied nature of marketing and look for fundamental concepts.

At Radio Shack, environmental analysis and marketing research are aided by a Store Operating System. This system uses microcomputers in 4,400 stores to transmit a steady stream of daily information to a large mainframe computer at company headquarters in Fort Worth, Texas. As a result, the company can respond quickly to changes in the environment, to customer demand, or to problems in particular stores.[2]

Stride Rite, a major U.S. shoe manufacturer, has been able to increase its sales and profits during a declining period for the U.S. shoe industry because of

---

[1] Maryann Mrowca, "Weather-Gear Firm Prospers on Idea of Handier Products," *Wall Street Journal* (August 11, 1983), p. 23.
[2] *Tandy Corporation Annual Report 1982*, p. 10.

Figure 1-2
**Herman Boots—by Stride
Rite**

Reprinted by permission.

its emphasis on consumer analysis. In the early 1970s, Stride Rite was almost exclusively a children's shoe company. Then, the firm noted the declining birth rate and decided to appeal to a number of market segments. Today, in addition to Stride Rite shoes, the company markets Herman boots, Keds sneakers, Grasshoppers women's casuals, and Sperry Top-Sider boat shoes.[3] Figure 1-2 shows several Herman boots, a great departure from children's shoes.

In 1980, IBM developed a product strategy to enter the personal computer market. Since the firm considered personal computers to be outside its normal product lines, IBM decided to set up a small, autonomous task force to develop its new product. Said one task force member, "IBM acted as a venture capitalist. It gave us management guidance, money, and allowed us to operate on our own." The task force devised what was later named the "IBM PC", the personal computer that now dominates the industry. After introduction, the management of the IBM PC was integrated back into the firm's regular organization structure. Due to

[3] Johnnie L. Roberts, "By Concentrating on Marketing, Stride Rite Does Well Despite Slump for Shoemakers," *Wall Street Journal* (February 23, 1983), p. 31.

the success of its nontraditional planning process for the IBM PC, the company now has 15 such new-product units operating.[4]

Hanes introduced a novel distribution approach for women's pantyhose in 1970. Until that time, pantyhose were marketed almost exclusively through department and discount stores. But, Hanes placed its L'eggs brand into supermarkets and achieved remarkable results. Annual sales of L'eggs are now $340 million. On the basis of L'eggs acceptance by women supermarket shoppers, Hanes believed that cosmetic products would attain similar purchase levels and began distributing L'erin lipstick and nail polish to supermarkets in 1977. By 1983, annual sales reached only $30 million. Hanes discovered that supermarkets wanted L'erin products stored in warehouses (not set up in store displays by Hanes' personnel), variety of color was more important than cost, and better advertising was needed. In late 1983, Hanes abandoned L'erin by selling the division to a group of entrepreneurs.[5]

Sales in the soft-drink industry are $27 billion a year; and a number of large firms (such as Coca-Cola, PepsiCo, and Philip Morris—the parent company of 7-Up) dominate the industry. Accordingly, aggressive promotion efforts have been undertaken, resulting in the "soda wars." For an example, see Figure 1-3. Among the tactics used are these:[6]

- Coca-Cola spends over $100 million annually on advertising for just four of its leading brands: Coke, diet Coke, Tab, and Sprite. Paul Newman, Susan Anton, and Bill Cosby are among the celebrities used in ads. Commercials for Sprite compare its lemon-lime flavor to that of 7-Up. In early 1984, a special promotion gave away free bottles and cans of diet Coke.
- PepsiCo spends about $100 million per year on advertising for four of its brands: Pepsi, Diet Pepsi, Pepsi Free, and Sugar Free Pepsi Free. In 1984, it launched a $40 million campaign featuring Michael Jackson; it also signed Lionel Richie to a multimillion dollar contract. These efforts followed the very successful "Pepsi Challenge" ads that showed taste comparisons with Coke.
- Philip Morris spends about $40 million annually on advertising for 7-Up and Diet 7-Up. It has actively promoted the slogans "no caffeine, no artificial color" and a "clean, crisp taste." 7-Up ads concentrate on its positioning as a cola alternative. A toll-free telephone number is now used to answer any consumer inquiries.

MCI Communications, founded in 1968, operates in the long-distance telephone service industry. It faces 200 competitors, including AT&T which has 96 per cent of industry sales. MCI is second with 2.5 per cent of sales. MCI has a base of over 1 million customers (including 200,000 business accounts) in 200 metropolitan areas.[7] MCI's marketing strategy relies upon aggressive pricing. Its

---

[4] "How the PC Project Changed the Way IBM Thinks," *Business Week* (October 3, 1983), pp. 86, 90.

[5] Bill Abrams, "Hanes Finds L'eggs Methods Don't Work with Cosmetics," *Wall Street Journal* (February 3, 1983), p. 33; and Bill Abrams, "How Several Ad Campaigns and Products Fared in 1983," *Wall Street Journal* (December 29, 1983), p. 15.

[6] Daniel Kahn, "Aggressive Action in Soft-Drink War," *Newsday* (October 23, 1983), p. 88; and John Koten, "PepsiCo Gambles Big on an Ad Campaign with Michael Jackson," *Wall Street Journal* (February 28, 1984), pp. 1, 16.

[7] Brian O'Reilly, "More Than Cheap Talk Propels MCI," *Fortune* (January 24, 1983), pp. 68–72; Robert Raissman, "MCI: Can Its Fabled Past Help Foretell Its Future?" *Advertising Age* (November 29, 1982), pp. 84–85; and Leslie Wayne, "MCI Loses Some Sparkle," *New York Times* (February 12, 1984), pp. 1, 8, 9.

Figure 1-3
7-Up—An Active Competitor in the Soda Wars

Reprinted by permission.

rates on long-distance calls are up to 50 per cent less than those of AT&T. When AT&T announced that its long-distance rates would drop after the final company breakup in January 1984, MCI quickly reported that it would lower its prices too. In late 1983, MCI entered the electronic mail business to compete with the U.S. Postal Service. MCI's ads claimed better, faster service at one tenth of the Postal Service's prices.

In mid-1983, Sears ended its operations in Brazil—after 34 years. Leaving Brazil was difficult for Sears because it represents the largest single consumer market in Latin America. However, Sears lost money in Brazil during 1981 and earned a very small profit in 1982. Worldwide, Sears lost $42 million in overseas markets in 1982. Sears' problems in Brazil included operating older stores in costly (yet declining) downtown areas, having a "fuddy-duddy" image, and not locating outlets in choice suburban shopping center sites. Sears sold its Brazilian stores to an Amsterdam-based retailer for $40 million.[8]

When Allegheny Industries acquired Sunbeam in 1981, top executives believed an integrated marketing-management structure would be relatively simple to implement. These executives felt that Allegheny's brands (such as Scripto pens, Wilkinson Sword razors, and True Temper hardware) would blend well with Sunbeam's brands (such as Sunbeam appliances, Oster appliances, and Northern Electric blankets). However, Allegheny did not realize that Sunbeam's marketing-management structure was complacent and very fragmented. To remedy the situation, Allegheny took drastic measures. Half of Sunbeam's senior managers were forced to retire or were fired. New managers were installed in the areas of marketing research, product development, and sales. Specific goals were set for return on investment, sales, cash flow, profit, and budgets. The presidents of each Sunbeam division were required to attend monthly meetings and cooperate with one another in planning and implementing strategies.[9]

The formal study of marketing requires an understanding of its definition, importance, scope, and functions, as well as the evolution of marketing and the marketing concept. These principles are discussed in the next three sections.

Definitions of Marketing

The definitions of marketing can be grouped into two major categories: classical (narrow) and modern (broad). In classical terms, marketing is defined as

the performance of business activities that direct the flow of goods and services from producer to consumer or user.[10]

or

the process in a society by which the demand structure for economic goods and services is anticipated or enlarged and satisfied through the conception, promotion, and physical distribution of such goods and services.[11]

These classical definitions of marketing are oriented toward the physical movement of economic goods and services. As such, they have several weaknesses. The role of physical distribution and marketing channels is overvalued. Government and nonprofit institutions, which are now frequently engaged in marketing, are omitted. The importance of exchange between buyers and sellers is overlooked. The strong impact on marketing by many publics—such as em-

The classical definitions of marketing overvalue distribution and economic goods.

[8] "Why Sears Roebuck Is Packing It In," *Business Week* (May 9, 1983), pp. 44–45.

[9] "How Allegheny Is Rebuilding Sunbeam," *Business Week* (May 16, 1983), pp. 142–144; and Janet Neiman, "Sunbeam Irons Out Problems, Now Allegheny's Bright Spot," *Advertising Age* (February 20, 1984), pp. 4, 71.

[10] Ralph S. Alexander (Chairman), *Marketing Definitions: A Glossary of Terms* (Chicago: American Marketing Association, 1960), p. 15.

[11] "Statement of the Philosophy of the Marketing Faculty," The Ohio State University, College of Commerce and Administration (Columbus, Ohio: 1964), p. 2. Reprinted in the *Journal of Marketing*, Vol. 29 (January 1965), pp. 43–44.

ployees, unions, stockholders, consumer groups, and government agencies—is not considered.

The modern definition is much broader.

A proper definition of marketing should not be confined to economic goods and services. It should cover organizations (Red Cross), people (political candidates), places (Hawaii), and ideas (the value of seat belts). A consumer orientation must be central to any definition. A company attains its objectives by satisfying consumers. Marketing is not just concerned with enlarging demand; it also attempts to regulate demand to match supply. For example, shortages in home heating oil, plastics, and in some natural fibers cause firms in these areas to regulate demand to match supply. The social nature of marketing, such as ethics and product safety, needs to be included in a definition. The organization needs to ask whether a product should be sold as well as whether it can be sold.

A broad, integrated definition of marketing will be used in this text:

Marketing is the anticipation, management, and satisfaction of demand through the exchange process.

Marketing involves products (durable and nondurable), services, organizations, people, places, and ideas. See Figure 1-4.

Figure 1-4
What Marketing Includes

PRODUCTS

SERVICES

ORGANIZATIONS

"Support our blood drive"

PEOPLE

PLACES

IDEAS

Hawaii

"Buckle your seat belt for safety."

Anticipation of demand requires a firm to do consumer research on a regular basis in order to develop and introduce offerings that are desired by consumers. Management of demand includes stimulation, facilitation, and regulation. Stimulation is arousing consumers to want the firm's offering through attractive product design, intensive promotion, and other strategies. Facilitation is the process whereby the firm makes it easy to buy its offering through convenient locations, availability of credit, well-informed sales people, and other strategies. Regulation is needed when there are peak periods for demand rather than balanced demand throughout the year or when demand is greater than the availability of the offering. Then, the goal is to spread demand throughout the year or to demarket a product or service (reduce overall demand). Satisfaction of demand involves actual product or service performance, safety, availability of options, aftersales service, and other factors. Consumer expectations must be satisfied through ownership or use of a product or service. See Figure 1-5.

Marketing activities can be directed to consumers and to publics. **Consumer demand** refers to the characteristics and needs of final consumers, industrial consumers, channel members (such as wholesalers and retailers), government institutions, international markets, and nonprofit institutions. A firm may appeal to one or a combination of these. **Publics' demand** refers to the characteristics and

Marketing involves anticipation, requiring the firm to conduct research; management, which involves stimulating, facilitating, and regulating demand; and satisfaction, fulfilling expectations.

Demand is affected by the characteristics and needs of both *consumers* and *publics*.

Figure 1-5
Anticipating, Managing, and Satisfying Demand

Exchange **completes the process.**

needs of employees, unions, stockholders, consumer groups, the general public, government agencies, and other internal and external forces that affect company operations.

The marketing process is not complete until consumers and publics *exchange* their money, their promise to pay, or their support for the offering of the firm, institution, person, place, or idea.

Some examples of the broadened definition of marketing are a person voting for a presidential candidate or selecting a college after seeing a television commercial, a museum selling art and art classes, a dairy trade association promoting the "Grade A Way" for milk, the change in a McDonald's storefront to accommodate area residents, product modifications to avoid recalls mandated by the government, the passage of state legislation pertaining to beverage container returns, and a retailer canceling a purchase because of dissatisfaction over the manufacturer's terms.

One study showed that 95 per cent of marketing educators believe the scope of marketing should be broadened to include nonbusiness activities.[12] Nonetheless, some marketers have criticized the broadened scope of marketing. Among the criticisms are that a broad definition does not limit marketing in terms of either institutions or the ultimate purpose of its activities, marketing must be categorized by buying and selling, marketing has a traditional domain that should be respected, not all exchanges are marketing exchanges (marketing should be limited to the study of economic needs and wants), a broad definition may lead to marketing inefficiency, and marketing principles are not applicable to all situations.[13]

Evolution of Marketing

The origins of marketing can be traced to people's earliest use of the exchange process: barter (trading one resource for another—for example, food for animal pelts). To accommodate the exchange process, trading posts, traveling salespeople, general stores, and cities evolved along with a national monetary system.

During the latter 1800s the Industrial Revolution marked the beginning of the modern concept of marketing. Until this time, exchanges were limited because people did not have surplus items to trade. With the onset of mass production, better transportation, and more efficient technology, products could be manufactured in greater quantities and sold at lower prices. People began to turn away from self-sufficiency (such as making all of their own clothes) to purchases (such as buying a new suit or dress). Improved transportation, densely populated

---

[12] William G. Nickels, "Conceptual Conflicts in Marketing," *Journal of Economics and Business,* Vol. 26 (Winter 1974), p. 142.

[13] David J. Luck, "Broadening the Concept of Marketing—Too Far," *Journal of Marketing,* Vol. 33 (July 1969), p. 53; Ben M. Enis, "Deepening the Concept of Marketing," *Journal of Marketing,* Vol. 37 (October 1973), p. 59; Johan Arndt, "How Broad Should the Marketing Concept Be?" *Journal of Marketing,* Vol. 42 (January 1978), pp. 101–103; Peter C. Bennett and Robert G. Cooper, "The Misuse of Marketing: An American Tragedy," *Business Horizons,* Vol. 24 (November–December 1981), pp. 51–61; and Elizabeth C. Hirschman, "Aesthetics, Ideologies, and the Limits of the Marketing Concept," *Journal of Marketing,* Vol. 47 (Summer 1983), pp. 45–55.

cities, and specialization also enabled more people to participate in the exchange process.

During the initial stages of the Industrial Revolution, output was limited and marketing was devoted to the physical distribution of products. Because demand was high and competition was low, companies did not have to conduct consumer research, modify products, or otherwise adapt to consumer needs. Their goal was to increase production to keep up with demand. This was known as the **production era** of marketing.

Once a company was able to maximize its production capabilities, it hired a sales force to sell its inventory. At first, while the company developed its products, consumer tastes or needs received little consideration. The role of advertising and the sales force was to make the desires of consumers fit the attributes of the products being manufactured. For example, a shoe manufacturer would produce brown wingtip shoes and use advertising and personal selling to convince consumers to buy them. The manufacturer would not determine consumer tastes before making shoes and adjust output to those tastes. This was known as the **sales era** of marketing.

As competition grew, supply began to exceed demand. A firm could not prosper without input from marketing. A marketing department was created. It conducted consumer research and advised management on how to design, price, distribute, and promote products. Unless the firm adapted to consumer needs, competitors might be better able to satisfy consumer demand and leave it with surplus inventory. Although the marketing department participated in company decisions, it remained in a subordinate or conflicting position to production, engineering, and sales departments during this period of evolution in marketing. This was known as the **marketing department era.**

In the past twenty years, the central role of marketing has been recognized by many firms; and the marketing department has become the equal of others in the company. At these firms, major decisions are made on the basis of thorough consumer analysis. Competition is intense and sophisticated. Consumers must be drawn and kept to the firm's brands. Company efforts are integrated and frequently re-evaluated. This is known as the **marketing company era.** Figure 1-6 shows the evolution of marketing at Pillsbury, a consumer-oriented company.

The marketing concept and marketing philosophy are the underpinnings of the marketing company era. They are examined here.

Marketing Concept

The **marketing concept** is a consumer-oriented, integrated, goal-oriented philosophy for a firm, institution, or person. See Figure 1-7.

In 1954 Peter Drucker emphasized the role of marketing in the success of a business. His words are just as valid today:

If we want to know what a business is we must start with its purpose. . . . There is only one valid definition of business purpose: to create a customer. What business thinks it produces is not of first importance—especially not to the future of the business or to its success. What the customer thinks he is buying, what he considers ''value'' is decisive—it determines what a business is, what it produces, and whether it will prosper.[14]

[14] Peter Drucker, *The Practice of Management* (New York: Harper & Row, 1954), p. 37.

The *production era* occurred when businesses increased production to keep up with demand.

In the *sales era* businesses manufactured and sold products without first determining consumers' desires.

The *marketing department era* occurred when research became necessary to determine the desires and needs of consumers.

The *marketing company era* integrates consumer research and analysis into all company efforts.

The *marketing concept* is consumer-oriented, integrated, and goal-oriented.

ERA

**PRODUCT
ORIENTATION
(1869 – 1930)**

**SALES
ORIENTATION
(1930s – 1950s)**

**MARKETING ORIENTATION
(1950s – 1960s)**

**MARKETING CONTROL
(1960s – PRESENT)**

CHARACTERISTICS AND GOALS

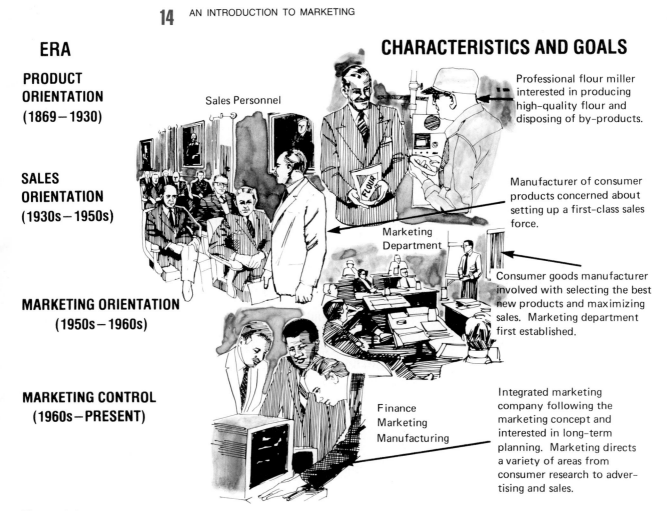

Sales Personnel

Professional flour miller interested in producing high-quality flour and disposing of by-products.

Manufacturer of consumer products concerned about setting up a first-class sales force.

Marketing Department

Consumer goods manufacturer involved with selecting the best new products and maximizing sales. Marketing department first established.

Finance
Marketing
Manufacturing

Integrated marketing company following the marketing concept and interested in long-term planning. Marketing directs a variety of areas from consumer research to advertising and sales.

**Figure 1-6
The Evolution of
Marketing at Pillsbury**

One of the first formal statements on the marketing concept was made in 1957 by John B. McKitterick, then president of General Electric. McKitterick told a meeting of the American Marketing Association (AMA) that the marketing concept was a customer-oriented, integrated, profit-oriented philosophy of business.[15]

During the past thirty years, many companies have publicized their reliance on marketing, as these illustrations show:

Instead of trying to market what is easiest for us to make, we must find out much more

---

[15] John B. McKitterick, "What Is the Marketing Management Concept?" in Frank M. Bass (Editor), *The Frontiers of Marketing Thought and Action* (Chicago: American Marketing Association, 1957), pp. 71–82.

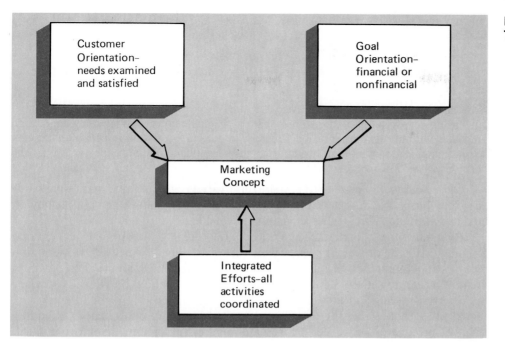

Figure 1-7
The Marketing Concept

about what the consumer is willing to buy. In other words, we must apply our creativeness more intelligently to *people* and their needs, rather than to *products*.[16] (General Foods)

Marketing is:

the process of defining, anticipating, and creating customer needs and wants and of organizing all the resources of the company to satisfy them at greater total profit to the company and to the customer.[17] (B.F. Goodrich)

Today, the thrust of our merchandising is more varied and complex, to meet the needs and desires of our customers. May [Department Stores] has diversified strategically to broaden and strengthen its position as a leading retailer, by growing through three distinct approaches to the market. Each of these operations serves the tastes, trends, and shopping patterns of significant segments of the consumer market.[18] (May Department Stores)

AT&T has become:

a high technology business applying advanced marketing strategies to the satisfaction of highly sophisticated customer requirements.[19]

We believe the strength of our results and the consistency of our growth reflect our dedication to anticipating and matching consumer desires with superior products. All of

---

[16] Charles G. Mortimer, "The Creative Factor in Marketing," Fifteenth Annual Parlin Memorial Lecture, Philadelphia Chapter, American Marketing Association, May 13, 1959.

[17] Don C. Miller, "Total Marketing—Management's Point of View," Third Regional Industrial Marketing Conference, American Marketing Association, Columbus, Ohio, March 31, 1960.

[18] May Company, *Annual Report for 1976*, p. 4.

[19] Ronald Nevans, "Ma Bell's New Look," *Financial World* (March 1, 1979), p. 12.

our marketing, operations, and financial strategies are dedicated to this goal.[20] (Philip Morris)

At Amcast Industrial Corporation, an automobile parts manufacturer whose customers include General Motors and other car makers, a new approach is being used to market its products:

No longer are its sales representatives mere glad-handers, skilled at wining and dining purchasing agents in hopes of getting a share of available orders. Today, they are college graduates with metalworking backgrounds, who not only deal with buyers but with customers' engineers, marketing specialists, and manufacturing personnel as well. The purpose: to get involved early on in the business plans of potential customers.[21]

These statements demonstrate that, for a variety of firms, the marketing company era has arrived; marketing is now seen as the underlying philosophy of business, around which other decisions are made.

The elements of the marketing concept are crucial to the ultimate success of a product, service, organization, person, place, or idea. A customer orientation requires an examination of market needs, not production capability, and development of a plan to satisfy them. Products and services should be viewed as means to accomplish ends and not the ends themselves. Under an integrated marketing focus, all activities relating to products and services are coordinated, including finance, production, engineering, research and development, inventory control, and marketing. The firm, organization, or person should be goal-oriented and employ marketing to achieve goals. The goals may be profit, a cure for a disease, increased tourism, the election of a political candidate, an improved corporate image, and so on. Marketing helps achieve goals by orienting the organization toward satisfying consumers and providing desirable products, services, or ideas.

> **Marketing goals may be profit, a cure for a disease, or an improved corporate image.**

While the marketing concept enables an organization to analyze, maximize, and satisfy consumer demand, it should realize that the concept is only a guide to planning. The organization must also consider its strengths and weaknesses in such functional areas as production, engineering, finance, and distribution. Marketing plans need to balance goals, customer needs, and resource capabilities. In addition, the impact of competition, government regulations, and other forces external to the firm must be evaluated. These factors are discussed in Chapters 2 and 3.

Selling Versus Marketing Philosophies

Figures 1-8 and 1-9 focus on the differences between selling and marketing philosophies. The benefits of a marketing, rather than a sales, orientation are many. Marketing stresses consumer analysis and satisfaction, directs the resources of the firm to making the products and services that consumers want, and is adaptive to changes in consumer characteristics and needs. Under a marketing philosophy, selling is used to communicate with and understand consumers; consumer dissatisfaction leads to changes in policy, not a stronger or different sales pitch. Marketing looks for real differences in consumer tastes and develops offerings to satisfy them. Marketing is oriented to the long run, and marketing goals reflect overall company goals. Finally, marketing views customer needs in a broad (for example, heating) rather than a narrow (for example, fuel oil) manner.

> **With a marketing orientation that stresses consumer satisfaction, selling is used to communicate with and understand consumers.**

---

[20] Philip Morris Incorporated, *Annual Report 1982*, p. 3.
[21] Gregory Stricharchuk, "Smokestack Industries Adopt Sophisticated Sales Approach," *Wall Street Journal* (March 15, 1984), p. 33.

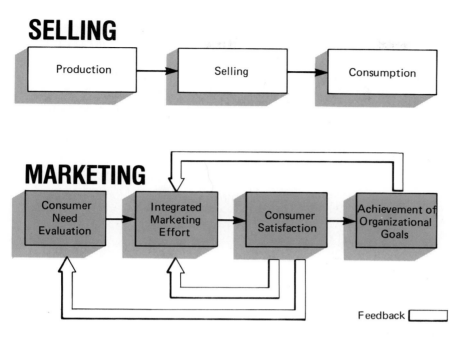

Figure 1-8
The Focus of Selling and Marketing Philosophies

Despite the advantages of a marketing approach, the widespread creation of marketing departments, and public acknowledgment of the importance of marketing, only a handful of large corporations really understand and practice sophisticated marketing. Among them are Procter & Gamble, Eastman Kodak, Avon, McDonald's, IBM, Xerox, General Electric, and Caterpillar.[22]

The existence of a large marketing department and marketing plans does not necessarily mean an organization is properly applying the marketing concept. For example, the chief executive of one of the world's largest automobile companies once said:

I thought we were doing marketing. We have a corporate vice-president, a skilled advertising department, and elaborate market planning procedures. These fooled us. When the crunch came, I realized that we weren't producing the cars that people wanted. We weren't responding to new needs. Our marketing operation was nothing more than a glorified sales department.[23]

Importance and Scope of Marketing

It is important to study the field of marketing for several reasons. Marketing stimulates demand. A basic task of marketing is to generate consumer enthusiasm for goods and services. The Gross National Product (GNP), the total market value of goods and services produced in a country during a year, in the United States is well over $3 trillion.

---

[22] Philip Kotler, "From Sales Obsession to Marketing Effectiveness," *Harvard Business Review,* Vol. 55 (November–December 1977), p. 68.
[23] Ibid.

Figure 1-9
Basic Differences Between Selling and Marketing Philosophies

SELLING

- Sales-oriented
- Output "sold" to consumers
- One-way process
- Short-run goals
- Volume-oriented
- Emphasis on single consumers
- Narrow view of consumer needs
- Informal planning and feedback
- Little adaptation to environment

Basic Differences

MARKETING

- Consumer-oriented
- Marketing research determines output
- Two-way process (interactive)
- Long-run goals
- Profit-oriented
- Emphasis on groups of consumers
- Broad view of consumer needs
- Integrated planning and feedback
- Appropriate adaptation to environment

Marketing generates consumer enthusiasm, involves a large part of each sales dollar, employs many people, supports entire industries, pertains to all consumers, and plays a major role in our daily lives.

A large amount of each sales dollar goes to cover marketing costs. Some estimates place the costs of marketing at 50 per cent or more of sales.[24] These costs should not be confused with marketing profits, nor should it be assumed that the elimination of marketing activities would lower prices. For example, could a consumer really save money by flying to Detroit to buy a new car directly from the manufacturer? Would a consumer buy clothing in bulk in order to save transportation and storage costs?

Between one fourth and one third of the civilian labor force in the United States is engaged in marketing activities. This includes people employed in the retailing, wholesaling, transportation, warehousing, and communications industries and those involved with marketing activities for manufacturing, financial, service, agricultural, mining, and other industries. For instance, more than 15 million people work in retailing, 5 million in wholesaling, and 5 million in transportation.

Marketing activities support entire industries, such as advertising and marketing research. Total annual U.S. advertising expenditures exceed $85 billion. Many agencies have worldwide billings of $1 billion or more including Young &

---

[24] See Reavis Cox, *Distribution in a High Level Economy* (Englewood Cliffs, N.J.: Prentice-Hall, 1965), p. 149; Paul W. Stewart and J. Frederick Dewhurst, *Does Distribution Cost Too Much?* (New York: Twentieth Century Fund, 1963), pp. 117–118; and Jules J. Schwartz, *Corporate Policy: A Casebook* (Englewood Cliffs, N.J.: Prentice-Hall, 1978), pp. 6–7.

Rubicam, J. Walter Thompson, McCann-Erickson, and Ogilvy & Mather. Approximately $1.5 billion is spent yearly in the U.S. on marketing research. Companies such as Nielsen, SAMI, Market Facts, and Audits and Surveys generate yearly revenues of several million dollars each.

All people serve as consumers for various products and services. By understanding the role of marketing, consumers can become better informed, more selective, and more efficient. Effective channels of communication with organizations can also be established and complaints resolved more easily and favorably. Consumer groups have a major impact on firms.

Because resources are scarce, marketing programs and systems must function at their peak. For example, optimization of store hours, inventory movement, advertising expenditures, product assortments, and other areas of marketing will better coordinate resources. As mentioned earlier in the chapter, some industries may actually require demarketing (lowering the demand for products and services). The latter include oil and gasoline.

Marketing has a strong impact on people's beliefs and life-styles. In fact, marketing has been criticized as developing materialistic attitudes, fads, product obsolescence, a reliance on gadgets, conspicuous consumption (status consciousness), and superficial product differences and wasting resources. Marketers reply that they merely respond to the desires of people and make the best products and services they can at the prices people will pay.

Marketing has a role to play in improving the quality of life. For example, marketers encourage firms to make safer products, such as low-tar cigarettes and child-proof bottle caps. They create public service messages on energy conservation, cures for diseases, driver safety, abuses of alcohol, and other topics. They help new products, ideas, and services (for example, microwave ovens, improved nutrition, automated banking) to be accepted and assimilated by people.

The scope of marketing is extremely wide. Among the areas in which marketing is involved are pricing, warehousing, packaging, branding, selling, sales force management, credit, transportation, social responsibility, retail site selection, consumer analysis, wholesaling, retailing, vendor appraisal and selection, advertising, public relations, marketing research, product planning, and warranties.

A knowledge of marketing is also valuable for those not directly involved with marketing. For example, marketing principles can be utilized by doctors, lawyers, management consultants, financial analysts, research and development personnel, economists, statisticians, city planners, nonprofit institutions, and others. Each of these professions and organizations requires an understanding and satisfaction of patient, client, consumer, taxpayer, or contributor needs.

Marketing Functions and Performers

The basic *marketing functions* are environmental analysis and marketing research, consumer analysis, product (service) planning, distribution planning, promotion planning, price planning, social responsibility, and marketing manage-

FUNCTION

DESCRIPTION

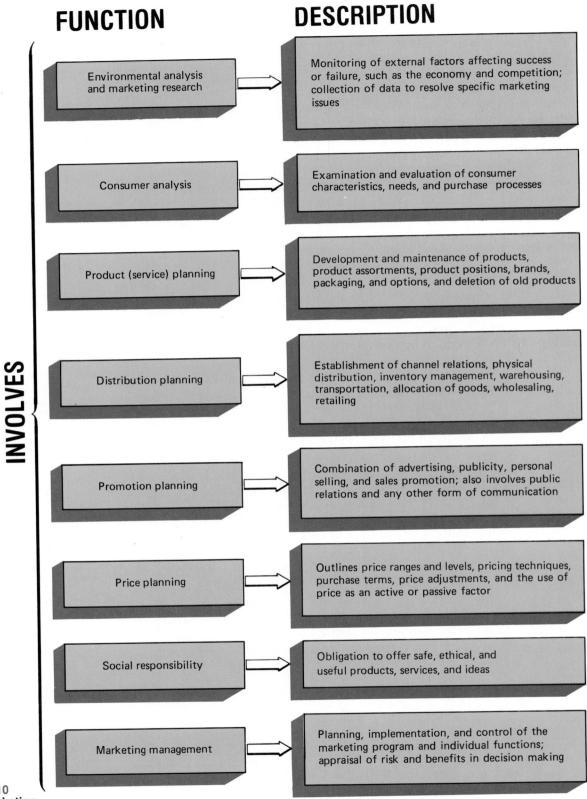

MARKETING INVOLVES

Function	Description
Environmental analysis and marketing research	Monitoring of external factors affecting success or failure, such as the economy and competition; collection of data to resolve specific marketing issues
Consumer analysis	Examination and evaluation of consumer characteristics, needs, and purchase processes
Product (service) planning	Development and maintenance of products, product assortments, product positions, brands, packaging, and options, and deletion of old products
Distribution planning	Establishment of channel relations, physical distribution, inventory management, warehousing, transportation, allocation of goods, wholesaling, retailing
Promotion planning	Combination of advertising, publicity, personal selling, and sales promotion; also involves public relations and any other form of communication
Price planning	Outlines price ranges and levels, pricing techniques, purchase terms, price adjustments, and the use of price as an active or passive factor
Social responsibility	Obligation to offer safe, ethical, and useful products, services, and ideas
Marketing management	Planning, implementation, and control of the marketing program and individual functions; appraisal of risk and benefits in decision making

Figure 1-10
Basic Marketing Functions

ment. These are described in Figure 1-10 and throughout the text. Although many transactions require the performance of similar marketing functions, such as consumer analysis, distribution, promotion, and pricing, there are a number of ways they can be carried out.

Marketing performers include manufacturers and service providers, wholesalers, retailers, marketing specialists, and organizational and final consumers. As shown in Figure 1-11, each of these performers has a different role. It is important to note that while the responsibility for fulfilling marketing functions can be shifted and shared in a variety of ways, the basic marketing functions must be completed by one performer or another. They cannot be eliminated in most situations.

For a number of reasons, one performer usually does not undertake all marketing functions. Many producers do not have the financial resources to engage in direct marketing. As an illustration, even General Motors, one of the world's

The basic *marketing functions* can be shifted among *performers*, but they cannot be eliminated.

One performer often does not have the resources or ability to undertake all marketing functions.

**Figure 1-11
Who Performs Marketing Functions**

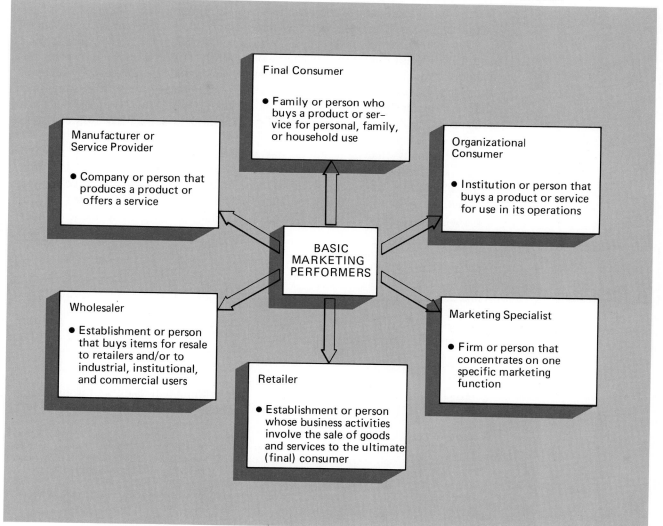

largest corporations, does not have the resources to undertake all the functions its dealers perform.

Direct marketing would often require producers to make complementary products or sell the complementary products of other manufacturers. For instance, there are about 200,000 U.S. grocery stores (comprised of supermarkets, superettes, small stores, and convenience stores), each carrying several thousand items. It would not be feasible for a producer of a limited line of foods to forego stores and sell directly to widely dispersed consumers.

A performer may be unable or unwilling to complete certain functions and seek a marketing specialist to fulfill them. For example, a firm may hire an advertising agency to develop its advertising campaign and mold a projected company image; utilize a marketing research firm to design a questionnaire, collect data, and evaluate the results; or use a credit bureau to assess consumers' credit ratings.

Many performers are too small to accomplish certain functions. For example, consumers are unlikely to be able to buy in bulk and independent retailers cannot purchase full trainloads of merchandise in order to minimize shipping costs; large wholesalers can. The overwhelming majority of retailers operate only one outlet.

For many products and services, established distribution methods are in force and it is difficult to circumvent them. A good illustration is the sale of packaged bakery products. Because of high delivery costs and the increase of one-stop shopping, these products must be sold in supermarkets (where it is sometimes difficult to gain shelf space). For similar reasons, items such as beer and soda also require distribution in supermarkets. High-volume sales almost always necessitate intensive, shared distribution.

While many final consumers may visit the nearest store (or shop via telephone), and expect the retailer or manufacturer to perform all marketing functions, others may undertake some functions themselves in order to save money. The latter may buy in quantity, purchase unfinished products or services, pick up merchandise, pay cash, use self-service outlets, and bargain with the retailer.

Marketing in Action

In this section, two different approaches to marketing, one successful and one unsuccessful, are presented and contrasted.

IBM: The Success of the PC[25]

IBM is the world's largest computer firm with annual sales well in excess of $40 billion. Of this amount, more than 5 per cent is generated from the IBM PC,

---

[25] "Personal Computers: And the Winner Is IBM," *Business Week* (October 3, 1983), pp. 76–90; Robert Sobel, "IBM: The Cautious Pacesetter," *Newsday* (October 16, 1983), p. 82; Peter D. Petre, "Meet the Lean, Mean New IBM," *Fortune* (June 13, 1983), pp. 68–82; Susan Chace, "IBM Unveils 2 More Personal Computers, Deals Blow to Office-Market Competition," *Wall Street Journal* (October 19, 1983), p. 2; Andrew Pollack, "The Debut of IBM's 'Junior,'" *New York Times* (November 2, 1983), pp. D1, D4; and Daniel Burstein, "Computer Marketing: No Longer Fun and Games," *Advertising Age* (March 5, 1984), pp. M–11—M–13ff.

introduced in August 1981. Despite a late entry into the personal computer market (several years after Apple and others started the industry), IBM is now clearly positioned as the industry leader. By the end of 1983, over 500,000 PCs had been sold; and IBM expected to market 2 to 3 million more in 1984, as production capacity and demand rose. The success of the PC is the result of a careful and well-executed marketing plan by IBM, and a willingness to undertake a different marketing approach than that normally used by the firm.

IBM regularly analyzes the environment in order to determine competitors' actions, economic changes, newer technology, and unserved markets. It also evaluates different consumer segments (e.g., small firms vs. large firms) to find out their characteristics and needs. Through its research, IBM discovered that a number of other firms, particularly Apple and Radio Shack, had developed inexpensive computers for the business market. IBM viewed this market as having significant potential and specific computer needs that were not being satisfied.

As noted at the beginning of the chapter, IBM set up an autonomous task force to produce the PC. By being a late entrant into the market, IBM's product planners were able to study the attributes of competitors' products and add their own special features, including compatibility with mainframe IBM computers. Components were purchased from a number of suppliers, rather than invented by IBM. A sophisticated 16-bit microprocessor was used (many competitors relied on slower 8-bit microprocessors). Finally, outside firms were encouraged to write software programs for the PC; so many companies began writing programs for the PC that the computer became the industry standard.

In order to market the PC properly, IBM recognized that it needed to modify the typical direct distribution system it used for more expensive products. IBM set up a three-tiered network. The sales force called on larger accounts interested in multiple units. IBM Product Centers were staffed with company personnel and operated nationwide. 800 major retailers, such as Computerland and Sears, were given distribution rights.

A multimillion dollar advertising campaign capitalizing on the IBM name concentrated on television and magazines. A Charlie Chaplin lookalike representing ''Modern Times'' demonstrated the versatility and simplicity of the PC. See Figure 1-12. After the PC was well established, IBM stimulated interest in its unveiled PC junior for many months and received great amounts of media publicity, because of the mystery surrounding the PC junior (which IBM did not acknowledge existed until formally introduced on November 1, 1983).

IBM established basic list prices for the PC and its components, such as monitors, disk drives, and printers. It suggested package variations (e.g., the PC, a monitor, one disk drive, a printer, and related interfaces) and a total price for the package. While prices were comparable to competitors', price cutting and deep discounting were discouraged. IBM brought price stability to an industry that frequently resorted to discounting.

IBM demonstrated its social responsibility by offering special discounts to nonprofit organizations. It worked with many schools and colleges to improve the level of computer literacy.

Finally, the marketing managers at IBM performed in an efficient, consumer-oriented manner:

In developing and offering the PC, IBM applied sound marketing principles and the marketing concept.

Figure 1-12
The IBM Personal
Computer

IBM is a registered trademark of the International Business Machines Corporation. Courtesy of IBM.

The PC's success was not accidental; rather, it was the result of new strategies put into place in 1979 and 1980. IBM did it by combining good timing, good luck, a new approach to product development, and an amazing flexibility for such a giant company.[26]

[26] ''Personal Computers: And the Winner Is IBM,'' p. 78.

Texas Instruments: Failure in the Home Computer Market[27]

On October 28, 1983, Texas Instruments (TI) announced that it was ceasing production of the 99/4A home computer four years after entering the market. During this period, between 1 and 1.5 million 99/4A computers were sold. Despite these sales, a number of marketing errors forced Texas Instruments to withdraw from the home computer field (after similar difficulties caused it to abandon hand-held calculators and digital watches in earlier years). Losses on the 99/4A were several hundred million dollars in 1983.

Texas Instruments' marketing problems with its home computers began when they were first introduced in 1979. TI had not correctly analyzed the environment and consumer needs. It produced an $1,100 computer aimed exclusively at the home market. In 1979, this market was extremely small; consumers did not yet know of the advantages and uses of home computers. And the high price tag discouraged many potential buyers. It was not until 1982 and 1983 that the market had grown enough and technology dropped prices enough to stimulate large-scale sales. Furthermore, TI did not monitor retailers' inventories to determine that they had excess 99/4As, which would have allowed it to reduce production.

Product planning was haphazard, in large part because of misjudging consumers. TI did not clarify who potential users were (parents, children, homeowners, etc.) and what features these users desired. TI also had difficulty differentiating its product from video-game consoles and very inexpensive home computers. As a result, its home computer was perceived as too similar to the Commodore VIC 20, a machine with much less computer memory. This caused TI to drop its less-expensive 99/2 model before it even reached the market. In addition, a defect in 99/4A's transformer required TI to stop shipments for a month. Only in the software programs did TI have an edge over competitors. Most observers rated TI's own software far superior to that of Commodore.

By 1981, Texas Instruments had lost significant control over the distribution of the 99/4A. It was sold in all types of outlets and was heavily discounted. During 1982 and 1983, a large amount of sales were made through discounters, toy stores (such as Toys "R" Us), and catalog showrooms. This situation contributed to TI's image problems.

Promotion emphasis underwent a number of changes. At various times, the 99/4A was advertised as a sophisticated video game console, a budget planner for adults, and an education tool for children. For an extended period, Bill Cosby was the corporate spokesperson. In all cases, TI positioned its computer at the low end of the market. It was not until mid-1983 that emphasis was placed on the software available for the 99/4A.

Probably the most crucial error Texas Instruments made was allowing itself to be drawn into a price war. While this raised revenues to record levels, it virtually eliminated profit margins. In December 1981, the 99/4A had a retail price of $399; by early 1983, the price had fallen to $99. TI used a rebate offer for six

Texas Instruments had a number of problems with the 99/4A computer because of poor marketing.

[27] Andrew Pollack, "Retreat Set by Texas Instruments," *New York Times* (October 29, 1983), pp. 35–36; Andrew Pollack, "Chaos for Texas Instruments," *New York Times* (November 1, 1983), pp. D1, D7; David Stipp, "Texas Instruments Is Seen as Getting a Boost from Move to Quit Home-Computer Field," *Wall Street Journal* (October 31, 1983), p. 2; and Bro Uttal, "Sudden Shake-up in Home Computers," *Fortune* (July 11, 1983), pp. 105–106.

months. The focus on price attracted the consumer looking for the least expensive model, not the model with the best value and features.

TI's method of withdrawing from the market was criticized by many as not being socially responsible. Until the day it announced its exit from the market, TI insisted it was in the home computer business to stay. It left questions about repairs and software that were unresolved. Schools which had made purchases of the 99/4A were particularly concerned.

In sum, TI's marketing managers did not perform well; and the firm did not recognize this until it was too late. A president of the consumer electronics division with a strong marketing background was not hired until August 1983. Said one observer about TI's price-cutting and mass-production strategy:

This is one of the worst displays of TI's mismanagement and poor planning. They opened the factory doors and flooded the market until the retailer couldn't take any more.[28]

IBM Versus Texas Instruments

Table 1-1 contrasts the approaches taken by IBM and Texas Instruments. Most significantly, IBM has been thoroughly involved with marketing planning and adaptation, while TI has not been. IBM has well applied the marketing concept—consumer orientation, integrated effort, and goal orientation.

Format of the Text

This book is divided into eight parts. The remainder of Part One concentrates on the environment of marketing, the developing of marketing plans, and the information needed for marketing decisions. These topics set the foundation for examining the specific components of marketing.

Part Two deals with the central orientation of marketing: understanding consumers. Consumer demographics, social and psychological factors, the decision process, organizational consumers, developing a target market, and sales forecasting are detailed.

Parts Three through Six describe the basic components of marketing (product, distribution, promotion, and price) and the decisions needed to carry out marketing plans.

Part Seven covers several topics that expand the scope of marketing, including international marketing, service and nonprofit marketing, and marketing and society.

Part Eight considers the marketing management implications of the topics raised throughout the text. Included are discussions on integrating and analyzing the marketing program as well as marketing in the future.

The text defines key terms, explains the significance of important concepts, studies the role of the marketing manager, and shows the scope of the field of marketing. In addition, numerous examples and illustrations of actual marketing

[28] Uttal, "Sudden Shake-up in Home Computers," p. 105.

Marketing Element	IBM PC	Texas Instruments 99/4A
Environmental analysis and marketing research	Regular monitoring of environment and use of research	Limited monitoring of environment and use of research; overestimate of market
Consumer analysis	Precise definition of market—inexpensive business computer users—and its reasons for using computers	Vague definition of home market—parents? children? homeowners?—and its reasons for using computers
Product planning	Autonomous task force, thorough planning, use of outside suppliers, 16-bit microprocessor, excellent software	Haphazard, product positioned too close to VIC 20, one new model never introduced, transformer problems, excellent software
Distribution planning	Three-tiered approach: sales force, product centers, and major retailers	Limited control due to distribution through any type of outlet, including toy stores
Promotion planning	Coordinated campaign based on Charlie Chaplin lookalike and IBM name	Varying campaign with changes in themes, too little distinctiveness
Price planning	Competitive, but stable, prices	Costly price wars
Social responsibility	Cooperation with nonprofit organizations, schools, etc.	Repair and software problems unresolved with announcement of withdrawal
Marketing management	Progressive planning, implementation, and control of marketing efforts	Disjointed planning, implementation, and control of marketing efforts

Table 1-1
IBM Versus Texas Instruments

practices by a variety of organizations are woven into the discussion of the framework of marketing and its components.

Summary

Marketing is an exciting and dynamic contemporary field that involves a wide variety of activities. The classical definition of marketing emphasizes the flow of goods and services from producer to consumer or user. In modern terms, marketing is defined as the anticipation, management, and satisfaction of demand through the exchange process.

The evolution of marketing can be traced to people's earliest use of the exchange process. Marketing has really developed since the Industrial Revolution, as mass production and improved transportation enabled more transactions to occur. For companies such as Pillsbury, marketing has evolved through four eras: production, sales, marketing department, and marketing company. The marketing concept requires a company to be consumer-oriented, have an integrated marketing program, and be goal-oriented.

When contrasting a marketing approach with a sales approach, marketing is found to be more involved with profit planning, analysis of trends, opportunities and threats, assessments of customer types and differences, and coordinated decision making.

The field of marketing is important for several reasons: stimulation and regulation of demand, marketing costs, the number of people employed in marketing, its support of entire industries such as advertising agencies and marketing research firms, the recognition that all people are consumers in some situations, the necessity of the efficient use of scarce resources, its impact on people's beliefs and life-styles, and its input into the quality of life. The scope of marketing is quite broad and diversified.

The major classifications of marketing functions are environmental analysis and marketing research, consumer analysis, product (service) planning, distribution planning, promotion planning, price planning, social responsibility, and marketing management. The responsibility for performing these functions can be shifted and shared in several ways among manufacturers and service providers, wholesalers, retailers, marketing specialists, and consumers. One party usually does not perform all the functions. This is due to costs, assortment requirements, specialized abilities, company size, established methods of distribution, and consumer interests.

The IBM PC has done so well because IBM has done an outstanding marketing job. The Texas Instruments 99/4A computer had to be removed from the market as a result of poor marketing performance.

Questions for Discussion

1. Despite its enormous success, Totes has had some product lines fail. For example, it developed a stainproof necktie for men. Commented Bradford Phillips, "We put the ties in a beautiful plastic box, and people thought the ties were made of plastic, too." How could Totes have made such an error?
2. What are the major differences between the classical (narrow) and modern (broad) definitions of marketing?
3. Explain the
   a. Anticipation of demand.
   b. Management of demand.
   c. Satisfaction of demand.
   d. Exchange process.
4. Distinguish between consumer and publics' demand.
5. Give an example of a product, service, organization, person, place, and idea that may be marketed.

6. Describe the four eras of marketing. Are any companies still able to operate in the production or sales era of marketing? Explain.
7. Define the marketing concept. How does your definition differ from that offered by McKitterick in 1957?
8. Describe at least five benefits of a marketing over a sales orientation.
9. Does the presence of a marketing department mean a firm is following the marketing concept? Explain your answer.
10. What would a nonmarketing major learn by studying marketing?
11. What are the basic functions performed by marketing?
12. Why do most consumers not buy products directly from manufacturers?
13. What must IBM do to maintain the dominance of the PC?
14. After withdrawing from the home-computer market, Texas Instruments said that it planned to continue making professional (business) computers. Evaluate this strategy.

Hints for Solving Cases

At the end of each chapter from 2 through 25, two short cases are presented—a total of forty-eight. These cases are intended to build on the material in the text, improve reasoning skills, and stimulate class discussions. At the end of each part, one longer case is presented—a total of eight. These cases are intended to improve reasoning skills, the ability to identify key points, and integrating skills.

The cases in *Marketing* describe actual marketing situations faced by a variety of organizations. The facts, circumstances, and people are all real. The questions following each case are designed to help identify the key issues encountered by the organization, evaluate its responses to these issues, outline additional courses of action, and develop appropriate marketing strategies. The information necessary to answer the questions is contained within the case or the chapter(s) to which the case relates.

These hints should be kept in mind when solving cases:

- Read the material carefully. Underline important data and statements.
- List the key issues, problems, and organizational responses.
- Read each question following the case. In outline form, write up tentative answers. Cover as many points as possible.
- Review the text. In particular, look for information pertaining to the case questions.
- Expand your tentative answers, substantiating them with data from the case and the chapter(s).
- Reread the case to be sure you have not omitted any important concepts in your answers.
- Integrate your answers. Consider their ramifications for the organization.
- Reread your solutions the next day. This ensures a more objective review of your work.
- Be sure your answers are not a summary of the case, but are analyses and recommendations.

Chapter 2

The Environment of Marketing

CHAPTER OBJECTIVES

1. To examine the environment of marketing and show why it is necessary for marketers to understand the total environment in which they operate

2. To view the environment in a systematic and integrated manner

3. To enumerate the controllable elements of a marketing plan and to differentiate between those elements controlled by top management and those controlled by marketers

4. To enumerate the uncontrollable elements that affect a marketing plan and how marketers may respond to them

5. To explain why feedback and adaptation to change are essential for marketers

*L*evi Strauss invented jeans in 1850. The firm he founded today accounts for about one quarter of total U.S. jeans sales, double the leading competitor (Wrangler). However, during the past few years, Levi Strauss & Co. has learned a lot about the effects of the environment within which it operates:

- Market share declined from over 30 per cent in 1979 to 25 per cent in 1983. This was caused by the boom in designer jeans and the aggressive behavior of traditional competitors such as Wrangler and Lee.
- The recession in 1981 and 1982 caused severe declines in profits.
- The company planned to outfit all U.S. athletes at the 1980 Olympics in Moscow and developed a multimillion dollar advertising campaign

built around the Olympic theme. The U.S. boycott of the Olympics eliminated Levi's strategy.

- Many attempts at diversification failed. These included the marketing of denim shirts, disposable sheets and towels, and belts and wallets. In most cases, the firm misread the market.
- Large loyal retailers, such as Macy's and Gap Stores, became disgruntled when Levi began selling jeans to Sears and J. C. Penney. This worsened a situation that had already been deteriorating because of the heavy discounting of jeans. Said one competitive jeans maker, "Levi seemed to think for many years that all it had to do was put its name on an item to be successful. It neglected the retailer."

Levi studied these events carefully and acted accordingly, "Success made us complacent, and our recent adversity was a great teacher." A number of changes in strategy have been enacted. A new and younger management team is in charge. The company's line of business is defined more broadly—as apparel. Among recent introductions were maternity clothes and two additional men's wear lines; and a contract for designer sportswear was signed with Perry Ellis. Senior executives have been assigned to major retail accounts to improve relations with these firms. To learn more about consumers, some Levi managers have actually operated cash registers in retail outlets.

Marketing operates in an environment with both controllable and uncontrollable elements. By better understanding its environment, Levi has been able to improve the performance of the elements it controls and respond better to those it cannot control. As a competitor noted, Levi "learned its lesson—and I'm sorry it did." [1] Figure 2-1 shows an advertisement keyed to Levi's participation in the 1984 Olympics.

Marketing and Its Environment

The environment within which marketing operates is depicted in Figure 2-2. This figure divides the ***marketing environment*** into five parts: controllable factors, uncontrollable factors, organization's level of success or failure in reaching its objectives, feedback, and adaptation.

Controllable factors are those directed by the firm and its marketers. A number of basic interrelated decisions are made by top management. These include choice of a line of business, overall objectives, the role of marketing, and the role of other business functions. Then, marketing managers make a number of deci-

The *marketing environment* consists of controllable factors, uncontrollable factors, organization's level of success or failure, feedback, and adaptation.

[1] Marilyn Chase, "Levi Emerges from Recession with Plan That Helps Boost Profit and Stock Price," *Wall Street Journal* (September 23, 1983), p. 16; Gurney Breckenfeld, "The Odyssey of Levi Strauss," *Fortune* (March 22, 1982), pp. 110–124; "Levi Strauss: A Touch of Fashion—And a Dash of Humility," *Business Week* (October 24, 1983), pp. 85, 88; "Levi Forms Unit to Make and Sell Designer Clothes," *Wall Street Journal* (January 19, 1984), p. 49; and Thomas C. Hayes," Hard Decisions Ahead for New Chief of Levi Strauss," *New York Times* (April 15, 1984), Section 3, p. 6.

Figure 2-1
The Levi's Message

LEVI STRAUSS & CO. COPYRIGHT 1982; reprinted by permission.

sions based on these guidelines. Included are the selection of a consumer market, marketing objectives, marketing organization, marketing plans, and control. In combination these factors result in an overall marketing strategy or offering (A in Figure 2-2).

The major uncontrollable factors are consumers, competition, government, the economy, technology, and independent media. They have an impact on how well the organization and its offering are accepted (B in Figure 2-2). For example, because of cultural beliefs, a product may not be popular. Competition may lower prices. The government may enact strict legislation. The inflation rate might slow down sales. Resource shortages might cause a necessary part to be unavailable. The media may present negative publicity about the firm.

Accordingly, the offering of the firm and the impact of the uncontrollable environment interact to determine the organization's level of success or failure in

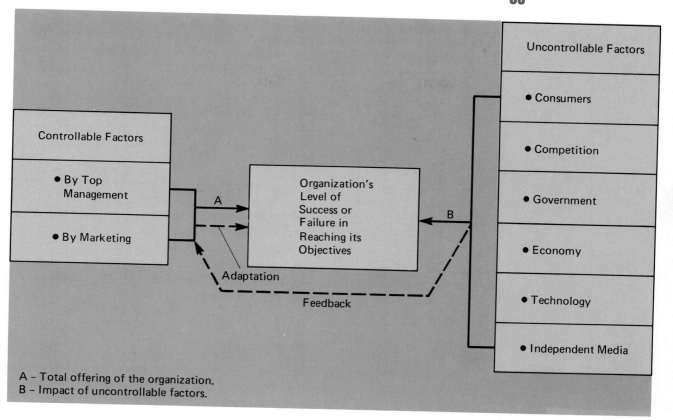

A – Total offering of the organization.
B – Impact of uncontrollable factors.

Figure 2-2
The Environment Within Which Marketing Operates

reaching its objectives. Feedback occurs when the firm makes an effort to monitor uncontrollable factors and assess its areas of strength and weakness. Adaptation refers to the changes in its marketing plan that an organization makes in order to comply with the uncontrollable environment.

If a firm is unwilling to consider the entire environment (controllable and uncontrollable factors) in a systematic manner, it increases the likelihood that the organization will have a lack of direction and not attain proper results. Consumers may be inadequately analyzed, some marketing functions may be omitted, and duplication of effort by departments and interdepartment rivalries may occur. Opportunities may be missed and undesirable products or services retained. The organization may be excluded from distribution (such as supermarkets refusing to carry a new brand of toothpaste), and have disputes with channel members. The wrong image may be generated through an inefficient promotion mix and prices that are not reflective of quality.

Without adequate analysis of the environment, the organization may also violate social or cultural taboos. It may not sustain a competitive edge over rivals. Existing legislation may be violated and consumer complaints incurred. There may be poor reactions to changes in inflation and unemployment, and failures to use new technology or plan for resource shortages. The environment may not be regularly monitored and poor adaptation to the environment and its changes may be undertaken.

Throughout this chapter, the various parts of Figure 2-2 are described and

Failure to consider the entire environment systematically may result in the organization's lack of direction and poor results.

drawn together so that a marketer can understand and operate in the complex environment he or she faces. In Chapter 3, the concept of strategic planning in marketing is presented. Strategic planning establishes a formal process for developing, implementing, and evaluating marketing programs in conjunction with the goals of top management.

Controllable Factors

Controllable factors are directed by the organization and its marketers.

Controllable factors are those elements that are directed by the organization and its marketers. Some of the controllable factors are directed by top management. These are not controllable by marketers, who must develop plans to satisfy organizational goals and work within the guidelines set by management. In situations involving small- or medium-sized institutions, both broad policy and marketing decisions are made by one person, usually the owner. Even in these cases, broad policy should be stated first and marketing plans must adjust to it.

Factors Directed by Top Management

Although top management is responsible for numerous decisions, four basic ones are of extreme importance to marketers: line of business, overall objectives, the role of marketing, and the role of other business functions. These decisions have an impact on all aspects of marketing. Figure 2-3 shows the types of decisions that are required in these four areas.

The line of business refers to the general product/service category, functions, geographic coverage, type of ownership, and specific business of a company. By analyzing these concepts, management becomes better able to generate and sustain its business.

The line of business refers to the general and specific business of a company.

The general product/service category is a broad definition of the kind of business a firm seeks to undertake. It may be energy, furniture, housing, education, or any number of others. The functions of the business outline a company's position in the marketing system, from supplier to manufacturer to wholesaler to retailer, and the tasks it seeks to undertake. It is important to note that a firm may want to undertake more than one of these functions. For example, Sherwin-Williams decided not only to perform production functions but also to market its paint products through its own retail outlets.

An organization must determine its span of geographic coverage. It can be neighborhood, city, county, state, regional, national, or international. The type of ownership arrangement ranges from a sole proprietorship, partnership, or franchise to a multiunit corporation. The specific business is a narrow definition of the firm, its functions, and its operations, such as McDonald's (fast-food, family-oriented chain) and Ed's Dry Cleaners (local full-service dry cleaner specializing in outerwear).

Top management outlines overall objectives.

Overall objectives are the measurable goals set by management. The success or failure of the firm may be determined by comparing objectives with actual performance. Usually a combination of sales, profit, and other objectives are

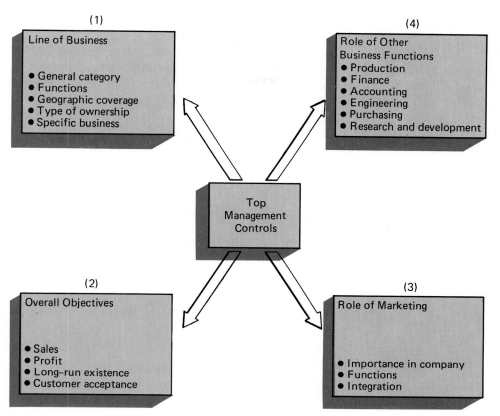

Figure 2-3
Factors Controlled by Top Management

stated by management for short-run (one year or less) and long-run (more than one year) time periods. Most firms recognize that customer acceptance is an important goal that has a strong effect on sales, profit, and long-run existence.

Management determines the role of marketing by noting its importance, outlining its functions, and integrating it into the overall operation of the firm. The importance of marketing in a firm is evident when marketing is given line (decision-making) authority, the rank of the chief marketing officer is equal to that of other areas (usually vice-president), and adequate resources are provided. Marketing is not considered important by a firm that gives marketing staff (advisory) status, places marketing in a subordinate position (such as reporting to the production vice-president), equates marketing with sales, and withholds the resources needed to research, advertise, and conduct other marketing activities.

The functions of marketing may be quite broad, including market research, new-product planning, inventory management, and many other marketing tasks; or they may be limited to selling or advertising but not include market research, planning, pricing, or credit. The larger marketing's role, the greater the likelihood of the firm having an integrated marketing organization. The smaller the role of marketing, the greater the possibility that the firm operates its marketing activities on a project, crisis, and fragmented basis.

The roles of other business functions and their interrelationships with marketing need to be delineated clearly in order to avoid overlaps, jealousy, and conflicts. Production, finance, accounting, engineering, purchasing, and research

The role of marketing refers to its importance, functions, and level of integration.

Cooperation between marketing and other functions is necessary.

and development departments each have different perspectives, orientations, and goals. This is discussed further in Chapter 3.

Mennen offers a good example of the impact of top management on marketers. At Mennen, two nonfamily members were recently hired to head the firm for the first time in its 100-year history. Mennen had fallen well behind its early competitors, particularly Procter & Gamble and Colgate-Palmolive, when the management team was shaken up. The new managers have redefined Mennen's line of business, from toiletries for men to a supplier of health and beauty aids for the family. An overall goal of doubling sales in four years was set. The role of marketing was elevated, as a group of marketing specialists was hired, the advertising budget was increased, and new-product planning was expanded. Conflicts among departments were resolved.[2]

After top management outlines the line of business, states overall company objectives, defines the role of marketing, and determines the role of other business functions, the marketing area begins to develop its controllable variables.

Factors Directed by Marketing

The major elements under the direction of the marketer are selection of a target market, marketing objectives, marketing organization, marketing plan, and control of the marketing plan. See Figure 2-4.

---

[2] "The Outsider's Touch That's Shaking Up Mennen," *Business Week* (February 1, 1982), pp. 58–59.

Figure 2-4
Factors Controlled by Marketing

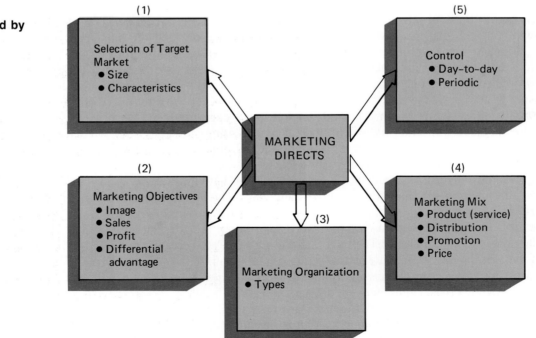

(1) Selection of Target Market
- Size
- Characteristics

(2) Marketing Objectives
- Image
- Sales
- Profit
- Differential advantage

MARKETING DIRECTS

(3) Marketing Organization
- Types

(4) Marketing Mix
- Product (service)
- Distribution
- Promotion
- Price

(5) Control
- Day-to-day
- Periodic

The selection of a ***target market*** (a defined customer group) involves two decisions, size and characteristics. A marketer can choose a very large target market, called mass marketing, or a small piece of the market, called market segmentation. In the latter instance, a marketing plan is tailored for a specific group of people; with mass marketing, a generalized marketing plan is developed. The marketer must also define the characteristics of people in the target market— such as male or female, married or single, and affluent or middle class—and key the marketing plan to these people.

> A ***target market*** is the customer group to which an organization appeals.

Marketing objectives are more customer-oriented than those set by top management. For example, marketers are extremely interested in the image consumers hold of the company and specific products. Sales objectives reflect a concern for brand loyalty (repeat purchase behavior), growth through new product introductions, and appeal to unsatisfied market segments. Profit objectives are set in per unit or total-profit terms. Last and most important, marketers seek to create a ***differential advantage,*** the set of unique features in a company's marketing program that causes consumers to patronize the company and not its competitors. Without a differential advantage, a company adopts a "me-too" philosophy and offers the consumer no reasons to select its offerings over a competitor's. A differential advantage can be achieved through a distinctive image, new products or features, product quality, availability, service, low prices, and other characteristics.

> ***Marketing objectives*** are highly consumer-oriented.

> A ***differential advantage*** consists of the firm's unique features that attract consumers.

A ***marketing organization*** is the structural arrangement for directing marketing functions. The organization outlines authority, responsibility, and tasks to be performed. Through the organization, functions are assigned and coordinated. An organization may be functional, with responsibility assigned on the basis of buying, selling, promotion, distribution, and other tasks; product-oriented, with product managers for each product category and brand managers for each individual brand in addition to functional categories; or market-oriented, with managers assigned on the basis of geographic markets and customer types in addition to functional categories. A single company may use a mixture of these forms. See Figure 2-5 for illustrations of the three organizational forms.

> A ***marketing organization*** may be functional, product-oriented, or market-oriented.

The ***marketing mix*** describes the specific combination of marketing elements used to achieve objectives and satisfy the target market. The mix consists of four major factors: product or service, distribution, promotion, and price. The marketer must select the combination of factors that is best for the firm. The marketing mix requires a number of decisions.

> The ***marketing mix*** consists of four elements: product or service, distribution, promotion, and price.

Product or service decisions involve determining what to sell, the level of quality, the number of items to sell, the innovativeness of the company, packaging, features (such as options and warranties), the level and timing of research, and when to drop existing offerings. Distribution decisions include whether to sell through middlemen or directly to consumers, how many outlets to sell through, whether to control or cooperate with other channel members, what purchasing terms to negotiate, selecting suppliers, determining which functions to assign to others, and identifying competitors.

Promotion decisions include the selection of a combination of tools (advertising, publicity, personal selling, and sales promotion), whether to share promotions and their costs with others, how to measure effectiveness, the image to pursue, the level of customer service, the choice of media (such as newspaper, television, radio, magazine), the format of messages, and ad timing throughout

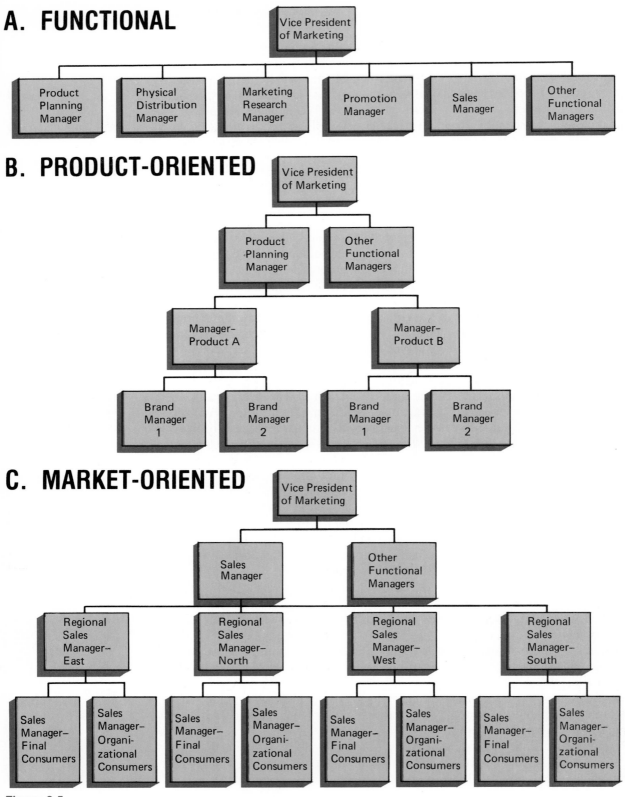

A. FUNCTIONAL

Vice President of Marketing

- Product Planning Manager
- Physical Distribution Manager
- Marketing Research Manager
- Promotion Manager
- Sales Manager
- Other Functional Managers

B. PRODUCT-ORIENTED

Vice President of Marketing

- Product Planning Manager
- Other Functional Managers

Manager– Product A
- Brand Manager 1
- Brand Manager 2

Manager– Product B
- Brand Manager 1
- Brand Manager 2

C. MARKET-ORIENTED

Vice President of Marketing

- Sales Manager
- Other Functional Managers

Regional Sales Manager– East
- Sales Manager– Final Consumers
- Sales Manager– Organizational Consumers

Regional Sales Manager– North
- Sales Manager– Final Consumers
- Sales Manager– Organizational Consumers

Regional Sales Manager– West
- Sales Manager– Final Consumers
- Sales Manager– Organizational Consumers

Regional Sales Manager– South
- Sales Manager– Final Consumers
- Sales Manager– Organizational Consumers

Figure 2-5
Illustrations of Marketing Organizations

the year or during peak periods. Price decisions include determining the overall level of prices (low, medium, or high), the range of prices (lowest to highest), the relationship between price and quality, the emphasis to place on price, how to react to competitors' prices, when to advertise prices, how prices are computed, and what billing terms to employ (such as a cash-only versus a credit policy).

In the development of a marketing mix, these four elements must be consistent with the selected target market and each other and be well integrated. For instance, neither a well-designed but poorly promoted product nor a well-promoted but overpriced product will normally be successful. Figure 2-6 shows three alternative marketing mixes available to a women's dress manufacturer.

An illustration of an appropriate marketing mix is one used by Canon for its cameras. The firm produces a complete line of camera products, with different models aimed at beginners, serious amateurs, and professional photographers. The simplest cameras have automatic focus and a built-in flash. They are sold through all types of retailers, including discounters and department stores. Advertising is concentrated on television and general magazines. These cameras retail for about $100. The most advanced cameras have superior features and a number of attachments. They are sold through camera stores and finer department stores. Advertising is concentrated on specialty magazines, with some television advertising. These cameras retail for several hundred dollars. Figure 2-7 shows one of Canon's simplest cameras.

The last, and extremely important, factor directed by a marketer involves *control:* monitoring and reviewing overall and specific performance. Evaluations should be conducted at regular intervals. The external environment and internal company data should be reviewed continuously. In-depth research and analysis of performance (marketing audits) should be completed at least once or twice each year. Revisions need to be accomplished when the external environment changes or the company encounters problems.

> A marketer's *control* involves monitoring and evaluating performance.

Uncontrollable Factors

Uncontrollable factors are those elements affecting an organization's performance that cannot be directed by the organization and its marketers. It must be recognized that any marketing plan, no matter how well conceived, may fail if adversely influenced by uncontrollable factors. Therefore, the external environment must be continually monitored and its effects incorporated into any marketing plan. Furthermore, contingency plans relating to uncontrollable variables should be an important part of a marketing plan. Uncontrollable variables that bear watching and anticipating are consumers, competition, government, the economy, technology, and independent media. See Figure 2-8.

> *Uncontrollable factors* influence an organization and its marketers, but cannot be directed by them.

Consumers

Although a marketer has control over the selection of a target market, he or she cannot control the characteristics of the population. Firms can react to but not

| ALTERNATIVES | PRODUCT | DISTRIBUTION | PROMOTION | PRICE |

High status/
high price

Moderate status/
moderate price

No status/
low price

Figure 2-6
Selected Alternative
Marketing Mixes for
Women's Dresses

Figure 2-7
**An Inexpensive Canon
Camera**

Reprinted by permission.

control these consumer characteristics: age, income, marital status, occupation, race, education, and place and type of residence. For example, although Gerber could develop new baby foods, it could not stop the decline in births. To continue growing, Gerber has had to expand into other products and services.

A marketer must understand the interpersonal influences on consumer behavior. The purchases that consumers make are affected by family, friends, religion, level of education, standards for performance, taboos, customs, and other factors

Organizations need to understand consumer characteristics, cultural and social factors, the decision process, and the impact of consumer groups.

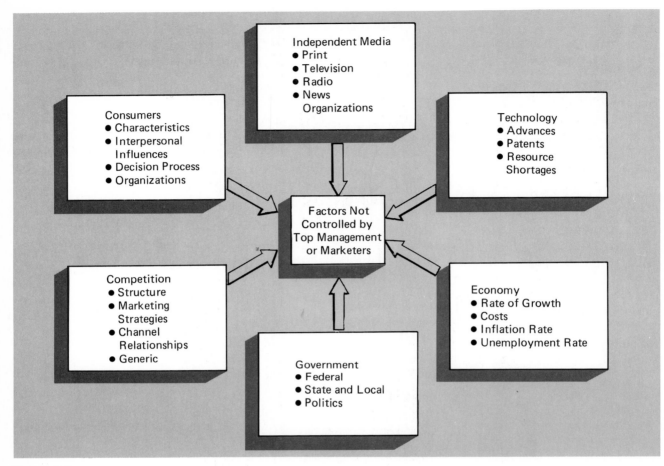

Figure 2-8
Uncontrollable Factors

that shape a culture and society. For instance, in some parts of the United States, stores are not allowed to open on Sundays, liquor sales are strictly regulated (as to prices, other goods that can be sold, days open, and who can buy alcoholic beverages), and movies are closely rated. In other parts of the United States, stores are regularly open seven days a week, liquor may be sold to eighteen-year-olds, and any movie can be shown uncut.

Because consumers act differently in purchasing various types of products and services, a marketer needs to comprehend the consumer's decision process. The decision process explains the steps a consumer goes through when buying a product. In the case of an automobile, the consumer carefully searches for information about a number of cars, ranks several alternatives, selects a favorite, negotiates terms, and finally completes the purchase. With a hamburger, the consumer looks at his or her watch, sees that it is lunchtime, and goes to a nearby fast-food outlet.

Today, consumer groups and organizations speak out on behalf of consumers at public hearings, stockholder meetings, and before the media. To avoid negative consequences brought on by active consumer groups, a marketer must communicate with consumers, anticipate problems, respond to complaints, and make sure that his or her company operates properly.

Competition

A firm's competitors frequently affect its marketing strategy and its success in attracting a target market. Therefore, the competitive structure facing a firm needs to be defined and analyzed. The four possible competitive structures are monopoly, oligopoly, monopolistic competition, and pure competition. Table 2-1 shows the characteristics of each of these structures.

In a ***monopoly,*** there is only one firm selling a particular product or service. This occurs in the United States when a firm has a patent (exclusive rights for seventeen years to a product it invented) or is allowed to be a public utility, such as a local power company. Depending on the product or service, the market may be small or large. Elasticity of demand (consumer sensitivity to price changes) depends on the need for the product. For public utilities, demand is usually relatively inelastic, meaning that people will continue to use the service no matter how high prices go.

One firm sells a product (service) and has control over marketing it in a *monopoly*.

A private-sector monopolist is able to control totally his or her marketing plan because of the unique nature of the product or service. Accordingly, the key marketing task is to maintain this uniqueness and not allow other firms to enter the market. As patents expire, competition generally increases. Public utilities are heavily regulated by government and must have their plans approved by it.

In an ***oligopoly,*** there are a few firms, generally large, that comprise most of an industry's sales. The automobile industry is a good illustration of this. The passenger car sales of General Motors, Ford, and Chrysler equal well over 90 per cent of all domestic automobiles sold in the United States. Other examples of

A limited number of large firms compete on nonprice factors in an *oligopoly*.

Table 2-1
Competitive Structures

Characteristics	Structures			
	Monopoly[a]	**Oligopoly**	**Monopolistic Competition**	**Pure Competition**
Number of firms	One	Few	Several	Many
Size of market for each firm	Small or large	Large	Small or large	Small
Elasticity of demand for each firm	Varies	Kinked	Varies	Elastic
Control of marketing plan	Total control of price, distribution, promotion, and product	Some control of price, distribution, promotion, and product	Some control of price, distribution, promotion, and product	No control of price; ineffective control of distribution, promotion, and product
Ease of entry	Difficult	Difficult	Easy	Easy
Differential advantage	Only source of product	Nonprice marketing factors	Any marketing factors	None
Key marketing task	Maintain unique product status	Differentiate product on nonprice factors	Differentiate product on any factors	Ensure supply of product at low prices and widespread distribution

[a] Characteristics of a private sector monopolist (e.g., a firm with a patent for a product). A public-sector monopolist is more closely regulated.

oligopolistic industries are flat glass, cereal breakfast foods, turbines and turbine engines, household refrigerators and freezers, electric lamps, and cigarettes.[3]

The market is often quite large and broken into various segments. Consumer elasticity of demand is kinked, which means that demand for one firm's offering will drop sharply if its prices are increased because other firms will not follow along and demand will increase only slightly if price is decreased because other firms will follow along. Because there are few firms, each is able to exert some control over its marketing plans. It is difficult for new firms to enter the market, because capital (factory and equipment) costs are usually high.

Oligopolistic firms seek to avoid price wars, which are costly and counterproductive. Instead, these firms offer similar prices and try to distinguish their products on the basis of image, options, color, delivery, and other features. To be successful, oligopolistic firms must get consumers to perceive their brands as distinctive: that is, that GE refrigerators really are better than Westinghouse or that Cheerios really taste better than Rice Chex.

Monopolistic competition occurs when there are several firms, each of which is trying to offer a unique marketing mix. In the U.S., monopolistic competition is the most common competitive structure, followed by oligopoly. Service stations, garment manufacturers, beauty salons, furniture manufacturers, and shoe retailers are examples of the firms operating under monopolistic competition. In each instance, a firm tries to attain a differential advantage through a mix of marketing variables that is different from competitors' and desirable to consumers.

Competition continues because a number of firms are making and/or selling essentially similar items. The size of the market depends on the necessity of the product. Control over price is based on how unique consumers view a particular brand or store to be. A firm can charge a higher price than the industry average and not lose sales if its product is viewed as distinct from the competition's. Through its combination of marketing variables, a firm is able to exert some control over its total marketing plan. However, in monopolistic competition, it is easy for new firms to enter the market because start-up costs are relatively low. For continued success, a company must continually revise its strategy and strive to remain differentiated.

Pure competition exists if there are many firms selling identical products or services. This situation occurs rarely in the United States and is most common for selected food items and commodities (and takes place only if there are a number of small firms competing with one another). The market for each firm is small; and demand is perfectly elastic, because price increases result in no sales and price decreases result in losses for the firm. There is no control over price and, because merchandise is standardized, little control over the other marketing variables. It is easy for new firms to enter the market.

In pure competition, no differential advantage is possible because prices and products are the same. It is essential that a firm develop a reputation for reliability, sell items at the lowest profitable prices, and convince as many distributors and retailers as possible to stock the merchandise.

After determining the characteristics of the market structure facing the firm, it must evaluate the marketing strategies of its competitors. Specifically, the firm

A number of firms offer a variety of marketing mixes in monopolistic competition.

Numerous firms sell the same items, without a differential advantage, in pure competition.

[3] See Paul MacAvoy, "Learning to Love Oligopolies," *New York Times* (September 28, 1980), p. F2.

must determine which markets are saturated and which are unfulfilled, the marketing plans and target markets of competitors, the images of competitors, the differential advantages of competitors, and the extent to which consumers are content with the level of service and quality provided by the competition.

The firm also needs to examine existing channel relationships. In well-established industries, such as the supermarket industry, long-run relationships have been built up among manufacturers, wholesalers, and retailers. These relationships become assets as much as any raw materials or equipment. New firms may be unable to place products in channels like these, and existing firms may find it easy to place even the most innovative of products. For a firm such as Procter & Gamble, a great asset is its ability to place a new soap or detergent product into virtually every supermarket across the United States.

Finally, the firm should define its competition in generic terms, which means as broadly as possible. For instance, the competition for a movie theater is not just other movie theaters, but also television, sporting events, operas, plays, amusement parks, schools (continuing education programs), radio, reading materials, and parties. The theater owner needs to ask, "What can I do to compete with a whole variety of entertainment and recreation forms, in terms of movie selection, prices, hours, refreshments, parking, and the like?"

> Competition should be defined in generic terms— meaning as widely as possible.

Government

For more than ninety years, the U.S. Congress has enacted a large amount of federal legislation that defines and controls the operations of business. During the early part of the twentieth century, this legislation was oriented toward protecting small businesses from large businesses. Laws involved antitrust, discriminatory pricing, and unfair trade practices. In the 1960s and 1970s, legislation was geared toward helping the consumer deal with deceptive and unsafe business practices. The late 1970s and early 1980s have seen a move toward greater deregulation of business.[4] Table 2-2 contains a listing of the main federal legislation affecting marketing. The *Federal Trade Commission (FTC)* is the major federal regulatory agency that monitors restraint of trade and enforces rules against unfair methods of competition.

> Federal legislation deals with issues pertaining to interstate commerce. The *Federal Trade Commission (FTC)* is most responsible for enforcing this legislation.

In addition to federal legislation and agencies, each state and local government has its own legal environment for firms operating within its boundaries. Laws regulate where a firm may locate, the hours it may be open, the types of items that may be sold, whether it may operate door-to-door, if unit pricing is required, and how merchandise must be labeled or dated.

> Every state and local government has regulations for firms.

State and local governments also provide incentives for companies to operate. Recently, *Inc.* magazine rated each of the fifty states' attractiveness for small business on the basis of capital resources, labor, taxes, state support (small business assistance), and business activity (such as population change, employment gain, personal income change). Texas, California, Colorado, New York, Minnesota, Florida, Massachusetts, New Mexico, Connecticut, and New Jersey were ranked the highest.[5]

---

[4] See Joel Blecke, "Deregulation: Riding the Rapids," *Business Horizons,* Vol. 26 (May–June 1983), pp. 15–25; "Deregulating America," *Business Week* (November 28, 1983), pp. 80–96; and "The Airlines' Dangerous Game with Fares," *Business Week* (March 5, 1984), pp. 33 ff.

[5] "Rating the States on Five Major Factors," *Inc.* (October 1983), pp. 140–142 ff. See also, Julien J. Studley Inc. "Rating the Cities," *Advertising Age* (January 23, 1984), pp. 16, 18.

Table 2-2 Key Federal Legislation Affecting Marketers

Year	Legislation	Major Purpose
A. Antitrust, Discriminatory Pricing, and Unfair Trade Practices		
1890	Sherman Act	To eliminate monopolies and sustain competition
1914	Clayton Act	To prohibit specific anticompetitive practices, such as tie-in sales, exclusive dealing, and price discrimination
1914	Federal Trade Commission (FTC) Act	To establish an independent regulatory agency to eliminate monopolies and restraint of trade and to enforce rules against unfair methods of competition
1936	Robinson-Patman Act	To prohibit price discrimination against channel members buying the same merchandise
1937	Miller-Tydings Act (repealed by Consumer Goods Pricing Act of 1975)	To permit retail price maintenance (price fixing) in order to protect small retailers against large chains and discounters
1938	Wheeler-Lea Amendment	To revise the FTC Act of 1914 to include unfair or deceptive practices
1946	Lanham Trademark Act	To protect and regulate trademarks and brand names
1950	Celler-Kefauver Antimerger Act	To limit or prohibit the acquisition of competitors or their assets if the effects of the acquisition would lessen competition
B. Consumer Protection		
1906	Food and Drug Act	To prohibit adulteration and misbranding of food and drugs, create the Food and Drug Administration, and regulate meat packing and shipping
1906	Meat Inspection Act	
1914	Federal Trade Commission Act	To establish an agency and provisions for protecting consumer rights
1938	Wheeler-Lea Amendment	
1939	Wood Products Labeling Act	To require wool products, fur products, and textile products to show contents and to prohibit sales of dangerous flammables
1951	Fur Products Labeling Act	
1953	Flammable Fabrics Act	
1958	Textile Fiber Identification Act	
1958	Food Additives Amendment	To prohibit food additives causing cancer, require the labeling of hazardous household products, and require drug manufacturers to demonstrate product effectiveness and safety
1960	Federal Hazardous Substances Labeling Act	
1962	Kefauver-Harris Drug Amendment	
1966	Fair Packaging and Labeling Act	To require packages to be labeled honestly and reduce package size proliferation

The political environment often signals legislation and government actions.

The political environment often affects legislation. Consumerism, nationalism, tax cuts, zoning, wage rates, unemployment, and other items are almost always discussed and debated through the political process before legislation is enacted. The issues of today frequently become the laws of tomorrow. A strength of the American political system is its continuity, which enables businesspeople to develop marketing strategies for long periods of time.

Economy

Economic growth is measured by changes in the *Gross National Product (GNP)*.

The rate of economic growth is the annual increase in a region's or country's economy. The *Gross National Product (GNP)* measures the annual volume of goods and services produced in a country. When certain industries, such as automobile and housing, slow down, repercussions are often felt in other areas, such

Table 2-2 Key Federal Legislation Affecting Marketers (Continued)

Year	Legislation	Major Purpose
1966	National Traffic and Motor Vehicle Safety Act	To set safety standards for automobiles and tires
1966	Child Protection Act	To ban hazardous products used by children, create standards for child-resistant packages for hazardous products, and provide drug information
1969	Child Protection and Toy Safety Act	
1970	Poison Prevention Labeling Act	
1972	Drug Listing Act	
1966	Cigarette Labeling Act	To require health warnings on cigarette packages and ban cigarette advertising on radio and television
1970	Public Health Smoking Act	
1967	Wholesome Meat Act	To mandate federal inspection standards
1968	Wholesome Poultry Products Act	
1968	Consumer Credit Protection Act	To have full disclosure of credit and loan terms and rates and regulate reporting and use of credit information
1970	Fair Credit Reporting Act	
1972	Consumer Product Safety Act	To create the Consumer Product Safety Commission and set safety standards
1975	Magnuson-Moss Consumer Product Warranty Act	To regulate warranties and set disclosure requirements
1975	Consumer Goods Pricing Act	To repeal the Miller-Tydings Act which permitted retail price maintenance
1980	Fair Debt Collection Act	To eliminate the harrassment of debtors and ban false statements to collect debts
1980	FTC Improvement Act	To reduce the power of the FTC to implement industrywide trade regulations (This Act reversed the trend toward increased federal government protection of consumers)
C. Industry Deregulation		
1978	Natural Gas Policy Act	To make the natural gas, airline, trucking, railroad, and banking industries more competitive
1978	Airline Deregulation Act	
1980	Motor Carrier Act	
1980	Staggers Rail Act	
1981	Depository Institutions Deregulatory Committee Act	
1981	Depository Institutions Act	

as insurance and home furnishings. A high rate of growth means the economy in the region or country is usually good and marketing potential large.

Of prime importance to marketers are the perceptions of consumers regarding the economy. If they believe the economy will be favorable, they will increase spending. If they believe the economy will be poor, they will cut back on spending. See Figure 2-9.

Several of the costs of doing business are generally beyond the control of the firm. These include raw materials, unionized labor wages, interest rates, machinery, and office (factory) rental. If costs rise by a large amount, marketing flexibility is limited and lower profit margins may be necessary. When costs are stable, marketers have much greater opportunities to differentiate their offerings and expand sales.

Business costs affect marketing flexibility.

When widespread cost increases drive prices up, the result is a high rate of

Figure 2-9
Consumer Optimism/
Pessimism Affects the
Economy

Reprinted by permission.

With high inflation or
unemployment, consumers
may cut back on some
purchases. *Real income*
describes earnings after
adjusting for inflation.

inflation; and the prices of some goods and services may go beyond the reach of many consumers; or consumers may be forced to alter their spending habits. For example, in 1981 the interest rate on mortgages reached 15 to 19 per cent, and the purchases of homes dropped dramatically.

Of importance to the marketer is what happens to ***real income,*** income adjusted for inflation, over time. For example, a marketer would not be concerned if a person's net income (after taxes) went from $15,000 to $20,000 per year while the price of food went from $100 to $120 per week. Income would have increased by 33⅓ per cent, while food prices rose 20 per cent. Therefore, real income would have increased, and there would be more money available for items other than food. On the other hand, if net income changed from $15,000 to $18,000 per year and food prices jumped from $100 to $150 per week, real income would decline (income up by 20 per cent; food up by 50 per cent) and there would be less money left for nonfood purchases.

A high rate of unemployment adversely affects marketers, because people cut back on luxuries wherever possible. Low unemployment leads to increased sales of large-ticket items, as consumers are optimistic and willing to spend their earnings. In recent years, it has been extremely difficult for the U.S. economy to achieve low rates of inflation and unemployment at the same time.

Technology

Technology refers to the development and use of machinery, products, and processes. Many technological advances are beyond the control of individual firms, especially smaller ones. For example, no firm has been able to develop a cure for the common cold, and small retailers are presently unable to afford the latest advances in physical distribution management.

Technology includes machinery, products, and processes.

Patents (exclusive rights to sell new products or services for seventeen years) have limited lifespans. When a company loses patent protection, competition may increase sharply because other firms are able to use the original firm's techniques. In the late 1970s Kodak entered the self-developing camera market because Polaroid's early patents had expired.

As organizations head into the end of the twentieth century, they must realize the need for improved technology in order to remain competitive in foreign markets and to minimize the impact of resource shortages. Oil, clean air, clean water, and skilled craftspeople are among the declining resources that must be rechanneled.

Independent Media

Independent media are not controlled by the firm; they can influence the government's, consumers', and public's perceptions of a company's products and overall image. The media can provide positive or negative coverage of a company when it produces a new product, pollutes the air, mislabels merchandise, contributes to charity, or otherwise performs a newsworthy activity. This coverage may be by print media, television, radio, or news organizations. For all of these reasons, the company should willingly distribute information to the independent press and always try to get the company's position written or spoken about.

Independent media can influence perceptions of a company's products and overall image.

It is important to note that, although the coverage of company information releases by independent media is uncontrollable, paid advertising is controllable by the marketer. Although media may reject advertising, if accepted it must be presented in the time interval and form stipulated by the firm.

Attainment of Objectives, Feedback, and Adaptation

Together, controllable and uncontrollable factors affect success or failure.

Feedback provides information, which enables an organization to adapt to the environment.

Marketing myopia is an inefficient, complacent marketing approach.

The organization's level of success or failure in reaching its objectives depends on how well it directs and implements its controllable factors and the impact of uncontrollable factors on the marketing plan. As shown in Figure 2-2, it is the interaction of the organization's total offering and the uncontrollable environment that determines its success or failure.

In order to improve the marketing effort and ensure long-run attainment of objectives, the organization needs to acquire **feedback** (information about the uncontrollable environment, the organization's performance, and how well the marketing plan is received). Feedback is obtained by measuring consumer satisfaction, looking at competitive trends, evaluating the relationship with government agencies, monitoring the economy and potential resource shortages, reading or viewing the independent media, analyzing sales and profit trends, talking with channel members, and employing other methods of obtaining and assessing information.

After evaluating feedback, the firm needs to **adapt** its strategy to the surrounding environment, while continuing to utilize its differential advantage(s). To ensure long-term success, the firm must continually look for new opportunities that fit into its overall market plan and are attainable by the firm and respond to potential threats by revising marketing policies.

Marketing myopia, a short-sighted, narrow-minded view of marketing and its environment,[6] must be avoided at all costs:

The DuPonts and Cornings have succeeded not primarily because of their product or research orientation but because they have been thoroughly customer-oriented also. It is constant watchfulness for opportunities to apply their technical know-how to the creation of customer-satisfying uses which accounts for their prodigious output of successful new products.[7]

Following are the adaptation approaches of two different organizations: General Foods and Greyhound. Each of these companies has had to modify its marketing approach in the face of a dynamic environment.

During the 1970s, General Foods followed a relatively conservative marketing philosophy. It emphasized moderate sales and profit growth for its processed meats, pet foods, cereals, coffee, instant beverages, and other lines. But this approach caused the firm to stagnate in 1980 and 1981, for a variety of reasons. The overall market for food grew by only 1 per cent annually; and General Foods was not represented in many growth segments, such as poultry, fresh baked goods, and low-calorie soft drinks. Coffee consumption in the U.S. had peaked, and Procter & Gamble's Folger's aggressively competed with General Foods' Maxwell House. The firm's Burger Chef restaurant chain and a number of products failed.

At this point, General Foods' management changed the course of the company, "from margin protection to volume building." Oscar Mayer, a meat proc-

---

[6] Theodore Levitt, "Marketing Myopia," *Harvard Business Review,* Vol. 53 (September–October 1975), pp. 26–44, 173–181.
[7] Ibid., p. 27.

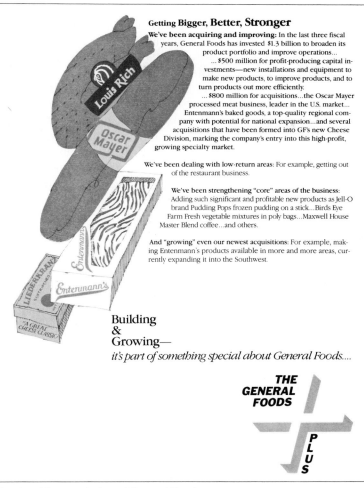

Figure 2-10
An Ambitious General Foods

Getting Bigger, Better, Stronger

We've been acquiring and improving: In the last three fiscal years, General Foods has invested $1.3 billion to broaden its product portfolio and improve operations...

...$500 million for profit-producing capital investments—new installations and equipment to make new products, to improve products, and to turn products out more efficiently.

...$800 million for acquisitions...the Oscar Mayer processed meat business, leader in the U.S. market... Entenmann's baked goods, a top-quality regional company with potential for national expansion...and several acquisitions that have been formed into GF's new Cheese Division, marking the company's entry into this high-profit, growing specialty market.

We've been dealing with low-return areas: For example, getting out of the restaurant business.

We've been strengthening "core" areas of the business: Adding such significant and profitable new products as Jell-O brand Pudding Pops frozen pudding on a stick...Birds Eye Farm Fresh vegetable mixtures in poly bags...Maxwell House Master Blend coffee...and others.

And "growing" even our newest acquisitions: For example, making Entenmann's products available in more and more areas, currently expanding it into the Southwest.

Building & Growing—
it's part of something special about General Foods....

THE GENERAL FOODS PLUS

Reprinted by permission of General Foods.

essor, and Entenmann's, a fresh baked goods maker, were acquired. New distribution systems were used, refrigerated goods shipped through Oscar Mayer and fresh goods through 800 Entenmann's trucks. Health-oriented cereals were developed. Frozen Jello-O Pudding Pops were introduced, with the potential for $100 million in annual sales. Sanka commercials no longer used Robert Young, but focused on more active people. New low-calorie Kool-Aid featured aspartame artificial sweetener. Marketing managers were encouraged to be more aggressive and take greater risks. It was no longer "relaxing" to work at General Foods.[8] See Figure 2-10.

In November 1982, the U.S. bus industry was deregulated by federal legislation. This meant that bus companies, like airlines before them, would be able to select the routes they served and change prices frequently. Until deregulation, the bus companies were required to serve unprofitable markets and could only revise prices after prior notification of the federal government. For Greyhound, the

[8] Jeremy Main, "General Foods Goes Back to Growing," *Fortune* (January 10, 1983), pp. 92–95; and Nancy Giges, "General Foods Sees Growth in Drink Mixes," *Advertising Age* (March 12, 1984), pp. 2 ff.

industry leader with 60 per cent of the passengers traveling on regularly scheduled intercity bus routes, deregulation meant substantial alterations in its environment and the marketing approach it employed.

Greyhound managers were encouraged to utilize "competitive thinking" to identify profitable and unprofitable markets. During 1983, Greyhound petitioned the Interstate Commerce Commission to add 2,200 miles of new routes in 44 states and to drop 1,100 points (markets) it served. In response to criticism that it was dropping some markets because of "greed," Greyhound commented that opportunities would now exist for smaller, regional bus lines. Management was decentralized by Greyhound to capitalize on the flexibility granted by deregulation. For example, pricing specialists in six regional offices were given the authority to instantly revise prices. This replaced a headquarters' pricing committee that required 60 to 90 days to act. Fleet maintenance, through regional centers, received highest priority. See Figure 2-11. Greyhound also planned to expand its package-delivery business via buses.

Three factors continue to concern Greyhound, and management is working to deal with each. First, price competition from airlines has increased due to the deregulation of that industry. Greyhound needs to underprice the airlines to maintain a competitive edge. Second, its labor costs are high. Greyhound has actively tried to reduce these costs, incurring a massive labor strike in late 1983 (which resulted in a total compensation reduction of 15 per cent for existing employees). Third, potential price wars, like one started by Trailways in 1982, could plague the bus line industry as they have airlines. Greyhound is seeking price stability.[9]

Summary

The environment of marketing encompasses all of the controllable factors that are utilized by a firm and its marketers to achieve established objectives as well as the uncontrollable factors that influence the ability of a firm and its marketers to achieve these objectives.

Controllable variables are the elements of a strategy that are determined by the firm and its marketers. Top management decides on the line of business, overall objectives, the role of marketing, and the role of other business functions. Marketing directs the selection of a target market, the marketing mix (product or service, distribution, promotion, and price), and the control function. In addition, it is the responsibility of marketing to create a differential advantage, the set of unique factors in a company's marketing program that causes consumers to patronize the company and not its competitors.

Uncontrollable variables are the elements affecting an overall strategy that cannot be directed by the firm and its marketers. Among the most important uncontrollable variables are consumers, competition, government, the economy, technology, and the independent media.

[9] Steven Greenhouse, "The Reshaping of Greyhound," *New York Times* (November 5, 1983), pp. 35–36; "Greyhound: A Big Sell-Off Leaves It Built for Better Speed," *Business Week* (July 25, 1983), pp. 88, 90; "Deregulation Will Take Bus Lines on a Tough Ride," *Business Week* (July 11, 1983), pp. 66, 68; and Agis Salpukas, "Bullish Views on Greyhound," *New York Times* (March 16, 1984), p. D4.

Figure 2-11
Fleet Maintenance at Greyhound
Round-the-clock maintenance of Greyhound's fleet of modern intercity buses receives the highest priority. The San Francisco facility, pictured here, is one of 11 major maintenance centers operated by the company nationwide.

Reprinted by permission.

An organization's level of success or failure is based on the interaction of controllable and uncontrollable factors. When implementing a marketing strategy, a marketer obtains feedback from the environment and adjusts the strategy to correct any deficiencies. Marketing myopia must be avoided.

Questions for Discussion

1. Explain the environment of marketing. Relate your answer to Levi Strauss.
2. What may occur if an organization does not analyze its entire environment in a systematic manner?
3. Why are the factors controlled by top management usually considered uncontrollable by marketers? How should marketers respond to this situation?
4. Why would top management in some companies give marketing only staff status, place it in a subordinate position, equate marketing with sales, and give it inadequate resources?
5. For each of the following, specify two to three overall management objectives and two to three marketing objectives. How do they differ?
   a. Newspaper publisher.
   b. Trucking firm.
   c. Florist.
   d. Public library.
6. How do marketing objectives influence the selection of a target market?

7. What is the differential advantage for each of these?
   a. McDonald's.
   b. *People* magazine.
   c. Sony televisions.
   d. Your college or university.
8. A manufacturer of women's watches, priced from $50 to $100, markets its products nationally through mail-order retailers and department stores. Draw an organization chart for the company and explain it.
9. Distinguish between the marketing mixes used by Cadillac and Chevrolet, two car lines of General Motors.
10. Since marketers can choose the target market to which they want their products or services to appeal, why are consumers considered to be uncontrollable?
11. Why do some industries become oligopolistic and others result in monopolistic competition? What does this mean for firms in these industries?
12. Deregulation represents both opportunities and potential problems for organizations. Offer several examples of both.
13. Differentiate between inflation and real income. Which concept is more crucial for marketers? Explain your answer.
14. If technological advances continue, how will smaller firms (unable to afford the advances) be able to compete with their more efficient, larger counterparts?
15. How should marketers interact with the independent media?
16. Comment on this statement: "By defining competition in generic terms, acquiring information about the uncontrollable environment, and modifying strategy when necessary, an organization will avoid marketing myopia and guarantee its long-term success."

Case 1 Good Humor: Marketing Ice Cream Products*

Good Humor began in the early 1920s, when a local confectioner introduced chocolate-covered ice cream on a stick. From one store in Youngstown, Ohio, Good Humor developed into a company marketing its products in 35 states. In 1982, 150 million frozen dessert items were sold.

But now, Good Humor (a division of Thomas J. Lipton since 1961) is moving away from its traditional novelty image, which relied on the "Good Humor man" and white ice-cream trucks. The company is seeking less seasonal sales, an image as a maker of quality ice cream, and a broader consumer market for its creations.

Good Humor's products are divided into four categories: ices, ice-cream cookies, traditional ice cream on sticks, and new items (such as Sunkist juice bars). During 1983, the company tested marketed Finger Bar water ice, Strawberry Colada (crushed strawberries and coconut), Jumbo Jet Star water ice, Banana Chuck (ice cream, chocolate, and peanuts), and King Cone (a chocolate-coated ice cream cone). In 1984, it added Fat Frog (green-colored vanilla ice cream with a chocolate back), Shark (grape ice), and other new products. Good

---

* The data in this case are drawn from Nancy Giges, "Good Humor Out to Shake Novelty Image," *Advertising Age* (August 15, 1983), pp. 4, 66; and "Good Humor Warms Up to Ice Novelties," *Advertising Age* (January 30, 1984), p. 70.

Humor decided not to become involved with frozen yogurt. "People eat Good Humor because they want a treat, and they are not thinking about calories. We don't want to change the image too much."

From 50 percent of sales in 1980, truck-and-street vending dropped to 15 per cent of sales in 1983 as Good Humor placed greater effort on distribution through grocery and convenience stores. This was consistent with the firm's intention to reduce seasonal sales and expand geographically. In 1983, Good Humor focused on 12 major markets in order to utilize network television advertising in those areas.

Good Humor products are often premium priced. The ice-cream cookies are sold four for $2.99. The Sunkist juice bars are sold four for $1.49.

Good Humor recognizes that ice-cream industry sales are relatively flat and competition is intense. It views its major competitors as Popsicle, Eskimo Pie, Chipwich, and Pudding Pops.

QUESTIONS

1. Based on the information contained in the case, what is the differential advantage of Good Humor? What is its current image?
2. Evaluate Good Humor's marketing mix. Can it be successful in the long run?
3. Has Good Humor defined its competition properly? Explain your answer.
4. Do you agree with Good Humor's decision not to market frozen yogurt? Why or why not?

Case 2 Kero-Sun: Reacting to an Uncertain Environment†

William Litwin founded Kero-Sun, which became the leading manufacturer of kerosene home heaters, in 1975 after seeing how a kerosene heater was used on a boat. After selling 50 heaters imported from Japan the first year, business rose so rapidly that Litwin left his job as an airline pilot to manage Kero-Sun. The sales boom was largely due to the high prices of oil heat and the relative value of kerosene heaters. During 1982, Kero-Sun's sales exceeded $150 million, representing over one million heaters (about 20 per cent of industry volume).

Despite its success, Kero-Sun faced an uncertain environment in 1982 and 1983. While the industry began to blossom less than a decade ago, by 1983 there were more than 70 competitors. Panasonic and Sears were just two of the larger firms marketing kerosene heaters. Many retailers started carrying competing brands in addition to Kero-Sun. For the most part, Kero-Sun's prices remained 10 to 30 per cent higher than competitors, since it stressed product quality and service. Its best-selling models had retail list prices of $249 and $289.

For a number of years, safety experts expressed concern about the risks of fire from tipped-over kerosene heaters. To combat this concern, kerosene heaters were improved significantly to minimize tip-overs and snuff out lighted wicks. Through intensive lobbying, several states removed restrictions on kerosene

† The data in this case are drawn from Maria Shao, "Kero-Sun, the Pioneer in Kerosene Heaters, Struggles as Growth Slows, Rivals Emerge," *Wall Street Journal* (December 17, 1982), p. 29.

home heaters as of mid-1981. However, a *Consumer Reports* cover story in October 1982 dealt a severe blow to the industry. The *Consumer Reports* story criticized kerosene heaters as a fire hazard, called them a "significant health hazard" as a result of air pollutants released by the heaters, and recommended that the heaters not be purchased. Kero-Sun filed a $41 million libel suit against the magazine, accusing it of 80 erroneous statements in the article. Kero-Sun also took out a number of newspaper ads and hired outside testing laboratories.

Throughout these developments, Kero-Sun remained detached from the rest of the industry, refusing to join the National Kerosene Heater Association. Said a spokesperson, "I hope it doesn't sound like ego, but we're more sophisticated than they are. They'd ride on our coattails."

In December 1983, after months of difficulties, Kero-Sun announced that it was filing for bankruptcy.

QUESTIONS
1. Evaluate Kero-Sun's approach to its environment.
2. Describe the risks taken by Kero-Sun in filing a libel suit against *Consumer Reports*.
3. Comment on the statement: "This company has been self-confident, almost smug in our perception of how people view us. The fact is, the first few years, we didn't have to sell. We just took orders."
4. Recommend a five-step plan Kero-Sun could have followed to operate better in the marketing environment it faced. Would it have been able to avoid bankruptcy if the plan was followed? Explain your answer.

Chapter 3

Strategic Planning in Marketing

1. To define strategic planning and consider its importance in marketing
2. To study the different types of marketing plans
3. To examine the relationships between marketing and the other functional areas in the organization
4. To thoroughly describe the steps in the strategic planning process: defining organizational mission, establishing strategic business units, setting marketing objectives, situation analysis, developing marketing strategy, implementing tactics, and monitoring results
5. To present examples of strategic marketing plans in diverse companies

*T*en years ago, Worth Sports Company concentrated on low-grade baseballs, whose market was virtually disappearing. Sales were about $4 million annually. Recognizing its shortcomings, Worth changed course and entered the expanding softball market. Today, annual sales exceed $30 million and Worth is the leading maker of softballs and softball bats— with a 40 per cent market share of softballs and 20 per cent for all kinds of bats. The firm is also recognized as a pioneer, having introduced a laser timing device (named Swing Ray) to record a player's bat speed and help the player determine his or her perfect bat. See Figure 3-1.

Figure 3-1
Worth Sports Company's
Swing Ray

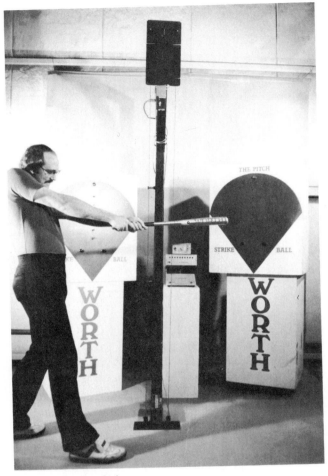

Reprinted by permission.

Worth's accomplishments are due to its adherence to a well-defined marketing strategy:

- Worth realizes that a distinctive strategy is necessary to compete with the larger firms making Louisville Slugger bats and Dudley softballs. It cannot employ a "me-too" philosophy.
- Worth engages in extensive new-product planning and development.
- Sales personnel spend time working in every phase of the manufacturing process; and they are given exclusive territorial rights, which increases their loyalty. They are more knowledgeable than competitors' salespeople.
- Continuous marketing research is used to measure customers' needs. Even though Worth has an 80 per cent market share for low-priced softballs, it developed a new polyurethane-core ball when research showed demand existed for high-quality softballs.
- Formal plans are devised and followed. By sticking to a five-year plan to introduce and improve an aluminum bat, Worth was able to revolu-

tionize the market (which consisted only of wood bats). Metal bats now account for two thirds of industry bat sales.
- New and broader distribution methods are sought. By adding Sears, J. C. Penney, and Montgomery Ward stores, Worth has expanded the size of its potential market.[1]

While strategic marketing plans are generally associated with large firms, Worth Sports Company illustrates that a small firm can also benefit by planning its strategy in a structured manner. Further, any organization must recognize that its long-term success depends on continually appraising its marketing plans, and not falling into the trap of marketing myopia.

The Importance of Strategic Planning in Marketing

As described in Chapter 2, the environment within which marketing operates includes a number of factors directed by top management and others directed by marketing. In order to coordinate these factors and provide guidance for decision making, it is quite useful to employ a formal strategic planning process. From a marketing perspective, a **strategic plan** outlines what marketing actions a firm should undertake, why these actions are necessary, who is responsible for carrying them out, where they will be accomplished, and how they will be completed.[2] It also determines a firm's current position, future orientation, and allocation of resources.

Strategic planning in marketing has several distinctive characteristics. A strategic marketing plan

Top management and marketing activities are guided and coordinated through a strategic plan.

1. Uses strategic business units (not product lines or company divisions) as the basis for planning efforts. The strategic business unit concept is discussed later in this chapter.
2. Focuses on the interaction of all strategic business units.
3. Relies on data from marketing information systems, marketing research, sales departments, the accounting department, and other areas.
4. Utilizes competitive analysis, productivity analysis, and planning models to apportion resources.
5. Capitalizes on an organization's ability to develop, maintain, and defend a specific position in the market.
6. Considers both short-term and long-term implications of decisions.
7. Incorporates environmental analysis and contingency plans, so that shifts or trends are adapted to in a timely manner.

A discussion of strategic planning in marketing is presented early in the text for several reasons. One, a strategic plan gives direction to an organization's

[1] Curtis Hartman, "Changing How the Game Is Played," *Inc.* (March 1983), pp. 94–96 ff.
[2] David W. Cravens, Gerald E. Hills, and Robert B. Woodruff, *Marketing Decision Making: Concepts and Strategy,* Revised Edition (Homewood, Ill.: Richard D. Irwin, 1980), p. 448.

efforts and better enables it to understand the dimensions of marketing research, consumer analysis, product planning, distribution planning, promotion planning, and price planning. Two, a strategic plan makes sure that each division in an organization has clear objectives that are integrated with overall company objectives. Three, different functional areas are encouraged to coordinate their efforts. Four, strategic planning forces an organization to assess its strengths and weaknesses in terms of competitors and opportunities and threats in the environment. Five, alternative actions or combinations of actions that an organization can take are outlined. Six, a basis for allocating resources is established. Seven, the value of enacting a procedure for assessing performance can be demonstrated.

The role of marketing in strategic planning is expanding at many organizations.

According to a recent study of chief executive officers, strategic planning is becoming more closely aligned with marketing:

> The future of the game appears to be marketing in one's own backyard and to obtain a bigger piece of an admittedly finite market. Planners are being forced down off their pedestals and into the organizational trenches.

One of every five firms with annual sales under $100 million has a formal planning department. Almost all companies with annual sales of $2 billion or more have them. In these firms, there is greater interest in fast-track marketing executives with strong operations experience.[3]

Types of Marketing Plans

Marketing plans can be categorized by duration, scope, and method of development. Plans range from short-run, specific, and department-generated to long-run, broad, and management-generated. See Figure 3-2.

Short-run marketing plans are quite precise; long-run plans outline needs.

Marketing plans may be short run (typically one year), moderate in length (two to five years), or long run (five to ten or even fifteen years). Many firms rely on a combination of these plans. Short-run and moderate-length plans are more detailed and operational in nature than long-run plans. For example, a one-year plan might describe precise marketing objectives and strategies for every product offered by the firm, while a fifteen-year plan might be confined to forecasting the environment during that period and determining the organization's long-term needs.[4]

Consumer products firms are most likely to employ separate plans for each line.

The scope of marketing plans also varies. There may be separate marketing plans for each of the firm's major products and services; a single, integrated marketing plan encompassing all products and services; or a broad business plan with a section devoted to marketing. Separate marketing plans for each product line are most often used by consumer products manufacturers; a single, integrated marketing plan is most often used by service firms; and a broad business plan is most often used by industrial products manufacturers.[5]

---

[3] Elizabeth M. Fowler, "A Need for Strategic Planners," *New York Times* (October 12, 1983), p. D25. See also, Richard Hise and Stephen McDaniel," CEOs' Views on Strategy: A Survey, *"Journal of Business Strategy,* Vol. 4 (Winter 1984), pp. 79–86.

[4] David S. Hopkins, *The Marketing Plan* (New York: Conference Board, 1981), p. 10.

[5] Ibid., p. 4.

Figure 3-2
Categorizing Marketing Plans

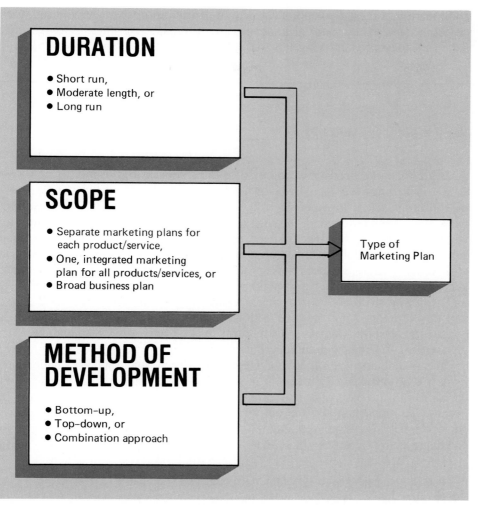

DURATION

- Short run,
- Moderate length, or
- Long run

SCOPE

- Separate marketing plans for each product/service,
- One, integrated marketing plan for all products/services, or
- Broad business plan

METHOD OF DEVELOPMENT

- Bottom-up,
- Top-down, or
- Combination approach

Type of Marketing Plan

Last, marketing plans can be developed through either a bottom-up or top-down approach. In the bottom-up approach, information from salespeople, product managers, advertising personnel, and other marketing areas is used to establish objectives, budgets, forecasts, timetables, and marketing mixes. Bottom-up plans are realistic (they are based on field reports) and good for morale (those who participate in the planning process are responsible for implementation). However, there may be difficulties in coordinating each bottom-up plan to attain one integrated plan and in incorporating different assumptions about the same concept, such as conflicting estimates about the impact of advertising on a new product's sales.

The problems of bottom-up plans are resolved in the top-down approach, which centrally directs and controls planning activities. Staff planners must seek approval of their rough plans from higher-level personnel. A top-down plan can utilize complex assumptions about competition or other external factors and provide a uniform direction for the marketing effort. Nonetheless, input from lower-level managers is not actively sought and morale may be diminished. A

Bottom-up plans foster significant employee input; top-down plans are set by senior management.

combination of these two approaches could be used if top management set overall objectives and policy, and sales, advertising, product, and other personnel established the plans for carrying out the policy.

Strengthening Relationships Between Marketing and Other Functional Areas in an Organization

The contrasting perspectives of marketing and other functional areas need to be reconciled.

Strategic planning needs to accommodate the distinct needs of marketing as well as the other functional areas in an organization. This is not always simple, due to the different orientations of each area, as shown in Table 3-1. For example, marketing seeks tailor-made products, flexible budgets, unique expenditures, a variety of product versions, frequent purchases, customer-driven new products, and aggressive actions against competitors. This conflicts with the goals of the other functional areas to seek mass production (production), well-established budgets (finance), routinized transactions (accounting), limited models (engineering), infrequent orders (purchasing), technology-driven new products (research and development), and passive actions against competitors (legal). Table 3-2 contains several illustrations of differences in perspectives between marketing and production, finance, and engineering.

Top management's role is to make sure that each functional area understands its desire for a balanced viewpoint in overall decision making and has input into decisions. In the case of a new-product decision, there must be a trade-off between sales opportunities, the ability of older products to substitute for newer ones, warehousing expenses, capital expenditures, growth potential, production and engineering expenses, and risks. Although a certain degree of tension among

Table 3-1
Orientations of Different Functional Areas

Functional Area	Major Strategic Orientation
Marketing	To attract and retain a loyal group of consumers through a unique combination of product, distribution, promotion, and price factors
Production	To utilize full plant capacity, hold down per-unit production costs, and maximize quality control
Finance	To operate within well-established budgets, focus on profitable items, control credit, and minimize the costs of loans to the company
Accounting	To standardize reports, fully detail costs, and routinize transactions
Engineering	To develop and adhere to exact product specifications, limit models and options, and concentrate on quality improvements
Purchasing	To acquire materials through large, uniform orders at low prices and maintain low inventories
Research and development	To seek technological breakthroughs, improvements in product quality, and recognition for innovations
Legal	To ensure that the strategy is defensible against challenges from the government, competitors, channel members, and consumers

Table 3-2 Illustrations of How Marketing, Production, Engineering, and Finance View One Another

Factor	Typical Marketing Comment	Typical Production Comment	Typical Finance Comment	Typical Engineering Comment
Technical service	"We need more engineering assistance on customer visits."	"Marketing has sold products for applications they were not designed to fulfill."	"Our technical service costs are higher than the industry average."	"Marketers don't need us as often as we're requested; they use us for credibility."
Promotion	"Our promotion is too technical."	"Product specifications and our quality control program should be stressed."	"Promotion should stress costs and benefits."	"Our promotion is not technical enough."
Design changes	"Design changes are too seldom."	"Design changes are too frequent."	"Design changes are generally very costly and therefore should be kept to a minimum."	"Design changes are too frequent."
Distributor selection	"We should select distributors based on their marketing savvy."	"We need distributors who can stock large inventory levels and provide steady orders."	"We should select distributors based on their financial resources."	"We need distributors who can provide high levels of technical service to clients."
Overseas markets	"Foreign markets represent excellent opportunities."	"Tailoring products to foreign needs and long lead times for shipments represent significant problems."	"While foreign markets represent excellent opportunities, we need to be concerned with foreign currency stability and nationalism."	"We must be careful not to give trade secrets to potential competitors."

Source: Adapted by the authors from Benson P. Shapiro, "Can Marketing and Manufacturing Coexist?" *Harvard Business Review,* Vol. 55 (September–October 1977), p. 105; and J. Donald Weinrauch and Richard Anderson, "Conflicts Between Engineering and Marketing Units," *Industrial Marketing Management,* Vol. 11 (October 1982), pp. 294–295.

departments is inevitable, it can be reduced if each area is encouraged to strongly present its position and then be willing to listen to other perspectives.

Departmental conflict can be reduced by[6]

1. Openly discussing differences and encouraging interfunctional contact. Managers from each functional area should attend the others' meetings on a regular basis.
2. Seeking employees who blend technical and marketing expertise. Managers should be encouraged to work in different functional areas to develop broader perspectives.
3. Establishing interfunctional task forces, committees, and management development programs.
4. Developing objectives for each department which take into account other departmental objectives, such as marketing managers being judged on the accuracy of sales forecasts (rather than by how far they can exceed them).

Cooperation among departments requires communications, broad employee backgrounds, interfunctional programs, and mutual objectives.

[6] Benson P. Shapiro, "Can Marketing and Manufacturing Coexist?" *Harvard Business Review,* Vol. 55 (September–October 1977), pp. 104–114; and J. Donald Weinrauch and Richard Anderson, "Conflicts Between Engineering and Marketing Units," *Industrial Marketing Management,* Vol. 11 (October 1982), pp. 291–301.

The Strategic Planning Process

The *strategic planning process* includes a number of steps ranging from defining organizational mission to monitoring results.

The **strategic planning process** in marketing consists of seven interrelated steps: defining organizational mission, establishing strategic business units, setting marketing objectives, situation analysis, developing marketing strategy, implementing tactics, and monitoring results. This process is depicted in Figure 3-3.

It is essential to realize that this process is applicable for small and large firms, product and service-based firms, and profit-oriented and nonprofit organizations. While planning at each step in the process differs by type of organization, the use of a thorough strategic plan is beneficial for any organization.[7]

The steps in the strategic planning process are discussed in the following sections.

Defining Organizational Mission

A firm commits itself to a specific business and place in the market through its *organizational mission*.

Organizational mission refers to a long-term commitment to a type of business and a place in the market. Mission can be defined in terms of customer groups served, customer functions, and technologies utilized. It is more comprehensive and formal than the line of business concept described in Chapter 2. Table 3-3 provides examples of alternate missions that could be employed by a watch manufacturer, an appliance repair service, and a college store.

Organizational mission is raised implicitly whenever a new product or service is introduced, an old product or service is deleted, a new customer group is sought, an existing customer group is abandoned, the business is diversified through acquisition, or part of the business is liquidated or sold.[8] Among the companies recently revising their organizational missions are Campbell and Yamaha.

Campbell Soup Company, best known for its soups and Pepperidge Farm, Swanson, Franco-American, and Godiva products, has undergone a rapid transformation as a result of its new organizational mission. This mission encourages the company "to be positioned with consumers as somebody who is looking after their well-being."[9] Consistent with the new mission, Campbell now operates a health and fitness business unit, which is involved with manufacturing related products. The health and fitness business would not be consistent with Campbell's mission if it were defined as a food and snack company.

Yamaha, a leading motorcycle manufacturer, has expanded its organizational mission to include products and services for leisure activities. Accordingly,

---

[7] See Philip H. Thurston, "Should Smaller Firms Make Formal Plans?" *Harvard Business Review,* Vol. 61 (September–October 1983), pp. 162 ff.

[8] Derek F. Abell, *Defining the Business: The Starting Point of Strategic Planning* (Englewood Cliffs, N.J.: Prentice-Hall, 1980), p. 6.

[9] "Campbell Soup: Cooking Up a Separate Dish for Each Consumer Group," *Business Week* (November 21, 1983), p. 102.

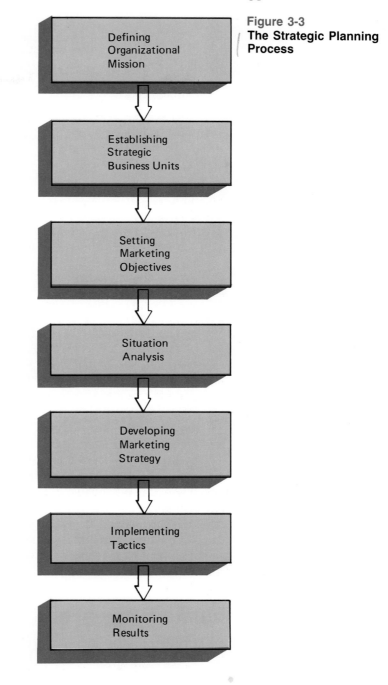

Figure 3-3
The Strategic Planning Process

Yamaha has diversified into archery and skiing equipment, boats, tennis rackets, and leisure parks.[10]

---

[10] Kenichi Ohmal, ''Setting the Options Before Planning Strategy,'' *Management Review* (May 1982), pp. 46–55.

Table 3-3
Examples of Alternate Organizational Missions

	Watch Manufacturer	Appliance Repair Service	College Store
Potential customer groups	Low-priced "disposable" watch market Status brands for upper-income market Consumer goods manufacturers Industrial goods manufacturers	Residential Commercial In-store In-home (office)	Students Faculty Alumni General public
Potential customer functions served	Stopwatch Camera shutter speed control Clock Timepiece	Basic warranty work Service contract work Fee-based repairs	Educational Personal care Food Clothing Gifts Financial Entertainment
Potential technologies served	Mechanical nonjewel movements Mechanical jewel movements Quartz digital movements Analog digital movements	Manual repairs Automated repairs Few appliances All kinds of appliances	Personal sale force Automatic teller machines Computerized checkouts Manual cash registers Mail-order sales

Note: Each of these organizations may define its mission narrowly (e.g., status brands of timepieces with quartz digital movements) or broadly (e.g., a college store for students, faculty, alumni, and the general public offering educational and personal-care items through a personal sales force and mail-order sales).

Overdiversification can result in a lack of organizational mission.

Organizations that diversify too much may not have a clear sense of mission. For example, Greyhound has been criticized by some analysts for becoming involved with computer leasing, car rentals, institutional feeding, soap manufacturing, insurance, and traveler's checks in addition to its traditional transportation services. The analysts regard all these business lines as making "too cluttered a plate." Greyhound's chief executive acknowledged this by commenting that "we are slimming down. We're defining business differently. We've sold off about 15 companies in recent years."[11]

Establishing Strategic Business Units

Strategic business units (SBUs) are established as separate operating entities within an organization.

After defining its mission, an organization establishes strategic business units (SBUs). Each **strategic business unit (SBU)** is a distinct part of the overall organization with a specific market focus and a manager with complete responsibility for integrating all functions into a strategy.[12] An SBU

may be a division, a product department, or even a product line or major market. It is designated as a business unit because it is a self-contained business for which a strategic

[11] Alexander Stuart, "Greyhound Gets Ready for a New Driver," *Fortune* (December 15, 1980), p. 59; and Steven Greenhouse, "The Reshaping of Greyhound," *New York Times* (November 5, 1983), pp. 35–36.
[12] Subhash C. Jain, *Marketing Strategy & Planning* (Cincinnati: South-Western, 1981), p. 142.

plan can be developed, balancing short- and long-term considerations; it also has an identifiable external competitor.[13]

An SBU may include all products with the same physical features or products that are bought for the same use by customers, depending on the mission of the organization.

SBUs are the basic building blocks of a strategic marketing plan, and each SBU has these general attributes:

1. A specific orientation.
2. A precise target market.
3. A senior marketing executive in charge.
4. Control over its resources.
5. Its own strategy.
6. Clear-cut competitors.
7. A distinctive differential advantage.

The SBU concept was developed by McKinsey & Co. for General Electric in 1971, and has enabled General Electric and other firms to identify those business units with the greatest earnings potential and allocate to them the resources necessary for their growth.

At General Electric, every SBU must have a unique mission within the company, identifiable competitors, and all of its major business functions (manufacturing, finance, and marketing) within the control of that SBU's manager. General Electric operates about 30 SBUs of various sizes. 16 of the SBUs (including major appliances, lighting, electrical motors, jet engines, medical equipment, electronics, and credit services) account for 87 per cent of sales and 92 per cent of profits; in all of these, GE is a leader. The other SBUs, such as transformer and television manufacturing, must improve their performance or they will be sold or closed down.[14]

It may be unmanageable for an organization to establish too many SBUs. For example, at one time, Westinghouse had 135 SBUs with each unit submitting its plans to top management on the same date. The result was a massive amount of reports that could be neither read nor digested. Westinghouse was subsequently reorganized into 26 business units, ranging from nuclear power to watches.[15]

On the other hand, if an organization has too few SBUs, it may be unable to recognize important differences in the planning requirements, marketing objectives, or strategy and tactics of each unit.

The proper number of SBUs depends on the mission of an organization, its resources, and the willingness of top management to delegate authority. One survey of the largest 1,000 industrial firms in the U.S. found that the typical company had about 30 SBUs.[16]

On average, large U.S. firms have about 30 SBUs.

---

[13] Ibid.

[14] William K. Hall, ''SBUs: Hot, New Topic in the Management of Diversification,'' *Business Horizons,* Vol. 21 (February 1978), pp. 17–25; and Howard Banks, ''General Electric—Going with the Winners,'' *Forbes* (March 26, 1984), pp. 97–106.

[15] ''Operation Turnaround: How Westinghouse's New CEO Plans to Fire Up an Old-Line Company,'' *Business Week* (December 5, 1983), p. 125.

[16] Philippe Haspeslagh, ''Portfolio Planning: Uses and Limits,'' *Harvard Business Review,* Vol. 60 (January–February 1982), p. 65. See also, Richard G. Hamermesh and Roderick E. White,'' Manage Beyond Portfolio Analysis,'' *Harvard Business Review,* Vol. 62 (January–February 1984), pp. 103–109.

Setting Marketing Objectives

Marketing objectives frequently encompass quantitative and qualitative measures.

Each strategic business unit in an organization needs to set its own objectives or expectations of marketing performance. Objectives are normally described in both quantitative terms (dollar sales, percentage profit growth, market share, etc.) and qualitative terms (image, level of innovativeness, industry leadership role, etc.).

There is an increasing tendency among organizations to integrate qualitative and quantitative goals. For instance, industry leadership may be evaluated on the basis of market-share growth and innovativeness assessed on the basis of the number of new patents registered. In this manner, qualitative objectives can be set without ambiguity.

Research has shown that, for industrial products manufacturers, the most important marketing objectives involve profit margins, field sales effort, new-product development, sales to major accounts, and pricing policy. For consumer products manufacturers, objectives center on profit margins, sales promotion, new-product development, pricing policy, field sales effort, and advertising expenditures. For service firms, objectives concentrate on field sales effort, advertising themes, customer service, and sales promotion.[17]

Situation Analysis

Situation analysis investigates opportunities and potential problems confronting an organization.

In *situation analysis,* an organization identifies the marketing opportunities and potential problems it faces. Situation analysis seeks answers to two general questions: Where is the firm now? In what direction is the firm headed? These questions are answered by studying the environment, searching for opportunities, assessing the organization's ability to capitalize on those opportunities, recognizing both strengths and weaknesses relative to competitors, and anticipating competitors' responses to company strategies.

For example, a situation analysis of RCA's major business units reveals the following:[18]

- Broadcasting—RCA owns and operates the NBC television network, five local television stations, and a number of radio stations. Although RCA earned $156 million in profit on this division in 1983, its television network and radio station earnings lag far behind ABC and CBS. Despite a number of personnel and programming changes, in 1984, NBC's chairman said that "we have not made (the kind of) progress . . . I thought we would."
- Commercial electronics—RCA makes commercial video cameras, television equipment, and tape recorders. The Japanese have taken over industry leadership in this category. In 1985, RCA plans to introduce a new high-technology television camera to recapture lost sales.
- Communications—While this business unit represents a small portion of overall RCA sales, it is extremely profitable. The division is very strong in meteorological satellites, commercial television satellites, and the Ground Wave Emer-

---

[17] Hopkins, *The Marketing Plan,* pp. 23–24.

[18] "RCA: Will It Ever Be a Top Performer?" *Business Week* (April 2, 1984), pp. 52–56; "The NBC Peacock Is Still Dragging Its Tail," *Business Week* (April 2, 1984), pp. 56–62; Laura Landro, "RCA Posts 73% Rise in First-Quarter Net, Will Phase Out Videodisc Player Business," *Wall Street Journal* (April 5, 1984), p. 3; and "Videodisc Dream Is Over: RCA," *Advertising Age* (April 9, 1984), pp. 3, 68.

gency Network (GWEN) program. It has also received approval to develop direct-broadcast satellites.

- Consumer electronics—This unit has had mixed success. RCA is the leading U.S. manufacturer of color television sets, recently regaining that position from Zenith. It is also the leader in videocassette recorders. However, in April 1984, RCA announced that it would phase out its videodisc player, following losses of over $500 million between 1979 and 1984.
- Government electronics—This is another profitable business unit. RCA has government contracts involving Navy cruisers, destroyers, and submarines. It plans to become more active in the defense area.
- Transportation services—RCA owns and operates Hertz, the largest automobile rental firm in the U.S. Despite mixed performance by Hertz, RCA plans to hold on to this business (despite years of rumors that it would sell Hertz).

Figure 3-4 shows the 1983 sales and profitability of RCA by business unit.

Sometimes, despite a company's best efforts, a situation analysis reveals that weaknesses cannot be overcome and the firm should leave the market. RCA

Situation analysis may reveal insurmountable difficulties.

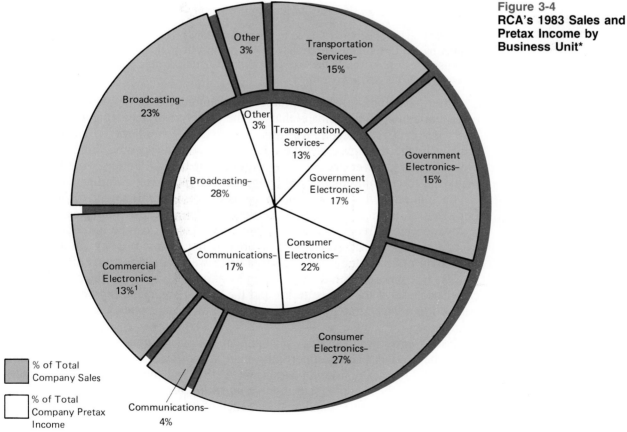

Figure 3-4
RCA's 1983 Sales and Pretax Income by Business Unit*

* Excluding CIT Financial Services, which was sold in 1984.

1 No pretax income, Commercial Electronics showed a loss in 1983.

Sources: RCA; and "RCA: Will It Ever Be a Top Performer?" *Business Week* (April 2, 1984), p. 53.

reached this difficult decision regarding its videodisc player for several reasons: the machine could play programs, but it could not record them; more movies, concerts, etc. were available for videocassette players; prices of videocassette recorders came down much faster than anticipated; price cuts eroded profit margins; and several retailers dropped the product. As RCA's chairman noted, "no matter how long we hung in there, we couldn't see it making a profit." [19]

Developing Marketing Strategy

A good *marketing strategy* provides a detailed framework for marketing activities.

A **marketing strategy** outlines the manner in which marketing is used to accomplish an organization's objectives. A separate strategy is necessary for each SBU in the organization.

A strategy should be as explicit as possible. For example, a plan for a continuing product should include priorities, responsibilities, dates, production schedules, promotion support, and service-training needs. A poor strategy would be too imprecise:

in order to increase the share of market for product 4, additional funds will be devoted to product design and advertising. [20]

A good strategy by the same organization would provide more guidance:

the market share of product 4 is to be increased from 6 per cent to 8 per cent within 12 months by (a) developing an attractive and functional package, (b) directing increased advertising effort to reach the top 200 users, (c) redesigning the product to improve appearance at no cost increase. [21]

Often, a firm must select a strategy from among two or more possible alternatives. For example, a company that has the objective of achieving a market share of 40 per cent may accomplish this objective in several ways. It can improve product image through extensive advertising, add salespeople, introduce a new product model, lower prices, or sell through more retail outlets. Another option would be to combine these marketing elements in a well-coordinated way.

Each alternative strategy emphasis has different ramifications for marketers. For instance, a price strategy may be very flexible, because a price can be raised or lowered more frequently than product modifications can be introduced. However, a strategy based solely on low price is the easiest to copy. In addition, a successful price strategy may lead to a price war, with disastrous effects on net profits. In contrast, a strategy based on locational advantages may be difficult to copy, because of long lease terms and the unavailability of appropriate sites for competitors. This strategy may be inflexible and adapt poorly to environmental changes.

Portfolio analysis, which investigates all of an organization's opportunities, products, and/or businesses, greatly aids strategy planning.

Four approaches to strategy planning are presented in the next several subsections: the product/market opportunity matrix, the Boston Consulting Group matrix, Profit Impact of Market Strategy (PIMS), and the Porter generic strategy model. All of these approaches involve *portfolio analysis,* by which an organization individually assesses and positions each of its opportunities, products, and/or

---

[19] Sandra Salmans, "RCA Defends Timing of Videodisc Canceling," *New York Times* (April 6, 1984), pp. D1, D15; and Landro, "RCA Posts 73% Rise in First-Quarter Net, Will Phase Out Videodisc Player Business."

[20] Hopkins, *The Marketing Plan,* p. 26.

[21] Ibid., p. 25.

businesses. Company efforts and resources are allocated and appropriate strategies developed on the basis of these assessments.

THE PRODUCT/MARKET OPPORTUNITY MATRIX

The ***product/market opportunity matrix*** is a broad method of strategy planning that offers an organization four alternative ways to maintain and/or increase sales: market penetration, market development, product development, and diversification.[22] See Figure 3-5.

In ***market penetration,*** a firm seeks to expand the sales of its present products in its present markets through more intensive distribution, aggressive promotion efforts, and highly competitive prices. It increases sales by attracting nonusers and competitors' customers and raising the usage rate among current customers. This strategy is effective when the market is growing or not yet saturated.

In ***market development,*** a firm seeks greater sales of present products from new markets or new product uses. It can enter new geographic markets, appeal to market segments it is not yet satisfying, and reposition existing products. New distribution methods may be tried; promotion efforts are more descriptive. This strategy is effective when a local or regional firm looks to widen its market, new market segments are emerging due to changes in consumer life-styles and demographics, and innovative uses are discovered for a mature product.

In ***product development,*** a firm develops new or modified products to appeal to present markets. It emphasizes new models, quality improvements, and other minor innovations closely related to established products and markets them to customers who are loyal to the company and its brands. Traditional distribution methods are used; and promotion stresses that the new product is made by a well-established firm. This strategy is effective when a company has a core of strong brands and a sizable consumer following.

The ***product/market opportunity matrix*** explains ***market penetration, market development, product development,*** and ***diversification*** strategy alternatives.

[22] H. Igor Ansoff, ''Strategies for Diversification,'' *Harvard Business Review,* Vol. 35 (September–October 1957), pp. 113–124.

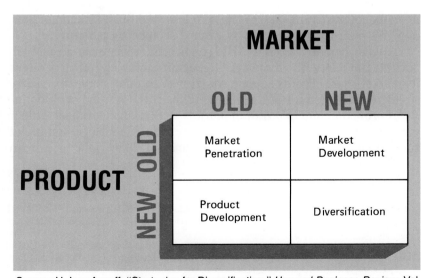

Figure 3-5
The Product/Market Opportunity Matrix

Source: H. Igor Ansoff, "Strategies for Diversification," *Harvard Business Review,* Vol. 35 (September–October 1957), pp. 113–124.

In *diversification,* a firm becomes involved with new products aimed at new markets. These products may be new to the industry or new only to the company (in the case of an acquisition of an ongoing firm). Distribution and promotion orientations are both different from those traditionally followed by the firm. This alternative is utilized so that an organization does not become overly dependent on one SBU.

Table 3-4 applies the product/market opportunity matrix to Coca-Cola, which uses a combination of strategies. Coca-Cola's strategic plan is a response to several factors: heavy soft drink users are aged thirteen to twenty-four and the relative size of this group is diminishing; sugar prices can be unstable; competition in the soda market is intense; and some current markets are saturated and offer little potential for long-term growth.[23]

THE BOSTON CONSULTING GROUP MATRIX

The *Boston Consulting Group matrix* uses market share and industry growth to describe *stars, cash cows, question marks,* and *dogs.*

The **Boston Consulting Group matrix** enables a company to classify each of its SBUs in terms of the SBU's market share relative to major competitors and the annual growth rate of the industry. By using the matrix, the firm can determine which of its SBUs are dominant compared with competitors and whether the industries in which it operates are growing, stable, or declining.[24]

The primary assumption of the Boston Consulting Group matrix is that the higher an SBU's market share, the lower its per-unit costs and the higher its profitability. This is the result of economies of scale (larger firms can mechanize and automate production and distribution), the experience curve (as projects and operations are repeated, time requirements are reduced), and improved bargaining power.

This matrix identifies four types of SBUs: star, cash cow, problem child (question mark), and dog, and suggests appropriate strategies for each. Figure 3-6 shows the Boston Consulting Group matrix.

A *star* is a leading SBU (high market share) in an expanding industry (high growth). It generates substantial profits but requires large amounts of resources to finance continued growth. Market share can be maintained or increased through price reductions, more advertising, product modifications, and/or greater distribution. As industry growth slows, a star becomes a cash cow.

A *cash cow* is a leading SBU (high market share) in a relatively mature or declining industry (low growth). It generates more cash than is required to retain its market share. Profits support the growth of other company SBUs. The firm's strategy is oriented toward maintaining the SBU's strong position in the market.

A *problem child* or *question mark* is an SBU that has made little impact in the marketplace (low market share) in an expanding industry (high growth). It needs substantial cash to maintain or increase market share in the face of strong compe-

[23] See William E. Schmidt, ''Putting the Daring Back in Coke,'' *New York Times* (March 4, 1984), Section 3, pp. 1, 8–9.

[24] See *Perspectives on Experience* (Boston: Boston Consulting Group, 1968); Bruce D. Henderson, ''The Experience Curve Reviewed: IV. The Growth Share Matrix of the Product Portfolio'' (Boston: Boston Consulting Group, 1973), Perspectives No. 135; George S. Day, ''Diagnosing the Product Portfolio,'' *Journal of Marketing,* Vol. 41 (April 1977), pp. 29–38; Richard Greene, ''Cash Cow into Prize Steer?'' *Forbes* (September 13, 1982), pp. 44 ff.; Betsy Gelb, ''Strategic Planning for the Underdog,'' *Business Horizons,* Vol. 25 (November–December 1982), pp. 8–11; Donald C. Hambuck and Ian C. MacMillan, ''The Product Portfolio and Man's Best Friend,'' *California Management Review,* Vol. 25 (Fall 1982), pp. 84–95; and Bruce D. Henderson, ''The Application and Misapplication of the Experience Curve,'' *Journal of Business Strategy,* Vol. 4 (Winter 1984), pp. 3–9.

Table 3-4
**The Product/Market
Opportunity Matrix
Applied to Coca-Cola**

Market Penetration
More adults used in commercials; "Coke is it" theme
Price discounts and sales promotions (such as Fun Caps) directed at current consumers
Continuing domination of in-store soda fountain market; increasing sales through fast-food chains
Greater promotion of nonCoke brands
Strengthened bottler (distribution) network

Market Development
World market divided into three parts, with an executive in charge of each: (1) U.S., Central America, and South America; (2) Europe, Africa, Southwest Asia, and Indian subcontinent; and (3) Canada, Far East, and Pacific
Changing image from children's drinks to family beverages

Product Development
Improving product quality
Adding new brands and flavors (such a diet Coke and decaffeinated versions of Coke, diet Coke, and Tab)
Introducing new container sizes (such as the 2-liter bottle)
Increasing the use of plastic bottles
Diet drinks reformulated with aspartame

Diversification
Producing juice, coffee, and tea
Manufacturing water-treatment and conditioning equipment
Making disposable plastic cutlery and straws for food-service chains and hospitals
Acquiring Columbia Pictures

tition. The company must decide whether to market more intensively or abandon the market. The choice of strategy depends on whether the company believes the SBU can compete successfully with adequate support and what that support will cost.

A *dog* is an SBU with limited sales (low market share) in a mature or declining industry (low growth). A dog usually has cost disadvantages and few growth opportunities. A company with such an SBU can attempt to appeal to a specialized market, harvest profits by cutting support services to a minimum, or leave the market.

Scott Paper Co. is one of the many firms that currently follow the strategy principles suggested by the Boston Consulting Group matrix. Scott makes paper towels, bathroom tissues, disposable mats, baby wipes, tissues, napkins, and other products. The company hired the Boston Consulting Group in 1980, after seeing its market share shrink and erratic earnings occur. These events were brought on by company complacency and inefficient, outdated equipment.

Now, Scott has developed the first overall strategic plan in its more than 100-year history. The strategy is straightforward: to pour money into businesses that have realistic chances to be industry leaders and to provide less resources for other businesses. This approach is not as easy as it seems. As a Boston Consulting Group vice-president observed, "I think the hardest thing for every company in the world is knowing when to limit your activity and not to do everything you want."

Scott's new strategy means that some well-known brands will be relatively neglected over the next few years. Included are Cottonelle and Soft 'n' Pretty

RELATIVE MARKET SHARE

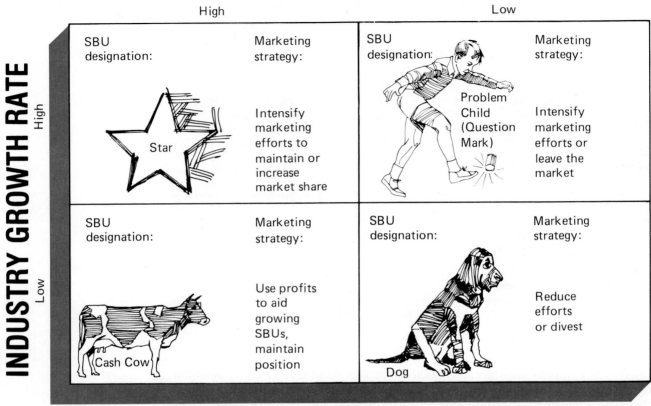

Relative market share is an SBU's market share in comparison to the leading competitors in the industry. Industry growth rate is the annual growth of all similar businesses in the market (such as sugarless gum).

Figure 3-6
The Boston Consulting Group Matrix

Source: Adapted from Bruce D. Henderson, "The Experience Curve Reviewed: IV. The Growth Share Matrix of the Product Portfolio," (Boston: Boston Consulting Group, 1973), Perspectives No. 135.

bathroom tissue, which were introduced in the 1970s to compete with Procter & Gamble's Charmin brand (the industry leader). Some of Scott's products will be "milked" for whatever cash they can produce. Others will be repositioned. Still others will probably be dropped (such as furniture and foam products).[25]

PIMS data describe the interaction between marketing factors and return on investment and cash flow.

PROFIT IMPACT OF MARKET STRATEGY (PIMS)

The *Profit Impact of Market Strategy (PIMS)* program, administered by the Strategic Planning Institute, gathers data from a number of corporations in order to establish relationships between a variety of business factors and two measures

---

[25] "Scott Paper Fights Back, at Last," *Business Week* (February 16, 1981), pp. 104, 106; Bernard Wysocki, "Torn Up by Rivals, Scott Paper Draws Up a Long-Term Strategy to Regain Its Stature," *Wall Street Journal* (May 11, 1981), p. 29; Paul Hemp, "Scott Makes Up Lost Ground," *New York Times* (August 31, 1983), pp. D1, D3; and Paul A. Engelmayer, "Scott Paper's Major Energy–Saving Plan Is Latest Effort to Help Company Compete," *Wall Street Journal* (October 18, 1983), p. 41.

of organizational performance: return on investment and cash flow. Information is collected by SBU and describes the characteristics of its business environment, competitive position, production process, budget allocation, strategic moves, and operating results. By examining PIMS data, an organization can determine the effects of various marketing strategies on performance. As of 1983, 2,000 SBUs, from 600 corporations, were participating in the PIMS program.[26]

According to PIMS' findings, these marketing-related factors have the greatest impact on return on investment (profitability): market share relative to the three largest competitors, the value added to a product by the company, industry growth, product quality, the level of innovation/differentiation, and vertical integration (ownership of other channel members). With respect to cash flow, PIMS' data suggest that growing markets drain company cash, high relative market share improves cash flow, and high levels of investment drain cash.[27] These conclusions are quite similar to those offered by the Boston Consulting Group matrix.

PIMS information is conveyed to participating firms through these reports:

- Par report—showing average return on investment and cash flow on the basis of market, competition, technology, and cost structure.
- Strategy analysis (sensitivity) report—showing effects of strategy changes on short-run and long-run return on investment and cash flow.
- Optimum strategy report—suggesting strategy that will maximize results.
- Look-alikes report—examining tactics of similar competitors, both successful and unsuccessful.

THE PORTER GENERIC STRATEGY MODEL

The *Porter generic strategy model* examines two major marketing planning concepts and the alternatives available with each: selection of a target market (industrywide or segmented) and strategic advantage (uniqueness or price).[28] By combining the two concepts, the Porter model identifies these basic strategies: overall cost leadership, differentiation, and focus. Figure 3-7 shows the Porter model.

With an overall cost leadership strategy, the firm appeals to a mass market and manufactures products in large quantities. Through mass production, the company is able to minimize per-unit costs and offer low prices. This allows the firm to have better profit margins than competitors, respond better to cost increases, and attract price-conscious consumers. Among the companies using cost leadership are Emerson Electric, DuPont, and Black & Decker.

With a differentiation strategy, the firm aims at a large market by offering a product viewed as quite distinctive. The company makes a product that has a broad appeal, yet is not available through competitors. As a result, price is not as important; and consumers become quite brand loyal. Among the firms using differentiation are McDonald's, Seiko, and Caterpillar Tractor.

The *Porter generic strategy model* distinguishes among overall cost leadership, differentiation, and focus strategies.

[26] Lynn W. Phillips, Doe R. Chang, and Robert D. Buzzell, "Product Quality, Cost Position, and Business Performance: A Test of Some Key Hypotheses," *Journal of Marketing,* Vol. 47 (Spring 1983), p. 33.
[27] *The PIMSLETTER on Business Strategy: Nine Basic Findings on Business Strategy* (Cambridge, Mass.: Strategic Planning Institute, 1980), p. 3.
[28] Michael E. Porter, *Competitive Strategy: Techniques for Analyzing Industries and Competitors* (New York: Free Press, 1980), pp. 34–46.

Figure 3-7
The Porter Generic Strategy Model

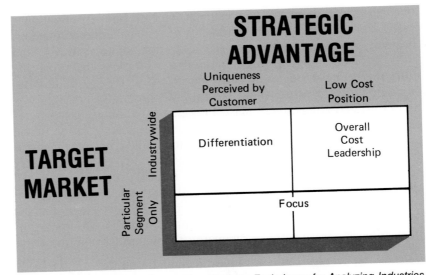

Source: Michael E. Porter, *Competitive Strategy: Techniques for Analyzing Industries and Competitors* (New York: Free Press, 1980), p. 39. Reprinted with the permission of The Free Press, a division of Macmillan Publishing Company. Copyright © 1980 by The Free Press.

The Porter model demonstrates that small firms can be successful through a focused strategy.

With a focus strategy, a company seeks a specific market segment through low prices or a unique offering. It is able to control costs by concentrating efforts, build a specialized reputation, or serve a market that may be unsatisfied by competitors. Martin-Brower is a low-cost food distributor servicing just eight fast-food chains. Porter Paint provides a unique combination of service, delivery, and quality paints for its market of professional painters.

According to the Porter model, the relationship between market share and profitability is U-shaped, as displayed in Figure 3-8. A firm with a low market share can succeed by developing a well-focused strategy. A firm with a high market share can succeed through overall cost leadership or a differentiated strategy. However, a company can become "stuck in the middle" if it has neither a strong and unique offering nor overall leadership. Unlike the Boston Consulting Group matrix and the PIMS program, the Porter model suggests that a small firm can profit by concentrating on one competitive niche, even though its total market share may be low.

EVALUATION OF STRATEGIC PLANNING APPROACHES

Portfolio planning is used by many firms.

The strategic planning approaches discussed in the previous subsections, as well as other portfolio models, are being used by many firms. Two studies of large industrial U.S. companies found that well over one third of the respondents had introduced some form of portfolio planning.[29]

Strategic models have strengths and weaknesses, and should be only one part of a planning process.

While an evaluation of each of the strategic approaches described is beyond the scope of this book, they do have some common strengths and weaknesses. The major strengths of the approaches are that each of the organization's opportunities, products, and/or businesses are identified and positioned, different strategies are recommended on the basis of this analysis, performance can be compared

---

[29] Haspeslagh, "Portfolio Planning: Uses and Limits," p. 59; and Bettis and Hall, "Strategic Portfolio Management in the Multibusiness Firm," p. 23.

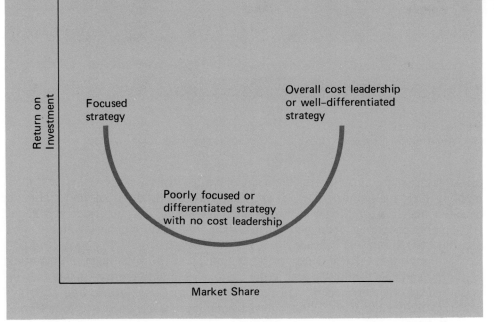

Source: Adapted from Michael E. Porter, *Competitive Strategy: Techniques for Analyzing Industries and Competitors* (New York: Free Press, 1980), p. 43. Reprinted with the permission of The Free Press, a division of Macmillan Publishing Company. Copyright © 1980 by The Free Press.

against designated goals, and principles for improving performance are noted. Competitors' actions and resource allocations can also be followed.[30]

The major weaknesses of the approaches are that they are difficult to implement, may be too simplistic and omit crucial factors, are extremely sensitive to changes in SBU definitions and modifications in rating criteria, do not adequately account for environmental conditions, and have been inadequately proven through research.[31]

The product/market opportunity matrix, Boston Consulting Group matrix, PIMS, and Porter generic strategy model should be viewed as one aspect of the strategic planning process, and not as the planning process in its entirety.

Implementing Tactics

Tactics are specific actions undertaken to implement a given marketing strategy. In the Coca-Cola example shown in Table 3-4, product development is one of the company's strategies. The enactment of a specific task, to reformulate diet

> The marketing strategy is enacted through a series of *tactics*.

---

[30] See Frederick Gluck, "The Dilemmas of Resource Allocation," *Journal of Business Strategy,* Vol. 2 (Fall 1981), pp. 67–71.

[31] See "The Future Catches Up with a Strategic Planner," *Business Week* (June 27, 1983), p. 62; and Yoram Wind, Vijay Mahajan, and Harold J. Swire, "An Empirical Comparison of Standard Portfolio Models," *Journal of Marketing,* Vol. 47 (Spring 1983), pp. 97–98.

Table 3-5 **Determining an Optimal Marketing Mix for a Company with a $2 Million Marketing Budget**

Alternative Marketing Mix	Selling Price	Unit Sales	Sales Revenue	Total Product Costs	Advertising Costs	Personal Selling Costs	Distribution Costs	Total Costs	Profit
Mass marketing	$10	1,000,000	$10,000,000	$6,000,000[a]	$850,000	$ 300,000	$850,000	$8,000,000	$2,000,000
Selective marketing	$20	400,000	$ 8,000,000	$4,800,000[b]	$750,000	$ 650,000	$600,000	$6,800,000	$1,200,000
Exclusive marketing	$40	250,000	$10,000,000	$5,500,000[c]	$400,000	$1,100,000	$500,000	$7,500,000	$2,500,000

[a] $6 per unit for labor, materials, and other production costs.
[b] $12 per unit for labor, materials, and other production costs.
[c] $22 per unit for labor, materials, and other production costs.

drinks with aspartame, involves tactics. Generally, firms that are skilled at implementing their marketing strategies are likely to provide direction and clarity to decision makers, offer a strong differential advantage and be concerned about consumers, encourage managers to use their ingenuity and be adaptable, and facilitate flexibility and latitude.[32]

Two important tactical decisions relate to the level of investment in marketing activities and the timing of marketing actions. Marketing investments can be classified as order processing and order generating. ***Order-processing costs*** are expenses associated with filling out and handling orders, such as order forms, computer time, and merchandise handling. The goal is to minimize those costs subject to obtaining a given level of service.

Order-generating costs, such as advertising and personal selling, are revenue producing. Reducing these costs may have a detrimental effect on a firm's sales and profits. Therefore, an organization needs to estimate revenues at various levels of costs and for various combinations of marketing functions. Table 3-5 shows how a company could allocate its $2 million marketing budget among advertising, personal selling, and distribution in a manner that maximizes profit. In this situation, the firm would choose an exclusive marketing mix that requires most marketing effort to be placed on personal selling.

Maximum profit rarely occurs at the lowest level of expenditure on order-generating costs. For example, the use of too few salespeople may result in inadequate coverage of a territory (since not all accounts can be visited as frequently as desired) and extensive travel time for each salesperson. Conversely, excessive costs will also rarely lead to maximum profit. Employing too many salespeople may limit their effectiveness, since the number of potential accounts available to each is reduced and some customers may be visited too frequently. See Figure 3-9.

The second major tactical decision deals with the timing of marketing activities. Proper timing may mean being the first to introduce a product, bringing out a product when the market is most receptive to it, or quickly reacting to a competitor's strategy to catch him or her off guard. The company must balance its desire to be an industry leader with a clear-cut competitive advantage against its concern

It is important to understand the distinction between *order-processing* **and** *order-generating* **costs.**

Marketing activities must be carefully timed, since opportunities exist only for specific periods.

[32] Thomas V. Bonoma, "Making Your Marketing Strategy Work," *Harvard Business Review,* Vol. 62 (March–April 1984), pp. 75–76.

Figure 3-9
**A Sales Response Curve
Based on the Number of
Salespeople**

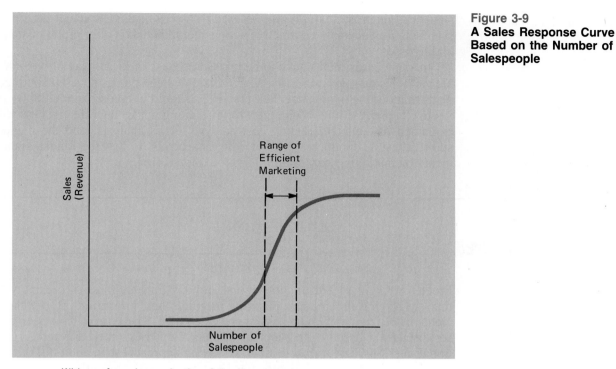

With too few salespeople, there is inadequate market coverage.
With too many salespeople, the market is saturated and the
effectiveness of each salesperson is inhibited.

about the risk of innovative actions. In any event, an organization must recognize that marketing opportunities exist for limited periods of time; it needs to act accordingly.

For example, firms need to plan carefully to capitalize on seasonal opportunities. When Coleco underestimated the demand for its "Cabbage Patch Kids" dolls during the 1983 December holiday season, the result was an extremely short supply. This caused customers to fight with one another in retail stores, sales clerks to be offered bribes to reserve dolls, and some store managers to arm themselves with baseball bats for protection against irate customers. A number of retailers set premium prices for the dolls and canceled advertising to dampen demand. Although Coleco ultimately shipped about 3 million dolls by the end of 1983, its inability to accurately forecast and satisfy holiday demand had negative short-term effects (in terms of lost sales) and long-term effects (in terms of poor credibility with consumers and retailers).[33]

Monitoring Results

Monitoring results involves the comparison of planned performance against actual performance for a specified period of time. Budgets, timetables, sales

Performance is evaluated
by *monitoring results*.

[33] Bob Davis, "Cabbage Patch Fever: Buyers Lose Heads over Homely Dolls," *Wall Street Journal* (November 29, 1983), p. 51; Philip Dougherty, "Behind the Cabbage Patch Kids," *New York Times* (December 1, 1983), p. D23; and "Trouble in the Cabbage Patch: Why Investors Are Down on Coleco," *Business Week* (January 9, 1984), pp. 93–94.

statistics, and cost analyses can be used to assess results. If actual performance lags behind plans, some corrective action should be taken after problem areas are highlighted.

In some cases, plans have to be revised because of the impact of uncontrollable variables on sales and costs. Many farsighted companies develop contingency plans that outline in advance their responses should unfavorable conditions arise.

In Chapter 24, three techniques for evaluating marketing effectiveness will be explained in depth: marketing cost analysis, sales analysis, and the marketing audit. These techniques are covered in Chapter 24 so that the fundamental elements of marketing can be thoroughly explored first.

Examples of Strategic Planning in Marketing

Strategic planning concepts are being applied by organizations in different industries and with diverse perspectives.

Procter & Gamble, Westinghouse, and Holiday Inns are three of the many firms that are relying on strategic planning to guide their marketing efforts. Selected elements of their strategic plans are presented here. These firms have been chosen for discussion because they are in different industries, have different organizational missions, and utilize distinct marketing approaches. In addition, the strategic plans of each of these companies have been revised recently to position them better for growth throughout the 1980s.

Procter & Gamble[34]

Procter & Gamble (P&G) is a leading maker of consumer-packaged goods, with about 70 brands including Ivory soap, Tide detergent, Pampers diapers, and Charmin bathroom tissue. Figure 3-10 shows several of P&G's brands. P&G's long-standing marketing objective has been to double unit sales volume every 10 years, a goal the firm wants to maintain.

However, in 1982, unit shipments declined for five of P&G's top six household brands. Furthermore, the company's market share fell significantly for laundry detergent, toothpaste, and disposable diapers from 1977 to 1983. Consumers became more responsive to competitors' price appeals, a strategy counter to P&G's focus on premium brands.

Procter & Gamble has launched a revised four-prong strategy in order to reach its unit sales volume objective. First, acquisitions are being used to break into new markets. P&G recently purchased Tender Leaf Tea, a portion of Crush (a soft drink manufacturer), the pharmaceutical division of Morton–Norwich, Ben Hill Griffin's citrus-processing operations, and a Coca-Cola bottler. Second, it is speeding up the product-development process. A record number of products are going through test marketing. Third, P&G is working to be the lowest-cost producer in its markets. Among its cost-cutting tactics are substituting plastic for glass in Crisco oil bottles and using animated cartoon characters in television commercials instead of actors and actresses. Fourth, P&G is placing a greater

[34] "Why Procter & Gamble Is Playing It Even Tougher," *Business Week* (July 18, 1983), pp. 176–177 ff; and Faye Rice, "Trouble at Procter & Gamble," *Fortune* (March 5, 1984), p. 70.

Figure 3-10
**Selected U.S. Products of
Procter & Gamble**

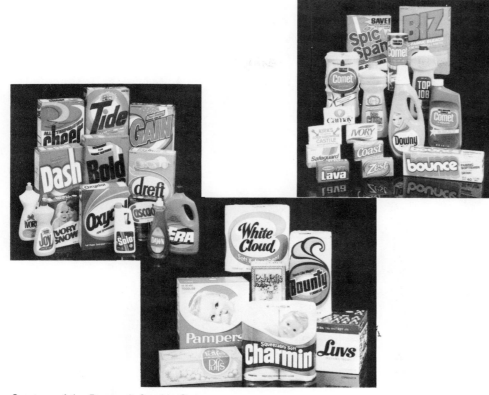

Courtesy of the Procter & Gamble Company.

emphasis on foreign markets. Major marketing efforts are underway in Latin America, Europe, Japan, and other regions.

This strategy is being continuously monitored. For example, products in test markets are judged by data gathered from retailers; and market shares for established products are regularly assessed.

Westinghouse[35]

As noted earlier in the chapter, Westinghouse is divided into 26 business units, ranging from nuclear power (Westinghouse is a major nuclear power-plant manufacturer) to watches (Westinghouse makes Longines and Longines-Wittnauer brands). Some of Westinghouse's businesses are in market areas with strong long-term outlooks, such as cable television, robotics, and defense electronics; others are in weak markets, such as nuclear power where no new U.S. plants are expected to be constructed during the 1980s. To reach the 1986 objectives set by management regarding annual sales growth, profit margins, foreign sales, and total income, Westinghouse is relying on a detailed strategic plan.

The company is placing less emphasis on mature businesses and placing greater effort on faster-growing businesses. It is also improving customer service,

[35] "Operation Turnaround: How Westinghouse's New CEO Plans to Fire Up an Old-Line Company," pp. 124–127 ff.

Figure 3-11
Electronic Testing of Generator Equipment at Westinghouse

Reprinted by permission.

upgrading product quality, and emphasizing better worker productivity. It has developed and is applying a more sophisticated strategic planning process. Tactics include utilizing a task force to examine ailing businesses, shifting focus from building U.S. nuclear plants to servicing existing ones and to foreign nuclear plant construction, establishing a quality control center in Pittsburgh, and inspecting all goods received from suppliers. A system for monitoring performance is in place. Figure 3-11 shows a technician working with electronic testing equipment at Westinghouse's large rotating apparatus (generator) division in East Pittsburgh, Pennsylvania.

Holiday Inns[36]

Holiday Inns is the world's largest hotel chain. It defines its mission as being a hospitality services provider, and seeks sales and profit growth consistent with

---

[36] "Holiday Inns Opens Doors for the Upscale Traveler," *Business Week* (April 25, 1983), pp. 100 ff.; and Subrata N. Chakravarty and Anne McGrath, "Room at the Top?" *Forbes* (March 12, 1984), pp. 58–61.

this mission. A situation analysis of the hospitality services market recently showed Holiday Inns that its traditional middle market for hotel facilities and services was saturated and that construction costs in desirable areas were too high for middle-priced hotel facilities. While Holiday Inns had strong brand recognition, it recognized that a ''middle of the road'' strategy would limit future growth.

On the basis of its situation analysis, Holiday Inns decided to launch two new hotel chains aimed at high-level executives who travel frequently and are willing to pay for specialized services, divest itself of more than 30 nonhospitality businesses, upgrade current Holiday Inn properties, and purchase/build hotels in all four important U.S. gambling centers.

At the new upscale hotel chains, Crowne Plaza and Embassy Suite, room rates are scheduled to be 50 per cent higher than those at regular Holiday Inn units. Crowne Plaza (shown in Figure 3-12) and Embassy Suite are planned to feature suite accommodations, luxurious rooms, plush upholstery in lobby areas, hardwood furnishings, and 18 hour/day maid service.

Holiday Inns monitors its strategic plan by analyzing sales by geographic market, sales by business and pleasure-traveler segments, traveler brand awareness, guest satisfaction, and room and facilities conditions.

Figure 3-12
The Holiday Inn Crowne Plaza Hotel
This is a top-of-the line hotel targeted primarily toward the frequent business traveler.

Reprinted by permission.

Summary

Strategic planning in marketing enables an organization to coordinate the factors directed by top management with those directed by marketing. Strategic marketing plans provide guidance, clarify objectives, encourage coordination among departments, focus on strengths and weaknesses, examine alternatives, help allocate resources, and point up the value of monitoring results.

Marketing plans may be short run, moderate in length, or long run. They may be developed for each major product or service, presented as one organizational marketing plan, or considered part of an overall business plan. A bottom-up or top-down management approach may be used.

The interests of marketing and the other key functional areas in an organization need to be accommodated in a strategic plan. Departmental conflict can be reduced by improving communications, employing personnel with broad backgrounds, establishing interdepartmental development programs, and blending departmental objectives.

The strategic planning process in marketing consists of seven interrelated steps. One, organizational mission, the long-term commitment to a type of business and a place in the market, is defined. Two, an organization divides itself into strategic business units (SBUs), which are distinct parts of the overall organization with specific markets and separate managers. Three, quantitative and qualitative marketing objectives are set. Four, through situation analysis, an organization identifies the marketing opportunities and potential problems it faces.

Five, a marketing strategy outlines the manner in which marketing is used to accomplish an organization's objectives. Four approaches to strategy planning are the product/market opportunity matrix, the Boston Consulting Group matrix, PIMS (Profit Impact of Market Strategy), and the Porter generic strategy model. All of these approaches involve portfolio analysis, by which each of an organization's opportunities, products, and/or businesses are individually assessed and positioned. Then company resources are allocated and appropriate strategies developed. These approaches should be viewed as one element in planning, not as the entire process.

Six, tactics (specific actions) are undertaken to implement the organization's marketing strategy. Of particular concern are the level of marketing investment and the timing of marketing actions. Seven, monitoring results compares planned performance against actual performance.

Questions for Discussion

1. Can an organization succeed without a strategic marketing plan? Why or why not?
2. Should a strategic plan be in writing? Explain your answer.
3. How would one- and five-year marketing plans differ for a daily newspaper?

4. Under what circumstances would it be advisable for an organization to have separate marketing plans for each product and service it offers? One integrated marketing plan?
5. Why are conflicts between marketing and other functional areas inevitable? How can these conflicts be beneficial?
6. Evaluate Yamaha's decision to expand its organizational mission.
7. What is a strategic business unit? Why is this concept so important to strategic planning?
8. Develop a list of five questions an organization could ask itself to determine the appropriate number of SBUs it should establish.
9. What issues should a small clothing manufacturer consider during situation analysis?
10. Create two market penetration and two market development strategies for a textbook publisher.
11. Give an example of a star, cash cow, question mark, and dog. Evaluate the current marketing strategy of each.
12. Compare the Porter generic strategy model with the Boston Consulting Group matrix and PIMS.
13. Explain the basic strengths and weaknesses of the portfolio approaches to strategy planning.
14. Comment on the statement that "maximum profit rarely occurs at the lowest level of expenditure on order-generating costs."
15. What are the similarities in the strategies of Procter & Gamble, Westinghouse, and Holiday Inn?

Case 1 Savin: Taking on Xerox in the Low-End Copier Market*

Savin Corporation is a relatively small manufacturer of photocopiers, with annual sales of $469 million. It is competing in an industry where the leader Xerox has annual sales of about $9 billion. As a result, Savin's organizational mission has been to "create a unique advantage in a niche." It has adhered to this mission by devoting all company resources to capturing a significant share of the low-end office-copier business from Xerox.

To accomplish its goals, Savin has relied on thorough and ongoing situation analysis. Through this analysis, Savin has identified the strengths and weaknesses of both Xerox and itself and developed a unique marketing strategy. Two kinds of competitive advantages are exploited: costs are lower and greater overall value is provided to small customers (who are most interested in a reliable, medium-quality copier). The strategy resulting from Savin's situation analysis is shown in Table 1.

---

* The data in this case are drawn from Ennius E. Bergsma, "In Strategic Phase, Line Management Needs 'Business' Research, Not Market Research," *Marketing News* (January 21, 1983), Section 1, p. 22.

Table 1 Marketing Low-End Office Copiers—Xerox Vs. Savin

	Technology	Product Design	Manufacturing	Distribution Channel	Terms/Pricing	Service
XEROX						
Strategy	Dry xerography	Feature rich High speed	United States Custom parts Backward integrated	Own sales force	Lease emphasis	Own technical service force
Attributes	High copy quality	Complex Relatively high failure rate	Higher costs/ prices	Limited outreach to small accounts	High fixed expense at low volume	Good service but thin coverage?
SAVIN						
Strategy	Liquid toner	Modular Low speed Human factors engineering	Japan Standard parts Subcontractors	Office supplies dealers	Sales emphasis	Dealers
Attributes	Medium quality Reliability	Reliability Foolproof	Lower costs/ prices	Good coverage of small accounts	One time capital cost—low expenses	Better service response time for small accounts?

Reprinted by permission of the American Marketing Association.

QUESTIONS

1. Evaluate the organizational mission stated by Savin.
2. Describe several marketing objectives that could be sought by Savin.
3. Comment on the strategies for Xerox and Savin outlined in Table 1. How can Savin have lower costs than Xerox?
4. Looking to the future, what growth opportunities should Savin consider (that would not place it head on against Xerox)?

Case 2 Gould Inc.: Selling a Cash-Cow Business[†]

Gould Inc. is an electronics manufacturer involved with minicomputers, custom-designed computer chips, medical instruments, and defense systems. During the past fifteen years, the firm has sold a number of its business units, such as engine parts and ball bearings, and used the funds received to acquire companies with leading positions in various electronics markets. Gould anticipates a 20 per cent compound annual growth rate throughout the 1980s.

In 1983, when Gould announced plans to sell its auto battery business, it surprised many analysts. At the time, Gould was the nation's third largest auto battery manufacturer, with a 15 per cent market share. Gould's auto battery business generated 1982 sales of $390 million, about 24 per cent of total company sales, and pretax operating profits of $31.5 million.

Furthermore, Gould had recently developed Cathanode, a new lightweight auto battery that provided 40 per cent greater starting power than conventional

[†] The data in this case are drawn from Jonathan Greenberg, "Getting Rid of a Good Thing," *Forbes* (May 9, 1983), p. 112.

batteries. This was important in cold weather and for compact cars needing more power to start. The Cathanode battery retailed for $90, twice the price of an ordinary battery, enabling Gould to achieve higher profit margins. After the Cathanode battery was introduced, demand consistently was twice the rate of sales (without significant advertising).

Gould's president offered two reasons for selling the auto battery business. First, the auto battery market grew by only 3 per cent in 1982. This was inconsistent with the company's desire to compete in faster-growing industries. Second, the development of the Cathanode battery boosted the selling price of the auto battery business. By selling this business at a high price, Gould would be better able to pursue other attractive opportunities.

In describing Gould, its president labeled it as a "honeycomb with a purpose in mind." And clearly, this purpose did not include an auto battery business.

QUESTIONS

1. Would you describe Gould's strategy as aggressive or conservative? Why?
2. What are the potential benefits and risks of Gould's divestiture strategy?
3. What questions should Gould consider in a situation analysis?
4. Examine Gould's approach in terms of the Boston Consulting Group matrix. Do you agree with Gould's tactics? Why or why not?

Chapter 4

Information for Marketing Decisions

CHAPTER OBJECTIVES

1. To explain why marketing information is needed

2. To define marketing research and its components

3. To examine the scope of marketing research

4. To describe the marketing research process: problem definition, examination of secondary data, generation of primary data (when necessary), analysis of data, recommendations, and implementation of findings

5. To explain the role and importance of the marketing information system

In the 1947 movie Magic Town, *opinion pollster James Stewart finds a town that is the perfect microcosm of America. Until the publicity goes to their heads, its inhabitants (including Jane Wyman, who captures Jimmy's heart) are typical American consumers, able with uncanny accuracy to forecast the success or failure of new products and politicians.*

Today, a real-life firm, Information Resources Inc. (IRI), is using techniques never dreamed of in *Magic Town* to research marketing practices and predict the success of products and their advertising campaigns. Among IRI's corporate clients are Searle (maker of aspartame artificial sweetener), Johnson & Johnson, Dart & Kraft, General Foods, Procter & Gamble, and Campbell Soup.

IRI attracts its clients through a service called BehaviorScan, which monitors television viewing habits and supermarket shopping behavior.

Figure 4-1
IRI's BehaviorScan
Consumer panelists in eight cities shop in supermarkets that use scanning equipment to relate consumer data with purchase behavior. This is just one portion of the overall BehaviorScan process.

Reprinted by permission.

20,000 consumer panelists in eight representative cities participate in BehaviorScan. Microcomputers are hooked up to their television sets and note all programs and commercials watched. The panelists shop in super-markets equipped with electronic scanning registers (shown in Figure 4-1), which provide printouts of purchases. Viewing and shopping behavior are then matched with consumer information, such as age and income, via computer analysis. Panelists are not compensated; they are given a $20 gift they select from a catalog once each year.

BehaviorScan enabled Searle to correctly project the first year national sales of Equal artificial sweetener. It allowed Johnson & Johnson to observe an upturn in Tylenol sales about one week after seven Chicago poisoning deaths were widely reported and publicized. At the same point, many other marketing consultants were incorrectly commenting that Tylenol would never recover. BehaviorScan also provided Heinz with data that 46 per cent of Heinz Ketchup buyers watching television at the time were tuned to the last episode of the 1983 television-movie *Winds of War*.[1]

By acquiring good marketing information, organizations are better able to make, implement, and evaluate decisions.

[1] Fern Schumer, "The New Magicians of Market Research," *Fortune* (July 25, 1983), pp. 72–74; Scott Hume, "BehaviorScan Links Purchasing, TV Viewing," *Advertising Age* (January 2, 1984), p. 33; and Kevin Higgins, "High-Tech Research Firm Is Hit with Advertisers and Investors," *Marketing News* (March 2, 1984), pp. 1, 28.

Why Information Is Needed

Marketers make better decisions when they have enough information.

To operate properly in the marketing environment, it is necessary to obtain adequate information before and after making decisions. There are many reasons why marketing information should be collected when constructing, implementing, and revising a firm's marketing plan or any of its elements. Reliance on intuition, executive judgment, and past experience is not sufficient. See Figure 4-2.

Risk is reduced, because potentially expensive failures can be avoided before cost outlays become too high and products or services that have a negative image

Figure 4-2
Reasons for Obtaining Information

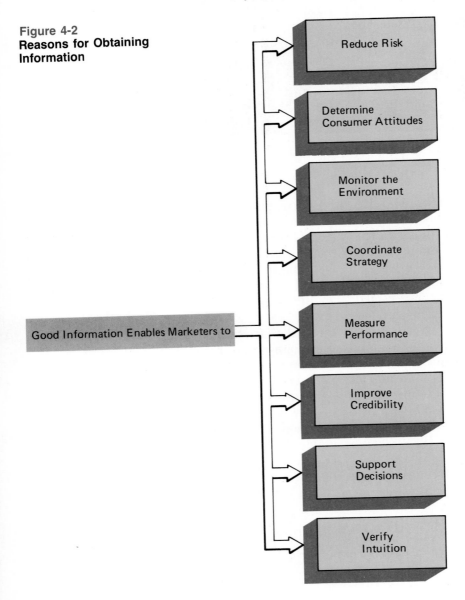

Good Information Enables Marketers to

- Reduce Risk
- Determine Consumer Attitudes
- Monitor the Environment
- Coordinate Strategy
- Measure Performance
- Improve Credibility
- Support Decisions
- Verify Intuition

can be modified or removed from the market before they hurt a company's overall image. Consumer attitudes, including likes and dislikes, are ascertained. The uncontrollable environment is monitored. The marketing strategy and each of its elements (product, distribution, promotion, and price) are coordinated; and the correct selection of one strategy alternative from among a number of choices is aided. Success or failure is measured by comparing actual performance with pre-established goals.

Marketing information is also helpful in selling a product because it can be used to enhance a firm's credibility. An advertisement or sales presentation that emphasizes factual information, such as the results of taste tests or the percentage of doctors recommending an item, has a higher level of customer acceptance than one that is merely entertaining. In addition, advertisements that make claims must be substantiated by research findings and companies promoting price reductions on merchandise must prove that it was originally sold at higher prices.

Marketing and top management often need information to gain support for a decision or to defend a decision already made. For example, a marketing manager may be better able to persuade top management to introduce a new product if a test market is favorable. After the new product is introduced, top management may explain its decision to stockholders by citing research results that indicate future success.

Finally, information can be gathered to verify intuition. In this case, a marketer may have a feeling about some aspect of the marketing plan or the overall plan itself but seek out further information to prove or disprove that intuition before implementing a decision.

Marketing Research Defined

Marketing research is

the systematic gathering, recording, and analyzing of data about problems relating to the marketing of goods and services. Such research may be undertaken by impartial agencies or by business firms or their agencies for the solution of their marketing problems.[2]

and:

the inclusive term which embraces all research activities carried on in connection with the management of marketing work.[3]

Several points in these definitions need to be emphasized. First, to be effective, marketing research must be systematic and not haphazard or disjointed. Second, marketing research involves a series of steps or a process. It is not a one-step activity; it includes data collection, recording, and analysis. Third, data may be available from different sources: the company itself, an impartial agency,

Marketing research in-volves the systematic collection, tabulation, and analysis of data needed to solve marketing problems.

---

[2] Ralph S. Alexander (Chairman), *Marketing Definitions: A Glossary of Marketing Terms* (Chicago, Ill.: American Marketing Association, 1960), pp. 16–17.
[3] Ibid., p. 17.

or a specialist in research working for the company. Fourth, marketing research may be applied to any aspect of marketing that requires information to aid decision making.

The *scientific method* requires objectivity, accuracy, and thoroughness.

When employing marketing research, the ***scientific method*** should be followed. The scientific method is based on objectivity, accuracy, and thoroughness.[4] Objectivity means that research is conducted in an unbiased, open-minded manner. Conclusions or opinions are not reached until after all data have been collected and analyzed. Accuracy refers to the use of research tools that are carefully constructed and utilized. Each aspect of research, such as the sample chosen, questionnaire format, interviewer selection and training, and tabulation of responses, needs to be carefully planned and implemented. For example, all questions in a survey should be pretested to ensure that the words are understood by prospective respondents. Thoroughness deals with the comprehensive nature of research. Mistaken conclusions may be reached if research does not probe deeply or widely enough.

A company's decision to use marketing research does not mean that it must undertake extensive, expensive studies like test marketing and national consumer attitude surveys. The firm may achieve its objectives through analysis of internal sales data or informal meetings with sales personnel. What marketing research does require is a systematic approach and adherence to principles of objectivity, accuracy, and thoroughness.

Marketing research may be formal or informal.

The amount and cost of marketing research depend, to a large extent, upon the amount of information required, the formality of research (informal discussions or structured surveys), the level of new data that must be collected, and the complexity of analysis (simple summaries or detailed statistical tests).[5]

Scope of Marketing Research

The use of marketing research varies widely by company and type of information required. Although most firms use some form of marketing research, large companies are more likely to have research departments than small firms. Typically, firms with annual sales of $25 million and more spend about 3.5 per cent of their marketing budgets on marketing research, while companies with sales less than $25 million spend about 1.5 per cent.[6]

Consumer goods companies have greater expenditures for marketing research than industrial firms. Nonetheless, there are many similarities in the kinds of research undertaken. Table 4-1 shows the types of marketing research conducted by both consumer goods and industrial firms.

[4] Harper W. Boyd, Jr., Ralph Westfall, and Stanley F. Stasch, *Marketing Research: Text and Cases,* Fifth Edition (Homewood, Ill.: Richard D. Irwin, 1981), pp. 31–32.
[5] Adapted from Donald R. Lehmann, *Marketing Research and Analysis* (Homewood, Ill.: Richard D. Irwin, 1979), p. 4.
[6] A. Parasuraman, "Research's Place in the Marketing Budget," *Business Horizons,* Vol. 26 (March–April 1983), pp. 25–29.

Table 4-1 Selected Research Activities by American Firms, 1983[1]

Type of Research	Consumer Companies, Per Cent Doing	Industrial Companies, Per Cent Doing
Advertising Research		
Copy research	78	55
Media research	72	57
Studies of ad effectiveness	86	67
Business Economics and Corporate Research		
Short-range forecasting (up to 1 year)	96	94
Long-range forecasting (over 1 year)	96	94
Studies of business trends	90	99
Corporate Responsibility Research		
Ecological impact studies	37	35
Studies of legal constraints on advertising and promotion	58	46
Product Research		
New product acceptance and potential	89	73
Competitive product studies	97	92
Packaging research: design or physical characteristics	91	61
Sales and Market Research		
Measurement of market potentials	99	99
Sales analysis	98	99
Establishment of sales quotas, territories	93	95
Distribution channel studies	89	83
Sales compensation studies	83	73
Promotional studies of premiums, coupons, sampling, deals, etc.	82	36

[1] Survey based on 143 consumer company responses and 124 industrial company responses.
Source: Dik Warren Twedt, *1983 Survey of Marketing Research* (Chicago: American Marketing Association, 1983), pp. 41, 43. Reprinted by permission of the American Marketing Association.

Marketing Research Process

The ***marketing research process*** is comprised of a series of activities: the definition of the problem or issue to be resolved; examination of secondary data (previously collected); generation of primary data (new), if necessary; analysis of information; recommendations; and implementation of findings.

Figure 4-3 presents the complete marketing research process. Each step is undertaken in order. For example, secondary data are not examined until the firm has stated the problem or issue to be studied, and primary data are not generated until secondary data are thoroughly reviewed. The dotted line around primary data means that primary data do not always have to be collected. In many instances a firm is able to solve its problem without gathering new data. Only when secondary data are insufficient should a firm generate primary data. The marketing research process is described next.

The *marketing research process* consists of six steps, ranging from problem definition to implementation of findings.

Figure 4-3
**The Marketing Research
Process**

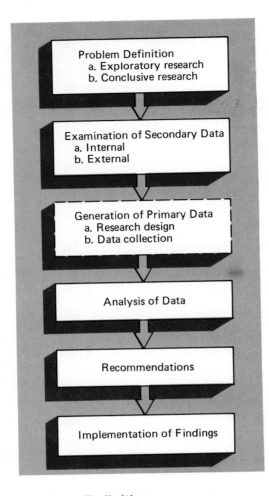

Problem Definition

The research topic is
described through
problem definition.

Problem definition is a statement of the topic to be investigated in marketing
research. Without a precise definition of the topic to be studied, a researcher may
collect irrelevant and expensive data and confuse rather than clarify issues. A
good problem definition directs the research process toward the collection and
analysis of specific information for the purpose of decision making.

Exploratory research is
used when the problem
is uncertain; *conclusive
research* is used to solve
a well-defined study.

When a researcher is uncertain about the precise topic to be investigated,
exploratory research should be employed. The purpose of exploratory research is
to develop a clear definition of the research problem by utilizing informal analysis. After the problem definition has been clarified, ***conclusive research*** should
be used. Conclusive research is structured data collection and analysis for the
solution of a specific problem or objective. Exploratory research techniques are
not as structured as conclusive research. Table 4-2 shows how exploratory and
conclusive research are used.

Secondary Data

Secondary data have been
previously gathered for
purposes other than the
current research.

Secondary data are those that have been previously gathered for purposes
other than solving the current problem under investigation. Whether secondary

Vague Research Problem	Exploratory Research	Precise Research Problem	Conclusive Research
1. Why are sales declining?	1. Discussions among key personnel to identify major cause	1. Why is turnover of sales personnel so high?	1. Survey sales personnel, interview sales managers
2. Is advertising effective?	2. Discussions among key advertising personnel to define effectiveness	2. Do customers recall an advertisement the day after it appears?	2. Survey customers and noncustomers to gauge advertising recall
3. Will a reduction in price increase sales volume?	3. Discussions among key personnel to determine the level of a price reduction	3. Will a 10 per cent price reduction have a significant impact on sales?	3. Run an in-store experiment to determine effects

Table 4-2
Examples of Exploratory and Conclusive Research

data completely solve the research problem of the firm or not, their low cost and relatively fast availability require that primary data not be collected until a thorough search of secondary data is completed. To assess the overall value of secondary data, the researcher needs to weigh low costs, speed, and access against accuracy and relevance.

ADVANTAGES

Many types of secondary data are inexpensive. Company records, trade publications, government publications, and general periodicals are each inexpensive to use. Data collection forms, interviewers, and experimental designs are unnecessary.

The assembly of secondary data is normally quick. Company, industry, government, and library records can be gathered and analyzed almost immediately, whereas the generation of primary data may take up to several months.

There frequently are several sources of secondary data. These allow a company to obtain various perspectives and large amounts of information and to verify data. With a primary study, limited data and only one perspective are usually obtained.

A secondary data source may contain information that the firm would be unable to get itself. For instance, the census data collected by the government could not be obtained by a single company.

When secondary data are assembled by an independent source such as *Fortune* or *Business Week,* the results are believable. Both of these sources have a high level of credibility and a reputation for thoroughness.

Secondary data are helpful in situations where exploratory research is needed. A search of secondary data also often enables the researcher to develop a specific problem definition before collecting primary data. Furthermore, background information about a problem can be gathered from secondary data.

Secondary data are usually quick and inexpensive to collect, and helpful in exploratory research.

DISADVANTAGES

Available secondary data may not suit the purposes of current research because they were collected for other reasons. For example, the units of measure-

Secondary data may not fit the purposes of current research, may be dated or imprecise, or may not be complete.

ment may be different from what are needed. The firm might require regional or local data, while secondary information is broken down by state or country. In addition, secondary data may not be complete enough for the company—e.g., industry sales not collected by age group, income level, and occupation of customers.

Secondary data may be dated or obsolete. Because the information was obtained for other purposes, it may have outlived its usefulness. Conclusions and statistics of a few years before may no longer be valid. For instance, the *Census of Population* is conducted only once a decade and the *Census of Retail Trade* is undertaken only once each five years.

The precision with which secondary data were collected, analyzed, and reported may be lacking. The firm must determine for itself whether the data were compiled in an unbiased, objective manner. The purpose, data collection technique, and method of analysis of the original study should each be examined for bias. This is especially important when the source of the study had a special interest in the results. Supporting evidence (actual data) should be read as well as summary reports.

The source of secondary data may not present all of its findings in a public report, because it may be hurt if competitors gain too much information. Generalities and omissions should be noted by the researcher. It is also important to distinguish among sources and rely on the one with the best reputation. Conflicting results reported by equally accurate sources may require the researcher to collect fresh (primary) data.

The reliability of secondary data is not always known. Many research projects are not retested. Therefore, the user of secondary data hopes that the results from one limited prior study can be applied to a current research problem.

SOURCES

There are two major forms of secondary data, internal and external. Internal secondary data are available within the company. External secondary data are available from sources outside the firm.

A firm's records or its own past studies comprise internal secondary data.

Internal Secondary Data. Before spending time and money searching for external secondary data or collecting primary data, the researcher should look at the information contained inside his or her company. Internal sources include budgets, sales figures, profit-and-loss statements, customer billings, inventory records, prior research reports, and written reports.

At the beginning of the business year, most firms develop budgets for the following twelve months. These budgets, based on sales forecasts, outline planned expenditures for every product and service during the year. The budget and the company's performance in the attainment of budgetary goals (adherence to the outlined plan of expenditures) are good sources for secondary data.

Sales figures are frequently used as indicators of success. By examining the sales of each division, product line, item, geographic area, salesperson, time of day, day of week, and other factors and comparing these sales with prior time periods, a marketer can measure performance. An overdependence on sales data may be misleading, because increased sales do not always reflect higher profits. Sales data should be used in conjunction with profit-and-loss statistics.

Profit-and-loss statements reveal a lot of information. Actual achievements can be measured against profit goals. Trends in company success over time can be determined. Profits can be analyzed by department, salesperson, and product. A detailed profit-and-loss breakdown can show strengths and weaknesses in the firm's marketing program and can lead to improvements.

Customer billings provide information about inventory movement, sales by region, peak selling seasons, sales volume, and sales by customer category. For example, credit customers can be examined by geographic area, size of outstanding balance, length of repayment time, products purchased, and demographic data.

Inventory records show the levels of merchandise bought, manufactured, stored, shipped, and sold throughout the year. Inventory planning is improved when the lead time for order processing is known and the proper level of safety stock (excess merchandise stored to avoid running out) is determined.

Prior research reports, based on the findings of past marketing research efforts, are often stored and retained for future use. When the report is used initially, it is primary data. Later reference to the report is secondary in nature, because the report is no longer employed for its primary purpose. The currency of the report must be noted in evaluating its worth.

Written reports (ongoing information stored by the company) may be compiled by management, marketers, sales personnel, and others. Among the information available from written reports are standards for marketing performance and customer complaints.

External Secondary Data. If the research problem has not been solved through internal secondary data, a firm should utilize external secondary data sources. External data are available from both government and nongovernment sources.[7]

The government collects and distributes a wide range of statistics and descriptive materials. Table 4-3 shows some selected government publications that should be available in any business library or medium-sized public library. In addition, government agencies publish a wide range of pamphlets on topics such as franchising, pricing, credit, product warranties, and deceptive sales practices. The materials are usually distributed free of charge or sold for a nominal fee. The *Monthly Catalog of United States Government Publications* contains a listing of these items. When using government data, particularly census statistics, the date of the project must be considered.

> Government and nongovernment sources outside the firm make available external secondary data.

There are three sources of nongovernment secondary data: regular publications; books, monographs, and other nonregular publications; and commercial research houses.

Regular publications contain articles on various aspects of marketing and are available in business libraries or via subscriptions. Some are quite broad in scope *(Business Week, Journal of Marketing);* others are more specialized *(Journal of Advertising, Journal of Consumer Research).* These periodicals are published by

---

[7] Valuable sources for anyone involved with collecting marketing information are C. R. Goeldner and Laura M. Dirks, "Business Facts: Where to Find Them," *MSU Business Topics,* Vol. 24 (Summer 1976), pp. 23–36; Jac L. Goldstucker (Editor) and Dennis W. Goodwin (Compiler), *Marketing Information: A Professional Guide* (Atlanta: Georgia State University, 1982); and James R. Fries, "Library Support for Industrial Marketing Research," *Industrial Marketing Management,* Vol. 11 (February 1982), pp. 47–51. Regularly published reference guides include *Business Periodicals Index, Funk & Scott, Monthly Catalog of United States Government Publications, Public Affairs Information Service Index,* and *Readers' Guide to Periodical Literature.* Computer-generated bibliographic searches are also available through many libraries and from firms such as Dun & Bradstreet.

Table 4-3
Selected Sources of Government Information

American Statistical Index (Congressional Information Service), annual with monthly updates
Annual Survey of Manufactures (Department of Commerce), annual
Bureau of the Census Catalog (Bureau of Census), biennial
Business Statistics (Office of Business Economics), biennial
Census of Manufactures (Bureau of Census), every five years ending in 2 and 7
Census of Population (Bureau of Census), every ten years ending in 0
Census of Retail Trade, Wholesale Trade, and Selected Service Industries (Bureau of Census), every five years ending in 2 and 7
Census of Transportation (Bureau of Census), every five years ending in 2 and 7
County and City Data Book (Department of Commerce), several times each decade
Federal Reserve Bulletin (Federal Reserve System), monthly
Monthly Labor Review (Bureau of Labor Statistics), monthly
Monthly Product Announcement (Bureau of Census), monthly
Statistical Abstract of the United States (Department of Commerce), annual
Survey of Current Business (Office of Business Economics), monthly
Vital Statistics Report (Health and Human Resources), monthly

professional associations, regular publishing companies, or trade associations. The orientation of these periodicals varies widely. Table 4-4 contains a listing of selected periodicals.

Books, monographs, and other nonrecurring literature are published by a number of organizations. Some groups, such as the American Marketing Association, provide information to increase knowledge and professionalism. Others, such as the Better Business Bureau, are involved with self-regulation and public opinion. Yet another type, such as the National Retail Merchants Association, functions as a spokesperson for an industry as well as an information disseminator. Each of these organizations distributes materials for a nominal fee or free of charge.

Commercial research houses conduct periodic and ongoing studies and make the results of the studies available to many clients for a fee. The fee can be quite

Table 4-4
Selected Periodicals

Advertising Age, twice weekly
Business, quarterly
Business Horizons, bimonthly
Business Marketing, monthly
Business Week, weekly
California Management Review, quarterly
Chain Store Age, monthly
Columbia Journal of World Business, quarterly
Editor & Publisher Market Guide, annual
Fortune, semimonthly
Graphic Guide to Consumer Markets, annual
Harvard Business Review, bimonthly
Industrial Marketing Management, quarterly
Journal of the Academy of Marketing Science, quarterly
Journal of Advertising, quarterly
Journal of Advertising Research, bimonthly
Journal of Business, quarterly

Journal of Business Research, quarterly
Journal of Business Strategy, quarterly
Journal of Consumer Research, quarterly
Journal of Marketing, quarterly
Journal of Marketing Research, quarterly
Journal of Personal Selling and Sales Management, quarterly
Journal of Retailing, quarterly
Journal of Small Business Management, quarterly
Marketing & Media Decisions, monthly
Nielsen Researcher, several times per year
Progressive Grocer, monthly
Rand McNally Commercial Atlas & Marketing Guide, annual
Sales & Marketing Management, monthly (annual *Survey of Buying Power*)
Standard Rate & Data Service, monthly
Stores, monthly
Wall Street Journal, daily

Other periodicals: Most trade associations distribute at least one regular publication.

low or range into the tens of thousands of dollars, depending on the extent of the data. This kind of research is secondary when the firm acts as a subscriber and does not request specific studies pertaining only to itself. Several large commercial houses specialize in selling secondary data and provide a number of services at lower costs than the company would incur if the data were collected for its sole use. Among the leading research firms are A. C. Nielsen, IMS International, SAMI, and Arbitron. Figure 4-4 describes one of the many services offered by Nielsen, retail store audits.

Primary Data

Primary data are those freshly collected to solve a specific problem or issue under investigation. Primary data are necessary when a thorough analysis of secondary data is unable to provide satisfactory information. To evaluate the overall value of primary data, the researcher must weigh precision, currentness, and reliability against high costs, time pressures, and limited access to materials.

Primary data are used to study a specific marketing issue.

ADVANTAGES

Primary data are collected to fit the precise purposes of the current research problem. Units of measure and level of detail are matched to the objectives of the company. The data are current, because obsolete information is not used or collected. Attitudes, consumer characteristics, and other factors are up to date.

Data are collected by the firm itself or by an outside source carrying out a tailor-made research study for the firm. The source is known and controlled, and the methodology is constructed for the specific study. There are no conflicting data from different sources, and the reliability of the research can be determined.

Primary data are precise, current, tailored to the company's needs, and private.

Reprinted by permission.

Figure 4-4
A. C. Nielsen's Retail Store Audits
On a regular basis, Nielsen monitors the performance of several thousand food, drug, mass merchandise, and other retailers. Full-time field auditors visit a national sample of stores, providing information about sales, inventories, brand distribution, out-of-stock conditions, prices, and displays.

Secrecy can be maintained if competitors do not see study results or know research is being conducted. This is not true with secondary data, which are more accessible.

When secondary data do not resolve all questions, the collection and analysis of primary data are the only way to acquire information.

DISADVANTAGES

The problems with primary data are collection time, expense, unavailability, and bias.

The collection of primary data may be quite time consuming. For example, a test market may require six months for the results to be accurate. Primary data may be expensive to obtain. For instance, a consumer survey may cost several thousand dollars.

Some types of information cannot be collected. Usually, accurate census data can only be gathered by the government. In addition, some respondents may not answer questions or may not treat the study seriously.

The company's perspective may be limited, because only one data source is used. The organization may be unable to collect or analyze primary data and need understandable secondary data.

RESEARCH DESIGN

The *research design* outlines the procedure for data collection.

If the company decides that primary data are necessary, it must develop a research design. The *research design* is the "framework or plan for a study used as a guide in collecting and analyzing data,"[8] and includes the following decisions.

Internal or outside research personnel can be used.

Who Collects the Data? The company can collect the data itself or hire an outside research firm for a specific project. The advantages of an internal research department are knowledge of company operations, total access to company personnel, ongoing assembly and storage of data, and high loyalty or commitment. The disadvantages of an internal department are continuous costs, narrow perspective, and too much support for management. The strengths and weaknesses of an outside research firm are the opposite of those for the inside department.

What Information Should Be Collected? The kinds and amounts of information to be collected will be based on the problem definition formulated by the company. Exploratory research requires less data collection than conclusive research. These are two examples of the range of information that might be gathered:

Problem Definition	Information to Be Collected
1. To evaluate the sales trend of brand A	1. Annual sales data on brand A for the last five years; industry sales data for the product category for the last five years; opinions of sales personnel, customers, and industry personnel regarding the future sales of the product category and brand A
2. To convert nonusers of brand A to users	2. Brand currently bought by nonusers of brand A; why nonusers do not purchase brand A; differences in characteristics of users and nonusers

[8] Gilbert A. Churchill, Jr., *Marketing Research: Methodological Foundations*, Third Edition (New York: Dryden Press, 1983), p. 56.

Who or What Should Be Studied? First, the researcher must stipulate the people or objects to be studied. This is known as the population. People studies generally involve customers (current, former, potential; light product users, heavy product users; customers categorized by demographic and life-style dimensions), company personnel (such as salespeople, sales managers), and/or channel members (wholesalers, retailers, brokers). Object studies usually center on company and/or product performance. Whether people or objects are analyzed, precise terms need to be employed:

A population is the people or objects studied.

Who or What Is to Be Investigated	Specifications
1. Target market of company	1. All single women in the Chicago area, ages eighteen to thirty
2. Product A	2. Model number 11, sales performance for 1985 calendar year by geographic region

Second, the manner in which people or objects are selected for investigation must be determined. Large and dispersed populations frequently are examined by *sampling* procedures. Sampling requires the analysis of selected people or objects in the specified population, rather than all of them. Sampling saves time and money; when used properly, the accuracy and representativeness of sampling can be measured.

Sampling the population can save time and money.

The two approaches to sampling are probability and nonprobability. In a probability (random) sample, every member of the specified population has an equal or known probability of being chosen for analysis. For example, a researcher may select every twenty-fifth person in a telephone directory. In a nonprobability sample, members of the population are chosen by the researcher or interviewer on the basis of convenience or judgment. For instance, a researcher may select the first 100 dormitory students entering the college cafeteria. A probability sample is more accurate; however, it is more costly and difficult than a nonprobability sample. Figure 4-5 illustrates probability and nonprobability sampling.

Third, the size of the sample to be investigated must be stated. Generally speaking, a large sample will yield greater accuracy and higher cost than a small sample. There are methods for assessing sample size in terms of costs and accuracy, but a description of them is beyond the scope of this text.[9]

What Technique of Data Collection Should Be Used? There are four basic methods for primary data collection: survey, observation, experiment, and simulation.

A *survey* systematically gathers information from respondents by communicating with them. It can uncover data about attitudes, past purchases, and consumer characteristics. Yet, it is susceptible to incorrect or biased answers. With a survey, the questionnaire is used to record responses. A survey can be conducted in person, over the telephone, or by mail.

A *survey* communicates with respondents in person, over the telephone, or by mail.

A personal survey is conducted face-to-face, is flexible, elicits lengthy replies, and reduces ambiguity. It is expensive, however, and interviewer bias is possible, because the interviewer may affect results by suggesting ideas to respon-

---

[9] See for example, Donald S. Tull and Del F. Hawkins, *Marketing Research: Measurement and Method,* Third Edition (New York: Macmillan, 1984), pp. 401–423.

Figure 4-5
Probability Versus
Nonprobability Sampling

PROBABILITY SAMPLING

Calvin Adams

Amy Adams

INTERVIEWS

Calvin Adams   Amy Adams

NONPROBABILITY SAMPLING

Any Patron

Johnson University Sampling Register here

Any Patron

Figure 4-5
Probability Versus
Nonprobability Sampling

dents or creating a certain mood during the interview. A telephone survey is fast and relatively inexpensive, especially with the growth of discount telephone services. Responses are usually brief, but nonresponse may be a problem. It must be verified that the desired respondent is actually contacted. Many people do not have a phone or utilize unlisted numbers. The latter problem may now be overcome through random digit-dialing devices. A mail survey can reach dispersed respondents, has no interviewer bias, and is relatively inexpensive. Nonresponse, slowness of return, and participation by incorrect respondents are the major problems. The technique that is chosen depends on the objectives and needs of the specific research project.

A nondisguised survey reveals its true purpose, while a disguised survey does not.

A survey may be nondisguised or disguised. In a nondisguised survey, the respondent is told the real purpose of the study. In a disguised survey, the respondent is not told the real purpose of the study. The latter is used to elicit honest attitudes or feelings and to avoid the respondent answering what he or she thinks the interviewer or researcher wants to hear or read. The left side of Figure 4-6 shows a nondisguised survey, which reveals the true intent of a study on sports car attitudes and behavior. The right side of Figure 4-6 shows how the survey can be disguised. By asking about sports car owners in general, the researcher is able to get more honest answers to personal questions than if he or she asks questions geared directly to the respondents. The real intent of the study is to uncover the respondents' actual reasons for buying a sports car.

NONDISGUISED

1. Why are you buying a sports car?

   _____

   _____

   _____

2. What factors are you considering in
   the purchase of a sports car?

   _____

   _____

   _____

3. Is status important to you in a
   sports–car purchase?

   — Yes

   — No

4. On the highway, I will drive my
   sports car

   — within the speed limit.

   — slightly over the speed limit.

   — well over the speed limit.

DISGUISED

1. Why do you think people buy sports cars?

   _____

   _____

   _____

2. What factors do people consider in the
   purchase of a sports car?

   _____

   _____

   _____

3. Are people who purchase sports cars
   status-conscious?

   — Yes

   — No

3. On the highway, sports car owners drive

   — within the speed limit.

   — slightly over the speed limit.

   — well over the speed limit.

Figure 4-6
Nondisguised and Disguised Surveys

The *semantic differential* is a list of bipolar (opposite) adjective scales. It is a survey technique that employs rating scales instead of, or in addition to, questions. It may be disguised or nondisguised, depending on whether the respondent is told the true purpose of the study. Each adjective in the semantic differential is evaluated along a bipolar scale, and average ratings for all respondents are computed. An overall company or product profile is then developed. This profile may be compared with competitors' profiles and consumers' ideal ratings. An example of a completed semantic differential appears in Figure 4-7.

The semantic differential surveys people through a list of rating scales.

Multidimensional scaling is another popular survey research tool that may be disguised or nondisguised. With multidimensional scaling, respondents' attitudes are surveyed for many product and company attributes. Then, computer analysis enables the firm to develop a single product or company rating, rather than a profile of several individual characteristics. A statistical description of the technique is beyond the scope of this text, but Figure 4-8 shows how it can be used to construct single overall ratings. In the figure, consumer attitudes about six brands of facial tissue and the consumers' ideal rating of facial tissue are depicted. Brand A most closely matches the consumers' ideal.

Multidimensional scaling analyzes attitudes and develops an overall product or company rating.

Observation is a research technique in which present behavior or the results of past behavior are observed and recorded. People are not questioned, and their cooperation is not necessary. Interviewer and question bias are minimized. Fre-

In *observation*, present behavior or the results of past behavior are viewed.

Figure 4-7
**A Semantic Differential
for a Color Television**

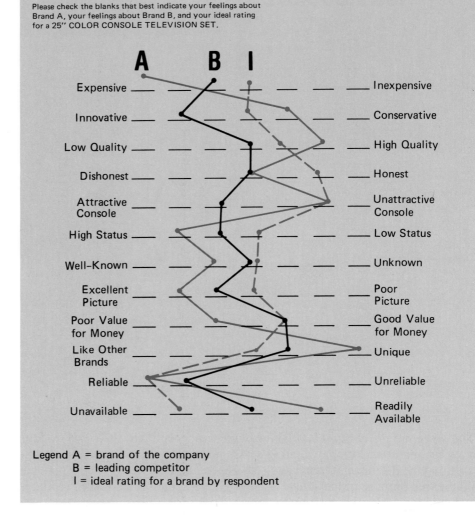

Figure 4-7
A Semantic Differential for a Color Television

quently, observation is used in actual situations. The major disadvantages are that attitudes cannot be determined and observers may misinterpret behavior.

In disguised observation, the consumer is not aware that he or she is being watched. A two-way mirror or hidden camera would be used. With nondisguised observation, the participant knows that he or she is being observed. Human observation is carried out by people; mechanical observation records behavior through electronic or other means, such as a movie camera filming in-store customer behavior.

An *experiment* is a type of research in which one or more factors are manipulated under controlled conditions. A factor may be any element of marketing from package design to advertising media. In an experiment just the factor under investigation is varied; all other factors remain constant. For example, in order to evaluate a new package design for a product, the manufacturer could send new

An *experiment* varies marketing factors under controlled conditions.

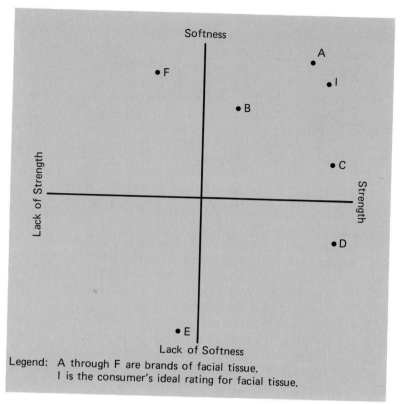

Figure 4-8
**Multidimensional
Scaling—Ratings for
Facial Tissues**

packages to five retail outlets and old packages to five similar retail outlets. All marketing factors other than packaging would remain the same. After one month, sales of the new package through the five test outlets would be compared with sales of the old package through the five similar outlets.

The major advantage of an experiment is that it is able to show cause and effect—for example, a new package design increases sales. It is also systematically structured and implemented. The major disadvantages are high costs, contrived settings, and the inability to control all factors in or affecting the marketing plan.

Simulation is a computer-based technique that recreates the use of various marketing factors on paper rather than in a real setting. First, a model of the controllable and uncontrollable factors facing the firm is constructed. Then different combinations of the factors are fed into a computer to determine their effects on the overall marketing strategy. Simulation requires no consumer cooperation and is able to handle many interrelated factors. However, it is complex and difficult to use.

Simulation enables marketing factors to be analyzed through a computer model rather than the marketplace.

Table 4-5 shows the most appropriate uses for each technique of primary data collection.

How Much Will the Study Cost? The overall and specific costs of the study must be clearly outlined. These costs include executive time, researcher time, support staff time, computer usage, respondents' incentives (if any), interview-

Research costs include everything from personnel time to marketing costs.

Table 4-5
Uses of Primary Data-Collection Techniques

Technique	Most Appropriate Uses
1. Survey	Determination of consumer attitudes and motivations, evaluation of commercials, measurement of purchase intentions, relation of consumer characteristics to attitudes
2. Observation	Examination under natural conditions, interest in behavior not attitudes
3. Experiment	Control of the research environment essential, cause-and-effect relationship important to establish
4. Simulation	Many interrelationships among variables to be derived and analyzed

ers, printing, pretesting, special equipment, and marketing costs (such as advertising).[10]

The costs of the study should be evaluated against the benefits to be derived from having better information. For example, a firm estimates that a new product can be introduced and earn the company a $100,000 profit during the first year. The firm also realizes that a consumer survey costing $10,000 will enable it to improve the marketing mix of the new product, particularly its package design and advertising. With the changes suggested by research, the firm will increase its first-year profit to $130,000. Therefore, the net increase as a result of research is $20,000 ($30,000 additional profit, $10,000 in research costs).

How Will the Data Be Collected? The personnel necessary to collect the data outlined in the research design must be determined. The attributes, skills, and training of the data collection force need to be specified. See Figure 4-9. Too often this important phase is improperly planned, and data are collected by unqualified personnel.

Data collection can be administered by others or self-administered. With administered questionnaires, interviewers are responsible for asking questions or observing behavior, noting responses or behavior, and explaining questions (if necessary) to a respondent. In self-administered questionnaires, respondents read the questions and write their own answers. In the choice of these techniques, there is a trade-off between control and interviewer probing (administered) versus privacy and limited interviewer bias (self-administered).

How Long Will the Data Collection Period Be? The researcher must stipulate the time frame within which data will be collected, or else a study can drag on. Too long a time frame may cause inconsistent responses and violations of secrecy. Short time frames are easy to set for personal and telephone surveys. Mail surveys, observation, and experiments require substantially more time. Nonetheless, time limits must be defined.

When and Where Should Information Be Collected? The day and time of data collection must be specified. In addition, it must be decided whether the study is undertaken on the firm's premises or off them. The researcher has to

Interviewers may administer questionnaires; or respondents may fill out questionnaires themselves.

---

[10] See David W. Flegal, ''How to Make Better Use of Dollars and Sense in Buying Market Research,'' *Management Review* (January 1983), pp. 49–51; David W. Flegal, ''Controlling Marketing Research Costs,'' *Management Review* (March 1983), pp. 52–55; and Alan R. Andreasen, ''Cost-Conscious Marketing Research,'' *Harvard Business Review*, Vol. 61 (July–August 1983), pp. 74–75 ff.

Figure 4-9
Interviewer Training
Walker Research is one of the largest commercial research companies in the United States. One of its operating divisions is the Custom Research Division, which conducts over 1,000 tailored studies annually. Prior to the start of each study, an interviewer training program is conducted using the most modern equipment: "Walker training programs include a unique three-level interviewer training, specialized study training, supervisor training, and traveling supervisor training."

weigh immediacy and convenience versus a desire to investigate hard-to-reach respondents at the proper time of the year.

DATA COLLECTION

After all aspects of the research design are thoroughly detailed, the data are actually collected. It is important that the personnel responsible for data collection be adequately supervised and follow directions exactly. Responses or observations must be entered correctly.

Data Analysis

In *data analysis,* forms are first coded and tabulated and then analyzed. Coding is the process by which each completed data form is numbered and response categories are labeled. Tabulation is the calculation of summary data for each response category. Analysis is the evaluation of responses, usually by statistical techniques, as they pertain to the specific problem under investigation. The relationship of coding, tabulation, and analysis is shown in Figure 4-10.

Data analysis consists of coding, tabulation, and analysis.

Partial Questionnaire	Total responses
1. Do you drink coffee? ☐ Yes 01	375
☐ No 02	125
2. Which of these brands have you heard of? Check all the answers that apply.	
☐ Brim 03	195
☐ Sanka 04	340
☐ Savarin 05	212
☐ None 06	63
3. Compared to tea, coffee is (Check only <u>one</u> answer)	
☐ more bitter 07	140
☐ better for your health 08	12
☐ more energizing 09	240
☐ more expensive 10	108

Coding: Questionnaires numbered A001 to A500.
Each response labeled 01 to 10 (e.g., Sanka is 04, more energizing is 09).
Question 2 is a multiple–response question.

Tabulation: Total responses as shown above right.

Analysis: 75% drink coffee; Sanka is the most well–known brand; only 39% are familiar with Brim; coffee is viewed as energizing; yet compared to tea, it is not seen as better for health; high prices may be a problem.

Recommendations: The advertising of Brim must be increased and concentrated on stimulating brand awareness; emphasis should be placed on good taste, energizing qualities, and low price per serving.

Implementation of findings: A new advertising campaign will be developed and the annual media budget expanded. Other suggestions will be accepted as noted above.

Figure 4-10 Data Analysis, Recommendations, and Implementation of Findings for a Study on Brim Coffee

Recommendations

Recommendations direct future actions.

Recommendations are suggestions for future actions by the company, based on the data collected by the researcher. They are generally presented in written (in some cases oral) form to management. The report must be written for the audience that will read it. For instance, terminology must be defined. Figure 4-10 shows recommendations flowing from completed research.

Implementation of Findings

Management determines how to respond to research.

The research report represents feedback to marketing management, which is responsible for utilizing findings. If management ignores weaknesses or company problems, research has little value. If marketing management bases decisions on research results, then marketing research has great value and the organization benefits in the short and long run.

Marketing managers are most likely to implement research findings when they participate in establishing the research design, they operate in a decentralized and informal organization with significant discretion over decision making, and research findings confirm their intuition.[11] Figure 4-10 provides an illustration of a company implementing research findings.

Marketing Information System

Companies should not approach marketing information collection as a haphazard, infrequent occurrence that is only necessary when the firm needs to generate data about a specific marketing topic. When marketing research alone is used, the company faces several risks:

1. Previous studies may not be stored in an easy-to-use format.
2. There may be a lack of awareness about environmental changes and competitors' actions.
3. Information collection may be disjointed.
4. Time lags may result whenever a new research study is required.
5. There may be no data to analyze over several comparable time periods.
6. Marketing plans and decisions may not be effectively reviewed.
7. Actions may be reactionary rather than anticipatory.

> When marketing information is seldom gathered, the firm may encounter several risks.

Marketing research should be considered as just one part of an ongoing, integrated information process. It is essential that a firm develop and utilize a system for scanning the environment in a continuous manner and for storing data, so that they may be reviewed in the future. A *marketing information system (MIS)* can be defined as

a set of procedures and methods designed to generate, store, analyze, and disseminate anticipated marketing decision information on a regular, continuous basis.[12]

> A *marketing information system (MIS)* generates, stores, analyzes, and disseminates information regularly.

Figure 4-11 presents a basic marketing information system. In this system, the firm begins with a statement of company objectives. These objectives are influenced by environmental factors, such as competition, government, and the economy. The objectives provide broad guidelines that direct marketing planning. Marketing plans involve the controllable factors explained in Chapters 2 and 3, including the selection of the target market, marketing objectives, the type of marketing organization, the marketing mix (product or service, distribution, promotion, and price), and control.

After marketing plans are outlined, the total information needs of the marketing department can be specified and satisfied through a *marketing intelligence*

---

[11] Rohit Deshpande, "The Organizational Context of Market Research Use," *Journal of Marketing,* Vol. 46 (Fall 1982), pp. 91–101; and Rohit Deshpande and Gerald Zaltman, "Factors Affecting the Use of Market Research Information: A Path Analysis," *Journal of Marketing Research,* Vol. 19 (February 1982), pp. 14–31.

[12] Robert A. Peterson, *Marketing Research* (Dallas: Business Publications, 1982), p. 16.

**Figure 4-11
A Basic Marketing
Information System**

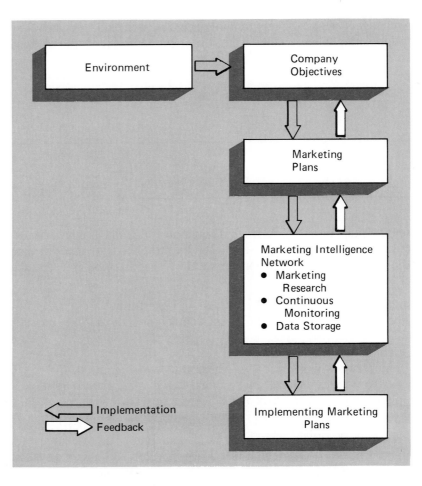

The *marketing intelligence network* **stage of an MIS consists of** *marketing research, continuous monitoring,* **and** *data storage.*

network, which consists of marketing research, continuous monitoring, and data storage. **Marketing research** is used to obtain precise information to solve research problems. It may acquire information from storage (internal secondary data) or collect external secondary data and/or primary data. **Continuous monitoring** is the procedure by which the changing environment is regularly viewed. Continuous monitoring can include subscriptions to business and trade publications, observing news reports, regularly obtaining information from employees and customers, attending industry meetings, and watching competitors' actions. **Data storage** involves the retention of all types of relevant company records (such as sales, costs, personnel performance, etc.) as well as the information collected through marketing research and continuous monitoring. These data aid decision making and are kept for future reference.

Depending on the resources of the firm and the complexity of information needs, the marketing intelligence network may or may not be computerized. Smaller firms can operate such systems very efficiently without computerization. The ingredients for the success of any system are consistency, thoroughness, and a good filing technique.

Marketing plans should be implemented on the basis of information obtained from the intelligence network. For example, by continuous monitoring, the firm may determine that the costs of raw materials will be rising by 7 per cent during the following year. This would give the company time to explore its marketing options (e.g., switch to substitute materials, pass along costs, absorb costs) and select one alternative to be implemented. If monitoring was not in effect, the firm might be caught by surprise and forced to absorb costs, without any choice.

In general, a marketing information system offers many advantages: organized data collection, broad perspective, retention of important data, avoidance of crises, coordination of the marketing plan, speed, quantifiable results, and cost-benefit analysis. However, developing a marketing information system may not be easy. Initial time and manpower costs are high, and setting up a system can be complex. Figure 4-12 shows how a marketing information system can assist a company in planning marketing strategies.

Figure 4-12
Using a Marketing Information System in Strategy Planning

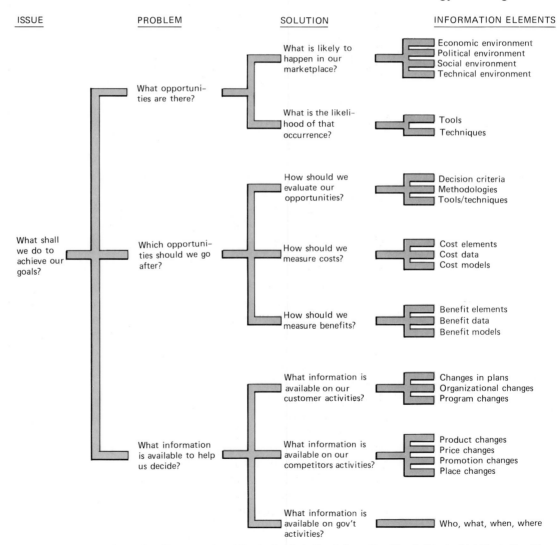

ISSUE	PROBLEM	SOLUTION	INFORMATION ELEMENTS

Source: M. Edward Goretsky, "Frameworks of Strategic Marketing Information Needs," *Industrial Marketing Management*, Vol. 12 (February 1983), p. 11. Reprinted by permission of the publisher. Copyright 1983—by Elsevier Science Publishing Co., Inc.

Recently, a major study examined the use of marketing information systems by the largest manufacturing firms in the U.S. These are some of the more important findings of this study:[13]

- Company records (data storage) are the most critical source of information, followed by continuous monitoring, and then by marketing research.
- In most instances, marketing intelligence data are transmitted to marketing managers by word-of-mouth rather than by computer.
- Customer, competitive, and government data are frequently collected on a regular basis.
- Company records and marketing research data that are stored are usually placed into a computer memory bank.
- About half of the marketing executives participating in the survey have a computer terminal in their office. Approximately one half of those executives use their terminals on a daily basis.
- Product decisions often rely on an MIS, while promotion decisions rarely depend on an MIS.
- Top management support for a marketing information system and its use in planning is growing.

Among the many companies with well-structured marketing information systems are GTE, Quaker Oats, Holiday Inns, and J. W. Robinson. Each devotes considerable time and resources to its system.

The Sylvania division of GTE is using its MIS in a rather unique way: it continuously monitors 51 leading competitors and feeds statistics into a complex computer data bank. The firm's MICS (Management Information of Competitor Strategies) coordinates data from industry publications, Securities and Exchange Commission filings, and reports from company personnel in the field. For every competitor, GTE studies as many as 17 factors, including management strategy, marketing strategy, and the backgrounds of top executives. Marketers work with 20-page forms and incorporate all types of "hearsay, rumor, and grapevine-intelligence" into the MCIS.[14]

Quaker Oats has had a computerized marketing information system for more than a decade. This system "plays a significant role in tracking of new products, provides top management with summary statistics and charts for strategy meetings, supports brand and industry forecasting, and supports customer analyses." The MIS has data storage of 20 million numbers. Any of these numbers can be retrieved in less than a minute. Computer simulations can also be undertaken. At Quaker, the MIS relies on simple English language commands (such as GET for retrieve) rather than complex computer programming; this makes the system easy to use by marketing executives. The firm calculates that millions of dollars have been saved because of the information gained through the MIS.[15]

Holiday Inns uses a computerized marketing information system to anticipate, monitor, and review business opportunities. At first, its system developed simple

[13] Raymond McLeod, Jr., and John Rogers, "Marketing Information Systems: Uses in the *Fortune* 500," *California Management Review,* Vol. 25 (Fall 1982), pp. 106–118.

[14] "GTE's Computer Records Secrets of 51 Competitors," *Marketing News* (September 16, 1983), Section 1, p.10; and Information Data Search Inc., "Intelligence Update".

[15] George A. Clowes, "Data Management Should Be No. 1 Priority in Developing On-Line MIS," *Marketing News* (December 12, 1980), pp. 1, 10.

models to measure lodging demand nationally and in several major markets. Now, the company is "building computer systems which combine internal and external data bases in order to have data bases on room supply, room-night sales, traveler characteristics, inspections, guest ratings, and prices." Some of the variables Holiday Inns examines are industry supply (rooms available), lodging demand as shown in consumer-tracking studies, and industry occupancy ratios.[16] Figure 4-13 highlights Holiday Inns' MIS.

J. W. Robinson is a California-based department store chain that is a division of Allied Stores Corporation. Robinson's MIS includes frequent secondary and primary marketing research studies, monitoring population changes and competitors' offerings, projecting long-term trends, obtaining information from in-store electronic sales registers, and storing a variety of data. The goal of Robinson's system is to engage in a constant examination of consumer attitudes and sales (market-share) potential in order to "maintain a balance of our growth with the future growth of the 500-mile market" in which the chain operates. Robinson's computerized MIS has been unique among Allied divisions. It represents what the parent firm wants to accomplish in these other divisions.[17]

Summary

Marketing information is necessary to reduce risk, obtain consumer attitudes, assess the uncontrollable environment, integrate the marketing strategy, and evaluate success or failure. It also helps to enhance credibility and meet legal requirements, gain support or defend a decision, and validate intuition.

Marketing research is the systematic gathering, recording, and analyzing of data about problems related to marketing. The scientific method requires objectivity, accuracy, and thoroughness. The use of marketing research varies by company and type of information required. Larger firms and consumer goods companies are most likely to engage in marketing research.

The marketing research process involves a series of actions: problem definition, examination of secondary data, generation of primary data (when necessary), analysis of data, recommendations, and implementation of findings. Many considerations and decisions are needed in each stage of the process.

Exploratory research is used to develop a clear problem definition. Conclusive research is structured data collection and analysis for the solution of a specific problem or objective. Secondary data, those previously gathered for purposes other than the solution of the current problem, are available from internal and external (government, nongovernment, commercial) sources. Primary data, those collected to solve a specific problem under investigation, are available through surveys, observation, experiments, or simulation. Primary data collection requires a research design: the specified framework for controlling data. Primary

---

[16] Thayer C. Taylor, "Computers That Plan." *Sales & Marketing Management* (December 7, 1981), special report.
[17] Isadore Barmash, "Research!" *Stores* (April 1981), pp. 23–24.

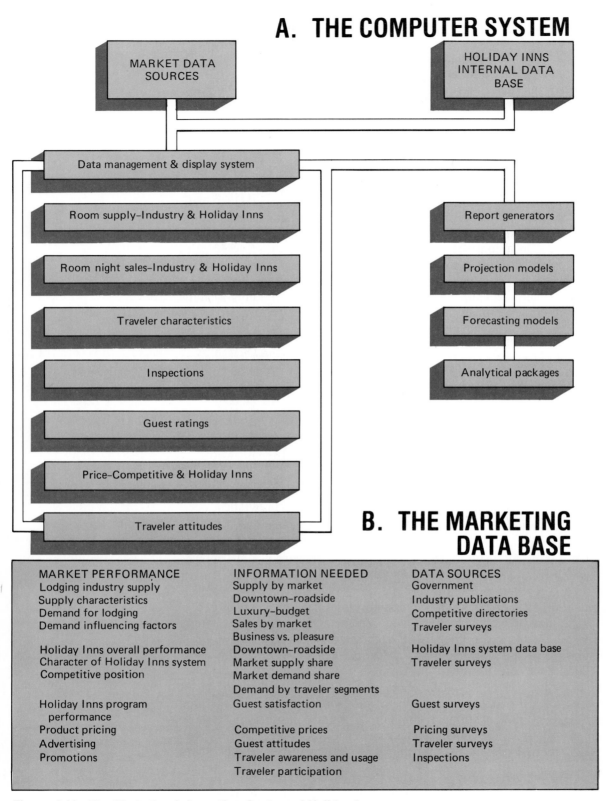

A. THE COMPUTER SYSTEM

MARKET DATA SOURCES

HOLIDAY INNS INTERNAL DATA BASE

Data management & display system

Room supply–Industry & Holiday Inns

Room night sales–Industry & Holiday Inns

Traveler characteristics

Inspections

Guest ratings

Price–Competitive & Holiday Inns

Traveler attitudes

Report generators

Projection models

Forecasting models

Analytical packages

B. THE MARKETING DATA BASE

MARKET PERFORMANCE	INFORMATION NEEDED	DATA SOURCES
Lodging industry supply	Supply by market	Government
Supply characteristics	Downtown-roadside	Industry publications
Demand for lodging	Luxury-budget	Competitive directories
Demand influencing factors	Sales by market	Traveler surveys
	Business vs. pleasure	
Holiday Inns overall performance	Downtown-roadside	Holiday Inns system data base
Character of Holiday Inns system	Market supply share	Traveler surveys
Competitive position	Market demand share	
	Demand by traveler segments	
Holiday Inns program performance	Guest satisfaction	Guest surveys
Product pricing	Competitive prices	Pricing surveys
Advertising	Guest attitudes	Traveler surveys
Promotions	Traveler awareness and usage	Inspections
	Traveler participation	

Figure 4-13 The Marketing Information System of Holiday Inns

Source: Thayer C. Taylor, "Computers That Plan," *Sales & Marketing Management* (December 7, 1981), special report. Reprinted by permission.

data are gathered only if secondary data are insufficient. Costs must be weighed against the benefits of research.

The concluding stages of marketing research are data analysis (including coding, tabulation, and analysis), recommendations, and the implementation of findings by management.

The marketing information system is an organized, interacting, continuous structure that directs the flow and uses of information for marketing decision making. The marketing intelligence phase of an MIS consists of marketing research, continuous monitoring, and data storage. An MIS can be used by both small and large firms, and the applications of marketing information systems are spreading rapidly. Today, many marketing executives are likely to have computer terminals in their offices.

Questions for Discussion

1. Why is marketing information necessary? What may result if managers rely exclusively on intuition?
2. Firms often have difficulties in applying the scientific method to marketing research. Why do you think this problem occurs?
3. Under which circumstances would informal, inexpensive research be acceptable? Unacceptable?
4. How could Polaroid use the marketing research process to determine consumer attitudes toward the quality of instant film?
5. What are several examples of exploratory and conclusive research that could be conducted by J. C. Penney?
6. When is primary data collection necessary?
7. 7-Eleven operates a national chain of convenience stores. Bob's 24-Hour Self-Serv is an independent neighborhood convenience store. Both retailers are interested in gathering information about their respective competitors' practices. How would the research design used by 7-Eleven differ from that of Bob's 24-Hour Self-Serv?
8. Develop a five-question disguised survey to determine attitudes toward shoplifting. Why use a disguised survey for this topic?
9. What can be learned from a semantic differential? From multidimensional scaling?
10. Comment on the ethics of disguised observation. Under which circumstances would you recommend its use?
11. Describe an experiment to evaluate the success or failure of a permanent price rise for a candy bar.
12. Explain the data analysis process of coding, tabulation, and analysis.
13. How can marketing managers be encouraged to implement marketing research findings?
14. Many companies have not yet set up marketing information systems. Why do you think this has occurred?
15. Evaluate the Holiday Inns' MIS shown in Figure 4-8. How could a smaller hotel chain adapt this system to its own needs and resources?

Case 1 Gillette: Actively Acquiring Marketing Information About Existing Products*

Gillette is a major manufacturer of shaving blades and razors, personal care products, writing instruments, and small appliances (overseas). Among its well-known brands are Trac II, Good News, Atra, and Daisy razors, Right Guard deodorant, Silkience shampoo, Paper Mate pens and pencils, and Braun small appliances.

As a marketing-oriented firm, Gillette is heavily engaged in a variety of marketing research activities—for new and continuing products. Its research program for existing products is particularly comprehensive and involves several activities.

Annually, national surveys of men and women determine the "last" brand of a product that has been purchased. Attitude questions center on brand loyalty, satisfaction, value for the money, impulsiveness, and company image. Respondents for these surveys are selected through probability sampling, and have not been questioned before by Gillette. To improve accuracy, questioning is done in participants' homes.

A constant panel of men and women receives an annual mail survey regarding the "last" brand purchased. The same people are questioned each year. Gillette's goals are to track brand loyalty and switching behavior, and to predict future market share. No attitude questions are asked of this panel.

Yearly brand awareness studies are conducted by telephone. These studies focus on brand recognition and recollections of advertising campaigns. Special life-style and image studies are also conducted.

Consumer use tests investigate whether Gillette products are "state of the art," performance standards, reactions to packaging and display claims, etc. These tests are used throughout the year, with a variety of brands. Participants are interviewed and reinterviewed.

Finally, trade activities are observed through continuous tracking of inventory, retail sales, displays, prices, local advertising, and out-of-stock situations.

QUESTIONS

1. Evaluate Gillette's marketing research program for existing products.
2. Why does Gillette conduct surveys with new respondents as well as with continuing panel members? Is this an instance of overkill? Explain your answer.
3. Suggest a variety of secondary data Gillette could use to supplement its primary research.
4. Gillette's research involves nondisguised surveys. Is this appropriate? Why or why not?

* The data in this case are drawn from Keith Dennis, "The Gillette Blade Market: The Role of Market Research," *Marketing Review* (April–May 1983), pp. 15–17.

Case 2 Randall's Supermarkets: Scanning for Profits[†]

Randall's is a moderate-sized supermarket chain based in Houston, with plans to open a number of larger superstores in the near future. These superstores will be more than twice the size of traditional supermarkets and carry double the items (including many nonfood goods).

A key part of Randall's marketing strategy revolves around the use of electronic scanning equipment in its newer stores. This equipment provides Randall's with better and faster information about product sales than regular cash registers. As a result, Randall's can redesign store shelves and allocate space on the basis of sales. Inventory turnover is improved, since the space allotted to weaker items is reduced, and so are profits.

One of Randall's new stores is a 52,000-square-foot unit in Sugar Land. In this store 24,000 items are manufacturer-coded with UPC (Universal Product Code) lines that designate size, color, price, and other product information. These lines are read by optical-scanning machines that are linked to central computers. Cashiers at 12 checkout counters pass items over their optical scanners, rather than ring up transactions. Instantly, information is processed and stored by the computer. Regular printouts are provided to management.

Because of the information from the scanner, the Sugar Land store is able to operate efficiently with a 9 days' supply of inventory. Other, older Randall's outlets require a 14 days' supply. This means that even popular items can be ordered in less quantity, since reordering can be done so rapidly; and the Sugar Land store can react faster to shifts in consumer demand. Said a Randall's executive,

The days when back rooms were loaded to the ceiling with products have long since disappeared. Most merchandise you'll find is for backup of specials. A corollary is that out-of-stocks are virtually eliminated. And the lost sales that result from those out-of-stocks.

QUESTIONS

1. Some manufacturers are not pleased with optical-scanning systems, since they result in retailers placing smaller, but more frequent orders. How would you answer this objection?
2. Randall's sells the scanning information it generates to commercial research firms, who assemble data from many sources and then make it widely available. Why would Randall sell its information? What are the risks of this approach?
3. What are the limitations to Randall's strong reliance on optical-scanning data?
4. What kinds of information should Randall's acquire in addition to inventory movement by product type?

[†] The data in this case are drawn from Robert E. O'Neill, ''Scanning for Profits: 'Free' Inventory Fuels Expansion,'' *Progressive Grocer* (May 1983), pp. 93, 96.

Part One Case AT&T: A New Era Begins*

On January 8, 1982, the American Telephone & Telegraph Company (AT&T) and the U.S. Justice Department signed a lengthy agreement. It stipulated that pending government antitrust charges and a previous settlement barring AT&T from participating in new businesses would be dropped; in return, AT&T would divest itself of its local Bell companies, which would become seven autonomous regional firms providing local telephone service ("selling dial tones"). The divestiture was to be completed on January 1, 1984. AT&T would gain greater freedom in its operations and be allowed to pursue emerging opportunities; the government would be able to further deregulate the telephone industry.

In 1983, AT&T had revenues of $100 billion, assets of $150 billion, and nearly 1 million employees. In 1984, it was expected to have revenues of $50 billion, assets of $35 billion, and 385,000 employees. Table 1 shows the anticipated 1984 revenues, assets, and employees for AT&T and the seven new regional telephone companies that were created out of the parent company.

The revamped AT&T is organized into two basic divisions: Communications and Technologies. AT&T Communications provides long-distance telephone service throughout the United States and around the world. AT&T Technologies is involved with the manufacture and marketing of telephones, computers, and other products. Technologies consists of AT&T Bell Laboratories, which fulfills research and development needs; AT&T Western Electric, which manufactures products; AT&T Information Systems, which markets products and services to residential and business customers; and AT&T International, which markets products and services overseas. Figure 1 shows AT&T's 1984 organization chart.

An overriding concern of many analysts is whether AT&T can develop a strong marketing orientation in its current highly competitive environment. Commented one management consultant,

Now that divestiture is over, the big issue this year is whether AT&T can marry manufacturing and marketing. Right now there appears to be a war, with the engineers from Western Electric versus the marketeers from Information Systems. IBM will flatten AT&T in the automated office and computer business unless the marketing types can gain more control.

---

* The data in this case are drawn from Charles L. Brown, "Recasting the Bell System," *Columbia Journal of World Business,* Vol. 18 (Spring 1983), pp. 5–7; "Changing Phone Habits: A New AT&T Sets Its Strategies to Keep up with Its Customers," *Business Week* (September 5, 1983), pp. 68–71; "Culture Shock Is Shaking the Bell System," *Business Week* (September 26, 1983), pp. 112–114, 116; Steven Flax, "The Orphan Called Baby Bell," *Fortune* (June 27, 1983), pp. 87–88; R. Edward Freeman, "Managing the Strategic Challenge in Telecommunications," *Columbia Journal of World Business,* Vol. 18 (Spring 1983), pp. 8–18; Virginia Inman, "AT&T Tells Everyone Its Long-Distance Calls Are Better than MCI's," *Wall Street Journal* (October 27, 1983), pp. 1, 21; Monica Langley, "AT&T Marketing Men Find Their Star Fails to Ascend as Expected," *Wall Street Journal* (February 13, 1984), pp. 1, 16; Brian O'Reilly, "Ma Bell's Kids Fight for Position," *Fortune* (June 27, 1983), pp. 62–68; Bro Uttal, "The Corporate Culture Vultures," *Fortune* (October 17, 1983), pp. 66–72; "What the Spinoff Will Mean to the Customer," *Business Week* (September 5, 1983), pp. 71–72; "Why AT&T Will Lose More Long Distance Business," *Business Week* (February 13, 1984), pp. 102, 106, 110; and Kathleen K. Wiegner, "Prometheus Unbound, And Seeking His Footing," *Forbes* (March 12, 1984), pp. 141–148.

Company	Service Area	Revenues (Billion $)	Assets (Billion $)	Employees
AT&T	U.S. and overseas	50	35	385,000
Ameritech	Illinois, Indiana, Michigan, Ohio, Wisconsin	8	16	79,000
Bell Atlantic	Delaware, Maryland, New Jersey, Pennsylvania, Virginia, West Virginia, District of Columbia	8	16	80,000
Bell South	Alabama, Florida, Georgia, Kentucky, Louisiana, Mississippi, North Carolina, South Carolina, Tennessee	10	21	99,000
Nynex	Connecticut, Maine, Massachusetts, New Hampshire, New York, Rhode Island, Vermont	10	17	98,000
Pacific Telesis	California, Nevada	8	16	82,000
Southwestern Bell	Arkansas, Kansas, Missouri, Oklahoma, Texas	8	16	75,000
U.S. West	Arizona, Colorado, Idaho, Iowa, Kansas, Minnesota, Montana, Nebraska, North Dakota, South Dakota, Oregon, Utah, Washington, Wyoming	7	15	75,000

Said a former AT&T marketing manager,

I left AT&T because the market-driven organization we were trying to achieve was losing out to the manufacturing mentality. The marketers want to supply the customers with what they need quickly, while the manufacturers want to take more time to make a product that's twice as expensive with half the options. It's a clash in corporate culture that produces battle after battle between these two segments.

In general, observers raise these issues. Historically, the telecommunications industry was always somewhat insensitive to external forces, since the industry was treated as a "natural monopoly" until recently. AT&T's providing "universal service" is contrary to the concept of segmenting markets and responding to distinct customer needs with different marketing mixes. AT&T's organization is dominated by people who have engineering and other technical backgrounds. Company managers have often been rewarded on the basis of service provided (or seniority) rather than because of their contributions to earnings. Some executives may be unable to make the transition from managing a telephone company to leading an information-systems firm. In the face of intensifying competition, AT&T may have less than five years to reorient its managers and its way of doing business.

Figure 1
AT&T's 1984 Organization Chart

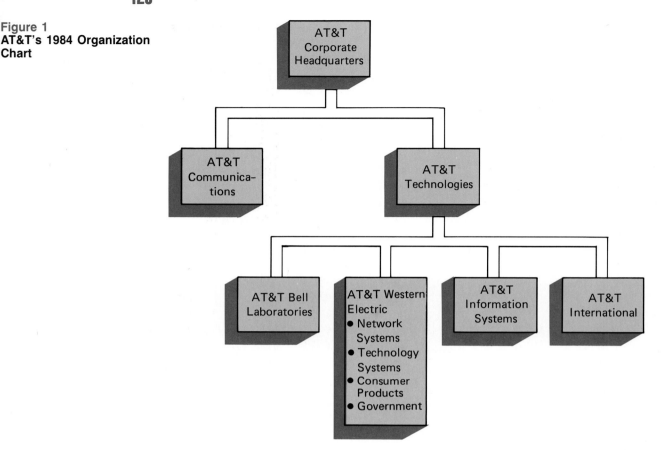

As one expert noted, a careful balance will be required: "If you move too slowly, the current culture moves around anything new and engulfs it. If you do it too quickly, you get a reject."

In reacting to its changed environment, AT&T must deal with a wide range of legal, technological, and competitive factors. As a result of Federal Communications Commission rulings, court decisions, and AT&T's agreement with the Justice Department, there is now competition in all phases of the telecommunications industry. For example, any company can manufacture and market telephones and accessory equipment, AT&T is excluded from local telephone services, firms can hook into the AT&T equipment network, and long-distance telephone service competition is encouraged.

Final consumers and business customers do not have to purchase equipment from Western Electric. Many are purchasing from AT&T's competitors. Western Electric no longer has a "captive market" for its products, most of which offer fewer features (at higher prices) than competitors'. In the final consumer market, competitors' telephones often include automatic redialing of the last number and a switch that temporarily disconnects the unit's bell; Western Electric phones without these features sell for twice the price. To compete with the extensive distribution of nonAT&T products, the company has entered into arrangements with retailers such as Sears, True Value Hardware Stores, and May Company. In the business segment, competitors are marketing more innovative and less expensive switching systems; AT&T has less than 30 per cent of the business switchboard market.

Greater coordination is required between AT&T and the regional telephone companies and among AT&T divisions, such as Western Electric, Bell Laboratories, and Information Systems. For example, the regional telephone companies no longer automatically route long-distance calls through AT&T. Instead, the companies are asking customers to specify their choice of long-distance service.

Technological advances are making it easier for competitors to enter the long-distance market. The advances include microwave, satellite, and fiber-optics transmission systems. Furthermore, in coming years, MCI, Sprint, and others will not have to require consumers to use push-button phones; and their consumers will not have to push two extra numbers to use a nonAT&T service. Technology also allows large business customers to bypass the local telephone company by installing their own satellite antennas or radio links. For example, when Heinz believed the rates it was charged were too high, it installed its own microwave radio link.

Most of AT&T's new business ventures are computer-based. The company was expected to introduce 30 computer-related products and services during 1984 alone, including a desktop office computer and a videotex service (allowing consumers to do banking and shopping and receive financial data bases and news information through a home computer terminal linked to a television monitor and a telephone modem). All of these new ventures place AT&T in direct competition with leading firms such as IBM and GTE, companies with well-established marketing divisions and considerable marketing skill. These companies are especially adept at product planning, distribution, promotion, and pricing.

QUESTIONS

1. Does AT&T practice the marketing concept and follow a marketing philosophy? Explain your answer.
2. Describe the various publics that have an impact on AT&T and how the company should deal with each of them.
3. Comment on the relationship between marketing and manufacturing and evaluate AT&T's organization chart (shown in Figure 1).
4. Describe AT&T on the basis of these strategic planning factors:
   a. Organizational mission.
   b. Definition of strategic business units.
   c. Marketing objectives.
   d. Situation analysis.
5. Apply portfolio analysis to AT&T.
6. In an AT&T marketing information system, what types of data should the company acquire through marketing research? Through continuous monitoring?

Understanding Consumers

Part Two provides an understanding of consumers and explains why consumer analysis is necessary. It discusses consumer profiles, characteristics, needs, and decision making and how companies can develop marketing programs that are responsive to consumers.

Chapter 5 is devoted to final consumer demographics, the easily identifiable and measurable statistics used to describe the population. Population size, gender, age, location, housing, mobility, income, expenditures, occupations, education, and marital status are examined. Trends and marketing implications are included. The limitations of demographics are noted.

Chapter 6 investigates final consumer life-styles and decision making. These concepts are useful in explaining how and why consumers act as they do. Life-styles are comprised of social and psychological factors. Social characteristics are culture, social class, performance, reference groups, family life cycle, and activities. Psychological characteristics are personality, attitudes, class consciousness, motivation, perceived risk, innovativeness, opinion leadership, and importance of purchase. In the decision process, consumers move through several stages: stimulus, problem awareness, information search, evaluation of alternatives, purchase, and postpurchase behavior. The interaction of demographics, social and psychological factors, and the decision process is shown. Marketing implications and limitations are noted.

Chapter 7 focuses on the organizational consumers that purchase products and services for further production, use in operations, or resale to other consumers. Organizational consumers are manufacturers, wholesalers, retailers, and government and nonprofit institutions. Their differences from final consumers, individual characteristics, buying objectives, buying structure, uses of purchases, and constraints on purchases are each described. The decision process for organizational consumers also is studied. Marketing implications are offered.

Chapter 8 examines the three alternative methods for developing a target market: mass marketing, market segmentation, and multiple segmentation. The factors considered in selecting these techniques are detailed, as are the strengths and weaknesses of each. Segmentation on the basis of geographic demographics, personal demographics, and consumer life-styles is explained. A six-step procedure for planning a segmentation strategy is presented. The requirements for successful segmentation and the limitations of segmentation are listed. Finally, because the development of a target market depends on future projections of sales and a corresponding marketing program, sales forecasting is discussed.

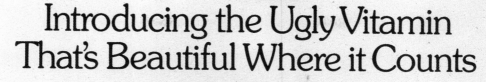

Introducing the Ugly Vitamin
That's Beautiful Where it Counts

New Lifestage® from Vicks is a whole new way to look at vitamins. Ours aren't radiant red or overwhelming orange. But that's because Lifestage is pure, no preservatives, sugar, artificial color or flavor like in most vitamins. And Lifestage meets your whole family's vitamin needs better than any other vitamin brand. There are 6 formulas, so every member of your family can get the best vitamin for each of them. Pure vitamins your family wants without the additives they don't.
That's the beauty of Lifestage.

Children
Lifestage Children's Chewables contain iron, plus even more vitamins than Flintstones. And Lifestage has a natural orange flavor that's sweet without sugar. So it tastes great, but won't promote tooth decay.

Teens
Created especially for teens, Lifestage Teens' Formula includes extra phosphorus and calcium to help ensure proper bone growth. And advanced levels of B complex and C vitamins to meet the special demands of active young lives.

Women
Because women need more iron than men, Lifestage Women's Formula contains even more iron than One-A-Day with Iron. 50% more. And Lifestage has higher potencies of B complex and C vitamins, so important for the energy systems of today's women.

Men
Lifestage Men's Formula has more vitamins than even Theragran-M. Plus Lifestage has 6 essential minerals. These include iron, zinc, and magnesium which are vital for energy production.

Women's Stress
Women under stress deplete higher quantities of all water-soluble vitamins. So Lifestage Women's Stress Formula provides advanced levels of these vitamins. Plus vitamin E and extra iron which are so valuable to women under stress.

Men's Stress
A high-potency formula with more water-soluble vitamins an active man needs. Plus magnesium, a mineral not in Stresstabs, so important for the proper metabolism of carbohydrates.

New Lifestage

Pure vitamins. Made to be best for each member of your family.
From Vicks.

© Richardson-Vicks Inc. 1983

Lifestage vitamins, a new product from Richardson-Vicks, appeal to consumers on the basis of two demographic factors—age and gender. Reprinted by permission.

As a diversified company, General Mills seeks to appeal to many different consumer life-styles. Its restaurants include Red Lobster and Casa Gallardo Mexican restaurants. Its toy divisions include Parker Brothers, Kenner, and Fundimensions. Consumer foods include Big G cereals and Yoplait yogurt. Fashion products include Izod clothes and Monet jewelry. Specialty retailing includes the Talbots and Eddie Bauer. Reprinted by permission. Photographs by Steve Umland.

Part Two   Consumer Life-Styles and Decision Making

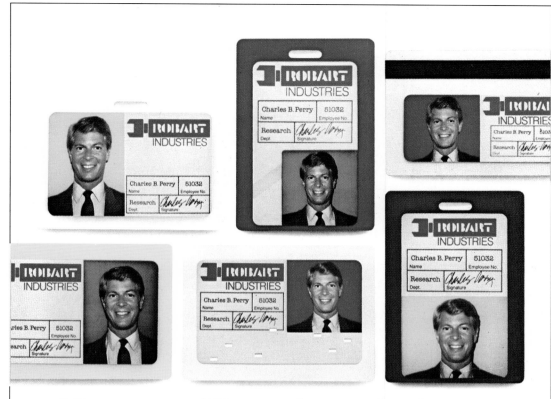

The many different faces of Polaroid's new, low-cost instant ID System.

Our new Model 710 instant ID system is a model of versatility as well as low cost.

Now you can make durable, tamper-resistant, PhotoSecure ID cards and badges in two minutes. With or without punch coding or magnetic encoding for access control. In a variety of configurations.

The modular, lightweight design lets you take the system from place to place easily.

The camera, die cutter and laminator can be set up quickly. The Model 710 is simple to operate, and for high volume situations, additional components may be added as needed.

Our service organization and reputation for reliability have made us the world leader in instant photo identification.

Send in the coupon, and permit us to present ourselves in person.

POLAROID

For more information and a demonstration return this coupon to: Polaroid Corp., Industrial Marketing Dept. 548, P.O. Box 5011, Clifton, N.J. 07015. Or call toll free from continental U.S.: (800) 526-7843, Ext. 400. For N.J. call: (800) 522-4503, Ext. 400.

Name _____

Title _____

Company _____

Address _____

City _____

State _____ Zip _____

Telephone _____

© 1982 Polaroid Corp. "Polaroid"® and "PhotoSecure"™

Although Polaroid is best known for its instant cameras for final consumers, the company has made products for industrial and professional markets since its earliest days. Today, nearly 40 per cent of Polaroid's sales come from products earmarked for industrial and professional use, such as the employee identification-card system shown here. Reprinted by permission.

After reviewing the VALS (Values and Life-Styles) classification, Dr. Pepper determined that its advertisements should be targeted toward inner-directed consumers. Scenes from several of its "Hold out for the out of the ordinary" television commercials are shown here. Reprinted by permission.

Consumer Demographics

1. To show the importance and scope of consumer analysis
2. To define and enumerate important demographics in the United States: population size, gender, and age; location, housing, and mobility of the population; income and expenditures of the population; occupations and education of the population; and marital status of the population
3. To examine trends and projections of important demographics and study their marketing implications
4. To describe several applications of consumer demographics and consider the limitations of demographics

*T*here are over 19 million single-person households in the U.S., with total annual income of $330 billion. One half of these households consists of people younger than 35. By 1990, almost 50 per cent of all U.S. households will be comprised of single persons, those never married, separated, divorced, or widowed. As such, this is a major market for companies to research and understand.

Analysis of singles reveals these findings:

- Expenditures are above average for eating out, vacations, and alcoholic beverages.
- Younger singles watch little prime-time television, but are attracted to later shows such as *Saturday Night Live* and rock concerts. They also do less than average newspaper reading. Radio and magazines are quite popular.

- Singles 25 to 35 have incomes that are 13 per cent above the U.S. average; this means significant expenditures on nonnecessities. 60 per cent of this group has attended some college. Housing, with easy maintenance, is important.
- Older singles watch more television and read newspapers more frequently.
- Young, middle-aged, and older singles are substantially different from one another.
- There are relatively more singles in Pacific states than in any others.
- Singles tend to locate in urban areas.

In sum,

the singles market tends to be affluent, well educated, highly mobile, fashion conscious, and active in leisure pursuits. Thus, this fertile, but diverse group presents a significant challenge to marketers.[1]

By developing a profile of the consumer demographics (statistical characteristics) of the market that a firm serves, it is better able to offer an appropriate marketing mix.

Consumer Analysis: Importance and Scope

As noted in Chapters 1 and 2, the central focus of marketing is the consumer. In order to develop successful marketing plans, it is necessary to determine the characteristics and needs of consumers, the social and psychological factors affecting consumers, and the process consumers go through when making a purchase.

The scope of consumer analysis includes the study of who buys, what they buy, why they buy, how they buy, when they buy, where they buy, and how often they buy.[2] Table 5-1 shows the scope of consumer analysis for different types of products and services.

Final consumers purchase for personal, family, or household use; *organizational consumers* purchase for production, operations, or resale.

In Chapters 5 through 8, the basic elements necessary for understanding and responding to consumers are detailed. Chapters 5 and 6 examine the demographics, social and psychological characteristics, and the decision process used by final consumers. **Final consumers** purchase products and services for personal, family, or household use. Chapter 7 centers on the characteristics and behavior of organizational consumers. **Organizational consumers** purchase products and services for further production, usage in operating the organization, or resale to other consumers. Chapter 8 explains how to develop a target market and the generation and uses of sales forecasts. By developing a profile of consumer characteristics, needs, and behavior patterns, an individual marketer is better able to satisfy the demands of consumers and remain ahead of the competition.

---

[1] Ronald D. Michman, ''The Challenge of the Singles Market,'' *The Collegiate Forum* (Spring 1983), p. 19. See also, Young & Rubicam, ''Singling Out Singles'' (1982).

[2] Adapted from Leon G. Schiffman and Leslie Lazar Kanuk, *Consumer Behavior,* Second Edition (Englewood Cliffs, N.J.: Prentice-Hall, 1983), p. 5.

Table 5-1 The Scope of Consumer Analysis

Who	What	Why	How	When	Where	How Often
Middle-aged male	Haircut	Messy hair	Use regular barber	Saturday morning	Regular shop	Every two months
Young female college graduate	Suit	Job interview	Read paper for sale, select conservatively	Next day	Store with low price and fast alterations	Once per year
Husband	Watch	Gift	Browse through a store	In two weeks	Local jeweler	Once
College student	College textbook	Required	Obtain book title from store list	By first class day	College store	Every term
Working woman, with husband and two children	Auto	Transportation	Talk to friends, read ads, test drive, thoroughly evaluate	In two months	Nearby authorized dealer	Every four years
Hospital	Hospital beds	Replacement	See salespeople, set specifications, thoroughly evaluate	In three months	Regular supplier	Every seven years

Demographics Defined and Enumerated [3]

Consumer demographics are statistics that are used to describe the population. They are easy to identify, collect, measure, and analyze. The demographics discussed in this chapter are population size, gender, and age; location, housing, and mobility; income and expenditures; occupations and education; and marital status.[4] By combining these demographics, a firm can establish consumer profiles that may pinpoint both attractive and declining market opportunities. See Figure 5-1.

For example, Safeway supermarkets used to appeal to the traditional family of four, with 85 per cent of shopping done by women on Saturday mornings. After recognizing the trend towards smaller families and working women, Safeway changed its approach to attract "the jogging generation"—two-income families with the adults aged 25 to 44. Stores are now open longer hours, many nonfood departments have been added, and the new motto is "Fresh and Full at 5" (signifying the shift to shopping after 5 P.M.).[5]

Several secondary sources provide a great amount of information about con-

Consumer demographics are easily identifiable and measurable population statistics.

---

[3] Good discussions of demographics in the 1980s are Gregory Spencer and John F. Long, "The New Census Bureau Projections," *American Demographics* (April 1983), pp. 24–31; George J. Stolnitz, "Our Main Population Patterns: Radical Shifts, Cloudy Prospects," *Business Horizons,* Vol. 25 (July–August 1982), pp. 91–99; and Paul C. Glick, "How American Families Are Changing," *American Demographics* (January 1984), pp. 21–25.

[4] The data presented in this chapter are all from the U.S. Bureau of Census, unless otherwise indicated.

[5] "Safeway Jilts the 'Family of Four' to Woo the Jogging Generation," *Business Week* (November 21, 1983), p. 98.

**Figure 5-1
Factors Determining a
Consumer's Demographic
Profile**

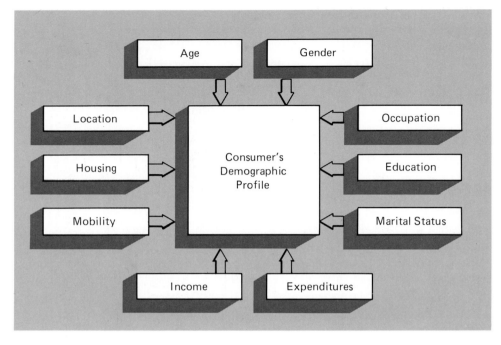

**Demographic data are
available from many
secondary sources.**

sumer demographics. The *Census of Population* is a federal government publication that presents a wide range of demographic data. In addition to providing total U.S. and statewide data, it breaks down geographic areas into blocks (about 200 households) and census tracts (about 1,200 households). A number of marketing research firms have developed computer-based systems which arrange census data by zip code, provide forecasts, and update information.[6] Since census data are gathered only once every ten years, they must be supplemented by statistics from chambers of commerce, public utilities, and building departments.

The *Survey of Buying Power* is published annually by *Sales & Marketing Management* magazine. It reports current data by metropolitan area and state. Many statistics not available from the *Census,* such as retail sales by merchandise category, personal disposable income, and five-year projections, are included. The *Survey* also measures each metropolitan area's sales potential through a buying power index (BPI) that weights the disposable income, retail sales, and population size of the area.

The *Editor & Publisher Market Guide* annually reports on citywide statistics. These range from population, households, auto registrations, and savings deposits to employment by industry and newspaper circulation. Other major secondary sources are *Rand McNally Commercial Atlas & Market Guide, Standard Rate & Data Service,* local newspapers, and regional planning boards.

---

[6] See Doris L. Walsh, ''Giving Demographics More Byte,'' *American Demographics* (April 1983), pp. 18–22; and ''Firm Sees Opportunity in Failure of Census Bureau to Provide Reliable Forecasts of Demographic Shifts,'' *Marketing News* (January 7, 1983), p. 8.

Population Size, Gender, and Age

As of 1983, the population of the United States was more than 235 million people; this is projected to grow to 268 million people by the year 2000. The population is increasing less than 1 per cent each year.

In the U.S., the population is growing slowly, there are many first-borns, there are more women than men, and average age is rising.

The annual number of births in the U.S. peaked at 4.3 million in 1957. During the 1980s and early 1990s, the annual birth rate is expected to be about 3.5–3.8 million. Unlike earlier decades, a large proportion of these births will be first-borns. 25 per cent of all babies born in the 1960s were firstborns; this figure will exceed 40 per cent throughout the 1980s and early 1990s.

Females comprise about 51.3 per cent of the population, with males accounting for 48.7 per cent. The life expectancy for newborn females is above 78 years; it is about 71 years for newborn males. The median age of the U.S. population is about 31, and expected to rise to 36.3 by the year 2000. Figure 5-2 shows the changing age distribution in the population from 1960 to 2000.

Marketing Implications

The large U.S. population offers a substantial market for all types of products and services. However, the low annual rate of population growth indicates that

Figure 5-2
The Age Distribution of the U.S. Population, 1960–2000

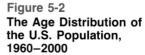

1960
1980
2000

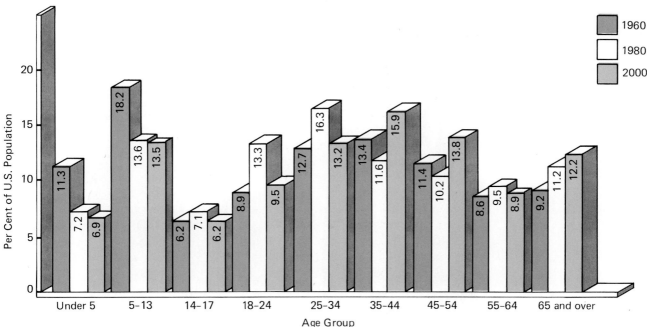

Source: U.S. Bureau of the Census, *Current Population Reports,* Series P-25, Nos. 310, 311, 519, 704, 721. Projections are based on Series II assumptions.

Companies need to focus efforts and actively appeal to more mature markets.

companies need to focus on specific opportunities, such as firstborns, females, and expanding age segments. There will be heightened battles among firms for market share in current markets.

The rise in firstborns is significant, since parents have many initial purchases to complete. They spend several hundred dollars on start-up costs for the first child, on items such as furniture, clothing, and a car seat.

There are six million more females than males in the total population. This has important implications for marketers of clothing, household services, appliances, and other items where there are differences in needs and buying behavior by gender. Accordingly, more and more companies are gearing their appeals to women, as illustrated in Figure 5-3. Special interest should be paid to female senior-citizens, who substantially outnumber their male counterparts.

The shifting age distribution points up many opportunities. For example, colleges and universities are increasing their recruitment of older, nontraditional

**Figure 5-3
E. F. Hutton: A Financial Services Ad Oriented Toward Women**

Some of the best minds in medicine listen to me.
I listen to E.F. Hutton.

Reprinted by permission—E. F. Hutton & Company Inc.

students, since their prime market (18–24 year olds) is declining. Sports and recreation companies are becoming more oriented toward the 35+ age group. The over-65 age group represents a growing market for food, medical care, utilities, vacation homes, travel, entertainment, and restaurants.

Location, Housing, and Mobility

During this century there has been a major movement of the U.S. population to large urban areas. Until mid-1983, the Bureau of the Census defined these urban centers as Standard Metropolitan Statistical Areas (SMSAs). Typically, an SMSA was comprised of a large central city and its surrounding suburbs, and contained at least 50,000 people. From 1960 to 1983, the number of SMSAs rose from 169 to over 300. By 1983, these SMSAs held about 75 per cent of the total U.S. population (in just 16 per cent of the land area).

The U.S. population is highly urbanized, with 75 per cent of the people concentrated in 16 per cent of the land area.

As of July 1, 1983, the Bureau of the Census developed a new classification system which eliminated the term SMSA. In large part, this was due to the broad definition of an SMSA. For example, both Fargo, North Dakota (55,000 population), and Los Angeles (7 million population) were classified as SMSAs. To remedy this problem, three new categories were created: Metropolitan Statistical Areas (MSAs), Primary Metropolitan Statistical Areas (PMSAs), and Consolidated Metropolitan Statistical Areas (CMSAs).[7]

A *Metropolitan Statistical Area (MSA)* is relatively free standing and not closely associated with other metropolitan areas. An MSA contains either a city of at least 50,000 population or an urbanized area of 50,000 population (with a total population of at least 100,000). There are 257 MSAs. New Haven–Meriden, Connecticut; Syracuse, New York; Fargo, North Dakota; and Sheboygan, Wisconsin, are examples are MSAs.

Urban areas are now categorized as *Metropolitan Statistical Areas (MSAs)*, *Primary Metropolitan Statistical Areas (PMSAs)*, and *Consolidated Metropolitan Statistical Areas (CMSAs)*.

A *Primary Metropolitan Statistical Area (PMSA)* consists of at least 1 million people and includes a large urbanized county or a cluster of counties that have strong economic and social links as well as ties to neighboring communities. There are 78 PMSAs. Gary-Hammond, Indiana; Kenosha, Wisconsin; and Arno-Elgin, Joliet, and Waukegan, Illinois, are illustrations of PMSAs.

A *Consolidated Metropolitan Statistical Area (CMSA)* contains several overlapping and interlocking PMSAs. They comprise the 23 largest metropolitan areas. For example, the Los Angeles CMSA is comprised of Anaheim–Santa Ana, Los Angeles–Long Beach, Oxnard–Ventura, and Riverside–San Bernardino.

The housing characteristics of the U.S. population are owner-oriented. About two thirds of American households reside in a home they own. This rate has increased over the last twenty years. Since 1960 there has been a change in the

Most Americans live in their own homes.

---

[7] See "Census Data to Reflect More Precise Geographic Definitions," *Marketing News* (January 21, 1983), Section 2, p. 20; John Herbers, "Major Cities Ringed by Suburbs Yielding to Sprawl of Small Metropolitan Areas," *New York Times* (July 8, 1983), p. A9; Eugene Carlson, "New Census Data Can Help—Or Hurt—Some Urban Areas," *Wall Street Journal* (January 10, 1984), p. 35; and Eugene Carlson, "Changes in Population Game Hurt Some Big-City Players," *Wall Street Journal* (February 14, 1984), p. 35.

mix of housing. The proportion of households residing in multiple-unit structures has grown from one quarter to more than one third. It is not a paradox for ownership to increase and the percentage of single-unit housing to decline at the same time; this trend is explained by the growth in condominiums and cooperatives (the ownership of a single unit in a multiple-unit dwelling) and the increase in smaller households.

12 to 17 per cent of the population changes residences each year.

The mobility of the U.S. population is quite high. According to the Bureau of the Census, about 12 to 17 per cent of the population moves each year. To properly understand mobility, its different forms should be noted: local, state-wide, regional, and foreign. For example, over 60 per cent of all residence changes are within the same county, over 80 per cent within the same state, and about 90 per cent within the same region. Less than 10 per cent of residence changes involve moves to a new region or abroad.

The mobility of the U.S. population varies by geographic region. Some regions are gaining in size, whereas others are declining. Figure 5-4 shows the regional distribution of the population for the period of 1970 to 2000. Major growth is occurring in South Atlantic, West South Central, and Mountain regions. Moderate growth exists in the Pacific region. The New England and East South Central regions are stable. The relative sizes of the Middle Atlantic, East North Central, and West North Central are declining.

Marketing Implications

Urban markets are highly concentrated, with opportunities for home-related products, well-known brands, and growing geographic regions.

The density of the U.S. population makes marketing programs more cost efficient and available to bigger groups of consumers. Opportunities for mass distribution and advertising are plentiful. Suburban shopping is growing, leading to branch outlets in suburbs and improved transportation and delivery services.

The continuing interest in home ownership offers sales potential for furniture, appliances, carpeting, etc. Specially modified products for apartment owners, such as space-efficient washers and driers, are growing in importance. Since home purchases are affected by the economy, marketers need to monitor economic conditions carefully.

Population mobility provides opportunities for highly advertised national or regional brands, retail chains and franchises, and major credit cards. Their names are well known when consumers relocate and represent an assurance of quality. For example, Old Style, a Midwestern beer, was successfully introduced in Arizona because many Midwesterners spend the winter there.[8] Macy's department stores were able to expand to Florida since a number of Northeasterners who were loyal customers relocated to Florida.[9] MasterCard and Visa credit cards are accepted and popular throughout the U.S.

As a result of the geographic growth of certain areas and the decline of others, marketing emphasis has shifted. The marketing efforts directed at consumers in states such as Texas, Florida, Georgia, and California have risen dramatically. Nevertheless, companies should be aware of the extensive competition in these

[8] Lawrence Ingrassia, "Heileman Plans Big Expansion into South, Setting Stage for Bruising Beer-Sales Fight," *Wall Street Journal* (February 3, 1983), p. 33.
[9] John Herbers, "Industrial Flight from North," *New York Times* (April 12, 1983), p. D1.

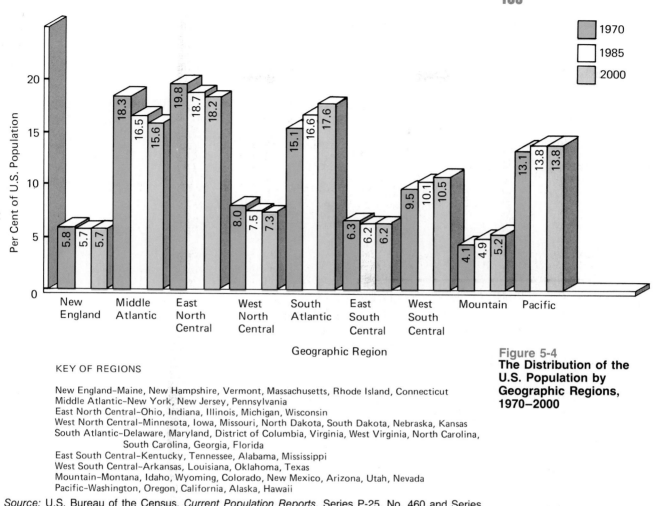

Per Cent of U.S. Population

Legend: 1970, 1985, 2000

Region	1970	1985	2000
New England	5.8	5.7	5.7
Middle Atlantic	18.3	16.5	15.6
East North Central	19.8	18.7	18.2
West North Central	8.0	7.5	7.3
South Atlantic	15.1	16.6	17.6
East South Central	6.3	6.2	6.2
West South Central	9.5	10.1	10.5
Mountain	4.1	4.9	5.2
Pacific	13.1	13.8	13.8

Geographic Region

Figure 5-4
The Distribution of the U.S. Population by Geographic Regions, 1970–2000

KEY OF REGIONS

New England–Maine, New Hampshire, Vermont, Massachusetts, Rhode Island, Connecticut
Middle Atlantic–New York, New Jersey, Pennsylvania
East North Central–Ohio, Indiana, Illinois, Michigan, Wisconsin
West North Central–Minnesota, Iowa, Missouri, North Dakota, South Dakota, Nebraska, Kansas
South Atlantic–Delaware, Maryland, District of Columbia, Virginia, West Virginia, North Carolina,
        South Carolina, Georgia, Florida
East South Central–Kentucky, Tennessee, Alabama, Mississippi
West South Central–Arkansas, Louisiana, Oklahoma, Texas
Mountain–Montana, Idaho, Wyoming, Colorado, New Mexico, Arizona, Utah, Nevada
Pacific–Washington, Oregon, California, Alaska, Hawaii

Source: U.S. Bureau of the Census, *Current Population Reports*, Series P-25, No. 460 and Series P-20, No. 324. Projections based on Series II assumptions.

states and the possibility of oversaturation. Regions that are being abandoned by some firms, such as the North, should be reappraised by comparing population trends with the level of competition.

Income and Expenditures

From 1960 to 1980, average real annual family income rose from $15,637 to $21,023 (expressed in 1980 dollars). Most of this rise occurred in the 1960s and early 1970s. Real income has gone up slightly since then.

The number of families with annual incomes under $5,000 dropped from

Real annual family income is above $21,000, with many families earning $25,000 or more.

about one in nine in 1960 to one in sixteen in 1980. In 1960, 30.5 per cent of all families had incomes of less than $10,000 per year. For 1980, less than 20 per cent fit in this category. At the upper end of the income scale, 51.3 per cent of all families had annual incomes of $15,000 or higher in 1960. This rose to over 67 per cent of all families in 1980; almost 40 per cent of all families had annual incomes of $25,000 and higher. Figure 5-5 shows the changing distribution of income in the United States from 1960 to 1980.

By 1990, even more families will have annual incomes of $25,000 and

Figure 5-5
The Distribution of the U.S. Population by Annual Family Income, 1960–1980*

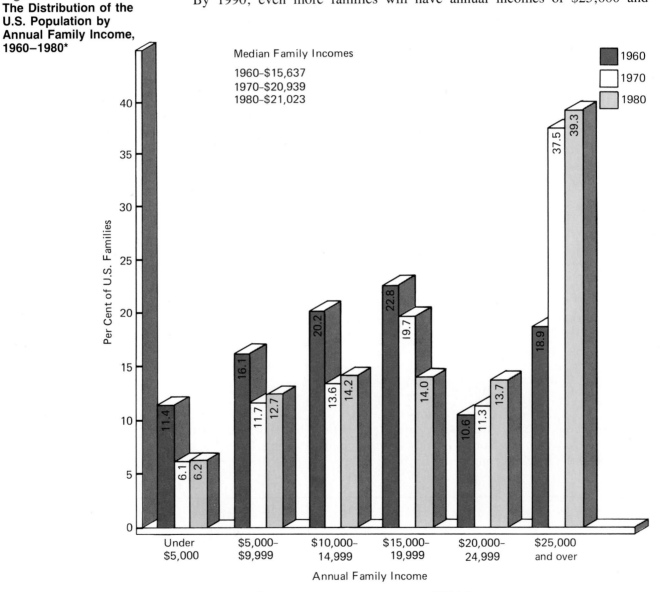

Median Family Incomes

1960–$15,637
1970–$20,939
1980–$21,023

*All percentages are based upon data in 1980 dollars.

Source: U.S. Bureau of the Census. *Current Population Reports,* Series P-60 and other Bureau of the Census data.

higher. Families with incomes over $50,000 will more than double, from 1.8 to 3.9 million. Although incomes will rise between 1980 and 1990, the real growth rate will be relatively low. Because of various economic factors (such as unemployment), real income growth will not approach that of the 1960s and early 1970s.

As income levels have changed, so have consumption patterns. The percentage of income spent on food, beverages, and tobacco, and on clothing, accessories, and jewelry has declined substantially. The percentage spent on housing, medical care, personal business, recreation, and, recently, transportation has increased substantially. Since 1960 total annual consumption expenditures have risen from $325 billion to about $2 trillion. Both **disposable income** (aftertax income to be used for spending and/or savings) and **discretionary income** (earnings remaining for luxuries, such as a vacation or dining out, after necessities such as food, clothing, and shelter are bought) have grown as the result of increases in family income. Table 5-2 shows the percentage of American households owning a wide range of necessary and discretionary products.

Although family income and expenditures have increased over the last two decades, the rate of inflation (the yearly percentage increase in the prices of products and services) has recently dampened the effects of higher income by causing rises in the cost of living (the total amount consumers annually pay for their products and services). The federal government monitors the cost of living through the **Consumer Price Index (CPI)**. The CPI measures the monthly and yearly changes in the prices of selected consumer items in different product categories, expressing the changes in terms of a base year.

At present the base year is 1967; and the price index for all items and individual items sold in 1967 is 100. Changes are measured against this base. For example, if monthly food costs were $200 in 1967 and $590 in 1984, the 1984 CPI for food would be 295 [100 × ($590/$200)]. This would represent a 195 per cent rise in food prices from 1967 to 1984. Since 1967 the greatest price increases have

Consumption patterns have changed to reflect the level of disposable income and discretionary income.

The Consumer Price Index (CPI) measures price fluctuations to determine the cost of living.

Product	Percentage of Households Reporting Ownership[a]
Automobile	90.7
Calculator	71.7
High-fidelity components	66.6
Smoke detector	56.5
Automobile stereo	49.1
Room air conditioner	35.7
Microwave oven	33.6
LCD watch	28.1
Videogame unit	19.5
Personal portable stereo (such as Walkman)	19.4
Air purifier	9.5
Videocassette recorder	9.2
Personal computer	5.6
Videocassette recorder camera	2.3

Table 5-2
U.S. Household Ownership of Selected Products, 1982

[a] Based on a sample of 1900 consumers.
Source: "10th Annual Consumer Survey," *Merchandising* (May 1982), pp. 17 ff.

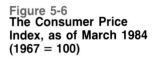

Figure 5-6
**The Consumer Price
Index, as of March 1984
(1967 = 100)**

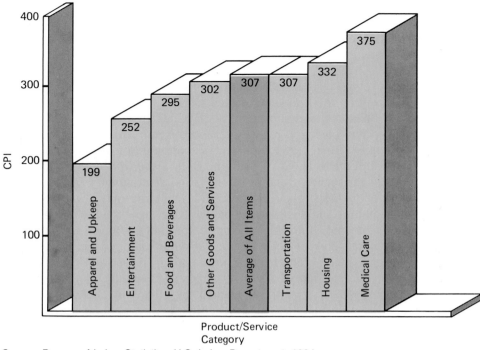

Source: Bureau of Labor Statistics, U.S. Labor Department, 1984.

occurred in medical care, housing, and transportation. The smallest increases have taken place for apparel and upkeep, and entertainment. See Figure 5-6.

Marketing Implications

Income trends have re-sulted in fewer purchases by some lower- and middle-income consumers, while upper-income consumers represent a prime market.

Two significant marketing implications can be drawn from the data on consumer income. First, many lower- and middle-income consumers are finding it difficult to keep pace with the cost of living. Their earnings have been eroded by the rate of inflation during the early 1980s. In great numbers, these consumers are holding on to durable products, such as automobiles and clothing, for longer periods; and it is hard for these consumers to purchase a home. For example, in 1983, 69 per cent of consumers could not afford the payments on a mortgage if they purchased a median-priced home.[10] This will remain a problem for several years, especially for 25–34 year olds. Overall, marketing responses include developing generic (no-frills) brands, do-it-yourself products, and smaller homes.

Second, on the other hand, affluent consumers represent a lucrative and expanding market. More than 30 million U.S. households have annual incomes of at least $40,000, with an average of $72,000 for these households.[11] By 1990, one third of all U.S. personal income will be accounted for by 15 per cent of all households. As one observer noted, ''The class market will become the mass market.'' This means substantial possibilities for luxury autos, vacation homes,

[10] ''Homebuilding's New Look,'' *Business Week* (November 17, 1983), pp. 93–94.
[11] Bill Abrams, ''More Affluence,'' *Wall Street Journal* (March 24, 1983), p. 35.

restaurants, and other items. For example, Neiman-Marcus department store customers have a median annual income of $50,000 to $65,000. General Electric is appealing to upscale customers by adding electronic features to major appliances.[12]

Occupations and Education

The labor force in the United States is continuing its steady movement toward white-collar and service occupations and away from blue-collar and farm occupations. Currently, the total labor force is over 100 million people. From 1960 to now, the percentage of those employed in professional, technical, and clerical white-collar jobs has risen substantially. The percentage of managers, administrators, and sales workers has remained relatively constant. Over the same period, the percentage of people employed as operatives (nonskilled workers) and nonfarm laborers has dropped substantially, while craft and kindred workers have been fairly constant. Only about 2.7 million people are employed as farm workers. See Figure 5-7.

The trend toward white-collar and service occupations is continuing.

For the 1980s the U.S. Bureau of Labor Statistics predicts strong gains in these occupational categories: engineering, science, medicine, computers, social science, buying, selling, secretarial, construction, refrigeration, health service, personal service, and protection. These categories will have limited growth or decline: education, office-machine operations, printing trades, baking, jewelry, shoe repair, tailoring, barbering, and farming.

Another important change in the U.S. labor force has been the increase in the number and percentage of working women. In 1960, 23 million women comprised 32 per cent of the total labor force. Today almost 50 million women account for 43 per cent of the total labor force, and 53 per cent of all adult women are in the labor force.

Women represent a large and growing percentage of the U.S. labor force.

The growth in the number and percentage of married women in the labor force has been substantial. In 1960, 12 million married women, 31 per cent of all married women, were employed. Today, over 25 million married women, 55 per cent of all married women, are in the labor force. The per cent of married women with children under six in the labor force has jumped from 19 per cent in 1960 to 50 per cent currently.

During 1981 and 1982, the U.S. labor force suffered the highest unemployment rates since the depression of 1932. At the end of 1982, the unemployment rate reached about 11 per cent, meaning that around one in nine people were out of work. Some of the unemployment was temporary, due to domestic and worldwide economic conditions. But in other industries, such as automobile and steel, many job losses were permanent. Overall, this meant severe cutbacks in discretionary purchases until the unemployment rate was reduced.

The educational attainment of Americans has sustained its upward trend. As of 1960, 58.8 per cent of all adults twenty-five years old and older had not

---

[12] Bruce Steinberg, "The Mass Market Is Splitting Apart," *Fortune* (November 28, 1983), p. 82.

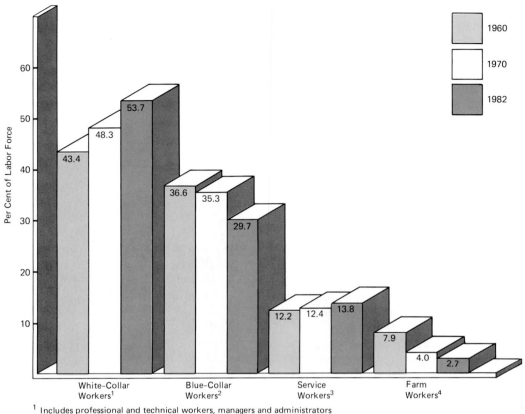

¹ Includes professional and technical workers, managers and administrators (except farm), sales workers, and clerical workers.

² Includes craft and kindred workers, operatives, and nonfarm laborers.

³ Includes private household and other service workers.

⁴ Includes farm managers and laborers.

Source: Bureau of Labor Statistics, U.S. Labor Department, 1983.

Figure 5-7
The Distribution of the U.S. Labor Force by Occupation, 1960–1982

One third of adults have received some college education; the figure is higher for young adults.

Marketing opportunities exist for job-related and time-saving products, and longer store hours.

graduated from high school. This figure had dropped to 29 per cent in 1982. As of 1960 only 16.5 per cent of all adults twenty-five years old and older had received some college education. This rose to 32.9 per cent in 1982. Of those adults aged twenty-five to thirty-four in 1982, 86.3 per cent had graduated high school, 45.1 per cent had received some college education, and 23.7 per cent were college graduates. See Figure 5-8.

The sharp increase in working wives and the increased educational attainment have contributed to the growing number of people in the upper-income brackets, while the relatively high unemployment rate and stagnant economy have caused other families to have low incomes.

Marketing Implications

The occupations and education of the population indicate these marketing implications. A greater number and percentage of the total population are working than ever before. The larger work force requires transportation, clothing, restau-

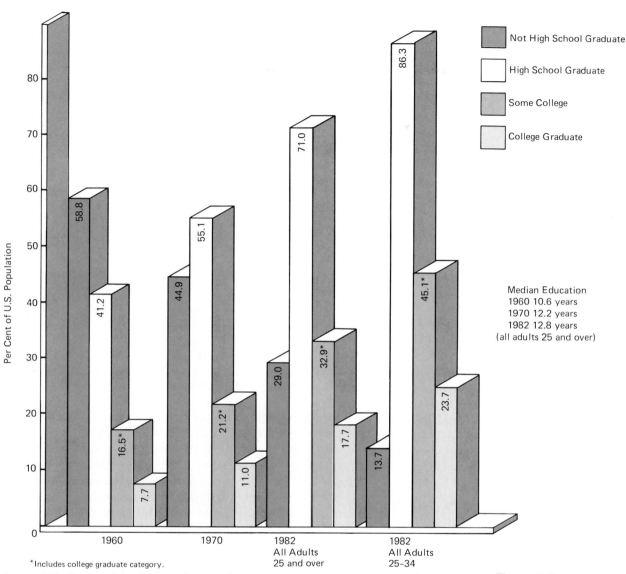

Not High School Graduate

High School Graduate

Some College

College Graduate

Median Education
1960 10.6 years
1970 12.2 years
1982 12.8 years
(all adults 25 and over)

*Includes college graduate category.

1960　　1970　　1982
All Adults
25 and over

1982
All Adults
25–34

Per Cent of U.S. Population

Source: U.S. Bureau of the Census, *Census of Population and Current Population Reports,* Series P-20, Nos. 207, 295, 314.

Figure 5-8
The Distribution of the U.S. Population by Educational Level, 1960–1982 (For persons 25 years old and over)

rants, and personal services. Stores have opportunities in major commercial centers. The market for job-oriented products and services is growing and the shift in occupations means different needs and aspirations in consumer purchases.

Working women have less time to spend shopping and operating the home. They may be unable to shop during regular retail hours and require longer store hours and mail-order purchases. Time-saving appliances (such as microwave ovens and food processors), prepared foods, prewrapped goods, and special services are also appealing to more working women. For example, Philadelphia ARA Services offers the workers who patronize employee cafeterias the option of taking home fully prepared dinners.[13] And, hotels attract women business travelers by providing special all-women's floors, additional security, pastel/feminine colors, special mirrors, and attractive bathroom vanities. This trend is essential, since the size of the woman business traveler market is growing three times faster than that of men.[14]

As the education level of the general population rises, marketers need to respond in terms of better information, better products and services, enhanced safety and environmental controls, greater accuracy in generating and meeting consumer expectations, and improved consumer-complaint departments.

Marital Status

The percentage of adults who are married has stayed constant, with the age at first marriage rising.

Despite some publicity to the contrary, the data indicate that marriage and family remain important in the United States. About 2.5 million couples get married each year. The percentage of the population 18 and older that is married has remained relatively stable over the past two decades at about two thirds of this population group. In 1960 the median age at first marriage was 23 years for males and 20 years for females. Today these figures are about 25 and 22 respectively. Therefore, in recent years adults have been waiting somewhat longer to be married. As a result, the size of the average family has declined slightly, from 3.7 members in 1950 to 3.3 now.

A *family* consists of related persons residing together. A *household* contains one or more persons who may or may not be related.

A *family* is defined as a group of two or more persons residing together who are related by blood, marriage, or adoption. A *household* is defined as a person or group of persons occupying a housing unit, whether related or unrelated. Figure 5-9 compares families and households. There have been two important changes in family and marital status. First, the number of single-person households has gone from 7.1 million in 1960 to 19.4 million in 1982. More than 23 per cent of all American households are now comprised of one-person units. Singles account for roughly one eighth of total consumer spending for goods and services.

Second, the size of the average household dropped from 3.3 in 1960 to 2.7 in 1982, because fewer single adults now live with their parents and divorces have risen substantially. From 1960 to 1982 the number of divorces jumped from 400,000 to 1.2 million annually.

Marketing Implications

Marital, family, and household trends offer diverse opportunities for marketers.

Marriage and family are important institutions in the United States, in spite of the high divorce level. The marketing implications of marital and family status include the following. There are opportunities for product and service industries associated with weddings (such as caterers and travel agents), family life (such as full-sized automobiles), and divorce (such as attorneys).

Because marriage is occurring slightly later in an individual's life, people

[13] "Marketing: The New Priority," *Business Week* (November 21, 1983), p. 96.
[14] Earl C. Gottschalk, Jr., "Hotel Industry Seems to Be Baffled on How to Please Businesswomen," *Wall Street Journal* (June 15, 1983), p. 37.

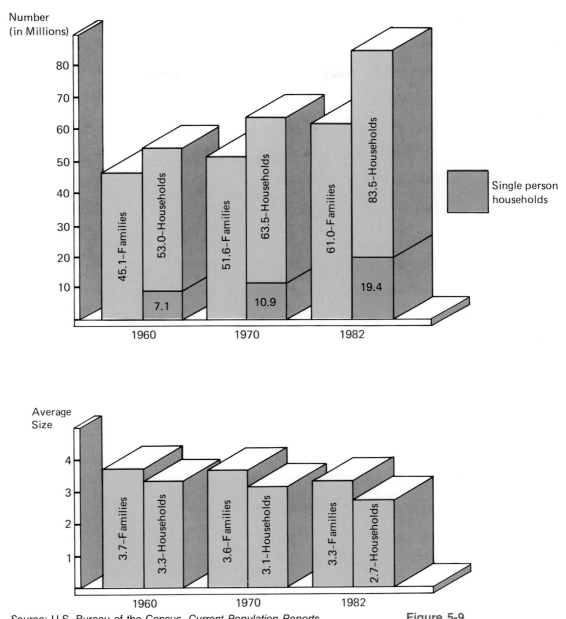

Source: U.S. Bureau of the Census, *Current Population Reports*.

Figure 5-9
Families Versus
Households, 1960–1982

have better financial resources and two-income families are prevalent. This leaves opportunities for organizations involved with travel, furniture, and entertainment.

The growth of single-person households provides opportunities for home and home furnishings industries and manufacturers who produce single-serving packages. These implications also apply to divorced and widowed persons.

For example, as noted earlier in the chapter, smaller households have created a demand for smaller homes. In the 1960s, homes frequently occupied 2,000 square feet of living space; now townhouse units containing as little as 900 square feet are commonplace. General Electric, among other companies, has reacted to this trend by producing a space-saving microwave oven (called the Space Maker) that can be installed above a range and function as a stove top and ventilator as well as an oven. See Figure 5-10.

Uses of Demographic Data

A consumer demographic profile combines several individual demographic factors.

After examining each of the demographics separately, a marketer would develop a consumer demographic profile that is a composite description of a consumer group based upon the most important demographics. Figure 5-11 summarizes the demographic characteristics of American consumers. In this section, several examples of demographic profiles are shown.

The Conference Board developed demographic profiles of U.S. heads of household by age, number and size of households, and income in 1982, as shown in Table 5-3. These profiles enable companies to learn a number of facts about potential consumers. For example, the under-25 market makes up 7.8 per cent of

Figure 5-10
General Electric Space-Saver Appliances for Smaller Homes

General Electric has the most intelligent solution to the problem of counter clutter—the GE Spacemaker™ appliances. Since they mount under your cabinets, they won't clutter up your counter.

ABOVE ALL, THEY SAVE YOU COUNTERSPACE

The Spacemaker™ drip coffeemaker is the newest member of the GE counter intelligence team. Simply set the timer the night before and wake up to great, freshly brewed coffee.

And when it's not brewing great coffee, it's not taking up counterspace.

OUT OF THE WAY, NOT OUT OF REACH

With the Spacemaker™ electric can opener, you can open up cans, bottles and even plastic bags— as well as your counterspace.

Then there's the Spacemaker™ electric knife with its own wall-mount storage bracket to help your countertop look sharp.

And the Spacemaker™ microwave oven helps you prepare meals in minutes while it sits snugly over your range.

The GE Spacemaker™ appliances;

● IS A TRADEMARK OF THE GENERAL ELECTRIC CO.

helping you fight counter clutter with counter intelligence.

WE BRING GOOD THINGS TO LIFE.

Reprinted by permission.

Table 5-3 Income by Age of Household Head, 1982

	Under 25	25–34	35–44	45–54	55–64	Over 64
Households (in millions)	6.4	19.2	14.5	12.7	12.7	16.9
Persons per household	2.23	2.94	3.66	3.26	2.32	1.72
Ave. household income	$14,227	$20,713	$26,052	$28,169	$23,504	$12,628
Distribution of households	7.8%	23.3%	17.6%	15.4%	15.4%	20.5%
Distribution of income	5.3%	22.9%	21.7%	20.6%	17.2%	12.3%

Source: Consumer Research Center of the Conference Board. Reprinted by permission.

all households but only 5.3 per cent of income. The 45–54 age group is the most affluent, representing 15.4 per cent of all households but 20.6 per cent of all income.

The increase in working women has greatly expanded the number of "two-earner" families. Today, half of all married couples fits into this category. Two-earner families have aftertax income that is 20 to 25 per cent higher than single-earner families. Unemployment has less impact on two-earner families, since one of the earners is usually able to maintain his or her position during weak economic times. In comparison to single-earner families, two-earner families spend substantially more on transportation, dry cleaning, clothing, home furnishings, and appliances.[15]

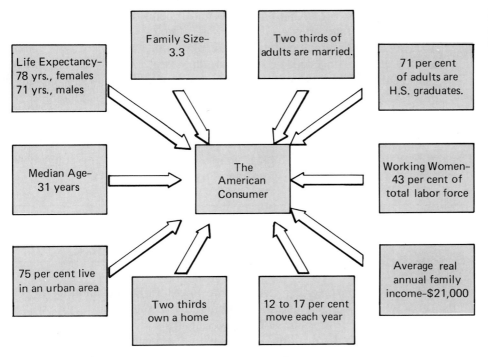

Figure 5-11
A Demographic Profile of the American Consumer

[15] "The Lasting Changes Brought by Women Workers," *Business Week* (March 15, 1982), pp. 61–64: Ronald D. Michman, "The Double Income Family: A New Market Target," *Business Horizons,* Vol. 23 (August 1980), pp. 31–37; and Arthur J. Norton, "Keeping Up with Households," *American Demographics* (February 1983), pp. 17–21.

B. Dalton Bookseller, a nationwide bookstore chain, uses demographic studies of 36,000 cities with information broken down by census tract. It defines heavy readers as those between twenty-one and forty-nine years of age, some college, high income, female, and employed in a management or professional position.[16]

Magazines frequently collect and update demographic data about consumers in order to set advertising rates and attract clients. For instance, *New York* magazine markets its real-estate ads (which feature homes, cooperatives, and vacation homes at prices up to $1,000,000) by listing reader demographics. According to *New York,* readers who are prospective real-estate buyers have a median household income of $52,275, and a median age of 42. Over half are married, 87 per cent have attended college, 75 per cent hold professional or managerial positions, and 62 per cent own a home (with an average value of $129,000).[17]

Limitations of Demographics

Demographic data may be dated, too general, require profile analysis, and not consider reasons for behavior.

When using demographic data, these limitations should be noted. One, demographic information may be dated. The national census is conducted only once every ten years. Regular statistical updates normally have time lags—for example, 1985 data will not be widely available until mid-1987. Two, summary data and trends may be too broad and hide opportunities and risks in small markets or specialized product categories.

Three, single demographic statistics are often not very useful. A consumer demographic profile is needed. Four, demographic data do not consider the psychological or the social factors influencing consumers. They do not explain the decision process consumers utilize when making purchases. Most importantly, demographics do not delve into the reasons why consumers make particular decisions; demographics are descriptive in nature. For example, why do people with similar demographic profiles buy different products or brands? For these reasons, Chapter 6 examines the psychological and social factors affecting consumer behavior and the decision process consumers use.

Summary

By understanding consumers, a firm is able to determine the most appropriate audience to which to appeal and the combination of marketing factors that will satisfy this audience. The scope of consumer analysis includes who, what, why, how, when, where, and how often. This chapter examined consumer demographics. Chapters 6 to 8 focus on social and psychological factors affecting behavior,

---

[16] John Mutter, "B. Dalton Bookseller: A Novel Approach to Retailing," *Sales & Marketing Management* (May 14, 1979), pp. 49–51.

[17] "Town & Country Properties Advertisers," *New York* (December 12, 1983), p. 169.

the consumer's decision process, organizational consumers, the development of a target market, and sales forecasting.

Demographics are the easily identifiable and measurable statistics that are used to describe the population. The U.S. population numbers about 235 million people, increasing less than 1 per cent each year. A large proportion of births is contributed by firstborns. There are slightly more women (who live longer) than men, with both having life expectancies into the seventies.

The Bureau of the Census recently redefined the urban areas that contain 75 per cent of the U.S. population into Metropolitan Statistical Areas (MSAs), Primary Metropolitan Statistical Areas (PMSAs), and Consolidated Metropolitan Statistical Areas (CMSAs). About two thirds of the population reside in homes they own, with the number occupying multiple-unit dwellings going up. About 12 to 17 per cent of the population moves every year. Major growth is occurring in the South Atlantic, West South Central, and Mountain regions.

Average annual real family income is over $21,000, up slightly since the early 1970s. Almost 40 per cent of families have incomes of $25,000 and higher. Total annual consumption exceeds $2 billion, and can be categorized in terms of disposable income and discretionary income expenditures. The rate of inflation and cost of living are measured through the Consumer Price Index (CPI).

The U.S. labor force of well over 100 million people continues its movement towards white-collar and service occupations. Women comprise a significant and rising portion of the labor force. In 1981 and 1982, U.S. unemployment reached a post-depression high of 11 per cent. Educational attainment has been maintained, with a greater percentage of Americans graduating high school and attending college than ever before.

The percentage of adults 18 and older who are married has remained stable, while men and women are waiting until they are older for marriage. A family consists of relatives residing together. A household consists of a person or persons occupying a housing unit, related or not. Both family and household size have declined, as single-person households have grown rapidly.

These limitations of demographics are noted: obsolete data, hidden trends or implications, limited use of single demographic statistics, and lack of explanation of the factors affecting behavior, consumer decision making, and motivation.

Questions for Discussion

1. How does the use of consumer demographics aid marketing decision making?
2. Develop a profile of the people residing in your census tract, using the *Census of Population*. What are the marketing implications of this profile?
3. Some companies have abandoned the market for baby products and oriented their offerings toward the senior-citizen market. Evaluate this strategy.
4. Explain and comment on the Census Bureau's revised procedure for defining metropolitan areas.
5. Why would a company be interested in the form of population mobility (e.g., local vs. regional)?
6. Since 1960, average real annual family income has increased by about 35 per cent. Comment on this trend and its marketing implications.

7. Distinguish between disposable income and discretionary income. During inflationary times, what happens to each?
8. Nearly all homes have radios, refrigerators, and televisions. What does this mean for marketers?
9. In mid-1984, the Consumer Price Index for energy was 450. What does this statistic signify?
10. In addition to the examples cited in the text, what products and services should grow as the number of working women and working mothers grows?
11. What marketing opportunities exist for serving college-educated consumers?
12. Which concept is more important to marketers, family or household? Why?
13. What is the value of a consumer demographic profile?
14. Describe at least three ways Burger King could gather data to develop a demographic profile of its customers.
15. Assess the limitations of demographics.

Case 1 Who Invests in the Stock Market? *

In 1983, the New York Stock Exchange sponsored a study that interviewed 4,549 adults selected at random. Of this sample, 1,537 owned shares of stock. From the survey, a profile of U.S. stockholders was developed on the basis of their demographic characteristics. Some highlights are detailed in Tables 1 and 2.

Table 1
Demographic Characteristics of Stockholders

Profile of Stockholders	1983 Survey	1981 Survey
Women stockholders (as per cent of total stockholders)	51.5	47.3
Men stockholders (as per cent of total stockholders)	48.5	52.7
Median age (all stockholders)	44.5	46.0
Median value of stock holdings	$ 5,100	$ 5,450
Median household income	$33,200	$29,200
Number of new stockholders (recently bought stock for the first time)	7,316,000	2,375,000

Reprinted by permission. Copyright © 1983 by the New York Times Company.

Table 2
Where Stockholders Live, 1983

State of Residence	Number of Stockholders
California	5,367,000
New York	4,695,000
Texas	2,606,000
Illinois	2,468,000
Pennsylvania	2,071,000
Florida	2,056,000
Ohio	1,884,000
New Jersey	1,674,000
Michigan	1,672,000
Massachusetts	1,292,000

Reprinted by permission. Copyright © 1983 by the New York Times Company.

* The data in this case are drawn from Michael Blumstein, "Who Invests What in the Market," *New York Times* (December 1, 1983), pp. D1, D22.

These conclusions were reached from the study:

- 42.4 million Americans, about 18 per cent of the population, own stock directly or through mutual funds.
- 7.3 million people who never before owned stock made purchases between July 1982 and June 1983. Of these, 80 per cent were under 45 years of age, 57 per cent were women, and 70 per cent invested less than $5,000.
- The number of stockholders residing in each of the 50 states increased between 1981 and 1983.
- The market is broadening, with many middle-income investors now making purchases.

Sears, which operates Dean Witter Reynolds stock brokerage outlets in a number of its larger retail stores, is encouraged by the trend to women and middle-income stock buyers. Other brokerage firms are not as pleased, because this trend is also resulting in lower stock holdings per customer.

QUESTIONS

1. Compare the demographic characteristics of stockholders (shown in Table 1) with the demographics of the U.S. population described in this chapter. Explain the differences.

2. Determine the 1983 population size of the ten states listed in Table 2 from *Current Population Reports*, Series P-25, in your college library. Compute the number of stockholders per 1,000 population for each of the states. What are the implications of this?

3. Why is Sears encouraged by the trend to women and middle-income stockholders? What should Sears' marketing approach emphasize to attract these buyers?

4. What other demographic data should be examined by stock brokerage firms?

_____ **Case 2 Coca-Cola: The Impact of Demographics** [†] _____

As the world's largest soft-drink manufacturer, Coca-Cola thoroughly examines the impact of demographic trends on its marketing strategy and reacts accordingly. During the early 1970s, the sales of carbonated beverages increased at an average rate of 10 per cent each year. Growth was propelled by the expanding number of "baby boomers" in the 10- to 24-year-old age group. Overall U.S. soft-drink consumption rose from 33 gallons per capita in 1975 to 40 gallons in 1983.

However, as those baby boomers became older and were not replaced due to the later age for first marriage and the decline in the birth rate, the growth in total sales of soda dropped considerably. By 1982, the soda beverage industry was growing by only 2 per cent annually. Most industry analysts expect sales growth to be 3 to 4 per cent each year throughout the rest of the 1980s.

In response to demographic factors, Coca-Cola has enacted a number of

---

[†] The data in this case are drawn from "Coke's Big Marketing Blitz," *Business Week* (May 30, 1983), pp. 58–64.

marketing plans. Diet Coke was launched in late 1982 to complement the firm's Tab. Coca-Cola recognized that demand for diet sodas was growing at a 10 per cent annual rate, compared with 1.4 per cent for sugared soft drinks. Diet Coke was aimed at weight-conscious adult males (Tab's appeal was to weight-conscious adult females) and placed into direct competition with Diet Pepsi. Initially, Coca-Cola worried that diet Coke sales would come at the expense of Tab, but it then discovered that only about one third of these sales were taken from Tab.

During 1983, three caffeine-free sodas were brought onto the market to attract health-conscious adults: caffeine-free Coke, caffeine-free diet Coke, and caffeine-free Tab. And, Coca-Cola intensified the volume discounts, price reductions, and free products offered to retailers buying in bulk in order to secure adequate shelf space.

Also, Coca-Cola continued its expansion into nonsoda beverages, which were gaining in popularity among adults. Among the firm's nonsoda beverage brands are: Minute Maid, Snow Crop, Five Alive, and Hi-C juices and fruit-based drinks; and Maryland Club and Butter-Nut coffee and tea. In late 1983, Coca-Cola sold its wine division, after generating impressive sales growth but unacceptable earnings.

QUESTIONS

1. Coca-Cola wants to raise per capita soda consumption to 50 gallons by 1990. How can it accomplish this?
2. Conduct an informal survey of 10 people regarding their perceptions of the markets for diet Coke and Tab. Are these perceptions consistent with the information in the case? Comment on this.
3. Evaluate Coca-Cola's rising interest in nonsoda beverages.
4. Only 35 per cent of Coca-Cola's soda sales are through supermarkets. The rest are through convenience stores, fast-food outlets, restaurants, hotels, bars and taverns, etc. From a demographics perspective, what does this signify?

Chapter 6

Consumer Life-Styles and Decision Making

1. To define and describe consumer life-styles and decision making
2. To demonstrate the importance of consumer life-styles and decision making for marketers and present appropriate marketing applications
3. To explain the interaction of consumer demographics, social concepts, psychological factors, and decision making
4. To point out the limitations of social, psychological, and decision-making analysis of consumers

*I*n 1964, Philip Knight became the U.S. distributor for Japan's Tiger running shoes. When Tiger ended Knight's exclusive selling rights in the United States, he formed his own company—Nike (named after the Greek goddess of victory)—in 1972. Today, Nike's total sales are nearing $1 billion annually.

Nike's prosperity is largely due to its identifying a new and growing American life-style (physical fitness) and enacting an appropriate marketing strategy to satisfy this life-style's emerging needs. Throughout the 1970s, Nike capitalized on the jogging boom in the U.S. where the total number of runners reached 20 million. Nike captured 50 per cent of the running-shoe market by offering quality products, social status, celebrity endorsements, a full line of shoes, and aggressive marketing. A strong appeal to "self-involved" and brand-conscious consumers was made.

Wisely, Nike foresaw a leveling off of jogging in the U.S. by the early

149

Figure 6-1
Nike Apparel and Running Shoes
In addition to its traditional running shoes, Nike now offers warmup suits (shown here), athletic shirts and shorts, and a variety of sports and recreational apparel.

Reprinted by permission.

1980s (as people diversified their physical-fitness efforts) and broadened its product lines, as illustrated in Figure 6-1. Its U.S. sales are now broken down as follows:

Running shoes	43%
Basketball shoes	24%
Racquetball shoes	18%
Children's shoes	8%
Apparel	3%
Other	4%
Total	100%

In addition, Nike has become active in the European running shoe market where Adidas and others are particularly strong. So far, consumer response in Europe has been limited. And, as one analyst observed, jogging is "not a national phenomenon. The English don't have the mad, ambitious striving . . . that it takes to make a whole country run. It's really a religion, this quest for self-perfection. People don't have that here." To this, replies Knight, "You are going to see guys jogging around Westminister Palace. It's happening."[1]

[1] Victor F. Zonana, "Jogging's Fade Fails to Push Nike Off Track." *Wall Street Journal* (March 5, 1981), p. 27; Myron Magnet, "Nike Starts the Second Mile," *Fortune* (November 1, 1982), pp. 158–166; "Nike Wins by Racing into New Markets," *Sales & Marketing Management* (January 17, 1983), pp. 23–24; and "Two U.S. Rivals Give Adidas a Run for Its Money," *Business Week* (July 18, 1983), p. 69.

By learning more about its consumers than just their demographics, any organization can better pinpoint market needs, the reasons for purchases, and changing life-styles and purchase-behavior patterns.

_____

Overview

The collection and analysis of demographic data are often not sufficient aids in the planning of marketing programs because demographics do not answer many questions. A selected list of these questions follows:

Many questions are usually unresolved after examining demographic data.

- Why do consumers act as they do?
- Why do consumers with similar demographic characteristics act differently?
- Why do consumers become brand loyal or regularly switch brands?
- Why do some consumers act as innovators and buy products before others?
- Under what situations do families employ joint decision making?
- How do consumers behave when shopping for a product?
- Why does status play a large role in the purchase of some goods and a small role in the purchase of others?
- How does risk affect consumer decisions?
- How do motives affect consumer decisions?
- How important is a purchase decision to a consumer?
- How long will it take for a consumer to reach a purchase decision?
- To whom does a consumer look for advice prior to purchasing a product or service?

In an attempt to answer these and other questions, marketers, in increasing numbers, are using demographic data in conjunction with and as part of social, psychological, and consumer decision-making analysis.

Social and psychological factors comprise a consumer's ***life-style,*** which is the pattern in which a person lives and spends time and money. A life-style combines the influences of personality and social values that have been internalized by an individual.[2] A person's demographic background has a strong influence on the life-style, or way of living, adopted.

Consumer life-styles *describe how people live, and can be measured through* psychographics.

Psychographics is the technique with which life-styles can be measured.[3] An AIO (activities, interests, and opinions) inventory is used in psychographic research to determine consumer life-styles. This inventory asks consumers to respond to a series of statements on their activities, interests, and opinions. Table 6-1 shows the range of topics covered in typical AIO inventories.

---

[2] James F. Engel and Roger D. Blackwell, *Consumer Behavior,* Fourth Edition (Hinsdale, Ill.: Dryden Press, 1982), p. 188.
[3] Ibid., p. 190.

Table 6-1
AIO Dimensions

Activities	Interests	Opinions
Work	Family	Themselves
Hobbies	Home	Social issues
Social events	Job	Politics
Vacation	Community	Business
Entertainment	Recreation	Economics
Club membership	Fashion	Education
Community	Food	Products
Shopping	Media	Future
Sports	Achievements	Culture

Source: Adapted from Joseph T. Plummer, "The Concept and Application of Life-Style Segmentation." *Journal of Marketing,* Vol. 38 (January 1974), p. 34. Reprinted by permission of the American Marketing Association.

The social aspects of life-style include culture, social class, performance, reference groups, family life cycle, and time expenditures (activities). Psychological aspects of life-style include personality, attitudes, level of class consciousness, motivation, perceived risk, innovativeness, opinion leadership, and importance of purchase. Social and psychological analysis overlap and complement each other; they are not independent or exclusive of one another.[4]

Consumers use a decision process consisting of several stages.

The consumer's decision process involves the steps a consumer goes through in purchasing a product or service: stimulus, problem awareness, information search, evaluation of alternatives, purchase, and postpurchase behavior. Demographics, social factors, and psychological factors affect the consumer's decision-making process.

By employing demographic, social, psychological, and decision-making analysis, a marketer can develop descriptive consumer profiles, answer each of the questions posed at the beginning of this chapter, and create consumer-oriented marketing plans.

Consumer Life-Styles

The social and psychological characteristics that form consumer life-styles are described next.

Social Characteristics of Consumers

The social profile of a consumer is comprised of a combination of culture, social class, performance, reference groups, family life cycle, and time expenditures (activities). See Figure 6-2.

American *culture* emphasizes success, materialism, freedom, and youthfulness.

A *culture* is a group of people sharing a distinctive heritage, such as Americans or Japanese. American culture has placed importance on achievement and success, activity, efficiency and practicality, progress, material comfort, individ-

---

[4] See William D. Wells (Editor), *Life Style and Psychographics* (Chicago: American Marketing Association, 1974).

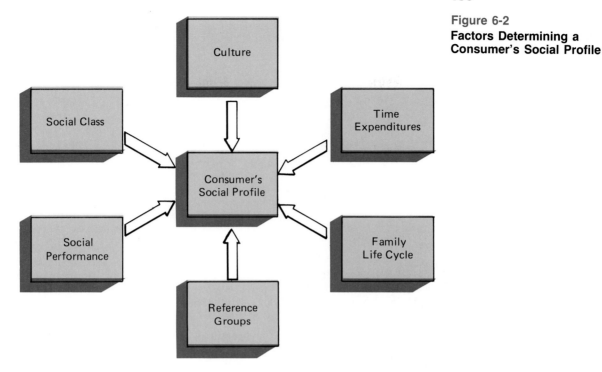

Figure 6-2
**Factors Determining a
Consumer's Social Profile**

ualism, freedom, external comfort, humanitarianism, and youthfulness.[5] Slower economic growth, the rising influence of foreign countries, and a maturing U.S. population may signal changes in these values. In Chapter 21, "International Marketing," the American culture is contrasted with other cultures.

A ***social class*** system is the ranking of people within a culture. Social classes are based on income, occupation, education, and type of dwelling. Social class systems separate society into divisions, grouping people with similar values and life-styles. Each social class may represent a distinct target market for a company. See Table 6-2.

Social performance is how a person carries out his or her roles as a worker, family member, citizen, and friend. At one extreme, a person may become a vice-president in a company, have a happy family life, be an active member of the community, and have many friends. At the other extreme, a person may never be promoted higher than assistant manager, be divorced, not participate in community affairs, and have few friends. It should be clear that many combinations of these performance criteria are possible—for example, vice-president and divorced. The advertisement shown in Figure 6-3 is oriented toward a person's interest in social performance.

A ***reference group*** is a group that influences a person's thoughts or actions. For many products and services, reference groups have an important impact on purchase behavior. A reference group may be aspirational, membership, or dissociative. An aspirational group is one to which a person does not belong but wishes to belong, such as a fraternity, professional society, or a social club. A member-

Social class **separates society into divisions.**

Social performance **describes how a person fulfills his or her roles.**

Reference groups **influence thoughts and behavior.**

[5] Leon G. Schiffman and Leslie Lazar Kanuk, *Consumer Behavior,* Second Edition (Englewood Cliffs, N.J.: Prentice-Hall, 1983), pp. 404–420.

**Table 6-2
The Social Class
Structure in the United
States**

Class	Size	Characteristics
Upper-upper	Less than 1%	Social elite; inherited wealth; exclusive neighborhood; summer home; children attend best schools; money not important in purchases; secure in status
Lower-upper	Combined with upper-upper equals 3%	Highest income level; earned wealth; often professionals; social mobility; "nouveaux riche"; college-educated but not at the best schools; seek the best for children; active in social affairs; value material possessions; not secure in position; "conspicuous consumption"; money not important in purchases
Upper-middle	12%	Career oriented; successful professionals and business people; earnings over $30,000; status based on occupation and earnings; education important; most educated in society, not from prestige schools; demanding of children; careful but conspicuous; attractive home; nice clothing; "gracious living"
Lower-middle	35%	"Typical American"; respectable; conscientious; obedient; church going; conservative; home ownership sought; do-it-yourselfers; neat; work at shopping; price sensitive; variety of lower-level white-collar occupations; incomes from $10,000–$25,000; purchases related to income and occupation; college for children
Upper-lower	40%	Routine existence; blue-collar occupations; limited education; seek job security; income can overlap with lower-middle; life of wife monotonous; child-oriented; impulsive for new purchases; brand loyal for regular items and "national brands"; little social contact; not status-oriented; protective against lower-lower
Lower-lower	10%	Present-oriented; impulsive; overpay; use credit; poor education; limited information; unemployed or work at most menial jobs; large market for foods; poor housing

Source: This table is derived, in part, from James F. Engel and Roger D. Blackwell, *Consumer Behavior,* Fourth Edition (Hinsdale, Ill.: Dryden Press, 1982), pp. 128–129; and Terrell G. Williams, *Consumer Behavior: Fundamentals and Strategies* (St. Paul: West Publishing, 1982), pp. 194–196.

ship group is one to which the person does belong, such as a family, union, or working women. A dissociative group is one to which the person does not want to belong, such as an unpopular social group, school dropouts, or a low-achievement group. Those reference groups that are face-to-face, such as family or fraternity, have the most influence on a person.

By pinpointing the reference groups that affect consumers, marketers can adapt their strategies. For example, commercials that show products and services being used by college students, successful professionals, and pet owners often ask viewers to join the "group" in making a similar purchase.

The *family life cycle* describes how a typical family evolves. Families often use *joint decision making*.

The *family life cycle,* shown in Table 6-3, describes how a typical family evolves from bachelorhood to marriage to children to solitary retirement. At each stage in the cycle, needs, experience, income, and family composition change. In addition, the use of *joint decision making*—the process whereby two or more consumers have input into purchases—changes throughout the cycle. The family life cycle is an excellent tool for market segmentation and for developing marketing campaigns. The number of people in different stages in the cycle can be obtained through a study of demographic data.

When utilizing family life cycle analysis, marketers should take note of the

Figure 6-3
A Hart Schaffner & Marx
Appeal to Social
Performance

Reprinted by permission.

growing numbers of people who do not marry, do not have children, or become divorced. These people are not reflected in Table 6-3, but may represent good marketing opportunities.[6]

Time expenditures refer to and involve the types of activities in which a person participates and the amount of time allocated to them. Since 1950 the average work week has declined by about five hours per week, from roughly 40 hours per week to 35. Two other trends are worth noting: urban Americans are spending significantly less time in family care, and leisure-time activities are increasing substantially. Americans are quite active in picnicking, driving for pleasure, swimming, sightseeing, walking activities, attending outdoor spectator events, and playing outdoor games and sports.

Time expenditures **reflect changes in the work week, family care, and leisure.**

---

[6] See for example, Patrick E. Murphy and William A. Staples, ''A Modernized Family Life Cycle,'' *Journal of Consumer Research,* Vol. 6 (June 1979), pp. 12–22.

**Table 6-3
The Traditional Family
Life Cycle**

Stage in Cycle	Characteristics	Relevance for Marketing
Bachelor, male or female	Independent; young; early stage of career; low earnings, low discretionary income	Clothing; automobile; stereo; travel; restaurants; entertainment; appeal to status
Newly married	Two incomes; relative independence; present- and future-oriented	Furnishing apartment; travel; clothing; durables; appeal to enjoyment and togetherness
Full nest I	Youngest child under 6; one income; limited independence; future-oriented	Products and services geared to child; family-use items; practicality of items; durability; safety; pharmaceuticals; appeal to economy
Full nest II	Youngest child over 6, but independent; one-and-a-half incomes; husband established in career; limited independence, future-oriented	Savings; home; education; family vacations; child-oriented products; some interest in luxuries; appeal to comfort and long-range enjoyment
Full nest III	Youngest child living at home, but independent; highest income level; independent; thoughts of retirement	Education; expensive durables for children; replacement and improvement of parents' durables; appeal to comfort and luxury
Empty nest I	No children at home; independent; good incomes; thoughts of self and retirement	Retirement home; travel; clothing; entertainment; luxuries; appeal to self-gratification
Empty nest II	Retirement; limited income and expenses; present-oriented	Travel; recreation; living in new home; pharmaceuticals and health items; little interest in luxuries; appeal to comfort at a low price
Sole survivor I	Only one spouse alive; actively employed; present-oriented; good income	Immersion in job and friends leading to opportunities in travel, clothing, health, and recreation areas; appeal to productive citizen
Sole survivor II	Only one person alive; retired; feeling of futility; poor income	Travel; recreation; pharmaceuticals; security; appeal to economy and social activity

Psychological Characteristics of Consumers

The psychological profile of a consumer combines personality, attitudes, class consciousness, motivation, perceived risk, innovativeness, opinion leadership, and importance of purchase. See Figure 6-4.

Personality describes the composite traits of a person.

A ***personality*** is the sum total of an individual's traits that make that individual unique. Self-confidence, dominance, autonomy, sociability, defensiveness, adaptability, and emotional stability are selected personality traits. Personality has a strong impact on an individual's behavior. For example, a self-confident and sociable person often will not purchase the same products and services as an inhibited and aloof person. It is necessary to remember that a personality is made up of many traits operating in conjunction with one another.

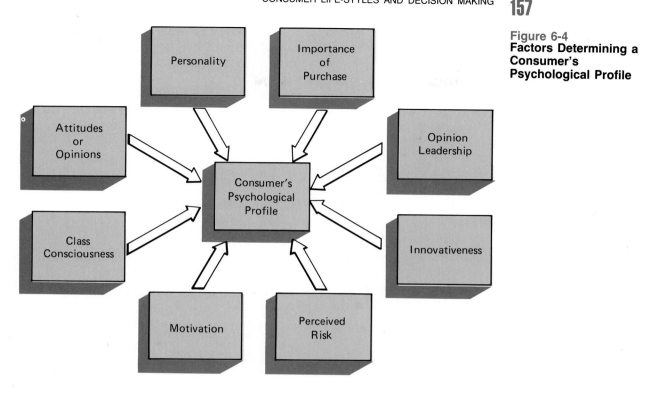

**Figure 6-4
Factors Determining a
Consumer's
Psychological Profile**

Attitudes (opinions) are a person's positive, neutral, or negative feelings about products, services, companies, issues, and/or institutions. Attitudes are shaped by demographics, social factors, and personality. One role of marketing is to generate favorable attitudes toward a company's products or services. Given the intensive competition in many industries, a firm cannot normally succeed without positive consumer attitudes.

When using attitude research, two concepts must be measured: the attitude itself and the purchase intent toward a company's brand. For example:

Attitudes (opinions) **can be positive, negative, or neutral.**

Attitude Evaluation	Purchase Intention
1. Are you familiar with brand A?	1. Have you ever purchased brand A?
2. Do you like brand A?	2. Would you buy brand A in the future?
3. Do you prefer brand A above other brands?	3. Do you regularly buy brand A?
4. How does brand A compare with other brands?	4. Would you buy brand A if it were priced higher than other brands?

Class consciousness is the extent to which social status is desired and pursued by a person. Class consciousness helps determine a consumer's use of reference groups, a person's concern about social class mobility, and the importance of prestige purchases. An *inner-directed person* is interested in pleasing him- or herself. This type of person is generally attracted by do-it-yourself products, products that perform well functionally, and products or services that are challenging and can be used when the person is alone. The inner-directed person relies

Class consciousness **is low for** *inner-directed persons* **and high for** *outer-directed persons*.

on his or her own judgment, is not involved with social mobility, and does not value prestige items. An **outer-directed person** is interested in pleasing the people around him or her. Approval by reference groups, upward social mobility, and the ownership of prestige items are sought. An outer-directed person is generally attracted by products or services that provide social visibility, well-known brands, competition with others, and uniqueness. Functional performance may be less important.

Motivation **is the drive impelling action; it is caused by** *motives.*

Motivation is

the driving force within individuals that impels them to action. This driving force is produced by a state of tension, which exists as the result of an unfulfilled need.[7]

By identifying and appealing to a consumer's **motives,** the reasons for behavior, a marketer can generate motivation. For example:

Motive	Marketer Actions That Motivate
Hunger	Television and radio commercials just before mealtime
Safety	Demonstration of a smoke detector
Sociability	Toothpaste and perfume commercials showing social success due to products
Achievement	Demonstration of knowledge obtained via a home computer
Economy	Newspaper coupons advertising sales

Each person has different motives for buying, and these change by situation and over time. Most consumers combine economic (price, durability) and emotional (status, self-esteem) motives when making a purchase.

Perceived risk **is the degree of uncertainty felt by the consumer. It must be minimized.**

Perceived risk is the level of risk a consumer believes exists regarding the outcome of a purchase decision; this belief may or may not be correct. Perceived risk can be divided into five major types:

1. Functional: the risk that the product will not perform adequately.
2. Physical: the risk that the product will be harmful.
3. Financial: the risk that the product will not be worth its cost or time commitment.
4. Social: the risk that the product will cause embarrassment before others.
5. Psychological: the risk that one's ego will be bruised.[8]

Figure 6-5 shows the different types of risk a consumer of a stereo system would face.

Marketers must deal with perceived risk, even if consumers are incorrect in their beliefs, because a high level of perceived risk usually dampens customer motivation. Perceived risk can be reduced by avoiding controversial ingredients, offering money-back guarantees, providing greater information, and developing and maintaining a reputation for quality products and services.

A consumer who is willing to try a new product or service that others perceive

[7] Schiffman and Kanuk, *Consumer Behavior,* p. 49.
[8] Ibid., p. 161.

Figure 6-5
Perceived Risk for a Stereo System

Functional Risk:
"Will the sound quality be superior?"

Physical Risk:
"Will the system be electrically safe?"

Financial Risk:
"Can I buy a comparable system for less?"

Social Risk:
"Will I be teased by my friends about the brand name?"

Psychological Risk:
"Will the system really help me to relax?"

as having a high degree of risk is said to exhibit ***innovativeness***. An innovator is likely to be well educated, literate, and have a high income and standard of living. This person is also apt to be knowledgeable, interested in change, achievement-motivated, business-oriented, open-minded, status conscious, mobile, venturesome, and have aspirations for his or her children.[9] It is essential for marketers to identify and appeal to innovators when introducing a new product or service.

Marketers are most interested in determining which innovators are ***opinion leaders***. Opinion leaders are people who influence the purchase behavior of other consumers through face-to-face interaction. Opinion leaders tend to be expert about a product or service category, socially accepted, longstanding members of the community, gregarious, active, and trusted, and tend to seek approval from others. Opinion leaders normally have an impact over a narrow range of products; they are perceived as more credible than commercial sources of information.

The ***importance of a purchase*** has a major impact on the time and effort a consumer will spend shopping for a product or service and on the amount of money allocated. An important purchase will involve careful decision making, high perceived risk, and probably a large amount of money. An unimportant purchase will receive little decision-making time (the product or service may be avoided altogether), have little perceived risk, and probably be inexpensive.

Innovativeness is a willingness to try a new product or service that others see as risky.

Opinion leaders influence other consumers through face-to-face contact.

The *importance of a purchase* determines the time, effort, and money a consumer will spend.

[9] Engel and Blackwell, *Consumer Behavior*, pp. 390–394.

Marketing Implications of Life-Style Analysis

During recent years, analysis of the social and psychological characteristics of consumers has increased dramatically. In this section, both general and specific applications of life-style analysis in marketing are presented.

Information on consumer life-styles is available from various sources.

Several organizations are involved with defining and measuring consumer life-styles. They sell this information to client firms, who use it to improve their marketing efforts. These are three of the best-known services:[10]

- Yankelovich Monitor, which tracks about 40 social trends, including upward mobility, female careerism, return to nature, and physical self-enhancement. Impermanent consumer profiles are developed, such as "successful adapters," "resistant adapters," and "traditional adapters"—which describe consumers in terms of their response to the changing 1980s environment.
- VALS (Values and Life-Styles), a research program sponsored by the Stanford Research Institute. It has categorized consumers into four basic life-style groups: need driven, those struggling to buy the basics; outer-directed, those heavily influenced by the opinions of others; inner-directed, those satisfying their own needs; and combined, those exhibiting maturity and flexibility.
- PRIZM (Potential Rating Index by Zip Market), a program that relies on census data and examines consumer life-styles by zip code. It uses 40 different neighborhood designations, such as blue blood ("old money") to describe life-styles.

These services have been used by firms marketing women's girdles, liquor, food, stock brokerage, automobiles, and other items.

Whirlpool sponsored a survey of 1,000 consumers to determine a variety of life-style factors. This study determined that [11]

- Consumers consider friends, relatives, and consumer reporters to be the most important sources of product information.
- Manufacturer and government information is believed by consumers.
- Consumers believe personal experience is the best way to evaluate a product.
- There are too many products and too much information available for consumers to make informed decisions.
- The overwhelming majority of consumers are satisfied with product quality; however they believe it is not improving.
- Most consumers feel they get good value for their money.
- The quality of supermarket services is viewed as improving, while auto services are deteriorating.
- Do-it-yourself activities are increasing. Those activities are related to education, age, gender, and family type, but not as much to economic conditions.

Said the president of Research and Forecasts, which conducted the study, "These results suggest that consumers' most trustworthy sources are not necessarily those with the best credentials, the most information, or the widest audience reach. Rather, direct human contact counts most."

[10] B. G. Yovovich, "It's 1982—Do You Know What Your Values Are?" *Advertising Age* (October 18, 1982), pp. M-28–M-31; and Leon G. Schiffman and Michael D. Jones, "Managerial Techniques for Implementing Psychographics," *Marketing Review* (November–December 1982), pp. 23–28.

[11] *America's Search for Quality: The Whirlpool Report on Consumers in the '80s* (Benton Harbor, Mich.: Whirlpool, 1983).

General Mills has developed a multifaceted marketing strategy to appeal to consumer life-styles that emphasize convenience, healthfulness, physical fitness, and social acceptance:[12]

- Yoplait yogurt and Nature Valley Granola bars are convenience foods that are healthy and can be eaten on the run.
- Traditional cereals fulfill the needs of vitamin-conscious consumers and natural cereals attract consumers concerned about additives.
- Izod sportswear focuses on status branding and physical fitness.
- Red Lobster Inns and other eateries are aimed at families dining out together.
- The Talbots mail-order business is oriented to consumers having little time for shopping.

Not long ago, Revlon revised its marketing approach for Charlie fragrances in response to changing consumer life-styles. For nine years, Charlie ads featured the "quintessential liberated woman." She was single, wore pants to the office, patronized clubs alone, dressed in tuxedos at night, signed restaurant checks, and walked in an independent, confident manner. Then, after a year of careful research and planning, a new Charlie commercial was released. In this ad, the woman wore an attractive evening gown, went out with a "wholesome-looking" man, and had the man propose marriage (without getting a definitive answer). See Figure 6-6. Said a Revlon executive, "Charlie hasn't changed. The world has changed." She "has proven her independence" and is waiting for "another dimension to her life."[13]

The social and psychological characteristics of consumers can also hold down sales, as well as increase them. For example, in the early 1980s, the U.S. automobile industry went through a major slowdown for many reasons. Among them were several consumer life-style factors. First, owning an older car was no longer socially unacceptable. As one consumer stated, "Instead of an ugly sight, it's a badge of honor." Second, consumers became more concerned about durability and economy and less interested in minor model changes and styling. Third, people reduced their driving mileage as a result of higher gasoline prices. Fourth, high new automobile prices encouraged consumers to invest in repairs for their existing cars. Fifth, consumers shifted spending to other items, such as housing, energy, food, and personal computers (which provided more status than autos). Sixth, as an American Motors executive commented, "In efforts to meet safety and fuel economy standards we all gravitated toward similar designs and styles." Another observer added that purchasing a car "is like buying a household appliance—you've got to have one, but you'll buy it only when you need it."[14]

Limitations of Life-Style Analysis

Unlike demographics, many social and psychological factors are difficult to measure, somewhat subjective, usually based on the self-reports of consumers,

Social and psychological factors can be hard to measure.

[12] Sandra D. Kresch, "The Impact of Consumer Trends on Corporate Strategy," *Journal of Business Strategy,* Vol. 3 (Winter 1983), pp. 58–63.

[13] Bill Abrams, "Why Revlon's Charlie Seems to Be Ready to Settle Down," *Wall Street Journal* (December 23, 1982), p. 11.

[14] Charles W. Stevens, "People Are Keeping Cars Longer as Costs Rise and Attitudes Change," *Wall Street Journal* (January 7, 1982), p. 23.

Figure 6-6
The Evolving Charlie
Life-Style

REVLON
Charlie

"AFTER THE PARTY" :30

RVCF 1143

(MUSIC UNDER)
HE: Nice party.

ANNCR: (VO) The best part of the party's when the party's over.

HE: Mmm, Charlie?
SHE: Uh huh.

HE: Would you cancel your trip to the coast if I proposed?

SHE: I wonder how much this lion weighs?

HE: Ciao!
SHE: Great bakery!

HE: Listen, I'm serious about what I said before.
SHE: Eat your breakfast.

HE: Even my mother thinks it's time for you to settle down.

SHE: Your mother's right.

ANNCR: (VO) Charlie. It's a great life.

Reprinted by permission of Revlon, Inc.

and sometimes hidden from view (to avoid embarrassment, protect privacy, convey an image, and other reasons). In addition, there are still ongoing disputes over terminology, misuse of data, and reliability.

Ten years ago, one of the pioneers in life-style analysis, William D. Wells, summarized the status of this research. His comments are just as valid today:

From the speed with which psychographics have diffused through the marketing community, it seems obvious that they are perceived as meeting a keenly felt need. The problem now is not so much one of pioneering as it is one of sorting out the techniques that work best. As that process proceeds, it seems extremely likely that psychographic methods will gradually become more familiar and less controversial, and eventually will merge into the mainstream of marketing research.[15]

The Consumer's Decision Process

The *consumer's decision process* is comprised of two parts: the process itself and factors affecting the process. The decision process consists of six basic stages: stimulus, problem awareness, information search, evaluation of alternatives, purchase, and postpurchase behavior. Factors that affect the process are a consumer's demographic, social, and psychological characteristics. The total consumer decision-making process is shown in Figures 6-7 and 6-8.

The *consumer's decision process* encompasses several stages, and can be affected by various factors.

[15] William D. Wells, "Psychographics: A Critical Review," *Journal of Marketing Research*, Vol. 12 (May 1975), p. 209.

Figure 6-7
The Consumer's Decision Process

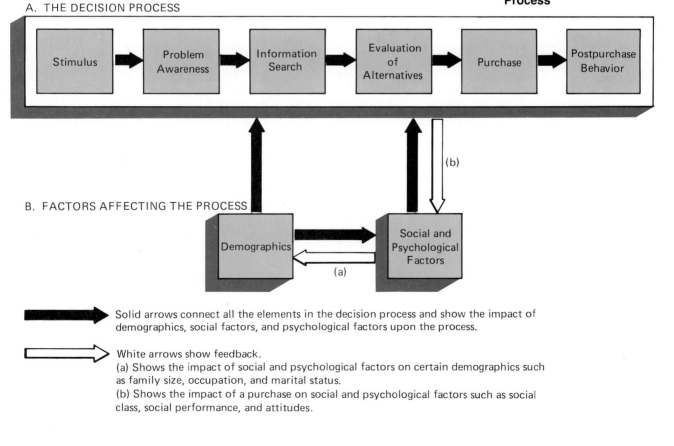

A. THE DECISION PROCESS

B. FACTORS AFFECTING THE PROCESS

Solid arrows connect all the elements in the decision process and show the impact of demographics, social factors, and psychological factors upon the process.

White arrows show feedback.
(a) Shows the impact of social and psychological factors on certain demographics such as family size, occupation, and marital status.
(b) Shows the impact of a purchase on social and psychological factors such as social class, social performance, and attitudes.

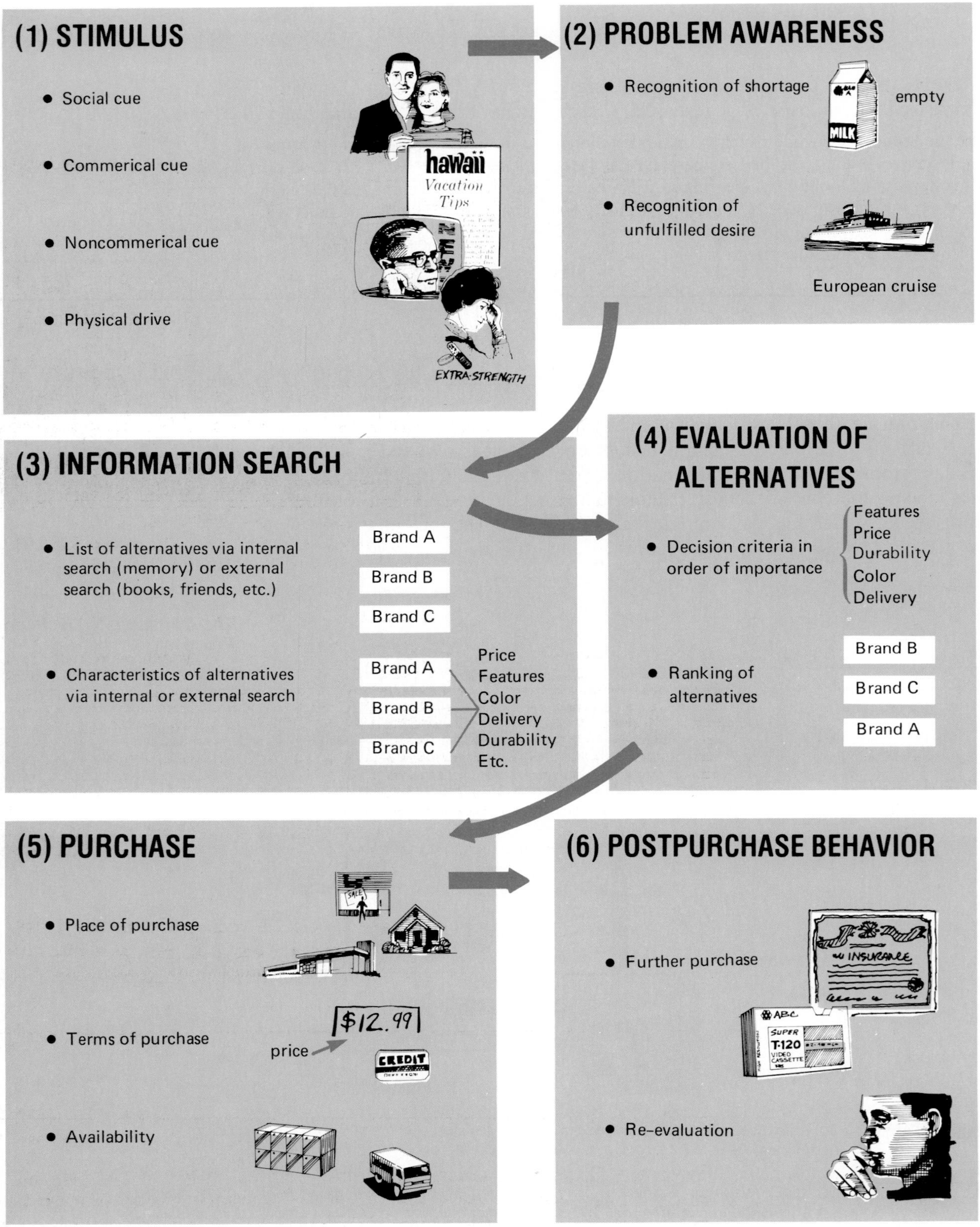
(1) STIMULUS
Social cue
Commerical cue
Noncommerical cue
Physical drive
hawaii
Vacation
Tips
EXTRA-STRENGTH
(2) PROBLEM AWARENESS
Recognition of shortage
MILK
empty
Recognition of unfulfilled desire
European cruise
(3) INFORMATION SEARCH
List of alternatives via internal search (memory) or external search (books, friends, etc.)
Brand A
Brand B
Brand C
Characteristics of alternatives via internal or external search
Brand A
Brand B
Brand C
Price
Features
Color
Delivery
Durability
Etc.
(4) EVALUATION OF ALTERNATIVES
Decision criteria in order of importance
Features
Price
Durability
Color
Delivery
Ranking of alternatives
Brand B
Brand C
Brand A
(5) PURCHASE
Place of purchase
SALE
Terms of purchase
price
$12.99
CREDIT
Availability
(6) POSTPURCHASE BEHAVIOR
Further purchase
INSURANCE
ABC
SUPER
T-120
VIDEO CASSETTE
Re-evaluation

Figure 6-8
Elements of the Consumer's Decision Process

When a consumer buys a product or service, he or she goes through this decision process. In some situations all six stages in the process are used; in others, only a few of the steps are utilized. For example, the purchase of an expensive stereo requires more decision making than the purchase of a new tie.

The decision process outlined in Figure 6-7 assumes that the end result is the purchase of a good or service by the consumer. However, it is important to realize that at *any* point in the process a potential consumer may decide not to buy and terminate the process. The product or service may turn out to be unnecessary, unsatisfactory, or too expensive.

Stimulus

A *stimulus* is a cue (social, commercial, or noncommercial) or a drive (physical) meant to motivate or arouse a person to act. When one talks with friends, fellow employees, family members, and others, social cues are received. The distinguishing attribute of a social cue is that it comes from an interpersonal source not affiliated with the seller.

A second type of stimulus is a commercial cue, which is a message sponsored by a manufacturer, wholesaler, retailer, or other seller. The objective of a commercial cue is to interest a consumer in a particular product, service, or store. Advertisements, personal selling, and sales promotions are forms of commercial stimuli. These cues may not be regarded as highly as social cues, because consumers realize they are seller-controlled. A consumer may react differently when a friend rather than a newspaper advertisement makes a suggestion.

A third type of stimulus is a noncommercial cue, which is a message received from an impartial source such as *Consumer Reports* or the government. This cue has higher credibility because it is not affiliated with the seller.

A fourth type of stimulus is a physical drive. This occurs when a person's physical senses are affected. Thirst, cold, heat, pain, hunger, and fear cause physical drives. If the drive is weak, it may be ignored. A strong drive requires further action.

A potential consumer may be exposed to any or all of these types of stimuli. If a person is sufficiently stimulated, he or she will go on to the next step in the decision process. If stimulation does not occur, the person will ignore the cue and delay or terminate the decision process for the given product or service.

> A *stimulus* is a social, commercial, noncommercial, or physical cue intended to motivate a consumer.

Problem Awareness

At the *problem awareness* stage, the consumer recognizes that the product or service under consideration may solve a problem of shortage or unfulfilled desire.

Recognition of shortage occurs when a consumer becomes alerted to the fact that a product or service needs to be repurchased. A product such as a suit, clock radio, or television may wear out. The consumer may run out of an item such as razor blades, coffee, or gasoline. Service may be necessary for a product such as an automobile or telephone. It may be time for a periodic service such as a haircut or an eye examination. In each of these examples, the consumer recognizes a need to replenish a product or service.

Recognition of unfulfilled desire occurs when a consumer becomes aware of a product or service that has not been purchased before. The product or service may

> *Problem awareness* entails recognition of a shortage or an unfulfilled desire.

improve a person's self-image, status, appearance, or knowledge in a manner that has not been tried before (cosmetic surgery, designer clothing, hair transplant, encyclopedia, luxury automobile), or it may offer new performance characteristics not previously available (videotape camera, talking magazine, tobacco-free cigarettes, outer-space travel). In either case the consumer is aroused by a desire to improve him- or herself and evaluates the utility of fulfilling this desire.

Many consumers are more hesitant to react to unfulfilled desires than to shortages because there are more risks, and the benefits may be hard to judge. There is less experience with new items than with the replacement of a product or service whose characteristics are well known. Whether the consumer becomes aware of a problem of shortage or a problem of unfulfilled desire, he or she will act only if the problem is perceived as worth solving. A strong stimulus does not mean the presence of a worthy problem. An unworthy problem will not be acted on, and the decision process is delayed or terminated at this point.

Information Search

Information search **involves determining alternatives and their characteristics through internal or external means.**

After the consumer decides that the shortage or unfulfilled desire is worth further consideration, information is gathered. The *information search* requires the assembly of a list of alternative products or services that will solve the problem at hand and a determination of the characteristics of each alternative.

The list of alternatives does not have to be very formal or even written. It can simply be a group of items the consumer thinks about. The key is that the consumer amasses a list of the products or services that are most likely to solve his or her problem. Normally, once the consumer has generated a list of alternatives, items (brands) not on the list do not receive further consideration.

This aspect of information search may be internal or external. Internal search takes place when the consumer has a lot of purchasing experience in the area under consideration and uses a search of his or her memory to determine the list of products or services that should be considered. A consumer with minimal purchasing experience will usually undertake external search to develop a list of alternatives. This type of search can involve commercial sources, noncommercial sources, and/or social sources. The consumer seeks information outside his or her memory.

The second type of information a consumer seeks deals with the characteristics of each alternative, as the attributes of each alternative under consideration are determined. This kind of information is gathered in the same manner as the list of alternatives was generated, internally or externally, depending on the expertise of the consumer and the level of perceived risk. As risk increases, the amount of information sought also increases.

Once the information search is completed, it must be determined whether the shortage or unfulfilled desire can be satisfied by any of the alternatives. If one or more alternatives are satisfactory, the consumer moves on to the next step in the decision process. The process is delayed or discontinued when no alternative provides minimal satisfaction.

Evaluation of Alternatives

At this point, the consumer has enough information to select one product or service alternative from the list of choices. Sometimes this is easy to do, when one alternative is clearly superior to the others across all characteristics. A product or service with excellent quality and a low price will be an automatic choice over an average quality, expensive one. Often the choice is not that simple, and the consumer must carefully *evaluate the alternatives* before making a decision. If two or more alternatives are attractive, the consumer needs to determine what criteria (attributes) to evaluate and their relative importance. Then the alternatives are ranked and a choice made.

Criteria for a decision are those product or service features that the consumer considers relevant. These may include price, color, style, options, quality, safety, durability, status, and warranty. The consumer sets performance standards for the features and evaluates (develops an attitude toward) each alternative according to its ability to meet the standards. In addition, the importance of each criterion is determined, because the multiple attributes of the product or service are usually of varying importance to the consumer. For example, a consumer may consider the price of a pair of shoes to be more important than style and act accordingly during a purchase by selecting inexpensive, nondistinctive shoes.

Next, the consumer ranks the alternatives from most desirable to least desirable and selects one product or service from among the alternatives. For some products or services, ranking is difficult because the items may be technical, poorly labeled, or new (the consumer has no experience with the brand or product type). These items are frequently ranked on the basis of brand name or price, which is used to indicate overall quality.

In situations where no alternative proves to be satisfactory, a decision to delay or not make the purchase is made.

Evaluating alternatives consists of determining important product features and then selecting the most desirable product.

Purchase

Following the selection of the best product or service from the list of alternatives, the consumer is ready for the *purchase act:* an exchange of money or a promise to pay for the acquisition of a product or service. Three important decisions remain: place of purchase, terms, and availability.

The place of purchase (where the product or service is bought) may be a store or nonstore location. The great majority of items (food, automobile, clothing, drugs, beauty services) are bought at stores (discount, department, boutique). Some items are purchased at school (books, stationery), work (health insurance), and home (mail, telephone, and door-to-door sales). The place of purchase is evaluated in the same manner as the product or service itself. Alternatives are listed, characteristics defined, and a ranking compiled. The most desirable place of purchase is then chosen.

The terms of purchase are the price and the method of payment. Price is the total dollar amount (including interest, tax, and other charges) a consumer pays to achieve ownership or use of a product or service. The method of payment is the manner in which the price is paid (cash, short-term credit, or long-term credit).

Availability refers to stock-on-hand and delivery. Stock-on-hand is the quantity of an item that the place of purchase has in its inventory. Delivery is the length of time from when an order is placed by the consumer until it is received and the ease with which an item is transported to its place of use.

The consumer will buy a product or service if these three elements of the

A consumer completes the purchase act *after deciding where to buy, agreeing to terms, and learning of availability.*

purchase act are acceptable. However, dissatisfaction with the place of purchase, terms, and/or availability may cause a consumer to delay or not buy the product or service, even though there is contentment with the product or service itself.

Postpurchase Behavior

Postpurchase behavior often embodies further purchases or re-evaluation.

After the purchase of a product or service, the consumer frequently is involved with ***postpurchase behavior***—either further purchases or re-evaluation. In many cases buying one product or service leads to further purchases. For example, the purchase of a house leads to the acquisition of fire insurance. The purchase of a suit leads to the purchase of a matching tie. The purchase of a home videotape system leads to the acquisition of blank and movie cassettes. In these and other situations, the purchase of one product or service provides the impetus for other purchases, and the decision process continues for these items until the last purchase is made.

The consumer may also re-evaluate the purchase of a product or service. Does the item perform as promised? Are the expectations of the consumer matched by actual product or service attributes? Satisfaction usually results in repurchase when the product or service runs out and there has been positive communication with other consumers interested in the same product or service. Dissatisfaction frequently results in brand switching and negative communications with other consumers.

Cognitive dissonance can be reduced by proper consumer aftercare.

Dissatisfaction with a purchase is often the result of ***cognitive dissonance,*** doubt that the correct decision has been made. The consumer may regret that the purchase was made at all or wish that another alternative had been chosen. To overcome cognitive dissonance and dissatisfaction, the firm must realize that the purchase process does not end with the purchase. Aftercare (follow-up telephone and service calls, advertisements aimed at purchasers as well as potential purchasers) is extremely important to reassure consumers, particularly for important and expensive decisions with many alternatives.

The coupling of a realistic promotion campaign, so that expectations are not raised too high, with consumer aftercare should reduce or eliminate cognitive dissonance and dissatisfaction.

Factors Affecting the Consumer's Decision Process

The decision process is affected by consumer demographics and life-style factors.

Demographic, social, and psychological factors have an important impact on the way consumers utilize the decision process. These factors are not only helpful for marketers in developing consumer profiles and adapting marketing strategies to them, but they also aid the firm in understanding how consumers use the decision process.

For example, a young male who participates in social activities and is outgoing would use the decision process differently from a middle-aged male who is a homebody and introverted. The former would place heavy emphasis on social sources of information, whereas the latter would not. An affluent consumer would move through the process more quickly than a middle-income consumer because the financial risk would be less. A person under tight time pressure would also move through the process more quickly than one who had sufficient time for shopping. An insecure consumer would spend more time making a decision than one who is secure.

By knowing how these factors affect the decision process, a company can fine tune its marketing strategies to cater to the target market and its purchase behavior; in addition, the company can answer these two questions: Why do two or more consumers use the decision process in the same way? Why do two or more people use the decision process in quite different ways?

Types of Decision Processes

Each time a consumer buys a product or service, he or she uses the decision process. Often, it is used subconsciously and the consumer is not even aware of its use. The decision process also is used differently in various situations. One situation may require the thorough use of each step in the process; another may allow the consumer to de-emphasize or skip certain steps. The three types of decision processes are extended, limited, and routine decision making. Their characteristics are shown in Figure 6-9.

Extended consumer decision making occurs when a consumer makes full use of the decision process shown in Figure 6-7. Considerable time is spent on information search and evaluation of alternatives before a purchase is made. Expensive, complex products or services with which the consumer has had little or no experience require this form of decision making. Perceived risk of all kinds is

Extended consumer decision making involves full use of the decision process and is applied to expensive, unique items.

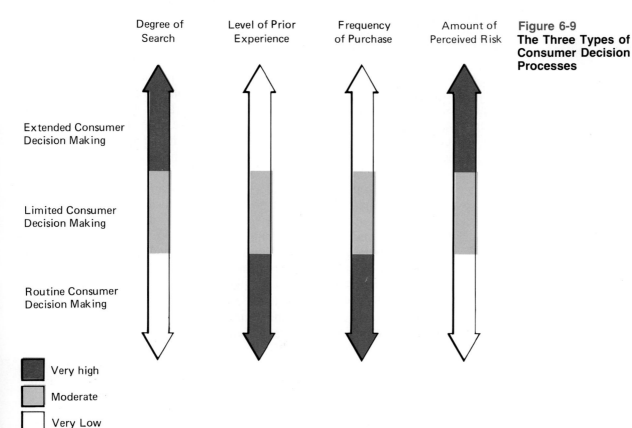

Figure 6-9
The Three Types of Consumer Decision Processes

Degree of Search | Level of Prior Experience | Frequency of Purchase | Amount of Perceived Risk

Extended Consumer Decision Making

Limited Consumer Decision Making

Routine Consumer Decision Making

■ Very high
▨ Moderate
☐ Very Low

generally high. Examples of products or services requiring extended decision making are college, a house, a first car, and a location for a wedding.

At any stage of the purchase process, a consumer can delay or terminate activity; this often occurs for expensive, complex items. The factors affecting the process have their greatest impact on extended decision making. Demographic, social, and psychological factors (age, income, education, activities, stage in family life cycle, experience, personality, and others) have a major influence on the use of extended decision making. High levels of perceived risk lead to increased information search, evaluation, and re-evaluation.

Limited consumer decision making involves the use of every step of the purchase process but not much time on any of them. It is used for items purchased infrequently.

Limited consumer decision making takes place when a consumer uses each of the steps in the purchase process but does not need to spend a great deal of time on any of them. This type of decision making normally requires less time than extended decision making, because the consumer has some past experience with the product or service under consideration. In this category are items the consumer has purchased, but not regularly. Perceived risk is moderate, and the consumer is willing to spend some time shopping. The thoroughness with which the process is used depends on the prior experience of the consumer and the importance of the purchase. Emphasis is usually on an evaluation of a list of known alternatives, based on desires or standards. An information search is important for some consumers. A second car, clothing, gifts, home furnishings, and a vacation are examples of items typically utilizing limited decision making.

The factors affecting the decision process have some impact on limited decision making. However, this impact lessens as experience increases and perceived risk decreases. Income, education, the importance of the purchase, motives, and the time available for shopping play strong roles in the uses of limited decision making.

Routine consumer decision making involves buying out of habit and skips many steps in the decision process. It is used for regularly purchased items.

Routine consumer decision making occurs when the consumer buys out of habit and skips steps in the decision process. The consumer seeks to spend no time in shopping and usually repurchases the same brands. In this category are items that are purchased regularly. These products have little or no perceived risk for the consumer because of the regular nature of their purchase (substantial experience by the consumer) and low purchase price. The key step for this form of decision making is problem awareness. Once the consumer realizes a product or service is depleted, a repurchase is made. Information search, evaluation of alternatives, and postpurchase behavior are normally omitted as long as the consumer is satisfied. Examples of routine purchases are the daily newspaper, a haircut by a regular barber, and weekly grocery items.

Factors affecting the process have little impact on routine behavior. Problem awareness almost always leads to a purchase.

Brand loyalty reduces consumer risk, time, and thought.

Because consumers like to reduce risk, the time spent shopping, and the use of detailed decision making, most purchases are made through routine or limited decision making. ***Brand loyalty*** is the consistent repurchase of and preference toward a brand. Through brand loyalty, consumers attempt to minimize risk, time, and thought. One recent study showed that in the U.S. about 60 per cent of consumers consider themselves likely to "try to stick to well-known brand names."[16] Where possible, consumers seek to avoid extended decision making.

---

[16] Bill Abrams, "Brand Loyalty Rises Slightly, But Increase Could Be Fluke," *Wall Street Journal* (January 7, 1982), p. 23.

Marketing Implications of the Consumer's Decision Process

Theories to explain the consumer's decision process began in the mid-1960s. The three leading theorists were Howard-Sheth,[17] Engel-Kollat-Blackwell,[18] and Nicosia.[19] Since that time, there has been considerable research on the marketing implications of the process. Today, the applications span many elements of marketing, as these illustrations demonstrate.

The purchase of a man's suit has symbolic meaning, potential social risk, and a wide range of attractive choices. Consumers for suits can be divided into four categories, based on the manner in which decisions are reached. High-status shoppers are somewhat older, relatively set in their ways, outgoing, make frequent purchases, exhibit low store loyalty, and spend minimal time seeking external information; they are influenced by spouses. Profashion shoppers tend to be older, open to change, more introverted, make infrequent purchases, exhibit low store loyalty, and spend a lot of time seeking external information; they are influenced by spouses. Single shoppers are younger, open to change, outgoing, make infrequent purchases, exhibit low store loyalty, and spend minimal time on external search; they are strongly influenced by peers. Uninvolved shoppers are somewhat older, set in their ways, relatively introverted, make infrequent purchases, exhibit very high levels of store loyalty, and spend little time on external search; they are less influenced by peers or spouses.[20]

Drugstore shoppers make almost 60 per cent of final purchase decisions after entering the store. The items for which specific buying plans are made in advance include prescriptions, photographic equipment, tobacco and alcohol, and nonprescription drugs. However, personal care items, magazines, snack foods, hardware, cosmetics, accessories, nonalcoholic beverages, jewelry, and automotive supplies are largely unplanned purchases that are greatly affected by store displays, advertisements, and coupons.[21]

The purchase process for houseware products (such as cook and bakeware, bathroom accessories, and small electrical appliances) is undergoing a number of changes. The importance of price is declining, with greater interest in color and design. Housewares are less frequently bought as gifts. Autonomous decision making is increasing. In-store displays have become the greatest source of information. There is a gradual movement away from discounters back to traditional department stores.[22]

The consumer's decision process has been examined in various settings.

Limitations of the Consumer's Decision Process

The limitations of the consumer's decision process for marketers lie in the hidden (unexpressed) nature of many elements of the process, the consumer's subconscious performance of the process or a number of its components, and the impact of demographic, social, and psychological factors on the process.

Much of purchase behavior is hidden or unconscious.

[17] John A. Howard and Jagdish N. Sheth, *The Theory of Buyer Behavior* (New York: John Wiley, 1969).
[18] James F. Engel, David T. Kollat, and Roger D. Blackwell, *Consumer Behavior* (New York: Holt, 1968).
[19] Francesco Nicosia, *Consumer Decision Processes* (Englewood Cliffs, N.J.: Prentice-Hall, 1966).
[20] David F. Midgley, "Patterns of Interpersonal Information Seeking for the Purchase of a Symbolic Product," *Journal of Marketing Research,* Vol. 20 (February 1983), pp. 74–83.
[21] "Pilot Study Finds Final Product Choice Usually Made in Store," *Marketing News* (August 6, 1982), p. 5.
[22] "Study Tracks Housewares Buying, Information Sources," *Marketing News* (October 14, 1983), p. 16.

Summary

Because demographic data alone are often inadequate for making marketing decisions, many firms analyze consumer social, psychological, and decision-making information in conjunction with demographics and then develop descriptive consumer profiles.

Social and psychological factors comprise a consumer's life-style, the pattern in which a person lives and spends time and money. Psychographics is the technique by which life-styles are measured. A consumer's social profile is made up of several elements, including culture, social class, performance, reference groups, family life cycle, and time expenditures. A psychological profile is based on a combination of these attributes: personality, attitudes, level of class consciousness, motivation, perceived risk, innovativeness, opinion leadership, and importance of purchase.

Even though social and psychological concepts have many marketing applications, they can be difficult to measure, somewhat subjective, based on self-reports by consumers, and sometimes hidden from view. There are disputes over terms, misuse of data, and reliability.

The consumer's decision process is composed of the process itself and the factors affecting it (demographics, social factors, and psychological factors). It can be delayed or terminated by the consumer at any point. The process consists of six steps: stimulus, problem awareness, information search, evaluation of alternatives, purchase, and postpurchase behavior. There are three types of consumer decision making: extended, limited, and routine. Brand loyalty, the consistent repurchase of and preference for a brand, is the consumer's attempt to minimize risk, time, and thought.

The limitations of the decision process for marketers lie in the unexpressed nature of many parts of the process, the subconscious nature of many actions by consumers, and the impact of demographic, social, and psychological factors.

Questions for Discussion

1. Why are demographic data alone frequently insufficient for marketing decisions?
2. American culture emphasizes achievement and success, freedom, and youthfulness. What are the implications of this emphasis for a company marketing soap? Automobiles?
3. How does social class affect an individual's life-style and purchases?
4. Give examples of advertising themes using a (n)
   a. Aspirational reference group.
   b. Membership reference group.
   c. Dissociative reference group.
5. What are the strengths and weaknesses of the traditional family life cycle?

6. How would a personal-selling approach aimed at self-confident, dominant consumers differ from one aimed at unsure, easily dominated consumers?
7. Develop a five-question survey to determine the attitudes of consumers toward exercise bicycles. What question must be included?
8. How does class consciousness differ for inner-directed and outer-directed people? What does this signify for marketers?
9. Distinguish between actual risk and perceived risk. How may a firm reduce perceived risk for a new cold remedy?
10. "Opinion leaders normally have an impact over a narrow range of products." Comment on this statement.
11. Differentiate among social, commercial, and noncommercial stimuli. Provide specific examples of each.
12. Under what circumstances is a consumer most likely to engage in external information search? Internal information search?
13. As a consumer, what criteria would you use to select from among three alternative newspapers? Three alternative apartments?
14. What causes cognitive dissonance? How may it be reduced?
15. Draw a flow chart showing the steps in routine behavior.
16. Define brand loyalty and explain its use by consumers.

Case 1 Nutri-Grain Cereal: Applying Life-Style Analysis*

Kellogg, now a company with $2.4 billion in annual sales and a 39 per cent market share of total cereal industry sales, was founded in 1906. It was Kellogg that pioneered the modern cereal industry. Of all major food-processing companies, Kellogg remains the most dependent on cereals. Some of Kellogg's leading cereal brands are Corn Flakes (its original product), Sugar Frosted Flakes, Raisin Bran, and Rice Krispies. Despite its prowess with cereals, Kellogg's sales growth in this category is about 2 per cent annually. Recent sales gains have come from other company product lines, such as Salada Foods.

In order to revitalize cereal sales, Kellogg has begun applying consumer life-style analysis in the introduction of new brands. Such analysis was undertaken in the planning of Nutri-Grain, a newer sugarless cereal with bits of whole grain that is offered in corn, wheat, and wheat-and-raisins varieties:

In no way, shape, or form is the target for Nutri-Grain those who are fanatics. We are going after those who are interested in nutrition, but we are really positioned beyond natural cereals. Natural cereals were a fad. We have gone beyond that by adding vitamins and minerals. Because of the addition, we cannot call it a natural food.

Kellogg's marketing efforts for Nutri-Grain are quite different from those it employs for other brands. The Nutri-Grain name is emphasized, rather than that of Kellogg. Its distinctive packaging uses the color white, signifying purity and

* The data in this case are drawn from Rebecca Fannin, "Daring to Be Different," *Marketing & Media Decisions* (May 1982), pp. 65–67, 162; "Kellogg Tells New Strategy," *Advertising Age* (February 28, 1983), pp. 1, 72; and John A. Maxwell, Jr., "Continued Growth Seen in Cold Cereal Market," *Advertising Age* (June 6, 1983), p. 42.

wholesomeness, and provides extensive product information and recipes. Nutri-Grain is aimed at both nutrition-conscious consumers as well as at younger adults (a relatively untapped group). Kellogg's goal has been to change the poor breakfast habits of younger adults. Advertising media are chosen on the basis of life-style appeal, instead of audience size. For the first time, Kellogg is advertising in *Self* and *Vogue* magazines. It also relies on longer, more informative ads in all types of media.

There are over 100 brands of cereal competing in the $3.5 billion U.S. ready-to-eat cereal industry, with the leading brand (General Mills' Cheerios) having a 6 per cent market share of dollar sales. Since its 1981 introduction, Nutri-Grain has achieved a 1 to 1.5 per cent market share, and its share has stabilized.

QUESTIONS

1. Thus far, Nutri-Grain has had little impact on the poor breakfast habits of young adults. Comment on this.
2. How could Kellogg apply life-style analysis to Rice Krispies?
3. Generic brands of cereal, containing only the retailer's name and priced well below manufacturer brands, are making a dent in the sales of Kellogg cereals. What life-style themes could Kellogg utilize in its advertising to minimize the effects of generics?
4. Kellogg believes that natural cereals represent a fad, because they are "too hearty." They contain brown sugar, cinnamon, and molasses—just like oatmeal cookies. Do you agree? Explain your answer.

Case 2 Life-Styles and Shopping Behavior: Learning About Two-Income Couples†

Two-income households account for one third of all U.S. households and earn a median income of just over $30,000. As such, these consumers are a prime target market for companies. To learn more about two-income couples, a national survey on the "Supermarket Shopping Strategies of Working Couples" was conducted in 1983. Participating couples were 25 to 54 years old.

Table 1 summarizes selected findings from this study. In general, two-income couples

want convenience and competitive pricing, but they also want quality, a variety of choices, and some sizzle.

Supermarkets should

appeal to the dual-income families' strong interest in quality. Both food and nonfood marketing thrusts should be geared to meeting their high expectations.

QUESTIONS

1. Evaluate the life-style findings in Table 1. What are the implications for marketers?

† "Changes Found in Attitudes, Shopping Behavior of U.S.'s Two-Income Couples," *Marketing News* (October 28, 1983), p. 12.

2. Evaluate the supermarket shopping-behavior findings in Table 1. What are the implications for supermarket executives?
3. Women shoppers are more likely to compile shopping lists before entering a supermarket than are men. How does this procedure affect the consumer's decision process?
4. If your company planned to market a new brand of toothpaste, who would be the target of an in-store display, the husband or the wife? Why?

Table 1

The Life-Styles and Shopping Behavior of Two-Income Couples

Only 2% are saving for retirement.

75% believe two incomes "are necessary."

Many activities are shared, such as vacation planning, supermarket shopping, and financial budgeting.

81% of husbands handle car maintenance. 90% of wives schedule children's appointments. 32% of men prepare one or more dinners each week.

50% dine out at least once a week.

Men visit the supermarket 3.7 times per month, wives 6.9 times. At least one trip is usually made together.

Women buy more health and beauty aids in supermarkets than men, and are more systematic and knowledgeable in this shopping.

Men often rely on signs and information in supermarkets. They are also twice as likely as women to make impulse purchases in supermarkets.

80% normally shop at the same supermarket. 75% shop at a chain store, rather than at an independent store.

Friday and Saturday are preferred shopping days.

Organizational Consumers

CHAPTER OBJECTIVES

1. To examine the characteristics of organizational consumers and show how they differ from final consumers

2. To describe the different types of organizational consumers and their buying objectives, buying structure, use of purchases, and purchase constraints

3. To explain the organizational consumer's decision process

4. To consider the marketing implications of organizational buyer types, characteristics, and behavior

Sensormatic Electronics Corporation manufactures and markets antishoplifting devices, which it sells to retailers. Sensormatic's plastic tags and magnetic strips are adhered to merchandise (such as clothing); an alarm is set off if the devices are not removed properly by store employees and a customer tries to leave the premises without paying for merchandise. The company has over a 70 per cent market share in the industry, with sales rising from $7.7 million in 1977 to $67 million in 1982.

Until recently, Sensormatic concentrated on general merchandise retailers, such as department stores, specialty stores, and discount and variety stores. But Ronald Assaf, Sensormatic's founder and chief executive, believes the time is ripe to market the firm's products to supermarkets. In the U.S., supermarket shoplifting is estimated at $1.2 billion annually; and supermarkets usually have extremely low profit margins (around 1 per cent). Therefore, a reduction in supermarket shoplifting could have a dramatic effect on profitability.

Earlier, Sensormatic's leading competitors, Knogo and Checkpoint, tested antishoplifting systems in supermarkets—with little success. They encountered too many false alarms and too much employee resistance. However, in 1982, Sensormatic introduced a new technology specifically aimed at high-turnover supermarket retailing. See Figure 7-1. Sensormatic's system is being heavily promoted by a 90-person national sales force personally calling on supermarket management. Midwestern supermarkets showed the greatest initial interest, as a result of above-average shoplifting during the recent recession. Stated one security manager, "If they can get the bugs out, the system will sell like wildfire."

Not all supermarket executives are convinced that electromagnetic antishoplifting devices will work in their industry. Regarding the possibility of false alarms, one executive commented that "Once a checkout clerk

Figure 7-1
SensorGate: Antishoplifting Devices for Supermarkets

SensorGate adhesive labels are adhered to supermarket items. Any items that pass through SensorGates without being checked out through supermarket electronic scanners set off an alarm or a flashing light. The gates swing freely and easily.

Reprinted by permission of Sensormatic.

has gone through a false alarm, it is almost impossible to rebuild confidence." On the cost of the devices, another executive said "Supermarket net profit margins are simply not enough to allow us to plug an expensive tag on a can of green beans." Sensormatic feels it can counter these and any other objections that are raised; nonetheless, two years after entering this market, sales remained relatively low.[1]

To improve its performance in marketing antishoplifting devices to supermarkets, Sensormatic is carefully reacting to the unique characteristics, needs, and buying patterns of this group of organizational consumers. Sensormatic realizes that it must overcome a resistance to its system, demonstrate real cost savings, and show how simple it is to train employees.

The Characteristics of Organizational Consumers

Companies involved with organizational consumers use industrial marketing.

As defined in Chapter 5, organizational consumers are formal entities that purchase products and services for further production, use in operating the organization, or resale to other consumers. In contrast, final consumers purchase products and services for personal, family, or household use. Organizational consumers are manufacturers, wholesalers, retailers, and government and other nonprofit institutions. When firms deal with organizational consumers, they are engaged in *industrial marketing,* as these illustrations demonstrate.

Dozier Equipment of Nashville, Tennessee, markets industrial maintenance, materials handling, and safety equipment to thousands of business customers. Dozier carries inexpensive supplies as well as $1,000 power paint stripers and $2,400 waste-barrel dumpers. Dozier employs a small sales force for local customers and uses a 196-page catalog to generate sales nationally. Said a company vice-president, "We can sell in California about as easily as in Tennessee."[2]

Advance Lifts is the leading company in the hydraulic loading dock market, with a 40 per cent market share. Sales are made to all types of organizational customers (retailers, mass merchandisers, wholesalers, etc.). Advance Lifts devotes 7 per cent of its gross sales to advertising its products to potential customers. It also develops new products for specific target markets. Said Advance Lifts' president, "Our entire company is geared to making it as easy as possible for people to buy our products. Everybody here is marketing-oriented."[3]

After many years of company growth through the sales of cameras, film, and related products aimed at final consumers, Polaroid has increased its focus on organizational consumers. In large part, this was a response to 1982 final-con-

---

[1] "Sensormatic: Out to Quadruple Revenue by Bagging Supermarket Thieves," *Business Week* (June 14, 1982), pp. 99–100; Phillip H. Wiggins, "Guarded Outlook for Sensormatic," *New York Times* (December 23, 1983), p. D4; and Jane Sasseen, "Stopping Roast Rustlers," *Forbes* (May 23, 1983), pp. 58–59.

[2] Steven Mintz, "Catalogues Get Down to Business-to-Business," *Sales & Marketing Management* (November 15, 1982), pp. 58–59.

[3] "Marketing Program Leads to Dominance," *Marketing News* (October 28, 1983), p. 6.

Differences in Purchases

1. Organizational consumers acquire for further production, use in operations, or resale to other consumers. Final consumers acquire only for personal, family, or household use.

2. Organizational consumers commonly purchase installations, raw materials, and semifinished materials. Final consumers rarely purchase these goods.

3. Organizational consumers purchase on the basis of specifications and technical data. Final consumers frequently purchase on the basis of description, fashion, and style.

4. Organizational consumers utilize multiple-buying and team-based decisions more often than final consumers.

5. Organizational consumers are more likely to apply value and vendor analysis.

6. Organizational consumers more commonly lease equipment.

7. Organizational consumers more frequently employ competitive bidding and negotiation.

Differences in the Market

1. The demand of organizational consumers is derived from the demand of final consumers.

2. The demand of organizational consumers is more subject to cyclical fluctuations than final-consumer demand.

3. Organizational consumers are fewer in number and more geographically concentrated than final consumers.

4. Organizational consumers often employ buying specialists.

5. The distribution channel for organizational consumers is shorter than for final consumers.

6. Organizational consumers may require special services.

7. Organizational consumers are more likely than final consumers to be able to make products and services as alternatives to purchasing them.

sumer camera sales falling to their lowest level since 1971. Today, one third of Polaroid's sales involve industrial marketing. It is producing specialty chemicals, industrial batteries, slide processors, and other items for business customers.[4]

Max Rubin Industries is a Baltimore, Maryland, menswear manufacturer that recently converted its business to government contracting. After ten unsuccessful bids on government contracts, Rubin finally received an order for 27,000 Marine Corps overcoats in May 1983. Since then, the firm has been awarded contracts for 80,000 Army coats, 77,600 pairs of trousers for the Marine Corps, and other apparel. In servicing government accounts, Rubin must purchase all materials from government-approved suppliers and meet exact product specifications. As Rubin's president stated, "Making the garment is the easiest part."[5]

In undertaking industrial marketing, a company must recognize that organizational consumers differ from final consumers in several important ways. These differences are due to the nature of products and services purchased and the nature of the market. See Table 7-1 and the discussion in the following subsections.

[4] William Bulkeley, "As Polaroid Matures, Some Lament a Decline in Creative Excitement," *Wall Street Journal* (May 10, 1983), pp. 1, 19; and Steven J. Marcus, "Polaroid Slide Setup Aimed at Businesses," *New York Times* (May 7, 1983), p. 31.
[5] Barbara Ettore, "The $4.59 Dress Shirt," *Forbes* (October 10, 1983), pp. 33–35.

Differences from Final Consumers Due to the Nature of Purchases

Organizational and final consumers vary in the way they use products and services and in the types of products and services they purchase. Organizational consumers use products and services in further production, operations, or for resale to other consumers. They purchase capital equipment, raw materials, semi-finished goods, and other products and services. Final consumers acquire products and services for personal, family, or household use. They usually buy finished items and are not involved with million-dollar purchases of plant and equipment.

Because of the nature of the products and services purchased by organizational consumers, such consumers are more likely to use specifications, multiple-buying decisions, value and vendor analysis, leased equipment, and competitive bidding and negotiation than are final consumers.

Product specifications must be met.

Many organizational consumers rely on ***product specifications*** in purchase decisions. Products are not considered unless they satisfy minimum specifications, such as engineering and architectural guidelines, purity and grade standards, horsepower, voltage, type of construction, and materials employed in construction. Final consumers often purchase on the basis of description, style, and color.

Multiple-buying responsibility is shared by two or more employees.

Organizational consumers often utilize ***multiple-buying responsibility,*** in which two or more employees participate in a decision for complex or expensive purchases. This procedure is formal, with duties fully outlined. For example, the decision to buy computer-based cash registers may involve input from computer personnel, marketing personnel, the operations manager, a systems consultant, and the controller. The firm's president might make the final choice about the characteristics of the system and the supplier. Although final consumers can use multiple-buying responsibility, they use it less frequently and less formally.

Value analysis eliminates unnecessary costs; vendor analysis rates specific suppliers.

In their well-defined decision processes, organizational consumers may apply value analysis and vendor analysis. ***Value analysis*** compares the benefits of different materials, components, and manufacturing processes in order to improve products, lower costs, or both.[6] Among the questions posed by value analysis are: What is an item's function? What is its present cost? What else could perform the function? Is the item's cost proportional to its usefulness? What features are necessary? Can a standard product be found?[7] ***Vendor analysis*** is the rating of specific suppliers in terms of quality (such as the per cent of defective merchandise), service (such as delivery speed and reliability), and price (such as credit and transportation terms). Figures 7-2 and 7-3 show examples of value analysis and vendor analysis.

Organizational consumers frequently lease major equipment. About 20 per cent of all capital goods, worth approximately $200 billion when new, are leased in the United States. Eight of ten U.S. companies are involved in leasing.[8] Final

---

[6] Michael D. Hutt and Thomas W. Speh, *Industrial Marketing Management* (Hinsdale, Ill.: Dryden Press, 1981), pp. 32–33.

[7] Anthony R. Tocco and Joseph Kaufman, "Value Engineering (Value Analysis)" in Carl Heyel (Editor). *The Encyclopedia of Management*. Third Edition (New York: Van Nostrand Reinhold, 1982), p. 1280.

[8] American Association of Equipment Lessors, "Leasing Means Business," *Fortune* (October 31, 1983), pp. 34–52.

	Definitely Yes	Probably Yes	Uncertain	Probably No	Definitely No
● Can plastic pipe be substituted for brass to reduce costs?	_____	_____	_____	_____	_____
● Can a standardized 1/3 horsepower motor be used?	_____	_____	_____	_____	_____
● Can an external float-triggered switch be used instead of an internal switch?	_____	_____	_____	_____	_____
● Can a noncorrosive base replace the current base which is easily corroded?	_____	_____	_____	_____	_____
● Is a Westinghouse motor more reliable than a GE motor?	_____	_____	_____	_____	_____
● Is a 5-year warranty acceptable?	_____	_____	_____	_____	_____

Figure 7-2
Value Analysis by a Purchaser of an Electrical Pump

consumers are less involved with leasing; it is most common in apartmental rentals. Figure 7-4 describes some of the reasons why organizational consumers are attracted to leasing.

Organizational consumers often utilize competitive bidding and negotiation in important contracts. In **competitive bidding** sellers are asked to submit independently price quotations for specific products, projects, and/or services. In **negotiation** the buyer uses bargaining ability and order size to set prices. Competitive bidding and negotiation are most applicable in situations where complex, custom-made products and services are involved.

In *competitive bidding* sellers submit price bids; in *negotiation* the buyer bargains to set prices.

	Superior	Average	Inferior
● Speed of normal delivery	_____	_____	_____
● Speed of rush delivery	_____	_____	_____
● Distinctiveness of merchandise	_____	_____	_____
● Availability of styles and colors in all sizes	_____	_____	_____
● Handling of defective merchandise	_____	_____	_____
● Per cent of merchandise defective	_____	_____	_____
● Ability for organizational consumer to make a profit when reselling merchandise	_____	_____	_____
● Purchase terms	_____	_____	_____

Figure 7-3
Vendor Analysis of a Sweater Supplier by a Purchaser

Figure 7-4
Leasing the Ryder Way

© 1984 Ryder Truck Rental, Inc.

Reprinted by permission

Differences from Final Consumers Due to the Nature of the Market

Organizational consumer demand is *derived* from final consumer demand.

Organizational consumer demand is ***derived*** from the demand of final consumers. For example, the demand for precision rivets used in aircraft construction is derived from the demand for new aircraft, which ultimately is derived from demand for air travel. Manufacturers utilizing channel members are aware that

Figure 7-5
**Derived Demand for
Major Appliances**

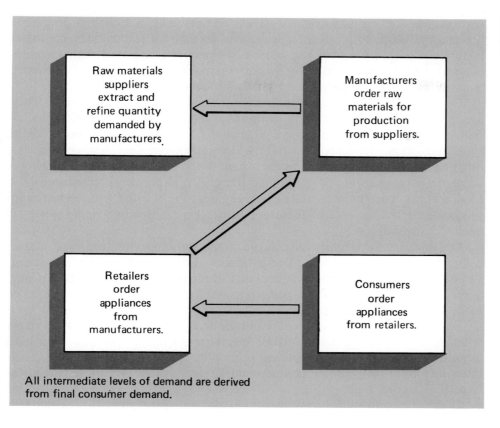

Raw materials suppliers extract and refine quantity demanded by manufacturers.

Manufacturers order raw materials for production from suppliers.

Retailers order appliances from manufacturers.

Consumers order appliances from retailers.

All intermediate levels of demand are derived from final consumer demand.

they sell through wholesalers and retailers and not to them. Unless demand is generated at the final consumer level, distribution pipelines become clogged quite quickly and channel members will not be able to purchase fresh goods and services. For this reason organizational consumers are less sensitive to price changes. As long as final consumers are willing to pay higher prices for goods and services, organizational consumers will not object to price increases. On the other hand, low final consumer demand will result in reduced purchases by organizational consumers, even if prices are drastically reduced. Figure 7-5 illustrates derived demand for major household appliances.

A good example of derived demand is the situation facing General Motors' Electro-Motive Division which produces locomotives for sale to railroad companies. Although General Motors, along with General Electric, dominates the locomotive market, recent sales have been low because of a sluggish railroad industry. However, the demand for new locomotives is expected to double by the late 1980s as the industry turns around. This will be due to the railroad's fuel efficiency, deregulation, and bulk shipments (such as coal).[9]

The demand of organizational consumers tends to be more volatile than that of final consumers. A small change in the final demand for highly processed goods and services can yield a large change in organizational consumers' demand. This is attributed to the ***accelerator principle,*** whereby final consumer demand affects

Through the accelerator principle, final consumer demand impacts on many organizational consumers.

9 Jeff Blyskal, "On the Siding," *Forbes* (May 1982), pp. 105–106.

several layers of organizational consumers. For example, a decline in automobile demand by final consumers reduces dealers' demand for automobiles, car manufacturers' demand for steel and other raw materials, and steel manufacturers' demand for iron ore. In addition, major purchases by organizational consumers (such as plant and equipment) are highly influenced by the economy.

Organizational consumers tend to be large and geographically concentrated.

Organizational consumers are fewer in number than final consumers. There are about 500,000 manufacturers, 600,000 wholesalers, and 2.5 million retailers in the United States, as compared with about 83.5 final consumer households. In some industries, the largest four firms dominate. The five most-concentrated oligopolistic industries and the market share of the largest four firms in each are domestic passenger cars (99 per cent), flat glass (92 per cent), cereal breakfast foods (90 per cent), turbines and turbine engines (90 per cent), and electric lamps (90 per cent).[10] The size of these companies gives them bargaining power in dealing with sellers.

Organizational consumers also are geographically concentrated. For example, eight states (California, New York, Illinois, Ohio, Pennsylvania, Michigan, Texas, and New Jersey) contain about half of the nation's manufacturing plants. Some industries (such as steel, petroleum, rubber, auto, and tobacco) are even more geographically concentrated.

Buying specialists are trained to purchase and negotiate with expertise.

Because of their size and the types of products and services purchased, many organizational consumers use **buying specialists.** These employees often have technical backgrounds and are trained in supplier analysis and negotiating. Their full-time jobs are to purchase products and services and analyze those purchases. Expertise is quite high.

Because organizational consumers are large and geographically concentrated, purchase complex products and services, require custom-made products and services, and use buying specialists, distribution channels tend to be shorter than those for final consumers. For example, a typewriter manufacturer would deal directly with a company interested in buying 100 typewriters, and a salesperson would call on the company's purchasing agent. A company marketing typewriters to final consumers would distribute the typewriters through retail stores and expect final consumers to visit those consumers.

Through *systems selling* **organizational consumers seek single-source accountability.**

Organizational consumers may require special services, such as extended warranties, a liberal return policy, cooperative advertising, and free credit. Two other such services are systems selling and reciprocity. In **systems selling,** a combination of goods and services is provided by a single source. This enables the buyer to have single-source accountability, one firm with which to negotiate, and assurance of the compatibility of various parts and components. Xerox employs systems selling for its main copiers, word processors, printers, typewriters, personal computers, and servicing. See Figure 7-6.

In *reciprocity,* **suppliers purchase as well as sell goods and/or services.**

Reciprocity is a procedure by which organizational consumers select suppliers who agree to purchase goods and services as well as sell them. The Justice Department and the Federal Trade Commission monitor reciprocity because it may substantially lessen competition. An example of reciprocity is the way the Canadian government purchased military aircraft from McDonnell Douglas (a U.S. firm). Canada agreed to buy $2.4 billion worth of aircraft. In return, McDonnell Douglas promised to find $2.9 billion of business for Canadian companies.[11]

---

[10] Paul MacAvoy, "Learning to Love Oligopolies," *New York Times* (September 18, 1980), p. F2.
[11] "New Restrictions on World Trade," *Business Week* (July 19, 1982), p. 119.

What can a growing business expect from Team Xerox?

When you're just starting out in business, it can seem like a big world out there.

Team Xerox can help.

We offer a wide range of small copiers including the incomparable 1020 Marathon copier. Perfect for places that are short on space. But still need perfect copies every time.

And since growing businesses like to leave a nice, big impression also, Team Xerox offers a way to obtain one. With error-free Xerox Memorywriter Typewriters. Each is state of the art. With memories and other capabilities that can grow as your needs grow.

If your organization is a little short on organization,

we offer the Xerox 860, a powerful word processor, and our personal computers, with a host of software packages that can increase the productivity of any office.

Of course, as far as the rest of our office equipment line goes, we've only just touched the tip of the iceberg. Team Xerox can fill your needs no matter how big you grow. Whether it's electronic printers that use laser technology to produce high-speed, letter-quality documents or a network to tie all your machines together, in your office, your building or across the country.

All of which brings us to another part of Team Xerox. The people.

From the first moment you come into contact with

the people of Team Xerox, you'll notice a pleasant difference. From our knowledgeable sales staff whose expertise can help you put together the system best for you. Right through to our well-trained, technical representatives who will keep your equipment up and running.

What's in it for us?

A lot. Because we know the better you feel about us, the longer you'll stay with us. And for a growing business, that can mean a long time.

So call Xerox at 1-800-833-2323, ext. 700.

And see how quickly the team that can grow with you will grow on you.

XEROX®, Marathon, 1020, and 860 are trademarks of XEROX CORPORATION.

Reprinted by permission

Figure 7-6
Systems Selling Through Team Xerox

Last, organizational consumers may be able to produce goods and services themselves, if they find purchase terms, the way they are treated, or available choices unacceptable. Sometimes, organizational consumers may suggest to suppliers that they will make their own goods in order to improve their bargaining positions.

Types of Organizational Consumers

In developing a marketing plan aimed at organizational consumers, it is necessary to research their attributes: areas of specialization, size and resources, location, and products and services purchased. Organizational consumers may be placed

The *Standard Industrial Classification (SIC)* provides information on the size and characteristics of organizational consumers.

into five broad categories: manufacturers, wholesalers, retailers, government, and nonprofit. See Figure 7-7.

For all but government, the **Standard Industrial Classification (SIC)** may be used to derive information about organizational consumers. The SIC, compiled by the U.S. Office of Management and Budget, has eight general industrial classifications: agricultural, forestry, and fishing; mining; construction; manufacturing; transportation, communication, electric, gas, and sanitary services; wholesale and retail trade; finance, insurance, and real estate; and services. Substantial data relating to SIC classifications are available from various government and commercial publications. For example, the Bureau of Industrial Economics' *Industrial Outlooks, Standard & Poor's Register, Dun & Bradstreet's Middle Market Directory,* and *Sales & Marketing Management's Survey of Industrial & Commercial Buying Power* list important information about industrial firms that is classified by SIC code and geographic area. Information on government organizations is available on a local, state, and federal level from many sources, such as *Census of Governments.*

In *end-use analysis* a seller discovers how much of its sales are made in different industries.

End-use analysis is one way in which SIC data can be employed. In end-use analysis a seller determines the proportion of its sales that are made to organizational consumers in different industries. Table 7-2(A) shows end-use analysis for a glue manufacturer. The manufacturer is able to ascertain the current relative importance of various categories of customers. The firm can then apply end-use analysis to make an overall sales forecast by estimating the expected growth of each customer category. See Table 7-2(B).

In the following subsections, the characteristics of manufacturers, wholesalers, retailers, government, and nonprofit organizations as consumers are described.

Manufacturers as Consumers

Manufacturers are firms that produce products for resale to other consumers. The *Standard Industrial Classification Manual* lists twenty major two-digit indus-

Figure 7-7
Types of Organizational Consumers

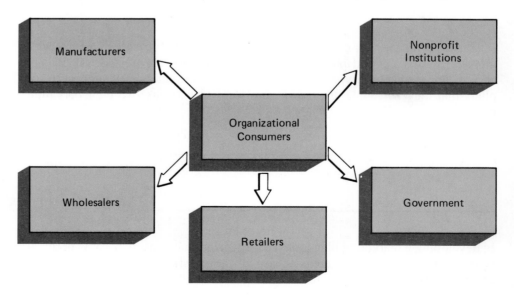

(A) Simple End-Use Analysis

Table 7-2
End-Use Analysis for a Glue Manufacturer

SIC Codes of Customers	Current Total Sales (in Per Cent)[a]
24 Lumber and wood products	25
25 Furniture and fixtures	20
27 Printing and publishing	17
30 Rubber and miscellaneous plastic products	15
31 Leather and leather products	10
Other SIC codes	13
	100

(B) Applying End-Use Analysis to Sales Forecasting

SIC Code of Customers	Per Cent of Current Total Sales	Estimated Annual Percentage Growth Rate of Industry[b]	Overall Sales Growth for Glue Manufacturer[c]
24 Lumber and wood products	25	+10	+2.50
25 Furniture and fixtures	20	+12	+2.40
27 Printing and publishing	17	+ 7	+1.19
30 Rubber and miscellaneous plastic products	15	+ 3	+0.45
31 Leather and leather products	10	− 2	−0.20
Other SIC codes	13	+ 5	+0.65
Total estimated sales increase			+6.99

[a] Firm examines sales receipts and categorizes them by SIC code.

[b] Firm estimates growth rate of each category of customer on the basis of trade association and government data.

[c] Firm multiplies per cent of current sales in each SIC code by expected growth rate in each industry to derive its own expected sales for the coming year. It expects sales to increase by 6.99 per cent during the next year.

try groups in manufacturing. See Table 7-3. Each of these major groups is divided into 150 industry groups; these industry groups are then further broken down into 450 four-digit subgroupings. For example, SIC 23 includes apparel and other textile products manufacturers; 223, women's, misses', and juniors' outerwear; and 2331, blouses.

In the United States, of the 500,000 manufacturers, more than one third of them have twenty or more employees. Approximately 20 million people work in manufacturing. The annual costs of materials to manufacturers exceeds $1 trillion. New capital expenditures for plant and equipment are about $100 billion each year. Manufacturers annually use 13 trillion BTUs of energy. Annual net sales exceed $2 trillion.[12]

Industry groups differ by geographic area. By knowing where different industries are located, a firm can concentrate its marketing efforts and not have to worry about covering dispersed geographic markets. Because the purchasing decisions of manufacturers can be made centrally at headquarters, the seller must identify the location of the proper decision maker.

As consumers, manufacturers purchase many products and services, including land and capital equipment, machinery, raw materials, component parts, trade

Manufacturers **produce products for resale to other consumers. They purchase equipment, parts, services, and other items.**

[12] U.S. Bureau of Economic Analysis, *Survey of Current Business, Current Business Reports,* and *Annual Survey of Manufactures.*

Table 7-3
U.S. Manufacturing Industries

Standard Industrial Classification Code	Industry Name
20	Food and kindred products
21	Tobacco products
22	Textile mill products
23	Apparel, other textile products
24	Lumber and wood products
25	Furniture and fixtures
26	Paper and allied products
27	Printing and publishing
28	Chemicals and allied products
29	Petroleum and coal products
30	Rubber and miscellaneous plastics products
31	Leather and leather products
32	Stone, clay, and glass products
33	Primary metal industries
34	Fabricated metal products
35	Machinery, exc. electrical
36	Electrical and electronic equipment
37	Transportation equipment
38	Instruments and related products
39	Miscellaneous manufacturing

Source: Standard Industrial Classification Manual (Washington, D.C.: Office of Management and Budget, 1972).

publications, accounting services, supplies, insurance, advertising, and delivery services. For example, in a typical year, General Foods purchases about $170 million of sugar, $1 billion of coffee, $18 million of raisins (80,000 pounds per day), $8 million of plastic bottles, and $35 million of corn sweeteners. It uses about 1.5 million jars and 500,000 corrugated cases each day.[13]

Wholesalers as Consumers

Wholesalers **buy or handle merchandise and its resale to retailers, merchants, and/or other users. They purchase warehouses, trucks, finished products, and other items.**

Wholesalers are organizations that buy or handle merchandise and its resale to retailers, other merchants, and/or industrial, institutional, and commercial users. They do not sell significant volume to final users. About 41 per cent of wholesale sales involve industrial, commercial, and government users; 37 per cent are made to retailers; 15 per cent are made to other wholesalers; 6 per cent are made to foreign buyers; and 1 per cent are made to final consumers and farmers.[14] Table 7-4 lists the major industry groups in wholesaling. Chapter 13 contains a comprehensive discussion of wholesaling.

In the United States there are about 600,000 wholesalers. More than 5 million people are employed in wholesaling. Wholesalers are prominent in New York, California, Illinois, Texas, Ohio, Pennsylvania, and New Jersey. Total annual wholesale sales (excluding agents and brokers) are well over $1 trillion. Sales are largest for groceries and related products; machinery, equipment, and supplies;

[13] N. R. Kleinfeld, ''How a Company Does Its Shopping,'' *New York Times* (January 17, 1982), Section 3, pp. 1, 27.
[14] Bert C. McCammon, Jr., and James W. Kenderine, ''Mainstream Developments in Wholesaling,'' paper presented at the 1975 Southwestern Marketing Association Conference, p. 3.

Table 7-4
**U.S. Wholesaling
Industries**

Standard Industrial Classification Code	o	Industry Name
50		Durables
		Motor vehicles and automotive equipment
		Furniture and home furnishings
		Lumber and construction materials
		Sporting, recreational, and photographic goods
		Metals and minerals, exc. petroleum
		Electrical goods
		Hardware, plumbing, and heating equipment
		Machinery, equipment, and supplies
51		Nondurables
		Paper and paper products
		Drugs, proprietaries, and sundries
		Apparel, piece goods, and notions
		Groceries and related products
		Farm-product raw materials
		Chemicals and allied products
		Petroleum and allied products
		Beer, wine, and distilled beverages
		Miscellaneous nondurable goods
73		Business services

Source: Standard Industrial Classification Manual (Washington, D.C.: Office of Management and Budget, 1972).

motor vehicles and automotive parts and supplies; electrical goods; lumber and other construction materials; and beer and liquor.

As consumers, wholesalers purchase or handle many products and services, including warehouses, trucks, finished products, insurance, refrigerators, trade publications, accounting services, supplies, and spare parts. A major task in dealing with wholesalers is getting them to carry the firm's product line for further resale, thereby placing the items into the distribution system. For new sellers or those with new products, gaining wholesaler cooperation may be difficult.

Sometimes, even well-established manufacturers can have problems with their wholesalers. As a case in point, Coors beer has seen 20 per cent of its wholesalers change ownership in the 1980s. In addition, over half of Coors wholesalers now carry other beer or wine brands, to make up for stagnant sales of Coors. During the 1970s, over two thirds of the wholesalers stocked only Coors beer.[15]

Retailers as Consumers

Retailers are firms that handle merchandise and services for sale to the ultimate (final) consumer. Retailers usually obtain their goods and services from a combination of manufacturers and wholesalers. Table 7-5 lists the major industry groups in retailing. Chapter 14 has a thorough discussion of retailing.

Retailers handle merchandise and services for sale to the final consumer. They purchase store fixtures, advertising, insurance, and other items.

[15] Brenton R. Schlender, "Heady Days Are Over for Coors Wholesalers as Sales Pace Drops," *Wall Street Journal* (October 6, 1982), p. 1.

Table 7-5
U.S. Retailing Industries

Standard Industrial Classification Code	Industry Name
52	Building materials, hardware, garden supply, and mobile home dealers
53	General merchandise stores
54	Food stores
55	Automotive dealers and gasoline service stations
56	Apparel and accessory stores
57	Furniture, home furnishings, and equipment stores
58	Eating and drinking places
59	Miscellaneous retail
60	Banking
63	Insurance
65	Real estate
70	Hotels, rooming houses, camps, and other lodging places
72	Personal services
75	Automotive repair, services, and garages
76	Miscellaneous repair services
78	Motion pictures
79	Amusement and recreation, except motion pictures
80	Health services
81	Legal services
82	Educational services
83	Social services
84	Museums, art galleries, botanical and zoological gardens

Source: Standard Industrial Classification Manual (Washington, D.C.: Office of Management and Budget, 1972).

In the United States there are about 2.5 million establishments that account for over $1 trillion in annual retail sales and employ 15 million people. More than 500,000 establishments are franchising arrangements (contractual agreements between central owners and local operators). Chain retailers (those operating two or more outlets) represent one fifth of all retailers but contribute about half of total sales. A large amount of retail sales involve automotive dealers, food stores, general merchandise group stores, gasoline service stations, eating and drinking places, and drug and proprietary stores.

As consumers, retailers purchase or handle a variety of products and services, including a store location, physical plant, interior design, advertising, items for resale, insurance, and trucks. On the average, retailers are more concerned about the composition and atmosphere of their stores than are wholesalers, who are more involved with the resale items themselves. This is because final consumers shop at retail stores, whereas wholesalers call on their customers. For the same reason retailers frequently buy fixtures, displays, and services to redecorate their stores. As an example, for the period from 1984 to 1988, Sears has allocated a total of $1.7 billion to renovate 600 existing stores and construct 62 new ones.[16]

Getting retailers to stock new items or continue handling current ones can be difficult because store space is limited. For instance, J. C. Penney decided not to sell home computers in its stores after February 1, 1984, because price discounting had reduced profitability and manufacturers were unable to supply sufficient

[16] Frank James, "Sears Sets Outlay at $1.7 Billion for Next 5 Years" *Wall Street Journal* (November 9, 1983), p. 4.

machines to satisfy demand.[17] And Coca-Cola lost $30 million in annual sales when Burger King restaurants dropped its beverages and switched to Pepsi-Cola in its 3,200 U.S. outlets.[18]

Sometimes retailers (and wholesalers) insist that manufacturers make products under the retailers' (wholesalers') names. For private-label manufacturers, the continued orders of these customers are essential. A few years ago, Star-Lite, a major producer of automotive softgoods such as mats and slip covers for seats, lost 41 per cent of its annual sales revenue (approximately $4 million) after Sears decided to phase it out as a supplier[19] It then took Star-Lite several years to establish its own brand name.

Government as Consumer

Government consumes products and services in the performance of its duties and responsibilities. Federal (1), state (50), and local (80,000) governmental units together account for the largest expenditures of any consumer group in the United States. In total, all branches spend over $1.5 trillion, half by the federal government. The greatest expenditures are on operations, capital outlays, military services, postal services, education, highways, public welfare, health, police, fire protection, sanitation, and natural resources. All levels of government employ 16 million people (excluding armed forces).

Statistics on state and local expenditures by item (education, highways, public welfare, health/hospitals, police and fire protection, housing and urban renewal) are reported in *Government Finances* and *City Government Finances* on an annual basis.

Governmental consumers purchase a wide range of products and services, including food, military equipment, office buildings, subway cars, office supplies, clothing, and automobiles. Many of the products purchased by these organizations are standard products offered to traditional consumers; others, such as armaments, are specially made for the federal government. While many large companies (such as Boeing and Lockheed) derive large percentages of their sales from government contracts, smaller firms now account for 25 to 35 per cent of federal purchases.[20]

Government purchases and uses a variety of routine and complex products and services.

Nonprofit Institutions as Consumers

Nonprofit institutions are those that operate in the public interest or to foster a cause and do not seek financial profits. Public hospitals, museums, most universities, political parties, civic organizations, and parks are examples of nonprofit institutions. They purchase products and services in order to run their organizations and also buy items for resale to generate additional revenues to offset costs. Nonprofit institutions are discussed in detail in Chapter 22.

Nonprofit institutions operate in the public interest. They purchase items for use in operations.

[17] Bob Davis, ''Penney Stores Won't Sell Home Computers After Feb. 1; Price Cuts and Supplies Cited,'' *Wall Street Journal* (December 16, 1983), p. 6.

[18] ''Burger King Converts to Pepsi from Coke in 3,200 Restaurants,'' *Wall Street Journal* (June 14, 1983), p. 20.

[19] Chuck Wingis, ''Sears Consolidates Vendors; Star-Lite Socked with Pink Slip,'' *Industrial Marketing* (October 1979), p. 22.

[20] David E. Gumpert and Jeffry A. Timmons, ''Penetrating the Government Procurement Maze,'' *Harvard Business Review,* Vol. 60 (May–June 1982), p. 15.

There are many national nonprofit institutions, such as the American Cancer Society, Democratic and Republican Parties, Boy and Girl Scouts, Chamber of Commerce, and the Red Cross. Hospitals, museums, and universities, because of their fixed locations, tend to be among the local nonprofit institutions.

Characteristics of Organizational Consumers

The consumer behavior of manufacturers, wholesalers, retailers, government, and nonprofit institutions depends on their buying objectives, buying structure, use of the purchase, and constraints.

Buying Objectives

Product availability, seller reliability, consistent quality, delivery, and price are crucial *organizational buying objectives*.

As stated at the beginning of this chapter, organizational buyers have several distinct objectives in purchasing goods and services. See Figure 7-8. In general, for all types of firms, these *organizational buying objectives* are important: availability of items, reliability of sellers, consistency of quality, delivery, and price.

Availability of items means that the buyer is able to secure an adequate supply of products throughout the year or whenever necessary. An organization's production or resales are not possible if purchases are unavailable at the appropriate time. Seller reliability is based on the seller's honesty in the reporting of bills or shipping orders, fairness to its customers, responsiveness to special requests, ongoing relationships, and reputation. Consistency of quality refers to the buyer's goal of obtaining similar items on a continuous basis. For example, drill bits should have the same degree of hardness, transistors the same level of durability, and employee uniforms the same color each time they are purchased. Delivery objectives include minimizing or stabilizing the length of time from the placing of an order to the receipt of items, minimizing the order size required by the supplier, having the seller maintain responsibility for shipments, minimizing costs, and adhering to an agreed-on schedule. Price considerations involve purchase price, discounts, availability of credit, and length of payment. As shown in Figure 7-9, Emery is an example of a firm that appeals to a variety of organizational consumer buying objectives to attract and retain business.

Manufacturer-consumers are also quite concerned about the minimum quality standards of raw materials, component parts, and equipment. Some manufacturers like to deal with a variety of suppliers to protect against shortages from a single supplier, to foster price and service competition, and to be exposed to new merchandise lines.

Saleability and exclusivity are keys for wholesalers and retailers.

Wholesalers and retailers consider the further saleability of items as the highest priority. Where possible, they seek exclusive buying arrangements, which limit the number of wholesalers and retailers who can carry merchandise in a geographic area. They also seek manufacturers' advertising, transportation, and warehousing support.

Government-consumers frequently require precise specifications for the prod-

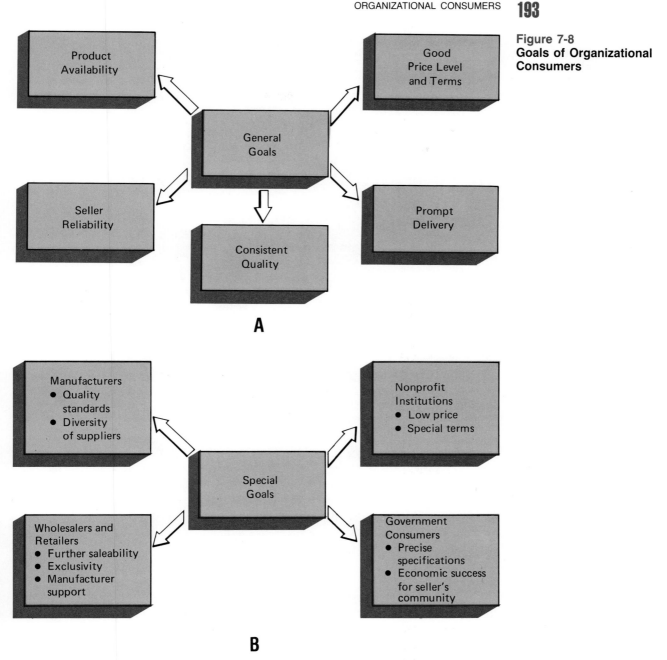

Figure 7-8
Goals of Organizational Consumers

A

B

ucts they purchase. For example, military tanks must be built to exact specifications. As large-volume, complex-product buyers, government-consumers are able to secure these specifications. In some cases government-consumers may also consider the economic conditions in the geographic areas of potential sellers when they make purchases. As an illustration, Grumman Aerospace of New York often bids against McDonnell Douglas of California for government contracts. Sometimes the contracts are awarded to the company that has the highest unemployment in its surrounding community.

Figure 7-9
Emery's Appeal to Organizational Consumer Buying Objectives

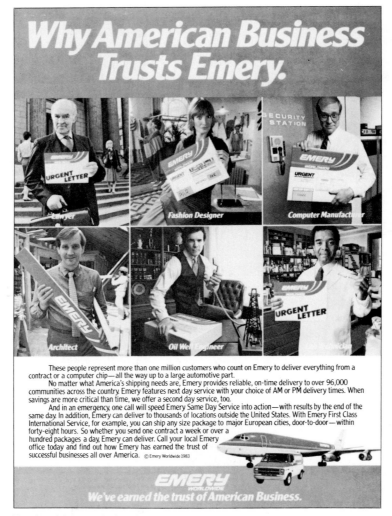

Reprinted by permission.

Nonprofit consumers place the most emphasis on price, availability, reliability, and consistency. They sometimes seek special purchase terms in recognition of their nonprofit status.

Buying Structure

The *buying structure of an organization* depends on its characteristics.

The *buying structure of an organization* refers to the level of formality and specialization used in the purchase process. It depends on an organization's size, resources, diversity, and level of specialization. The buying structure is likely to be formalized (separate department or function) for a large, corporate, resourceful, diversified, and specialized organization. It will be less formalized for a small, independently owned, financially limited, and general organization.

Large manufacturer-consumers will normally have specialized purchasing agents who work with engineers, the production department, or the plant general manager. Large wholesaler-consumers tend to have a single purchasing department or a general manager in charge of operations. Large retailer-consumers tend to be extremely specialized and have buyers for each narrow product category. These buyers are supervised by group managers. Small manufacturers, wholesalers, and retailers have their buying functions completed by the owner-operator.

Each governmental unit (federal, state, and local) and division has a purchasing department. The General Services Administration (GSA) is the federal office responsible for centralized procurement and coordination of purchases. Each federal unit may receive merchandise from the GSA's Bureau of Federal Supply or buy directly from suppliers.[21] In a nonprofit organization, there is usually one purchasing department or a member of the operations staff performs the buying function.

Use of Purchases

As mentioned earlier, organizational consumers have different uses for their products. Manufacturer-consumers buy items that are used in the production process or for the operation of the company. Wholesaler-consumers purchase component parts, items for further resale, or items used in the operation of the company. Retailer-consumers buy for further resale or use in operations. Government-consumers buy items for use in the operation of the government and the enactment of various programs. Nonprofit consumers primarily buy items to be used in operations; they sometimes purchase for resale.

The various types of organizational consumers use their purchases differently from one another.

Constraints on Purchases

For manufacturer-consumers, wholesaler-consumers, and retailer-consumers, derived demand is the major constraint on purchase behavior. Without the demand of final consumers, production halts and sales disappear as the backward chain of demand comes into play (final consumer→retailer→wholesaler→manufacturer).

Manufacturer-consumers also are constrained by the availability of raw materials and their ability to pay for large-ticket items. Wholesaler-consumers and retailer-consumers are usually unwilling and unable to buy merchandise that does not meet minimum profit margins (profits as per cents of sales), regardless of sales potential. They are also limited by the finances available to make purchases and the level of risk they are willing to take. In this case, risk refers to the probability that wholesalers or retailers will be able to sell the merchandise they buy in a reasonable time period. Product categories such as fashion clothing have higher risks than staple merchandise such as panty hose, children's underwear, and men's leather-palm woolen gloves.

Government-consumers are constrained by the budget-setting process. Approval for categories of purchases must normally be secured well in advance, and deviations must be fully explained. Budgets must be certified by various legislative bodies. For nonprofit consumers, cash flow (timing of money coming into the organization versus money spent by it) is the major concern.

Final consumer demand is the major constraint on organizational purchase behavior.

---

[21] See Gumpert and Timmons, "Penetrating the Government Maze," pp. 14–20.

The Organizational Consumer's Decision Process

The *organizational consumer's decision process* is like the final consumer's.

Organizational consumers use a decision-making procedure in much the same manner as final consumers. Figure 7-10 shows the ***organizational consumer's decision process,*** which has four major components: expectations, buying process, conflict resolution, and situational factors.[22]

[22] The material in this section is drawn from Jagdish N. Sheth, "A Model of Industrial Buyer Behavior," *Journal of Marketing,* Vol. 37 (October 1973), pp. 50–56.

Figure 7-10
The Organizational Consumer's Decision Process

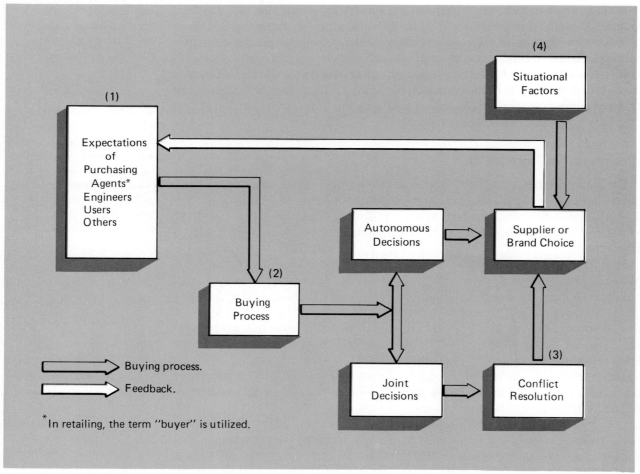

Source: Adapted from Jagdish N. Sheth, "A Model of Industrial Buyer Behavior," *Journal of Marketing,* Vol. 37 (October 1973), p. 51. Reprinted from *Journal of Marketing,* published by the American Marketing Association.

Expectations

Purchasing agents, engineers, and users bring a set of *organizational consumer expectations* to any buying situation:

Expectations refer to the *perceived* potential of alternative suppliers and brands to satisfy a number of explicit and implicit objectives.[23]

In order for a purchase to be made, the buyer must have favorable expectations about a supplier's product quality, availability, reliability, delivery time, and service.

Expectations are derived from a variety of factors: background of individuals, information sources, search, perception, and satisfaction with past purchases.[24]

The background of the buyer includes his or her educational training, job orientation, life-style, and personal objectives. The background of a manufacturer's purchasing agent will usually be different from that of a retailer's buyer. For the former, emphasis is on technical training, knowledge of product specifications, interaction with engineers, and a conservative life-style. For the latter, emphasis is on marketing training, knowledge of final consumer demand, interaction with other buyers, and a contemporary life-style. In addition, manufacturers frequently rely on team decision making involving both engineers and purchasing agents.

Information sources provide knowledge about suppliers and their offerings. Among the available sources are exhibitions and trade shows, direct mail, press releases, journal advertising, professional and technical conferences, salespeople, trade news, and others in the same business.

In situations where a purchase decision must be made, but enough information is not at hand, the organizational consumer will make an active search of information sources. This usually involves a search for answers to specific questions.

All information that is processed by organizational consumers is filtered by their perceptions, which are interpretations they place on that information. For example, a $10,000 lathe may be perceived as economical and efficient by one buyer and cheap and susceptible to breakdowns by another.

Not all perceptions are positive, as this example shows. Some retailers have perceptions that suppliers oversell without regard to production and delivery capability, lack an understanding of retail goals and merchandising philosophy, do not give adequate in-store service, and do not offer a planned approach to promoting and merchandising products. Some suppliers have perceptions that retailers are preoccupied with "chiseling" for the best price, lack decision-making autonomy, ignore or move too slowly in accepting promotional deals and other allowances, handle too many product lines to be effective product managers, ignore merchandise after an order is placed, and refuse to cooperate for fear of being locked to a supplier.[25] Through improved communications, these negative perceptions can be resolved.

Purchase *expectations* are based on factors such as buyers' backgrounds, information, perception, and past experience.

[23] Ibid., p. 52.

[24] See Lowell E. Crow and Jay D. Lindquist, "Buyers Differ in Evaluating Suppliers," *Industrial Marketing Management*, Vol. 11 (July 1982), pp. 205–214.

[25] Ronald L. Ernst, "'Distribution Channel Detente' Benefits Suppliers, Retailers, and Consumers," *Marketing News* (March 7, 1980), p. 19.

The level of satisfaction with past purchases also has an impact on the buyer's expectations that a supplier or brand will perform at the required standard in the future. Satisfaction is improved when the supplier provides assistance in reselling goods.

Buying Process

The use of autonomous or joint decision making is based on product-specific buying factors and company-specific buying factors.

The buying process may involve autonomous (independent) or joint decision making. The type of decision making depends on product-specific and company-specific factors.

Product-specific buying factors leading to autonomous decision making are low perceived risk, routine products, and time pressures. Joint decision making is the result of high perceived risk, unique or seldom-purchased products, and a lead time for purchases.

Company-specific buying factors leading to autonomous decision making are technology or production orientation, small size, and high centralization. Joint decision making is the result of low technology or production orientation, large size, and little centralization.

During the buying process, a decision to buy is initiated, information gathered, alternative suppliers evaluated, and conflicts among the different representatives of the buyer resolved. The process itself is similar to the consumer buying process shown in Figure 6-7.

As noted at the beginning of the chapter, competitive bidding is frequently used with organizational consumers: the potential seller specifies in writing all the terms and conditions of the purchase in addition to product or service attributes. With open bidding, the proposed contract can be seen by competitors. With closed bidding, contract terms are kept secret and the sellers are asked to make their best presentation in their first bids. Bidding is most often used in government purchases in order to avoid charges of unfair negotiations or bias. For these reasons, bids for government purchases are generally closed. Chapter 20 (''Applications of Pricing Techniques'') contains an example of how competitive bidding is used.

Conflict Resolution

Problem solving, persuasion, bargaining, and politicking are the basic methods of conflict resolution.

Because of the different training, role orientation, goals, and life-styles of purchasing agents, engineers, and users, joint decision making sometimes results in conflicts. ***Conflict resolution*** is then necessary to make a purchase decision. Four methods of resolution are possible: problem solving, persuasion, bargaining, and politicking. Figure 7-11 provides examples of each.

Problem solving occurs when the members of the purchasing team decide to acquire further information before making a decision. This is the best procedure for the company. Persuasion takes place when each member of the team presents his or her reasons why a particular supplier or brand should be selected. In theory, the most logical presentation should be chosen. However, the most dynamic speaker often persuades others to follow his or her lead.

Under bargaining, team members agree to support each other's recommendations in different situations, regardless of merit. For example, one member is allowed to select the supplier of the current item. In return, another member

Figure 7-11
**Conflict Resolution by
Organizational
Consumers**

PROBLEM SOLVING   PERSUASION

Futher information is
acquired by joint decision
makers before a purchase
is made.

One decision maker convinces
the others as to the correctness
of his/her alternative.

BARGAINING   POLITICKING

One decision maker agrees
to support another now in
return for the latter's support
for a subsequent purchase.

One decision maker campaigns
to have his/her alternative selected.

chooses the vendor for the next item. The last, and least desirable, method of
conflict resolution is politicking. With politicking, team members seek to persuade outside parties and superiors to back their positions and then seek to win at
power plays.

Situational Factors

A number of ***situational factors*** can interrupt the decision process and the
actual selection of a supplier or brand:

temporary economic conditions such as price controls, recession, or foreign trade; internal
strikes, walkouts, machine breakdowns, and other production-related events; organizational changes such as merger or acquisition; and ad hoc changes in the market place, such
as promotional efforts, new product introduction, price changes, and so on, in the supplier
industries.[26]

Situational factors **are
external variables that
affect organizational
consumers.**

[26] Sheth, "A Model of Industrial Buyer Behavior," p. 56.

Purchase and Feedback

After the decision process is complete and situational factors are eliminated or adapted to, a choice of supplier or brand is made and the purchase undertaken. The level of satisfaction with the purchase is fed back to the purchasing agent or team, and this information is stored for future use. To maintain customer satisfaction and ensure continued purchases, regular service and follow-up calls are essential:

Companies will find technological differentiation increasingly difficult to maintain in the years ahead because of the ever-higher costs of doing so. Differentiation will soon be prohibitively expensive for all but the largest firms. So customers will not buy a specific brand because of what it does; all brands will be able to do the same thing. Rather they'll buy from a company they feel will support it and give maximum postsale satisfaction.[27]

Types of Purchases

Organizational consumers use *new task* purchases for unique items, *modified rebuys* for infrequently purchased items, and *straight rebuys* for regularly purchased items.

As with final consumers, organizational buyers have three types of decision processes. A ***new task purchase process*** is needed for an expensive product the firm has not bought before. A large amount of decision making is undertaken. This is similar to extended decision making for a final consumer. A ***modified rebuy purchase process*** is employed for medium-priced products the firm has bought infrequently before. A moderate amount of decision making is needed. This is similar to limited decision making for a final consumer. A ***straight rebuy purchase process*** is used for inexpensive items bought on a regular basis. Reordering, not decision making, is applied. This is similar to a routine purchase for a final consumer. See Figure 7-12.

Marketing Implications

There are many similarities, as well as differences, between organizational and final consumers.

Organizational and final consumers have substantial differences, as was noted at the beginning of this chapter. They also have substantial similarities. Both can be described in demographic terms, and statistical and descriptive data can be gathered and analyzed.[28] Both consumers have different categories of buyers, each of whom has separate needs and requirements. Both can be defined by using social and psychological factors, such as operating style, buying structure, use of the purchase, expectations, perceived risk, and conflict resolution among buyers or purchasing agents. Both organizational and final consumers use a decision process, employ joint decision making, and face different kinds of purchase situations.

[27] Milind M. Lele, "Product Service: How to Protect Your Unguarded Battlefield," *Business Marketing* (June 1983), p. 69.
[28] See Norman Wiener, "Customer Demographics for Strategic Selling," *Business Marketing* (May 1983), pp. 78–82.

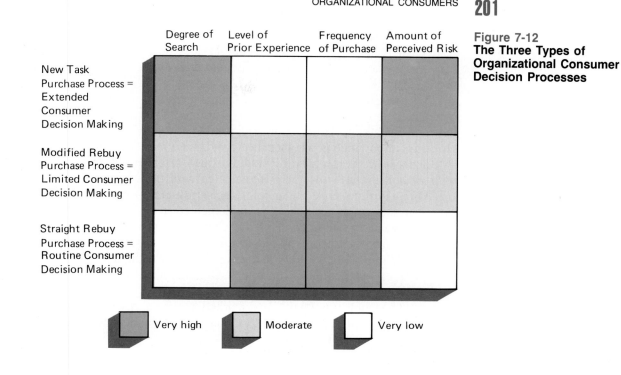

Figure 7-12
**The Three Types of
Organizational Consumer
Decision Processes**

Marketers must understand the similarities as well as the differences between organizational and final consumers and develop their plans accordingly. Furthermore, it must be realized by manufacturers and wholesalers that they need two marketing plans—one for the intermediate buyer and another for the final consumer.

Finally, marketers need to see that organizational purchasing agents or buyers have personal as well as company goals. These buyers seek status, approval, promotion, bonuses, and other rewards. And, as noted in Figure 7-10, these individuals bring distinct backgrounds and expectations to each buying situation, just as final consumers do.

Summary

An organizational consumer is a formal entity that purchases products or services for further production, for use in operating the entity, or for resale to other consumers. Organizational consumers seek supplier reliability and consistency and specific product attributes. They are influenced by derived demand and utilize formal purchasing departments. They are geographically concentrated, expect sellers to visit them, use joint decision making, make large purchases, require personal selling, and look for favorable purchase items.

Organizational consumers may be classified by area of specialization, size and resources, location, and products and services purchased. The major organizational consumers are manufacturers, wholesalers, retailers, government, and nonprofit. The SIC system provides much information on nongovernment consumers.

Organizational consumers can be characterized by buying objectives, buying structure, use of the purchase, and constraints. Their decision process includes buyer expectations, buying process, conflict resolution, and situational factors. Of prime importance is whether the organization uses joint decision making and, if it does, how. Some form of bidding, open or closed, is frequently employed with organizational consumers (most often with the government).

When conflicts arise under joint decision making, problem solving, persuasion, bargaining, or politicking is implemented to arrive at a purchase decision. Situational factors can intervene between decision making and a purchase. These factors include strikes, economic conditions, and organizational changes.

New task, modified rebuy, and straight rebuy are the different purchase situations facing organizational consumers. Organizational consumers and final consumers have many similarities and differences. It is important for marketers to understand and adapt to them. Dual marketing campaigns are necessary for manufacturers and wholesalers who sell to intermediate buyers and have their products resold to final consumers.

Purchasing agents and buyers have personal goals, such as status, promotion, and bonuses, which have a large impact on their decision making.

Questions for Discussion

1. Explain five differences between organizational and final consumers of furniture.
2. As a government purchasing agent, what criteria would you consider in vendor analysis for air conditioners?
3. How can derived demand be increased?
4. Under what circumstances would systems selling be undesirable to an organizational consumer?
5. How is the Standard Industrial Classification useful for marketers?
6. Large manufacturers dominate the tobacco, motor vehicle, and soap industries. What does this mean for suppliers to these companies?
7. Comment on this statement: "For new sellers or those with new products, gaining wholesaler cooperation may be difficult."
8. Develop a plan for marketing surgical gowns to hospitals.
9. What factors that make up organizational buying expectations can be influenced by marketers? Which cannot? Why?
10. Many firms are supporters of autonomous decision making. Others favor joint decision making. Why are there opposing views?
11. When is conflict resolution likely to be most difficult? Explain your answer.
12. How can situational factors facilitate an organizational consumer's purchase?
13. Describe the organizational consumer's decision process for office staplers. Compare it with that for final consumers.
14. "Marketers need to see that organizational purchasing agents or buyers have personal as well as company goals." Comment on this statement.

Case 1 Boeing: Marketing Aircraft During Tough Times*

In 1978, Boeing began a $3+ billion program to develop and market two new aircraft, the single-aisle 757 and the wide-body 767. But after a large sale of 757s to Delta in 1980, orders for the new jets fell drastically. Companywide aircraft deliveries in 1982 were 176 planes (compared with a high of 368 planes in 1968). Said one Boeing executive, "I feel like a basketball coach whose team is running hard, shooting well, and rebounding beautifully. But the auditorium is on fire."

Boeing produced the 757 and 767 jets with specific objectives in mind: to greatly improve fuel consumption, to reduce cockpit personnel from three to two, to share interchangeable parts, and to service different capacity needs of airlines (the 757 seats 186 people; the 767 seats 211 to 289 people).

Despite success in achieving these goals, a number of factors caused Boeing's customers to avoid or postpone purchases of the 757 and 767. The entire airline passenger market in the U.S. performed poorly; and because passenger travel was down, airlines were reluctant to purchase new planes. During 1982, the U.S. airline industry lost about $2 billion. Those airlines not canceling orders let them "slide," industry slang for postponing delivery dates.

Airlines became less concerned about fuel consumption, since their costs dropped from $1.10 to $1.00 a gallon and stabilized at that level, and more concerned about aircraft costs ($35 million for a 757 and $50 million for a 767).

In a poor passenger market, the 186-seat 757 proved to be too large for many airlines; a competitor offered a 150-passenger plane. Also, a number of airlines were buying used aircraft, for as little as 10 per cent of the price of new aircraft. Finally, airlines saw some traditional lenders retreat, drying up funds for aircraft purchases.

Boeing believes its 757 and 767 jets will succeed in the long run, as the airlines improve their profitability and passenger travel takes an upturn. As a financially strong company, it has the resources to ride out the current situation. After all, the 727 had limited sales for more than two years. Then, the 727 became the best-selling and most profitable plane ever.

After virtually no customer deliveries of 757s and 767s in 1982, Boeing delivered a total of about 80 of them in 1983. From 1984 to 1987, combined sales of the two aircraft were projected to range from 50 to 75 planes each year.

QUESTIONS

1. In 1982, Boeing could have dropped the prices of its new aircraft by 25 per cent and generated almost no additional sales. Why?
2. What airline characteristics should Boeing examine to determine the prime prospects for its aircraft?
3. Describe the organizational consumer's decision process for the purchase of a 757.
4. What marketing tactics should Boeing utilize to maximize the sales of 757s and 767s over the next two years?

* The data in this case are drawn from Alexander Stuart, "Boeing's New Beauties Are a Tough Sell," *Fortune* (October 18, 1982), pp. 114–120; Tom Incantalupo, "A Pinch Is Felt as Boeing Tightens Its Belt," *Newsday* (September 12, 1983), Business, pp. 1, 17; and Gary Putka, "Boeing Rise Bucks Market Trend on Buy Signal by Analysts Expecting Jet Replacement Orders," *Wall Street Journal* (February 16, 1984), p. 61.

Case 2 Susan Davis: A Buyer for Bloomingdale's[†]

In 1978, Susan Davis entered the Bloomingdale's executive-training program, following graduation from Hamilton College in Clinton, New York. Davis had developed an interest in retailing while working at a store in her hometown (Springfield, Massachusetts) during the summers of her college years. After progressing through a variety of jobs at Bloomingdale's, Davis became a buyer of "traditional gifts" in 1981, responsible for purchasing these items for Bloomingdale's 13 department stores.

Davis' buying responsibility centers around ceramic and decorative accessories for the home, such as wall plaques, cake plates, planters, and baskets. For the holiday season, Davis adds "real gift items" that consumers would not buy for themselves. These include brass plates, rag place mats, and other more unusual products. Davis expects 20 per cent of her department's annual sales to be made during December.

Buying plans, made several months in advance, incorporate both traditional and trendier items. The needs of each of Bloomingdale's 13 stores are evaluated separately. Then, a key-item list is developed. This list details the 20 items Davis believes will account for 50+ per cent of her business in each store. These items are always maintained in stock.

Travel is a major part of Davis' job. She attends trade shows in New York and Europe on a regular basis. She also goes to Europe and the Far East to negotiate exclusive purchases for Bloomingdale's; on these trips, a fashion expert accompanies Davis to offer input on color and styling. Price, availability, assortment, and reliability are crucial criteria for assessing vendors.

Davis is also strongly involved with store relations:

You have to make a decision and stand by it. If you don't buy something good, some other buyer will. If you don't buy it in depth, your stores in the field won't tend to back it. If you do, they see that you are serious and will give the merchandise front-and-center treatment.

QUESTIONS
1. As a new manufacturer of wall plaques, how would you convince Davis to buy from you?
2. On a trip overseas when Davis is accompanied by a fashion expert, which decisions would you expect Davis to make? The fashion expert? How should conflicts be resolved?
3. What situational factors could affect Davis' purchase decisions?
4. As a manufacturer, under what circumstances would you decide to make a product exclusively for Bloomingdale's?

[†] The data in this case are drawn from Isadore Barmash, "Buying for Bloomingdale's," *New York Times* (November 19, 1983), pp. D1, D5.

Chapter 8

Developing a Target Market

CHAPTER OBJECTIVES

1. To explain and contrast mass marketing, market segmentation, and multiple segmentation and to describe the factors to be considered in selecting a target market strategy

2. To present several applications of each method for developing a target market

3. To discuss the bases of segmentation, steps in planning a segmentation strategy, organizational consumer segments, requirements for successful segmentation, and the limitations of segmentation

4. To examine sales forecasting and its role in developing a target market

Huffy Corporation manufactures and sells more bicycles than any other U.S. company, including Schwinn. However, Huffy has had a difficult time in expanding its market beyond children's bikes. As one observer noted, "Status-conscious adults would no more ride a Huffy tenspeed than wear a polyester leisure suit."

Huffy has discovered that a marketing approach oriented toward children's bikes is significantly different from one appealing to "sophisticated adults." Huffy's children's bikes are inexpensive and distributed through discount and department stores. Adult bikes are priced at $200 and more and distributed through bicycle stores. These outlets are unwilling to carry Huffy bicycles, because of their limited status and lower quality and the company's acceptance of price discounting. Huffy considers sales through bike stores to be imperative for its continued growth.

205

**Figure 8-1
Raleigh Bicycles for
Adults**

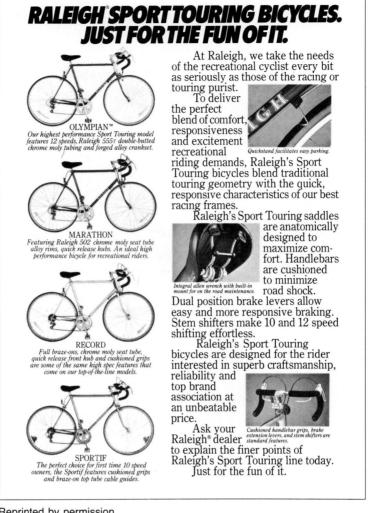

RALEIGH® SPORT TOURING BICYCLES.
JUST FOR THE FUN OF IT.

OLYMPIAN™

Our highest performance Sport Touring model features 12 speeds, Raleigh 555T double-butted chrome moly tubing and forged alloy crankset.

MARATHON

Featuring Raleigh 502 chrome moly seat tube alloy rims, quick release hubs. An ideal high performance bicycle for recreational riders.

RECORD

Full braze-ons, chrome moly seat tube, quick release front hub and cushioned grips are some of the same high spec features that come on our top-of-the-line models.

SPORTIF

The perfect choice for first time 10 speed owners, the Sportif features cushioned grips and braze-on top tube cable guides.

At Raleigh, we take the needs of the recreational cyclist every bit as seriously as those of the racing or touring purist.

To deliver the perfect blend of comfort, responsiveness and excitement recreational riding demands, Raleigh's Sport Touring bicycles blend traditional touring geometry with the quick, responsive characteristics of our best racing frames.

Quickstand facilitates easy parking.

Raleigh's Sport Touring saddles are anatomically designed to maximize comfort. Handlebars are cushioned to minimize road shock.

Integral allen wrench with built-in mount for on the road maintenance.

Dual position brake levers allow easy and more responsive braking. Stem shifters make 10 and 12 speed shifting effortless.

Raleigh's Sport Touring bicycles are designed for the rider interested in superb craftsmanship, reliability and top brand association at an unbeatable price.

Cushioned handlebar grips, brake extension levers, and stem shifters are standard features.

Ask your Raleigh® dealer to explain the finer points of Raleigh's Sport Touring line today. Just for the fun of it.

Reprinted by permission.

While the shops sell only 25 per cent of all bikes, they contribute 40 per cent of industry sales revenue.

As a result, Huffy has added a second marketing strategy targeted at adults. In 1982, it acquired exclusive rights to market Raleigh bikes in the U.S. from TI Raleigh Industries, a British bicycle manufacturer. Raleigh bikes have the recognition, image, product features, and consumer acceptance among adults that Huffy wants. For example, these bikes have alloy frames, lugged joints, and imported parts. Prices for Raleigh bikes start at just under $200, and they are distributed through bicycle stores. Figure 8-1 shows a variety of Raleigh touring bicycles.

For this target market approach to succeed, Huffy Corporation must continue to use two separate strategies—one for children's bikes and one for adult bikes; and it must be careful that the Huffy and Raleigh brands are kept distinct. Customers must be convinced that Raleighs are not "only painted-over Huffys." The company must also reassure bicycle shops that Raleigh bikes will not be distributed by discount and department stores, and that discounting will not be permitted.[1]

Huffy Corporation illustrates how developing a target market requires that an organization understand the alternatives available, evaluate a number of company and market characteristics, and enact a systematic (and appropriate) strategy.

Developing a Target Market Strategy

Mass marketing, market segmentation, and multiple segmentation are the three alternative methods a firm has for developing a target market. These methods are summarized in Table 8-1.

Table 8-1 Methods for Developing a Target Market

Marketing Approach	Mass Marketing	Market Segmentation	Multiple Segmentation
Target market	Broad range of consumers	One well-defined consumer group	Two or more well-defined consumer groups
Product or service	Limited number of products or services under one brand for many types of consumers	One product or service brand tailored to one consumer group	Distinct product or service brand for each consumer group
Price	One "popular" price range	One price range tailored to the consumer group	Distinct price range for each consumer group
Distribution	All possible outlets	All suitable outlets	All suitable outlets—differs by segment
Promotion	Mass media	All suitable media	All suitable media—differs by segment
Strategy emphasis	Appeal to various types of consumers through a uniform, broad-based marketing program	Appeal to one specific consumer group through a highly specialized, but uniform, marketing program	Appeal to two or more distinct market segments through different marketing plans catering to each segment

In **mass marketing,** a company seeks to appeal to a broad range of consumers by utilizing a single basic marketing program. In **market segmentation,** a company seeks to appeal to one well-defined consumer group by one marketing plan. In **multiple segmentation,** a company seeks to appeal to two or more well-defined consumer groups by different marketing plans. See Figure 8-2.

Mass marketing seeks a range of consumers, market segmentation one segment, and multiple segmentation diverse segments.

---

[1] Damon Darlin, "Huffy Trying to Sell More Bikes to Adults," *Wall Street Journal* (April 8, 1983), pp. 29, 48; and "Maker of Bicycles Turning Optimistic," *New York Times* (February 27, 1984), pp. D1, D4.

Figure 8-2
Contrasting Target Market Approaches

Mass Marketing

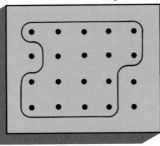

The firm tries to reach a wide range of consumers with one basic marketing plan. These consumers are assumed to have a desire for similar product or service attributes.

Market Segmentation

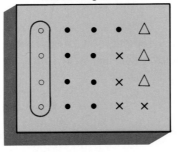

The firm concentrates on one group of consumers with a distinct set of needs and uses a tailor–made marketing plan to attract this single group.

Multiple Segmentation

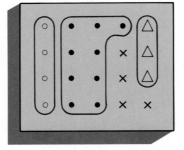

The firm aims at two or more different market segments, each of which has a distinct set of needs, and offers a tailor–made marketing plan for each segment.

Mass Marketing

A mass-marketing approach aims at a large, broad consumer market through one basic marketing plan. The firm believes that consumers have very similar desires regarding product/service attributes. An early practitioner of mass marketing was Henry Ford, who created and sold one standard automobile model at a reasonable price to a large number and variety of people. The original Model T had no options and came only in black.

Mass marketing was a popular method for developing a target market when large-scale production started, but the number of companies using a pure mass-marketing approach has declined rapidly over the last several years. Among the factors contributing to its fall from use are that competition has grown, demand is stimulated by an appeal to specific market segments, improved marketing research is able to pinpoint the desires of different segments, and total production and marketing costs can be reduced by segmentation.

Before an organization undertakes mass marketing, it must examine several factors. Substantial total company resources and abilities are needed to mass produce, mass distribute, and mass advertise. There are per unit production and marketing savings because a limited number of products or services are offered, and different brand names are not employed. These savings may allow low competitive prices.

A major objective of mass marketing is to maximize sales—that is, a company attempts to sell as many units of an item as possible. National goals are usually set. Diversification is not undertaken.

Mass marketing seeks to maximize sales without diversifying.

For successful mass marketing, a large group of consumers must have the desire for the same product or service attributes, so that the company can appeal to them through one marketing program. As an example, suppose all consumers buy Morton's salt because of its freshness, quality, storability, availability, and fair price. Then, a pure mass-marketing strategy is appropriate. However, if some consumers want attractive decanters, larger crystals, and smaller-sized packages, then Morton would be unable to appeal to all consumers through one marketing plan. Under mass marketing, different consumer groups are not identified and sought.

With mass marketing, the firm pursues an intensive channel strategy. Its offerings are sold at all possible outlets. Channel requirements (the needs of wholesalers and retailers) must be evaluated. Some channel members may not be pleased if the company's brand is sold at several nearby locations and may insist on carrying additional brands to fill out their product lines. It is very difficult to persuade channel members not to carry competing brands. The shelf space given to the company depends on the popularity of its brand and the promotional support given. Channel members often set final selling prices.

A mass-marketing strategy should consider total profits and long-run profits. Sometimes firms become too involved with sales and lose sight of profits. For example, for a number of years, the sales of A&P rose as the company continued its competition with Safeway for leadership in supermarket sales. Unfortunately, A&P incurred large losses during that period. Only when A&P began to close some unprofitable stores and stop pursuing sales at any cost did it start to show profits.

A company can ensure a consistent, well-known image with a mass-marketing approach. Consumers have only one image when thinking of a firm, and it is retained for a number of years.

TV Guide magazine and Sears are good examples of mass-marketing appeals. *TV Guide* is a weekly television magazine that was established over thirty years ago. It contains television program listings, descriptions, and evaluations as well as current events and articles on personalities, shows, and the industry. *TV Guide* has a circulation of more than 17 million copies per week. It is advertised on television and in newspapers and stores. *TV Guide* is relatively inexpensive and is available at several types of stores and newsstands. Many sales are through subscription. The product itself, the magazine, has undergone few changes since its inception and is recognized as the standard in the field. Consumers of varying backgrounds buy *TV Guide* for its listings and stories.

Sears is the country's largest retailer, with total annual company sales of more than $36 billion and well over 400,000 employees.[2] In addition to retail stores, Sears owns and operates Allstate insurance, Dean Witter stock brokerage, and Coldwell Banker realty. Its long-time slogan is "Sears, Where America Shops." Through its product and service assortments, middle-range prices, heavy promotion ($631 million in media in 1982),[3] and geographically dispersed store locations, Sears seeks a wide range of consumers.

Other illustrations of mass-marketing approaches are Commodore home computers priced at $80 to $200 and sold at all types of outlets (including toy stores),[4] National Liberty Corporation selling insurance through television and direct mail advertising,[5] and the broad and varied uses of Riunite wines:

Riunite can be used as a table wine to accompany food. It can be used as an apertif before the meal, and also as a refreshment wine that is used—apart from any food—at bars, at home, in the backyard.[6]

Market Segmentation

A market-segmentation approach aims at a narrow, specific consumer group (market segment) through one, specialized marketing plan that caters to the needs of that segment.

With market segmentation, a firm can succeed with limited resources by specializing.

Market segmentation has emerged as a popular technique, particularly for small or specialized firms. With market segmentation a firm does not have to mass produce, mass distribute, or mass advertise. The firm can succeed with limited resources and abilities by specializing. A market segmentation strategy is not normally a sales-maximization approach. Instead, the firm's objective is efficiency, attracting a large portion of one market segment at controlled costs. The firm wants recognition as a specialist. It does not try to diversify.

In evaluating competition the firm must determine whether it wants to attract a market segment with no competitors or one with several strong competitors. It is essential that the company do a better job of tailoring a marketing program for its segment than competitors. Competitor strengths should be avoided and weaknesses exploited. For instance, a new fast-food restaurant that sells hamburgers would have a more difficult time in differentiating itself from competitors than a fast-food restaurant selling French onion soup and crepes.

Rather than fall victim to the majority fallacy, a company may be better off entering a smaller but untapped segment.

If there are two or more available consumer groups, the firm must select the one segment that offers the greatest opportunity. While criteria for selecting a segment are detailed later in this chapter, the firm should be alert to two factors. One, the largest segment may not provide the best opportunity because of heavy competition or high consumer satisfaction with competitor offerings (for example, the medium-size segment of the auto market). A company selecting the largest segment may regret it because of the **majority fallacy,** which asserts that

[2] "Corporate Scoreboard," *Business Week* (March 21, 1984), p. 52; and "The 50 Largest Retailing Companies," *Fortune* (June 13, 1983), pp. 168–169.

[3] "Sears, Roebuck & Co." *Advertising Age* (September 8, 1983), p. 140.

[4] Laura Landro and James A. White, "Computer Firms Push Prices Down, Try to Improve Marketing Tactics," *Wall Street Journal* (April 29, 1983), p. 35.

[5] Cynthia Saltzman, "Troubled Life-Insurance Companies Try Mass-Marketing Tactics to Increase Sales," *Wall Street Journal* (December 19, 1980), p. 50.

[6] Jeanne Toomey, "A Citadel of Success," *Advertising Age* (July 27, 1981), p. S-43.

companies sometimes fail when they go after the largest market segment because competition is intense. See Figure 8-3. Two, a potentially profitable market segment may be one that is ignored by other firms. As an illustration, Frank Perdue is very successful in the poultry business. This has occurred because Perdue was the first chicken producer to see a market segment that desired quality, an identifiable brand name, a guarantee, and would pay premium prices. Others sold chickens as unlabeled commodities.

Market segmentation can enable a company to maximize per unit profits but not total profits, because only one segment is sought. It also enables a firm with low resources to compete effectively with larger firms for specialized markets. For example, there are many regional soda producers who can effectively compete with national manufacturers in a given region but who do not have the resources to compete on a national level. On the other hand, small shifts in population or consumer tastes can sharply affect a segmenter.

1. Without studying the competition in Segment A, a company decides to develop a product for this segment since it is much larger.

**Figure 8-3
How the Majority Fallacy Occurs**

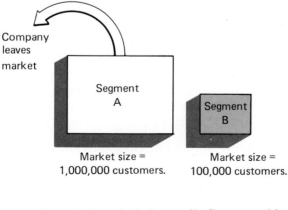

Company enters market

Segment A

Segment B

Market size = 1,000,000 customers.

Market size = 100,000 customers.

2. The company is forced out of the market due to heavy competition. It mistakenly ignored Segment B, which had no competition.

Company leaves market

Segment A

Segment B

Market size = 1,000,000 customers.

Market size = 100,000 customers.

There are 12 competitors, including 3 national firms. (each with a 20 per cent market share).

No firms serve this market.

A segmenter is able to generate a specialized image for a particular brand. This encourages brand loyalty for the current offering and may be helpful if the company develops a product line under one name (such as Hellman's). As long as the firm stays within its perceived area of expertise, the image of one product (mayonnaise) will rub off on another (tartar sauce).

House of Patou and Video Air Express are two examples of companies employing market segmentation. House of Patou makes expensive perfume that appeals to up-scale, affluent women. Its leading brand is Joy, "the world's costliest fragrance." In the U.S., Joy sells for $175 an ounce; and it is distributed through only 1,000 outlets. Said House of Patou's director general, "We don't want our fragrance to be killed by over-sell, like certain competitors. Every time someone tries to steal our position at the top, they either fade away or come down in price."[7]

Video Air Express (VAX) is an express-delivery firm that concentrates on shipping video film and artwork for advertising agencies and graphic-arts studios. By focusing its business, VAX is able to "make the customer feel like he's getting a customized product." Unlike Federal Express and other general express-delivery firms, VAX understands and caters to the unique shipping needs and problems of its customers. For example, if advertising copy does not arrive at a newspaper due to bad weather, VAX will call the paper and describe the ad's layout and space requirements.[8]

Others using market segmentation include Sharper Image mail-order catalogs, which cater to affluent consumers with items such as $179 pocket knives and $2,395 motorized surfboards;[9] retailers such as San Francisco's The Short Stop and Detroit's Napoleon's Closet, which concentrate on clothes for small men;[10] and *Working Woman* magazine, aimed at career-minded women.[11]

Multiple Segmentation

With multiple segmentation, two or more different marketing plans are enacted.

Under a multiple-segmentation approach, a company tries to combine the best attributes of mass marketing and market segmentation. The method is similar to market segmentation, except that the firm appeals to two or more distinct market segments, with a different marketing plan for each segment. Some firms, such as General Motors, employ multiple segmentation to attract all the segments in the market and achieve the same effect as mass marketing. General Motors has five car brands (Cadillac, Buick, Oldsmobile, Pontiac, Chevrolet) and a truck brand. Other firms, such as Batus, use multiple segmentation to attract two or more, but not all, of the potential market segments. Batus operates Saks Fifth Avenue (status conscious, high-income market) and Gimbels (middle-income market) but

---

[7] Carolyn Pfaff, "House of Patou Carefully Spreads Its Joy," *Advertising Age* (February 27, 1984), pp. M–42—M–43.

[8] Sara Delano, "A Niche in Time," *Inc.* (April 1984), pp. 190–195.

[9] Bill Abrams, "Entrepreneur's Slick Catalog for Affluent Is Pacing the Growing Direct-Mail Business," *Wall Street Journal* (March 1, 1984), p. 31.

[10] Jeffrey H. Birnbaum, "Little Guys' Shops Separate the Men from the Boys' Dept.," *Wall Street Journal* (February 3, 1981), p. 1.

[11] Neal Hirschfeld," *Working Woman* Caters to the Career-Minded," *Advertising Age* (April 2, 1984), p. M–22.

does not pursue discount-oriented customers. Batus uses a selective strategy in choosing market segments, General Motors an all-inclusive strategy.

In some cases, companies actually use both mass-marketing and segmentation approaches in their multiple-segmentation strategy. These firms have one or more major brands aimed at a wide range of consumers (the mass market) and secondary brands geared toward specific market segments. For example, Time Inc. publishes *Time, Life,* and *People* for very broad audiences and *Fortune, Money,* and *Discover* for specialized segments. Coca-Cola markets Coke to a broad spectrum of consumers, while its diet Coke, Tab, Fresca, Sprite, Mr. Pibb, Mello Yello, and other brands appeal to narrower groups of customers.

As with the other techniques, multiple segmentation requires a thorough analysis. Company resources and abilities must be able to produce and market two or more different sizes, brands, or products. This can be costly. Such is the case in the automobile industry. On the other hand, if the company sells its own and retailer brands, added costs are small.

Multiple segmentation should enable the firm to achieve many company objectives. It is possible to maximize sales, when a number of segments are addressed. For example, Procter & Gamble has a 50 percent market share in the laundry and cleaning products field. This is made possible through a number of detergent brands such as Tide, Bold, Dash, Cheer, Gain, Oxydol, and Duz.

Recognition as a specialist can continue as long as the firm markets a narrow product line, or uses different brand names for products aimed at different segments. For instance, Whirlpool maintains a distinct image under its own label; few consumers know it also makes products for Sears. Multiple segmentation also allows a firm to diversify and minimize its risks, because all the emphasis is not placed on one segment. Gerber life insurance provides an excellent hedge against a drop in the sales of baby products for that company.

Multiple segmentation does not mean that a firm has to enter markets where competitors are strongest and be subjected to the majority fallacy. Its objectives, strengths, and weaknesses must be measured against competitors. The firm's philosophy should be to choose and develop only those segments that it can handle. The company should note that the majority fallacy also works in reverse. If the firm enters a market segment before a competitor, it may prevent the competitor from successfully entering that segment in the future.

Multiple segmentation requires the existence of two or more sizable consumer markets, with distinctive desires by each. For example, a firm that sells both designer jeans and store-brand jeans appeals to two distinct market segments (status conscious and affluent versus functionally oriented and price conscious). The more unique segments facing the firm, the greater the opportunity for multiple segmentation. In many cases, a firm that begins as a market segmenter is able to use multiple segmentation and pursue underdeveloped consumer segments after it becomes firmly established in one segment.

Channel members usually find multiple segmentation to be highly desirable. It enables them to reach different consumer groups, offers some degree of brand exclusivity, allows orders to be concentrated with one seller, and encourages them to carry their own private brands. From the selling firm's perspective, several channel benefits exist. Items can be sold to competing stores under different labels. Store shelf space must be provided to display each size, package, or brand. Price differentials among brands can be maintained. Competition may be kept out

Chances are better for successful multiple segmentation when many unique segments exist.

of the channel. Overall, multiple segmentation places the seller in a good bargaining position.

Multiple segmentation can be extremely profitable, because total profits should rise as the firm increases the number of segments it services. Per unit profits should also be high, if the firm does a good job of developing a unique market plan for each segment. Then, consumers in each segment are willing to pay a premium price for the tailor-made product or service.

Because the firm diversifies its markets under multiple segmentation, risks from a decline in any one segment are lessened. However, the firm can incur extra costs from making many product variations, selling through different channels (a separate sales force for each channel may be necessary), and promoting more brands. A firm must balance the additional revenues obtained from selling to multiple segments with the additional costs.

Under multiple segmentation, a company must also be careful to maintain product distinctiveness in each consumer segment and guard its image. A firm's reputation can be hurt if it sells similar products and services at different prices to different segments under separate brand names and consumers find out about it. A few years ago, General Motors had such a problem when a number of Oldsmobile and Buick customers discovered that their automobiles had engines from the less-expensive Chevrolet division.

Other companies using multiple segmentation include Club Med, with separate resorts for couples only and families;[12] the Clinique division of Estee Lauder, which makes skin care products for women and for men;[13] and Johnson & Johnson, which markets Johnson & Johnson's Baby Shampoo and Affinity shampoo (for women over 40).[14]

Applying a Segmentation Approach

In this section, several aspects of segmentation are discussed: bases, steps in planning, organizational consumer segments, requirements for success, and limitations.

Bases of Segmentation

Market segments can be based on geographic demographics, personal demographics, and consumer life-styles. See Table 8-2.

GEOGRAPHIC DEMOGRAPHICS

Geographic demographics describe towns, cities, states, and regions.

Geographic demographics are the basic identifiable characteristics of towns, cities, states, and regions. A company can use one or a combination of geographic demographics to segment its market. Segmentation strategies emphasize and cater to geographic differences.

---

[12] Alan Rosenthal, "Club Med: Taking Aim at the Family," *Advertising Age* (March 15, 1982), pp. M-2–M-3.
[13] "Cosmetics Makers Are Luring Men," *New York Times* (January 7, 1982), p. D3.
[14] "The Lather Wars Have Shampoo Makers Hunting for Niches," *Business Week* (January 9, 1984), p. 124.

Table 8-2
Bases for Segmentation

Base	Examples of Possible Segments
Geographic demographics	
Population	
Location	North, South, East, West
Size	Small, medium, large
Density	Urban, suburban, rural
Transportation network	Mass transit, vehicular, pedestrian
Climate	Warm, cold
Type of commerce	Tourist, local worker, resident
Retail establishments	Downtown shopping district, shopping mall
Media	Local, regional, national
Competition	Underdeveloped, saturated
Growth pattern	Stable, negative, positive
Legislation	Stringent, lax
Rate of inflation	Low, moderate, high
Personal demographics	
Age	Child, teenager, adult, senior citizen
Gender	Male, female
Education	Less than high school, high school, college
Mobility	Same residence for 2 years, changed residence in last 2 years
Income	Low, middle, high
Occupation	Blue-collar, white-collar, professional
Marital status	Single, married, divorced, widowed
Family size	1, 2, 3, 4, 5, 6, or more
Nationality or race	European, Hispanic, American, Asian; black, white
Consumer life-styles	
Social class	Lower-lower to upper-upper
Family life cycle	Bachelor to solitary survivor
Usage rate	Light, medium, heavy
Usage experience	None, some, extensive
Brand loyalty	None, some, total
Personality	Introverted-extroverted, persuasible-nonpersuasible
Attitudes	Neutral, positive, negative
Class consciousness	Inner-directed, outer-directed
Motives	Benefit segmentation
Perceived risk	Low, moderate, high
Innovativeness	Innovator, laggard
Opinion leadership	None, some, a lot
Importance of purchase	Little, a great deal

Geographic population traits include an area's location, population, and density. The locations of areas may reflect differences in income, culture, social values, and other consumer factors. For example, one region may be more conservative than another. Population size and density indicate whether an area has enough people to generate sales and the ease of mounting a marketing campaign. Figure 8-4 shows a demographic map of the United States.

An area's transportation network is its mass transit and highway mix. A locale with a limited mass transit system is likely to have different marketing needs from an area with an extensive system. For instance, in California, there are nearly 18 million registered motor vehicles (with a population of 23.7 million) compared with about 8 million in New York (with a population of 17.6 million).

A firm may segment on the basis of an area's climate. As an illustration, 55 per cent of all U.S. homes are air conditioned. Yet, in Houston, 95 per cent of the

States	1980 Population Ranking	2000 Projected Population	1982 Per Capita Income Ranking	1980 Geographic Size Ranking	1980 Urbanization Ranking*
Alabama	22	24	47	29	36
Alaska	50	48	1	1	29
Arizona	29	15	32	6	9
Arkansas	33	32	49	27	42
California	1	1	4	3	1
Colorado	27	21	7	8	12
Connecticut	25	29	2	48	15
Delaware	47	49	13	49	20
Florida	7	3	20	22	8
Georgia	12	11	36	21	34
Hawaii	40	42	14	47	4
Idaho	41	39	42	13	39
Illinois	5	6	9	24	11
Indiana	13	14	34	38	30
Iowa	28	30	25	25	37
Kansas	32	34	12	14	27
Kentucky	24	25	43	37	43
Louisiana	18	19	31	31	22
Maine	39	41	41	39	45
Maryland	19	22	8	42	13
Massachusetts	11	16	10	45	9
Michigan	8	8	21	23	19
Minnesota	21	23	18	12	26
Mississippi	31	31	50	32	46
Missouri	15	20	33	19	23
Montana	45	44	37	4	40
Nebraska	36	38	23	15	32
Nevada	44	36	11	7	5
New Hampshire	43	40	27	44	41
New Jersey	9	9	3	46	2
New Mexico	38	37	39	5	18
New York	2	4	6	30	7
North Carolina	10	10	40	28	48
North Dakota	46	47	24	17	44
Ohio	6	7	29	35	17
Oklahoma	26	27	17	18	25
Oregon	30	26	30	10	24
Pennsylvania	4	5	22	33	21
Rhode Island	41	45	28	50	3
South Carolina	24	28	48	40	38
South Dakota	45	46	35	16	47
Tennessee	17	17	44	34	35
Texas	3	2	16	2	14
Utah	36	33	45	11	6
Vermont	48	50	38	43	50
Virginia	14	12	19	36	28
Washington	20	13	15	20	16
West Virginia	34	35	46	41	49
Wisconsin	16	18	26	26	30
Wyoming	49	43	5	9	33

*% of population living in urban areas.

Sources: Bureau of the Census, and Bureau of Economic Analysis.

Figure 8-4
A Demographic Map of the United States

homes are air conditioned, due to the high average temperature and humidity. This has created a market for 700 air-conditioner firms to install 90,000 new units annually. Along with repair companies, these businesses account for 44 pages in the Houston Yellow Pages.[15]

An area's commerce mix involves its orientation toward tourists, local workers, and residents. Tourist product and service needs in New Orleans are distinct from worker needs in Detroit and from resident needs in a Detroit suburb. For example, tourists are attracted to unique restaurants, workers to fast-food outlets, and residents to supermarkets.

Central cities are more apt to have downtown shopping districts; suburbs are more likely to have shopping centers. Each shopping district or center generally has its own distinctive image and combination of retailers. For instance, Reading, Pennsylvania, features a large factory-outlet shopping district, while Philadelphia contains the largest urban mall in the U.S. (the Gallery), anchored by Gimbels and Strawbridge & Clothier. The Gallery is an integral part of Philadelphia's redevelopment plan.

The availability of media varies by area. This has an important impact on a company's ability to segment. For example, one city may have its own local television station, another may not. This would make it difficult for a retailer in the second city to reach only customers in its vicinity. Many national publications, particularly magazines, now print regional issues to allow companies to advertise to selected geographic audiences.

An area may be underdeveloped or saturated in competition for the sale of a particular product or service. A firm may be able to succeed by entering smaller but underdeveloped markets. As an illustration, Ames Department Stores operates 127 discount outlets in towns such as Ossipee, New Hampshire, and North Tonawanda, New York. By locating in these markets, Ames is able to be "the big fish in a small pond" and competition is "slim."[16]

The growth pattern of a region may be stable, negative, or positive, as discussed in Chapter 5. A company is most likely to find an underdeveloped market in a growing area and a saturated market in a stable or declining area (although it must beware of the majority fallacy). For example, L. Luria & Son (a retail catalog showroom specializing in jewelry, cameras, and brand-name items such as toasters) has achieved annual sales of $125 million in 26 stores situated in Florida—one of the fastest-growing states in the U.S. Now, saturation is causing Luria to consider expansion into New Orleans, Dallas, or Washington, D.C.[17]

Legal restrictions vary by municipality and state. A firm may choose not to enter an area that restricts its operations. If it does enter, it must abide by legal requirements. For example, automobile emissions are more stringently controlled in California than elsewhere in the United States. Oregon also has strict environmental laws. In both of these states, firms offer modified products from those marketed in other states. Delaware is an attractive state for many firms because they do not have to charge customers sales tax; this draws shoppers from other states.

[15] Bryan Burrough, "In Houston, the Ubiquitous Air Conditioner Makes Tolerable an Otherwise Muggy Life," *Wall Street Journal* (September 21, 1983), p. 35.

[16] Aaron Bernstein, "Cornering the Market," *Forbes* (May 23, 1983), p. 46.

[17] "L. Luria & Son: A Cataloger Whose Profits Match Its Classy Image," *Business Week* (July 11, 1983), p. 98.

The rate of inflation can vary by area; and this can affect marketing strategy. For instance, in January 1984, the average cost of housing was $75,000 in Akron, Ohio; $88,000 in Peoria, Illinois; $110,000 in Fort Worth, Texas; and $147,000 in Anchorage, Alaska.[18]

Toys "R" Us, the largest toy store chain in the U.S., is an example of a company that considers several factors when applying geographic segmentation. Toys "R" Us operates more than 100 outlets in 26 markets (in 17 states). Its expansion strategy involves entering one new market, with several outlets, each year. In the evaluation of new locations, Toys "R" Us specifies that the areas must each have at least 250,000 people, including 25 to 28 per cent children. Toys "R" Us wants to operate stores in the largest 25 markets in the U.S.; it is now located in 15 of them.[19]

PERSONAL DEMOGRAPHICS

Personal demographics describe individual people.

Personal demographics are the basic identifiable characteristics of individual people. They are often used as the basis for segmentation, because people with different backgrounds frequently have different purchase requirements. Personal demographics may be viewed singly or in combinations.

Consumers can be divided into several age categories, such as child, teenager, adult, and senior citizen. Age is frequently used as a segmentation factor:

● Health-Tex makes infant and children's clothing, ranging from polo shirts and dresses to swim suits and sweatpants. It distributes through department and children's stores only under its own name.[20]
● Castle & Cook runs ads in *Seventeen* magazine featuring recipes and instructions for throwing parties, using its Dole pineapples and bananas and Bumble Bee tuna.[21]
● The Petersen Company publishes nine magazines, including *Motor Trend* and *Photographic,* aimed at 18- to 34-year-old males.[22]
● Revlon uses Joan Collins as advertising spokesperson for Scoundrel, a perfume targeted at over-30-year-old women.[23] See Figure 8-5.

Gender is a major segmentation variable for a number of products and services, such as clothing, personal-care products, jewelry, and personal services. For example, Timex sells both men's and women's watches, department stores have separate men's and women's departments, and the Hardy Boys and Nancy Drew novels appeal to boys and girls respectively. During the 1970s, a counter-trend developed: unisex products and services; and many hair stylists, clothing manufacturers, and others began offering items that would attract a combination

[18] Robert Guenther, "Uneven Pattern of Housing Prices Is Mainly Tied to Local Conditions," *Wall Street Journal* (March 15, 1984), p. 33.

[19] "Simplified Growth: One Market Per Year," *Chain Store Age* (September 1981), p. 18; and Janet Neiman, "Retailers Should Know Their Place," *Advertising Age* (November 1, 1982), p. M-22.

[20] Jeff Blyskal, "Filling Up the Table," *Forbes* (December 6, 1982), pp. 100–101.

[21] Mark N. Dodosh, "Widely Ignored Teen Market Has a Lot of Spending Power," *Wall Street Journal* (June 17, 1982), p. 31.

[22] "We Deliver the Men for You," (Los Angeles: Petersen Publishing Company).

[23] Pat Sloan, "Cosmetics Chase Older Consumers," *Advertising Age* (July 25, 1983), pp. 3, 77.

Figure 8-5
**Scoundrel: A Perfume
Aimed at Women over 30**

Reprinted by permission of Revlon, Inc.

of men and women. Today, companies are placing a heightened emphasis on marketing products to women that were previously geared towards men:

- American Express is addressing some of its ads to the 10 million women who qualify for its card, but do not yet own one.[24]
- Chrysler is offering a test-drive program in shopping malls for its Dodge Caravan and Plymouth Voyager minivans. Women are the prime market for this program.[25]

---

[24] Bill Abrams, ''American Express Is Gearing New Ad Campaign to Women,'' *Wall Street Journal* (August 4, 1983), p. 23.
[25] Jesse Snyder, ''Chrysler Aims Minivan Promos at Women, Via Shopping Malls,'' *Advertising Age* (December 12, 1983), pp. 1, 70.

Figure 8-6
An Upscale Refrigerator from Magic Chef
Magic Chef refrigerators feature ice cream and cold soup makers, water and ice service, wine chiller racks, and wide shelves.

Reprinted by permission.

Educational level can be used to distinguish among market segments. A poorly educated consumer is likely to spend less time shopping, read less, and rely more on well-known brands than a college-educated consumer. The latter is likely to comparison shop, read noncommercial sources of information, and purchase the product perceived as best, whether it is well known or not.

A person's mobility refers to the degree to which he or she changes residence.[26] A mobile consumer relies on national brands and stores and nonpersonal information. A stationary consumer relies on an acquired knowledge of differences among various brands and stores (national and local) and personal trust and information.

Consumers can be divided into low-, middle-, and high-income categories. Each category has different resources with which to buy products and services. The price a company charges helps determine which income group buys its offerings. For example, clothing can be sold at thrift stores, discount and department stores, or specialty clothiers. With the growth in the size of the high-income market segment in the U.S., more companies are aiming at this group. As an illustration, Magic Chef is now marketing $1,000 to $1,400 refrigerators that can make ice cream, cold soups, and slush drinks.[27] See Figure 8-6.

The consumer's occupation may affect purchases. For instance, a construction

---

[26] For a good discussion on the characteristics of mobile people, see Gerald Albaum and Del I. Hawkins, "Geographic Mobility and Demographic and Socioeconomic Market Segmentation," *Journal of the Academy of Marketing Science,* Vol. 11 (Spring 1983), pp. 97–113.

[27] "Magic Chef's New Recipe Calls for Upscale Appliances," *Business Week* (June 20, 1983), p. 73; and John Koten, "Innovative Upscale Iceboxes Mark a Sales Coup for Admiral," *Wall Street Journal* (April 19, 1984), p. 33.

worker has different clothing and lunch requirements than a computer technology salesperson. The former wears flannel shirts, dungarees, and work shoes and brings lunch. The latter wears a three-piece suit and wing-tip shoes and takes clients to restaurants for lunch.

Marital status and family size provide bases for segmentation. Many firms orient their products or services either to single (sports car) or married (sedan) people. Hotels constantly advertise singles weekends or vacations for honeymooners. Family-size segmentation has resulted in different package sizes, such as single-serving and family size, and special offerings such as discounts for large purchases.

Nationality or race represents another segmentation variable. For example, ethnic products or services may be aimed at persons of Italian, German, and other backgrounds. As the black (12 per cent of the U.S. population) and Hispanic (5 per cent of the U.S. population) markets have grown, specialized newspapers, beauty products firms, magazines, and other items have evolved to satisfy them.[28] Goya Foods has been able to top $150 million in annual sales by concentrating on 700 food items aimed at the Hispanic market.[29]

Personal-demographic profiles combining several factors are frequently used in planning a segmentation strategy, as this example shows. Until recently, the Chevrolet Camaro was marketed as a "slab-sided boxy" car to single, young consumers with annual incomes of $20,000. Now, the redesigned Camaro offers a stylish look, a European appearance, interior comfort, good acceleration, and family roominess. As a result, the new Camaro attracts slightly older, married consumers with annual incomes of $35,000.[30]

CONSUMER LIFE-STYLES

As defined in Chapter 5, life-styles are the patterns in which people live and spend time and money. They include social and psychological factors. By developing life-style profiles, companies may be able to appeal to distinct market segments. Table 8-2 shows life-style segmentation for a wide range of social and psychological factors.

Segments can be described on the basis of social and psychological factors.

Consumers can be segmented by social class and stage in the family life cycle. For example, American Motors markets the Renault Encore to a "trendy, image-conscious individual, young, well-educated, and white collar" with above average income; the Renault Alliance to a "more conservative, practical, and family-minded" buyer with average income and education and a more blue-collar background; and the AMC Eagle (a station-wagon-like, four-wheel-drive vehicle) to larger families described as "middle America."[31]

Market segments can be based on usage rate, usage experience, and brand loyalty. The usage rate refers to the amount of a product or service that a consumer buys. A consumer may use very little, some, or a great deal. In the 1960s

[28] See B. G. Yovovich, "Marketing to Blacks," *Advertising Age* (November 29, 1982), pp. M-9–M-10; Danny N. Bellenger and Humberto Valencia, "Understanding the Hispanic Market," *Business Horizons,* Vol. 25 (May–June 1982), pp. 47–50; and Liz Murphy, "Hispanic Gets Manic," *Sales & Marketing Management* (November 14, 1983), pp. 39–42.

[29] Nancy Giges, "Hispanic Marketer Goya Plans Mass-Market Bid," *Advertising Age* (October 11, 1982), pp. 4, 61.

[30] Douglas R. Sease, "Camaro, Firebird Become Fast-Selling Cars for GM, Helping Profit and Lifting Morale," *Wall Street Journal* (June 8, 1982), p. 37.

[31] Ralph Gray, "Smaller Jeeps Create Big-Size Marketing Woes," *Advertising Age* (August 22, 1983), p. 14.

Figure 8-7
Applying the Heavy-Half Theory to Fast-Food Restaurants

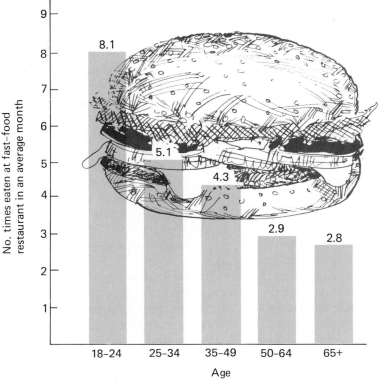

No. times eaten at fast-food restaurant in an average month

Age

Fast-food restaurants do very well with young adults; however, older adults are much less likely to be regular patrons.

Source: R. H. Bruskin, "Checking Out the Consumer," *Advertising Age* (November 21, 1983), p. M-10. Reprinted by permission of *Advertising Age*. Copyright 1983 by Crain Communications, Inc.

The *heavy-half* segment represents a much larger percentage of sales than the light-half segment.

Dik Warren Twedt coined the term ***heavy-half*** to describe the market segment accounting for a large proportion of a product or service's total sales. For a wide variety of products, such as soda and shampoo, Twedt found that a heavy-user segment existed. In some cases, less than 20 per cent of the market made 80+ per cent of purchases.[32] Figure 8-7 applies the heavy-half theory to fast-food restaurants.

Other applications of the heavy-half theory include the following.[33] Singles represent 12.5 per cent of total adult consumers, yet account for 15.5 per cent of "eating-out" spending and car sales, and 20 per cent of alcohol sales. Consumers 55 years of age and older represent one fifth of the population, but purchase nearly 50 per cent of decaffinated coffee. Four per cent of the U.S. population consumes 53 per cent of all wine bought. When pursuing the heavy-half segment, a firm must be careful not to engage in the majority fallacy. Perhaps the "light" half has been underdeveloped.

[32] Dik Warren Twedt, "How Important to Marketing Is the 'Heavy User'?" *Journal of Marketing,* Vol. 28 (January 1964), pp. 71–72.

[33] Gay Jervey, "Y & R Study: New Life to Singles," *Advertising Age* (October 4, 1982), p. 14; "Catering to Older Age Groups," *New York Times* (February 23, 1984), p. D3; and "Creating a Mass Market for Wine," *Business Week* (March 15, 1983), p. 109.

Usage experience refers to the amount of prior experience a consumer has with a product or service. A consumer with no prior experience operates much differently from one with substantial experience. In addition, the firm should distinguish between nonusers, potential users (those evaluating the product or service for possible purchase), and regular users. Each segment has different needs.

Consumer brand loyalty can take one of three forms: none, some, or total. If no brand loyalty exists, the consumer has no real preference for a brand, is attracted by sales, switches brands frequently, and is willing to try new products or services. If some brand loyalty exists, the consumer has a preference for a few brands, is attracted by discounts for these brands, switches brands infrequently, and is usually not willing to try new brands. If total brand loyalty exists, the consumer insists on one brand, is not attracted by discounts for other brands, never switches brands, and will not try a new brand.

Consumers can be segmented by personality type, such as introverted-extroverted or persuasible-nonpersuasible. The introverted consumer will tend to be more conservative and systematic in his or her purchasing behavior than an extroverted consumer. A nonpersuasible person reacts adversely to heavy personal sales efforts and is skeptical of advertising claims. A persuasible person can be convinced to buy an item because of a strong sales pitch and is easily swayed by advertising claims.

Consumers can be categorized by their attitudes toward the firm and its offering. For instance, neutral attitudes (''I've heard of brand X, but I don't really know about it'') require heavy informative and persuasive promotion. Positive attitudes (''Brand X is the best product on the market'') require such reinforcement as follow-up advertising and personal contacts with consumers. Negative attitudes (''Brand X is far inferior to brand Y'') are difficult to change and require substantiation of advertising claims, product improvements, an upgraded company image, and other tactics. It may be worthwhile for a firm to ignore this segment and concentrate on the first two. It is important to remember that with segmentation a firm does not seek to please all groups with one effort.

Segmentation by class consciousness is possible for socially visible products and services such as clothing, automobiles, restaurants, travel, and real estate. Inner-directed consumers buy to satisfy themselves and are not impressed with fancy labels and high price tags. Outer-directed consumers seek social acceptance, regularly buy items with fancy labels, and pay higher prices. As one outer-directed consumer noted: ''Professional persons, whether they're doctors, lawyers, or ballplayers, get Mercedes. They can afford it, and they think they should have one.''[34]

Consumer motives (reasons for purchases) can be broken down into benefit segments. **Benefit segmentation** was popularized by Russell Haley in 1968:

Benefit segmentation **assumes that consumers may be grouped on the basis of their reasons for using products or services.**

The belief underlying this segmentation strategy is that the benefits which people are seeking in consuming a given product are the basic reasons for the existence of true market segments.[35]

---

[34] Charles W. Stevens, ''European Luxury Cars Capturing a Growing Share of U.S. Market,'' *Wall Street Journal* (May 6, 1983), p. 31.

[35] Russell I. Haley, ''Benefit Segmentation: A Decision-Oriented Research Tool,'' *Journal of Marketing,* Vol. 32 (July 1968), p. 31.

Figure 8-8
Applying Benefit
Segmentation to Shampoo

Haley studied the toothpaste market and was able to divide it into four segments. The sensory segment sought flavor and product appearance, had children, used spearmint toothpaste, favored brands like Colgate, had a degree of self-involvement, and was pleasure-oriented. The sociable segment sought bright teeth, was young, smoked, favored brands like Ultra Brite, and was highly sociable and active. The worrier segment sought decay prevention, had large families, used toothpaste heavily, favored Crest, had hypochondria, and was conservative. The independent segment sought low prices, was male, used toothpaste heavily, bought the brand on sale, and was autonomous and value-oriented.[36] Figure 8-8 applies benefit segmentation to shampoo.

Perceived risk can inhibit the purchase of a product or service. To attract risk avoiders, the marketer needs to reduce their perception of risk. Some techniques for accomplishing this are extensive informative advertising, well-known brands, low introductory prices, trial package sizes, money-back guarantees, and in-store demonstrations. Risk takers are attracted to new, distinctive items.

Innovators have low perceived risk and are the first to try new products. They are interested in unique and different ideas. Laggards have high perceived risk and are the last to try new products. They hold onto existing products for a long time and wait for new items to be perfected and come down in price. Some innovators are opinion leaders who can influence fellow consumers. Other innovators are not opinion leaders, because they do not have the respect and confidence of their peers. As noted earlier, a person can be an opinion leader for one product and an opinion follower for another product category.

[36] Ibid., p. 33.

In a major study of fashion behavior, innovators described themselves as much more sophisticated, modern, different, willing to take chances, confident, creative, sociable, and distinctive than followers described themselves. The two groups were very similar in demographic terms (age, income, and education), although innovators were more often single.[37]

The importance of a purchase also differs by consumer. For example, a suburban commuter would probably consider the purchase of an automobile to be more important than a city worker with access to mass transit. The purchase of a refrigerator would be more important for a family with a broken machine than one with a well-functioning model. This factor should be acknowledged in a firm's strategy.

Life-style segmentation often is based on a combination of factors, as this illustration shows.[38] In the 1950s,

Dad worked, Mom stayed home with the kids, and in the evenings the whole clan might hunker down in front of the TV and eat from prepackaged tin trays. Fried chicken and spaghetti were the favorites. The emphasis was simply on belly filling, and the food was heavy, fatty, and salty.

Now, the market for frozen dinners is ''wealthier, more health-conscious, and more demanding.'' Consumers are looking for ''lighter, more nutritious, more flavorful'' dinners. As a result, Campbell's Swanson division is marketing lobster thermador and other fancy dishes; one commercial for its Le Menu entrees takes place aboard a yacht. Said a Campbell spokesperson:

Until now, the average American shopper would be mortified to be seen with more than three or four TV dinners in her cart. Our job is to make it all right.

See Figure 8-9.

BLENDING DEMOGRAPHIC AND LIFE-STYLE FACTORS

A firm should normally use a mix of demographic and life-style factors to determine and describe its market segments. A richer and more valuable analysis takes place when a variety of factors is reviewed.

An extremely useful classification system for segmenting consumers in terms of a broad range of demographic and life-style factors has been developed by the Stanford Research Institute. Its *VALS (Values and Life-Styles) program* divides American life-styles into nine major categories, based on the responses of more than 1,600 adults to a 1980 mail survey containing over 800 questions:[39]

VALS describes nine major American market segments on the basis of both demographic and life-style factors.

- Need-driven
    (1) Survivors—old, poor, fearful, removed from cultural mainstream.
    (2) Sustainers—angry, resentful, streetwise, poor.
- Outer-directed
    (3) Belongers—aging, conventional, content, traditional Middle Americans, patriotic.

[37] Jonathan Gutman and Michael K. Mills, ''Fashion Life Style, Self-Concept, Shopping Orientation, and Store Patronage: An Integrative Analysis,'' *Journal of Retailing,* Vol. 58 (Summer 1982), pp. 64–86.
[38] Paul A. Engelmayer, ''Food Concerns Rush to Serve More Quality Frozen Foods,'' *Wall Street Journal* (October 20, 1983), p. 33.
[39] Arnold Mitchell, *The Nine American Lifestyles: Who We Are & Where We Are Going* (New York: Macmillan, 1983).

Figure 8-9
**A Changing Image for
Frozen Dinners**

Reprinted by permission.

    (4) Emulators—young, ambitious, flashy, trying to break into the system.

    (5) Achievers—middle-aged, prosperous, self-assured, the leaders and builders of the American dream.

• Inner-directed

    (6) I-am-me—very young, impulsive, exhibitionist, self-centered.

    (7) Experiential—youthful, seeking experience, oriented to inner growth, artistic.

    (8) Societally conscious—mission-oriented, mature, successful, out to change the world.

• Combined

    (9) Integrated—mature, tolerant, understanding, flexible, able to see ''the big picture.''

Table 8-3 shows selected demographic and life-style characteristics for these nine segments.

Table 8-3

The Nine American Life-Styles, Selected Characteristics (Based on VALS Program Research)

Segment	% of Adult Population	Characteristics		
		Demographics	Life-Style	Consumption Patterns
Need-driven				
Survivors	4	Overrepresented in South, most over 65, 77% female, income under $7,500, median 8th-9th grade education.	Many bake bread, eat vegetarian meals, like store brands, are concerned with ingredients, smoke cigarettes, have no credit cards, use the phone often, visit doctors, watch television, listen to radio, do not own a car.	Many emphasize convenience, price, safety; buy clothing, personal products, pet food, pain relievers, cleaning products, beverages, hot cereal, gelatin.
Sustainers	7	Numerous in New England, 58% under 35, 55% female, $11,000 median income, median 11th grade education.	Many are active in sports and entertainment, eat while watching television, eat breakfast out, are concerned with nutrition, smoke cigarettes, phone friends, shop in convenience stores, have no credit cards, watch a lot of television, listen to radio, read tabloid magazines, own a small car.	Many purchase used cars, jeans, casual clothes, personal care products, cleaning products, snack foods, canned soup, frozen TV dinners.
Outer-directed				
Belongers	35	Numerous in South, median age of 52, 68% female, $17,300 median income, high-school education.	Many garden and bake, smoke, watch television; are very stable; are not active in sports, entertainment, learning, business travel.	Purchases of durables, recreational equipment, electronic products, clothing, personal care products, and beverages are below average.
Emulators	9	Overrepresented in South Atlantic, median age of 27, 53% male, $18,000 median income, high-school education plus.	Many are active in bowling, billiards, entertainment, playing cards, eating dinner while watching television, eating at fast-food outlets, smoking cigarettes, watching television.	Many purchase electronic products, jeans, personal products, alcoholic beverages, soft drinks, pet food; are interested in a home computer.

By reviewing the VALS classification, a company is better able to determine the size of different market segments, their characteristics and behavior, and product and service needs and to maximize its marketing efforts. For example, Dr. Pepper is targeted toward inner-directed consumers, those "likely to be responsive to a distinct message."[40] Its slogan is "Hold out for the out of the ordinary."

[40] Laura Konrad Jereski, "Do You Know Your Consumers?" *Marketing & Media Decisions* (February 1984), p. 142.

Table 8-3
The Nine American Life-Styles, Selected Characteristics (Continued)

Segment	% of Adult Population	Characteristics		
		Demographics	Life-Style	Consumption Patterns
Achievers	22	Overrepresented in Pacific region, median age of 43, 60% male, $31,400 median income, college graduate or more.	Many are active in sports, eat out, smoke cigarettes, travel, spend time in learning experiences, have several credit cards, own insurance, read newspapers and business magazines, own 3+ cars.	Many purchase new cars, durables, recreational equipment, electronic products, clothing, personal products, pet food, alcoholic beverages.
Inner-directed I-am-me	5	Overrepresented in Mid Atlantic, South Atlantic, and East North Central; 91% under 25; 64% male; $8,800 median income; some college.	Many are active in sports, outdoor life, the arts, entertainment, playing cards, do-it-yourself projects, eating snacks, a second job, pleasure travel, attending movies, magazine reading.	Many purchase specialty cars, recreational equipment, electronic products, jeans, personal products, alcoholic beverages, soft drinks, snack food.
Experiential	7	Numerous in Pacific region, median age of 27, 55% female, $23,800 median income, 38% college graduate or more.	Many are active in sports, outdoor life, the arts, cultural events, entertainment, meditation, health foods, working a second job, phoning friends, learning, travel, shopping, credit cards, newspaper and book reading.	Many purchase compact cars, durables, recreational equipment, electronic products, cameras, clothing, personal products, alcoholic beverages, sugarless gum.
Societally conscious	8	Numerous in New England and Pacific regions, median age of 39, 52% male, $27,200 median income, 58% college graduate (39% graduate school).	Many are active in sports, the arts, cultural events, health foods, learning, travel; have stopped smoking; have several credit cards; watch educational television, read newspapers, books, and magazines; own 2+ cars.	Many purchase durables, recreational equipment, electronic products, clothing, pet food, alcoholic beverages, seafood.
Combined Integrated	2	Most middle age or older, slightly more males, $30,000 median income, well educated.	People combine the decisiveness of outer-direction (achievers) with the introspection of inner-direction (societally conscious).	People combine the consumption patterns of outer-direction (achievers) and inner-direction (societally conscious).

Source: Adapted by the authors from Arnold Mitchell, *The Nine American Lifestyles: Who We Are & Where We Are Going* (New York: Macmillan, 1983).

Planning a Segmentation Strategy

A segmentation strategy follows a series of stages.

The development of a ***segmentation strategy*** involves the six steps shown in Figure 8-10 and described in the following subsections.

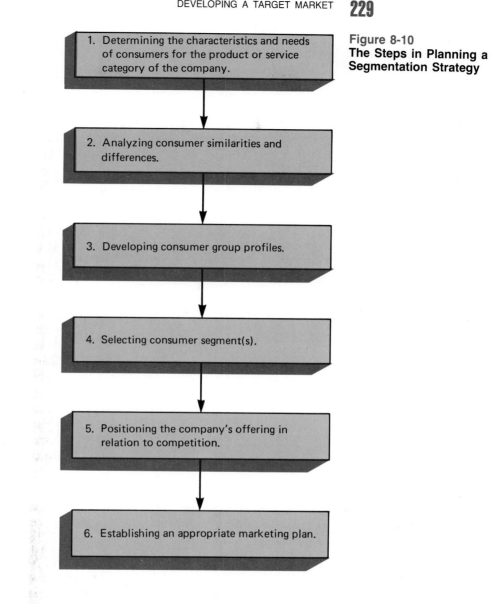

Figure 8-10
**The Steps in Planning a
Segmentation Strategy**

1. Determining the characteristics and needs of consumers for the product or service category of the company.

2. Analyzing consumer similarities and differences.

3. Developing consumer group profiles.

4. Selecting consumer segment(s).

5. Positioning the company's offering in relation to competition.

6. Establishing an appropriate marketing plan.

CHARACTERISTICS AND NEEDS OF CONSUMERS

A company should determine the characteristics and needs of consumers when it specifies the broad nature of its business. The exact product or service (such as, ladies' leather handbags or discount dental plans) should not be defined until after consumer research is undertaken. Step one is a data-collection stage.

For illustrative purposes, a hypothetical beer manufacturer named Brewers Beer will be taken through the segmentation process. Table 8-4 shows some of the information the firm would obtain in step one.

CONSUMER SIMILARITIES AND DIFFERENCES

After determining and characterizing consumer needs, individual similarities and differences among consumers are analyzed. Where similarities exist, the firm knows it must respond to them in its marketing plan regardless of the segment(s)

Table 8-4
Selected Characteristics and Needs, Beer Consumers in Model City, U.S.A.

Characteristics	Description
No. of beer drinkers	100,000—80,000 male, 20,000 female; 60% under 35; 70% under $20,000/year income; 27% white-collar workers; 24% college-educated
Beer consumption	8 million units (including bars and restaurants); 7 million by males, 1 million by females; 20% by under 35; 72% by under $20,000/year; 22% by white-collar workers; 20% by college-educated
Types of beer consumed	60% regular domestic, 25% light domestic, 10% imported, 5% domestic premium
Occasions for consumption	40% for relaxing, 27% with meals, 24% for social activities, 9% other
Place of purchase	52% at supermarket or grocery store, 22% at bar or restaurant, 18% at discount or specialty store, 8% other

Needs	Description
Product taste	45% prefer a strong, heavy beer; 30% a strong, light beer; 15% a moderate, light beer; 10% a strong, tangy beer
Caloric content	35% concerned, 65% unconcerned
Price	30% comparison shop, 50% indifferent to price, 20% prefer cheapest brand
Image	45% prefer macho image, 30% quality image, 20% socially acceptable image, 5% other
Package, type of container	68% prefer bottles, 32% cans (in bars and restaurants, 36% prefer bottles, 30% cans, 34% tap)
Package size	98% prefer regular 12-oz. size, 2% smaller size

chosen. As an example, Table 8-4 reveals that 98 per cent of all beer drinkers prefer regular-sized bottles or cans. Therefore, package size should not be used to differentiate consumers. The firm must sell beer in regular-sized bottles or cans.

Where differences exist among consumers, the choice of a market segment will determine how the firm devises its marketing plan. For instance, 68 per cent of beer drinkers prefer bottles and 32 per cent prefer cans. Each segment is large enough (68,000 versus 32,000 people) for at least one firm to respond to it. By appealing to consumer differences, the company is able to create a differential advantage.

CONSUMER GROUP PROFILES

After assessing the individual similarities and differences among consumers, the firm is ready to assemble consumer profiles. These profiles define market segments by aggregating consumers with similar characteristics and needs and separating them from consumers with different characteristics and needs.

Table 8-5 shows the consumer profiles for the market segments from which Brewers can select. This table follows the benefit segmentation format introduced by Haley.[41]

[41] Haley, ''Benefit Segmentation: A Decision-Oriented Research Tool,'' p. 31.

Table 8-5 **Beer Consumer Profiles for Model City, U.S.A.**

Factor	Segments				
	He-Man	**Traditionalist**	**Sociable**	**Sophisticate**	**Health Conscious**
No. of people	25,000	23,000	20,000	17,000	15,000
Principal benefits sought	Good taste; "macho" image; strong, heavy beer	Good taste, domestic brand, low price, freshness	Status of brand, attractive package	Status of brand, imported brand	Low calories, good taste
Demographic traits	Male, under 35, under $20,000/year income, high school education, blue collar	Male, 35–50, under $20,000/year income, family, high school education, blue collar	Male (70%) and female (30%), under 35, about $20,000/year income, some college, white collar	Male, under 35, over $20,000/year income, college education, white collar	Male and female, 18–50, about $20,000/year income, some college, white collar
Life-style traits	Physically active, patronizes taverns and bars, outgoing	Secure, conservative, brand loyal, family-oriented	Outgoing, leisure activities, socially aggressive, patronizes restaurants	Socially mobile, intellectual, cosmopolitan, domineering, likes uniqueness	Watches bad habits, secure, not status conscious, self-centered
Level of beer consumption	Heavy	Heavy	Moderate	Moderate	Moderate
Favorite brand	Schmidts	Budweiser	Michelob	Lowenbrau	Miller Lite

Five distinct market segments are available to Brewers Beer: he-man, traditionalist, sociable, sophisticate, and health conscious. A different marketing strategy is necessary to appeal to each of the segments.

SELECTING CONSUMER SEGMENTS

At this point, Brewers Beer has two decisions to make: Which segment(s) offer the greatest opportunities for the company? How many segments should the firm pursue?

In deciding which segment(s) contain the greatest potential, Brewers must consider company objectives, company strengths, the level of competition, the size of the markets, channel relations, profits, and company image. Table 8-6 contains a rating form developed by Brewers Beer. On the basis of the ratings, the sociable, sophisticate, and health-conscious segments offer the best opportunities, the he-man and traditionalist segments the poorest. Brewers ranks the three favorable segments: health conscious, sophisticate, and then sociable. This decision is made on the basis of competition and company objectives and secondarily on the other factors shown in Table 8-6.

Because Brewers is entering a new geographic region with its beer, the company decides to employ market segmentation. It will market beer only to the health-conscious market. In this way, company strengths will be fully exploited, consumer desires met, one type of competition faced, and costs controlled. If Brewers does well, it will expand into the sophisticate market in two years.

Table 8-6 Brewers Beer Assessment of Market Segments

Factor	Segments				
	He-Man	Traditionalist	Sociable	Sophisticate	Health Conscious
Consistency with company objectives	Fair	Fair	Excellent	Good	Excellent
Match with company strengths	Fair	Fair	Excellent	Good	Good
Level of competition	Heavy	Heavy	Heavy	Heavy	Moderate
Size of segment	Excellent	Excellent	Good	Good	Good
Match with present distribution channel	Fair	Fair	Good	Good	Good
Profitability	Fair	Fair	Fair	Good	Good
Fit with present company image	Poor	Poor	Good	Good	Good

POSITIONING THE COMPANY'S OFFERING

Once the company selects a market segment, it must identify the attributes and images of each competitor's products and select a position for its own product or service.

Brewers Beer identifies its leading competitors as Miller Lite, Natural Light (by Anheuser Busch), Michelob Light (by Anheuser Busch), and Schlitz Light. Miller Lite appeals to male, blue-collar drinkers. Natural Light appeals to active consumers who do not want additives in their beer. Michelob Light draws young, upscale drinkers. Schlitz Light attracts taste-conscious, middle-class consumers.

On the basis of its analysis, Brewers believes it can challenge its four competitors by introducing a dark, heavy, imported beer that is also low in calories. This beer, to be called Imported Light, would attract young, college-educated, white-collar males, who favor a rich taste and would treat themselves to imported beer.

ESTABLISHING A MARKETING PLAN

The last stage in the segmentation process is for the firm to develop its marketing plan. The overall marketing plan for Brewers Beer is

1. Product: dark, heavy, rich beer; attractive bottle; named Imported Light.
2. Distribution: all types of outlets, emphasis on supermarkets, restaurants, and hotels.
3. Price: premium.
4. Promotion: regional television, in-store displays, emphasis on imported taste without the calories.

Organizational Consumer Segments

When segmenting, a firm should examine organizational consumers as well as final consumers. The same segmentation criteria are used for both.

In Chapter 7, the characteristics and behavior of organizational consumers (manufacturers, wholesalers, retailers, government, and nonprofit institutions) were discussed and contrasted with final consumers. A firm engaging in a segmentation strategy should first examine and choose between final and organizational consumer markets. Then it should develop segments within either or both of these markets.

As noted in Chapter 7, organizational consumers require precise items, normally have strict price limits, frequently utilize joint decision making, buy in quantity, rate reliability and service very high, expect salespeople to visit them, and rely on trade publications. In contrast, final consumers frequently have flexibility in purchases, can vary price limits, often act alone, buy single units, may be relatively unconcerned about the future reliability of a vendor, usually go to a store, and rely on commercial media. The two markets require entirely different marketing approaches. For example, a firm selling vacuum cleaners to hospitals as well as to final consumers would need vastly different marketing plans for each.

When segmenting the organizational consumer market, a company should use the same criteria it would use for a final consumer. Geographic demographics include the features of the area in which the organizational consumer resides. Personal demographics refer to the consuming organization and its personnel, including size, area of specialization, resources, existing contracts, past purchases, order size, and the demographics of decision maker(s). Life-style factors include the way in which the organization operates (centralized or decentralized), brand loyalty, reasons for purchases, and the social and psychological attributes of decision maker(s). These characteristics are potential bases for segmentation.

The procedure for segmenting organizational consumers is the same as that for final consumers and a company may decide on a market or multiple-segmentation strategy.

The segmentation of organizational consumer markets can be applied to many different situations, as these examples demonstrate:

- The office photocopier market is segmented according to machine speed, volume, and price range. The leading companies offer models for multiple segments. See Table 8-7.
- The *Farm Journal* offers over 1,100 versions of its publications to its one million subscribers. It services five kinds of farmers (cotton, dairy, beef, hog, and livestock) in 26 regions of the U.S. Each version of the *Farm Journal* has a different combination of the basic magazine and 32 supplements.[42]
- Citytrust bank of Connecticut concentrates its efforts on servicing the financial needs of companies with $1 million to $25 million in annual sales. Says its chairman, "We want to treat the head of a $5 million company the way Morgan Guarantee treats General Electric."[43]
- The Ford Tractor division is actively seeking to attract women as customers for its farm tractors, since many women use these products or have a major impact on decisions. Ford has redesigned its large tractors to make it easier for women to operate them, trained dealers to act more business-like with women customers, and developed ads specifically directed at women.[44]

Requirements for Successful Segmentation

In order for segmentation planning to be successful, consumer groups must meet five criteria:

1. There must be *differences* among consumers, or else mass marketing would be an appropriate strategy.

Effective segmentation requires segments that are large, distinct, homogenous, measurable, and reachable.

[42] Jeffrey N. Birnbaum, "With 1,134 Editions, *Farm Journal* Labors to Please All of Its Readers," *Wall Street Journal* (January 21, 1983), p. 25.

[43] Julie Salamon, "Bank in Connecticut Recovers by Ignoring the Big Companies and Small Consumers," *Wall Street Journal* (August 16, 1983), pp. 35, 42.

[44] Jesse Snyder, "Ford Cultivating Larger Tractor Market," *Advertising Age* (February 27, 1984), p. 57.

2. Within each segment there must be enough consumer *similarities* to develop an appropriate marketing plan for the entire segment.

3. The firm must be able to *measure* the characteristics and needs of consumers in order to establish groups. This may be difficult for life-style factors.

4. The segments must be *large* enough to generate sales and cover costs.

5. The members of a segment must be *reachable* in an efficient manner. For example, young women can be reached through *Seventeen* magazine. It is efficient because males and older women do not read the magazine.

Table 8-7
Segmentation of the Office Photocopier Market

Market Segment	Speed (copies/min.)	Volume (copies/mo.)	Price Range	Examples
1	to 12	to 5,000	to $2,500	Canon PC-10, PC-20 Panasonic FP-1300 Ricoh FW 420 Royal 110 Sharp SF-755 Xerox 1020
2	to 20	to 10,000	to $3,500	Minolta 320 Panasonic FP-1801 Ricoh FT 4030 Savin 765, 770 Sharp SF-771, SF-781 Xerox 1035
3	20-30	to 25,000	to $5,000	Panasonic 2520 Royal 130R Savin 760, 790 Sharp SF-815 Xerox 3300 Canon NP-270 Pitney Bowes 9600
4	30-45	to 50,000	to $10,000	Sharp SF-900 Xerox 1045 Savin 5030, 5040 Canon NP-300, NP-400 Ricoh FT 6600 FDS Royal 145, 145R
5	45-70	to 75,000	to $50,000	Canon NP-500 Kodak Ektaprint 100 Xerox 1075, 7000
6	70-90	to 100,000	to $100,000	Kodak Ektaprint 150 Kodak Ektaprint 200 Xerox 8200 IBM Series III
7	90-120 +	100,000 +	$100,000 +	Xerox 9200 Series Kodak Ektaprint 250 IBM Series III

Note: In the fast-moving copier market, traditional classification criteria are less definitive than they were in recent years. Thus, some of the listed products may not satisfy all the criteria of the product segments in which they were grouped.
Source: Adapted from "Business Equipment In the '80s," *Forbes* (March 26, 1984), p. Advertisement 18. Reprinted by permission.

Limitations of Segmentation

Although segmentation is usually a consumer-oriented, efficient, and profitable marketing technique, it should not be abused. Firms can divide markets into segments that are too small, misinterpret consumer similarities and differences, become cost inefficient, spin off too many imitations of original brands, become myopic in research, be unable to use certain media, try to compete in too many disparate segments, confuse consumers, or become locked into a market segment that is declining.

Sales Forecasting

As a company develops its target market, it should forecast the short-run (one-year) and long-run (five-year) sales of its product or service to that market. A *sales forecast* outlines expected company sales for a specific product or service to a specific consumer group over a specific period of time under a well-defined marketing program. By accurately forecasting sales, the firm is able to pinpoint areas of growth, develop a marketing budget, allocate marketing resources, measure success, analyze sales productivity, monitor the external environment, monitor competition, and modify marketing plans.

In order to estimate company sales, a firm should first look at industry forecasts, because they usually have a strong bearing on the sales of an individual company. Next, sales potential outlines the upper sales limit for the firm, based on marketing and production capacity. Then a sales forecast details a firm's realistic sales level. The forecast is based on the expected environment and performance of the firm. Figure 8-11 shows the sales-forecasting process.

A *sales forecast* predicts company sales over a specified period of time.

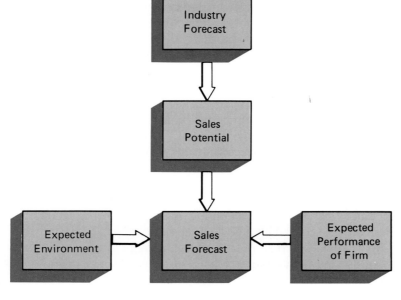

Figure 8-11
Developing a Sales Forecast

A sales forecast should take into account demographics (such as per capita income and number of households), economic conditions (such as the GNP and the rate of inflation), the competitive environment (such as price and advertising levels), last year's sales, and other variables. When constructing a sales forecast, precision is required. The forecast should break sales down by specific product or service (model 123), specific consumer group (adult female), time period (January through March), and type of marketing plan (market segmentation).

Data Sources

Data for forecasts may be obtained from government sources and industry and business publications.

A company has several available sources to generate the data needed for a sales forecast. The government collects and stores information on national and local population trends, past sales by industry and product type, and economic conditions. Industry trade associations put out publications and maintain libraries dealing with a variety of sales statistics. For example, the Conference Board publishes widely and maintains an extensive library for member firms. General business publications, such as *Business Week* and *Fortune,* conduct a variety of forecasts on a regular basis.

The firm can also obtain data from present and future customers, executives, sales personnel, and internal records. This information will usually center on company rather than industry predictions.

Methods of Sales Forecasting

Various methods of sales forecasting can be undertaken by a firm. The methods range from simple and unsophisticated to complex and quite sophisticated. Among the simple methods are trend analysis, market share analysis, jury of executive or expert opinion, sales force surveys, and consumer surveys. Among the more complex methods are the chain-ratio technique, market buildup method, and statistical analyses. At the end of this section, Table 8-8 contains illustrations of each of these forecasting methods. By combining two or more of these techniques, the firm can develop a better sales forecast and minimize the weaknesses inherent in any one technique.

With *simple trend analysis,* a firm extends past sales into the future.

Under ***simple trend analysis,*** the firm forecasts future sales on the basis of recent or current performance. For example, if the company's sales have increased an average of 10 per cent each year over the past five years, it forecasts next year's sales to be 10 per cent higher than this year's. While this technique is the easiest to use, the problems with simple trend analysis are that past sales fluctuations, the economy, changing consumer tastes, changing competition, and market saturation are not considered. A firm's growth rate may change as a result of these factors. In addition, all firms in an industry do not progress at the same rate.

With *market share analysis,* a constant market share is assumed.

Market share analysis is similar to simple trend analysis, except that the company bases its forecast on the assumption that its share of industry sales will remain constant. Although market share analysis has the same weaknesses as simple trend analysis, it does enable an aggressive or declining firm to adjust its forecast and marketing efforts.

The *jury of executive or expert opinion* is a forecasting method used when the management of a company or other well-informed persons meet, discuss the future, and set sales estimates based on the group's experience and intuition. By itself, this method excludes statistical data and relies too heavily on informal analysis. In conjunction with other methods, it is effective because it enables experts to direct, interpret, and respond to concrete data. Because management establishes objectives, sets priorities, and guides an organization's destiny, its input is mandatory.

The firm's employees most in touch with consumers and the external environment are sales personnel. *Sales force surveys* enable the company to obtain input in a structured way. Sales personnel are frequently able to pinpoint coming trends, strengths and weaknesses in the company's offering, competitive strategies, customer resistance, and the traits of heavy users. They can also break sales forecasts down by product category, customer grouping, and geographic area. On the other hand, sales personnel can have a limited perspective, offer biased replies, and misinterpret consumer desires.

Many market researchers believe that the best indicators of future sales are consumer attitudes. By conducting *consumer surveys,* a company can obtain a variety of information: purchase intentions, future expectations (optimistic-pessimistic), rate of consumption, brand switching, time between purchases, and reasons for purchases. Consumers are not always willing to reply to company surveys and may act differently from what they believe or state.

Under the *chain-ratio method,* the firm starts with general market information and then computes a series of more specific market information. These combined data yield a sales forecast. The chain-ratio method is only as accurate as the data plugged in for each market factor. Nonetheless, it is a useful tool because it requires management to think through the sales forecast and obtain different kinds of information.

The opposite approach to the chain-ratio method is the *market buildup method.* With the market buildup method, the firm gathers data from small, separate market segments and aggregates them. For example, the market buildup method enables a company operating in four metropolitan areas to develop a forecast by first estimating sales in each area and then adding the areas.

When using the market buildup method, a marketer must note that consumer tastes, competition, population growth, and media differ by geographic area. Areas or consumer groups of equal size may offer entirely dissimilar sales opportunities. They should not be lumped together indiscriminately on the basis of simple demographics.

Test marketing provides a form of market buildup analysis in which the firm estimates total future sales from the short-run, geographically limited sales of a product or service. In test marketing, the company usually introduces a new product or service into one or a few markets for a short period of time. The full marketing campaign of the firm is carried out during the test. After the test is completed, the company forecasts future sales from test market sales. The firm must remember that test areas may not be representative of all locations. Furthermore, test market enthusiasm may not carry over into national distribution. Test marketing is discussed in greater depth in Chapter 10.

A number of detailed statistical analyses are available for sales forecasting.

The *jury of executive* or *expert opinion* method has well-informed people estimate sales.

Sales force surveys use input from personnel who are most in touch with consumers.

Through *consumer surveys*, attitudes and intentions are assessed.

With the *chain-ratio method,* the firm uses general data and develops specific information.

The *market buildup method* compiles data from segments to make a prediction.

In test marketing the firm estimates total future sales from short-run, geographically limited sales.

Table 8-8 Sales Forecasting Techniques

Technique	Illustration	Selected Potential Shortcomings with Technique
Simple trend analysis	This year's sales = $2 million; company trend indicates 5 per cent growth per year; sales forecast = $2,100,000	Economic decline not considered
Market share analysis	Current market share = 18 per cent; company seeks stable market share; industry forecast = $10,000,000; company sales forecast = $1,800,000	New competitors and increased marketing efforts by current competition not considered
Jury of executive opinion	In a meeting of six top executives, three see strong growth (12 per cent) and three see limited growth (2 per cent); executives compromise on 6 per cent growth on this year's sales of $11 million; sales forecast = $11,660,000	Change in consumer attitudes not uncovered
Jury of expert opinion	Groups of wholesalers, retailers, suppliers, and consultants meet to predict sales growth. Each group confers and reaches a consensus; top management utilizes each group's forecast in formulating final expert opinion forecast	Each group has different assumptions about economic growth
Sales force survey	Sales personnel report that competitor's price drop of 10 per cent will cause company sales to decline 3 per cent from this year's $7 million; sales forecast = $6,790,000	Sales force unaware that competitor's price cut will be temporary
Consumer survey	85 per cent of current customers (1 million) say they will repurchase next year; 3 per cent of noncustomers (10 million) say they will purchase next year; sales forecast = 1,150,000 customers, an increase of 15 per cent	Consumer intentions may not reflect actions
Chain-ratio method	Sales forecast (units) for introductory marketing text = number of college students $\times$ per cent annually enrolled in introductory marketing $\times$ per cent purchasing a new book $\times$ expected market share = (10,000,000) $\times$ (.07) $\times$ (.87) $\times$ (.11) = 66,990	Inaccurate estimate of enrollment in introductory marketing course
Market buildup method	Total sales forecast = region 1 forecast + region 2 forecast + region 3 forecast; sales forecast = $2,000,000 + $7,000,000 + $13,000,000 = $22,000,000	Incorrect assumption that areas will behave similarly in the future
Test marketing	Total sales forecast = (Sales in test market A + sales in test market B) $\times$ (25); sales forecast = ($1,000,000 + $1,200,000) $\times$ (25) = $55,000,000	Test markets not representative of all locations
Detailed statistical analyses	Simulation, complex trend analysis (time-series analysis), regression, and correlation	Lack of understanding by management; not all factors affecting demand can be quantified

Simulation allows a company to enter several market factor statistics into a computer-based model and forecast under varying conditions and marketing plans. With complex trend analysis (time-series analysis), the firm includes past sales fluctuations (seasonal and long term), cyclical factors (such as economic conditions), and other factors when developing short-run and long-run sales trends. Regression and correlation techniques seek to explore the mathematical relationships between future sales and market factors, such as total family income. These methods depend on reliable data and the ability of personnel and management to use them correctly. A deeper discussion is beyond the scope of this text.

Detailed statistical analyses use the methods of simulation, complex trend analysis (time-series analysis), regression, and correlation.

Additional Considerations

The method and accuracy of sales forecasting depend a great deal on the newness of a firm's offering. A forecast for a continuing product or service should utilize trend analysis, market share analysis, executive and expert opinion, and sales force surveys. Barring major changes in the economy, competition, or consumer tastes, the sales forecast should be relatively accurate.

A forecast for a continuing product should be the most accurate, while one for a completely new product should be the least.

A sales forecast for a product or service that is new to the firm but continuing in the industry should utilize trade association data, executive and expert opinion, sales force surveys, consumer surveys, and test marketing. The sales forecast for the first year should be somewhat accurate, the following years more accurate. It is difficult to estimate first-year sales, because consumer acceptance and competitive reactions are difficult to gauge precisely.

A sales forecast for a product or service that is new to both the firm and the industry needs to rely on consumer surveys, test marketing, sales force surveys, executive and expert opinion, and simulation. The sales forecast for the first two to three years may be highly inaccurate, because the speed of consumer acceptance is difficult to measure precisely. Later forecasts will be more accurate. Even though the initial sales forecast may be inaccurate, it is necessary for the reasons cited earlier: pinpointing growth, budgeting, allocating resources, measuring success, monitoring the environment and competition, and setting market plans.

The firm must also consider sales penetration when forecasting future sales. **Sales penetration** is the degree to which a company achieves its sales potential. It is expressed as:

Sales penetration describes whether a company has reached its potential. Diminishing returns may result if a firm seeks nonconsumers.

Sales penetration = Actual sales ÷ Sales potential.

A firm with a high sales penetration level must realize that ***diminishing returns*** may occur if it attempts to convert the remaining nonconsumers of its products, because the costs of attracting these people may outweigh the revenues. Other products or segments may offer better opportunities. An illustration of sales penetration and diminishing returns is shown in Table 8-9.

Again, the company must remember that a number of factors may change and cause the sales forecast to be inaccurate unless revised. These include economic conditions, industry conditions, company performance, competition, and consumer tastes.

**Table 8-9
An Illustration of Sales
Penetration and
Diminishing Returns**

Year 1	Year 2
Sales potential = $1,000,000	Sales potential = $1,000,000
Actual sales = $600,000 (60,000 units)	Actual sales = $700,000 (70,000 units)
Selling price = $10/unit	Selling price = $10/unit
Total marketing costs = $100,000	Total marketing costs = $150,000
Total production	Total production
costs (at $8/unit) = $480,000	costs (at $8/unit) = $560,000

$$\text{Sales penetration} = \frac{\$600,000}{\$1,000,000} = \underline{\underline{60\%}} \qquad \text{Sales penetration} = \frac{\$700,000}{\$1,000,000} = \underline{\underline{70\%}}$$

$$\begin{aligned} \text{Total profit} &= \$600,000 - \\ &\quad (\$100,000 + \$480,000) \\ &= \underline{\underline{\$20,000}} \end{aligned} \qquad \begin{aligned} \text{Total profit} &= \$700,000 - \\ &\quad (\$150,000 + \$560,000) \\ &= \underline{\underline{-\$10,000}} \end{aligned}$$

In Year 1, sales penetration is 60 per cent and the firm earns a $20,000 profit. In Year 2, the firm raises its marketing expenditures drastically in order to increase sales penetration to 70 per cent; as a result it suffers diminishing returns—the additional $100,000 in actual sales are more than offset by a $130,000 rise in total costs (from $580,000 in Year 1 to $710,000 in Year 2).

Summary

Mass marketing (appealing to many customers through one basic marketing plan), market segmentation (appealing to one, well-defined consumer group through one marketing program), and multiple segmentation (appealing to two or more well-defined consumer groups through different marketing plans) are the alternative methods by which a firm can develop a target market. In choosing a method, the company must examine its resources and abilities, objectives, competition, consumer characteristics and needs, channel requirements, profits, and image. In recent years, pure mass marketing has declined, whereas market and multiple segmentation have grown.

When segmenting, a company must be careful to understand the majority fallacy: selecting the largest consumer segment, which also has the greatest number of competitors and brands. Untapped, smaller segments may offer greater potential.

Segmentation can be based on one or a combination of geographic demographics, personal demographics, social factors, and psychological factors. The heavy-half theory, benefit segmentation, and the VALS classification are useful ways of defining market groups.

Six steps are necessary to create a segmentation strategy: determining consumer characteristics and needs, analyzing consumer similarities and differences, developing consumer group profiles, selecting consumer segment(s), positioning the company's offering in relation to competition, and establishing the marketing plan. Organizational consumer segments deserve separate analysis and planning by firms, even though the procedure for developing a target market is similar to that for final consumers. Successful segmentation planning requires large enough segments, differences among segments, similarities within segments, measurable consumer traits and needs, and efficiency in reaching segments.

Marketers should forecast short-run (one-year) and long-run (five-year) sales in conjunction with the development of target markets. This will enable them to pinpoint growth, compute budgets, allocate resources, measure success, analyze productivity, monitor the external environment and competition, and adjust marketing plans. A sales forecast describes the expected company sales of a specific product or service to a specific consumer group over a specific time period under a well-defined marketing program.

The company can obtain the data needed for sales forecasting from the government, industry trade associations, general publications, present and future customers, executives, experts, sales personnel, and internal records. A number of simple and complex methods are available for sales forecasting. These include simple trend analysis, market share analysis, jury of executive and expert opinion, sales force surveys, consumer surveys, chain-ratio method, market buildup method, and detailed statistical analyses. The best results are obtained when several methods and forecasts are combined.

The sales forecast should take into account the level of newness of the firm's offering, sales penetration, diminishing returns, and the changing nature of many variables.

Questions for Discussion

1. Evaluate Huffy's strategy for marketing adult bicycles.
2. Why has the use of a pure mass-marketing approach declined? Does this mean there is no place for mass marketing? Explain your answer.
3. Compare market segmentation and multiple segmentation.
4. Provide an example of a company that has had problems because it ignored the majority fallacy when marketing a new product.
5. How could a furniture manufacturer utilize geographic-demographic segmentation?
6. Develop a personal-demographic profile of the students in your marketing class. For what products and services would the class be a good market segment?
7. What are the benefits and risks of appealing to the heavy-half market segment?
8. Describe several potential benefit segments for telephones.
9. Develop a marketing strategy to appeal to the traditionalist segment of the beer market shown in Table 8-5. How does this differ from Brewers' strategy for the health-conscious market?
10. The Johnston Company wants to sell elastic bandages to both hospitals and final consumers. Create marketing strategies for each.
11. Apply the requirements for successful segmentation to Trident sugarless gum.
12. What factors affect the accuracy of a sales forecast?
13. Distinguish between the chain-ratio and market buildup methods of sales forecasting.
14. Why are long-run sales forecasts for new products more accurate than short-run forecasts.
15. A firm has a sales potential of $1,000,000 and attains actual sales of $950,000. What does this signify? What should the firm do next?

Case 1 Seeking New Markets for Gatorade*

Gatorade was developed by Dr. Robert Cade, a professor of medicine at the University of Florida, in 1965. Dr. Cade created the salt, water, and glucose drink to enable the university's football players to withstand the intense Florida sun. Gatorade initially tasted "like steel and salt water."

Then in 1967, Stokely obtained the rights to Gatorade. First, it improved the drink's taste by adding orange and lemon-lime flavors. Next, it sent samples to professional and school athletic teams and coaches throughout the U.S. Sales grew rapidly. Vince Lombardi (then the legendary coach of the Green Bay Packers football team) endorsed Gatorade.

After reaching a high level of sales penetration in its prime market segment (athletes), Stokely broadened its approach and targeted construction and factory workers and "anyone in a high-temperature environment." A powdered Gatorade was added in 1979. By 1982, Gatorade revenues had reached about $100 million annually.

In mid-1983, Quaker Oats purchased Gatorade from Stokely and immediately stated plans to increase Gatorade's market geographically and demographically. Said Quaker Oats' president, "Gatorade has been undermarketed, especially outside of the Sunbelt." At that time, these were the characteristics of Gatorade's target market:

- The Southeast and Southwest accounted for over 60 per cent of sales, in large part due to the high level of outdoor exercise and the "brutal" sun.
- Heavy users represented one third of customers, yet contributed 85 per cent of sales volume.
- The customer base was still largely limited to people engaged in sports activities.
- Few women or children consumed Gatorade.

Quaker is determined to expand U.S. Gatorade sales outside the Sunbelt, enter international markets, and attract women and children as consumers, despite some observers' belief that Gatorade's market is saturated and cannot be broadened. This is a particularly important product to the company, since it complements Quaker's traditional winter-oriented product lines.

QUESTIONS

1. Evaluate the target market served by Gatorade at the time it was purchased by Quaker Oats. Relate your answer to the heavy-half theory.
2. How can Gatorade attract women and children?
3. What are the risks of Quaker Oats' plans to broaden Gatorade's market?
4. Quaker Oats planned to advertise extensively during the 1984 Summer Olympics. Comment on this plan.
5. What technique(s) should be used to forecast next year's sales of Gatorade?

* The data in this case are drawn from Janet Neiman, "Quaker to Push Gatorade Outside the Sunbelt," *Advertising Age* (November 7, 1983), p. 20; and "Quaker Sees New Markets for Gatorade," *New York Times* (August 8, 1983), p. D4.

Case 2 A New Target Market Approach for the Yellow Pages[†]

"Let your fingers do the walking through the Yellow Pages" is a long-standing advertising slogan, aimed at maximizing final consumer and business use of the Yellow Pages. Until recently, one Yellow Pages directory in a geographic area serviced both groups of consumers. Now, in some areas, the slogan might be changing to, "Your fingers have two Yellow Pages directories to walk through."

In Cincinnati, as in a number of cities, there are Consumer Yellow Pages and Business-to-Business Yellow Pages. The consumer directory, which is provided to residential telephone customers, does not include listings geared mostly to business (such as machine tools and abrasives companies). The business directory, which is provided to commercial telephone customers, does not include listings geared mostly to final consumers (such as beauty salons and dry cleaners). Advertisers that appeal to both final consumers and business accounts must buy space in each of the directories.

This multiple-segmentation strategy is highly desired by directory publishers, who are able to increase their profits. However, many advertisers are not happy with this approach and are complaining bitterly about it. In Cincinnati, for example, Howard Mees is disturbed that his ceramic-tile and marble business must take out ads in both directories. Previously, Mees placed one ad under the "Tile-Ceramic" heading. Albert Lane is even more upset. Although he sells commercial and industrial properties to individuals and to businesses, he is not allowed to advertise in the Consumer Yellow Pages. "My customers could live in an apartment and they can't find me in the Yellow Pages."

In response, a spokesperson for the directories' publisher said this about the business-to-business directory: "The number of complaints aren't enough to make us drop it. [The company] gets calls from people who say they use it and would be lost without it." Furthermore, the costs of advertising in one specialized directory are less than the costs of an ad in a combined directory.

Business-to-business directories have done well in a number of cities, such as New York. They have failed in many others, including Denver, Dallas, Phoenix, and Portland.

QUESTIONS
1. Why do some advertisers like two Yellow Page directories, while others want a single directory?
2. What geographic-demographic factors would favor a successful multiple segmentation strategy for Yellow Pages?
3. Apply benefit segmentation to Yellow Pages directories.
4. Explain the development of Business-to-Business Yellow Pages in terms of sales penetration and diminishing returns.

---

† Sanford L. Jacobs, "Split Yellow Pages Highlight Problems in Phone-Book Ads," *Wall Street Journal* (December 5, 1983), p. 31.

Part Two Case General Electric: Serving Diverse Consumer Markets*

General Electric (GE) is one of the largest industrial corporations in the United States, with annual sales of about $30 billion. GE is a highly diversified company, involved with such products and services as major appliances, out-of-warranty appliance repair, hospital diagnostic equipment, electrical manufacturing, computer information service, aircraft engines, televisions, and audio electronics.

As a marketing-oriented firm, GE understands that the characteristics and needs of consumers differ for each of its businesses, and enacts marketing plans accordingly. This is illustrated by GE's separate approaches to the marketing of major consumer appliances and military aircraft engines.

Major Consumer Appliances

GE produces a full range of major consumer appliances, including electric and gas ranges, dishwashers, refrigerators, freezers, ovens, washers, and dryers. Its annual appliance sales are about $3 billion.

The major appliance industry is characterized by efficient production, consistently ranking in the top ten of all industries monitored by the Department of Labor. A basic refrigerator costs less today (in inflation-adjusted dollars) than it did ten years ago; the present model is also likely to be frost-free and use about 35 per cent less energy.

GE is a leader in an industry that has been so competitive that less than 25 firms now make major appliances, down from about 230 U.S. manufacturers at the end of World War II. Among the companies that have abandoned the major appliance business because of high losses are General Motors, Ford, and United Technologies.

The differences among competing brands are relatively small. According to the president of White Consolidated (marketer of brands such as Kelvinator, Westinghouse, Frigidaire, Gibson, and private-label appliances), "The quality spread from best to worst has become very narrow." Said a Whirlpool executive, "It's a marketing game. We all know how to make these things, and we all have pretty good quality."

About 80 per cent of major appliance sales are made directly to final consumers. As a result of the small growth rate of the U.S. population, most of the purchases are made by consumers already owning appliances rather than first-time purchases by new customers. The average life span for major appliances is 12 to 15 years; and according to experts, about one third of refrigerators and

* The data in this case are drawn from ''Ninth Annual Major Appliance Statistical and Marketing Report,'' *Merchandising* (November 1983), pp. 15–16 ff; Lisa Miller Mesdag, ''The Appliance Boom Begins,'' *Fortune* (July 25, 1983), pp. 52–57; Walter S. Mossberg and Edward T. Pound, ''How Pratt & Whitney Gains from the Way U.S. Buys Spare Parts,'' *Wall Street Journal* (October 3, 1983), pp. 1, 25; ''Pratt & Whitney: Revving Up to Offset Its Military Disappointments,'' *Business Week* (February 20, 1984), pp. 48, 53–54; Gerald F. Seib, ''Competition to Win Air Force Engine Job Splits Pentagon, Angers Some Legislators,'' *Wall Street Journal* (January 12, 1984), p. 27; Stratford P. Sherman, ''Casualty in the Engine War,'' *Fortune* (March 5, 1984), pp. 59–60; and Winston Williams, ''How GE Won Engine War,'' *New York Times* (February 15, 1984), pp. D1, D5.

ranges currently in use are over ten years old. For example, one observer has stated that 25 million refrigerators are on the verge of collapse. The remaining 20 per cent of major appliance sales are made to builders of traditional housing and mobile homes.

Final consumers require a distinct set of product, distribution, promotion, price, and service characteristics. They desire

- An extensive range of product features and options from which to choose. Thus, General Electric makes models with different capacities, functions, colors, prices, etc. It offers products for all consumer segments, such as its Hotpoint "value" line and its GE "quality" line.
- Space-efficient products. To satisfy this need, General Electric offers items such as microwave ovens that are installed above kitchen ranges instead of on countertops.
- Distribution through a number of convenient outlets that stock a wide product assortment. In response, General Electric sells through many different retailers and suppliers, as shown in Table 1. Its Hotpoint and GE brands are both stocked by most of these retailers.
- Information from noncommercial sources. Favorable *Consumer Reports* evaluations have contributed to GE dishwashers maintaining industry leadership with a 22 per cent market share of sales.
- Information from commercial sources. General Electric sponsors company ads and participates in cooperative advertising with retailers. Salespeople may receive $5 to $20 each time a GE appliance is sold. As White Consolidated's president noted, "Once the customer is in the store, the salesman is in control."
- Fair prices. General Electric offers competitive prices and a wide selection of price ranges.
- Credit availability. To accommodate this, GE has offered its own credit plans, such as a Christmas promotion providing "no payments until February."
- After-purchase service. General Electric provides an 800-number "hotline," regular warranty service, and out-of-warranty service (for a fee).

Table 1 Major Appliance Sales by Type of Outlet, 1983

Outlet	Per Cent of Sales by Product Category					
	Dishwashers	Dryers	Electric Ranges	Freezers	Refrigerators	Washers
Builder/contractor	31	5	12	1	14	4
Appliance/television store	24	34	39	14	32	34
Catalog store (e.g., Sears, J. C. Penney)	24	38	21	48	29	39
Kitchen remodeler	6	—	12	1	2	—
Discount store	6	8	3	14	5	8
Home improvement center	3	—	4	2	3	—
Plumbing contractor	2	—	—	—	—	—
Department store	2	8	4	14	6	8
Furniture store	1	4	3	4	5	4
Catalog showroom	1	3	1	—	—	3
Other	—	—	1	2	4	—
Total	100	100	100	100	100	100

Source: "Ninth Annual Major Appliance Statistical and Marketing Report," *Merchandising* (November 1983), pp. 16, 18, 21, 22.

Builders usually require appliance manufacturers to submit competitive bids for kitchen packages, based on builder specifications. GE exerts high control over this market segment. For example, several years ago, GE introduced a new almond color for its appliance line. Since all appliances had to be color-coordinated, and the other manufacturers' almond color did not match GE's, these firms were quickly forced to accept the GE color as the industry standard.

Military Aircraft Engines

Overall, GE has annual aircraft engine sales (both military and commercial) of more than $3 billion, and it is quite aggressive in this area. In early 1984, GE won significant new long-term contracts for military aircraft engines. The Air Force decided to purchase GE engines for F-15 and F-16 fighter jets; and the Navy agreed to buy the engines for F-14 fighter jets. Until GE received these contracts, Pratt & Whitney (a division of United Technologies) had manufactured all the engines for the F-14, F-15, and F-16 jets. GE was producing engines for two other aircraft, the B-1 bomber and the C-5 cargo plane.

For a number of reasons, GE was asked to submit competitive bids with Pratt & Whitney for F-14, F-15, and F-16 engine contracts. Each firm was given one year to prepare its proposal:

- Competition was desired between contractors to reduce the price of jet engines.
- The Pentagon was concerned about a single firm providing engines for the major fighter jets of both the Air Force and Navy. However, there was also uncertainty about maintenance and spare-parts complications if two manufacturers supplied engines.
- Pratt & Whitney engines faced product quality questions. The company had been slow to correct problems. Greater reliability and durability were desired.
- Pratt & Whitney had been accused of overcharging for spare parts.

In bidding for the contracts, Pratt & Whitney and GE each offered a unique combination of advantages. Pratt & Whitney's engine was a derivative of one used by the Air Force for many years, thus reducing spare parts and maintenance problems as well as development costs. The new engine would readily fit the fighter jets. In addition, the Pratt & Whitney engine was 600 pounds lighter than the GE version.

General Electric had invested $100 million annually for several years to improve its aircraft engine performance. It was perceived as the lowest-cost manufacturer. Its engine was more powerful than that of Pratt & Whitney. GE would allow spare parts to be purchased directly from suppliers (instead of adding a distribution layer by forcing the government to buy from General Electric). A 1,000-hour engine warranty was proposed.

The bids were submitted to the Secretaries of the Air Force and the Navy. They consulted with experts, and passed on their recommendations to the Secretary of Defense. The latter made the final selection, with budget approval from Congress. GE won contracts to produce three quarters of the engines for the F-15 and F-16 and all of the F-14 engines. Commented a Pratt & Whitney spokesperson, "We are surprised the Navy has chosen the [GE engine] without competition, particularly since the Air Force and the Defense Department have been so strongly advocating competing purchases of engines."

QUESTIONS

1. What consumer demographic and life-style factors have the greatest impact on major appliances? How should GE react to these factors?
2. One major appliance industry observer notes that manufacturers have been unsuccessful at convincing people to trade in working models for units that are more fashionable or have more functions. Comment on this.
3. How would the consumer's decision process (Figure 6-7) for a major appliance differ for a replacement customer than for a first-time customer?
4. Interpret the data in Table 1. What are the implications for GE?
5. Use the organizational consumer's decision process (Figure 7-10) to explain the government's behavior in selecting between GE and Pratt & Whitney military aircraft engines.
6. Evaluate the statement of the Pratt & Whitney spokesperson regarding the Navy's decision to select GE as the sole supplier of F-14 engines.
7. Differentiate between the military aircraft engine market segment and the commerical aircraft engine market segment (e.g., Eastern, Delta).

In order to carry out the marketing concept (consumer satisfaction, integrated effort, and attainment of company goals), a firm must develop, implement, and monitor a systematic marketing plan. This plan centers on the four elements of the marketing mix: product, distribution, promotion, and price. Parts Three through Six examine each of these four elements in detail and show their interrelationship. Part Three describes product planning and its components.

Chapter 9 offers an overview to product planning, the systematic decision making pertaining to all aspects of the development and management of a firm's products. Tangible, extended, and generic products are defined and different types of consumer and industrial products are distinguished. Width and depth of product assortment are considered and the various types of product management forms are detailed. The use of product positioning, the analysis of consumer perceptions of the firm's and competitors' products, is explained. The product life cycle concept is described and evaluated.

Chapter 10 deals with the development and management of products from their inception to their deletion. The coverage of new products includes a description of new product types, why new products fail, and the new-product-planning process: idea generation, product screening, concept testing, business analysis, product development, test marketing, and commercialization. The growth of products is shown in terms of the adoption and diffusion processes. Several methods for extending the lives of mature products are described. Finally, product deletion decisions and strategies are detailed.

Chapter 11 consists of two sections, branding and packaging. Branding is the procedure followed in researching, developing, and implementing brand names, brand marks, trade characters, and trademarks. Branding decisions include corporate symbols, branding philosophy, choice of brand name, and the use of trademarks. Packaging involves a product's physical container, label, and inserts. Packaging serves six basic functions: containment, usage, communication, market segmentation, channel cooperation, and new-product planning. Several packaging decisions are examined. A number of criticisms of packaging are addressed.

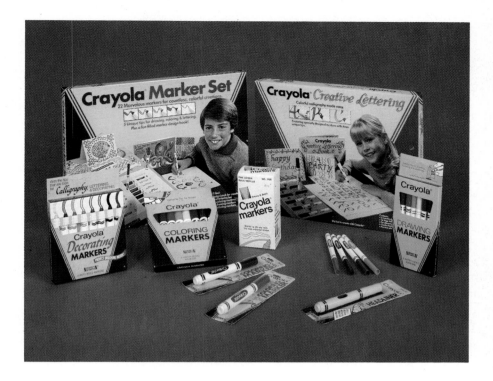

Binney & Smith has made Crayola crayons for more than eighty years. Today, Binney & Smith's Crayola product lines include crayons, markers, activity books, and lettering sets. Under the Liquitex brand, Binney & Smith offers a full range of materials and supplies for artists. Reprinted by permission.

Now it's easier to leave word anywhere.

Press on a 3M Post-it® Note anywhere you want it noticed. It stays put without tape, tacks, paper clips or staples. The secret is a unique 3M adhesive that holds on almost any surface, then peels away easily.

The idea was born of a 3M employee's need to mark pages in a choir book. But it's become a communications medium that's creating a minor revolution among note-leavers everywhere.

By listening to people's needs, 3M has pioneered over 700 products for office, training and business problems. We've developed everything from correction tape for typists to microfilm systems that file 20,000 lines a minute and laser systems that find any of 108,000 computer data frames in just 3 seconds.

And it all began by listening.

3M hears you...

For a free brochure on all 3M products and capabilities write: Dept. 061811/3M P.O. Box 22002, Robbinsdale, MN 55422.

Name_____

Address_____

City_____State_____Zip_____

Or call toll-free: **1-800-33M-HEAR** or 1-800-336-4327.

© 1983, 3M

3M is widely recognized for its new-product development process, which encourages open communication, an entrepreneurial spirit, and a willingness to take risks. As indicated in this advertisement, 3M developed Post-it note paper after an employee suggested the idea, because his place mark kept falling out of his hymn book. Courtesy of 3M, St. Paul, MN.

Health·tex

Bradlees

Stop & Shop   **Medi Mart**

An important aspect of branding involves an organization's use of corporate symbols. These symbols have a strong impact on a firm's image and on consumer recognition of the firm. Each of the symbols on this page is relatively new and presents the organization's desired current image. They were developed by Selame Design of Newton, Mass. Reprinted by permission of the organizations shown. The Kodak trademark is courtesy of Eastman Kodak Company.

COMEnergy
COMGas
COMElectric

Amoco

Certicare

PRODUCTS BY
Kodak

GENERAL CINEMA CORPORATION

goodwill

Mister Donut

Campbell is phasing out its famous soup cans and replacing them with plastic containers. The containers are lighter, do not require a can opener, and can be used to heat soup in microwave ovens. Reprinted by permission.

Combibloc manufactures aseptic packages that are used with a number of beverage products. Aseptic packages enable beverages to be shipped, displayed, and stored without refrigeration. They also allow the shelf lives of beverages to be extended. Reprinted by permission.

Chapter 9

An Overview of Product Planning

1. To define product planning and differentiate among tangible, extended, and generic products
2. To examine the various types of consumer and industrial products, product mixes, and product management organization forms from which a firm may select
3. To discuss product positioning and its usefulness for marketers
4. To study the different types of product life cycles that a firm may encounter and the stages of the traditional product life cycle (introduction, growth, maturity, and decline)

A chemist for the Rocket Chemical Company invented WD-40 as a lubricant and rust and corrosion preventative for the U.S. government's Atlas missiles in the 1950s. WD-40 was applied to the stainless steel skins of the missiles to protect them. Soon thereafter, company employees began informally experimenting with WD-40 on their personal property. They used the product on items such as squeaky chairs, engines, and rifles. Rocket Chemical "realized it had a diamond in the rough."

Then in the 1960s, cans of WD-40 were sold to an organization that sent gift packs to American soldiers in Vietnam. The soldiers rubbed WD-40 on their rifles, cooking utensils, etc., and they became the biggest fans of the product. Upon their return home, these users of WD-40 quickly found new applications for it, lubricating and protecting tools, equipment, and even home appliances.

While WD-40 was gaining popularity in the late 1960s, John Barry (who formerly worked in new products for 3M) became Rocket's chief executive and changed the company's name to WD-40. Since Barry has been in charge, the firm has not developed or marketed any products other than WD-40. Worldwide, more than 50 million people use WD-40; and sales have increased for 20 straight years—to about $50 million in 1982. Each dollar of WD-40's sales is divided as follows: 44 cents for ingredients and packaging, 23 cents for overhead and advertising, 17 cents for earnings, and 16 cents for taxes.

WD-40 has 36 employees. It operates one manufacturing facility in San Diego, "where the secret ingredients are mixed in a single vat." WD-40 works with independent contractors who package the product in blue-and-yellow cans and bottles and send it to wholesalers and distributors. A large amount of sales are through mail orders. Figure 9-1 shows three of WD-40's package sizes.

Recently, WD-40 has begun broadening its market and distributing through supermarkets. Said one company executive: "We're trying to position the product to one that is found under the kitchen sink as well as in the garage and the workshop. It's a process of education."

When questioned about his one-product strategy, Barry replied:

Figure 9-1
WD-40: An Impressive Success Story
Although WD-40 Company makes only one basic product, it has more than 50 million loyal customers throughout the world. WD-40 is available in a variety of sizes, from a 2-ounce spray can to a 5-gallon pail.

Reprinted by permission.

We're already breaking all the Harvard Business School rules. You're not even supposed to have a one-product company. How can we follow this act? There's fabulous female potential out there. I dream of being under the kitchen sink, I dream of being in the back closet. . . .[1]

While it is highly unusual for a company to grow for 20 years on the strength of just one product, WD-40 certainly has not broken "all the Harvard Business School rules." Whether it be the result of entrepreneurial ingenuity or systematic planning, WD-40 has clearly defined its product, positioned it well relative to competitors, attracted a loyal following, and expanded its market as the product moves through its maturity stage. Can this one-product company continue to grow in the future? That remains to be seen.

The Framework of Product Planning

Product planning is systematic decision making relating to all aspects of the development and management of a firm's products, including branding and packaging. A *product* consists of a basic offering and an accompanying set of image features that seek to satisfy consumer needs. A well-structured product-planning process enables a company to pinpoint potential opportunities, develop appropriate marketing programs, coordinate a mix of products, maintain successful products as long as possible, reappraise faltering products, and delete undesirable products.

Product planning involves developing and managing *products*, the basic offerings of the firm.

A firm should define its products in three distinct ways: tangible, extended, and generic. By combining all three definitions, the firm is better able to identify consumer needs, competitive offerings, and distinctive product attributes. This is illustrated in Figure 9-2.

A *tangible product* is the basic physical entity, service, or idea, which has precise specifications and is offered under a given description or model number. Heinz ketchup, an IBM business computer, a Nikon EM camera, a manicure, a seven-day European cruise on the QE2 (Queen Elizabeth 2), and cutting state income taxes by 3.5 per cent are examples of tangible products. Color, style, taste, size, weight, durability, quality of construction, and efficiency in use are some tangible product features.

A *tangible product* has precise specifications.

An *extended product* includes not only the tangible elements of a product, service, or idea, but also the accompanying cluster of image and service features. For example, one political candidate may receive more votes than another because of his or her charisma, despite identical platform issues (tangible product). The sales of the Cadillac are substantially greater than those of the Lincoln, predominantly due to the image of luxury and status it is able to convey. The purchase of a washing machine involves technical advice, warranty, credit, return

An *extended product* includes image and service features.

---

[1] Ellen Paris, "The One-Mystique Company," *Forbes* (April 26, 1982), p. 103; and "WD-40 Tries Sight-of-Hand," *Sales & Marketing Management* (July 4, 1983), pp. 14, 16.

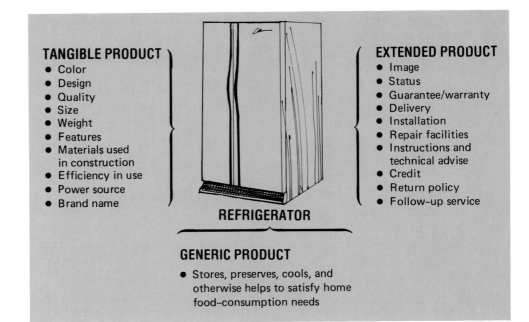

TANGIBLE PRODUCT
- Color
- Design
- Quality
- Size
- Weight
- Features
- Materials used
  in construction
- Efficiency in use
- Power source
- Brand name

EXTENDED PRODUCT
- Image
- Status
- Guarantee/warranty
- Delivery
- Installation
- Repair facilities
- Instructions and
  technical advise
- Credit
- Return policy
- Follow-up service

REFRIGERATOR

GENERIC PRODUCT
- Stores, preserves, cools, and
  otherwise helps to satisfy home
  food-consumption needs

policy, delivery, and instruction in use. The extended product for a computer includes software packages, instructions for users, maintenance, and promptness of service. Service features are often used to distinguish suppliers of undifferentiated products.

A *generic product* centers on consumer benefits.

A ***generic product*** focuses on what a product means to the customer, not the seller. It is the broadest definition of a product. Thus, a buyer of an IBM computer is acquiring an information-processing tool, not a piece of machinery. A generic definition of a product is consistent with the marketing concept that considers the consumer as having a problem-solving orientation:

- ''In the factory we make cosmetics, and in the drugstore we sell hope'' (Charles Revson of Revlon).
- ''One million quarter-inch drills were sold not because people wanted quarter-inch drills, but because they wanted quarter-inch holes'' (Theodore Levitt, Harvard professor).
- ''People no longer buy shoes to keep their feet warm and dry. They buy them because of the way the shoes make them feel—masculine, feminine, rugged, different, sophisticated, young, glamorous, in. Buying shoes has become an emotional experience. Our business now is selling excitement rather than shoes'' (President of Melville Corp., owner of Thom McAn).

This chapter provides an overview of product planning. It examines the basic decisions facing the firm: product type(s), product mix, product management organization, and product positioning. It also describes the product life cycle and its importance for marketers.

Chapter 10 presents an in-depth discussion of product planning from finding new product ideas to deleting existing products. Chapter 11 concentrates on two specialized aspects of product planning: branding and packaging.

Types of Products

The initial decision in product planning is the choice of the type(s) of products to offer. Products can be categorized on the basis of the buyer: consumer or industrial. Categorization is important because it focuses on the differences in the characteristics of products and the resulting implications for marketers.

Consumer Products

Consumer products are goods or services destined for the ultimate consumer for personal, family, or household use. The use of the good or service (not the tangible nature of it) designates it as a consumer product. For example, a calculator, dinner at a restaurant, telephone service, a file cabinet, a vacuum cleaner, and an electric pencil sharpener are consumer products only if they are purchased for personal, family, or household use. The range of consumer products is shown in Figure 9-3 on page 256.

Consumer products are final consumer goods and services.

CONSUMER GOODS

Consumer goods were first classified more than sixty years ago by Melvin T. Copeland.[2] His three-category system of convenience, shopping, and specialty goods is widely employed today. The system is based on shoppers' awareness of alternative products and their characteristics prior to the shopping trip and the degree of search shoppers will undertake. It is important to recognize that placing a product into one of these categories depends on the shopper's behavior. See Table 9-1.

[2] Melvin T. Copeland, "Relation of Consumers' Buying Habits to Marketing Methods," *Harvard Business Review*, Vol. 1 (April, 1923), pp. 282–289.

Table 9-1 Characteristics of Consumer Goods

Consumer Characteristics	Type of Good		
	Convenience	Shopping	Specialty
Awareness of product alternatives and their attributes prior to purchase	High	Low	High
Effort expended to acquire good	Minimal	Moderate to high	As much as necessary
Willingness to accept substitutes	High	Moderate	None
Frequency of purchase	High	Moderate or low	Varies
Information search	Low	High	Varies
Major desire	Availability without effort	Comparison shopping to determine best choice	Brand loyalty regardless of price and availability

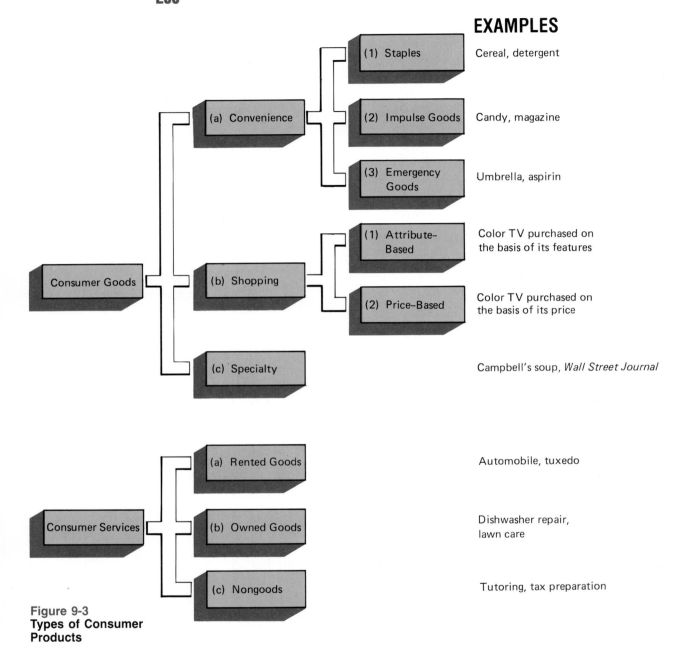

EXAMPLES

(1) Staples — Cereal, detergent

(2) Impulse Goods — Candy, magazine

(3) Emergency Goods — Umbrella, aspirin

(1) Attribute-Based — Color TV purchased on the basis of its features

(2) Price-Based — Color TV purchased on the basis of its price

Specialty — Campbell's soup, *Wall Street Journal*

(a) Rented Goods — Automobile, tuxedo

(b) Owned Goods — Dishwasher repair, lawn care

(c) Nongoods — Tutoring, tax preparation

Figure 9-3
Types of Consumer Products

Convenience goods are purchased with minimum effort and are categorized as *staples*, *impulse goods*, and *emergency goods*.

Convenience goods are those purchased with a minimum of effort, because the buyer has knowledge of product characteristics prior to shopping. The consumer does not want to search for additional information (because the item has been bought before) and will accept a substitute (Libby's instead of Green Giant canned corn) rather than have to frequent more than one store.

The tasks of marketing center on intensive distribution (all available outlets), convenient store locations, evening and weekend store hours, heavy use of mass advertising and in-store displays, well-designed store layouts, and self-service to minimize purchase time. Retailers often carry a number of brands for convenience goods.

Convenience goods can be further divided into staples, impulse goods, and emergency goods. *Staples* are low-priced items that are routinely purchased on a regular basis. *Impulse goods* are items that the consumer does not plan to buy on a specific trip to a store. There are four kinds of impulse purchase:[3]

1. Pure: novelty or escape buying out of the normal routine.
2. Reminder: previous experience remembered.
3. Suggestion: an item seen and evaluated for the first time in the store.
4. Planned: purchase based on a sale or coupon offer.

According to one study, only 35 per cent of grocery store purchases are specifically planned, 18 per cent generally planned, and 47 per cent unplanned.[4] *Emergency goods* are items purchased out of urgent need, such as an umbrella during a rainstorm or a tire to replace a flat.

Shopping goods are those for which consumers lack sufficient information about product alternatives and their attributes, and therefore must acquire further knowledge in order to make a purchase decision. The two major kinds of shopping goods are attribute-based and price-based. For ***attribute-based shopping goods,*** consumers get information about and then evaluate product features, warranty, performance, options, and other factors. The good with the best combination of attributes is purchased. For ***price-based shopping goods,*** consumers judge product attributes to be similar and look around for the least expensive item/store. Consumers will exert effort in searching for information, because shopping goods are bought infrequently.

Attribute-based shopping goods and *price-based shopping goods* require an information search.

The marketing emphasis for shopping goods is on depth of assortment (such as many colors, sizes, options), knowledgeable and persuasive sales personnel, the communication of competitive advantages, informative and persuasive advertising, well-known brands, channel enthusiasm to sell the goods, and customer warranties and follow-up service to reduce perceived risk. Shopping centers and downtown business districts ease shopping behavior by placing several stores in close proximity.

Specialty goods are those to which consumers are brand loyal. They are fully aware of these products and their attributes prior to making a purchase decision. They are willing to make a significant purchase effort to acquire the brand desired and will pay a higher price than competitive products, if necessary. For specialty goods, consumers will not make purchases if their brand is not available.

Consumers are loyal to *specialty goods* and will pay more and exert more effort to acquire them.

The marketing emphasis for specialty goods is on maintaining the product features that make the items so unique to loyal consumers, reminder advertising, distribution appropriate for the product (Hellman's mayonnaise and *Business Week* require different distribution to loyal customers: supermarkets versus home subscriptions), extension of the brand name to related products (such as Hellman's tartar sauce), product improvements, ongoing customer contact (such as *Friends* magazine, published for owners of Chevrolet cars), and monitoring the performance of channel members.

[3] Hawkins Stern, "The Significance of Impulse Buying Today," *Journal of Marketing*, Vol. 26 (April 1962), pp. 59–62.
[4] "Display Effectiveness: An Evaluation," *Nielsen Researcher* (Number 2, 1983), pp. 2–8.

The consumer goods classification system recognizes that many customers view the same products differently. It is an excellent basis for segmentation. For example, Sure deodorant may be a convenience good for some consumers (who will buy Ban or Right Guard if Sure is unavailable), a shopping good for others (who read ingredient labels before selecting a brand), and a specialty good for still others (who insist on Sure regardless of price or availability). Procter & Gamble, maker of Sure, must understand how Sure fits into these different categories to plan its marketing strategy accordingly. Finally, it should be noted that this classification system can be applied to consumer services.

CONSUMER SERVICES

Consumer services involve rented goods, owned goods, and *nongoods.*

There are three broad categories of consumer services: rented goods, owned goods, and nongoods. A *rented-goods service* involves the leasing of a product for a specified period of time. Examples include car, hotel room, apartment, and boat rentals. An *owned-goods service* involves an alteration or repair of a product owned by the consumer. Examples include repair services (such as automobile, watch, and plumbing), lawn care, car wash, haircut, and dry cleaning. A *nongoods service* provides personal service on the part of the seller; it does not involve a product. Examples include accounting, legal, and tutoring services. Services are fully discussed in Chapter 22.

The marketing characteristics of services differ significantly from those of goods:[5]

1. The intangible nature of many services makes the consumer's choice more difficult than with goods.
2. The producer and his or her services are often inseparable.
3. The perishability of services prevents storage and increases risks (for example, the revenues from an unrented hotel room are lost forever).

Industrial Products

Industrial products are organizational consumer goods and services.

Industrial products are goods or services purchased for use in the production of other goods or services, in the operation of a business, or for resale to other consumers. Industrial products include heavy machinery, raw materials, typewriters, janitorial services, and cash registers. An industrial buyer may be a manufacturer, wholesaler, retailer, or government or other nonprofit organization. Figure 9-4 shows the range of industrial products.

INDUSTRIAL GOODS

Industrial goods are categorized by the degree of decision making that is necessary in making a purchase, costs, rapidity of consumption, role in production, and change in form. Because industrial-goods sellers normally seek out potential purchasers, store shopping behavior is not a useful classification method. Installations, accessory equipment, raw materials, component materials, fabricated parts, and supplies are types of industrial goods. Table 9-2 describes these goods.

[5] Richard M. Bessom and Donald W. Jackson, Jr., "Service Retailing: A Strategic Marketing Approach," *Journal of Retailing*, Vol. 51 (Summer 1975), pp. 75–84; and William R. George, "The Retailing of Services—A Challenging Future," *Journal of Retailing*, Vol. 53 (Fall 1977), pp. 85–98.

Installations and *accessory equipment* are capital items. They are used in the production process and do not become part of the final product. Installations involve a high degree of decision making (usually by several upper-level executives), are very expensive, last for many years, and do not change form. The major marketing tasks are direct selling from the manufacturer to the purchaser, lengthy negotiations about features and terms, providing complementary services such as maintenance and repair, tailoring products to the desires of the buyer, technical expertise, and team selling (in which various salespeople have different areas of expertise and interact with specialized executives of the buyer). Examples of installations are buildings, assembly lines, major equipment, large machine tools, and printing presses.

Accessory equipment requires a moderate amount of decision making, is less

Installations and *accessory equipment* are expensive capital items that do not become part of the final product.

Figure 9-4
Types of Industrial Products

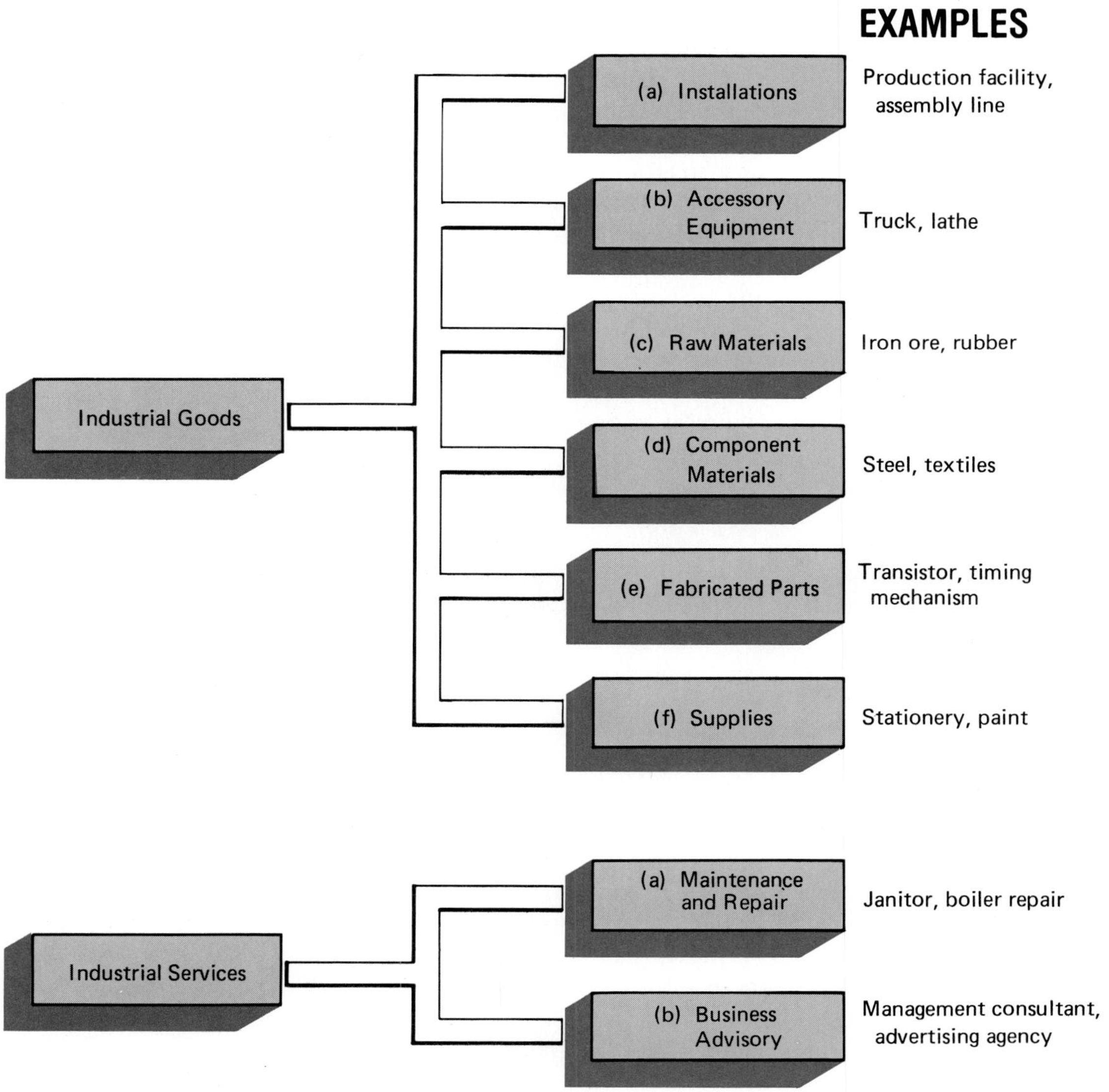

EXAMPLES

	EXAMPLES
(a) Installations	Production facility, assembly line
(b) Accessory Equipment	Truck, lathe
(c) Raw Materials	Iron ore, rubber
(d) Component Materials	Steel, textiles
(e) Fabricated Parts	Transistor, timing mechanism
(f) Supplies	Stationery, paint
(a) Maintenance and Repair	Janitor, boiler repair
(b) Business Advisory	Management consultant, advertising agency

Industrial Goods
Industrial Services

expensive than installations, lasts a number of years, and does not become part of the final product or change its form. The major marketing tasks are tying sales to those of installations; providing a variety of choices in price, size, and capacity; employing a strong channel or sales force; stressing durability and efficiency; and providing technical and maintenance support. Examples of accessory equipment are drill presses, motor trucks, and lift trucks.

Raw materials, component materials, and *fabricated parts* are consumed in production and are considered expense items.

Raw materials, component materials, and ***fabricated parts*** are used in production or become part of final products. They are expense rather than capital items. They require limited decision making by the buyer, are inexpensive on a per unit basis, and are rapidly consumed. Raw materials are unprocessed primary materials from extractive and agricultural industries—minerals, crude petroleum, crops, and iron ore, for example. Component materials are semimanufactured goods that undergo further changes in form—steel, cement, wire, textiles, and basic chemicals, for example. Fabricated parts are placed into a product without further changes in form—electric motors, automobile batteries, refrigerator thermostats, and microprocessors, for example.

The major marketing tasks for materials and parts are to ensure continuity in shipments, quality items, and prompt delivery; actively pursue reorders; implement standardized pricing; employ active channel members or sales personnel; seek long-term contracts; and satisfy specifications set by buyers.

Industrial supplies are used in daily operations.

Industrial supplies are convenience goods that are necessary for the daily operation of the firm. These goods can be maintenance supplies, such as lightbulbs, cleaning materials, and paint; repair supplies, such as rivets, screws, nuts, and bolts; or operating supplies, such as stationery, pens, and business cards.

Industrial supplies do not require extensive decision making by the buyer, are very inexpensive on a per unit basis, are rapidly consumed, and do not become part of the finished product. Marketing emphasis is on availability, promptness, and ease of ordering.

Table 9-2   Characteristics of Industrial Goods

	Type of Good					
Characteristics	**Installations**	**Accessory Equipment**	**Raw Materials**	**Component Materials**	**Fabricated Parts**	**Supplies**
Degree of consumer decision making	High	Moderate	Low	Low	Low	Very low
Per unit costs	High	Moderate	Low	Low	Low	Very low
Rapidity of consumption	Very low	Low	High	High	High	High
Item becomes part of final product	No	No	Yes	Yes	Yes	No
Item undergoes changes in form	No	No	Yes	Yes	No	No
Major consumer desire	Long-term production facility	Modern equipment	Continuous, cost-efficient, graded materials	Continuous, cost-efficient, specified materials	Continuous, cost-efficient, fabricated materials	Continuous, cost-efficient supplies

INDUSTRIAL SERVICES

Industrial services are of two general types: maintenance and repair, and business advisory. *Maintenance and repair services* include painting, machinery repair, and janitorial services. *Business advisory services* include management consulting, advertising agency services, accounting services, and legal services.

Industrial services are intangible, the producer and his or her service are inseparable, and services are perishable. They are frequently purchased on a contract or retainer basis, and some firms undertake the services internally. A general principle is that services can be performed by others, but not eliminated.

Industrial services are classified as *maintenance and repair*, and *business advisory*.

Elements of a Product Mix

After determining the type(s) of products it will offer, a firm needs to outline the variety and assortment of those products. A *product item* is a specific model, brand, or size of a product that the company sells, such as a 4-door Cutlass, Polaroid One-Step camera, or 12-ounce can of Pepsi-Cola.

Usually, a company sells many product items. A *product line* is a group of closely related items. For example, Noxell markets Cover Girl lipstick, eye makeup, and other cosmetics. Campbell makes many varieties of canned soup. Macmillan publishes a number of college textbooks in marketing. A local lawn care firm offers lawn mowing, landscaping, and tree-trimming services.

The *product mix* consists of all the different product lines a firm offers. For instance, Lever Brothers (a subsidiary of Unilever) operates household products, personal products, and foods divisions. Among its well-known brands are All and Wisk detergents, Close-Up and Aim toothpaste, and Promise margarine. Figure 9-5 shows selected brands in Lever's product mix.

A product mix can be described by its *width* (based on the number of different product lines it has), *depth* (based on the number of product items within each product line), and *consistency* (based on the relationship among product lines in terms of their sharing a common end-use, distribution outlets, consumer group[s], and price range). Figure 9-6 shows product mix alternatives in terms of width and depth.

A wide mix enables a firm to diversify its products, appeal to different consumer needs, and encourage one-stop shopping. It also requires resource investments and expertise in different product categories. A deep mix can satisfy the needs of several consumer segments for the same product, maximize shelf space, prevent competitors, cover a range of prices, and sustain dealer support. It also imposes higher costs for inventory, product alterations, and order processing. In addition, there may be some difficulty in differentiating between two similar product items. A consistent mix is generally easier to manage than an inconsistent one. It allows the company to concentrate on marketing and production expertise, create a strong image, and generate solid channel relations. However, excessive consistency may leave the firm vulnerable to environmental threats (such as resource shortages), cyclical or seasonal fluctuations, or decreased growth poten-

A *product item* is a specific model, brand, or size of a product; a *product line* is a group of closely related items; a *product mix* is all the firm's product lines.

A product mix can be explained in terms of its *width, depth,* and *consistency.*

Figure 9-5
**Selected Brands in
Lever's Product Mix**

Reprinted by permission.

tial, because all the emphasis is on a limited product assortment. Figure 9-7 shows the wide/deep mix of General Mills.

Product-mix decisions can have both positive and negative effects on companies, as these examples demonstrate:

- In 1967, Crayola crayons accounted for 87 per cent of Binney & Smith's sales. By 1980, this figure fell to 45 per cent. Binney & Smith has maintained impressive sales growth by adding coloring activity books for children, Crayola markers, artists' materials, and other related products.[6] Figure 9-8 shows some of the newer children's products developed by Binney & Smith.
- In 1978, color televisions contributed nearly 80 per cent of Zenith's sales. By

[6] Gay Jervey, "New Products Painting Rosy Future for Crayola," *Advertising Age* (January 11, 1982), pp. 4, 85.

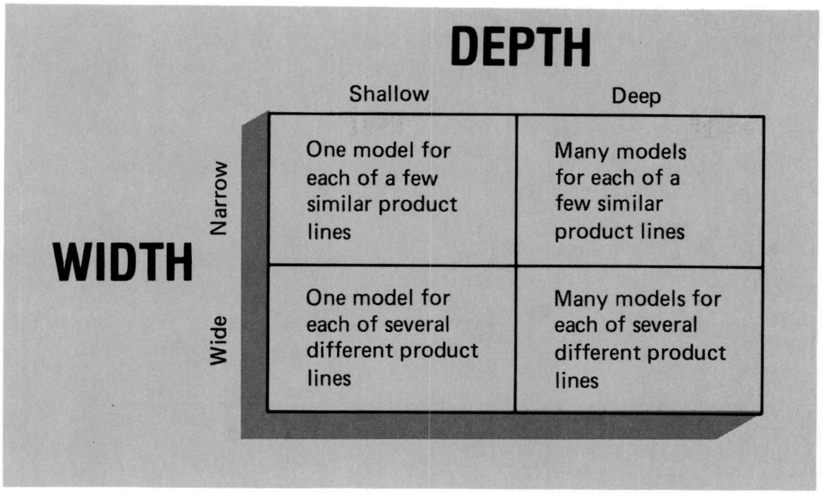

Figure 9-6
Product Mix Alternatives

DEPTH / Shallow / Deep

WIDTH / Narrow / Wide

	Shallow	Deep
Narrow	One model for each of a few similar product lines	Many models for each of a few similar product lines
Wide	One model for each of several different product lines	Many models for each of several different product lines

1982, 60 per cent of sales were devoted to televisions. Zenith's computer and cable television revenues rose dramatically. However, its consumer electronics did not do so well.[7]

- Time Inc. spun off its forest products business into a separate company in 1983. Although forest products yielded 32 per cent of Time's revenues, there were no common characteristics between the marketing of these items and the firm's communications businesses.[8]

- Gillette had to abandon its smoke alarm, pocket calculator, and digital watch product lines when it found it did not possess competence in these areas. Most of Gillette's products are low-cost, repeat-purchase items.[9]

Product Management Organizations

There are several organizational forms of product management from which a firm may choose: marketing manager, product manager, product-planning committee, new-product manager, and venture team. See Table 9-3.

Under a *marketing-manager system* all the functional areas of marketing report to one manager. These areas include sales, advertising, sales promotion, and product planning. This type of system works well for companies with a line of similar products or one dominant product line. It may be less successful when there are many products and brands and each requires a different marketing mix. Pepsi, Purex, Eastman Kodak, and Levi Strauss are companies using some form of marketing-manager system.

All marketing areas report to one manager with a *marketing-manager system*.

[7] Michael Blumstein, "Zenith Regaining Strength," *New York Times* (July 20, 1983), pp. D1, D4.
[8] Sandra Salmans, "Time to Spin Off Forest Unit," *New York Times* (May 20, 1983), pp. D1, D15; and "Humbled and More Cautious, Time Inc. Marches On," *Business Week* (February 13, 1984), pp. 62–63ff.
[9] Pamela G. Hollie, "Gillette's Deodorant Drive," *New York Times* (February 15, 1984), pp. D1, D4.

A. WIDTH AND DEPTH OF PRODUCT LINES[1]

Depth
of
Product
Lines

Big G cereals
Betty Crocker desserts
Bisquick baking mix
Gold Medal flour
Nature Valley granola
  snacks
Betty Crocker specialty
  potatoes
Hamburger Helper
  dinner mixes
Gorton's seafood
Yoplait yogurt
	The Good Earth
	  restaurants
	Darryl's "Turn of
	  the Century"
	  restaurants
	Casa Gallardo Mexican
	  restaurants
	York Steak Houses
	Red Lobster Inns
		Fundimensions
		Kenner Products
		Parker Brothers
			Lark luggage
			Foot-Joy golf shoes
			Monet Jewelers
			Ship'n Shore
			Izod
				Eddie Bauer
				Wild West
				Wallpaper to Go
				Lee Wards
				Talbots
				Pennsylvanian House
				Kittinger
				Dunbar

Consumer Foods— 1983 sales of $2.8 billion	Restaurants— 1983 sales of $728 million	Toys— 1983 sales of $985 million	Fashion— 1983 sales of $616 million	Specialty Retailing and Furniture— 1983 sales of $429 million

Width
of
Product
Lines

[1]Within many product categories, there are several more specific brands.
For example, General Mills' cereals include Cheerios, Total, Wheaties,
Kix, Trix, and Golden Grahams.

Source: *General Mills 1983 Annual Report*

B. CONSISTENCY OF PRODUCT LINES—SELECTED COMPARISONS

FACTOR	LOW CONSISTENCY	HIGH CONSISTENCY

End use
Distribution
  outlets
Consumer groups
Price range
	Consumer Foods—Fashion
	Restaurants—Toys
	
	Toys—Fashion
	Consumer Foods—Specialty
	  Retailing and Furniture
		Consumer Foods—Restaurants
		Fashion—Specialty Retailing
		  and Furniture
		Consumer Foods—Toys
		Restaurants—Toys

Figure 9-7
General Mills' Product Mix

A manager handles new and existing products in one or a group of categories in the *product (brand) manager system*.

With a ***product (brand) manager system*** there is a middle manager who focuses on a single product or a small group of products. This manager handles new and existing products and is involved with everything from marketing research to package design to advertising. The product-manager system allows each product or brand to receive adequate attention. It works well when there are many distinct products or brands, each requiring individual expertise and marketing decisions. There are two problems with this system: lack of authority for the product manager and inadequate attention to new products. Nabisco, Pillsbury, General Mills, Procter & Gamble, Colgate-Palmolive, Lever Brothers, and Lehn-Fink are companies using product managers.

A *product-planning committee* has executives who handle product development part-time.

A ***product-planning committee*** is staffed by executives from functional areas, including marketing, production, engineering, finance, and research and development (R&D). The committee handles product approval, evaluation, and development on a part-time basis. Once a product is introduced in the market, the committee usually disbands and gives it over to a product manager. This system enables management to have a strong input into product decisions; however, it

Figure 9-8
Selected Products in Binney & Smith's Expanding Mix

Reprinted by permission.

meets on an irregular basis and must pass projects on to line managers. The product-planning committee functions best as a supplement to other methods.

A **new-product manager system** utilizes product managers for existing products and new-product managers for new products. This ensures adequate time, resources, enthusiasm, and expertise for new products. After a new product is introduced, it is managed by the product manager. The new-product manager system can be costly, lead to conflicts, and cause discontinuity when the product is introduced. General Foods, General Electric, NCR, and Johnson & Johnson use new product managers.

A **venture team** is a small, independent department consisting of a broad range of specialists who manage a new product's entire development process from idea generation to market introduction. Team members work on a full-time basis and function as a separate unit within the company. The team disbands when the product is introduced. A venture team provides adequate resources, a flexible environment, expertise, and continuity. It is also expensive to establish and operate. Xerox, IBM, Polaroid, Monsanto, Westinghouse, and Texas Instruments use venture teams.

The correct organizational form depends on the diversity of the firm's offerings, the number of new products introduced, the level of innovation, company resources, and management expertise. A combination of forms may also be highly desirable. According to one recent study, almost one half of the firms studied use more than one product management organization; and most of these companies linked organizational format to product-specific factors. As one manager in an information-processing company commented:

In a *new-product manager system*, there are separate managers for new and existing products.

A *venture team* is an autonomous department that manages new-product development.

**Table 9-3
Comparing Product
Management
Organizations**

Organization	Characteristics		
	Staffing	**Ideal Use**	**Permanency**
Marketing-manager system	All functional areas of marketing report to one manager.	A company makes a line of similar products or has one dominant line.	The system is ongoing.
Product (brand) manager system	A middle manager focuses on a single product or group of products.	A company makes many distinct products, each requiring managerial expertise.	The system is ongoing.
Product-planning committee	Executives from various functional areas participate.	The committee should supplement another product manager organization.	The committee meets irregularly.
New-product manager system	Separate managers direct new products and existing products.	A company makes several existing products and substantial management time, resources, and expertise are needed for new product decisions.	The system is ongoing, but new products are shifted to product managers after production.
Venture team	An independent group of specialists guides all phases of a new product's development.	A company is interested in creating vastly different products than those currently made, and needs to set up an autonomous structure to aid development.	The team disbands after a new product is introduced, turning responsibility over to a product manager.

New products related to one of our existing businesses are developed within an existing division. New products that represent a shift in direction for the company are developed by a separate venture group.[10]

After studying why certain companies are more successful than others in product planning, Peters and Waterman (authors of *In Search of Excellence*) reached this conclusion:

[10] *New Product Management for the 1980s* (New York: Booz, Allen & Hamilton, 1982), p. 13.

Perhaps the most important element of their enviable track record is an ability to be big and yet to act small at the same time. A concomitant essential apparently is that they encourage the entrepreneurial spirit among their people, because they push autonomy remarkably far down the line.[11]

Product Positioning

Product positioning enables the firm to map its offerings in terms of consumer perceptions and desires, competition, other company products, and environmental changes.[12] Consumer perceptions are the images consumers have of products, both a company's and competitors'. Consumer desires refer to the attributes consumers would like products to possess—that is, their *ideal points.* Competitive product positioning refers to the perceptions consumers have of a firm relative to its competitors. Company product positioning shows a firm how consumers perceive the firm's different brands within the same product line and the relationship of those brands to each other. A company must also monitor environmental changes that would alter the manner in which its products are viewed. These changes include new products by competitors, changing consumer profiles, new technology, negative publicity, and resource availability.

An illustration of product positioning is shown in Figure 9-9. A number of brands of ice cream are rated by consumers on the basis of price and richness (level of butterfat content).[13] Godiva, Häagen-Dazs, Frusen Glädjé, and Alpen Zauber are perceived as expensive and very rich (high in butterfat content). Breyer's, Sealtest, Dolly Madison, and Louis Sherry are perceived as medium in price and richness. Weight Watcher's and Light n' Lively are perceived as medium in price and not rich (low in butterfat content). Supermarket brands are perceived as low in price and moderate in richness.

Each of these brand groups has carved out a distinctive product position that matches an ideal point (market segment): I_1—super premium, I_2—regular, I_3—low calorie, and I_4—economy. There is no overlap among these categories. Demand is greatest for regular ice cream.

An examination of competitive product positioning reveals that the super-premium segment is relatively small and highly saturated. There is a lot of competition in the regular ice cream segment; however, the size of the segment merits this level of competition. The low-calorie and economy segments are relatively small and have fewer competitors.

Breyer's, Sealtest, and Light n' Lively are all marketed by Kraft. From an analysis of company product positioning, Kraft sees that it well serves the regular

Product positioning uses consumer perceptions and product attributes to describe products. *Ideal points* represent consumers' preferred product attributes.

---

[11] Thomas J. Peters and Robert H. Waterman, Jr., *In Search of Excellence: Lessons from America's Best-Run Companies* (New York: Harper & Row, 1982), p. 201.

[12] See David A. Aaker, "Positioning Your Product," *Business Horizons*, Vol. 25 (May–June 1982), pp. 56–62.

[13] See Kendall J. Wills, "The Scoop War's Gourmet Battle," *New York Times* (September 11, 1983), Section 3, p. 8.

Figure 9-9
Product Positioning of Selected Ice Cream Brands

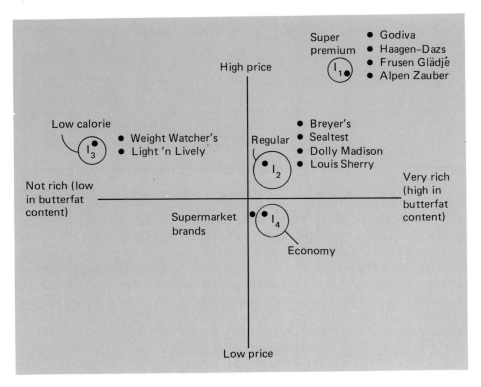

and low-calorie market segments, and that it has no brands appealing to the super-premium and economy segments. It has two brands catering to the largest segment. Kraft has no plans to enter the super-premium market (too crowded) or the economy market (not in keeping with the image it portrays for ice cream). Kraft will continue to carefully differentiate between Breyer's (the ''all natural'' ice cream) and Sealtest (the ''ice-cream parlor'' ice cream).

By undertaking product-positioning analysis, a company can learn a great deal and plan marketing efforts accordingly, as these examples show:

- Snuggle fabric softener is positioned ''as offering softness comparable to the leading brand (Downy) but at a lower price.''[14]
- Hasbro Industries makes traditional toys and dolls, such as Mr. Potato Head, G.I. Joe soldiers, and ''hug me'' toys. It has avoided video and electronic games (whose markets are now saturated). Says a Hasbro executive, ''When we're not on the leading edge and we don't have a breakthrough, we stay out of it.''[15]
- When Hewlett-Packard introduced a $300 programmable business calculator that could be connected to personal computers, test instruments, and video screens, it removed the name ''calculator'' from the product. To position the item properly, Hewlett-Packard calls it a ''handheld computer.''[16] Figure 9-10 shows the HP-75, one of the firm's handheld computers.
- Chrysler's marketing department tracks the company's product positioning by

[14] Nancy Giges, ''Snuggle Targets Downy,'' *Advertising Age* (September 26, 1983), pp. 1, 84.
[15] Bob Davis, ''Hasbro Toys Find Profits in Tradition,'' *Wall Street Journal* (December 12, 1983), pp. 29, 40.
[16] ''When 'Calculator' Is a Dirty Word,'' *Business Week* (June 14, 1982), p. 62.

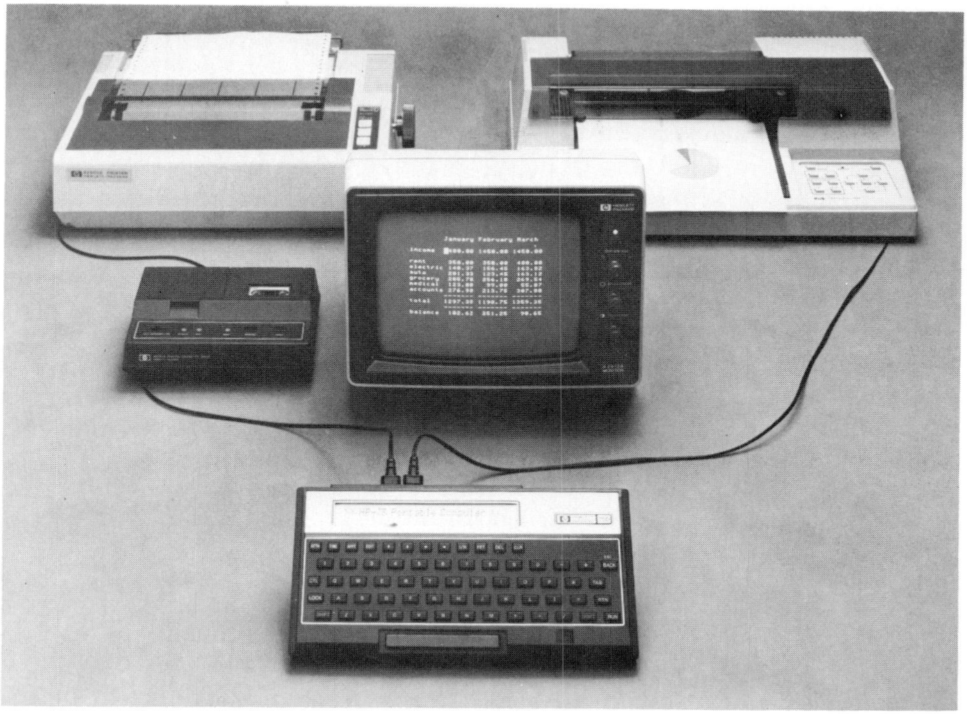

Figure 9-10
**Hewlett-Packard's
Handheld Computer**

Photo courtesy of Hewlett-Packard Company.

surveying consumers three times a year. Questions deal with youthfulness, luxury, practicality, etc. Figure 9-11 shows a recent product positioning map developed by Chrysler. After examining this map, Chrysler executives determined that its car lines (Chrysler, Dodge, and Plymouth) needed to present younger images and that Dodge and Plymouth needed to improve their rating for luxury ("a touch of class").[17]

Product Life Cycle

The ***product life cycle*** is a concept that attempts to describe a product's sales, profits, customers, competitors, and marketing emphasis from its beginning until it is removed from the market. The product life cycle was popularized by Theodore Levitt in 1965.[18]

Marketers are interested in the product life cycle for several reasons. One, some analysts have found that product lives are shorter now than previously. Two, new products are requiring increased investments. Three, the product life

The ***product life cycle*** describes each stage in its life.

---

[17] John Koten, "Car Makers Use 'Image' Map as Tool to Position Products," *Wall Street Journal* (March 22, 1984), p. 33.
[18] Theodore Levitt, "Exploit the Product Life Cycle," *Harvard Business Review*, Vol. 43 (November–December 1965), pp. 81–94.

Figure 9-11
A Product Positioning Map Generated by Chrysler

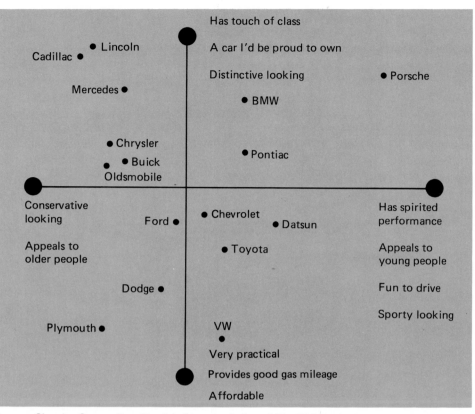

cycle enables a marketer to anticipate changes in consumer tastes, competition, and channel support and adjust the marketing plan accordingly. Four, the product life-cycle concept enables the marketer to consider the mix of products the firm will offer; many firms seek to attain a ***balanced product portfolio,*** whereby a combination of new, growing, and mature products is maintained (Portfolio analysis was explained in Chapter 3).

Companies often desire a *balanced product portfolio*.

The product life-cycle concept may be applied to a product class (watches), a product form (quartz watches), and a brand (Seiko quartz watches). However, product forms generally follow the traditional product life cycle more faithfully than product classes or brands.

Product life-cycle types are traditional, boom or classic, fad, extended fad, seasonal or fashion, revival or nostalgia, and bust.

Product life-cycle patterns vary a lot, both in length of time and shape.[19] Figure 9-12 shows several product life-cycle patterns. The traditional curve contains distinctive periods of introduction, growth, maturity, and decline. The boom, or classic, curve describes an extremely popular product that receives steady sales over a long period of time. A fad curve represents a product that has quick popularity and a sudden decline. An extended fad is like a fad, except that residual sales continue at a fraction of earlier sales after the initial success. A seasonal or fashion curve results when a product sells well during nonconsecutive

[19] See John E. Swan and David R. Rink, ''Fitting Marketing Strategy to Varying Product Life Cycles,'' *Business Horizons*, Vol. 25 (January–February 1982), pp. 72–76.

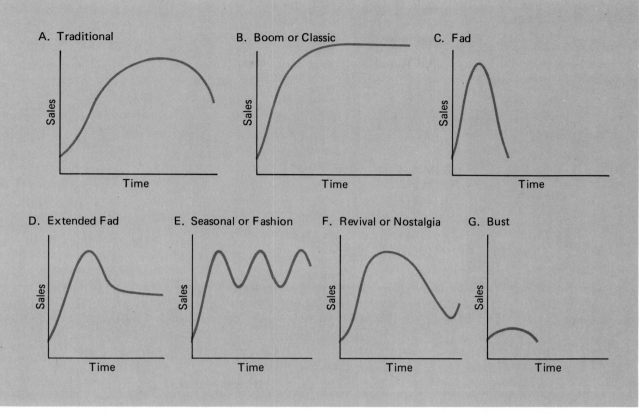

Figure 9-12
Selected Product Life Cycle Patterns

time periods. With a revival or nostalgia curve, a seemingly obsolete product achieves new popularity. A bust curve occurs for a product that is not successful at all.

Stages in the Product Life Cycle

The stages and characteristics of the traditional product life cycle are shown in Figure 9-13 and Table 9-4, which refer to total industry performance during the cycle. The performance of an individual firm will vary from that of the industry, depending on its specific goals, resources, marketing plans, location, competitive environment, level of success, and stage of entry.

During the ***introduction stage,*** the objective is to develop a customer market for a new product. The rate of sales growth depends on the newness of the product as well as its desirability. Generally, a product modification generates faster sales than a major innovation. At this stage, only one firm has entered the market and competition is limited. Losses are taken because of high production and marketing costs; similarly, profit margins (unit profits) are low. Initial customers are innovators who are willing to take risks, can afford to take them, and like the status of buying first. Because only one firm dominates the market and costs are high, one basic model of the product is sold. For a convenience item, like a new cereal, distribution is extensive. For a luxury item, like a new boat, distribution is

In *introduction*, the goal is to establish a consumer market.

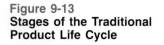

Figure 9-13
**Stages of the Traditional
Product Life Cycle**

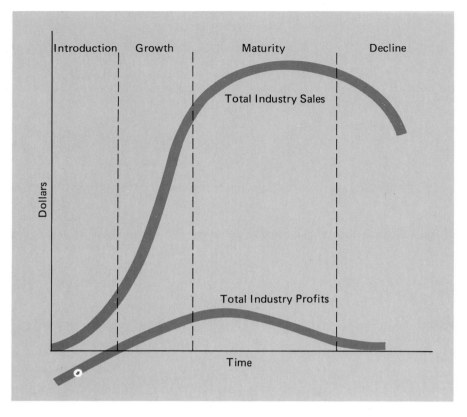

exclusive. Depending on the product and choice of consumer market, the firm may start with a high status price or a low mass-market price. Promotion must be informative and free samples may be desirable.

During *growth*, firms expand distribution, enlarge the market, and offer alternatives.

In the ***growth stage,*** the marketing objective is to expand distribution and the range of available product alternatives. Industry sales increase rapidly as a few more firms enter a highly profitable market that has substantial potential. Unit profits are high because an affluent mass market buys distinctive products from a limited group of firms and is willing to pay for them. To accommodate the growing market, modified versions of the basic model are offered, distribution is expanded, a range of prices is available, and persuasive mass advertising is utilized.

In *maturity*, companies work hard to sustain a differential advantage and stabilize sales.

During the ***maturity stage,*** companies try to maintain a differential advantage (such as a lower price, product features, or extended warranty). Industry sales stabilize as the market becomes saturated and many firms enter to capitalize on the still sizable demand. Competition is at its highest level. Therefore, total industry and unit profits decline because discounting becomes popular. At this stage, the average-income mass market makes its purchases. A full line of products is made available at many outlets and many price levels. Promotion becomes very competitive.

During *decline*, companies reduce marketing, revive the product, or terminate the product.

In the ***decline stage,*** firms have three alternate courses of action. They can cut back on their marketing programs, thereby reducing the number of products they make, the outlets they sell through, and the promotions they use; they can revive

Table 9-4 **Characteristics of the Traditional Product Life Cycle**

Characteristics	Stage in Life Cycle			
	Introduction	Growth	Maturity	Decline
Marketing objective	Attract innovators and opinion leaders to new product	Expand distribution and product line	Maintain differential advantage	(a) Cut back, (b) revive, (c) terminate
Industry sales	Increasing	Rapidly increasing	Stable	Decreasing
Competition	None or small	Some	Many	Few
Industry profits	Negative	Increasing	Decreasing	Decreasing
Profit margins	Low	High	Decreasing	Decreasing
Customers	Innovators	Affluent mass market	Mass market	Laggards
Product mix	One basic model	Expanding line	Full product line	Best sellers
Distribution	Depends on product	Expanding number of outlets	Expanding number of outlets	Decreasing number of outlets
Pricing	Depends on product	Greater range of prices	Full line of prices	Selected prices
Promotion	Informative	Persuasive	Competitive	Informative

the product by repositioning, repackaging, or otherwise remarketing it; or they can terminate the product. At this stage, industry sales decline and many firms leave the market because customers are fewer and they have less income to spend. The product mix concentrates on best sellers, selected outlets and prices, and promotion that stresses, in an informative way, availability and price.

The pocket calculator is a good example of a product that has recently moved through the life cycle. It went from an exclusive, expensive item to a widespread, moderately priced item to a mass-marketed, inexpensive item in just a few years. Its characteristics during the life cycle closely paralleled those in Table 9-4.

Evaluating the Product Life-Cycle Concept

As mentioned earlier, the product life cycle is an interesting and useful concept for marketers; but, although it provides a good framework for product planning, it has not proven useful in forecasting.[20] First, the stages of the life cycle, the time span of the entire life cycle, and the shape of the cycle (such as flat, erratic, or sharply inclined) vary by product.

Second, external factors such as the economy, rate of inflation, and consumer life-styles may have a major impact on the performance of a product and shorten or lengthen its life cycle.

Third, a company may not only be able to manage the product life cycle, it may also be able to extend it. Effective marketing may attract a new market segment, find a new use for the product, or generate increased dealer support.

Fourth, some companies may engage in *self-fulfilling prophecies,* whereby

A self-fulfilling prophecy may occur when a firm reduces marketing.

[20] A good synopsis of the controversy surrounding the product life cycle is George Day, "The Product Life Cycle: Analysis and Applications Issues," *Journal of Marketing,* Vol. 45 (Fall 1981), pp. 60–67.

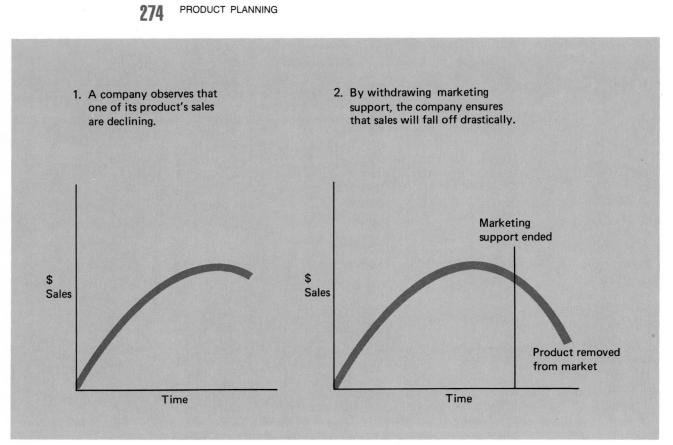

1. A company observes that one of its product's sales are declining.

2. By withdrawing marketing support, the company ensures that sales will fall off drastically.

$
Sales

Time

$
Sales

Marketing support ended

Product removed from market

Time

Figure 9-14
A Self-Fulfilling Prophecy

they predict sales will decline and then ensure this will occur by removing marketing support. With adequate support, these products might not fail. See Figure 9-14.

One major study of four diverse products (cigarettes, makeup, toilet tissue, and cereal) revealed that[21]

1. It is difficult to predict when the next stage will appear, how long it will last, and what levels sales will reach.
2. A product's stage in the life cycle cannot be judged accurately.
3. The four major phases of the cycle do not divide themselves into clear-cut stages. At certain points, a product may appear to attain maturity when it has actually reached temporary plateaus in the growth stage.

Summary

Product planning is systematic decision making pertaining to all aspects of the development and management of a firm's products. It allows the firm to pinpoint opportunities, develop marketing programs, coordinate a product mix, maintain

---

[21] Nariman Dhalla and Sonia Yuspeh, "Forget the Product Life Cycle Concept," *Harvard Business Review*, Vol. 54 (January–February 1976), pp. 102–112.

successful products, reappraise faltering products, and delete undesirable products.

Products should be defined in a combination of ways. A tangible product is the basic physical entity, service, or idea, which has precise specifications and is offered under a given description or model number. An extended product includes not only tangible elements, but also the accompanying cluster of image and service features. A generic product focuses on the benefits a buyer desires.

Consumer products are goods or services for the final consumer. They can be classified as convenience (staples, impulse, emergency), shopping, and specialty items. These are products that are differentiated on the basis of consumer awareness of alternatives and their characteristics prior to the shopping trip and the degree of search and time spent shopping. Consumer services can be categorized as rented-goods, owned-goods, or nongoods services.

Industrial products are goods or services used in the production of other goods or services, in the operation of a business, or for resale. Industrial goods are divided into installations, accessory equipment, raw materials, component materials, fabricated parts, and supplies. They are differentiated on the basis of decision making, costs, rapidity of consumption, role in production, and change in form. Industrial services are maintenance/repair and business advisory.

A product item is a specific model, brand, or size of a product that the company sells. A product line is a group of closely related items sold by the firm. A product mix consists of all the different product lines a firm offers.

A firm may choose from among or combine several product management organizations: marketing-manager system, product (brand) manager, product-planning committee, new-product manager system, and venture team.

Product positioning enables the firm to map its offerings in terms of consumer perceptions, consumer desires (ideal points), competition, its own products within the same line, and the changing environment.

The product life cycle is a concept that seeks to describe a product's sales, profits, customers, competitors, and marketing emphasis from its inception until its removal from the market. Many firms desire a balanced product portfolio, with products in various stages of the life cycle. There are several derivations of the product life cycle: traditional, boom or classic, fad, extended fad, seasonal or fashion, revival or nostalgia, and bust. The traditional life cycle goes through four stages: introduction, growth, maturity, and decline. During each stage, the marketing objective, industry sales, competition, industry profits, profit margins, customers, and marketing plan change. Although the life cycle is useful as a planning tool, it should not be employed as a forecasting tool.

Questions for Discussion

1. Evaluate WD-40's product strategy.
2. For each of the following, describe the tangible, extended, and generic product:
   a. Wedding ring.
   b. Contact lenses.

    c. Refrigerator.

    d. Ticket to a concert.

3. How are convenience and specialty goods similar? How are they dissimilar?

4. How can one product be a convenience, shopping, *and* specialty good? What does this mean to marketers?

5. Which is more intangible, an owned-goods service or a nongoods service? Why?

6. Why is the consumer goods classification not useful for industrial products?

7. What are the similarities and differences between raw materials and fabricated parts?

8. Evaluate the product mix for General Mills.

9. Would a firm ever seek a wide, shallow product mix? Explain your answer.

10. Under what circumstances is a product manager system appropriate? A new-product manager system?

11. Frusen Glädjé and Dolly Madison are both owned by Richard Smith. Comment on this (refer to Figure 9-9).

12. How do competitive positioning and company positioning differ?

13. Explain the basic premise of the product life cycle. What is the value of this concept?

14. Give an example for each of the following product life cycles:

    a. Boom.

    b. Fad.

    c. Extended fad.

    d. Fashion.

    e. Bust.

15. For the pocket calculator, describe the consumer market and marketing plan during each stage of the product life cycle.

Case 1 Mattel: Problems with a Product Mix*

Mattel revised its product mix significantly between 1980 and 1983. In 1980, the toy and hobby products division dominated the company and electronics represented less than 10 per cent of total sales. By 1983, electronics (mostly Intellivision videogames and Mattel videogame cartridges) accounted for 41 per cent of sales and publishing represented another 18 per cent of sales. Table 1 shows Mattel's 1983 product mix and several of its leading brands.

In 1982, Mattel earned more than $200 million in total profits, including over $100 million from electronics. But during 1983, the situation changed dramatically and Mattel lost $300 million overall, with electronics contributing losses of $400 million (toys and hobby products earned about $100 million in profits). This was due to the intense competition in and saturation of the videogame market, which caused a severe cycle of price discounting and left many retailers with excessive

---

* The data in this case are drawn from "Mattel Struggles to Fix Its Product Woes," *Business Week* (May 9, 1983), pp. 76, 78; "Mattel Inc." *Advertising Age* (September 8, 1983), p. 112; Stephen J. Sansweet, "Troubles at Mattel Seen Extending Beyond Fallout in Electronics," *Wall Street Journal* (December 1, 1983), pp. 31, 34; Thomas C. Hayes, "Mattel Is Counting on Its Toys," *New York Times* (February 4, 1984), pp. 35, 37; and Stephen J. Sansweet, "Mattel Will Concentrate on Making Toys After Decision to Leave Two Other Lines," *Wall Street Journal* (February 6, 1984), p. 32.

Table 1
Mattel's 1983 Product Mix

Division	Sales (millions)	Per Cent of Company Sales	Leading Brands
Electronics	$556	41.4	Intellivision videogames, Mattel video cartridges, Aquarius home computers,[b] Synsonics electronic drums
Toy and hobby	528	39.3	Barbi dolls, Hot Wheels cars, He Man-Masters of the Universe action play figures
Publishing and printing	246	18.3	Western Publishing (Golden Books)
Entertainment[a]	12	0.9	Circus World Theme Park in Florida
	$1,342	100.0[c]	

[a] In 1980, Mattel sold Ringling Bros. and Barnum & Bailey Circus, which it had acquired in 1971.
[b] This product was abandoned in late 1983.
[c] Rounding error.

inventory on their shelves. In addition, many consumers turned to home computers, as their prices dropped; Mattel had no product for this market until its unsuccessful Aquarius brand was introduced in mid-1983. Several observers were critical of Mattel's product planning:

- "I think they are totally confused about the direction they are going. Mattel is a superb marketer of toys, but they are not adaptable to the electronics industry."
- "Product life cycles are very short [for consumer electronics]. You have to move quickly or develop a proprietary product that gives you an edge. That's what Mattel hasn't understood. [Product development] in their old business and their new business is very different."
- "[Aquarius home computer] is a day late and a dollar short. It doesn't offer any special features, extraordinary graphics, or a lot of software. Mattel is in a defensive, reactive mode in which other game makers and computer companies are setting the pace."

After Aquarius was introduced in 1983, sales were very poor; and the product was quickly withdrawn from the market. Then in early 1984, Mattel announced that it was leaving electronics, publishing, and entertainment. The firm planned to concentrate on toys and hobby products by selling its other businesses to interested buyers. For example, Intellivision was sold to a small company headed by a former Mattel senior vice-president.

QUESTIONS
1. Evaluate Mattel's 1983 product mix and its decision to leave the electronics, publishing, and entertainment businesses.
2. What product management organization should Mattel employ now? Explain your answer.
3. Why would another company buy Intellivision if Mattel suffered such large losses and encountered so many difficulties with it?
4. Do you agree that product life cycles are shorter for consumer electronics than for toys? Explain your answer.

Case 2 Nabisco Brands: "Almost Home" Enters the Cookie Market[†]

Nabisco Brands is the leading manufacturer of packaged, store-bought cookies with $800 million in sales (over one third of industry sales). Its cookie brands include Oreo and Chips Ahoy! Oreo, a chocolate sandwich cookie with a vanilla cream filling, is the world's best-selling cookie. More than 100 billion Oreos have been sold, enough "to reach to the moon and back. Twice!" Chips Ahoy! is the leading chocolate-chip cookie.

While industry dollar sales of packaged cookies rose consistently from 1967 to 1982, unit sales dropped by 10 per cent over this period. In fact, per capita annual cookie consumption fell from 11.9 pounds in 1967 to 8.9 pounds in 1982. One market observer cited these reasons for the consumption decline: (1) fewer 5 to 13 year olds, (2) increased nutritional concerns, and (3) competition from fresh-baked cookies.

In an attempt to revitalize the packaged-cookie market, Frito-Lay introduced sixteen types of Grandma's cookies ("So fresh, they taste suspiciously close to homemade") in May 1982. Next, Procter & Gamble brought out five varieties of Duncan Hines chocolate-chip cookies ("crispy outside and chewy inside") in early 1983. Shortly thereafter, Frito Lay marketed five varieties of Rich 'N Chewy chocolate-chip cookies.

Until these competitive developments, Nabisco seemed pretty complacent. For example, it spent only 1 per cent of sales ($8 million) on cookie advertising in 1982. And Nabisco's major innovation was adding more chocolate chips to Chips Ahoy! But once Nabisco saw the early success of Grandma's cookies, it invested heavily in new product development.

In August 1983, Nabisco launched Almost Home cookies ("The moistest, chewiest, most perfectly baked cookies the world has ever tasted . . . well, almost") in 15 varieties, from chocolate chip to cream sandwich to granola and brownies. At the same time, Nabisco increased its 1983 advertising budget for cookies to $30 million. Commented one company salesperson, "It's the best thing Nabisco has done in a long time and we're happy to see it. We can't be told we taste like hockey pucks anymore."

Frito-Lay and Procter & Gamble are keeping the pressure on Nabisco. Grandma's cookies had a $70 million promotion budget in 1983; while 40 per cent of the sales of Duncan Hines' cookies were devoted to their promotion. The battle for retailers' shelf space will be intense over the next several years.

QUESTIONS

1. Comment on this statement. "There are no chocolate-chip cookies which are store-bought that taste like a real cookie."

[†] The data in this case are drawn from Al Urbanski, "On with the $2.1 Billion Cookie War," *Sales & Marketing Management* (June 6, 1983), pp. 37–40; and Janet Guyon, "Nabisco's New Cookie Line Marks the Beginning of a Fierce Sales War," *Wall Street Journal* (October 17, 1983), pp. 33, 51.

2. Draw and explain a product positioning map showing traditional packaged, store-bought cookies; the newer packaged, store-bought cookies; bakery cookies; and home-made cookies.
3. Develop a product positioning strategy for Oreo cookies. Should Nabisco reposition Oreo? Why or why not?
4. Evaluate Nabisco's strategy in terms of the product life-cycle theory.

Product Planning: From New Products to Product Deletion

CHAPTER OBJECTIVES

1. To examine the different types of new products available to a firm
2. To detail the importance of new products and determine why new products fail
3. To study the stages in the new-product planning process: idea generation, product screening, concept testing, business analysis, product development, test marketing, and commercialization
4. To analyze the growth and maturity of products, including the adoption process, the diffusion process, and extension strategies
5. To examine product deletion decisions and strategies

*T*he search for successful products is not limited to manufacturers. It involves all types of firms in all kinds of industries. Nowhere is this more apparent than in the fast-food industry.

Said Wendy's president, "Four years ago we didn't even have a research and development staff. Today we've got 42 people in that area." Wendy's uses food economists and microbiologists to evaluate new products and product ingredients. It has a marketing staff to gauge consumer opinion. At one point, Wendy's was concerned that it did not attract enough women. To remedy this, it added a salad bar and a variety of baked potatoes. Wendy's is currently working on more than 50 new-product ideas.

Burger King examined the soft-drink industry for two years before deciding to switch to Pepsi from Coke. For this and other decisions, Burger King uses a computer to determine the labor time and costs involved with a menu change. In evaluating product ingredients, Burger King strives for price stability. Noted one Burger King executive, "Just deciding to have three strips of bacon on a burger can have one heck of an effect on the supply of pork bellies." Burger King also recognizes that regional customer differences can exist. In one case, it successfully introduced a mustard burger in Texas, but was unable to market it elsewhere. It spent more than four years in researching its salad bar and salad-in-a-pita products. See Figure 10-1.

At McDonald's, there are usually at least 20 new products in some stage of development. McDonald's employees are encouraged to offer new-product ideas. The Big Mac, Fillet-o-Fish sandwich, and Egg McMuffin were each suggested by individual franchise operators. Chicken McNuggets was proposed in an elevator conversation between McDonald's chairman and its head chef. Company researchers also read cookbooks and visit supermarkets in search of ideas. Customers are not asked for their ideas, because the company is afraid of lawsuits regarding potential royalties. Once McDonald's decides to go ahead with a new product, it

Figure 10-1
Burger King: From Research to Salad Bar
Burger King's salad bar was thoroughly researched and test marketed before national introduction. The salad-in-a pita concept was developed during a brainstorming session of company officials, then tested with consumers. Each of the salad bar's twenty-plus ingredients was subjected to consumer tests, as were all the salad dressings.

Reprinted by permission.

must be sure that supply sources are readily available. For example, Chicken McNuggets require enough chicken to sell more than 5 million pounds of McNuggets every week. Sometimes, despite careful planning, new products fail—as occurred when McDonald's had to withdraw McRib barbeque sandwiches. They just did not meet company expectations.[1]

Through trial and error, fast-food companies have learned two valuable product-planning lessons: innovation is necessary to stay ahead in a competitive industry; and all products need to be thoroughly developed and managed throughout their life cycles.

Developing and Managing Products

Product planning involves both new and continuing products.

In this chapter the development of new products and their management throughout the product life cycle are discussed. Emphasis is placed on new-product development, growing and mature products, and the termination of undesirable products.

As previously defined, a product is a basic offering with an accompanying set of image features that seeks to satisfy consumer needs. A ***new product*** involves a modification of an existing product or an innovation that the consumer perceives as meaningful. For a new product to succeed, it must have desirable attributes, be unique, and be able to have its features communicate to consumers. Full marketing support is necessary.

A *new product* is perceived as such by the consumer and may be a *modification*, a *minor innovation*, or a *major innovation*.

Modifications are alterations in a company's existing products and include new models, styles, colors, product improvements, and brands. ***Minor innovations*** are items that have not been previously sold by the firm but have been sold by others (such as Kodak's introducing a self-developing camera). ***Major innovations*** are items that have not been previously sold by the company or any other firm (such as the first home computer). As a company moves from modifications to major innovations, costs, risks, and time required for profitability all increase. Among large U.S. firms, 70 per cent of new products are modifications, 20 per cent are minor innovations, and 10 per cent are major innovations.[2]

New products may be developed by the company itself or purchased from another firm. In the latter case the company may buy a firm outright, purchase the product, or enter into a licensing agreement (whereby it pays the founder a royalty fee based on sales). Acquisitions reduce risks and time requirements but rely on outside parties for innovations and require large investments.

After introduction, products are managed during their growth, maturity, and decline.

During the course of a product's life, there is usually a solid period of strong sales growth, as more and more consumers purchase and repurchase it. This is an exciting and profitable period. Next, the market becomes saturated, and competition intensifies. At this point, the company can maintain a high level of sales by adding features that provide convenience and durability, using new materials in

---

[1] John Koten, ''Fast-Food Firms' New Items Undergo Exhaustive Testing,'' *Wall Street Journal* (January 5, 1984), p. 25.

[2] *New Product Management for the 1980s* (New York: Booz, Allen & Hamilton, 1982), p. 9.

product construction, emphasizing new packaging and product safety, offering a range of models, and adding customer services. It can also reposition the product, enter untapped geographic markets, demonstrate new product uses, offer new brands, set lower prices, use new media, and appeal to new market segments. Then, at some point, the company must determine whether the product has outlived its usefulness and is a candidate for deletion.

Importance of New Products

A firm's product policy must always look to the future and recognize that all products, no matter how successful, are mortal—that is, they will eventually have to be withdrawn from the market. Therefore, replacements need to be constantly planned. According to a recent Booz, Allen & Hamilton survey, major consumer and industrial goods companies expect new products (those less than five years old) to account for about 35 per cent of their total sales by 1986. Between 1981 and 1986, these companies expected to double the number of new products they introduced each year.[3]

New products account for a large percentage of total company sales.

Companies have several objectives in introducing new products: sales, profits, less dependence on one product or product line, use of an existing distribution system, use of waste materials from current production, and image.[4]

For companies with cyclical or seasonal sales, new products can stabilize sales and costs throughout the year. Union Carbide diversified into agriculture, fish, and medical-testing equipment in an attempt to reduce its dependence on the cyclical chemicals business. Black & Decker, the world's largest maker of power tools, cut back sharply on lawn mowers and hedge trimmers and looked for new opportunities in more traditional, stable product lines (such as acquiring the small appliance division of General Electric):

New products can stabilize sales or contribute to sales growth.

Business could collapse if it rained during the key months and you can't use that as an excuse to your stockholders if you call yourself a growth company. So Black & Decker cut back sharply on outdoor products.[5]

Planning for sales growth must take into account the time required for a new product to move from the idea stage to full commercialization. For instance, in 1965, a scientist for Searle first discovered that aspartame could be used as a nonsugar, low-calorie sweetener. After years of product development and thorough testing, Searle filed for Food and Drug Administration (FDA) approval of aspartame in 1973. Yet, while aspartame was approved by countries around the world, it was not permitted to be marketed in the U.S. until the end of 1981 (and then only in tablets and powder form and as a food additive). Not until July 1983 did the FDA allow aspartame to be used in diet soda. Then Coca-Cola and others quickly signed agreements with Searle. 1984 sales of Searle's NutraSweet brand

---

[3] Thomas D. Kuczmarksi and Steven J. Silver, ''Strategy: The Key to Successful New Product Development,'' *Management Review,* Vol. 71 (July 1982), pp. 26–40.
[4] Adapted from George A. Steiner, *Top Management Planning* (New York: Macmillan, 1969).
[5] Paul W. Sturm, ''Keep 'Em Coming,'' *Forbes* (February 5, 1979), p. 56.

Figure 10-2
Selected Products Using NutraSweet

Reprinted by permission.

of aspartame were expected to reach $400 million.[6] Figure 10-2 shows some of the many brands using NutraSweet.

New products can increase profits and control over price.

New products can lead to large profits and enable the firm to gain control over price. For example, General Motors spent about $150 million in developing its Seville model Cadillac. In return, initial pretax profit on each Seville was $4,000 (as compared with $1,250 profit for each Chevrolet Malibu).[7] Since their intro-

---

[6] Leslie Wayne, "Searle's Push into Sweeteners," *New York Times* (October 24, 1982), Section 3, p. 4; Jennifer Alter, "Something Old, Something New Sweeten Searle's Sales Picture," *Advertising Age* (February 14, 1983), pp. 4, 64; and Carolyn Phillips, "Success of G. D. Searle's NutraSweet Buoys Sales and Cushions Problems," *Wall Street Journal* (November 4, 1983), pp. 37, 43.

[7] "The Mark of Dominance," *Forbes* (April 1, 1977), pp. 62–64.

duction in 1975, several hundred thousand Sevilles have been sold. Today, their retail selling price is over $25,000.

To limit risk, many firms seek to reduce dependence on one product or product line, as these illustrations show. Ocean Spray now makes a variety of beverage and fruit products; it no longer depends exclusively on cranberry products. Stride Rite produces Keds sneakers as well as its traditional line of children's shoes. Bic markets disposable razors in addition to its inexpensive pens.

Some companies look to maximize the efficiency of their established distribution systems by introducing new products into them. This enables the firms to spread sales, advertising, and distribution costs among several products, obtain dealer support, and preclude potential competitors from entering the distribution network. Companies such as Nabisco, Dart & Kraft, and Revlon are able to place new products in many outlets quickly and obtain dealer support for them.

A number of firms seek to find uses for waste materials from existing products. For example, fish packers determined that by-products could be used for cat food. Cosmetics firms and dairy-products companies discovered that by-products could result in new cosmetic and dairy products. Vasoline is a by-product of petroleum.

Frequently, new products enhance a firm's image, as this example shows. Long known only for its Crayola crayons, Binney & Smith is now viewed as a "company in the business of providing assorted products that are fun to use and inspire self-expression." Binney & Smith currently markets coloring books, markers, and more than 30 other children's activity items. Just 45 per cent of sales are from crayons.[8]

Good, long-run new-product planning requires systematic research and development, matching the requirements of new-product opportunities against company abilities, emphasis on consumers' perceived product attributes, sizable expenditures of time and money, and defensive as well as offensive planning. In addition, a firm must be willing to accept that some new products will fail because of competition and changing customers; a progressive firm will take risks.

> **Risk may be lessened through product diversity.**

> **Often, companies add new products into established channels.**

> **Waste materials may be used for new products.**

> **New products can build up and broaden a firm's image.**

Why New Products Fail

Despite improved marketing technology, the failure rate of new products remains as high as it was thirty years ago. A comprehensive Booz, Allen & Hamilton survey completed in 1981 found an overall failure rate of 35 per cent for a combination of industrial and consumer products.[9]

Product failure can be defined in absolute and relative terms. ***Absolute product failure*** occurs when a company is unable to regain its production and marketing costs. It incurs a financial loss. ***Relative product failure*** occurs when a company is able to make a profit on an item but the product does not reach profit objectives and/or adversely affects the firm's image. In computing profits and

> Under *absolute product failure,* costs are not regained. Under *relative product failure,* goals are not met.

---

[8] Gay Jervey, "New Products Painting Rosy Future for Crayola," *Advertising Age* (January 11, 1982), p. 4.
[9] *New Product Management for the 1980s,* p. 7.

Table 10-1 Examples of Modern Product Failures

Food Items	Health and Beauty Aids	Other Products
Campbell's Red Kettle Soups	Colgate's Cue Toothpaste	Texas Instruments' 99/4A computer
Best Foods' Knoor Soups	Aerosol Ipana Toothpaste	Real cigarettes
Post Cereals with Freeze-Dried Fruit	Bristol-Myers' Resolve Analgesic	RCA's videodisc players
Gablinger's Beer	Scott Paper's Babyscott Diapers	Susan B. Anthony dollar coin
Hunt-Wesson's Suprema Spaghetti Sauce	Nine Flags Men's Cologne	Edsel
Heinz's Great American Soup	Warner-Lambert's Reef Mouthwash	Dupont's Corfam (leather substitute)
Rheingold's California Gold Label Beer	Colgate's 007 Men's Cologne	Laker Airways
Seagram's Four Roses Premium Light Whiskey	Revlon's Super Natural Hairspray	Gillette's calculators and watches
McRib sandwiches by McDonald's	Procter & Gamble's Hidden Magic Hairspray	Westinghouse's white goods[a]
	Crazy Legs (shaving cream for women)	Prestone Long-Life Coolant
	Us (unisex deodorant)	Corvair
	Rely tampons	DuPont's 270 Material Dye Products
	Johnson & Johnson's disposable diapers	*TV-Cable Week*

[a] White goods are major home appliances, such as refrigerators, washing machines, dishwashers, ranges, and dryers.

losses, the impact of the new product on the sales of other company items must be measured.

Even firms with good new-product performance records have had failures along with their successes.[10] Dow Chemical has done well with Saran Wrap and Handi-Wrap food wraps and has done poorly with Dowgard antifreeze and Handi-Wrap sandwich bags. Procter & Gamble, maker of Crest, failed with Teel (a liquid toothpaste). General Foods, manufacturer of Jell-O, Sanka, and Maxwell House, failed with its Gourmet Food line and Post Cereals with freeze-dried fruit. Table 10-1 lists some examples of modern product failures.

Factors leading to product failure include lack of a differential advantage, poor planning and timing, and excessive enthusiasm.

There are a number of factors that lead to new product failure or unsatisfactory performance. Among the most important are lack of a differential advantage, poor planning, poor timing, and excessive enthusiasm by the product sponsor. Illustrations of failures or weak performance caused by these factors follow.

Johnson & Johnson disposable diapers were unable to compete with Procter & Gamble's Pampers and Luvs, and Kimberly-Clark's Huggies. Consumers observed no differential advantage, since Johnson & Johnson diapers represented a ''Cadillac,'' while Pampers was seen as a ''Chevy'' and Luvs and Huggies were perceived as ''Mercedes.'' Johnson & Johnson was outpositioned.[11] The product had to be withdrawn from the market.

Poor planning by Nimslo International resulted in significant problems for its new 3-D camera. Executives did not realize ''the amount of education required to get customers interested in 3-D.'' The company first tried to distribute the cameras itself, then sought to attract large retail chains. Too high an initial price was set ($269); this soon dropped to $100. There were production difficulties that led to stock shortages. Although sales of the Nimslo 3-D camera were under $10 million in 1983, the company's management remained confident: ''If the thing is marketed correctly, I don't think there's a problem convincing customers it's worth buying.''[12]

[10] See Robert F. Hartley, *Marketing Mistakes,* Second Edition (Columbus, Ohio: Grid, 1981).
[11] ''Diaper Rash at Johnson & Johnson,'' *Business Week* (June 16, 1980), pp. 63–64.
[12] George Anders, ''Developing a 3-D Camera Isn't Enough, Nimslo Learns After Marketing Failure,'' *Wall Street Journal* (October 21, 1983), p. 32.

Boeing introduced its new $50 million 767 jet in 1981 during a very poor period for the airline industry. The timing of Boeing's introduction resulted in the sales of only two 767s over the first two years. Boeing has been willing to wait until the airline industry turns around, which could be quite a while longer.[13]

Excessive enthusiasm caused Procter & Gamble to lose over $200 million on Pringle's potato chips—and still keep them on the market. After reducing advertising costs to $340,000 in 1980, the company spent $8 million on advertising in 1981. Although introduced in 1968, Pringle's had just a 5 per cent market share by 1980 (compared to 30 per cent for Frito-Lay). Among the problems encountered by Pringle's were a bland, processed taste; consumer perceptions of a high price and fewer potato chips than in competitors' bags; and an advertising campaign by competitors that stressed their natural ingredients. 1981's ''new'' Pringle's featured a better flavor; regular, light, and rippled potato chips; and no artificial ingredients (which had been removed in 1977.)[14]

New-Product Planning

The **new-product planning process** involves seven steps: idea generation, product screening, concept testing, business analysis, product development, test marketing, and commercialization. See Figure 10–3. During the process, the company generates several potential opportunities, evaluates them, weeds out the least attractive ones, obtains consumer perceptions, develops the product, tests it, and introduces it into the marketplace. The termination of an idea can occur at any point; costs increase the further into the process the company goes.

*The **new-product planning process** includes all the stages from idea generation to commercialization.*

In 1968, U.S. manufacturing companies reported that it took 58 product ideas to yield one successful new product. In 1981, these firms stated that it took only 7 product ideas to produce one successful new product. This improvement was due to more systematic and careful product planning.[15] Now, companies spend more time and money during the early stages of product planning and are therefore able to spend much less at the later stages.[16]

Idea Generation

Idea generation is the continuous, systematic search for new product opportunities. It involves delineating the sources of new ideas and methods for generating them.

Idea generation is the search for new product opportunities.

Sources of new product ideas may be employees, channel members, competitors, government, and others.[17] It is important to distinguish between market-

---

[13] Alexander Stuart, ''Boeing's New Beauties Are a Tough Sell,'' *Fortune* (October 18, 1982), pp. 114–120.

[14] Dean Robert, ''In Spite of Huge Losses, Procter & Gamble Tries Once More to Revive Pringle's Chips,'' *Wall Street Journal* (October 7, 1981), pp. 29, 42.

[15] *Product Management in the 1980s,* p. 6.

[16] John R. Rockwell and Marc C. Particelli, ''New Product Strategy: How the Pros Do It,'' *Industrial Marketing* (May 1982), pp. 49–50 ff.

[17] See Leigh Lawton and A. Parasuraman, ''So You Want Your New Product Planning to Be Productive,'' *Business Horizons,* Vol. 23 (December 1980), pp. 29–34; and Tom W. White, ''Use Variety of Internal, External Sources to Gather and Screen New Product Ideas,'' *Marketing News* (September 16, 1983), Section 2, p. 12.

Figure 10-3
**The New-Product Planning
Process**

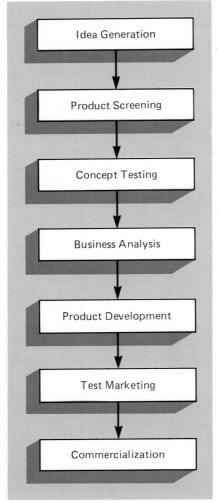

oriented and laboratory-oriented sources. Market-oriented sources identify opportunities on the basis of consumer needs and wants; then laboratory research is directed to satisfying defined consumer requirements. Filter cigarettes, roll-on deodorants, and easy opening beer and soda cans evolved from market-oriented sources. Laboratory-oriented sources identify opportunities on the basis of pure research (which seeks to gain knowledge and indirectly leads to specific new-product ideas) or applied research (which uses existing scientific techniques to develop new-product ideas). Penicillin, antifreeze, teflon, and synthetic fibers evolved from laboratory-oriented sources.

Methods for generating new ideas include brainstorming (small-group sessions where open discussions encourage a wide range of ideas), analysis of existing products, and surveys. When new ideas are being compiled, these points should be followed: ideas should not be criticized, no matter how foolish they may seem; creative concepts should be sought; a large number of ideas should be generated; and the ideas of different people should be combined. Many marketing analysts suggest that an open perspective is essential for generating new ideas. For example, a 3M employee came up with the idea for note paper that could be stuck to telephones, desks, paper, and walls by a small adhesive strip on the back. The employee thought of the idea because his place mark kept falling out of his hymn book during choir practice. Today, annual sales of Post-it notes are around $40 million.[18]

Product Screening

After the firm has identified a set of potential products, it must screen them. In **product screening**, poor, unsuitable, or otherwise unattractive ideas are weeded out from further consideration. Today, many companies use a new-product screening checklist for preliminary evaluation. In the checklist, the firms list the attributes of new products they consider most important and compare each product idea with those attributes. The checklist is a standardized form that allows product ideas to be measured against each other.

Product screening weeds out undesirable ideas, often using a special checklist.

Figure 10-4 contains an illustration of a new-product screening checklist. It has three major categories: general characteristics, marketing characteristics, and production characteristics. Within each category there are several product attributes to be assessed. These attributes are scored on the basis of 1 (outstanding) to 10 (very poor) for every product idea. In addition, the importance of each product attribute is weighted, since the attributes vary in their impact on new-product success. This is an example of how a firm would develop overall ratings for two potential new-product ideas:

1. Product idea A receives a rating of 53 on its general characteristics, 50 on its marketing characteristics, and 47 on its production characteristics. Product idea B receives ratings of 50, 60, and 40 respectively.
2. The company assigns an importance weight of 4 to general characteristics, 5 to marketing characteristics, and 3 to production characteristics. The poorest possible overall rating is 780 [(70 × 4) + (70 × 5) + (50 × 3)].
3. Product idea A obtains an overall rating of 603 [(53 × 4) + (50 × 5) + (47 × 3)]. Product idea B obtains an overall rating of 620 [(50 × 4) + [(60 × 5) + (40 × 3)].
4. Product idea A's overall rating is better than that for B because of its significantly better marketing evaluation (the characteristics judged most important by the firm for new-product success).

During the screening stage the potential for product patentability must be determined. A **patent** grants the inventor of a useful product or process exclusive selling rights for a period of 17 years. In the United States any product or process can be patented through the Patent Office if it is novel and useful and plans for a working model are provided. A patent holder has the right to sell his or her invention or receive licensing fees from it. When patents are filed, the information pertaining to them becomes public.

A patent permits exclusive selling rights for 17 years.

As an illustration, Scovill considers these questions regarding patents in its new-product development procedure: Can a proposal be patented? Are competi-

---

[18] Lawrence Ingrassia, ''By Improving Scratch Paper, 3M Gets New-Product Winner,'' *Wall Street Journal* (March 31, 1983), p. 31.

**Figure 10-4
A New-Product Screening
Checklist**

GENERAL CHARACTERISTICS OF NEW PRODUCT   Rating*

Profit potential   _____
Existing competition   _____
Potential competition   _____
Size of market   _____
Level of investment   _____
Patentability   _____
Level of risk   _____

MARKETING CHARACTERISTICS OF NEW PRODUCTS

Fit with marketing capabilities   _____
Effect on existing products (brands)   _____
Appeal to current consumer markets   _____
Potential length of product life cycle   _____
Existence of differential advantage   _____
Impact on image   _____
Resistance to seasonal factors   _____

PRODUCTION CHARACTERISTICS OF NEW PRODUCTS

Fit with production capabilities   _____
Length of time to commercialization   _____
Ease of product manufacture   _____
Availability of labor and material resources   _____
Ability to produce at competitive prices   _____

*Each characteristic is rated on a 1-10 scale.
  1 = outstanding; 10 = very poor.

Note: Companies will usually weight these
         characteristics, since they are not all
         of equal value.

tive items patented? When do patents expire? Are patents on competitive items available under a licensing agreement? Are we free of patent liability (infringement)?[19]

Concept Testing

Concept testing determines customer attitudes before high investment in product development.

A firm needs to acquire consumer feedback about its product ideas. **Concept testing** presents the consumer with a proposed product and measures purchase intention at this early stage of development.

Concept testing is a quick and inexpensive tool for measuring consumer enthusiasm. It involves asking potential consumers to react to a picture, written statement, or oral description of a product, thus enabling the firm to determine initial attitudes prior to expensive, time-consuming prototype development. Fig-

[19] Scovill, "New Product Development Procedure," Section #20–100, Exhibit #2, p. 1.

A leading air conditioner manufacturer is developing a completely portable room model. This air conditioner is expected to weigh 8 pounds, operate on regular electrical current, be adaptable to most home windows (the only tool needed will be a screwdriver), and cool rooms up to 12 X 20 feet. Consumers will be able to move the air conditioner from room to room and install it in less than five minutes.

Would you please answer some questions to give us a better idea of the air conditioner's marketability?

1. React to the concept of a portable room air conditioner.
_____
_____
_____
_____

2. Under what circumstances would you consider buying a portable room air conditioner?
_____
_____
_____

3. What would be a fair price for a portable room air conditioner?
_____
_____

4. Do you have any suggestions about the design or features of the air conditioner?
_____
_____
_____
_____

5. How likely would you be to buy a portable room air conditioner within the next year? Check one answer.

Very likely   _____
Somewhat likely   _____
Don't know   _____
Somewhat unlikely   _____
Very unlikely   _____

Figure 10-5
A Brief Concept Test for a Proposed Portable Room Air-Conditioner

ure 10-5 shows a concept test for a proposed portable room air conditioner. Among the many companies using concept testing are Kodak, CPC (Best Foods, etc.), and Minnetonka (Softsoap, etc.).

In general, concept testing should ask these types of questions of consumers:[20]

1. Is the idea easy to understand?
2. Do you perceive distinct benefits for this product over those products currently on the market?
3. Do you find the claims about this product believable?

---

[20] Adapted from Philip Kotler, *Marketing Management: Analysis, Planning, and Control*, Fifth Edition (Englewood Cliffs, N.J.: Prentice-Hall, 1984), p. 325. See also, David A. Schwartz, "Concept Test *Can* Be Improved—And Here's How to Do It," *Marketing News* (January 6, 1984), Section 1, pp. 22–23, 25.

4. Would you buy the product?
5. Would you replace your current brand with this new product?
6. Would this product meet a real need?
7. What improvements can you suggest in various attributes of the concept?
8. How frequently would you buy the product?
9. Who would use it?

Business Analysis

Business analysis
**investigates demand,
costs, competition, and
other factors.**

Business analysis for the remaining product ideas centers on demand projections, costs, competition, investment requirements, and profits. Business analysis is much more time consuming and detailed than product screening. Following are some of the factors to be considered in business analysis:

Factors	Considerations
Demand projections	Potential sales at different prices; short- and long-run sales potential; speed of consumer acceptance; seasonality in sales; rate of repurchases; channel intensity
Cost projections	Total and per unit fixed and variable costs; use of existing facilities and resources; start-up vs. continuing costs; estimates of future raw materials and other costs; economies of scale; channel needs; break-even point
Competition	Short-run and long-run market shares of company and competitors; time until competitor introduces new product; strengths and weaknesses of competitors; potential competitors; likely competitive strategies in response to new product by firm
Required investment	Product planning (engineering, patent search, product development, testing); promotion (advertising, sales personnel, promotions, samples); production (facilities, maintenance, materials, financing); distribution (shipping, storing, selling, dealer support)
Profitability	Time to recoup initial costs; short- and long-run total and per unit profits; channel needs; control over price; return on investment (ROI); risk

Because the next step is the expensive and time-consuming product-development stage, critical use of business analysis is essential to eliminate marginal items.

Product Development

Product development
**focuses on manufacturing
and outlines a marketing
strategy.**

The **product development** stage converts a product idea into a physical form and identifies a basic marketing strategy. Product development involves product construction, packaging, branding, product and brand positioning, and attitude and usage testing.

Product-construction decisions include the type and quality of materials comprising the product, the method of production, costs and production time requirements per unit, the level of plant capacity, alternative sizes and colors, and the time needed to move from development to commercialization.

Packaging decisions include the materials to be used, the functions to be performed (such as promotion and storage), costs, and alternative sizes and colors. Branding decisions include the choice of a new or existing name, exclusivity, trademark protection, and the image sought. Packaging and branding are discussed in depth in Chapter 11.

Product and brand positioning involve the selection of a market segment, positioning the new item against competitors, and positioning the new item against other company offerings. Attitude and usage testing center on consumer perceptions of and satisfaction with the product.

Product development can be quite costly. Innovative consumer products often cost a million dollars or more for development. For example, Ford invested several years and over $1 billion to develop its Ford Tempo and Mercury Topaz cars, advertised as "a remarkable combination of driving and handling features in a 5-passenger car."[21] See Figure 10-6.

Sometimes product development is a difficult process. For example, Gillette developed Dry Idea, a new roll-on antiperspirant that "goes on dry," after concept testing attracted consumer interest. Consumers liked the idea of a strong antiperspirant that was dry on application.

Gillette's problem was to develop the product as desired by consumers. It had to find a replacement for water in the antiperspirant formulation. One ingredient dissolved the ball in the applicator. Another was too oily. A third had a short shelf-life—it became rock-hard after four months. Finally, a proper ingredient was found and tested with women who sat in a 100-degree "hot room" for several hours. It was also smeared on rabbits' skins and fed to rats to test its safety.

Next, packaging was needed. The first packaging developed was egg-shaped; it made the product feel too dry when applied and allowed the contents to leak. Engineers gave the applicator a texture and built a clicking noise into it to enable consumers to know it was working. After all this, Gillette decided to continue with a modified conventional roll-on bottle.

Last, a brand name had to be determined. More than a dozen names were tested on consumers. Among those rejected were Dry a Mite (sounded to much like a drain cleaner), Feel Free (sounded like a tampon), and Omni and Horizon (automobile names). Dry Idea was selected, and positioned for women aged twenty to forty-five.[22]

Test Marketing

Test marketing involves placing a product for sale in one or more selected areas and observing its actual performance under the proposed marketing plan. The purpose of the test is to evaluate the product and pretest the firm's marketing plan prior to a full-scale introduction of the product.[23]

Test marketing enables the product to be analyzed in a real setting. Rather than inquire about intentions, test marketing allows actual consumer behavior to be observed. The firm can also learn about competitive reactions and the response

Test marketing places a product in selected areas and observes its performance.

[21] Douglas R. Sease, "Ford Awaits the Payoff on Its 4-Year Gamble on New Compact Car," *Wall Street Journal* (May 4, 1983), pp. 1, 24.

[22] Neil Ulman, "Sweating It Out: Time, Risk, Ingenuity All Go into Launching New Personal Product," *Wall Street Journal,* (November 17, 1978), pp. 1, 41.

[23] *Advertising Age* annually publishes a special section on the latest developments in test marketing. For example, see "Special Report: Test Marketing," *Advertising Age* (February 20, 1984), pp. M–9—M–44.

Reprinted by permission.

of channel members. On the basis of test marketing, the firm can go ahead with its plans on a larger scale, modify the product and then expand its effort, modify the marketing plan and then expand its effort, or drop the product. Procter & Gamble, Levi Strauss, and McDonald's are among the companies who use test marketing.

The test-marketing process requires several decisions: when, where, how long, what information to acquire, and how to apply results. See Figure 10-7. When the market test is conducted depends on speed and timing. In a highly competitive environment, companies seek to bring a product into test marketing as quickly as possible. In some cases, particularly for seasonal items, timing is more important than speed. For example, summer fashions would not test well in New York during December.

Where to test market consists of how many and which cities in which to

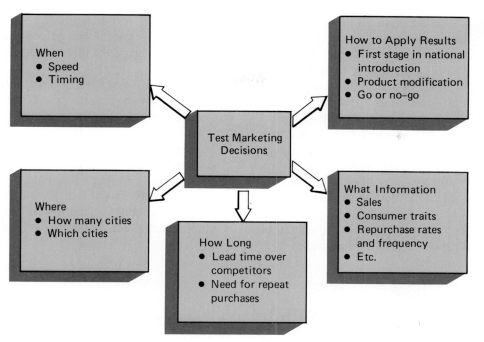

Figure 10-7
Test Marketing Decisions

introduce the product. Usually companies test market in two or three cities. A two-city test can cost $250,000 or more. The choice of which city to use depends on its representativeness relative to the national market, the degree of retailer cooperation, costs, the level of competition, and the ability to control and measure the marketing program. One expert classifies Cedar Rapids and Des Moines, Iowa; Cincinnati, Ohio; Omaha, Nebraska; Portland, Oregon; South Bend, Indiana; Springfield, Illinois; and Syracuse, New York, as ideal test market cities. They are the "most average of the average."[24]

The length of a market test typically runs from two months to two years. This depends on the company's lead time over competitors, the objectives of the test, the product's rate of repurchase, and the desire for secrecy. The test should be long enough to show sales after initial enthusiasm has worn off. The percentage of repeat purchases, the frequency of repeat purchases, and product or marketing deficiencies should be carefully monitored. For frequently purchased items, a six-month test is normally adequate.

The firm must determine what information it seeks from a test market and measure results against company objectives. Some types of information sought are sales, characteristics of consumers, rate of purchase, frequency of repurchase, distribution strengths and weaknesses, dealer enthusiasm, market share, effect of the new product on other company products, competitive reactions, the effectiveness of the marketing strategy, and reactions to the product itself.

Last, the firm must consider how it will use test results. For some firms, test marketing is only used to gain consumer acceptance and is a first step in national introduction. Others use it to determine necessary modifications in product and

[24] Eugene Carlson, "Peoria Isn't Average Enough for One Ad Agency Anymore," *Wall Street Journal* (September 27, 1983), p. 37.

marketing plans. Still others use test marketing for final go or no-go decisions; these will drop products not performing up to company expectations before commercialization. In order to make test marketing efficient, only information that will be used by the firm should be collected.

There are some major limitations to test marketing.

Although test marketing has been successful in many cases, some companies now question its effectiveness and downplay or skip this stage in the new-product planning process. Dissatisfaction with test marketing arises from its costs, the time delays before full introduction, information being provided to competitors, an inability to predict national results based on one or two test market cities, and the impact of external factors, such as the economy and competition, on test results.

Frequently test marketing allows nontesting competitors to catch up with the innovative firm by the time the product is ready for national distribution. In these five cases, test marketing actually enabled competitors to reach the national market before the original firm:[25]

Test Market Brand	First in National Introduction
Arm in Arm Deodorant (Helene Curtis)	Arm & Hammer Deodorant (Church & Dwight)
Maxim (General Foods)	Taster's Choice (Nestlé)
High Yield Coffee (Hills Brothers)	Folgers' Flakes (Procter & Gamble)
Prima Salsa Tomato Sauce (Hunt-Wesson)	Ragu Extra Thick & Zesty (Chesebrough-Pond)
Cooking Ease (Clorox)	Mazola No-Stick (CPC International)

Commercialization

Commercialization involves a major marketing commitment.

After all testing is completed, the firm is ready to introduce the product to its full target market. This is known as ***commercialization*** and corresponds to the introductory stage of the product life cycle. Commercialization involves implementation of a total marketing plan and full production.

The commercialization stage often requires considerable expenditures and rapid decision making. For example, Campbell began regional marketing of Prego bottled spaghetti sauce in 1981, with an advertising budget of $15 million. Advertising was increased to $25 million for 1982, when Campbell started national marketing; this amounted to about 25 per cent of sales. In response to Campbell, Chesebrough-Pond (maker of the leading spaghetti sauce, Ragu) added a new Ragu Homestyle spaghetti sauce, spent $20 million to promote it, and distributed 75-cent discount coupons for regular Ragu in 1982. Chesebrough-Pond then introduced Ragu Chunky Garden-style sauce in late 1983, and budgeted $22 million for first-year advertising. Said an observer, "These two brands are beating each other's brains out."[26]

Sometimes, commercialization of a new product must overcome consumer

---

[25] Geoffrey E. Meredith, "Test Markets Succumb to the Defense," *Advertising Age* (February 4, 1980), pp. SS–24—S–25.

[26] Betsy Morris, "New Campbell Entry Sets Off a Big Spaghetti Sauce Battle," *Wall Street Journal* (December 2, 1982), p. 31; and Nancy Giges, "Ragu Grows Via Garden Plot," *Advertising Age* (September 26, 1983), p. 10.

resistence because of ineffective prior company offerings. This occurred with American Motors' Renault Alliance. A preintroduction survey of potential customers indicated that most would not consider an AMC or Renault product. Nonetheless, AMC was able to make 90 per cent of the sales of the new Alliance to customers who had never owned an AMC car before by focusing on ''European technology, now built in America to be affordable'' during early advertising. Now, the Alliance is AMC's best success since the 1950 Rambler.[27]

Among the factors to be considered in the commercialization stage are the speed of acceptance by consumers, the speed of acceptance by channel members, the intensity of distribution (how many outlets), production capabilities, the promotional mix, prices, competition, the time period until profitability occurs, and the costs of commercialization.

Growing Products

The growth rate and total sales level of new products rely heavily on two related consumer behavior concepts: the adoption process and the diffusion process.

The *adoption process* is the procedure an individual consumer goes through when learning about and purchasing a new product. It includes the mental and behavioral sequence through which consumers progress, potentially leading to the acceptance and continued use of a product or brand.[28] The adoption process is in six stages:[29]

> The *adoption process* explains the new-product purchase behavior of individual consumers.

1. Awareness: the person learns of the existence of a product but does not have information about it.
2. Interest: the person is motivated to seek information.
3. Evaluation: the person decides whether to try the product.
4. Trial: the person buys the product and tests its usefulness.
5. Adoption: the person uses the product on a regular basis.
6. Confirmation: the person seeks reinforcement and may reverse the decision if exposed to conflicting messages.

The rate (speed) of adoption depends on the traits of consumers, the product, and the firm's marketing effort. The rate of adoption will be faster if consumers have high discretionary income and are willing to try new offerings; the product presents little physical, social, or financial risk; the product has an advantage over other items already on the market; the product is a modification of an existing idea and not a major innovation; the product is compatible with current consumer life-styles; the attributes of the product can be easily communicated; the impor-

---

[27] Bill Abrams, ''Careful Study, Good Product Making AMC's Alliance a Hit,'' *Wall Street Journal* (April 21, 1983), p. 35.

[28] Leon G. Schiffman and Leslie Lazar Kanuk, *Consumer Behavior* (Englewood Cliffs, N.J.: Prentice-Hall, 1978), p. 262.

[29] Everett M. Rogers, *Diffusion of Innovation* (New York: Free Press, 1962), pp. 81–86; and Everett M. Rogers and F. Floyd Shoemaker, *Communication of Innovations,* Second Edition (New York: Free Press, 1971), p. 103.

tance of the product is low; the product can be tried in small quantities; mass advertising and distribution are used; the product is consumed quickly; the product is easy to use; and the marketer responds to the changing needs of the consumer as he or she moves through the adoption process and seeks to satisfy those needs.

The *diffusion process* describes when different market segments are likely to purchase a product.

The ***diffusion process*** describes the manner in which different members of the target market often accept and purchase a product. The process spans the time from product introduction until market saturation. It is in five stages:[30]

1. Innovators are the first consumers to accept a new product. They are venturesome, willing to accept risk, socially aggressive, communicative, and cosmopolitan. As detailed in Chapter 6, it is necessary to determine which innovators are opinion leaders—those who influence others to purchase. This group represents 2.5 per cent of the target market.
2. Early adopters are the next group of consumers to accept a new product. They enjoy the leadership, prestige, and respect that early purchases bring. These consumers tend to be opinion leaders. They adopt new ideas early but use discretion. This group represents 13.5 per cent of the target market.
3. The early majority is the first part of the mass market to buy a product. They have status in their social class and are outgoing, communicative, and attentive to information cues. This group represents 34 per cent of the target market.
4. The late majority is the second part of the mass market to buy a product. They are less cosmopolitan and responsive to change. The late majority includes people with lower economic and social status, those past middle age, and skeptics. This group represents 34 per cent of the target market.
5. Laggards are the last people to purchase a product. They are price conscious, extremely suspicious of novelty and change, low in income and status, tradition bound, and conservative. Laggards do not adopt a product until it reaches maturity. From a profit perspective, it may be wise for some firms to ignore laggards because it could be extremely expensive to reach and market a product to this small group. On the other hand, a market segmenter might do well to concentrate on a line of products for laggards. This group represents 16 per cent of the target market.

The adoption and diffusion processes operate slowly for major innovations.

The rate and level of growth for a major innovation may be slow at first because there is an extended adoption process and the early majority may be hesitant to purchase. It may then rise quite quickly. Figure 10-8 shows the growth of color televisions in the United States from 1950 to 1984. These sets were first marketed in the early 1950s. Yet only 340,000 households (less than 1 per cent of all U.S. households) owned one by 1960. At this point, sales began to expand rapidly, because of reduced prices, better-quality sets, improved programming, increased competition, and the transition from innovators to early majority. As of 1984, almost 91 per cent of U.S. households had at least one color set.

The home video recorder, another major innovation, succeeded much more quickly than color television, although sales penetration was not immediate. Sony mastered the technology for the home video recorder in 1976. The recorders were priced at well over $1,000 each; and only 30,000 units were sold in 1976.

[30] Rogers, *Diffusion of Innovation*.

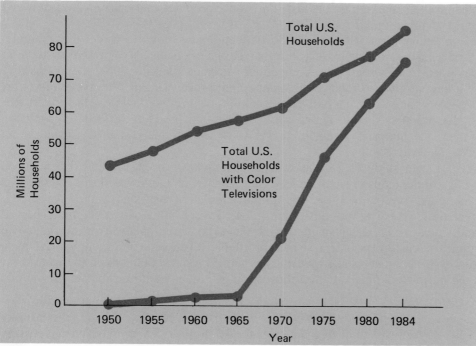

Figure 10-8
**The Growth of Television
Sets in the U.S.
(1950–1984)**

Source: "Trends in Television, 1950 to Date," Television Bureau of Advertising, Inc. (March 1984), p. 3.

200,000 recorders were sold in 1977. In 1980, 800,000 recorders were sold. During 1983, 4 million recorders were sold in the U.S. There are over a dozen major competitors, a wide variety of models, and prices starting as low as $300.

For minor innovations or product modifications, growth is even quicker. As an example, Polaroid has sold self-developing cameras for more than thirty years and is the recognized leader in the field. In 1981, it introduced a new automatic-focus Sun camera. Because of its past reputation, intensive distribution, and multimillion dollar advertising campaign, Polaroid was able to generate high initial sales for the new camera and expected saturation in fewer than two years.

Among the many products now in the growth stage, personal home computers, national newspapers (*USA Today*), and large-screen rear-projection television sets will be interesting to observe over the next several years.

Mature Products

When products reach the late majority and laggard markets, they are in the maturity stage of the product life cycle. Company goals turn from growth to maintenance. Because new products are so costly and risky, more and more firms are

Proper marketing can enable mature products to maintain high sales.

placing their marketing emphasis on mature products that offer steady sales and profits with minimal risk.[31]

In the analysis of mature products, a company should consider these factors: the size of the existing market, the characteristics and needs of present customers, untapped market segments, competition, product modifications, the availability of a new product to replace the mature one, profit margins, the marketing effort necessary for each sale, channel satisfaction, the promotional mix, the importance of the products in the overall product line, the products' effects on company image, the number of remaining years for the products, and the management effort needed.

A recent study of 25 market-leading brands from 1923 found that nineteen were still the industry sales leaders, four were second, one was third, and one was among the top five in 1983. These brands include Ivory soap, Lipton tea, Goodyear tires, Sherwin-Williams paints, Life Savers mints, Swift Premium bacon, and Coca-Cola.[32] Each of the brands provides its company with a large, loyal group of customers and a stable, profitable position in the market. The most successful companies and industries generate products that remain in maturity for long periods of time, as the following illustrations demonstrate:

- Until 1969, Arm & Hammer baking soda (which was developed in 1846) was marketed simply as a baking soda to be used in cooking. Changing consumer life-styles resulted in stagnant sales for the product. Then, intensive advertising was begun. The baking soda was repositioned to include new product uses: refrigerator freshener, kitchen drain deodorizer, bath water additive, plaque remover for dental plates, cat litter deodorizer, etc. New products, such as detergents, were introduced under the Arm & Hammer name. Between 1969 and 1982, yearly sales rose from $15.6 million to $150 million.[33] Figure 10-9 shows a number of products now marketed under the Arm & Hammer name.
- The first Corvette was marketed in 1953; and it quickly appealed to a loyal group of customers with "an image of adventure, excitement, with-it-ness, virility." Except for a brief period during and after the 1973 oil embargo, the 1970s were strong years for the Corvette (with sales of nearly 50,000 cars per year). When the U.S. auto industry declined in 1981 and 1982, the Corvette also declined (1982 sales were 23,000 units). Then, General Motors redesigned the Corvette and introduced a new $22,000 model. Reviewers called it the "most advanced production car on the planet," "an authentic American hero," and "one of the supercars of the world." Sales are expected to be constrained only by production capacity (37,000 cars per year as of 1983).[34]
- The telephone was invented by Alexander Graham Bell in the 1870s. Until 1977, telephones could be manufactured and sold only by AT&T. At that time, the Federal Communications Commission ruled that any company could make and sell phones. As a result, more than 100 firms entered this mature market and developed a wide assortment of products, from designer phones to hand-held phones, to stimulate sales. Recently, there has been a boom in cordless

---

[31] See Roger W. Hearne, "Fighting Industrial Senility: A System for Growth in Mature Industries," *Journal of Business Strategy*, Vol. 3 (Fall 1982), pp. 3–20.

[32] "'Old Standbys' Hold Their Own," *Advertising Age* (September 19, 1983), p. M–20.

[33] Jack J. Honomichl, "The Ongoing Saga of 'Mother Baking Soda,'" *Advertising Age* (September 20, 1982), pp. M–2, M–3, M–22.

[34] Bernice Kanner, "Betting on the 'Vette," *New York* (May 16, 1983), pp. 18 ff.

Figure 10-9
Arm & Hammer: Stronger Than Ever

ARM & HAMMER is a registered trademark of Church & Dwight Co., Inc. This picture was reproduced with permission of Church & Dwight Co., Inc.

telephone sales—from under 1 million units in 1981 to an estimated 6.6 million units in 1984. Telephone sales are expected to remain high for the next several years.[35]

There are several strategies available for extending the mature stage of the product life cycle. Table 10-2 presents seven such strategies and provides examples of each.

Not all mature products can be revitalized or extended. The consumer's need may disappear, as occurred when frozen orange juice replaced orange juice squeezers. Better, cheaper, and more convenient products may be developed, such as electronic calculators to replace mechanical ones and plastic furniture moldings to replace wooden ones. Competitors may secure a strategic advantage, such as IBM getting a large government order for traditional electric typewriters. Finally, the market may be saturated and additional marketing efforts may be unable to generate sufficient sales to justify time and cost expenditures.

Product Deletion

When products offer limited sales and profit potential, involve large amounts of management time, tie up resources that could be used for other opportunities,

---

[35] James A. White, "Sales of Telephones Are Expected to Boom as More Consumers Realize They Can Buy," *Wall Street Journal* (January 28, 1983), p. 33; and Phil Mintz, "Cordless Phones Wired for Success This Season," *Newsday* (December 18, 1983), p. 118.

Table 10-2
Strategies for Extending the Mature Stage of the Product Life Cycle

Strategy	Examples
1. Develop new uses for the product	Jell-O used in garden salads Arm & Hammer baking soda used as a refrigerator deodorant
2. Develop new product features and refinements	Zoom lenses for 35mm cameras Battery-powered televisions Campbell's Chunky soups
3. Increase market segmentation	Family and individual sizes for food products Regional editions of major magazines
4. Find new classes of consumers for the present product	Nylon carpeting for institutional markets Johnson & Johnson's baby shampoo used by adults Coca-Cola and Pepsi-Cola in less-developed nations
5. Find new classes of consumers for the modified product	Breakfast menu at McDonald's Industrial power tools altered for the do-it-yourself market Inexpensive copy machines for home offices
6. Increase product usage among current users	Multiple packages for soda and beer Jeans promoted for wear at social gatherings Season tickets for sports and entertainment events
7. Change marketing strategy	Hosiery sold in supermarkets Electronic games priced at $30 or less (down from $100) *Reader's Digest* advertising on television

Products need to be deleted if they have consistently poor sales, tie up resources, and cannot be revived.

create channel dissatisfaction due to low turnover, reflect poorly on the company, and divert attention from long-term goals, these products should be deleted from the firm's offerings.

However, there are a number of factors to consider before deleting a product:

1. As a product matures, it blends in with existing items and becomes part of the total product line.
2. Customers and channel members may be hurt if the item is withdrawn.
3. The firm may not want competitors to have the only product for customers.
4. Poor current sales and profits may be only temporary.
5. The marketing strategy, not the product, may be the cause of poor results.

Ralph S. Alexander, the first marketer to write in depth about product deletion, proposed a systematic, four-step procedure for eliminating products: (1) select products that are candidates for deletion, (2) gather and analyze information about these products, (3) make deletion decisions, and (4) remove products from the line.[36]

Low-margin or rapidly declining products are often dropped or de-emphasized, as these recent examples show:

- Zenith decided to drop its Beta-format video recorders and concentrate on VHS models. Although Sony popularized the video recorder using the Beta-format, only 35 per cent of U.S. recorder sales were contributed by Beta-format models in 1983.[37]

[36] Ralph S. Alexander, "The Death and Burial of 'Sick' Products," *Journal of Marketing*, Vol. 28 (April 1964), pp. 1–7. See also, George J. Avlonitis, "The Product-Elimination Decision and Strategies," *Industrial Marketing Management*, Vol. 12 (February 1983), pp. 31–43.

[37] Heywood Klein, "Zenith Radio to Sell VHS Video Recorder and Drop Beta Line Made by Sony Corp.," *Wall Street Journal* (January 3, 1984), p. 4.

A COMPANY PLANS TO DELETE ITS LINE OF TYPEWRITERS.

IT MUST CONSIDER:

1. REPLACEMENT PARTS

- Who will make them?
- How long will they be made?

2. NOTIFICATION TIME

NOTICE:
We are no longer making typewriters

- How soon before the actual deletion will an announcement be made?
- Will channel members be alerted early enough so that they can line up alternate suppliers?

3. GUARANTEES

GUARANTEE

- How will guarantees be honored?
- After guarantees expire, how will repairs be handled?

Figure 10-10
Product Deletion Considerations

- Bell & Howell, which started as a camera manufacturer, abandoned its photography products (cameras, projectors, and accessories). It was unable to compete with Kodak, Polaroid, Nikon, Minolta, Canon, and others. Said one executive, "We were losing market share and facing intense competition in almost every line." Now, Bell & Howell concentrates on specialized business equipment, and technical education and training.[38]
- In 1980, Ford removed the Pinto from its product line. Although almost 3 million Pintos were sold during the decade it was on the market, sales declined rapidly after the mid-1970s. There was a lot of negative publicity about safety problems. Ford decided the product could not be revitalized and moved ahead with other models.[39]

When discontinuing a product, the firm must remember to consider replacement parts, notification time for customers and channel members, and honoring of guarantees/warranties. See Figure 10-10.

Summary

Management of the product life cycle deals with the creation and supervision of products over their life. A new product involves a modification or an innovation that the consumer perceives as substantive. A modification is an alteration in an

[38] Eric N. Berg, "Bell & Howell's New Direction," *New York Times* (July 26, 1983), pp. D1, D5; and Bell & Howell: Sharpening Its Focus on Video, Technical Schools, and Office Machines," *Business Week* (April 16, 1984), pp. 104–105.
[39] Ralph Gray, "Putting the Pinto out to Pasture After a Decade," *Advertising Age* (April 7, 1980), p. 64.

existing product. A minor innovation is an item that has not been previously sold by the firm but has been sold by others. A major innovation is an item that is new to the firm and has not been sold by others.

Company objectives for introducing new products relate to sales, profits, less dependence on one product or product line, use of an established company distribution system, use of waste materials, and/or image.

When the company suffers a financial loss, a product is an absolute failure. When the company makes a profit but does not attain its objectives, a product is a relative failure. Failures occur because of a lack of a significant competitive advantage, poor planning, poor timing, and excessive enthusiasm by the product sponsor.

Proper new-product planning involves a comprehensive, seven-step process. During idea generation, new-product opportunities are sought and emphasis is placed on sources and methods. In product screening, unattractive ideas are weeded out by the use of a new-product screening checklist. At concept testing, the consumer reacts to the proposed idea and states a purchase intention. Business analysis requires a detailed evaluation of demand, costs, competition, investment, and profits. Product development converts an idea into a physical form and outlines a basic marketing strategy. Test marketing, a much-disputed technique, involves placing a product for sale in one or more selected areas and observing its performance under actual conditions. Commercialization is the sale of the product to the full target market. It should be noted that a new product can be aborted or modified at any point in the process.

The growth rate and level of a new product are highly dependent on the adoption process, which describes how a single consumer learns about and purchases a product, and the diffusion process, which describes how different members of the target market learn about and purchase a product. The adoption and diffusion processes are quicker for certain consumers, products, and marketing strategies.

Mature products provide companies with stable sales and profits and loyal consumers. They do not require the risks and costs of new products. There are several factors to consider and alternative strategies from which to choose when planning to sustain mature products. It may not be possible to retain these products if consumer needs disappear, new products make them obsolete, competitors exhibit too much strength, or the market becomes too saturated.

Product deletion is necessary for weak products. It may be difficult because of the interrelation of products, lost jobs, the impact on customers and channel members, and other factors. Product deletion should be conducted in a systematic manner.

Questions for Discussion

1. Give two current examples of a product modification, a minor innovation, and a major innovation. Explain your choices.
2. New products are expected to account for 35 per cent of total company sales by 1986. What are the pros and cons of this?

3. Comment on the following statement: "We never worry about relative product failures, because we make a profit on them. We only worry about absolute product failures."

4. A Nimslo executive stated that the firm's 3-D camera would sell well as long as it was marketed correctly; there would be no problem convincing customers the camera is worth buying. Do you agree or disagree? Why?

5. In 1981, it took only 7 product ideas to produce one successful product, compared with 58 ideas for one successful product in 1968. Yet, the new-product failure rate remains as high as ever. Explain this.

6. During idea generation, should the firm's objective be to discover as many ideas as possible or to concentrate on the best three to five ideas? Why?

7. Develop a ten-item new-product screening checklist for a proposed microwave oven. How would you weight each item?

8. Construct a 50-word concept test for a product which reduces the need for weekly lawn cutting by slowing down grass growth. What would you expect to learn from this test?

9. How does business analysis differ from product screening?

10. What is the major task during product development? Under which circumstances would a company decide to abandon a new product during this stage?

11. For what types of products is test marketing most helpful? Least helpful? Explain your answer.

12. Differentiate between the commercialization strategies for a product modification and a major innovation. Relate your answers to the adoption process and the diffusion process.

13. How can a firm speed a product's growth?

14. Is the maturity stage a good or bad position for a product to occupy? Why?

15. Select a product that has been in existence for ten or more years and explain why it cannot be rejuvenated.

16. Why is a product deletion decision so difficult?

Case 1 *TV-Cable Week:* A Major New-Product Failure*

In September 1983, Time Inc. announced that it was terminating *TV-Cable Week*, only five months after the magazine was introduced. Time estimated that $47 million was lost on the venture, which had begun with expectations for *TV-Cable Week* eventually to become the company's best-selling magazine (ahead of *Time*) and to challenge *TV Guide*. Although Time devoted a year to detailed planning before the magazine was launched and had a corporate commitment to invest $100 million to commercialize it over a 5-year period, the company (which is the successful publisher of *Time, People, Life, Sports Illustrated, Fortune*, etc.) was unable to overcome a number of serious problems.

Analysts pinpointed these difficulties:

* The data in this case are drawn from "Some Top Products of '83 Won't See '84," *Advertising Age* (January 2, 1984), p. 3; Stuart J. Elliott, "Time Gives Up on Cable Book," *Advertising Age* (September 19, 1983), pp. 1, 96; "Right Decision Given Problems, Observers Say," *Advertising Age* (September 19, 1983), pp. 1, 96; Daniel Machalaba, "Time Inc. to End Its 5-Month-Old *TV-Cable Week*," *Wall Street Journal* (September 16, 1983), p. 4; and Ronald Alsop, "Time Inc.'s *TV-Cable Week* Said to Fail Because It Neglected Operator Interests," *Wall Street Journal* (September 19, 1983), p. 8.

- *TV-Cable Week* had to satisfy three distinct target markets—readers, cable system operators, and advertisers. The magazine was able to attract less than 400,000 readers (compared with a combined 4 million audience for *Cable Today* and *Cable Guide*) and a declining group of advertisers, because few cable system operators agreed to have their programs listed. These operators believed that the magazine did not offer them enough control, did not enable them to highlight premium services, and helped Time Inc.'s own divisions (Home Box Office and Cinemax).
- *TV-Cable Week* had too much national and network television coverage. It did not adequately promote cable television and specific programs. "The guides have to help market the pay services, make them look extra special so that the viewer believes they're worth $30 or $35 a month."
- *TV-Cable Week* was published weekly, while other cable magazines were distributed monthly. Its newstand price was $.95 (*TV Guide* was $.50). Since it came out weekly, a home subscriber would pay $2.95 per month (compared to $1.00 for many cable guides).
- *TV Guide* was quite aggressive in its response to *TV-Cable Week*. It expanded cable listings by 25 per cent. It also boosted promotional expenditures substantially.

QUESTIONS

1. Comment on this statement, "You're talking about an entirely new kind of magazine. It was almost impossible to gauge how it would be received. And it was almost as impossible to test."
2. How could Time have attracted more cable system operators?
3. *TV Guide* is well entrenched. It has been around for over 30 years. Did Time withdraw *TV-Cable Week* too quickly? Explain your answer.
4. *Life* magazine was removed from the market for many years. Then, Time redesigned *Life* and reintroduced it. Should Time consider the same strategy for *TV-Cable Week?* Why or why not?

Case 2 The IBM Selectric Typewriter: Still Going Strong[†]

A 1981 advertisement for Olympia typewriters asserted that "Olympia Electronics are to the future what IBM Selectrics were to the past. Goodby, old friend." Selectric typewriter customers must not have read this ad, because they purchased 450,000 machines in 1982. In contrast, the total sales of all brands of electronic typewriters involved 260,000 units in 1982. IBM spent $1.5 million on promotion for the Selectric in 1982, up 31 per cent from 1981.

The Selectric typewriter, with its unique "golfball printer," was introduced in 1961. Yet, nearly twenty-five years later the Selectric remains the dominant typewriter on the market. In addition to strong current sales of new machines, more

---

[†] The data in this case are drawn from James A. White, "IBM's Selectric Typewriter Still Sells Well as Many Offices Shun Electronic Machines," *Wall Street Journal* (February 8, 1983), pp. 35, 45; and Franklin Whitehouse, "I.B.M.'s Typewriters Miss a Stroke," *New York Times* (March 28, 1982), Section 3, p. 4.

than eight million Selectrics remain in use. The Selectric enables IBM to retain an 80 per cent market share of electric typewriter sales (several hundred million dollars a year in sales for IBM).

The Selectric is a large business typewriter that is priced at around $1,000. Its users are fiercely brand loyal, feel comfortable with the typing format, feel electronic typewriters provide many unneeded features, and think electronics are too expensive (at $1,000 to $6,000 for office models). IBM predicts that it will sell several million more Selectrics in the future as they continue to be "the most popular typewriters for a long time to come." IBM is now the only U.S. manufacturer of heavy-duty typewriters.

The desktop electronic typewriter was introduced in 1978, promising easier, faster, and more efficient typing along with the ability to form communications systems by interfacing with a company's computer. This typewriter contained a built-in correction feature, positioned paper and set margins, had a memory bank for storing and reusing correspondence, and other features. While IBM had a 94 per cent share of the electronic typewriter market in 1978, this figure dropped to less than 50 per cent during 1982 as twenty competitors entered the market. Competitors forecast large increases in electronic sales in the near future, as the economy improves and computerization expands.

Although IBM is confident that Selectric typewriter sales will remain high for many years, the company is not complacent. IBM has begun marketing the $695 "Personal Typewriter," the first typewriter it has aimed at the home market; and new electronic typewriter models were marketed in 1983.

QUESTIONS

1. Explain the Selectric's long-run popularity in terms of the adoption process.
2. The Selectric typewriter has undergone only minor modifications over the past several years. For example, a self-correcting feature was added. However, IBM has not added a memory bank or other substantial new features. Evaluate this strategy.
3. Develop a marketing strategy for the new Personal Typewriter.
4. At what point should IBM say, "Goodby, old friend?" Is it possible that this time will never come? Why or why not?

Chapter 11

Branding and Packaging

CHAPTER OBJECTIVES

1. To define and distinguish among branding terms and to examine the importance of branding

2. To study the branding decisions a firm must consider regarding corporate symbols, branding philosophy, choice of brand names, and the use of trademarks

3. To define and distinguish among packaging terms and to examine the importance of packaging

4. To study the basic functions of packaging, factors considered in packaging decisions, and criticisms of packaging

*W*orldwide, Nissan Motor Corporation was the fourth largest motor company (behind General Motors, Ford, and Toyota) in 1981, with 2.6 million vehicles produced. It sold 500,000 vehicles in the U.S. during 1981. Nonetheless, in mid-1981, Nissan announced that it would phase out its highly popular Datsun name, the only one used in the U.S., and replace it with the corporate name (which was used in many other markets). This decision raised a number of doubts among observers and analysts.

Nissan believed that its new strategy was vital to long-term growth: "It's essential to unify the name of the company and the brand name in order to pursue our global strategy and to fulfill the kind of social responsibility requested [of us] by society and governments." Worldwide, Nissan had ventures with Italy's Alfa Romeo, Germany's Volkswagen, Spain's

Figure 11-1
The Nissan 200SX
The 1984 Nissan 200SX was the last Datsun model to switch to the Nissan name plate. There is a Datsun logo above the left tail lights.

Motor Iberica, and plans for a $500 million plant in Great Britain. It was also concerned that consumers did not link the brand Datsun with the company.

Nissan has used a gradual approach. Ads for 1982 Datsun models mentioned Nissan as the manufacturer. The 1982 Nissan Stanza and Sentra contained a Datsun logo. Existing car models retained the Datsun name until 1984. See Figure 11-1. New models all used the Nissan name. Both the Nissan and Datsun names are still prominently mentioned in dealer ads (many dealers continue to view themselves as Datsun dealers). It is estimated that a total of $150 million would eventually be spent in advertising the name change in the U.S.

A number of U.S. Datsun dealers have not been happy about Nissan's approach. They feel the Datsun name represents quality at a good price and that it has a high level of recognition. One Japanese competitor also has criticized Nissan, saying "I'd change the name of the company to Datsun." This strategy was followed by Sony and Olympus.

A vice-president of Datsun U.S.A. summarized the positions: "Some dealers feel that the name of Datsun has been part of their success and are concerned about losing their image. Others feel that one name identification will be better for everybody. Only time will tell. . . ."

Thus far, the concerns have been unwarranted. In 1982, Nissan's worldwide sales were about the same as in 1981, despite a poor year for the auto industry. 1983 sales were significantly better, as the economy improved throughout the world. Nonetheless, a 1984 consumer survey in the U.S. indicated that only 6 per cent of those interviewed recognized the Nissan name.[1]

---

[1] "A Worldwide Brand for Nissan," *Business Week* (August 24, 1981), p. 104; and "Datsun Name Shift Is Costly for Nissan," *New York Times* (January 23, 1984), pp. D1, D5.

The Nissan experience demonstrates how important corporate symbols and brand names are in a firm's long-run marketing strategy. In this chapter, both the branding and packaging aspects of product planning are examined. Branding and packaging decisions are complex and involve billions of dollars in expenditures.

Branding

A *brand* is a name, design, or symbol; the four types of brand designation are *brand name, brand mark, trade character,* and *trademark.*

An important part of product planning is branding, the procedure a firm follows in researching, developing, and implementing its brand(s). A *brand* is a name, design, or symbol (or combination of these) that identifies the products and services of a seller or group of sellers. By using or establishing well-known brands, companies are usually able to obtain public acceptance, extensive distribution, and higher prices.

There are four types of brand designation:

1. A *brand name* is a word, letter, group of words, or letters that can be spoken. Examples are Lite Beer, Lipton Cup-a-Soup, and Yankee Stadium.
2. A *brand mark* is a symbol, design, or distinctive coloring or lettering. Examples are Ralston-Purina's checkerboard and Prudential's rock.
3. A *trade character* is a brand mark that is personified. Examples are Ronald McDonald, Borden's Elsie the Cow, and Morton Salt's umbrella girl.
4. A *trademark* is a brand name, brand mark, or trade character or combination thereof that is given legal protection. When it is used, a registered trademark is followed by ®. Examples are Scotch® Brand tape, Scrabble®, and Master-Card®.

Brand names, brand marks, and trade characters are marketing designations for products and services. They do not offer legal protection against use by competitors, unless they are registered as trademarks (which all of the above examples have been). Trademarks ensure exclusivity for trademark owners or those securing their permission and provide legal remedies against firms using ''confusingly similar'' names, designs, or symbols. Trademarks are discussed more fully later in the chapter.

Branding started during the Middle Ages, when craft and merchant guilds were created to control both the quantity and quality of production. The guilds required that each producer mark goods so that output could be restricted and inferior goods traced to the producer. The marks also served as standards for quality because items were sold outside the local markets in which the guilds operated. In the fifteenth, sixteenth, and seventeenth centuries, guilds appeared throughout the cloth and cutlery trades.[2] The earliest and most aggressive promoters of brands in the United States were patent medicine manufacturers. Examples of current U.S. brands that started more than one hundred years ago are Borden's Condensed Milk, Quaker Oats, Vaseline, Pillsbury's Best Flour, and Ivory Soap.

[2] Dorothy Cohen, *Advertising* (New York: Wiley, 1972), pp. 48–49.

In the U.S., there are now over 300,000 brand names in circulation. Each year, the top 100 advertisers spend about $20 billion advertising their brands. Permanent media expenditures (such as a company logo, stationery, brochures, business forms and cards, and vehicular and building signs) for brands are another major cost.

A major goal of companies is to develop brand loyalty, a consumer's consistent repurchase of and preference for a brand. This allows them to maximize sales and maintain a strong brand image. Brand loyalty for supermarket products is particularly high. For example, a recent study showed that at least 75 per cent of supermarket shoppers were "exclusive one-brand users" of products such as salt, vinegar, dinner rolls, popcorn, waxed paper, oven cleaner, yogurt, and doughnuts.[3]

The use of popular brands can speed up public acceptance and gain dealer cooperation for new products. For instance, Murjani (a company unknown to many consumers) hired well-known Gloria Vanderbilt to design status jeans and called them Vanderbilt by Murjani. Soon after introduction, the basic denim jean was carried by 5,500 stores across the United States and sold for $36.[4]

The acceptance of new and continuing products is improved by popularizing brand names.

Re-establishing existing brand names is also often a top priority for companies. As an illustration, Heinz purchased Ore-Ida (a food processor) in the mid-1960s when Ore-Ida was near bankruptcy. Ore-Ida made french-fried potatoes that were treated as a commodity; there was limited brand recognition and sales were moderate. By aggressively advertising the Ore-Ida brand of french-fried potatoes, Heinz has been able to develop a stronger differential advantage (quality image). Today, Ore-Ida french fries have a market share of 55 per cent; the leading competitor has 3 per cent.[5]

In countries that do not use brand names, consumers and sellers both suffer. For example, in the past, the absence of brands for television sets in the Soviet Union meant customers could not identify the factory that habitually produced "lemons." The sales of all television sets suffered as a result.[6]

These are several reasons why branding is important:

- Product identification is facilitated. A customer can order a product or service by name instead of description. A brand name is substituted for a standard or specification.
- Customers are assured that a product or service has a certain level of quality and that they will obtain comparable quality if the same brand is reordered.
- The firm responsible for the product is known. The producer of unbranded items cannot be directly identified.
- Price comparisons are reduced as customers perceive brand distinctiveness. This is especially true when buyers attribute special characteristics to different brands.
- A firm is able to advertise its products and services and associate a brand and its characteristics in the buyer's mind.
- Product prestige is increased, as social visibility becomes meaningful.

Branding eases product identification, assures customers of a level of quality, and performs other valuable functions.

[3] "Progressive Grocer's Guide to Usage of Supermarket Products," *Progressive Grocer* (July 1983), pp. 39–41.

[4] Francesca Stanfill, "The Marketing of Gloria Vanderbilt," *New York Times Magazine* (October 14, 1979), pp. 29–31.

[5] Eamonn Fingleton, "Potato Peel and Prime Time," *Forbes* (October 11, 1982), p. 114.

[6] Theodore Levitt, "Branding on Trial," *Harvard Business Review*, Vol. 44 (March–April 1966), p. 28.

- Consumers feel less risk when purchasing a brand with which they are familiar and toward which they have a favorable attitude.
- Branding helps segment markets and create a distinctive image. By using multiple brands, different market segments are attracted.
- Channel cooperation is greater for well-known brands. A strong brand enables the producer to exert greater control in the channel.
- A brand can be used to sell an entire line of products, such as Polaroid cameras.
- A brand can be used to enter a new product category, such as Arm & Hammer detergent.

There are four branding decisions a firm must undertake. These involve corporate symbols, branding philosophy, choice of brand name, and the use of trademarks. See Figure 11-2.

Corporate Symbols

Corporate symbols help establish and maintain a company's overall image.

Corporate symbols are a firm's name, logo, and trade characters. These symbols are significant parts of overall company image. When a company first begins a business, expands or diversifies product lines, seeks new geographic markets, or finds its name to be unwieldy, nondistinctive, or confusing, it needs to evaluate

**Figure 11-2
Branding Decisions**

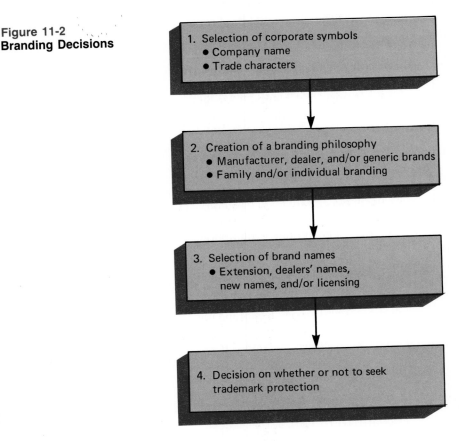

1. Selection of corporate symbols
   - Company name
   - Trade characters

2. Creation of a branding philosophy
   - Manufacturer, dealer, and/or generic brands
   - Family and/or individual branding

3. Selection of brand names
   - Extension, dealers' names, new names, and/or licensing

4. Decision on whether or not to seek trademark protection

and possibly change its corporate symbols. In 1983, 1,055 U.S. corporations adopted new names.[7] Following are examples of companies operating under each of these situations.

Rana Systems, a small manufacturer of computer software, first began business in October 1981. In selecting the company logo, a futuristic graphic design of the company's initials (RS), Rana Systems set these guidelines:

From Day One we wanted to be seen in the marketplace as a professional company with the look of an IBM or Radio Shack. We wanted whatever design we adopted to work from the start and to last. We didn't want to change as new products were introduced.[8]

Addressograph-Multigraph became AM International because only a small portion of its business dealt with mailing plate equipment. National Cash Register switched to NCR because it believed the old name was too restrictive. Other firms have retained parts of their original names (Georgia Pacific Plywood becoming Georgia Pacific) or developed acronyms from their former names (General Shoe Corporation becoming Genesco).

Allegheny Airlines changed its name to US Air, because the old name suggested a small regional airline. The Exxon name was developed, since the company's regional brands such as Esso and Humble could not be used nationwide and others had unfortunate foreign connotations (for example, Enco means "stalled car" in Japanese).

The National Railroad Passenger Corporation was an unwieldy name; it became Amtrack. The First National City Bank of New York was a nondistinctive name; it became Citibank. The United Biscuit Company of America changed its name to Keebler to avoid confusion with the Nabisco name.[9]

While some firms have developed abstract, less personal names and logos, others have found that personal impact is necessary. After negative experiences with the impersonal "N" (for NBC) and "RCA," RCA has returned to the colorful peacock and Nipper (the dog who listens to the company phonograph). In a similar vein, Campbell reintroduced the Campbell Kids as corporate symbols in 1983 after a five-year absence.[10]

Corporate symbols should not be developed in isolation, since they can impact on all aspects of a firm's marketing effort. An illustration of a well-integrated image is projected by Rusty Jones, the largest automobile rust proofer. Originally the firm was known as Matex and called its product Thixo-Tex. Research indicated poor consumer acceptance. The firm then developed the name Rusty Jones and associated it with the theme "Hello Rusty Jones, Goodbye Rusty Cars." A trade character, a smiling, red-haired man with a cowlick and mustache, was introduced as Rusty Jones. This allowed the consumer to see Rusty Jones as the man down the street who had worked on cars all his life and knew everything about them.[11] See Figure 11-3.

Corporate symbols need to be integrated with a firm's marketing strategy.

[7] "AT&T Sets Pace in Name Change," *Advertising Age* (January 16, 1984), p. 39.

[8] Norm Sklarewitz, "If the Corporate Image Calls for a Facelift," *Inc.* (December 1982), pp. 112.

[9] Hal Goodman, "Name-Dropping," *Across the Board* (May 1983), pp. 35–39.

[10] Nancy Giges, "Campbell Kids Back at Age 80," *Advertising Age* (January 16, 1984), p. 67.

[11] Madeleine Dreyfack, "A Red Mustache Makes Millions," *Marketing & Media Decisions* (November 1982), pp. 68 ff.

Figure 11-3
Rusty Jones From Matex International

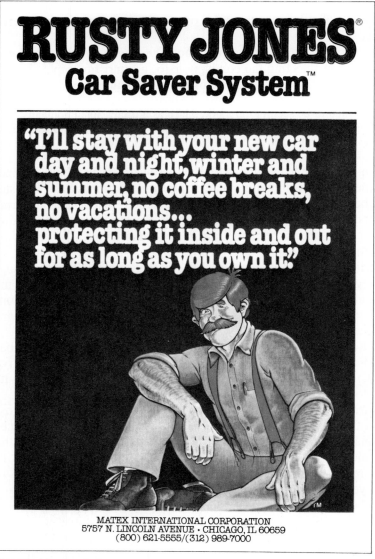

Reprinted by permission.

Branding Philosophy

When developing a brand strategy, a firm needs to state its branding philosophy. This philosophy outlines the use of manufacturer, dealer, and/or generic brands as well as the use of family or multiple branding.

MANUFACTURER, DEALER, AND GENERIC BRANDS

Manufacturer (national) brands are those items that contain the name of the manufacturer. *Dealer (private) brands* are those items that contain the name of the wholesaler or retailer. *Generic brands* are those items that contain the names of the products themselves and do not emphasize manufacturer or dealer names. See Table 11-1.

Table 11-1 **Manufacturer, Dealer, and Generic Brands**

Characteristic	Manufacturer Brand	Dealer Brand	Generic Brand
Target market	Risk avoider, quality conscious, brand loyal, status conscious, quick shopper	Price conscious, comparison shopper, quality conscious, moderate risk taker, store loyal	Price conscious, careful shopper, willing to accept lower quality, large family
Product	Well-known, trusted, best quality control, clearly identifiable, deep product line	Same overall quality as manufacturer, less emphasis on packaging, less assortment, not known to nonstore shoppers	Usually less overall quality than manufacturer, little emphasis on packaging, very limited assortment, not well known
Distribution	Usually sold at many competing retailers	Usually only available in the outlets of a single retailer	Varies
Promotion	Manufacturer-sponsored advertisements, cooperative advertisements	Dealer-sponsored advertisements	Few advertisements, secondary shelf space
Price	Highest, usually controlled by manufacturer	Moderate, usually controlled by dealer	Lowest, usually controlled by dealer
Marketing focus	To generate brand loyalty and manufacturer control	To generate store loyalty and control	To offer a low-priced, lesser-quality item to those desiring it

Manufacturer brands represent the vast majority of sales for most product categories, such as 70 per cent in food items, all automobiles, more than two thirds of major appliances, and more than 80 per cent of gasoline. These brands appeal to a wide range of consumers who desire low risk of poor product performance, good quality, routinized purchase behavior, status, and convenience shopping. Manufacturer brands are quite well known and trusted because quality control is strictly maintained. The brand name is identifiable and presents a distinctive image to shoppers. Manufacturers normally produce a number of product alternatives under their brands.

Manufacturer brands, **which are well known and heavily promoted, account for the bulk of sales in most industries.**

Manufacturer brands are sold at many competing retailers. For each individual retailer, purchases (and therefore inventory investments) may be low. In addition, the presold nature of these brands makes turnover high. Manufacturers spend large sums promoting their brands and frequently run cooperative advertisements with dealers, so that costs are shared. Prices are the highest of the three brands, with the bulk going to the manufacturer (who also receives the greatest profit). The major marketing focus for manufacturer brands is to attract and retain consumers who are loyal to the firm's offering and to control the marketing effort for the brands.

Dealer brands account for significant levels of sales in many product categories, such as 50 per cent in shoes, about a third of tires, 30 per cent of food items, and almost a third of appliance sales. Also, many retailers, such as Sears and McDonald's, generate 75 per cent or more of sales from their own brands. Dealer brands appeal to price-conscious consumers. These shoppers compare prices and ingredients with manufacturer brands. When they believe dealer brands offer good quality at a lower price, they purchase them. They are willing to accept some risk regarding quality, but store loyalty causes these consumers to believe the products are reliable. Usually, dealer brands are similar in quality to manufac-

Dealer brands **enable wholesalers and retailers to generate customer loyalty and to control the marketing effort.**

turer brands, although packaging is less important. In some cases, these brands are made to dealer specifications. Assortments are limited and the brands are unknown to shoppers who do not patronize the store.

Dealers secure exclusive rights for their brands and are responsible for their distribution. Dealer brands require large total investments and purchases by retailers. Turnover is lower than that of manufacturer brands. Promotion is also the responsibility of the dealer and prices are controlled by the retailer. Because per unit distribution and promotion costs are less for dealer brands, retailers are able to sell these items at lower prices and still obtain higher per unit profits (their share of the final selling price is higher than for manufacturer brands). The marketing focus of dealer brands is to attract and retain customers who are loyal to the store and to exert control over the marketing plan for these brands. Large retailers now advertise their brands extensively. Some, such as Sears' Kenmore brand, have become as well known as manufacturer brands. Furthermore, some companies (e.g., Sherwin-Williams) operate as both manufacturers and retailers.

Generic brands are low-priced goods that receive little advertising. They appeal to price-conscious consumers.

Generic brands started in the drug industry as low-cost alternatives to expensive, heavily promoted manufacturer brands. Generic food items began in a French supermarket chain in 1976, and Jewel of Chicago brought the idea to the United States. Today, generics have expanded into cigarettes, coffee, flashlight batteries, tennis shoes, underwear, beer, Scotch, and motor oil. Nationally, generics represent over 4 per cent of grocery sales. In those stores carrying generics, they account for 8 to 10 per cent of grocery sales.[12] Generics appeal to price-conscious, careful shoppers, who are sometimes willing to accept lower quality and purchase for large families.

Generic brands are seldom advertised and receive secondary shelf space (for example, floor level). Consumers must search out these brands. Prices are less than manufacturer or dealer brands by anywhere from 10 to 50 per cent. The low prices are due to quality, packaging, assortment, distribution, and promotion economies. The major marketing goal with generics is to offer low-priced, lower-quality items to consumers interested in price savings.

A *mixed-brand strategy* combines manufacturer and dealer brands, and offers advantages for each channel member.

Many manufacturers and retailers employ a **mixed-brand strategy,** whereby they sell a combination of manufacturer and dealer brands (and sometimes generic brands). A mixed-brand strategy provides benefits for manufacturers and retailers:

1. There is control over the brand bearing the seller's name.
2. Two or more market segments can be reached.
3. Exclusive rights to a brand can be obtained.
4. Brand and store loyalty are encouraged, shelf space and locations are coordinated, and assortments are increased.
5. Production is stabilized and excess capacity utilized.
6. Channel member cooperation is enhanced.
7. Profits are equitably shared.
8. Distinct images and offerings are maintained.
9. Sales are maximized.
10. Long-run planning is coordinated.

[12] J. O. Peckham, "Brand Marketing in Low-Growth Grocery Categories and an Expanding Private Label Economy," *Nielsen Researcher* (Number 3, 1983), p. 16; and J. L. Parks, *Generics in Supermarkets: Myth or Magic?* (Chicago: A. C. Nielsen, 1981).

Sometimes, manufacturer, dealer, and generic brands engage in a ***battle of the brands,*** in which each attempts to obtain a greater share of the consumer's dollar. In particular, this is a battle between manufacturers and retailers. Each wants to control the marketing strategy of a brand, obtain consumer loyalty, maintain exclusive rights to a brand, maximize shelf space and locations, acquire a large share of profits, create a distinctive image and offering, limit competition, optimize total costs, and maximize sales.

Although dealer brands began in the early 1900s, it was not until the 1950s that department-store retailers found these brands useful in gaining price concessions from name-brand manufacturers and increasing store loyalty and profits. The battle is normally between large manufacturers and large retailers (supermarkets, department stores, discount stores, and franchises) that seek to dominate each other. In recent years, the power of many retailers has grown and put them on more equal footing with manufacturers.[13]

In the battle of the brands, *manufacturer, dealer, and generic brands compete for sales.*

FAMILY AND MULTIPLE BRANDING

Under ***family (blanket) branding*** one name is used for several products. Some companies, such as Xerox, utilize family branding for their entire product mixes. Other firms employ a family brand for each category of products. For example, Sears has Kenmore appliances and Craftsman tools. Family branding can be applied to both manufacturer and dealer brands.

Family branding applies one name to many products.

Family branding is most effective for specialized firms or those with specialized product lines. It enables companies to capitalize on a uniform image and promote the same name continually. Accordingly, promotion costs are kept down. The major disadvantages of family branding are that a company's image may be adversely affected when widely different products (such as cereal and pet food, or luxury and economy cars) carry one name and multiple segmentation efforts are minimized.

Family branding is particularly effective for firms introducing new products. ***Brand extension*** is a strategy by which an established brand name is applied to new products. Quick customer acceptance is gained because people are already familiar and happy with existing products bearing the same name. For example, by applying the Jell-O name to its Pudding Pops, General Foods was able to generate first year sales of more than $100 million for the product. Consumer recognition and retailer cooperation were quite high, because of the Jell-O name.[14] See Figure 11-4.

Brand extension gains quick acceptance for new products; but it may blur image.

With ***multiple (individual) branding,*** separate brands are used for each item or product category sold by the firm. As an example, Ralston-Purina markets Purina Dog Chow, Bran Chex cereal, and Chicken of the Sea tuna, and owns Jack's restaurants. In these cases not only does each have distinct images and appeals, each must be marketed differently. Ralston-Purina must be careful not to have people confuse pet and human products.

Multiple branding applies distinct brands to each item or product.

For firms that use a mixed-brand strategy, multiple branding is necessary to

---

[13] See Theodore J. Gage, "The Labels May Be Private—But the Demand Isn't," *Advertising Age* (October 11, 1982), pp. M-44–M-45; Lewis A. Spalding, "Private Label or National Brand Men's Wear," *Stores* (March 1983), pp. 34–37 ff.; and Fred Gardner, "The Generics Threat," *Marketing & Media Decisions* (February 1982), pp. 59–61 ff.

[14] Janet Guyon, "General Foods Gets a Winner with Its Jell-O Pudding Pops," *Wall Street Journal* (March 10, 1983), p. 33.

**Figure 11-4
Jell-O Pudding Pops,
a Successful Line
Extension**

Reprinted by permission of General Foods.

secure control and secrecy. In addition, multiple branding allows a manufacturer to secure greater shelf space in a retail store. On the negative side, multiple brands require large promotional costs and there may be a loss of continuity. Economies due to mass production are lessened. New products do not benefit from an established identity.

To obtain the advantages of family and multiple branding, several companies combine the two. For example, Dodge is a family brand used by Chrysler to designate one product line that contains several automobile models. The division has an overall image and appeals to a specific market segment. New models benefit from the Dodge label, and there is an interrelationship among the models. Individual brands are also used with each model so that product differences can be identified. Among the Dodge models are Charger, 600ES, Omni, and Aries.

Choosing a Brand Name

When a firm chooses the brand name for a product, there are several potential sources:

Sources of brand names range from existing names to *licensing agreements* with other firms.

1. Under a brand extension policy, the existing name is applied to a new product (Cracker Jacks popcorn, *Rocky IV*).
2. For a dealer's brand, the dealer specifies the name.
3. When a new name is sought, these alternatives are available:
   - Initials (IBM, ABC, J&B Whisky).
   - Invented name (Kleenex, Exxon).
   - Numbers (Chanel No. 5, Century 21).
   - Mythological character (Atlas tires).
   - Personal name (Lipton, Heinz, Ford).

Figure 11-5
An E.T. Licensing Agreement
In early 1984, Squibb introduced a chewable children's multivitamin featuring a three-dimensional E.T. E.T. Vitamins were produced under a licensing agreement with Universal City Studios. The package was designed by Gerstman & Meyers, Inc.

Reprinted by permission.

- Geographical name (Pittsburgh paints, Utica sheets).
- Dictionary name (Sunbeam appliances, Whirlpool appliances).
- Foreign word (Nestlé, Lux).
- Combination of words (Head and Shoulders shampoo).

4. A name can be licensed from a firm that holds the trademark to it. Under a *licensing agreement,* the company pays a fee to use a name. Examples of licensed names are Sesame Street, Mickey Mouse, Strawberry Shortcake, Smurf, Superman, E.T., Cabbage Patch Kids, and Care Bears. In 1983, licensed names and characters accounted for $27 billion in retail sales.[15] See Figure 11-5.

A good brand name: suggests something about a product's use, benefit, or attributes (Beauty Rest mattress, Wash 'n Dry, Budget Rent-a-Car); is easy to spell and remember, and pronounceable in only one way (Bic, Tang, *Time* magazine); can be applied to a whole line of products (Gerber baby foods, Calvin Klein clothing, General Electric appliances); is capable of legal protection from use by others (Mr. Coffee, Big Mac, Equal artificial sweetener); and has a pleasant or at

Among other things, a brand name should be suggestive, easy to remember, and flexible.

[15] Stephen Williams, "Big-Name Hunts Make a Killing," *Newsday* (February 19, 1984), p. 120.

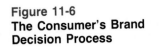
Figure 11-6
The Consumer's Brand
Decision Process

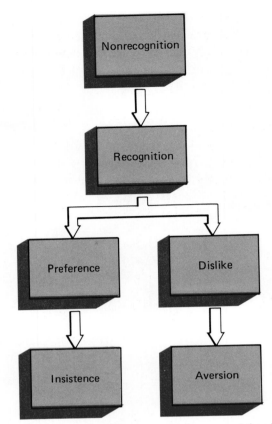

The marketer's goal is to gain consumer preference and then insistence (brand loyalty). He/she wants to avoid customer dislike or aversion.

least neutral meaning in foreign countries or international markets (Exxon, Kodak, IBM).

The process of developing and testing a new brand name can involve extensive research. Procter & Gamble chose the name Pampers for its disposable diaper after eliminating many other names. Unacceptable names included Tenders, Dri Wees, Winks, Solos, and Zephyrs. Pampers represented the tender, loving care given by parents to their babies.[16]

The consumer's *brand decision process* moves from nonrecognition to recognition to preference (or dislike) to insistence (or aversion).

In choosing a brand name, it is essential that a firm understand and plan for the consumer's ***brand decision process,*** which is shown in Figure 11-6. For a new brand, the consumer begins with nonrecognition of the name, and the seller must make the consumer aware of the brand. Then the consumer moves to recognition, wherein the brand and its attributes are known, and the seller emphasizes persuasion. Next, the consumer develops a preference (or dislike) for the brand and purchases it; the seller's task is to achieve brand loyalty. Last, some consumers exhibit an insistence (or aversion) for the brand and become loyal to it; the seller's role is to maintain this loyalty. In many cases, consumers develop preferences toward several brands, but do not buy or insist upon one brand exclusively.

[16] "The Pampers Story: A P&G Success," *Consumer Choice* (Cincinnati, Ohio: Procter & Gamble, 1977).

With a brand-extension strategy, the product begins at the preference or insistence stage, because of the carryover effect of the established name. Consumers who dislike the existing product line are unlikely to try a new product under a brand-extension strategy, but may try another company product under a different brand.

Use of Trademarks

Finally a company must determine whether to apply for trademark protection under the federal Lanham Act of 1946. Trademark protection gives a firm exclusive use of a brand for as long as the brand is marketed. The protection is voluntary and requires a registration procedure.

Any aspect of a product or its package may be registered as a trademark if the feature is nonfunctional (a functional feature may be patented for seventeen years). For example, Haig & Haig's ''pinch bottle'' for Scotch is a registered trademark. Identification marks of services (such as Weight Watchers), certification marks (such as Wool Bureau label), and trade characters (such as Elsie the Cow) can also be registered.

There are requirements for making a trademark legally protectable: it must be adhered to the product, its label, or its container; it must not be confusingly similar to other trademarks; it must be used in interstate commerce; and it cannot imply characteristics that the product does not possess. A surname by itself cannot be registered, because anyone can do business under his or her name.[17] However, a surname can be registered if used to describe a specific business (e.g., Roy Rogers' Restaurants).

The registration and administration of trademarks can be time consuming, complex, and expensive (a successful challenge of a competitor may require large legal fees and many years in court). A multinational firm must register trademarks in every country in which it operates.

When brands become too popular, they run the risk of becoming public property. Then a firm loses its trademark position. Brands that are fighting to remain exclusive trademarks include Xerox, Levi's, Frigidaire, Formica, Kleenex, and Teflon. Brands of former trademarks that are now considered generic and therefore public property are cellophane, aspirin, shredded wheat, kerosene, cola, linoleum, and monopoly.

DuPont used careful research to retain a trademark for Teflon. A company survey showed that 68 per cent of the consumers questioned identified Teflon as a brand name. This enabled DuPont to win a court case against a Japanese firm using the name Eflon.[18] On the other hand, in 1983, the U.S. Supreme Court ruled that ''Monopoly'' was a generic term that could be used by any game maker.[19]

Trademark protection is essential to many firms because exclusive use of

Trademark protection legally grants a firm exclusive use of a brand or symbol for as long as it is marketed.

---

[17] Joe L. Welch, *Marketing Law* (Tulsa, Okla.: PPC Books, 1980), pp. 136–137; and Frank Delano, ''Keeping Your Trade Name or Trademark out of Court,'' *Harvard Business Review,* Vol. 60 (March–April 1982), pp. 72–74.

[18] Sidney A. Diamond, ''DuPont's Teflon Trademark Survives Attack,'' *Advertising Age* (July 14, 1975), p. 93.

[19] Richard L. Gordon, ''Monopoly Name Doesn't Pass Go,'' *Advertising Age* (February 28, 1983), pp. 3, 69.

brands and symbols enables firms to maintain long-established images and market shares. For example, Xerox vigorously polices its brands. It realizes that a loss of brand recognition would be extremely harmful. See Figure 11-7.

Packaging

A *package* consists of a physical container, label, and inserts.

Packaging is the part of product planning in which a firm researches, designs, and produces its package(s). A *package* is a product's physical container, label, and inserts. The physical container may include a cardboard box, cellophane wrapper, glass, aluminum, or plastic jar or can, paper bag, styrofoam, or a combination of these. Products frequently have more than one physical container. For example, cereal is shipped in large cardboard boxes and individually packaged in smaller cardboard boxes. Watches are shipped in plastic boxes and covered in inner cloth linings. A label contains the product's brand name, the company logo, ingredients, promotional messages, inventory control codes, and instructions for use. Inserts are (1) detailed instructions and safety information for complex or dangerous products that are carried in drug, toy, and other packages or (2) coupons, prizes, or recipe booklets.

Prior to the advent of the modern supermarket and department store, manufacturers shipped merchandise in bulk containers, such as cracker barrels, sugar sacks, and butter tubs. The retail merchants repackaged the contents into smaller, more convenient units to meet each customer's needs. With the growth of mass merchants and self-service, manufacturers came to realize the value of packaging as a marketing tool.

Packaging is expensive and requires complex decisions.

Today packaging is a vital part of a firm's product-development strategy; the package may even be an integral part of the product itself (for example, the aerosol can for shaving cream). Well over $50 billion is annually spent on packaging. On the average, packaging costs 10 per cent of a product's retail price. This amount is higher for such products as cosmetics (up to 40 per cent and more). The complete package redesign of a major product might cost several million dollars for machinery and production.

Packaging decisions are generally complex. They must serve both channel member and ultimate consumer needs. Plans are often made in conjunction with production, logistics, and legal personnel. Errors in packaging decisions can be quite costly.

For these and other reasons, many firms exert a large effort in package design. As an example, Coca-Cola rejected 150 package designs for its new diet Coke before selecting a satisfactory package. Diet Coke's package contains red lettering on a white-striped and silver-reflective background. Among the package colors turned down by Coca-Cola executives were blue (associated with Pepsi), silver (associated with Diet Rite), and a red background (too confusing due to its similarity to Coke's design). The packaging of diet Coke was so important to the company because no other new Coca-Cola product had ever used the Coke name in the firm's 95 years of existence.[20]

[20] Nancy Giges, "After 150 Tries Comes a Winning Design," *Advertising Age* (October 18, 1982), pp. M-4–M-5.

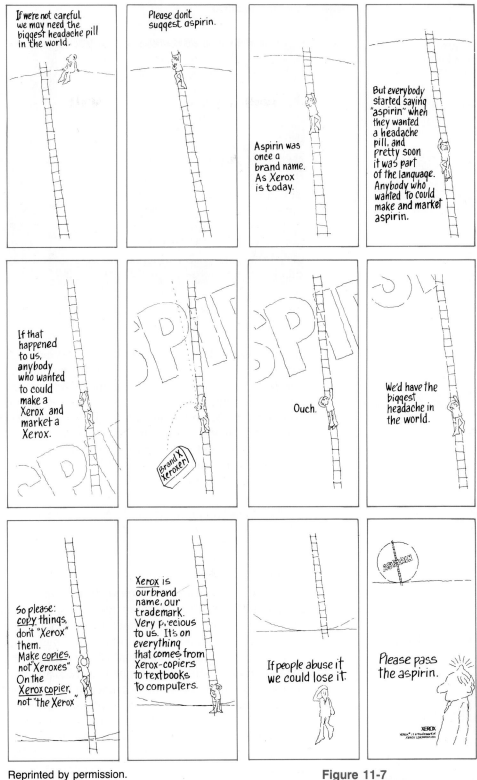

Reprinted by permission.

Figure 11-7
Trademark Protection by Xerox

Figure 11-8
Package Redesign for Fig Newtons

Source: Information provided by Charles Moldenhauer, Lefkowith, Inc. Package design for Nabisco Brands, Inc. Reprinted by permission.

Package redesign frequently occurs when a firm's current packaging is too expensive, receives a poor response from channel members and customers or the company seeks a new market segment, reformulates a product, or changes product positioning. For instance, demographic changes and increasing competition convinced Nabisco Brands that its Fig Newtons cookies needed redesigned packaging. The new package incorporates a bolder and more eye-catching logo, a more colorful and interesting design, an appetizing photograph, a switch to the word cookies (instead of cakes), elimination of ''Big Fig,'' and greater emphasis on moistness.[21] Figure 11-8 shows the before and after packaging of Fig Newtons.

The basic functions of packaging, factors considered in packaging decisions, and criticisms of packaging are described next.

Basic Packaging Functions

Packaging functions **range from containment and protection to new-product planning.**

There are six basic ***packaging functions:*** containment and protection, usage, communication, market segmentation, channel cooperation, and new-product planning. Figure 11-9 illustrates these functions.

For liquid, granular, and other divisible products, containment is needed to secure the items in a given quantity and form. The package also creates protection for the product while it is shipped, stored, and handled. Containment and protection must be undertaken in a manner that is safe to the consumer and the environment. For example, early pop-top cans had to overcome the dual problems of consumers' cutting their fingers and littering. The pop-tops were then produced more safely and made inseparable from the cans, thus solving both problems. In all cases, the package must protect the product against the effects of light, infestation, shock, vibration, breakage, evaporation, and spilling.

[21] Charles A. Moldenhauer, ''Packaging Designers Must Be Cognizant of Right Cues if the Consumer Base Is to Expand,'' *Marketing News* (March 30, 1984), p. 14.

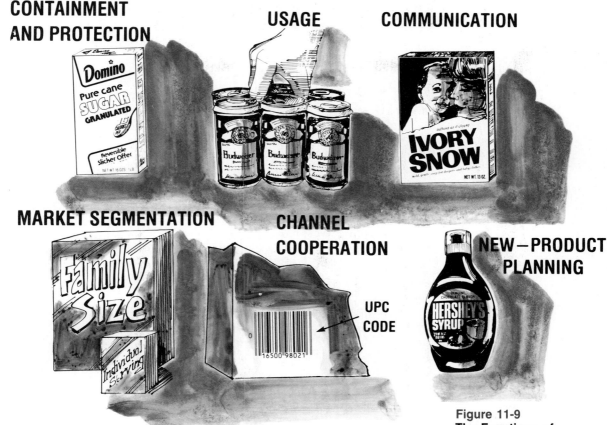

CONTAINMENT AND PROTECTION

USAGE

COMMUNICATION

MARKET SEGMENTATION

CHANNEL COOPERATION

UPC CODE

NEW—PRODUCT PLANNING

Figure 11-9
The Functions of Packaging

The package must facilitate product usage. Multiple packaging and larger sizes encourage increased product usage. Beer and soda increased sales by these techniques. Product dispensement may be eased through a no-drip spout, self-applicator, flip-top, squeeze tube, boil bag, oven-ready container, or other package design. For divisible products, the package needs to accommodate storage after the item is initially used. For example, a plastic margarine container with a snap-on lid makes continued storage simple. Finally, some manufacturers find that they can raise sales by making packages that are reusable once the product is depleted. For many years Welch's jellies have been sold in decorative jars that can be used as drinking glasses once the jellies are finished.

The package is an important method of communication with the customer. It identifies the brand, provides ingredients and directions, represents an image of the brand, and displays the product. It also serves as a promotional tool; and the package is the final form of promotion the consumer sees prior to making a purchase decision. This is particularly significant in self-service operations. The package differentiates the product from competitors by its design, color, shape, and materials. Packaging is particularly valuable for firms concentrating on impulse purchases, such as candy. The package also serves a promotional purpose after a purchase is made, because a reusable package is a constant reminder of the product.

Packaging can be used for market segmentation (or multiple segmentation). A package can be tailor-made for a specific market group. For example, gift boxes appeal to shoppers buying presents. Single-serving containers attract one-person households. Unusual packages are sought by risk takers or status seekers. Similarly, when a company offers two or more package shapes, sizes, colors, or designs it may employ multiple segmentation. In the examples noted here, companies may also sell plain boxes and family-serving containers.

In developing a packaging strategy, a firm must consider the needs of its wholesalers and retailers in order to secure channel cooperation. The package should make the product easy to ship, handle, and store. It should be durable and have a reasonable shelf life. It should fit into pre-existing dealer facilities and displays. It should facilitate price marking by providing a convenient place for the price. It should make inventory control easier by applying computer codes to labels. The package should minimize shoplifting by special tagging or coding. As an illustration, a West Coast lumber company obtained a competitive advantage with its dealers by shipping construction lumber in reinforced paper wrapping. This made the lumber dry, bright, and easy to handle. It could be stored outdoors. Color coding identified the size and type of wood. Pilferage and short-order claims were reduced.

Finally, packaging should be a major element of new-product planning. Many firms have been able to position existing products as new by changing their packages. Examples of products that were successfully modified and presented as new because of packaging innovations are aerosol cans for shaving cream, deodorants, and hair sprays; disposable containers for milk, soda, and beer; aluminum containers for television dinners; multiple packages for cereal, soda, and beer; pop-up tissues; self-sealing food packages; flip-top cigarette boxes; see-through meat packages; vacuum-packed tennis balls; individually wrapped sticks of chewing gum; and child-proof medicine bottles. Recently, oil companies began marketing motor oil in plastic containers, as shown in Figure 11-10.

Not all new packaging strategies have proven successful, as these illustrations show. A new scouring pad package would not stock and fell off dealer shelves. A new cigarette package could not protect the contents in hot weather and the cigarettes dried out. A dog food discolored on store shelves. In cold weather, baby food separated into a clear liquid and a sludge. Excessive settling in a box of paper tissues caused the boxes to be one third empty at purchase.[22]

Factors Considered in Packaging Decisions

Several key factors must be considered in making packaging decisions. A discussion of each follows.

What image is sought?

Package design has an impact on the image a company seeks for its products. Color, shape, and material all influence the consumer's perception of a company and its products. For example, when Mobil and Exxon introduced their high-priced synthetic oils they developed packages of silver and gold/white, respectively. As noted previously, plain packaging fosters a lower-quality image for generics.

[22] Jay E. Klompmaker, G. David Hughes, and Russell I. Haley, "Test Marketing in New Product Development," *Harvard Business Review,* Vol. 54 (May–June 1976), pp. 135–136.

Figure 11-10
Plastic Motor Oil Containers
These containers, such as that used by Quaker State, eliminate the need for greasy oil funnels and dirty rags. The containers are easy to use, spill-proof, and reusable.

Reprinted by permission.

In family packaging a firm uses a common element on each package in its product line. Family packaging parallels family branding. Campbell Soup has virtually identical packages for every soup. The only difference is flavor or content identification. Procter & Gamble, maker of Charmin and White Cloud toilet tissues, does not use family packaging and has significantly different packages for each brand to attract different segments.

Should family packaging be used?

An international or multinational firm must determine whether a standardized package can be used throughout the world (with only a language change on the label). Standardization increases worldwide recognition. For this reason, Coke and Pepsi utilize standard packages in all parts of the world. With the United States converting to the metric system (already used by other countries) in the 1980s, standardization will be easier. Nonetheless, some colors, symbols, and shapes have negative connotations in certain countries. For example, white can represent purity or mourning, two vastly different images.

Should a standard package be used throughout the world?

Package costs must be considered on both a total and per unit basis. As noted earlier, total costs can run into the millions of dollars. Per unit costs can go as high as 40 per cent of a product's retail price, depending on the purpose and extent of packaging.

What should costs be?

The firm has a number of packaging materials from which to choose, such as paperboard, plastic, metal, glass, styrofoam, and cellophane. In the selection,

What materials should be used? How innovative should the package be?

trade-offs are probably necessary. For instance, cellophane allows products to be displayed, but it is highly susceptible to tearing; paperboard is relatively inexpensive, but it is difficult to open. Also, a company must determine how innovative it wants its packaging to be. For example, Ocean Spray and other companies have introduced paper bottles (aseptic packages) for beverages that allow them to be displayed and stored without refrigeration. Previously, most fruit juices and milk had to be kept cold and could be preserved only for short periods.[23]

What features should the package incorporate?

There is a wide range of package features from which to choose, depending on the product. These features include pour spouts, hinged lids, screw-on tops, pop-tops, see-through bags, tuck- or seal-end cartons, carry handles, product testers (for items like batteries), freshness dating, and blister cards (products are placed under a plastic dome mounted on a card with a hole in it and hung on a metal rack). Any one or combination of these features provides a firm with a differential advantage over its competition.

What size(s), color(s), and shape(s) should be used?

Next, the firm selects the size(s), color(s), and shape(s) of its packages. Included in this decision is the question of how many different packages it should offer. In selecting a package size, shelf life (how long a product retains its freshness), convenience, tradition, and competition must be considered. In the food industry, new and larger sizes have captured high sales. The choice of package color depends on the image sought for the brand. Mello Yello, a citrus soft drink by Coca-Cola, has bright orange and green lettering on a lemon-yellow background for its label. Package shape also affects a product's image. Hanes created a mystique for L'eggs pantyhose by creating the egg-shaped package. The number of packages for any one product depends on competition and the company's use of multiple segmentation. The sales of small, medium, large, and family packages of current detergents make it difficult and expensive for a new firm to enter, ensure maximum shelf space, and appeal to different consumers. Size, color, and shape are an integral part of a package's promotional value.

How should the label and inserts appear?

The placement, content, size, and prominence of the label must be determined. The company and brand names need to appear on the label. Package inserts range from recipes to directions for use to safety tips to coupons for future purchases. Cracker Jacks has for some time inserted toys and puzzles to boost its sales.

Should multiple packaging be used?

Multiple packaging is the coupling of two or more products in one container. This coupling may involve the same item (such as razor blades, soda, or socks) or a combination of different items (such as comb and brush, first aid kit, and tool set). The goals of multiple packaging are to increase consumption of the same item (hoarding may be a problem), get the consumer to buy an assortment of items, or have the consumer try a new item (such as a new automatic pencil packaged with an established ball-point pen).

Should items be individually wrapped?

Individually wrapping portions of a divisible product may offer a competitive advantage. It may also be quite costly. Kraft has done well with its individually wrapped cheese slices. Alka-Seltzer sells its tablets in individually wrapped tin-foil containers, as well as in a bottle without wrapping.

Should the package be versatile?

The versatility of the package must be determined. For example, soda cans do not have to be stored in a refrigerator until they are served. Some items need to fit

[23] See "Who'll Buy a Drink in a Box?" *Marketing & Media Decisions* (April 1982), pp. 74–75 ff; and " 'Paper Bottles' Are Coming On Strong," *Business Week* (January 6, 1984), pp. 56–57.

Figure 11-11
**Pepsi's Resealable
Aluminum Beverage
Containers**

Reprinted by permission. © Pepsico, Inc. 1984

into vending machine spaces (long cigarettes are troublesome here). Packages must be sturdy enough for shelf displays, yet easy enough to open. Most multiple packs, like cereal, are versatile because they can be sold as they are shipped or broken into single units.

For certain items, preprinted prices are desired by dealers. These include shirts, magazines, watches, and candy. The dealers have the option of charging those prices or adhering their own labels. Many retailers prefer only a space for the price on a package and insert their own price labels automatically. With improved computer technology for handling inventory control, more channel members are insisting on premarked inventory codes. The *Universal Product Code (UPC)*, used in the food industry, and *Optical Character Recognition (OCR-A)*, used in department stores, are industrywide systems for coding information onto merchandise. The UPC requires manufacturers to premark items with a series of thick and thin vertical lines; price and inventory data are contained but are not readable by employees and customers. OCR-A is readable by both machines and humans and can handle more information than the UPC. With the UPC, prices must still be marked on merchandise; OCR-A is slower to process.[24]

> Should the package have a preprinted price and use the *Universal Product Code (UPC)* or *Optical Character Recognition (OCR-A)?*

A variety of firms offer reusable packages, containers that can be utilized after the product is depleted. For example, Pepsi recently began test marketing an "aluminum bottle." It offered the combined benefits of a resealable package and quick chilling. See Figure 11-11. Resealing is quite important to consumers, according to a recent Package Designers Council survey.[25]

> Should the package be reusable?

[24] See Barry Berman and Joel R. Evans, *Retail Management: A Strategic Approach*, Second Edition (New York: Macmillan, 1983), pp. 175–176, 339–341.
[25] "Consumers Want Food Packaging That Can Be Easily Resealed: Survey," *Marketing News* (May 28, 1982), p. 9.

How does the package interrelate with other marketing variables?

Finally, a company must be certain that package design fits in with the rest of the marketing mix. When Borden repackaged its super glue, it overcame prior problems with the package bursting and the glue drying out. The new package stood upright, was placed on attractive in-store displays, and was backed by an extensive, multimillion-dollar promotion campaign. The name was changed from Wonder Bond to Wonder Bond Plus.[26]

Criticisms of Packaging

Packaging has been faulted for waste, misleading labels, and lack of safety.

Packaging has been criticized and regulated in recent years because of its impact on the environment and scarce resources, rising costs, questions about the honesty of labels and confusion caused by inconsistent package sizes (e.g., large, family, super), and inadequate package safety.[27]

For example, when Lever Brothers introduced Sunlight dishwashing liquid with lemon juice, it designed a package similar to Minute Maid Lemon Juice. As a result, a number of adults and children drank Sunlight. Lever Brothers responded that the misperception was very minor and continued with the Sunlight package. Said a Lever Brothers spokesperson:

We feel we've leaned over backwards with our labeling to try to avoid this type of problem. Sunlight contains 10% real lemon juice, an attribute that sets it apart from other dishwashing liquids. We would be doing ourselves a disservice if we didn't call attention to this fact.[28]

The consumer must also bear responsibility for some of the negative results of packaging. For example, the more than $1 billion worth of shoplifting annually adds to packaging costs by causing firms to add security tags and otherwise alter packages. Throwaway bottles (highly preferred by consumers) use 2.7 times the energy of returnable bottles.[29] In planning a packaging program, both the benefits and costs of providing environmentally safer, less confusing, and tamper-resistant packages must be weighed. Many firms are responding positively to the criticisms raised here; they will be examined in Chapter 23, "Marketing and Society."

Summary

Branding is the procedure a firm follows in formulating its brand(s). A brand is a name, design, or symbol (or combination of these) that identifies a product or service. A brand name is a word, letter, or group of words or letters that can be

---

[26] "Marketing Facelift Corrects Elmer's Problem," *Marketing News* (February 8, 1980), p. 8.

[27] For example, see Bill Abrams, "Packaging Often Irks Buyers, But Firms Are Slow to Change," *Wall Street Journal* (January 28, 1982), p. 29; Tom Masloski, "An Understanding of Overpackaging," *Advertising Age* (August 9, 1982), p. M-10; and "Consumers Examine Packages Very Closely Since Tylenol Tragedy," *Wall Street Journal* (November 5, 1982), pp. 1, 31.

[28] Lynn G. Reiling, "Consumer Misuse Mars Sampling for Sunlight Dishwashing Liquid," *Marketing News* (September 3, 1982), pp. 1, 12.

[29] R. Bruce Holmgren, "Product Packaging in an Era of Scarce Resources," *Journal of Contemporary Business,* Vol. 4 (Winter 1975), p. 20.

spoken. A brand mark is a symbol, design, or distinctive coloring or lettering. A trade character is a personified brand mark. A trademark is a brand given legal protection.

Four decisions are necessary in branding. First, corporate symbols are determined and, if applicable, revised. The company name, logo, and trade characters set its overall image. Second, a branding philosophy is set, which includes the proper use of manufacturer, dealer, and/or generic brands as well as family or multiple branding. In addition, a mixed-brand strategy, the battle of the brands, and brand extension are assessed. Third, a brand name is chosen from one of several sources. A firm may license a name from another company. The consumer's brand decision process moves from nonrecognition to recognition to preference (dislike) to insistence (aversion). Fourth, the use of trademarks is evaluated and planned.

Packaging is the procedure a firm follows in formulating its package(s). A package consists of a product's physical container, label, and inserts. Packaging has six basic functions: containment and protection, usage, communication, market segmentation, channel cooperation, and new-product planning.

Packaging decisions involve image; family packaging; standardized packaging; package costs; packaging materials and innovativeness; package features; package size(s), color(s), and shape(s); the label and package inserts; multiple packaging; individual wrapping; package versatility; preprinted prices and inventory codes (such as UPC and OCR-A); reusable packages; and integration with the marketing plan. Packaging has been criticized on the basis of environmental, safety, and other issues.

Questions for Discussion

1. Evaluate Nissan's decision to gradually drop the Datsun brand name and replace it with the Nissan name.
2. Differentiate among brand name, brand mark, trade character, and trademark.
3. The Michigan Seamless Tube Company changed its name to Quanex (an abbreviation for quality and nexus). Why do you think this name change was necessary?
4. Appraise RCA's decision to reintroduce its Nipper (the dog) symbol.
5. Why do manufacturer brands have such a large percentage of sales in so many product categories? Will private brands and generic brands eventually displace manufacturer brands? Explain your answer.
6. Contrast a mixed-brand strategy with the battle of the brands.
7. Is it a good strategy to combine family and individual branding? Why or why not?
8. Under what circumstances is brand extension a poor method of branding?
9. Describe the basic characteristics of a good brand name.
10. "Even though a company wants a brand to be popular, it must not be used to describe an entire product category." Explain this.
11. What are the three components of a package?
12. Describe the six major functions of packaging.
13. Give several examples of existing products that have recently modified their packaging to create distinctiveness.

14. How can poor packaging cause problems with channel members?
15. Compare and contrast family packaging and standardized packaging.
16. How many packaging innovativeness have a negative impact?
17. Analyze Lever's decision not to modify the packaging of its new Sunlight dishwashing liquid.

Case 1 Fieldcrest: Protecting the Company Name*

In recent years, most towel manufacturers, in their unbounded appetite for market share, have fought hard to increase volume in a depressed market. In the process, they moved the industry closer to a commodity business in which brand names were neglected. Even designer towels and sheets were sold to bargain-hungry consumers at rock-bottom prices.

To Fieldcrest, the third largest towel manufacturer in the U.S., this situation is unacceptable. It believes that manufacturers must maintain strong national brands and display and promote them accordingly. Fieldcrest therefore follows a branding philosophy that is different from that of its leading competitors.

Cannon Mills (the largest towel maker), Springs Industries, West Point–Pepperell, and others stitch their company names as well as individual brand names on all the grades of towels they make. These towels are marketed through department stores, discount stores, and other mass merchandisers. In contrast, Fieldcrest attaches its company name only to the top-quality towels it distributes through department stores. Also, Fieldcrest brand towels are not sold in discount stores. There is a separate line of St. Mary's towels, which do not carry the Fieldcrest name, that are distributed through mass merchandisers.

Fieldcrest believes its brand philosophy is quite effective. The Royal Velvet by Fieldcrest towel is considered the best-selling branded department store towel of all time. Currently, this towel is offered in three textures, a wide variety of colors, and at a range of prices. Fieldcrest's goal is to "have family groupings built around the Royal Velvet brand, which is widely known for its color leadership, broad department store exposure, and quality."

In addition to its Fieldcrest and St. Mary's lines, Fieldcrest manufactures private-label towels for Sears. These towels' sales are $75 million per year, making Fieldcrest the leading towel supplier for Sears.

QUESTIONS

1. Why is Fieldcrest so concerned about towels having commodity status?
2. Some of St. Mary's managers are attempting to get the Fieldcrest name to appear on their towels. Comment on this.
3. How should Fieldcrest's marketing strategies for Royal Velvet and St. Mary's towels differ?
4. Evaluate Fieldcrest's strategy of making private-label towels for Sears.

* The data in this case are drawn from "Fieldcrest: Saving Its Name for a Luxury Image," *Business Week* (January 9, 1984), pp. 112–113.

Case 2 Plastic Containers Come of Age[†]

Glass containers protect contents well for indefinite periods of time, can withstand extreme temperatures, are relatively inexpensive to manufacture, leave no odor or aftertaste, and are easy to recycle. However, glass containers have several short-comings: they are heavy, breakable, and potentially dangerous. Breaking and exploding glass bottles result in more than 20,000 serious injuries every year.

For many years, plastic containers have been used in place of glass containers for shampoos, detergents, industrial chemicals, and other nonfood products. However, early plastic containers had an odor, left an aftertaste, and could not protect carbonation. Then, DuPont introduced a new plastic container material in 1977. This material was named PET, short for polyester terephthalate. PET bottles were 11 times lighter than similar-size glass bottles, nonbreakable, left no odor or aftertaste, and could protect carbonation for three months. Although slightly more expensive than glass bottles to manufacture, PET bottles enabled companies to reduce shipping costs by 40 per cent.

The first container company to capitalize on this packaging breakthrough was Dorsey Corporation, a company one tenth the size of the industry leaders such as Owens-Illinois and Continental. Because of that, Dorsey was able to innovate and become the low-cost producer in the industry. Today, Dorsey has a 28 per cent market share of plastic container sales, compared with 22 per cent for Owens-Illinois and 16 per cent for Continental. Within five years, plastic containers represented 15 per cent of total U.S. beverage packages.

The switch to plastic has not been easy for container manufacturers. While the 2-liter plastic bottle is now the standard for this size container, smaller plastic bottles are still much more expensive to make than glass bottles. Plastic container sales, with relatively low profit margins, have replaced glass container sales; they have not expanded sales. Some manufacturers have built new plants to make plastic containers; this has left them with unused capacity.

To stimulate plastic container sales, manufacturers are developing plastic beer, wine, and liquor bottles; cost-efficient one-half liter (single serving) plastic soda bottles; and plastic bottles for food items, such as cooking oil.

QUESTIONS
1. If given a choice between a 2-liter bottle of soda and a six-pack of soda cans, why would customers select one over the other?
2. Do you think plastic beer, wine, and liquor bottles will be successful? Explain your answer.
3. From a consumer's perspective, what are the image differences between glass and plastic containers? Explain your answer.
4. As a container manufacturer, how would you differentiate your packages from those of competitors?

[†] The data in this case are drawn from Edward Boyer, ''Turning Glass to Plastic to Gold,'' *Fortune* (April 4, 1983), pp. 172–176; and Jean A. Briggs, ''Packaging,'' *Forbes* (January 4, 1982), pp. 220–221.

Part Three Case Kodak: Evaluating a Product-Planning Strategy*

At the Eastman Kodak Company, about 80 per cent of the firm's $11 billion in annual revenues are derived from the sales of photography equipment, supplies, and services. Kodak is the world's leading photography firm, well ahead of Japan's Fuji (the number two firm).

In order to maintain its leadership position in the photography field, Kodak regularly modifies its cameras and film and periodically introduces major new products. Kodak realizes that amateur photographers tend to use less film as their cameras get older. So the firm brings out new cameras that are increasingly more convenient to use and more reliable, thus stimulating a greater level of picture taking.

Over the past twenty years, Kodak has marketed these major new camera products:

- 1963—Instamatic, with the first film cartridge.
- 1972—110 Instamatic, a pocket camera.
- 1976—Colorburst, a self-developing camera.
- 1982—Disc, the easiest to use and best pocket camera yet produced by Kodak.

The new disc camera took more than five years to commercialize and cost over $600 million. The camera offered consumers an automatic built-in flash (guaranteed for five years), automatic film advance and exposure control, closer-range pictures, and a very high rate of good pictures (about 95 per cent). In addition, the pocket-size camera relied on a revolutionary film disc cartridge. The camera's models had list prices ranging from $70 to $140.

Each time Kodak successfully introduces a new product for the mass market, it earns profits not only from camera sales but from film chemicals, photographic paper, and film-processing sales. For example, it estimated that an average of 130 film discs would be purchased by each disc camera owner within five years after the camera was bought; and Kodak makes a 50 per cent gross profit on the sales of color film.

Despite its long-run leadership in the photography field, Kodak has recently begun experiencing several major problems. These difficulties caused Kodak to lay off 2,700 workers in 1983 and to plan for further cuts through attrition (not filling positions when certain employees retire or leave).

---

* The data in this case are drawn from Eric N. Berg, "Shrinking a Staff the Kodak Way," *New York Times* (September 4, 1983), Section 3, pp. F1, F6; Lydia Chavez, "Why Kodak Went for the Disc," *New York Times* (December 26, 1982), Section 3, pp. 1, 22; Ann Hughey, "Kodak Names New Chairman President, Tells Annual Meeting of Economy Drive," *Wall Street Journal* (May 12, 1983), p. 12; Gay Jervey, "GE, Kodak, RCA Bracing for 8mm Camera Battle," *Advertising Age* (January 9, 1984), p. 56; Gay Jervey, "Kodak, Minolta Efforts Picture Big Disc Market," *Advertising Age* (April 1, 1983), pp. 3, 66; "Kodak Employees Were Instrumental in Successful Introduction of Disc Camera," *Marketing News* (April 16, 1982), p. 11; "Kodak Fights Back," *Business Week* (February 1, 1982), pp. 48–54; Steve Lohr, "Fuji's Joust With Kodak San," *New York Times* (October 30, 1983), pp. F1, F27; Thomas Moore, "Embattled Kodak Enters the Electronic Age," *Fortune* (August 22, 1983), pp. 120–122, 126, 128; John J. Powers, "Credit Success of Disc Camera to Research," *Marketing News* (January 21, 1983), Section 1, pp. 8–9; and "Kodak Takes a Risky Leap into Consumer Video," *Business Week* (January 16, 1984), pp. 92–93.

The growth in picture taking has slowed considerably in comparison with previous years. From 1959 to 1969, the growth was 13 per cent annually. From 1969 to 1979, it was 12 per cent annually. Since 1979, the growth in picture taking has been under 4 per cent per year. In addition, the U.S. camera market is saturated, since the average household already owns 1.5 cameras.

Japanese and other manufacturers are going after Kodak's conventional film and photographic markets. In particular, Fuji has improved its manufacturing capabilities and product quality in the amateur photography market and has taken away some of Kodak's domestic and foreign market share. One analyst, in contrasting the productivity of Kodak and Fuji, points out that Kodak's sales are about $80,000 per employee while Fuji's are $160,000. The increase in competition is affecting Kodak's ability to maintain profit margins on its film and camera products. Table 1 shows the market shares for the leading producers of color film.

After 1982 sales of 8 million units, the Kodak Disc cameras have not fulfilled early optimistic sales forecasts in the U.S., Europe, or Japan. Despite high development costs and initial consumer enthusiasm, the camera seems unlikely to enjoy the 8- to 10-year product life of its Instamatic predecessors. Many experts believe the camera will actually have a 4- to 5-year economic life. These experts also feel that Kodak has not earned any profits on its line of self-developing cameras, after nearly a decade on the market; Polaroid remains dominant in this market. And Kodak is facing intensive competition from firms marketing inexpensive 35-mm cameras. While Kodak does well with 35-mm color film, it does not have an inexpensive camera to compete with Canon, Minolta, Nikon, and others.

Finally, Kodak's present photography products may eventually be replaced by electronic cameras that use magnetic tape or discs. Table 2 shows some of the electronics developments threatening Kodak's products. A number of competitors in the camera and film market have better expertise than Kodak in electronics. For example, Fuji is among the world's largest makers of videotape, a product not made by Kodak as of early 1984; in fact, videotape is Fuji's fastest-growing product. Canon, Minolta, Olympus, and Pentax already market television cameras.

Because of its limited growth potential with traditional photography products, Kodak is now expanding its involvement with a variety of electronics businesses. As its research director acknowledged, "we have a mandate to integrate electronics into the fiber of the company over the next five years."

Among the electronics products thus far introduced by Kodak, business pho-

Company	Market Share in Per Cent		
	U.S.	Japan	Worldwide
Kodak	85	18	60
Fuji	7	70	14
Agfa Gavaert	2	—	15
Konishiroku (Konica)	3	12*	3
3M	3	—	8
Total market share	100	100	100
Total market size	$1.1 bil	$500 mil	$2.75 bil

Table 1
Market Shares for Consumer Color Film Sales, 1983 (Amateur Photography)

*Includes Konishiroku and all other Japanese firms except Fuji
Sources: Smith, Barney, Harris Upham & Company; Dean Witter Reynolds; and Photographic Trade News.

**Table 2
Developments in
Electronics Threatening
Kodak's Traditional
Product Lines**

New Electronic Products	Kodak's Traditional Product Lines
1. Electronic imaging cameras	1. Conventional still cameras
2. Magnetic tape or disc	2. Silver halide film
3. Video display	3. Photographic paper
4. Videotape cameras	4. Super 8 movie cameras
5. Television sets and video playback systems	5. Slide and movie projection equipment

Source: Reprinted from the February 1, 1982 issue of *Business Week* by special permission, © 1982 by McGraw-Hill, Inc.

tocopiers and blood analysis machines typify the success and problems encountered by the firm. High-speed Ektaprint photocopiers are doing extremely well, due in large part to their high quality and reliability. Photocopiers have become Kodak's fastest-growing product line. On the other hand, Ektachem blood analysis machines (which are marketed mostly to hospitals) have had poor sales, because of the limited number of tests they can perform and their unreliability. A newer model is expected to do better, since it performs more tests and can be tied to a computer having access to patient records and clinical data sources.

Kodak's riskiest new venture is its entry into the videotape and video recorder market, planned for summer 1984. The venture is considered risky for three basic reasons:

• Kodak is relying on the technology of Matsushita, the Japanese firm which is manufacturing the video recorders. While Kodak has stated that a joint venture is desirable because "our capital investment is practically nil," a number of observers believe the company is being used by Matsushita (which will "jump in" with its own brand if Kodak succeeds). Kodak is marketing blank videotape made by TDK.

• The video market is extremely competitive, other firms are well entrenched, and profit margins are low. Some experts "wonder if Kodak knows how to compete in a market where it is not the dominant supplier, the technological leader, or the low-cost producer—in short, where margins will be far less than in film, the standard by which Kodak has judged all opportunities until now." There are more than 20 videotape brands, battling for retail shelf-space.

• Kodak's video recorder is an 8-mm "camcorder," a combination video camera and recorder. A special magnetic tape allows the camcorder to be much lighter and more compact than videocassette camera/recorders; 8-mm videotape is about a third of an inch wide, compared to one half an inch for regular videotape. However, this also means Kodak is marketing a product that cannot use VHS or Beta videotape; it is an incompatible system for the millions of U.S. households that already own video recorders. Nonetheless, Kodak projected 1984 sales at 100,000 units, priced from $1,600 to $1,900.

QUESTIONS

1. Draw and explain product life cycle charts for Kodak's Instamatic, Colorburst, and Disc cameras.
2. The Disc camera underwent substantial planning and marketing research, including an analysis of 64 different camera configurations, testing by 500 Kodak employees, and in-home testing by 1,000 consumers. Therefore, why was Kodak unable to accurately anticipate the camera's sales performance?

3. Develop a new-product screening checklist for Kodak's camcorder.
4. Evaluate Kodak's decision to market products made by Matsushita and TDK.
5. Comment on this statement: ''Kodak's various projects to merge photographic and electronic technologies still seem to lack an underlying strategy. Kodak's current plan seems to be to participate in as many technologies as possible, on the chance that one will become a big market.''
6. Kodak's brand name and its distinctive packages contribute to its photography sales. Why?

Distribution Planning

Part Four deals with the second major element of marketing, distribution. Chapter 12 presents an overview of distribution planning, the systematic decision making relating to the physical movement and transfer of ownership of a product or service from producer to consumer. The chapter explores the functions of distribution, types of channels, manufacturer/channel member contracts, channel cooperation and conflict, and the industrial channel of distribution. The elements of physical distribution, especially transportation and inventory management, are also discussed in detail.

Chapter 13 examines the wholesaling aspect of distribution. Wholesaling involves the buying or handling of merchandise and its subsequent resale to retailers, organizational users, and/or other wholesalers—but not the sale of significant volume to final consumers. The impact of wholesaling on the economy, its functions, and its relationships with suppliers and customers are shown. The major types of company-owned and independent wholesalers are described: manufacturer wholesaling, merchant wholesaling, and agents and brokers. Recent trends in wholesaling are detailed.

Chapter 14 concentrates on the retailing aspects of distribution. Retailing encompasses those business activities that involve the sale of goods and services to the ultimate (final) consumer for personal, family, or household use. The impact of retailing on the economy, its functions in distribution, and its relationship with suppliers are shown. Retailers are categorized by ownership, strategy mix, and nonstore operations. Four key factors in retail planning are described: location, atmosphere, scrambled merchandising, and the wheel of retailing. Recent trends in retailing are noted.

Tandy Corporation maintains strong control of its distribution channel by manufacturing products and then selling them through 8,700 Radio Shack stores that are company owned or franchised. Included are 500 specialized Radio Shack Computer Centers (like the one shown here) that it stocks and operates. Reprinted by permission.

Despite increased competition from motor trucks, waterways, pipelines, and airways, railroads remain the leading transportation form in the U.S. They are particularly effective in carrying heavy, bulky items over long distances. This photo shows a freight train passing through downtown Washington, D.C.

American Hospital Supply is the largest wholesaler in its field. Its product mix is divided into 41 divisions. American Hospital Supply operates 159 warehouses, such as the one shown here. It also offers personal and computerized services for its hospital customers (see the photo on the right). Reprinted by permission.

Many supermarket chains are opening superstore outlets that carry a variety of nonfood items in addition to traditional supermarket offerings. The Safeway superstore shown above is located in Arlington, Texas and occupies 61,000 square feet (compared with 20,000 for an average supermarket). The store exterior is quite distinctive. Reprinted by permission of Safeway Stores, Inc. © 1984.

Some food stores, such as the Grand Union supermarket in Monmouth, New Jersey that is depicted here, are reviving bulk selling to appeal to consumers. In bulk selling, consumers pay lower prices, select their items, and buy the exact quantity desired. Reprinted by permission of *Supermarket Business.*

Specialty stores concentrate sales on one merchandise line. The Limited stores, shown here, specialize in medium-priced fashion apparel for fashion-conscious contemporary women, ages 20 to 40. Store design and merchandise displays in The Limited differentiate it from competitors and create an exciting shopping environment. Reprinted by permission.

J. C. Penney is one of the leading department store chains in the U.S. Penney places great emphasis on its store exteriors in recognition of their impact on atmosphere. At this mall store, Penney features an open, two-tiered look with an attractive escalator in front of the store. Reprinted by permission.

Chapter 12

An Overview of Distribution Planning and Physical Distribution

1. To define distribution planning, examine distribution functions, describe the different types of distribution channels, and consider the factors used in selecting a channel of distribution

2. To consider cooperation and conflict in a channel of distribution

3. To show the special considerations relating to a distribution channel for industrial products

4. To discuss physical distribution and demonstrate its significance for marketing

5. To study transportation alternatives and inventory management

*T*he Adolph Coors Company, maker of Coors Beer, was started in 1873 and reached its peak in 1980, when 13.8 million barrels of beer were shipped. For a long while, Coors Beer was only distributed in Western states, which resulted in the beer being "bootlegged" to other regions by loyal customers such as Paul Newman. In "Smokey and the Bandit," Burt Reynolds spread the Coors myth by sneaking it into Atlanta.

Coors became so popular because of its unique brewing and distribution process. The beer contains only natural ingredients (no preservatives), features "pure Rocky Mountain spring water," and is not pasteurized. Coors is produced in only one brewery, located in Colorado, and shipped via refrigerated trucks and refrigerated railroad cars. Beer not sold within 60 days must be destroyed.

At one time, Coors dominated the Western market. For example,

341

during the mid-1970s, Coors had a 50 per cent market share in California. This meant that wholesalers were anxious to distribute the beer; there was a waiting list for new territories. As a result, Coors dominated its wholesalers and dictated strict policies. Said one wholesaler, "They were more interested in policing your inventory than helping you move it."

Between 1980 and 1983, Coors sales fell nearly two million barrels to 11.9 million barrels in 1983. It slipped from third to sixth in market share. These events were spurred on by the expansion of Anheuser-Busch and Miller into Coors' Western strongholds. In California, Anheuser-Busch now has a 52 per cent market share.

To reverse its sales decline, Coors decided to distribute its beer in more states. It now operates in 34 states, compared with 16 in 1980. But, this growth brought a whole range of distribution problems to Coors:

- It tried to expand into Louisiana and Tennessee through newly established wholesalers. These wholesalers had to spend up to $500,000 each for refrigerated warehouses and trucks, leaving limited funds to market the beer. Other beers do not require refrigeration because they contain preservatives. This venture failed. Coors now enters areas through established wholesalers, who have existing facilities.
- Refrigerated shipping from Colorado to Southeastern states costs $7 to $8 per barrel (the cost for nonrefrigerated beer is about $3 per barrel).
- All competitors have a sunbelt brewery. It will cost Coors $500 million to build a satisfactory second plant.

Coors has discovered that the beer strategy that made it so successful is the same strategy that has made distribution planning and physical distribution so difficult—and costly.[1]

Distribution Planning

Distribution planning involves physical movement and ownership transfer in a channel of distribution, consisting of the channel members in the process.

Distribution planning is systematic decision making regarding the physical movement and transfer of ownership of a product or service from producer to consumer. It includes transportation, storage, and customer transactions.

Distribution functions are carried out through a **channel of distribution**, which is comprised of all the organizations or people involved with the movement and exchange of products or services. The organizations or people in the distribution process are known as **channel members** or **middlemen.**

A channel of distribution can be simple or complex. It can be based on a handshake agreement between a small manufacturer and a local retailer or require detailed written contracts among a number of manufacturers, wholesalers, and retailers.

[1] Robert Reed, "Coors Charts Path over a Rocky Road to Growth," *Advertising Age* (July 11, 1983), pp. 4, 59, 60; Robert McGough, "A Difference of Perspective," *Forbes* (October 24, 1983), p. 88; and Brenton R. Schlender, "Heady Days Are over for Coors Wholesalers as Sales Pace Drops," *Wall Street Journal* (October 6, 1982), pp. 1, 27.

Many firms, such as Commodore and General Foods, are interested in wide-spread distribution. They need independent retailers to carry their merchandise and improve their cash flow. Other firms, like Avon and Electrolux, desire direct contact with consumers and do not use independent channel members. Industrial channels of distribution usually have more direct contact between manufacturers and customers than do final consumer channels.

This chapter presents an overview of distribution and the role of physical distribution. Chapter 13 discusses the role of wholesaling in the process. Chapter 14 covers the area of retailing.

Importance of Distribution Planning

Distribution decisions have a broad impact on the operations and marketing program of a firm. For example, a decision to use independent channel members and the kind of distribution channel employed both affect a firm's marketing efforts. Because middlemen can provide a wide variety of marketing functions, the firm's marketing plan will differ if it sells direct rather than through channel members. Similarly, a decision to sell through retail stores rather than through the mail requires a different marketing orientation and tasks.

In many cases the choice of a channel of distribution is the most important one a firm will make. This occurs for several reasons. First, good relations with channel members take a long time to develop and are difficult to change. Second, where established channels exist, it is hard for a new firm to enter. Third, once a firm generates good channel relationships, suitable new products are easier to place into distribution. Fourth, channel members need to plan and implement strategies in a coordinated manner. Fifth, strong distributors greatly enhance manufacturers' marketing capabilities. Sixth, consumers like to purchase products or services in the same manner over time.

The choice of a distribution channel may be the most important one a company makes.

Operating costs as well as profits are affected by the selection of a channel. A firm undertaking all channel functions must pay for these functions; in return, the firm reaps whatever profits are earned. A firm that uses independent (outside) channel members is able to reduce its per unit distribution costs; however, it also reduces its per unit profits because channel members must receive their share. With the latter type of channel, total profits can rise if channel members help bring in higher sales than the firm could accomplish itself.

Channels of distribution tend to be traditional in a number of product categories. For example, in the beverage and food industry, manufacturers normally sell through wholesalers who deal with retailers. Automobile makers sell through franchised dealers. Mail-order firms line up products, print catalogs, and sell directly to consumers. Firms must conform to these channel patterns.

The size and nature of a firm's market are influenced by the location of channel members, the number of channel members, geographic penetration, channel members' image and product selection, channel services provided, and the overall marketing program of channel members. In addition, the more middlemen a firm employs, the less customer contact it achieves and the lower its control over the marketing mix.

These examples show the scope and importance of distribution planning:

- Sherwin-Williams, the world's largest paint producer, operates over 1,500 company-owned stores. Sherwin-Williams determines the stores' product as-

Figure 12-1
Sherwin-Williams: From Manufacturing to Final Consumers
This photo depicts one of the 1,500 + stores owned by Sherwin-Williams, the largest paint manufacturer in the world.

Reprinted by permission.

sortments, sets their prices, and spends more than $25 million annually advertising the stores. In competing with Sears (the leading paint retailer), Sherwin-Williams recognizes that it must pick new markets carefully, fill them with outlets, and advertise extensively. "It's Modern Retailing 101."[2] See Figure 12-1.

- Lawson Products is a wholesaler of spare parts (such as screws and bolts) which are marketed to organizational consumers. The company handles 17,000 different items. It operates five regional warehouses and employs 1,100 salespeople. The warehouses are able to immediately meet 99 per cent of customer requests. Lawson's ability to deliver quickly and its complete product assortment enables it to charge prices that are two to three times higher than competitors.[3]

- The distribution system for automobile parts (such as spark plugs and shock absorbers) is quite complex. It is estimated that these parts are distributed through 22 different channels, including service stations, specialty stores, and mass merchandisers; each requires a different marketing strategy. In all, there are over 540,000 outlets marketing parts to consumers owning motor vehicles. This creates substantial difficulties for parts manufacturers.[4]

- Radio Shack (a division of Tandy Corporation) unlike almost all of its competitors, performs every channel function—from manufacturing to retailing—for the electronics and computer products it markets. Others in the industry operate as either manufacturers or as retailers. As a Radio Shack vice-president noted:

---

[2] Paul Ingrassia, "Sherwin-Williams Makes Big Turnaround Under Chairman's Aggressive Leadership," *Wall Street Journal* (December 14, 1983), p. 33.
[3] William Baldwin, "Dollars from Doodads," *Forbes* (October 11, 1982), pp. 51-52.
[4] "Automotive Aftermarket Is Confronted with Turbulent Times," *Marketing News* (February 18, 1983), p. 24.

Figure 12-2
**Entenmann's: From
Bakery to Grocery Store**
Unlike most bakery
companies that rely on
independent wholesalers to
call on accounts,
Entenmann's has its own
sales force that distributes
directly to grocery stores.

Reprinted by permission of General Foods.

If we manufacture a product . . . we are already assured that we will be able to distribute it to an established, nationwide chain of retail outlets. If RCA or G.E. or any of our other competitors comes up with a product, they have to put together a distribution system store by store.[5]

- Entenmann's, a wholly owned subsidiary of General Foods, uses its own employees to distribute bakery products to grocery stores. 750 route salespersons (a few earning up to $50,000 per year) call on stores to deliver merchandise and to pick up unsold bakery products with expired code dates and transport them to Entenmann's more than 40 thrift shops. Many other bakery companies distribute products through independent wholesalers and do not operate thrift shops.[6] See Figure 12-2.

Channel Functions and the Role of Middlemen

For the great majority of products and services, these **channel functions** (shown in Figure 12-3) must be provided:

1. Marketing research—analyzing customer characteristics and needs.
2. Buying—purchasing arrangements and terms for items acquired by channel members.
3. Promotion—advertising, personal selling, and special sales and events.

Basic *channel functions* must be performed by at least one member of the distribution channel.

[5] Craig Reiss, ''Advantages of Being Self-Contained,'' *Marketing & Media Decisions* (Spring 1982, Special Edition), pp. 69–70.
[6] ''The Sweet Smell of Success at Entenmann's,'' *Fortune* (August 8, 1983), p. 82.

**Figure 12-3
Channel Functions**

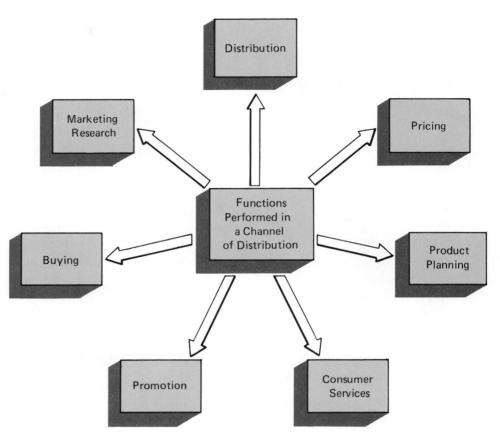

4. Consumer services—delivery, credit, in-home purchases, etc.
5. Product planning—product testing, product positioning, and product deletion.
6. Pricing—setting intermediate and final prices.
7. Distribution—transporting, warehousing, and customer contact.

These functions must be completed by some member of the distribution channel (the manufacturer, if no middlemen are used) and responsibility for them assigned.

When they are used, independent middlemen have a major role in distribution. Due to their closeness to the market, they have good insights into the characteristics and needs of customers. This customer contact eases the marketing research process.

Middlemen can reduce costs, provide early payments, offer expertise, open new markets, and lower risks.

In some cases, wholesalers and retailers purchase merchandise upon its receipt; in others, the middlemen are consigned the items and do not pay for them until after a sale has been made. Furthermore, purchase terms may range from net cash (payment due immediately) to net sixty days (payment not due for sixty days) or longer. Ownership and credit arrangements are key areas in channel arrangements. When the middleman does not pay for merchandise from the manufacturer until after its resale, the manufacturer risks a poor cash flow, high merchandise returns, product obsolescence, spoilage, multiple transactions with wholesalers and retailers, and potentially low sales to customers.

In assigning promotion responsibility, manufacturers usually take care of national advertising. Wholesalers sometimes motivate and train a retailer's sales staff and help coordinate local promotion among retailers. Retailers undertake local advertising, personal selling, and special events.

Consumer services include delivery, credit, in-home purchases, warranties and guarantees, and return policies. Again, these services can be provided by a channel member or a combination of channel members.

Channel members contribute to product planning in several ways. Channel personnel provide advice on new and existing products. Test marketing requires the cooperation of channel members. Finally, middlemen can be quite helpful in properly positioning products against competitors and suggesting which products to delete.

Channel members usually have strong input into pricing decisions. They stipulate their required markups and generally prefer to price mark their own merchandise. Court decisions have severely restricted manufacturers' ability to control final prices. Therefore, channel members have great flexibility in setting final prices and their methods of payment.

Distribution incorporates three factors: transporting, warehousing, and customer contact. Merchandise must be shipped from the manufacturer to channel members and then to final consumers. Because production frequently exceeds immediate demand, items need to be warehoused. Last, products and services are sold to consumers. This requires a store or seller location, hours of operation, fixtures, and inventory management.

Through the sorting process, middlemen can help manufacturers complete the distribution function. The **sorting process** consists of accumulation, allocation, sorting, and assorting.[7] It resolves the differences in the goals of manufacturers and final consumers.

The *sorting process* coordinates the goals of manufacturers and consumers; it includes accumulation, allocation, sorting, and assorting.

Accumulation is the wholesaler function of collecting small shipments from several manufacturers so that they can be transported more economically. Allocation is the wholesaler/retailer function of distributing items to various consumer markets; it apportions goods. Sorting is the wholesaler/retailer function of separating merchandise into grades, colors, and sizes. Assorting is the retailer function of acquiring a broad range of merchandise so that the consumer is able to choose from among different brands, price ranges, and models.

Often, manufacturers would like to produce a limited variety of an item in large quantity and make as few transactions as possible to sell their entire production output. However, a final consumer would like a variety of brands, colors, sizes, and qualities from which to choose and wants to buy a small amount of an item at a time. In addition, manufacturers would prefer to sell merchandise from the factory, maintain nine-to-five hours and spartan fixtures, and have a limited sales force. The consumer wants to shop at a nearby location, wants to be able to visit a store on weekends and evenings, appreciates store atmosphere, and frequently desires sales help. With the sorting process, middlemen eliminate these differences between manufacturers and consumers.

---

[7] Wroe Alderson, *Marketing Behavior and Executive Action* (Homewood, Ill.: Richard D. Irwin, 1957), Chapter 7.

Selecting a Channel of Distribution

The choice of a channel depends on consumers, the company, the product (service), competition, existing channels, and legalities.

In the selection of a channel of distribution, several key factors must be considered:

- Consumer.

  1. Characteristics—number, concentration, average purchase size.
  2. Needs—store locations and hours, assortment, sales help, credit.
  3. Segments—size, purchase behavior.

- Company.

  1. Goals—control, sales, profit, timing.
  2. Resources—level, flexibility, service needs.
  3. Expertise—functions, specialization, efficiency.
  4. Experience—distribution methods, channel relationships.

- Product or service.

  1. Value—price per unit.
  2. Complexity—technical nature.
  3. Perishability—shelf life, frequency of shipments.
  4. Bulk—weight per unit, divisibility.

- Competition.

  1. Characteristics—number, concentration, assortment, customers.
  2. Tactics—distribution methods, channel relationships.

- Distribution channels.

  1. Alternatives—direct, indirect.
  2. Characteristics—number, functions performed, tradition.
  3. Availability—exclusive arrangements, territorial restrictions.

- Legalities—current laws, pending laws.

While assessing these factors, the firm makes decisions about the type of channel employed, contractual arrangements or administered channels, channel length and width, channel intensity, and the use of dual channels.

In a *direct channel*, the manufacturer performs all functions. In an *indirect channel*, independents are used.

There are two basic types of channel of distribution: direct and indirect. A ***direct channel of distribution*** involves the movement of goods and services from manufacturer to consumer without the use of independent middlemen. An ***indirect channel of distribution*** involves the movement of goods and services from manufacturer to independent channel member to consumer. Figure 12-4A shows a direct channel for final and organizational goods. Figure 12-4B shows the most common indirect channels for consumer and organizational goods.

Figure 12-5 shows the transactions necessary for the sale of 200,000 men's umbrellas under a manufacturer-direct-to-consumer channel and under an indirect channel. In Figure 12-5A, the manufacturer is required to make 200,000 transactions, one with each individual consumer. In Figure 12-5B, the manufacturer makes four transactions, one with each regional wholesaler. Each wholesaler sells through 50 retailers. Finally, each retailer sells to 1,000 final consumers.

A direct channel is most frequently used by companies that want to control

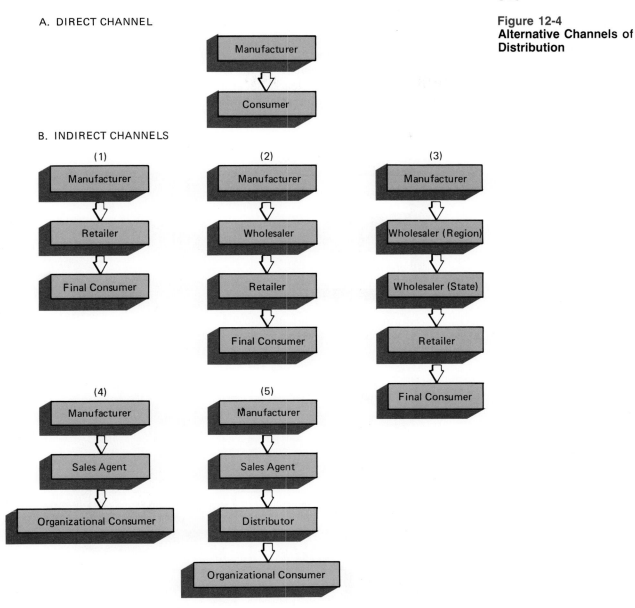

**Figure 12-4
Alternative Channels of
Distribution**

their entire marketing program, desire close customer contact, and have limited target markets. An indirect channel is usually used by companies that want to enlarge their markets, increase sales volume, give up many distribution functions and costs, and are willing to relinquish some channel control and customer contact.

Two points are important. First, when a manufacturer sells to consumers through company-owned outlets (for example, Texaco-owned gas stations or Singer-owned home products stores), this is a direct channel of distribution. Second, with an indirect channel, a manufacturer may employ several layers of wholesalers (for example, regional, state, and local) and sell through different kinds of retailers (such as discount, department, and specialty stores).

A *contractual channel arrangement* outlines all terms for each member.

**Figure 12-5
Transactions in a Direct Versus an Indirect Channel**

Because an indirect channel has independent members, a method for developing an overall marketing plan and assigning responsibilities is needed. This may be accomplished by a contractual arrangement or an administered channel. With a ***contractual channel arrangement***, all the terms regarding distribution functions, prices, and other factors are clearly specified in writing for each member. For example, a manufacturer and a retailer would sign an agreement stating delivery

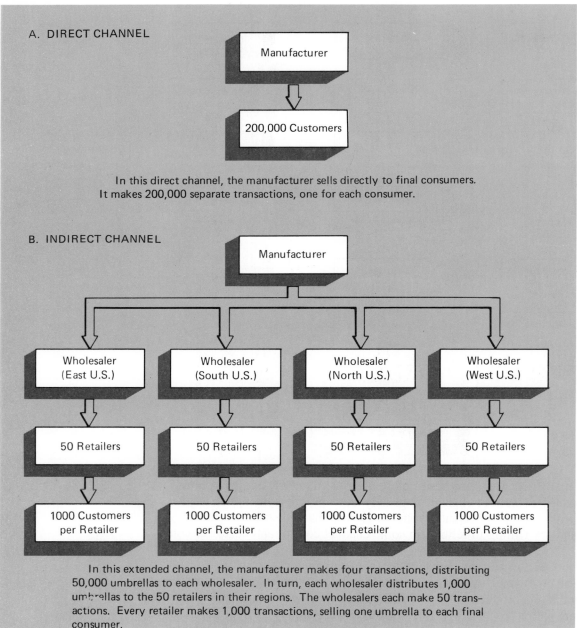

A. DIRECT CHANNEL

Manufacturer

200,000 Customers

In this direct channel, the manufacturer sells directly to final consumers. It makes 200,000 separate transactions, one for each consumer.

B. INDIRECT CHANNEL

Manufacturer

| Wholesaler (East U.S.) | Wholesaler (South U.S.) | Wholesaler (North U.S.) | Wholesaler (West U.S.) |

| 50 Retailers | 50 Retailers | 50 Retailers | 50 Retailers |

| 1000 Customers per Retailer | 1000 Customers per Retailer | 1000 Customers per Retailer | 1000 Customers per Retailer |

In this extended channel, the manufacturer makes four transactions, distributing 50,000 umbrellas to each wholesaler. In turn, each wholesaler distributes 1,000 umbrellas to the 50 retailers in their regions. The wholesalers each make 50 transactions. Every retailer makes 1,000 transactions, selling one umbrella to each final consumer.

dates, quantity discounts, commissions, payment terms, promotional support, and merchandise handling, marking, and displays.

In an **administered channel,** the dominant firm in the distribution process plans the marketing program and itemizes responsibilities. Depending on their relative strength, a manufacturer, wholesaler, or retailer could be the channel leader. For example, a manufacturer of a strong national brand would set its image, price range, and method of selling. It could refuse to sell through uncooperative channel members. Similarly, a powerful retailer could decline to stock an item because its suppliers did not conform to its requests.

The most powerful firm sets policy in an administered channel.

In describing distribution, **channel length** refers to the number of independent members along the channel. In Figure 12-4, *A* represents a short channel, while *B2, B3,* and *B5* show long channels. When a firm shortens its channel by acquiring a company at another stage in the channel, such as a manufacturer merging with a wholesaler, it is involved with **vertical integration.**[8] This enables the firm to be more self-sufficient, ensure supply, lower middleman costs, control channel members, and coordinate timing of products through the channel. Critics of vertical integration believe that it limits competition, fosters inefficiency, and does not result in lower prices to consumers.

Channel length describes the levels of independents; it can be reduced by vertical integration.

Channel width refers to the number of independent middlemen at any stage of the distribution process. A narrow channel is one in which the manufacturer sells through few channel members; in a wide channel the manufacturer sells through many channel members. When a company wants to strengthen its position at its stage of the channel, it may undertake horizontal integration. With **horizontal integration** the firm acquires other businesses like itself. For example, one radio manufacturer would purchase another. Horizontal integration or expansion enables a company to increase its size and share of the market, improve bargaining power with outside channel members, enlarge its consumer market, and utilize mass media and distribution techniques more efficiently.

Channel width refers to the number of independents at any level. Horizontal integration can strengthen a firm.

In conjunction with its choice of a distribution channel, the consumer goods firm must determine the intensity of its channel coverage. Three possibilities are available: exclusive, selective, and intensive. The characteristics of each are shown in Table 12-1.

Under **exclusive distribution,** the firm severely limits the wholesalers and retailers it utilizes in a geographic area, perhaps employing only one or two retailers within a specific shopping district. Unit sales are low and unit profits are high. With **selective distribution,** the firm employs a moderate number of wholesalers and retailers. It tries to combine channel control and a prestige image with good sales volume. In **intensive distribution,** the firm uses a large number of wholesalers and retailers. Its objectives are to obtain widespread market coverage, channel acceptance, and high-volume sales. Unit sales and total profits are high and per unit profits are small. Intensive distribution is a channel strategy aimed at the mass market, particularly at consumers interested in convenience.

The use of exclusive, selective, or intensive distribution depends on company objectives, channel members, customers, and marketing emphasis.

Some additional factors are important in studying channel coverage. First, a firm may use a **dual channel of distribution.** Under this system, the firm appeals to different market segments or diversifies its business by selling through two or

[8] See Kathryn Rudie Harrigan, "A Framework for Looking at Vertical Integration," *Journal of Business Strategy,* Vol. 3 (Winter 1983), pp. 30–37; and Robert D. Buzzell, "Is Vertical Integration Profitable?" *Harvard Business Review,* Vol. 61 (January–February 1983), pp. 92–102.

Table 12-1 Intensity of Channel Coverage

Characteristics	Exclusive Distribution	Selective Distribution	Intensive Distribution
Objectives	Strong image, channel control and loyalty, price stability	Moderate market coverage, solid image, some channel control and loyalty	Widespread market coverage, channel acceptance, volume sales
Channel members	Few in number, well-established, reputable stores	Moderate in number, well-established, better stores	Many in number, all types of outlets
Customers	Few in number, trend setters, willing to travel to store, brand loyal	Moderate in number, brand conscious, somewhat willing to travel to store	Many in number, convenience-oriented
Marketing emphasis	Personal selling, pleasant shopping conditions, good service	Promotional mix, pleasant shopping conditions, good service	Mass advertising, nearby location, items in stock
Examples	Automobiles, designer clothes, caviar	Furniture, clothing, watches	Groceries, household products, magazines

A *dual channel of distribution* allows the company to reach different segments of the market or to diversify its offerings.

more different channels. For example, a manufacturer may use selective distribution for a prestige brand of watches and intensive distribution for a discount brand, or use both indirect and direct channels (such as oil companies selling gasoline through independent stations and company-owned stations). Second, a firm may move from exclusive to selective to intensive distribution as a product passes through its life cycle. However, it would be extremely difficult to go from intensive to selective to exclusive distribution. As an example, designer jeans moved rapidly from prestige stores to better stores to all types of outlets. This process would not have worked in reverse. Third, a company may distribute its products in a new way and achieve considerable success. L'eggs, a division of Hanes, revolutionized the sale of women's hosiery by placing the product in supermarkets.

Manufacturer/Channel Member Contracts

Manufacturer/channel member contracts cover prices, conditions of sale, territories, service/ responsibility mix, duration, and termination.

Manufacturer/channel member contracts focus on five components: price policy, conditions of sale, territorial rights, services/responsibility mix, and contract length and conditions of termination. The highlights of a basic contract follow.

Price policy largely deals with the discounts provided to channel members for performing trade functions, quantity purchases, and cash payments and with commission rates. Trade (functional) discounts are deductions from list prices given to channel members for performing storage, handling, transportation, selling, and other activities. Sometimes, commissions are paid to channel members (such as agents and brokers) for performing functions. Quantity discounts are deductions for large-volume purchases. Cash discounts are deductions for immediate or early payment of goods.

Conditions of sale cover price and quality guarantees, payment and shipping terms, reimbursement for unsaleable merchandise, and return allowances. Of particular importance is the guarantee against a price decline. With this guarantee, a channel member is protected against paying a high price for an item that is then offered to other firms at a lower price. If prices are reduced, the original buyer receives a rebate so that the cost of its merchandise is similar to that of competitors. Otherwise, it could not meet the prices competitors charge customers.

Territorial rights outline the geographic areas (such as greater San Diego) in which channel members may operate and/or the target markets (such as small business accounts) that may be contacted by these firms. In some cases, wholesalers and retailers receive exclusive territories, such as McDonald's franchisees; in others, many competitive firms are granted territorial rights for the same areas, such as retailers selling Sharp calculators.

The services/responsibility mix describes the services and responsibilities each channel member provides to the others. Included in the mix are sales force training, accounting systems assistance, inventory level requirements, delivery standards, and communication. Frequently, manufacturers/suppliers employ full-line forcing, whereby wholesalers and retailers are required to carry an entire line of products. This is legal as long as wholesalers and retailers are not prevented from purchasing competitive products from other suppliers. A hold-harmless agreement protects wholesalers and retailers in product liability cases. Under it, manufacturers assume responsibility for legal suits arising from poor product design or negligence in production.

The length of the contract and conditions of termination protect a wholesaler or retailer against a manufacturer/supplier prematurely bypassing it after a territory has been built up. The manufacturer is protected by limiting the duration of the contract and specifying the factors leading to termination.

It should be remembered that not all relationships among channel members are formal. Sometimes firms operate with handshake agreements. However, without a contract, the danger exists that there will be misunderstandings regarding objectives, compensation, services to be provided, and the length of the agreement. The one constraint of a written contract may be its inflexibility under changing market conditions.

Channel Cooperation and Conflict

All channel members have the same general objectives: profitability, access to products and services, efficient distribution, and customer loyalty. However, the way these and other objectives are accomplished frequently leads to differing views. For example: How are profits allocated along the channel? How can manufacturers sell products through many competing retailers and expect the retailers not to carry other brands? Who coordinates channel decisions? To whom are consumers loyal, manufacturers or retailers?

Channel member goals need to be balanced and differences settled in an equitable manner.

It should be recognized that there are natural differences among channel members by virtue of their positions in the channel, the functions performed, and the desire of every firm to maximize its own profits and control its strategy. The successful channel will be able to maximize cooperation and minimize conflict. Table 12-2 shows several potential causes of channel conflict. Table 12-3 shows how channel cooperation can reduce conflict.

In the past, manufacturers tended to dominate channels because they had national market coverage and recognition, and retailers were small and localized. Today, with the growth of large national retail chains and private-label merchandise, the balance of power has shifted somewhat toward retailers. Now, the control in any given channel depends on the attributes of its members.

Retailers are becoming more powerful and demanding.

Table 12-2 Potential Causes of Channel Conflict

Factor	Manufacturer's Goal	Wholesaler's/Retailer's Goal
Pricing	To establish final price consistent with product image	To establish final price consistent with channel member's image
Purchase terms	To ensure prompt, accurate payments and minimize discounts	To defer payments as long as possible and secure discounts
Shelf space	To obtain plentiful shelf space with good visibility in order to maximize brand sales	To allocate shelf space among many brands in order to maximize total product sales
Exclusivity	To hold down the number of competing brands a channel member stocks while selling through many channel members	To hold down the number of competing members carrying the same brands while selling different brands itself
Delivery	To receive adequate notice before deliveries are required	To obtain quick service
Advertising support	To secure advertising support from wholesalers and retailers	To secure advertising support from manufacturers
Profitability	To maintain adequate profit margins	To maintain adequate profit margins
Continuity	To receive orders on a regular basis	To receive shipments on a regular basis
Order size	To maximize order size	To have order size conform with consumer demand to minimize inventory investment
Assortment	To standardize production	To secure a full variety
Risk	To have wholesalers and retailers assume risks	To have manufacturers assume risks
Branding	To sell products under the manufacturer's label	To sell products under dealer labels as well as manufacturer labels
Channel access	To be able to distribute items wherever desirable by manufacturer	To carry only those items desired by channel member
Importance of account	To not allow any single wholesaler or retailer to dominate	To not allow any single manufacturer to dominate
Consumer loyalty	To have consumers loyal to the manufacturer	To have consumers loyal to the channel member
Channel control	To make the key channel decisions	To make the key channel decisions

If conflicts arise, they may be resolved in a cooperative manner in which channel members discuss their problems and accept mutual responsibility for solving them, or conflicts may lead to confrontations. These may result in a manufacturer shipping late, refusing to deal with certain middlemen, limiting financing, withdrawing promotional support, and other tactics. Similarly, a retailer may make late payments, provide poor shelf space, refuse to carry items, return many products, and apply other tactics. A channel cannot function well within a confrontational framework.

Following are some recent examples of channel conflict:

- When videocassette retailers found that consumers would not pay $75 to $100 to buy a cassette of a movie, they began renting them for $2 to $5 per night. This resulted in little consumer demand to buy cassettes. Accordingly, movie

Table 12-3 **Methods of Channel Cooperation**

Factor	Manufacturer Action	Wholesaler/Retailer Action
New-product introduction	Thorough testing, adequate promotional support	Good shelf location and space, enthusiasm for product, assistance in test marketing
Delivery	Prompt filling of orders, adherence to scheduled dates	Proper time allowed for delivery, shipments immediately checked for accuracy
Marketing research	Data provided to wholesalers and retailers	Data provided to manufacturers
Pricing	Prices to wholesalers and retailers enable them to achieve reasonable profits, dealer flexibility allowed	Infrequent sales from regular prices, maintenance of proper image
Promotion	Sales force training, sales force incentives, development of national advertising campaign, cooperative advertising programs	Attractive in-store displays, knowledgeable salespeople, participation in cooperative programs
Financing	Liberal financial terms	Adherence to financial terms
Product quality	Product guarantees	Proper installation and servicing of products
Channel control	Shared and specified decision making	Shared and specified decision making

studios became dissatisfied. They dropped the prices of many cassettes to $29 to $39 and started releasing movies to cable television much earlier.[9]

- Anheuser-Busch prohibited its beer distributors from selling company products outside their territories. Discount retailers were thus unable to shop around for the lowest distributor's prices. As a result, beer prices to final consumers rose.[10]
- Jordache filed a lawsuit against K mart, claiming that the retailer was selling counterfeit Jordache jeans. In response, K mart ordered the removal of Jordache jeans from its shelves.[11]
- When Porsche (the West German auto maker) announced that it would market cars in the U.S. through company-owned distribution centers and no longer rely on independent dealers, the independents charged that Porsche was violating franchising laws. Porsche then backed off, and continued to use the independents as it had previously.[12]

An existing manufacturer is usually able to secure dealer support and enthusiasm when introducing a new product. This occurs because the dealer knows the manufacturer's past track record, the type of promotional support that will be provided, and the manufacturer's reliability in future deliveries. Accordingly, the channel members cooperate in what is a ***pushing strategy***.[13]

On the other hand, it may be difficult for a new manufacturer to break into an

In a *pushing strategy*, a manufacturer and channel members cooperate. In a *pulling strategy*, a manufacturer generates demand before channel support.

[9] Laura Landro, "Movie Studios' Cuts in Videocassette Prices Stir Battle with Retailers on Video Rentals," *Wall Street Journal* (September 23, 1983), pp. 33, 57.
[10] Richard Sandomir, "King Bud's New Rules," *Newsday* (October 18, 1982), Business section, pp. 1, 13.
[11] "Jordache Sues K mart in Its Battle to Halt Jeans Counterfeiting," *Wall Street Journal* (December 13, 1982), p. 38.
[12] John Holusha, "The Porsche Franchise Fight," *New York Times* (March 14, 1984), pp. D1–D2; and David B. Tinnin, "Porsche's Civil War with Its Dealers," *Fortune* (April 16, 1984), pp. 63–68.
[13] See Michael Levy, John Webster, and Roger A. Kerin, "Formulating Push Marketing Strategies: A Method and Application," *Journal of Marketing*, Vol. 47 (Winter 1983), pp. 25–34.

Figure 12-6
**Pushing Versus Pulling
Strategies**

PUSHING

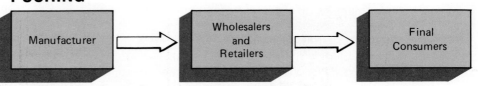

An established manufacturer has acceptance and cooperation from channel members. Together, they promote new and continuing products to final consumers.

PULLING

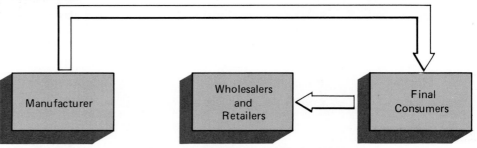

A new manufacturer cannot gain interest from channel members without first showing final consumer demand. The manufacturer promotes products directly to final consumers, who pull on channel members until they carry the items.

existing channel. The dealer will be unfamiliar with the manufacturer, be unable to gauge its sales potential, and wonder about its support and future deliveries. Because of these factors, the new firm must embark on a ***pulling strategy.*** With that approach, the company first develops consumer demand and then secures dealer support. This requires heavy promotional expenses, paid entirely by the manufacturer; frequently, it must offer retailers guarantees of minimum sales or profits (and make up any shortages from these guarantees). Figure 12-6 contrasts pushing and pulling strategies.

During the 1970s one of the most successful pulling strategies was carried out by Frank Perdue. Perdue had the idea to label his chickens and guarantee customer satisfaction. No chickens were branded at that time. Because supermarkets were content to sell unlabeled chickens and had no consumer demand for changing this policy, they initially decided not to handle Perdue products. After a massive advertising campaign, Perdue products were in great demand. Supermarkets rushed to stock them and generated high sales volume at a premium price.

Industrial Channel of Distribution

An industrial channel has several unique characteristics.

The distribution channel for industrial products differs from that for consumer products in the following ways:[14]

---

[14] See Donald M. Jackson, Robert F. Krampf, and Leonard J. Konopa, ''Factors That Influence the Length of Industrial Channels,'' *Industrial Marketing Management,* Vol. 11 (October 1982), pp. 263–268; and James D. Hlavacek and Tommy J. McCuiston, ''Industrial Distributors—When, Who, and How?'' *Harvard Business Review,* Vol. 61 (March–April 1983), pp. 96–101.

1. Retailers are usually not employed.
2. Direct channels are more readily used.
3. Transactions are fewer and orders are larger.
4. Specification selling is more prevalent.
5. Independent channel members are more knowledgeable.
6. Team selling (two or more salespeople) may be necessary.
7. Different channel members specialize in industrial products from those in consumer products.
8. Leasing, rather than selling, may be required.

Physical Distribution

Physical distribution describes the broad range of activities concerned with the efficient movement of finished goods from the end of the production line to the consumer, and in some cases includes the movement of raw materials from the source of supply to the beginning of the production line.[15]

Physical distribution involves deliveries to the right place, at the right time, and in good condition.

Physical distribution is involved with delivering goods (raw materials, parts, semifinished items, and finished goods and services) to the designated place, at the designated time, and in proper condition. It is undertaken by manufacturers, wholesalers, and retailers.

Physical distribution includes customer service, warehousing, shipping, inventory controls, private trucking fleet operations, packaging, receiving, materials handling, and plant, warehouse, and store location. Figure 12-7 illustrates the physical distribution activities involved in a typical *order cycle* (the period of time that spans the customer's placing an order and its receipt).

An *order cycle* covers many distribution activities.

Importance of Physical Distribution

Physical distribution is important for a number of reasons: its costs, the value of distribution service in obtaining and keeping customers, and the relationship of physical distribution to the other functional areas of a company.

COSTS

Distribution costs vary widely by industry. For example, in the food industry these costs account for nearly one third of the retail price, whereas for wood products and textiles the costs are closer to one sixth of the retail price.[16]

As energy costs continued to rise, expenditures on transportation increased sharply. According to one report, from 1972 to 1981, physical distribution costs doubled,[17] before stabilizing during 1982 and 1983.

---

[15] National Council of Physical Distribution Management, 307 North Michigan Avenue, Chicago.

[16] Ronald H. Ballou, *Basic Business Logistics* (Englewood Cliffs, N.J.: Prentice-Hall, 1978), pp. 17–18.

[17] "New Distribution Strategies Needed to Combat Skyrocketing Energy Costs," *Marketing News* (February 8, 1980), p. 14.

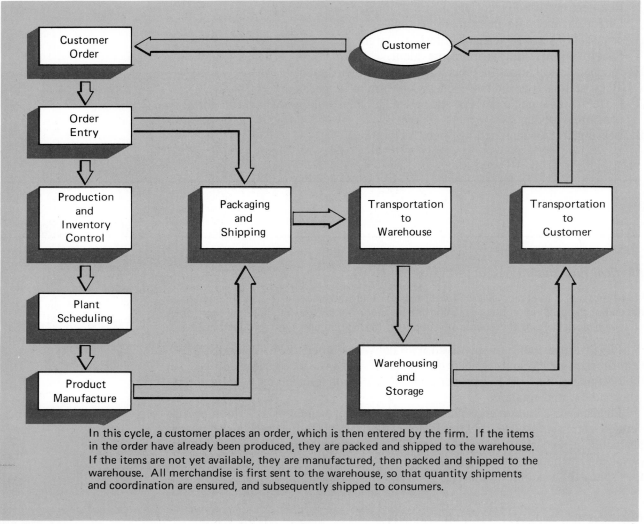

In this cycle, a customer places an order, which is then entered by the firm. If the items in the order have already been produced, they are packed and shipped to the warehouse. If the items are not yet available, they are manufactured, then packed and shipped to the warehouse. All merchandise is first sent to the warehouse, so that quantity shipments and coordination are ensured, and subsequently shipped to consumers.

Figure 12-7
Physical Distribution Activities Involved in a Typical Order Cycle

Source: Adapted from Stephen B. Oresman and Charles D. Scudder. "A Remedy for Maldistribution," *Business Horizons,* Vol. 17 (June 1974), pp. 61–72. Copyright, 1974, by the Foundation for the School of Business at Indiana University. Reprinted by permission.

It is essential for marketers to be able to identify the symptoms of a poor physical distribution system, since it could result in high costs and/or poor customer service. These symptoms are shown in Table 12-4.

CUSTOMER SERVICE

Efficient customer service is vital. Therefore, *distribution standards* are needed.

A major part of any firm's distribution program is its level of customer service. Physical distribution services include frequent deliveries, the speed and consistency of deliveries, emergency shipment policies, the acceptance of small orders, warehousing, coordination of assortments, and the provision of order progress reports. Poor performance in these areas can result in lost customers.

Accordingly, ***distribution standards,*** clear and measurable goals regarding

Table 12-4 Symptoms of a Poor Physical Distribution System

Symptom	Explanation
1. Slow-turning inventories	Inventory turnover should be comparable to that of similar firms.
2. Inefficient customer service	Costs are high compared with the value of shipments; warehouses are poorly situated; inventory levels are not tied to customer demand.
3. A large number of interwarehouse shipments	Merchandise transfers increase physical distribution costs because they must be handled (packed, unpacked, stored, and verified) at each warehouse.
4. Frequent use of emergency shipments	Extra charges add significantly to physical distribution costs.
5. Erratic customer service	Large variations in the order cycle exist; customers cannot depend on the supplier for consistent delivery times.
6. Too-high inventory levels	Too much capital is tied up in inventory. The firm must bear high insurance costs, interest expense, and high risks of pilferage and product obsolescence. Merchandise may not be fresh.
7. No backhaul opportunities	The firm uses its own trucking facilities; however, trucks are only full one way.
8. Peripheral hauls	The firm uses its own trucking facility; however, many hauls are peripheral or too spread out.
9. Large group of small orders	Small orders often are unprofitable. Many distribution costs are fixed.

service levels in physical distribution, must be developed. Examples are filling 90 per cent of orders from existing inventory, responding to customer requests for order information within three hours, filling orders with 99 per cent accuracy, and limiting merchandise damaged in transit to 3 per cent.

One way to determine the optimal customer service level is through the ***total-cost approach.*** Under this approach, the distribution service level with the lowest total costs—including freight (shipping), warehousing, and the cost of lost business—is the optimal service level. The ideal system seeks a balance between low distribution costs and high opportunities for sales. Seldom will this balance be achieved at the lowest level of distribution costs; lost sales will be too great. Figure 12-8 illustrates the total-cost approach.

Research has shown the importance of physical distribution services in obtaining and retaining customers. An analysis of retailers found that quick and easy ordering, return privileges, delivery provided when needed, and small-order delivery were important factors in selecting suppliers.[18] An investigation of industrial purchasing managers showed that physical distribution ranked second only to product quality as a major reason for buying from a particular firm.[19] A study of purchasing managers in small firms revealed these problem areas with vendors: failure to deliver on time, the quantity and quality of items delivered not the same as those ordered, and the unwillingness of some sellers to call on and sell to smaller firms.[20]

*The **total-cost approach** considers both costs and opportunities.*

[18] James R. Brown and Prem C. Purwar, "A Cross-Channel Comparison of Retailer Supplier Selection Factors" in Richard P. Bagozzi et. al (Editors), *Marketing in the 80's* (Chicago: American Marketing Association, 1980), p. 219.

[19] William D. Perreault, Jr., and Frederick A. Russ, "Physical Distribution Service in Industrial Purchase Decisions," *Journal of Marketing,* Vol. 40 (April 1976), p. 5.

[20] Monroe Murphy Bird, "Small Industrial Buyers Call Late Delivery Worst Problem," *Marketing News* (April 4, 1980), p. 24.

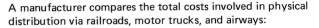

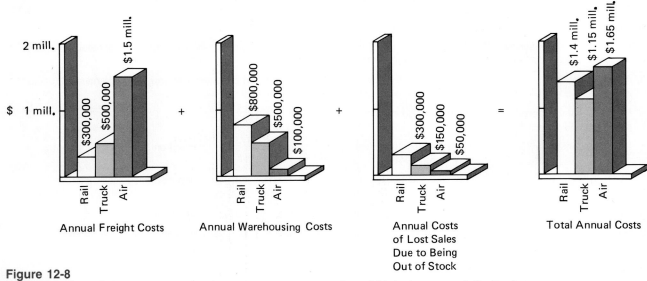

A manufacturer compares the total costs involved in physical distribution via railroads, motor trucks, and airways:

Annual Freight Costs   Annual Warehousing Costs   Annual Costs of Lost Sales Due to Being Out of Stock   Total Annual Costs

Figure 12-8
An Illustration of the Total-Cost Approach in Distribution

The firm selects motor trucks because they yield the lowest total distribution costs.

PHYSICAL DISTRIBUTION AND OTHER FUNCTIONAL AREAS

Physical distribution interacts with every aspect of marketing as well as other functional areas within the company.

Physical distribution must be coordinated with other marketing and nonmarketing areas.

Product differentiation—which adds many different product variations in color, size, features, quality, and style—imposes a heavy burden on a company's distribution facilities. Greater variety means lower volume per item, which increases unit shipping and warehousing costs. The stocking of a broader range of replacement parts also becomes necessary.

The high costs of transportation have motivated some manufacturers to seek methods for reducing the water concentration in products like soft drinks, beer, canned juice, and fresh meat. For example, Procter & Gamble has developed a dry mix which, when reconstituted with water, will produce a carbonated beverage.[21]

Distribution policy must be closely aligned with promotions. Because promotion campaigns are often planned weeks in advance, it is essential that distribution to wholesalers and retailers be carried out at the proper times to ensure ample stocks of goods. Retailers may receive consumer complaints for not carrying or having sufficient quantities of the items they advertise, even though the manufacturer is at fault. Some new products fail because of poor initial distribution.

Physical distribution is related to overall channel strategy. A firm seeking extensive distribution needs many dispersed warehouses. One involved with perishables needs to be sure that a large proportion of a product's selling life is not spent in transit.

Physical distribution also plays an important part in pricing decisions. A firm with quick, reliable delivery and an ample supply of replacement parts that will

---

[21] Rudolf Struse, "High Cost of Shipping Water to Spur Dry Mix Food Forms," *Marketing News* (December 28, 1979), p. 1.

ship small orders and provide emergency shipments may be able to charge higher prices than a company that provides less service.

A distribution strategy has an important overlap with production and financial functions. For example, many meat processors are able to reduce transportation costs by centralizing their cutting operations because less waste is shipped to each store. High freight costs and the uncertainty of continuous fuel supplies encourage firms to locate plants closer to markets. Low average inventories in stock enable companies to reduce finance charges. Public warehouse receipts can be used as collateral for loans, and the utilization of bonded warehouses defers the payment of excise taxes and import duties until goods are sold.

There are many decisions to be made in the development of a ***physical distribution strategy:*** the transportation form or forms to be used, inventory levels and warehouse form(s), and the number and locations of plants, warehouses, and retail locations.

> A *physical distribution strategy* involves transportation, inventory, and facilities.

A physical distribution strategy can be fairly simple. A firm can have one plant, focus attention on one geographic market, and ship directly to customers without the use of decentralized warehouses. At the other extreme, a physical distribution strategy can include multiple plants, assembly locations in each geographic market, thousands of customer locations, and the integration of many transportation modes.

The remainder of this chapter deals with the two central components of physical distribution strategy: transportation and inventory management (which includes warehousing).

Transportation

Since 1950, the relative importance of railroads has declined substantially, despite their continuing leadership in ton miles. Motor trucks have increased their share of ton miles by 50 per cent during this period. Waterway shipments have had a stable share for the last thirty years. The share of ton miles shipped via pipelines has more than doubled since 1950. Despite the growth of airlines, freight deliveries through the airways remain at less than 1 per cent of all shipments.

Over the last several years, the deregulation of transportation industries has greatly expanded the competition in and among these industries. In general, deregulation allows transportation firms greater flexibility in entering new markets, expanding their businesses, the products they carry, price setting, and the functions they perform.[22]

Figure 12-9 ranks the transportation forms on the basis of six operating statistics. Airways have the best rating for speed. Pipelines are superior in dependability (schedules met), frequency (shipments per day), and cost per ton mile. Waterways are able to handle the most different products. Motor trucks have the highest availability in terms of number of geographic points served.

> Transportation forms may be rated on speed, availability, dependability, capability, frequency, and cost.

Each transportation form and such transportation services as parcel post are studied next.

---

[22] Bill Paul, ''Freight Transportation Is Being Transformed in Era of Deregulation,'' *Wall Street Journal* (October 20, 1983), pp. 1, 18; and Peter Brimelow, ''Where Those Hybrid Haulers Are Headed,'' *Fortune* (March 19, 1984), pp. 114–120.

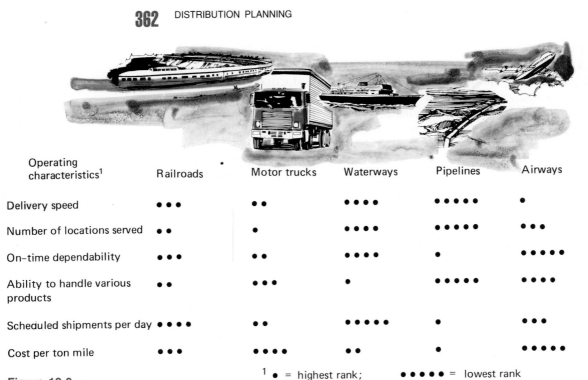

Operating characteristics[1]	Railroads	Motor trucks	Waterways	Pipelines	Airways
Delivery speed	•••	••	••••	•••••	•
Number of locations served	••	•	••••	•••••	•••
On–time dependability	•••	••	••••	•	•••••
Ability to handle various products	••	•••	•	•••••	••••
Scheduled shipments per day	••••	••	•••••	•	•••
Cost per ton mile	•••	••••	••	•	•••••

[1] • = highest rank; ••••• = lowest rank

Figure 12-9
The Relative Operating Characteristics of Five Basic Transportation Forms

Source: Adapted from Donald J. Bowersox, *Logistical Management,* Second Edition (New York: Macmillan, 1978), p. 120. (Copyright © 1978, Donald J. Bowersox); reprinted by permission.

Railroads transport mostly heavy items over long distances.

RAILROADS

Railroads usually carry heavy, bulky items that are low in value (relative to their weight) over long distances. Railroads ship items too heavy for trucks.

Despite their dominant position in ton miles shipped, railroads have been beset by a variety of problems in recent years. Fixed costs are high because of investments in facilities. Shippers face railroad car shortages during high demand months for agricultural goods. Some tracks and railroad cars are in serious need of repair. Trucks are faster, more flexible, and are packed more easily. In response to these difficulties, the railroads are relying on three solutions to improve their outlook: new shipping techniques, deregulation, and mergers.

Motor trucks handle small shipments over short distances.

MOTOR TRUCKS

Motor trucks predominantly transport small shipments over short distances. Motor carriers handle about 80 per cent of the country's shipments of less than 500 or 1,000 pounds. Seventy per cent of all trucks are used for local deliveries and 50 per cent of total truck miles are local.

Trucks are more flexible than rail because they can pick up packages at the factory or warehouse and deliver them to the customer's door. For example, General Motors moves half its total shipments by trucks, which carry parts from one plant right to the assembly area of another.[23] In addition, trucks are faster than rail for short distances. Like railroads, the trucking industry has been deregulated since 1980.

[23] "Getting Ready: Businessmen Brace for a Trucking Strike, But There's a Limit to What They Can Do," *Wall Street Journal* (March 29, 1979), p. 46.

WATERWAYS

Waterways involve the movement of goods on barges via inland rivers and on tankers and general merchandise freighters through the Great Lakes, intercoastal shipping, and the St. Lawrence Seaway. Waterways are used primarily for transporting low-value, high-bulk freight (such as coal, iron ore, gravel, grain, and cement). Although this transportation is slow, and may be closed by ice during the winter, the rates are extremely low.

Various improvements in vessel design have recently occurred. For example, many "supervessels" are now operating on the Great Lakes. These supervessels can each carry 61,000 gross tons of iron-bearing rock in one trip. The conveyor system is twice as efficient as the one on older boats. One supervessel can annually deliver three and one-half million gross tons of rock along a route from Lake Superior to Gary, Indiana. This is enough to keep Gary's blast furnaces operating for 160 days.[24]

Waterways **specialize in low-value, high-bulk items.**

PIPELINES

Within *pipelines,* there is continuous movement and there are no interruptions, inventories (except those held by a carrier), and intermediate storage locations. Thus, handling and labor costs are minimized. Even though pipelines are very reliable, only certain commodities can be moved through them. In the past, emphasis was on gas and petroleum-based products. Recently, pipelines have been modified to accept coal and wood chips, which are transported in a semiliquid state. Nonetheless, lack of flexibility limits the potential of pipelines.

Some pipelines are enormous in size. For example, the Alaska Natural Gas Transportation System (ANGTS) will eventually cover 4,800 miles and deliver 2.4 billion cubic feet of natural gas per day to the lower 48 states.[25] It has been estimated that this pipeline will cost $10 billion to construct.

Pipelines **center on liquids, gases, and semiliquids.**

AIRWAYS

Airways are the fastest, most expensive form of transportation. As a result, high-value products, perishable goods, and emergency goods dominate air shipments. Even though air transit is costly, it may lower other costs, such as the need for outlying or even regional warehouses. The costs of packing, unpacking, and preparing goods for shipping are lower than for other transportation forms.

Airfreight has been deregulated since late 1977. As a result, some airlines have stepped up cargo operations, while others have curtailed them. Many carriers now employ wide-bodied jets that can handle large containers. In addition, modern communications and sorting equipment have been added to airfreight operations. Firms specializing in air shipments have done well by emphasizing fast, guaranteed service at reasonable prices.

Airways **stress valuable, perishable, and emergency items.**

TRANSPORTATION SERVICES

Transportation service companies handle the shipments of moderate-sized packages. Some pick up packages from the shipping firm's office and deliver direct to the addressee. Others require packages to be brought to a service company outlet. The three major kinds of service companies are government parcel post, private parcel, and express.

These *transportation service companies* **ship medium- and small-sized packages: government parcel post, private parcel, and express.**

---

[24] Seth Cropsey, "King of the Ore Boats," *Fortune* (March 10, 1980), pp. 104–106.
[25] "McMillian: A Tough Pipeliner Vs. the Producers," *Business Week* (March 31, 1980), pp. 62, 65.

Government parcel post operates out of post offices and utilizes rates based on postal zones, of which there are eight. Parcel post can be insured or sent COD (collect on delivery). Special handling is available to expedite shipments. Express mail is available for next-day service from a post office to an addressee.

Private parcel services specialize in small-package delivery, usually less than 50-pound shipments. Most services ship from manufacturers, wholesalers, distributors, and retailers to their customers within a several-state area. The largest private firm is United Parcel Service (UPS), a multibillion dollar, national company.

Express companies, such as Federal Express, Emery Air Freight, Burlington Northern Air Freight, and Purolator Courier Corporation, generally provide guaranteed nationwide delivery of small packages for the morning after pickup. The average express delivery is 10 pounds.

COORDINATION OF TRANSPORTATION

Because a single shipment may involve a combination of transportation forms, coordination is necessary. Two major innovations that improve a firm's ability to coordinate shipments are containerization and freight forwarding.

With *containerization*, nonbreakable containers are sealed until the final destination.

Under **containerization,** goods are placed into sturdy containers that can be placed on trains, trucks, ships, or planes. These marked containers are sealed until delivered, thereby reducing damage and pilferage. Their progress and destination are frequently monitored. The containers are mobile warehouses that can be moved from manufacturing plants to receiving docks, where they remain until the contents are needed.

***Freight forwarders* accumulate shipments from several companies.**

Freight forwarders consolidate small shipments (usually less than 500 pounds each) from several companies. They pick up merchandise at the shipper's place of business and arrange for delivery at the buyer's door. Freight forwarders prosper because less than carload (lcl) rates are sharply higher than carload (cl) rates. Freight forwarders also provide traffic management services, such as selecting the best transportation form at the most reasonable rate.

LEGAL STATUS OF TRANSPORTATION FIRMS

Carriers are classified as *common*, *contract*, *exempt*, or *private*.

Transportation firms are categorized as common, contract, exempt, or private carriers. **Common carriers** must transport the goods of any firm interested in their services; they cannot refuse any shipments unless the carrier's rules are broken (such as packing requirements). Common carriers provide service on a fixed and publicized schedule between designated points. A regular fee schedule is also published. All railroads and petroleum pipelines and some air, motor truck, and water transporters are common carriers.

Contract carriers provide one or a few shippers with transportation services based on individual agreements. Contract carriers are not required to maintain fixed routes or schedules, and rates may be negotiated. Many motor-truck, inland-waterway, and airfreight transporters are contract carriers.

Exempt carriers are excused from legal regulations and must only comply with safety requirements. Exempt carriers are specified by law. Some commodities moved by water, such as coal, and most agricultural goods are exempt from economic restrictions.

Private carriers are shippers who possess their own transportation facilities. They are subject to safety rules. Private carriers are common in the automobile industry.

Inventory Management

The intent of **inventory management** is to provide a continuous flow of goods and to match the quantity of goods kept in inventory with sales demand. When production or consumption is seasonal or erratic, this can be difficult.

Therefore, inventory management (including warehousing) has broad implications for the firm. It is vital that sufficient quantities be on hand when they are advertised by a retailer. A producer cannot afford to run out of a crucial item that could put a halt to production. On the other hand, inventory should not be too large, since the costs of storing products for a year (floor space, insurance, supervision, and credit) are estimated by one source to be 36 per cent of the goods' costs.[26] In situations where models change yearly, as with automobiles, large inventories of year-old cars can adversely affect new-car sales. Finally, large inventories may result in stale goods, cause the firm to mark down prices due to product obsolescence, and tie up working capital.

In order to improve inventory management, a number of U.S. firms are now applying a **just-in-time (JIT) inventory system,** a procedure used most by the Japanese. With a JIT system, the purchasing firm reduces the amount of inventory it keeps on hand by ordering more frequently and in lower quantity. This requires better planning and information on the part of the purchaser, geographically closer sellers, improved buyer-seller relationships and stability, and better production and distribution facilities. JIT systems are being used by automobile firms, Hewlett-Packard, Motorola, General Electric, Deere, Black & Decker, and others.[27] Figure 12-10 describes the Whirlpool JIT system, in use for over thirty years. As one analyst noted,

For too long we have been building inventories on overtime and reducing them with idle time—hardly an efficient practice. By focusing on lowering inventory you will force attention on the reasons for the wrong inventory, with enormous benefits to your business.[28]

Four aspects of inventory management are explained in the following subsections: stock turnover, when to reorder, how much to reorder, and warehousing.

STOCK TURNOVER

The balance between sales and inventory on hand is expressed by **stock turnover,** which represents the number of times during a specified period (usually one

> *Inventory management* deals with the steady and efficient flow and allocation of products.

> A *just-in time (JIT) inventory system* relies on small, frequent orders.

> *Stock turnover* shows the ratio between annual sales and average inventory on hand.

[26] Richard F. Janssen and John Koten, "Leaner Inventories Than in Prior Slumps Could Lessen Severity of This Recession," *Wall Street Journal* (May 23, 1980), p. 48.

[27] Richard J. Schonberger and James P. Gilbert, "Just-In-Time Purchasing: A Challenge for U.S. Industry," *California Management Review*, Vol. 26 (Fall 1983), pp. 54–68; Craig R. Waters, "Why Everybody's Talking About 'Just-In-Time,'" *Inc.* (March 1984), pp. 77–90; and Ralph E. Winter, "Firms Cut Inventories Down to Low Levels, But Major Test Looms," *Wall Street Journal* (March 29, 1984), pp. 1, 25.

[28] Hal F. Mather, "The Case for Skimpy Inventories," *Harvard Business Review*, Vol. 62 (January-February 1984), p. 46.

Figure 12-10
Whirlpool's Just-in-Time
Inventory System

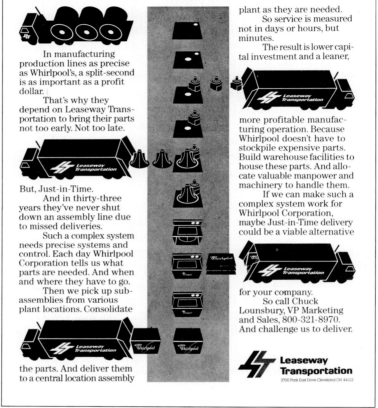

Reprinted by permission.

year) that the average inventory on hand is sold. Stock turnover is calculated in units or dollars:

$$\begin{array}{c} \text{Annual rate of} \\ \text{stock turnover} \\ \text{(in units)} \end{array} = \frac{\text{Number of units sold during year}}{\text{Average inventory on hand (in units)}}$$

$$\begin{array}{c} \text{Annual rate of} \\ \text{stock turnover} \\ \text{(in dollars)} \end{array} = \frac{\text{Net yearly sales (in retail dollars)}}{\text{Average inventory on hand (in retail dollars).}}$$

Annual stock turnover rates range from 3.0 in jewelry stores to 16.0 in grocery stores.

There are many advantages to high inventory turnover: inventory investments are productive, merchandise is fresh, losses from changes in styles and fashion

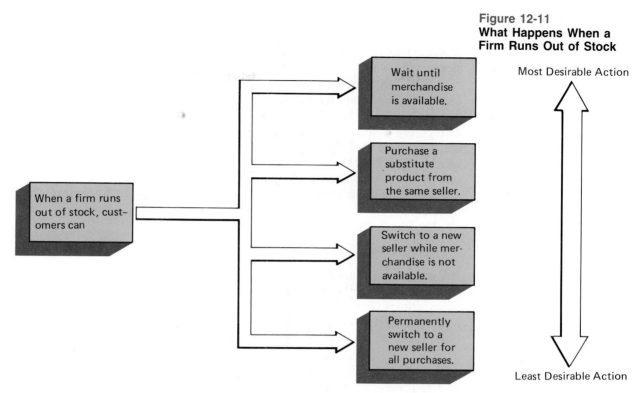

Figure 12-11
What Happens When a
Firm Runs Out of Stock

The firm's objective is to minimize the percentage of customers that switch to other sellers because of stock-outs.

are reduced, and the costs of maintaining inventory (such as insurance, breakage, warehousing, and credit) are lessened.

Turnover can be improved by reducing assortments, eliminating slow-selling items, maintaining minimal inventories for some items, and purchasing from suppliers who deliver on time. According to the purchasing manager for U.S. Borax and Chemical Corp. in Los Angeles:

While people think of inventories as ''something in a warehouse'' . . . 65% of our inventory is in conveyance somewhere—the biggest warehouse in the world is on wheels.[29]

Too high a turnover can negatively affect a firm for several reasons. Small-quantity purchases can cause the loss of volume discounts. Low product assortment can reduce sales if consumers are unable to compare brands or related items are not carried. Low prices may be necessary to stimulate sufficient sales. The chances of running out of stock increase when average inventory size is lowered. As the purchasing chief at Pfizer commented: ''If you have too much inventory, you get yelled at; if you shut the plant because you don't have it, you get fired.''[30] Figure 12-11 shows how customers can react if a firm runs out of stock.

Knowing when to reorder merchandise helps protect against stockouts while minimizing inventory investments.

---

[29] Janssen and Koten, ''Leaner Inventories Than in Prior Slumps Could Lessen Severity of This Recession.''
[30] Ibid.

WHEN TO REORDER INVENTORY

The ***reorder point*** sets a level at which orders must be placed—based on lead time, usage, and safety stock.

The ***reorder point*** establishes an inventory level at which new orders must be placed. The reorder point depends on order lead time, usage rate, and safety stock.

Order lead time is the period from the date an order is placed until the date merchandise is ready for sale (received, checked against the order, and altered, if necessary). Usage rate refers to the average sales in units per day (for a wholesaler or retailer) or the rate at which a product is used in a production process (for a manufacturer). Safety stock is the extra merchandise kept on hand to protect against out-of-stock conditions resulting from unexpectedly high demand, greater-than-anticipated production volume, and delivery delays. Safety stock must be planned in accordance with the marketer's policy toward running out of merchandise.

The reorder point formula is

Reorder point = (Order lead time × Usage rate) + (Safety stock).

A firm that needs four days for an order to be completed, sells 10 items per day, and wants to have 10 extra items on hand in case of a delivery delay of one day has a reorder point of 50[(4 × 10) + 10)]. Without the safety stock, the firm will lose 10 sales if it orders when inventory is 40 items and the order is completed in 5 days. Figure 12-12 shows reorder points and their results under four situations.

Figure 12-12
Reorder Points under Different Assumptions

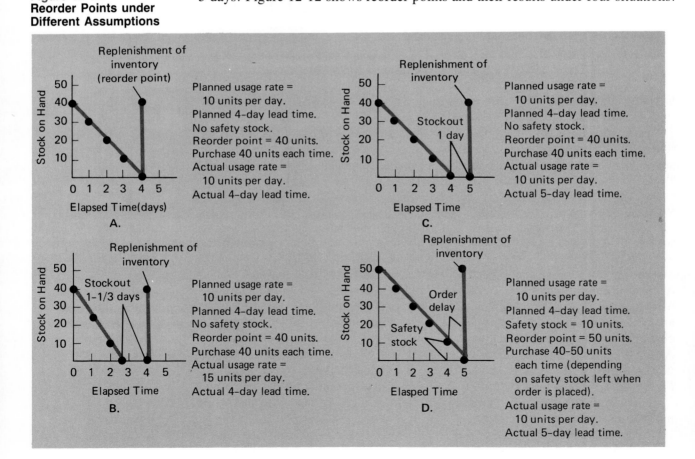

HOW MUCH TO REORDER

Firms must determine their *order size,* the appropriate amount of merchandise, parts, etc. to purchase at one time. Order size depends on several factors: the availability of quantity discounts, the resources of the firm, inventory turnover, the costs of processing each order, and the costs of maintaining goods in inventory. When orders are large, quantity discounts are usually available, a large portion of a firm's finances are tied up in inventory, stock turnover is relatively low, per-order processing costs are reduced, and inventory costs are generally high. The firm is also less likely to run out of goods. The opposite is true for small orders.

Order size depends on discounts, company resources, stock turnover, and costs.

Many companies seek to balance their order-processing costs (filling out forms, computer utilization, and merchandise handling) and their inventory-holding costs (warehouse expenses, interest charges, insurance, deterioration, and pilferage). Processing costs per unit decline as orders get bigger while inventory costs rise. The *economic order quantity (EOQ)* is the order volume corresponding to the lowest sum of order-processing and inventory-holding costs.

Economic order quantity (EOQ) balances ordering and inventory costs.

Table 12-5 demonstrates three ways to compute EOQ. In this illustration a firm faces an annual demand of 3,000 units; their wholesale unit cost is $1, order processing costs are $3, and holding costs equal 20 per cent of the average inventory on hand. The economic order quantity is 300 units. Therefore, 300 units should be ordered at a time.

WAREHOUSING

Warehouses receive, identify, and sort merchandise. They store goods, implement product-recall programs, select goods for shipment, coordinate shipments, and dispatch orders.

Private and public warehouses store and dispatch goods.

Private warehouses are owned and operated by firms which store and distribute their own products. Private warehouses are most likely to be used by companies with stable inventory levels and long-run expectations to serve the same geographic markets.

Public warehouses provide storage and related physical distribution services to any interested individual or firm on a rental basis. Public warehouses are used by firms that desire additional storage space (because their private warehouses are filled) or firms entering new geographic markets (where test marketing or preopening space is needed). If a product is recalled, a public warehouse can be utilized as a collection point, where products are segregated, disposed of, or salvaged.

Public warehouses can provide transportation economies for users by allowing carload shipments to local markets before warehouse distribution to customers. Firms are able to reduce capital expenditures and maximize flexibility by using public warehouses, which are adapted easily to new or expanding markets. Public

**Table 12-5
Economic Order Quantity
Computation**

Background Data

Annual demand = 3,000 units per year

Unit cost = $1 per unit (at wholesale)
Costs to place an order = $3
Holding costs (as per cent of unit cost) = { Interest cost on inventory = 17%
Insurance cost on inventory = 1%
Warehouse expense on inventory = 2%
20%

A.

Order Quantity in Units	Average Inventory on Hand[a] = 1/2 (Order Quantity)	Holding Costs[b] = .20 ($1) × Average Inventory on Hand	Order Placement Costs[c] = $\dfrac{\text{Annual Demand}}{\text{Order Quantity}} \times \$3$	Total Costs = Holding Costs + Order Processing Costs
50	25	5	180	185
100	50	10	90	100
150	75	15	60	75
200	100	20	45	65
250	125	25	36	61
EOQ → 300	150	30	30	60
350	175	35	27	62
400	200	40	24	64
450	225	45	21	66
500	250	50	18	68

B.

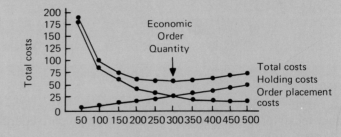

Order Quantity in Units

C. The Economic Order Quantity Can Also be Solved Mathematically[d]

$$EOQ = \sqrt{\frac{2DS}{IC}}$$

Where: EOQ = Order quantity
(in units)
D = Annual demand
(in units)
S = Costs to place
an order
(in dollars)
I = Annual holding costs
(as a % of unit costs)
C = Unit cost of an item
(in dollars)

$$EOQ = \sqrt{\frac{2\,(3000)\,(\$3)}{.20\,(\$1)}} = \sqrt{\frac{\$18,000}{\$.20}} = \sqrt{90,000} = 300$$

[a] Inventory is assumed to equal the order quantity when an order is received and to approach zero, because of sales throughout the order cycle, just prior to a new order being received. Therefore, the average inventory on hand is assumed to be 1/2 × order quantity.

[b] Holding costs = holding costs as a per cent of unit cost × average inventory on hand.

[c] Order placement costs = number of orders × costs to place an order.

[d] The economic order quantity computation may be further complicated by changes in demand, quantity discounts, variable order processing costs, variable holding costs, multiple warehouse locations, and loss in sales revenues due to stock-outs.

warehouses are available in major urban areas and in many smaller cities; there are about 15,000 public warehouses in the United States.

Bonded warehousing and field warehousing are also available through public warehouses. In a **bonded warehouse,** imported or taxable merchandise is stored and can be released for sale only after the appropriate taxes are paid. A bonded warehouse allows firms to postpone tax payments until they are ready to make deliveries to customers. Cigarettes, liquor, and various imported products are often stored in a bonded warehouse.

With *field warehousing* a receipt is issued by the public warehouse for goods stored in a private warehouse or in transit to consumers. These goods are usually placed in a special area, and the field warehouser takes responsibility for the merchandise. A firm uses field warehousing because the warehouse receipt serves as collateral for a loan.

For many firms a combination of private and public warehouses may be optimal. This enables the private warehouse to be full at almost all times and the public warehouse to stock items for peak seasons, bonded goods, and merchandise for geographic areas with low concentrations of customers.

The coordination of a firm's transportation and inventory management strategies is known as a *physical distribution system.*

> A *bonded warehouse* can store imported or taxable goods. *Field warehousing* provides receipts for private or in-transit items.

Summary

Distribution planning is systematic decision making relating to the physical movement and transfer of ownership of a product or service from producer to consumer. A channel of distribution contains the organizations or people involved with the movement and exchange of products or services.

Regardless of who performs them, channel functions include marketing research, buying, promotion, customer services, product planning, price planning, and distribution. Independent channel members can play an important role by performing various functions and resolving the differences between manufacturers' and consumers' goals.

A direct channel requires the manufacturer to perform all distribution functions, while in an indirect channel these activities are carried out by both the manufacturer and independent middlemen. In comparing the two methods, the firm must balance its costs and abilities against control and total sales. An indirect channel may use a contractual arrangement or an administered agreement.

A long channel has a number of levels of independent middlemen; it can be shortened if the firm increases the functions it performs. A wide channel has a large number of firms at any stage in the channel, such as retailers. The distribution channel may be exclusive, selective, or intensive, depending on the firm's goals, channel members, customers, and marketing emphasis. A dual channel allows a company to operate through two or more distribution methods.

In contracts between manufacturers and other channel members, price policy, conditions of sale, territorial rights, services/responsibility mix, and contract length and conditions of termination are specified. Cooperation and conflict both occur in a channel of distribution. Conflicts need to be settled fairly, since confrontation leads to hostility and negative actions by all parties. A pushing strategy, based on channel cooperation, is available to established, successful firms. A pulling strategy, based on proving the existence of consumer demand prior to channel support or acceptance, must be used by many new companies.

The channel of distribution for industrial products normally does not use retailers but tends to be direct, involve few transactions and large orders, require specification selling and knowledgeable channel members, utilize team selling and different channel members, and include leasing arrangements.

Physical distribution is involved with getting goods delivered to the designated place, at the designated time, and in proper condition. There are a number of reasons for studying physical distribution: costs, importance of customer service, and its relationship with other functional areas of the organization.

In a physical distribution strategy, decisions are made regarding transportation, inventory levels, warehousing, and location of facilities. Railroads typically carry goods for long distances and ship bulky items that are low in value in relation to their weight. Motor trucks dominate in transporting small shipments over short distances. Waterways are used primarily for the shipment of low-value freight. Pipelines provide reliable and continuous movement of liquid, gaseous, and semiliquid products. Airways offer fast, expensive movement of perishables and high-value items.

Inventory management is needed to regulate product supplies and distribution. Stock turnover is the number of times during a year that the average inventory on hand is sold. The reorder point is based on a pre-established minimum inventory level at which merchandise must be reordered. The economic order quantity formula determines the optimal quantity of goods to order based on total order-processing and holding costs. Warehousing decisions include selecting a private or public warehouse and examining the availability of public warehouse services.

Questions for Discussion

1. What distribution decisions would a new manufacturer of women's dresses have to make?
2. Explain the sorting process. Provide an example in your answer.
3. How do these product factors influence the selection of a channel of distribution?
   a. Value.
   b. Complexity.
   c. Perishability.
   d. Bulk.
4. Under what circumstances should a firm engage in direct distribution? Indirect distribution?
5. Distinguish between vertical integration and horizontal integration. What is the goal of each?
6. Give an illustration of a product moving from exclusive to selective to intensive distribution.

7. Texaco distributes its gasoline through its own stations and independently operated stations. Is this system inefficient? Explain your answer.
8. Should manufacturer/channel member contracts be formal or informal? Why?
9. Comment on this statement: "It should be recognized that there are natural differences among channel members."
10. Devise distribution channels for the sale of a weekly family magazine, office furniture, and diamond jewelry.
11. Develop a list of distribution standards for a firm delivering floral products to florists and other retailers.
12. Compare railroad and airfreight deliveries on the basis of the total-cost approach.
13. Average stock turnover in grocery stores is 16.0. What does this mean?
14. Two stores sell identical merchandise. Yet, one plans a safety stock equal to 10 per cent of expected sales, while the other plans no safety stock. Explain this difference.
15. Why would a firm use both private and public warehouses?

Case 1 Xerox: A Distribution Strategy Fails*

For many decades, Xerox has been the leading manufacturer of photocopiers. Over the years, it has expanded the company's product mix to include word processors, electronic typewriters, computers, and other information-oriented items. In the face of intensive competition, especially from Japanese firms, Xerox still accounted for 45 per cent of all copier sales during 1983. However, competitors have forced prices down and made significant inroads in the small copier market.

Until 1980, Xerox employed only a direct channel of distribution. A company sales force visited large and medium-size business accounts. Xerox had no store outlets and did not market through independent channel members. The small-business and home-office markets were virtually ignored. Then, Xerox determined that a dual channel of distribution would enable it to increase the market for the firm's products. The Xerox sales force would continue to visit larger customers, and company-owned stores would attract small-business customers.

The first Xerox store was opened in a Dallas shopping center in 1980, with Xerox announcing plans to add 50 new stores each year. The stores would carry the company's full product mix: copiers, word-processing equipment, printers, small computers, electronic typewriters, and telephone-answering machines. The target market was defined as doctors, lawyers, accountants, and other small businesses, including any people with home offices.

In mid-1983, Xerox reached agreement with Businessland, Inc. (an independent chain of business centers) to distribute its copiers and typewriters in thirteen stores in California, Arizona, and Texas. This was Xerox's first move toward establishing a nationwide network of independent distributors. At the same time, Xerox

* The data in this case are drawn from Susan Chace, "Xerox Plans to Sell Most of Its Retail Stores to New Concern Headed by Texas Group," *Wall Street Journal* (October 25, 1983), p. 60; Andrew Pollack, "Xerox Will Sell Retail Outlets," *New York Times* (October 25, 1983), p. D4; and "Xerox to Sell Copiers, Typewriters in Stores of Outside Retailer," *Wall Street Journal* (August 30, 1983), p. 50.

began marketing a portable computer to bank customers by inserting ads with their monthly bank statements.

At the end of October 1983, Xerox decided to sell off its retail stores and concentrate on direct distribution and independent channel members. Xerox was unsuccessful with its stores for a number of reasons: only 54 outlets had been opened (compared with 3,000 independent business centers); operating costs were higher than anticipated; competitors offered a better variety of products and brands; and its computer line was weak. As one expert noted, "A manufacturer can't do everything. He needs to get distribution, the quickest and widest possible."

QUESTIONS

1. Evaluate Xerox's decision to become involved with dual distribution.
2. What are the pros and cons of company-owned versus independent channels of distribution?
3. Tandy (Radio Shack) operates a company-owned distribution channel. It owns manufacturing, wholesaling, and retailing facilities. Why has Tandy succeeded, where Xerox has failed?
4. What criteria should Xerox consider when examining potential channel members (independent business centers)?

Case 2 United Parcel Service: The Unsung Giant of Package Delivery[†]

United Parcel Service (UPS) is a low-profile package-delivery company. UPS is privately owned by its 10,000 managers and engages in very little advertising (unlike Federal Express and other express delivery firms). For more than 75 years, UPS has specialized in the highway delivery of packages that weigh less than 50 pounds. Today, it delivers more than 1.6 billion packages annually (10 million on a busy day). UPS has annual revenues of $5.2 billion. It owns about 40 planes and 62,000 motor vehicles. In comparison, Federal Express ships 225,000 packages a day, has annual revenues of $1 billion, and owns 65 planes and 5,000 motor vehicles.

The success of UPS is based upon several factors:

- Its reputation for reliability (on-time delivery) is outstanding.
- Two-day delivery service is available anywhere in the continental U.S.
- Prices are significantly lower than those offered by the U.S. Postal Service and air-express firms.
- 85,000 company drivers call on 600,000 stores, factories, and offices every day. There are also over 100 highly mechanized distribution hubs throughout the U.S.

[†] The data in this case are drawn from "Behind the UPS Mystique: Puritanism and Productivity," *Business Week* (June 6, 1983), pp. 66–73; and Phil Mintz, "The Courier Express," *Newsday* (December 12, 1983), Business section, pp. 1, 17.

- Mail-order and catalog firms believe that UPS provides the best combination of speed and price for their needs. 45 per cent of UPS deliveries are made to residential dwellings.
- Drivers are well paid, averaging $13.50 per hour. Virtually all management positions are filled from within.
- Productivity is closely monitored. For example, driver performance is regularly evaluated against specific standards.

During late 1982, UPS entered the next-day air-express delivery business for the first time. UPS recognized that the air-express industry had become very lucrative, growing from virtually no revenue in 1973 to $2.4 billion in revenue for 1982. Since beginning its air-express business, UPS' greatest success has been with existing large customers who want one company to handle all their shipping requirements.

QUESTIONS

1. Assess the overall strengths and weaknesses of UPS.
2. What important differences are there between regular package delivery and express delivery? UPS believes customers have been oversold on air express. Do you agree?
3. What changes in marketing strategy will UPS have to make to further develop its air-express business?
4. Could a new package-delivery firm compete with UPS in its main business (two-day delivery throughout the U.S.)? Explain your answer.

Wholesaling

CHAPTER OBJECTIVES

1. To define wholesaling and show its importance
2. To describe the three broad categories of wholesaling (manufacturer wholesaling, merchant wholesaling, and agents and brokers) and the specific types of firms within each category.
3. To examine recent trends in wholesaling

Figure 13-1
Marketing Mr. Coffee Filters Through Food Stores
Mr. Coffee filters are now sold in thousands of food stores throughout the U.S. North American Systems advertises to these stores that "The big deal with genuine Mr. Coffee filters is repeat profitability. Genuine Mr. Coffee filters are the leader in a market that's expected to double quickly."

North American Systems introduced Mr. Coffee, the electric-drip coffeemaker featuring Joe DiMaggio in its advertising, in the 1960s. At that time, the company sold both Mr. Coffee and its replacement coffee filters through the same appliance retailers and department stores. The filters were also distributed through mail order.

After closely monitoring the sales of the coffeemaker and the filters, North American soon realized that Mr. Coffee users did not visit appliance and department stores as frequently as they needed filters. This method of distribution made the purchase of replacement filters inconvenient. The most logical outlets for selling filters were those carrying coffee, not coffeemakers.

However, adding new distribution channels was not easy for North American:

- 165,000 retail food outlets had to be reached and served on a regular basis.
- The company had only one product to distribute through food outlets, so the costs of sales calls could not be divided among a wide number of products.

- It did not want to alienate manufacturers' representatives who sold Mr. Coffee machines and filters to appliance and department stores.

North American made the decision to hire a national network of food brokers, the Association of Independent Marketing Services, to sell coffee filters to supermarkets and grocery stores. According to a North American vice-president, "Brokers offer the store coverage and already have relationships with [store] headquarters executives that are important in the grocery business."

By 1982, Mr. Coffee filters had become the industry leader with $80 million in annual sales. About 65 per cent of these filter sales are now made through food outlets.[1] Figure 13-1 shows a box of Mr. Coffee filters.

North American Systems has discovered that employing a group of independent wholesalers can enable a firm to gain access to new markets, maximize efficiency, and improve channel relations.

Wholesaling Defined

As noted in Chapter 12, wholesaling undertakes many vital functions in the sorting process. **Wholesaling** involves the buying or handling of merchandise and its subsequent resale to retailers, organizational users, and/or other wholesalers but not the sale of significant volume to final consumers.[2] All independent wholesalers do not take title to or physical possession of goods, as shown later in the chapter. Some wholesalers perform limited functions, such as contacting retailers or employing a personal sales force. Others perform the full range of distribution functions, including buying and transporting. Wholesaling does not include retailing.

According to one study, wholesale sales are divided as follows: 40.7 per cent to industrial, commercial, and government users; 37.2 per cent to retailers; 15.0 per cent to other wholesalers; and 7.1 per cent to others.[3]

Wholesaling **is the buying or handling of merchandise and its resale to organizational consumers.**

Importance of Wholesaling

Among the major reasons for studying wholesaling are its impact on the economy, functions in distribution, and relationships with suppliers and customers.

---

[1] Nancy Giges, "Grocers 'Middlemen' Step to the Forefront," *Advertising Age* (October 11, 1982), pp. M-18–M-19 ff.

[2] Adapted from Ralph S. Alexander (Chairman), *Marketing Definitions: Report of Definitions Committee* (Chicago: American Marketing Association, 1960), p. 47.

[3] Bert C. McCammon, Jr., and James W. Kenderine, "Mainstream Developments in Wholesaling," paper presented at the 1975 Conference of the Southwestern Marketing Association, p. 3.

Impact on the Economy

Wholesale sales are high; wholesalers greatly affect final prices.

There are about 600,000 wholesalers with total sales above $1 trillion. Although wholesale revenues are higher than those in retailing, there are more than four times as many retailers as wholesalers.

High wholesale sales occur because some products move through several levels of wholesalers; there is only one level of retailing. Therefore, an item can be sold twice or more at the wholesale level (e.g., regionally, then locally), yet just once at the retail level. There are more retailers because they service small and geographically dispersed final consumer groups; wholesalers deal with fewer, larger, more geographically concentrated customers.

From a cost perspective, wholesalers have a significant impact on the price of merchandise. Table 13-1 shows the per cent of wholesale prices that go to wholesalers to cover their operating expenses and pretax profits. For example, 30.4 per cent of the price an automobile-equipment wholesaler charges its retailers covers the wholesaler's operations and other expenses (28.0 per cent) and pretax profit (2.4 per cent). Operating costs include inventory charges, sales force salaries, advertising, and rent.

Wholesaler costs and profits depend on the rate of inventory turnover, the dollar value of products, functions performed, efficiency, and competition.

Functions of Wholesalers

Wholesalers are capable of providing a variety of functions, depending on manufacturer and retailer needs.

Among the important functions typically performed by wholesalers are the following. Wholesalers[4]

- Enable a manufacturer or supplier to have local distribution with a minimum of customer contacts.
- Provide a ready-made sales force.
- Provide marketing and technical assistance for the manufacturer or supplier and the retail or business customer.
- Purchase goods in large quantities, enabling carload quantities to be shipped and delivery costs to be reduced.
- Provide warehouse, field storage, and delivery facilities.
- Offer financial assistance for the manufacturer or supplier (by paying for goods when they are shipped, not when they are sold) and retail or business customer (by granting trade credit).
- Handle credit and accounting records.
- Handle returns and allowances and adjust for defective merchandise.
- Take risks by being responsible for theft, damage, spoilage, and obsolescence of inventory.

Those wholesalers who take title to and possession of goods usually perform several or all of these functions. Those who facilitate sales, but do not take title or possession, are agents and brokers that generally carry out the first three functions. Agents and brokers allow manufacturers/suppliers to substitute a predetermined, straight commission rate for general administrative expenses and sales force salaries.

[4] Adapted from Paul L. Courtney, "The Wholesaler as a Link in the Distribution Channel," *Business Horizons*, Vol. 4 (February 1961), p. 92.

Table 13-1   Gross Margins, Operating Expenses, All Other Expenses (Net), and Profit Before Taxes for Wholesalers by Product Category[a]

Product Category of Wholesaler	Gross Margins (As Per Cent of Sales)[b]	Operating Expenses (As Per Cent of Sales)	All Other Expenses (As Per Cent of Sales)	Profit Before Taxes (As Per Cent of Sales)
Automobile equipment	30.4	27.0	1.0	2.4
Chemicals and allied products	24.8	22.2	0.5	2.1
Drugs and related items	27.5	24.3	0.3	3.0
Electronic parts and equipment	30.6	27.6	0.8	2.2
Flowers and florists' supplies	33.3	29.2	1.6	2.4
Coffee, tea, and spices	22.6	20.2	0.6	1.8
Fish and sea foods	14.7	12.3	0.9	1.5
General groceries	15.7	14.1	0.3	1.3
Wine, liquor, and beer	22.5	19.6	0.6	2.2
General merchandise	32.5	28.6	1.0	2.9
Hardware and paints	30.3	27.8	1.1	1.4
Jewelry	29.7	26.0	1.7	2.0
Building materials	23.9	22.2	0.7	1.0
Fuel oil	10.2	9.1	0.1	1.0
Cotton	10.6	7.1	1.1	2.5

[a] RMA does not recommend the Statement Studies figures be considered as absolute norms for a given industry. Rather the figures should be used only as general guidelines and in addition to other methods of financial analysis. RMA makes no claim as to the representativeness of its figures.
[b] Total costs of wholesaling, which include expenses and profit. There are some rounding errors.
Source: Adapted from *'83 Annual Statement Studies* (Philadelphia: Robert Morris Associates, 1983). © 1983, Robert Morris Associates; reprinted by permission.

The use of wholesalers varies by industry. For example, most consumer products, food items, replacement parts, and office supplies are funneled through independent channel members. In other industries, including heavy equipment, computers, and gasoline, many manufacturers bypass independent wholesalers and retailers. In either case, wholesaling activities must be completed, regardless of whether wholesale institutions are involved.

Without wholesalers, retailers and other organizational consumers would have to deal with a number of manufacturers and coordinate shipments, develop supplier contacts, perform more distribution functions, stock greater quantities, and place more emphasis on an internal purchasing agent or department. In addition, many small retailers and organizational customers might be avoided because they would not be profitably reached by a manufacturer/supplier; and these small retailers and organizational customers might not be able to purchase necessary items elsewhere.

As an illustration of the importance of wholesaling, in the auto parts industry there is now an orderly system of independent distributors (wholesalers) to perform functions for manufacturers and their retailer customers. Before this system was introduced, there were thousands of manufacturers producing a wide range of products and marketing them through a multitude of selling organizations. Customers, mostly garages and service stations, were constantly interrupted by salespeople. Sales costs were high for the manufacturers. A smoother, less costly arrangement exists today with the organized use of a moderate number of independent distributors.

Relationships with Suppliers and Customers

Wholesalers have obligations to their suppliers and to their customers.

Wholesalers are very much "in the middle," not fully knowing whether their allegiance should be to the manufacturer/supplier or their own customer. The comments of two manufacturers (one industrial and the other consumer) show the dilemma faced by many wholesalers:[5]

While I don't dictate to my distributors, I darn well want them to be cooperative. We pay them well but we don't seem to gain the support we need.

If I could gain more help from my distribution channels, we could substantially increase volume and have an even greater impact on profits. But when I press the button which says, "Get the distributors to increase sales of product A immediately," all too often I get a push on product C in three months.

Wholesalers take a different view and feel it is they who receive inadequate support from manufacturers/suppliers. They desire training, technical assistance, product literature, and advertising. Wholesalers dislike vendors altering territory assignments, shrinking territory size, adding new distributors to cover an existing geographic area, or deciding to change to a direct channel and perform wholesale functions themselves.

Wholesalers want manufacturers/suppliers to sell to them and not through them. Selling to the wholesaler means the distributor is viewed as a customer who must be researched and satisfied. Selling through the wholesaler means the retailer or final consumer is the object of the manufacturer's/supplier's interest and that the needs of the wholesaler are unimportant.

Coca-Cola's past practices in dealing with its wholesalers (bottlers) illustrate the conflict that can occur between manufacturers and wholesalers:

- All bottlers were given the same commercials for their local advertising. While this was less expensive than customized ads and helped Coca-Cola reinforce a national image, the advertisements were often viewed by the bottlers as inappropriate for their markets.
- Coca-Cola implemented a program that provided bottlers with a $100 contribution toward their advertising efforts for each new display rack they placed in stores. The bottlers felt the racks were unnecessary.
- The bottlers believed that Coca-Cola was less interested in U.S. operations than in overseas markets. They questioned the company's U.S. investment plans.

The bottlers pressed Coca-Cola for a number of changes, which have now been enacted. The bottlers can select commercials and promotions for their areas. Coca-Cola field representatives meet regularly with the bottlers and are aided by computer routing and other systems. Domestic operations are now more valued.[6]

---

[5] Benson P. Shapiro, "Improve Distribution with Your Promotional Mix," *Harvard Business Review,* Vol. 55 (March–April 1977), pp. 115–116.

[6] "Coke's New Program to Placate Bottlers," *Business Week* (October 12, 1981), p. 48.

_____ **Types of Wholesalers** _

The three broad categories of wholesaling are outlined in Figure 13-2: manufacturer wholesaling, merchant wholesaling, and agents and brokers. Table 13-2 contains detailed descriptions of each type of independent wholesaler and shows their functions and special features.

Figure 13-2
The Broad Categories of Wholesaling

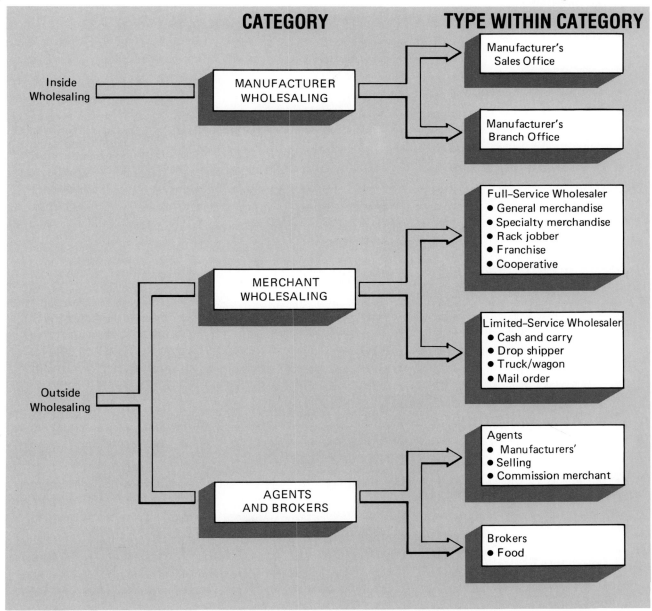

CATEGORY

TYPE WITHIN CATEGORY

Inside Wholesaling

MANUFACTURER WHOLESALING

Manufacturer's Sales Office

Manufacturer's Branch Office

Outside Wholesaling

MERCHANT WHOLESALING

Full–Service Wholesaler
• General merchandise
• Specialty merchandise
• Rack jobber
• Franchise
• Cooperative

Limited-Service Wholesaler
• Cash and carry
• Drop shipper
• Truck/wagon
• Mail order

AGENTS AND BROKERS

Agents
• Manufacturers'
• Selling
• Commission merchant

Brokers
• Food

Table 13-2 Characteristics of Independent Wholesalers

Wholesaler Type	Major Functions						Special Features
	Provides Credit	Stores and Delivers Goods	Takes Title to Goods	Provides Merchandising and Promotion Assistance	Provides Personal Sales Force	Performs Research and Planning	
I. Merchant wholesaler							
A. Full service							
1. General merchandise	Yes	Yes	Yes	Yes	Yes	Yes	Carries nearly all the items normally needed by a retailer
2. Specialty merchandise	Yes	Yes	Yes	Yes	Yes	Yes	Specializes in a narrow range of products, extensive assortment
3. Rack jobber	Yes	Yes	Yes	Yes	Yes	Yes	Furnishes racks and shelves, consignment sales
4. Franchise	Yes	Yes	Yes	Yes	Yes	Yes	Use of common business format, extensive management services
5. Cooperative							
a. Producer-owned	Yes	Yes	Yes	Yes	Yes	Yes	Farmer controlled, profits divided among members
b. Retailer-owned	Yes	Yes	Yes	Yes	Yes	Yes	Wholesaler owned by several retailers
B. Limited service							
1. Cash and carry	No	Stores, no delivery	Yes	No	No	No	No outside sales force, wholesale store for retailer and business needs
2. Drop shipper	Yes	Delivers, no storage	Yes	No	Yes	Sometimes	Ships items without physically handling them
3. Truck/wagon	Rarely	Yes	Yes	Yes	Yes	Sometimes	Sales and delivery on same call
4. Mail order	Rarely	Yes	Yes	No	No	Sometimes	Catalogs used as sole promotion tool
II. Agents and brokers							
A. Agents							
1. Manufacturers'	No	Sometimes	No	Yes	Yes	Sometimes	Sells selected goods for several manufacturers
2. Selling	Sometimes	Yes	No	Yes	Yes	Yes	Markets all the goods of a manufacturer
3. Commission (factor) merchants	Sometimes	Yes	No	No	Yes	Yes	Handles goods on a consignment basis
B. Brokers							
1. Food	No	Sometimes	No	Yes	Yes	Yes	Brings together buyers and sellers

Manufacturer Wholesaling

With *manufacturer wholesaling,* the producer undertakes all wholesaling functions itself. This occurs when the firm believes it is most able to reach its retailers and other organizational customers effectively by assuming responsibility and completing wholesaling tasks. Examples of companies selling at least some of their products directly to final and organizational consumers and bypassing independent wholesalers and retailers are Fuller Brush, Avon, Electrolux, IBM, NCR, Grumman Aerospace, and Hazeltine.

Manufacturers' wholesale sales volume is between 35 and 40 per cent of total wholesale revenues; they operate approximately 45,000 to 50,000 outlets. Wholesale activities by manufacturers may be conducted in either a sales office or branch office. A *manufacturer's sales office* is located at the company's production facilities or a site close to the market. No inventory is carried at the sales office. In contrast, a *manufacturer's branch office* includes facilities for warehousing goods as well as for selling them.

According to recent research, manufacturer wholesaling is most likely when there are no available middlemen, few customers to service, the product is considered a major purchase by customers, orders are very large, customers are geographically concentrated, and regulations limit arrangements with independent channel members (particularly in overseas markets).[7]

Manufacturer wholesaling is often necessary when no satisfactory independent wholesaler is available. This took place for both R. J. Reynolds and Philip Morris, who found no existing wholesale channel for marketing their tobacco products in Brazil. And their wholesaling activities proved costly. According to the president of Philip Morris' Brazilian subsidiary, "Selling direct is cheap if you have a large share of market, but with 8 per cent its expensive."[8]

> In *manufacturer wholesaling,* a firm completes all wholesaling activities through its own *sales* or *branch offices.*

Merchant Wholesaling

Merchant wholesalers buy, take title, and take possession of products for further resale. They represent the largest category of wholesalers in terms of sales—roughly 50 per cent of the total—and establishments—more than three quarters of the total.

For example, Wetterau is a merchant wholesaler in the food industry. Wetterau handles several thousand products for its 1,500 supermarkets. It helps the retailers design their stores, trains employees, provides credit, installs computerized inventory-control systems, and offers private-label items.[9] Figure 13-3 shows Wetterau's automated distribution warehouse in Pennsylvania.

Merchant wholesalers may be full service or limited service. *Full-service merchant wholesalers* assemble an assortment of products in a given place. They provide trade credit, store and deliver merchandise, offer merchandising and promotion assistance, provide a personal sales force, and offer research and planning support. Information is available for suppliers and customers. Installation and

> *Merchant wholesalers purchase products for resale. They may be full service or limited service.*

---

[7] Donald J. Jackson, Robert F. Krampf, and Leonard J. Konopa, "Factors That Influence the Length of Industrial Channels," *Industrial Marketing Management,* Vol. 11 (October 1982), pp. 263–268; and S. Tanner Cavusgil, "Exporters Wrestle with Market and Distributor Selection Problems in Penetrating New Markets," *Marketing News* (December 23, 1983), p. 10.

[8] "Marketing Observer," *Business Week* (October 4, 1976), p. 104.

[9] "A Food Supplier's Bigger Bite," *Business Week* (February 22, 1982), p. 136.

Figure 13-3
Mechanized Food
Distribution at Wetterau
Wetterau operates a large automated food distribution warehouse in Reading, Pennsylvania. Because of Wetterau's efficiency, its supermarket customers pay less for delivered merchandise.

Reprinted by permission.

repair services are given. Full-service merchant wholesalers act like the sales arms of their manufacturers. They are prevalent for grocery products, tobacco, alcoholic beverages, hardware, plumbing equipment, and drugs.

Limited-service merchant wholesalers buy and take title to merchandise. However, they do not perform all the functions of full-service merchant wholesalers. For example, they may not provide credit, merchandising assistance, or marketing research data. Limited-service wholesalers are popular for construction materials, coal, lumber, perishables, and specialty foods.

On the average, full-service merchant wholesalers require higher compensation than limited-service merchant wholesalers, because they perform greater functions. Table 13-3 contrasts the marketing strategies of the two kinds of merchant wholesalers for medical supplies.

FULL-SERVICE MERCHANT WHOLESALERS

Full-service merchant wholesalers can be divided into general merchandise, specialty merchandise, rack jobber, franchise, and cooperative types. See Figure 13-4.

Table 13-3
Contrasting Strategies of Full-Service and Limited-Service Medical-Supply Merchant Wholesalers

Full-Service Medical-Supply Wholesaler

Provides special services for physicians, such as frequent sales calls, emergency and small-order delivery, and liberal credit terms

Guarantees zero out-of-stock policy for key health care items through an inventory control system

Prepares an ideal inventory model for accounts and agrees to manage inventory to maintain appropriate stock levels

Uses a sales contract or prime vendor contract whereby the hospital agrees to do the majority of its purchasing through the contracting wholesaler

Maintains an inventory of 8,000–10,000 items

Is paid, on average, every 50 days

Limited-Service Medical-Supply Wholesaler

Offers the lowest market price as the primary means of generating sales; gross profit margin is 10% of sales, compared with the industry average of 20%

Uses multiyear supply contracts with hospitals, reducing need for field sales support; average selling costs as a per cent of new sales are 2.0%, compared with the industry average of 5.5%

Seeks sales contracts only from largest-volume hospitals

Deals only in high-volume medical commodities

Uses high levels of computer cost controls and accounting controls

Maintains an inventory of 1,500–3,000 items

Is paid, on average, in fewer than 30 days

Source: Adapted from P. Ronald Stephenson, "Wholesale Distribution: An Analysis of Structure, Strategy and Profit Performance," in Arch G. Woodside *et al.* (Editors), *Foundations of Marketing Channels* (Austin, Texas: Lone Star Publishers, 1978), pp. 103–107. © Lone Star Publishers, 1978; reprinted with permission.

General-merchandise (full-line) wholesalers carry a wide assortment of products, nearly all the items needed by the retailer to which they cater. For example, general-merchandise hardware, drug, and clothing wholesalers stock many items for their retailers, but not much depth within any specific product line. These wholesalers seek to sell their retailers or other organizational customers all or most of their products and develop strong loyalty and exclusivity with them.

Specialty-merchandise (limited-line) wholesalers concentrate efforts on a relatively narrow range of products and have an extensive assortment within that range. These wholesalers offer expertise and many sizes, colors, and models in their product categories. The specialty wholesaler provides functions similar to general-merchandise and other full-service merchant wholesalers. Specialty wholesaling is popular for health foods, seafood, retailers' store displays, and frozen foods.

Rack jobbers furnish the racks or shelves on which merchandise is displayed. The rack jobber owns the merchandise on its racks, selling the items on a consignment basis, so that the retailer pays after the goods are sold. Unsold merchandise is taken back. The jobber sets up displays, refills shelves, price marks merchandise, maintains inventory records, and computes the amount due from the retailer. Heavily advertised, branded merchandise that is sold on a self-service basis is most frequently handled. Included are health and beauty aids, drugs, cosmetics, magazines, hand tools, toys, housewares, and stationery.

Rack jobbing began after World War II, because general merchandise wholesalers were unable to sell nonfood items to supermarkets because of potential conflicts with their regular drugstore and hardware store customers and their

General-merchandise wholesalers **sell a wide range of items, and try to secure exclusivity.**

Specialty-merchandise wholesalers **concentrate efforts on a narrow but deep product line.**

Rack jobbers **set up displays, price mark merchandise, receive payments after sales, and take returns.**

General-merchandise (full-line) wholesaler—wide assortment, little depth.

Rack jobber—supplies merchandise and display racks.

Specialty-merchandise (limited-line) wholesaler—narrow assortment, great depth.

Franchise wholesaling—wholesaler helps independent retailers to develop a common name, storefront, etc.

Wholesale cooperative—owned by producers or retailers to economize functions.

**Figure 13-4
Full-Service Merchant
Wholesalers**

**All full—service merchant wholesalers purchase goods
and provide a broad range of functions.**

inability to stock a wide range of nonfood items for supermarkets. Over time, rack jobbers started to serve drugstores, hardware stores, variety stores, service stations, and restaurants, in addition to supermarkets. Recently some large retail chains have begun to bypass rack jobbers and assume their functions in order to increase profit margins.

In *franchise wholesaling,* independent retailers affiliate with an existing

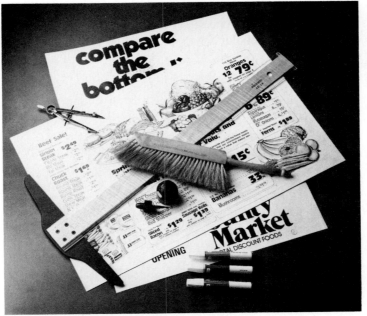

Figure 13-5
Advertising Support from Super Valu
Super Valu furnishes advertising copy and artwork for affiliated stores.

Reprinted by permission of Super Valu Stores, Inc.

wholesaler in order to use a standardized storefront design, business format, name, and purchase system. In many instances, suppliers produce goods according to specifications set by the franchise wholesaler. This form of wholesaling is utilized for hardware, auto parts, and groceries.

With *franchise wholesaling,* retailers join with a wholesaler.

Major franchise wholesalers include Independent Grocers Affiliate (IGA), Ben Franklin Stores, Western Auto, Walgreen, and Super Valu Stores. As an illustration, retailers affiliated with Super Valu are supplied with a variety of food and nonfood services, such as site selection, store engineering, interior design, and merchandising assistance (furnishing of advertising formats and point-of-sale promotional materials).[10] See Figure 13-5.

A *wholesale cooperative* is owned by its member firms to economize functions and offer broad support. Producer-owned wholesale cooperatives are popular in farming. For example, Land O'Lakes had 350,000 member firms and sales of $3.8 billion in 1982. It handles food products and farm commodities, and provides agricultural services. In 1982, cooperatives marketed 30 per cent of all U.S. agricultural commodities, 41 per cent of all raisins, 70 per cent of all milk, and 92 per cent of all cranberries.[11] Producer cooperatives not only market, transport, and process farm products; they also manufacture and distribute farm supplies. In many cases, cooperatives sell to supermarkets under their own names, such as Ocean Spray, Sunkist, Land O'Lakes, and Welch's. Figure 13-6 shows several Land O'Lakes products.

A number of manufacturers or retailers can establish a *wholesale cooperative.*

Retailer-owned wholesale cooperatives appear when independent retailers

[10] Bill Saporito, "Super Valu Does Two Things Well," *Fortune* (April 18, 1983), pp. 114–117.
[11] James Cook, "Dreams of Glory," *Forbes* (September 12, 1983), pp. 92, 94.

form associations that purchase, lease, or build wholesale facilities. The cooperative takes title to merchandise, handles cooperative advertising, and negotiates with suppliers. Retailer-owned cooperatives are used by hardware and grocery stores.

LIMITED-SERVICE MERCHANT WHOLESALERS

Limited-service merchant wholesalers can be divided into cash and carry, drop shipper, truck/wagon, and mail-order types. See Figure 13-7.

With *cash-and-carry wholesaling,* a small businessperson is able to drive his

Figure 13-6
Land O'Lakes Products
These are just some of the many products marketed through the Land O'Lakes producer-owned wholesale cooperative.

Reprinted by permission.

Cash-and-carry wholesaling— businessperson drives to wholesaler and buys items.

Drop shipper (desk jobber)—operates via telephone to buy and ship heavy goods.

Truck/wagon wholesaler–sells and delivers goods over a regular route.

Mail-order wholesaler—offers merchandise through catalogs.

All limited-service wholesalers buy goods, but they provide only some functions.

Figure 13-7
Limited-Service Merchant Wholesalers

or her truck to a wholesaler, order products, and take them back to the store or business. Cash-and-carry wholesaling emerged in the 1920s and 1930s as a result of the growing threat of chain stores against independent retailers. Cash-and-carry wholesalers offer no credit or delivery, provide no merchandising and promotion assistance, have no outside sales force, and do not aid in marketing research or planning. They are important for fill-in items, have low prices, and allow immediate product availability. Cash-and-carry wholesalers are common for construc-

In *cash-and-carry wholesaling*, the customer drives to a wholesaler, orders products, and takes them back.

tion materials, electrical supplies, office supplies, auto supplies, hardware products, and groceries.

Drop shippers (desk jobbers) purchase goods from manufacturers or suppliers and arrange for their shipment to retailers or industrial users. While the drop shipper has legal ownership of the products, it does not take physical possession of them and has no facilities for storing them. A drop shipper buys items, leaves them at manufacturers' plants, contacts customers by telephone, coordinates carload shipments from manufacturers directly to its customers, and assumes responsibility for items that cannot be sold. Trade credit, a personal sales force, and some research and planning assistance are provided; merchandising and promotional support are not. Drop shippers are frequently used for coal, coke, and building materials. These goods have high freight costs in relation to their unit value, because of their weight. Therefore, direct shipments from suppliers to customers are needed.

Drop shippers **buy goods and arrange for their shipment to customers. They do not take possession of goods.**

Truck/wagon wholesalers generally have a regular sales route, offer items from the truck or wagon, and deliver goods at the same time they are sold. They also provide merchandising and promotion support. This wholesaler is considered to offer limited service because it usually does not extend credit and offers little research and planning help. High operating costs are required because of the personalized services performed and low average sales. A truck or wagon wholesaler often deals with goods requiring special handling or those that are highly perishable. These include bakery products, tobacco, meat, candy, potato chips, and dairy products.

Truck/wagon wholesalers **offer items from their vehicles and deliver goods on a sales route.**

Mail-order wholesalers utilize catalogs, instead of a personal sales force, to promote products and communicate with their customers. Generally, they do not provide credit or merchandising and promotion support. They do store and deliver goods and offer some research and planning assistance. Mail-order wholesaling is found with jewelry, cosmetics, auto parts, specialty food product lines, business supplies, and small office equipment.

Mail-order wholesalers **sell through catalogs.**

Agents and Brokers

Agents and **brokers** provide various wholesale functions, but they do not take title to goods. Unlike merchant wholesalers, who receive profits from the sales of goods they own, agents and brokers work for commissions or fees as payment for their services. Roughly 10 to 12 per cent of wholesale sales and 8 to 10 per cent of wholesale establishments are contributed by agents and brokers. The principal difference between agents and brokers is that agents are more likely to be used on a permanent basis, whereas brokers are employed on a temporary basis. See Figure 13-8.

Agents **and** *brokers* **do not take title to goods; relationships with agents are usually more permanent.**

Agents and brokers offer three major advantages: they allow a manufacturer or supplier to expand sales despite limited resources; their selling costs are a predetermined per cent of sales; and they provide a trained sales force.[12]

Agents are comprised of manufacturers' agents, selling agents, and commission (factor) merchants. **Manufacturers' agents** are organizations that work for

---

[12] Edwin E. Bobrow, "Suddenly, An Urge to Boost Their Potential," *Sales & Marketing Management* (June 1982), Special Report.

Selling agent—acts as a marketing department for sellers.

Manufacturers' agent—carries noncompetive products of several manufacturers.

sets prices

negotiates terms

provides merchandising support

arranges delivery

Commission (factor) merchant works on consignment, accumulates goods, and arranges central market sales.

Food broker—brings buyers and sellers together.

All agents and brokers receive commissions or fees for the functions they perform; they do not own goods.

Figure 13-8
Agents and Brokers

several manufacturers and carry noncompetitive, complementary products in exclusive territories. By selling noncompetitive items, agents are able to eliminate conflict-of-interest situations. By selling complementary goods, agents are able to stock a fairly complete line of products for their market areas. These agents do not offer credit but sometimes store and deliver products and provide limited research and planning aid. Merchandising and promotion support are given.

Manufacturers' agents may supplement the sales efforts of producers, help introduce new products, enter geographically dispersed markets, and sell products with low average sales. They usually carry only a portion of a manufacturer's products. A manufacturer may employ many agents, each with a unique product-territorial mix. Larger firms might use a different agent for every major product line. Agents have limited input into the manufacturer's marketing program and price structure.

Manufacturers' agents are major wholesalers of automotive products, iron, steel, footwear, and textile products. It is estimated that there are almost 50,000 manufacturers' agents in the U.S., many of which employ two or more salespeo-

Manufacturers' agents **work for several manufacturers and carry noncompetitive, complementary products in exclusive territories.**

Selling agents **market all the products of a manufacturer under contractual agreement. They offer many services.**

ple.[13] Manufacturers' agents generally earn commissions of 5 to 10 per cent of sales.

Selling agents assume responsibility for marketing the entire output of a manufacturer under a contractual agreement. In effect, selling agents become the marketing departments for their manufacturers/suppliers and are empowered to negotiate price and other conditions of sale, such as credit and delivery. They perform all wholesale functions except taking title to merchandise. While a manufacturer may use several manufacturers' agents, it may employ only one sales agent.

Selling agents are more likely to work for small manufacturers than large ones. These agents are common for textile manufacturing, canned foods, metals, home furnishings, apparel, lumber, and metal products.

Commission merchants **assemble goods from local markets and sell them in a large market.**

Commission (factor) merchants receive goods on consignment from producers, accumulate them from local markets, and arrange for their sale in a central market location. These merchants sometimes offer credit, store and deliver goods, provide a sales force, and offer research and planning help. They normally do not assist in merchandising and promotion.

Commission merchants can negotiate selling prices with buyers, providing the prices are not below the seller's stated minimums. They may operate in an auction setting. The merchants deduct their commission, freight charges, and other expenses after the products are sold. The balance is sent to the producer or supplier. Commission merchants are used for agricultural and seafood products, furniture, and art.

Food brokers **unite buyers and sellers in the food industry to conclude sales.**

Brokers are very common in the food industry. ***Food brokers*** introduce buyers and sellers of food and related general-merchandise items to one another and bring them together to complete a sale. They are well informed about market conditions, terms of sale, sources of credit, price setting, potential buyers, and the art of negotiating. They do not actually provide credit but sometimes store and deliver goods. Brokers also do not take title to goods and usually are not allowed to complete a transaction without formal approval. Brokers generally represent the seller, who pays their commission.[14]

Food brokers, like manufacturers' agents, operate in specific geographic locations and work for a limited number of food producers within these areas. Their sales force calls on chain-store buyers, store managers, and institutional purchasing agents. Brokers work closely with advertising agencies. The average commission for food brokers is 5 per cent of sales.

Nabisco, Heinz, and Dairymen's Inc. are examples of companies using food brokers. At Nabisco, cookies and crackers are sold directly to retail stores; but, margarines, candies, and Planters peanuts are sold through brokers. Heinz employs brokers in sparsely populated states. Dairymen's Inc., a cooperative, uses brokers for its new nonrefrigerated milk packages, because they provide a "sales force in place that would take us months to duplicate."[15]

---

[13] "Selling Through Independent Representatives: Getting Them to Work for You," *Sales & Marketing Management* (June 1982), Special Report.

[14] See Steven Mintz, "S&MM Spends a Day in the Field with a Food Broker," *Sales & Marketing Management* (June 1982), Special Report; and Richard Edel, "Tracking Local Developments," *Advertising Age* (October 10, 1983), pp. M-44–M-45.

[15] Nancy Giges, "Grocers' 'Middlemen' Step to the Forefront," *Advertising Age* (October 11, 1982), p. M-19.

Recent Trends in Wholesaling

Over the last several years, competition among independent wholesalers has increased dramatically due to numerous factors, including the growth of manufacturer wholesaling through branch offices, the emergence of wholesaler chains, the development of retailer/user buying groups, the expansion of cooperatives, and the existence of unauthorized "master" distributors (who buy in large volume and then allocate smaller quantities to individual retailers).[16] The following activities show a range of wholesaler responses to these trends that are intended to protect the independent wholesaler's place in the distribution channel.

Competition in wholesaling has risen significantly.

In large numbers, wholesalers are diversifying the markets they serve. For example, Wetterau, the fourth-largest food wholesaler in the U.S., originally concentrated on small, independent supermarkets. Today, its customers include supermarket chains consisting of 10 to 20 units, in addition to its traditional customers.[17] Farm and garden machinery wholesalers now sell to florists, hardware dealers, and garden supply stores. Plumbing wholesalers have added industrial accounts, contractors, and builders to their markets. Grocery wholesalers deal with hotels, airlines, hospitals, schools, and restaurants.

Independent wholesalers are aggressive in protecting their position in the channel.

Many wholesalers are also broadening their product mixes, as these illustrations show. Super Valu, the nation's largest food wholesaler, has moved into apparel retailing; Malone & Hyde, the third largest food wholesaler, has opened auto-parts stores.[18] Rexall, a distributor of vitamins and plastic products (such as toothbrushes and hair brushes) to retail outlets is currently distributing health foods.[19]

Some wholesalers are taking the opposite approach and turning to special-line wholesaling. For example, several hardware and drug wholesalers now specialize in order to have sufficient product depth for large retailers and other customers. This specialization has thus far stopped manufacturers from selling directly to retailers. One highly specialized hardware wholesaler is S&T Industries. S&T used to have 2,000 customers in 11 states. Today, it derives 80 per cent of its total sales volume from 600 retailers. S&T is a primary supplier of merchandise and services for its stores.[20] Williams Drug Co. is a pharmaceutical wholesaler that specializes in patent medicines, rural and ethnic products, and other difficult-to-obtain products. As a result, its customers are other wholesalers around the country.[21]

Because of increased costs many wholesalers have begun to service small accounts through telephone selling and automatic reorder systems. For example,

---

[16] Lynn Brown and Bob Garda, "Changes in Distribution Channels Spell Opportunity for Those Who Fathom Them," *Marketing News* (February 4, 1983), p. 12.

[17] "A Food Supplier's Bigger Bite."

[18] Ibid.

[19] "The Rexall Rx: Dropping Out of Retailing to Be a Distributor," *Business Week* (March 1, 1982), pp. 85–86.

[20] Ronald L. Ernst, " 'Distribution Channel Detente' Benefits Suppliers, Retailers, and Consumers," *Marketing News* (March 7, 1980), p. 19.

[21] Frederick C. Klein, "Wholesale Drug Firm Thrives on Nostalgia, Buyer's Loyalty," *Wall Street Journal* (June 20, 1983), p. 29.

J. Fegely & Son is a distributor of industrial supplies. It has a telephone sales staff of 13 that generates $1.4 million in annual sales from 1,850 active accounts in four states. The best telephone salesperson makes 40 to 50 calls per day.[22]

Summary

Wholesaling is the buying or handling of merchandise and its resale to retailers, organizational users, and/or other wholesalers but not the sale of significant volume to final consumers. Approximately 600,000 wholesalers sell over $1 trillion of merchandise annually.

Wholesale functions encompass distribution, personal selling, marketing and technical assistance, financial assistance, recordkeeping, returns and allowances, and risk taking. These functions may be assumed by the manufacturer or shared with an independent wholesaler. Wholesalers are sometimes in a precarious position because they are located between manufacturers and retailers and must determine their responsibilities to each.

Manufacturer wholesaling can be conducted through sales or branch offices. The sales office carries no inventory. Through either or both offices, manufacturers carry out all wholesale functions.

Merchant wholesalers buy, take title, and possess products for their own accounts. Full-service merchant wholesalers assemble an assortment of products, provide trade credit, store and deliver merchandise, offer merchandising and promotion assistance, provide a personal sales force, and offer research and planning support. Full-service merchant wholesalers fall into general merchandise, specialty merchandise, rack jobber, franchise, and cooperative types. Limited-service merchant wholesalers take title to merchandise but do not provide all wholesale functions. Limited-service merchant wholesalers are divided into cash and carry, drop shipper, truck/wagon, and mail-order types.

Agents and brokers negotiate purchases and expedite sales but do not take title to goods. Agents are used on a more permanent basis than brokers. Types of agents are manufacturers' agents, selling agents, and commission (factor) merchants. Food brokers dominate brokerage.

Competition among independent wholesalers has grown over the last several years. To protect their place in the channel, some wholesalers are diversifying their markets and product mixes, while others are specializing more. To reduce costs, telephone sales are rising.

Questions for Discussion

1. Now that its coffee filters are accepted by supermarkets, should North American Systems drop its wholesalers and sell directly to the stores? Explain your answer.
2. Why does wholesale sales volume exceed retail sales volume?

[22] Sara Delano, "Turning Sales Inside Out," *Inc.* (August 1983), pp. 99–101.

3. "Wholesalers are very much in the middle, often not fully knowing whether first allegiance should be to the manufacturer/supplier or the customer." Comment on this statement.
4. Differentiate between selling to a wholesaler and selling through a wholesaler.
5. The marketing vice-president of a large camera manufacturer has asked you to outline a support program for its wholesalers. Prepare this outline.
6. Under what circumstances should a firm avoid manufacturer wholesaling?
7. Which wholesale functions are performed by merchant wholesalers? Which are performed by agents and brokers?
8. As a rack jobber, how would you determine which retail outlets should stock your magazines?
9. Distinguish between franchise wholesaling and wholesale cooperatives.
10. What are the unique features of cash-and-carry and mail-order merchant wholesalers?
11. Why are drop shippers frequently used for coal, coke, and building materials?
12. Contrast the advantages and disadvantages of merchant wholesalers and agents and brokers.
13. How do manufacturers' agents and selling agents differ?
14. Develop a short checklist a manufacturer could use to evaluate independent wholesalers.
15. Evaluate the activities undertaken by independent wholesalers to protect their channel position. Will independent wholesalers eventually disappear from distribution channels? Explain your answer.

Case 1 American Hospital Supply: Efficiency Pays Off*

According to an industry consultant, hospital-supply wholesaling is not a glamorous field: "It's a no-technology business—basically a lot of warehouse shelves and a truck. There's no product differentiation because all the distributors sell the same things. Add to that, the margins are low."

One wholesaler is an exception to that statement: American Hospital Supply. Its sales have increased about 400 per cent since the early 1970s; and pretax profits average 10 per cent of sales, about four times the industry average. American Hospital Supply has done so well because of a strategy that is efficient and distinctive.

It manufactures many of its products and is sole distributor for them. For example, a subsidiary introduced the first artificial heart valve. In all, American produces 28,000 products, accounting for 45 per cent of its dollar sales.

American has a product mix that is divided into 41 divisions. While other distributors specialize in narrow product lines, American can satisfy 60 per cent of an average hospital's total purchasing requirements. To handle its product lines, American operates 159 warehouses and owns more trucks than any competitor. It can deliver supplies to a hospital within 24 hours, 90 per cent of the time. Hospital customers are told by American to "let our warehouse be your warehouse."

Until 1977, each of American's many manufacturing divisions operated as separate firms. Every division sent its own salesperson to call on hospitals and

* The data in this case are drawn from Anne B. Pillsbury, "The Hard-Selling Supplier to the Sick," *Fortune* (July 26, 1982), pp. 56–61.

negotiate agreements with them. Then, American revised its strategy, after determining that it would be more efficient to have a single salesperson represent all company products when calling on a hospital.

Since 1978, American has installed thousands of computer terminals in hospitals. This reduces the paperwork for hospital purchasing agents, bookkeepers, and administrators. It also makes it easier and faster for hospitals to place orders with American than with a competitor. American's ASAPC (analytical systems automated purchasing) computer system allows 3,000 hospitals to order supplies directly from its distribution centers.

QUESTIONS
1. How has American Hospital Supply converted hospital-supply wholesaling from a no-technology business with no product differentiation to a high-technology business with high product differentiation?
2. Comment on the statement, "Let our warehouse be your warehouse."
3. Evaluate American's decision to have a single company salesperson call on a hospital.
4. How can a specialty-merchandise (limited-line) wholesaler compete against American?

Case 2 Super Valu: A Franchise Wholesaler[†]

Super Valu is the largest food wholesaler in the U.S. with 2,300 affiliated stores. While Super Valu is a franchise wholesaler, it would rather be called a "retail support company." And by helping retailers expand their businesses, Super Valu can increase its own sales (85 per cent of which are represented by grocery wholesaling).

Super Valu is convinced that the leading food wholesalers are beginning to drive the retail market, rather than merely supplying it. On the basis of this philosophy, Super Valu helps its independent retailers find appropriate store locations, designs store interiors and exteriors, finances equipment, trains supermarket employees, develops advertising plans, operates warehouses, offers pricing suggestions, and monitors store performance. These are examples of some of the services Super Valu provides for affiliated stores:

- Site selection—A computer program called SLASH (Store Location Analysis Strategy Heuristic) performs a total location evaluation, including market share analysis and competitor vulnerability assessment. The program also considers the impact of store size on a location decision.
- Store design—A computer-assisted store design program contains over 100 different interior store plans. They can be viewed individually on a monitor.
- Warehousing—Super Valu warehouses are fully automated and can quickly respond to order requests by individual supermarkets.
- Retail counseling—Super Valu counselors regularly visit stores, uncover potential problems, and offer helpful suggestions.

[†] The data in this case are drawn from Bill Saporito, "Super Valu Does Two Things Well," *Fortune* (April 18, 1983), pp. 114–117.

Super Valu's services enable affiliated store owners to derive many benefits normally reserved for large chains: centralized buying, specialized staff assistance, and computerized operating systems. However, unlike traditional chains, Super Valu stores have no national marketing plan and no single image. A store affiliated with Super Valu can usually earn a profit that is twice the industry average.

QUESTIONS

1. What criteria should Super Valu consider when examining potential affiliates? What criteria should potential affiliates consider when examining Super Valu?
2. Evaluate the statement "The leading wholesalers are beginning to drive the retail market, rather than merely supplying it."
3. Independent supermarkets affiliated with Super Valu earn a profit that is much higher than that earned by most supermarket chains. Explain this.
4. From a manufacturer's perspective, what are the pros and cons of selling to Super Valu?

Chapter 14

Retailing

CHAPTER OBJECTIVES

1. To define retailing and show its importance
2. To examine the different types of retailing categorized by ownership, strategy mix, and nonstore operations
3. To describe four major considerations in retail planning: store location, atmosphere, scrambled merchandising, and the wheel of retailing
4. To explore recent trends in retailing

J. C. Penney, in an effort to improve sluggish sales performance (sales rose only 4.4 per cent from 1977 to 1982), signed an exclusive contract with the noted fashion designer Halston in 1983 under which he would produce a collection of men's and women's clothing and accessories. This collection would be known as Halston III and would be sold at Penney's 600 largest suburban mall locations. Figure 14-1 shows a selection of Halston III clothing sold at J. C. Penney.

The marketing of Halston fashions is consistent with Penney's goal to trade up its customer base and upgrade its image. In the past, Penney's principal competitors were mass merchandisers such as Sears and K mart. It is now planning to compete with traditional department stores for their fashion-conscious customers.

While Penney is placing greater emphasis on men's, women's, and children's clothing, it has decided to stop selling major appliances, paint and hardware, lawn and garden supplies, fabrics, and automotive goods and repair services. It has allocated over $1 billion to renovate 450 stores. Remodeled stores have wood parquet floors, carpeting, wide aisles, and partitioned departments to suggest separate boutiques.

Figure 14-1
**Halston III: Designer
Clothing at J. C. Penny**

Reprinted by permission.

While impressive sales gains have been recorded in Penney's newly renovated stores, the success of this retail strategy is not assured. One marketing analyst commented that the "biggest problem is the Penney name. It's going to be a tough one." Others believe that Penney will encounter difficulties in purchasing fashion items for a wider geographic area (Penney operates well over 2,000 stores nationwide), as department stores increase their pressure on fashion designers. For example, Bergdorf Goodman department stores have stopped carrying Halston merchandise.[1]

The J. C. Penney illustration shows some of the numerous decisions retailers must make regarding their strategy mix, image, and store atmosphere.

[1] Isadore Barmash, "Penney's $1 Billion Gamble on Chic," *New York Times* (July 10, 1983), Section 3, p. 4; "Penney to Spend Over $1 Billion on 450 Stores," *Wall Street Journal* (February 1, 1983), p. 5; Claudia Ricci, "J. C. Penney Goes After Affluent Shoppers, But Store's New Image May Be Hard to Sell," *Wall Street Journal* (February 15, 1983), p. 35; "J. C. Penney Shops for a Trendier Image," *Business Week* (February 6, 1984), p. 58; and Pat Sloan, "Penney's Saying 'Ciao' to Staid Image," *Advertising Age* (April 9, 1984), pp. 4, 69.

Retailing Defined

Retailing, the last stage in a channel, includes the activities in selling to final consumers.

Retailing encompasses those business activities that involve the sale of goods and services to the ultimate (final) consumer for personal, family, or household use. It is the final stage in a channel of distribution.

Retailing includes products, such as automobiles and televisions, as well as services, such as life insurance and appliance repair. It involves store and non-store (vending machine, direct-to-home, mail order) sales. Manufacturers, importers, and wholesalers act as retailers when they sell products directly to the ultimate consumer.

The average size of a retail sale is small, about $21.00 for department stores and $39.00 for specialty stores.[2] Convenience stores, like 7-Eleven, have average sales of about $2.25.[3] Medium-sized chain supermarkets average $18.00.[4] Accordingly, retailers need to increase sales through one-stop shopping appeals, broadened merchandise assortments, increased frequency of shopping, and attracting more family members to go on shopping trips. Inventory controls, automated material handling, and electronic cash registers are needed to reduce transaction costs.

Despite low average sales, 63 per cent of department store and 54 per cent of specialty store sales are on credit.[5] For example, Sears has more than 25 million households with active credit card accounts; they buy over $6 billion of merchandise on credit each year.[6] The use of credit necessitates bank or store credit plans and reasonable credit terms but leads to increased sales.

Whereas salespeople regularly visit organizational consumers to initiate and conclude transactions, most final consumers patronize stores. This makes the location of the store, product assortment, store hours, store fixtures, sales personnel, delivery, and other factors critical tools in drawing customers to the store.

Final consumers make many unplanned purchases. In contrast, those who buy for resale or use in manufacturing are more systematic in their purchasing. Therefore, retailers need to place impulse items in high-traffic locations, organize store layout, train sales personnel in suggestion selling, place related items next to each other, and sponsor special events.

Importance of Retailing

Among the major reasons for studying retailing are its impact on the economy, functions in distribution, and relationships with suppliers.

---

[2] David P. Schulz, "FOR: Financial & Operating Results," *Stores* (December 1983), p. 48.
[3] *1982 Major Market Study* (Dallas: 7-Eleven Research Department, 1982).
[4] "51st Annual Report of the Grocery Industry," *Progressive Grocer* (April 1984), p. 98.
[5] Schulz, "FOR: Financial & Operating Results."
[6] "For Sears Shoppers, New Bag of Money Items," *Marketing & Media Decisions* (September 1982), pp. 156–159.

Table 14-1
Sales and Income Data on Selected Retailers, 1983

Name	Sales ($ Million)	Net Income ($ Million)	Net Income (As a Percentage of Sales)
A. Food Retailers			
Safeway	18,585	183	1.0
Kroger	15,236	127	0.8
Southland (7-Eleven)	8,805	132	1.5
Lucky Stores	8,277	113	1.4
American Stores	7,804	110	1.4
Winn-Dixie	7,133	114	1.6
Jewel	5,662	83	1.5
Great Atlantic & Pacific (A&P)	5,017	27	0.5
Albertson's	4,230	66	1.6
Supermarkets General	3,467	42	1.2
B. Nonfood Retailers			
Sears Roebuck	35,883	1,342	3.7
K mart	18,310	409	2.2
J. C. Penney	11,681	441	3.8
Federated Department Stores	8,412	308	3.7
Dayton Hudson	6,510	219	3.4
F. W. Woolworth	5,336	107	2.0
Wal-Mart	4,215	167	4.0
May Department Stores	4,040	170	4.2
Melville	3,923	176	4.5
R. H. Macy	3,602	195	5.4

Source: Adapted from ''Corporate Scoreboard,'' *Business Week* (March 21, 1984), pp. 50–53.

Impact on the Economy

Retail sales and employment comprise substantial amounts of total U.S. sales and employment. Annual retail store sales volume exceeds $1 trillion; this does not include nonstore sales (vending machines, direct-to-home sales, and mail-order sales) and retail services. See Table 14-1 for sales and income data for selected retailers.

Retailing is also a major source of employment. According to the Department of Labor, about 17 per cent of the nation's total nonagricultural workforce is employed in 2.5 million retail establishments in the United States. A wide range of retailing career opportunities is available, including store management, merchandising, and owning one's own retail business.[7]

From another perspective—costs—retailing is a significant field of study. For example, on the average, about 42 cents of every dollar a consumer spends in a department store goes to the store as compensation for the functions it performs.[8] The corresponding figures for other stores are 44 cents for specialty stores[9] and 20 cents for independent supermarkets.[10] This compensation, known as gross margin, is for rent, taxes, fuel, advertising, inventory management, personnel, and other retail costs, as well as profits.

Retailing involves high annual sales and employment.

[7] A further discussion of careers in retailing can be found in Barry Berman and Joel R. Evans, *Retail Management: A Strategic Approach,* Second Edition (New York: Macmillan, 1983), pp. 7–14.
[8] David P. Schulz, ''NRMA's New MOR,'' *Stores* (October 1983), p. 24.
[9] Ibid.
[10] ''51st Annual Report of the Supermarket Industry,'' p. 96.

Figure 14-2
Key Retailing Functions

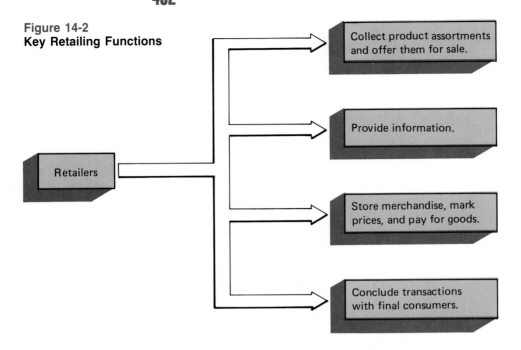

Retailers

Collect product assortments and offer them for sale.

Provide information.

Store merchandise, mark prices, and pay for goods.

Conclude transactions with final consumers.

Retail Functions in Distribution

Chapter 12 outlined the basic roles of retailers and wholesalers in distribution. In general, retailers perform four functions: they collect an assortment of products and services from a wide variety of suppliers and offer them for sale; they provide information to consumers, as well as to other channel members; they frequently store merchandise, mark prices on it, and pay for items prior to selling them to final consumers; and they conclude transactions with final consumers. These functions are summarized in Figure 14-2.

Relationship of Retailers and Suppliers

Retailers have suppliers for products they use and for those they resell.

Retailers deal with two broad categories of suppliers: those selling products or services for use by the retailers and those selling products or services which are resold by the retailers. Examples of products and services purchased by retailers for their use are store fixtures, data-processing equipment, management consulting, and insurance. Resale purchases depend on the lines sold by the retailer.

Suppliers must have knowledge of a retailer's goals, strategies, and methods of business operation in order to sell and service accounts effectively. Frequently, retailers and their suppliers have divergent viewpoints, which must be reconciled:

- Commodore announced a new computer, code-named TED, to be marketed in 1984. As designed, TED is not able to operate with Commodore 64 software. This limitation may force retailers to expand shelf space to accommodate TED and its software packages or to choose to stock only the 64 or TED.[11]

[11] "Commodore International Plans to Unveil a Home Computer with Built-in Software," *Wall Street Journal* (December 27, 1983), p. 2.

- Imported merchandise such as cameras, watches, and electronics is usually sold to retailers through authorized U.S. distributors. However, some U.S. retailers have chosen to bypass these distributors and purchase goods from international dealers; they import the goods into the U.S. on their own. These ''gray-market'' products are then marketed to final consumers at low prices, but without the guarantees of U.S. distributors. Both authorized distributors and the retailers who buy from them are troubled because of lost sales and the loss in goodwill when they refuse to honor manufacturers' guarantees. They want manufacturers to not allow gray-market goods.[12]
- A number of department-store chains have stated that they will drop manufacturers and other suppliers which sell in-season merchandise to off-price merchants in their trading areas. Federated Department Stores, the leading department-store chain in the U.S., is one of the retailers most upset by manufacturers' sales to off-price outlets.[13]

Types of Retailers

Retailers can be categorized by ownership, strategy mix, nonstore operations, and service retailing.[14] The categories are overlapping; that is, a retailer can be correctly placed in more than one grouping. For example, 7-Eleven can be classified as a chain, a franchise, and a convenience store.

An examination of retailers by category provides information about their attributes, relative sizes and importance, different strategies, and the impact of environmental factors.

By Ownership

Retail ownership can be independent, chain, franchise, leased department, and/or cooperative, as shown in Figure 14-3 and described in Table 14-2.

An *independent retailer* operates only one retail outlet. It offers personal service, a convenient location, and close customer contact. Dry cleaners, butcher shops, furniture stores, independent service stations, barber shops, and many neighborhood stores are independents. About 80 per cent of all retailers are independents. This large number is the result of the ease of entry in retailing. For many kinds of retailing, investment requirements, state licensing standards, and technical knowledge requirements are low, and, therefore, competition is plentiful. Many retailers may fail because of ease of entry, poor management skills, and inadequate capital. Annually, several thousand firms fail, including about one

An *independent retailer* operates one retail outlet and offers personal service and a good location.

---

[12] Tamar Lewin, ''Gray Area for Imports,'' *New York Times* (November 1, 1983), p. D2.

[13] Daniel Kahn, ''Stores Toughen on Designer Tactics,'' *Newsday* (July 17, 1983), p. 76; and Claudia Ricci, ''FTC Studying Whether Large Retailers Are Discriminating Against Discounters,'' *Wall Street Journal* (August 31, 1983), p. 8.

[14] Service retailing is discussed fully in Chapter 22. Types of services were classified in Chapter 9. This chapter does not deal with service retailing.

Figure 14-3
Retail Ownership Forms

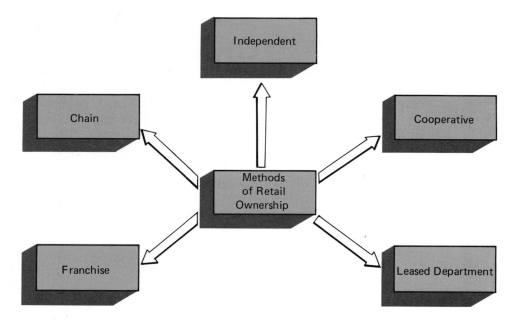

third of those in business three years or less. In 1982, over 9,000 retail stores went out of business due to the weak economy, the highest figure in at least twenty years.[15]

A *chain* involves common ownership of multiple retail units. It usually employs centralized purchasing and decision making. Independents have simple organizations, but chains have specialization, standardization, and elaborate control systems. Because of these factors, chains are able to serve a large, geographically dispersed target market and maintain a well-known company name. Although chains represent only about 20 per cent of all retailers, they account for over 50 per cent of total retail store sales. Only a few hundred chains operate one hundred or more units, yet they are responsible for over one quarter of total store sales. Chains are widespread for supermarkets, department stores, variety stores, and fast-food restaurants, among others. Examples of large chains are Sears, K mart, and Safeway.

Retail franchising is a contractual arrangement between a franchisor (who may be a manufacturer, wholesaler, or service sponsor) and a retail franchisee, which allows the franchisee to conduct a certain form of business under an established name and according to a specific set of rules. It is a form of chain ownership. Franchising allows a small businessperson to benefit from the experience, buying capabilities, and image of a large multiunit chain retailer. The franchisee also receives management training, participates in cooperative buying and advertising, and acquires a well-established company name. The franchisor benefits by obtaining franchise fees and royalties, fast payments for goods and services, strict controls over operations, consistency among outlets, and motivated owner-operators. Annually, franchises account for more than $430 billion in sales through

In a *chain*, one firm operates multiple outlets. Chains account for 50 per cent of store sales, yet are only 20 per cent of retailers.

Retail franchising **involves an arrangement to employ an established name and operate under certain rules.**

---

[15] Claudia Ricci and John Curley, "Small Stores Struggle as Consumers Scrimp; Failures Are Up by 40 Per Cent," *Wall Street Journal* (December 17, 1982), p. 1.

Table 14-2 Key Characteristics of Retail Ownership Forms

Ownership Form	Distinguishing Features	Major Advantages	Major Disadvantages
		Characteristics	
Independent	Operates one outlet, easy entry	Personal service, convenient location, customer contact	Much competition, poor management skills, little capital
Chain	Common ownership of multiple retail units	Central purchasing, strong management, specialization of tasks, larger market	Inflexibility, high investment costs, less entrepreneurial
Franchising	Contractual arrangement between central management (franchisor) and independent businesspersons (franchisees) to operate a specified form of business	To franchisor: investments from franchisees, faster-growth, entrepreneurial spirit of franchisees To franchisee: established name, training, experience of franchisor, cooperative ads	To franchisor: some loss of control, franchisees not employees, harder to maintain uniformity To franchisee: strict rules, limited decision-making ability, payments to franchisors
Leased Department	Space in a store leased to an outside operator	To lessor: expertise of lessee, little risk, diversification To lessee: less investment in store fixtures, customer traffic, store image	To lessor: some loss of control, poor performance reflects on store To lessee: strict rules, limited decision-making ability, payments to store
Cooperative Retail	Purchases, advertising, planning, and other functions shared by independent retailers	Independence maintained, efficiency improved, enhances competitiveness with chains	Different objectives of participants, hard to control members, some autonomy lost
Consumer	Purchases, advertising, planning, and other functions shared by consumer owners	Savings to members, social experience, improves consumer leverage against retailers	Difficult to organize, member turnover, dwindling interest in performing functions

about 500,000 establishments.[16] Franchising is particularly popular for auto and truck dealers, fast-food outlets, health spas, and convenience-foods stores. Examples of franchises are McDonald's, Jack LaLanne health spas, and Chevrolet dealers.

A *leased department* is a department in a retail store (usually a department, discount, or specialty store) that is rented to an outside party. The manager of a leased department is responsible for all aspects of its operation and pays a percentage of sales as rent. As in franchising, the leasing retailer places strict rules on the leased department operator. Lessors benefit because of the expertise of department operators, reduced risk and inventory investment, lucrative lease terms, increased store traffic, and an appeal to one-stop shopping convenience. Lessees benefit from the existence of an established location, the prestige of the lessor's name, the store traffic generated by the lessor, the one-stop customers attracted by the store as a whole, and whatever services (advertising, accounting, etc.) the lessor provides by mutual agreement. Leased departments are popular for beauty salons, jewelry, photographic studios, shoe repairs, and cosmetics. On average, leased departments contribute 7.0 per cent of department store sales and 11.0 per cent of specialty store sales.[17]

A *leased department* in a store is rented to an outside party that provides expertise and management skills.

---

[16] See ''Franchising: A Tool for Growth in the '80s,'' *Forbes* (June 7, 1982), pp. 63 ff; Curtis Hartman, ''The Conversion of Skip Kelley,'' *Inc.* (February 1984), pp. 41–48; ''Franchise Marketing,'' *Marketing News* (February 17, 1984), Special Issue; and *Franchising in the Economy* (Washington, D.C.: U.S. Department of Commerce, January 1984).

[17] ''Leased Departments,'' *Stores* (December 1977), p. 44.

With a *retail cooperative*, independent stores organize to share costs, functions, and planning.

A cooperative is a retail organization that is operated by several independent retailers or by a group of consumers. In a **retail cooperative**, independent retailers share purchases, storage and shipping facilities, advertising, planning, and other functions. The individual stores retain their independence but agree on broad, common policies. Retail cooperatives are growing in response to the domination of independents by chains. Retail cooperatives are common for liquor stores, hardware stores, and some grocery stores. Ace Hardware, Associated Food Stores, and Western Auto are retail cooperatives. As pointed out earlier, wholesalers frequently aid retailers in setting up cooperatives.

With a *consumer cooperative*, consumer members invest in and operate a retail firm.

In a **consumer cooperative**, a retailer is owned and operated by consumer members. A group of consumers invests, receives stock certificates, elects officers, manages operations, and shares profits or savings. The goal is to offer reduced prices to members. Consumer cooperatives have been most prevalent with food products, particularly produce items. However, the cooperatives represent less than 1 per cent of total supermarket sales or supermarket produce sales. They have not grown further because they involve a lot of consumer initiative, profits have been low, and consumer expertise as owner-operators has been lacking.

By Strategy Mix

The *retail strategy mix* is the combination of prices, products, etc. that a retailer offers.

Retailers can be classified by **retail strategy mix,** the combination of prices, products, sales personnel, hours, and other factors they employ. Retail strategy mixes differ for convenience stores, supermarkets, superstores, specialty stores, variety stores, department stores, full-line discount stores, and retail catalog showrooms. See Figure 14-4 and Table 14-3.

Figure 14-4
Retail Strategy Mixes

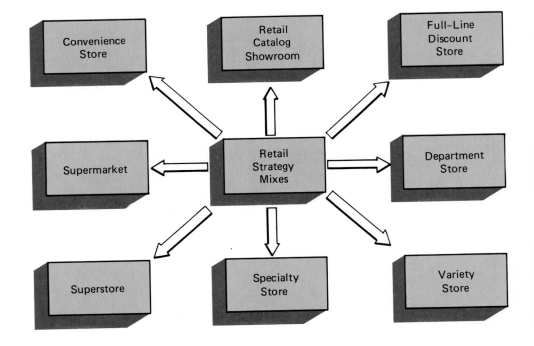

Table 14-3 Key Characteristics of Retail Strategy Mixes

Retailer	Strategy Mix					
	Convenience of Hours	Convenience of Location	Width of Assortment	Depth of Assortment	Service[a]	Price Level
Convenience store	High	High	Moderate	Low	Low	Average to above average
Supermarket	High	High	High	High	Low	Competitive
Superstore	High	Moderate	Very high	High	Low	Competitive on food items, average to above average on nonfood items
Specialty store	Moderate	Moderate	Low	High	Varies	Varies
Variety store	Moderate	Moderate	Moderate to high	Moderate	Moderate	Average
Department store	High	Moderate	Very high	High	High	Average to above average
Full-line discount store	High	Moderate	High	High	Low to moderate	Low
Retail catalog showroom	Moderate	Low	High	Low to moderate	Low	Low

[a]Includes availability of sales personnel, credit, delivery, custom orders, etc.

A *convenience store* is a store featuring food items that is open long hours and carries a limited number of items. In the U.S., convenience stores have annual sales of $25 billion, including gasoline. They account for 6 per cent of U.S. grocery sales. The average convenience store has sales that are less than one fifth of those of the average supermarket.[18] Consumers use a convenience store for fill-in merchandise, often at off-hours. Bread, milk, ice cream, newspapers, and gasoline are popular items at convenience stores (with gasoline contributing 40 per cent of all sales). 7-Eleven, Arco, and Dairy Barn operate convenience stores. See Figure 14-5.

A *supermarket* is a departmentalized food store with minimum annual sales of $2 million. The supermarket originated in the 1930s, when food retailers realized that a large-scale operation would enable them to combine volume sales, self-service, low prices, impulse buying, and one-stop food shopping. The automobile and refrigerator contributed to the supermarket's success by lowering travel costs and adding to the life span of perishable items. During the past twenty years, supermarket sales have stabilized at about 72 to 75 per cent of total grocery sales. Annually, supermarkets have sales of about $190 billion, 69 per cent of which is provided by chains.[19] In response to convenience stores, some supermarkets have lengthened their hours of operation. The largest supermarkets are Safeway, Kroger, and Lucky Stores.

A *superstore* is a large food-based retailer that is much more diversified than a

A *convenience store* has long hours and carries a limited number of items.

A *supermarket* is a large food store, with annual sales of at least $2 million. It is self-service and offers low prices.

18 "1982 Convenience Store Industry Report," *Convenience Store News;* Craig Endicott, "Life in the Fast-Food Lane," *Advertising Age* (October 10, 1983), p. M-32; and Carol E. Curtis, "Mobil Wants to Be Your Milkman," *Forbes* (February 13, 1984), pp. 44–45.
19 "51st Annual Report of the Grocery Industry," p. 44.

Figure 14-5
A Typical 7-Eleven
Convenience Store

Reprinted by permission of the International Franchise Association.

A *superstore* stocks supermarket items and a variety of other products to attract one-stop shoppers.

supermarket. Superstores typically carry garden supplies, televisions, clothing, wine, boutique items, bakery products, and household appliances—in addition to a full line of supermarket items. For example, Kroger generally carries everything from flowers to auto parts in its superstores. Kroger is also testing pasta parlors, sausage boutiques, tortilla shops, beauty salons, and adjacent restaurants for its superstores.[20] While the average supermarket occupies 20,000 square feet of space, the typical superstore utilizes at least 30,000 square feet. Several factors are causing a number of supermarkets to switch to superstores: an interest in total one-stop shopping, the leveling off of food sales as a result of population stability and competition from restaurants and fast-food stores, improved transportation networks, and the higher margins on general merchandise (more than double those of food items). Safeway has more than 500 superstores.[21]

A *specialty store* emphasizes one type of merchandise.

A *specialty store* concentrates on the sale of one merchandise line, such as apparel and its accessories, sewing machines, or high-fidelity equipment. Consumers like specialty stores because they are not confronted with racks of merchandise, do not have to walk or search through several departments, can select from tailored assortments, and usually avoid crowds. Specialty stores are most successful in the apparel, gourmet food, appliance, toy, electronics, and sports product lines. In some cases department stores have reacted by creating boutiques and specialty shops within their stores. Specialty store sales exceed $50 billion per year. Successful specialty stores include Radio Shack, The Limited, and Toys "R" Us.

A *variety store* sells an assortment of lower-priced merchandise.

A *variety store* sells a wide assortment of low and popularly priced merchandise. It features stationery, gift items, women's accessories, toilet articles, light hardware, toys, housewares, and confectionaries. Variety-store sales are about $9 billion per year. With the growth of other retail strategy mixes, variety stores have

[20] Brian S. Rogers, "Kroger: From Bisquick to Auto Parts. . . ," *Advertising Age* (October 10, 1983), p. M-48.
[21] Bill Saporito, "Shopping Cart Battle in Winn-Dixieland," *Fortune* (October 3, 1983), p. 212.

fallen on hard times. In the mid-1970s W. T. Grant went bankrupt, the largest bankruptcy in retailing history. F. W. Woolworth, the country's thirteenth largest retailer, dominates the variety-store category.[22]

A *department store* is a large retailer that employs at least 25 people and usually sells a general line of apparel for the family, household linens and dry goods, and furniture, home furnishings, appliances, radios, and television sets. It is organized into separate departments for purposes of buying, promotion, service, and control. A department store has the greatest assortment of any retailer, provides many customer services, is a fashion leader, and dominates the stores around it. Because most department stores are parts of chains, they have high name recognition and can utilize all forms of media. In recent years department stores have set up many boutiques, theme displays, and designer departments to compete with other retailers. Annual total department store sales including mail order, are over $110 billion. Examples of department store chains are Federated, Dayton Hudson, May, Carter Hawley Hale, and R. H. Macy.

> A *department store* offers the broadest assortment of goods and customer services of any retailer, and dominates nearby stores.

A *full-line discount store* has low prices, a relatively broad merchandise assortment, low-rent location, self-service, brand-name merchandise, wide aisles, shopping carts, and most merchandise displayed on the selling floor. Annually, full-line discount stores sell over $60 billion in merchandise. These stores are the largest retailers of linens, domestic goods, toys and games, housewares, gifts, small electric appliances, and infants' wear. Sixty per cent of their sales are from hard goods, forty per cent from apparel.[23]

> A *full-line discount store* has a broad assortment, self-service, and features popular brands.

Another discount retailer is a *retail catalog showroom,* in which consumers select merchandise from a catalog and shop at a warehouse location. Customers frequently write up their own orders, products are usually stocked in a back room, and there are limited displays. Catalog showrooms specialize in national brands. Annual sales are about $9 billion.[24] Best Products, Service Merchandise, and Consumer Distributing are among the largest catalog showrooms.

> In a *retail catalog showroom,* consumers shop from a catalog at a warehouse location.

During recent years, a number of other forms of low-price retailing have grown. These include limited-line and warehouse food stores, factory outlet stores, off-price chains, discount drugstores, and flea markets. These retailers reduce prices by limiting inventory, using plain store fixtures, locating at inexpensive sites, and offering few customer services.[25] Table 14-4 shows the basic differences between most discount and department store strategies.

By Nonstore Operations

Nonstore retailing refers to retailers who do not utilize conventional store facilities. It includes vending machines, direct-to-home sales, and mail order. Figure 14-6 highlights the characteristics of nonstore retailing.

> *Nonstore retailing* is nontraditional.

[22] See Jacquelyn Bivins, "F. W. Woolworth: Turning Back the Clock?" *Chain Store Age,* Executive Edition (October 1983), pp. 29–39; and Pamela G. Hollie, "Variety—and Profits—at Woolworth," *New York Times* (February 5, 1984), Section 3, p. 6.

[23] "Retailing: Basic Analysis," *Standard & Poor's Industry Analysis* (January 26, 1984), Section 2, p. R119.

[24] Jody Long, "Catalog Firms Faring Well in Recession," *Wall Street Journal* (March 23, 1982), pp. 37, 43; and "The Number of Catalog Showroom Companies," *Marketing News* (July 8, 1983), p. 7.

[25] Ann M. Morrison, "The Upshot of Off-Price," *Fortune* (June 13, 1983), pp. 122–124; Kenneth Wylie, "A Perspective on Today's Grocer," *Advertising Age* (October 10, 1983), pp. M-9–M-12 ff; Susan Carey, "Pechin's Mart Breaks Many Rules, But Not the One on Pricing," *Wall Street Journal* (March 5, 1984), pp. 1, 26; and "'Super Warehouses' Chomp into Food Business," *Business Week* (April 16, 1984), p. 72.

Table 14-4 Retail Strategy Mixes—A Discount Store Versus a Department Store

Discount-Store Strategy	Department-Store Strategy
1. Inexpensive rental location—low level of pedestrian traffic (Note: full-line discount stores are increasingly using more expensive locations)	1. Expensive rental location in shopping center or district—high level of pedestrian traffic
2. Simple fixtures, linoleum floor, centralized dressing room, few interior or window displays	2. Elaborate fixtures, carpeted floor, individual dressing rooms, many interior and exterior displays
3. Promotional emphasis on price. Some discounters do not advertise brand names, but state "famous brand"	3. Promotional emphasis on full service, quality brands, and fashion leadership
4. No alterations, telephone orders, delivery, or gift wrapping; limited credit	4. Alterations included in clothing prices, telephone ordering, and home delivery at little or no fee; credit widely available
5. Reliance on self-service, dump-bin displays (plain cases with piles of merchandise), and rack displays; all merchandise visible	5. Extensive sales force assistance, attractive merchandise displays, most storage in back room
6. Emphasis on branded merchandise. Selection probably not complete (not all models and colors); featuring "seconds," removal of labels from merchandise if required by manufacturer, and stocking of low-price nonbranded items	6. Emphasis on a full selection of branded and privately branded first-quality merchandise; will not stock closeouts, discontinued lines, or seconds
7. Year-round use of low prices	7. Sales limited to end-of-season clearance and special events

Vending machines eliminate a sales force, allow 24-hour sales, and can be placed outside a store.

A *vending machine* uses coin-operated machinery, eliminates the need for sales personnel, allows around-the-clock sales, and can be placed outside rather than inside a store. Vending-machine sales are concentrated in a narrow product line. Cigarettes, candy, and beverages yield 80 per cent of sales. Less than 10 per cent of sales come from nonfood items. Machines require intensive servicing because of breakdowns, stock-outs, and vandalism. Although annual sales exceed $15 billion, vending machines have limited growth potential.[26]

Direct-to-home retailers use canvassing, referrals, or party plans to sell to consumers in their homes.

Direct-to-home retailers sell directly to consumers in their homes. Cosmetics, vacuum cleaners, encyclopedias, dairy products, and newspapers are successfully sold direct-to-home. This form of retailing can be either on a cold canvass (Fuller Brush), referral (Avon), or party (Tupperware) basis.[27] In a cold canvass the salesperson goes through an area and knocks on each door in search of customers. With a referral system, past buyers recommend friends for the salesperson to call on. In the party method one consumer acts as host and invites friends and acquaintances to a sales demonstration in his or her home. It is estimated that direct-to-home sales are about $10 billion per year.

With mail order retailing, a seller seeks orders through the media and ships merchandise to the consumer at home.

Mail order retailing occurs when the seller seeks orders through television, radio, printed media, or the mail, receives orders through the mail or telephone, and ships merchandise to the customer's home. Annually, 45 per cent of U.S. adults make a mail-order purchase—mostly because of availability and conven-

---

[26] "Review 1983," *Vending and Food Services Management* (1983); and "Retailing: Food, Supermarkets, Restaurants, Food Service: Basic Analysis," *Standard & Poor's Industry Surveys* (May 26, 1983), p. R171.

[27] See M. Howard Gelfand, "Fuller Still Keeps a Foot in the Door," *Advertising Age* (November 28, 1983), pp. M-51–M-53; Pat Sloan, "Avon Ladies Toughen Up Sales Pitch," *Advertising Age* (March 12, 1984), p. 12; Gwen Kinkead, "Tupperware's Party Times Are Over," *Fortune* (February 20, 1984), pp. 113–120; and Dean Rotbart and Laurie P. Cohen, "The Party at Mary Kay Isn't Quite So Lively, As Recruiting Falls Off," *Wall Street Journal* (October 28, 1983), pp. 1, 12.

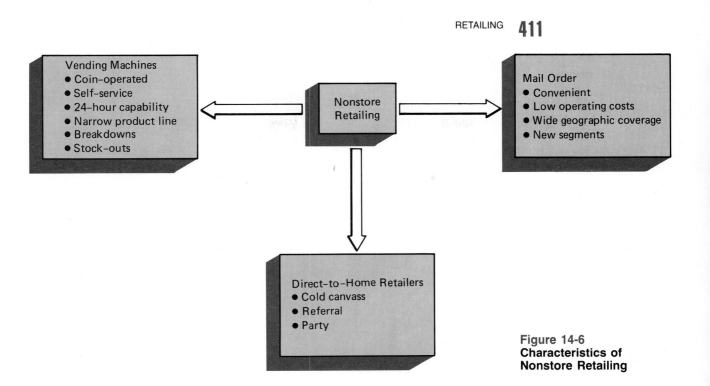

Figure 14-6
Characteristics of
Nonstore Retailing

ience.[28] There are general-merchandise mail-order firms, stores offering mail order as a supplement to regular business, and novelty or specialty mail-order firms. The most popular mail-order items are ready-to-wear clothing, insurance, magazines, and books. Annual mail-order sales are approximately $40 billion. This form of retailing offers convenience for consumers, low operating costs, coverage of a wide geographic area, and new market segments. Large mail-order firms are Spiegel, L. L. Bean, Montgomery Ward, and Sears (the leader). Figure 14-7 shows an advertisement for Lands' End, a mail-order retailer of clothing and other quality products.

Considerations in Retail Planning

There are many factors for retailers to consider when developing and implementing their marketing plans. Four of the most important factors are store location, atmosphere, scrambled merchandising, and the wheel of retailing.

Store Location

Store location is important to retailers because it helps determine the customer mix and competition. It is also highly inflexible. These are the basic forms of

[28] "Direct Marketing: Now a Bigger Bargain," *Advertising Age* (May 30, 1983), p. M-28.

**Figure 14-7
Lands' End, a Mail-Order
Retailer**

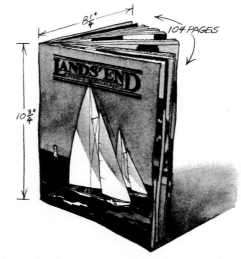

The Store We Mind

Our store is 10¾ inches tall, 8¼ inches wide, and 104 pages deep.**
It has no crowded parking lots, clogged elevators, or hidden rest rooms.

It displays over 600 pieces of merchandise. And by the time you count colors and sizes and shapes and variations, you are up to 8,300 items you can shop from—assembled under one "roof" from the four corners of the earth, wherever quality calls.

Most of these items are shown on or with models so much like you they could live in your neighborhood. Every item is unconditionally guaranteed by the world's shortest guarantee. In two words: **GUARANTEED. PERIOD.**

We mind our store 24 hours a day, 7 days a week. You can buy from us in the comfort of your own home.

But first, remember, we're only a phone call away—wherever you live. The toll-free telephone number: 800-356-4444. Or fill in the coupon below.

Oh, yes—we accept AX, MC, or VISA. And we deliver by United Parcel Service or U.S. Mail. You name it.

** *This describes our "store" for the Spring of 84. The dimensions may vary by season, but you can always count on the quality, price, and service.*

☐ **Please send free catalog.**
Lands' End Dept. **K-10**
Dodgeville, WI 53595

Name_____
Address_____
City_____
State_____ Zip_____

Or call Toll-free:
800-356-4444
(Except Alaska and Hawaii call 608-935-2788)

Reprinted by permission.

store location: the isolated store, the unplanned business district, and the planned shopping center. They are contrasted in Figure 14-8.

An ***isolated store*** is a free-standing retail outlet located on either a highway or side street. This type of store location is sometimes used by discount or warehouse stores because of low rent and manufacturers' desires for them to be far enough away from traditional specialty and department stores that sell goods at full prices. Although there are no adjacent stores with which the firm must com-

An *isolated store* is a free-standing outlet on a highway or side street. There are no other stores next to it.

ISOLATED STORE

—Free-standing outlet on a highway or side street
- Low rent
- No competition
- Flexibility in operations
- Difficult to attract customers
- No shared costs

UNPLANNED BUSINESS DISTRICT

—Combination of stores located together without prior planning

- Near consumers' work or residence and commercial, social, and cultural facilities
- Access to public transportation
- Few restrictions on merchandise carried and operations
- Crowding
- Lack of parking
- Old buildings

PLANNED SHOPPING CENTER

—Centrally owned or managed facility where the combination of stores is based on prior planning
- Balanced tenancy and shared costs
- Plentiful parking
- Good product assortment
- Unified image
- Restrictions on merchandise carried and operations
- Domination by largest store

Figure 14-8
Contrasting Store Locations

pete, there are also no stores to help draw consumer traffic. The difficulty of attracting and holding consumers is the reason why large retailers are usually best suited for an isolated location. Customers are unwilling to travel to an isolated store that does not have a wide assortment of products and an established reputation.

In an unplanned business district, stores locate together with no planning.

An **unplanned business district** exists where a group of stores are located close to one another and the combination of stores is not based on prior planning. There are four kinds of unplanned business district: central business district, secondary business district, neighborhood business district, and string.

A central business district (CBD) is the largest "downtown" area of a city.

A central business district (CBD) is the hub of retailing in a city and is synonymous with the term downtown. It contains the largest commercial and shopping facilities in a city. Cultural, employment, and entertainment facilities surround it. There is at least one major department store and a broad grouping of specialty and convenience stores. CBDs have had some problems with crowding, lack of parking, old buildings, limited pedestrian traffic when offices close, non-standardized store hours, crime, and other factors. However, CBD sales remain strong. Among the innovations used to strengthen CBDs are closing streets to vehicular traffic, modernizing storefronts and equipment, developing strong merchant associations, planting trees to make the area more attractive, improving transportation, and integrating a commercial and residential environment.

A secondary business district (SBD) has a junior department store.

A secondary business district (SBD) is a shopping area that is usually bounded by the intersection of two major streets. Cities generally have several SBDs, each having at least one junior department store, a variety store, and several small service shops. In comparison with the CBD, the SBD has less merchandise assortment, a smaller trading area (the geographic area from which a store draws its customers), and sells more convenience items.

A neighborhood business district (NBD) satisfies local needs.

A neighborhood business district (NBD) satisfies the convenience shopping needs of a neighborhood. The NBD contains a number of small stores, with the major retailer being a supermarket or variety store. An NBD is located on the major street in a residential area.

A string contains closely grouped stores on a highway or street.

A string is usually composed of a group of stores with similar or compatible product lines. However, because this location is unplanned, various store combinations are possible. It is located along a street or highway. Car dealers, antique stores, and clothing stores are retailers that frequently locate in a string.

A planned shopping center is centrally planned and has balanced tenancy.

A **planned shopping center** is centrally owned or managed, planned and operated as an entity, surrounded by parking, and based on balanced tenancy. **Balanced tenancy** means that the type and number of stores within any planned center are related to the overall needs of the surrounding population. The various stores complement each other in the quality and variety of merchandise. To ensure balance, a center may limit the merchandise lines any store carries. Planned centers account for approximately 43 per cent of total retail store sales; isolated stores and unplanned business districts account for the remaining 57 per cent. The three types of planned center are regional, community, and neighborhood.

A regional shopping center sells shopping goods to a large market.

A regional shopping center sells mostly shopping goods to a geographically dispersed market. A regional center has at least one or two department stores and up to one hundred or more small retailers. Customers are willing to drive up to a half hour to reach a regional center. As in the case of central business districts, many regional shopping centers (especially those built 25 years ago or earlier) require renovation. Among the improvements being undertaken in regional shopping centers are enclosing malls, redesigning storefronts, making storefronts more uniform, erecting new store directories, adding more plants, and modernizing concrete in parking lots, etc.

A community shopping center has a variety store and/or small department store as its major retailer, with several smaller stores. This center sells both convenience and shopping items. A neighborhood shopping center sells mostly convenience products. The largest store is a supermarket and/or drugstore, with a few smaller stores.

A community center has some variety of stores; a neighborhood center sells convenience goods.

Atmosphere

Atmosphere is the sum total of the physical characteristics of a retail store that are used to develop an image and draw customers. The overall atmosphere of a store helps determine the customers it will attract, sets the mood for shopping, encourages impulse purchases, and sets a long-term image for the store. Atmosphere is closely related to the strategy mix a retailer selects, as described earlier in the chapter. For example, a discounter will have linoleum floors, crowded displays, centrally located cash registers, and shopping carts. A prestige department store will have carpeted floors, wide aisles and attractive displays, recessed cash registers, and sales personnel to help carry purchases.

There are four components of a store's atmosphere: exterior, general interior, store layout, and interior displays. The exterior of a store encompasses its storefront, marquee, entrances, display windows, visibility from the street or highway, uniqueness, surrounding area, surrounding stores, and traffic congestion. The general interior includes a store's flooring, colors, scents, lighting, fixtures, wall textures, temperature, width of aisles, dressing facilities, vertical transportation, personnel, and placement of cash registers.

Store layout refers to the floor space allocated for customers, selling, and storage, the groupings of products, department locations, and arrangements within departments. Interior (or point-of-purchase) displays involve the types of cases and racks used to show merchandise, mobiles, in-store advertising, mannequins, and wall decorations.

Recently, Safeway opened an innovative 61,000-square-foot food and general merchandise store in Arlington, Texas. A major objective set by Safeway was to change the atmosphere consumers faced when entering traditional food stores. According to the store's designer:

We set out to create something with pizazz, something that isn't mundane and something which puts some fun and interest into shopping. There's a little less merchandise per square foot than Safeway normally would get into a store, but we've made it more inviting for people to come into the store.[29]

To establish the atmosphere it sought, Safeway created a number of small shops in the center of the store, used photos as aisle signs, and set up a simulated sidewalk cafe (with seating for 36 customers) inside the store. The store cost $3 million to build.

Atmosphere refers to the physical characteristics of a store. It consists of a store's exterior, general interior, layout, and displays.

[29] Kevin Higgins, "Safeway Enters Quest for Supermarket of Future," *Marketing News* (January 7, 1983), pp. 1, 6.

Scrambled Merchandising

Scrambled merchandising occurs when a retailer adds products or product lines that are unrelated to each other and the retailer's original business. Examples of scrambled merchandising are supermarkets carrying nonfood items like toys, panty hose, nonprescription drugs, and magazines; gasoline service stations selling food items; and drugstores selling film and gift items.

There are three reasons for the popularity of scrambled merchandising: retailers seek to convert their stores to one-stop shopping centers; scrambled merchandise is often fast selling, generates store traffic, and yields high profit margins; and impulse purchasing is increased. For example, convenience stores have added self-service food centers (with items such as frozen fountain drinks, hot beverages, hot sandwiches, and other fast foods). These food-counter items have the highest gross profit margins of any of the product categories sold in convenience stores.[30]

Scrambled merchandising spreads quickly and frequently leads to competition among unrelated stores. For example, when supermarkets branched into nonfood personal care items, they created a decline in drugstore sales. Drugstores were then forced to scramble into small appliances and toys. This had an impact on specialty store sales, and so on.

There are limits to scrambled merchandising, especially if the addition of unrelated items lowers buying, selling, and servicing expertise. Furthermore, a low turnover of certain products can occur, should the retailer expand into too many diverse product categories. Finally, store image may become fuzzy as consumers fail to see a retailer stressing any one product category or group.

Sears provides a good example of scrambled merchandising. In addition to the regular goods and services that department stores offer, Sears now provides insurance (Allstate), real estate brokerage (Coldwell Banker), and stock brokerage (Dean Witter) in many stores. While some observers refer to Sears as "Socks 'n' Stocks," the firm has been quite successful with its strategy.[31] See Figure 14-9.

Wheel of Retailing

The ***wheel of retailing*** describes how low-end (discount) strategies can turn into high-end (full service, high price) strategies and thus provide opportunities for new firms to enter as discounters. According to the wheel, retail innovators often first appear as low-price operators with low profit-margin requirements. As time passes, these innovators look to increase sales and their customer base. They upgrade product offerings, facilities, and services and develop into more traditional retailers. They may expand sales force support, utilize a more costly location, and introduce delivery, credit, and alterations. These improvements lead to higher costs, which in turn lead to higher prices. This creates opportunities for new retailers to emerge by appealing to price-conscious consumers.[32]

Figure 14-10 shows the wheel of retailing in action.

---

[30] Endicott, "Life in the Fast-Food Lane," p. M-32.

[31] Tim Carrington, "Socks 'n' Stocks," *Wall Street Journal* (November 19, 1982), pp. 1, 21; and John R. Dorfman, "Surprise!" *Forbes* (March 26, 1984), p. 210.

[32] The pioneering works on the wheel of retailing are Malcolm P. McNair, "Significant Trends and Developments in the Postwar Period," in A. B. Smith (Editor), *Competitive Distribution in a Free High Level Economy and Its Implications for the University* (Pittsburgh: University of Pittsburgh Press, 1958), pp. 17–18, and Stanley Hollander, "The Wheel of Retailing," *Journal of Marketing,* Vol. 25 (July 1960), pp. 37–42.

Figure 14-9
Financial Services at Sears

Reprinted by permission of Sears, Roebuck and Co.

Recent Trends in Retailing

Retailers are affected by consumer demographics and life-styles, costs and price levels, and technological advances. This section presents a variety of retailers' responses to these elements.

Responses to Consumer Demographics and Life-Styles

The slowdown in overall population growth in the U.S. and geographic population shifts are causing a number of retailers to develop more regional and cross-country branches. For instance, Federated Department Stores' Los Angeles-based Bullock's is considering opportunities anywhere in the western United States. Macy's is planning to become a national department store chain. It already has outlets in Florida, California, and other states, in addition to its New York stronghold; a major store was recently opened in Houston. Geographic expansion requires more decentralized planning and budgeting; otherwise management personnel will be stretched to the limit, local adaptations overlooked, and the popularity of individual store names diminished.

The saturation of many prime markets has resulted in some retailers placing stores in nontraditional locations in an attempt to reach more consumers. For example, Baskin-Robbins operates over 40 outlets on U.S. Navy exchange facili-

More retailers are expanding geographically and satisfying consumers with shopping time pressure.

Figure 14-10
The Wheel of Retailing in Action

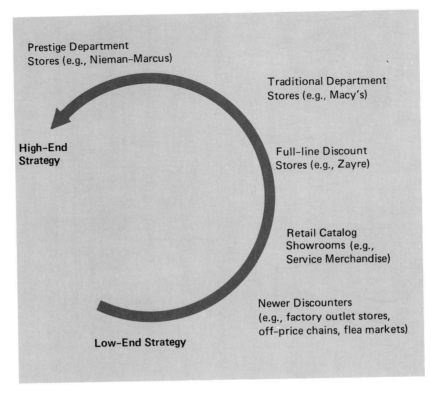

Prestige Department Stores (e.g., Nieman–Marcus)

Traditional Department Stores (e.g., Macy's)

High-End Strategy

Full-line Discount Stores (e.g., Zayre)

Retail Catalog Showrooms (e.g., Service Merchandise)

Newer Discounters (e.g., factory outlet stores, off-price chains, flea markets)

Low-End Strategy

ties. Burger King has stores inside Woolworth outlets. McDonald's has a store in a Montreal train depot.[33]

Retailers have developed a range of strategies to meet the shopping needs and time constraints of the growing number of working women and others with limited free time. They are stocking labor-saving devices, such as microwave ovens and ready-to-eat foods; lengthening store hours and opening additional days; expanding catalog sales efforts; prewrapping gift items to eliminate waiting lines; setting up comprehensive specialty boutiques to minimize the number of departments a consumer must visit; and adding special services, such as fashion coordinators. Pizza Hut is an example of a firm that has gone to great effort to attract customers under time pressure. For its lunchtime consumers, Pizza Hut now offers an individual-serving pizza with a guarantee that the pizza is received within five minutes after an order is placed (or the next pie is free).[34]

Retailers are reacting to the increased sophistication of consumers with regard to their purchases. For instance, Shopwell has opened 17 premium stores, known as Food Emporiums. These gourmet food outlets feature tanks of live fish, full-time butchers to cut meat to customer requirements, hand-dipped chocolates, truffles, and 75 kinds of mustard.[35]

[33] Scott Hume, "Fast-Foods Stalk Locations," *Advertising Age* (November 28, 1983), pp. 1, 5.
[34] Walter E. Gates, "Pizza Hut Asserts Presence in Lunch Market," *Marketing News* (April 29, 1983), p. 4.
[35] Aaron Bernstein, "Truffles, Anyone?" *Forbes* (April 25, 1983), pp. 132–134.

Responses to Costs and Price Levels

The high inflation of the late 1970s and early 1980s has had a dramatic effect on the way many retailers do business. These retailers are much more concerned with merchandise and business operating costs than ever before. They are also interested in the price levels that confront final consumers; the retailers recognize that high prices influence consumer attitudes and buying habits. During periods when price levels rise rapidly, people feel that their standard of living goes down; they stock up on bargains and lower-priced brands, and buy replacement products less frequently.

One of the most successful drugstores in the U.S. is Shulman's, an independent store in suburban Cleveland. During an average week, 30,000 people go through the store; a typical drugstore would need 5 months of business to do what Shulman's does in one week. Shulman's buys goods only when manufacturers offer discounts. It does little advertising, has plain linoleum floors, and sets prices at only 20 per cent above merchandise costs. Shulman's approach has attracted a following across the U.S.[36]

Some supermarkets are reviving bulk selling, by which consumers select the exact quantities of items that are displayed in bulk and not prepackaged (such as jelly beans, rice, dog biscuits, and dried fruits). Goods bought from bulk displays generally are priced 30 per cent less than comparable packaged items; consumers also buy the precise amounts needed. Giant Food has bulk displays in all of its supermarkets. Said a Giant spokesperson, "We've found out just by the old cash register that people want it."[37]

Today, retailers are much more cost and price conscious.

Responses to Technological Advances

During the past several years, a number of technological advances have emerged in retailing, many as the result of growing computerization. The most important advance involves the computerized-checkout (electronic point-of-purchase) system.

With a computerized-checkout system, a cashier passes an item over or past an optical scanner and a computer system instantly records and displays a sale. The customer is given a receipt, and all inventory information is stored in the computer's memory bank.

A computerized checkout lowers costs by reducing checkout time and employee training, decreasing misrings, and eliminating the need for price marking on merchandise. In addition, the system generates a current listing of the types and quantities of merchandise in stock without taking a physical inventory, improves inventory control, reduces spoilage, and improves ordering. The system is also able to verify and change transactions, provide instantaneous sales and profit reports, compute discounts, and determine the prices of items with missing tags. The major obstacles to computerized checkouts are their high purchase costs and consumers' insistence that price tags be adhered to each item.

Technological advances in retailing are improving efficiency and performance.

---

[36] Bill Abrams, "Discount Drugstores Thriving with Tricky Buying Strategy," *Wall Street Journal* (March 17, 1983), p. 29.
[37] Bill Johnson, "Supermarkets Bring Back Bulk Selling," *Wall Street Journal* (July 18, 1982), p. 21.

The following are illustrations of other technological advances that are being used by retailers:

- Antishoplifting tags that are attached to merchandise and set off an alarm if not properly removed by employees.
- Automatic energy-control systems that carefully monitor store temperature and reduce fuel costs.
- Computerized site-selection programs that are able to evaluate the characteristics of many potential store locations.
- Improved credit systems that allow faster processing of credit authorizations and efficient transfers of funds.
- Computerized inventory systems that reduce the need for physical inventory counts.

Sanger-Harris, a regional division of Federated Department Stores, uses a complex computer system that includes computerized checkouts, credit authorization, and inventory control. Through its system, Sanger-Harris is able to keep track of 9,000 inventory items; record transactions, deliveries, returns, and purchase orders; and locate merchandise within warehouses.[38]

Summary

Retailing encompasses those business activities involved with the sale of goods and services to the ultimate (final) consumer for personal, family, or household use. Average retail sales are small, yet the use of credit is widespread. Final consumers make many unplanned purchases and generally visit a retail store to make a purchase.

Retailing has an impact on the economy because of its total sales and the number of people employed. Retailers provide a variety of functions, including gathering a product assortment, providing information, handling merchandise, and completing transactions. Retailers deal with one group of suppliers that sell products the retailers use in operating their businesses and a second group selling items the retailers will resell.

Retailers may be categorized in several ways. Ownership types are independent, chain, franchise, leased department, and cooperative. The ease of entry into retailing fosters competition and results in many new firms failing. Different strategy mixes are used by convenience stores, supermarkets, superstores, specialty stores, variety stores, department stores, full-line discount stores, and retail catalog showrooms. Nonstore retailing involves vending machines, direct-to-home, and mail order. Service retailing is discussed in Chapters 9 and 22.

---

[38] "Inventory Management: Sanger-Harris," *Stores* (June 1983), pp. 27–28.

In retail planning, store location, atmosphere, scrambled merchandising, the wheel of retailing, and technological advances need to be considered. Locational alternatives are isolated stores, unplanned business districts, and planned shopping centers. Only the planned centers utilize balanced tenancy. Atmosphere is the sum total of a store's physical characteristics that help develop an image and attract customers. Scrambled merchandising is the addition of products unrelated to the retailer's original business. The wheel of retailing explains low-end and high-end retail strategies and how they emerge.

Retailers have adapted their strategies in response to recent trends regarding consumer demographics and life-styles, costs and price levels, and technological advances.

Questions for Discussion

1. What are the implications of small average sales for such retailers as convenience stores and supermarkets?
2. Sears has more than 25 million households with active credit card accounts who buy over $6 billion of merchandise each year. What are the advantages and disadvantages of this?
3. Table 14-1 shows net income as a per cent of sales for 20 leading retailers. How can the percentages be so low if 42 cents of every customer dollar spent in department stores and 20 cents of every customer dollar spent in supermarkets go to the retailers?
4. Explain how a restaurant owner and one of his or her suppliers could have different goals.
5. What are the strengths and weaknesses of independent retailers who compete against chains?
6. At one time most of McDonald's outlets operated under franchise agreements. Today one quarter of all McDonald's outlets are owned by the firm itself.
   a. Why was franchising a correct strategy for McDonald's in its early years?
   b. Why would McDonald's want to operate its own outlets now?
7. Why have consumer cooperatives not become a more important factor in food marketing?
8. Compare the strategies of convenience stores, supermarkets, and superstores.
9. Develop a discount store strategy for high-fidelity equipment. How would it compete with a high-priced specialty store?
10. Select an unplanned business district near your college or university and evaluate it.
11. Why do car dealers often situate in string locations? Doesn't this increase competition? Explain your answer.
12. Describe the atmosphere in a retail catalog showroom. Does it lend itself to the selling of fine jewelry. Why or why not?
13. Discuss two examples of scrambled merchandising in action in your area.
14. Evaluate Baskin-Robbins' decision to operate stores on naval facilities.
15. Explain many retailers' heightened interest in cost control and price levels in terms of the wheel of retailing.

Case 1 Off-Price Retailing: The Battle Heats Up*

Off-price retailers are now flourishing, particularly in the apparel area. These retailers usually purchase manufacturers' overruns, canceled orders, irregulars, and end-of-season merchandise at very low prices (sometimes at one quarter to one fifth of the wholesale price paid by traditional retailers for in-season, first-quality merchandise). Off-price apparel chains include Marshalls, Zayre, T. J. Maxx, Hit or Miss, and Loehmann's. Ten of the top 50 retailers in the U.S., such as K mart, operate off-price chains.

Off-price retailing is extremely profitable. Annual sales per square foot, the industry's measure of productivity, can be $200 and more; this is double the average sales per foot for conventional department and discount stores. Off-price retailers have an inventory turnover rate of 9 times per year, compared with 3.3 times for department stores. In addition, off-price stores have markups that are similar to department stores; their lower selling prices are due to reduced merchandise, operating, and property costs.

Until recently, department stores privately complained about the off-price chains; but, as long as they only carried noncompeting items, the department stores took no actions. However, two factors have led to a more aggressive position by department stores: the high sales level attained by off-price chains and some manufacturers selling in-season, first-quality goods to off-price stores. Department stores recognize that most off-price business is at their expense.

Increasingly, department stores are confronting their suppliers. The chief executive of Houston's Sakowitz department stores stated

These manufacturers who sell to seven stores within a two-block area and also to Loehmann's and Marshall's we've already told good-bye—like Ralph Lauren.

An executive vice-president at Carter Hawley Hale (a large department store chain) said

We're not going to hold up price umbrellas for brands that are being discounted every day.

Manufacturers who sell to off-price chains must make a choice. They can deal only with department stores, continue to do business with department stores and off-price retailers (and risk poor relations with traditional retailers), or they can develop different brands for off-price chains (and receive lower prices for these brands). One major manufacturer, Van Heusen, has already announced that it intends to eliminate off-price retailers as customers.

QUESTIONS

1. If they are so opposed to off-price retailing, why do 10 of the top 50 retailers operate off-price chains?

2. How can department stores compete against off-price chains?

* The data in this case are drawn from Ann M. Morrison, ''The Upshot of Off-Price,'' *Fortune* (June 13, 1983), pp. 122–124 ff; Walter McQuade, ''The Man Who Makes Millions on Mistakes,'' *Fortune* (September 6, 1982), pp. 106–108 ff; and Steve Weiner, ''Caught in a Cross-Fire, Brand-Apparel Makers Design Their Defenses,'' *Wall Street Journal* (January 24, 1984), pp. 1, 17

3. Explain this statement: "We're not going to hold up price umbrellas for brands that are being discounted every day."
4. As a manufacturer, what would you do if there is excess production and traditional retailers resent dealings with off-price chains?

Case 2 McDonald's: A Long-Running Franchise Strategy[†]

McDonald's is the largest restaurant organization in the U.S. Its $8 billion in annual sales account for 6 per cent of total meals away from home and 42 per cent of all sales at fast-food hamburger outlets. McDonald's consists of 7,500 restaurants. 68 per cent are franchised, 26 per cent company-owned, and 6 per cent affiliated (McDonald's Corporation is a part owner).

A 20-year franchise agreement for a McDonald's restaurant costs about $325,000. Rent and royalty payments by franchisees average 11.5 per cent of sales. Franchisees are also responsible for property tax payments, insurance, and maintenance. In return, franchisees receive training at Hamburger U, business advice, location planning, and other services—in addition to the right to operate under the McDonald's name. Existing franchisees are so satisfied with this arrangement that they are involved with 50 per cent of the new outlets McDonald's opens each year.

McDonald's has a reputation for innovativeness. For example, drive-through service was introduced in 1975. Today, drive-through service is featured at more than 5,000 McDonald restaurants; its sales represent about 40 per cent of overall company revenues. McDonald's breakfast menu, begun only a few years ago, contributes 18 per cent of sales; new items, such as ham and pork sausage "Bisquit Breakfast" sandwiches, are regularly tested. A number of outlets have McDonald's Playland facilities for children.

McDonald's worldwide advertising expenditures amount to 4.5 per cent of corporate sales. Worldwide advertising in 1982 was $368 million; it was $266 million in the U.S. alone. McDonald's also sponsors promotions such as "Quality in the Bag," "Happy Meal," and "Camp Snoopy."

In evaluating McDonald's strategy, one expert noted

McDonald's hasn't separated marketing from food services. What they've done is taken an intangible service and made it very tangible . . . They have eliminated human judgment in the system of service . . . McDonald's gives the customer clean, speedy service and a tasty product.

QUESTIONS
1. Some retail analysts feel that the fast-food industry has limited growth potential. Discuss several opportunities for McDonald's.

[†] The data in this case are drawn from Steve Raddock, "The Mammoth, Marvelous Money Machine: McDonald's," *Marketing & Media Decisions* (Spring 1982, Special Edition), pp. 111–114 ff; *McDonald's Corporation 1982 Annual Report;* and "The Fast-Food War: Big Mac Under Attack," *Business Week* (January 30, 1984), pp. 44–46.

2. What are the pros and cons of owning a McDonald's franchise?
3. Describe McDonald's store atmosphere. Differentiate it from that of a local fast-food outlet.
4. When asked the criteria he used to evaluate prospective franchise owners, Ray Kroc (the late founder of McDonald's) said he looked "for somebody who's good with people; we'd rather get a salesman than an accountant or even a chef." Comment on this.

Part Four Case Sears: A Growth Strategy for the Nation's Largest Retailer*

Sears, Roebuck & Company is the largest retailer in the United States, far ahead of K mart, J. C. Penney, and Federated Department Stores; 1983 total sales were nearly $36 billion. While Sears derives about 70 per cent of its revenues from traditional retailing and credit operations, it is also involved with Allstate Insurance (the second largest U.S. insurance company), Coldwell Banker (the leading residential real-estate firm), Dean Witter (the fifth largest brokerage firm), and World Trading Company (a small international financier). Figure 1 shows Sears' 1983 organization chart. Table 1 shows Sears' 1983 sales and profit performance by division.

1983 was a record-breaking year for Sears, after several lackbuster years. Sales increased by almost 20 per cent over 1982, while profit rose by over 50 per cent and amounted to 3.7 per cent of sales. In comparison, sales growth aver-

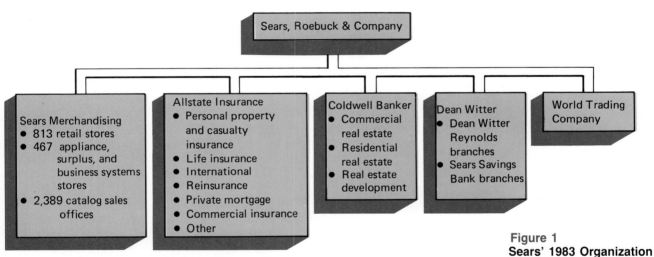

Source: Adapted from "Sears Roebuck: A Corporate Anatomy," *New York Times* (February 12, 1984), Section 3, p. 6.

**Figure 1
Sears' 1983 Organization Chart**

---

* The data in this case are drawn from Tim Carrington, "Socks 'n' Stocks," *Wall Street Journal* (November 19, 1982), pp. 1, 21; "For Sears Shoppers, New Bag of Money Items," *Marketing & Media Decisions* (September 1982), pp. 156–159; Daniel Kahn, "Retail Giant Launches a Change in Strategy," *Newsday* (October 3, 1983), Business Section, pp. 12–13; Ann M. Morrison, "Sears' Overdue Retailing Revival," *Fortune* (April 4, 1983), pp. 133–134 ff; "Sears Opens Its First 'Store of the Future' in Philadelphia Area," *Marketing News* (August 19, 1983), p. 8; Isadore Barmash, "Shaping a Sears Financial Empire," *New York Times* (February 12, 1984), Section 3, pp. 1, 6; Isadore Barmash, "At the Heart of the Plan—Merchandising Muscle," *New York Times* (February 12, 1984), Section 3, p. 6; Michael Blumstein, "Dean Witter: Cashing in on the Retail Connection," *New York Times* (February 12, 1984), Section 3, p. 7; Tim Jarrell, "Allstate: A Financial Role Model," *New York Times* (February 12, 1984), Section 3, p. 7; Thomas C. Hayes, "Coldwell: A Burst of Growth," *New York Times* (February 12, 1984), Section 3, p. 7; Winston Williams, "Wins and Losses in Trade and Bits," *New York Times* (February 12, 1984), Section 3, p. 7; Teresa H. Barker, "Allstate Jumps at Fitness," *Advertising Age* (February 6, 1984), pp. 1, 60; and Steve Weiner and Frank E. James, "Sears, a Powerhouse in Many Fields Now, Looks into New Ones," *Wall Street Journal* (February 10, 1984), pp. 1, 16.

Table 1
Sears' 1983 Sales and Profit Performance

Overall Company	1983	
Sales	$35.9 billion	
Profit	$1.34 billion	

Division	% of 1983 Sales	% of 1983 Profit
Sears Merchandising	69.6	53.1
Allstate Insurance	22.4	37.7
Coldwell Banker	2.0	3.3
Dean Witter	5.9	6.8
World Trading Company	0.2	(0.08)
	100.0[a]	100.0[a]

[a] Rounding error

Sources: Isadore Barmash, "Shaping a Sears Financial Empire," *New York Times* (February 12, 1984), Section, 3, p. 1; and Steve Weiner and Frank E. James, "Sears, a Powerhouse in Many Fields Now, Looks into New Ones," *Wall Street Journal* (February 10, 1984), p. 16.

aged 13.5 per cent from 1977 to 1982; and profit fell from 4.9 per cent of sales in 1977 to 2.9 per cent of sales in 1982.

Sears' difficulties during the 1977 to 1982 period were due to

- Frequent changes in strategy.
- Increased competition from discounters, department stores, and specialty stores.
- Inadequate analysis of product lines.
- Weak assortments for some product lines.
- An overreliance on private-label brands to the exclusion of national manufacturers' brands.
- Many older and unattractive stores.
- A weak economy.
- Inefficient operations.
- The high costs of acquiring Coldwell Banker and Dean Witter and integrating them into the company.

Following is a discussion of how Sears addressed each of these issues.

In the recent past, Sears was unsure whether it wanted to project an image as a mass merchant, an upscale department store chain, or a discounter. This resulted in confused customers and employees and frequent changes in strategy. Sears now understands that its original strategy of offering "moderately priced general merchandise for America's heartland" is the proper approach. Two thirds of all American adults visit a Sears store at least once a year. By adding financial services and more carefully assessing its merchandise mix, Sears intends "to increase the number of lines each customer buys from us without increasing the number of lines we carry."

When Sears revamped its strategy several times, it drew heightened competition because it no longer had a distinctive niche. For example, its upscale strategy placed it head on against traditional department stores and its discount strategy positioned it against the rapidly growing class of off-price retailers. Both of these approaches failed. Today, Sears has returned to its long-running distinctive niche, positioned between department stores and discounters. Sears has accomplished this by offering a broad merchandise assortment; emphasizing value; providing credit, delivery, and other services; encouraging one-stop shopping; maintaining its lines of appliances, furniture, and automotive goods (which some department stores have dropped); featuring mainstream fashions; and continuing strong catalog sales.

Sears now regularly evaluates each of the 800 product lines that are carried in its stores and catalogs. Products that do not sell well are dropped. Thus far, Sears has eliminated 30 product lines and replaced them with others. Sears plans to maintain those hard goods (such as radial tires, car batteries, washers, and dryers) with which it is a market leader. 65 per cent of Sears' retailing sales come from durable goods. In contrast, J. C. Penney eliminated its home furnishings and automotive lines.

Sears has improved its assortments in many lines, particularly home furnishings and apparel. In home furnishings, Sears has introduced an extensive range of "country look" fashions for products such as furniture, sheets, and dinnerware as well as a full line of designer Diane Von Furstenberg textiles, wall coverings, dinnerware, and bathroom furnishings. In apparel, Sears is offering Cheryl Tiegs sportswear, Evonne Goolagong Cawley tennis and warm-up clothes, and Arnold Palmer "Arnie" menswear. Despite these changes, Sears clearly knows its position in the clothing market; it is not aiming at the trendy consumers targeted by many department stores. As one Sears executive acknowledged, "We're aiming for the middle market, not for high fashion."

While many of Sears' own brands (e.g., Craftsman tools and Kenmore appliances) are extremely popular, the company now also recognizes that many consumers desire manufacturers' brands. As a result, today, Sears' stores carry Levi Strauss and Wrangler clothes, Wilson and Spaulding sporting goods, Adidas running shoes, and Black & Decker tools along with private-label merchandise. Said Sears' chief executive, "A few years ago we would have sat and talked and not dreamed that Sears should get into [manufacturers' brands]. But obviously by not doing so for years we passed up a lot of business."

Sears has allocated $1.7 billion to modernize over 660 existing stores and to construct 62 new ones. This approach "recognizes a dramatic decline in the number of desirable new shopping mall locations and the competitive importance of upgrading existing facilities to generate sales and growth." Sears' "stores of the future" feature indirect lighting, vaulted ceilings, spotlighted key interest areas, extensive use of computer technology for inventory planning and credit verification, and new merchandising techniques. Among the merchandising tools used in revitalized stores is the "store within a store concept" by which merchandise is grouped in self-contained clusters, such as a lawn and garden center; photography, audio, and video products; and apparel by life-style. Previously, some related merchandise was displayed not only in separate departments, but on different floors. About 200 product lines were moved to new locations. Stated one retail analyst, "Sears has put a lot of planning into the merchandise mixture, layout, presentation, and price-quality equation and feels it has it right."

In 1983, the U.S. economy improved substantially over previous years. Consumers had more discretionary income and were able to make purchases of costly durable goods. By offering a better merchandise mix and retaining its strength in hard goods, Sears was able to capitalize on the economic upturn.

Furthermore, Sears earned a profit of $144 million from credit-card operations in 1983. During 1981, Sears had lost $144 million, because finance charges to customers were far less than Sears' cost of borrowed funds (due to extremely high interest rates).

At the same time, Sears enacted a number of cost-cutting and other measures to raise efficiency. For example, headquarters personnel was reduced from 9,000 to 7,000. Stores were realigned into four regions instead of five. The New York buying office was closed. Overall, costs were reduced by about 2.5 per cent of annual sales (between $750 million and $1 billion per year).

Coldwell Banker and Dean Witter were acquired by Sears for over $800 million in fall 1981. By 1983, these divisions were fully integrated into the company. As of December 1983, the "Sears Financial Network" (Coldwell Banker, Dean Witter, and Allstate Insurance) was operating in 133 stores. As of December 1984, Sears expected to have full-service financial networks in 283 of its stores. Sears believes its financial networks have a number of competitive advantages:

- A base of 36 million regular customers, with 25 million households actively using Sears' credit cards (including 70 per cent of all U.S. households with $36,000+ in annual income and 73 per cent of all stock market investors making yearly transactions worth $25,000 or more).
- A strong image as an honest, reliable merchant that offers good value.
- Convenient locations throughout the U.S.
- One-stop shopping for a variety of financial services and merchandise.
- Long hours of operation, 10:00 A.M. to 9:30 P.M. daily and noon to 5:00 P.M. Sundays.
- The resources to support many company ventures. "If you make a mistake and you've got a (rich) parent, then you're going to be more aggressive. That's the difference; that's how you win." For example, during 1984, Sears developed a $30 million "shape up and save" advertising campaign for Allstate life insurance. The campaign was keyed to the Olympics and provided discounts for consumers who worked to improve their physical fitness.
- Sears hopes eventually to gain approval to operate savings banks in all its financial networks. Now, its savings banks are restricted to California by law.

QUESTIONS

1. Assess Sears' current strategy.
2. Evaluate the information in Table 1.
3. How will Sears' relations with firms such as Levi Strauss and Adidas differ from those with manufacturers making products under the Sears brand name?
4. Sears sells refrigerators in stores as well as through catalogs. Distinguish between the physical distribution strategies of these two selling methods.
5. Sears buys many of its products directly from manufacturers rather than through wholesalers.
   a. Why does Sears use this approach?
   b. For what items would direct buying be ineffective? Explain your answer.
6. Comment on this statement: "Sears still sells sportswear next to tires and men's suits next to vacuum cleaners."

PART

Promotion Planning

Part Five deals with the third major element of marketing, promotion. Chapter 15 provides an overview to promotion planning, the systematic decision making relating to the communication used by a firm to inform, persuade, or remind people about its products, services, image, ideas, community involvement, or impact on society. The basic types of promotion are described: advertising, publicity, personal selling, and sales promotion. The channel of communication, the mechanism through which a company sends a message to its audience, is fully explained. Next, the steps in the development of an overall promotion plan are described. These include establishing objectives, setting a budget, and developing a promotion mix. The chapter concludes with discussions regarding the legal environment of promotion and the criticisms and defenses of promotion.

Chapter 16 examines the two mass communication forms of promotion, advertising and publicity. Advertising is defined as the paid, nonpersonal presentation and promotion of ideas, goods, and services by an identified sponsor. Publicity is defined as the nonpaid, nonpersonal presentation and promotion of ideas, goods, and services by an independent source. The scope of advertising and publicity and their positive and negative attributes are detailed. There are comprehensive descriptions of the development of advertising and publicity plans, from objectives to evaluating success or failure.

Chapter 17 concentrates on personal selling and sales promotion. Personal selling is defined as that part of promotion involving an oral presentation in a conversation with one or more prospective buyers for the purpose of a sale. Sales promotion consists of the marketing activities, other than advertising, publicity, or personal selling, that stimulate consumer purchases and dealer effectiveness. In this chapter the scope, characteristics, and stages in planning are described for both personal selling and sales promotion.

Although Beatrice is one of the largest consumer-goods firms in the U.S., the company believes that too few consumers are familiar with the corporate name. Consumer recognition has been limited to the brands shown here and others such as Tropicana orange juice, La Choy foods, and Stiffel lamps. To remedy this, Beatrice spent almost $30 million in 1984 on corporate ads. Reprinted by permission.

TITLE: "FLUFFY BUN"

LENGTH: 30 SECONDS
COMM'L NO.: WOFH-3386

CUST. #1: It certainly is a big bun.
CUST. #2: It's a very big bun.

CUST. #1: A big fluffy bun.

CUST. #2: It's a very...big...fluffy... bun.

CUST. #3: Where's the beef?
ANNCR: Some hamburger places give you a lot less beef on a lot of bun.

CUST. #3: Where's the beef?

ANNCR: At Wendy's, we serve a hamburger we modestly call a "Single" — and Wendy's Single has more beef than the Whopper or Big Mac. At Wendy's, you get more beef and less bun.

CUST. #3: Hey, where's the beef? I don't think there's anybody back there!

ANNCR: You want something better, you're Wendy's Kind of People.

One of the most popular and effective ads in recent years was this humorous 1984 television commercial by Wendy's restaurants. The "where's the beef?" campaign increased Wendy's sales dramatically and reinforced the perception that Wendy's hamburgers were bigger than those of competitors. Intensive media coverage of the campaign resulted in substantial favorable publicity for the company. Reprinted by permission.

Hallmark advertising is characterized by its emphasis on themes (particularly how to convey feelings) and holidays (such as Father's Day). Its effective use of advertising enables Hallmark to continue as the leading greeting card company in the U.S. Reprinted by permission.

Postsales customer service is a vital component of Pitney Bowes' marketing effort. After having assisted in the redesign of a Citicorp mailroom and the related purchase of new equipment, the Pitney Bowes Sales Team Manager (at left) reviews the facility's improved operating efficiency with its assistant manager. Reprinted by permission from *Pitney Bowes 1983 Annual Report/* Photographer: Gabe Palmer.

In 1983–1984, Toro ran a sales promotion that offered consumers a rebate on the purchase of a snow blower if it snowed lightly in their areas. The promotion increased sales dramatically; and Toro had to provide rebates in only 2 of 172 markets. Reprinted by permission.

If it snows less than	You keep the Toro and you receive:
20% * AVERAGE SNOWFALL	**100%** REFUND of suggested retail price
30% * AVERAGE SNOWFALL	**70%** REFUND of suggested retail price
40% * AVERAGE SNOWFALL	**60%** REFUND of suggested retail price
50% * AVERAGE SNOWFALL	**50%** REFUND of suggested retail price

Chapter 15

An Overview of Promotion Planning

1. To define promotion and show its importance
2. To describe the general characteristics of advertising, publicity, personal selling, and sales promotion
3. To explain the channel of communication and how it functions
4. To examine the components of a promotion plan: objectives, budget, and mix of elements
5. To study the legal environment and the criticisms and defenses of promotion

FTD (Florists' Transworld Delivery) is a retail delivery service of floral products that works with 20,000 participating florists. Under the FTD system, a customer places an order for an out-of-town delivery with a local participating florist. This florist then transmits the order to FTD, which arranges with a florist in the delivery area to complete the transaction. In addition to delivery service, FTD offers its own products through participating florists: Wish 'n Well bouquets for hospital patients, birthday party bouquets, and Tickler bouquets for any occasion.

Because of its unique business, FTD's promotion strategy is aimed at both final consumers and florists. According to FTD's director of advertising and public relations:

Our strategy is to convince consumers they will be recognized as warm, caring people who demand the highest quality if they specify FTD. Our tactics are to maximize memorability and maintain high visibility through

431

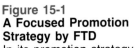

Figure 15-1
A Focused Promotion Strategy by FTD
In its promotion strategy, FTD is using a well-known spokesperson and a clear, identifiable series of messages, such as this one for the Wish 'N Well Bouquet, ® registered trademark of Florists' Transworld Delivery Association.

Reprinted by permission.

key commercial cues like a unique product, music, a personality, or a distinctive situation.

On the florist side, our strategy is to prove to florists that FTD remains a powerful industry leader, and our tactics are to increase consumer requests for FTD products, maintain a communication program which is highly visible to florists as well as consumers, and continue a strong trade campaign reminding florists of FTD's value and importance in generating additional floral sales.

To accomplish its promotion goals, in 1983, FTD hired Merlin Olsen (the television personality and former professional football player) to be its celebrity spokesperson. FTD's research showed Olsen to be well liked, believable, and respected by consumers and florists. By featuring Merlin Olsen in its promotion mix, FTD hopes to foster a competitive advantage, add credibility to messages, stress the FTD brand name, provide continuity over time, and instill pride in participating florists.[1] See Figure 15-1.

This illustration demonstrates that a company needs to employ careful analysis and planning in order to enact a focused promotion strategy. Promotion involves much more than a one-time television or newspaper ad.

---

[1] "Research Suggests Using Celebrity Spokesperson as Focal Point for Floral Group's Consumer, Trade Ads," *Marketing News* (November 11, 1983), p. 10.

Characteristics and Importance of Promotion

Promotion planning is systematic decision making relating to all aspects of the development and management of a firm's promotional effort. *Promotion* is any form of communication used by a firm to inform, persuade, or remind people about its products, services, image, ideas, community involvement, or impact on society. The components of this definition are explained in the following paragraphs.

A firm can communicate through brand names, packaging, store marquees and displays, a personal sales force, trade shows, sweepstakes, messages in mass media (newspapers, television, radio, direct mail, billboards, magazines, and transit), and other forms. Communication can be company sponsored or controlled by independent media. Messages may emphasize information, persuasion, fear, sociability, product performance, humor, and/or comparisons with competitors.

With new products, customers must be informed about the items and their attributes before developing favorable attitudes toward them. For products that have a solid level of consumer awareness, the promotional thrust is on persuasion—converting product knowledge to product liking. For well-entrenched products, the emphasis is on reminder promotion—reinforcing existing consumer beliefs.

The people to whom a firm's promotional effort is addressed fall into several categories: consumers, stockholders, consumer organizations and lobbies, government, channel members, employees, and the general public. It is important to realize that communication goes on between a firm and each of these groups, not just with its consumers. In addition, the communication with each will be different because the groups have distinct goals, knowledge, and needs. Within groups, a firm must identify and appeal to opinion leaders. It needs to understand the mechanisms of *word-of-mouth communication,* the process by which people express their opinions and product-related experiences to one another. Without sustained positive word-of-mouth, it is difficult for a company to succeed in the long run.

A firm's promotional plan usually stresses individual products and services, with the objective of moving consumers from awareness to purchase. However, a company may also seek to communicate its overall image (such as industry innovator), views on ideas (such as nuclear energy), community involvement (such as publicizing the funding of a new hospital), or impact on society (for example, by citing the number of workers employed).

Promotion enables a company to establish an image, generate sales, interact with channel members, provide customer afterservice, and perform other activities. See Table 15-1. A good promotion plan complements the product, distribution, and price components of marketing. For example, a manufacturer of quality stereo equipment would distribute merchandise through finer specialty stores and maintain high prices (avoiding discounting). It would advertise in

Promotion planning focuses on the total promotion effort— including information, persuasion, and reminding.

Word-of-mouth communication occurs when people state opinions to one another.

Promotion has an effect on image, sales, channel relations, and customer satisfaction.

Table 15-1
The Value of Promotion

Promotion
Establishes a company or product/service image, such as prestige, discount, or innovative.
Communicates product or service features.
Creates awareness for new products or services.
Keeps existing products or services popular.
Can reposition the images or uses of faltering products or services.
Generates enthusiasm from channel members.
Explains where products or services can be purchased.
Convinces consumers to trade up from one product or service to a more expensive one.
Alerts consumers to sales.
Justifies product or service prices.
Answers consumer questions.
Closes transactions.
Provides afterservice for consumers.
Places the company and its products or services in a favorable light, relative to competitors.

magazines such as *Stereo Review* and expect its retailers to provide a significant level of personal selling. Ads would be full color and emphasize product features.

These are illustrations of several well-conceived promotion plans:

- For more than 25 years, Pepsi has communicated the ''Pepsi generation'' message to its customers. Although the themes used by Pepsi have changed over the years, the general message has remained the same:[2]

1958–1961	''So young at heart''
1961–1962	''Now it's Pepsi for those who think young''
1963–1968	''Come alive. You're in the Pepsi generation''
1969–1973	''You've got a lot to live. Pepsi's got a lot to give''
1974–1976	''Join the Pepsi people, feeling free''
1977–1979	''Have a Pepsi day''
1980–1983	''Catch that Pepsi spirit! Drink it in''
1983–1984	''Pepsi Now''
1984–	''Pepsi: The choice of a new generation''

These themes appear in advertisements, sales promotions, and in-store displays. They provide Pepsi with a well-defined, stable image. Pepsi also aggressively promotes its ''Pepsi Challenge'' taste test, comparing its product with Coke.

- The International Apple Institute developed a promotion plan to increase the consumption of apples in the U.S. To encourage consumers to treat apples as a snack product, the theme ''Crunch an Apple Instead'' was adopted. Other themes were devised for nonsnack uses, such as ''Serve a Baked Apple Instead.'' *Family Circle, Woman's Day*, and other magazines were encouraged to run feature articles describing apples and apple recipes. 30,000 kits containing apple uses, recipes, and case histories of successful applications were distributed to hotel chains, school cafeterias, restaurants, and other food-service companies. As a result of the efforts of the International Apple Institute, U.S. per capita apple consumption rose almost 24 per cent between 1980 and 1983.[3]

[2] James P. Forkan, ''Pepsi Generation Bridges Two Decades,'' *Advertising Age* (May 5, 1980), pp. 41–43; and Nancy Giges, ''Time-and-Theme-Is-Now for Pepsi,'' *Advertising Age* (March 7, 1983), pp. 2, 62.
[3] Kevin Higgins, ''Marketing Becoming Essential for Commodity Producer Groups,'' *Marketing News* (April 29, 1983), pp. 1, 4.

- Beatrice is a large consumer-goods company. It makes such brands as Tropicana orange juice, Cutty Sark Scotch, La Choy foods, Samsonite luggage, and Swiss Miss cocoa and puddings. While consumers are familiar with these brands, few recognize the Beatrice name. To remedy this, Beatrice spent $29 million on corporate advertising during 1984, using the slogan "Beatrice, you've known us all along." Beatrice's goal was to "enhance consumer respect for any product in the Beatrice line." Television commercials were keyed to the 1984 Winter and Summer Olympics. Magazine ads were distributed throughout the year in publications such as *Fortune, Seventeen, House Beautiful,* and *Ebony.* Coupon inserts were sent to 30 million consumer homes. Point-of-purchase displays included take-home scorecards for the Olympics containing the Beatrice name. A new corporate logo was designed and adhered to all company products.[4]
- J.M. Smucker, a manufacturer of jellies and jams, created a two-pronged strategy—one aimed at children and one at adults. For children, Smucker had a tie-in with Walt Disney movies (offering items such as free drinking mugs containing characters from the films) and ran other sales promotions. For adults, Smucker gave away cookbooks and other premiums. All the promotions were related to product purchases by consumers.[5]

The importance of promotion is also evident from the expenditures and employment of people in this area, as these figures indicate. Annually, auto makers spend $1.6 billion, airlines about $500 million, and pharmaceuticals manufacturers over $1.5 billion on advertising in the U.S. Almost 7 million people are employed in some aspect of sales. Over 140 billion coupons are annually distributed. The yearly sales volume for trading stamps exceeds $530 million.[6]

In this chapter an overview of promotion planning is provided. Included are discussions on the types of promotion, channel of communication, promotion planning, the legal environment, and criticisms and defenses of promotion. Chapter 16 covers advertising and publicity—the paid and nonpaid forms of mass communication. Chapter 17 deals with personal selling and sales promotion—the individual and supplemental forms of promotion.

Types of Promotion

In its communications program, a firm can utilize one or a combination of four basic types of promotion: advertising, publicity, personal selling, and sales promotion.

---

[4] Janet Neiman, "Beatrice Seeks Respect in Huge Corporate Push," *Advertising Age* (January 9, 1984), pp. 3, 62; and JoEllen Goodman and Paul Merrion, "Overhauling a $9-Billion Giant," *Advertising Age* (February 27, 1984), pp. M-4–M-5, M-48.

[5] "How Four Companies Used Strategic Promotion Planning," *Marketing News* (October 30, 1981), p. 13.

[6] Marion L. Elmquist, "100 Leaders Parry Recession with Heavy Spending," *Advertising Age,* (September 8, 1983), p. 166; *Employment and Earnings* (Washington, D.C.: U.S. Bureau of Labor Statistics, 1980); "Analyzing Promotions," *Nielsen Researcher* (Number 4, 1982), p. 17; "Marketing Briefs," *Marketing News* (April 29, 1983), p. 11; and "1983 Report: A Cautious Year as Buyers Wait for the Recovery," *Incentive Marketing Magazine* (February 1984), p. 13.

Advertising and *publicity* are nonpersonal types of promotion. *Personal selling* involves one-to-one contact. *Sales promotion* includes supplemental techniques.

Advertising is any paid form of nonpersonal presentation and promotion of ideas, goods, and services by an identified sponsor. ***Publicity*** is the nonpersonal stimulation of demand for a product, service, or business by placing commercially significant news about it in a published medium or obtaining favorable presentation on radio, television, or stage that is not paid for by an identified sponsor. ***Personal selling*** is an oral presentation in a conversation with one or more prospective buyers for the purpose of making sales. ***Sales promotion*** involves marketing activities, other than advertising, publicity, or personal selling that stimulate consumer purchases and dealer effectiveness. Included are shows, demonstrations, and various nonrecurrent selling efforts not in the ordinary promotion routine.[7]

The general characteristics of each type of promotion are shown in Table 15-2. As discussed later in the chapter, many firms combine these four types in an integrated promotional blend. This enables them to reach the entire target market, present both persuasive and believable messages, have personal contact with customers, sponsor special events, and balance the promotional budget.

Channel of Communication

A message is sent to an audience through a *channel of communication.*

In order to develop a promotion mix properly and communicate effectively with consumers, a firm must understand the channel of communication shown in Figure 15-2. Through the ***channel of communication (communication process),*** a source sends a message to its audience. A communication channel consists of the source, encoding, the message, the medium, decoding, the audience, feedback, and noise. These are discussed next.

[7] Ralph S. Alexander (Chairman), *Marketing Definitions: A Glossary of Marketing Terms* (Chicago: American Marketing Association, 1960), pp. 9, 18, 19, 20.

Figure 15-2
Channel of Communication

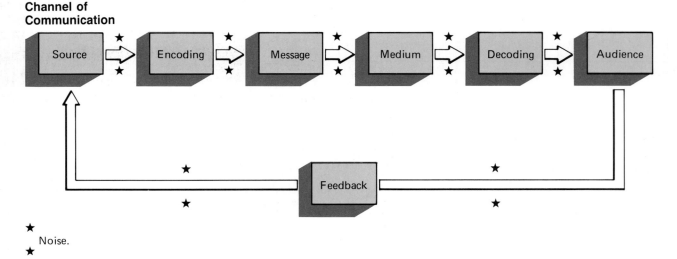

★ Noise.
★

Table 15-2 Characteristics of Promotional Types

Factor	Advertising	Publicity	Personal Selling	Sales Promotion
Audience	Mass	Mass	Small (one-to-one)	Varies
Message	Uniform	Uniform	Specific	Varies
Cost	Low per viewer or reader	None for media space and time; can be moderate costs for press releases and publicity materials	High per customer	Moderate per customer
Sponsor	Company	No formal sponsor in that media are not paid	Company	Company
Flexibility	Low	Low	High	Moderate
Control over content and placement	High	None	High	High
Credibility	Moderate	High	Moderate	Moderate
Major goal	To appeal to a mass audience at a reasonable cost, and create awareness and favorable attitudes	To reach a mass audience with an independently reported message	To deal with individual consumers, to resolve questions, to close sales	To stimulate short-run sales, to increase impulse purchases
Example	Television ad for the Kodak video camera	Newspaper article reporting on the unique features of the Kodak video camera	Retail sales personnel explaining how the Kodak video camera works	The Kodak video camera displayed at consumer photography shows

Source

The *source* of communication is the company, independent institution, or opinion leader that seeks to present a message to an audience. The company communicates through a company spokesperson, celebrity, actor playing a role, representative consumer, and/or salesperson.

A company spokesperson is usually a high-ranking employee of the firm who represents it in advertisements. The spokesperson provides an aura of sincerity, commitment, and expertise. Chrysler's Lee Iacocca, Remington's Victor Kiam, Tom Carvel, and Frank Perdue have been particularly effective.[8]

A celebrity is used to gain the attention of the audience and improve product awareness. Problems can arise if consumers perceive the celebrity as insincere or unknowledgeable. Among the most popular celebrity sources are Jim Palmer for Jockey, Cheryl Tiegs for Cover Girl, and Bill Cosby for Jell-O Pudding Pops. To reach younger consumers, some companies are using music stars such as Michael Jackson (Pepsi-Cola), Hall & Oates (Canada Dry), and the Who (Schlitz).[9]

Many advertisements use actors playing roles rather than celebrity spokespeople. In these commercials emphasis is placed on presenting a message about a product or service, rather than on the consumer recognizing a celebrity. The hope is that the consumer will learn more about product or service attributes.

The source presents a message.

Company sources are spokespersons, celebrities, actors playing roles, representative consumers, and salespersons.

[8] Madeleine Dreyfack, "Four Who Dared," *Marketing & Media Decisions* (April 1982), pp. 64–65 ff; "Putting the Boss in TV Commercials," *New York Times* (August 8, 1982), Section 3, p. 21; and Ann Morrison, "The Boss as Pitchman," *Fortune* (August 25, 1980), pp. 66–73.

[9] For an analysis of celebrity sources, see Mitchell J. Shields, "Putting Wine to the Test-imonial," *Advertising Age* (January 16, 1984), p. M-43.

A representative consumer is one who likes the product and recommends it in an advertisement. This person is shown with his or her name and general address. The intent is to show a real consumer in an actual situation. A hidden camera or blind taste test is often used with the representative consumer. Today a number of viewers are skeptical about how ''representative'' the endorser is.

Finally, the company may be represented by a salesperson who communicates with consumers. Most salespeople are knowledgeable, aggressive, and persuasive. However, consumers question their objectivity and fairness. Car salespeople rate particularly low in consumer surveys.

An independent institution is not paid by the firm on which it reports.

An independent institution is not controlled by the companies on which it reports. It evaluates and presents information on the operations and products of companies in a professional, nonpaid (by the companies) manner. Consumers Union, Consumers' Research, and the local newspaper food critic are examples of independent sources. They usually have great credibility for their readers because they point out both good and bad points, but large segments of the population may not be exposed to these sources. The information presented may differ from that contained in a firm's commercials.

Opinion leaders influence others through the *two-step flow of communication*. These leaders are also influenced in a *multistep flow*.

Opinion leaders are people who have face-to-face contact with and influence potential consumers. Because they deal on a personal level, opinion leaders usually have strong persuasive impact and believability. They are able to offer social acceptance and status for followers. The firm should address its initial messages to opinion leaders, who then provide word-of-mouth communication about the product to other consumers. This is the **two-step flow of communication** (company to opinion leader to target market). Marketers further believe that opinion leaders not only influence but also are influenced by the general public (opinion receivers); they need approval for their decisions. This is the **multistep flow of communication**.

In assessing the qualities of a source, these questions are most critical: Is the source believable? Is the source convincing? Does the source present an image consistent with the firm? Do consumers value the message of the source? Is the source perceived as knowledgeable? Does the source complement the product or service it communicates about or does the source overwhelm it? Do significant parts of the market dislike the source? Figure 15-3 shows an ad aimed at enhancing the status of pharmacists as a source for information about medications.

Encoding

During *encoding*, the source translates a thought or idea into a message.

Encoding is the process whereby a thought or idea is translated into a message by the source. At this stage, preliminary decisions are made regarding message content, such as the use of symbolism and wording. It is vital that the thought or idea be translated exactly as the source desires. For example, a firm wanting to stress the prestige of its product would include the concepts of status, exclusive ownership, and special features in a message. It would not emphasize a price lower than competitors, availability in discount stores, or the millions of people who have already purchased it.

Message

A *message* combines words and symbols, and contains various information features.

The **message** is the combination of words and symbols transmitted to an audience. The focus of message content depends on whether the firm's goal is to inform, persuade, or remind its audience. This is examined later in the chapter.

Figure 15-3
**Pharmacists—An
Important Source of
Information About
Medications**

Reprinted by permission.

Almost all messages would include information on the company name, product/service name, desired image, differential advantage, and product/service attributes and benefits. Additionally, a firm would provide information about availability and price somewhere in the communication process.

Most communication involves *one-sided messages,* in which the firm mentions only the benefits of its product or service. Few companies use *two-sided messages,* in which both benefits and limitations are discussed. Companies are not anxious to point out their own shortcomings, even though consumer perceptions of honesty are improved through two-sided messages. For example, a few years ago a new deodorant named Stay Dry was marketed. In the commercials for the product, the spokesperson said it should have been called Stay Drier. He explained that although Stay Dry could keep people drier than any other deodorant, no deodorant could keep them dry. The product did not sell well.

Many messages use symbolism and try to relate safety, social acceptance, or

With *one-sided messages,* only benefits are mentioned; *two-sided messages* describe both benefits and limitations.

Symbolism relates the message to a product's safety, social value, or sexual appeal.

sexual appeal to the purchase of a product. For example, in commercials, life insurance provides safety for family members; clothing styles offer acceptance by peers; and toothpaste brightens teeth and makes a person more sexually attractive. With symbolic messages the firm stresses psychological benefits rather than tangible product performance, such as miles per gallon.

One type of symbolism, the use of fear appeals, has had mixed results. Although consumers respond to moderate fear appeals, strong messages may not yield favorable responses. For example, the Highway Traffic and Safety Commission found that a commercial for safety belts showing mangled cars and broken bones was too overpowering for people, causing them to avoid viewing it. A subsequent campaign based on "If you love me, you'll show me" sent out the same message, but in a milder way. On the other hand, Prudential recently switched to a relatively strong fear appeal in its television ads for life insurance. In these ads, people are shown being revived from near-death situations (such as drowning), followed by the remark "At Prudential we know that most of us don't get a second chance." Preliminary tests of audience reactions to these ads have been quite positive.[10] Detergents, toothpaste, and deodorants are among the many products that have successfully used moderate fear appeals based on social factors, rather than physical ones.

Humor in messages can attract attention, but it should not detract from image.

Humor is sometimes used to gain audience attention and retain it. Some examples of humor are Wendy's "Where's the Beef?" commercial showing a large bun and a small hamburger offered at other fast-food chains, Federal Express ads with the slogan "When it absolutely, positively has to get there the next morning," and George Steinbrenner (New York Yankees owner) telling Billy Martin (the three-time former Yankee manager) he is fired again in a Miller Lite commercial. The firm needs to be careful to get across the intended message when using humor. The humor should not make fun of the company, its products, or services; and it should not dominate the message so that the brand name or attributes of the item go unnoticed.[11] Figure 15-4 shows a parody of the "Where's the Beef?" commercial by Frank Perdue.

Comparative messages position the firm's offerings versus competitors'.

Comparative messages contrast the firm's offerings with those of competitors. In recent years, comparative messages have substantially increased in number. They now account for 35 per cent of all television commercials.[12] Some comparative messages use a brand X or leading brand campaign (such as "Our fabric softener is more effective than other leading brands"). Others utilize direct comparisons (such as Burger King asserting that its process of flame broiling hamburgers is superior to McDonald's frying process). Salespeople frequently compare the characteristics of their products with those of competitors.

A message must be in desirable, exclusive, and believable terms.

The content of a message must be presented in a desirable, exclusive, and believable manner. The product, service, or idea needs to be perceived by the audience as something worth purchasing or accepting. It also needs to be considered unique to the company—that is, it cannot be obtained elsewhere. Finally, the message must contain believable statements and claims.

---

[10] Bill Abrams, "New Prudential Ads Portray Death as No Laughing Matter," *Wall Street Journal* (November 10, 1983), p. 31.

[11] Tamar Lewin, "Behind 'Where's the Beef?'" *New York Times* (March 8, 1984), pp. D1, D18; and John Koten, "After Serious '70s, Advertisers Are Going for Laughs," *Wall Street Journal* (February 23, 1984), p. 31.

[12] John Koten, "More Firms File Challenges to Rivals' Comparative Ads," *Wall Street Journal* (January 12, 1984), p. 27.

Figure 15-4
Humor in Advertising

WHO CARES
WHERE THE BEEF IS?
Frank Perdue

Reprinted by permission.

The timing of messages must be carefully planned. First, during what periods in the year should the firm advertise, add salespeople, or run promotions? With **massed promotion,** communication is concentrated in peak periods, like holidays. With **distributed promotion,** communication is spread throughout the year. See Figure 15-5.

Second, the **wearout rate** (the period of time it takes for a message to lose its effectiveness) must be determined. Some messages wear out quickly, while others may last for months or years. The wearout rate depends on the frequency of communications, the quality of the message, the number of messages used by the company, and other factors. When measuring wearout, it must be noted that effective messages can be used over a long period of time. For example Wisk's ''ring around the collar'' message has been around since 1967; and as the slogan's author noted:

The use of *massed* or *distributed promotion* and the *wearout rate* must be carefully planned.

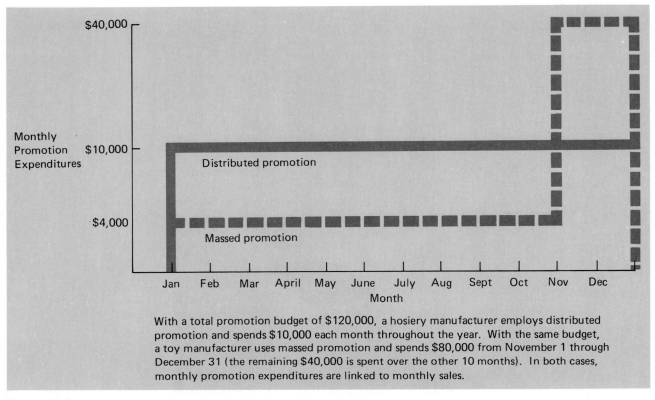

With a total promotion budget of $120,000, a hosiery manufacturer employs distributed promotion and spends $10,000 each month throughout the year. With the same budget, a toy manufacturer uses massed promotion and spends $80,000 from November 1 through December 31 (the remaining $40,000 is spent over the other 10 months). In both cases, monthly promotion expenditures are linked to monthly sales.

Figure 15-5
Massed Versus
Distributed Promotion

It would be fair to call that commercial a screeching commercial, an abrasive commercial, an intrusive commercial. But the one thing you can't call it is a bad commercial because the purpose of a commercial is to do a commercial job.[13]

Medium

The *medium* is the personal or nonpersonal channel for a message.

The ***medium*** is the personal or nonpersonal channel used to send a message. Personal media are company salespeople and other representatives as well as opinion leaders. Nonpersonal media include newspapers, television, radio, direct mail, billboards, magazines, and transit.

Personal media offer one-to-one contact with the audience. They are flexible, able to adapt messages to individual needs, and can answer questions. They also appeal to a small audience and work best with a concentrated target market.

Nonpersonal (mass) media provide a large audience and low per customer costs. They are inflexible and not as dynamic as one-to-one presentations. They work best with a dispersed target market.

When deciding between personal and nonpersonal media, the firm should consider total and per unit costs, product or service complexity, audience attributes, and communication goals. The two types of media also work well together, because nonpersonal media generate consumer interest and personal media help close sales.

[13] Bill Abrams, " 'Ring Around the Collar' Ads Irritate Many Yet Get Results," *Wall Street Journal* (November 4, 1982), p. 33.

Decoding

Decoding is the process by which the message sent by the source is interpreted by the audience. Members of the audience interpret the message according to their background and the clarity of message content. As noted earlier in the chapter, it is essential that a message be decoded in the manner desired by the source (encoding = decoding).

The background of the audience—demographics and life-styles—affects the way it decodes messages. For example, a housewife and a working woman might have different interpretations of a message on the value of day-care centers. An upper-class consumer would view Cadillac commercials differently from a middle-class consumer.

Clarity of message content also influences decoding. Usually, as symbolism increases, clarity decreases. Some ambiguous messages are "We circle the world (MasterCard)," "Out front. Pulling away (Goodyear)," "Think what we can do for you (Bank of America)," and "A powerful part of your life (Westinghouse)." Clearer messages are "Now is the closest thing to a tar-free cigarette" and "C&C is half the price of Coke and Pepsi."

Finally, *subliminal advertising* is a highly controversial type of promotion because it does not enable a consumer to consciously decode a message. In subliminal advertising, visual or verbal messages are presented so quickly that consumers do not see or hear them or remember them. Yet, consumers are expected to buy goods and services because of subconscious impulses. Ads of this type stress symbolism, and sometimes sexual themes, to increase sales. The overwhelming evidence shows that subliminal advertising cannot get consumers to buy products they do not want. In addition, subliminal ads are often misinterpreted; and clear, well-labeled ads are much more effective.[14] In the U.S., self-regulation by advertising associations (such as the National Association of Broadcasters) has all but eliminated subliminal ads.

In decoding, the audience translates the message sent by the source.

Subliminal advertising aims at the consumer's subconscious.

Audience

The *audience* is the object of the source's message. In most marketing situations, the audience is the target market. However, the source may also want to communicate an idea, build an image, or provide information to stockholders, consumer groups, independent media, the public, or government officials.

The types of communication channels used by a firm depend on the size and dispersion of the audience, demographic and life-style audience traits, and the availability of media appropriate for the audience. The total communication process must be keyed to the audience.

The findings of a 1983 survey of the American public show that[15]

The *audience* is usually the target market; but it can also be investors, government officials, or others.

1. 88 per cent feel the overall quality of advertising is excellent, good, or fair. 9 per cent feel it is poor.
2. 44 per cent believe advertising is not generally honest or trustworthy.
3. Newspapers provide the most information regarding day-to-day purchases. Personal communication is more important for major purchases.

[14] See Timothy E. Moore, "Subliminal Advertising: What You See Is What You Get," *Journal of Marketing,* Vol. 46 (Spring 1982), pp. 37-47; and Eric J. Zanot, J. David Pincus, and E. Joseph Lamp, "Public Perceptions of Subliminal Advertising," *Journal of Advertising,* Vol. 12 (Number 2, 1983), pp. 39–45.
[15] Nancy Millman, "Consumers Rate Advertising High," *Advertising Age* (October 24, 1983), pp. 1, 18.

One California car dealer has found the right way to interact with his customers and is representative of the new orientation of business:

My sales techniques and service philosophies are founded upon the ways I'd like to be treated if I was buying a car. I've adopted a more consumer-oriented approach to selling cars. There was a time when high-pressure selling and leader ads worked. But today you must have respect for the intelligence of the consumer.[16]

Feedback

Feedback consists of purchase, attitude, or nonpurchase responses to a message.

Feedback is the response the audience makes to the firm's message. It may take one of three forms: purchase, attitude change, or nonpurchase. A company must understand that each of these three alternative responses is possible and develop a procedure for monitoring them.

The most desirable kind of feedback occurs when a consumer purchases a product or service after communications with or from the firm. This means the message is effective enough to stimulate a transaction.

A second type of feedback takes place when the firm determines that its promotional efforts have elicited a favorable attitude change toward the company or its offerings by the audience. For new products or services, favorable attitudes must be created prior to consumer purchases (awareness→favorable attitude→purchase). For existing products, consumers may have bought a competing brand before the message was received or be temporarily out of funds. The generation of favorable attitudes in these consumers may lead to future purchases.

The least desirable feedback is when the audience neither purchases an item nor develops a favorable attitude. This may happen for one of several reasons: no recall of message, contentment with present product, message not believed, or no differential advantage shown.

Following are selected techniques for monitoring or obtaining feedback. Several of these techniques can be combined:

- Pretest/posttest—Sales or attitudes are examined prior to new promotional effort, re-examined after effort; differences are then studied. Example—Prior to ad, 68% liked product; after ad, 75% liked product; favorable attitude increase: 7%.
- Aided recall—Recall of promotional effort is based on multiple-choice questions or selection of ads seen from a list. This method inflates recall but approximates a consumer's actual shopping experience. Example—Which products did you see advertised in yesterday's paper? (a) *Reader's Digest*, (b) Levitz Furniture, (c) Close-up toothpaste.
- Unaided recall—Recall of promotional effort is based on open-ended questions. This method measures true recall but places too much emphasis on unaided memory. Example—Which products did you see advertised in yesterday's paper?
- Physiological test—Reactions to promotional efforts are measured through skin responses and eye movements. Example—Consumer is hooked by electrode to a monitor and watches a commercial; physical responses are tracked.

[16] "Car Dealer Increases Sales with Honest Ads, Respect for Shoppers," *Marketing News* (August 24, 1979), p. 12.

- Monadic test—Single commercial or sales presentation is evaluated. Example—Consumer is shown an ad of a brand of shoes and asked to comment on it.
- Comparison test—Two or more commercials or sales presentations are evaluated at the same time. Example—Consumer listens to the sales presentations of both Bob and Don and is then asked to comment on them.

Noise

Noise is interference at any stage along the channel of communication. Because of noise, messages are sometimes encoded or decoded incorrectly or weak responses are made. Examples of noise are

Noise may interfere with the communication process at any stage.

- A telephone call interrupting the company's marketing manager while he or she is developing a promotional theme.
- A salesperson misidentifying a product and giving the wrong sales presentation.
- An impatient customer interrupting a sales presentation.
- Conversation between two consumers during a television commercial.
- A direct-mail ad being opened by the wrong person.
- A consumer seeing a sale on a competitor's item while waiting at a supermarket checkout counter.

Promotion Planning

After a firm has gained an understanding of the communication process, it is ready to develop an overall promotion plan. The plan consists of three parts: objectives, budget, and mix of elements.

Objectives

The objectives of promotion can be divided into two general categories: stimulating demand and enhancing company image.

In setting specific demand objectives (such as increasing sales by 12 per cent through a $1 million promotion campaign), a firm should understand the ***hierarchy-of-effects model.*** This model outlines the intermediate and long-term promotional objectives the firm should pursue: awareness, knowledge, liking, preference, conviction, and purchase.[17] Obtaining a consumer purchase is based on achieving each of the steps before it. Figure 15-6 shows the hierarchy-of-effects model and relates it to promotional objectives and tools.

The *hierarchy-of-effects model* outlines demand objectives.

By using the hierarchy-of-effects model, a firm can move from informing to persuading and then to reminding consumers about its offerings. At the early

[17] Robert J. Lavidge and Gary A. Steiner, "A Model for Predictive Measurements of Advertising Effectiveness," *Journal of Marketing*, Vol. 25 (October 1961), pp. 59–62. See also, Ivan L. Preston, "The Association Model of the Advertising Communication Process, *Journal of Advertising*, Vol. 11 (Number 2, 1982), pp. 3–15; and Robert E. Smith and William R. Swinyard, "Information Response Models: An Integrated Approach," *Journal of Marketing*, Vol. 46 (Winter 1982), pp. 81–93.

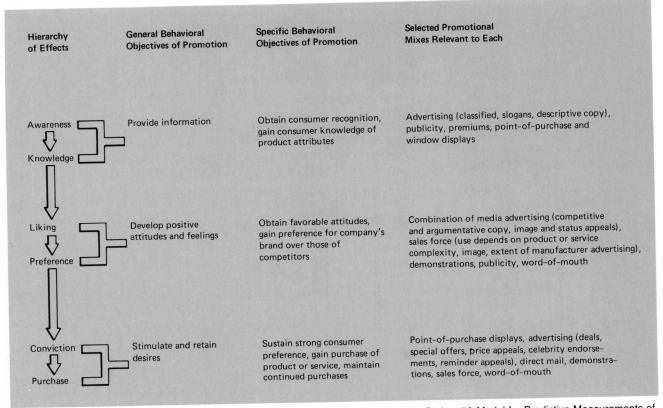

**Figure 15-6
Promotion and the
Hierarchy-of-Effects
Model**

Source: Adapted from Robert Lavidge and Garry A. Steiner "A Model for Predictive Measurements of Advertising Effectiveness," *Journal of Marketing,* Vol. 25 (October 1961), p. 61. Reprinted by permission of the American Marketing Association.

Primary demand is for a product category; *selective demand* is for a brand.

stages of the model, when the product or service is little known, primary demand should be sought. ***Primary demand*** is consumer demand for a product category, such as canned peaches or dietetic candy. At later stages, when preference is the goal, selective demand should be sought. ***Selective demand*** is consumer demand for a particular brand of a product. Sometimes, companies use the hierarchy-of-effects model to revitalize interest in mature products. As an example, Campbell uses the theme "soup is good food" to increase overall consumer demand for soup. It advertises specific brands of soup, such as Vegetable Beef, to generate selective demand for Campbell products. See Figure 15-7.

Institutional advertising is involved with image objectives.

Enhancing company image is the second major promotional objective. In this case firms utilize ***institutional advertising,*** for which the goal is improved corporate image and not the sales of products or services. About one half of the large companies in the U.S. engage in some form of institutional advertising.[18] These are two illustrations of institutional advertising:

● TRW runs a number of television and magazine ads focusing on its technological innovations in electronics and space systems, industrial and energy projects, and automotive products. All of these ads have the phrase "Tomorrow is taking

---

[18] Thomas F. Garbett, "When to Advertise Your Company," *Harvard Business Review,* Vol. 60 (March–April 1982), pp. 100–106.

Reprinted by permission.

shape at a company called TRW.'' In 1984, TRW planned to spend $7 million on this campaign in order to ''create [a] friendly image for a diverse multinational [company] with 85,000 employees in 25 countries, which doesn't market consumer products or services, which does a great deal of defense-related work for the U.S. government, and is located in Cleveland.''[19] See Figure 15-8.

- Gulf Oil has sponsored a series of National Geographic specials on public television since 1975. By the end of 1985, Gulf's cumulative investment in the production and advertising of these specials will exceed $36 million. Gulf's hope ''is that opinion leaders will think better of Gulf Oil as a result of our support . . . . According to a national opinion poll, Gulf's underwriting of these specials has been a leading factor in increased positive attitudes toward the company.''[20]

[19] Jack Hafferkamp, ''TRW Shapes Up Today for Tomorrow,'' *Advertising Age* (January 23, 1984), p. M-14.
[20] Kevin Higgins, ''Underwrite Bolsters the Image of Gulf Among Opinion Leaders,'' *Marketing News* (April 1, 1983), p. 9.

Figure 15-8
Institutional Advertising by TRW Inc.

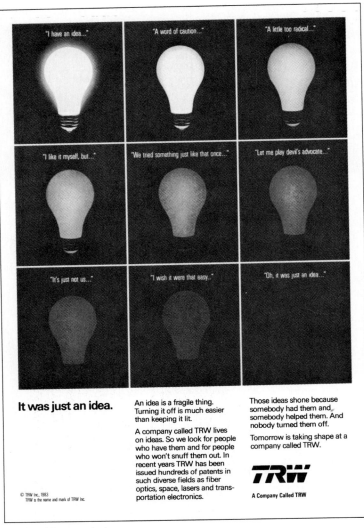

Reprinted by permission.

Promotion Budget

The different techniques for setting a total promotion budget are *all you can afford, incremental, competitive parity, percentage of sales,* and *objective and task.*

There are five alternative techniques for setting a total promotion budget: all you can afford, incremental, competitive parity, percentage of sales, and objective and task. The selection of a technique depends on the requirements and constraints of the individual firm. Table 15-3 illustrates each method.

In the ***all-you-can-afford technique,*** the firm first allocates funds for every element of marketing except promotion. Whatever funds are left over are placed in a promotion budget. This method is the weakest of the five and is used most frequently by small, production-oriented companies. Its shortcomings are little importance given to promotion, expenditures not linked to objectives, and the risk of having no promotion budget if no funds are left over.

With the ***incremental technique,*** the company bases its new budget on previous expenditures. A percentage is either added to or subtracted from this year's budget in order to determine next year's budget. This technique is also used by small firms. It offers these advantages: provision of a reference point, a budget based on a firm's feelings about past successes and future trends, and easy calculations. Important disadvantages do exist: budget size is rarely tied to objectives, "gut feelings" are overemphasized, and there is difficulty in evaluating success or failure.

In the *competitive parity technique,* the company's promotion budget is raised or lowered according to the actions of competitors. It is useful to both large and small firms. The benefits of the method are that it provides a reference point, it is market-oriented, and it is conservative. The shortcomings are that it is a following and not a leadership position, it is difficult to obtain competitors' promotion data, and there is the assumption of a similarity between the firm and its competitors (years in business, products or services, image, prices). The last point is particularly important; firms usually have basic differences from competitors.

With the *percentage-of-sales technique,* the company ties the promotion budget to sales revenue. In the first year a promotion-to-sales ratio is established. During succeeding years, the per cent of promotion to sales dollars remains constant. The benefits of this procedure are the use of sales as a base, adaptability, and the interrelationship of sales and promotion. The weaknesses are that there is no relationship to objectives, promotion is used as a sales follower and not a sales leader, and automatic promotion decreases are applied in poor sales periods (when increases could be beneficial). This technique provides too large a budget during high sales periods and too small a budget during low sales periods.

Under the *objective-and-task technique,* the firm clearly outlines its promotional objectives, determines the tasks needed to satisfy those objectives, and then establishes the appropriate budget. It is the best of the five methods. The advantages are that objectives are clearly stated, expenditures are related to the completion of goal-oriented tasks, it offers adaptability, and it is relatively easy to evalu-

Technique	Illustration
All you can afford	The firm has a $110,000 marketing budget: $50,000 is allocated for distribution costs, $40,000 for product testing, and $8,000 for consumer surveys. The remaining $12,000 is left for advertising, sales force, and sales promotions.
Incremental	The current year's promotion budget is $30,000. Next year is expected to be a good year; therefore, 10 percent is added to the budget. The new budget is $33,000.
Competitive parity	The current year's promotion budget is $50,000. The leading competitor is expected to increase its promotion budget by 2 per cent. The firm follows this strategy and establishes a budget of $51,000 for next year.
Percentage of sales	The promotion-to-sales ratio is 20 per cent (one dollar of promotion for every five dollars of sales). Next year's sales are forecast to be $1 million. The promotion budget will be $200,000.
Objective and task	The firm has three goals for next year: increase sales of brand A by 5 per cent, introduce brand B and attain recognition by 15 per cent of the target market, and improve the public's positive rating of the company from 60 to 75 per cent (based on a standardized attitude measure). The promotional tasks and tools needed to achieve these goals will result in a budget of $73,000.

Table 15-3
Illustrations of Promotional Budgeting Techniques

ate success or failure. The major weakness is the complexity of setting goals and specific tasks, especially for small companies. A recent industrial marketing survey found that 43 per cent of the respondents use the objective-and-task method, while another 39 per cent use that method in conjunction with the percentage-of-sales technique.[21]

The *S-curve effect* and *marginal return* should be understood.

While a promotion budget is being developed, the firm should consider the S-curve effect and marginal return. The **S-curve effect** occurs if the sales of a product rise sharply after it is introduced because of a heavy initial promotion effort (ads, coupons, samples, etc.), drop slightly as promotional support is reduced, and then rise again as positive word-of-mouth communication takes place. A more balanced budget may be able to minimize the S-curve effect. The **marginal return** is the amount of sales each increment of promotion will generate. When a product is new, the marginal return is high because the market is expanding. As a product becomes established, the marginal return is lower, because each additional increment of promotion will have less of an impact on sales (the target market is saturated). Figure 15-9 shows how the S-curve effect and marginal return operate.

Promotion Mix

The *promotion mix* is a combination of advertising, publicity, personal selling, and/or sales promotion.

After establishing a total promotion budget, the company must determine its promotion mix. The **promotion mix** is the overall and specific communication program of the firm, consisting of a combination of advertising, publicity, personal selling, and/or sales promotion.

It is rare for a company to use only one type of promotion—for example, a mail-order firm relying on advertising, a hospital on publicity, or a flea market vendor on personal selling. In most cases a mix of promotion types is used. For example, General Foods has a sales force that visits every supermarket in which its products are stocked, advertises in newspapers and magazines and on television, and distributes cents-off coupons. IBM has a large technical sales force, advertises heavily in business and trade publications, and sends representatives to trade shows.

It is important to remember that each type of promotion serves a different function, and therefore complements the other types. Advertisements appeal to large audiences and create awareness; without them, the personal sales effort is much more difficult, time consuming, and expensive. Publicity provides credible information to a wide audience, but its content and timing cannot be controlled by the firm. Personal selling offers one-to-one contact, flexibility, and the ability to close sales; without it, the initial interest caused by ads would be wasted. Sales promotion stimulates short-run sales and supplements advertising and selling.

The promotion mix varies by type of company. A small firm is restricted in the kinds of ads it can afford or use efficiently. It would emphasize personal selling. A large firm covers a sizable geographic area and would stress advertising as well as personal selling. A nonprofit firm would seek as much publicity as possible. A consumer company would feature the advertising of its brands. An industrial company would count on a major personal selling effort.

In general, these factors should be considered when developing a promotion mix:

[21] "'84 Ad Budgets Leap Nearly 20%," *Business Marketing* (January 1984), p. 8.

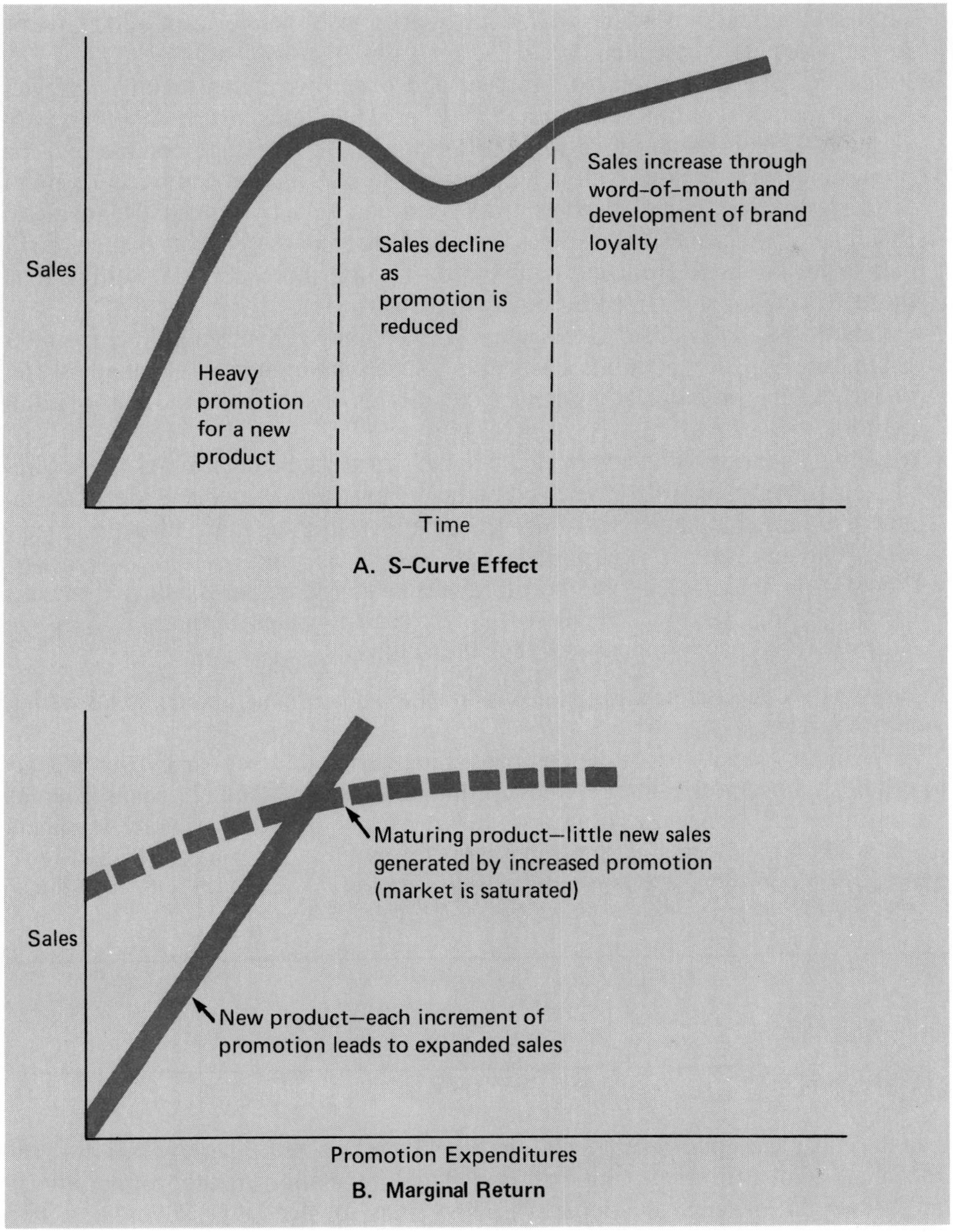

Figure 15-9
The S-Curve Effect and Marginal Return

Sales

Heavy promotion for a new product

Sales decline as promotion is reduced

Sales increase through word-of-mouth and development of brand loyalty

Time

A. S-Curve Effect

Sales

Maturing product—little new sales generated by increased promotion (market is saturated)

New product—each increment of promotion leads to expanded sales

Promotion Expenditures

B. Marginal Return

- Consumers—A large, dispersed target market favors advertising; a small, concentrated market favors personal selling. Organizational consumers require more personal attention than final consumers. Channel members often ask for promotional support (cooperative advertising, displays, coupons). Some consumers are more persuadable than others. Some react poorly to personal selling and prefer self-service. Media use can be determined through demographic profiles.
- Budget—A limited budget eliminates advertising via TV or magazines and directs efforts at personal selling and local newspapers. A large budget makes

full use of all tools possible. After the budget is set, its per cent allocation by promotion type is needed.

- Products—Highly technical (complex) and expensive items require a greater level of personal selling than simple, inexpensive items which depend on advertising. As products move through the life cycle, message content and the promotional mix change. Initial emphasis is on information and the creation of primary demand. Then, persuasion is used and selective demand generated. Finally, reminder messages are used to sustain demand. Products that are difficult to differentiate from the competition require more personal selling than those with distinct differential advantages.
- Competition—Each firm establishes its own long-run promotion mix, after examining the competition, based on its particular needs. Companies frequently match short-run advertising expenditures or special promotions of competitors.
- Media—The media that are available to the firm must be determined (for example, cigarettes cannot be advertised on television). Some media (such as magazines) require the placement of advertisements well in advance of their appearance. Others (such as newspapers) need short lead time.
- Place of purchase—Distribution through discount stores or direct mail means extensive advertising and self-service purchases. Sales through full-service stores combine advertising and personal selling.

Figure 15-10 contrasts promotion mixes in which advertising and personal selling would dominate.

It is the responsibility of the company's marketing director (or vice-president) to establish a promotion budget and a promotion mix and then allocate resources and effort to each aspect of promotion. In large firms, there are separate managers for advertising, personal selling, and sales promotion. They report to and have their efforts coordinated by the marketing director.

Legal Environment of Promotion

Federal and local governments and agencies have enacted a variety of laws and rules that affect a firm's promotional mix. These regulations range from prohibiting billboards in many locations to issuing fines for deceptive advertising and sales practices. The major federal agency involved with promotion is the Federal Trade Commission. Table 15-4 outlines the impact of the legal environment on promotion.[22]

---

[22] A substantial number of articles have been written on the legal environment of promotion. For example, see Mary Jane Sheffet, "An Experimental Investigation of the Documentaton of Advertising Claims," *Journal of Advertising*, Vol. 12 (Number 1, 1983), pp. 19–29; John S. Healy and Harold H. Kassarjian, "Advertising Substantiation and Advertiser Response: A Content Analysis of Magazine Advertisements," *Journal of Marketing*, Vol. 47 (Winter 1983), pp. 107–117; Gary M. Armstrong, George R. Franke, and Frederick A. Russ, "The Effects of Corrective Advertising on Company Image," *Journal of Advertising*, Vol. 11 (Number 4, 1982), pp. 39–47; and Dorothy Cohen, "Unfairness in Advertising Revisited," *Journal of Marketing*, Vol. 46 (Winter 1982), pp. 73–80.

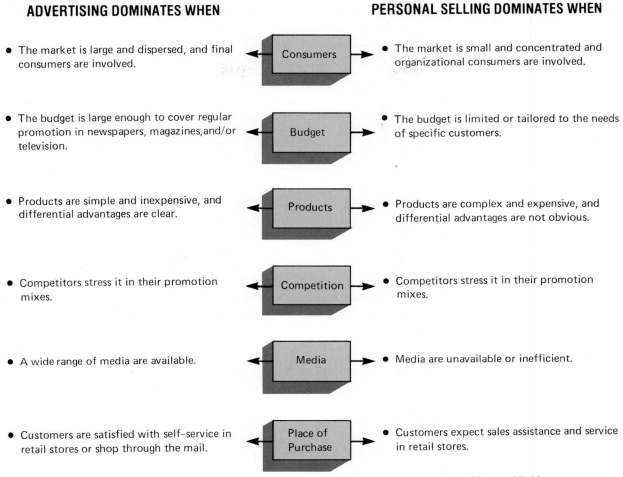

ADVERTISING DOMINATES WHEN

- The market is large and dispersed, and final consumers are involved.
- The budget is large enough to cover regular promotion in newspapers, magazines, and/or television.
- Products are simple and inexpensive, and differential advantages are clear.
- Competitors stress it in their promotion mixes.
- A wide range of media are available.
- Customers are satisfied with self-service in retail stores or shop through the mail.

PERSONAL SELLING DOMINATES WHEN

- The market is small and concentrated and organizational consumers are involved.
- The budget is limited or tailored to the needs of specific customers.
- Products are complex and expensive, and differential advantages are not obvious.
- Competitors stress it in their promotion mixes.
- Media are unavailable or inefficient.
- Customers expect sales assistance and service in retail stores.

(boxes: Consumers, Budget, Products, Competition, Media, Place of Purchase)

Figure 15-10
Contrasting Promotion Mixes

There are five major ways in which the legal environment protects consumers and competing firms against unsatisfactory promotion practices: full disclosure, substantiation, cease-and-desist orders, corrective advertising, and fines.

Full disclosure requires that all data necessary for a consumer to make a safe and informed decision be provided. For example, Alka Seltzer must mention that its regular product contains aspirin, and diet products must note that they include saccharin. In this way consumers are able to assess the overall benefits and risks of a purchase.

Substantiation requires a firm to be able to prove all the claims it makes. This means thorough testing and evidence of performance are need prior to making claims. For example, a tire company that says its brand will last for 70,000 miles must be able to prove this assertion with test results.

Under a *cease-and-desist order,* a firm must discontinue deceptive practices and modify its promotion messages. It is not forced to admit guilt or pay fines. For example, Sears agreed not to use bait-and-switch practices (whereby sales personnel try to pressure consumers to buy high-priced goods instead of heavily advertised low-priced items) to sell large home appliances.

Full disclosure, substantiation, cease-and-desist orders, corrective advertising, and *fines* are major governmental limits on promotion activities.

Table 15-4
Legal Environment of Promotion

Factor	Legal Environment
Access	Cigarettes, liquor, and billboards have restricted access. Legal, medical, and other professions have been given the right to advertise.
Deception	It is illegal to use messages that would mislead reasonable consumers and potentially harm them.
Bait-and-switch	It is illegal to lure a customer to a store with an advertisement for a low-priced item and then, after the customer is in the store, to use a strong sales pitch intentionally to switch the shopper to a more expensive item.
Direct-to-home sales	Many locales restrict direct-to-home sales practices. A cooling-off period allows a consumer to cancel a direct-to-home sale up to three days after an agreement is reached.
Promotional allowances	Promotional allowances must be available to channel members in a fair and equitable manner.
Comparative advertisements	Claims must be substantiated. The Federal Trade Commission favors naming competitors in ads (not citing a competitor as brand X).
Testimonials or endorsements	The celebrity or expert endorser must actually use the product if advertisements make such a claim.

Corrective advertising requires a firm to run new advertisements to correct the false impressions left by previous ones. For example, Listerine was told to spend $10.2 million on advertising to correct previous messages claiming the product was a cold remedy. Listerine decided to run the ads after learning that it would not be able to continue any advertising without them.

The last major remedy is *fines,* which are dollar penalties levied on a firm for deceptive promotion. A company may be required to pay a large sum to the government, as in the case of STP, or forced to provide consumer refunds, as in the case of mail-order firms who do not meet delivery dates. STP was fined $700,000 for misrepresenting the effectiveness of its product in raising auto gas mileage.

In addition to government restrictions, the media place voluntary controls on promotion. For example, the National Association of Broadcasters monitors the ads placed on television and radio. General groups, such as the Better Business Bureau, also contribute to self-regulation.

In 1983, the FTC made two significant changes in the way it regulates promotion. First, it made it easier for companies to substantiate claims made in ads and sales presentations by requiring less evidence in some cases.[23] Second, it altered the definition of deceptive advertising to include only claims that would mislead a "reasonable" consumer and result in "injury" (physical, financial, or other).[24]

[23] Jeanne Saddler, "FTC Easing Rules Requiring Firms to Support Ad Claims," *Wall Street Journal* (July 21, 1983), p. 29.
[24] Richard L. Gordon, "FTC Tells Congress Ad Deception Plans," *Advertising Age* (October 24, 1983), pp. 1, 98; and "Does the New FTC Deception Policy Fill the Bill?" *Advertising Age* (February 13, 1984), pp. M-22–M-28.

Criticisms and Defenses of Promotion

Promotion is probably the most heavily criticized area of marketing. Following are a number of these criticisms and the defenses of marketers to them:

Promotion controversies center on materialism, honesty, prices, symbolism, and expectations.

Detractors Feel Promotion	Marketers Answer That Promotion
Creates an obsession with material possessions.	Responds to consumer desires for material possessions. In an affluent society, these items are plentiful and paid for with discretionary earnings.
Is basically dishonest.	Is basically honest. The great majority of companies abide by all laws and set strict self-regulations. A few dishonest firms give a bad name to all.
Raises the prices of products and services.	Holds down prices. By increasing consumer demand, promotion enables manufacturers to utilize mass production and reduce per unit costs. Employment is higher when demand is stimulated.
Overemphasizes symbolism and status.	Differentiates products and services through symbolic and status appeals. Consumers desire distinctiveness and product benefits.
Causes excessively high expectations.	Keeps expectations high; it thereby sustains consumer motivation and worker productivity in order to satisfy expectations.

In 1984, the American Association of Advertising Agencies began a campaign to "change consumer perceptions that 'advertising makes people buy things they don't want, increases the costs of goods, and helps sell inferior products.'"[25] See Figure 15-11.

Summary

Promotion informs, persuades, or reminds people about a firm's products, services, ideas, community involvement, or impact on society. Its major elements are advertising, publicity, personal selling, and sales promotion.

Through the channel of communication, a source sends a message to its audience. The channel consists of source, encoding, message, medium, decoding,

[25] Nancy Millman, "Four A's Tackles Ad Image with Ads," *Advertising Age* (March 12, 1984), pp. 1, 62.

**Figure 15-11
A Strong Defense of
Promotion**

THIS AD IS FULL OF LIES.

LIE #1: ADVERTISING MAKES YOU BUY THINGS YOU DON'T WANT.
Advertising is often accused of inducing people to buy things against their will.

But when was the last time you returned home from the local shopping mall with a bag full of things you had absolutely no use for? The truth is, nothing short of a pointed gun can get *anybody* to spend money on something he or she doesn't want.

No matter how effective an ad is, you and millions of other American consumers make your own decisions. If you don't believe it, ask someone who knows firsthand about the limits of advertising. Like your local Edsel dealer.

LIE #2: ADVERTISING MAKES THINGS COST MORE.
Since advertising costs money, it's natural to assume it costs *you* money. But the truth is that advertising often brings prices down.

Consider the electronic calculator, for example. In the late 1960s, advertising created a mass market for calculators. That meant more of them needed to be produced, which brought the price of producing each calculator down. Competition spurred by advertising brought the price down still further.

As a result, the same product that used to cost hundreds of dollars now costs as little as five dollars.

LIE #3: ADVERTISING HELPS BAD PRODUCTS SELL.
Some people worry that good advertising sometimes covers up for bad products.

But nothing can make you like a bad product. So, while advertising can help convince you to try something once, it can't make you buy it twice. If you don't like what you've bought, you won't buy it again. And if enough people feel the same way, the product dies on the shelf.

In other words, the only thing advertising can do for a bad product is help you find out it's a bad product. And you take it from there.

LIE #4: ADVERTISING IS A WASTE OF MONEY.
Some people wonder why we don't just put all the money spent on advertising directly into our national economy.

The answer is, we already do.

Advertising helps products sell, which holds down prices, which helps sales even more. It creates jobs. It informs you about all the products available and helps you compare them. And it stimulates the competition that produces new and better products at reasonable prices.

If all that doesn't convince you that advertising is important to our economy, you might as well stop reading.

Because on top of everything else, advertising has paid for a large part of the magazine you're now holding.

And that's the truth.

ADVERTISING.
ANOTHER WORD FOR FREEDOM OF CHOICE.
American Association of Advertising Agencies

Reprinted by permission.

audience, feedback, and noise. The source is the company, independent institution, or opinion leader that seeks to present a message to an audience. In choosing a source, credibility, expertise, and other factors must be considered.

Encoding is the process by which a thought or an idea is translated into a message by the source. The message is the combination of words and symbols transmitted to the audience; it must be presented in a desirable, exclusive, and believable manner. Timing must be carefully planned. The medium is the personal or nonpersonal channel used to convey a message. Decoding is the process through which the message sent by the source is translated by the audience.

The audience is the object of the source's message. Although it is usually the target market, it may also be stockholders, consumer groups, independent media, the public, or government officials. Feedback is the response the audience makes to the firm's message: purchase, attitude change, or nonpurchase. Noise is the interference at any stage along the channel of communication.

Promotion objectives may be demand- or image-oriented. Demand objectives should parallel the hierarchy-of-effects model, moving from awareness to purchase. Primary demand is total product demand; selective demand is for the company's brand. Institutional advertising is used to enhance company image.

There are five methods for setting a promotion budget: all you can afford, incremental, competitive parity, percentage of sales, and objective and task. The weakest is the all-you-can-afford technique. The best is the objective-and-task technique. The S-curve effect and marginal return should be considered when setting a budget.

The promotion mix is the overall and specific communication program of the firm, combining advertising, publicity, personal selling, and/or sales promotion. Consumer, budget, product, competition, media, and place-of-purchase factors should be considered in the development of a promotion mix.

There are many laws and rules affecting promotion. The major ways unsatisfactory promotion is guarded against are full disclosure, substantiation, cease-and-desist orders, corrective advertising, and fines. Critics are strong in their complaints about promotion. Marketers are equally firm in their defenses.

Questions for Discussion

1. What is word-of-mouth? Why is it so important?
2. Distinguish among advertising, publicity, personal selling, and sales promotion.
3. Evaluate the use of Frank Borman as the company spokesperson for Eastern Airlines. Is it a good long-run strategy for Borman to continue as spokesperson? Why or why not?
4. Analyze the use of John McEnroe (the tennis star) as a celebrity endorser of Bic razors.
5. Distinguish between the multistep flow and two-step flow of communication.
6. Comment on Prudential's ''most of us don't get a second chance'' life-insurance commercials that use a strong fear appeal.
7. Give a recent example of a comparative message and evaluate it.
8. What are the advantages and disadvantages of using the same message (theme) for an extended period of time?
9. Describe a recent advertisement that you saw which could be misunderstood by the audience.
10. What audience attributes should be considered in using the channel of communication?
11. A consumer listens to a sales presentation but does not make a purchase. Has the presentation failed? Explain your answer.
12. Explain the hierarchy-of-effects model. How is it related to demand objectives?
13. Why are many companies likely to reduce promotion expenditures after a new product is introduced successfully? Is this a proper approach? Explain your answer.
14. Develop a promotion mix for
    a. A local movie theater.
    b. Burger King.

c. International Harvester (tractor division).

d. Revlon (cosmetic products).

15. Comment on this statement: "Full disclosure only confuses consumers by giving them too much information. It also raises costs."

16. Evaluate the criticisms and defenses of promotion.

Case 1 Vermont Castings: A Stove Maker's Promotion Strategy*

Vermont Castings Inc. is a manufacturer of wood- and coal-burning stoves. Founded in 1975, the company now sells more than 50,000 stoves (priced at $400 to $800) each year. It accomplishes this despite almost no distribution in retail stores and a sales force operating only in Randolph, Vermont, where the firm is located. Vermont Castings Inc.'s success is due to a well-organized promotion effort and extensive referrals by satisfied customers.

The company opened just after the 1973–1974 oil embargo, at a time when consumers began purchasing stoves for heating their homes. Initial advertising was placed in New England magazines and drew tremendous responses. Expanded direct mail advertising eliminated the need for retailers and a field sales force. Instead, telephone sales personnel were used to handle all inquiries and resolve outstanding questions. Past customers helped out by providing leads.

To maintain customer loyalty and generate further referrals, Vermont Castings Inc. publishes a quarterly newsletter; each customer is given a lifetime subscription. The newsletter reports on such topics as the manufacturing of stoves, employee profiles, recreational activities, letters from stove owners, and advice on stove maintenance. The firm also makes customers feel welcome at its Randolph showroom by giving away apples or zucchini, and selling maple syrup made by employees in their free time.

Not long ago, the company sponsored a picnic attended by 10,000 people, from as far way as Michigan and Texas. The picnic included plant tours, lectures on wood and coal burning, square dancing, barbequed chicken, ballooning, woodchopping demonstrations, and lots of conversation among stove owners. Said Duncan Syme, the firm's founder, "When was the last time your refrigerator maker invited you to a picnic?"

Occasionally, Vermont Castings has problems. For example, the company was unable to fill customer orders when it first added coal-burning stoves; the stoves were not ready for shipment until the spring (customers had been promised winter delivery). Another time, a customer drove from New Hampshire to Vermont to pick up a stove that was not yet ready, after receiving a letter from the company stating that it was. To accommodate the customer, Vermont Castings paid his 200-mile gas bill.

---

* The data in this case are drawn from William L. Bulkeley, "Wood-Stove Maker Has Hot Love Affair with Its Customers," *Wall Street Journal* (September 9, 1981), pp. 1, 25; and Anne Bagamery, "The Problems of Growing Up," *Forbes* (January 16, 1984), p. 55.

QUESTIONS

1. Evaluate the promotion strategy of Vermont Castings.
2. Why would customers buy through the mail or drive to Vermont if they could purchase a stove locally that is made by a competitor?
3. Will Vermont Castings be able to expand if it retains its current promotion strategy? Explain your answer.
4. Since stoves are extremely durable, why does Vermont Castings spend so much effort communicating with people who have already bought them? Rather than a "lifetime subscriber" newsletter, wouldn't the firm be better off placing magazine ads aimed at prospective customers?

Case 2 DuPont: A Promotion Strategy Aimed at Final Consumers[†]

Although DuPont is one of the leading companies in the U.S. (consistently ranking among the top ten industrial firms according to *Fortune* magazine), its product mix is one that does not easily lend itself to final consumer promotion. DuPont's most important products, such as nylon and dacron polyester fibers, are used in the production of clothing, carpets, etc. It is the clothing manufacturers and others who promote extensively and achieve final consumer loyalty.

Until recently, DuPont did little communicating directly with final consumers. Then, in 1983, DuPont revised its promotion strategy. As one analyst observed, "There is a reawakening to the role consumer-oriented advertising can have. There may also be a fear that consumer awareness of DuPont brands has dropped."

DuPont's final-consumer promotion efforts included

- Giving away 50,000 home computers to consumers who purchased carpeting woven with DuPont nylon.
- Sponsoring a tennis tournament to display apparel made with DuPont fibers.
- Offering Acapulco honeymoon trips to sweepstakes winners to feature suitcases made with DuPont fibers.
- Expanding the advertising budget substantially.

Some experts believe DuPont waited too long to re-orient its promotion strategy, and thereby allowed Monsanto, Celanese, Allied, the Wool Bureau, and Cotton Inc. (representing cotton growers) to move ahead in final consumer recognition and loyalty. Furthermore, Celanese was able to get its polyester stretch yarn used in Levi and Lee denim jeans, a product category DuPont was having difficulty in penetrating. DuPont planned a $1 million spring 1984 advertising campaign to obtain greater acceptance for its "Denimotion," a stretch polyester-cotton blend.

[†] The data in this case are drawn from Ronald Alsop, "DuPont Steps Up Promotions to Prove Its Selling Ability," *Wall Street Journal* (December 1, 1983), p. 31.

As one DuPont executive acknowledged, "A lot of our products are maturing, and we have to be better marketers."

QUESTIONS

1. Evaluate DuPont's giving away 50,000 home computers to consumers buying carpeting with DuPont fibers.
2. Describe at least five promotion objectives for DuPont.
3. Should DuPont use comparative advertising? Why or why not?
4. How can DuPont measure the effectiveness of its final-consumer promotion strategy?

Chapter 16

Advertising and Publicity

After nearly 8 years of development and an investment of $100 million, Stouffer's introduced its Lean Cuisine line of frozen low-calorie foods in 1981. Lean Cuisine features nutritious, tasty entrees that have less than 300 calories each. This enables consumers to eat a salad or vegetable with a Lean Cuisine entree and still adhere to the 500 calories recommended for the main daily meal by the American Dietetic Association.

To support Lean Cuisine, Stouffer's enacted a detailed advertising and publicity campaign:

- Test marketing was conducted in Cleveland, Cincinnati, and Columbus, Ohio; and in Omaha, Denver, and Philadelphia. $2 million was spent on television, print, and direct mail advertising in these markets.

461

- When Lean Cuisine was launched nationally during September 1981 to April 1982, $7 million was allocated to advertising. Ads were placed in magazines and newspapers, coupons were mailed to consumers, and television commercials were heavily used. Radio was not employed: "Taste kind of goes along with the sense of sight, and you can't show food on the radio."
- Advertising aimed at retailers was used in every market Lean Cuisine entered. Food retailers were also invited to formal dinners that served Lean Cuisine.
- Stouffer's employed three 2-person "Lean Teams," consisting of nutritionists, former woman marathoners, etc., who toured the country. In addition, 300,000 free copies of the booklet "On the Way to Being Lean" were distributed to consumers and medical professionals.
- Publicity for Lean Cuisine was received when "Lean Team" members appeared on local television and radio shows to discuss the product line. Newspaper and magazine articles describing Lean Cuisine were also written after interviews with "Lean Team" members.

During 1982, its first year in national distribution, Lean Cuisine sales were $125 million—in large part due to Stouffer's creative combination of advertising and publicity.[1] Figure 16-1 shows a recent advertisement for Lean Cuisine.

Overview

This chapter examines the two mass communication forms of promotion available to a firm, advertising and publicity. As defined in Chapter 15, advertising is the paid, nonpersonal presentation and promotion of ideas, goods, and services by an identified sponsor. The distinguishing features of advertising are that the firm pays for its message, a set format is delivered to the entire audience through mass media, the name of the sponsor is clearly presented, and the company controls the message.

Publicity is the nonpaid, nonpersonal presentation and promotion of ideas, goods, and services by an independent source. Its unique features are that the firm does not pay for a message, a set format is delivered to the entire audience through mass media, the message is presented by a source not affiliated with the company, and the independent source controls the message.

The differences between advertising and publicity are in part shown by the statement, "Advertising is paid for, publicity is prayed for."

---

[1] Kevin Higgins, "Meticulous Planning Pays Dividends at Stouffer's," *Marketing News* (October 28, 1983), pp. 1, 20.

Figure 16-1
Stouffer's Lean Cuisine

Reprinted by permission.

Scope and Importance of Advertising

It was estimated that more than $85 billion would be spent on advertising in 1984, an increase of almost 14 per cent from 1983 and about 56 per cent from 1980. Table 16-1 shows advertising expenditures by medium and the changing emphasis since 1960. The leading medium throughout this period has been newspapers;

The leading advertising media are newspapers, television, and direct mail.

Table 16-1
Advertising Expenditures, 1960–1984, by Medium (in Billions)

Medium	1960 $	1960 %	1970 $	1970 %	1980 $	1980 %	1984[a] $	1984[a] %
Newspapers	3.69	30.8	5.70	29.2	15.62	28.5	23.02	26.9
Magazines	.91	7.6	1.29	6.6	3.23	5.9	4.80	5.6
Farm publications	.07	0.6	.06	0.3	0.14	0.3	0.18	0.2
Television	1.63	13.6	3.60	18.4	11.33	20.7	18.21	21.3
Radio	.69	5.8	1.31	6.7	3.69	6.7	5.91	6.9
Direct mail	1.83	15.3	2.77	14.2	7.65	14.0	13.41	15.7
Business papers	.61	5.1	.74	3.8	1.69	3.1	2.16	2.5
Outdoor	.20	1.7	.23	1.2	0.61	1.1	0.90	1.1
Miscellaneous	2.34	19.5	3.85	19.7	10.79	19.7	16.83	19.7
Total	11.96[b]	100.0	19.55	100.0[b]	54.75	100.0	85.42	100.0[b]

[a] Estimated
[b] Rounding error
Source: McCann-Erickson, Inc., and *Advertising Age* (September 1979); (January 5, 1981), p. 56; and (January 2, 1984), p. 31.

however, newspapers' share of advertising has dropped substantially since 1960 (from 30.8 to 26.9 per cent). The second leading medium is now television, whose relative size has grown significantly since 1960 (from 13.6 to 21.3 per cent). After a fall in advertising share between 1960 and 1980, direct mail expenditures have risen significantly since 1980 (from 14.0 to 15.7 per cent). Radio's share of advertising has remained constant since 1970, up slightly from 1960 (6.9 per cent in 1984). Magazines, business papers, outdoor ads, and farm publications have all declined in relative importance since 1960. Miscellaneous advertising continues to represent a steady one fifth of expenditures.

Large firms spend a little more than 2 per cent of sales on advertising.

Advertising as a per cent of sales varies by industry and company. This is shown in Tables 16-2 and 16-3, which present data for selected industries and the 10 leading national advertisers in 1982. Overall, advertising as a per cent of sales is quite low. For example, during 1982, the 100 leading national advertisers in the U.S. (excluding the federal government) had advertising expenditures that averaged 2.3 per cent of their sales.[2]

Ads are most important for new and existing consumer products that have a low selling price.

A comprehensive study involving more than one thousand consumer and industrial products investigated the conditions under which a strong emphasis is placed on advertising. It found that standardized products with large markets and small average purchase amounts receive substantial advertising. Companies are likely to advertise if they have high gross margins, relatively small market shares, and/or surplus production capacity. In addition, new products and those sold through independent channel members obtain high advertising support.[3]

Another advertising research study, by Joseph E. Seagram & Sons and Time Inc., was conducted over a three-year period and involved 20,000 consumers. It found that[4]

- Behavior is easier to change than attitudes.
- Recall is a weak measure of advertising effectiveness.

[2] Marion L. Elmquist, "100 Leaders Parry Recession with Heavy Spending," *Advertising Age* (September 8, 1983), p. 1.
[3] Paul W. Farris and Robert D. Buzzell, "Why Advertising and Promotional Costs Vary: Some Cross-Sectional Analyses," *Journal of Marketing,* Vol. 43 (Fall 1979), p. 120.
[4] Stuart Emmrich, "Major Study Details Ads' Effect on Sales," *Advertising Age* (June 21, 1982), pp. 1, 80.

Industry	Advertising as a Per Cent of Sales
Mail order	15.7
Phonograph record	13.0
Toy	10.5
Perfume	8.4
Drug	8.2
Furniture store	7.2
Soap and detergent	6.8
Soft drink	5.7
Radio and television	4.0
Auto dealer	1.3
Chemical	1.2
Sheet metal	0.6
Savings and loan association	0.5
Aircraft	0.3
Hospital	0.3
Management consulting	0.2
Wholesale lumber	0.0

Table 16-2
Advertising in Selected Industries, 1982

Source: Schonfeld & Associates, "Advertising-to-Sales Ratios, 1982," *Advertising Age* (August 15, 1983), p. 20. Reprinted by permission of *Advertising Age.* Copyright 1983 by Crain Communications Inc.

- One ad can have a strong effect on brand awareness.
- It is easier to improve the favorable rating for a little-known product by extended advertising than a well-known product.
- Advertising effectiveness grows during extended campaigns.

A third research project, by A. C. Nielsen, examined 25 food and drugstore product categories. The leading brands in 17 of the categories had higher shares of total advertising expenditures in their categories than shares of sales. On average, a 10 per cent market share of sales required a 12 per cent share of advertising expenditures:

For some brands, this rule does not hold true, *but in each case inspection reveals a strong compensating factor.* This factor might be price, or quality that assures brand loyalty, or a strong ethical connotation, for example.[5]

[5] "Advertising and Sales Relationships: A Current Appraisal," *Nielsen Researcher* (Number 1, 1980), p. 9.

Company	Advertising Expenditures	Advertising as a Per Cent of Sales
Procter & Gamble	$726,100,000	5.8
Sears	631,100,000	2.1
General Motors	549,000,000	0.9
R. J. Reynolds	530,300,000	4.1
Philip Morris	501,700,000	4.3
General Foods	429,100,000	5.2
AT&T	373,600,000	0.6
K mart	366,100,000	2.2
Nabisco Brands	335,200,000	5.7
American Home Products	325,400,000	7.1

Table 16-3
Ten Leading U.S. Advertisers, 1982

Source: "100 Leaders: Advertising as a Per Cent of Sales," *Advertising Age* (September 8, 1983), p. 166. Reprinted by permission of *Advertising Age.* Copyright 1983 by Crain Communications Inc.

Characteristics of Advertising

Advertising attracts a large audience, has low per customer costs, offers many media, is controllable, may be surrounded by noncommercial information, and aids selling.

Advertising offers a number of positive and negative characteristics. On the positive side, advertising attracts a large and geographically dispersed market. For print media, circulation is supplemented by the passing of a copy from one reader to another.

The costs per viewer or listener are low. For example, a single television ad may cost $150,000 to air and reach thirty million viewers, a cost of $.005 per watcher (this figure includes media time only and not commercial production costs).

A broad range of media is available: from national television to local newspapers. Therefore, the objectives of a firm and its resources may be matched with the most appropriate medium.

The firm has control over all aspects of advertising, including message content, graphics, timing, size or length of message, and the demographics of the audience. In addition, a uniform message is delivered to all members of the audience. And, with print media, consumers can study and restudy messages.

With advertising, editorial content (a news story or segment of a television show) often surrounds an advertisement. This will increase readership or viewing, enhance the company's or product's image, and create the proper mood for the advertisement. It is for these reasons that firms seek specialized media or sections of media (such as the sports section of a newspaper for a men's clothing ad).

Advertising eases the way for personal selling by obtaining audience awareness and liking for a firm's brands. In addition, advertising both allows reduced-service and self-service retailers to operate and sustains an entire industry—mail order. With a pulling strategy, advertising enables a firm to show its channel members that consumer demand exists.

Advertising is inflexible and has high total costs, wasted audience segments, limited information, and weak feedback.

On the negative side, because advertising messages are standardized, they are inflexible. This makes it difficult to adapt to consumer needs and differences. Furthermore, questions consumers have about a product or service cannot be answered. Because the audiences for most mass media are quite diverse, inflexibility is a significant problem.

Some types of advertising require high total expenditures, even though costs per viewer or reader are low. This may exclude smaller firms from utilizing certain media. In the preceding example, a television ad cost $.005 per viewer. Nonetheless, total costs (excluding production expenses) are $150,000 and this is for one ad placed once.

Many media appeal to large geographical areas. This may result in wasted viewing or circulation for a small or moderate-sized firm. For example, a single-unit discount store or a beer manufacturer distributing locally might find that only 60 per cent of a newspaper's readers live within its shopping area. Also, because audiences for advertisements are diversified, a large amount of readership or viewership may be wasted. A manufacturer of clothes designed for fifteen- to eighteen-year-old females might find only magazines with broader readership profiles, for example, thirteen- to twenty-five-year-old females.

Mass media attract many people who do not view or listen to commercials, read advertisements, or keep circulars or mail ads. These people watch television, read magazines and newspapers, and keep up with first-class mail; but they do not pay attention to advertising.

The majority of advertisements do not provide the audience with much information, because high costs lead to brief messages. In particular, television commercials are short, averaging thirty or fewer seconds; few are longer than one minute.

Last, because advertising is nonpersonal, feedback is difficult to obtain and usually it is not immediately available.

Developing an Advertising Plan

The development of an advertising plan consists of the nine steps shown in Figure 16-2 on page 468. The steps are highlighted in the following subsections.

Setting Objectives

The advertising objectives set by a firm guide its entire advertising plan. As described in Chapter 15, objectives can be divided into demand and image types. Table 16-4 outlines several specific objectives a firm may set in each category. Usually, a number of these objectives are combined and pursued through the advertising plan.

Table 16-4
Illustrations of Specific Advertising Objectives

Type of Objective	Illustrations
Demand-Oriented	
Information	To create brand awareness of a new product by the target market
	To explain the characteristics of a new product or service
	To acquaint consumers with new store hours
	To reduce the time it takes for salespeople to answer basic questions
	To expand the existing base of customers by appealing to new geographic areas or market segments
Persuasion	To improve brand ratings
	To gain brand preference
	To increase store traffic
	To increase sales
	To achieve brand loyalty
Reminding (retention)	To stabilize sales
	To maintain brand loyalty
	To sustain brand recognition and image
	To reinforce customers' brand preferences
Image-Oriented	
Industry	To develop and maintain a favorable industry image
	To generate primary demand for products or services
Company	To develop and maintain a favorable company image
	To generate selective demand for products or services

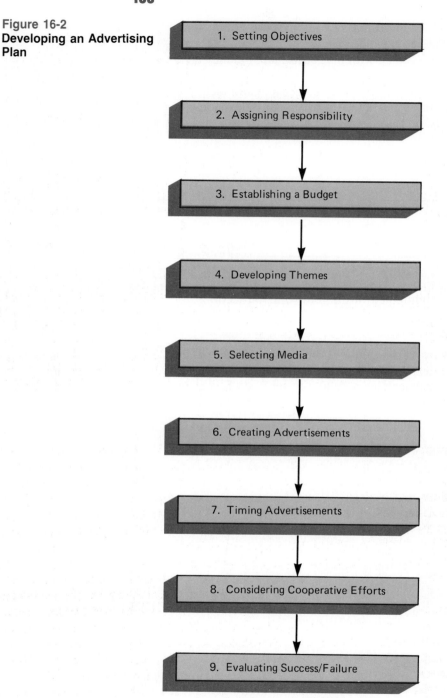

Figure 16-2
Developing an Advertising Plan

1. Setting Objectives

2. Assigning Responsibility

3. Establishing a Budget

4. Developing Themes

5. Selecting Media

6. Creating Advertisements

7. Timing Advertisements

8. Considering Cooperative Efforts

9. Evaluating Success/Failure

As an example, AT&T seeks to achieve a variety of objectives through advertising. It informs consumers of new telephone services and products, persuades them to increase long-distance calling, uses reminder advertising to retain business customers, and places institutional ads detailing the overall value of the company.

Assigning Responsibility

In assigning responsibility for the advertising plan, the firm has two options. It can undertake the plan through an in-house advertising department or hire an outside advertising agency. Although a number of companies have in-house departments, most of those involved with advertising on a sizable or continuous basis employ outside agencies (many in addition to their own departments). Diversified firms frequently employ a different advertising agency for each of their product lines.

An *advertising agency* offers a variety of functions. It usually works with the firm in the development of its advertising plan. This includes themes, media selection, copywriting, and other tasks. The large agencies offer a full complement of market research, product planning, consumer research, public relations, and other services. As an example, J. C. Penney now has an advertising agency (N. W. Ayer) perform a full range of functions, after conducting research and media tasks in-house for several years.[6]

For many years, advertising agencies received commissions equal to 15 per cent of the advertising expenditures of their clients for performing basic functions. They added charges for additional services. Since the 15 per cent rate is no longer mandatory, new compensation arrangements have developed. According to a 1982 study of the Association of National Advertisers, 52 per cent of agencies used the 15 per cent commission rate, 29 per cent allowed a fee arrangement (by which flat fees are set for services and not tied to ad expenditures), and 19 per cent used a negotiated commission rate (which varies by client).[7]

The firm's decision to use an outside advertising agency depends on its own expertise and resources, and the role of advertising for the firm. Table 16-5 shows the billings, gross income, and selected clients for the largest ten advertising agencies in the United States.

> An *advertising agency* may work with a firm to develop its advertising plan, conduct research, or provide other services.

Establishing a Budget

After determining the overall expenditures to be allocated to advertising by the all-you-can-afford, incremental, competitive parity, percentage-of-sales, or objective-and-task method, the firm establishes a detailed advertising budget. It must delineate the funds for each type of advertising (such as product and institutional messages) and each medium (such as newspapers and radio). Table 16-6 shows the 1982 advertising budget of CBS, which operates broadcast and publishing divisions, owns television and radio stations, makes records and films, runs a mail-order business, etc.

Several points should be considered in the budgeting process. What are the costs for different alternatives (a 30-second national television spot versus a full-page magazine ad)? How many placements of an ad are necessary for it to be effective (if four telecasts of a single television ad are needed to make an impact, the budget must provide for four placements)? How have media prices risen in recent years? How should the company react during a recession (research shows that firms which maintain advertising during a recession do better than those who do not)?[8] Which channel member is assigned promotional tasks? Do channel

---

[6] Pat Sloan, ''Ayer Sells Penney on Full Service,'' *Advertising Age* (January 16, 1984), pp. 3, 74.
[7] ''The 15% Media Commission Is on the Way Toward Becoming a Relic in Ad Agency Compensation Plans,'' *Marketing News* (June 10, 1983), p. 9.
[8] ''Study Supports Recession Ads,'' *Advertising Age* (April 28, 1980), p. 4.

Table 16-5
The Ten Largest Advertising Agencies in the United States, 1983

Agency	Worldwide Gross Income (Millions)	Worldwide Billings (Millions)	Selected Clients
Young & Rubicam	$414	$2,761	AT&T, Hallmark, Canada Dry, Del Monte, Gillette, CBS, Merrill Lynch, Southland
Ted Bates	388	2,586	Colgate-Palmolive, Mars, Warner-Lambert, Dr. Scholls, R. J. Reynolds, Warner Amex
J. Walter Thompson	378	2,524	Toys "R" Us, Lever Bros., Eastman Kodak, Ford, Quaker Oats, *Reader's Digest*
Ogilvy & Mather	346	2,360	Gallo, Mattel, Baskin-Robbins, Pepperidge Farms, Chem Lawn, General Foods, Sears
McCann-Erickson	299	1,993	Exxon, Mitsubishi, Nabisco Brands, Pabst, Coca-Cola, General Electric, General Motors
BBD & O	289	1,949	Chrysler, Firestone, Wrigley, Pillsbury, Pfizer, Dow Jones, DuPont, Pepsi, Armstrong Cork
Saatchi & Saatchi Compton	253	1,711	Paine Webber, K mart, British Airways, CIT Financial, American Cyanamid, *Ladies Home Journal*
Leo Burnett	217	1,485	Miller, Allstate, Green Giant, Kellogg, Maytag, Procter & Gamble
Foote, Cone & Belding	208	1,406	Embassy Pictures, Cinzano, Eaton, Clairol, Hughes Aircraft, Levi Strauss, Sunkist, Zenith
Doyle Dane Bernbach	199	1,321	Murjani, Borden, Bulova, Citicorp, IBM, Hershey, Litton, Polaroid, Volkswagen of America

Sources: "Some Major Agencies and Their Longtime Clients," *Advertising Age* (July 12, 1982), p. 41; and "U.S. Agency Income Profiles," *Advertising Age* (March 28, 1984).

members require contributions toward their advertising? What does it cost to produce an ad?[9]

A firm must proceed very carefully before reducing advertising expenditures for a product. As an example, the tobacco industry has been able to sustain the sales of cigarettes despite long-running bans against television advertising. Instead of reducing expenditures when excluded from certain media, total advertising increased as more magazine, newspaper, and other print ads were used.

Developing Themes

The basic *advertising themes* are the product or service appeal, the consumer appeal, and/or the nonconsumer appeal.

Next, the firm develops ***advertising themes,*** the overall appeals for its campaign. A product or service appeal centers on the item and its attributes. A consumer appeal describes the product or service in terms of consumer benefits rather than product or service characteristics. A nonconsumer or nonproduct or nonser-

[9] For an interesting article on promotional budgeting, see Malcolm A. McNiven, "Plan for More Productive Advertising," *Harvard Business Review*, Vol. 58 (March–April 1980), pp. 130–136.

	Advertising Budget	Per Cent of Budget
Media costs		
Newspapers	$ 38,896,000	24.5%
Magazines	22,008,000	13.8
Business publications	4,331,000	2.7
Television	22,944,000	14.4
Radio	13,653,000	8.6
Point-of-purchase	6,628,000	4.2
Direct mail	18,051,000	11.4
Outdoor/transit	2,543,000	1.6
Other	2,076,000	1.3
Production costs	27,857,000	17.5
Total costs	$158,987,000	100.0%
Advertising as a per cent of sales = 3.9.		

Table 16-6
Advertising Budget for CBS, 1982

Source: "CBS Inc.," *Advertising Age* (September 8, 1983), p.44. Reprinted by permission of *Advertising Age.* Copyright 1983 by Crain Communications Inc.

vice appeal deals with institutional advertising and corporate image.[10] Table 16-7 presents the full range of advertising themes from which the firm may select.

Selecting Media

The firm has a wide variety of media from which to choose. The characteristics of the leading media are shown in Table 16-8 on pages 474–475.

When selecting media, these factors should be considered: cost, waste, reach, frequency, message permanence, persuasive impact, clutter, and lead time.

Advertising costs should be assessed in two ways. First, the total costs of a medium are calculated—for example, $30,000 for a full-page color ad in a national magazine. Second, per reader or viewer costs are computed. Costs are expressed on a per thousand basis, except by newspapers which use a cost per million base. If the $30,000 ad is placed in a magazine with a circulation of 500,000, the cost per thousand is $60.

Advertising costs must be examined on the basis of total and per person costs.

Waste is the portion of the audience that is not in the firm's target market. Because media appeal to mass audiences, waste is a significant factor in advertising. This can be demonstrated with a continuation of the magazine illustration. The publication is a special-interest magazine for amateur photographers. Through marketing research, the firm knows that 450,000 readers will have an interest in a new fast-speed film; 50,000 have no interest in the film. The latter represents the wasted audience for an ad on fast-speed film. Therefore, the real cost of an ad is $66.67 ($30,000/450,000 × 1000 = $66.67) per thousand circulation. A general-interest magazine also advertises photographic film. It has a circulation of one million and the cost of a full-page ad is $40,000, $40 per thousand. However, only 200,000 people have an interest in photography. Therefore, the real cost of an ad is $200 ($40,000/200,000 × 1000 = $200) per thousand circulation. See Figure 16-3.

Waste is the audience segment that is not part of the company's target market.

[10] This classification method was developed by William M. Weilbacher, *Advertising,* Second Edition (New York: Macmillan, 1984), pp. 198–213.

Table 16-7 Advertising Themes

Theme	Explanation	Example
Product- or Service-Related		
1. Product or service features	Dominant features described	Maytag washers emphasize dependability and durability.
2. Product or service competitors' advantages	Competitive advantages cited	Ford stresses the quiet ride of its cars versus competitors' cars.
3. Product or service prices	Price used as dominant feature	Suave beauty products advertise low prices.
4. Product or service news	News or information domination	New-model cars point out improvements in gas mileage.
5. Product or service popularity	Size of market detailed	Hertz emphasizes its leading position in car rentals.
6. Generic	Primary demand sought	Grapes are advertised.
Consumer-Related		
1. Consumer uses	Product or service uses explained	Pillsbury ads show cake recipes.
2. Savings through uses	Cost benefits of product or service shown	Owens-Corning shows how consumers reduce heating bills with fiberglas insulation.
3. Consumer self-enhancement	Emphasis on how product or service helps consumer improve	Listerine advertises that it eliminates bad breath.
4. Fear	Threatening situation displayed	American Express points out the risks of carrying cash.
5. Subsidized product or service trials	Incentives given to encourage product or service purchases	An ad mentions $1 off the purchase as an introductory offer for a new brand of coffee.
Nonconsumer or Nonproduct/ Service-Related		
1. Corporate citizenship	Favorable image sought	Exxon shows how it is searching for new energy sources.
2. Investor solicitations	Growth, profits, and potential described to attract investors	Full-page ads are taken in business sections of major newspapers.

Reach refers to the total audience size. It includes circulation and passalongs.

Reach refers to the number of viewers or readers in the audience. For television and radio, reach is the total number of people who are exposed to an advertisement. For print media, reach has two components, circulation and passalong rate. Circulation is the number of copies sold or distributed to consumers. Passalong rate is the number of times each copy is placed with another reader. For example, each copy of *Newsweek* is read by about six people. The passalong rate for magazines is much higher than for daily newspapers.

Frequency is highest for newspapers, radio, and television.

Frequency is how often a medium can be used. It is greatest for newspapers, radio, and television, where ads may appear daily and advertising strategy may be easily changed. Telephone directories, outdoor ads, and magazines have the poorest frequency. A Yellow Pages ad may be placed or changed only once per year.

Exposures per ad involve *message permanence.*

Message permanence refers to the number of exposures one advertisement generates and how long it remains with the audience. Outdoor ads, transit ads, and telephone directories yield many exposures per message. In addition, magazines are retained by consumers for long periods of time. On the other hand, radio and television ads last only 5 to 60 seconds and are over.

Persuasive impact is the ability of a medium to stimulate consumers. Television often has the highest persuasive impact because it is able to combine audio, video, color, animation, and other appeals. Magazines also have high persuasive impact. Many newspapers are improving their technology in order to feature 4-color ads and increase their persuasive impact.[11]

Persuasive impact is highest for television.

Clutter involves the number of ads that are contained in a single program, issue, etc. of a medium. Clutter is low when a limited number of ads is presented, such as Hallmark placing a few scattered commercials on its television specials. Clutter is high when many ads are presented, such as the large number of supermarket ads in the Wednesday issue of a newspaper. Increasingly, television networks are being criticized for permitting too much clutter, particularly in allowing companies to sponsor very brief commercials (e.g., 15 seconds or shorter). Between 1967 and 1982, the number of television ads rose by 140 per cent.[12] Figure 16-4 illustrates the problem of clutter.

Clutter is highest when a single program/issue has many ads.

Lead time is the time required by the medium for placing an advertisement. It is shortest for newspapers and longest for magazines and telephone directories. A long lead time means a firm must plan its advertising program six months or more in advance, and risk incorrect messages in a changing environment. Television

Lead time is needed by a medium for placing an advertisement.

[11] David Schulz, ''Strategies for Using ROP Newspaper Color,'' *Stores* (February 1983), pp. 38–44.
[12] Bill Abrams, ''More Ads Are Squeezed into Less Time,'' *Wall Street Journal* (October 23, 1983), p. 33. See also, Richard Kostyra, ''The Votes Are Still Out on 'Split-30' Commercials,'' *Advertising Age* (November 7, 1983), p. M–36; and James P. Forkan, ''Clutter Crunch to Hurt Impact,'' *Advertising Age* (March 5, 1984), pp. 3, 74.

**Figure 16-3
Waste in Advertising**

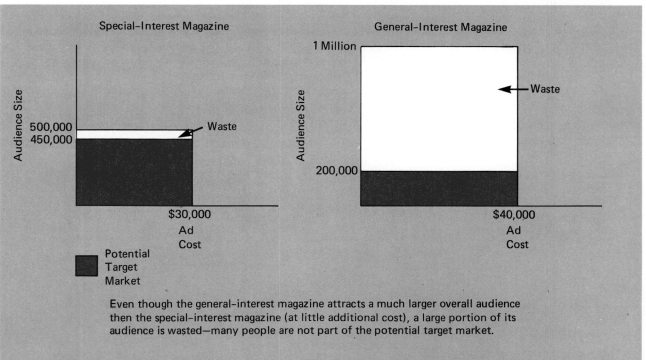

Even though the general-interest magazine attracts a much larger overall audience then the special-interest magazine (at little additional cost), a large portion of its audience is wasted—many people are not part of the potential target market.

Table 16-8 **Advertising Media**

Medium	Market Coverage	Typical Costs[a]	Best Uses	Advantages	Disadvantages
Daily newspaper	Entire metropolitan area, local editions sometimes used	$.25–$2.50 per agate line, depending on audience size	Large retailers	Short lead time, concentrated market, flexible, passalongs, surrounded by content	General audience, heavy ad competition, limited color, limited creativity
Weekly newspaper	One community	$.25–$1.25 per agate line, depending on audience size	Local retailers	Same as daily	Heavy ad competition, limited color, limited creativity, small market
Commercial television	Regional or national	$50.00–$250,000 for a 30-second commercial, depending on audience size	Regional manufacturers and large retailers; national, large manufacturers and largest retailers	Reach, low cost per viewer, persuasive impact, creative options, flexible, surrounded by programs	High minimum total costs, general audience, lead time, short message, limited availability
Cable television	Local, regional, or national	$5.00–$3,500 for a 30-second commercial, depending on audience size	Local, regional, and national manufacturers and retailers	More precise audience and more creative than commercial television	Limited number of consumers hooked up, ads not yet fully accepted on programs
Direct mail	Advertiser selects market	$.30 and up per person, depending on audience size and message characteristics	New products, book clubs, financial services, catalog sales	Precise audience, flexible, personal approach, no clutter from other messages	High throwaway rate, receipt by wrong person, low credibility
Magazines	National (most with regional editions) or local	$300 (small ad) up to $50,000 (for a full-color page in a national magazine)	National manufacturers; local service retailers and mail-order firms	Color, creative options, affluent audience, permanence of message, passalongs, flexible, surrounded by content	Long lead time, poor frequency, ad clutter, geographically dispersed audience
Radio	Entire metropolitan area	$50.00–$500 for a 60-second commercial	Local or regional retailers	Low costs, selective market, high frequency, immediacy of messages, surrounded by content	No visual impact, commercial clutter, channel switching, consumer distractions
Business paper	National or regional	$300–$10,000, depending on audience and ad size	Corporate advertising, industrial manufacturers	Selective market, high readability, surrounded by content, permanence of message, passalongs	Restricted product or service applications, not final consumer oriented

Table 16-8 Advertising Media (*Continued*)

Medium	Market Coverage	Typical Costs[a]	Best Uses	Advantages	Disadvantages
Outdoor	Entire metropolitan area or one location	$200–$10,000 per month, depending on audience and sign size	Brand-name products, nearby retailers, reminder ads	Large size, color, creative options, frequency, no clutter of competing messages, permanence of message	Legal restrictions, consumer distractions, general audience, inflexible
Transit	Urban community with a transit system	$50.00–$10,000 per month, depending on number of placements and audience size	Firms located along transit route	Concentrated market, permanence of messages, frequency, action orientation, color, creative options	Clutter of ads, consumer distractions, limited audience
Telephone directories	Entire metropolitan area (with local supplements)	$15.00–$100 per half column per month, depending on audience size	All types of retailers, professionals, service companies	Low costs, permanence of message, coverage of market, specialized listings, action oriented	Clutter of ads, limited creativity, long lead time, low appeal to passive consumers
Flyers	Single neighborhood	$.05 per flyer plus distribution costs	Local retailers	Low cost, market coverage, little waste, flexible	High throwaway rate, poor image

[a] A column inch of a newspaper (1 inch deep by 2 inches wide) contains 14 agate lines.

may also require a long lead time, because the number of ads it can carry is limited.

In recent years there have been many media innovations. These include regional editions and zip-code marketing (ads placed in specific geographic areas) to revive magazines; newspapers improving their computer skills in placing ads; advertising on cable television; televised commercials in supermarkets, movie theaters, and airplanes; specialized Yellow Pages; more radio stations handling ads in stereo; and better quality in outdoor signs (billboards).[13]

Creating Advertisements

Creating advertisements involves four fundamental decisions:

1. Message content must be determined. Each advertisement needs a headline or opening that creates consumer interest, such as "We look like Hertz and Avis. Until you see the bill" and copy that presents the message:

Creating advertisements involves message content, production schedule, message variations, and placement in the medium.

[13] See *Zip*, the monthly magazine for zip-code marketing; Cindy Ris, "Electronic Newspapers Could Alter Shape of the $4.6 Billion Classified Ad Market," *Wall Street Journal* (August 11, 1980), p. 15; "Only Use Cable to Reach Narrow Audience, Experiment, or Improve Coverage," *Marketing News* (May 28, 1982), p. 1; Bernard F. Whalen, "On-Line Markets New Mass Advertising Medium," *Marketing News* (December 28, 1979), pp. 1, 4; Richard Kreisman, "Airlines Deciding on In-Flight Ad Formats," *Advertising Age* (June 28, 1982), p. 10; Richard Davis, "Specialty Yellow Pages Making Debut," *Advertising Age* (August 17, 1981), p. 26; J. Fred McDonald, "New Tools, New Tunes," *Advertising Age* (July 11, 1983), pp. M-9—M-11; and "Fiber Optics and Other Technologies Add 'Wow Appeal' to Outdoor Ads," *Marketing News* (July 22, 1983), p. 10.

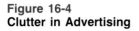

Figure 16-4
Clutter in Advertising

Copyright © 1983 by The New York Times Company. Reprinted by permission.

Our cars are the same as their cars. And our convenient locations in major airports are the same as their convenient locations in major airports. We also give you the same attention they do. The big difference is that Dollar Cars simply cost less.

So rent from Dollar for a change. You'll be pleasantly surprised when you see the bill. (See Figure 16-5).[14]

Content decisions also involve the use of color and illustrations, ad size or length, the source, and the use of symbolism. The role of these factors depends on the firm's goals and resources.

2. A production schedule must be outlined. This schedule should allow for all copy and artwork and be based on the lead time needed for the chosen medium.

[14] Dollar Rent a Car advertisement, *Fortune* (February 6, 1984), p. 67.

3. The firm needs to determine how many variations of its basic message to utilize. This depends on the frequency of presentation and the quality of the ad.
4. The location of an ad in a broadcast program or print medium must be determined. For men, newspaper placement in the sports section increases readership. Women read the entertainment and food and cooking sections more frequently. As costs have risen, more and more companies have become concerned about improved ad placement.

Timing Advertisements

Timing advertisements requires two major decisions: how often a particular ad is shown and when to advertise during the year. In the first decision the firm must balance audience awareness and knowledge versus irritation if it places an ad a

Timing advertisements involves how often an advertisement is shown and when to advertise during the year.

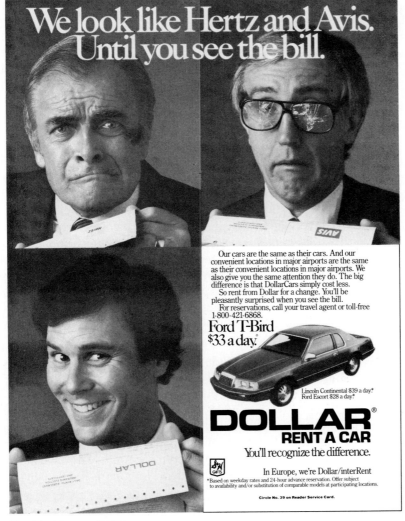

Figure 16-5
Message Content

Reprinted by permission.

number of times in a short period. For example, McDonald's runs its ads repeatedly, but changes them very often.

Second, the firm determines whether to advertise throughout the year or in concentrated periods. Distributed advertising maintains company and brand recognition, balances sales, and increases sales in nonpeak periods. It is used by most manufacturers and general-merchandise retailers. Massed advertising concentrates advertising during peak periods, maximizes returns, generates short-run consumer enthusiasm, and ignores sales in nonpeak periods. Specialty manufacturers and retailers use this method.

Other timing considerations are when to advertise new products, when to stop advertising existing products, how to coordinate advertising and other promotional tools, when to change basic themes, and how to space messages throughout the hierarchy-of-effects process.

Considering Cooperative Efforts

With a *cooperative advertising plan*, costs are shared by channel members. Cooperative arrangements may be vertical or horizontal.

In order to stimulate channel members and expand advertising efforts, the firm should consider cooperative efforts. Under a ***cooperative advertising plan,*** channel members share the costs of some aspects of advertising. In a vertical cooperative-advertising agreement, channel members at different stages share costs (for example, manufacturer and retailer). With a horizontal cooperative-advertising agreement, two or more channel members at the same stage share costs (for example, two retailers).

Good cooperative agreements state the share of costs paid by each party, functions and responsibilities of each party, advertisements to be covered, and basis for termination. They also benefit each participant.

It is estimated that approximately $8 billion in vertical-cooperative advertising support was made available by manufacturers in the U.S. during 1983. However, retailers actually used only about $5 billion of this amount. The nonuse of cooperative advertising by many retailers was due to their perceptions of manufacturer inflexibility involving messages and media, the costs of cooperative advertising to retailers, restrictive provisions (such as high minimum purchases to be eligible), and the emphasis on the manufacturer's name in advertising. To remedy this, a number of manufacturers are now more flexible in the messages and media they will support, paying for a larger percentage of advertising costs, easing restrictive provisions, and featuring retailer names more prominently in ads.

These are examples of cooperative advertising in action, involving vertical and horizontal arrangements:[15]

- Straus, a Fargo, North Dakota, men's clothing retailer, allocates 1 per cent of its $3.5 million in annual sales ($35,000) for cooperative advertising arrangements. This represents one third of its advertising budget.
- Computer Mart, a chain of 15 retail computer stores based in Troy, Michigan, develops its own ads and seeks manufacturer funds for them. Apple pays 75 per cent of media costs for ads featuring its products.
- Levi Strauss allows retailers to receive cooperative advertising dollars for messages placed in magazines, outdoor billboards, statements enclosed with

[15] Sara Delano, "How to Get a Fix on Free Ad Dollars," *Inc.* (July 1983), pp. 94, 96; Renee Blakkan, "Savory Deals Tempt Hungry Retailers," *Advertising Age* (March 7, 1983), pp. M-9–M-11; and Martin Everett, "Just the Weapon for a Tough Fight," *Sales & Marketing Management* (May 17, 1982), pp. 62–82.

monthly bills sent to charge customers, neighborhood newspapers, and many other media. Previously, Levi was very strict about the media it would sponsor.

- Vivitar (camera lenses and accessory equipment), Fram (automotive filters), and American Express participate in plans involving both vertical and horizontal cooperative advertising. They cover most of the costs of display ads emphasizing their companies; and a group of retailers share the remaining costs for listing their names in these ads.
- Franchise operators (such as Lincoln/Mercury dealers), retail cooperatives (such as Ace Hardware), and noncompeting independent retailers (such as local liquor stores) are often involved with horizontal cooperative advertising. This enables them to reach a large audience in an efficient manner; waste is reduced.

Evaluating Success or Failure

The general methods for evaluating promotional success or failure were detailed in Chapter 15. The firm should select one or a combination of these methods to evaluate its advertising campaign. The success or failure of advertising depends on how well it helps the company achieve promotion objectives. Creating customer awareness and increasing sales are two distinct goals; success or failure in attaining them must be measured differently. Furthermore, advertising is extremely difficult to isolate as the single factor leading to a certain image or sales level.

In 1982, 21 of the largest advertising agencies in the U.S. reached a consensus on the basic principles to be followed in measuring the effectiveness of advertising messages. *PACT* (Positioning Advertising Copy Testing) describes these principles:[16]

1. A good testing system examines data that are relevant to the objectives of the advertising under consideration.
2. A good testing system requires agreement about how results will be used before the analysis is conducted.
3. A combination of measurement methods is desirable, because single methods are generally inadequate.
4. A good testing system is based on the consumer's decision process, particularly reception of a stimulus, comprehension of a message, and behavior response.
5. The use of repetitious advertising is studied in a good testing system.
6. When comparing alternative messages, each requires the same degree of support.
7. Biases are to be avoided.
8. Audience sampling is to be carefully specified.
9. Good tests are valid (accurate) and can be repeated with similar results (reliable).

Following are a variety of examples dealing with the evaluation of advertising success or failure:

- In 1983, for the third straight year, Miller Lite beer commercials were rated the ''most outstanding'' on television according to a survey of 20,000 adults. This rating was based on the total number of consumers who remembered and liked Miller Lite ads. However, when advertising efficiency (the number of con-

> **Evaluation of success or failure must relate performance to objectives.**

---

[16] *PACT* (Positioning Advertising Copy Testing), 1982.

Figure 16-6
A Miller Lite Beer
Television Commercial
After many years, the Miller Lite Beer television commercials remain extremely popular and well received.

Reprinted by permission.

sumers recalling an ad per dollar of advertising expenditures) was measured, Miller Lite commercials did not score as well. It cost $30.06 to reach each 1,000 consumers who remembered Miller Lite commercials. In comparison, it cost $8.01 to reach each 1,000 consumers who remembered Calvin Klein jeans commercials. The high recall of Miller Lite ads was partly the result of large expenditures ($50.1 million).[17] Figure 16-6 shows one of the commercials used by Miller.

● Igloo, a division of Anderson, Clayton, & Co., tested an advertising campaign for its Playmate personal-size ice chest. It found that the campaign increased

[17] John Koten, ''Creativity, Not Budget Size, Is Vital to TV-Ad Popularity,'' *Wall Street Journal* (March 1, 1984), p. 31.

igloo®

30-SECOND "CAVEMAN" TELEVISION COMMERCIAL

Figure 16-7
**The Igloo Playmate
Personal-Size Ice Chest**
After thorough testing in
several market areas, Igloo
introduced this television
commercial nationally in
1983.

ANNCR: (VO) In the beginning...

...man struggled to carry...

food and drink...

Then Igloo created the Playmate
ice chest.

It was easy to carry...

and it carried a lot.

SFX: Prehistoric bird cry

Reprinted by permission.

Playmate by Igloo.

Built to Survive the Real World.

brand awareness by 300 to 400 per cent, and sales rose by 75 per cent.[18] As a result of the successful test, Igloo decided to run the national television campaign shown in Figure 16-7 during 1983.

• Country Fresh advertised its chocolate milk on outdoor billboards and found

[18] Tom Bayer, "Igloo Is Taking Its Case to Consumer in Ad Drive," *Advertising Age* (June 21, 1982), p. 4; and Igloo Corporation, 1984.

that sales increased by over 100 per cent during a 4-week period in several Michigan markets.[19]

- A study on two AT&T commercials revealed that "cost of visit" ads (which stressed the economy of long-distance calls) generated greater revenues than "reach out and touch someone" ads.[20]
- An analysis of more than 800 commercials found that celebrities were not overly effective in gaining brand preference, but they did contribute to higher levels of recall about the ads in which they appeared.[21]

Scope and Importance of Publicity

Every company would like to receive favorable publicity about its offerings or the company itself, such as "This television reporter rates Panasonic portable color televisions as a superior effort" or "State Farm Insurance is considered one of the five best homeowners' insurance companies by this magazine."

Accordingly, the competition for publicity is intense. After all, there are only four national television networks (ABC, CBS, NBC, and PBS) and a few national periodicals. It is difficult to make the network news. However, there are numerous opportunities for publicity because there are 4,600 AM radio stations, 4,300 FM radio stations, 1,100 television stations, and 10,000 newspapers and periodicals located throughout the United States. In addition, the number of cable television stations is rising rapidly.

Unfortunately, many firms have poor or ineffective policies for dealing with the independent media or developing a sustained publicity campaign. Table 16-9 shows a variety of publicity-related situations and the alternate ways a firm could deal with them. From this table it should be clear that unfavorable as well as favorable publicity can occur and the firm must be prepared to handle it in the best way possible. Negative publicity can happen to any company, but the successful one will have a contingency plan to handle it.

Public relations is image-directed—paid or non-paid. Publicity is nonpaid and may be demand- or image-oriented.

It is important for the relationship of advertising, public relations, and publicity to be understood. Advertising is paid mass communication that is demand- or image-directed. *Public relations* is mass and personal communication that is image-directed. Public relations efforts include institutional advertising, publicity, and personal appearances to enhance a firm's image.[22] Publicity is nonpaid mass communication that is demand- or image-directed. Figure 16-8 contains examples of the three concepts.

[19] Bill Wilkens, "Advertising in the Great Outdoors," *Progressive Grocer* (August 1983), p. 128.
[20] Robert Raissman, "Study Says 'Reach Out' Not AT&T's Best," *Advertising Age* (November 1, 1982), p. 20.
[21] David Ogilvy and Joel Raphaelson, "Research on Advertising Techniques That Work—And Don't Work," *Harvard Business Review*, Vol. 60 (July–August 1982), p. 15.
[22] For example, see James McN. Stancill, "Upgrade Your Company's Image—and Valuation," *Harvard Business Review*, Vol. 62 (January–February 1984), pp. 16–18ff.

Characteristics of Publicity

Publicity offers several benefits. There are no costs for message time or space. An advertisement in prime-time television may cost $250,000 to $500,000 or more per minute, whereas a five-minute report on a network newscast would not cost anything. However, publicity should not be viewed as entirely cost free. There are costs for news releases, a publicity department, and other items.

Publicity has no space or message costs, high credibility, an attentive audience, and a mass audience.

Credibility about messages is high, because they are reported in independent media. A newspaper review of a movie has a higher level of believability than an ad in the same paper, because the reader knows the review is not sponsored by the movie producer. The audience associates independence with objectivity.

Similarly, people are more likely to pay attention to news reports than to clearly identified ads. For example, *Women's Wear Daily* has many fashion reports and advertisements. Readers spend time reading the stories, but they flip through the ads. In the same vein, there may be ten commercials during a half-hour television program or hundreds of ads in a magazine. Feature stories are much fewer in number and stand out clearly.

As with advertisements, publicity reaches a mass audience. Within a short period of time, new products or company policies can be known by most of the target market.

Publicity also has some significant limitations. A firm has little control over messages, their timing, their placement, or their coverage by a given medium. A company may issue detailed news releases and find only portions cited by the

Publicity cannot be controlled, planned, or timed accurately by the firm.

Table 16-9 Publicity-Related Situations and How a Firm Could Respond to Them

Situation	Poor Response	Good Response
Fire breaks out in a company plant	Requests for information by media are ignored.	Company spokesperson explains the cause of the fire and company precautions to avoid it and answer questions.
New product introduced	Advertising is used without publicity.	Preintroduction news releases, product samples, and testimonials are used.
News story about product defects	Requests for information by media are ignored, blanket denials are issued, hostility is exhibited toward reporter of story.	Company spokesperson states that tests are being conducted on products, describes procedure for handling defects, and answers questions.
Competitor introduces new product	The advertising campaign is stepped up.	Extensive news releases, statistics, and spokespeople are made available to media to present company's competitive features.
High profits reported	Profits are rationalized and positive effects on the economy are cited.	Profitability is explained, data (historical and current) are provided, uses of profits are detailed: research, community development.
Overall view of publicity	There is an infrequent need for publicity; crisis fighting is used when bad reports are circulated.	There is an ongoing need for publicity, strong planning, and contingency plans for bad reports.

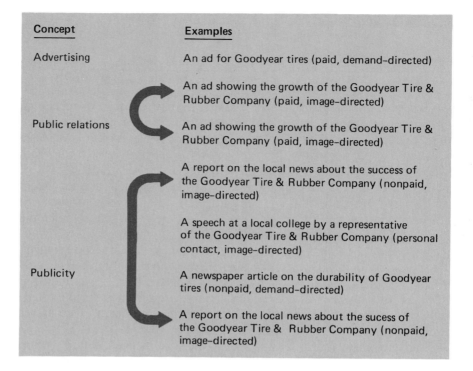

Figure 16-8
Relationship of Advertising, Public Relations, and Publicity

Concept	Examples
Advertising	An ad for Goodyear tires (paid, demand-directed)
Public relations	An ad showing the growth of the Goodyear Tire & Rubber Company (paid, image-directed)
	An ad showing the growth of the Goodyear Tire & Rubber Company (paid, image-directed)
Publicity	A report on the local news about the success of the Goodyear Tire & Rubber Company (nonpaid, image-directed)
	A speech at a local college by a representative of the Goodyear Tire & Rubber Company (personal contact, image-directed)
	A newspaper article on the durability of Goodyear tires (nonpaid, demand-directed)
	A report on the local news about the sucess of the Goodyear Tire & Rubber Company (nonpaid, image-directed)

media. In particular, media have the ability to be much more critical than a company would like. Furthermore, media often find disasters (fires, auto crashes, product side effects) more newsworthy than routine statements distributed by the firm.

For example, in 1982, Procter & Gamble faced a substantial publicity problem over the meaning of the firm's 123-year-old company logo. A small number of ministers and other private citizens believed that the symbol was based on Satanism and therefore sacrilegious. These beliefs were covered extensively by the media and resulted in the firm receiving 15,000 phone calls about the rumor in June alone. To combat this negative publicity, Procter & Gamble issued news releases featuring prominent clergy (such as Jerry Falwell) that refuted the rumors, threatened to sue those people spreading the stories, and had a spokesperson appear on *Good Morning America*. The media cooperated with the company and ultimately the false rumors were put to rest, with no adverse affect on sales.[23]

A firm may want publicity during certain periods, such as when a new product is introduced or a new store opened, but the media may not cover the introduction or opening until after the time it would aid the firm. Similarly, media determine the placement of a story; it may follow a report on crime or sports. Finally, the media ascertain whether to cover a story at all and the amount of coverage to be devoted to it. A company-sponsored jobs program might go unreported or receive three-sentence coverage in a local newspaper.

It is difficult to plan publicity in advance, because newsworthy happenings take place quickly. Therefore, short-run plans are most applicable. Publicity must

[23] Sandra Salmans, "P&G's Battles With Rumors," *New York Times* (July 22, 1982), pp. D1, D4; and "P&G's Rumor Blitz Looks Like a Bomb," *Advertising Age* (August 9, 1982), pp. 1, 68–69.

be viewed as complementary to advertising and not a substitute for it. The characteristics of both (credibility and low costs for publicity, control and coverage for advertising) are needed for an effective communications program.

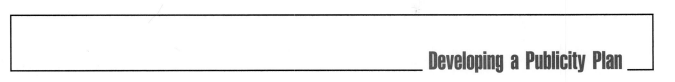

Developing a Publicity Plan

Developing a publicity plan is much like developing an advertising plan. It consists of the steps shown in Figure 16-9 and is described in the following subsections.

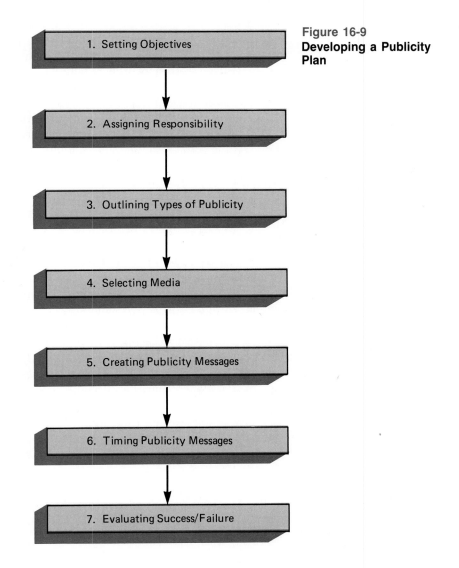

Figure 16-9
Developing a Publicity Plan

1. Setting Objectives

2. Assigning Responsibility

3. Outlining Types of Publicity

4. Selecting Media

5. Creating Publicity Messages

6. Timing Publicity Messages

7. Evaluating Success/Failure

Setting Objectives

The objectives of publicity are the same as those for advertising—they are demand-oriented (information, persuasion, reminding) and image-oriented (industry, company). The objectives guide the entire publicity plan.

As an example, the publicity objectives for the *American Heritage Dictionary* when it was first introduced were inclusion on national best-seller lists for as long as possible, placement of company personnel on leading broadcast interview programs, publication of print interviews in major daily newspapers in twelve key cities, placement of stories and book reviews on a national basis, and acceptance by editors as a worthwhile, innovative working tool.[24]

Assigning Responsibility

A firm can use an in-house department, hire an outside ad agency, or hire a specialist.

A firm has three options for assigning publicity responsibility: it may employ an in-house public relations or publicity department to enact the entire publicity plan; it may have its outside advertising agency handle publicity; or it may hire a specialized public relations or publicity firm. The in-house department ensures greater secrecy until releases are distributed. The outside firm has better contacts and expertise. Each approach is popular.

Recently, mergers between advertising agencies and public relations firms have risen and questions about conflicts of interest over clients have also grown. For example, J. Walter Thompson, then the second largest ad agency in the United States, and Hill & Knowlton, the largest public relations firm, merged in 1980. At the time of the merger, Thompson accounts included Goodyear, Chevron, Lever Brothers, Ford, and Hyatt. Hill & Knowlton accounts included Goodrich, Texaco, Procter & Gamble, Mazda, and Marriott.[25]

Outlining Types of Publicity

Publicity types involve news, features, releases, background material, and emergency information.

There are several general ***publicity types*** available to a firm, as shown in Table 16-10.[26] News publicity deals with events of national, regional, or local interest. Spontaneous news publicity is a result of a fire, union strike, or other major occurrence. Planned news publicity is based on news releases prepared and distributed by the firm on a regular basis.

Business feature articles are detailed stories about the company or its offerings that are distributed to business media. Service feature articles are lighter stories that focus on personal care, household items, and recipes and are distributed to newspapers and magazines. Finance releases are stories aimed at business sections of newspapers and magazines. Product releases deal with new products and product improvements. They are aimed at all forms of media.

Pictorial releases are illustrations or pictures supplied to media. Background editorial material is extra information provided to media writers and editors; it enhances standard releases and provides filler for stories (such as the biography of

---

[24] Arthur M. Merims, "Marketing's Stepchild: Product Publicity," *Harvard Business Review,* Vol. 50 (November–December 1972), p. 110.

[25] Jeffrey H. Birnbaum, "Merger of Thompson, Hill & Knowlton Could Produce Conflict Over Clients," *Wall Street Journal* (June 4, 1980), p. 10.

[26] H. Frazier Moore, *Public Relations: Principles, Cases, and Problems,* Eighth Edition (Homewood, Ill.: Richard D. Irwin, 1981), pp. 163–167.

Table 16-10
Types of Publicity

Publicity Type	Example
News publicity	Macy's describes its decision to open stores in Houston and New Orleans.
Business feature article	Kodak explains its goals and objectives for the 1980s.
Service feature article	A trade association offers 10 tips on how to reduce home heating costs.
Finance release	E. F. Hutton distributes quarterly financial data about the company.
Product release	RCA announces its new, fast-speed film.
Pictorial release	IBM distributes photos showing all of its personal computer products and related software.
Background editorial release	K mart presents a biography of its president and his rise through the company.
Emergency publicity	The Red Cross makes a request for aid to tornado victims.

the chief executive of the company). Emergency publicity consists of special releases keyed to disasters or serious problems.

Each of these types of publicity plays a role in a good, well-planned publicity program.

Selecting Media

The media available for publicity are newspapers, television, magazines, radio, and business papers. Because of the infrequent nature of many magazines and some business papers, publicity is usually aimed at those media that appear daily or weekly.

It is important that company representatives understand how to interact with the media. For example, Dataspeed Inc., a manufacturer of high-technology products such as portable stock-quotation devices, hired a public relations firm to teach its executives how to deal with the media. To prepare for a major news conference, Dataspeed's chief executive was briefed on the types of questions that were likely to be asked, engaged in a mock interview, and was shown how and when to relate significant company information during the conference.[27]

Creating Publicity Messages

Creating publicity messages involves the same factors as in advertising—message content, message variations, and a production schedule. Publicity messages can be conveyed in one or a combination of forms: news conference, press or news release, phone calls or personal contacts, press kit (a combination of materials about a story), special events (Macy's Thanksgiving Parade, an appearance on the *Today* show), or films.

[27] Bro Uttal, "The Man Who Markets Silicon Valley," *Fortune* (December 13, 1982), p. 136.

Timing Publicity Messages

Publicity should precede the introduction of new products and generate excitement for them. For emergencies, press releases and spokespeople should be immediately available. For ongoing publicity, messages should be properly spaced throughout the year. As noted previously, a company may have difficulty anticipating the timing of both unanticipated and planned publicity since the media control timing.

Evaluating Success or Failure

There are several straightforward methods for evaluating the success or failure of a publicity campaign. The firm can count the media covering each story, analyze the length and placement of coverage, correlate desired with actual timing, evaluate audience reactions to publicity, and/or compute the cost of comparable advertising.

By any measure, the most successful use of publicity in recent years involved Coleco's 1983 campaign for its Cabbage Patch Kids dolls. Coleco spent nearly a year and $500,000 to stimulate the publicity blitz that began in October 1983. These are some of the highlights of Coleco's Cabbage Patch Kids 1983 campaign:[28]

- November issues of many women's magazines (on sale in late October) described the dolls in stories about holiday gift ideas. Coleco had worked on the placement of these stories for six months.
- Jane Pauley had a five-minute report on the dolls during the November 18 *Today* show.
- Coleco representatives appeared on television and radio shows in 12 major markets.
- Throughout the U.S., news programs reported on the number of shoppers waiting in store lines for the dolls on the day after Thanksgiving.
- During December, the dolls were featured on the *Tonight* show several times and in a skit on the Bob Hope Christmas special (with Brooke Shields and Catherine Bach depicted as Cabbage Patch Kids).
- Just before Christmas, the media reported on children's hospitals giving out the dolls to patients.

As a result of this campaign, the demand for Cabbage Patch Kids dolls was overwhelming; Coleco's production could not keep up with this demand (as discussed in Chapter 3). Figure 16-10 shows a collection of Cabbage Patch Kids dolls attired in their "sporting outfits."

Summary

Advertising and publicity are the two forms of mass communication available to a firm. Advertising expenditures exceed $85 billion annually through such media as

28 "Behind-Scenes Look at Cabbage Patch PR," *Advertising Age* (December 26, 1983), pp. 2, 18.

Figure 16-10
Coleco's Cabbage Patch Kids™

newspapers, magazines, farm publications, television, radio, direct mail, business papers, and outdoor.

The advantages of advertising are appeal to a large and geographically dispersed audience, low per customer costs, availability of a broad variety of media, control over all aspects of a message, surrounding editorial content, and how it complements personal selling. Disadvantages are inflexibility of messages, high total expenditures for some media, wasted viewers or readers, low audience involvement and high throwaway rates, limited information provided, and difficulty in obtaining audience feedback.

An advertising plan has nine steps: (1) setting objectives, (2) assigning responsibility, (3) establishing a budget, (4) developing themes, (5) selecting media, (6) creating advertisements, (7) timing advertisements, (8) considering cooperative efforts, and (9) evaluating success or failure.

Firms seek to obtain favorable publicity and avoid or minimize negative publicity. Competition is intense for placing publicity releases. The advantages of publicity are no costs for message time and content, high level of credibility, audience attentiveness, and mass audience. The disadvantages are lack of control by the firm and the difficulty of planning in advance. Public relations is mass and personal communication aimed at company image. It uses advertising, publicity, and personal contact.

A publicity plan has seven steps: (1) setting objectives, (2) assigning responsibility, (3) outlining types of publicity, (4) selecting media, (5) creating publicity messages, (6) timing publicity messages, and (7) evaluating success or failure.

Questions for Discussion

1. Explain the statement "Advertising is paid for, publicity is prayed for."
2. Comment on the advertising-as-a-percentage-of-sales data in Tables 16-2 and 16-3.
3. Under what circumstances is advertising most likely to be used?
4. Why do you think recall is a weak measure of advertising effectiveness?
5. List five objectives of advertising and give an example of how each may be accomplished.
6. A firm has an overall annual budget of $50,000 for advertising. What specific decisions must it make in allocating the budget?
7. A refrigerator manufacturer has determined that a full-page ad in a general-interest magazine would cost $50,000; the magazine's total audience is 3 million, of which 750,000 are potential consumers of a refrigerator. A full-page ad in a food magazine would cost $25,000; its total audience is 400,000, of which 300,000 are potential consumers. Which magazine should be selected? Why?
8. Do consumers respond differently to advertising clutter on television than in magazines? Explain your answer.
9. What are the pros and cons of cooperative advertising?
10. Describe *PACT* and its components.
11. Present an example of a company utilizing advertising, public relations, and publicity.
12. Why do so many firms handle publicity situations poorly?
13. "Publicity should not be viewed as entirely cost free." Comment on this.
14. How could a firm increase media coverage of its publicity releases?
15. What criteria would you use to evaluate Procter & Gamble's reaction to the negative publicity about its company logo?

Case 1 American Home Products: An Expensive Advertising Strategy*

American Home Products manufactures and markets four categories of products:

1. Prescription drugs and medical supplies (47 per cent of company sales)—including Ativan and Serax tranquilizers, Inderal heart medication, and the Sherwood Medical Group.
2. Household products and housewares (22 per cent)—including Woolite clothing cleaner, Black Flag insecticides, Easy-Off oven cleaner, Sani-Flush toilet tank cleaner, and Ekco pots and pans.
3. Food products (18 per cent)—including Chef Boy-Ar-Dee pasta products, Gulden's mustard, Jiffy popcorn, and Crunch 'n Munch snacks.
4. Package medicines and related items (13 per cent)—including Anacin, Dristan, Preparation H, Denorex medicated shampoo, Sleep-Eze, and Youth Garde cosmetics.

* The data in this case drawn from Susan Fraker, "American Home Products Battles the Doubters," *Fortune* (July 25, 1983), pp. 59–64; "American Home Products," *Advertising Age* (September 8, 1983), pp. 12, 14; and Bill Abrams, "Anacin's New, Intense TV Ads Try to Avoid 'Sanitized Look,'" *Wall Street Journal* (October 13, 1983), p. 31.

It is one of the leading advertisers in the U.S. For example, in 1982, American Home Products had the 10th highest advertising investment of any firm, $325.4 million. This amounted to 7.1 per cent of company sales; an advertising-to-sales ratio that ranked sixteenth among the 100 largest advertisers in the U.S.

In the past, American Home Products had a relatively conservative, noncreative reputation for its advertising. The company was known as "Anonymous Home Products." Previous commercials for Dristan and Anacin had messages that emphasized clogged nasal passages, pulsating headaches, and medical information. They were produced inexpensively. In addition, if a new product did not do well quickly, its ad budget was cut drastically.

Now, American Home Products is more creative and spending greater sums to produce commercials. In 1983, the focus of Anacin ads was changed. A series of television commercials featuring actors portraying a miner, farmer, waitress, teacher, and housewife was begun. And French model/actress Catherine Deneuve was hired as a celebrity spokesperson for Youth Garde cosmetics, at an annual fee of over $200,000. The Deneuve message is very low key, "Come closer. I've done a lot of living and I've nothing to hide. I use Youth Garde. See what the years haven't done."

QUESTIONS

1. How would American Home Products' advertising differ for each of its four product lines?
2. Why would American Home Products have had an "Anonymous Home Products" reputation despite such a large advertising-to-sales ratio?
3. The new Anacin ads are people-oriented rather than data-oriented. American Home Products is reacting to the view that "consumers want honesty; they don't want a lot of mumbo jumbo. If you don't reach out and get their attention, they're not going to watch you." However, some critics feel that the commercials are appealing, but "wonder if they can sell aspirin." Comment on these views.
4. In terms of marginal return, how should American Home Products determine which brands deserve more advertising?

Case 2 Artesia Waters: Using Publicity to Compete with Perrier[†]

In early 1980, Rick Scoville entered the sparkling water business, after obtaining a $25,000 loan and acquiring an aging, small bottling plant in San Antonio, Texas. Scoville attracted his first customers by loading cases of Artesia water in his van and personally visiting grocery chains and discos, pushing his brand's "pure Texas spirit." He began to develop a loyal following in selected markets. However, Scoville's goal was to have Artesia compete head on with Perrier throughout Texas. And Scoville had a major problem—he had no money to advertise.

To make up for his inability to advertise, Scoville mounted an aggressive publicity campaign to secure media attention, following the plan outlined in Table 1. Initially, Scoville wrote letters to media describing his product; this resulted in

[†] The data in this case are drawn from John Sharkey, "Kicking Perrier in the Derriere," *Inc.* (September 1981), pp. 165–166.

Table 1
Artesia Water's Guidelines for Generating Publicity

1. Place stories directly with newspapers, trade magazines, and radio and television stations.
2. Send letters to the editors and program directors for local media. They are frequently on the lookout for interesting stories.
3. Write short pieces, emphasizing newsworthy factors.
4. Reproduce and forward copies of early stories that have been placed in the media to news organizations. This establishes credibility and leads to further placements.
5. Create an angle (e.g., small company makes good).
6. Design product packaging for maximum attention.
7. Be patient, flexible, and persistent.

newspaper stories in Dallas, Houston, and San Antonio. He reproduced a story from a Houston paper and mailed it to other publications. A follow-up telephone call to the *Wall Street Journal* led to a one-paragraph article on page one.

The *Texas Monthly* printed a feature story on Artesia. This earned Scoville an invitation to a bottled water taste test; and Artesia won the test. Coverage on Texas television stations increased rapidly, and sales tripled the day after the first telecast.

Artesia's image was carefully developed, "We tell Perrier drinkers, 'We're chic. We're American. We're Texan. We're good. *And* we cost less.'" Scoville played up the theme of the small American firm versus the large foreign firm. And fancy bottling and labeling added to Artesia's image.

Sales during 1980 were $102,000; they jumped to $1.5 million in 1981. Artesia gained a strong market share in Texas, taking up to 30 per cent of Perrier's sales. Based upon his early success, Scoville started advertising in 1981, setting a budget of $270,000. Advertising centered on direct mail, outdoor, and print media.

QUESTIONS

1. Evaluate Table 1.
2. Why would the *Wall Street Journal* carry a story on a small, unknown bottled water company?
3. What would have happened to Artesia Waters if it lost the televised taste test?
4. In 1981, Scoville decided to reduce the role of publicity and began advertising. Why? Was this action correct?

Chapter 17

Personal Selling and Sales Promotion

CHAPTER OBJECTIVES

1. To examine the scope, importance, and characteristics of personal selling

2. To study the elements in a personal selling plan: objectives, responsibility, budget, type(s) of sales positions, sales techniques, sales tasks, and implementation

3. To examine the scope, importance, and characteristics of sales promotion

4. To study the elements in a sales promotion plan: objectives, responsibility, overall plan, types of sales promotion, coordination, and evaluation of success or failure

Sales managers frequently have doubts about their ability to select personnel properly on the basis of interviewing. As one sales manager commented, "People razzle-dazzle me in an interview. But how do I know if they have drive, if they can handle rejection, or if they can be self-disciplined enough to go out and sell in the boonies. Good vibes are okay, but how do I get inside a guy's head?"

A variety of testing devices are available to help managers evaluate prospective salespersons. At one extreme is a simple test such as the Wesman Personnel Classification Test. It takes 25 minutes to administer, measures verbal and numerical ability, is self-scoring, and costs $9 for 25 copies. At the other extreme is a complex test such as the Personnel Dynamics Inc. (PDI) profile. It consists of 181 questions, measures

493

personality, and costs $125 per job applicant to be scored. These are two of the questions included in the PDI personality profile:

If performing the following activities paid the same compensation and carried equal status, which would you choose: a) representing clients in court; b) performing as a concert pianist; c) commanding a ship; d) advising on electronics problems?

Among these statements, which best describes you: a) I don't need to be the focus of attention at parties; b) I have a better understanding of what politicians are up to than most of my associates do; c) I don't delay making decisions that are unpleasant?

Personnel experts believe that the most important factors in a salesperson's success are his/her motivation to persuade others, empathy with clients, and resiliency after losing a potential sale. In particular, behavior during a sales call (including listening, handling objections, and closing the presentation) affects results. Demographic data, such as gender, experience, and education, are less important.

These experts also point out that many companies make mistakes when they promote a superior salesperson to a sales manager's job, without analyzing the unique features that should be possessed by a good manager. Said one analyst, "They've taken their best producer—who's a doer not a delegator—and ended up with a mediocre or worse manager."[1]

Sales force selection is just one of the many tasks facing marketers with regard to their personal selling and sales promotion efforts.

Scope and Importance of Personal Selling

Personal selling utilizes oral presentations to prospective buyers.

As defined in Chapter 15, personal selling is that part of promotion involving an oral presentation in a conversation with one or more prospective buyers for the purpose of making a sale. Unlike advertising and publicity, selling relies on personal contact. The goals of personal selling are similar to other promotion types: information, persuasion, and/or reminding.

In the United States, almost seven million people are employed in the sales positions defined by the Bureau of Labor Statistics. Included are professional sales personnel and clerical sales personnel. Salesworkers may be involved with complex selling arrangements or perform routine tasks.

Professional sales personnel build accounts; clerical sales personnel complete transactions.

Professional sales personnel generate customer accounts, ascertain needs, interact with consumers, emphasize knowledge as well as persuasion, and provide substantial service. Top salespeople can earn more than $100,000 per year. Examples of professional sales personnel are stockbrokers, manufacturing sales representatives, insurance agents, and real estate brokers.

Clerical sales personnel answer telephone inquiries, obtain stock from inventory, recommend the best brand in a product category, and complete transactions

---

[1] Sara Delano, "Improving the Odds for Hiring Success," *Inc.* (June 1983), pp. 145–150.

by receiving payments and packing products. Examples are retail, wholesale, and manufacturer sales clerks.

Personal selling goes far beyond the workers identified by the Bureau of Labor Statistics, because every contact between a company representative and a current or potential customer entails some degree of personal interaction. For example, lawyers, plumbers, hairdressers, and cashiers are not defined as sales workers. Yet, each occupation involves a great degree of customer contact.

In a variety of situations, a strong emphasis on personal selling is usually needed. Large-volume customers require special attention and handling. With direct company to consumer sales, channel members are not hired to complete transactions; the company is responsible for personal selling. Geographically concentrated consumers may be more efficiently served by a sales force than through advertisements in mass media. Custom-made, expensive, and/or complex products or services require detailed consumer information, demonstrations, and follow-up calls. Tangential sales services, such as gift wrapping, delivery, and installation, may be requested. If ads do not provide enough information, questions can be resolved only through personal selling. New products may require personal selling to gain channel acceptance. Finally, organizational customers expect a high level of personal contact and service. In general, the decision to stress personal selling rather than other promotion tools should be based on costs, audience size, audience needs, and the desire for flexibility.

> **Personal selling is stressed when orders are large, special handling is needed, a direct channel is used, consumers are concentrated, items are expensive or new, or service is required.**

The costs of personal selling are much greater than advertising for most companies. With consumer-goods companies, selling expenses (compensation, travel, lodging, meals, and entertainment) range from 3.5 per cent of sales for food manufacturers to 16.9 per cent for pharmaceutical firms. With industrial-goods companies, selling expenses range from 1.6 per cent of sales for containers-and-packaging-materials manufacturers to 10.7 per cent for computer makers. The cost of a single sales call is over $150; and it takes 5 visits to complete a typical sale. On average, a salesperson's weekly (5 day) expenditures on meals, lodging, and an automobile are $700. The median annual compensation for a senior field salesperson is over $36,000 (not including expenses).[2]

> **Personal selling costs are high. This has led to a heightened concern for efficiency.**

In order to keep selling costs down and improve sales force efficiency, a number of firms have developed specific strategies, as these examples show:

- Pitney Bowes, a manufacturer of mailing machines and other office products, has a national sales force of 3,500. It uses print and direct mail advertisements to generate leads for its sales force. It also utilizes telephone calls to prescreen customers, before having salespeople make field visits. Pitney Bowes' system works far better than cold canvassing, which is able to obtain sales from only 3 per cent of the customers visited. By 1990, it is expected that many companies will rely on telephone sales personnel to contact customers; outside sales personnel will be more involved with promotion and technical assistance.[3]
- Nabisco Brands employs several thousand salespeople who sell directly to supermarkets. In 1980, Nabisco began looking for new methods to deploy "the capabilities of its vast sales and distribution organization," which it believed

[2] *Sales & Marketing Management's 1984 Survey of Selling Costs* (February 20, 1984); and *Sales Force Compensation—Dartnell's 22nd Biennial Survey* (Chicago: Dartnell Corporation, 1984).
[3] Mary McCabe English, "Following Its Own (Sales) Lead," *Advertising Age* (June 20, 1983), pp. M-22–M-23; and "Rebirth of a Salesman: Willy Loman Goes Electronic, "*Business Week* (February 27, 1984), p. 104.

Figure 17-1
Cameron & Barkley's Computerized Customer Ordering System
Through a computerized ordering system, a customer of Cameron & Barkley is able to type in an order at a computer located in his (her) office. The customer immediately receives price and availability information, as well as order confirmation.

Reprinted by permission.

was underutilized. It decided to use its sales force to conduct marketing research, promotional services, and pickups of recalled products for other smaller companies. It also tested a program in which Nabisco salespeople would sell nonfood products for companies with limited resources.[4] For instance, Nabisco's Life Savers salespeople service accounts for Tums antacids.

- Cameron & Barkley is a Charleston, South Carolina, wholesaler of electrical and industrial supplies, with customers in over 30 states. To facilitate customer orders, Cameron & Barkley has a mainframe IBM computer hooked up with its 20 branch offices; these branch offices are connected to more than 200 computer terminals located with customers. Computerization enables customers to check merchandise availability, obtain price quotes, place orders, and monitor delivery. Bills are automatically sent out.[5] See Figure 17-1.

- Skil's Power Tool Group has implemented a number of changes in its personal selling approach. The sales force was reduced from 144 to 97 people by eliminating many trainees in support positions and redesigning sales territories. In addition, assistant regional sales managers were eliminated; this allows the regional managers better control over a smaller sales force. Finally, more salespeople now work on a commission-only basis. As a result of these practices, sales per salesperson have risen almost 150 per cent and the expense-to-sales ratio has dropped from 11.5 to 4.5 per cent.[6]

[4] Gay Sands Miller, "Nabisco Sees Its Sales Force Providing Promotional Services for Other Firms," *Wall Street Journal* (April 21, 1980), p. 20.
[5] Sara Delano, "Turning Sales Inside Out," *Inc.* (August 1983), p. 100.
[6] Lad Kuzela, "Slicing Costs with Smarter Selling," *Industry Week* (February 22, 1982).

Characteristics of Personal Selling

Personal selling has a number of positive and negative attributes. On the positive side, personal selling provides individual attention for each consumer and is able to pass along a lot of information. There is a dynamic, rather than passive, interaction between buyer and seller. This enables the firm to apply the concept of a **buyer-seller dyad,** which is a two-way flow of communication between both parties. This is not possible with advertising. See Figure 17-2.

Personal selling approaches can be flexible and adapted to the needs of specific consumers. For example, a real estate broker would use a different sales presentation for a couple buying a home for the first time than for a couple that has previously purchased a home. The salesperson can use as much persuasion as necessary and balance it against the need for information.

There is less waste with most forms of selling than with advertising. Personal selling centers on a more defined and concentrated target market. In addition, customers who walk into a store or who are contacted by a salesperson are more likely to purchase a product or service than those watching an advertisement on

The *buyer-seller dyad* is the two-way flow of communication.

Personal selling is flexible, has little waste, closes sales, and provides fast feedback.

Figure 17-2
The Buyer-Seller Dyad

Customer   Salesperson

Communication is freely exchanged between the salesperson and the customer.

television. Finally, because advertising stimulates consumers, those who make it to the personal selling stage are key members of the target market. Direct-to-home selling, where unsolicited, has the highest amount of wasted audience in personal selling.

Personal selling clinches sales and is often the last stage in the consumer's decision process, taking place after an information search and exposure to advertisements. It holds on to repeat customers and customers already convinced by advertising and resolves any doubts or concerns of undecided consumers. Personal selling answers any remaining questions about price, warranty, and other factors. It also settles service issues, such as delivery and installation.

Feedback is immediate and clear-cut with personal selling. Consumers may be asked about company policies or product attributes, or they may register complaints about the firm or its products. Salespeople are able to determine the strengths and weaknesses of a marketing program, such as a firm's advertising campaign or new product features.

Personal selling reaches a limited audience, has high per customer costs, creates little awareness, and has a poor image to some.

On the negative side, personal selling can accommodate only a limited number of consumers. For example, a retail furniture salesperson may be able to handle less than twenty consumers per day if the average length of a presentation is 15 minutes to a half hour. Sales personnel who call on customers can handle even fewer accounts, due to travel time.

As mentioned in the previous section, personal selling costs per customer are high. This is because of the one-on-one nature of selling. An in-store furniture salesperson who interacts with 20 customers per day might cost a company $3 per presentation ($60/day compensation divided by 20), an amount much higher than that for advertising. For outside sales personnel, expenses associated with travel such as hotel, meals, and car rental can easily amount to more than $100 per day per salesperson, and compensation must be added to these costs.

Personal selling is an ineffective tool for generating consumer awareness about a product or service. This role is better assumed by advertising. Similarly, many consumers attracted by advertising desire self-service. This is discouraged by some aggressive salespeople.

Finally, personal selling, particularly on the retail level, has a poor image in the eyes of a number of consumers. It is criticized for a lack of honesty, strong-pressure sales pitches, and pushing consumers to make premature decisions. These criticisms may be overcome by improved sales force training and the use of modern marketing (consumer-oriented) rather than selling (seller-oriented) practices.

Developing a Personal Selling Plan

The development of a personal selling plan can be broken down into the seven steps shown in Figure 17-3. The steps are highlighted in the following subsections.

Setting Objectives

Personal selling objectives are demand- or image-oriented. Illustrations of each type of objective appear in Table 17-1.

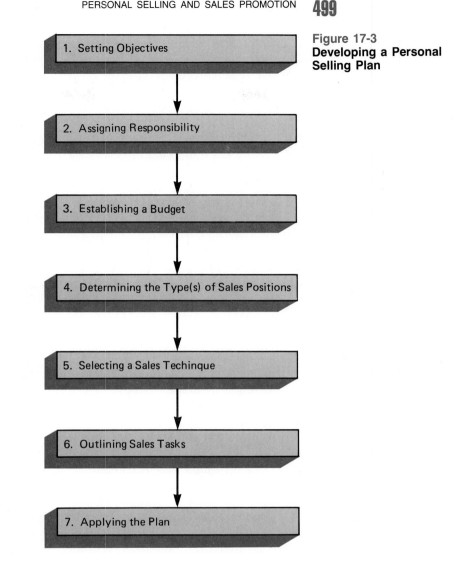

Figure 17-3
**Developing a Personal
Selling Plan**

1. Setting Objectives

2. Assigning Responsibility

3. Establishing a Budget

4. Determining the Type(s) of Sales Positions

5. Selecting a Sales Techinque

6. Outlining Sales Tasks

7. Applying the Plan

Although most firms have information, reminding, and image goals for personal selling, the major goal is persuasion: converting consumer interest into a sale.

Assigning Responsibility

Depending on the size of the company, there may be one or more sales managers who are responsible for all aspects of personal selling, including budgeting, types of selling, types of salespeople, selling tasks, and sales force management.

For a small or specialized firm, there is usually one sales manager. For a large or diversified firm, there are generally several sales managers, classified by geographic area (east, west), customer type (organizational consumer, final consumer), and/or product line (furniture, appliances).

Table 17-1
Specific Personal Selling Objectives

Type of Objective	Illustrations
Demand-Oriented	
Information	To explain fully all product and service attributes
	To answer any questions
	To probe for any further questions
Persuasion	To distinguish clearly product or service attributes from those of competitors
	To maximize the number of sales as a per cent of presentations
	To convert undecided consumers into buyers
	To sell complementary items, e.g., film with a camera
	To placate dissatisfied customers
Reminding	To ensure delivery, installation, etc.
	To follow up after a product or service has been used
	To follow up when a repurchase is near
	To reassure previous customers when making a new purchase
Image-Oriented	
Industry and company	To maintain a good appearance by all personnel in contact with consumers
	To follow acceptable sales practices

These are the basic responsibilities of a sales manager:

- To understand the company's objectives, strategies, market position, and basic marketing plan and to convey them to the sales force.
- To identify a sales philosophy, sales force characteristics, selling tasks, a sales organization, and methods of customer contact.
- To develop and update sales forecasts.
- To allocate selling resources based on sales forecasts and customer needs.
- To select, train, assign, compensate, and supervise sales personnel.
- To synchronize sales functions with advertising, product planning, distribution, marketing research, and production.
- To assess sales performance by salesperson, product, product line, customer, customer group, and geographic area.
- To continuously monitor competitors' actions.

Establishing a Budget

A *sales-expense budget* apportions expenditures for a specific time.

A **sales-expense budget** allocates expenditures among salespeople, products, customers, and geographic areas for a given period of time. A budget is usually based on a sales forecast and relates selling tasks to the achievement of sales goals. It should have some flexibility in the event the forecasted sales level is not reached or is exceeded.

These items should be covered in a sales-expense budget: projected sales, overhead (manager's compensation, office costs), sales force compensation, sales expenses (travel, lodging, meals, entertainment), sales meetings, selling aids, and sales management (employee selection and training) costs. Table 17-2 contains two sales-expense budgeting illustrations, one for a small, specialized firm and one for a large, diversified firm.

In Table 17-2A, the company is a small, single-product firm. It expects yearly sales to be $3 million, and the total sales-expense budget to be $149,800. In Table 17-2B, the company is large and has two separate product lines, each having a separate budget. Toy sales are forecast to be $10 million, with a $500,000 sales-expense budget. Small appliance sales are forecast to be $8 million, with a sales-expense budget of $386,000. The total sales-expense budget is $886,000 on sales of $18 million. For both companies, production and other marketing costs need to be included before profits can be computed. As an example, in Table 17-2A, the company has a $180,200 profit because production costs are $2 million and other marketing costs are $670,000.

The size of the sales-expense budget depends on many factors. It will tend to be larger if customers are geographically dispersed and extensive travel is necessary. Complex products and services require time-consuming sales calls and result in fewer calls per salesperson. An expanding sales force needs expenditures for the recruitment and training of new salespeople.

Table 17-2
Two Sales Budgets

A. Small, Specialized Firm

Sales Budget, 1985 (Based on Expected Sales of $3 Million)	
Overhead (1 sales manager, 1 office)	$ 60,000
Sales force compensation (2 salespeople)	54,000
Sales expenses	30,000
Sales meetings	1,000
Selling aids	1,500
Sales management costs	3,300
Total sales budget	$149,800

B. Large, Diversified Firm

Sales Budget, 1985—Toy Division (Based on Expected Sales of $10 Million)	
Overhead (2 regional sales managers, 2 offices)	$130,000
Sales force compensation (10 salespeople)	250,000
Sales expenses	80,000
Sales meetings	20,000
Selling aids	10,000
Sales management costs	10,000
Total divisional sales budget	$500,000

Sales Budget, 1985—Small Appliances Division (Based on Expected Sales of $8 Million)	
Overhead (2 regional sales managers, 2 offices)	$105,000
Sales force compensation (6 salespeople)	200,000
Sales expenses	55,000
Sales meetings	10,000
Selling aids	8,000
Sales management costs	8,000
Total divisional sales budget	$386,000
Total sales budget (based on total expected sales of $18 million)	$886,000

Determining Type(s) of Sales Positions

Salespeople can be broadly classified as order takers, order getters, or support personnel. Some companies utilize one type of salesperson, others a combination of all three types.

An **order taker** processes routine orders and reorders. The job is more clerical than creative selling. The order taker usually handles products or services that are presold. He or she arranges displays, restocks merchandise, answers simple questions, writes up orders, and completes transactions. An order taker may work inside a store (retail clerk or cashier) or call on customers (a field salesperson dealing with liquor stores).

The order taker offers several advantages to the employer: compensation is low, little training is required, a variety of selling and nonselling functions are performed, and the sales force can be expanded or contracted quickly. There are also a number of disadvantages. Order takers are not appropriate for products and services requiring creative selling or information. Turnover of personnel is high. Enthusiasm is often limited because of the low salary and nature of routine tasks.

An **order getter** is involved with generating customer leads, providing information, persuading customers, and closing sales. The order getter is the creative salesperson. High-priced, complex, or new products generally require an order getter. There is less emphasis on clerical work. Like the order taker, an order getter may be inside (automobile salesperson) or outside (Xerox salesperson). Table 17-3 presents the profile of an average order getter. Figure 17-4 contrasts order takers and order getters.

The order getter provides expertise and enthusiasm. This salesperson expands company sales; the order taker maintains sales. The order getter is frequently able to convince undecided customers to make purchases or decided customers to add peripheral items, such as carpeting and appliances along with a new house. On the negative side, for many consumers, the image of the order getter is one of high pressure and limited honesty. The order getter may also require expensive and

An order taker *handles routine orders and sells items that are presold.*

An order getter *obtains customer leads, provides information, persuades customers, and closes sales.*

Table 17-3
Profile of an Average Order-Getter Salesperson, 1983

Personal Characteristics
37 years of age
College graduate or some college education
7 years average length of service with the same company

Job Characteristics
Training costs (including compensation and training expenses) of $20,000
Training period of 6.7 months
$152 cost per sales call
6–10 sales calls per day
16 hours per week in nonselling activities

Compensation
Trainee—$22,000 per year
Semiexperienced salesperson—$28,000 per year
Senior salesperson—$36,000 per year
Sales manager—$46,000 per year
Travel expenses and medical and life insurance paid by company

Sources: Sales & Marketing Management's 1984 Survey of Selling Costs (February 20, 1984); and *Sales Force Compensation: Dartnell's 22nd Biennial Survey* (Chicago: Dartnell Corporation, 1984).

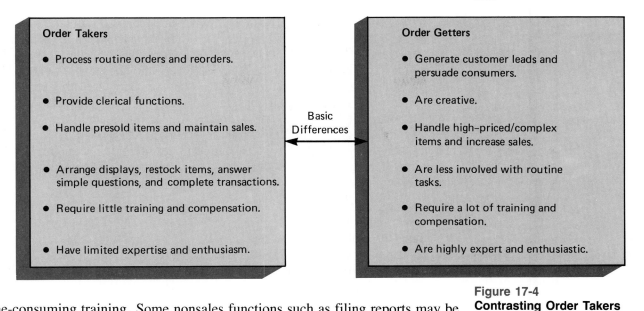

Order Takers

- Process routine orders and reorders.

- Provide clerical functions.

- Handle presold items and maintain sales.

- Arrange displays, restock items, answer simple questions, and complete transactions.

- Require little training and compensation.

- Have limited expertise and enthusiasm.

Basic Differences

Order Getters

- Generate customer leads and persuade consumers.

- Are creative.

- Handle high-priced/complex items and increase sales.

- Are less involved with routine tasks.

- Require a lot of training and compensation.

- Are highly expert and enthusiastic.

Figure 17-4
Contrasting Order Takers and Order Getters

time-consuming training. Some nonsales functions such as filing reports may be avoided, because they take away from the salesperson's time with customers and are seldom rewarded by the firm. Compensation can be very high for salespersons who are effective order getters.

Support personnel supplement the basic sales force by providing a variety of functions. A ***missionary salesperson*** is used to distribute information about new products or services. This person does not sell but describes the attributes of the new item, answers questions, and leaves written material. The missionary salesperson paves the way for later sales. This is most commonly used with pharmaceuticals and other medical products. A ***sales engineer*** may accompany an order getter when a highly technical or complex item is being sold. This salesperson explains product specifications, alternatives, and long-range uses. The order getter initially contacts customers and closes sales for these products. A ***service salesperson*** usually interacts with customers after sales are completed. Delivery, installation, or other follow-up tasks are undertaken.

Missionary salespersons, sales engineers, **and** *service salespersons* **are support personnel.**

Selecting a Sales Technique

There are two basic techniques for selling: the canned sales presentation and the need-satisfaction approach. The ***canned sales presentation*** is a memorized, repetitive presentation given to all customers interested in a particular item. This approach does not adapt to customer needs or traits but presumes that a general presentation will appeal to all customers. Although the method has been criticized for its inflexibility and nonmarketing orientation, it still retains some value:

The *canned sales technique* **is a memorized, nonadaptive presentation made to all customers.**

Logically, inexperienced salespeople who are lacking in selling instinct and confidence will benefit from the professionalism, anticipation of questions and objections, and other fail-safe mechanisms that are often inherent in a company-prepared memorized, audiovisual, or flip chart presentation. Consequently, this method should be considered when qualified new salespeople are scarce and when brevity of training is essential.[7]

[7] Marvin A. Jolson, "The Underestimated Potential of the Canned Sales Presentation," *Journal of Marketing,* Vol. 39 (January 1975), p. 78.

The *need-satisfaction approach* adapts the sales presentation to suit the needs and wants of individual consumers.

The ***need-satisfaction approach*** is a higher-level method based on the principle that each customer has different characteristics and wants, and therefore the sales presentation should be adapted to each individual consumer. With need satisfaction, the salesperson first asks questions of the consumer, such as: What type of product are you looking for? Have you ever purchased this product before? What price range are you considering? Then the sales presentation can be more responsive to the particular customer. Under this method a new shopper would be treated quite differently from an experienced shopper. The need-satisfaction approach is the most popular and customer-oriented technique; however, it requires more training and better-skilled sales personnel. The need-satisfaction approach includes[8]

- Generating mutual respect.
- Listening aggressively.
- Making thoughtful presentations.
- Spending time on presales visit research.
- Exhibiting timeliness (and a willingness to leave when appointment time is over).
- Letting the customer talk.
- Showing competence.
- Admitting ''I don't know,'' but ''I'll find out.''
- Not wasting a prospect's time.

The canned sales presentation works best with inexpensive, routine items that are heavily advertised and usually presold. The need-satisfaction approach works best with more expensive, more complex items that have moderate advertising and require substantial additional information for consumers. Figure 17-5 shows the two techniques.

Outlining Sales Tasks

The *selling process* consists of seven steps.

The tasks to be performed by the personal sales force need to be outlined. The ***selling process*** involves prospecting for customer leads, approaching customers, determining customer wants, giving a sales presentation, answering questions, closing the sale, and following up. Figure 17-6 shows examples for each of these stages.

Prospecting creates customer leads.

Outside selling requires a procedure for generating a list of customer leads. This procedure is known as ***prospecting.*** Blind prospecting relies on telephone directories and other general listings of potential customers. With blind prospecting a small percentage of the people contacted will be interested in the firm's offering. Lead prospecting depends on past customers and others for referrals. With lead prospecting a greater percentage of people will be interested because of the referral from a person they know and respect. Inside selling usually does not involve prospecting, because customers have already been drawn into the store or office as a result of advertisements or past purchase experience.

The preapproach and greeting are each part of *approaching customers.*

Approaching customers is a two-stage procedure: preapproach and greeting. During the preapproach, the salesperson tries to obtain information about the customer's characteristics from census and other secondary data, as well as from

[8] Kenneth A. Meyers, ''The Selling Professional of the 1980s,'' *Business*, Vol. 32 (October–December 1982), pp. 44–46.

A. CANNED PRESENTATION

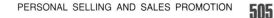

Sales Manual

The salesperson uses a repetitive presentation for all customers.

B. NEED–SATISFACTION APPROACH

"What are you looking for?"
"Have you purchased this before?"
"How much do you want to spend?"

The salesperson determines customers needs, and then offers a tailor–made present-ation.

**Figure 17-5
Selling Techniques**

referrals. In this way the salesperson is better equipped to interact with the customer. Inside retail salespeople are frequently unable to use a preapproach; and therefore they know nothing about a consumer until he or she enters the store. In the greeting the salesperson begins a conversation with the customer. The intention is to put the customer at ease and build a rapport.

The next step is to ascertain customer wants by asking the consumer a variety of questions regarding past experience, price, product or service features, intended uses, and the kinds of information still needed.

The *sales presentation* includes a description of the product or service, its benefits, available options and models, price, associated services such as delivery and warranty, and a demonstration (if necessary). As explained earlier, the presentation may involve a canned sales or need-satisfaction method. The purpose of the sales presentation is to be thorough and convert an undecided consumer into a purchaser.

The *sales presentation* converts an uncertain consumer.

After the presentation the salesperson usually must answer questions from the consumer. These questions are of two kinds: the first require further information, and the second raise objections that must be settled before a sale is made.

Once the questions have been answered, the salesperson is ready for the major goal: ***closing the sale.*** This involves getting the customer to agree to a purchase. The salesperson must be sure that no major questions remain before attempting to close a sale. In addition, the salesperson should not argue with the consumer.

The *closing* clinches the sale.

Finally, for major purchases, salespeople should follow up after the sale to

Figure 17-6
The Selling Process

STAGES

EXAMPLES

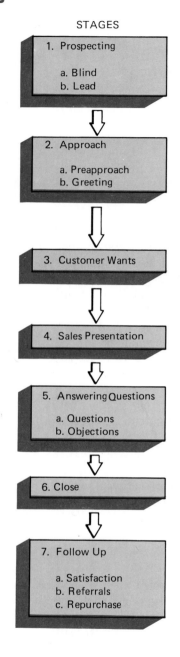

a. Send a direct mail piece to all people residing in an area. Wait for replies.
b. Ask each customer within the last six months for the names of two friends who would be interested in the product or service.

a. Determine customer demographics from available census data.
b. "Good morning. I'm Bill Case from the American Camera House, the area's largest seller of camera equipment. Your next-door-neighbor, Jack Dean, just bought a camera from us. Jack said you were over at his house last night and remarked that you were interested in a similar camera. May we talk?"

"Do you have a specific camera in mind?" "For what purpose is it to be used?" "What price range are you considering?" "Have you ever bought a camera of this type before?" "What would you like to know about the different brands?"

"This camera comes in three models, for beginners, intermediates, and experts. The beginner model is the least complex and costs $120. The others are more complex and take better pictures. Their prices are $200 and $400. Each camera has a one-year limited warranty."

a. "The beginner model has fewer parts and a simple focusing mechanism. These are the basic differences."
b. "I understand that you feel $400 is expensive for this type of camera, but it is comparable to competitors' prices and takes excellent pictures."

"I agree with your choice. The expert camera is best suited to your ability and interests. Would you like to pay cash or charge it?"

a. "Hi. This is Jack from the American Camera House. How are you enjoying the camera you bought two weeks ago?"
b. "We are running a workshop for camera buffs. Would you like to come and bring two or three of your friends?"
c. "Hi. This is Jack from American Camera. We just got in an upgraded model of the camera you bought last year. If you are interested, we will give you a $140 trade-in on your present camera."

ensure that the customer is satisfied. This accomplishes three objectives: the customer gains short-run satisfaction, referrals are stimulated, and, in the long run, repurchases are more likely. "To keep buyers happy, vendors must maintain constructive interaction with purchasers—which includes keeping up on their complaints and future needs. Repeat orders will go to those sellers who have done the best job of nurturing these relationships."[9]

[9] Theodore Levitt, "After the Sale Is Over . . .," *Harvard Business Review*, Vol. 61 (September–October 1983), p. 87.

Besides the tasks accomplished through the selling process, the firm must clearly delineate the nonselling tasks it wants the sales force to perform. Among the nonselling tasks that may be carried out by the sales force are setting up displays, writing up information sheets, pricing merchandise, checking competitors' strategies, conducting such marketing research as test marketing and consumer surveys, and training new employees.

Sales personnel may be required to perform nonselling tasks.

Applying the Plan

The application of the plan is accomplished through the firm's sales management structure. **Sales management** is the planning, analysis, and control of the personal sales function.[10] It covers employee selection, training, territory allocation, compensation, and supervision.

Sales management ranges from employee selection to supervision.

In the selection of sales personnel, a number of factors needed to be considered. First, a combination of personal attributes should be assessed. The major attributes are mental (intelligence, ability to plan), physical (appearance, speaking ability), experience (education, sales and business background), environmental (group memberships, social influences), personality (ambition, enthusiasm, tact, resourcefulness, stability), and willingness to be trained and to follow instructions.[11] Contrary to earlier beliefs, it is now generally accepted that good salespeople are not necessarily born; they are carefully selected and trained. Figure 17-7 shows a semantic differential comparing the traits of successful and unsuccessful salespeople, according to a study of sales managers at 71 manufacturing and wholesaling firms.

Sales force selection involves an analysis of several personal attributes.

Second, the traits of salespeople must be matched with those of customers. As noted earlier in the chapter the buyer-seller dyad is the interaction between the customer and the salesperson. The two relate better when their characteristics are similar. A recent study showed that buyer-seller similarities were most important for high financial purchases and for racial backgrounds.[12]

Third, the traits of salespeople must be matched to the requirements of the product or service being sold. For example, an automobile salesperson would have different traits from a computer salesperson. The latter would need much more formal education, technical training, and utilize a longer, more informational sales process.

After these factors are studied, the firm would develop a formal selection procedure. It would outline the personal attributes sought, sources of employees (such as colleges and employment agencies), and methods for selection (such as interviews, application forms, and testing). This procedure would be based on the firm's overall sales program and needs.

The training of sales personnel may take one or a combination of forms. A formal program utilizes a trainer, classroom setting, lectures, and printed materials. This program may also include role playing, in which trainees act out parts to

Sales training must cover selling skills and company characteristics and requirements.

[10] Two good overview articles on sales management are Alan J. Dubinsky, "A Survey of Sales Management Practices," *Industrial Marketing Management*, Vol. 11 (April 1982), pp. 133–141; and G. David Hughes, "Computerized Sales Management," *Harvard Business Review*, Vol. 61 (March–April 1983), pp. 102–112.

[11] Adapted from William J. Stanton and Richard H. Buskirk, *Management of the Sales Force*, Sixth Edition (Homewood, Ill.: Richard D. Irwin, 1983).

[12] Ishmael P. Akaah, "Dyadic Similarity and Its Influence on Customer Preferences: An Experimental Study," in Richard P. Bagozzi et al. (Editors), *Marketing in the '80s* (Chicago: American Marketing Association, 1980), pp. 114–117.

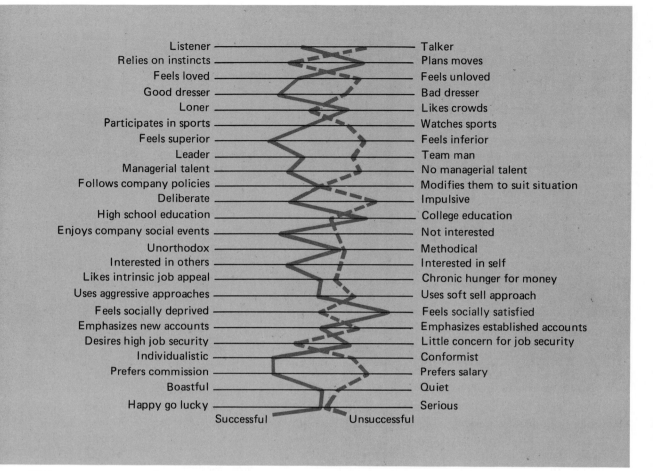

Successful	Unsuccessful
Listener	Talker
Relies on instincts	Plans moves
Feels loved	Feels unloved
Good dresser	Bad dresser
Loner	Likes crowds
Participates in sports	Watches sports
Feels superior	Feels inferior
Leader	Team man
Managerial talent	No managerial talent
Follows company policies	Modifies them to suit situation
Deliberate	Impulsive
High school education	College education
Enjoys company social events	Not interested
Unorthodox	Methodical
Interested in others	Interested in self
Likes intrinsic job appeal	Chronic hunger for money
Uses aggressive approaches	Uses soft sell approach
Feels socially deprived	Feels socially satisfied
Emphasizes new accounts	Emphasizes established accounts
Desires high job security	Little concern for job security
Individualistic	Conformist
Prefers commission	Prefers salary
Boastful	Quiet
Happy go lucky	Serious

Figure 17-7
Successful and Unsuccessful Salespeople Profiles

Source: Bradley D. Lockeman and John H. Hallaq, "Who Are Your Successful Salespeople?" *Journal of the Academy of Marketing Science,* Vol. 10 (Fall 1982), p. 466. Reprinted by permission.

improve skills, and case analysis. Field trips take trainees out on actual calls so they can observe skilled salespeople in action. On-the-job training places trainees in their own selling situations under the close supervision of the trainer or senior salesperson.

Training usually covers a wide range of material. It should teach necessary selling skills and also include information about the company and its offerings, the industry, and employee responsibilities. In addition to initial training, many companies use continuous training or retraining of sales personnel in order to teach new techniques, explain new products, or improve performance. This is particularly important for highly technical products and services.

Next, territory size and salesperson allocation are determined. A territory consists of the geographic area, customers, and/or product lines assigned to a salesperson. When territories are assigned on the basis of customer type (such as large or small) or product type (such as computers or photocopiers), two or more salespeople may cover the same geographic area. Territory size depends on the geographic concentration of customers, order size, travel time and expenses, the

A territory contains the area, customers, and/or products assigned to a salesperson; salesperson allocation depends on ability, seniority, etc.

time needed for each sales call, the number of yearly visits for each account, and the amount of hours per year each salesperson has available for selling tasks. The allocation of a salesperson to a specific territory depends on his or her ability, the buyer-seller dyad, the mix of selling and nonselling functions (for example, one salesperson may do a lot of training of new employees), and seniority.

Proper territory size and allocation provide adequate coverage of customers, minimize territory overlap and salesperson conflict, recognize natural geographic boundaries, minimize travel expenses, encourage solicitation of new accounts, provide a large enough sales potential for a good salesperson to be well rewarded, and offer equity among salespeople in terms of territorial sales potential and workload.[13]

Sales compensation can take one of three general formats: straight salary, straight commission, or a combination of salary and commission. Under the ***straight-salary plan,*** the salesperson is paid a flat fee per week, month, or year. Earnings are not tied to sales. The advantages of the plan are that both selling and nonselling tasks are specified and controlled, there is security for salespeople, and expenses are known in advance. The disadvantages of the plan are low sales force incentive to increase sales, expenses not tied to productivity, and continued costs even if there are low sales. Order takers are usually paid straight salaries.

> **Sales compensation may be *straight salary, straight commission,* or a *combination* of the two.**

With a ***straight-commission plan,*** a salesperson's earnings are directly related to sales or profits. The commission rate is often keyed to a quota, which is a performance standard for the salesperson. A quota can be based on total sales, total profit, customers serviced, products sold, or some other criterion. The advantages of this plan are motivated salespeople, no fixed costs, and expenses tied to productivity. The disadvantages of the plan are lack of control over nonselling tasks performed, instability of a company's dollar expenses and employee earnings, and the risk to employees. Real estate, insurance, and direct-to-home order getters are often paid on a straight commission basis. For example, a real estate salesperson might receive a 3 per cent commission of $3,000 for selling a $100,000 house.

To combine the advantages of salary and commission plans, many companies use ***combination compensation plans.*** These plans balance control, flexibility, and employee incentives. Sometimes bonuses are stipulated for outstanding individual or company performance. All types of order getters work on a combination basis.

The combination plan is used by 57 per cent of the firms analyzed in *Dartnell's 22nd Biennial Survey*. Straight salary is utilized by 22 per cent of the firms. Straight-commission plans are used by 21 per cent. On average, sales personnel paid via a combination plan earn the most and those on a straight-salary plan the least.

Supervision incorporates four aspects of sales management: sales force motivation, measurement of performance, completion of nonselling tasks, and initiating behavior changes. First, sales personnel must be motivated to fulfill their jobs. Research shows that motivation is related to task clarity (what must be done), the salesperson's need for achievement, task variety, the incentive provided for each task (such as compensation), good management (such as all sales

> **Sales force supervision involves motivation, performance measurement, nonselling tasks, and modifying poor behavior.**

---

[13] See A. Parasuraman, ''An Approach for Allocating Sales Call Effort,'' *Industrial Marketing Management,* Vol. 11 (February 1982), pp. 75–79.

personnel treated equitably and outstanding performance recognized), and flexibility.[14]

Second, performance must be measured. To do this, achievements must be gauged against objectives such as total sales and calls per day. This analysis should take into account territory size, travel time, experience, and other factors. Third, the sales manager must ensure that all nonselling tasks are completed, even if sales personnel are not rewarded for them. Fourth, poor behavior should be modified. For example, salespeople go through career cycles similar to those of products—that is, at the maturity and decline stages, enthusiasm and productivity fall. The manager should rekindle enthusiasm through increased compensation, retraining, new territories, added responsibilities, or promotion.[15]

Scope and Importance of Sales Promotion

Sales promotion consists of activities that stimulate customer purchases and dealer effectiveness.

As defined in Chapter 15, sales promotion involves the marketing activities, other than advertising, publicity, or personal selling, that stimulate consumer purchases and dealer effectiveness. Types of sales promotion described later in this section include samples, coupons, special sales, contests, trading stamps, trade shows, and many additional activities. Annual sales promotion expenditures are over $70 billion.[16]

The level of sales promotion activities can be shown through the following:

- More than 140 billion coupons are distributed annually (1,500 per U.S. household). For example, during the week preceding the 1984 Super Bowl, 16 firms offered $11 million in coupons through 40 million newspaper inserts. Although 80 per cent of American households use coupons, redemption rates are relatively low (ranging from 2.1 per cent for Sunday supplements to 10.5 per cent for direct mail.)[17]
- Each year, more than $530 million worth of trading stamps are given out. About 20 per cent of U.S. supermarkets now handle trading stamps, down from a peak of 65 per cent.[18] Consumers have become more price conscious and less interested in stamps.

[14] Stephen X. Doyle and Benson P. Shapiro, "What Counts Most in Motivating Your Sales Force," *Harvard Business Review,* Vol. 58 (May–June 1980), pp. 133–140; Richard C. Becherer, Fred W. Morgan, and Lawrence M. Richard, "The Job Characteristics of Industrial Salespersons: Relationship to Motivation and Satisfaction," *Journal of Marketing,* Vol. 46 (Fall 1982), pp. 125–135; Thomas N. Ingram and Danny N. Bellenger, "Motivational Segments in the Sales Force," *California Management Review,* Vol. 24 (Spring 1982), pp. 81–88; and R. Kenneth Teas, "Performance-Reward Instrumentalities and the Motivation of Retail Salespeople," *Journal of Retailing,* Vol. 58 (Fall 1982), pp. 4–26.

[15] Marvin A. Jolson, "The Salesman's Career Cycle," *Journal of Marketing,* Vol. 38 (July 1974), pp. 39–46.

[16] Don E. Schultz, "Why Marketers Like the Sales Promotion Gambit," *Advertising Age* (November 7, 1983), p. M-52.

[17] B. G. Yovovich, "Stepping into a New Era," *Advertising Age* (August 22, 1983), p. M-9; "Analyzing Promotions," *Nielsen Researcher* (Number 4, 1982), p. 17; and "Insert Keyed to Super Bowl," *Advertising Age* (January 9, 1984), p. 60.

[18] Daniel Kahn. "Trading Stamps Make LI Comeback." *Newsday* (May 12, 1981), p. 35; Jeffrey H. Birnbaum. "Industry Blues Fail to Deter S&H Stamps." *Wall Street Journal* (August 5, 1980), p. 29; and "1983 Report: A Cautious Year as Buyers Wait for the Recovery," *Incentive Marketing Magazine* (February 1984), p. 13.

Reprinted by permission.

Figure 17-8
ITT Trade Show Displays
ITT is one of the many firms that regularly participate in trade shows throughout the U. S. and the world. In this photo, the high-technology nature of ITT displays is shown. ITT is interested in serious presentations.

- Trade show attendance exceeds 35 million people per year; there are more than 8,000 shows containing ten exhibits or more. The average attendee spends 7.5 hours at a show and visits 19 exhibits.[19] See Figure 17-8.
- There are about 1,000 nationally advertised sweepstakes each year. They award well over $150 million in prizes. For example, a 1983 sweepstakes sponsored by Kraft Foods and Chevrolet attracted almost 1.5 million entries. This sweepstakes awarded a Chevrolet Cavalier and a trip to Walt Disney World's EPCOT Center as a grand prize; autos were also given to retailers with the best displays and ads featuring the sweepstakes.[20]
- About $6 billion per year is spent on point-of-purchase displays in retail stores. In supermarkets, promotional displays are utilized most frequently for carbonated beverages, laundry detergents, shampoo, and toilet tissue. They are least frequently used for canned fruit drinks, hand and body lotions, trash bags, headache remedies, and salad dressings. However, when they receive special promotion displays, the latter group of products have large sales increases.[21] Figure 17-9 shows a BMW auto dealership display that won a 1984 award from the Point-of-Purchase Advertising Institute (POPAI).

[19] "Trade Show Industry Still Growing, But at Slower Rate." *Marketing News* (April 30, 1982), p. 1; and Richard K. Swandby and Jonathan (Skip) Cox, "How Trade Shows Served the '70s," *Industrial Marketing* (April 1980), pp. 72–78.
[20] Franklynn Peterson and Judi Kesselman-Turkel, "Catching Customers with Sweepstakes," *Fortune* (February 8, 1982), p. 84; and "Tie-In Promotions Prove Mutually Beneficial for Advertisers and GM," *Marketing News* (January 20, 1984), p. 8.
[21] "Display Effectiveness: An Evaluation, Part II," *Nielsen Researcher* (Number 3, 1983), pp. 2–10.

Figure 17-9
A BMW Point-of-Purchase Display
This point-of-purchase display was used in BMW automobile dealer showrooms. The display appeals to prospective purchasers by playing up BMW's "Ultimate Driving Machine" image. It positions the BMW as an imported luxury sports car. Consumers are also encouraged to buy BMW accessories.

Reprinted by permission of Point-of-Purchase Advertising Institute, Inc.

Several factors have contributed to the growth of sales promotion. The various forms of promotions are now more acceptable to firms and consumers. Executives are better qualified to direct sales promotion. Quick returns are possible. As competition increases, promotions increase. During economic recessions consumers look for promotions, and channel members put more pressure on manufacturers for promotions.[22]

Characteristics of Sales Promotion

Sales promotion lures customers, maintains loyalty, provides value, increases impulse purchases, creates excitement, is often keyed to patronage, and appeals to channel members.

Sales promotion has a number of advantages for the firm. It helps attract customer traffic and maintain brand or store loyalty. For example, new-product samples or trial offers draw customers. A manufacturer can retain brand loyalty through gifts to regular customers or coupons for its brands. A retailer can retain store loyalty by giving store trading stamps or store coupons. Quick results can be achieved.

Some forms of sales promotion provide value to the consumer and are retained

[22] Roger A. Strang, "Sales Promotion—Fast Growth, Faulty Management." *Harvard Business Review,* Vol. 54 (July–August 1976), pp. 117–119.

by them. They provide a reminder function. These include calendars, matchbooks, T-shirts, pens, and posters with the firm's name.

Impulse purchases can be increased through in-store displays. For example, an attractive display for batteries in a supermarket can significantly increase sales. In addition, a good display can lead to a larger-volume purchase than originally intended by the consumer.

Excitement is created through certain short-run promotions involving gifts, contests, or sweepstakes. In particular, high-value items or high payoffs encourage consumers to participate. Contests offer the further benefit of customer involvement (through the completion of a puzzle or some other skill-oriented activity).

Many types of sales promotion are keyed to customer patronage. Some promotions, such as coupons, trading stamps, and referral gifts, are directly related to sales. In these cases the promotions are a fixed percentage of sales and their costs are not incurred until sales are completed.

Finally, channel members cooperate better with manufacturers when sales-promotion support is provided in the form of displays, manufacturers' coupons, manufacturers' rebates, joint training of the retail sales force, and trade allowances.

There are also several limitations to sales promotion. The image of the firm may be lessened if it continuously runs special deals. Consumers may view the discounts as representing a decline in product or service quality and believe the firm could not sell its offerings without them.

Sales promotion may hurt image, cause consumers to wait for special offers, and shift the focus from the product.

When coupons, rebates, or other special deals are used frequently, consumers may not make purchases if the items are sold at regular prices. Instead, they will stock up each time there is a special offer. In addition, consumers may interpret the regular price as a price hike for items that are heavily promoted.

Sometimes sales promotions shift the focus away from the product or service onto secondary factors. Consumers may be attracted by calendars, coupons, or sweepstakes instead of by the product or service's quality, functions, and durability. In the short run this generates consumer enthusiasm. In the long run this may have adverse effects on a brand's image and on sales, because a product-related differential advantage has not been developed.

It must be remembered that sales promotion is a supplement to the other forms of promotion. It enhances, but does not replace, advertising, personal selling, and publicity.

Developing a Sales Promotion Plan

The development of a sales promotion plan consists of the steps shown in Figure 17-10 and explained in the following subsections.

Setting Objectives

Sales promotion objectives are almost always demand-oriented. These objectives may be related to channel members or consumers.

Figure 17-10
Developing a Sales Promotion Plan

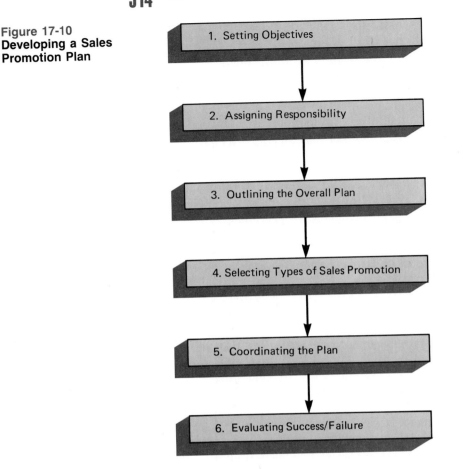

Objectives pertaining to channel members include obtaining distribution, receiving adequate store shelf space, increasing dealer enthusiasm, increasing sales, and cooperation in sales promotion expenditures.[23]

Objectives pertaining to customers include increasing brand awareness, increasing trial of a product or service, increasing average purchases, stimulating repurchases, obtaining impulse sales, emphasizing novelty, and supplementing other promotional tools.

Assigning Responsibility

The responsibility for sales promotion is usually shared by advertising and sales managers. Each directs the promotions regarding his or her area. For example, the advertising manager would be involved with coupons, contests, trading stamps, matchbooks, calendars, and other mass-promotion tools. The sales manager would be involved with trade shows, special sales, trade allowances, cooper-

---

[23] See John A. Quelch, "It's Time to Make Trade Promotion More Productive," *Harvard Business Review,* Vol. 61 (May–June 1983), pp. 130–136.

ative promotions, special events, demonstrations, and other efforts requiring individualized attention directed at channel members or final consumers.

In some cases companies that utilize sales promotion employ specialized inside departments or outside sales promotion firms, such as Donnelly Marketing (a division of Dun & Bradstreet). Many outside firms tend to operate in narrow areas, such as coupons, stamps, or gifts, and generally are able to produce promotional items for less than the user company could. These firms offer expertise, fast service, flexibility, and, when requested, distribution.

Outlining the Overall Plan

The overall sales promotion plan should be outlined and include a budget, an orientation or theme, conditions, media, duration or timing, and cooperative efforts.

When establishing the sales promotion budget, it is important to include all costs. For example, the average face value of a coupon is about 20 cents; in addition, manufacturers have to pay retailers a 7 to 10 cent handling charge for each coupon they redeem. Other coupon costs involve printing, mailing, advertising, and manufacturer handling.

Sales promotion orientation refers to its focus: channel members or final consumers. Promotions directed at channel members should increase product knowledge, provide sales support, offer rewards for sales, and aim to increase cooperation and productivity. Promotions directed at final consumers should stimulate impulse and larger-volume sales, sustain brand-name recognition, and gain audience participation. The theme of sales promotion refers to its underlying message, such as a special sale, store opening, new-product introduction, holiday celebration, or new-customer recruitment.

Sales promotion conditions are the stipulations channel members or final customers must meet to be eligible for a sales promotion. These may include minimum purchases, performance provisions, and minimum age. For example, a channel member may have to stock merchandise and set up advertising displays in order to receive a display case from a manufacturer. A final consumer may have to send in proofs of purchase in order to receive a refund or gift. In most situations, strict time limits are set that define the closing dates for participation in a sales promotion.

The media are the vehicles through which sales promotions reach channel members or final consumers. Media include direct mail, newspapers, television, personal selling, and group meetings.

The duration of a sales promotion may be short or long. Supermarket and fast-food coupons usually have quick closing dates. Trading stamps normally have no closing dates. The duration must be keyed to objectives. Coupons are used to increase store traffic, and trading stamps are used to maintain loyalty. As noted earlier, when sales promotions are lengthy or are offered frequently, consumers may come to expect them as a basic part of the purchase. Some promotions are seasonal, and for these timing is crucial. The promotions must be tied to the introduction of seasonal activities such as school openings or model or style changes.

Finally, the firm should determine the feasibility of shared sales promotions.

Sales promotion orientation **may be toward channel members and/or final consumers.**

The *conditions of sales promotion* specify eligibility requirements that must be met.

Sales promotions may be shared by channel members.

With cooperative efforts, each channel member pays part of the promotion cost and receives benefits. In retailing, cooperative sales promotions are frequently sponsored by merchants via shopping-center associations. For example, a group of merchants may share the costs of running a children's petting zoo located in a regional shopping center.

Selecting Types of Sales Promotion

There is a wide range of sales promotion tools available to a firm. The characteristics of channel-member sales-promotion tools are shown in Table 17-4. The characteristics of final-consumer sales-promotion tools are displayed in Table 17-5. Examples for each tool are provided in these tables.

A variety of sales promotion tools can be offered to channel members and shoppers.

In general, sales promotion budgets have been allocated as follows: direct mail, 15 per cent; trade shows and exhibits, 6 per cent; promotion advertising space, 8 per cent; printing and audiovisuals, 7 per cent; point-of-purchase displays, 14 per cent; business meetings and conventions, 31 per cent; premiums, incentives, and specialties, 16 per cent; and coupon redemption, 3 per cent.[24]

The selection of sales promotions should be based on company image, objectives, costs, participation requirements, and channel or customer enthusiasm.

Coordinating the Plan

In coordinating the plan, advertising and sales promotion should be integrated.

It is essential that sales promotion activities be well coordinated with other elements of the promotion mix. In particular, advertising and sales promotion plans should be integrated. The sales force should be notified of all promotions well in advance and trained to implement them. For special events, such as the appearance of a major celebrity, publicity should be generated. Sales promotions should also be consistent with channel-member activities.

Evaluating Success or Failure

The success or failure of sales promotions is often simple to measure.

The success or failure of many types of sales promotions is relatively straightforward to measure because promotions are so closely linked to performance or sales. By analyzing before-and-after data, the usefulness of promotions should be apparent.

For example, trade show effectiveness can be measured by counting the number of leads generated from a show, examining the sales from these leads and the cost per lead, getting customer feedback about a show from the sales force, and determining the amount of literature given out at a show.[25]

Likewise, companies are able to verify changes in their sales as a result of dealer-training programs. Firms using coupons examine sales and compare redemption rates with industry averages. Attitudinal surveys of channel members and final consumers indicate satisfaction with various kinds of promotions, suggestions for improvements, and the effect of promotions on image.

Some promotions, such as calendars, pens, and special events, are more difficult to evaluate because objectives are less definite.

---

[24] Yovovich, "Stepping into a New Era," p. M-30.
[25] Thomas V. Bonoma, "Get More out of Your Trade Shows," *Harvard Business Review,* Vol. 61 (January–February 1983), p. 78.

Table 17-4   Types of Sales Promotions Directed at Channel Members

Type	Characteristics	Illustration
Trade shows or meetings	One or a group of manufacturers invites channel members to attend sessions where products are displayed and explained.	The annual National Home Center Show attracts more than 1,200 exhibitors and thousands of attendees.
Training	The manufacturer provides training for channel members' personnel.	Apple trains retail salespeople how to operate and use its computers.
Trade allowances or special offers	Channel members are given discounts or rebates for performing specified functions or purchasing during certain time periods.	A local retailer receives a discount for setting up a special display for GE lightbulbs.
Point-of-purchase displays	The manufacturer or wholesaler gives the retailer a fully equipped display for its products and sets it up.	Coca-Cola provides refrigerators with its name on them to retailers carrying minimum quantities of Coca-Cola products.
Push money	Channel members or their salespeople are given bonuses for pushing the brand of a particular manufacturer. Retailers may not like this practice if salespeople shift their loyalty to the manufacturer.	A salesperson in a television store is paid an extra $50 for every console of a particular brand that is sold.
Sales contests	Prizes or bonuses are distributed if certain performance levels are met.	A retailer receives an extra $1,000 for selling 1,000 radios in a month.
Free merchandise	Discounts or allowances are provided in the form of merchandise.	A retailer gets one case of ballpoint pens free for every ten cases purchased.
Demonstration models	A free item is given to the wholesaler or retailer for demonstration purposes.	A vacuum-cleaner manufacturer offers retailers a floor demonstrator.
Gifts	Channel members are given gifts for carrying items or performing functions.	During one two-month period, Sherwood Medical Industries offered wholesalers purchasing a $6,000 syringe package a choice of a color television, microwave oven, or freezer filled with steaks.
Cooperative promotions	Two or more channel members share the costs of a promotion.	A manufacturer and retailer each pay part of the costs for pens with the retailer's name embossed.

Summary

Almost seven million people are employed in personal-selling occupations. This number understates the value of personal selling, because every contact between a company representative and a customer involves some amount of personal selling. Selling costs as a percentage of sales fall between 1.6 and 16.9 per cent. The average cost of one sales call can be as high as $150 or more.

Personal selling establishes a buyer-seller dyad (the two-way flow of communication between both parties), offers flexibility and adaptability, results in little waste in terms of audience, clinches sales, and provides immediate feedback. However, personal selling can handle only a limited number of customers, has

Table 17-5 Types of Sales Promotions Directed at Final Consumers

Type	Characteristics	Illustration
Coupons	Manufacturers or retailers advertise special discounts for customers who redeem coupons.	P&G mails consumers a 25-cents-off coupon for Sure deodorant, which can be redeemed at any supermarket.
Refund or rebate	A consumer submits proof-of-purchase (usually to the manufacturer) and receives an extra discount.	First Alert home fire alarms provides $5 rebates to consumers submitting proof of purchase.
Samples	Free merchandise or services are given consumers, generally for new items.	When Sunlight dishwashing liquid was introduced, free samples were mailed to consumers.
Trading stamps	Consumers are given free stamps based on dollar purchases. Stamps are accumulated and exchanged for gifts or money.	Some A&P supermarkets distribute S&H trading stamps.
Contests or sweepstakes	Consumers compete for prizes by answering questions (contests) or filling out forms for random drawings of prizes (sweepstakes).	Publishers Clearinghouse sponsors annual sweepstakes and awards automobiles, houses, and other prizes.
Bonus or multipacks	Consumers receive discounts for purchasing in quantity.	Some stores run one-cent sales, whereby the consumer buys one item and gets a second one for a penny.
Shows or exhibits	Many manufacturers cosponsor exhibitions for consumers.	The Auto Show is annually scheduled for the public in New York.
Point-of-purchase displays	In-store displays remind customers and generate impulse purchases.	Chewing gum sales in supermarkets are high because displays are placed at checkout counters.
Special events	Manufacturers or retailers sponsor celebrity appearances, fashion shows, and other activities.	Virtually every major league baseball team has an annual "Old Timers' Day," which attracts large crowds.
Gifts	Consumers are given gifts for making a purchase or opening a new account.	Savings banks offer a range of gifts for consumers opening new accounts or expanding existing ones.
Referral gifts	Existing customers are given gifts for referring their friends to the company.	Tupperware awards gifts to the woman hosting a Tupperware party in her home.
Demonstrations	Products or services are shown in action.	The Evelyn Woods' reading course technique is demonstrated in a complimentary lesson.

high costs per customer, is ineffective for creating consumer awareness, and has a poor image for some consumers.

A personal selling plan involves (1) setting objectives, (2) assigning responsibility, (3) establishing a budget, (4) determining the type(s) of sales positions, (5) selecting a sales technique, (6) outlining sales tasks, and (7) applying the plan.

Sales promotion encompasses all forms of promotion not defined as advertising, publicity, and personal selling. Sales promotion has annual expenditures of over $70 billion. The growth of sales promotion is the result of greater firm and consumer acceptance, better management, quick payoffs, competition, economic conditions, and demands by channel members.

Sales promotion helps attract customer traffic and loyalty, provides value to consumers and is sometimes retained by them, increases impulse purchases, creates excitement, is keyed to customer patronage, and improves channel-member cooperation. On the other hand, sales promotion may hurt the firm's image, encourage consumers to wait for promotions before making purchases, and shift the focus away from product or service attributes. Sales promotion cannot replace other forms of promotion.

A sales promotion plan includes (1) setting objectives, (2) assigning responsibility, (3) outlining the overall plan, (4) selecting types of sales promotion, (5) coordinating the plan, and (6) evaluating success or failure. Types of sales promotion include trade shows, training, allowances, free merchandise, and cooperative promotions for channel members and coupons, refunds, samples, stamps, and gifts for final consumers.

Questions for Discussion

1. The Bureau of Labor Statistics lists nearly seven million people in sales positions. Why does this figure understate the importance of personal selling?
2. Can computerized order-processing systems replace a personal sales force? Explain your answer.
3. Why is personal selling an ineffective tool for generating consumer awareness about a product or service?
4. Compare personal-selling objectives with those for advertising.
5. In what situations should a firm employ order takers? Order getters?
6. When is a canned sales presentation acceptable? When is it not acceptable?
7. How would you handle these objections raised at the end of a sales presentation?
   a. "The price is too high."
   b. "Your warranty period is much too short."
   c. "None of the alternatives you showed me is satisfactory."
8. What characteristics are desirable in a salesperson? Are they the same for all categories of sales personnel?
9. Why do so many firms use a combination plan for sales force compensation?
10. How would you motivate a retail sales clerk? A life insurance salesperson?
11. Some observers believe that sales promotion is more important to a firm than advertising. Comment on this.
12. Evaluate sweepstakes as a sales promotion tool.
13. What are the risks associated with sales promotion?
14. Differentiate between sales promotion orientation and conditions.
15. List several sales promotion techniques that would be appropriate for Zenith televisions. List several that would be inappropriate. Explain your answer.
16. How could the effectiveness of a point-of-purchase display be determined?

Case 1 Ray Henderson: A Pharmaceutical Salesperson*

Ray Henderson is a traveling salesperson who regularly visits doctors' offices and medical centers in northeast Tennessee for his employer, Merck & Co. (a leading pharmaceutical company). He is a "detail man," one of 25,000 such medical

---

* The data in this case are drawn from Michael Waldholz, "How a 'Detail Man' Promotes New Drugs to Tennessee Doctors," *Wall Street Journal* (November 8, 1982), pp. 1, 25.

representatives in the U.S., who provides information (details) about and promotes new and existing medicines to doctors and tries to convince them to prescribe Merck products to their patients. In many cases, "Whether a new drug becomes well accepted by physicians can depend as much on the salesmanship of a man like Ray Henderson as on the qualities of the medicines themselves."

Ray began with Merck in 1960, after working for a medical-supply house. He travels about 25,000 miles each year and distributes large amounts of drug samples to the doctors in his territory. Twice, Ray has been the highest-producing salesperson at Merck. He is at the top of the company's $25,000 to $50,000 annual compensation range.

The communication between Ray Henderson and his doctors is highly interactive. In a quiet manner, Ray explains the uses and benefits of Merck's medicines. The doctors raise questions about adverse side effects and the circumstances under which certain drugs should or should not be used. They expect Henderson to be completely honest with them, and not make inaccurate or exaggerated statements. If a new Merck drug would not serve their purposes, they expect Henderson to say so. To aid the process, Ray also helps to set up medical symposiums, bringing together local doctors with invited guest lecturers from outside the geographic area.

Henderson works hard to ensure that doctors respect him and his company. He spends many hours learning about Merck's new products and refreshing his memory about existing products (at Merck, a detail person spends 12 weeks during his or her first year in formal courses and in rounds with interns and residents at a teaching hospital). Every year, all sales personnel are tested four times and must attend four regional tutorials conducted by medical experts.

Despite Henderson's high standards and low-key approach, some doctors and others criticize the general role of the detail person in promoting drugs. They fear that overzealous salesmanship can sometimes overstate actual product effectiveness. Nonetheless, "Even the critics of detail men agree that most drug salespeople are ethical and straightforward"; and many companies have clear policies that tone down the sales presentations of detail persons.

Ray Henderson really enjoys his job. He likes providing the "best-educated members of the community with a real service." He even goes on hunting trips with some of his clients. Responding to one of his job's limitations, Ray remarked, "Nobody likes to spend his day waiting in a doctor's waiting room. If it weren't fun, I couldn't think of doing anything worse than waiting all day to see a doctor."

QUESTIONS

1. Describe at least five objectives Merck would set for its detail salespeople.
2. What criteria should Merck consider when selecting new detail salespeople?
3. Comment on this doctor's statement: "I know I should know about drugs before Ray tells me. If it were physically possible to keep up with all the literature, I would. But family practice sees a lot of drugs. I shouldn't have to depend on it, but I must admit when a detail man tells me something I didn't know, I appreciate it."
4. Evaluate Ray Henderson's attitude toward his job. How much does this attitude affect his performance? Explain your answer.

Case 2 The Coupon Craze: Has It Gone Too Far?[†]

Between 1978 and 1983, the number of coupons annually distributed in the U.S. grew by 92 per cent, from 73 billion to 140 billion. The value of all coupons redeemed by consumers has risen to over $1.7 billion per year. In addition to food products, which have traditionally offered coupons, a number of other items are now involved with couponing, including liquor, tobacco, and clothing (such as Wrangler jeans).

The couponing craze has developed for several reasons: consumer responses are rapid; consumers are becoming extremely price conscious; television and other advertising media have become so expensive; and store traffic and inventory turnover are increased. Said a Sara Lee food executive, "If we place a coupon in someone's hand, we give them more reason to buy." Added a Kroger supermarket spokesperson, "We'll do whatever the consumer wants to be competitive."

Nonetheless, many companies are beginning to question whether couponing has gone too far. They point to these problems:

- Less than 10 per cent of all coupons are redeemed.
- Coupons cause lower levels of brand loyalty, as consumers switch among brands—depending on which has a coupon.
- Consumers become conditioned to wait for coupons and not make purchases at regular prices.
- Retailers are competing with each other through "double coupons," by which the retailers match manufacturers' price discounts.
- With so many coupons in circulation, handling them has become more difficult. Also, coupon fraud is at an alltime high. Some experts estimate that 20 per cent or more of all coupon refunds are either fraudulent or incorrect (e.g., expired coupons redeemed); this amounts to $350 million annually. Some firms have eliminated expiration dates to reduce mishandling.

Many retailers have other complaints about coupons. They believe the 7- to 10-cent handling fee per coupon paid by manufacturers does not cover their costs. They often find refunds from manufacturers being processed too slowly, which results in a long lag between the time they give consumers the coupon reductions and the date they receive reimbursement. They would also like to see more permanent price cuts and less reliance on coupons. But as the sales promotion director of Pillsbury commented, couponing is the "most effective way to generate trials, brand-continuity, and brand-switching."

[†] The data in this case are drawn from "Retailing May Have Overdosed on Coupons," *Business Week* (June 13, 1983), pp. 147 ff; Jennifer Alter and Nancy Giges, "Industry Losing $350 Million on Coupon Misredemption," *Advertising Age* (May 30, 1983), p. 1; and "Marketing Briefs," *Marketing News* (April 27, 1984), p. 16.

QUESTIONS

1. Virtually all supermarkets are heavily involved with coupons, yet only 20 per cent give out trading stamps. Comment on this.
2. Evaluate Wrangler's decision to occasionally offer coupons for its jeans.
3. Despite the rapid growth of coupons, less than 10 per cent of the coupons distributed are redeemed by consumers. Explain this low redemption rate. What can be done to increase it?
4. Why are manufacturers reluctant to institute permanent price cuts instead of coupons?

Part Five Case Chrysler Corporation: A Good Promotion Plan Aids Its Recovery*

In 1982, Chrysler Corporation reported a net profit of $170 million, the first profit for the company since 1977; during 1983, it earned about $700 million as the firm and the U.S. auto industry made a strong recovery from previous years. Company car and truck market shares both rose. As a result, Chrysler was able to fully repay $1.2 billion in federally guaranteed loans in 1983—several years early. Some analysts predicted that Chrysler would earn over $2 billion in 1984 (compared with a $1.7 billion loss in 1980).

Chrysler's recovery is due to the successful revision of the company's entire marketing strategy, including an appeal to younger consumers, an extended warranty plan, attractive and fuel-efficient new cars, better quality control (few recalls), cars built to buyer specifications (rather than mass-produced prior to determining consumer desires), better inventory control, and aggressive pricing. Yet, despite these major strategy revisions, many observers believe that the innovative and daring promotion plan that was developed when the firm was near bankruptcy has keyed Chrysler's recovery. In recognition of Chrysler's promotional prowess, Lee Iacocca was selected as Adman of the Year for 1983 by the editors of *Advertising Age*.

One of Iacocca's first actions after he became Chrysler chairman in late 1978 was to drop the firm's long-time advertising agency, BBD&O, and give the entire Chrysler account to Kenyon & Eckhardt. Iacocca had worked with Kenyon & Eckhardt when he was the president of Ford, and convinced the agency to give up its Lincoln-Mercury account with Ford in exchange for a five-year no-cut Chrysler contract. At the time, Chrysler's annual media expenditures were between $120 million and $150 million.

From 1979 to fall 1980, Chrysler's major promotional objective was to assure the public that it would not go bankrupt and would be able to replace parts and honor service warranties. Kenyon & Eckhardt developed the theme, "Trust us, support us, and we'll be around." Lee Iacocca was not the agency's first choice as Chrysler advertising spokesperson. Walter Cronkite, then the CBS television news anchorman, was the personality who came out best in consumer research; however, he would not accept a Chrysler offer. Instead, a reluctant Iacocca was used in ads, saying only "I'm not asking you to buy any car on faith. I'm asking you to compare" or "If you buy any car without considering Chrysler, that'll be too bad for both of us."

At first, Kenyon & Eckhardt felt the Iacocca ads were not effective enough and

---

* The data in this case are drawn from Ralph Gray, "Chrysler Corporation," *Advertising Age* (September 8, 1983), p. 50; John Holusha, "Blunt Talk from the Chief of Chrysler," *New York Times* (January 29, 1984), Auto section, pp. 1, 14; "How Chrysler Does More with Less," *Marketing & Media Decisions* (March 1982), pp. 62–65, 148, 150; "Lee Iacocca of Chrysler: Crisis Plans Paying Off," *Advertising Age* (January 2, 1984), pp. 1, 30–31; Steve Raddock, "Chrysler: Back from the Brink," *Marketing & Media Decisions* (Spring 1983), pp. 27–30, 34–36, 40–41; *Standard Rate & Data Service: Consumer Magazines and Agricultural Media Rates and Data* (January 27, 1984), various pages; and Urban C. Lehner, "Chrysler Seen Spending $350 Million or More on Minivan, But Step Is Careful," *Wall Street Journal* (March 23, 1984), p. 8.

hired Joe Garagiola (the sports personality) to replace him as the corporation spokesperson in order to "sell cars, not image." But after Chrysler received its federal loan guarantees in January 1980, Kenyon & Eckhardt decided to use Iacocca more prominently in commercials. As Iacocca himself noted, he gave the Chrysler ads a tremendous amount of credibility: "If people saw somebody on TV who, after making certain promises, would go back and make the cars, sales might not erode."

Chrysler's promotional efforts during this period were considered to be a "holding action," while the firm revamped its product line (which took about two years). For example, a sales-incentive program offered consumers $50 for taking a test drive; a 30-day, 1000-mile money-back guarantee (if a new car buyer was dissatisfied for any reason whatsoever); a no-cost scheduled maintenance program for two years or 24,000 miles; and a free two-year membership in the Amoco Motor Club. At the same time, Kenyon & Eckhardt sought to improve advertising effectiveness by increasing Chrysler's use of spot (local) television and radio, newspapers, and direct mail. This also built stronger relations between Chrysler and its dealers.

In fall 1980, Chrysler introduced its long-awaited, fuel-efficient "K" cars, the Dodge Aries and Plymouth Reliant. These were Chrysler's first new cars since 1978. The company generated a huge amount of publicity for the K cars. Stories appeared on network news programs; there were magazine articles; and newspapers ran features. Advertising stressed the patriotism involved with the purchase of an American-made K car.

With the beginning of the 1982 model year (fall 1981), Chrysler began to place greater focus on product advertising, as it switched away from the institutional advertising which was designed to convince consumers that the company was financially sound. Chrysler started using celebrities in commercials. They included Ricardo Montalban for Chrysler LeBaron, Kelly Harmon for Dodge cars, Walt Garrison for Dodge trucks, and John Houseman for Plymouth Reliant. Because 1982 was a difficult year for U.S. auto makers, sales promotions were used throughout the year. Among Chrysler's promotions were a "February Bonus Rebate" ($300–$2,000), a "Spring Rebate" ($300–$500), "Value Coupons" ($300–$600), and 10.9 per cent financing (far below the market interest rates at the time). These promotions relied heavily on the use of spot (local) radio, because it required a short lead time and was quite flexible.

At the same time, Chrysler perfected its use of a "target audience matrix" as a tool for evaluating media. This matrix outlined the relative importance of each demographic market segment for a particular automobile model; media would then be evaluated on the basis of how well their audiences matched the target market(s) sought. Table 1 shows the target audience matrix developed for the Chrysler LeBaron. The most likely purchasers of the LeBaron were 25- to 34-year-old males and females with incomes of $35,000 and above, and 35- to 54-year-old females with incomes of $35,000 and above. The least likely purchasers were males and females ages 55 and older with incomes below $35,000. Table 2 shows the costs and circulations of selected magazines actually used for LeBaron advertising.

In analyzing media, Chrysler used other measures of effectiveness in addition to the target audience matrix. It examined market-by-market differences, competitors, car inventory on hand, and sales patterns by product category (e.g., imports

Table 1
**Chrysler LeBaron
Target Audience Matrix**[a]

Male	Income Below $35,000	Income of $35,000 and Above
18–24	112	138
25–34	87	276
35–44	123	159
45–54	81	172
55–64	74	169
65 and over	51	114
Female	**Income Below $35,000**	**Income of $35,000 and Above**
18–24	94	105
25–34	105	282
35–44	86	211
45–54	102	207
55–64	78	154
65 and over	32	158

[a] 100 equals an average probability of purchase. Under 100 means a less than average probability of purchase. Above 100 means a greater than average probability of purchase.

Source: "How Chrysler Does More with Less," *Marketing & Media Decisions* (March 1982), p. 65. Reprinted by permission.

versus domestic cars). Table 3 compares 1981 and 1982 advertising expenditures by medium for the Chrysler Corporation.

During spring 1982, Chrysler began promoting an important competitive advantage, its "5/50 Three-Way Protection Plan" (providing five years or 50,000 miles protection against powertrain problems, free scheduled maintenance, and protection against outer body rust-through). To date, no other auto manufacturer has offered such a plan, while Chrysler continues to stress it in advertising.

Table 2   Selected Costs and Circulations of Magazines in Which the Chrysler LeBaron Was Advertised, 1984

Magazine	Annual Frequency of Publication	Per Ad Cost of 1 Full-Page 4-Color Ad in a Single Issue[a]	Per Ad Cost of 1 Full-Page 4-Color Ad in 12 Issues[b]	Total Paid Circulation per Issue	Subscription Circulation	Single-Issue Newsstand Circulation
Autoweek	52	$ 4,563	$ 4,010[c]	122,893	120,824	2,069
Bon Appetit	12	22,315	19,160	1,300,703	1,109,686	191,017
Car & Driver	12	29,760	24,955	784,521	543,517	241,004
Discover	12	24,500	22,540	932,013	794,942	137,071
New York	50	17,100	16,420[c]	422,819	383,824	38,995
People	51	49,200	47,725	2,700,515	1,029,969	1,670,546
Self	12	19,690	19,690	1,085,141	492,694	592,447
Science Digest	12	14,555	13,100	532,381	324,780	207,601
Sunset	12	25,262	25,262	1,422,618	1,328,941	93,677
Time	52	101,825	957,155	4,464,228	4,188,212	276,016
Travel & Leisure	12	22,530	19,151[c]	934,093	926,360	7,733
Working Woman	12	15,100	13,892	565,340	539,935	25,405

[a] An ad is placed once in the magazine during the year. This does not include production costs.
[b] Ads are placed in 12 separate issues of the magazine during the year sometimes resulting in a discount; ad content may differ in each issue. This does not include production costs.
[c] Discounts given for placement in 13 issues.

Source: Standard Rate & Data Service: Consumer Magazines and Agricultural Media Rates and Data (January 27, 1984), various pages.

Table 3
Chrysler Corporation Advertising Expenditures by Medium

Medium	1982		1981	
	$	%	$	%
Newspapers	29,600,000	17.1	30,955,700	16.0
Magazines	25,582,200	14.8	25,197,200	13.1
Farm publications	733,500	0.4	864,000	0.4
Spot television	23,538,900	13.6	17,430,600	9.0
Network television	68,219,500	39.4	54,874,400	28.4
Spot radio	11,997,200	6.9	50,760,500	26.3
Network radio	2,919,300	1.7	2,084,800	1.1
Outdoor	874,700	0.5	152,800	0.1
Unmeasured (e.g., direct mail, production costs)	9,556,100	5.5	10,680,000	5.5
Total	$173,021,400	100.0[a]	$193,000,000	100.0[a]
Advertising expenditures as per cent of sales		1.7		1.9

[a] Rounding error

Source: Ralph Gray, "Chrysler Corporation," *Advertising Age* (September 8, 1983), p. 50. Reprinted by permission of *Advertising Age.* Copyright 1983 by Crain Communications Inc.

Late in 1982, Chrysler established separate marketing groups (comprised of advertising, merchandising, and marketing planning) for Chrysler/Plymouth and Dodge. BBD&O was rehired to handle Dodge advertising. Kenyon & Eckhardt opened a division in Los Angeles to promote Chrysler's distribution and sale of Mitsubishi imports.

As a result, 1983 promotion stressed more distinctive images for Chrysler, Dodge, Plymouth, Dodge trucks, and Mitsubishi vehicles. Ricardo Montalban became the spokesperson for the entire Chrysler line. Dodge expanded on its theme as "America's driving machine," but dropped Kelly Harmon. Plymouth used the theme "the American way to get your money's worth," but dropped John Houseman. Dodge trucks relied on the "Ram tough" theme and continued to use Walt Garrison. Mitsubishi retained its "master car builders of Japan" theme.

Chrysler's 1984 promotion efforts capitalized on previous themes, with a strong emphasis on its popular new minivans (the Dodge Caravan and Plymouth Voyager)—called "a transportation revolution" by Chrysler. Said Lee Iacocca, "You hate to be carried away, but I believe (the minivan's) going to be that hot. . . . Everywhere I go, people go wild." However, Iacocca also stated that he would appear in no more than one Chrysler television commercial in 1984; his real goal was not to appear at all.

QUESTIONS
1. Evaluate Chrysler's use of Lee Iacocca as company spokesperson. Will Chrysler's sales or image suffer when he no longer appears in ads? Explain your answer.
2. Why did Chrysler emphasize institutional advertising from 1979 to 1981, and then switch to product advertising?
3. Determine the audience characteristics of three of the magazines listed in Table 2 (use W. R. Simmons data or a comparable reference source available in the library). Then, analyze each magazine as a LeBaron advertising medium on the basis of the information contained in Table 1 and Table 2.

4. Compare Chrysler's 1981 and 1982 media advertising expenditures. Explain the basic differences. Next, review Chrysler's listing in the most recent "100 Leading National Advertisers" issue of *Advertising Age,* published every September, and contrast the expenditures with those from 1981 and 1982.
5. How can Chrysler continue to generate favorable publicity? How can it avoid negative publicity?
6. Should Chrysler salespeople use a canned sales presentation or a need-satisfaction approach? Why?
7. Chrysler no longer offers $50 to consumers who test drive its cars or money-back guarantees to those who buy them. Explain this. Would you recommend a return to these sales promotions? Why or why not?

PART **SIX**

Price
Planning

Part Six covers the fourth and final major element of marketing, pricing. Chapter 18 presents an overview of price planning, the systematic decision making pertaining to all aspects of pricing by the organization. The role of pricing in allocating goods and services among purchasers, its importance in transactions, and its interrelation with other marketing variables are described. The differences between price and nonprice competition are explained. Each of the factors affecting price decisions are studied: consumers, government, channel members, competitors, and costs. Included are discussions of consumer sensitivity to price, legal restrictions, channel requirements, types of competitive environments, and the impact of costs on prices.

Chapter 19 details how a pricing strategy is developed. It distinguishes among sales, profit, and status quo objectives. The use of a broad price policy and the utility of the multistage approach to pricing are studied. The three basic types of pricing strategy are outlined: cost, demand, and competition. A number of pricing tactics, such as customary and odd pricing, are examined. The various methods for adjusting prices are noted.

Chapter 20 shows how cost, demand, and competition techniques of pricing may be applied. The attributes and variations of each technique are evaluated. Mathematical illustrations are used to demonstrate the techniques. These illustrations all rely on data about the Phase III bicycle, a futuristic product that will travel 55 miles per hour. Finally, it is explained why cost, demand, and competition techniques must be integrated.

SUAVE
MOISTURIZING SHAMPOO & CONDITIONER

"BOARDROOM" :30

HCSU 1023

WOMAN: When I started working,

Suave was the only shampoo I could afford.

I kept thinking, "Someday I'll be successful and I'll try some of those expensive shampoos."

But they weren't better than Suave. Just more expensive.

In fact, one of the best ways I've found to protect against blow-drying

is Suave's new Moisturizing Shampoo and Conditioner.

Today I could spend a fortune on my hair. I don't.

Suave just makes me look as if I do.

MALE (VO): Suave makes you look as if you spent a fortune on your hair.

Suave personal care products by Helene Curtis rely on an aggressive low-price strategy to generate sales. This approach has been very successful. Recently, Helene Curtis introduced high-priced Finesse shampoo and conditioner products. By offering two distinct brands, Helene Curtis can appeal to elastic (Suave) and inelastic (Finesse) consumer demand. Reprinted by permission.

Summer and the Great American You Store:

It's our light and airy Summer Sandal collection. All with comfortable leather uppers. And all from $14.99 to $18.99. So come browse. The Great American You Store has your summer sandals now.

Kinney
The Great American Shoe Store

All colors not available in all stores.

Kinney shoe stores use a penetration price strategy intended to capture the mass market that is price- and value-conscious. The above advertisement features shoes priced from $14.99 to $18.99. Kinney's slogan ("The Great American Shoe Store") reflects its mass-market orientation. Reprinted by permission.

The Florsheim Shoes pricing strategy shown in this advertisement is intended to attract an affluent market segment that is more interested in product quality, comfort, and style than in price. The ad itself is quite elegant. Reprinted by permission.

At one hundred twenty-five dollars the pair, it's a very comfortable investment.

Putting money into a Royal Imperial shoe from Florsheim is not only smart fashion, it's a wise investment. Take the Ritz moccasin shown above. It's magnificently crafted from the finest kangaroo leather so it's supple, lightweight and durable. Retains its elegance with normal care. When combined with the premium calfskin lining, the Ritz moccasin provides a personalized fit of unparalleled comfort.

The Royal Imperial Collection by Florsheim. An investment that pays dividends.

Royal Imperial by FLORSHEIM®
an INTERCO company

*Retail price quoted herein is suggested only. Independent retailers are free to determine their own retail prices. See the Yellow Pages for the Florsheim dealer nearest you. For free style brochure, write: Florsheim, Dept. #56, 130 S. Canal Street, Chicago, Illinois 60606.

Once you taste
West Virginia Brand Thick-Sliced Bacon,
you'll know why all the others
are priced lower.

Only the finest quality center slabs are chosen for West Virginia Brand Thick-Sliced Bacon. Because the center is the part of the bacon with the leanest, the widest, and the tenderest ribbons of lean meat. It's like keeping only the filet and discarding all the rest. Most other bacons don't do this because it costs more. Nor do they slow-cure and deep-smoke their bacon.

This also costs more. We do it because it adds more flavor. Sweet, smoky flavor that you get to taste so much more of, 'cause the slices are extra-thick. West Virginia Brand Thick-Sliced Bacon. You'll notice the difference when you pay for it. And every luscious bite thereafter.

West Virginia Brand Thick-Sliced Bacon.

Hormel, the maker of West Virginia bacon, combines cost, demand, and competitive considerations when setting prices. West Virginia bacon costs a lot to produce, because only center cuts are used and a slow-curing process is utilized. Consumers are willing to pay more for the bacon's sweet, smoky flavor. Competitors charge less; their bacon is of lower quality. Reprinted by permission.

Chapter **18**

An Overview of
Price Planning

CHAPTER OBJECTIVES

Kroger is the fourth largest retailer in the U.S., behind only Sears, Safeway, and K mart. It operates about 1,200 supermarkets in 19 states and a 560-unit drugstore chain. Kroger has a reputation as an aggressive pricer that responds quickly to competitor attempts at underpricing it.

In several of its geographical areas, warehouse stores have opened to compete with Kroger supermarkets. The warehouse stores typically carry fewer items and costs are less than Kroger; their emphasis is on low prices. Warehouse stores hold down costs through low rent (due to nonprime locations), fewer employees, and scant services and amenities. For example, warehouse stores usually do not unpack items from their shipping boxes and consumers must package their own purchases; this saves money by eliminating unpacking, shelving, and repacking functions and reducing the need for store displays.

When the prices at a warehouse store endanger business at a Kroger supermarket, it matches the store's prices item for item and advertises "Warehouse Prices in a Complete Store". To avoid an area-wide price

531

war, Kroger only reduces prices at the one or two supermarket outlets nearest a warehouse store. This situation has occurred in Nashville, Tennessee, where one of Kroger's 29 area supermarkets has been matching the prices of a warehouse store for over two years. The competing supermarket even uses advertising circulars separate from those distributed by the other 28 Kroger outlets in Nashville (who have maintained regular prices) to list its discount prices.

Kroger calls this practice zone pricing; competitors claim Kroger is trying to destroy them. Waremart (the Nashville warehouse store) appealed to the Federal Trade Commission for relief, asserting that Kroger's pricing strategy as illegal. However, the FTC took no action. As a result, Waremart decided not to open any other stores in Nashville. Said Waremart's president, "Kroger is just denying me an opportunity to sell low-cost generics."

Recently, Kroger started four warehouse stores of its own in Cleveland. Kroger wants to learn the economics of the business and how best to compete against these stores.[1] It recognizes that a good pricing strategy must take consumers, government, channel members, competition, and costs into consideration.

Price Planning Defined

A price places a value on a product or service. Price planning deals with all the elements of pricing.

A **price** represents the value of a product or service for both the seller and the buyer. **Price planning** is systematic decision making by an organization regarding all aspects of pricing.

The value of a product or service to an organizational or final customer can involve both tangible and intangible factors. An example of a tangible factor is the cost savings obtained by the purchase of a new bottling machine by a soda manufacturer. An example of an intangible factor is a consumer's pride in the ownership of a Nikon rather than another brand camera.

Many words are substitutes for the term price: admission fee, membership fee, rate, tuition, service charge, donation, rent, salary, interest, retainer, and assessment.

A price can be expressed in monetary or nonmonetary terms.

A price can also refer to a nonmonetary exchange of goods and services: the price of a new iron may be ten books of trading stamps; an airline may offer plane tickets to pay for advertising space and time.[2] Monetary and nonmonetary exchange may be combined. This is common with automobiles, where the consumer gives the seller money plus a trade-in. This combination allows a reduction in the monetary price.

A price contains all the terms of purchase: monetary and nonmonetary charges, discounts, handling and shipping fees, credit charges and other forms of interest, and late-payment penalties.

[1] Bill Saporito, "Kroger, The New King of Supermarketing," *Fortune* (February 21, 1983), pp. 74–76 ff.
[2] Jack G. Kaikati, "Marketing Without Exchange of Money," *Harvard Business Review*, Vol. 60 (November–December 1982), pp. 72, 74.

For an exchange to take place, both the buyer and seller must feel that the price of a product or service provides an equitable value. To the buyer, the payment of a price reduces purchasing power available for other items. To the seller, receipt of a price is a source of revenue and an important determinant of sales and profit levels.

From a broader perspective, price is the mechanism for allocating goods and services among potential purchasers and for ensuring competition among sellers in an open market economy. If there is an excess of demand over supply, prices are usually bid up by consumers. If there is an excess of supply over demand, prices are usually reduced by sellers. See Figure 18-1.

In this chapter, the importance of price and its relationship to other marketing variables, price and nonprice competition, and the factors affecting price decisions are examined. Chapter 19 deals with the components and development of a price strategy. Chapter 20 concentrates on applying the techniques for setting prices.

Exchange takes place only when the buyer and the seller are satisfied with the price.

Figure 18-1
The Role of Price in Balancing Supply and Demand

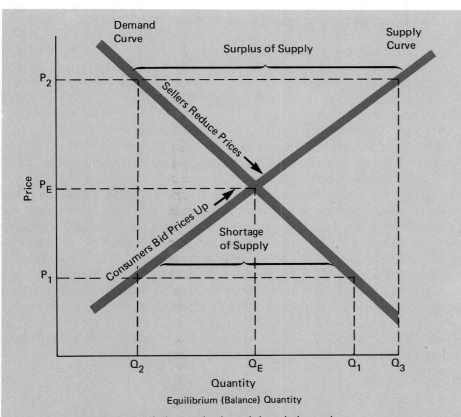

At equilibrium (balance), the quantity demanded equals the supply.
At price P_1, consumers demand Q_1 of an item. However, at this price, suppliers will make available only Q_2. There is a shortage of supply of $Q_1 - Q_2$. The price is bid up as consumers seek to buy greater quantities than offered at P_1.
At price P_2, suppliers will make available Q_3 of an item. However, at this price, consumers demand only Q_2. There is a surplus of supply of $Q_3 - Q_2$. The price is reduced by sellers in order to attract greater demand by consumers.

Importance of Price and Its Relationship to Other Marketing Variables

The significance of price has risen because of cost increases, greater price awareness, product shortages, deregulation, and foreign competition.

The importance of price to marketing executives has risen substantially over the past 20 years. In a 1964 study, they ranked pricing as the sixth most important of twelve marketing factors, behind product planning, marketing research, sales management, advertising and sales promotion, and customer services. Half of the executives did not consider pricing to be one of the five most vital areas.[3] However, in a 1983 survey of executives at 125 U.S. corporations, pricing was cited as the most critical "pressure point" for 1984. It was rated ahead of new product introductions, internal staffing and training, product differentiation (differential advantage), and 12 other factors.[4]

There are several reasons for the rise in the relative importance of pricing. During the 1970s and early 1980s, costs and prices rose rapidly. This has led to companies and consumers being more price conscious. Shortages of some products, such as petroleum, have caused prices to remain high (even though increases have slowed significantly). Deregulation of communications, banking, transportation, and other industries has resulted in greater price competition. In addition, a strong U.S. dollar with respect to foreign currencies has given many foreign competitors a price advantage in U.S. markets. Finally, because price in a monetary or nonmonetary form is a key component of exchange, it appears in every marketing transaction.

Pricing must be interrelated with product, distribution, and promotion decisions to ensure consistency.

Since a price places a value on the overall combination of marketing variables offered to consumers (such as product features, image, store location, customer service, etc.), pricing decisions must be made in conjunction with product, distribution, and promotion plans. An incorrect price can misstate the value of a product or service and result in diminished sales and profits. A correct price can present an equitable value to consumers and maximize sales and profits. For example, General Systems Company originally marketed a $4,000 computer printer that also cost the buyer $3,250 to operate and service (total ownership costs of $7,250). By upgrading the quality of the printer, General Systems was able to raise the item's selling price to $5,000, because the buyer's operating and service costs of the machine were reduced to $1,250 (total ownership costs of $6,250). Sales of the new model have been four times those of the original.[5] See Figure 18-2.

Following are the basic ways in which pricing is related to other marketing and firm variables:

- Prices frequently vary over the life cycle of a product, from high introductory prices to gain status-conscious innovators to low prices to attract the mass market.
- Customer service levels are affected by prices. Low prices are usually associated with little customer service.

[3] Jon G. Udell, "How Important Is Pricing in Competitive Strategy?" *Journal of Marketing*, Vol. 28 (January 1964), pp. 44–48.

[4] Richard Fleming, "Pricing Competition Is Shaping Up as '84's Top Marketing Pressure Point," *Marketing News* (November 11, 1983), p. 1.

[5] "Quality: The U.S. Drives to Catch Up," *Business Week* (November 1, 1982), pp. 66–67.

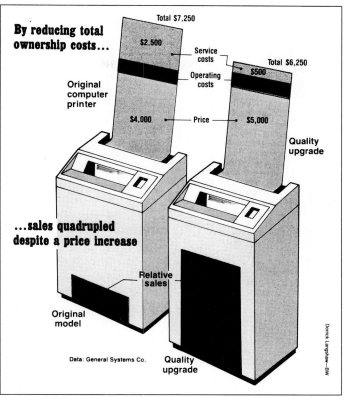

Figure 18-2
How Better Quality Helped One Manufacturer—and Its Customers

Reprinted from the November 1, 1982 issue of *Business Week* by special permission, © 1982 by McGraw-Hill, Inc.

- From a distribution perspective, the prices charged to channel members must adequately compensate them for their functions, yet be low enough to be competitive with other brands at the retail level.
- There may be channel conflict if the manufacturer tries to control or suggest final prices.
- Product lines with different prices attract different market segments.
- The personal sales force needs some flexibility in negotiating prices and terms.
- The efforts of marketing and finance personnel need to be coordinated. Marketers usually begin with final consumer prices and work backward to determine channel member prices and acceptable production costs. Finance people typically start with costs and add desired profits to come up with selling prices.

Price and Nonprice Competition

With *price competition,* sellers influence demand primarily through changes in price levels. *Nonprice competition* minimizes price as a factor in consumer demand. This is accomplished by creating a distinctive product or service as ex-

Figure 18-3
Price and Nonprice Competition

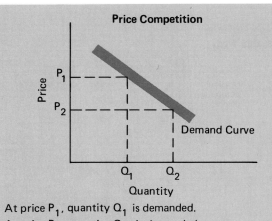

Price Competition

At price P₁, quantity Q₁ is demanded.
At price P₂, quantity Q₂, is demanded.

A company operating at P_1 Q_1 may increase sales by lowering its price to P_2. This increases demand to Q_2. A firm relying on price competition must lower prices to increase sales.

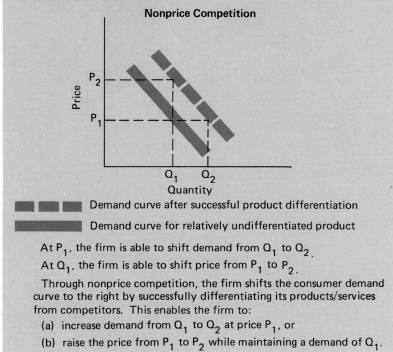

Nonprice Competition

Demand curve after successful product differentiation

Demand curve for relatively undifferentiated product

At P_1, the firm is able to shift demand from Q_1 to Q_2.
At Q_1, the firm is able to shift price from P_1 to P_2.

Through nonprice competition, the firm shifts the consumer demand curve to the right by successfully differentiating its products/services from competitors. This enables the firm to:
(a) increase demand from Q_1 to Q_2 at price P_1, or
(b) raise the price from P_1 to P_2 while maintaining a demand of Q_1.

Price competition occurs when sellers influence demand through price changes; *nonprice competition* emphasizes marketing factors other than price.

pressed through promotion, packaging, delivery, customer service, availability, and other marketing factors. The more unique a product or service offering is perceived to be by consumers, the greater is the freedom of a marketer to set prices above competitors'.

In price competition, sellers move along a demand curve by raising or lowering their prices. Price competition is a flexible marketing tool because prices can be adjusted quickly and easily to reflect demand, cost, or competitive factors.

Figure 18-4
The Strategies of Generic and Manufacturer Brands
Goldline Laboratories markets Genapap acetaminophen tablets to compete with Tylenol and Genprin aspirin tablets to compete with Bayer.

However, of all the controllable marketing variables, a pricing strategy is the easiest for a competitor to duplicate. This may result in a "me-too" strategy or even in a price war. Furthermore, the government monitors price strategies.

In nonprice competition, sellers shift the demand curves of consumers to the right by stressing the distinctive attributes of their products or services. This enables firms to increase unit sales at a given price or to sell their original supply at a higher price. The risk with a nonprice strategy is that consumers may not perceive the seller's product or service attributes as better than the competition's. In this case the consumer will buy the lower-priced item he or she believes is similar to the higher-priced item. See Figures 18-3 and 18-4 for illustrations of price and nonprice competition.

Helene Curtis and Quaker State illustrate the difference between price and nonprice strategies. Helene Curtis makes a number of personal care products under the Suave brand name and follows a price competition strategy with this brand. Suave products, which are priced just above private-label brands, include shampoo, hair conditioner, skin lotion, deodorant, and hair spray—about 25 items in all. See Figure 18-5. Suave is the market leader in shampoo unit sales (10 per cent market share) and second in hair conditioner unit sales (7 per cent market share). Suave is not a unique or innovative brand: "We don't try to create any trends. We simply wait for them to develop." Helene Curtis recently changed its long-running advertising slogan from "Suave does what yours does for a lot less" to "Suave makes you look as if you spent a fortune on your hair."[6]

Quaker State produces a variety of motor oils and related products. For more

---

[6] Jennifer Alter, "Curtis Finesses Way into High-End Care," *Advertising Age* (January 31, 1983), p. 12.

Figure 18-5
Suave by Helene Curtis

Reprinted by permission.

than 70 years, it has maintained a nonprice strategy that stresses quality. Despite competition from a number of companies, large and small, Quaker has been able to keep the price for a quart of its motor oil about ten cents higher than its competitors. Quaker has the loyalty of almost one of every five American motorists, leading to annual sales of almost $1 billion. Quaker State sells its products through mass merchandisers (such as K mart, Zayre, and Target) as well as through service stations. These retailers are particularly happy about Quaker's quality image, since it enables them to obtain higher price margins or use the motor oil as a sale item to increase store traffic.[7] Figure 18-6 illustrates Quaker's quality image.

Factors Affecting Pricing Decisions

The outside factors affecting price should be studied before enacting a price strategy.

Before a firm develops a pricing strategy (which will be described in Chapter 19), it should analyze the outside factors affecting price decisions. Like channel-of-distribution decisions, price decisions depend heavily on elements external to the firm. This contrasts with product and promotion decisions, which are more directly controlled by the firm.

The major factors affecting price decisions are consumers, government, channel members, competitors, and costs. Sometimes the factors greatly influence the company's ability to set prices; in other instances, the factors have little impact. Figure 18-7 outlines the factors.

[7] Jean A. Briggs, "Hurray for Cheaper Oil," *Forbes* (March 28, 1983), pp. 141–142.

Figure 18-6
**Quaker State DeLuxe
Motor Oil**
NASCAR racing champion
Bobby Allison is sponsored
by Quaker State. Here,
Allison (in a tuxedo) is
shown outside New York's
exclusive Club 21 holding a
container of Quaker State
DeLuxe Motor Oil.

Reprinted by permission.

Consumers

A marketer should understand the relationship between price and consumer purchases and perceptions. This relationship is explained by two economic principles—the law of demand and price elasticity of demand—and market segmentation.

The **_law of demand_** states that consumers usually purchase more units at a low price than at a high price. The **_price elasticity of demand_** defines the sensitivity of buyers to price changes in terms of the quantities they will purchase.[8]

Price elasticity is computed by dividing the percentage change in quantity demanded by the percentage change in price charged:

$$\text{Price elasticity} = \frac{\dfrac{\text{Quantity 1} - \text{Quantity 2}}{\text{Quantity 1} + \text{Quantity 2}}}{\dfrac{\text{Price 1} - \text{Price 2}}{\text{Price 1} + \text{Price 2}}}$$

This formula shows the percentage change in quantity demanded for each 1 per cent change in price. Because quantity demanded usually decreases as price in-

According to the *law of demand*, more is bought at low prices; *price elasticity of demand* explains reactions to changes.

[8] See Scott A. Neslin and Robert W. Shoemaker, ''Using a Natural Experiment to Estimate Price Elasticity: The 1974 Sugar Shortage and the Ready-to-Eat Cereal Market,'' *Journal of Marketing,* Vol. 47 (Winter 1983), pp. 44–57.

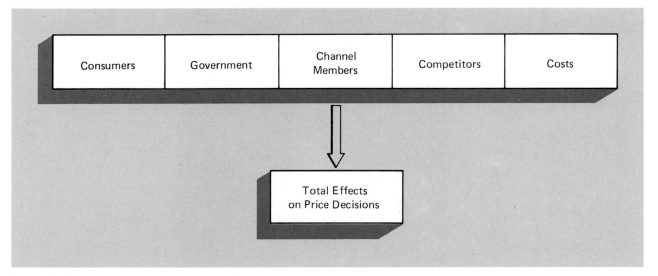

Figure 18-7
Factors Affecting Price Decisions

Demand may be *elastic*, *inelastic*, or *unitary*.

creases, elasticity is a negative number. However, for purposes of simplicity, the elasticity calculations in this section are expressed as positive numbers.

Elastic demand occurs if relatively small changes in price result in large changes in quantity demanded. Numerically, price elasticity is greater than one. With elastic demand, total revenue goes up when prices are decreased and goes down when prices rise. *Inelastic demand* takes place if price changes have little impact on quantity demanded. Price elasticity is less than one. With inelastic demand, total revenue goes up when prices are raised and goes down when prices decline. *Unitary demand* exists if changes in price are exactly offset by changes in quantity demanded, so that total sales revenue remains constant. Price elasticity is one.

The type of demand depends on availability of substitutes and urgency of need.

The type of demand that exists is based on two criteria: availability of substitutes and urgency of need. When the consumer believes there are many similar products or services from which to choose or there is no urgency to make a purchase, demand is elastic and highly influenced by price changes. A price increase will lead to the purchase of a substitute or a delayed purchase. A price decrease will expand sales as customers are drawn from competitors or move up the date of their purchases. For many customers the airfare for a vacation is highly elastic. If prices go up the consumer may travel by car or postpone the trip.

When the consumer believes the firm's product or service offering is unique or that there is an urgency to make a purchase, demand is inelastic and little influenced by price changes. Neither a price increase nor a price decline will have much impact on demand. For example, in most communities, if home heating oil prices are increased or decreased, demand remains relatively constant because there is often no viable substitute and people must have their homes properly heated. Brand loyalty also generates inelastic demand because consumers perceive their brand as distinctive and may not accept substitutes. Finally, emergency conditions increase demand inelasticity. A consumer with a flat tire would pay more for a replacement than a consumer with time to shop around. Figure 18-8 shows elastic and inelastic demand.

It should be noted that demand elasticity varies over a wide range of prices for the same product or service. At very high prices, sales of essential items decline (transit ridership would drop if fares rose from 60 cents to $2; this would allow cars to become a more reasonable substitute). At very low prices, demand cannot be stimulated further as market saturation is reached and consumers begin to perceive quality to be inferior.

Table 18-1 shows the price-elasticity calculations for an appliance repair service. There is a clear relationship between price and demand. At the lowest price, $8, demand is greatest: 10 service calls. At the highest price, $20, demand is least: 5 service calls. Demand is inelastic between $8 and $14, and total revenue (price × quantity) increases as price increases. Demand is unitary between $14 and $16, and total revenue remains the same ($112). Demand is elastic between $16 and $20, and total revenue declines as the price rises within this range.

Figure 18-8
Demand Elasticity for Two Models of Automobiles

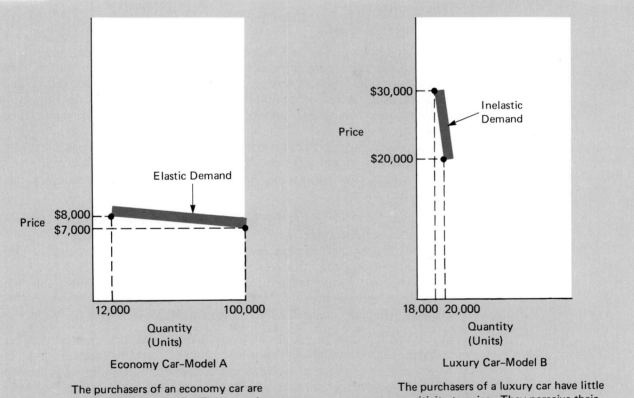

Price — $8,000 / $7,000

Elastic Demand

Quantity (Units) — 12,000 / 100,000

Economy Car–Model A

The purchasers of an economy car are highly sensitive to price. They perceive many models as interchangeable and demand will suffer significantly if the car is priced too high. At $7,000, 100,000 models may be sold (revenues are $700 million). A small increase to $8,000 will cause demand to fall to 12,000 units (revenues are $96 million).

Price — $30,000 / $20,000

Inelastic Demand

Quantity (Units) — 18,000 / 20,000

Luxury Car–Model B

The purchasers of a luxury car have little sensitivity to price. They perceive their model as quite distinctive and will pay a premium price for it. At $20,000, 20,000 models may be sold (revenues are $400 million). A large increase in price, to $30,000, will have a small effect on demand, 18,000 units (revenues are $540 million).

Table 18-1
Price Elasticity for an Appliance Repair Service

Price of Service Call	Service Calls Demanded per Day	Revenues From Service Calls	Price Elasticity of Demand[a]	Type of Demand
$ 8.00	10	$ 80.00		
$10.00	10	$100.00	$E = \left(\dfrac{10 - 10}{10 + 10}\right)\bigg/\left(\dfrac{\$\,8 - \$10}{\$\,8 + \$10}\right) = 0$	Inelastic
$12.00	9	$108.00	$E = \left(\dfrac{10 - 9}{10 + 9}\right)\bigg/\left(\dfrac{\$10 - \$12}{\$10 + \$12}\right) = 0.58$	Inelastic
$14.00	8	$112.00	$E = \left(\dfrac{9 - 8}{9 + 8}\right)\bigg/\left(\dfrac{\$12 - \$14}{\$12 + \$14}\right) = 0.76$	Inelastic
$16.00	7	$112.00	$E = \left(\dfrac{8 - 7}{8 + 7}\right)\bigg/\left(\dfrac{\$14 - \$16}{\$14 + \$16}\right) = 1.00$	Unitary
$18.00	6	$108.00	$E = \left(\dfrac{7 - 6}{7 + 6}\right)\bigg/\left(\dfrac{\$16 - \$18}{\$16 + \$18}\right) = 1.31$	Elastic
$20.00	5	$100.00	$E = \left(\dfrac{6 - 5}{6 + 5}\right)\bigg/\left(\dfrac{\$18 - \$20}{\$18 + \$20}\right) = 1.73$	Elastic

[a] Expressed as positive numbers

Although a price of $14 or $16 yields the highest total revenue, $112, other criteria must be evaluated before selecting a price. The appliance firm in Table 18-1 should consider costs per service call; total sales at each service call, including parts and additional labor; travel time; the percentage of satisfied customers at the different price levels, as expressed by repeat business; and the potential for referrals of new customers.

It is also necessary to understand the importance of price by market segment. Not all consumers are equally price conscious. On the basis of a classic study, consumers can be divided into four categories or segments, depending on their shopping orientation:[9]

Consumers can be divided into four categories: economical, personalizing, ethical, and apathetic.

1. Economical shopper: Primarily interested in shopping for values and extremely sensitive to price, quality, and merchandise assortment.
2. Personalizing shopper: emphasizes product or service image, personal service, and treatment by firms; less concerned with price.
3. Ethical shopper: willing to sacrifice low prices and wide assortments in order to patronize a small firm.
4. Apathetic shopper: major concern for convenience, whatever the price.

Research confirms that not all consumers use price as the dominant purchase determinant. One study showed that price is not an overriding factor for products for which consumers have a strong brand preference.[10] Another study demonstrated that a convenient store location and a close relationship with local merchants are significant determinants in a purchase.[11] A third study determined that most consumers who shop at food warehouse outlets do so because of prices; however, supermarket shoppers rate store location, product quality, and selection

[9] Gregory P. Stone, "City Shoppers and Urban Identification: Observation on the Social Psychology of City Life," *American Journal of Sociology*, Vol. 60 (July 1954), pp. 36–45.
[10] Evan E. Anderson, "The Effectiveness of Retail Price Reductions: A Comparison for Alternative Expressions of Price," *Journal of Marketing Research*, Vol. 11 (August 1974), pp. 327–330.
[11] Robert F. Hartley, "The Importance of Price in Small Town Shopping Behavior," *Southern Journal of Business*, Vol. 5 (April 1970), pp. 24–32.

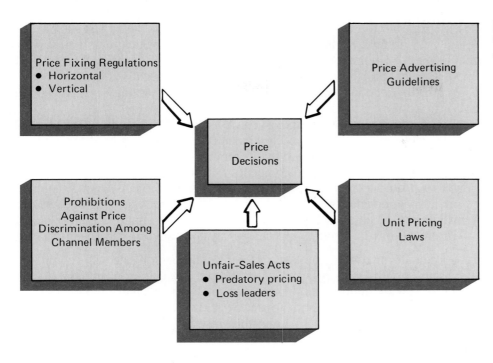

Figure 18-9
**Government Actions
Affecting Price Decisions**

as more important than prices.[12] A fourth study found that a consumer's perception of price as high or low, *subjective price*, may be more important than actual price.[13] For example, a consumer may believe that a low price represents a good buy or inferior quality or that a high price represents status or poor value, depending on his/her perception.

The consumer's perception of a price level is the *subjective price*.

Government

Government actions relating to price can be divided into five major areas: price fixing, price discrimination, minimum prices, unit pricing, and price advertising. Each of these is discussed in the following subsections and shown in Figure 18-9.

PRICE FIXING

The government places limitations on horizontal and vertical price fixing. *Horizontal price fixing* results from agreements among manufacturers, among wholesalers, or among retailers to set prices at a given stage in a channel of distribution. Such agreements are illegal according to the Sherman Antitrust Act and the Federal Trade Commission Act, regardless of how "reasonable" the price is.

Horizontal price fixing is illegal and results from agreements among companies at the same stage in a channel.
1890

An example of a horizontal price agreement and its legal ramifications occurred in the folding-carton industry. The Justice Department charged that a widespread conspiracy, mainly among plant managers, existed east of the Rocky Mountains. The managers were said to have fixed the prices of corrugated card-

---

[12] "Resistance Noted to Removal of Food Item Prices," *Marketing News* (September 30, 1983), p. 7.
[13] Kent B. Monroe, "Buyers' Subjective Perceptions of Price," *Journal of Marketing Research,* Vol. 10 (February 1973), pp 73–80.

board boxes and folding cartons. The criminal case was the largest such antitrust action ever brought by the Justice Department. Companies representing 70 per cent of the $1.5 billion in annual industry sales were convicted. A federal judge imposed fines, probation, or jail terms on 47 of 48 executives in 22 companies. One company reported that legal fees alone exceeded earnings over the previous five-year period.[14]

A similar case is now pending in court. In July 1983, six firms were indicted for allegedly conspiring to rig electrical contract bids at eight U.S. Steel plants in the Pittsburgh area. According to the indictments, U.S. Steel invited the contractors to submit bids "to promote competition in order to obtain the lowest possible price"; instead the firms were accused of allocating projects among themselves by predesignating one company as the low bidder for each project. The remaining firms then refrained from bidding on that project or submitted high bids.[15]

In order to avoid price-fixing charges, a company must be careful not to[16]

1. Coordinate discounts, credit terms, or conditions of sale with competitors;
2. Discuss prices, markups, and costs at trade association meetings;
3. Arrange with competitors to issue new price lists at the same date;
4. Arrange with competitors to rotate low bids on contracts;
5. Agree with competitors to uniformly restrict production to maintain high prices; or
6. Exchange information with competitors, even on an informal basis.

Under *vertical price fixing*, manufacturers or wholesalers try to control retail prices. Today this practice is limited.

Vertical price fixing occurs when manufacturers or wholesalers are able to control the retail prices of their products or services. Until 1975 the Miller-Tydings Act (in conjunction with the McGuire Act) enabled firms to strictly set and enforce retail prices if they desired. This practice was known as fair trade. It protected small retailers and maintained brand images by forcing all retailers within fair-trade states to charge the same price for affected products.

Fair trade was heavily criticized by consumer groups, many retailers, and a number of manufacturers for being noncompetitive, keeping prices artificially high, and rewarding retailer inefficiency. On December 12, 1975, President Gerald Ford signed the Consumer Goods Pricing Act. This law terminated all interstate utilization of fair trade or resale price maintenance as of March 11, 1976.[17]

Today, retailers cannot be required to adhere to list prices developed by manufacturers or wholesalers. In most cases, retailers are free to establish final selling prices. Manufacturers or wholesalers may control retail prices only through one of these methods:

1. Manufacturer or wholesaler ownership of retail facilities.
2. Consignment selling, whereby the manufacturer or wholesaler owns items until they are sold and assumes all costs normally associated with the retailer, such as advertising and selling.

[14] Winston Williams, "Cardboard Makers to Pay $300 Million to End Pricing Suit," *New York Times* (May 2, 1979), pp. 1, D4; and Jeffrey Sonnenfeld and Paul R. Lawrence, "Why Do Companies Succumb to Price Fixing?" *Harvard Business Review,* Vol. 56 (July–August 1978), p. 147.
[15] "Six Electrical Concerns Indicted," *New York Times* (July 5, 1983), p. D5.
[16] "Price Fixing: Crackdown Under Way," *Business Week* (June 2, 1975), pp. 42–48.
[17] See L. Louise Luchsinger and Patrick M. Dunne, "Fair Trade Laws—How Fair?" *Journal of Marketing,* Vol. 42 (January 1978), pp. 50–53; and Richard Sandomir, "Retailers Fear Price-Fixing Return," *Newsday* (October 3, 1982), p. 92.

3. Careful screening of the retailers through which products or services are sold.
4. Suggesting realistic retail list prices.
5. Preprinting prices on products.
6. Establishing a customary price (such as 25 cents for a newspaper) that is accepted by consumers.

PRICE DISCRIMINATION

The ***Robinson-Patman Act*** prohibits manufacturers and wholesalers from price discrimination in dealing with different channel-member purchasers of products of "like quality" if the effect of such discrimination is to injure competition. Covered by the Robinson-Patman Act are prices, discounts, rebates, premiums, guarantees, delivery, warehousing, and credit terms. Terms and conditions of sale must be made available to all competing channel members on a proportionately equal basis.[18]

The Robinson-Patman Act was enacted in 1936 in order to protect small retailers from unfair price competition from large chains. It was feared that small retailers would be driven out of business due to the superior bargaining power of large chains with product suppliers. The Robinson-Patman Act required price differences to be limited to a manufacturer's cost savings in dealing with different retailers. The Robinson-Patman Act remains a major legal restriction on pricing.

There are some exceptions to the Robinson-Patman Act. Price discrimination within a channel is permissible if each buyer purchases products with substantial physical differences, if noncompeting buyers are involved, if prices do not injure competition, if price differences are justified by costs, if market conditions change (such as production costs rising), or if the seller reduces price to meet another supplier's bid.

Discounts are acceptable if the seller demonstrates that they are available to all competitive channel buyers on a proportionate basis, that they are sufficiently graduated so that small as well as large buyers can qualify, or that they are cost-justified. For example, the seller must prove that discounts for cumulative purchases (total volume during the year) or multistore purchases by retail chains are based on cost savings.

Although the Robinson-Patman Act is oriented toward sellers, it provides specific liabilities for purchasing firms under Section 2(F):

it shall be unlawful for any person engaged in commerce, in the course of such commerce, knowingly to induce or receive a discrimination in price which is prohibited in this section.

Channel members should attempt to obtain the lowest prices charged to any competitor in their class. Yet they should not bargain so hard that the discounts received cannot be explained by one of the acceptable exceptions to Robinson-Patman.

MINIMUM PRICES

A number of states have enacted **unfair-sales acts (minimum price laws)** that prevent retailers from selling merchandise for less than the cost of the product plus a fixed percentage that covers overhead and profit. Approximately half the states have unfair-sales acts that cover all types of products and retail situations.

The *Robinson-Patman Act* prohibits manufacturers and wholesalers from discriminating in price when selling to channel members.

Unfair-sales acts protect small firms from *predatory pricing* by large companies, and limit the use of *loss leaders*.

[18] Kent B. Monroe, *Pricing: Making Profitable Decisions* (New York: McGraw-Hill, 1979), p. 253.

About two thirds of the states have laws that involve specific products, such as bread, dairy items, cigarettes, and liquor.[19] Unfair-sales acts are intended to protect small firms from predatory pricing by larger competitors and to limit the use of loss leaders by retailers.

Under **predatory pricing,** large companies cut prices on products below their cost in selected geographic areas in order to eliminate small, local competitors. At the federal level, predatory pricing is banned by the Sherman and Clayton Acts. Manufacturers, wholesalers, and retailers are all subject to these acts. There is some evidence that predatory price enforcement is now being relaxed in terms of cost calculations and in the definitions of affected market areas.[20]

Loss leaders, items priced below cost to draw customer traffic into a store, are also restricted by unfair-sales acts. Retailers use loss leaders, typically well-known and heavily advertised brands, to increase overall store sales. They assume that customers who are drawn by loss leaders will also purchase nonsale items. Because consumers normally benefit from loss leaders, the laws are rarely enforced.

UNIT PRICING

> With *unit pricing*, consumers can easily compare price per quantity for different-size packages.

The lack of uniformity and consistency in package sizes has led to the enactment of unit-pricing legislation in a number of states. **Unit pricing** enables consumers to compare price per quantity for competing brands and for various sizes of the same brand.

Food stores are most affected by unit pricing. In many cases the stores must express price per unit of measure as well as total price. For example, unit pricing would show that a 12-ounce can of soda selling for 30 cents is priced at 2.5 cents per ounce, whereas a 67.6-ounce (2 liter) bottle of the same brand of soda selling for $1.39 is priced at 2.1 cents per ounce. The larger size is cheaper than the smaller.

The costs of unit pricing to retailers include per unit price computations, printing of shelf labels, and computer records. Costs are influenced by the number of stores in a chain, sales per store, the number of items under unit pricing, and the frequency of price changes.

When unit-pricing legislation was first enacted just over a decade ago, a number of studies showed it to be ineffective. These studies found that consumers in general did not use the information and that low-income consumers (for whom the laws were most intended) were least likely to use unit-price data. Accordingly, critics stated that the legislation was costly without providing consumer benefits.

More recent research shows that unit pricing is, in fact, effective and suggests consumer learning about unit pricing and the resulting behavior changes take time. Early critics may have been too quick to disagree with the practice. How-

---

[19] Michael J. Houston, ''Minimum Markup Laws: An Empirical Assessment,'' *Journal of Retailing,* Vol. 57 (Winter 1981), p. 98.

[20] See William M. Carley, ''Laws Against 'Predatory Pricing' by Firms Are Being Relaxed in Many Court Rulings,'' *Wall Street Journal* (July 14, 1982), p. 52; Richard L. Gordon, ''FTC Pricing Squeeze Is off ReaLemon,'' *Advertising Age* (March 7, 1983), pp. 6, 62; and Margaret Garrard Warner, ''FTC to Relax 1978 Order Against Borden on Pricing Practices for ReaLemon Juice,'' *Wall Street Journal* (March 21, 1983), p. 54.

ever, urban residents (who have lower educational and income levels) are still less likely to use unit-pricing data than suburban residents, as the results of one study indicate:[21]

	Per Cent of City Residents	Per Cent of Suburban Residents
Aware of unit pricing	73.5	90.4
Comprehending unit pricing	36.7	73.6
Using unit pricing	33.1	59.9
Used unit pricing within the last month	26.0	59.5
Find unit pricing helpful	29.8	59.5

PRICE ADVERTISING

Guidelines for price advertising have been developed by the Federal Trade Commission (FTC) and various trade associations, such as the Better Business Bureau. The FTC's guidelines specify standards of permissible conduct in five broad categories:[22]

FTC guidelines establish standards for price ads.

- A company may not claim or imply that a price has been reduced from a former level unless the original price was offered to the public on a regular basis during a reasonable, recent period of time.
- A firm may not claim that its price is lower than that of competitors or the manufacturer's list price without verifying, through price comparisons involving large quantities of merchandise, that the price of an item at other outlets in the same trading area is in fact higher.
- A suggested list price or a premarked price cannot be advertised as a reference point for a sale or a comparison with other products unless the advertised product has actually been sold at the list or premarked price.
- Bargain offers such as "free," "buy one, get one free," "two-for-one sale," "half-price sale," and "one-cent sale" are frequently used by companies. These practices are considered deceptive by the FTC if the terms of the offer are not disclosed at the beginning of a sales presentation or advertisement, the stated regular price of an item is inflated to create an impression of savings, or the quality or quantity of the merchandise is reduced without informing the consumer of the change. In addition, a firm may not continuously advertise the same product as being on sale.
- *Bait-and-switch advertising* is an illegal procedure in which a retailer lures customers into a store by advertising items at exceptionally low prices and then tells the customers that the items are out of stock or are of inferior quality. The salesperson attempts to switch the customers to more expensive substitutes, and there is no intention of selling the advertised item. Signs of bait-and-switch are refusal to demonstrate requested products, disparagement of products, insufficient quantity to meet reasonable demand, refusal to take orders, demonstration of defective products, and a compensation plan encouraging salespeople to engage in the practice.

Under *bait-and-switch advertising,* retailers illegally draw customers into a store with no intention of selling the advertised product.

---

[21] David A. Aaker and Gary T. Ford, "Unit Pricing Ten Years Later: A Replication," Vol. 47, *Journal of Marketing* (Winter 1983), pp. 118–122.

[22] Earl W. Kintner, *A Primer on the Law of Deceptive Practices* (New York: Macmillan, 1978), pp. 213–230.

Each of the FTC's guidelines requires careful record keeping and documentation for all claims that are made.

Channel Members

Every channel member seeks a major role in setting prices in order to meet its specific goals.

Each channel member seeks to play a significant role in setting prices in order to generate sales volume, obtain adequate profit margins, derive a suitable image, ensure repeat purchases, and meet specific goals.

There often are conflicts among manufacturers, wholesalers, and retailers regarding price policies. The manufacturer wants to cover production costs and make a profit, establish a brand image, and have input into final selling prices. It is particularly fearful of continued discounts or price cutting that may hurt brand image. The wholesaler wants to cover selling costs and make a profit, be competitive with other wholesalers, and have input into final selling prices. Wholesale prices are based on the costs, goals, and strengths of individual wholesalers. The retailer wants to cover selling costs and make a profit, be competitive with other retailers, and control final selling prices. It sets prices based on individual image, objectives, method of operations, and cost considerations.

A manufacturer can gain stronger control over price by using an exclusive distribution system or minimizing sales through price-cutting retailers, preticketing prices on merchandise, opening his or her own retail outlets, offering goods on consignment, providing adequate margins to channel members, and most importantly by developing strong national brands that consumers have brand loyalty toward and for which they will pay whatever final price is charged.

To increase private brand sales, some retailers *sell against the brand.*

A wholesaler or retailer can gain stronger control over price by stressing his or her importance as a customer to the manufacturer, linking resale support (displays, personal selling) to the profit margins allowed by the manufacturer, refusing to carry unprofitable products, stocking competitive items, and developing strong wholesaler or retailer brands so that consumers are loyal to the seller and not the manufacturer. Sometimes retailers engage in **selling against the brand,** whereby they stock merchandise, place high prices on it, and then sell other brands for lower prices. This is often done to increase the sales of private (store) brands. The practice is disliked by manufacturers because the sales of their brands decline.

To ensure channel member cooperation with price decisions, the manufacturer needs to consider four factors: channel member profit margins, price guarantees, special deals, and the impact of price increases.

Wholesalers and retailers require specific profit margins in order to cover their costs (shipping, storage, advertising, credit, etc.) and earn reasonable profits. Therefore, the prices manufacturers charge their channel members must take these profit margins into account. An attempt by a manufacturer to reduce traditional margins for wholesalers or retailers may lose their cooperation and perhaps find them unwilling to carry a product. Pricing through the channel is discussed further in Chapter 20.

Price guarantees reassure channel members.

In some cases, wholesalers and retailers seek price guarantees to maintain inventory values and profit. As explained in Chapter 12, **price guarantees** assure wholesalers or retailers that the prices they pay are the lowest available. Any discount given to competitors will also be given to the original purchasers. Guarantees are most frequently provided by new firms or new products that want to gain entry into an established channel of distribution.

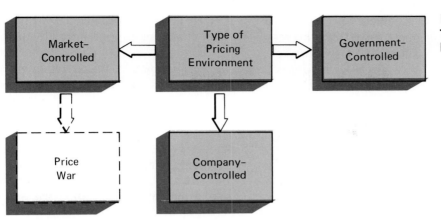

Figure 18-10
**The Competitive
Environments of Pricing**

Often, manufacturers present special deals to channel members. Special deals usually consist of limited-time volume discounts, price reductions, and/or free merchandise to stimulate purchases by wholesalers and retailers. These deals require channel members to pass their savings on to final consumers to increase the latter's demand. For example, soda bottlers normally give retailers large price discounts, up to 50 per cent off list price, on new products to encourage retailers to make purchases and to offer low introductory prices to consumers.[23]

Finally, the effect of price increases on channel-member behavior should be evaluated. Usually, when manufacturers raise prices to channel members, the increases are passed along to final consumers. This practice is more difficult for items with customary prices, such as candy or newspapers, where small cost rises may be absorbed by the channel members. In any event, cooperation depends on an equitable distribution of costs and profit within the channel.

Competition

Another element contributing to the degree of control a firm has over prices is the competitive environment within which it operates: market-controlled, company-controlled, and government-controlled. See Figure 18-10.

A *market-controlled price environment* is characterized by a high level of competition, similar products and services, and little control over price by individual companies. Firms attempting to charge more than the going competitive price would attract few customers, because demand for any single firm is weak enough that customers would switch to a competitor if prices were raised. Similarly, a firm would gain little by selling for less than its competition, because competitors would match any price cuts.

A *company-controlled price environment* is characterized by a moderate level of competition, well-differentiated products and services, and strong control over price by individual firms. In this environment firms may succeed with high prices because consumers view their offerings as unique. Differentiation may be based on brand image, features, associated services, assortment, or other factors.

*A firm may face a
market-controlled,
company-controlled, or
government-controlled
price environment.*

[23] "Coke's Big Marketing Blitz," *Business Week* (May 30, 1983), p. 61. Also see Robert C. Blattberg, Gary D. Eppen, and Joshua Lieberman, "A Theoretical and Empirical Evaluation of Price Deals for Consumer Nondurables," *Journal of Marketing*, Vol. 45 (Winter 1981), pp. 116–129.

Discounters also can carve out a niche in this environment by attracting consumers interested in low prices. The choice of a price depends on the firm's strategy and target market.

A **government-controlled price environment** is characterized by prices set by the government. Examples are public utilities, buses, taxis, and state universities. In each of these cases, government bodies determine prices after obtaining input from the affected companies, institutions, or industries as well as other interested parties (such as consumer groups).

Firms may have to adapt to changes in the competitive environment in their industry. For example, the price environment facing transportation (airlines, trucking, railroads, and intercity bus services), telecommunications (phone systems), and financial markets (banking and brokerage firms) has shifted from government-controlled to market-controlled.

Because price strategies are relatively easy and quick to copy, the reaction of competition is predictable if the firm initiating price changes is successful. Accordingly, a marketer should view price from both short-run and long-run perspectives.

Price wars occur when competing firms frequently lower prices.

Excessive price competition may lead to long and costly **price wars,** in which various firms continually try to undercut each other's prices to draw customers. These wars usually result in low profits or even losses for the participants and in some companies being forced out of business.

A good example of this is the long-running price war among U.S. insurance companies in the highly fragmented commercial insurance market.[24] Beginning in the mid-1970s, deregulation of the insurance industry by state agencies enabled firms to earn large profits, fueled by a strong economy in the late 1970s. At this point, a number of major companies entered the insurance field and actively promoted prices. In some insurance categories, rates fell by 35 per cent in two years. Price competition has been heaviest in the commercial market for three reasons. Commercial accounts are more price sensitive, since a rate change can mean hundreds of thousands of dollars. Two, many commercial accounts are quite sizable, and they can exert pressure on their insurance companies. Three, "there is no Big 3 or even Big 10" in the commercial end of the insurance industry, which means competition is heavy. The personal insurance market has fewer firms operating and consumers are less price sensitive. As DeRoy Thomas, chairman of Hartford Insurance commented, "I am sleeping like a baby . . . I sleep for two hours and then wake up and cry for two hours."

Costs

The costs of raw materials, supplies, labor, advertising, transportation, and other items are frequently beyond the control of the firm. Yet, these costs have a great influence on final prices.[25]

---

[24] "Price-Cutting Bleeds the Casualty Insurers," *Business Week* (November 8, 1982), pp. 88, 91, 95.

[25] See, for example, Mary Louise Hatten, "Don't Get Caught with Your Prices Down: Pricing in Inflationary Times," *Business Horizons*, Vol. 22 (March–April 1982), pp. 23–28; Carol J. Loomis, "How GE Manages Inflation," *Fortune* (May 4, 1981), pp. 121–124; Michael L. King, "Inflation Forces Mortgage Lenders to Find New Pricing Methods That Prevent Losses," *Wall Street Journal* (January 5, 1982), p. 33; Ralph E. Winter, "Like Inflation, Disinflation Is Affecting Specific Goods, Services Very Differently," *Wall Street Journal* (May 28, 1982), p. 38; and Arthur A. Thompson, Jr., "Strategies for Staying Cost Competitive," *Harvard Business Review*, Vol. 62 (January–February 1984), pp. 110–117.

From the early 1970s through 1981, many costs rose rapidly and pushed prices to high levels. For example,

For a decade, costs increased dramatically in many areas, before leveling off in 1982.

- Fuel costs went up almost 500 per cent. This placed pressure on airlines, the trucking industry, and the automobile industry.
- Silver and gold prices were extremely volatile. Silver went from $6 per ounce to more than $50 per ounce, before settling at $10 to $15 per ounce. This created difficulties for the photography industry which used silver as a prime ingredient in film. Gold went from $45 per ounce to about $1,000 per ounce, before settling at $300 to $600 per ounce. This had an effect on dentists and jewelers.
- The minimum wage rose from $1.60 per hour in 1970 to $3.35 per hour on January 1, 1981. This affected fast-food retailers and other firms who rely on unskilled labor.
- Mortgage interest rates more than doubled between 1977 and 1981. This severely dampened the housing market.
- The cost of prime-time television commercials went up dramatically. As an illustration, a 30-second commercial on the 1973 Super Bowl cost $103,500. In 1983, the cost was $400,000.

In 1982, cost increases tapered off. For the year, wholesale prices increased by only 3.5 per cent, the lowest amount in over a decade. Lower costs continued through 1983 and 1984. This meant better cost control for marketers and more stable prices.

During periods of rapidly rising costs, companies can react in one or more ways. They can leave their products and services unchanged and pass along all of their cost increases to consumers, leave their products and services unchanged and pass along part of their increases and absorb part of them, modify products and services to hold down costs and maintain prices (by reducing size, offering fewer options, or using lesser-quality materials), modify products and services to gain consumer support for higher prices (by increasing size, offering more options, or using better-quality materials), and/or abandon unprofitable products and services.

In the face of rising costs, companies pass along increases, alter products or services, or delete some items.

Sometimes, despite a company's or industry's best intentions, it may take several years to get runaway costs (and prices) under control. A good illustration is the automobile industry, where costs and prices have gone up drastically since 1970. At that time, an average U.S. automobile had a retail price of under $4,000; today, the average price is about $10,000. Among the costs auto executives have had to deal with are

1. $80 billion in retooling from large to small cars.
2. High fixed costs—plant, equipment, unionized labor.
3. Hundreds of millions of dollars for antipollution devices and safety features.
4. $1,500 per car higher costs for U.S. cars than for Japanese cars.
5. Up to $1 billion or more to develop a single major new car model.

As a result, pricing decisions have to be made well in advance; little flexibility is possible.[26] Figure 18-11 shows the costs and sticker price of a 1982 U.S. compact car.

---

[26] "Why Detroit Can't Cut Prices," *Business Week* (March 1, 1982) pp. 110–111; John Holusha, "Detroit Bows to Sticker Shock," *New York Times* (August 5, 1982), pp. D1, D5; and John Holusha, "Detroit Battle: The Cost Gap," *New York Times* (May 28, 1983), pp. 35, 37.

Figure 18-11
How a Small Car's Price Grows from the Assembly Line to the Showroom

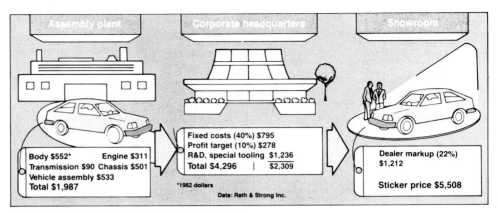

Assembly plant Corporate headquarters Showroom

Body $552* Engine $311
Transmission $90 Chassis $501
Vehicle assembly $533
Total $1,987

Fixed costs (40%) $795
Profit target (10%) $278
R&D, special tooling $1,236
Total $4,296 | $2,309

*1982 dollars

Data: Rath & Strong Inc.

Dealer markup (22%) $1,212

Sticker price $5,508

Reprinted from March 1, 1982 issue of *Business Week* by special permission, © 1982 by McGraw-Hill, Inc.

Cost decreases can have positive benefits for marketing strategies.

It should be noted that cost declines also can occur and enable firms to lower selling prices or raise profit margins, as these illustrations show:

- The use of microprocessors in personal computers has reduced their costs significantly by requiring less wiring and assembly time during production, improving durability, and enlarging information-processing capability. Prices have been steadily lowered, thus expanding the market considerably.[27]
- The drop in sugar prices during 1981 and 1982 allowed candy manufacturers to increase package size (and profits) without raising prices.

Summary

A price represents the value of a product or service for both the seller and the buyer. Price planning is systematic decision making relating to all aspects of pricing by a company; it involves tangible and intangible factors and can refer to the nonmonetary exchange of goods and services. A price contains all the terms of a purchase. Exchange does not take place unless both the buyer and seller agree that a price represents an equitable value. Price also balances supply and demand. The increased importance of price is the result of cost rises, consumer awareness, product shortages, deregulation, and foreign competition.

Under price competition, sellers influence demand primarily through changes in price levels. With nonprice competition, sellers minimize price and emphasize other marketing characteristics such as image, packaging, and features.

Several factors affect a firm's pricing decisions: consumers, government, channel members, competition, and costs. The law of demand states that consumers usually purchase more units at a low price than at a high price. Price elasticity of demand explains the sensitivity of buyers to price changes in terms of the quantities they purchase. Elastic demand occurs if relatively small changes in

---

[27] William M. Bulkeley, "New, Powerful Personal Computers Force Price Cuts and Alter Market," *Wall Street Journal* (May 11, 1982), p. 33.

price result in large changes in quantity demanded; inelastic demand results if price changes have little impact on quantity demanded; and unitary demand occurs if price changes offset quantity changes. Demand is influenced by the availability of substitutes and urgency of need. Consumers can be divided into economical, personalizing, ethical, and apathetic market segments.

Government is active in a broad variety of pricing areas. Price fixing, both horizontal and vertical, is subject to severe restrictions. The Robinson-Patman Act bans most forms of price discrimination to channel members that are not justified by costs. A number of states have unfair-sales acts (minimum price laws) to protect small firms against predatory pricing. Unit pricing requires specified retailers to post prices in terms of quantity. The Federal Trade Commission has a series of guidelines for price advertising.

Each channel member seeks a major role in setting prices in order to generate sales, obtain adequate profit margins, sustain a suitable image, ensure repeat purchases, and meet its own goals. Manufacturers exert control through exclusive distribution, preticketing, opening their own outlets, offering goods on consignment, providing adequate margins, and having strong brands. Wholesalers and retailers exert control by making large purchases, linking sales support to margins, refusing to carry items, stocking competitive brands, and developing their own brands. Manufacturers need to consider channel member profit margins, price guarantees, special deals, and the ramifications of price increases.

A market-controlled price environment has a high level of competition, similar products and services, and little control over price by individual firms. A company-controlled price environment has a moderate level of competition, well-differentiated products and services, and strong control over price by individual firms. In a government-controlled price environment, the government sets prices. Some competitive actions may result in price wars, in which firms try to undercut each other's prices.

The costs of raw materials, supplies, labor, advertising, transportation, and other items affect prices. During the past decade, costs have risen significantly in many areas. This has caused companies to pass along increases to consumers, modify products and services, and abandon some offerings. Cost declines can benefit marketing strategies by improving the firm's ability to plan prices.

Questions for Discussion

1. Explain the role of price in balancing supply and demand. Refer to Figure 18-1.
2. A survey of executives at U.S. corporations rated pricing as a more critical "pressure point" than new product introductions. Comment on this.
3. Describe how a local typewriter repair shop can utilize both price and nonprice competition strategies.
4. Distinguish between elastic and inelastic demand. Why is it necessary for a marketer to understand these differences?
5. How could a firm estimate price elasticity for a new product?
6. Why would a manufacturer want to control retail prices if it receives the same amount from a retailer regardless of the price charged the final consumer?

7. Is the Robinson-Patman Act consumer-oriented? Explain your answer.
8. Differentiate between predatory pricing and loss leaders. Should they be covered by the same legislation? Why or why not?
9. Present five examples of price advertising for a men's clothing store that would violate FTC guidelines.
10. What are a retailer's risks in selling against the brand?
11. Under which circumstances could a manufacturer successfully decline to offer price guarantees to retailers?
12. How can a firm turn a market-controlled price environment into a company-controlled one?
13. What conditions are necessary for a price war to develop and continue?
14. Describe the benefits and costs of a price war to the winner.
15. When would you pass along a cost decrease to consumers? When would you not pass the decrease along?

Case 1 Premier Industrial: Using a Nonprice Strategy*

Premier Industrial is a Cleveland-based distributor of electronic components, maintenance products (such as nuts, bolts, lubricants, and welding supplies), and fire-fighting equipment. Premier's 1983 sales were $317 million, with a pretax net profit margin of about 18 per cent. In electronic components, its profit margin is twice that of competitors. Remarked Premier's chief executive,"We make uncommon profits in a common line of products."

In an industry where discounting is traditional, Premier does not cut prices. It has been successful in converting a commodity-based business into a value-added business. Said a company senior vice-president, "We've picked a niche that gives us the appropriate return and our customers the appropriate value."

Premier's nonprice strategy involves such tactics as offering high product availability, servicing small accounts, providing custom-made items, presenting a large product assortment, and emphasizing customer service. These tactics are illustrated through the following:

- High product availability—Deliveries are made shortly after orders are received. An order from Zenith for 102 different items resulted in 99 being delivered within a few hours.
- Servicing small accounts—Premier's average electronic components order is $100, compared with $400 and more for a leading competitor. Premier sales personnel get referrals from other distributors who do not handle small accounts.
- Custom-made items—Premier distributes products that are not carried by competitors. Its Apollo Lightweight Deluge Gun weighs substantially less than conventional fire-fighting equipment and is popular in large cities with female fire fighters.
- Product assortment—Premier encourages "one-stop shopping." It carries

---

* The data in this case are drawn from Susan Fraker, "Making a Mint in Nuts and Bolts," *Fortune* (August 22, 1983), pp. 131–137 ff.

about 200 product lines of electronic components, about double the number stocked by competitors.

Customer service—Extra service is provided. For customers purchasing premium diesel oil, Premier offers computer analysis of the oil after it has been used in a vehicle. An oil sample that shows too much copper indicates worn engine bearings; excessive chrome in the oil means piston ring problems.

In summing up Premier's strategy, its chief executive stated "We discovered that by finding a niche and doing well in it, we could compete with anyone. We didn't get involved in things where we were amateurs, like distributing brand-name spark plugs."

QUESTIONS

1. Comment on the statement that Premier has "picked a niche that gives us the appropriate return and our customers the appropriate value."

2. How can Premier profitably handle small accounts that its competitors are unable to service?

3. Do you agree that Premier should not carry brand-name spark plugs? Explain your answer.

4. Develop a price-oriented strategy to compete with Premier.

Case 2 Cuisinart: A Price-Fixing Settlement[†]

Cuisinart, the food processor and gourmet cooking-utensil manufacturer, has been the subject of several vertical price-fixing complaints since the mid-1970s. Cuisinart has been accused of illegally setting prices at the retail level and making its food processor products unavailable to retailers who discount Cuisinart products.

Cuisinart's problems began when the owner of Zabar's food emporium (a large New York retail store) complained to the Federal Trade Commission that Cuisinart had cut off the store's supply of food processors, after Zabar's advertised a machine with a $190 list price for $135. Zabar's took customer orders for 1,163 food processors; however, it only had 200 units on hand. After Zabar's was turned down for more machines by Cuisinart, it tried to purchase the food processors from other retailers. But no one would sell to Zabar's, because Cuisinart told these retailers that it would stop selling merchandise to any merchants who resold items to discounters. Two years after the alleged infraction, Cuisinart reached an out-of-court settlement with Zabar's.

In December 1980, Cuisinart pleaded no contest to a Justice Department charge that the firm had conspired to fix prices on its food processors throughout the country. Cuisinart paid a $250,000 fine and agreed to abide by the law in the future. The fine was the largest ever imposed on a company for vertical price fixing.

Cuisinart's difficulties were not over. In 1981, consumers filed a class-action lawsuit to recover what they had overpaid as a result of Cuisinart's alleged price

---

[†] The data in this case are drawn from Bernice Kanner, "Cuisinart Cuts a Deal," *New York* (August 1, 1983), pp. 10–11; and Tamar Lewin, "Cuisinart's Deal in Pricing Suit," *New York Times* (July 20, 1983), pp. D1, D25.

fixing. The lawsuit was filed on behalf of the more than one million consumers who had purchased Cuisinart food processors between 1973 and 1981, and contended that each consumer had been overcharged by $32 to $75. After contesting this lawsuit for two years, Cuisinart developed a proposal for an out-of-court settlement (while still denying any wrongdoing) in 1983. According to the Cuisinart plan, every consumer who had purchased a food processor between 1973 and 1981 would be mailed a coupon entitling him or her to a 50 per cent discount from list price on new purchases of Cuisinart products. The coupon would be worth up to $100 and could be used to buy pots and pans, knives, or food-processor accessories— but not a food processor. If the consumer so desired, the coupon could be transferred to another person. Purchases would be made directly from Cuisinart.

Cuisinart critics are not satisfied with the company's settlement of the class-action suit. They believe the coupons are not worth much, because a number of retailers are currently offering Cuisinart products at 25 to 50 per cent off list price. They also question whether a company charged with price fixing should be allowed to give out coupons that encourage affected consumers to buy more of its products.

QUESTIONS

1. Evaluate Cuisinart's approach in dealing with discounters such as Zabar's.
2. Comment on Cuisinart's settlement plan.
3. What is the effect of the half-price settlement plan on traditional retailers who sell Cuisinart products? On discounters?
4. How can Cuisinart legally control its products' retail selling prices? Describe the pros and cons of this strategy.

Chapter **19**

Developing a Pricing Strategy

CHAPTER OBJECTIVES

1. To study the overall process of developing a pricing strategy
2. To analyze sales-based, profit-based, and status quo-based pricing objectives
3. To examine the aspects of a broad price policy, including the multistage approach, and to consider the alternative pricing techniques
4. To show how a pricing strategy can be implemented
5. To present the major ways that prices can be adjusted

For the last several years, Sony has experienced a tough time, despite steadily growing sales. Although sales rose from $3.6 billion in 1980 to nearly $5 billion in 1983, net income declined from $279 million to about $100 million during the same period. Much of Sony's current difficulties can be traced to its strategy of investing heavily in new products and maintaining high prices for both new and continuing products, an approach that was extremely successful for decades. However, the environment facing Sony has changed:

Sony is producing premium products for a market where it can no longer charge a premium price. With most of its innovations, it simply doesn't have time. For whenever Sony innovates, its competitors come to market with a me-too product of comparable quality and lower price.

557

Sony pledges to be first, with the best, in the relentlessly competitive consumer electronics market. But being first no longer carries much of a premium, either in price or in exclusivity.

A good illustration of this phenomenon is the competition that the Sony Walkman now encounters. The first Walkman was introduced in mid-1979. Since that time, Sony has sold millions of Walkmans at relatively high prices. Because of the Walkman's popularity, more than 50 competitors have entered the market. Almost all of these companies offer their versions at prices that are substantially lower than those of the Walkman. In response, Sony has developed a full line of Walkman products, but it has not entered into price competition. There are similar levels of competition for Sony televisions, video recorders, and other products.

Sony is confident that its pricing orientation is correct, and that the company's strength is in innovation and product quality. As a result, it plans to continue spending 8 to 10 per cent of sales on research and development, compared with the 3 to 5 per cent spent by competitors, and to maintain prices above the market average.[1]

Sony's pricing strategy is consistent with the overall marketing philosophy of the company. For the strategy to succeed in the future, Sony must convince consumers that its products are indeed innovative and superior to any others on the market. This will be a difficult task. Ultimately, Sony may be forced into a more active pricing strategy.

A Pricing Strategy Framework

Developing a pricing strategy involves objectives, broad policy, strategy, implementation, and adjustments.

There are five stages in developing a pricing strategy: objectives, broad policy, strategy, implementation, and adjustments. See Figure 19-1. It is important to recognize that all aspects of the process are affected by the external factors discussed in Chapter 18.

Like any planning activity, pricing strategy begins with a clear statement of objectives and ends with an adaptive or corrective mechanism. It is essential that pricing decisions be integrated with the firm's overall marketing program. This is done in the broad price-policy phase shown in Figure 19-1.

The construction of a pricing strategy is not a one-time occurrence. The strategy needs to be re-examined when a new product is developed, a product is revised, the competitive environment changes, a product moves through its life cycle, a competitor initiates a price change, costs rise, or the firm's prices come under government scrutiny. These are some indications that a pricing strategy is performing poorly:

- Prices are changed too frequently.
- Pricing policy is difficult to explain to consumers.
- Channel members complain that profit margins are inadequate.

[1] Michael Cieply, ''Sony's Profitless Prosperity,'' *Forbes* (October 24, 1983), pp. 129–134.

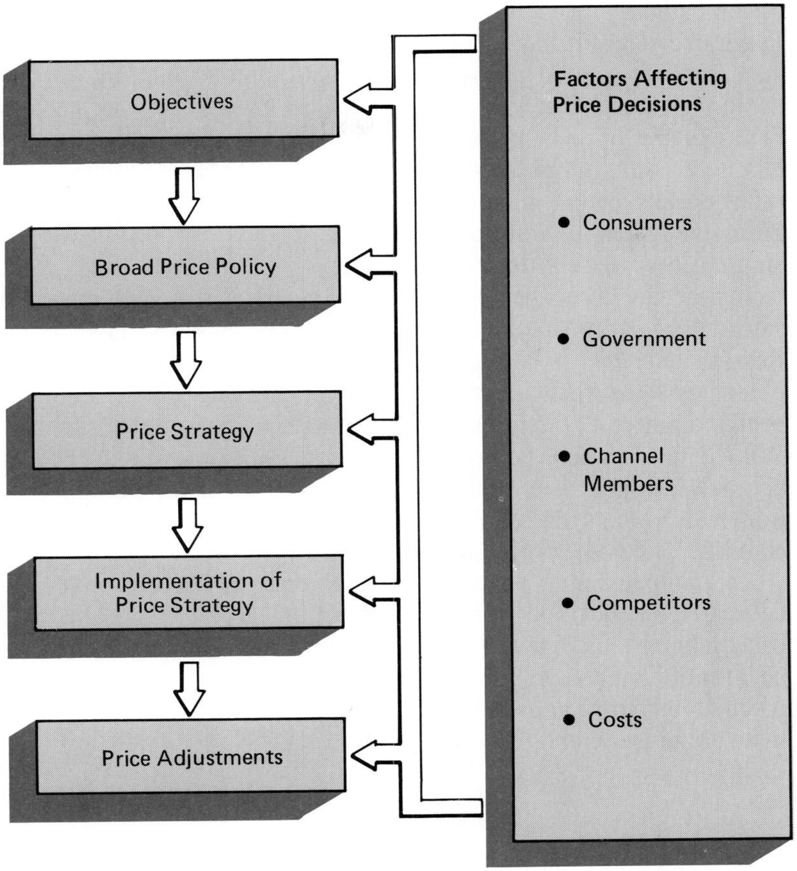

Figure 19-1
**A Framework for
Developing a Pricing
Strategy**

- Price decisions are made without adequate market research information.
- Too many different price options are available.
- Too much sales personnel time is spent in bargaining.
- Prices are inconsistent with the target market.
- A high proportion of goods are marked down or discounted late in the selling season in order to clear out surplus inventory.
- Too high a proportion of customers are price-sensitive and are attracted by competitors' discounts. Demand is elastic.
- The firm has major problems conforming with pricing legislation.

  This chapter describes each of the components of a pricing strategy shown in Figure 19-1 in detail.

Pricing Objectives

A pricing strategy should be consistent with and reflect overall company objectives. It is possible for different firms in the same industry to have dissimilar objectives and, therefore, different pricing strategies. For example, in the ice cream industry, Baskin-Robbins appeals to middle-class families and seeks to maximize sales. It has 2,500 franchised outlets, offering more than 500 rotating ice cream flavors (31 are sold each month) and accounting for over $400 million in annual sales. For the most part, Baskin-Robbins' stores have no sit-down facilities and price a single-dip cone at $.85. In contrast, Häagen-Daz caters to a "largely adult, more sophisticated, and better-heeled market" through its 200 retail outlets, which have annual sales of $60 million. Häagen-Daz stores have attractive sit-down facilities and feature 23 flavors of top-of-the-line ice cream. A single-dip cone sells for $1.25 and up.[2]

Pricing objectives can be sales-, profit-, and/or status quo-based.

There are three general pricing objectives from which a firm may select: sales-based, profit-based, and status quo-based. With sales-based objectives, the firm is interested in sales growth or maximizing market share. With profit-based objectives, the firm is interested in maximizing profit, earning a satisfactory profit, optimizing the return on investment, or securing an early recovery of cash. With status quo-based objectives, the firm seeks to avoid unfavorable government actions, minimize the effects of competitor actions, maintain good channel relations, discourage the entry of competitors, reduce demands from suppliers, or stabilize prices. See Figure 19-2.

A company may pursue more than one pricing objective at the same time, such as General Foods managers being told to increase sales by 3 to 5 per cent each year and to achieve a 15 per cent return on capital investments.[3] A firm may also set different short-run and long-run objectives. For example, in the short run, it may want to secure an early recovery of cash; in the long run, it may seek to discourage the entry of competitors.

Sales-Based Objectives

Sales-based objectives seek high sales volume or increased market share.

A company with **sales-based objectives** is oriented toward high sales volume or expanding its share of sales relative to competitors. A firm would focus on sales-based objectives for either of three reasons. One, it is interested in market saturation or sales growth as a major step leading to market control and sustained profits. Two, it seeks to maximize unit sales and is willing to trade low per unit profits for larger total profits. Three, it assumes that higher sales will enable the firm to have lower per unit costs.

A penetration price is a low price aimed at the mass market.

In order to achieve high sales, a penetration pricing strategy is frequently used. A **penetration price** is a low price intended to capture the mass market for a product or service. It is a proper strategy when customers are highly sensitive to price, low prices discourage actual and potential competitors, there are economies of scale (per unit production and distribution costs decrease as sales increase), and a large consumer market exists. Penetration pricing also recognizes that a high price may leave a product vulnerable to competition.

A penetration strategy was followed when the Commodore VIC-20 was originally priced at $299, compared with $600 for the Atari 400 and $500 for the Texas Instruments' 99/4A. Atari and Texas Instruments then dropped their prices; but they were unable to match Commodore, which kept reducing its prices. By 1983, the VIC-20 was selling for $80 (with Commodore earning a profit at that price),

---

[2] "The Scoop on Ice Cream Sales," *Business Week* (September 20, 1982), p. 73; and Kendall J. Wills, "The Scoop War's Gourmet Battle," *New York Times* (September 11, 1983), Section 3, p. 8.
[3] Jeremy Main, "General Foods Goes Back to Growing," *Fortune* (January 10, 1983), p. 93.

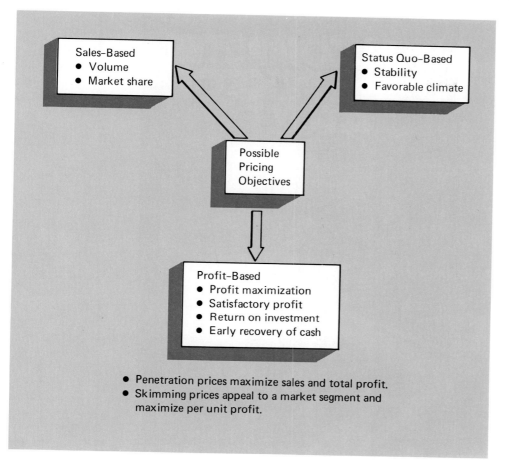

Figure 19-2
Pricing Objectives

while the Atari 400 and Texas Instruments' 99/4A were forced out of the market. Over 1.5 million VIC-20s were sold within the first two years.[4] See Figure 19-3.

In many cases, penetration pricing may tap markets that were not originally anticipated. For example, few people forecast that electronic hand-held calculators would reach the sales volume attained during their peak. The market expanded rapidly after prices fell below $100. It grew again as new models were introduced for $20 and less.

Profit-Based Objectives

A company with ***profit-based objectives*** orients its strategy toward some type of profit goal. Profit-maximization objectives are used when a firm designates high dollar profit as a goal, such as $1 million before taxes. Satisfactory-profit objectives are used by a firm seeking stable profits over a period of time. Rather than maximize profits in any given year, which could result in declines in non-peak years, the firm sets a steady profit goal for a number of years, such as

*Profit-based objectives
seek maximization, satis-
factory profit, return on
investment, and/or
recovery of cash.*

4 Laura Landro and James A. White, "Computer Firms Push Prices Down, Try to Improve Marketing Tactics," *Wall Street Journal* (April 29, 1983), p. 35.

Figure 19-3
The Commodore VIC-20,
Penetration Pricing

Courtesy of Commodore Electronics Limited.

$700,000 per year for five years. With return-on-investment objectives, the firm states that profits must relate to investment costs. This objective is frequently used by regulated utilities as a means of justifying rate-increase requests. Early-recovery-of-cash objectives are used by firms that desire high initial profits because they are short of funds or uncertain about the future.

Profit goals can be related to per unit profit or total profit.

Profit may be expressed in per unit or total terms. Per unit profit equals the revenue a seller receives for one unit sold minus costs. An item like perfume would have a high unit profit. Total profit equals the revenue a seller receives for all items sold minus costs. It is computed by multiplying per unit profit times the number of units sold. An item like milk would have a low unit profit. Its profitability is based on the number of units that are sold (turnover). High per unit profits usually rely on skimming prices. High total profits usually involve penetration pricing.

A *skimming price* **is aimed at consumers interested in quality. It can be followed by a penetration price.**

A *skimming price* is a high price intended to attract the market segment that is more concerned with product quality, uniqueness, or status than price. It is a

Figure 19-4
Mercedes-Benz, Skimming Prices
Mercedes-Benz offers a line of luxury cars aimed at upscale consumers. The cars are attractively styled and feature the latest in technological innovations and plush interiors. The 190 model is the newest car in the line.

proper strategy if competition can be kept out or minimized (through patent protection, brand loyalty, raw material control, or high capital requirements), funds are needed for early recovery of cash or further expansion, the market is insensitive to price or willing to pay a high initial price, and unit production and distribution costs remain equal or increase as sales increase (economies of scale are absent).

Mercedes-Benz, a producer of automobiles and trucks, employs skimming prices for the cars it markets in the U.S. By establishing and retaining a luxury image for its vehicles, Mercedes-Benz is able to set high prices for them. The company earns at least a 20 per cent margin on these vehicles. It discourages discounting and sales. Advertising emphasizes styling, status, handling, and other product-related features; television commercials never mention prices. These were the U.S. base prices for selected 1984 models: 190E (sedan), $24,000; 300TD (station wagon), $34,000; and 380SL (sports car), $44,500.[5] Figure 19-4 shows the new 190 model.

In some situations, companies first employ a skimming price and then apply penetration pricing. There are several advantages to this strategy. One, a high price is charged when competition is limited. Two, a high price helps defray research and development and introductory advertising costs. Three, the first group of customers to purchase a new product is usually less sensitive to price than later groups. Four, a high initial price portrays a high-quality image for a product. Five, raising an initial price often encounters market resistance; lowering a price is viewed favorably. Six, after the initial market segment is saturated, penetration pricing can be used to appeal to the mass market and expand total sales volume.

[5] John Holusha, ''Mercedes-Benz U.S. Strategy,'' *New York Times* (October 12, 1983), pp. D1, D5.

For example, Xerox usually introduces new photocopiers at relatively high prices and later lowers them to meet competition. Its model 3109 was first priced at $7,495. Eventually the price dropped to $4,175—and less.[6]

Status Quo-Based Objectives

Status quo-based objectives seek stability and favorable business conditions.

Status quo-based objectives are sought by a firm interested in stability or in continuing a favorable climate for its operations. Pricing strategy is oriented toward avoiding declines in sales and minimizing the impact of such outside parties as government, competitors, and channel members.

It should not be inferred that status quo objectives require no effort on the part of the firm. For example, a manufacturer would instruct salespeople not to offer different terms to competing retailers, or else the government may accuse the company of a Robinson-Patman Act violation. In order to retain customers, a wholesaler may have to match the price cuts of its competitors. To maintain channel cooperation, a manufacturer may have to lower its markup in the face of rising costs. A retailer may have to charge low prices to discourage competitors from stocking certain product lines.

Broad Price Policy

A *broad price policy* links prices with the target market, company image, and other marketing elements.

A **broad price policy** coordinates pricing decisions with the firm's target market, image, and marketing mix. It generates a coordinated series of actions, a consistent image, and a strategy that incorporates short- and long-term goals. For example, a high-income market purchasing status brands at prestigious stores would expect high prices. A moderate-income market purchasing private brands at discount stores would expect low prices. The role of pricing can range from achieving customer loyalty via superior service, convenience, and quality to loyalty via low prices through extensive price cutting.

The company outlines its broad price policy by placing individual price decisions into an integrated framework. For example, the firm would decide on the interrelationship of prices for goods within a product line, how often special discounts are used, how prices compare to competition, the frequency of price changes, and the method for setting the prices of new products.

The *multistage approach to pricing* can help set a broad price policy.

A popular technique for developing a broad price policy is the **multi-stage approach to pricing,** which divides price planning into six successive steps, with each placing constraints on the next step: identifying the target market, examining brand image, analyzing the other components of the marketing mix, outlining a broad price policy, determining a pricing strategy, and arriving at a specific price.[7] The first four steps concentrate on the enactment of a broad price policy; the last two steps center on specific decisions and their implementation, which are discussed later in this chapter.

[6] Dylan Landis, "Xerox Slashes Copier Prices," *New York Times* (July 1, 1982), p. D5.
[7] Alfred R. Oxenfeldt, "Multi-Stage Approach to Pricing," *Harvard Business Review,* Vol. 38 (July–August 1960), pp. 125–133.

A price strategy may be cost-based, demand-based, or competition-based. See Figure 19-5. With a *cost-based price strategy,* the marketer sets prices by computing merchandise, service, and overhead costs, and then adding the desired profit to these figures. Demand is not analyzed. For example, an item may cost

Figure 19-5
The Alternative Ways of Developing a Price Strategy

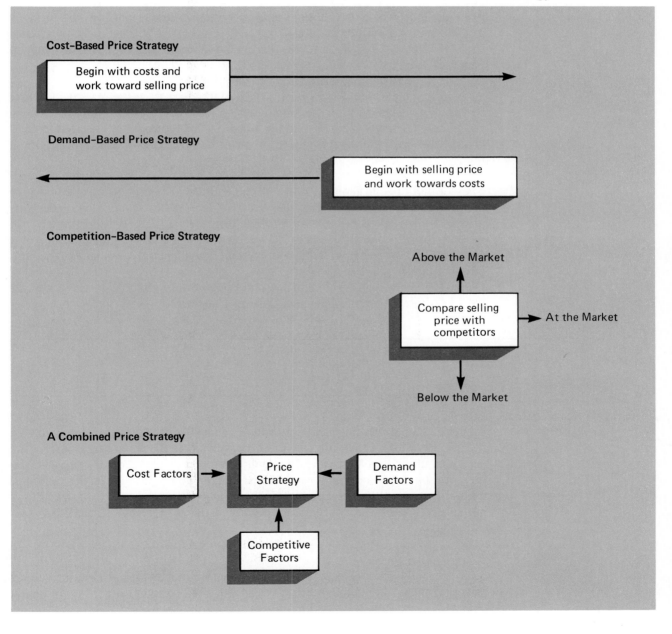

Cost-Based Price Strategy

Begin with costs and work toward selling price

Demand-Based Price Strategy

Begin with selling price and work towards costs

Competition-Based Price Strategy

Compare selling price with competitors

Above the Market

At the Market

Below the Market

A Combined Price Strategy

Cost Factors → Price Strategy ← Demand Factors

Competitive Factors

Under a *cost-based price strategy*, costs are computed and a *price floor* is set.

Under a *demand-based price strategy*, final consumers are researched and a *price ceiling* is determined.

$10 to manufacture and sell, and the firm may seek a $1 profit per unit. Selling price is then $11. Cost-based pricing is often used by companies whose objectives are stated in terms of profit or return on investment. It sets the prices a firm must charge in order to attain its level of profitability. The **price floor** is the lowest acceptable price the firm can charge and attain its profit goal.

In a **demand-based price strategy,** the marketer sets prices after researching consumer desires and ascertaining the range of prices acceptable to the target market. For example, if the firm finds that its customers will pay $10 for an item and it needs a $3 margin to cover profit and selling expenses, production costs must not exceed $7. Demand-based pricing is used by marketers who believe that price is a key factor in consumer decision making. These marketers identify the **price ceiling,** which is the maximum amount consumers will pay for a given product or service. If the ceiling is exceeded, consumers will not make purchases. Its level depends on the elasticity of demand (availability of substitutes and urgency of need).

Setting prices on the basis of competitors is a *competition-based price strategy*.

Under a **competition-based price strategy,** the marketer sets prices in accordance with competitors. Prices may be below the market, at the market, or above the market, depending on customer loyalty, services provided, image, real or perceived differences between brands or stores, and the competitive environment. Competition-based pricing is applied by firms that face competitors selling similar items.

All three approaches should be considered when establishing a price strategy. They do not operate independently of one another. These questions demonstrate the interrelation of cost-, demand-, and competition-based methods of deriving prices. Will a given price level allow a firm to attain the desired profit (cost-based)? If prices are increased by 10 per cent, how much will unit sales decrease (demand-based)? What will competitors do if a company gives quantity discounts (competition-based)?

The attributes of cost, demand, and competitive pricing and how they are calculated are covered in greater depth in Chapter 20.

Implementing Price Strategy

Implementing a price strategy involves a wide variety of separate but related specific decisions in addition to the broad concepts discussed previously. The decisions involve customary and variable pricing, a one-price policy versus flexible pricing, odd pricing, the price-quality association, leader pricing, multiple-unit pricing, price lining, geographic pricing, and terms. In the following subsections, these concepts are described in detail. See Figure 19-6.

Customary and Variable Pricing

With *customary pricing*, one price is maintained over an extended period of time.

Customary pricing occurs when a channel member sets product or service prices and seeks to maintain them over an extended period of time. Prices are not changed during this time period.

CUSTOMARY PRICING

Price maintained over time

VARIABLE PRICING

POOR ORANGE CROP — PRICES ↑

Prices respond to costs and demand

ONE-PRICE POLICY

ALL BLOUSES $12.95

One price for all customers

FLEXIBLE PRICING

SPECIAL SALE MAKE US AN OFFER

Prices depend on customer bargaining

ODD PRICING

GOLD BRACELETS $299

Pricing below even dollar values

PRESTIGE PRICING

SHOP THE BEST OUR PRODUCTS ARE BETTER, SO OUR PRICES ARE HIGHER

Appealing to quality

LEADER PRICING

Kodak

Film, no one beats our prices!

Low prices to attract customer traffic

MULTIPLE-UNIT PRICING

Campbells SOUP

Campbells Soup 3 for $1.

Price discounts given for quantity purchases

PRICE LINING

RUNNING SHOES $12.95 $22.95 $35.95

Distinct price points set within a specific range

Figure 19-6
Selected Pricing Strategies

Customary pricing is used for items like candy, gum, magazines, restaurant food, and mass transit. Instead of modifying prices to reflect cost increases, organizations reduce package size, change ingredients, or "impose a stricter transfer policy among bus lines." The assumption is that consumers prefer one of these modifications over a price hike.

Between 1971 and 1983, Wrigley raised the price of its chewing gum only three times, from 10 to 15 cents, from 15 to 20 cents, and from 20 to 25 cents, despite steadily higher costs for sugar, gum base, and wrapping material. In order to minimize consumer resistance to the first increase from 10 to 15 cents, Wrigley changed the package size from five- to seven-stick packs. Wrigley could have raised prices without changing package size and incurring the expense of modifying its wrapping machines, but it was concerned with consumer perceptions about value.

Under *variable pricing*, prices reflect cost changes or differences in demand.

With ***variable pricing,*** the firm intentionally alters prices to respond to cost fluctuations or differences in consumer demand. When costs fluctuate, prices are lowered or raised to reflect the changes; cost fluctuations are not absorbed and product quality is not modified in order to maintain customary prices. Through price discrimination, a company offers distinct prices to appeal to different market segments. In this case, the prices charged to various consumers are not based on costs. Most firms use some form of variable pricing. Demand-based variable pricing is examined further in Chapter 20 under the topic of price discrimination.

It is possible to combine customary and variable pricing. For example, a magazine may be priced at $2 per single copy and be available for $20 per year's subscription ($1.67 an issue). Under this strategy two customary prices are charged, and the consumer selects the offer that he or she finds most attractive.

One-Price Policy and Flexible Pricing

All customers buying the same product or service pay the same price under a *one-price policy*.

With a ***one-price policy*** a firm charges the same price to all customers who seek to purchase a product or service under similar conditions. Price may vary according to quantity purchased, time of purchase, and services obtained (such as delivery, installation, and an extended guarantee); but all consumers are given the opportunity to pay the same price for identical combinations of product and service. A one-price policy builds consumer confidence, is easy to administer, eliminates bargaining, and permits self-service and catalog sales.

The one-price policy was begun by John Wanamaker, who was the first merchant to mark prices clearly on each item in stock. Throughout the United States, one-price policies are the rule for most retailers. In industrial marketing, a firm with a one-price policy would not permit its sales personnel to deviate from a published price list.

With *flexible pricing*, different customers may pay different prices for the same product or service.

Flexible pricing allows the marketer to adjust prices based on the consumer's ability to negotiate or on the buying power of a large customer. Consumers who are knowledgeable or who are good bargainers pay lower prices than those who are not knowledgeable or are poorer bargainers. Jewelry stores, automobile dealers, flea markets, real estate brokers, antique shops, and industrial marketers frequently use flexible pricing. In some cases, commissions are paid to sales personnel on the basis of the profitability of each order. This encourages sales personnel to solicit higher prices. Flexible prices to channel members are subject to the Robinson-Patman restrictions explained in Chapter 18.

Odd Pricing

An *odd-pricing strategy* is used when final selling prices are set at levels below even dollar values, such as 49 cents, $4.95, and $199. Odd pricing has proven popular for several reasons. Consumers like receiving change. And because the cashier must make change, employers ensure that transactions are properly recorded and money is placed in the cash register. Consumers gain the impression that the firm thinks carefully about its prices and sets them as low as possible. Consumers may also believe that odd prices represent price reductions; a price of $8.95 may be viewed as a discount from $10.[8]

Odd prices that are one or two cents below the next even price (29 cents, $2.98) are common up to $4. Beyond that point and up to $50, five-cent reductions from the highest even price ($19.95, $49.95) are more usual. For expensive items, odd endings are in dollars ($499, $5995).

Odd prices help a number of consumers to stay within their price limits and still buy the best items available. A shopper willing to spend ''less than $10'' for a tie will be attracted to a $9.95 tie and be as likely to purchase it as a tie selling for $9, because it is within the defined price range. The imposition of sales tax in most states has the effect of raising odd prices into higher dollar levels and may reduce the effectiveness of odd pricing as a selling tool.

Price-Quality Association

The *price-quality association* is a concept stating that consumers may believe high prices mean high quality and low prices mean low quality. In setting prices, the price-quality association is particularly important for situations where quality is difficult to judge on bases other than price, buyers perceive large differences in quality among brands, buyers have little experience or confidence in judging quality (as in the case of a new product), high prices exclude the mass market, brand names are unknown, or brand names require certain price levels to sustain their images. It is essential that prices properly reflect the quality and image the company seeks for its offerings.[9]

With *prestige pricing,* a theory drawn from the price-quality association, it is assumed that consumers do not buy products or services at prices considered too low. Consumers set price floors and will not make purchases at prices below those floors. They feel quality and status are inferior at extremely low prices. Consumers also set upper limits for prices they consider acceptable for particular products or services. Above the price ceilings, the items are perceived as too expensive. For each product or service, the firm must set its price within the acceptable range between the floor and ceiling. See Figure 19-7.

When consumers are perceptually sensitive to certain prices and departures from these prices in either direction result in decreases in demand, they are responding to *psychological pricing.* Customary, odd, and prestige pricing are all forms of psychological pricing.

In an *odd-pricing strategy,* prices are set below even-dollar values.

The *price-quality association* indicates consumers often believe there is a relationship between price and quality.

Prestige pricing indicates consumers may not buy when a price is too low.

In *psychological pricing,* certain prices are most effective.

---

[8] See Bernard F. Whalen, ''Strategic Mix of Odd, Even Prices Can Lead to Increased Retail Profits,'' *Marketing News* (March 7, 1980), p. 24.

[9] See John J. Wheatley, John S. Y. Chiu, and Arieh Goldman, ''Physical Quality, Price, and Perceptions of Product Quality: Implications for Retailers,'' *Journal of Retailing,* Vol. 57 (Summer 1981), pp. 100–113; V. K. Venkataraman, ''The Price-Quality Relationship in an Experimental Setting,'' *Journal of Advertising Research,* Vol. 21 (August 1981), pp. 49–52; and ''Study Product Quality/Profit Relationship so Firms Can Leapfrog over Foreign Competitors,'' *Marketing News* (January 21, 1983), Section 2, pp. 4–5.

Figure 19-7
Demand for Designer Jeans under Prestige Pricing

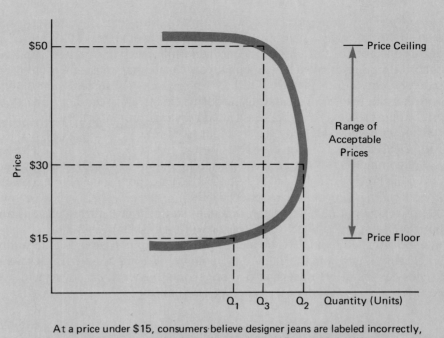

At a price under $15, consumers believe designer jeans are labeled incorrectly, an old style, seconds, or otherwise of poor quality. Demand is negligible.

At $15, consumer demand is Q_1. A small group of discount-oriented consumers will buy the jeans. This is the minimum price they will pay for a good pair of designer jeans.

As the price goes from $15 to $30, demand rises continuously as more consumers perceive the jeans as a high-quality, status product. At $30, sales peak at Q_2.

As the price goes from $30 to $50, consumer demand drops gradually to Q_3. During this range, some consumers begin to see the jeans as too expensive. But, many will buy the jeans until they reach $50, their ceiling price.

At a price over $50, consumers believe designer jeans are too expensive. Demand is negligible.

Leader Pricing

Selling key items at lower than usual prices to attract customers is *leader pricing*.

Under ***leader pricing,*** a firm advertises and sells key items in its product assortment at less than their usual profit margins. For a retailer the objective of leader pricing is to increase customer traffic into a store. For a manufacturer the objective is to gain greater consumer interest in its overall product line. In both cases it is hoped that consumers will purchase regularly priced merchandise in addition to the specially priced items that drew them to the store or manufacturer's display.

Leader pricing is most often used with nationally branded, high-turnover, frequently purchased products. For example, in drugstores, the best-selling items in terms of dollar sales are Kodak and Polaroid film. In order to stimulate customer traffic into their stores, druggists price film at very low markups; in some cases, it is sold at close to cost. According to a vice-president at Peoples, a drugstore chain with annual sales of $800 million and 600 stores in several states:

We sell it at less than a 20 per cent markup and near 5 per cent or cost when it is on sale.

Our position is that we offer some kind of photo-related item—film, flash bulbs, and so forth—every week in our ads.[10]

Film is a good item for leader pricing because consumers are able to detect low prices and they are attracted into a store by a discount on the item, which regularly sells for several dollars.

There are two kinds of leader pricing: loss leaders and prices higher than cost but lower than regular prices. As described in Chapter 18, the use of loss leaders is closely regulated or illegal in a number of states.

Multiple-Unit Pricing

Multiple-unit pricing is a practice whereby a company offers final consumers discounts for buying in quantity in order to increase sales volume. For example, by offering items at two for 99 cents or six for $1.39, the firm attempts to sell more units than at 50 cents or 25 cents each.

With multiple-unit pricing, quantity discounts are intended to result in higher overall sales volume.

There are four major reasons for using multiple-unit pricing. First, customers may increase their immediate purchases if they believe a bargain is achieved through a multiple-unit purchase. Second, customers may increase their overall consumption if they make quantity purchases. For instance, the multiple-unit pricing of soda may encourage greater consumption. Third, competitors' customers may be attracted by the firm's discounts. Fourth, the firm may be able to clear out slow-moving and end-of-season merchandise.

Multiple-unit pricing will not achieve its goals if consumers merely shift their purchases and do not increase consumption of a company's brand. For example, multiple-unit pricing for Heinz ketchup will probably not result in consumers using more ketchup with their meals. It will not raise total dollar sales, but will cause consumers to buy ketchup less frequently because it can be stored.

Price Lining

Price lining involves selling merchandise at a range of prices, with each price representing a distinct level of quality. Instead of setting one price for a single model of a product, the firm sells two or more models (at different quality levels) at different prices. Price lining involves two decisions: defining the price range of the firm's offerings (floor and ceiling) and establishing specific price points within the price range.

Price lining establishes a range of selling prices and price points within that range.

The price range may be defined as low, intermediate, or high. For example, inexpensive radios may be priced from $8 to $20, moderately priced radios from $22 to $50, and expensive radios from $55 to $120. After the range is determined, a limited number of price points is set. These prices must be distinct and not too close together. Inexpensive radios could be priced at $8, $12, and $20. They should not be priced at $8, $9, $10, $11, $12, $13, $14, $15, $16, $17, $18, $19, and $20. This will confuse consumers and be inefficient for the firm. Figure 19-8 illustrates price lining for inexpensive radios.

When developing a price line, the marketer must consider the following factors. One, price points must be spaced far enough apart so that customers perceive

[10] Barbara Ettorre, ''A New Picture at Drugstores,'' *New York Times* (August 2, 1980), p. 27; and Alan Freeman, ''Imasco Seeks Peoples Drug at $320 Million,'' *Wall Street Journal* (February 28, 1984), p. 8.

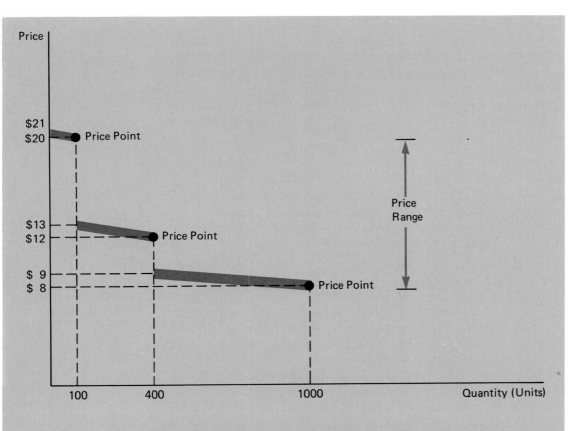

At $8, 1000 radios can be sold. A price of $9 is perceived as substantially more expensive.

Between $9 and $12, demand remains at 400 radios since consumers consider the prices within this range to be similar. Therefore, the price point should be $12, since this price provides the same unit sales as could be obtained at $9, $10, or $11 and total revenues are highest. A price of $13 is perceived as substantially more expensive.

Between $13 and $20, demand remains at 100 radios since consumers consider the prices within this range to be similar. Therefore, the price point should be $20, since the price provides the same unit sales and higher total revenues then any other price above $12. A price of $21 is perceived as substantially more expensive.

If the firm uses a price line of $8, $12, and $20, it will maximize total revenues. It will sell 100 radios at $20, 300 radios at $12, and 600 radios at $8, Total revenues are $10,400 (with only one price, $8, the same thousand radios would be sold, but revenues would be $8,000).

Figure 19-8
Price Lining for an Inexpensive Radio

quality differences among models, otherwise consumers will view the price floor as the price they should pay and believe that there is no difference among models. Two, price points should be spaced farther apart at higher prices, because consumer demand becomes more inelastic. Three, the relationships of price points must be maintained when costs rise, so that clear differences are retained. For example, if radio costs rise 25 per cent, prices should be $10, $15, and $25.

Price lining benefits both channel members and consumers. Channel members are able to offer an assortment of products, attract market segments, trade up consumers within a price range, control inventory by price point, exclude competitors from the channel by offering models throughout the price range, and increase overall sales volume. Consumers are given an assortment from which to choose, confusion is minimized, comparisons may be made, and quality alternatives are available within the desired price range.

Price lining also has several constraints. One, consumers may perceive the gaps between prices as too large. For example, a $25 handbag may be too inexpensive, whereas the next price point of $100 may be too expensive. Two, rising costs may put a squeeze on individual prices and make it difficult for a firm to maintain the proper relationship among prices. Three, markdowns or special sales may disrupt the balance in a price line, unless all items in the line are proportionately reduced in price.

Geographic Pricing

Geographic pricing outlines the responsibility for transportation charges. Generally, geographic pricing is not negotiated but depends on the traditional practices in the industry in which the firm operates. All firms in an industry normally conform to the same geographic pricing format. FOB mill (factory) pricing, uniform delivered pricing, zone pricing, and base-point pricing are the most common methods of geographic pricing.

In *FOB mill (factory) pricing,* the buyer selects the transportation form and pays all freight charges. The seller pays the costs of loading the goods (hence, "free on board"). The delivered price to the buyer depends on freight charges. Under *uniform delivered pricing,* all buyers pay the same delivered price for the same quantity of goods, regardless of their location. The seller pays for shipping. *Zone pricing* provides for a uniform delivered price to all buyers within a geographic zone. In a multiple-zone system, delivered prices vary by zone. In *base-point pricing,* firms in an industry establish basing points from which the costs of shipping are computed. The delivered price to a buyer reflects the cost of transporting goods from the basing point nearest to the buyer, regardless of the actual site of supply. These forms of pricing are summarized in Figure 19-9.

Geographic pricing alternatives are FOB mill (factory), uniform delivered, zone, and base-point pricing.

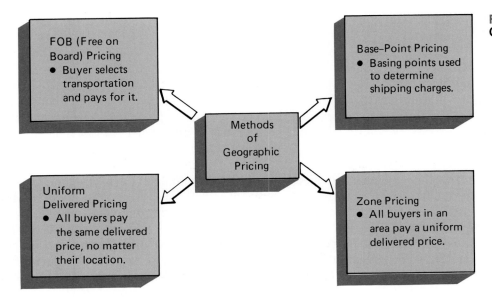

Figure 19-9
Geographic Pricing

Terms

Terms outline all pricing provisions.

Discounts **are reductions from final price for performing functions, paying in cash, quantity buying, and off-season purchases.**

Terms are the provisions of price agreements, including discounts, timing of payments, and credit arrangements. Discounts may be functional, cash, quantity, seasonal, or promotional. Payments may be made immediately, upon receipt of merchandise, after a bill is received, or spread over time. The firm may insist on cash, allow open credit accounts, or accept revolving credit.

Discounts are reductions from final selling price that are available to channel members and final consumers for performing certain functions, paying cash, buying large quantities, purchasing in off-seasons, or enhancing promotions. For example, a wholesaler could purchase goods at 40 per cent off the manufacturer's suggested list price. This would cover the wholesaler's selling expenses, profit, and discount to the retailer. The retailer could purchase goods for 25 per cent off list (the wholesaler would retain 15 per cent for costs and profit).

Functional or trade discounts are the traditional discounts provided to wholesalers and retailers to compensate them for the distribution tasks they perform. Cash discounts are reductions in invoice amounts that are given to stimulate immediate or early payments.

Quantity discounts are price reductions related to efficiencies that result from large-volume purchases. Noncumulative quantity discounts are based on the size of individual orders. Cumulative quantity discounts are based on total purchases for a given period (usually one year).

Seasonal discounts are used to encourage off-peak purchases or advance orders. These purchases often receive forward dating, so that the customer does not pay for goods until after the order is received. The benefits to the manufacturer are that storage costs are held down, risks are minimized, and production peaks can be eliminated.

Promotional discounts reimburse channel members for promoting products. They may involve free merchandise, cash selling incentives, cooperative advertising allowances, or other methods for attaining channel cooperation. These discounts may be permanent or geared to specific promotions. When computing any type of discount, the firm must be sure that discounts are proportionately available to all competing channel members to avoid violation of the Robinson-Patman Act.

The total discounts a firm offers its customers are typically quoted in the form of a chain. Cash, quantity, seasonal, and promotional discounts are deducted after the functional or trade discount has been determined. Transportation costs are not discounted; they are added to the final price to the channel member or consumer.

The timing of payments needs to be specified in a purchase agreement. Final consumers may make payments immediately or after delivery of merchandise. In credit transactions, payments are not made until bills are received; they may be spread over time.

Channel members are quite interested in the timing of payments and negotiate for the best terms. For example, terms of net 30 mean that goods do not have to be paid for until thirty days after receipt. At that point, they must be paid for in full. Terms of 2/10, net 30 mean that a buyer receives a 2 per cent discount if the full bill is paid within ten days after receipt of merchandise. The buyer must pay the face value of the bill within thirty days after receipt of goods. Terms of 2/10 EOM, net 30 mean the buyer receives a 2 per cent discount if the full bill is paid within ten days after the end of the month in which an order is placed or pays the face value within thirty days after the end of the month. A wide variety of time terms is available.

A firm that allows credit purchases may use an open account or revolving credit. With an *open credit account,* the buyer receives a monthly bill for goods bought during the preceding month. The account must be paid in full each month. With a *revolving credit account,* the buyer agrees to make minimum payments during an extended period of time and pays interest on outstanding balances.

A credit account may be open or revolving.

Price Adjustments

After a price strategy is implemented, it usually requires continuous fine tuning to reflect changes in costs, competitive conditions, and demand considerations. Prices can be adjusted through changes in list prices, escalator clauses and surcharges, added markups, markdowns, and rebates. It is important that price be used as an adaptive mechanism.

List prices are the regularly quoted prices provided to customers. They are preprinted on price tags, in catalogs, and in dealer purchase orders. Modifications in list prices are necessary if there are sustained changes in labor costs, raw material costs, and market segments and as a product moves through its life cycle. Because these events are long term in nature, they enable customary prices to be revised, new catalogs to be printed, and adjustments to be completed in an orderly fashion.

In some cases, costs or economic conditions are so volatile that revised list prices cannot be printed or distributed efficiently. Then, escalator clauses or surcharges can be used.[11] Each of these allows prices to be adjusted quickly. With an *escalator clause,* the firm is contractually allowed to raise the price of an item to reflect higher costs in the item's essential ingredients without changing printed list prices. Through an escalator clause, a firm may be allowed to determine its selling prices at the time of delivery. *Surcharges* are across-the-board published price increases that supplement list prices. These are frequently used with catalogs because of their simplicity; an insert is distributed with the catalog.

When list prices are not involved, *additional markups* can be used to raise regular retail prices because demand is unexpectedly high or costs are rising. There is a risk to additional markups. For example, supermarkets have received adverse publicity for relabeling low-cost existing inventories at higher prices so that they match those of newer merchandise purchased at higher costs.

Markdowns are reductions from the original selling prices of items. Both manufacturers and retailers use markdowns to meet the lower prices of competi-

When costs, competition, or demand changes, price strategy must be modified.

List prices, escalator clauses, surcharges, additional markups, markdowns, and rebates must be used properly.

[11] See Robert J. Dolan, ''Pricing Strategies That Adjust to Inflation,'' *Industrial Marketing Management,* Vol. 10 (July 1981), pp. 151–156; Barbara Bund Jackson, ''Manage Risk in Industrial Pricing,'' *Harvard Business Review,* Vol. 58 (July–August 1980), pp. 121–133; and Dale Varble, ''Flexible Price Agreements: Purchasing's View,'' *California Management Review,* Vol. 23 (Winter 1980), pp. 44–51.

tors, counteract overstocking of merchandise, clear out shopworn merchandise, deplete assortments of odds and ends, and increase customer traffic.[12]

While manufacturers give discounts to wholesalers and retailers on a regular basis, they may periodically offer cash rebates to customers to stimulate consumption of an item or a group of items. **Rebates** are flexible, do not alter basic list prices, and increase direct communication between consumers and manufacturers (because rebates are sent to consumers by manufacturers). Price cuts by individual retailers do not generate the same kind of consumer enthusiasm. The recent popularity of rebates can be traced to their usage by the auto industry to help cut down on inventory surpluses. Rebates have also been used by Fedders, Gillette, Polaroid, Minolta, and a number of other companies, in addition to all the U.S. auto makers.

Whenever price adjustments are necessary, channel members should cooperatively determine their individual roles. Price hikes or cuts should not be unilaterally imposed.

Summary

Developing a pricing strategy consists of objectives, broad policy, strategy, implementation, and adjustments. Pricing objectives may be sales-, profit-, or status quo-based. Sales objectives center on growth or market share. A penetration price is a low price intended to capture the mass market. Profit objectives center on profit maximization, satisfactory profits, optimizing return on investment, or early cash recovery. Profit can be expressed in per unit or total dollar terms. A skimming price is a high price intended to capture the market segment less concerned with price than quality or status. A firm may use a skimming and then a penetration pricing strategy. Status quo objectives are geared toward avoiding declines in business and minimizing the impact of outside parties. Objectives may be combined.

A broad price policy integrates pricing decisions with the firm's target market, image, and marketing mix. Within its broad price policy, the company determines whether it is price- or nonprice-oriented. A popular technique for planning a broad policy is the multistage approach to pricing.

A price strategy may be cost-, demand-, or competition-based. With cost-based pricing, prices are computed by adding desired profits to the costs of production and selling. In demand-based pricing, final prices are based on consumer research. The firm works backward to determine the costs it can afford to incur and still sell an item at the price sought by consumers. Under competition-based pricing, prices are set below, at, or higher than those of competitors. All three approaches should be integrated when establishing a price strategy.

Implementing a price strategy involves a variety of separate but interlocking specific decisions. Customary pricing exists when a channel member maintains prices for an extended period of time. With variable pricing the marketer alters

[12] See Phillip G. Carlson, "Fashion Retailing: The Sensitivity of Rate of Sale to Markdown," *Journal of Retailing*, Vol. 59 (Spring 1983), pp. 67–76.

prices to coincide with fluctuations in costs or consumer demand. With a one-price policy, all consumers making a purchase under similar conditions pay the same price. Flexible pricing allows the marketer to vary prices based on the consumer's ability to negotiate or the buying power of a large customer.

An odd-price strategy is used when final selling prices are set at levels below even-dollar values. The price-quality association states that consumers believe there is a correlation between price and quality. With prestige pricing, it is assumed that consumers do not buy products or services at prices that are considered too low. They set price floors as well as price ceilings. Under leader pricing, key items are sold at less than their usual profit margins in order to increase consumer traffic.

Multiple-unit pricing is a practice in which a company offers final consumers discounts for buying in quantity. Price lining is the sale of merchandise at a range of prices, with each price representing a distinct level of quality. Geographic pricing outlines the responsibility for transportation charges. Terms are the provisions of price agreements, including discounts, timing of payments, and credit arrangements.

After a price strategy is implemented, it usually requires regular fine tuning to reflect cost, competition, or demand changes. Prices can be adjusted by changing list prices, including escalator clauses and surcharges in contracts, marking prices up or down, and offering direct manufacturer rebates.

Questions for Discussion

1. Evaluate Sony's pricing strategy.
2. One indication that a pricing strategy is performing poorly is that prices are changed too frequently. Why is this a bad sign?
3. Explain how two pricing objectives could be in conflict with each other.
4. Under what circumstances should a stationery manufacturer pursue a penetration price strategy? A skimming price strategy?
5. Why would a marketer be unable to set a penetration price and then a skimming price?
6. Apply the multistage approach to pricing to your college bookstore.
7. What problems are associated with the use of customary pricing? How can they be overcome?
8. Why do most U.S. firms apply a one-price policy? Should more companies utilize flexible pricing? Explain your answer.
9. Compare and contrast the law of demand and the price-quality association. Are those theories in disagreement? Why or why not?
10. Under what circumstances would multiple-unit pricing be a poor strategy?
11. How does price lining benefit manufacturers? Retailers? Consumers?
12. Distinguish between uniform delivered pricing and zone pricing.
13. Describe the major purposes of each of these types of discounts: functional (trade), seasonal, and promotional.
14. Distinguish between escalator clauses and surcharges. When should each be used?
15. What are the advantages and disadvantages of rebates? Why not just offer price discounts (sales)?

Case 1 Cover Girl Cosmetics: A Penetration Pricing Strategy*

Noxell Corporation markets its Cover Girl cosmetics at popular prices to a large mass market, consisting mostly of teenagers and young adults. Cover Girl products project an image of "fresh-faced, natural beauty." For more than a decade, the Cover Girl image has been promoted by model/actress Cheryl Tiegs.

Cover Girl cosmetics are widely distributed through chains such as K mart and F. W. Woolworth. The products are displayed on self-service racks, with retailers depending on fast turnover (with low profit per unit) for success. The Cover Girl product line is deliberately limited to maximize turnover for both Noxell and retailers, to make it easier for self-service shoppers, and to give the company cost savings in manufacturing. As a Noxell executive explained, "We don't want to burden the storekeeper with too many shades." For example, Cover Girl markets only 7 shades of liquid face makeup.

In comparison, competitors such as Maybelline and Revlon distribute their products through department and specialty stores. They usually lease store space, set up elaborate displays, and employ commissioned salespeople. A large product assortment is emphasized. For example, Maybelline offers 20 shades of liquid face makeup.

Cover Girl products are priced from $1.25 to $3.75, in keeping with Noxell's low-price, mass-market philosophy. Other cosmetic makers, who are more oriented toward marketing status brands and gift items, set prices that are higher than those for Cover Girl. The Noxell approach is particularly attractive to cost-conscious consumers.

To maintain its strong brand image for Cover Girl, Noxell consistently spends about 22 per cent of Cover Girl's sales on advertising; the industry average is 7 to 9 per cent of sales. Cover Girl accounts for over 50 per cent of Noxell's overall sales, and has a 14 per cent share of the market for low or medium-priced cosmetics. It has been steadily gaining on industry leader Maybelline, which has an 18 per cent market share. Revlon's Natural Wonder line has a 5 per cent market share. Cover Girl is becoming particularly strong with young working women who want an "active, attractive girl-next-door image" for themselves.

QUESTIONS
1. Describe several pricing objectives Noxell could set for Cover Girl cosmetics.
2. Evaluate Cover Girl's broad price policy using the multistage approach to pricing.
3. Are the use of Cheryl Tiegs as a spokesperson and the expenditure of 22 per cent of revenues proper for low-price, mass-market products such as Cover Girl cosmetics?
4. Examine Cover Girl's penetration pricing strategy in terms of the price-quality association.

---

* The data in this case are drawn from "Noxell Glows in the Mass Market," *Business Week* (February 14, 1983), pp. 148 ff.

Case 2 The Van Bortel Auto Dealership Plan: Pricing GM Cars at $49 Above Costs[†]

Howard Van Bortel operated a General Motors automobile dealership featuring Chevrolets and Oldsmobiles in Palmyra, New York, for more than twenty years. For most of that time, Van Bortel offered the same combination of service, personal selling, selection, and price as his fellow auto dealers. He sold about 800 cars a year. Then, in 1977, Van Bortel implemented a new plan, which

- Set selling prices at $49 above factory invoice cost to the dealership.
- Lowered the number of cars maintained in inventory on the premises.
- Reduced the size of the sales force and discarded the high commission rate system.
- Eliminated price bargaining.
- Stressed dealer-installed services, such as paint striping and rustproofing (These services are very profitable).
- Paid bills promptly to GM, resulting in a 3 per cent savings (which then becomes dealer profit).

By 1979, Van Bortel was selling 8,000 cars per year. At that time, General Motors decided not to renew his franchise. Van Bortel believes that his dealership was not extended because he was taking too much business away from conventional dealers. Since losing his dealership, Van Bortel has marketed his plan to dealerships in small towns near big metropolitan markets. He earns a living by charging each auto dealer a fee for teaching him or her the program as well as a $15 commission on each car sold under his plan.

About 12 GM dealers are currently utilizing the Van Bortel plan. One of these is John Peterson of Lake City, Minnesota. Peterson offers every type of GM car from the cheapest Chevette to the most expensive Cadillac at $49 over factory invoice. There is no pressure selling, no dickering over price, and price quotes (and even orders) are possible by telephone. Deposits are refundable at any time before a customer takes delivery. John Peterson's customers are able to save $420 to $700 on each auto purchased. However, they must be willing to wait 6 to 8 weeks or longer for delivery, because Peterson places his orders only after receiving customer deposits. In the first seven months after he began using the Van Bortel plan, Peterson was able to increase sales from 20 cars a month to nearly 200.

General Motors acknowledges that traditional dealers have complained about the Van Bortel plan. But GM responds that, once it sells a car to a dealer, the dealer is free to sell it at any price he/she wishes.

QUESTIONS

1. On a car selling for $10,000, a typical auto dealer makes a profit of $600 to $800, of which 25 per cent is paid to the salesperson. A Van Bortel dealer sells the same car for

---

[†] The data in this case are drawn from Douglas R. Sease, "You Can Buy a Car at $49 Over Invoice, But It'll Take Time," *Wall Street Journal* (September 21, 1983), p. 23.

$9,500 and makes $49 (plus dealer-installed services and a prompt payment discount from GM). Compare these two approaches.

2. How can a traditional dealer compete with a Van Bortel dealer?
3. Why does Van Bortel look for dealers in small towns near large metropolitan markets?
4. Of several thousand GM dealers, only about 12 use the Van Bortel plan.
   a. Will this number grow in the future? Why or why not?
   b. What is the potential size of the consumer market for cars sold under this plan? Explain your answer.

Chapter 20

Applications of Pricing Techniques

CHAPTER OBJECTIVES

1. To examine and evaluate various cost-, demand-, and competition-based pricing techniques
2. To present applications of cost-, demand-, and competition-based pricing techniques
3. To explain the mathematics of pricing techniques
4. To demonstrate why cost-, demand-, and competition-based pricing techniques must be integrated

In 1981, a severe financial crisis caused Chicago's Regional Transit Authority to raise city mass transit fares by 50 per cent and suburban commuter train fares by 100 per cent. As a result, city ridership has fallen by 12 per cent and suburban ridership has declined by 25 per cent. The situation in Chicago is similar to that of transit systems in large cities throughout the U.S. Nationwide, fares have gone up by more than 65 per cent in the past five years, the quality of service has worsened, and the number of riders has dropped substantially. Said Chicago's transit chief, "I'm firmly convinced that headlines year after year about fare hikes and service cuts had a very dampening effect on the public's attitude toward transit."

To begin to win back people who turned away from Chicago mass transit, a fare reduction plan was implemented in 1984. For example, suburban riders were able to save $49 to $228 annually through the revised price structure begun on February 1, 1984. The fare cuts cost

Chicago's mass transit authority about $9 million for the year; but transit executives believe these losses would be far exceeded by the increased revenues generated by higher ridership.

Chicago's transit chief also worked hard to cut costs. He tightened the annual budget, gave up his own chauffeur-driven limousine, tried to eliminate duplicate service (where areas were served by both city and suburban lines), and sought to control labor costs. The Chicago legislature passed a transit reform bill prohibiting cost-of-living pay hikes for transit workers and encouraging the hiring of part-time employees. However, the transit union has been lobbying to change the law. Chicago wages are much higher than the national average. Bus drivers earn a base pay of $13 per hour; and they are guaranteed 40 hours of work each week, 52 weeks a year. They earn about $10,000 a year more than their counterparts in other cities.

Many transit experts do not feel reduced fares can be effective. The mayor of Glencoe (a Chicago suburb) stated, "It took years to build up suburban rail traffic, and I think it will be very, very slow to come back after the 1981 debacle." The research director at Northwestern University's Transportation Center commented that "lower fares never make up for loss of revenues. Even when losing riders by increasing fares, revenues usually go up. It's a law of economics." And, it is pointed out, although bus fare reductions in Los Angeles increased ridership by 30 per cent, they decreased revenues by 35 per cent (the fares were lowered from 85 to 50 cents in 1980).

In the future, the Chicago transit system hopes to implement gradual fare increases, unlike the big jump in 1981: "What we need are small but regular inflation-driven increases. I'm convinced that fare increases of that magnitude won't drive riders away."[1] If the transit system can achieve this goal it will be because it has properly combined cost-, demand-, and competition-based pricing techniques.

Techniques of Pricing

This chapter examines in depth the cost-, demand-, and competition-based techniques for setting prices outlined in Chapter 19. Each technique is described and applications shown.

Competitive pricing is used by the majority of firms.

A classic study of the pricing techniques employed by the manufacturers of 485 consumer and industrial products found that competitive pricing is used by more than half the firms, cost-based policies by more than 25 per cent, and demand-based methods by about 15 per cent. Pricing according to government rules and regulations accounts for the balance of the firms.[2]

---

[1] Harlan S. Byrne, "Chicago's Troubled Transit System Takes Unorthodox Steps to Attract Consumers," *Wall Street Journal* (January 17, 1984), pp. 33, 47.

[2] Jon G. Udell, "The Pricing Strategies of United States Industry," in Thomas V. Greer (Editor), *Combined Proceedings of the American Marketing Association, 1973* (Chicago: American Marketing Association, 1974), p. 152.

Throughout the chapter, applications of pricing techniques will be tied to the Phase III bicycle. This is a high-performance bicycle capable of speeds of 55 miles per hour, with three or more wheels and a fiberglas shell reinforced with crossbars for protection in accidents. It is streamlined to glide through the air. Although the technology is available to build such a bicycle on a mass-production scale, Phase III has not yet been made commercial.[3]

Cost-Based Pricing

With cost-based pricing, the firm determines prices by computing merchandise, service, and overhead costs and then adding an amount to cover the firm's profit goal.

Cost-based prices are relatively easy to implement, because there is no need to estimate elasticity of demand or competitive reactions to price changes. There is also more certainty about costs than demand or competitor responses to prices. Finally, cost pricing seeks to attain reasonable profits, because it is geared to covering all types of costs.

Cost-based pricing does have some significant limitations. It does not consider market conditions, the existence of excess plant capacity, competitive prices, the product's phase in its life cycle, market share goals, consumers' ability to pay, and other factors.[4] For example, U.S. Steel passes cost increases on to consumers no matter how large the increases are. According to an outside marketing expert, U.S. Steel "kept prices high enough to allow 10 to 12 smaller companies to take a substantial share of the market." From 1910 to the mid-1950s, U.S. Steel's market share dropped from 48 to 34 per cent. As of 1983, it had fallen to 17 per cent.[5]

In some situations it is difficult to calculate the overhead costs that should be attributed to individual products. When a company makes or sells a variety of products, it must determine how rent, lighting, personnel, and other general costs are allocated to each product. Overhead costs are often assigned on the basis of product sales or personnel time associated with each item. For instance, if product A accounts for 10 per cent of company sales, it might be allocated 10 per cent of overhead costs. If product B receives 20 per cent of personnel time, it might be allocated 20 per cent of overhead costs. Problems may arise because there are different methods for ascertaining overhead costs and they may yield different results; how would the costs be allocated if Product A yields 10 per cent of company sales and requires 20 per cent of personnel time?

In the following subsections, the basic concepts surrounding cost-based pricing are described, and four cost-based pricing techniques are discussed in detail: cost-plus, markup, target, and traditional break-even analysis. See Figure 20-1.

> Cost-based pricing is simple to use, based on relative certainty, and tied to a reasonable profit. However, it does not consider market conditions, plant capacity, competitors, and other factors.

[3] See Barney Cohen, "Future Bikes," *New York Times Magazine* (August 10, 1980), pp. 14–20ff; and John Holusha, "Pedal Power: High Speeds Achieved," *New York Times* (February 28, 1984), pp. C1, C3.
[4] See Seymour E. Heymann, "Consider Other Factors Than Cost When Pricing Industrial Products," *Marketing News* (April 4, 1980), p. 11.
[5] "Flexible Pricing," *Business Week* (December 12, 1977), p. 84; and Agis Salpukas, "A Restructured Steel Industry," *New York Times* (February 2, 1984), pp. D1, D6.

Figure 20-1
Cost-Based Pricing Techniques

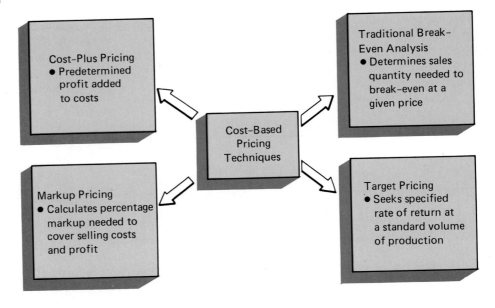

Cost Concepts

Table 20-1 defines the key concepts needed in cost-based pricing and shows how they may be used for Phase III bicycles. Table 20-2 presents hypothetical cost data for Phase III bicycles for each of the concepts shown in Table 20-1. Several important cost relationships can be drawn from Table 20-2:

Fixed, variable, and marginal costs are essential elements of cost-based pricing.

1. Total fixed costs remain constant over the entire range of production. Average fixed costs fall as the quantity produced increases, because overhead costs are spread over more units.
2. Total variable costs rise over the entire range of production. Average variable costs remain constant at $2,600 per unit produced.
3. Total costs rise over the entire production range, since total fixed costs are constant and total variable costs increase. Average total costs decline, because average fixed costs drop and average fixed costs are constant, as production grows.
4. The marginal costs of producing additional bicycles are $2,600 (average variable costs) over the entire range of production, because fixed costs are constant throughout.

Cost-Plus Pricing

Cost-plus pricing is the easiest form of pricing, based on units produced, total costs, and profit.

With *cost-plus pricing*, prices are determined by adding a predetermined profit to costs. It is the simplest form of cost-based pricing.

In general the steps for computing cost-plus pricing are to estimate the number of units to be produced, calculate fixed and variable costs, and add a predetermined profit to costs. The formula for cost-plus pricing is

$$\text{Price} = \frac{\text{Total fixed costs} + \text{Total variable costs} + \text{Projected profit}}{\text{Units produced}}$$

Table 20-1 **Key Cost Concepts and How They May Be Applied to Phase III Bicycles**

Cost Concept	Definition	Examples[a]	Sources of Information	Method of Computation
Total fixed costs	Ongoing costs that are unrelated to volume. These costs are generally constant over a given range of output within a specified period of time.	Rent, administrative salaries, electricity, real estate taxes, plant, and equipment.	Accounting data, bills, cost estimates.	Addition of all fixed cost components.
Total variable costs	Costs that change with increases or decreases in output (volume).	Bicycle parts (such as gears, fiberglas panels, wheels, brakes, tires), hourly employees who assemble bicycles, and sales commissions.	Cost data from suppliers, estimates of labor productivity, sales estimates.	Addition of all variable cost components.
Total costs	Sum of total fixed and total variable costs.	See above.	See above.	Addition of all fixed and variable cost components.
Average fixed costs	Average fixed costs per unit.	See above under total fixed costs	Total fixed costs and sales estimates.	Total fixed costs/quantity produced in units.
Average variable costs	Average variable costs per unit.	See above under total variable costs.	Total variable costs and sales estimates.	Total variable costs/ quantity produced in units.
Average total costs	Sum of average fixed costs and average variable costs.	See above under total fixed and total variable costs.	Total costs and sales estimates.	Average fixed costs + average variable costs or Total costs/quantity produced in units.
Marginal costs	Costs of producing an additional unit.	See above under total fixed and total variable costs.	Accounting data, bills, cost estimates of labor and materials.	Total costs of producing additional quantity − total costs of producing current quantity.

[a] Marketing costs, such as advertising and distribution, are often broken down into both fixed and variable components.

As an illustration, if 300 Phase III bicycles are produced and the company desires a profit of $50,000, its per unit selling price to retailers would be

$$\text{Price} = \frac{\$175,000 + \$780,000 + \$50,000}{300} = \$3,350.$$

Although the cost-plus method is easy to compute, it has several shortcomings. Profit is not expressed as a per cent of sales but as a per cent of cost, and price is not tied to consumer demand. Adjustments for rising costs are poorly conceived, and there are no plans for using excess capacity. There is little incentive for the firm to improve efficiency to hold down costs, and marginal costs are rarely analyzed.

Cost-plus pricing is most effective when price fluctuations have little influence on sales and when the manufacturer is able to control price. For example, the prices of custom-made furniture, airplanes, ships, heavy machinery, and extracted minerals depend on the costs that are necessary to produce these items. Manufacturers set prices by determining costs and adding a reasonable profit. In

Table 20-2 Computing Key Cost Concepts for Phase III Bicycles (in Multiples of 100 Units)

Col. 1	Col. 2	Col. 3	Col. 4 = Col. 2 + Col. 3	Col. 5 = Col. 2 ÷ Col. 1	Col. 6 = Col. 3 ÷ Col. 1	Col. 7 = Col. 5 + Col. 6	Col. 8
Quantity Produced (in Units)	Total Fixed Costs	Total Variable Costs	Total Costs	Average Fixed Costs	Average Variable Costs	Average Total Costs	Marginal Costs (per Unit)[a]
100	$175,000	$ 260,000	$ 435,000	$1,750.00	$2,600	$4,350.00	$2,600
200	175,000	520,000	695,000	875.00	2,600	3,475.00	$2,600
300	175,000	780,000	955,000	583.33	2,600	3,183.33	$2,600
400	175,000	1,040,000	1,215,000	437.50	2,600	3,037.50	$2,600
500	175,000	1,300,000	1,475,000	350.00	2,600	2,950.00	$2,600
600	175,000	1,560,000	1,735,000	291.67	2,600	2,891.67	$2,600
700	175,000	1,820,000	1,995,000	250.00	2,600	2,850.00	$2,600
800	175,000	2,080,000	2,255,000	218.75	2,600	2,818.75	$2,600
900	175,000	2,340,000	2,515,000	194.44	2,600	2,794.44	$2,600
1,000	175,000	2,600,000	2,775,000	175.00	2,600	2,775.00	$2,600

[a] No increase in fixed costs is needed to produce quantities above 100 units. Therefore, for this example, marginal costs per unit equal average variable costs.

many instances, cost-plus pricing allows manufacturers to receive orders, produce items, and then derive prices after total costs are known. This protects sellers against cost increases during time-consuming production periods and where the prices of raw materials fluctuate widely.

Markup Pricing

Markup pricing considers per unit merchandise costs and the markups required to cover selling costs and profits.

In *markup pricing* the firm sets prices by calculating per unit merchandise costs and then determining the markup percentages that are needed to cover selling costs and profit. Markup pricing is most commonly used by wholesalers and retailers. The formula for markup pricing is[6]

$$\text{Price} = \frac{\text{Merchandise costs}}{(100 - \text{Markup per cent})/100}.$$

For example, if a retailer pays $3,350 for a Phase III bicycle and needs a 40 per cent markup to cover selling costs and profit, the final selling price is $3,350/[(100 − 40)/100] = $5,583.33. The retailer receives 40 per cent, or $2,233.33, for expenses and profit. Merchandise costs are covered by $3,350. As in this illustration, markup is usually expressed as a percentage of selling price not cost.

Markups are expressed in terms of selling price rather than cost.

There are several reasons why markups are stated in terms of selling price instead of cost. First, expenses, markdowns, and profits are always computed as percentages of sales. When markups are per cents of sales they aid in profit planning. Second, manufacturers quote their selling prices and trade discounts to channel members as percentage reductions from retail list prices. Third, retail sales price information is more readily available than cost information. Fourth,

---

[6] Markup can be calculated by transposing the above formula into

$$\text{Markup percentage (at retail)} = \frac{\text{Retail selling price} - \text{Merchandise cost}}{\text{Retail selling price}} \times 100.$$

profitability appears to be smaller if based on price rather than cost. This can be useful in avoiding criticism over high profits.

The size of a markup depends on traditional profit margins, retail expenses, manufacturers' suggested list prices, inventory turnover, competition, the extent to which products must be altered or otherwise serviced, and the effort needed to complete sales.

In order to respond to differences in selling costs among products, firms sometimes use a ***variable markup policy***, whereby separate categories of goods and services receive different percentage markups. Variable markups recognize that some items require greater personal selling efforts, customer service, alterations, and end-of-season markdowns than others. For example, computer stores often have two price levels. A full-service price level offers consumers an analysis of their individual needs, computer installation, and training assistance. A "no-frills" price level provides no need analysis, installation, or training. See Figure 20-2 for a department store illustration.

Markup pricing, while having many of the limitations of cost-plus pricing, remains very popular for wholesalers and retailers. It is fairly simple, especially for firms that use the same markup for a number of items. It offers channel members equitable profits. Price competition is reduced when retailers adhere to

A *variable markup policy* responds to differences in selling costs among products by using distinct markups.

Figure 20-2
An Illustration of a Variable Markup Policy in a Department Store

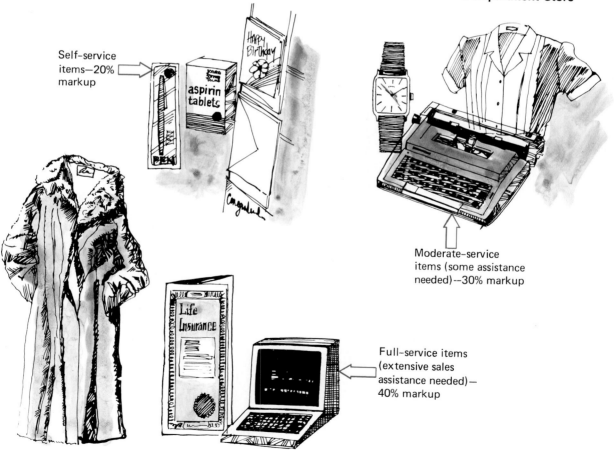

Self-service items—20% markup

Moderate-service items (some assistance needed)--30% markup

Full-service items (extensive sales assistance needed)— 40% markup

similar markups. Channel members are able to compare their prices with manufacturers' suggested list prices. Price adjustments can be made when costs rise. Variable markups are responsive to selling cost differences among products or channel members.

Target Pricing

Target pricing sets prices that enable a rate of return on investment to be earned for a standard volume of production.

In ***target pricing***, prices are set to provide a specified rate of return on investment for a standard volume of production, which is the level of production the firm anticipates achieving. For example, in the paper industry, the standard volume of production is usually set at around 90 per cent of plant capacity.[7] In order for target pricing to operate properly, the company must sell its entire standard volume at specified prices.

Target pricing was introduced by General Motors in the 1920s and worked well for the company through the 1960s. Then during the 1970s and early 1980s, problems with target pricing occurred because costs rose rapidly, competition expanded and forced lower prices, and demand leveled off. General Motors saw inventories rise and was unable to sell its entire standard volume at specified prices.

Target pricing is used by capital-intensive firms (such as auto makers) and public utilities (such as power and light companies). The prices charged by public utilities are based on fair rates of return on invested assets and must be approved by regulatory commissions.

Mathematically, target price is computed as

$$\text{Price} = \left(\frac{\text{Investment costs} \times \text{Target return on investment (\%)}}{\text{Standard volume}} \right. $$
$$\left. + \left(\text{Average total costs (at standard volume)} \right) \right).$$

A Phase III bicycle example demonstrates how target pricing works. If Phase III must build a new factory at a cost of $2 million in order to mass produce bicycles, it might set target return on investment as a goal because investment costs represent such a large portion of expenses. Phase III projects standard volume of production to be 700 units and desires a target return of 20 per cent. At this volume, average total costs are $2,850 (from Table 20-2). Selling price to retailers is then

$$\text{Price} = \left(\frac{\$2,000,000 \times .20}{700} \right) + \$2,850 = \$3421.43.$$

Of this amount, $2,850 per unit goes for regular fixed and variable costs, and $571.43 per unit is used to pay off the capital investment. At a 20 per cent rate of return, this is accomplished in five years. These calculations are shown in Table 20-3.

Target pricing has four major limitations. One, it is not useful for firms with low capital investments because it will undervalue selling price. Two, because

---

[7] Stuart U. Rich, "Price Leadership in the Paper Industry," *Industrial Marketing Management*, Vol. 12 (April 1983), p. 101.

(1) Capital investment for new plant	$2,000,000	
(2) Target return on investment	20%	
(3) Target income for year: (1) × (2)	$ 400,000	
(4) Standard volume for year in units	700	
(5) Target return per unit: (3) ÷ (4)		$ 571.43
(6) Average fixed costs at standard volume[a,b]	$ 250.00	
(7) Average variable costs at standard volume[b]	$ 2,600.00	
(8) Average total costs: (6) + (7)		$2,850.00
(9) Selling price to retailers: (5) + (8)		$3,421.43

Table 20-3
Target Pricing for Phase III Bicycles

[a] Does not include capital investment.
[b] See Table 20-2 for average fixed costs and average variable costs at standard volume (700 units).

Source: This method is explained in Douglas G. Brooks, "Cost-Oriented Pricing: A Realistic Solution to a Complicated Problem," *Journal of Marketing,* Vol. 39 (April 1975), p. 73.

prices are not keyed to demand, the entire standard volume may not be sold at the target price. Three, production problems may hamper output and the standard volume may not be attained. Four, price reductions to handle overstocked inventory are not planned under this approach. Therefore, inventory may be priced too high at peak production levels and too low at limited production levels.

When a firm has excess (unused) capacity, it may use price-floor pricing, in which the company determines the lowest price at which it is economical to offer additional units for sale. The general principle in price-floor pricing is that additional units will contribute to overhead costs and profits if incremental (marginal) revenues are greater than incremental costs. For manufacturers, price floors should be ascertained along with target prices for different levels of sales (production).

Price-floor pricing may be used when there is excess capacity.

An interesting case of price-floor calculations was Continental Airlines' decision to run an extra daily flight. Continental knew its average total costs for the flight would be $4,500, of which $2,500 was for fixed costs and $2,000 for variable costs. Without the flight, fixed costs would still be incurred, and Continental would lose $2,500. Continental realized that by setting prices that generated more than $2,000 per flight (the figure for variable costs) in revenues it could reduce the loss of having an idle plane. Prices were set so that Continental was able to receive $3,100 in revenues, thus contributing $1,100 to overhead.

As a result of deregulation, many airlines have been setting prices at just above variable costs, rather than total costs, in order to increase demand during slack periods.[8] Although a firm cannot survive in the long run unless its average total costs are met, it can reduce short-run losses on selected products or services through price-floor pricing.

Traditional Break-Even Analysis

Like target pricing, traditional break-even analysis examines the relationship among costs, revenues, and profits. While target pricing yields the price that results in a specified return on investment, *traditional break-even analysis* determines the sales quantity in units or dollars that is necessary for total revenues (price × units sold) to equal total costs (fixed and variable) at a given price. When sales exceed the break-even quantity, the firm earns a profit. When sales are less than the break-even quantity, the firm loses money. Traditional break-

Traditional break-even analysis describes the unit or dollar sales needed to break even at a specific price.

[8] "Deregulating America," *Business Week* (November 28, 1983), p. 86.

even analysis does not consider return on investment or the dollar value of investment. It can be extended to take profit planning into account, and it is used by all types of channel members.

The break-even point can be computed in terms of units or sales dollars:

$$\text{Break-even point (units)} = \frac{\text{Total fixed costs}}{\text{Price} - \text{Variable costs (per unit)}}$$

$$\text{Break-even point (sales dollars)} = \frac{\text{Total fixed costs}}{1 - \dfrac{\text{Variable costs (per unit)}}{\text{Price}}}$$

These formulas are derived from the equation: Price × Quantity = Total fixed costs + (Variable costs per unit × Quantity).

Table 20-4 and Figure 20-3 show the costs, revenues, and profits for Phase III bicycles priced at $2,950 to retailers. At quantities below 500 units, the firm would lose money. At quantities above 500 units, it would make a profit. At exactly 500 units, Phase III would break even. By using a break-even formula, the firm is able to find its break-even point without all the computations in Table 20-4 and Figure 20-1:

$$\text{Break-even point (units)} \doteq \frac{\$175,000}{\$2,950 - \$2,600} = 500 \text{ units.}$$

$$\text{Break-even point (sales dollars)} = \frac{\$175,000}{1 - \left(\dfrac{\$2,600}{\$2,950}\right)} = \$1,475,000.$$

Break-even analysis can be adjusted to take into account the profit sought by a firm:

Table 20-4   Break-Even Analysis for Phase III Bicycles—Priced at $2,950 Each to Retailers

Col. 1 Production Quantity (Units) (Q)	Col. 2 Total Fixed Costs	Col. 3 Total Variable Costs	Col. 4 = Col. 2 + Col. 3 Total Costs	Col. 5 Price per Unit (P)	Col. 6 = Col. 1 × Col. 5 Total Revenue (P × Q)	Col. 7 = Col. 6 − Col. 4 Total Profit (Loss)[a]	
100	$175,000	$ 260,000	$ 435,000	$2,950	$ 295,000	$(140,000)	
200	175,000	520,000	695,000	2,950	590,000	(105,000)	Loss
300	175,000	780,000	955,000	2,950	885,000	(70,000)	
400	175,000	1,040,000	1,215,000	2,950	1,180,000	(35,000)	
500	175,000	1,300,000	1,475,000	2,950	1,475,000	0	Break-even point
600	175,000	1,560,000	1,735,000	2,950	1,770,000	35,000	
700	175,000	1,820,000	1,995,000	2,950	2,065,000	70,000	
800	175,000	2,080,000	2,255,000	2,950	2,360,000	105,000	Profit
900	175,000	2,340,000	2,515,000	2,950	2,655,000	140,000	
1,000	175,000	2,600,000	2,775,000	2,950	2,950,000	175,000	

[a] Total profit = Total revenue − Total costs

$$\text{Break-even point (units)} = \frac{\text{Total fixed costs} + \text{Projected profit}}{\text{Price} - \text{Variable costs (per unit)}}$$

$$\text{Break-even point (sales dollars)} = \frac{\text{Total fixed costs} + \text{Projected profit}}{1 - \dfrac{\text{Variable costs (per unit)}}{\text{Price}}}$$

In the preceding Phase III example, if the firm seeks a $100,000 profit, the break-even point is

$$\text{Break-even point (units)} = \frac{\$175,000 + \$100,000}{\$2,950 - \$2,600} = 785.71 \text{ units.}^*$$

$$\text{Break-even point (sales dollars)} = \frac{\$275,000}{1 - \left(\dfrac{\$2,600}{\$2,950}\right)} = \$2,317,857.^*$$

There are some limitations to traditional break-even analysis. One, as with all forms of cost-based pricing, it does not consider demand. The assumption is that wide variations in quantity can be sold at the same price, and this is highly unlikely. Two, traditional break-even analysis assumes all costs can be divided into fixed and variable categories. Some costs, like advertising, are difficult to define as fixed or variable because they can be placed in either category, depending on the situation. Advertising can be fixed or a per cent of sales. Three, traditional break-even formulas presume that variable costs per unit are constant over a range of quantities. However, quantity and shipping discounts or overtime wages may alter these costs. Fourth, it is assumed that fixed costs remain constant. Yet, increases in production may lead to higher costs for lighting, salaried employees, and other items.

By including demand considerations, each of the cost-based techniques can be improved. Demand-based pricing techniques are discussed next.

Demand-Based Pricing

With demand-based pricing, the firm determines the prices final consumers and channel members will pay for products and services, calculates the markups needed to cover selling expenses and profits, and then determines the maximum it can spend to produce its offering. In this way, prices and costs are linked to consumer preferences and channel needs, and a specific product image is sought.

Under demand-based pricing, prices are linked to consumer desires, channel needs, and product image.

Demand-based techniques require consumer research regarding the quantities that will be purchased at various prices, the elasticity of demand (sensitivity to price changes), the existence of market segments, and consumers' ability to pay for products or services. It must be realized that demand estimations are usually

---

* These numbers would be rounded off to 786 units and $2,318,700, because the firm could not sell part of a bicycle.

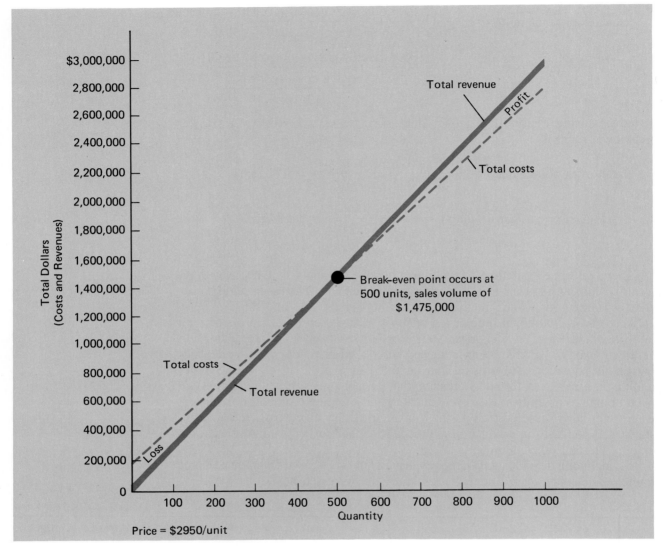

Figure 20-3
A Graphical
Representation of
Traditional Break-Even
Analysis for Phase III
Bicycles

less precise and more subject to change than cost estimations. In addition, firms that do inadequate research on costs and rely on demand-oriented data may end up losing money, because they make unrealistically low assumptions about costs.

With demand pricing, highly competitive situations result in small markups and low prices because consumers will purchase substitutes. In these cases it is necessary for costs to be held down or else prices will be too high. For example, if a firm desires a 50 per cent markup on selling price and it knows from research that consumers will pay $10 for an item, the costs of producing the item must be $5 or less. At a lower cost, the firm will be satisfied; markup will be greater than 50 per cent. Costs above $5 are not satisfactory because customers will not accept a price above $10 and markup will be less than 50 per cent. In the latter situation the firm would either switch to a more profitable item, substitute cheaper materials to reduce costs, or decide to tolerate lower per cent profits.

Noncompetitive situations allow firms to achieve large markups and high prices because demand is relatively inelastic. Companies could place little emphasis on costs when setting prices in these situations. For example, a firm that knows consumers will pay $20 for an item costing $7 will achieve a 65 per cent markup on selling price and receive a large profit per unit. With cost-based pricing, the firm would be likely to set prices that are too low in noncompetitive markets.

In the following subsections, four demand-based pricing techniques are examined: demand-minus, chain-markup, modified break-even, and price discrimination. See Figure 20-4.

Demand-Minus Pricing

In **demand-minus (demand-backward) pricing,** the firm ascertains the appropriate final selling price and works backward to compute costs. This approach stipulates that price decisions revolve around consumer demand rather than internal company operations. It is used by companies that sell directly to consumers.

Demand-minus pricing is comprised of three steps. One, final selling price is determined through consumer surveys or other research techniques. Two, the markup percentage is derived from selling expenses and desired profits. Three, maximum acceptable merchandise costs are computed.

The formula used in demand-minus pricing is

Maximum merchandise costs = Price × [(100 − Markup per cent)/100].

As noted, this formula shows that costs are calculated after selling price and markup are set.

For example, a retailer for Phase III bicycles would first conduct a survey to measure consumer demand. Then, it would compute selling expenses and desired profit. Finally, the maximum acceptable costs of a Phase III bicycle to the retailer would be derived. If the retailer finds that consumers would spend $6,000 for the bicycle and selling expenses plus profit are 40 per cent, then

In demand-minus pricing, final selling price, then markup, and finally maximum merchandise costs are computed.

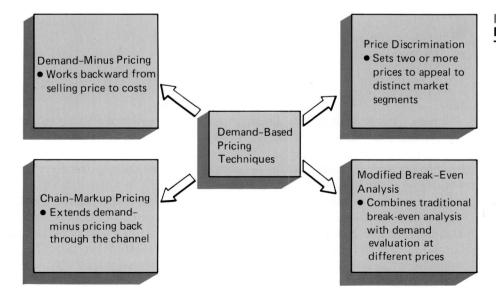

Figure 20-4
Demand-Based Pricing Techniques

Maximum merchandise costs = $6,000 × [(100 − 40)/100] = $3,600.

At per unit costs of $3,600 or less, the retailer would stock Phase III. At costs above $3,600, the bicycles would not be stocked, because the retailer knows higher costs could not be passed along to consumers and profits would be too low.

The difficulty in demand-minus pricing is that marketing research may be time-consuming or complex, particularly if many items are involved. Also, new-product pricing research may be particularly inaccurate.

Chain-Markup Pricing

Chain-markup pricing traces demand-minus calculations from the retailer to the manufacturer.

Chain-markup pricing extends demand-minus calculations from the retailer all the way back to the manufacturer. With chain-markup pricing, final selling price is determined, markups for each channel member are examined, and the maximum acceptable costs to each member are computed.

In a traditional channel, the chain is composed of

1. Maximum selling price to retailer = Final selling price × [(100 − Retailer's markup)/100].

2. Maximum selling price to wholesaler = Selling price to retailer × [(100 − Wholesaler's markup)/100].

3. Maximum merchandise costs to manufacturer = Selling price to wholesaler × [(100 − Manufacturer's markup)/100].

If the manufacturer of Phase III bicycles decides to market the product through wholesalers and retailers, all three parties would share marketing costs and profits; and each would seek a markup of 20 per cent. Since they know the consumer will pay $6,000 for a Phase III bicycle, the chain markup is

1. Maximum selling price to retailer = $6,000 × [(100 − 20)/100] = $4,800.

2. Maximum selling price to wholesaler = $4,800 × [(100 − 20)/100] = $3,840.

3. Maximum merchandise costs to manufacturer = $3,840 × [(100 − 20)/100] = $3,072.

Several conclusions can be drawn from this illustration. First, the selling prices of manufacturers, wholesalers, and retailers must be equal to or less than the amounts their respective customers are willing to pay. Second, cost increases should be controlled. In the preceding example, a manufacturing cost rise of $100 to $3,172 would result in a final selling price rise of $195.31 to $6,195.31, if each channel member maintains its 20 per cent markup. Third, by sharing cost increases, final prices can be stabilized. The original price of $6,000 could be maintained despite a manufacturing cost increase of $100 if the manufacturer, wholesaler, and retailer each reduce markup by less than 1 per cent. Fourth, changes in final demand have a major impact on all channel members. For instance, if consumers would be willing to pay $6,500, there would be an extra

$500 that could be allocated throughout the channel. This could cover higher costs or lead to higher profits.

Through chain-markup pricing, price decisions are related to consumer demand and each channel member is able to see the effects of price changes on the total system. The interdependence of members becomes clear; channel members cannot set prices independently of one another.

Modified Break-Even Analysis

Modified break-even analysis combines traditional break-even analysis with an evaluation of demand at various levels of price. Traditional analysis focuses on the sales needed to break even at a given price. It does not indicate the likely level of demand at that price, examine how demand responds to different levels of price, consider that the break-even point can vary greatly depending on the price the firm happens to select, or calculate the price that maximizes profits.

Whereas traditional analysis defines the sales needed to break even at a specific price, modified analysis reveals the price-quantity mix that maximizes profits. It demonstrates that profits do not necessarily rise as quantity sold increases, because lower prices are needed to increase demand. It also verifies that a firm should examine various levels of price and select the one that maximizes profits. Finally, it relates demand to price, rather than assuming that the same volume could be sold at any price.[9]

Table 20-5 shows the quantities that Phase III would be able to sell under different prices from $4,500 to $7,000. This table assumes that sales are made from the manufacturer to the wholesaler to the retailer to the customer. The cost data are reproduced from Tables 20-2 and 20-4. Profits are maximized at a retail price-quantity mix of $6,000 and 300 units.

> **Combining traditional break-even analysis with demand evaluation at various prices is *modified break-even analysis*.**

[9] An analysis of the methods for estimating demand at various prices can be found in Kent B. Monroe, *Pricing: Making Profitable Decisions* (New York: McGraw-Hill, 1979), pp. 31–35.

Table 20-5   Modified Break-Even Analysis for Phase III Bicycles—Priced from $4,500 to $7,000

Col. 1	Col. 2	Col. 3	Col. 4 = Col. 2 × Col. 3	Col. 5	Col. 6 = Col. 4 − Col. 5
Retail Selling Price	Quantity Demanded	Price Received by Manufacturer[a]	Manufacturer's Total Revenue	Manufacturer's Total Cost[b]	Manufacturer's Profit (Loss)
$7,000	100	$4,480	$ 448,000	$ 435,000	$ 13,000
6,500	200	4,160	832,000	695,000	137,000
6,000	300	3,840	1,152,000	955,000	197,000 ←——— Maximum profit
5,500	400	3,520	1,408,000	1,215,000	193,000
5,000	500	3,200	1,600,000	1,475,000	125,000
4,500	600	2,880	1,728,000	1,735,000	(7,000)

[a] The Phase III manufacturer receives 64 cents of every retail dollar ($1.00 × .8 × .8) using the traditional chain-markup involving the retailer, wholesaler, and manufacturer.
[b] From Table 20-2.

Price Discrimination

Price discrimination enables a firm to set two or more distinct prices for a product or service in order to appeal to different final consumer or organizational consumer market segments. With price discrimination, higher prices are established for inelastic consumer segments and lower prices for elastic segments. Price discrimination can be customer-based, product-based, time-based, or place-based.

In customer-based price discrimination, prices differ by customer category for the same product or service. Price differentials may relate to a consumer's ability to pay (physicians, lawyers, and accountants partially set prices in this manner), negotiating ability (the final price of a new or used car is usually established by bargaining), or buying power (discounts are given for large purchases).

Under product-based price discrimination, the firm offers a number of features, styles, qualities, brands, or sizes of a product or service and sets a different price for each one. Price differentials are greater than cost differentials for the various product or service versions. For example, one type of haircut may be priced at $7 and take 20 minutes to complete (35 cents per minute); another may be priced at $12 and take 30 minutes to complete (40 cents per minute). A dishwasher may be priced at $300 in white and $320 in brown, although the brown color costs the manufacturer only $3 more. In both situations there is inelastic demand by customers desiring special features or services, and the product or service versions are priced accordingly.

With time-based price discrimination, the company varies prices by day versus evening (movie theater tickets), time of day (telephone and utility rates), or season (hotel rates). Consumers that insist on prime time use of a product or service pay higher prices than those who are willing to make their purchases during nonpeak times.

In place-based price discrimination, prices differ by seat location (sports and entertainment events), floor location (office buildings, hotels), or geographic location (resort cities). The demand for locations near the stage, elevators, or warm climates drives the prices of these locations up. General admission tickets, basement offices, and moderate-temperature resorts are priced lower in order to attract consumers to make otherwise less desirable purchases.

Price discrimination methods can be combined. For example, automobile prices are frequently different on the West Coast from those on the East Coast. Profit margins on accessory equipment are generally greater than on basic car prices. Different body styles (two-door, hatchback, station wagon) have different profit margins. Also, final prices are agreed on after bargaining between buyers and sellers.

Figure 20-5 shows how a firm benefits from a price discrimination strategy. It was established in Table 20-5 that Phase III would maximize profits for one model of bicycle if it sold 300 units at $6,000 each to consumers. However, Phase III could increase profits by selling its bicycles under three different models and offering distinct features for each model.

Before employing price discrimination, the marketer should consider these points. Are there distinct market segments? Do consumers communicate with each other about product features and prices? Can product versions be differentiated? Will some consumers choose low-priced models when they might otherwise buy high-priced models if they are the only ones available? How do marginal costs of creating additional product alternatives compare with marginal revenues? Will channel members stock all models? How difficult is it to explain product differences to consumers? Under what conditions is price discrimination legal (the firm would not want to violate the Robinson-Patman Act)?

When product-based price discrimination is used, the additional production, inventory management, and distribution costs involved with offering multiple versions of the same product must be considered. For example, the 1984 Ford Thunderbird was available in more than 69,000 versions, the Chevrolet Citation in over 32,000 varieties (based on the different combinations of engines, transmissions, optional accessories, etc.). In contrast, Honda marketed only 32 variations of its Accord model (including colors). The overutilization of product-based price discrimination in U.S. cars adds about $1,000 in overhead costs to each unit produced. According to a GM marketing vice-president,

Price discrimination may substantially increase costs.

the challenge for all of us is to figure out what product differences the consumer is willing to pay for and which ones are spurious and too expensive.[10]

Competition-Based Pricing

In competition-based pricing the firm uses competitors' prices rather than demand or cost considerations as its primary guideposts. With this approach, the company may not respond to changes in demand or costs unless they have an effect on competitors' prices. A company may set prices below the market, at the market, or above the market, depending on its customers, image, overall marketing mix, consumer loyalty, and other factors.

Setting prices on the basis of competition is competition-based pricing.

Competition-based pricing is popular for several reasons. It is simple, with no calculations of demand curves, price elasticity, or costs per unit. The ongoing market price level is assumed to be fair for both consumers and companies. Pricing at the market level does not disrupt competition and, therefore, does not lead to retaliations. It may lead to complacency.

Two aspects of competition-based pricing are discussed in the following subsections: price leadership and competitive bidding.

Price Leadership

Price leadership exists in situations where one firm is usually the first to announce price changes and the other companies in the industry follow. The role of the price leader is to adjust prices to reflect changing market conditions, without precipitating a price war with competitors.[11] Price leaders are firms that have significant market shares, well-established positions, respect from competitors,

In *price leadership*, one or a few firms initiate price changes in an industry; they are effective when other firms follow.

---

[10] John Koten, "Giving Buyers Wide Choices May Be Hurting Auto Makers," *Wall Street Journal* (December 15, 1983), p. 37.
[11] Rich, "Price Leadership in the Paper Industry," p. 101.

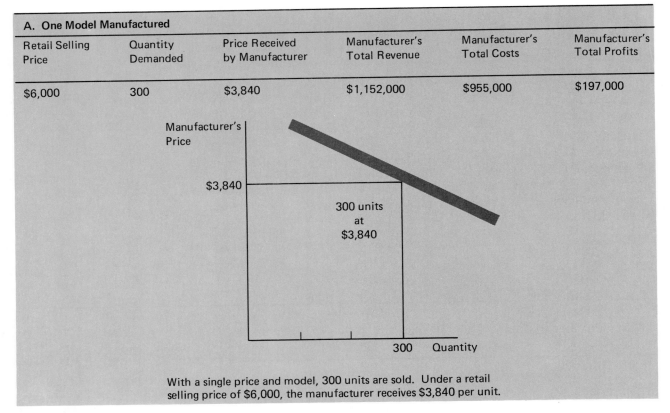

A. One Model Manufactured					
Retail Selling Price	Quantity Demanded	Price Received by Manufacturer	Manufacturer's Total Revenue	Manufacturer's Total Costs	Manufacturer's Total Profits
$6,000	300	$3,840	$1,152,000	$955,000	$197,000

With a single price and model, 300 units are sold. Under a retail selling price of $6,000, the manufacturer receives $3,840 per unit.

Figure 20-5
Price Discrimination for Phase III Bicycles

and the desire to implement price changes, such as IBM and General Motors. Sometimes, price leadership is rotated among several leading firms in an industry.

A frequent price leader in the newsprint industry is Abitibi-Price. It is the largest producer, has the greatest manufacturing capacity, and has the dominant market share, 14.3 per cent (versus 9.7 per cent for International Paper and 9.6 per cent for Bowater). Since over half of company sales are in newsprint, Abitibi-Price has a strong commitment to maintain price stability.[12]

During the past several years, the role of the price leader has been substantially reduced in many industries, including steel, chemical, and glass container. For example, when Owens-Illinois (larger than its next five competitors combined) raised list prices by 4.5 per cent, its competitors offered huge discounts on glass bottles. The smaller firms feared the higher prices would hurt sales to breweries that had just begun to switch to glass bottles. Said one glass company president, "In effect, the smaller companies become the price leaders in order to entice the brewers."[13] This action also showed that the smaller firms were after Owen-Illinois' market share.

Announcements of price changes by industry leaders must be communicated through independent media or company publicity releases. It is illegal for firms to confer with one another regarding price setting.

[12] Ibid., p. 103.
[13] "Flexible Pricing," p. 81.

B. Three Models Manufactured

Model	Retail Selling Price	Quantity Demanded	Price Received by Mfr.	Mfr.'s Total Revenue	Mfr.'s Variable Costs*	Mfr.'s Fixed Costs+	Mfr.'s Total Costs	Mfr.'s Total Profit
AA	$7,000	100	$4,480	$ 448,000	$300,000	$58,333	$ 358,333	$89,667
BB	6,500	100	4,160	416,000	280,000	58,333	338,333	77,667
CC	6,000	100	3,840	384,000	260,000	58,333	318,333	65,667
Total		300		$1,248,000	$840,000	$175,000[1]	$1,015,000[1]	$233,000[1]

*The materials for models AA and BB are upgraded by $400 and $200, respectively.

+The fixed costs of $175,000 are allocated to each model.

[1]Rounding errors

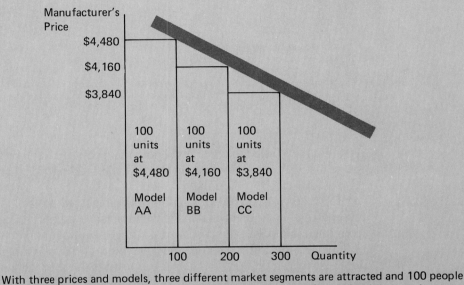

With three prices and models, three different market segments are attracted and 100 people buy each model. The manufacturer's revenue is increased by $96,000, while costs increase by only $60,000. Therefore, profits rise by $36,000.

**Figure 20-5
Price Discrimination for
Phase III Bicycles
(Continued)**

Competitive Bidding

With competitive bidding, two or more companies independently submit prices for specific products, projects, and/or services. Generally, sealed bids are offered in response to precise government or organizational consumer requests, and each seller has one chance to make its best offer.

Various mathematical models have been applied to competitive bidding.[14] All of them utilize the ***expected profit concept,*** which states that as the bid price increases the profit to a firm increases but the probability of its winning the contract decreases. The long-run average expected profit at each bid amount equals the company's profit times its probability of obtaining the contract at this

*Competitive bidding re-
lies on the* expected profit
concept.

[14] See Wayne J. Morse, "Probabilistic Bidding Models: A Synthesis," *Business Horizons,* Vol. 18 (April 1975), pp. 67–74; and Stephen Paranka, "Question: To Bid or Not to Bid? Answer: Strategic Prebid Analysis," *Marketing News* (April 4, 1980), p. 16.

Table 20-6

Application of Expected Profit Concept in Competitive Bidding to Government Machinery Contracts[a]

Company's Bid Amount	Costs of Fulfilling Contract	Profit (Loss)	Probability of Winning Bid[b]	Long-Run Average Expected Profit (Loss) at Each Bid Amount[c]	
$6,500	$7,500	$(1,000)	.99	$(990)	
7,000	7,500	(500)	.95	(475)	
7,500	7,500	0	.85	0	
8,000	7,500	500	.75	375	
8,500	7,500	1,000	.60	600	
9,000	7,500	1,500	.50	750 ←	Best average long-run bid
9,500	7,500	2,000	.30	600	
10,000	7,500	2,500	.15	375	
10,500	7,500	3,000	.10	300	
11,000	7,500	3,500	.05	175	

[a] The highest long-run average expected profit occurs at a bid amount of $9,000. The firm will earn $1,500 on each bid it wins, win half the contracts it bids on, and receive an average profit of $750 on all the contracts it bids on (.5 × $1,500).

[b] The probability of having the winning (lowest) bid must be estimated by analyzing past bids, current competitive conditions, and the cost relationships of the company in contrast with its competitors.

[c] Average expected profit (loss) = Profit (loss) × Probability of winning bid.

bid amount. While the company's potential profit is usually measured accurately, the probability of getting a contract (or underbidding all other qualified competitors) is difficult to determine.

Table 20-6 shows an application of the expected profit concept in competitive bidding for government machinery contracts. A number of points can be drawn from this table. One, the costs of fulfilling a contract remain the same regardless of the bid. Two, a firm should study the impact of a wide range of bids (as done in Table 20-6). Three, long-run expected profit is the average yield for a bid amount used over a sustained period of time, not the actual profit on a single bid. Four, small errors in cost estimates or the probability of winning a bid may cause the firm to select a wrong bid. For example, if there is really a 40 per cent chance of winning contracts with a bid of $9,500, the long-run average expected profit at this amount would be $800 ($2,000 × .4).

Combining Techniques

It is beneficial for companies to combine cost, demand, and competitive pricing techniques.

Although cost-, demand-, and competition-based pricing techniques have been discussed separately throughout this chapter, in practice the three approaches are often combined. The cost method sets a price floor and outlines the various costs incurred in doing business. It establishes profit margins, target prices, and/or break-even quantities. The demand approach determines the appropriate final price and the ceiling prices for each channel member. It develops the price-quantity mix that maximizes profits and allows a firm to reach different market seg-

Cost-Based

What profit margin does a price level allow?

Do markups allow for differences in product investments, installation and servicing, and selling effort and merchandising skills?

Are there accurate and timely cost data by product, service, project, process, and/or store?

Are cost increases monitored and prices adjusted accordingly?

Are there specific profit or return-on-investment goals?

What are the break-even points for each product, service, project, process, and/or store?

What is the price floor for each product, service, project, process, and/or store?

Demand-Based

What type of demand does each product, service, project, process, and/or store face?

Have price elasticities been estimated for various price levels?

Are demand-minus, chain-markup, and modified break-even analyses utilized?

Has price discrimination been considered?

How loyal are customers?

Competition-Based

How do prices compare with those of competitors?

Is price leadership used in the industry? By whom?

How do competitors react to price changes?

How are competitive bids determined?

Is the long-run expected profit concept used in competitive bidding?

ments. The competition approach examines the appropriate price level for the firm in relation to competitors.

Unless the techniques are combined, critical decisions are likely to be overlooked. Table 20-7 provides a broad list of questions a firm should consider when setting prices; it expands the questions presented in Chapter 19.

Summary

With cost-based pricing, the firm computes merchandise, service, and overhead costs and then adds an amount to cover profit. Cost-based prices are relatively easy to implement, are founded on comparative certainty, and incorporate profitability. They also disregard market conditions, plant capacity, competitive prices, the product's phase in its life cycle, market share, and the consumer's ability to pay. Overhead costs may be difficult to allocate. When using cost-based techniques, it is necessary to understand several cost concepts, including fixed costs, variable costs, total costs, average costs, and marginal costs.

Cost-plus pricing is the simplest cost method. It adds costs and a desired profit rate to determine price. It is most effective when the manufacturer is able to control selling price. In markup pricing, the firm sets prices by determining the markup percentages needed to cover selling costs and profit and calculating per unit merchandise costs. Markup pricing is common among wholesalers and retailers. A variable markup policy allows a company to use different markups for distinct products or services. In target pricing, prices are set to provide a specified rate of return on investment for a standard volume of production. Standard volume is the level of production the firm anticipates achieving. When a firm has excess capacity, it may use price-floor pricing, in which prices are set to cover variable costs and contribute to overhead. Traditional break-even analysis determines the sales quantity at which total costs equal revenues for a chosen price. It can be extended to include profit analysis.

For demand-based pricing, the company first determines the prices final consumers and channel members will pay, then figures the mark-ups needed to cover selling expenses and profits, and finally derives the maximum merchandise costs that can be incurred. Prices are linked to consumer preferences, channel needs, and product image. Demand techniques require consumer research, are predicated on imprecise data, and sometimes are not keyed to profitability.

In demand-minus pricing, the firm works backward from final selling price to costs. Chain-markup pricing extends demand-minus calculations from the retailer back to the manufacturer, and assures a proper final selling price and equitable markups throughout the channel. Modified break-even analysis combines traditional break-even analysis with an evaluation of demand at various levels of price. It helps select the price-quantity mix that optimizes profit. Price discrimination is a technique with which a firm sets two or more prices for a product or service in order to appeal to different market segments. Price discrimination may be based on customers, products, time, and/or place.

In competition-based pricing, the firm uses competitors' prices as its main guideposts. Prices may be below, at, or above the market. It is simple, provides equity for customers and companies, and minimizes price confrontations. A firm must determine whether it has the ability and the interest to be a price leader or price follower. Under competitive bidding, two or more companies independently submit prices in response to precise customer requests. The expected profit concept states that as the bid price increases, the profit to a firm increases, but the probability of the firm's winning the contract decreases.

Cost-, demand-, and competition-based pricing techniques should be combined so that all necessary factors are considered. Otherwise, critical decisions are likely to be overlooked.

Questions for Discussion

1. Why are overhead costs sometimes difficult to assign to specific products and services?
2. What are the advantages and disadvantages of cost-plus pricing?
3. Why are markups usually computed on the basis of selling price?

4. When should a firm consider a variable markup policy?
5. A firm requires a 20 per cent return on a $600,000 investment in order to produce a new electric can opener. If the standard volume is 40,000 units, fixed costs are $200,000, and variable costs are $4.00 per unit, what is the target price?
6. Given the limitations of target pricing, why do auto manufacturers still rely on this technique?
7. A movie theater has weekly fixed costs (land, building, and equipment) of $1,000. Variable weekly costs (movie rental, electricity, ushers, etc.) are $1,100. From a price-floor pricing perspective, how much revenue must a movie generate during a slow week for it to be worthwhile to open the theater?
8. A company making office desks has total fixed costs of $1 million per year, and variable costs of $400 per desk. It sells the desks to retailers for $500 apiece. Compute the traditional break-even point in both units and dollars.
9. What is the fundamental difference between demand-based and cost-based pricing?
10. A retailer determines that its customers are willing to spend $15.95 on a Julia Child cookbook. The publisher charges the retailer $12.00 for each copy. The retailer wants a 30 per cent markup. Comment on this situation.
11. A clock manufacturer knows consumers will pay $60 for a radio/alarm clock with a digital face and extra options. If the chain markup is 30, 30, 30, what is the maximum the clock can cost the manufacturer? What if the clock costs less than the maximum amount?
12. An industrial wholesaler of small tools has fixed costs of $800,000, variable costs of $1 per tool, and faces this demand schedule:

Price	Quantity Demanded
$10	100,000
$12	85,000
$15	70,000
$20	50,000

At what price is profit maximized?
13. If the company in Question 12 decides to sell 50,000 tools at $20 and 20,000 at $15, what will its profit be? What are the risks of this approach?
14. Can a small firm become a price leader? Explain your answer.
15. Compute the best average long-run competitive bid from among the following. The costs of fulfilling a contract are $9,000:

Bid Amount	Probability of Winning Bid
$10,000	.60
10,500	.50
11,000	.40
11,500	.30
12,000	.20
12,500	.10

Case 1 7-Eleven Stores: Pumping Up Profits with Gasoline Sales[*]

Well over one third of Southland Corporation's 7,400 7-Eleven stores now market gasoline. Of the 2,000 new 7-Elevens opened in the last 10 years, almost all carry gas. Annually, 7-Eleven pumps more than 1.2 billion gallons. This represents about one sixth of Southland's total company sales, which were almost $9 billion in 1983.

7-Eleven's prowess in gasoline retailing is due to two crucial factors: its costs are lower than those of conventional outlets, and customers make other purchases when they enter the store to pay for gas. At many neighborhood service stations, the repair business and accessory sales have declined; as a result, a greater proportion of overhead costs are charged against gasoline sales. In contrast, at 7-Eleven, overhead costs are distributed among many productive product categories. gas pumps are self-service, and the regular cashier collects gas receipts.

While 7-Eleven can earn a profit on gasoline with a 2 cents per gallon markup, full-service neighborhood service stations may only break even at 10 cents per gallon. 7-Eleven stores could easily win price wars, but it does not start them. Instead, they strive to match the lowest prices in the market area. In some locations, 7-Eleven managers actually change gasoline prices as often as three or four times a day.

Any calculation of Southland's gasoline profits must also consider the carry-over sales in 7-Eleven outlets. The firm estimates that one in three customers makes an extra purchase worth about $1. Since 7-Eleven's gross margin (markup) is about 30 per cent, the average gasoline customer contributes another 10 cents to gross profits (one third of customers making an additional purchase multiplied by 30 cents markup).

7-Eleven's biggest investment is for gas pumps, tanks, and related equipment, about $80,000 for a typical outlet. In addition, each store has annual fixed operating costs of $10,000 for gasoline. The average 7-Eleven store pumps about 500,000 gallons a year. The extra profit from gasoline sales is approximately $25,000 per store.

Sun Oil, Tenneco, and Arco have begun to add grocery products at their retail stores that formerly featured only gasoline to compete with 7-Eleven. This tactic is proving popular with consumers. For example, Arco's AM/PM stores pump 50 per cent more gas than previously, nongasoline sales are growing, and markup requirements have been reduced from 5.5 to 4 cents a gallon (as overhead is spread over more products).

QUESTIONS

1. Compute a target price for gasoline at 7-Eleven, if each store seeks a 30 per cent return on its investment. Assume that the $80,000 investment is paid in full when the pumps

---

[*] The data in this case are drawn from Shawn Tully, "Look Who's Champ of Gasoline Marketing," *Fortune* (November 1, 1982), pp. 149–150 ff; and Pamela G. Hollie, "Southland's Successful Mix," *New York Times* (March 25, 1983), pp. D1, D3.

are installed, gasoline costs 7-Eleven $1.03 a gallon, and average total costs are based on both operating costs and the cost of gasoline.
2. Determine the break-even point for gasoline at a 7-Eleven store in terms of number of gallons, based on the target price from Question 1. Include a projected profit of $25,000 in your calculation. (Do not include the pump investment)
3. What kind of price discrimination strategy is most appropriate for 7-Eleven?
4. Explain how 7-Eleven combines cost-, demand-, and competition-based pricing.

Case 2 Aspartame: Pricing a Low-Calorie Sweetener†

Aspartame is the low-calorie sweetener manufactured and marketed by G. D. Searle under the brand names NutraSweet (as an ingredient used in beverages and food) and Equal (as a separate product that consumers use in coffee, tea, cooking, etc.). Searle's exclusive patent for aspartame extends until 1987.

In some ways, the characteristics of aspartame are too good to be true. It is generally judged to taste about as good as sugar, has only a fraction of sugar's calories, and has been approved by the Food and Drug Administration as "absolutely safe." Thus, it has desirable qualities for diet- and health-conscious consumers, particularly for those who complain of saccharin's aftertaste and/or feel it is too dangerous to consume.

The most profitable segment of the sweetener market is the low-calorie end. For the ten-year period before aspartame entered the market in 1983, the unit sales of saccharin increased by 40 per cent, despite the health warning on labels. The sales potential of aspartame is considered to be even higher, because of its better taste and relative safety.

To capitalize on the demand for aspartame, Searle placed a high price on it. During 1983, aspartame sold for $90 a pound, contrasted with $4 a pound for saccharin. A box of 100 packets of Equal sweetener sold for $3.50, about three times the price of a similar box of Sweet 'n Low (saccharin). Searle expected aspartame prices to drop by 50 per cent by the end of 1984. A comparison of aspartame, sugar, saccharin, and high-fructose corn syrup sweeteners is shown in Table 1 on page 606.

QUESTIONS
1. Evaluate the data in Table 1.
2. Develop a long-term pricing strategy for Equal and NutraSweet. Would you price Equal differently from NutraSweet? Why or why not?
3. Should the pricing of aspartame be more related to cost, demand, or competition? Explain your answer.
4. Soda makers are using aspartame in combination with saccharin in diet beverages. Although this improves product taste and holds down costs, health warnings about saccharin are still required on container labels. Assess this strategy.

---

† The data in this case are drawn from Gene Bylinsky, "The Battle for America's Sweet Tooth," *Fortune* (July 26, 1981), pp. 28–32; Daniel Kahn, "Aggressive Action in Soft-Drink War," *Newsday* (October 23, 1983), p. 88; and Carolyn Phillips, "FDA Clears Searle's Aspartame for Use in Carbonated Soft Drinks and More Foods," *Wall Street Journal* (July 5, 1983), p. 12.

Table 1
Characteristics of Sweeteners

Sweetener	Calories[a]	Undiluted Sweetness (Compared with Sugar)	Price per Pound	Comparative Price[b]
Aspartame	2 (powder) .4 (tablet)	200 times as sweet	$90.00	$.45
Sugar	16	—	.29	.29
Saccharin	1.35 (powder) 0 (tablet)	300 times as sweet	4.00	.013
High-fructose corn syrup	15	same	.18	.18

[a] Sweetening equivalent of 1 teaspoon of sugar.
[b] Sweetening equivalent of 1 pound of sugar.

Source: Reprinted with permission from *Inc.* magazine, January 1984. Copyright © 1984 by INC. Publishing Company, 38 Commercial Wharf, Boston, MA 02110.

Part Six Case People Express:
An Airline Soars on a Low-Price Strategy*

In 1978, Congress enacted the Airline Deregulation Act. This act made it easier for new airlines to enter the industry, and allowed existing airlines to determine and revise their routes and prices without the severe restrictions and time delays that had been imposed by the Civil Aeronautics Board (CAB). By 1983, the eleven well-established U.S. airlines (each with $1 billion in yearly sales) had been joined by ten new jet-operating airlines. The new airlines accounted for about 2.5 per cent of industry revenues during 1983. Today, airlines are completely deregulated; they can fly anywhere in the U.S. and set any prices they would like.

Because of deregulation and a variety of other factors, the period since 1978 has been an extremely tumultuous one. Deregulation has resulted in frequent fare wars, heavy competition for passengers in large markets, overcapacity (more seats available than warranted by demand), and extreme financial difficulties for some airlines (such as Eastern, Braniff, and Continental). Many airlines did not adapt well to the deregulated marketing environment they faced; they were unable to protect their existing markets from new competitors, have enough control over prices, contain costs adequately, encourage flexibility in decision making, or establish differential advantages that were not based on prices. In addition, the industry was adversely affected by rising fuel prices, a high rate of inflation, an air controller's strike, and the worst recession in decades. For example, between 1978 and 1982, operating costs went up by 58 per cent, while airline fares rose by only 48 per cent.

By far the most successful of the airlines started since the Airline Deregulation Act went into effect is People Express, which has been the fastest-growing airline in the history of the industry. People Express began flying on April 30, 1981. At that time it had three planes and offered flights between Newark, New Jersey, and Buffalo, New York; Columbus, Ohio; and Norfolk, Virginia (a total of 24 flights daily). By 1983, People Express owned over 20 jets and offered flights between Newark and 20 other cities, including London (a total of 264 daily nonstop flights). People Express had revenues of $38 million and losses of $9.2 million during 1981; its revenues rose to almost $300 million and profits to over $10 million in 1983. By 1985, People Express expects revenues to be $750 million, as it expands to 67 planes and services even more cities (including Chicago and Atlanta).

---

* The data in this case are drawn from Daniel F. Cuff, "How to Start an Airline: People Express Poised to Fly," *New York Times* (April 26, 1982), Section 3, pp. 8–9; Agis Salpukas, "Poised for a Steep Lift-off at People Express," *New York Times* (June 5, 1983), Section 3, pp. 8–9; John D. Williams and Barry Kramer, "U.K. Clears $149 People Express Service from Newark; Rivals Seem Unconcerned," *Wall Street Journal* (May 27, 1983), p. 8; Lucien Rhodes, "That Daring Young Man and His Flying Machine," *Inc.* (January 1984), pp. 42–52; John D. Williams, "Major Airlines, Stung by the Competition of No-Frills Carriers, Are Fighting Back," *Wall Street Journal* (March 1, 1983), p. 56; Thomas S. Robertson and Scott Ward, "Management Lessons from Airline Deregulation," *Harvard Business Review*, Vol. 61 (January–February 1983), pp. 40–44; "Airlines in Turmoil," *Business Week* (October 10, 1983), pp. 98–102; William M. Carley, "Some Major Airlines Are Being Threatened by Low-Cost Carriers," *Wall Street Journal* (October 12, 1983), pp. 1, 23; Charles W. Stevens, "US Air, Shaking Its 'Agony Air' Past, Profits from Routes Others Avoid," *Wall Street Journal* (February 28, 1984), p. 35; and William M. Carley, "People Express Flies into Airlines' Big Time in Just 3 Years Aloft," *Wall Street Journal* (March 30, 1984), pp. 1, 18.

People Express entered the airline industry with a simple philosophy, "to knock the price down so low that it fills the plane." As one industry expert noted in 1981:

Airlines seats are essentially a commodity product. If you can produce cheaper than the competition, you are in a position of price leadership. I think the Northeast is a ripe market. Higher productivity and lower wage scales can produce cheap seats. That's it in a nutshell.

People Express' price-oriented strategy is based on a combination of factors:

- Used planes are purchased at very low prices. It initially bought 17 737s from Lufthansa for $76.5 million; these planes would have cost $289 million if new. In 1983, People agreed to buy 37 727s from Braniff (then in bankruptcy) for $4.2 million apiece; they would have cost $7.5 million each if new.
- By redesigning plane interiors, more passenger seats are made available. People's 727s and 737s have only coach-class seats; there are no first-class seats. As a result, its 727s can hold 118 passengers (up from 90) and its 737s can hold 185 passengers (up from 150).
- Each plane has a cockpit crew of two and is in the air an average of 10.4 hours per day. Major airlines often have cockpit crews of three and their planes are in the air an average of 7.1 hours per day.
- There are no unions; employees are treated well and own an average of more than $46,000 in company stock (all employees are required to buy stock). The Airline Pilots Association has twice tried to unionize People's pilots and failed both times. By not having to contend with unions, People has more flexibility in operations (a pilot may help load baggage) and wages are lower (about half the industry average). People's passenger miles per employee are double the average of the industry. Employees are also quite loyal.
- Headquarters are located in Newark Airport's North Terminal, which was nearly abandoned before People took occupancy. Office rent is about $6 per square foot annually, compared with $50 per square foot in the Pan Am Building at New York's Kennedy Airport. Newark is also used as the "hub" at which most of People's flights depart or land; this reduces costs and gives People greater control (it is Newark's leading airline). Automobile parking fees are much lower than at Kennedy or LaGuardia airports. Furthermore, bus, minibus, and limousine service to Manhattan is frequent and inexpensive.
- Passengers are ticketed on board or pay in advance. There are extra charges for baggage checking, snacks, and beverages. People Express reasons that passengers are most interested in safety, a convenient flight schedule, and clean aircraft at low prices. Therefore, it charges separately for all "frills."
- A simple fare system is used. There are only off-peak rates (nights and weekends) and peak rates (regular coach) for domestic flights, unlike some major competitors. In one People Express television commercial, a reservation clerk at a fictitious competitor tells a customer: "You want the BSA Airlines super low-price special. OK? You simply fly one way and pay the price you pay the other way if you fly two ways. OK? Simply put, each way costs of either way, both ways, some days. OK?"

People Express has been able to earn a profit with its discount fare structure because it is the low-cost leader in the industry. Its operating costs per available seat are about 5 cents per mile. Thus, People Express can earn a profit by charging as little as 8 cents per passenger mile. At that rate, People would break even with a load factor (average per cent of seats filled per flight) of 60 per cent while Eastern and Delta flights would have to be filled just to break even. US Air could not cover its costs at that price even if flights are filled. Furthermore, 95 per cent of every sales dollar People receives above the break-even point contributes to net profit. Table 1 shows revenue per passenger mile, operating expenses, and load factors for People and four leading competitors. Table 2 shows selected airfares during March 1984.

Airline	Revenue per Passenger Mile		Operating Expenses per Available Seat Mile		Load Factor	
	1982	1983[a]	1982	1983[a]	1982	1983[a]
People Express	$ 8.90	$ 8.00	$ 5.00	$ 5.60	60.9%	77.5[b]
Delta	13.67	12.03	7.97	8.11	52.7	58.3
Eastern	13.01	12.39	8.21	8.42	56.7	60.9
Piedmont	15.87	15.29	9.26	8.91	55.6	53.5
US Air	19.51	17.69	11.07	10.64	57.2	60.5

Table 1
Operating Data for People Express and Four Major Competitors

[a] First six months.
[b] This rose to over 80 per cent during the second half of 1983; the industry average was 60 per cent.

Source: Lucien Rhodes,"That Daring Young Man and His Flying Machines," *Inc.* (January 1984), p. 46. Reprinted by permission.

Airline	Type of Service	Round-trip Airfares			
		Newark to Pittsburgh, Pa.	Newark to Houston, Tx.	Newark to West Palm Beach, Fl.	Newark to London, Eng.
People Express	Regular coach	$76	$198	$198	$298
	Nights/weekends	50	150	150	—
	First class	—	—	—	878
Delta	Regular coach	—	660	560	—
	Super-saver	—	288	329	—
Eastern	Regular coach	—	660	358	—
	Super-saver	—	198	338	—
Piedmont	Regular coach	—	640	—	—
	Super-saver	—	269	—	—
TWA	Regular coach	—	660	—	786
	Super-saver	—	259	—	—
	First class	—	—	—	3,858
US Air	Regular coach	138	298	512	—
	Super-saver	76	259	329	—

Table 2
Selected Airline Fares, March 1984

Sources: Airline ticket offices.

People Express' strategy is not without flaws. It has the highest rate of complaints in the industry, 6.91 per 100,000 passengers; this compares with 2.35 for American Airlines and 0.77 for Southwest Airlines (the industry leader in this category). Some consumers desire more services and less waiting at airports. Phone lines are frequently busy. Overbooking occurs twice as often as the industry average; and other airlines do not honor People's tickets if flights are overbooked or canceled. The major airlines believe People should be penalized more severely for overbooking or lost baggage. By law, the majors must offer up to $400 to passengers bumped off flights (People provides 2 free tickets) and $750 for each lost bag (People pays $250).

Competitors are responding to People Express in a number of ways. They are matching (but not undercutting) fares on specific flights, adding flights, advertising heavily, and cutting costs drastically. For example, during 1983, about 80 per cent of all passengers on domestic flights were paying discount fares averaging 45 per cent off regular coach prices. Eastern and American Airlines won major concessions from their unions. And American placed a large order for low-cost planes. The major airlines recognize that they must cut costs to prosper in the future; they cannot tolerate this situation: "Either we don't match and we lose customers, or we match and then, because costs are so high, we lose buckets of money."

QUESTIONS

1. Does the airline industry face elastic or inelastic consumer demand regarding prices? Why have there been so many price wars since 1978? Explain your answer.
2. What types of customers are likely to fly with People Express? With Delta or United?
3. Evaluate the data in Tables 1 and 2. What conclusions should be reached for People Express and its competitors?
4. Describe how People Express integrates cost-, demand-, and competitive-pricing techniques.
5. People Express operates one flight daily each way between Newark and London. British Airways offers about 5 (35 per week). People's fares are about half those of British Airways. Comment on this.
6. Assess People Express' approach of charging separately for baggage check-in, meals, and beverages.
7. Given the reactions of competitors (such as reducing costs), will People Express be able to continue as the discount fare leader in the future? Why or why not?
8. As a major airline, what differential advantages should you stress?

In Part Seven, the scope of marketing is broadened. Chapter 21 examines international marketing and how marketing principles can be applied in foreign markets. International and multinational marketing are defined, and the factors behind the growth of international marketing are explored. The cultural, economic, political and legal, and technological factors facing international marketers are assessed. The stages in the development of an international marketing strategy are detailed. These are company organization, degree of standardization, and product, distribution, promotion, and price planning.

Chapter 22 extends marketing to service and nonprofit organizations. The first half of the chapter deals with the marketing of services. The differences in service and product marketing are explained. The characteristics of services, their role in the economy, and special considerations for service marketing are noted. Service-marketing strategies are discussed for hotels, car repair and maintenance services, and legal services. The second half of the chapter concentrates on nonprofit marketing. The differences between nonprofit and profit marketing are described, and the characteristics of nonprofit marketing and its role in the economy are enumerated. Nonprofit marketing strategies are discussed for the United States Postal Service, colleges and universities, and public libraries.

In Chapter 23 the interaction of marketing and society is examined. The chapter is divided into two sections. The first section evaluates the concept of social responsibility and its meaning for marketers. The depletion of natural resources, marring of the landscape, planned obsolescence, ethics, and the benefits and costs of social responsibility are discussed. The second section describes consumerism and its meaning for marketers. Consumer information and education, consumer safety, consumer choice, consumers' right to be heard, and the responses of business to consumer issues are each detailed. The trend toward greater deregulation and the maturity of consumerism are noted.

In order to accommodate the special features of European washing machines, Procter & Gamble developed Ariel laundry detergent to operate at high temperatures and with little water. In Spain, a new ingredient was added to bleach white fabrics during drying. Reprinted by permission.

Gillette double-edge razor blades are manufactured in twenty countries. Shown at right are local brands made in Morocco, China, Egypt, the Phillipines, and Indonesia. Reprinted by permission.

3M Philippines developed Scotch Brite pads for floor scrubbing. They are used underfoot in the same way coconut husks were traditionally used. Reprinted by permission.

Hotels such as Hyatt are among the service organizations that are expanding their use of marketing. In this advertisement, Hyatt indicates its services that are particularly oriented toward women. Reprinted by permission.

COMFORTABLY HYATT.

In an unfamiliar city, it's important to find a truly comfortable hotel. That's why so many frequent travelers find their way to Hyatt.

For women, as for all our guests, our comforts are many. A room with the location you prefer. A thoughtful, professional staff with a gift for anticipating your next request. The small touches are never overlooked. Like imported soap, shampoo, skirt hangers, even hair dryers in many rooms. And our sunny atrium lounges are wonderful places to brighten your spirits throughout the day.

For us the greatest comfort is to see so many guests return, again and again. A comfortable touch of Hyatt. Don't you **WISH YOU WERE HERE**℠

ATLANTA
Discover magnificent Peachtree Center, 15 minutes from Atlanta International Airport.

CHICAGO
In Illinois Center overlooking Michigan Avenue and Lake Michigan.

NEW YORK
Grand Hyatt on fashionable Park Avenue at Grand Central.

SAN FRANCISCO
Hyatt Regency soars above the Embarcadero Center business complex.

WASHINGTON, D.C.
Walk to Capitol Hill, government agencies, art galleries and museums.

HYATT HOTELS

For reservations, call your travel planner or 800 228 9000. © 1984 Hyatt Hotels Corp.

The San Diego Zoo is one of the most popular and well known zoos in the world. These outdoor billboards encourage visitors to come and enjoy the zoo. They were recognized by the Institute of Outdoor Advertising in *The Best of Outdoor, Book II.* Reprinted by permission.

Breathe free.

So far, we've created 27 types of comfortable, economical masks that help people breathe free of contaminated air. They filter out dusts, pollens, germs and toxic fumes.

3M developed these lightweight, disposable masks over 20 years ago at the request of one company with a bad-air problem.

By listening to people's needs, we've developed many innovative safety and security products. We've made a fire extinguisher foam that floats on oil, gas and solvent fires and smothers them. And we've made clothing that reflects at night.

3M has pioneered over 100 safety and security products. And it all began by listening.

3M hears you...

For your free brochure on 3M's safety and security products plus all other 3M products, write: Dept. 040103MM5, P.O. Box 22002, Robbinsdale, MN 55422.

Name_____

Address_____

City_____State_____Zip_____

Or call toll-free: **1-800-336-4327.**

©1984, 3M

3M

Many U.S. firms regularly engage in practices that are beneficial to society. An illustration of this is the antipollutant mask developed by 3M that is shown above. Courtesy of 3M, St. Paul, MN.

Chapter 21

International Marketing

1. To define international and multinational marketing

2. To explain why international marketing has developed

3. To study the scope of international marketing

4. To explore the cultural, economic, political and legal, and technological environments facing international marketers

5. To analyze the stages in the development of an international marketing strategy: company organization, degree of standardization, and product, distribution, promotion, and price planning

IBM Japan, a subsidiary of U.S.-based IBM, has a computer market share of 20.2 per cent in Japan; this places the firm second behind the Japanese firm Fujitsu, which has a 22.3 per cent share of the market. Until 1979, IBM Japan was the industry leader. As in the U.S., the greatest degree of competition among computer manufacturers involves the personal computer aimed at the office segment of the Japanese market.

Significant opportunities exist for personal computer sales in Japan, because of their ability to master the thousands of characters that comprise the written Japanese language. A typewriter is inadequate to communicate in Japanese; personnel in offices without computers must correspond through handwritten memos. The potential for similar personal computer applications exists in Korea, Taiwan, Singapore, and China. See Figure 21-1.

Figure 21-1
IBM Japan
The IBM Japan 5550 Multistation, shown here, is a small, high-performance multifunction computer system. The Multistation has Japanese and English language processing capability, a large memory (256k to 512k), a high-speed printer, plentiful software, and a high-resolution monitor.

Reprinted by permission.

While IBM's equipment often sells at above-market prices in the U.S. and other markets, it has been difficult for the company to win market share away from Japanese firms in Japan. To regain the position of market leader and increase market share, IBM Japan needs to overcome these difficulties:

- In Japan, extensive distribution is needed to market personal computers. For example, Hitachi (a major Japanese competitor) markets its products through 10,000 exclusive retail dealers, who do not carry competing brands. This represents more retail outlets than IBM uses in the U.S., where sales are far greater. To expand its limited distribution network in Japan, IBM has solicited assistance from independent channel members such as Nissan Motors dealers and a large sake distributor (to gain sales to liquor retailers needing computers).
- Japanese competitors are often willing to sacrifice immediate earnings in return for market share gains; they set prices accordingly. Many provide support and service levels for customers that are beyond those offered by IBM Japan.
- IBM Japan is viewed as a foreign company despite the fact that 13,800 of its 14,000 employees are Japanese, including the president. Furthermore, almost all the components for the IBM computers that are marketed in Japan are manufactured in Japan.

- The IBM name is not as valued in Japan as in other markets: "In the U.S., IBM can sell good but less than extraordinary equipment at a premium price simply because of those famous initials. In Japan, IBM is more like any competitor, forced to keep its manufacturing efficient, strive for broad distribution, and price carefully."[1]

For IBM or any firm to succeed in international marketing, it must study the cultural, economic, political and legal, and technological environments of the countries in which it seeks to market products and services—and implement appropriate strategies.

Overview

International marketing involves the marketing of goods and services outside an organization's home country. *Multinational marketing* is a complex form of international marketing that involves an organization engaged in marketing operations in many foreign countries. Multinational firms include Nestlé, Unilever, Shell, ITT, Exxon, and Coca-Cola. These companies have brand names that are known throughout the world and extensive worldwide operations. Large multinational organizations often allocate company resources without regard to national boundaries, even though they have a home country in terms of ownership and top management.

The watch industry typifies the international approach to marketing:

A watch might be designed in Switzerland, have its electronic parts manufactured in Japan, have its timekeeping module assembled in Hong Kong, its watch case produced in the U.S., its face produced in Japan, and its final assembly completed in the Virgin Islands before being sold in the U.S.

Thus, a brand name which formerly represented the perceived excellence of Swiss or American craftsmanship now stands for managerial excellence in coordinating labor and logistics in many nations to assure high standards of quality and service.[2]

International efforts vary widely. At one end, a firm may limit itself to one or a few foreign markets, manufacture goods domestically, and market them to foreign countries with little or no adaptation of the domestic marketing plan. At the opposite end, a multinational firm has a global orientation, operates in many different countries, and uses foreign manufacturing and marketing subsidiaries to cater to individual markets.

For international companies to prosper in the 1980s, it is vital that they research and understand the similarities and differences among countries and adapt their plans accordingly. No longer can small or large American firms succeed by merely exporting to foreign markets products that have sold well in the United States. Competition is too severe and cultures too distinct.

Marketing outside the firm's home country is *international marketing; multinational marketing* includes many foreign countries.

---

[1] Lee Smith, "IBM's Counteroffensive in Japan," *Fortune* (December 12, 1983), pp. 97–98, 102.
[2] Russell M. Moore, "International Marketing's Competitive Arena Now Features Battle of World Firms, World Brands," *Marketing News* (October 17, 1980), Section 1, p. 10.

This chapter focuses on how to adapt modern marketing principles to foreign markets. The chapter examines the development and scope of international marketing, its environment, and the components of an international marketing strategy.

Why International Marketing Has Developed

There are several reasons why countries and individual firms engage in international marketing, including: comparative advantage, economic trends, demographic conditions, competition at home, the stage in the product life cycle, and tax structures.[3] See Figure 21-2.

Countries trade items in which they have a *comparative advantage* for those in shortage.

The concept of ***comparative advantage*** states that countries have different rates of productivity for different products because of resources, specialization, mechanization, or climate. Therefore, countries can benefit by exchanging goods in which they have relative production advantages for those in which they have relative disadvantages. For example, the United States exports computer technology, wheat, and aircraft. It imports petroleum, coffee, and clothing.

International marketing may minimize unfavorable domestic conditions or appeal to growing populations.

Economic trends vary by country. A firm may minimize adverse domestic conditions such as high inflation or unemployment by marketing goods and services in countries with good economic conditions. In this way annual sales can be stabilized. During the late 1970s and early 1980s, the economic climate in some parts of Europe and Asia was better than that in the United States, thus increasing the importance of those markets.

Demographic conditions also differ by country. A firm in a country with a small or stagnant population base can find new business by entering foreign markets with undersatisfied market segments. In the 1980s, more than 90 per cent of the world's population growth will occur in developing countries.[4] This is causing firms to intensely examine these markets. For example, the president of H. J. Heinz commented that

Much of our planning stems from an awareness that we serve only 15 per cent of the world's population. There's huge potential to expand our markets to the remaining 85 per cent.[5]

International expansion may result from competition at home.

Heinz believes that improved living conditions in less-developed nations will increase consumer demand for Western-style food.

Competition in the domestic market may become intense, thereby leading to international expansion. As an example, Safeway's most profitable geographic

---

[3] See Douglas G. Norvell and Sim Raveed, "Eleven Reasons for Firms to 'Go International,'" *Marketing News* (October 17, 1980), Section 1, pp. 1–2.

[4] Doris L. Walsh, "Demographic Trends, Transition Phases Suggest International Marketing Opportunities, Strategies," *Marketing News* (September 16, 1983), Section 1, p. 16.

[5] Carol Hymowitz, "Heinz Sets Out to Expand in Africa and Asia, Seeking New Markets, Sources of Materials," *Wall Street Journal* (September 27, 1983), p. 37.

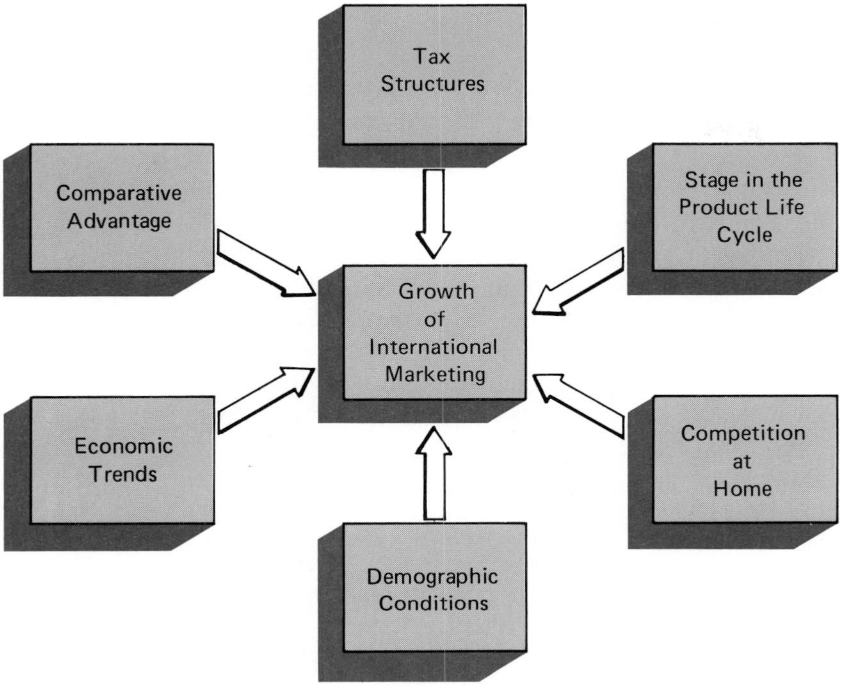

Figure 21-2
**Why International
Marketing Has Developed**

market for its food stores is Great Britain, where its net profit margin is 3.4 per cent of sales, compared with a profit margin of 1.0 per cent in the U.S. Its profit margins are also higher in Canada, Australia, and West Germany than in the U.S. The U.S. market for supermarkets is a highly saturated one.[6]

In many instances products are in different stages in the life cycle in different countries. Exporting may provide opportunities for prolonging product growth. For example, foreign manufacturers of small refrigerators found that those units could be sold in the United States for dens, bars, dormitories, and studio apartments. In their home countries, they were used only as the major refrigerators for families.

International marketing may extend the product life cycle or dispose of discontinued items.

International marketing can provide for the disposal of discontinued merchandise, seconds, and manufacturer remakes (products that have been repaired). These items can be sold abroad without spoiling the domestic market for full-price, first-quality merchandise. However, companies must be careful not to dump unsafe products on foreign markets. This creates ill will and diminishes a firm's image.

There may be some tax advantages through international marketing. A number of countries entice new business from foreign companies by offering tax incentives in the form of reduced property, import, and income taxes for an initial period. In addition, multinational firms may adjust prices so that the largest profits are recorded in the countries with the lowest tax rates.

Some firms are attracted to international marketing because of tax benefits.

[6] Howard Sharmon, "Safeway Holds U.K. Expansion Course," *Advertising Age* (September 5, 1983), pp. 32, 34.

Scope of International Marketing

The United States accounts for 10 per cent of world exports.

The United States is the largest exporter in the world. In 1983 U.S. exports totaled $201 billion, about 10 per cent of total world exports. During the same period West German exports were about $180 billion, and Japanese exports about $150 billion. U.S. exports represent roughly 6 per cent of the American gross national product. Leading U.S. exports are chemicals, industrial equipment, motor vehicles, tobacco, and earth-moving machinery. Services make up one third of exports. These include air travel, tourist expenditures in the United States, ocean shipping, insurance, management fees, and military expenses.[7]

The involvement of United States firms in international marketing varies greatly. One Department of Commerce study found that 92 per cent of United States companies confined themselves to domestic markets.[8] Nonetheless, well over 20,000 U.S. companies with fewer than 100 employees export goods and services to international markets. During 1982, the fifty largest United States exporters accounted for almost $59 billion in foreign sales.[9] The latter figure is deceptively low because it does not include returns on foreign investments and sales by foreign subsidiaries. Among major U.S. firms, exports range from 1 per cent of sales (Exxon) to 43 per cent of sales (Boeing). Table 21-1 shows the ten largest U.S. exporters.

By the end of 1982, U.S. firms had cumulatively invested over $221 billion to develop subsidiaries, conduct joint ventures, build facilities, or acquire property in foreign countries. The greatest proportion of these investments has been in Western Europe, Canada, and Latin America. See Table 21-2.

The United States is also the world's largest importer. In 1983, imports totaled $270 billion. Examples of other major importers are West Germany, France, and Japan. Leading U.S. imports are petroleum, machinery, transport equipment, and iron and steel mill products.

In 1983, U.S. imports exceeded exports by $69 billion, creating a large *trade deficit*.

During 1983, the United States had a ***trade deficit*** of $69 billion. This means that the value of imports exceeded the value of exports by $69 billion. Trade deficits are recent in the United States. Between 1888 and 1970 the balance of trade was positive in every year.[10] Since 1971, there has been a trade deficit every year. The 1983 trade deficit was by far the largest in U.S. history (the previous record was $43 billion in 1982). Some experts expected the trade deficit in 1984 to reach $100 billion.[11]

The trade deficit is attributable to a variety of factors, including: huge increases in foreign oil prices, the dollar's convertability into gold, increased

---

[7] Bureau of Economic Analysis, U.S. Commerce Department, 1984; and Office of Planning and Research, U.S. Commerce Department, 1984.

[8] Deborah A. Randolph, "Small Firms Go Multinational, Find Niches in Foreign Markets," *Wall Street Journal* (September 8, 1980), p. 33.

[9] Andrew Kupfer, "The 50 Leading Exporters," *Fortune* (August 8, 1983), pp. 88–89.

[10] Bureau of Economic Analysis, U.S. Commerce Department, 1984; and Philip R. Cateora, *International Marketing*, Fifth Edition (Homewood, Ill.: Richard D. Irwin, 1983), p. 27.

[11] Alan Murray, "Trade Deficit Set High in 1983 of $69.39 Billion," *Wall Street Journal* (January 30, 1984), p. 4; and Alfred L. Malabre, Jr., "That Smaller Deficit Is Awesome," *Wall Street Journal* (February 27, 1984), p. 1.

Table 21-1   The Ten Largest U.S. Exporters, 1982

Rank 1982	Company	Products	Export Sales ($000)	Total Company Sales ($000)	Exports as Per Cent of Total Company Sales
1	General Motors	Motor vehicles and parts, locomotives, diesel engines	4,673,800	60,025,600	7.8
2	General Electric	Aircraft engines, generating equipment, locomotives	3,921,000	26,500,000	14.8
3	Boeing	Aircraft	3,879,000	9,035,000	42.9
4	Ford Motor	Motor vehicles and parts	3,733,000	37,067,200	10.1
5	Caterpillar Tractor	Construction equipment, engines	2,619,000	6,469,000	40.5
6	E. I. DuPont de Nemours	Chemicals, fibers, polymer products, petroleum, coal	2,559,000	33,331,000	7.7
7	United Technologies	Aircraft engines, helicopters	2,271,721	13,577,129	16.7
8	McDonnell Douglas	Aircraft, missiles, space systems	2,076,500	7,331,300	28.3
9	International Business Machines	Information-handling systems, equipment, and parts	1,875,000	34,364,000	5.5
10	Eastman Kodak	Photographic equipment and supplies	1,853,000	10,815,000	17.1

Source: Andrew Kupfer, "The 50 Largest Exporters," *Fortune* (August 8, 1983), p. 89. Reprinted by permission. © 1983 Time Inc. All rights reserved.

competition in foreign markets, less than optimal quality control for U.S. products, incentives by some foreign countries that encourage their industries to export products to the U.S., improving productivity in many foreign countries, and the U.S. dollar's rise in value. The dollar's high value makes U.S. exports more costly overseas and foreign goods cheaper in the U.S. Between 1980 and 1983, the dollar's value rose 30 per cent in relation to other countries' currencies, or as an observer noted: "American firms have a 30 per cent cost disadvantage in world markets."[12] Furthermore, the U.S. market has been and remains a very

[12] Ibid.

Table 21-2
U.S. Investment Abroad, Cumulative Through 1982

Region/Country	Investment	
	U.S. Billions ($)	Per Cent of Total
Developed countries		
Western Europe	99.9	45.1
Canada	44.5	20.1
Other	18.7	8.5
Developed subtotal	163.1	73.7
Developing countries		
Latin America	33.0	14.9
Other	20.1	9.1
Developing subtotal	53.1	24.0
International and unallocated	5.1	2.3
Total	221.3	100.0

Source: Bureau of Economic Analysis, U.S. Commerce Department, 1983.

lucrative one for foreign companies; its per capita consumption is the highest of any country in the world for most products and services.

Because U.S. trade deficits have been so high over the past few years, many American companies have called for tighter controls on imports and more open access to restricted foreign markets. The U.S. government has been negotiating with foreign governments to improve the situation. For example, Japan has agreed to a number of trade provisions to improve its balance of trade with the U.S.[13] In 1983, the U.S. had a trade deficit of $18 billion with Japan.

Many non-U.S. firms are becoming much more active in international marketing. For example, in 1964 only twelve of the world's fifty largest industrial companies were European. By 1982 this figure had risen to twenty-nine.[14] Among the largest non-U.S. firms are Royal Dutch/Shell Group, British Petroleum, ENI, IRI, and Unilever.

Of the ten leading firms in the world, eight are U.S.-based.

Despite these trends the U.S. remains a dominant force in international marketing. In 1982, of the world's fifty largest industrial firms, American companies comprised twenty-one. Eight of the ten leaders were American, and these eight had worldwide sales of over $400 billion. Furthermore, in a 1983 survey, European executives continued to rank the U.S. as the worldwide technological leader—ahead of Japan and West Germany.[15]

Environment of International Marketing

Although the basic marketing principles described in this text apply to international marketing, there are significant environmental differences between domestic and foreign markets, and marketing practices should be adapted accordingly. Each market should be evaluated separately:

There is no such thing as a multinational market. We have domestic markets worldwide but no multinational markets. Each market is unique, unlike any other market, and therefore each is a domestic market.[16]

The major cultural, economic, political and legal, and technological environments facing international marketers are discussed in the succeeding subsections. See Figure 21-3.

Cultural Environment

International marketers need to be aware of each market's cultural environment. As defined in Chapter 6, culture refers to a group of people sharing a

---

[13] Masayoshi Kanabayashi and Urban C. Lehner, "Japanese Adopt Another Package to Open Market," *Wall Street Journal* (January 14, 1983), p. 26; Douglas R. Sease and Amal Nag, "Third Year of U.S. Curbs on Japan's Cars Likely to Raise Prices, Delay New Entries," *Wall Street Journal* (February 14, 1983), p. 3; and "Japan Reports '83 Trade Surplus Nearly Tripled," *Wall Street Journal* (January 16, 1984), p. 31.

[14] Michael McFadden and Ann Goodman, "The World's 50 Largest Industrial Corporations," *Fortune* (August 22, 1983), pp. 170–171.

[15] Ibid; and "European Executives Pick Technological Leaders," *Wall Street Journal* (February 1, 1984), p. 28.

[16] Warren J. Keegan, "A Conceptual Framework for Multinational Marketing," *Columbia Journal of World Business*, Vol. 7 (November 1972), p. 67.

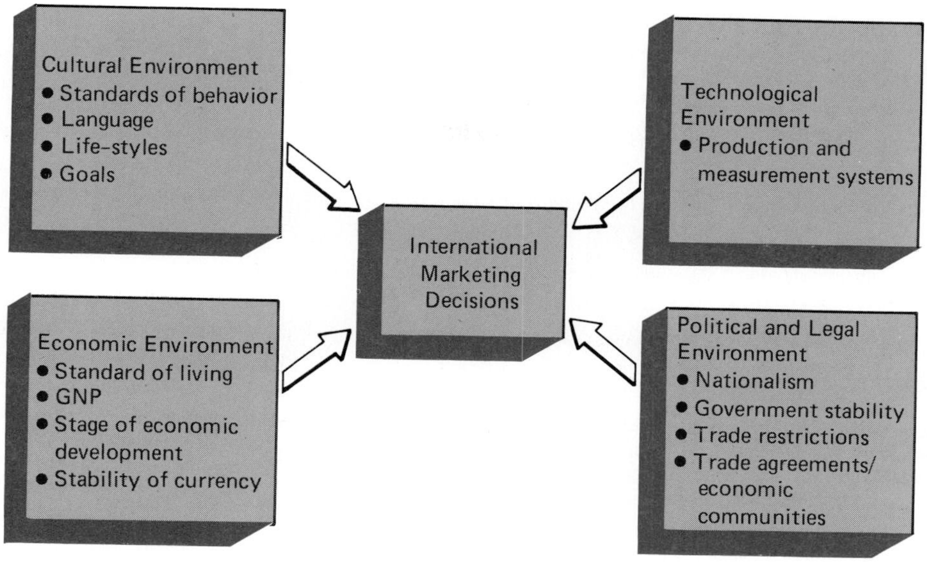

Figure 21-3
The Environment Facing International Marketers

distinctive heritage. This heritage teaches behavior standards, language, life-styles, and goals. A culture is passed down from generation to generation and is not easily changed. Almost every country in the world has a different culture, and continental differences exist as well. A domestic firm unfamiliar with or insensitive to a foreign culture may try to market products or services that are unacceptable to or misunderstood by that culture. For example, beef or pork products are rejected by some cultures.

Table 21-3 illustrates the errors a firm engaged in international marketing may commit as a result of a lack of awareness about foreign cultures that is rooted in inadequate data. In some cases the firm is at fault because it functions out of a domestic home office and receives little local foreign input. In other cases, such

Inadequate information about foreign cultures is a common cause of errors.

Table 21-3   Illustrations of Errors in International Marketing Because of Lack of Cultural Awareness

In Japan, photograph frames aimed at the office market have done poorly, because photos of a person's family are not kept on desks (which are viewed as places of work). The Japanese put photos into albums and show them only to friends.

Pepsodent was unsuccessful in Southeast Asia because it promised white teeth to a culture where black or yellow teeth are symbols of prestige.

In Quebec, a canned fish manufacturer tried to promote a product by showing a woman dressed in shorts, golfing with her husband, and planning to serve canned fish for dinner. These activities violated cultural norms.

Maxwell House advertised itself as the "great American coffee" in Germany. It found out that Germans have little respect for American coffee.

In Puerto Rico, the Chevrolet Nova (meaning "star") was translated as "no va"—"it doesn't go."

General Motors' "Body by Fisher" slogan became "Corpse by Fisher" when translated into Japanese.

In Brazil, Gerber could not convince mothers that baby food was a good alternative to food the mothers made themselves.

African men were upset by a commercial for men's deodorant that showed a happy male being chased by women. They thought the deodorant would make them weak and overrun by women.

Sources: David A. Ricks, *Big Business Blunders* (Homewood, Ill.: Richard D. Irwin, 1983); Ann Helming, "Culture Shocks," *Advertising Age* (May 17, 1982), pp. M-8–M-9; and Heywood Klein, "Firms Seek Aid in Deciphering Japan's Culture," *Wall Street Journal* (September 1, 1983), p. 27.

Table 21-4 Examples of Cultural Opportunities for International Marketers

Since Brazilians have an extremely high per capita rate of sugar consumption, Dunkin' Donuts is investing heavily in outlets there, rather than selling licensing rights to others. It recognizes that it will take time to win Brazilians' approval for donuts.

Hong Kong is said to have the world's highest per capita consumption of Cognac. "The belief has been established that it's good for you. You'll have old ladies who get up in the morning and have a glass of it."

In Germany, beer communicates, "Let's meet over a beer." The average annual per capita consumption of beer is 153.4 quarts, about 68 six packs of twelve-ounce cans, in West Germany. It is 97.2 quarts in the United States.

In China, the most popular color is red; it indicates happiness. Black with gold lettering also elicits a positive response, because it denotes age and stability.

In France, chocolate is used in cooking. Italians serve chocolate as a snack for children, placing it between two slices of bread.

Tropical area residents apply Vicks Vaporub as a mosquito repellant.

Sources: Laurel Wentz, "New Donut Snack Has Brazilians Confused," *Advertising Age* (March 25, 1983), p. 54; Nicole Seligman, "Be Sure Not to Wear a Green Hat If You Visit Hong Kong," *Wall Street Journal* (May 10, 1979), p. 41; John M. Gross, "The Germans Drink a Great Deal of Beer, But Not Enough to Suit the Beer Makers," *Wall Street Journal* (August 28, 1980), p. 38; George Fields, "How to Scale the Cultural Fence," *Advertising Age* (December 13, 1982), pp. M-11–M-12; and Saul Sands, "Can You Standardize International Marketing Strategy?" *Journal of the Academy of Marketing Science,* Vol. 7 (Winter–Spring 1979), p. 120.

as marketing in less-developed countries, information is limited because a low level of population data or marketing research skill exists, and people are reluctant to participate in surveys. Sometimes, mail and telephone service are poor. Thus, marketing research, which could determine the hidden meanings and the ease of pronunciation of brand names and slogans, the rate of product consumption, and reasons for purchases, is not fully utilized.

Cultural awareness can be improved by employing foreign personnel in key positions, hiring foreign marketing research specialists, locating company offices in each country of operations, actively studying cultural differences, and being responsive to cultural changes. Table 21-4 shows several cultural opportunities.

Economic Environment

A country's economic environment indicates its present and potential capacities for consuming goods and services. Measures of economic performance include the standard of living, Gross National Product (GNP), stage of economic development, and stability of currency.

The quality of life in a country is measured by its *standard of living*.

The ***standard of living*** refers to the average quantity and quality of goods and services consumed in a country. Not long ago, the United Nations studied the per capita consumption of goods and services in countries throughout the world. It gave the United States an index number of 100 and rated the other countries in relation to this figure. The ratings were 68 for France, 66 for West Germany, 57 for Great Britain, 56 for Japan, and 46 for Italy. The report concluded that the United States has the highest standard of living for any main industrial country.[17] Figure 21-4 shows the results of a 1982 study sponsored by the National Federation of Independent Business.

The total value of goods and services produced in a country each year is the *Gross National Product (GNP)*.

The ***Gross National Product (GNP)*** indicates the total value of goods and services produced in a country each year. Total and per capita GNP are the most frequently used measures of a country's wealth, because they are regularly pub-

---

[17] Alfred L. Malabre, Jr., "Despite the Dollar's Decline, U.S. Retains Top Living Standard Among Major Nations," *Wall Street Journal* (May 1, 1979), p. 48.

lished and easy to calculate and compare with other countries. However, per capita GNP figures may be misleading for two reasons. First, these figures represent means and not income distributions. A few wealthy citizens may boost the per capita GNP even though the bulk of the population has low income. Second, incomes purchase different standards of living in each country; an income of

What's the Difference?

Commodity	Washington	Moscow	London	Paris	Munich
Weekly food basket, *selected items:*	*Minutes of worktime unless otherwise specified*				
Bread *1 kg*	16	17	16	18	27
Hamburger meat, beef *1 kg*	37	123	63	80	70
Sausages *1 kg*	33	160	51	75	75
Cod *1 kg*	61	47	72	118	45
Sugar *1 kg*	9	58	11	9	10
Butter *1 kg*	55	222	50	47	52
Milk *1 liter*	6	22	9	8	7
Cheese *1 kg*	100	185	65	59	65
Eggs *10*	8	55	16	13	12
Potatoes *1 kg*	7	7	3	4	4
Cabbage *1 kg*	9	12	10	9	7
Carrots *1 kg*	11	19	13	7	10
Apples *1 kg*	10	92	23	15	15
Tea *100 g*	10	53	5	17	10
Beer *1 liter*	11	16	18	7	8
Vodka *.7 liter*	61	452	131	107	74
Cigarettes *20*	9	15	25	8	16
Weekly basket *family of 4 (hours)*	18.6	53.5	24.7	22.2	23.3
Cosmetics, Drugs, etc.					
Toilet soap *150 g, small bar*	4	20	5	7	6
Toothpaste *125 ml*	16	27	13	29	28
Aspirin *100, cheapest*	5	246	9	21	64
Lipstick *one*	30	69	60	76	80
Clothing, Household items and services					
T-shirt *cotton, white*	19	185	66	53	50
Panty hose *one pair*	18	366	18	17	18
Jeans *Levi's (hours)*	3	46	6	6	7
Men's shoes *(hours)*	8	25	7	7	5
Men's office suit *2-piece, rayon, dacron (hours)*	25	109	22	13	15
Refrigerator *cheapest (hours)*	44	155	40	53	42
Television *color, 56-cm (hours)*	65	701	132	106	143
Electricity *1/12 annual bill*	253	246	198	265	242
Gas *1/12 annual bill*	290	39	568	369	125
Water *1/12 annual bill*	32	123	97	95	37
Telephone rent *per month*	119	154	190	119	136
Television and radio license *annual, color television (hours)*	nil	nil	20	15	13
Shirt laundered *white, cotton*	10	25	16	18	13
Dry cleaning *one men's overcoat*	79	92	53	91	54
Haircut *men, no extras*	63	37	34	108	60
Transportation					
Small car *Ford Escort (months)*	5	53	11	8	6
Gasoline *regular, 10 liters*	32	185	85	87	61
Taxi fare *2mi./3km*	21	37	52	27	35
Bus fare *2mi./3km*	7	3	11	9	8
Miscellaneous					
Morning paper	3	3	5	7	5
Suburban movies *best seat*	42	31	53	38	40

NFIB National Federation of Independent Business Research and Education Foundation
150 West 20th Avenue, San Mateo, CA 94403

Figure 21-4
Comparing Standards of Living
Shown are the approximate worktimes (in minutes) for an average manufacturing employee to buy selected commodities in retail stores in Washington, D. C., London, Paris, and Munich and at state-fixed prices in Moscow during March 1982.

Source: Keith Bush, *Retail Prices in Moscow and Four Western Countries in March, 1982* (San Mateo, California: National Federation of Independent Business Research and Education Foundation, 1982). Reprinted by permission.

$10,000 in the United States may represent the same standard of living as an income of $5,000 in another country.

Marketing opportunities often can be highlighted by evaluating a country's stage of economic growth. One method for categorizing the economic growth of countries is to divide them into industrialized, developing, and less-developed classes. See Figure 21-5. ***Industrialized countries*** include the United States, Canada, Japan, the USSR, and nations in Oceania and Western Europe. These countries have high literacy, modern technology, and per capita income of several thousand dollars. ***Developing countries*** include many Latin American nations. Education and technology are rising, and per capita income is about $1,500. Developing countries have 20 per cent of the world's population and almost one third of its income. ***Less-developed countries*** include a number of countries in Africa and South Asia. Literacy is low, technology limited, and per capita GNP is generally below $500. These countries have two thirds of the world's population but less than 15 per cent of world income.

The greatest marketing opportunities generally occur in industrialized countries because of their higher discretionary income and standard of living. However, industrialized countries usually have stable population bases, and sales of some product categories may already be saturated. Developing and less-developed countries have expanding population bases and currently purchase limited amounts of imports. There is long-run potential for international marketers in these nations.

By examining product ownership per thousand population, a marketer can obtain a good estimate of the current size of consumer demand in a country. Table 21-5 shows consumption per 1,000 people of cars, televisions, meat, gasoline,

Countries can be classified as *industrialized*, *developing*, and *less-developed*.

The size of consumer demand can be estimated by studying product ownership. Untapped markets should also be noted.

Figure 21-5
The Stages of Economic Development

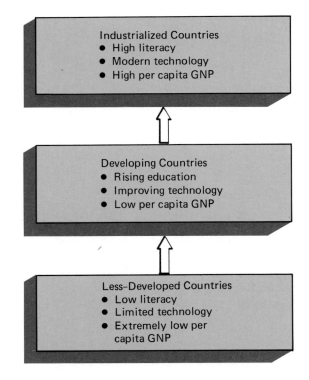

Industrialized Countries
• High literacy
• Modern technology
• High per capita GNP

Developing Countries
• Rising education
• Improving technology
• Low per capita GNP

Less-Developed Countries
• Low literacy
• Limited technology
• Extremely low per capita GNP

Table 21-5
**Product and Service
Consumption in Nine
Major Industrialized
Countries, 1981**

	Cars (per 1,000 People)	Televisions (per 1,000 People)	Meat (Lbs. per Year Eaten per Person)	Gasoline (Lbs.[a] per Year Used per Person)	Electricity (Kilowatt Hours Used per Year per Person)	Telephones (per 100 People)
United States	507	571	211	2,968	9,456	69
Britain	260	315	163	622	4,934	38
Denmark	260	308	146	904	4,710	45
France	300	235	172	659	3,900	26
Italy	283	213	68	454	2,865	26
Japan	164	233	15	423	4,470	40
Sweden	350	348	113	1,131	9,970	66
Switzerland	271	264	133	886	5,670	61
West Germany	307	297	133	734	5,710	32

[a] Standard unit of international measure
Source: United Nations

electricity, and telephones for nine major industrialized countries. As already noted, there is usually long-run potential in countries where consumers presently have few products and services. For example, Argentina has 100 automobiles per 1,000 population, Nigeria has 3 per 1,000, and India has fewer than 3 per 1,000. The one-billion-plus people of China own only 50,000 cars. Of all the automobiles in the world, 40 per cent are in the United States; 83 per cent of the global population has only 12 per cent of the cars.[18]

Currency stability is another economic factor a firm would consider in international marketing, because sales and profits could be affected if a foreign country revalues its currency in relation to the company's home currency. For example, in 1982, an extremely weak Mexican economy caused that country's peso to be devalued by 160 per cent. This meant that Mexican goods became much cheaper for consumers in other countries, while making it very expensive for Mexican consumers to purchase any foreign products. As a result, U.S. firms had great difficulties exporting products to Mexico during this period, because their prices were relatively high.[19]

Stability of currency is important because re-evaluation could affect a firm's foreign sales and profit.

Political and Legal Environment

In each country, a unique political and legal environment exists.[20] Among the key political and legal factors to examine are nationalism, government stability, trade restrictions, and trade agreements and economic communities.

Nationalism refers to a country's efforts to become self-reliant and raise its status in the eyes of the world community. Frequently, nationalism leads to tight restrictions on foreign companies and fosters the development of domestic indus-

Nationalism involves a host country's attempts to promote its interests.

---

[18] Thomas A. Staudt, "Rise of World Automobile Companies, Expanding Overseas Markets, New Vehicles to Mark 1980s," *Marketing News* (July 11, 1980), p. 8.

[19] Kenneth Labich, "The So-Far-So-Good Mexican Recovery," *Fortune* (January 9, 1984), pp. 97–99 ff. See also, Ike Mathur, "Managing Foreign Exchange Risk Profitably," *Columbia Journal of World Business,* Vol. 16 (Winter 1982), pp. 23–30.

[20] See Pravin Banker, "You're the Best Judge of Foreign Risks," *Harvard Business Review*, Vol. 61 (March–April 1983), pp. 157–165; and Jeffrey D. Simon, "Political Risk Assessment," *Columbia Journal of World Business*, Vol. 16 (Fall 1982), pp. 62–71.

try at their expense. In recent years some countries have seized the assets of multinational firms, revoked their licenses to operate, prevented the transfer of funds from one currency to another, increased taxes, or unilaterally changed contract terms.

For continued success in a foreign market, government stability is needed.

Government stability should be examined on the basis of two factors: consistency of policies and orderliness in installing leaders. First, do government policies regarding taxes, company expansion, profits, and so on remain relatively unchanged over time? Second, is there an orderly process for selecting and empowering new government leaders? Companies will be unable to function properly unless both of these factors are positive.

For example, although food producers such as Nestlé, Carnation, and CPC International have made large investments in developing nations, many other food companies are staying away from less-developed and developing countries. H. J. Heinz has ruled out additional investments in Latin America because of currency devaluations and political turmoil. Said an executive of another U.S.-based food company,

There's a long list of countries on the economic critical list, and another long list threatened with political upheaval. The risks you face as an investor are enormous.[21]

An international firm can protect itself against the adverse effects of nationalism and political instability. It can measure domestic instability (riots, government purges, excessive strikes), foreign conflict (diplomatic expulsions, military activity), the political climate (stability of political parties, manner of selecting government officials), and the economic climate (currency stability, economic strength, extent of government intervention) prior to entering a foreign market.[22]

Investments may also be protected through insurance. The U.S. government's Overseas Private Investment Corporation (OPIC) insures investments in friendly underdeveloped countries against such perils as war damage and inconvertibility of earnings. In addition, private underwriters insure foreign investments. See Figure 21-6.

Last, the risks of nationalism and political unrest can be reduced by taking foreign partners, borrowing money from foreign governments or banks, and/or utilizing one of various organizational modes such as licensing, contract manufacturing, and management contracting. These modes are discussed later in this chapter.

Tariffs, trade quotas, and local content laws are forms of trade restrictions.

Another aspect of the political and legal environment encompasses trade restrictions. The most common form of restriction is a *tariff,* which is a tax placed on imported goods by a foreign government. The second major restriction is a *trade quota,* which sets limits on the amounts of goods that can be imported into a country. The strictest form of trade quota is an *embargo,* which disallows entry of specified products into a country. The third major regulation involves *local content laws,* which require foreign-based manufacturers to establish local plants and use locally produced components; the goal of these laws is to promote domestic employment. These trade restrictions are illustrated in Figure 21-7.

Other nontariff barriers also restrict trade. For example, West German law

[21] Hymowitz, "Heinz Sets Out to Expand in Africa and Asia, Seeking New Markets, Sources of Materials."
[22] R. J. Rummel and David A. Heenan, "How Multinationals Analyze Political Risk," *Harvard Business Review,* Vol. 56 (January–February 1978), p. 71.

Figure 21-6
**Foreign Investments May
Be Protected by
Insurance**

Reprinted by permission

specifies that beer sold in that country must contain only barley malt, hops, and water:

Since brewers in France, Belgium, and the Netherlands, like those in the United States, now use other grains or additives, this means that not a single bottle of Kronenbourg, Stella Artois, or Heineken can be sent across the [German] Rhine.[23]

In many cases, economic barriers among nations have been reduced or eliminated through multilateral trade agreements and economic communities. In 1948 twenty-three nations, including the United States, accepted the idea of multilateral agreements by signing the ***General Agreement on Tariffs and Trade (GATT).*** The main contribution of GATT is the ***most-favored nation principle,***

**Trade agreements can
reduce or eliminate trade
barriers.** *GATT* intro-
duced the *most-favored
nation principle.*

[23] Robert Ball, "The Common Market's Failure," *Fortune* (November 14, 1983), p. 195.

Figure 21-7
Types of Trade Restrictions

Tariff—tax placed on imported goods

Trade Quota—quantity of imports limited by a country

Embargo—products not allowed into a country

Local Content Law—requires production in country where item is sold

which allows every nation covered by the agreement to obtain the best contract terms received by any single nation. GATT members agree to meet every two years and to negotiate for tariff reductions. By 1982, 88 nations representing more than 90 per cent of the total volume of international trade participated in GATT.

In November 1982, GATT member countries met in Geneva, Switzerland to try to overcome their differences due to nationalism, the worldwide recession, and trade barriers. A consensus was reached that free trade was desirable and needed to be promoted through more cooperation among countries. Despite this understanding, some trade tensions are expected to continue, as countries seek to protect their self-interests.[24]

Since its founding, GATT has allowed a few exceptions to the most-favored-nation principle. For example, regional trade associations or economic communities can be established by GATT members provided that such communities do not result in increased discrimination against other GATT members.

The ***European Community (EC)*** joins several countries in trade and other agreements.

The most important economic community is the ***European Community (EC),*** the Common Market. EC members are Belgium, Denmark, France, Great Britain, Greece, Ireland, Italy, Luxembourg, the Netherlands, and West Germany. Spain and Portugal were scheduled to join in 1984 or later. The Common Market

[24] See David B. Tinnin, "Trying to Restart the Engine," *Fortune* (November 29, 1982), pp. 52–56.

agreement calls for no tariffs among members and a uniform tariff with nonmember nations. In addition, the agreement encourages common standards for food additives, labeling requirements, and package sizes and a free flow of labor and capital. The combined GNP of Common Market members is about three quarters that of the United States. The combined population is roughly 120 per cent of the U.S. population. Although the European Community has been relatively beneficial for its members, there have been some problems in recent years. These problems center around the use of nontariff barriers to limit trade, customs restrictions, production and agricultural disagreements, budget contributions, and time wasted in getting goods through customs at a country's border.[25]

Other significant economic communities are the Latin American Integration Association, Central American Common Market, Council for Mutual Economic Assistance (made up of Eastern European countries), Andean Common Market, Asian Common Market, Caribbean Common Market, and Economic Community of West African States.

Technological Environment

Technological factors such as production and measurement systems influence international marketing. Foreign workers must frequently be trained to operate and maintain unfamiliar equipment. Problems occur if maintenance standards or practices vary by country or adverse production conditions exist, such as high humidity, extreme hot or cold weather, or air pollution. Furthermore, electrical power needs may vary by country and require modifications in products. For example, U.S. appliances work on 110 volts; in Europe, appliances work on 220 volts.

International marketing may require adjustments in production or measures.

Although the metric system has been adopted by most of the world, the United States, Borneo, Burma, Liberia, and South Yemen still use ounces, pounds, inches, and feet. At the present time the United States is in the process of converting to the metric system in order to be consistent with its major trading partners. General Motors, major tire manufacturers, all large soda and liquor bottlers, and other U.S. firms have recently converted or begun conversion to metric standards. As the United States converts to the metric system, the American market will have to be re-educated about measurement and learn the value of meters, liters, and other metric standards. This process will be a slow one.[26]

Developing an International Marketing Strategy

In the following subsections, the vital parts of an international marketing strategy are explored: company organization, the degree of standardization, and product, distribution, promotion, and price planning.

[25] Ball, "The Common Market's Failure," pp. 188–190 ff; Paul Lewis, "Common Market Showdown Today," *New York Times* (March 19, 1984), p. A3; and Thomas Kamm," EC Achieves Broad Accord on Farm Policy," *Wall Street Journal* (April 2, 1984), p. 34.

[26] See Philip M. Boffey, "Experts to Study Crawl Toward Metric System," *New York Times* (April 25, 1983), p. A10.

Company Organization

There are three international organizational formats from which a company may choose: exporting, joint venture, and direct ownership. They are compared in Figure 21-8.

Exporting **enables a domestic manufacturer to reach international markets without foreign production.**

With **exporting,** a company reaches international markets by selling directly through its own sales force or indirectly through foreign merchants or agents. In direct selling, the firm situates its sales force in a home office or foreign branch offices. This technique is prominent when customers are easy to locate or come to the seller. In indirect selling, the firm hires outside specialists to search out and contact customers. These specialists are based in the home or foreign country. Indirect selling is applied in situations where customers are hard to locate, the exporting company has limited resources, or local customs are unique.

An exporting structure requires minimal investment in foreign facilities. There is no foreign production by the firm. The exporter may modify its packages, labels, or catalogs at its domestic facilities in response to foreign market needs. Exporting represents the lowest level of commitment to international marketing. As an illustration, Paul Masson wines are made in California and exported to many European countries. Foreign wholesalers market the wines through grocery stores and wine shops.[27]

In a **joint venture,** the firm agrees to combine some aspect of its manufacturing or marketing efforts with those of a foreign company in order to share expertise, costs, and connections with important persons. For example, Philips, a large

[27] "Masson Leads Cal. Wines in Europe," *Advertising Age* (September 13, 1982), p. 26.

Figure 21-8
Alternative Company Organizations for International Marketing

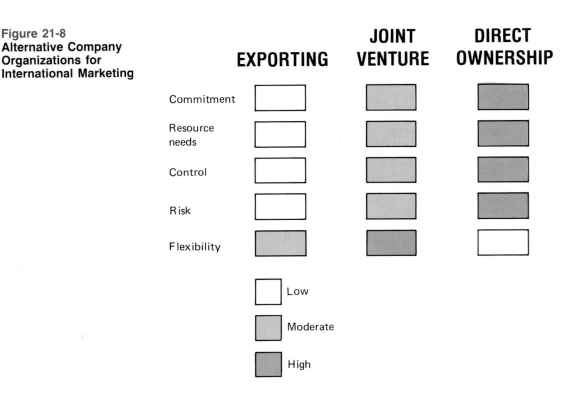

Netherlands-based manufacturer of electronics products, appliances, etc., has recently entered into a number of joint ventures. Philips is [28]

- Manufacturing a version of the Victor Company of Japan's VHS videocassette recorder in Europe.
- Marketing AT&T's digital telephone switching systems in Europe.
- A major owner of Grundig of West Germany, a leading electronics company. It also manages the firm.
- Cooperating with CIT-Alcatel of France to develop microwave transmission systems and other high-technology products.

A joint venture may also result in reduced costs and favorable trade terms from a foreign government if products are produced locally and foreign ownership is established. For example, the number of joint ventures between Japanese and U.S. companies is growing, because Japanese firms see them as reducing the possibility of U.S. trade restrictions (such as local content laws) and as a method of easing political tension. U.S. firms view these ventures as a means of establishing operations in the Japanese market and as a way to restrict the operations of potential competitors. [29]

A joint venture can take the form of licensing, contract manufacturing, management contracting, or joint ownership. Licensing gives a foreign firm the rights to a manufacturing process, trademark, patent, and/or trade secret in exchange for a commission, fee, or royalty. Coca Cola and PepsiCo license their products. Under contract manufacturing, the firm agrees to have a foreign company make its products locally. The firm markets the products itself and provides management expertise. This arrangement is common in book publishing.

In management contracting, the firm acts as a consultant to foreign companies. Many hotel chains, such as Hilton, engage in management contracting. With joint ownership, a firm agrees to manufacture and market products in partnership with a foreign company in order to reduce costs and spread risk. As an illustration, in February 1983, General Motors and Toyota announced plans to jointly operate a small-car plant in California, beginning in 1984. In some instances, a foreign government may require joint ownership with local businesses as a condition for entry. For example, in Canada, outsiders must use joint ownership arrangements with Canadian firms for new ventures.

Direct ownership involves the full undertaking and control of all international operations. The company owns production, marketing, and other facilities in foreign countries without any partners. In some cases international operations are organized into wholly owned subsidiaries. For example, Atari operates wholly owned subsidiaries for its video games in the United Kingdom, France, Germany, and the Netherlands. [30] The firm has all the benefits and risks associated with ownership. There are savings in labor, and marketing plans are more sensitive to local needs. Profit potential is high, although costs are also high. The possibility

> In a *joint venture*, a firm shares efforts with a foreign company. It can be based on licensing, contract manufacturing, management contracting, or joint ownership.

> *Direct ownership* involves total control of foreign operations and facilities by a firm.

---

[28] John Tagliabue, ''The New Philips' Strategy in Electronics,'' *New York Times* (January 15, 1984), Section 3, pp. 8–9.

[29] Ann Hughey and Masayoshi Kanabayashi, ''More U.S. and Japanese Companies Decide to Operate Joint Ventures,'' *Wall Street Journal* (May 10, 1983), p. 37.

[30] Howard Sharman, ''Atari's Pac-Man Gobbling Up Interest in U.K.,'' *Advertising Age* (June 7, 1982), p. 62.

of nationalistic acts is raised, and government restrictions are likely to be more stringent. This is the riskiest form of organization.

Frequently, companies combine organizational formats. For instance, a firm could use an exporting organization in a country that has a history of taking over the assets of foreign firms and a direct ownership organization in a country that provides tax advantages for plant construction. In the case of McDonald's, international expansion is carried out by opening company-operated stores (367 in 1982), franchisee-operated stores (493 in 1982), and affiliate-operated stores (481 in 1982). With affiliate-operated stores, the McDonald's Corporation usually owns 50 per cent or less of their assets; the rest are owned by resident nationals. Company stores are mostly in Canada, West Germany, and Australia; franchisee outlets are concentrated in Canada and Western European countries; and affiliate restaurants are common in Japan, Great Britain, and Hong Kong.[31]

Standardizing Plans

A firm engaged in international marketing activities must determine the degree to which its plans should be standardized. Both standardized and nonstandardized plans have benefits and limitations.

With a ***pure standardized approach,*** the company utilizes a common marketing plan for all countries in which it operates. There are usually marketing and production economies because product design, assembly, advertising, packaging, and other costs are spread over a large product base. A uniform image is presented, training of foreign personnel is reduced, and centralized control is applied. It works best when few foreign markets are involved and they are similar to the home country. However, this approach is not sensitive to individual market needs, and the input from foreign personnel is limited.[32] For example, Campbell tried to market its soups in Brazil in the same way that they were marketed in the U.S. This strategy failed, since Brazilians were used to dehydrated soup mixes or homemade soup. One critic commented on "The Campbell Syndrome":

> Campbell thought "All Brazilians have to eat my soups because they're the finest soups in the world and I'm the biggest soup manufacturer."

After selling "the wrong product too expensively" for three years, Campbell withdrew from the Brazilian market.[33]

A ***pure nonstandardized approach*** assumes that each market is different and requires a distinct marketing plan. This strategy is sensitive to local needs and provides opportunities for the development of foreign managers. Decentralized control is undertaken. It works best when distinctive major foreign markets are involved and/or the company has many product lines. For example, Massey-Ferguson is a Canadian-based manufacturer of farm and industrial equipment. It operates nine relatively autonomous subsidiaries in major foreign markets.[34] The pure nonstandardized approach can result in increased design and promotion costs, different company images throughout the world, and limited centralized direction.

Under a *pure standardized approach*, a common marketing plan is used in each country in which a firm operates. Under a *pure nonstandardized approach*, each country is given a separate marketing plan. A *mixed approach* is a combination strategy.

[31] *McDonald's Corporation 1982 Annual Report*, pp. 11–12.
[32] See William H. Davidson and Phillipe Haspeslagh, "Shaping a Global Product Organization," *Harvard Business Review*, Vol. 60 (July–August 1982), pp. 125–133.
[33] Laura Wentz, "How Big Advertisers Flopped in Brazil," *Advertising Age* (July 5, 1982), p. M-25.
[34] Cateora, *International Marketing*, p. 385.

Figure 21-9
Illustrations of
International Product
Planning

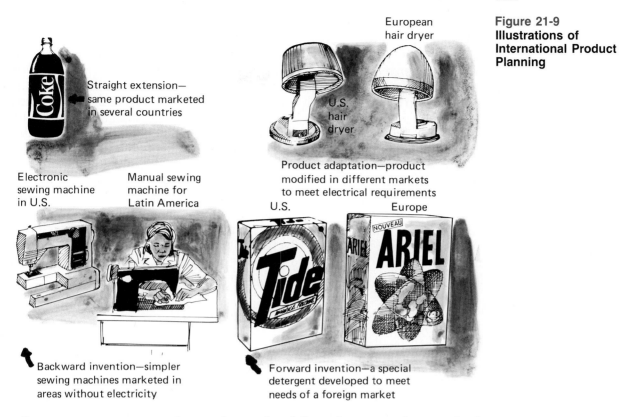

Straight extension—
same product marketed
in several countries

European
hair dryer

U.S.
hair
dryer

Product adaptation—product
modified in different markets
to meet electrical requirements

Electronic
sewing machine
in U.S.

Manual sewing
machine for
Latin America

U.S.

Europe

Backward invention—simpler
sewing machines marketed in
areas without electricity

Forward invention—a special
detergent developed to meet
needs of a foreign market

In recent years, more and more international firms have turned to a ***mixed approach*** for marketing planning. Under a mixed approach, a combination of standardized and nonstandardized efforts enable companies to maximize production efficiencies, maintain a consistent image, exercise home-office control, and yet be sensitive and responsive to local needs. As an illustration, at U.S. factories, 3M manufactures in semifinished or bulk form many of the products it markets internationally. It then ships these products to countries around the world, where production is completed and the goods are packaged and labeled according to the specific needs of the consumers in the particular country or region.[35]

When determining a marketing approach, a firm would evaluate whether differences among countries are sufficiently great to warrant changes in marketing plans, which elements of marketing can be standardized, whether the size of each foreign market will result in profitable adaptation, and if modifications can be made on a regional rather than a country basis.

Product Planning

International product planning can be based on straight extension, product adaptation, backward invention, and/or forward-invention strategies.[36] These strategies are illustrated in Figure 21-9.

---

[35] James A. Thwaits, "Global Marketing Success Is Contingent on a Solid Bank of Foreign Market Intelligence," *Marketing News* (December 23, 1983), p. 12.

[36] See Warren J. Keegan, "Multinational Product Planning: Strategic Alternatives," *Journal of Marketing*, Vol. 33 (January 1969), pp. 58–62.

Straight extension, product adaptation, backward invention, and *forward invention* are the basic methods of international product planning.

In a ***straight-extension*** strategy, the company manufactures the same products for domestic and foreign sales. The firm is confident that successful products can be sold abroad without any modifications in the product, its brand name, package design, or ingredients. It is a simple, straightforward approach, which allows costs to be minimized through economies of scale in production. However, it does not take into account differences in laws, customs, technology, and other factors. Soda companies, such as Coca-Cola and PepsiCo, use a straight-extension strategy; and "both successfully cross multitudes of national, regional, and ethnic taste buds trained to a variety of deeply ingrained local preferences of taste, flavor, consistency, effervescence, and aftertaste."[37] Beer companies also apply straight-extension strategies. In fact, imported beer often has a higher status than domestic beer.

With a ***product-adaptation*** strategy, domestic products are modified to meet taste preferences, foreign conditions, electrical requirements, water conditions, or legal regulations. This is a relatively simple way to plan products for international markets, because it is assumed that new products are not necessary and minor changes are sufficient. Product adaptation is the most frequently used strategy in international marketing.[38]

In some cases, a product's flavor is modified to satisfy local tastes, as occurred when Dunkin' Donuts opened a store in Brazil. While the store retained the classical shape of the donut, local fruit fillings (such as papaya and quava) were used.[39] A product-adaptation strategy is also appropriate for gasoline formulations, which must vary according to a country's weather conditions; detergent formulations, which must be changed to satisfy a country's water hardness; and electrical appliances, which are changed to accommodate voltage requirements. Sometimes adaptation is needed because a product's function differs by country. For example, a consumer lawn mower would be modified if it were to be used as a commercial mower in a foreign country.

With ***backward invention,*** the firm appeals to developing countries by making products that are less complex than the ones it sells in its domestic market. An example of backward invention is the sale of manual cash registers and nonelectric sewing machines in countries without widespread electricity. Singer markets nonelectric sewing machines in rural, foreign communities throughout the world (such as Iturbide, Mexico). This enables residents to create products that generate income and improve the local economy.[40]

In ***forward invention*** the company develops new products for its international markets. This plan is more risky and time-consuming and requires higher capital investments than the other strategies. It also provides the firm with profit potential and, in some situations, worldwide recognition for its beneficial practices. An illustration of forward invention is Procter & Gamble's development of Ariel laundry detergent, which is marketed in Europe where washload requirements differ from those in the U.S. In West Germany, the typical washload is presoaked

[37] Theodore Levitt, "The Globalization of Markets," *Harvard Business Review*, Vol. 61 (May–June 1983), pp. 92–102.
[38] See John S. Hill and Richard R. Still, "Adapting Products to LDC Tastes," *Harvard Business Review*, Vol. 62 (March–April 1984), pp. 92–101.
[39] Laurel Wentz, "New Doughnut Snack Has Brazilians Confused," *Advertising Age* (March 25, 1983), p. 54.
[40] *The Singer Company 1981 Annual Report*, p. 22.

at a temperature of 95 degrees for an hour and then washed at 140–200 degrees (U.S. machines operate at 95 degrees) in front-load machines holding only 3.5 gallons of water (U.S. machines hold 17 gallons of water). Ariel is the top-selling powder detergent in Europe.[41]

Distribution Planning

International distribution planning encompasses the selection of channel members and the physical movement of products. As noted earlier in this chapter, a firm may sell products directly through its own sales force or hire outside middlemen to complete transactions.[42] In the selection of a distribution channel, the company would examine traditional relationships, the availability of appropriate middlemen, differences in wholesaling and retailing patterns from those in the home country, government restrictions, and costs.

International distribution planning involves channel members, transportation, storage, and special arrangements.

For example,

Powerful Japanese trading companies *(sogo shosha)* stand ready to help U.S. exports enter the Japanese market. . . . They have enormous capabilities in international trade, in that they collect and process information, and organize business projects. However, *soga shosha* generally have dealt in bulk commodities; they only recently have started to emphasize consumer goods imports and now are organizing operations aimed at handling such goods, which normally involve small lot shipments of a great variety of merchandise.[43]

And in Europe, Nike (the athletic goods and sportswear marketer) had to adjust to a distribution system that centered on small, independently owned stores that carry little inventory.[44]

The physical distribution of products into international markets often requires special planning. The processing of marine insurance, government documents, and other papers may be time consuming, and transportation modes may be unavailable or inefficient. For example, a foreign country may have inadequate docking facilities, poor highways, or too few motor vehicles. Finally, distribution by ship is lengthy and subject to schedule delays.

Inventory management should take into account the value and availability of warehousing and the costs of shipping in small quantities. For example, Champion spark plugs had difficulties because it had to airfreight its products to Japan to service the Honda Motors account properly. At that time Champion had no facilities in Japan. The costs of shipping were several times the value of the spark plugs.[45] Champion now has warehouse facilities in Japan.

---

[41] Dennis Kneale, ''New Foreign Products Pour into U.S. in Increasing Numbers,'' *Wall Street Journal* (November 11, 1982), p. 22.

[42] For a discussion of how a small firm set up a strong network of overseas sales representatives, see Sara Delano, ''When in Rome,'' *Inc.* (September 1983), pp. 126 ff.

[43] Frank Meissner, ''Americans Must Practice the Marketing They Preach to Succeed in Japan's Mass Markets,'' *Marketing News* (October 17, 1980), Section 1, p. 5.

[44] ''Nike Pins Hope for Growth on Foreign Sales and Apparel,'' *New York Times* (March 24, 1983), p. D5.

[45] Kenneth H. Bacon, ''U.S. Auto-Parts Firms Face Tough Time in Japan Despite Tariff-Bar Removal,'' *Wall Street Journal* (December 9, 1980), p. 30.

Promotion Planning

Promotional campaigns can be standardized, mixed, or nonstandardized (as shown in Figure 21-10). For companies marketing in different European countries, some degree of standardization in promotion is usually important because of the overlap of readership and viewers in these nations. For instance, West German television broadcasts are received by about 40 percent of Dutch homes with televisions. The magazine *Paris Match* has substantial readership in Belgium, Switzerland, Luxembourg, Germany, Italy, and Holland.

There are also reasons for utilizing more nonstandardized promotion tools. Many countries have cultural differences that are not satisfied through a single promotion campaign. These differences include customs, language, the meaning of colors and symbols, and the level of literacy. Media may be unavailable or inappropriate. In a number of countries there are few televisions in operation, no advertising is permitted, or mailing lists are not current. Finally, national pride sometimes requires that individual promotions be used.

Tire and jeans manufacturers are among the firms using nonstandardized promotion. Tire advertisers emphasize safety in Britain, durability and mileage in the United States, and agile performance in Germany.[46] Wrangler markets its European jeans through three regional divisions: "Our strategy is not to have [one] European advertising campaign. By doing so there's a danger of losing specific appeal."[47]

Most companies combine standardized and nonstandardized tools into mixed promotion plans. For example, Exxon's "Put a Tiger in Your Tank" campaign has been widely used. The tiger represents an internationally recognized symbol of power. Avis Rent-A-Car has used its "We Try Harder" theme throughout Europe as well as the United States.[48] Both companies also create commercials and messages for individual foreign markets.

In 1981, total annual advertising expenditures in the noncommunist world exceeded $118 billion (about one half of it spent in the United States). Ten countries accounted for over 80 per cent of international expenditures. While overall per capita expenditures averaged $42, U.S. expenditures were over $260 per resident and many European countries averaged over $100 per resident. The lowest per capita expenditures were in Africa and Asia. They were ten cents per person in Ethiopia.[49]

Media habits vary by country. For example, 36 per cent of the French population watches less than one hour of television per week. Only 9 per cent of the U.S. population watches this little television. French residents subscribe to 2.4 magazines, while U.S. residents subscribe to 3.7.[50] Table 21-6 shows advertising expenditures by medium for eight countries.

[46] Kneale, "New Products Pour into U.S. Market in Increasing Numbers," p. 22.

[47] Anika Michalowska, "Jeans Stretch Across Europe," *Advertising Age* (April 12, 1982), p. M-3.

[48] Saul Sands, "Can You Standardize International Marketing Strategy?" *Journal of the Academy of Marketing Science*, Vol. 7 (Winter–Spring 1979), p. 130.

[49] "International Ad Spending: 1981 By Country," *Advertising Age* (June 20, 1983), p. 72.

[50] Robert T. Green and Eric Langeard, "A Cross-National Comparison of Consumer Habits and Innovator Characteristics," *Journal of Marketing*, Vol. 39 (July 1975), p. 39.

(a)

(b)

Figure 21-10
Approaches to Advertising in Foreign Countries

(a) Standardized—Jou Jou in Canada. This English language ad is used in many countries.

(b) Mixed—Dunkin' Donuts in Asia. This ad combines the Dunkin' Donuts English logo and slogan with Korean.

(c) Nonstandardized— Eastern Air Lines in Latin America. This ad was especially prepared for the Latin American market.
Reprinted by permission.

**Table 21-6
Comparison of Eight
Countries' Advertising
Expenditures by Medium,
1980 (in Per Cent)**

	Advertising Expenditures (Percentage)							
	United States	Brazil	Britain	France	Greece	Japan	Norway	West Germany
Cinema	NA	1	1	1	2	NA	2	1
Radio	7	20	2	6	5	5	*	3
Television	20	40	24	9	47	35	*	11
Print	38	31	61	39	45	37	78	65
All other (outdoor, direct, etc.)	35	8	12	45	1	23	20	20
Total	100	100	100	100	100	100	100	100

NA Statistics not available.
* Advertising prohibited.

Source: International Advertising Association

Price Planning

Major decisions in international price planning involve standardization, levels, currency, and sales terms. *Dumping* is disliked by host countries.

The basic considerations in international price planning are whether prices should be standardized, the level at which prices are set, the currency in which prices are quoted, and terms of sale.

Standardization of prices is difficult unless a firm operates within an economic community, such as the Common Market. Taxes, tariffs, and current exchange charges are among the added costs a company incurs when engaged in international marketing. As an example, in Japan, domestic beers are priced at about $.79 per can, while Budweiser is priced at $1.28 per can. The higher price is due to taxes and shipping costs.[51]

When setting a price level, a firm would consider local economic conditions such as per capita GNP. For this reason, many firms try to hold down prices in developing and less-developed countries by marketing simplified product versions or employing less-expensive local labor. On the other hand, prices in industrialized countries such as West Germany reflect product quality and the added charges of international marketing.

Some marketers set lower prices in foreign countries in order to dispose of outmoded products or remove excess supply from the home market and preserve the home market's price structure. In the latter case, dumping is involved. ***Dumping*** is defined as selling a product in a foreign country at a price lower than that prevailing in the exporter's home market, below the cost of production, or both. In the United States and other countries, duties may be levied on products that are dumped by foreign companies. In the steel industry, the Commerce Department monitors a trigger-price program in which imported steel prices are investigated automatically once they fall below minimum levels.

A third fundamental pricing decision relates to the currency in which prices are quoted. If a firm sets prices on the basis of its own nation's currency, the risk of a foreign currency devaluation is passed on to the buyer and better control is maintained. However, this strategy also has limitations. For example, consumers

---

[51] Jack Burton, "Japan Agrees: When You Say Bud, You've Said It All," *Advertising Age* (March 28, 1983), p. M-23.

may be confused or unable to convert the price into their currency, or a foreign government may insist that transactions be quoted and completed in its currency.

Finally, terms of sale need to be determined. This involves such judgments as what middlemen discounts are needed, when ownership is transferred, what form of payment will be required, how much time customers will have to pay bills, and what constitutes an appropriate refund policy.

Summary

International marketing involves the marketing of goods and services outside the organization's home country. Multinational marketing is a complex form of international marketing that engages an organization in marketing operations in many countries. For international companies to succeed in the 1980s, it is vital that they research and understand the similarities and differences among countries and adapt their strategies accordingly.

International marketing has developed for several reasons. Countries are interested in exchanging products with which they have comparative advantages for those with which they do not. Firms seek to minimize adverse economic conditions, attract growing markets, avoid intense domestic competition, extend the product life cycle, dispose of discontinued items, and utilize tax breaks.

The United States accounts for 10 per cent of the world's exports. Yet, more than 90 per cent of United States firms do not engage in international marketing. The United States also imports $270 billion in goods annually, causing a substantial trade deficit. Non-U.S. firms are rapidly increasing their role in international marketing.

International marketers work within several environments. The cultural environment includes the behavior standards, language, life-styles, and goals of a country's citizens. The economic environment incorporates a country's standard of living, GNP, stage of economic development, and stability of currency. The political and legal environment encompasses nationalism, trade restrictions, and trade agreements such as the European Community. The technological environment refers to a country's production and measurement systems. These environments create opportunities as well as problems and vary by country.

In the development of an international marketing strategy, the firm may emphasize exporting, engage in joint ventures, or directly own foreign subsidiaries. It may adopt a standardized, nonstandardized, or mixed approach to marketing.

Product planning would extend existing products into foreign markets, modify existing products to local needs, produce less sophisticated items for developing nations, or invent new products specifically for foreign markets. Distribution planning would investigate channel relationships and establish a formal network for direct sales or middlemen. In addition, physical distribution features would be analyzed and the proper modifications made. Promotion planning would stress standardized, mixed, or nonstandardized campaigns. Mixed strategies combine the best standardized and nonstandardized promotion tools. Price planning would outline whether prices should be standardized, the level at which prices are set, the currency in which prices are quoted, and terms of sale.

Questions for Discussion

1. Comment on this statement: "No longer can small or large American firms succeed by merely exporting to foreign markets products that have sold well in the United States."
2. Present three examples of the principle of comparative advantage.
3. Why has the U.S. had such large trade deficits? How can the annual deficit be reduced?
4. Evaluate this statement: "There is no such thing as a multinational market. We have domestic markets worldwide but no multinational markets. Each market is unique, unlike any other market, and therefore each is a domestic market."
5. What environmental factors might affect a U.S. company marketing televisions in Latin America?
6. Why do companies make culture-based marketing errors? How can these errors be avoided?
7. How can a country's GNP be a misleading indicator of marketing opportunities?
8. In Italy, there are 26 telephones per 100 people, compared with 69 per 100 per people in the U.S. What are the ramifications of this from a marketing perspective?
9. Develop a plan for limiting the negative consequences of nationalism.
10. What are the advantages and disadvantages of a country belonging to an economic community such as the Common Market?
11. Under what circumstances should a firm engage in exporting? A joint venture? Direct ownership?
12. Why do pure standardized plans sometimes fail?
13. Distinguish among straight extension, product adaptation, backward invention, and forward-invention product planning.
14. Develop a 10-question checklist by which a magazine publisher could determine its most effective overseas distribution system.
15. Provide a current example of an international ad that combines standardized and nonstandardized elements.

Case 1 Gillette: Marketing Razors in Europe*

The international division of the Gillette Company operates 31 factories in 22 countries overseas and accounts for well over one third of the firm's total sales. Gillette has had considerable experience in developing marketing strategies that fit European life-styles. The company carefully analyzes and plans everything from choosing a product's name to its promotional strategy, as the company has done with its Trac II razors.

---

* The data in this case are drawn from Jamie Talan, "Yankee Goods—and—Know-How Go Abroad," *Advertising Age* (May 17, 1982), pp. M-14 ff.

For the European market, Gillette decided on the brand name of G II for the razors known as Trac II in the U.S., after detailed research studies showed that in some Romance languages "trac" means fragile. Said a Gillette vice-president, "We wanted our target audience—men—to know that they could count on a good strong razor and not one that would easily break." Gillette verifies all brand translations for accuracy at the international division's London office.

In promoting the G II razor in Europe, Gillette has relied on print advertising, because many consumers do not have televisions. The promotion theme for G II features a sports analogy showing the importance of coordinating movements to reach a goal (in G II's case, the goal is a clean, close shave). The sports analogy is understood by Europeans and it is readily adaptable to print media. In all, Gillette has prepared more than 50 advertisements focusing on tennis players, boxers, and, of course, soccer players. These ads are adapted to individual cultures, pretested by market, and monitored for effectiveness.

The Trac II is promoted quite differently in the U.S., where television commercials are used extensively. The U.S. theme centers on the razor's construction. An animated sequence shows the first blade raising the whiskers on a man's face and the second blade shaving the whiskers closely.

While the G II razor has been quite popular in Europe, its success in other parts of the world, such as Latin America, the Middle East, and Africa, is more doubtful. Many consumers in these regions consider razors to be a luxury, and a number of countries restrict the import of razors by placing high tariffs or embargos on them.

Gillette is also facing difficulties in the marketing of some of its products in Europe. For example, it has been unable to stimulate demand for deodorants, because "the people of the European continent have a cultural resistance toward anything that impedes perspiration. They see it as unhealthy."

QUESTIONS

1. Describe the advantages and disadvantages of Gillette's mixed approach to the marketing of razors.
2. As a result of a sound marketing strategy, Gillette has done well in Europe with razors. Yet, Gillette has not succeeded with deodorants, despite careful planning. Explain this.
3. In the U.S., Gillette markets Daisy brand razors to women. What information should the firm acquire before marketing Daisy in Europe?
4. What are some of the problems Gillette may encounter when conducting marketing research in Europe?

Case 2 American Motors Corporation: A Joint Venture with China[†]

In 1983, American Motors Corporation (AMC) and the Chinese government signed a contract for a joint venture involving the production of a four-wheel-drive jeep-type vehicle. At that time, the four-wheel-drive vehicle being produced in

[†] The data in this case are drawn from Amanda Bennett, "Four Years of Tortuous Negotiations Led to AMC Jeep Venture with China," *Wall Street Journal* (May 6, 1983), p. 34; and Christopher S. Wren, "A.M.C. and China Sign Jeep Plan Pact," *New York Times* (May 6, 1983), p. D3.

China (called the "Jipu" in Chinese slang) was based on the design of the military jeep supplied to the Chinese by the Soviet Union during the 1950s.

According to the joint-venture agreement, the new vehicles will be manufactured in China for use in China and for export to other countries in the Far East. Although China's poorly developed road system offers probably the world's largest potential market for four-wheel-drive vehicles, the Chinese government plans to export 10,000 of the 40,000 vehicles that will eventually be produced each year.

Overall, the joint-venture contract took four years to negotiate. Interestingly, some major concepts, such as each party's investment (AMC is contributing $8 million in cash and $8 million in technology; China is contributing an automobile plant and cash valued at about $35 million) and target profit levels, were agreed upon relatively easily. However, there were difficulties in these areas which had to be resolved:

- Both AMC and the Chinese had limited awareness of the other's business practices. For example, the Chinese were unfamiliar with the process of adjusting parts prices to reflect the inflation rate.
- AMC was concerned about the value and stability of the currency in which its profits would be earned. It was finally agreed that a special fund would be set up from which AMC would draw its profits.
- The Chinese insisted that their managers be paid a salary similar to that of AMC managers working in China (about $45,000 per year). The Chinese managers are to receive only a fraction of this salary; the rest goes to the government.

The contract took so long to complete that negotiators on the AMC side remembered only one Chinese official who remained with the project from start to finish. In addition, AMC's chairman retired during negotiations and Renault (AMC's new partner) added its own representatives as talks dragged on.

QUESTIONS

1. What general principles can be learned from AMC's negotiations for a firm wanting to enter into a joint venture with China?
2. American Motors sold 314,000 vehicles in the U.S. during 1983. Why would it enter into such time-consuming negotiations (that required significant compromises) to reach an agreement regarding the "eventual" production of 40,000 vehicles per year?
3. What are the benefits of a joint venture versus other organizational forms to AMC?
4. Describe several potential problems that AMC could still encounter in this joint venture with China.

Chapter 22

Service and Nonprofit Marketing

1. To differentiate between the marketing of services and products
2. To describe the characteristics of services, their role in the U.S. economy, special considerations for service marketers, and applications of service marketing
3. To distinguish between nonprofit and profit-oriented marketing
4. To discuss the characteristics of nonprofit marketing, its role in the U.S. economy, and applications of nonprofit marketing

Generally, American homeowners are quite concerned about the appearance of their lawns. They want the lawns to be uniformly green and free of weeds and fungi. Lawn care can be undertaken by the homeowners themselves (who buy the proper chemicals and apply them), local lawn-maintenance services (who supply and apply chemicals and also mow lawns), and franchised lawn-care firms (who specialize in fertilization and weed/fungus prevention, but do not mow lawns).

Over the past decade, franchised lawn-care firms, such as Chem Lawn and Lawn Doctor, have grown rapidly. Annually, about $500 million is spent on residential lawn care. The popularity of these lawn-care firms is due to several factors. Reliability is provided through well-known and regularly promoted company names and money-back guarantees. Service applications and prices are standardized; prices are relatively low. Service is available in virtually all major residential areas in the U.S. Consistent quality is offered, since service representatives are thoroughly trained and

643

chemicals are constantly checked for effectiveness. Lawn-care information is given to customers in the form of brochures, checksheets, etc. Free reapplications are offered if customers are dissatisfied.

The leading lawn-care firm is Chem Lawn, which had sales of more than $200 million in 1983 (about 40 per cent of the residential lawn-care market). Chem Lawn services 1.2 million residential and commercial lawn-care customers, 80 per cent of which renew each year. This shows a very high level of customer satisfaction. See Figure 22-1.

In addition to its main lawn-care business, Chem Lawn has offered tree and shrub care since 1977. It is now considering adding new services such as pest control and carpet cleaning. Chem Lawn believes these services are consistent with those it already offers; they are neither overly complicated nor labor intensive, but they require some expertise. Like

Figure 22-1
Lawn Care Services from Chem Lawn

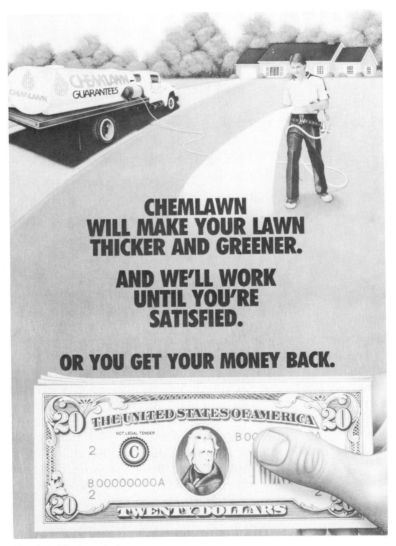

Reprinted by permission.

lawn care, pest control and carpet cleaning are repeat businesses, appeal to Chem Lawn's large base of existing residential and commercial customers, and rely on service operators as a sales force. As a Chem Lawn vice-president noted, "We don't have some people making all the promises and a bunch of others trying to live up to them."[1]

Chem Lawn is one of an expanding number of service firms which recognize the importance of marketing principles. These principles are equally applicable to nonprofit organizations.

Overview

This chapter examines the marketing of services as well as the marketing activities of nonprofit organizations. Service and nonprofit marketing are distinct and different from product- and profit-oriented marketing. These differences require separate chapter coverage of these areas.

There is a substantial interaction between service and nonprofit marketing, because many nonprofit organizations are involved with services. Examples are colleges and universities, health clinics, and libraries.

Service Marketing: Definition and Scope

As defined in Chapter 9, **service marketing** encompasses the rental of products, the alteration or repair of products owned by consumers, and personal services. According to a senior vice-president at Bankers Trust,

> People confuse services with products and with good manners. But a service is not a physical object and cannot be possessed. When we buy the use of a hotel room, we take nothing away with us but the experience of the night's stay. . . . Although a consultant's product may appear as a bound report, what the consumer bought was mental capability, not paper and ink.[2]

Generally, services have four characteristics that distinguish them from products: intangibility, perishability, inseparability from the service provider, and variability in quality. Table 22-1 contrasts these characteristics for services and products.

The **intangibility** of services means they often cannot be displayed, transported, stored, packaged, or inspected before buying. This occurs for repair services and personal services. The service operator can only describe the benefits

Service marketing **consists of personal services and the rental and repair of products.**

Intangibility, perishability, inseparability, **and** *variability* **differentiate service from product marketing.**

---

[1] Laura Saunders, "Snug as a Bug in a Rug?" *Forbes* (May 23, 1983), p. 64; and Gary Levin, "Chem Lawn Branches Out So Profits Grow," *Advertising Age* (June 4, 1984), pp. 4, 65.
[2] G. Lynn Shostack, "Designing Services That Deliver," *Harvard Business Review,* Vol. 62 (January–February 1984), p. 134.

Table 22-1
Basic Differences Between Services and Products

Services	Products
1. *Services are often intangible.* Services are acts, deeds, performances, efforts. Most services cannot be physically possessed. The value of a service is based on an experience; there is no transfer of title.	1. *Products are tangible.* Products are objects, things, materials. The value of a product is based on ownership; transfer of title takes place.
2. *Services are usually perishable.* Unused capacity cannot be stored or shifted from one time to another.	2. *Products can be stored.* Product surpluses in one period can be applied against product shortages in another period.
3. *Services are frequently inseparable.* One cannot separate the quality of many services from the service provider.	3. *Products can be graded or built to specifications.* The quality of a product can be differentiated from a channel member's quality.
4. *Services may vary in quality over time.* It is difficult to standardize some services because of their labor intensiveness and the involvement of the service user in diagnosing his or her service needs.	4. *Products can be standardized.* Mass production and quality control can be used.

that can be derived from the service experience.[3] The **perishability** of many services means they cannot be stored for future sale. Unused capacity cannot be shifted from one time to another. For example, if a house painter who needs eight hours to paint a single house is idle on Monday, he or she will not be able to paint two houses on Tuesday. Monday's idle time is just lost. The service supplier must try to regulate consumer usage so there is consistent demand throughout various periods.

Services are usually **inseparable** from the service provider. Customer contact is often considered an integral part of the service experience. For example, the quality of a car repair depends on the skill of the mechanic, and the quality of legal services depends on the skill of an attorney. Except for repair and maintenance services, there are usually no traditional physical distribution channels for services.[4] **Variability in quality** often occurs even if services are completed by the same operator. Variations may be due to the difficulty in diagnosing a problem (for repairs), the inability of the customer to verbalize his or her service needs, and the lack of standardization and mass production for most services.

The impact of these characteristics is greatest for personal services. They are more intangible, more perishable, more inseparable from the service provider, and have more quality variations than product-rental services or owned-goods services.

Although services have different characteristics from products, their sales are often connected. In service marketing, the service dominates the offering and the product augments it. For example, the major cost of a hair-cut service is the time of the operator, not the machinery used. Repair-service firms exist to install, modify, or fix all types of products from televisions to plumbing. Other independ-

[3] See Theodore Levitt, ''Marketing Intangible Products and Product Intangibles,'' *Harvard Business Review,* Vol. 59 (May–June 1981), pp. 96–102.

[4] Christopher H. Lovelock and John A. Quelch, ''Consumer Promotions in Service Marketing,'' *Business Horizons,* Vol. 26 (May–June 1983), p. 67.

ent service firms aid consumers in their purchases. These include credit card companies such as American Express and Visa and delivery firms such as United Parcel and Emery. In some instances, such as car rental and leasing, an alternative to product purchase is provided.

Service marketing can be examined in terms of a classification system, the extent of services in the economy, and the use of marketing by service firms.

Classification of Services

Figure 22-2 shows a detailed, seven-way classification system for services. Services are categorized by market, degree of tangibility, skill of the service provider, goal of the service provider, degree of regulation, labor intensiveness, and amount of customer contact. The classification system is a useful way of showing the diversity of service marketing.

In selecting a market, a firm should recognize that consumer and organizational segments have similarities as well as differences, as detailed in Chapter 7. The same basic service (for example, carpet cleaning, typewriter repair, lawn care, and air travel) may be offered to each market. Both markets use consumer decision making to select a service, although buying influences may be different. Each segment can counter high prices or poor service levels by performing some tasks themselves. The major differences between the segments are the reasons for the service, the quantity of service required, and the complexity of the service performed.

Services differ significantly in terms of their tangibility. In general, the less tangible the service, the less service marketing resembles product marketing. For nongoods services, performance can be judged only after the service is completed; and a consistent service level is difficult to maintain. Rentals and owned-goods services involve physical products and are more tangible than nongoods services; thus they may be marketed in a manner similar to products.

Services may be provided by persons of greatly varying skills. For services requiring high levels of skills, customers are quite selective in their choice of provider. That is why professionals often achieve customer loyalty. For services requiring low levels of skill, the range of acceptable substitutes is usually much greater.

Service marketing may be profit or nonprofit-oriented. Nonprofit-service marketing may be undertaken by government or private organizations. Nonprofit marketing is discussed in depth in the second part of this chapter.

Service marketing also varies by the extent of regulation. Some firms, such as insurance companies, are highly regulated. Others, such as caterers and house painters, are subject to limited regulation.

The traditional view of services has been that they are something performed by one individual for another. However, this view is too narrow. Services do differ in their labor intensity—for example, an automated versus a manual car wash or teller-oriented versus automated bank services. Labor intensity increases when highly skilled personnel are involved and/or services must be provided at the customer's home or place of business (as a result of the inability to transport heavy equipment and the amount of time necessary for travel, the basic service, and follow up). Some labor-intensive services may be performed by do-it-yourself consumers—for example, home repair.

Services are classified on the basis of market, tangibility, skill, goals, regulation, labor intensiveness, and customer contact.

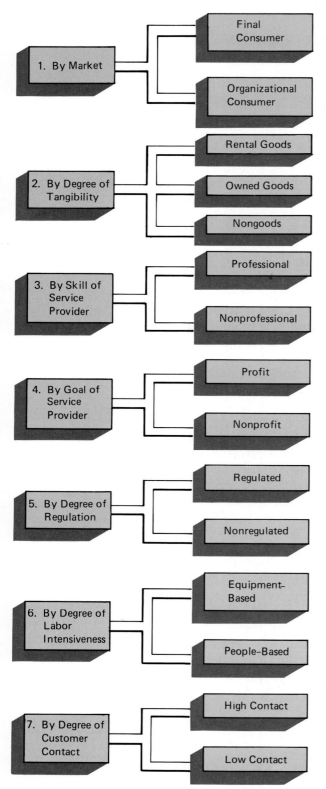

Examples

Tutoring, taxi, car wash, life insurance

Management consulting, machinery repair, accounting services, legal services

Car rental, boat rental, hotel room rental, tool rental

Television repair, watch repair, plumbing repair

College education, tutoring, legal services

Legal services, medical services, accounting services, management consulting

Taxi, uniformed security, janitorial, shoe shining

United Parcel Service, insurance firms, executive recruiting, airlines

U.S. Postal Service, universities, libraries, museums

Mass transit, hospitals, insurance firms, utilities

Computer time sharing, catering, lawn care, house painting

Automated car wash, computer time sharing, dry cleaning, air travel

Executive recruiting, tennis instruction, accounting, uniform security

Universities, large appliance repair, air travel, hotels

Lawn care, motion picture entertainment, janitorial service, automated car wash

Figure 22-2
A Classification System for Services

Last, service marketing can be classified by the degree of customer contact. When customer contact is high, training personnel in interpersonal skills is essential. This is in addition to the technical training needed to properly perform a service. Many service providers mistakenly ignore interpersonal training. They must realize that appliance repairpeople, car mechanics, and other service personnel also function as salespeople and complaint handlers. They may be the only contact a consumer has with the firm. When customer contact is low, technical skills are most essential.

It is important to note that an organization would normally be classified on the basis of a combination of the factors listed in Figure 22-2. For example, a firm that tutors students for college-board exams appeals to final consumers, offers an intangible service, requires skill by the service provider, is profit-oriented, is not regulated, employs many trainers, and has high customer contact. A company can operate in more than one part of a category. For example, an accountant may deal with both final and organizational consumer markets.

Extent of Services in the Economy

The United States has been described as the leading service economy in the world. In the private sector two thirds of the labor force is now employed in a service capacity. During 1960, the typical family spent 40 per cent of its budget on services. By 1982, the figure was just under 50 per cent. Over this period, annual service expenditures rose from $131 billion to almost $1 trillion. Housing, medical care, and household operations account for almost 70 per cent of consumer service spending.[5]

> The average American family spends almost half of its budget on services.

Various reasons have been cited for the growth of final consumer-related services, such as the increased prosperity of the population, complex products requiring specialized installation and repair, and the leisure orientation of U.S. society.

In the industrial sector the original value of equipment being leased accounts for 20 per cent of all capital goods in the U.S. As purchase prices have risen, leasing has become more attractive. Among the types of equipment that can be leased are communication satellites, supertankers, oil rigs, and computers.[6]

Despite these sizable figures, the data on services are underestimated. They do not include the **hidden service sector** that encompasses the systems planning, preinstallation support, software, repair, maintenance, delivery, collection, and bookkeeping of firms that emphasize product sales. For example, although Caterpillar Tractor and John Deere are classified as manufacturing companies, many of their employees are involved in dealer- and user-training programs, product servicing, parts delivery, and warranty repairs.[7]

> The *hidden service sector* includes services offered by product-oriented firms.

The following illustrations show the scope of service marketing:

- The Department of Health and Human Services predicts a surplus of 70,000 doctors by 1990. As a result, physicians are beginning to learn marketing skills.

---

[5] Bureau of Economic Analysis, U.S. Commerce Department, 1983.
[6] Paul F. Anderson, ''Industrial Leasing Offers Economic and Competitive Edge,'' *Marketing News* (April 4, 1980), p. 20; and American Association of Equipment Lessors, ''Leasing Means Business,'' *Fortune* (December 31, 1983), pp. 34–52.
[7] Milind M. Lele and Uday S. Karmarkar, ''Good Product Support Is Smart Marketing,'' *Harvard Business Review*, Vol. 61 (November–December 1983), pp. 124–125.

Many of them attend seminars, employ marketing consultants, analyze census data when opening offices, mail medical columns to patients and prospective patients, offer extended office hours, and send thank-you notes after payments are received. While most doctors are opposed to advertising, attitudes are slowly changing. Said one young physician, "Word of mouth isn't adequate in these times. If you've got an advantage, you ought to let people know."[8]

- Stanley Works (a large toolmaker) owns and operates Taylor Rental Corporation, a chain of 562 stores that rents tools and equipment. U-Haul and Winnebago have a joint venture that rents mobile homes. Gran-Tree Corporation runs 80 furniture rental showrooms in eight Western and Southwestern states as well as in Canada; its sales are $70 million per year.[9]
- In order to train consumers in how to use their new computers, hundreds of service firms are entering the market. They provide seminars, classroom instruction, and on-site company courses. The role of training in computer literacy is significant. As one potential customer said, "I would love to buy a personal computer for my business if I weren't so intimidated by it and someone could show me how to use it." Between 1983 and 1986, it is expected that $3 billion will be spent on computer training.[10]
- Eastern Cruise Lines specializes in 3- and 4-day Caribbean cruises between Miami and the Bahamas. In 1983, it carried over 71,000 passengers. The average age of its passengers is 35; and they are drawn mostly from the Southern U.S. The company's Emerald Seas ship features large cabins that accommodate two full-fare passengers and two free passengers. Cruise fares range from $265 to $755. Eastern spends $2 million annually on newspaper advertising. After decades of complacency, cruise line firms (such as Eastern) are aggressively involved in marketing: "These days, we're in combat."[11]
- Citibank offers a broad assortment of banking services for final and business consumers. Citibank makes extensive use of advertising, has implemented a huge automatic teller system, and is an innovator in services (such as money market funds for small investors). Recently, Citibank introduced a segmentation strategy aimed at wealthy consumers, emphasizing convenience and personal service.[12] See Figure 22-3.

Use of Marketing by Service Firms

The lower use of marketing is due to an emphasis on technical expertise, small size, limited competition, and negative attitudes toward marketing.

Service firms have typically lagged behind manufacturing firms in developing and using marketing. This is explained by several factors. One, many service firms stress technical expertise. Often, these firms were started because of specialized skills, such as repairing plumbing systems, preparing food, or having knowledge of the law. Two, most service firms are so small that marketing specialists cannot be used. Three, strict licensing provisions sometimes limit

[8] Susan Tompor, "Doctors Turn to Marketing to Get Patients," *Wall Street Journal* (September 1, 1981), p. 33; and Laurel Sorenson, "Hospitals and Doctors Compete for Patients, With Rising Bitterness," *Wall Street Journal* (July 19, 1983), pp. 1, 12.

[9] Jeff Blyskal, "An Expensive Way to Borrow," *Forbes* (July 18, 1983), pp. 126–127.

[10] "Training: A Built-In Market Worth Billions," *Business Week* (November 1, 1982), pp. 84–85.

[11] Lori Kessler, "A Cruise Line Docks at the Isle of Marketing," *Advertising Age* (January 9, 1984), pp. M-30–M-31.

[12] Jeremy Main, "How Banks Lure the Rich," *Fortune* (November 1, 1982), pp. 60–64.

Figure 22-3
A Citibank Appeal to Upscale Consumers

A WORD TO THE WEALTHY.

HAVING ONE'S CAKE AND EATING IT TOO IS LARGELY A MATTER OF PROPERLY MANAGING THE ENTREPRENEUR'S COMPLETE CYCLE OF WEALTH. FROM ITS CREATION, TO ITS INVESTMENT, TO ITS CONSERVATION FOR ONE'S ESTATE.

© 1982 Citibank, N.A., Member FDIC

CITIBANK
PRIVATE BANKING & INVESTMENT

Reprinted by permission.

competition and the need for marketing. Four, consumers have held a variety of service professionals, particularly doctors and lawyers, in such high esteem that marketing has not been needed. Five, in the past a number of associations prohibited advertising by their members. This was changed by Supreme Court rulings in the late 1970s that permitted advertising by professionals. Finally, there are still a number of service professionals who have a dislike for marketing, lack a full understanding of it, or question the use of marketing practices, such as advertising, in their fields.

Over the next several years, it is expected that the use of marketing by service firms will increase dramatically, as a result of deregulation in many industries (such as banking, transportation, and communication), growing competition among service providers (such as dental services in retail stores versus traditional dentists), the recent growth in the do-it-yourself market segment due to the rising costs of services, and the expanding number of service professionals with formal business training.

Applying Marketing to Services

The first part of this section assesses some of the special considerations in applying marketing to services. The second part contains illustrations of service marketing in three different areas: hotels, car repair and servicing, and legal services.

Special Considerations for Service Marketers

Services cannot be stored for later sale; therefore, demand must be carefully matched with supply.

The marketing of services involves a variety of special considerations, several of which are discussed in this subsection.[13] Generally, services cannot be stockpiled. For example, if a movie theater has 500 seats, it cannot admit more than 500 customers to a Saturday night showing even though a Wednesday matinee had 400 empty seats. It is clear that the empty seats during a Wednesday movie cannot be used to increase theater capacity during the Saturday peak demand period. In order to match demand with supply, a service firm must alter the timing of demand and/or exert better control over the supply of the service offering. It should avoid excess demand that goes unsatisfied as well as excess capacity that results in an unproductive use of resources. Following are a number of methods for matching demand with supply:[14]

Balance the timing of demand by
- Adding attractive services in off-peak periods, such as a hotel providing convention-meeting rooms at reduced prices.
- Utilizing a reservation system to spread out demand.
- Employing price discrimination, with lower prices for off-peak periods.
- Providing customers with peripheral services while they are waiting, such as a cocktail lounge in a restaurant.

Balance supply by
- Using part-time employees at peak periods.
- Training employees in different skills so they can be shifted to whatever task has the greatest demand at any point in time, thus avoiding a bottleneck.
- Increasing consumer participation in the completion of services, such as self-service buffets and direct dialing for long-distance calls.

---

[13] For a good overview of service planning, see J. Patrick Kelley and William R. George, "Strategic Management Issues for the Retailing of Services," *Journal of Retailing*, Vol. 58 (Summer 1982), pp. 26–43.

[14] W. Earl Sasser, "Match Supply and Demand in Service Industries," *Harvard Business Review*, Vol. 54 (November–December 1976), pp. 133–140.

Sharing capacity with other service providers, such as hospitals sharing expensive, but seldom-used, diagnostic equipment.

For some services, only a small portion of the service mix is visible to the consumer. As an example, in-store repairs are normally not seen by consumers. Although the repairperson may spend three hours on a television and insert two parts priced at $6, the consumer sees a bill for $37 and does not realize the amount of service involved. Therefore, service time and functions must be explained to customers.

The intangibility of services makes pricing difficult. For example, should an automobile mechanic set a price for the repair of a transmission on the basis of a standardized price list or place a value on his or her time and set a specific price after the transmission is repaired? How should the price be broken down into problem analysis and service components? Should prices vary among repairs performed by the head mechanic and regular mechanics? In setting routine prices, what is covered in the basic service? Services that are equipment-based and routine in nature may be suited to cost-oriented pricing. Other services should rely on competitive pricing.[15]

The intangibility of services also makes promotion difficult. Unlike product promotion, which may stress tangible attributes and consumer analysis prior to a purchase, much service promotion must rely on performance attributes, which can be measured only after a purchase is made. There are three fundamental ways to promote a service:[16]

- Develop a tangible representation of the service. For example, a credit card, although not a financial service itself, still serves as a physical product with its own image and benefits.
- Associate the intangible service with a tangible object more easily perceived by the customer.
  For example: "You're in good *hands* with Allstate."
  "I've got a piece of the *rock*."
  "Under the Traveler's *umbrella*."
  "The Nationwide *blanket* of protection."
- Focus on the relationship between the seller of the service and the user of the service and away from the intangible itself. Sell the competence, skill, and concern of the agent or service employee to develop a client relationship.

As noted earlier, the existence of a close service provider-consumer relationship makes employee interpersonal skills important. The workforce must be trained to interact well with consumers and be consistent in responses. Employee appearance and mannerisms have a much greater impact on service firms than on product firms. All employee-customer contacts should be performed properly, including sales, credit, delivery, and repair. This was confirmed in a study of 521 retail and organizational salespeople which found that more personal involve-

Consumers see only a small portion of the service mix for some services.

The intangibility of services makes pricing and promotion decisions more complex.

Interpersonal skills are important due to the relationship between consumer and service provider.

[15] Dan R. E. Thomas, "Strategy's Different in Service Businesses," *Harvard Business Review,* Vol. 56 (July–August 1978), p. 163.

[16] James H. Donnelly, Jr., "Use Three Methods to Help Market Intangible Service," *Marketing News* (October 19, 1979), p. 5.

ment, personal contact, and customer input are required in selling services than are needed to sell goods.[17]

Many services have high costs and low reliability. One solution to this problem is the **industrialization of services** using hard, soft, and hybrid technologies.[18] **Hard technologies** substitute machinery for people, such as the implementation of an electronic credit authorization system instead of manual credit checks. Hard technologies cannot be applied to services requiring extensive personal skill and contact such as medical, legal, and hairstyling services.

The industrialization of services can involve hard technologies, soft technologies, or hybrid technologies.

Soft technologies substitute preplanned systems for individual services. For example, many travel agents sell prepackaged vacation tours. This standardizes transportation, accommodations, food, and sightseeing. **Hybrid technologies** combine hard and soft technologies. Examples include computer-based truck routing and specialized low-priced repair facilities, such as muffler repair shops. Figure 22-4 presents examples of hard, soft, and hybrid technologies.

In greater numbers, service firms are now recognizing the value of industrializing their offerings. New technology investment reached nearly $47 billion in 1982, up from $19.1 billion (adjusted for inflation) in 1975. As an illustration, Merrill Lynch (the financial services company) spent $100 million on computers and their installation between 1979 and 1983 in order to better coordinate the efforts of its 438 branch offices. Today, Merrill Lynch headquarters can send information about financial planning and stock offerings directly to its 10,200 account executives throughout the U.S. via computer terminals.[19]

Service reliability can also be improved by setting higher-level standards and by tying employee pay, promotions, and retention to performance levels. As an example, American Airlines developed a series of standards that enabled the company to become the preferred domestic airline, according to one Airline Passengers Association survey:[20]

- Reservation phones must be answered within 20 seconds.
- 85 per cent of passengers should not have to stand in line more than 5 minutes.
- Flights must take off within 5 minutes of scheduled departure time.
- Cabins must have their proper supply of magazines.
- 85 per cent of flights should land within 15 minutes of scheduled arrival time.
- Doors are to be opened 70 seconds after the plane stops rolling.
- The last baggage should reach the terminal not more than 17 minutes after passengers begin to disembark from the plane.

Peripheral services add to the basic offering and can create a competitive advantage.

Peripheral services are complementary services that are needed to supplement the basic service offering. For example, while a tourist hotel markets rooms for travelers, it will also need an adequate reservation system, cleaning personnel, parking facilities, recreation facilities, restaurants, and connections to transportation terminals. Peripheral services increase a service firm's investment, require additional employee and management skills, and may be time consuming. However, they may also enable the company to create and sustain a competitive advantage.

[17] William R. George and J. Patrick Kelly, ''The Promotion and Selling of Services,'' *Business*, Vol. 33 (July–August–September 1983), pp. 14–20.

[18] Theodore Levitt, ''The Industrialization of Services,'' *Harvard Business Review*, Vol. 54 (July–August 1976), pp. 63–74.

[19] ''A Productivity Revolution in the Service Sector,'' *Business Week* (September 5, 1983), p. 108.

[20] Jeremy Main, ''Toward Service Without a Snarl,'' *Fortune* (March 23, 1981), p. 61.

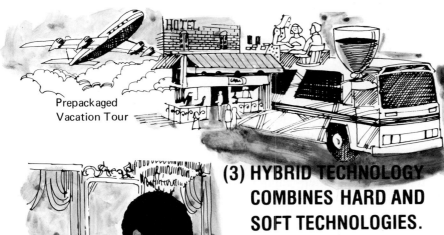

Figure 22-4
Industrializing Services

(1) HARD TECHNOLOGY SUBSTITUTES MACHINERY FOR PEOPLE.

Computerized Credit Authorization System

(2) SOFT TECHNOLOGY SUBSTITUTES PREPLANNED SYSTEMS FOR INDIVIDUAL SERVICES.

Prepackaged Vacation Tour

(3) HYBRID TECHNOLOGY COMBINES HARD AND SOFT TECHNOLOGIES.

Computer-Based Hotel Reservation System

Illustrations of Service Marketing

This subsection examines service marketing for hotels, car repairs and servicing, and legal services. These three examples represent a rented-goods service, an owned-goods service, and a nongoods service. They differ by degree of tangibility, skill of service provider, degree of labor intensiveness, and level of customer contact.

Hotels may appeal to one or more consumer segments from among business travelers, through tourists (who stay one night), regular tourists (who stay two or more nights), and conventioneers. Each segment would require different services. The business traveler seeks efficient service, a desk in the room, and convenient meeting rooms. The through tourist seeks a convenient location, low prices, and fast-food service. The regular tourist seeks a nice room, recreational facilities, and connections for sightseeing. Conventioneers seek large meeting rooms, pre-planned sightseeing, and hospitality suites.[21]

To attract and retain customers, hotels have been adding new services and improving their marketing efforts. First-run movies that can be viewed in the room, an indoor health spa, and casino gambling (where legal) are some of the services being added. Marketing efforts involve more television advertising, the use of well-conceived slogans, such as Holiday Inn's "no excuses guarantee," and greater personal attention for consumers.[22]

Hotels are also trying to resolve consumer complaints more effectively. For example, frequent business travelers are most concerned about overbooking—even those with guaranteed reservations could get turned away; long waiting lines; late check-in times; and unresponsive or discourteous staffs. In addition, female business travelers are concerned about personal safety and are reluctant to eat alone in restaurants. Some of these complaints have been caused by elements over which hotels have control, such as inadequate or poorly trained staff. Others are uncontrollable, such as guests overstaying their reservations.[23]

Hotels are responding in several ways. Many offer express checkouts, whereby bills are mailed to guests' businesses or homes. Some hotels place women traveling alone on certain floors and patrol those floors more frequently. A number of hotels are increasing the lighting in lobbies so that women will be more comfortable. Also, questionnaires are used to measure consumer satisfaction with hotel performance. Figure 22-5 shows a Hyatt Hotels computerized terminal.

Automobile repairs and servicing are carried out through two basic formats: manufacturer-owned or sponsored dealerships or independent service centers. Annually, more than $75 billion is spent on auto repairs, about one third through manufacturer dealerships and two thirds through independents. About 50 per cent of new-car buyers buy service contracts, priced from $200 to $800 per year, from manufacturer dealerships.[24]

For example, General Motors cars can be repaired and serviced through the company's "Mr. Goodwrench" program, which is available at approved dealerships. To qualify for the Mr. Goodwrench program, dealers must satisfy a number of specific quality standards. General Motors supports this program by providing

[21] See "Hyatt Hotels: Putting out the Welcome Mat for a Broader Clientele," *Business Week* (October 31, 1983), pp. 68, 70; "Days Inns: Looking for a Berth in a Crowded National Field," *Business Week* (October 31, 1983), pp. 70–72; and Scott Hume, "Segmentation Holds Key to Hotel Battle," *Advertising Age* (October 17, 1983), p. 50.

[22] Susan Spillman, "Movie Outlets Checking into Hotel Market," *Advertising Age* (August 16, 1982), p. 50; "Hilton Hotels: Ready to Grow Again After Years of Caution," *Business Week* (July 5, 1982), pp. 91–92; Daniel F. Cuff, "Wake-Up Call at Quality Inns," *New York Times* (September 13, 1981), Section 3, p. 8; Holiday Inn advertisements; and Sanford L. Jacobs, "Hotel Chain Exploits Its Size to Compete with Big Rivals," *Wall Street Journal* (January 9, 1984), p. 21.

[23] "As Hotel Rates Climb, Service Keeps Falling, Many Travelers Gripe," *Wall Street Journal* (June 9, 1980), pp. 1, 26 and "Women Travelers Find Safety and Harassment Can Be Major Problems," *Wall Street Journal* (March 5, 1980), pp. 1, 32.

[24] Phil Mintz, "Auto Repair Is No Longer the Domain of the Gas Station," *Newsday* (April 18, 1983), Business section, p. 3; and Roger Rowand, "Keeping the Marketing Securely Covered," *Advertising Age* (June 6, 1983), pp. M-38–M-39.

Figure 22-5
A Self-Service Computer Terminal at Hyatt Hotels
With Hyatt Hotel's computerized terminal, travelers are able to check-in and check-out in about 90 seconds. Bills are processed by inserting a major credit card; receipts are provided through short computer printouts.

Reprinted by permission.

mass advertising, supervising the dealers, and improving service techniques.[25] General Motors cars can also be repaired and serviced through independent repair shops; tire, muffler, and battery outlets; mass merchandisers (such as Sears); and service stations. The independents handle a wide variety of makes and models. They emphasize a convenient location, personalized service, more flexible prices, faster service time, and longer hours.

The growth in foreign car sales and the increased period of time that consumers hold on to their cars have resulted in more independent servicing of automobiles. Some firms specialize in foreign car work because of higher profit margins. Others accept imports only grudgingly, because of difficulties with getting parts, the metric system, and the relatively small working space under the hood.

Long waiting lists at car dealers and relatively high prices have also shifted many car owners from dealer service centers to independent firms. In an attempt to gain this business back, many manufacturers have urged their dealers to accept credit cards, promote specials, stress quality control, extend service hours, and provide more accurate repair estimates. They advertise their repair and maintenance services extensively.

In 1977 the Supreme Court ruled that attorneys could not be prohibited from advertising their services and fee structures.[26] Since then, the advertising of legal services has increased significantly and a number of marketing innovations have been implemented. Lawyers now advertise on television and radio and in newspapers and magazines.

[25] Gregory D. Upah, "Mass Marketing in Service Retailing: A Review and Synthesis of Major Methods," *Journal of Retailing,* Vol. 56 (Fall 1980) pp. 73–75.
[26] Today all professionals are able to advertise their services.

Law clinics and franchised law firms have developed. These operations feature a large staff of attorneys, convenient locations (such as in shopping centers), standardized fees and services (such as $100 for a simple will), plain fixtures and furniture, and word-processing systems. The companies concentrate on routine legal services.

One leading law chain is Hyatt Legal Services, a division of H&R Block. Hyatt:[27]

- Operates offices in 17 states and the District of Columbia. It plans to expand to 400–500 offices by 1988 (up from 117 in 1983).
- Offers the services of over 250 attorneys.
- Has a base of several thousand clients, adding 15,000 new clients each month.
- Has very low prices (e.g., $275 for a divorce compared with $750 to $1,500 for traditional competitors).
- Spends more than $2 million per year on television advertising.
- Sets fees in advance and in writing.
- Pays new lawyers $17,000 annually.
- Shares administrative services and office space with H&R Block outlets.
- Provides prepaid legal services to workers in several labor unions.

The marketing of legal services has been met with resistance and objections from many attorneys. They criticize price advertising for stressing price at the expense of quality and mass-marketing techniques as eliminating personalized counseling. They also believe the public's confidence in the profession will decline, information in ads may not be accurate, and overly high consumer expectations will be created. Attorneys applying marketing techniques state that they are making legal services available to new groups of consumers and those who could not otherwise afford them.[28] The majority of attorneys still do not advertise; they rely on referrals.

Nonprofit Marketing: Definition and Scope

Nonprofit marketing serves the public interest and does not seek profits.

As defined in Chapter 7, **nonprofit marketing** is conducted by organizations that operate in the public interest or to foster a cause and do not seek financial profits. It may involve organizations (religious groups, labor unions, trade associations), people (political candidates), places (resorts, convention centers, industrial sites), and ideas (''stop smoking''), as well as products and services. Although nonprofit organizations conduct exchanges, they are not necessarily in the form of dollars for goods and services. Politicians request votes in exchange for promises of

---

[27] Tamar Lewin, ''Chain of Legal Clinics Is No. 1,'' *New York Times* (May 9, 1983), pp. D1, D10.

[28] For perspectives on both sides of the issue of legal advertising, see Robert F. Dyer and Terence A. Shimp, ''Reactions to Legal Advertising,'' *Journal of Advertising Research,* Vol. 20 (April 1980), pp. 43–51; Larry T. Patterson and Robert A. Swerdlow, ''Should Lawyers Advertise? A Study of Consumer Attitudes,'' *Journal of the Academy of Marketing Science,* Vol. 10 (Summer 1982), pp. 314–326; ''Lawyers Ease ABA Ad Code,'' *Advertising Age* (August 8, 1983), p. 14; ''A Bigger Peek Inside the Top Law Firms,'' *Business Week* (October 24, 1983), p. 156; and Richard Greene, ''Lawyers Versus the Marketplace,'' *Forbes* (January 16, 1984), pp. 73–77.

better and more effective government services. The Postal Service wants increased use of zip codes in exchange for improved service and lower rate hikes. The American Cancer Society seeks funds for cancer research and treatment programs.

In many cases the prices charged by nonprofit organizations have no relationship to the cost or value of services. For example, the Girl Scouts of America sells cookies to raise funds, but only part of the purchase price goes for the cookies. On the other hand, the price of a chest X ray at a local health clinic may be below its cost or even free.

Nonprofit marketing can be examined in terms of a comparison with profit-oriented marketing, a classification system, and its extent in the economy. Three examples of nonprofit marketing are examined in depth: the U.S. Postal Service, colleges and universities, and public libraries.

Nonprofit Versus Profit-Oriented Marketing

It is important to recognize that there are a number of significant similarities between nonprofit and profit-oriented marketing, as well as many differences. And, in today's uncertain and competitive environment, it is becoming increasingly necessary for nonprofit organizations to learn and apply appropriate marketing concepts.[29]

Nonprofit marketing has both similarities with and distinctions from profit-oriented marketing.

Both nonprofit and profit-oriented marketing offer products/services to consumers; consumers typically can choose among the offerings of competing organizations; the benefits provided by competing organizations differ; various consumers may have distinctive reasons for their product/service choices; and consumers experience either satisfaction or dissatisfaction with product/service performance.[30]

The manager of research for the Direct Marketing Association (DMA), a large nonprofit trade association, stated:

Running an association is just like running a commercial business; members are the customers, services are the products, and dues are the prices put on the services.[31]

The DMA is interested in determining the needs of member firms, developing appropriate new services, and improving the value of the association to members, the perceptions of members, and the awareness of the services it does provide. These goals are similar to those of profit-oriented marketers.

There are also a number of basic marketing differences between nonprofit and profit-oriented organizations. These differences are outlined in Table 22-2 and described in the following paragraphs.

[29] See Christopher H. Lovelock and Charles B. Weinberg, "Public and Nonprofit Marketing Comes of Age," *Review of Marketing 1978* (Chicago: American Marketing Association, 1978), pp. 413–452; Alan R. Andreasen, "Nonprofits: Check Your Attention to Customers," *Harvard Business Review,* Vol. 60 (May–June 1982), pp. 105–110; Edward Skloot, "Should Not-for-Profits Go for Business?" *Harvard Business Review,* Vol. 61 (January–February 1983), pp. 20–26; Robert E. Gruber and Mary Mohr, "Strategic Management for Multiprogram Nonprofit Organizations," *California Management Review,* Vol. 24 (Spring 1982), pp. 15–22; and Christopher H. Lovelock and Charles B. Weinberg, "Retailing Strategies for Public and Nonprofit Organizations," *Journal of Retailing,* Vol. 59 (Fall 1983), pp. 93–115.

[30] Bruce I. Newman, "Political Candidates Can Use Marketing Research Tools to Build Comprehensive Campaign Strategy," *Marketing News* (May 13, 1983), Section 2, p. 14.

[31] Glenda Shasho, "Method May Vary, But Goals Don't When 'Nonprofits' Conduct Research," *Marketing News* (May 13, 1983), Section 2, p. 24.

**Table 22-2
Basic Differences
Between Nonprofit and
Profit-Oriented Marketing**

Nonprofit Marketing	Profit-Oriented Marketing
1. Nonprofit marketing is concerned with organizations, people, places, and ideas, as well as products and services.	1. Profit-oriented marketing is largely concerned with goods and services.
2. Exchanges can be in the form of votes in return for better government or the use of a zip code in return for improved service and lower rate increases.	2. Exchanges are generally in the form of dollars for goods and services.
3. Objectives are more complex because success or failure cannot be measured strictly in financial terms.	3. Objectives are generally stated in terms of sales, profits, and recovery of cash.
4. The benefits of nonprofit services are often not related to consumer payments.	4. The benefits of profit-oriented marketing are usually related to consumer payments.
5. Nonprofit organizations may be expected or required to serve economically unfeasible market segments.	5. Profit-oriented marketing seeks to serve only those market segments that are profitable.
6. Nonprofit organizations typically have two constituencies: clients and donors.	6. Profit-oriented marketing has one constituency: clients.

Nonprofit marketing often relies on fundraising efforts.

Nonprofit marketing may not generate revenues in day-to-day exchanges. Instead it may rely on infrequent fund-raising efforts. In addition, a successful marketing campaign may actually lose money if services or products are provided at less than cost. It is necessary for operating budgets to be large enough to serve the number of anticipated clients, so that none is poorly treated or turned away.

Objectives are not necessarily financial.

Objectives for nonprofit organizations are sometimes complex, because success or failure cannot be measured strictly in financial terms. There is also less accountability, because there are no owners. A nonprofit organization might have this combination of objectives: raise $300,000 from government grants, increase client usage, find a cure for a disease, change public attitudes, and raise $500,000 from private donors. Objectives must include the number of clients to be served, the amount of service to be rendered, and the quality of service to be provided.

Nonprofit marketing is broad in scope and is frequently involved with *social marketing*.

Nonprofit marketing includes organizations, people, places, and ideas, as well as products and services. It is much more likely to promote social programs and ideas than is profit-oriented marketing. Examples include recycling, highway safety, family planning, gun control, and energy conservation. The use of marketing to increase the acceptability of social ideas is referred to as ***social marketing***.[32] Table 22-3 contains illustrations of the exchange process for organizations, people, places, and ideas.

While the general public supports nonprofit organizations, benefits may be distributed unequally.

The benefits of nonprofit organizations are often not distributed on the basis of consumer payments. Only a small portion of the population contracts a disease, requires humanitarian services, visits a museum, uses a public library, or goes to a health clinic in a given year; yet, the general public pays to find cures, support fellow citizens, or otherwise assist nonprofit organizations. In many cases the group that would benefit most from a nonprofit organization's activities may be the one least prone to seek or use them. This occurs for libraries, health clinics,

[32] See Paul N. Bloom and William D. Novelli, "Problems and Challenges in Social Marketing," *Journal of Marketing*, Vol. 45 (Spring 1981), pp. 79–88.

Exchange Process		
Organizations		
College fraternities	Benefits to members: social experience, convenient place to live, assistance from upper classmen and graduates	Benefits to fraternities: membership dues, greater on-campus exposure, improved facilities
People		
Political candidates	Benefits to voters: efficient government, better services, election of candidates with similar views	Benefits to candidates: election, prestige, power
Places		
Major cities as sites for conventions	Benefits to attendees: central locations, cultural facilities, superior accommodations and transportation	Benefits to cities: revenues, prestige, lessening of tax burdens for residents
Ideas		
Nonsmoking campaigns	Benefits to smokers: improved health, better self-image, increased social acceptance	Benefits to nonsmokers: cleaner environment, longer life span for loved ones, lower costs for medical system

**Table 22-3
Illustrations of Exchange Process for Organizations, People, Places, and Ideas**

remedial programs, and other nonprofit organizations and activities. With profit organizations, benefits are usually distributed equitably, based on consumers' direct payments in exchange for products or services.

Nonprofit organizations often serve markets that are uneconomical.

Nonprofit organizations are frequently expected, or even required, to serve market segments that a profit-oriented organization would find uneconomical. For example, the U.S. Postal Service must maintain rural post offices and Amtrak must provide passenger rail service on routes across sparsely populated areas. This may give profit-oriented firms an advantage, because they can concentrate their efforts on the most lucrative market segments.

Nonprofit organizations have two primary constituencies: *clients* and *donors*.

While profit-oriented firms have one primary constituency to which they offer goods and services and from which they receive payment, the typical nonprofit organization has two constituencies: *clients*—for whom it provides membership, elected officials, locations, ideas, products, and services—and *donors*—from whom it receives resources (which may be time from volunteers or money from foundations and individuals). Often, there is little overlap between clients and donors.

Private nonprofit organizations have also been granted a number of legal advantages over their profit-oriented counterparts. These include tax-deductible contributions, exemptions from most sales and real-estate taxes, and special reduced postal rates.

Classification of Nonprofit Marketing

Nonprofit marketing may be classified on the basis of tangibility, organization structure, objectives, and constituency. This four-way classification is shown in Figure 22-6. As in the service-marketing classification, a nonprofit organization

EXAMPLES

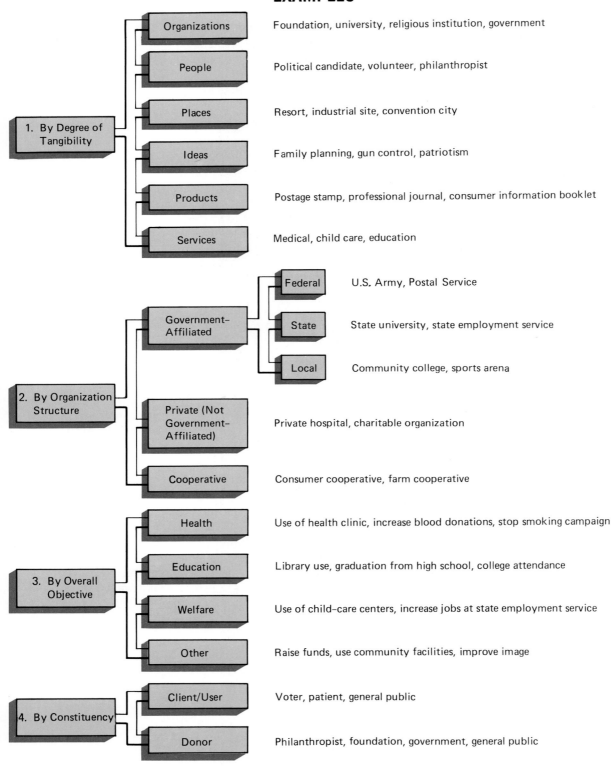

	EXAMPLES
Organizations	Foundation, university, religious institution, government
People	Political candidate, volunteer, philanthropist
Places	Resort, industrial site, convention city
Ideas	Family planning, gun control, patriotism
Products	Postage stamp, professional journal, consumer information booklet
Services	Medical, child care, education

1. By Degree of Tangibility

2. By Organization Structure

Government-Affiliated		
Federal	U.S. Army, Postal Service
State	State university, state employment service
Local	Community college, sports arena

| Private (Not Government-Affiliated) | Private hospital, charitable organization |
| Cooperative | Consumer cooperative, farm cooperative |

3. By Overall Objective

Health	Use of health clinic, increase blood donations, stop smoking campaign
Education	Library use, graduation from high school, college attendance
Welfare	Use of child-care centers, increase jobs at state employment service
Other	Raise funds, use community facilities, improve image

4. By Constituency

| Client/User | Voter, patient, general public |
| Donor | Philanthropist, foundation, government, general public |

Figure 22-6
A Classification System for Nonprofit Marketing

would be categorized by a combination of these factors. For example, postage stamps for collectors are tangible products, distributed by the federal government, intended to reduce the yearly deficit of the Postal Service, and aimed at a market segment of the general public.

As noted previously, nonprofit marketing may involve organizations, people, places, ideas, products, and services. For example, organizations include foundations, universities, religious institutions, and government; people include politicians and volunteers; places include resorts and industrial centers; ideas include family planning and patriotism; products include postage stamps and professional journals; and services include medical care, child care, and education.

Nonprofit organizations may have one of three alternate structures: government (federal, state, local), private, or cooperative. For example, the federal government markets military service to potential recruits, postal services, and other products and services. State governments market universities and employment services. Local governments market colleges, libraries, and sports arenas. In addition, government marketing is often used to increase voter registration, secure approval of bonds, and obtain passage of school and library budgets. Private organizations market hospitals, charities, social services, and other products and services. They also use marketing to increase membership and donations. Cooperative organizations aid people such as consumers and farmers. The success of cooperatives depends on their ability to attract and maintain a large membership base and on their efficiency in performing distribution functions.

Overall nonprofit marketing objectives can be divided into health (increase the number of nonsmokers), education (increase usage of the local library), welfare (list more job openings at a state employment office), and other components (increase membership in the Boy Scouts).

Last, nonprofit organizations must remember that they usually require the support of two distinct constituencies: clients/users and donors. Clients/users are interested in the direct benefits they obtain from participation in an organization, such as their improved health, education, or welfare. Donors are concerned about efficiency of operations, success rates, availability of products and services, and recognition of their contributions. For each constituency, the organization must correctly pinpoint its target market. As an example, the League of Women Voters might concentrate on unregistered voters during an enrollment drive, and seek funds from corporate foundations. Figure 22-7 shows some of the differing interests between clients and donors.

> The classification of nonprofit marketing is based on tangibility, organization structure, objectives, and constituency.

Extent of Nonprofit Marketing in the Economy

Thousands of nonprofit organizations operate in the United States, and their use of marketing varies widely, as these examples show:

> Nonprofit organizations are diverse in their focus and use of marketing.

- During 1982–1983, the Public Broadcasting Service (PBS) engaged in a nine-city test that allowed advertising during the programs of seven television stations. Until that time, corporate sponsors (who contribute $35 million to PBS each year) were only identified before and after programs. The PBS experiment generated $3 million in added revenues: ''The bottom line is that public television's future is in jeopardy, and one way or another we may have to accept advertising.'' As a result of the test, a federal commission recommended in late

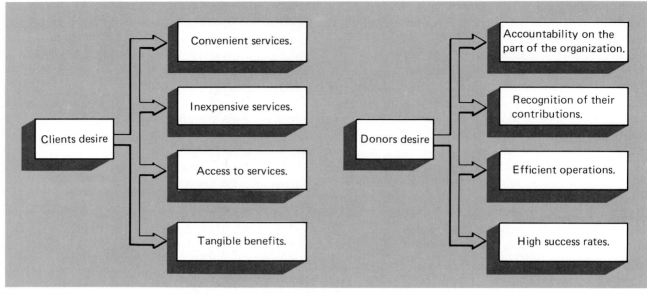

Figure 22-7
Clients Versus Donors

1983 that brand names, slogans, and brief institutional ads be allowed during programs.[33]

● The American Association of the Red Cross was founded in 1881. Throughout its existence, the Red Cross has actively promoted its humanitarian goals. In World War I, it produced 2,000 parades and advertised in many media to raise funds. In World War II, movie and Broadway stars made announcements and appearances. In 1982–1983, The Red Cross used a sophisticated television, radio, newspaper, and magazine ad campaign. It received free advertising space valued at more than $35 million during 1982–1983.[34]

● In 1982, the U.S. government spent about $206 million for national advertising, making it the twenty-ninth largest advertiser in the country.[35] The federal government spent more on advertising than firms such as Gillette, General Electric, Revlon, and American Express. The largest federal expenditures were for military recruitment, the Postal Service, and Amtrak. See Figure 22-8.

● In 1976, visitors to New York State spent $5.2 billion on tourism. As a result of the popular "I Love New York" campaign, this figure rose to $10.5 billion in 1981. Resort occupancy rose by nearly 70 per cent, while Broadway ticket sales doubled during this time. The campaign ran on television and radio and in print media, and featured celebrities and New York landmarks.[36] New York was the first state to promote itself so aggressively. Others have now followed.

● In 1982, the winning candidate in an election for the U.S. Senate spent an average of $1.7 million; the winning candidate in a House of Representatives election spent an average of $214,000. Overall, $314 million was expended on congressional races in 1982 (up 37 per cent from 1980). A large amount of these funds went for television and direct-mail advertising. It was estimated

---

[33] "PBS May Get a Few More Words from Its Sponsors," *Business Week* (October 10, 1983), pp. 70–71.
[34] Jamie Talan, "Getting a Message of Help Across," *Advertising Age* (August 2, 1982), p. M-29.
[35] "U.S. Government," *Advertising Age* (September 8, 1983), p. 153.
[36] Rob Howe, "Luring 'Em with Brass and Class," *Marketing & Media Decisions* (Spring 1982, Special Edition), pp. 189–200.

that more than $1 billion would be spent on advertising by state, congressional, and presidential candidates in 1984 election campaigns.[37]

A conservative estimate would place the total annual advertising expenditures of nonprofit organizations at over $10 billion. This estimate does not include the costs of marketing research such as political polling, point-of-sale displays, and sales personnel, nor the value of volunteers and free advertising.

Illustrations of Nonprofit Marketing

This subsection examines nonprofit marketing for the Postal Service, colleges and universities, and public libraries. The activities of these organizations differ because of their degree of tangibility, structure, objectives, and constituency.

[37] Adam Clymer, "Campaign Costs Soar as Median Spending for Senate Seat Hits $1.7 Million," *New York Times* (April 3, 1983), p. 20; and Stuart Emmrich, "Political Ad Spending to Top $1 Billion Record," *Advertising Age* (December 5, 1983), p. 1.

The Postal Reorganization Act of 1970 created the U.S. Postal Service as an independent agency and called on it to become a self-supporting enterprise. Previously, it was a government agency with no mandate to improve its marketing efforts. While postage increases have occurred with some regularity since 1970, the agency has made significant progress. For fiscal 1982, the Postal Service earned a surplus of $800 million; in the past, it consistently reported deficits.[38]

New services have been developed and established services have been expanded. For example, Express Mail delivers packages and letters to distant cities overnight; these items can be dropped at specially designated collection boxes (thus eliminating waiting lines). Self-service stamp vending machines are available in shopping centers. A commemorative stamp program was started in 1975; annual sales now exceed $170 million. Many post offices sell inexpensive hand-held scales, padded envelopes for small packages, airmail markers, and a device for adhering stamps to envelopes.[39]

The Postal Service had an advertising budget of $20 million in 1982, with a large portion of this going to Express Mail, direct mail ads for business accounts, and commemorative stamps. Young & Rubicam was used as an advertising agency. Despite these efforts, the Postal Service faces strong competition from a number of express delivery firms and others (such as Western Union).[40] Figure 22-9 shows a recent Postal Service ad.

Colleges and universities are aware that the years of rapid growth in overall enrollments are over. Between 1980 and 1985, the annual number of high school graduates was expected to decline by almost 20 per cent. In the Northeast, it is forecast that there will be 30 per cent fewer high school graduates in the year 2000 than in 1981. Accordingly, new markets are being sought and marketing is being used more aggressively.[41]

Many schools are actively seeking the adult market. The National Center for Educational Statistics estimates that about 20 million adults are now involved in some types of higher education program at colleges, universities, and private companies. The adult market requires class times that do not infringe on work commitments and convenient locations (at work, at a neighborhood library, in a business district).

Traditional students are also being actively pursued. In 1973 public institutions spent $113 per new student on admissions. This figure more than doubled by 1982. Annually, over 1,000 schools purchase direct-mailing lists of prospective students from the Educational Testing Service (the organization that administers college-board examinations); the number of schools purchasing lists in 1971 was only 125.

The expansion of marketing in higher education is not confined to poor- or

[38] Jayne A. Pearl, "Good News Department," *Forbes* (August 1, 1983), p. 33.

[39] Richard L. Gordon, "USPS Sees Stamp Sales Booming," *Advertising Age* (April 4, 1983), p. 71.

[40] Fred Gardener, "Squeeze of Federal Ad Budgets," *Marketing & Media Decisions* (January 1982), pp. 62–63ff; and "U.S. Government."

[41] Bruce Allen and William H. Peters, "College Presidents Are Receptive to Strategic Planning Techniques," *Marketing News* (October 15, 1982), p. 9; William M. Bulkeley, "'Baby Bust' Enrollment Drop Seen Having an Uneven Effect," *Wall Street Journal* (December 14, 1982), p. 33; D.C. Denison, "Selling College in a Buyer's Market," *New York Times Magazine* (April 10, 1983), pp. 48–50ff.; Bruce H. Allen and William H. Peters, "The Status of Strategic Marketing in Higher Education: College Presidents' Viewpoints" in Patrick E. Murphy et al. (Editors), *1983 AMA Educators Proceedings* (Chicago: American Marketing Association, 1983), pp. 354–359; and Eugene Carlson, "High School Student Falloff Worries College Presidents," *Wall Street Journal* (February 28, 1984), p. 35.

Figure 22-9
**Marketing the Postal
Service**

average-quality institutions. For example, Barnard College in New York has spent more than $100,000 for mailings, posters, and an 18-minute slide presentation. The campaign has helped draw more applications.

In 1982, the Higher Education Research Institute of the University of California at Los Angeles conducted a nationwide survey of 1,600 students at four-year colleges and universities. Overall, the Institute found that two thirds of the students would definitely or probably enroll at the same school if they were starting college again. More specifically, students expressed their greatest satisfaction with courses in the major, the quality of instruction, extracurricular activities, library resources, science classes, and interaction with professors. Their greatest dissatisfaction was with career advising, academic advising, and job-placement services.[42]

This is a crucial period for public libraries. About three quarters of U.S. adults

[42] Beverly T. Watkins, "Students Like Classes, Dislike Campus Services," *Chronicle of Higher Education* (July 27, 1983).

visit a public library one or fewer times during a typical year. Juvenile use in many public libraries has declined by 50 per cent or more over the past 12 to 15 years.[43] Also, demographic trends are not favorable for long-run increases in the library's market, because libraries have been most successful with children (a declining proportion of the population).

To satisfy donors (the local communities that fund them) and respond to the changing composition of the market, many public libraries are becoming more marketing-oriented. Some are turning into multimedia centers, where even tools, toys, and videogames can be borrowed. Others are changing into community centers, by providing meeting rooms for neighborhood groups. Still other libraries are appealing to markets they have served poorly in the past by implementing literacy programs, offering specialized collections for minority groups, accommodating disabled persons, and reaching out to senior citizens.[44] Table 22-4 contains examples of innovative marketing programs for attracting people to public libraries.

More public libraries are beginning to utilize strategic marketing planning. For example, they are using clear consumer-oriented mission statements, such as: to promote increased awareness, acceptance, and use of public libraries; to secure and maintain adequate funding; and to provide the materials which are wanted by the most people in the service area. They also use marketing research during the planning process and regularly conduct satisfaction studies.[45]

Summary

Service marketing involves product rental, product alteration and repair, and personal services. In general, services are less tangible, more perishable, less separable from their provider, and more variable in quality than products that are sold. Service and product marketing may be interconnected.

Services can be categorized by market, degree of tangibility, skill of the service provider, goal of the service provider, degree of regulation, labor intensiveness, and amount of customer contact. An organization would be classified on the basis of a combination of these factors.

The United States is the leading service economy in the world, with two thirds of the American private labor force employed in services. United States families

[43] "Americans Read and Use Libraries: Says Gallup," *Library Journal* (December 15, 1978), p. 2466; and Lowell A. Martin, "The Public Library: Middle-Age Crisis or Old Age?" *Library Journal* (January 1, 1983), pp. 17–22.

[44] Ibid; "Oklahoma Reaches Out to Minorities with Rotating Ethnic Collections," *Library Journal* (June 1, 1983), pp. 1084–1085; "North York Library Uses Apple II to Develop Literacy Program," *Library Journal* (April 15, 1983), p. 786; and "Brooklyn's SAGE Program: Providing Library Service to *All* the Elderly," *Library Journal* (March 15, 1983), p. 556.

[45] Mary Jo Detweiler, "Planning—More Than Process," *Library Journal* (January 1, 1983), pp. 23–27; and George D'Elia and Sandra Walsh, "User Satisfaction with Library Service—A Measure of Public Library Performance," *Library Quarterly*, Vol. 53 (April 1983), pp. 109–133.

I. General Population
Piano and organ practice room
Calisthenics
Swap discount coupon room
Lend-out reproduction of sculptures
Tax return help by accounting students
Drive-in book pick-up station
Home delivery of books
Extension of library hours
Operation of a year-round store for used books

II. Children
Lend a guinea pig (for a week)
Use of children's advisory council to help run juvenile section
Lend-out toys
Dial library for a 3-minute recorded story
Karate instruction
Bicycle-safety programs
Guitar sessions in library rooms

III. Other Populations
Special programs for bicultural constituents
Tool lending for artisans
Instruction in "survival English"
Improvement of staff expertise in dealing with inner-city residents
Handling requests for transportation for physically handicapped persons
Bookmobile service to hospitals, nursing homes, and institutions
Exercise programs for senior citizens

Source: Adapted from Barry Berman and Joel R. Evans, "The Marketing Audit: A New Tool for Public Libraries," *LJ Special Report 18*. Reprinted from *Library Journal Special Report,* March 15, 1981. Published by R. R. Bowker Co. (a Xerox company), copyright © 1981 by Xerox Corporation.

spend almost 50 per cent of their income on services. Twenty per cent of all industrial capital goods are leased.

Service firms have lagged behind manufacturing firms in the use of marketing because of technical emphasis, small size, less competition, the lack of a need for marketing, past prohibitions on advertising, and a dislike of marketing by some service professionals. Special considerations in service marketing are an inability to stockpile, lack of visibility of effort, difficulties in pricing and promotion, importance of customer relations, the cost/reliability mix, and peripheral services.

Nonprofit marketing is conducted by organizations that operate in the public interest or to foster a cause and do not seek financial profits. It may involve organizations, people, places, ideas, products, and services. Exchanges do not have to involve money, and objectives can be difficult to formulate. Benefits are often distributed unequally, and economically unfeasible market segments may be served. Two constituencies must be satisfied: clients and donors.

Nonprofit marketing can be classified on the basis of tangibility, organization structure, objectives, and constituency. In 1982, the U.S. government spent about $206 million for national advertising. Total advertising for nonprofit institutions is estimated at over $10 billion per year.

Questions for Discussion

1. What are the pros and cons of Chem Lawn entering the pest-control and carpet-cleaning businesses?
2. Explain the statement: "Although a consultant's product may appear as a bound report, what the consumer bought was mental capability, not paper and ink."
3. Why are services usually more intangible than products? How can services be made more tangible?
4. Why does variability in quality often occur even if services are completed by the same service operator?
5. Classify a tutoring service and a computer-repair firm using the seven factors shown in Figure 22-2.
6. What impact will the do-it-yourself market have on the hidden service sector?
7. Why have service firms lagged behind manufacturers in the development and use of marketing?
8. Present three ways a beauty salon can match demand and supply on days following holidays.
9. Show how a fast-food franchise can use hard and soft technologies to industrialize its services.
10. What peripheral services are needed for an indoor tennis center?
11. What are some of the similarities in the marketing efforts of nonprofit and profit-oriented organizations?
12. Present five objectives that could be used to evaluate the effectiveness of a state employment office.
13. Differentiate between the clients and donors of a local hospital. What are the goals and potential conflicts between the two?
14. Classify the Boy Scouts of America and the Smithsonian Institution using the four factors shown in Figure 22-6.
15. Present five innovative programs for your state's tourist office to utilize.

Case 1 Firestone: Marketing the MasterCare Service Program*

During the 1980s, the annual sales in the automobile service industry have increased to $75 billion, because consumers are keeping their cars for longer periods. Today, the average car on U.S. roads is about seven years old.

Despite its image as a tire manufacturer, Firestone is the second largest auto service company in the U.S., behind Sears. Firestone operates approximately 12,000 service bays in 1,500 outlets. Sears has 12,800 service bays in 850 outlets. However, Sears has 25 million active credit-card households (through its department stores), versus 2 million for Firestone.

In 1984, Firestone planned to introduce its new MasterCare service program

---

* The data in this case are drawn from "Firestone Tries the Service Business Again," *Business Week* (June 20, 1983), pp. 70–71.

and convert each of its 1,500 service centers to MasterCare centers. The Master-Care program is based upon these concepts:

- Customers will be given guarantees which are valid at all centers.
- A computer, called MasterMind, will analyze a car's performance level in 8 to 12 minutes.
- After repairs are made, the center's manager will call each customer who has spent more than $100 to determine if he/she is satisfied. Cars will be repaired again if necessary. A toll-free emergency number will also be made available to customers.
- Private-label shock absorbers and mufflers will be stocked to enable Firestone centers better to compete with mass merchants and specialty muffler shops.
- Firestone purchased 300 auto service centers from J. C. Penney, which decided it would no longer service cars or sell car accessories.

Firestone recognizes that the success of its MasterCare program will not come easily. First, many of its dealers feel that the $25,000 price for the Master-Mind computer is too high. To remedy this, Firestone has agreed to lease the computer to dealers for $600 per month on a five-year basis. Second, Firestone uses its own training centers for mechanics. As a result, these mechanics are not certified by the National Institute for Automotive Service Excellence (as competitors' mechanics are). Third, several oil companies are beginning to place greater emphasis on repair guarantee programs, computer analysis of car problems, and specialized tune-up centers. Amoco, Shell, and Arco are among the large oil firms stepping up their service efforts.

QUESTIONS
1. How does the marketing of auto repair services differ from the marketing of tires?
2. What are the key factors consumers consider in the selection of an auto service center? How well does Firestone's MasterCare program address these factors?
3. Evaluate Firestone's use of private-label shock absorbers and muffler systems.
4. Identify and describe the characteristics of each of the types of competitors Firestone faces in the auto service industry. What is Firestone's differential advantage in each instance?

Case 2 Marketing: No Longer a Dirty Word for Museums[†]

According to Sandra Horrocks, manager of public relations for the Philadelphia Museum of Art, "Marketing is no longer a dirty word. We use it freely." Until recently, this was a far different view from that held by most people associated with museums. Instead, they believed that museums were "treasure houses of culture that should not be sullied with crass sales techniques."

What has caused the change in attitude toward marketing? There are several

[†] The data in this case are drawn from Alan Rosenthal, ''Museums Jump into the Marketing Game,'' *Advertising Age* (September 27, 1982), pp. M-2–M-3; and Sandra Salmans, ''Holiday Sales Thriving at Met Museum,'' *New York Times* (December 19, 1983), p. C11.

reasons. New museum professionals have had more formal training in marketing and are more interested in it. The value of marketing in communicating with the public and with donors is now recognized. Museum directors realize that their target markets must be broadened. Operating and other costs have increased rapidly, while traditional funding from government, foundations, corporations, and individuals has leveled off (for example, cuts in federal programs are expected to amount to $27 million between 1982 and 1986). There is rising competition from other leisure-time activities, such as amusement parks, sporting events, and home gardening.

A number of museums have become quite aggressive in their marketing approaches, as these illustrations show:

- The Metropolitan Museum of Art in New York has a museum store that generates annual sales of about $30 million and profits of $2.5 million. The store operates in the Metropolitan Museum and has "branch" outlets in the New York Public Library, Macy's Herald Square, and Macy's in Ventura, Florida. The museum receives a royalty on branch-store sales.
- The Philadelphia Museum of Art has a five-year marketing plan intended to raise attendance and persuade the public that the museum is a fun place to visit.
- The Boston Museum of Fine Arts (known as "the old gray lady on Huntington Avenue") uses marketing surveys, advertises widely, has a publicity program, and sponsors special events.
- The Henry Ford Museum and Greenfield Village in Dearborn, Michigan has a department of marketing and public relations. In addition to its regular advertising program, the museum has sales exhibitions at shopping malls and hotel lobbies, promotes food sales on museum grounds, and offers products in museum shops and through a mail-order catalog. In 1981, $60,000 was spent on television advertising.
- The Children's Museum of Denver generates 95 per cent of its revenues from publications, traveling exhibits, special promotions, admissions, and memberships. It has used shopping bag tie-ins with Safeway supermarkets, promoted a booklet titled "The Baby Sitter's Guide," published a monthly family newspaper (with a nationwide circulation of 2 million), and participated in cooperative efforts with the media and business.

While museums have adopted a number of marketing practices, they recognize that "Dignity and decorum have to be maintained. We have to remember to maintain good taste when we sell, but still get across the idea that this is a place for fun. For example, we wouldn't create a musical jingle for a museum, as we might for a theme park." (Tom Murray, a consultant for Henry Ford Museum and Greenfield Village)

Museums must also be concerned about their tax-exempt status. For their stores to be tax exempt, they must sell merchandise with an educational or cultural function that is related to the museum's purpose. There is a fine line between what is educational and what is merely a souvenir. The Internal Revenue Service examines the merchandise sold by museums, prices, and the impact on profit-oriented competitors when determining tax-exempt status.

QUESTIONS

1. Four donor categories were mentioned in the case (government, foundations, corporations, and individuals).
   a. Why would these donors contribute to museums?
   b. What do they expect in return for their contribution?
   c. How do their expectations differ from clients/users of museums?
2. Identify five market segments of clients/users that a museum could seek and present a brief marketing plan aimed at each.
3. Would you create a musical jingle for a museum? Explain your answer.
4. Is a museum store a fair competitor for a traditional retailer marketing paintings by well-known artists? Why or why not?

Chapter 23

Marketing and Society

CHAPTER OBJECTIVES

1. To provide an overview of marketing and society
2. To study social responsibility and consider its benefits and costs
3. To define consumerism and examine the consumer bill of rights
4. To discuss the responses of manufacturers, retailers, and trade associations to consumerism
5. To explore the future of consumerism

*M*any businesses are discovering that community involvement and public service have dual rewards. First, the firms are able to make real contributions to the quality of life of the people in the areas in which they operate. Second, the companies receive recognition, and usually increased customer interest, because of their involvement; often, this recognition is better than any visibility that could be obtained through extensive advertising. Community involvement and public service can be undertaken by small firms, not just large ones, as these illustrations show:

- Cookies Cook'n is a Massachusetts chain of six retail cookie stores. Unable to donate cash to charitable organizations, Cookies Cook'n arranged to give away more than 100 pounds of its cookies and brownies to the Muscular Dystrophy Association (MDA). These products were awarded to volunteers who participated in the MDA's annual telethon. Also, several giant chocolate chip cookies were auctioned off on television. In return, Cookies Cook'n's president appeared on the telethon to be publicly recognized; and the firm received a $440 tax deduction for its cookies.

- Dedham Racquet Time Sports and Health Club is located in Dedham, Massachusetts. When the company expanded from a tennis and racquetball club to a full-service health and fitness club, it co-sponsored a Health and Fitness Fair with WEEI-FM, a Boston radio station. The fair raised $5,000 for Ronald McDonald House (a living facility for terminally ill children and their parents). Dedham provided courts and a gym, which were available free to the public during the fair. A number of donated prizes were raffled off. Over a one-month period, WEEI-FM publicized the fair hundreds of times on the air; and it broadcast the fair live.
- Instant Copy, a printing company with 10 outlets in northern Indiana, has sponsored various community projects. It offered a $10,000 prize to any person who achieved a hole-in-one on the ninth hole of the Hoosier Celebrities Golf Tournament (the company insured itself against a hole-in-one for $500 with Lloyd's of London). Well-known speakers are regularly hired to address business audiences on management techniques. "Instant News" letters featuring local news and sports are distributed free to more than 20 restaurants. Instant Copy receives substantial media coverage and customer acknowledgment for its efforts.

Some companies do not participate in community programs, because it is difficult to prove a direct relation between financial rewards and such participation. But as Instant Copy's president noted,

Right now, we're a depressed town. We've lost 19,000 jobs in the last year, and our biggest employer, International Harvester, recently closed its doors and moved to Springfield, Ohio. I look for opportunities that will help the community. In the end, that helps us too.[1]

Overview

Marketing can have both a positive and a negative impact on society.

Marketing has a strong impact on the society which it serves. It has the potential for both positive and negative consequences regarding areas such as

- The quality of life (standard of living).
- Consumer expectations and satisfaction with goods and services.
- Consumer choice.
- Product design and safety.
- Product durability.
- Product and distribution costs.
- Final prices.
- Competition.
- Natural resources, the landscape, and environmental pollution.
- Communications with consumers.

[1] Sara Delano, "Give and You Shall Receive," *Inc.* (February 1983), pp. 128, 130.

- Employment.
- Innovation.
- Deceptive practices.

For example, in the U.S., marketing practices have made a wide variety of goods and services available at relatively low prices and through convenient locations. These include food products, transportation products and services, clothing, entertainment, books, insurance, banking, television sets, furniture, and personal computers. On the other hand, marketing activities can sometimes create unrealistic consumer expectations, result in costly minor product design changes, or adversely affect the environment.

People's perceptions of marketing are mixed, at best. An Opinion Research Corporation survey in 1983 found that the general public's estimate of the average U.S. manufacturer's after-tax profit was 37 per cent of sales (up from 31 per cent in 1981)—almost ten times the actual profit. More specifically, people believed that oil companies earned a profit of 60 per cent (almost 14 times the actual profit), insurance companies a profit of 55 per cent (almost 8 times the actual profit), and food companies a profit of 38 per cent (about 11 times the actual profit).[2]

A large number of persons feel that marketing practices are not always satisfactory.

Studies by R. H. Bruskin and A. C. Nielsen show that at least one third of Americans feel cheated by purchases. The figure may actually approach two thirds of Americans. Others have reported that consumers may believe they are being "ripped off" when prices rise. Finally, marketers need to recognize that consumer dissatisfaction is not always transmitted to the firm. Consumers can boycott a product and privately complain to friends. Only 3 per cent of disgruntled consumers actually take the time to write to offending companies. The true level of dissatisfaction may be "hidden."[3]

In this chapter the discussion of marketing and society is broken into two broad categories: social responsibility as it involves the general public, competition, employees, stockholders, and others; and consumerism as it involves consumers of a firm's offering.

Social Responsibility

Social responsibility involves marketing that benefits society.

Social responsibility is the "possession of a 'corporate conscience' or a response to social problems based on a sense of moral obligation."[4] Social responsibility requires that a marketing decision not only serve the interests of business but also

[2] "ORC Study Finds Public's View of Corporate Profits Highly Exaggerated," *Marketing Review* (November–December 1983), p. 7.

[3] Dik Twedt, "Irate Buyer Needs Quick Reply," *Marketing News* (April 6, 1979), pp. 1, 5; Shelby D. Hunt and John R. Nevin. "Why Consumers Believe They Are Being Ripped Off," *Business Horizons,* Vol. 24 (May–June 1981), pp. 48–52; Ralph L. Day, Klaus Grabicke, Thomas Schaetzle, and Fritz Staubach, "The Hidden Agenda of Consumer Complaining," *Journal of Retailing,* Vol. 57 (Fall 1981), pp. 86–106; Kevin Higgins, "Mail Order Industry Is Fighting the Old, Sleazy Image on Several Fronts," *Marketing News* (July 8, 1983), pp. 1, 12; William O. Bearden and Jesse E. Teel, "Selected Determinants of Consumer Satisfaction and Complaint Reports," *Journal of Marketing Research,* Vol. 20 (February 1983), pp. 21–28; and Alan J. Resnick and Robert R. Harmon, "Consumer Complaints and Managerial Response: A Holistic Approach," *Journal of Marketing,* Vol. 47 (Winter 1983), pp. 86–97.

[4] Robert C. Albrook, "Business Wrestles with Its Social Conscience," *Fortune* (August 1968), p. 90.

protect and enhance society's interests.[5] This calls for business to be accountable to society for its actions and for consumers to act responsibly.

The ***socioecological view of marketing*** includes all the stages of a product's life span from raw materials to junkpile and incorporates the interests of all consumers who are influenced by the use of a product or service, including involuntary consumers who must share the consequences of someone else's consumption.[6]

There are times when social responsibility poses dilemmas for the marketer, because various products and services may have potential adverse effects on the consumer's or society's well-being. Examples of items that offer such dilemmas are cigarettes, no-return bottles, food with high taste appeal but low nutritional content, shoes with high heels, crash diet plans, and liquor.

Until the 1960s it was accepted that the marketer's role was limited to satisfying consumers and generating profits. Environmental resources, such as air, water, energy, and paper, were viewed as limitless. Responsibility to the general public was rarely considered. Now the marketer realizes that he or she must respond to the general public, environment, employees, channel members, stockholders, and competitors, as well as consumers.[7] Table 23-1 contains examples of marketing's social responsibility in these areas.

Both business and consumer activities have a significant impact on natural resources, the landscape, pollution, planned obsolescence, and standards of ethics. Each of these areas is discussed in the following subsections.

The socioecological view of marketing considers the environment and involuntary consumers.

Natural Resources

In the last several years, there has been a growing awareness that the supply of natural resources is not unlimited. Both consumers and marketers have contributed to some resource shortages.

Packaging materials absorb large amounts of natural resources. Since World War II the consumption of these materials has increased several times faster than the population. Packaging now accounts for 30 to 40 per cent of all refuse. Annual packaging costs exceed $50 billion; yet, 90 per cent of packaging is thrown away. In addition, over $2 billion is spent to collect and dispose of packaging materials.

Americans throw out more than 160 million tons of materials yearly, about 1,400 pounds for every man, woman, and child. The United States has 5 per cent of the world's population but generates more than half of the world's trash. Included in the United States' annual refuse are 85 billion cans, 40 billion glass bottles, 45 million tons of paper, 5 million tons of plastic, 200 million tires, 10 million tons of appliances, 200,000 tons of copper, 1 million tons of aluminum, and 20 million tons of grass and leaves.[8]

Depletion of resources can be slowed by reducing consumption, improving efficiency, limiting disposable packages, and lengthening products' lives.

---

[5] Keith Davis, "Five Propositions for Social Responsibility," *Business Horizons,* Vol. 18 (June 1975), p. 20.
[6] Etienne Cracco and Jacques Restenne, "The Socio-ecological Product," *MSU Business Topics,* Vol. 19 (Summer 1971), pp. 27–34.
[7] See Kenneth E. Goodpaster and John B. Matthews, Jr., "Can a Corporation Have a Conscience?" *Harvard Business Review,* Vol. 60 (January–February 1982), pp. 132–141; and "J & J Shows Civic Service Pays," *Advertising Age* (February 13, 1984), p. 53.
[8] Stuart Diamond, "Garbage: Our Wasted Resource," *Newsday Long Island Magazine* (May 6, 1979), pp. 43–44.

Table 23-1
Examples of Socially Responsible Marketing Practices

Regarding the General Public and the Environment
Recycling of products
Elimination of offensive signs and billboards
Proper disposal of waste
Use of products and services requiring low levels of environmental resources
Hiring of hard-core unemployed
Involvement in community
Donations to nonprofit organizations

Regarding Employees
Ample internal communications
Input into decisions
Training about social issues and the appropriate responses to them
No reprisals for uncovering questionable company policies
Recognition of socially responsible employees

Regarding Channel Members
Honoring verbal as well as written commitments
Fair distribution of scarce goods
Adherence to fair requests of channel members
Not forcing channel members to act irresponsibly
No coercion
Cooperative programs addressed at the general public and the environment

Regarding Stockholders
Honest reporting and financial disclosure
Publicity of company activities
Participation in setting socially responsible policy
Explanation of social issues affecting the company
Earning a responsible profit

Regarding Competitors
Adherence to high standards of performance
No illegal or unethical acts to hinder competitors
Cooperative programs for the general public and environment
No actions that would lead competitors to waste resources

In general the depletion of natural resources can be reduced if the consumption of scarce materials is lessened and more efficient alternatives are purchased; fewer throwaway or disposable items such as soda bottles and cans, pens, cigarette lighters, and carbon typewriter ribbons are bought; products are given longer life spans; and styles are changed less frequently. Convenient recycling and repair facilities, better trade-in arrangements, common facilities such as apartments, and less packaging also contribute to more efficient use of resources. For example, it has been estimated that a returnable container system would save 40 to 45 per cent of the glass, 6 to 11 per cent of the aluminum, and 0.5 to 2 per cent of the steel produced in the U.S.[9] See Figure 23-1.

Progressive actions require cooperation among business, stockholders, government, employees, the general public, consumers, and others. They also

---

[9] W. Kent Moore and David L. Scott, "Beverage Container Deposit Laws: A Survey of the Issues and Results," *Journal of Consumer Affairs,* Vol. 17 (Summer 1983), pp. 60–61.

Figure 23-1
Aluminum Can Recycling
"Reverse vending machines" are located in or adjacent to more than 2,300 retail stores throughout the U.S., including many large supermarket chains. A single machine can process about 3,000 pounds per week.

Source: "'Reverse Vending Machines' Turn Recycling into Profit for Retailers," *Marketing News* (November 25, 1983), Section 2, p. 4. Reprinted by permission.

involve changes in life-styles and values.[10] For instance, since 1978 Americans have reduced their automobile driving by more than 5 per cent in response to rising gasoline prices and shortages. In addition, the use of mass transit has risen.

The Landscape

No-deposit beverage containers and abandoned automobiles are examples of items that mar the landscape. Thirty years ago virtually all beverage containers were recycled. Then manufacturers developed no-return bottles and cans. As a result, littering at roadsides and other areas became a major problem. In an attempt to reduce litter, many states, including Oregon, Vermont, Maine, Iowa, Connecticut, and Michigan, have enacted laws requiring beverage containers to have deposit fees that are refunded to consumers when they return empty containers. Many manufacturers and retailers believe these laws unfairly hold them responsible for the disposal of their products; littering is conducted by consumers.

Littering has become a major factor in marring the landscape. Various states and municipalities have introduced regulations to lessen it.

[10] See Phillip E. Downs and Jon B. Freiden, 'Investigating Potential Market Segments for Energy Conservation Strategies," *Journal of Public Policy & Marketing*, Vol. 2 (1983), pp. 136–152; Chris T. Allen, Roger J. Calantone, and Charles D. Schewe, "Consumers' Attitudes about Energy Conservation in Sweden, Canada, and the United States, with Implications for Policy Makers," *Journal of Public Policy & Marketing*, Vol. 1 (1982), pp. 57–68; and "Energy-Guzzling: Most Consumers Are Cured," *Business Week* (April 4, 1983), p. 16.

Also, labor and recycling costs associated with container returns have caused beverage prices to rise slightly. Nonetheless, a consumer study in Michigan found that, on balance, beverage container returns work very well.[11]

Cars are frequently abandoned on highways and streets, where they are subsequently stripped of usable parts. One suggestion is to include an amount to cover the disposal of the car in its original price or in a transfer tax. For example, Maryland imposes a small fee on title transfers to aid in the removal of abandoned cars.

Other means of reducing the marring of the landscape include bans on billboards and roadside signs, fines for littering, and better trade-ins for automobiles and appliances. Neighborhood block associations, merchant self-regulation, area planning and zoning, and consumer education may increase appreciation for the landscape. Maintaining an attractive landscape is a cooperative effort. A merchant clean-up patrol cannot overcome pedestrians who throw litter on the street rather than in waste baskets.

Environmental Pollution

Both government and business actions are needed to reduce dangerous environmental pollution.

Dangerous pollutants need to be eliminated from the environment and safe substitutes found. The Environmental Protection Agency (EPA) is the major federal organization involved with pollution. A number of state agencies are also quite active in this area.

For example, until the late 1970s fluorocarbon propellants were used in most spray cans, such as insecticide, deodorant, hairspray, and paint. Scientists found that these propellants drifted into the upper atmosphere where they could decompose and destroy the ozone layer that shields the earth from most of the sun's ultraviolet radiation. A 5 per cent reduction in the ozone layer could lead to several thousand additional cases of skin cancer in the United States each year. Socially conscious companies, such as S. C. Johnson (maker of Raid), voluntarily discontinued fluorocarbon use. Ban deodorant, by Bristol-Myers, introduced pump-spray deodorants without fluorocarbons. Eventually, the EPA prohibited the use of fluorocarbon propellants.

Pesticides often threaten the environment. As an illustration, in February 1979, the EPA issued a ban on 2,4,5T and 2,4,5TP herbicides which were widely used along roadways and under rights-of-way of power lines, in forests to kill hardwood trees, in rangelands to give cattle more grass, and in rice fields to kill a weed called curly indigo. In early 1984, problems were discovered with EDB, a pesticide that had been sprayed on farm grains. Some food products, such as Duncan Hines cake mix, had to be recalled, because they were contaminated with excessive amounts of EDB (which was banned as a pesticide). In both cases, the pesticides were believed to have cancer-causing potential.

Another major source of pollution is industrial waste. The EPA estimates that heavy industry and the chemical, electroplating, textile, rubber, refining, and plastics industries generate the greatest amounts of hazardous waste. According to the EPA, most of the forty million tons of annual dangerous waste in the United

---

[11] Lawrence A. Crosby and James R. Taylor, ''Consumer Satisfaction with Michigan's Container Deposit Law–An Ecological Perspective,'' *Journal of Marketing*, Vol. 46 (Winter 1982), pp. 47–60. See also Moore and Scott, ''Beverage Container Deposit Laws: A Survey of the Issues and Results,'' pp. 57–80.

States is disposed of inadequately. In many cases the problem of industrial waste is compounded by porous soil and dependence on underground water supplies. The potential dangers of nuclear power were shown at Three Mile Island. During 1983, the EPA stepped up its enforcement activity regarding industrial waste; several executives and their firms were fined (up to $500,000) and some of the executives received prison sentences.[12] There are now over 30 states that have their own laws regarding proper waste disposal and dump sites.[13]

Even though reducing pollution is difficult, many firms have made notable attempts to do so. For instance, Allied Corporation recycles waste byproducts from chemical manufacturing into materials used in fluorine-based items, such as toothpaste. Dow Chemical has developed a product stewardship concept in which it anticipates and attempts to solve a product's environmental problems by performing toxicological studies.[14]

Planned Obsolescence

Planned obsolescence is a practice that encourages short-run material wearout, style changes, and functional product changes. See Figure 23-2. It is supported by marketers as a means of satisfying consumer demand and criticized by consumer advocates for increasing resourage shortages, waste, and environmental pollution.

Planned obsolescence **can involve materials, styles, and functions.**

In material planned obsolescence, manufacturers choose materials and components that are subject to comparatively early breakage, wear, rot, or corrosion. For example, the makers of disposable lighters and razors use this form of planned obsolescence in a constructive manner by offering inexpensive, short-life, convenient products.

There is increasing resistance to all types of material planned obsolescence, particulary with raw-material shortages. For example, the Canadian government

---

[12] Robert E. Taylor, ''U.S. Increases Prosecutions of Polluters,'' *Wall Street Journal* (October 27, 1983), pp. 33, 39.
[13] ''When States Talk Tougher than the EPA,'' *Business Week* (May 30, 1983), pp. 33, 37.
[14] Steven J. Marcus, ''The Recycling of Chemical Waste,'' *New York Times* (January 8, 1984), Section 3, p. 4.

**Figure 23-2
Forms of Planned
Obsolescence**

Material
Planned Obsolescence

Style Planned
Obsolescence

Functional Planned
Obsolescence

has set rust protection guidelines that call for three-year warranties against rust in new cars sold in Canada. Similarly, Fiat and Peugeot-Citröen, European automakers whose cars already have long lives, are conducting research in order to produce a twenty-year car.

In style planned obsolescence, the manufacturer makes some minor changes to clearly differentiate this year's model from last year's. Because consumers, particularly in the United States, are style conscious, they are willing to discard old items while they are still functional in order to acquire new items with more status. This is common with fashion items.

With functional planned obsolescence, the manufacturer introduces new product features or improvements to generate consumer dissatisfaction with a currently owned product. These features or improvements were withheld from the original model in order to obtain faster repurchases. Companies using this approach risk competitors' introducing the features or improvements first. Frequently, a change in style accompanies a functional change in order to heighten the consumer's awareness of the "new" product.

Marketers reply to the criticisms of planned obsolescence with the following justifications: planned obsolescence is a response to consumer demands regarding prices, features, and styles and is not coercion; without rapid product turnover, consumers would be disenchanted by the lack of available choices; consumers like disposable items and frequently discard products before they lose their effectiveness; manufacturers use materials that hold down prices during inflationary periods; competition requires companies to produce the best products they can, companies cannot hold back on improvements; and, for many product categories, such as clothing, consumers desire continuous style changes.

Ethics

Ethical behavior **involves** *process-related* **and** *product-related issues.*

In any marketing situation, ***ethical behavior*** based on honest and proper conduct should be followed. Figure 23-3 shows the code of ethics for the National Food Brokers Association. Ethical issues can be divided into two categories: process-related and product-related.[15] ***Process-related ethical issues*** "involve the unethical use of marketing strategies or tactics." Examples include bait-and-switch advertising, price fixing, selling products overseas that have been found unsafe in the U.S., and bribing purchasing agents of large customers.

Product-related ethical issues involve "the ethical appropriateness of marketing certain products." For example, how should tobacco products, intimate personal hygiene items, sugar-coated cereals, political candidates, and nonprofit organizations be marketed? More specifically, should cigarettes be manufactured? Should there be restrictions on their sales? Should advertising for cigarettes be limited? Should taxes on cigarettes be raised to discourage use? Should cigarette smoking be banned in offices, restaurants, and planes?

These examples show the varying company responses to ethical issues:

- The Center for Science in the Public Interest (CSPI) and other organizations are calling for bans on alcohol ads on broadcast media, eliminating ads aimed at heavy drinkers and young people, warnings on alcoholic beverage labels, and

[15] Gene R. Laczniak, Robert F. Lusch, and William A. Strang, "Ethical Marketing: Perceptions of Economic Goods and Social Problems," *Journal of Macromarketing,* Vol. 1 (Spring 1981), p. 49.

Figure 23-3
A Code of Ethics

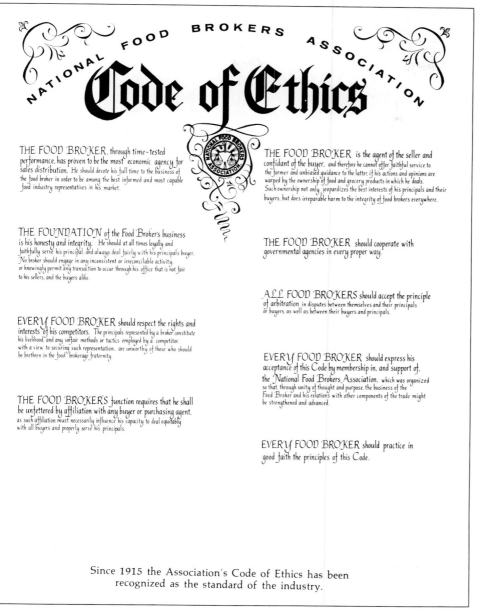

NATIONAL FOOD BROKERS ASSOCIATION

Code of Ethics

THE FOOD BROKER, through time-tested performance, has proven to be the most economic agency for sales distribution. He should devote his full time to the business of the food broker in order to be among the best informed and most capable food industry representatives in his market.

THE FOUNDATION of the Food Brokers business is his honesty and integrity. He should at all times loyally and faithfully serve his principal, and always deal fairly with his principals buyer. No broker should engage in any inconsistent or irreconcilable activity, or knowingly permit any transaction to occur through his office that is not fair to his sellers, and the buyers alike.

EVERY FOOD BROKER should respect the rights and interests of his competitors. The principals represented by a broker constitute his livelihood, and any unfair methods or tactics employed by a competitor, with a view to securing such representation, are unworthy of those who should be brethren in the food brokerage fraternity.

THE FOOD BROKER'S function requires that he shall be unfettered by affiliation with any buyer or purchasing agent, as such affiliation must necessarily influence his capacity to deal equitably with all buyers and properly serve his principals.

THE FOOD BROKER is the agent of the seller and confidant of the buyer, and therefore he cannot offer faithful service to the former and unbiased guidance to the latter, if his actions and opinions are warped by the ownership of food and grocery products in which he deals. Such ownership not only jeopardizes the best interests of his principals and their buyers, but does irreparable harm to the integrity of food brokers everywhere.

THE FOOD BROKER should cooperate with governmental agencies in every proper way.

ALL FOOD BROKERS should accept the principle of arbitration in disputes between themselves and their principals or buyers, as well as between their buyers and principals.

EVERY FOOD BROKER should express his acceptance of this Code by membership in, and support of, the National Food Brokers Association, which was organized so that, through unity of thought and purpose, the business of the Food Broker and his relations with other components of the trade might be strengthened and advanced.

EVERY FOOD BROKER should practice in good faith the principles of this Code.

Since 1915 the Association's Code of Ethics has been recognized as the standard of the industry.

Reprinted by permission.

the restriction of distribution channels for alcohol.[16] Seagram is one of a number of alcoholic beverage makers that are revising their ad messages to encourage moderation. See Figure 23-4.

- Allied Tube & Conduit Corporation of Harvey, Illinois, markets metal piping used to contain and protect electrical wiring in buildings. To combat the success of PVC (plastic) tubing, Allied has embarked on a campaign to publicize the

---

[16] Kevin Higgins, "Debate Rages Over Marketing and Alcohol Problems," *Marketing News* (September 30, 1983), pp. 1, 4; and Albert R. Karr, "Liquor Sellers Pushed to Stop Drunk Drivers," *Wall Street Journal* (January 23, 1984), p. 25.

Figure 23-4
A Socially Responsible Ad

These one oz. jiggers of 80 proof spirits, 10 oz. glasses of beer, and 3 oz. glasses of wine are equal in alcohol content.

Surprised?

We can understand if you are. It seems hard to believe that the alcohol content in the three groups of glasses above is, in fact, equal. And so it's true that sometimes when you think you're drinking less, you may actually **THE HOUSE OF SEAGRAM** be drinking more. Because any alcoholic beverage should be used only in moderation, it's important that you know what you're drinking as well as how much. Remember, even though it may look light, it shouldn't be taken lightly.

FOR REPRINTS PLEASE WRITE ADVERTISING DEPT. CU-184, THE HOUSE OF SEAGRAM, 375 PARK AVE., N.Y., N.Y. 10152

Reprinted by permission.

fire hazards of plastic piping. To gain greater credibility, Allied has established the nonprofit Foundation for Fire Safety and pays 75 per cent of its annual budget. The foundation sends officials around the country criticizing PVC piping. Many observers believe this practice is misleading (since Allied sponsors the foundation) and unethical, and feel Allied's claims are greatly exaggerated.[17]

- A few large airlines, including United and American, have installed computer terminals in the offices of travel agents. Together, United and American systems are in use in 65 per cent of the travel agencies. These terminals provide agents with flight times, fares, and other pertinent information. However, the systems were set up to emphasize the flights of the airline which supplied the terminals; many other flights, particularly those of discounters, were downplayed or ignored. After considerable government pressure and negative pub-

[17] Steven Flax, ''The Dubious War on Plastic Pipe,'' *Fortune* (February 7, 1983), pp. 68–74.

licity in 1983, the Civil Aeronautics Board developed a plan in 1984 to make the systems more equitable.[18]

- Stride Rite has chosen to exceed industry quality standards in the production of its children's shoes. Commented one observer: "They're fanatics about the health of children's feet. Part of that company's culture is putting a leather lining inside children's shoes, even though the industry standard is now plastic lining, which costs less. They do it because they believe it's better. Business ethics is largely a question of corporate character."[19]

- In 1984, R. J. Reynolds ran a print advertisement asking "Can we have an open debate about smoking? . . . Studies which conclude that smoking causes disease have regularly ignored significant evidence to the contrary." This advertisement was one in a series sponsored by R. J. Reynolds. Critics quickly responded that "Reynolds has adopted a marketing strategy that attempts to seduce smokers and potential smokers into a false security at the expense of their own health. This is callous and irresponsible."[20] Figure 23-5 shows one of R. J. Reynolds' ads.

During 1983, the *Wall Street Journal* commissioned the Gallup Poll to conduct a survey on ethical behavior in the U.S. A national sample of more than 1,500 adults and almost 400 middle-level executives at large companies was questioned. In general, 65 per cent of the respondents believed that the overall level of ethics had declined over the previous decade; only 9 per cent thought it had risen. Higher levels of ethical behavior were reported by older adults, women, and high-school graduates than by younger adults, men, and college graduates. The honesty and ethics of business executives was rated as very high or high by only 18 per cent of the general public. However, business executives were much more likely than the general public to apply stiff ethical standards to their employees' behavior.[21] Table 23-2 shows selected findings from the Gallup survey.

The general public believes ethics have declined in the last decade.

When making decisions, these broad ethical questions should be considered:[22]

Ethical decisions should consider the consequences of actions, the public good, honesty, and humanity.

1. What are the probable consequences of alternative proposals?
2. Which policy will result in the greatest possible good for the greater number?
3. Is a practice right? Is it just? Is it honest?
4. Does the policy put people first?
5. Is humanity treated as an end and not merely as a means?
6. What will relieve the conflicts and tensions of the situation?
7. Does the proposed strategy or solution anticipate consequences in the larger environment as well as in the immediate situation?

[18] "Do Airlines Play Fair with Their Computers?" *Business Week* (May 23, 1983), pp. 143 ff; and Christopher Conte, "CAB Accepts Outline of Plan to Regulate Airline Computer-Reservation Systems," *Wall Street Journal* (February 10, 1984), p. 4.
[19] Tamar Lewin, "Business Ethics' New Appeal," *New York Times* (December 11, 1983), Section 3, p. 4.
[20] Burt Schorr, "R. J. Reynolds' Ads on Smoking Debate Ignite Sharp Protest," *Wall Street Journal* (February 17, 1984), p. 19.
[21] Roger Ricklefs, "Ethics in America," *Wall Street Journal* (October 31, 1983), pp. 33, 42; (November 1, 1983), p. 33; (November 2, 1983), p. 33; and (November 3, 1983), pp. 33, 37.
[22] Adapted from James M. Patterson, "What Are the Social and Ethical Responsibilities of Marketing Executives?" *Journal of Marketing*, Vol. 31 (July 1966), pp. 12–15. See also, Laura L. Nash, "Ethics Without the Sermon," *Harvard Business Review*, Vol. 59 (November–December 1981), pp. 78–79; and the Winter 1984 issue of the *Marketing Educator*.

Figure 23-5
A Controversial
Advertising Campaign

Reprinted by permission.

Benefits and Costs of Social Responsibility

Social responsibility has costs as well as benefits.

The performance of socially responsible actions has both benefits and costs. Among the benefits are improved worker and public safety, as reflected in fewer and less severe accidents, longer life spans, and less disease; cleaner air; more efficient use of resources; economic growth; a better image for business; government cooperation; public education; an attractive and safe environment; and self-satisfaction for a firm. Many of these benefits cannot be quantified. Furthermore, although costs are borne by all, the benefits of worker safety programs and many industrial environmental programs are enjoyed primarily by workers and their families.

The costs of socially responsible actions vary. The cumulative costs of pollution control devices are estimated at well in excess of $50 billion since 1973. Pollution control and worker safety programs account for up to one quarter of the capital budgets for some chemical, petroleum, nonferrous metals, steel, and paper companies. Some environmentally questionable products that are efficient have

Table 23-2   Ethics in America, a 1983 *Wall Street Journal*/Gallup Survey

Activity	A. Reported Behavior (Per Cent Who Have Ever Done Each Activity)	
	Business Executives	General Public
Taken home work supplies	74	40
Called in sick to work when not ill	14	31
Used company telephone for personal long-distance calls	78	15
Overstated deductions somewhat on tax forms	35	13
Driven while drunk	80	33
Saw a fellow employee steal something at work and did not report it	7	26

Activity	Reported Behavior (Per Cent Who Have Ever Done Each Activity)					
	General Public					
	Under 50 Years Old	Over 50 Years Old	Men	Women	College Graduate	High School Graduate
Taken home work supplies	50	26	47	33	58	21
Called in sick to work when not ill	40	18	Not reported		36	21

Group	B. How the General Public Rates the Honesty and Ethical Standards of Various Groups (by Per Cent)		
	Very High, High	Average	Low, Very Low
Medical doctors	53	35	10
Lawyers	24	43	27
Business executives	18	55	20
Representatives in Congress	14	43	38

Issue	C. Attitudes Toward Ethical Issues (by Per Cent Responding Yes)	
	Business Executives	General Public
Is it all right for a purchasing agent to accept a *case* of liquor from a supplier at Christmas time?	25	71
Is it all right for a purchasing agent to accept a *bottle* of liquor from a supplier at Christmas time?	75	84
Is it all right to charge an employer $5 for a cab ride when the employee actually walks?	24	48
Is it all right to use a company photocopier for personal reasons?	80	75
Should an employer hire the best-qualified job applicant if he or she earned only $18,000 a year on the last job, but claimed to have earned $28,000?	47	63
Should an employer dismiss an employee who has done a good job for a year if it is found that the employee falsely claimed to have earned a college degree?	50	22
Should an employee report a water pollution problem to the company if it will cost $100,000 to fix and presently represents *no* health hazard?	70	63

Source: Roger Ricklefs, "Ethics in America," *Wall Street Journal* (October 31, 1983), pp. 33, 42; (November 1, 1983), p. 33; (November 2, 1983), p. 33; and (November 3, 1983), pp. 33, 37.

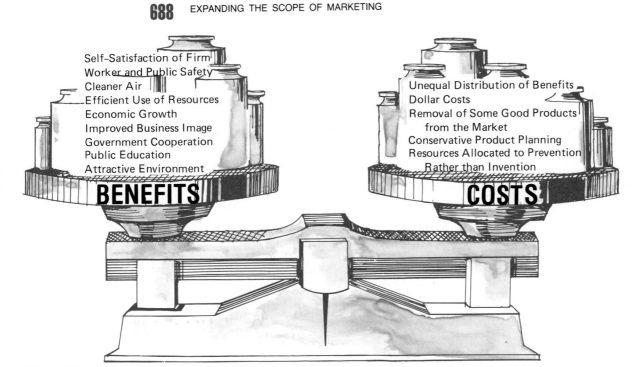

Figure 23-6
The Benefits and Costs
of Social Responsibility

been removed from the marketplace or greatly modified. Product planning is more conservative; and resources are often allocated to prevention rather than invention. Figure 23-6 weighs the benefits and costs of social responsibility.

The controversy over the introduction of automobile air bags offers a good illustration of the benefits and costs associated with social responsibility. Advocates of a passive restraint system that would not require any action by consumers (such as air bags that automatically inflate in an auto crash) state that a passive system would save the country $4.5 billion yearly in medical costs, insurance costs, and lost wages due to deaths and injuries. They believe the usefulness of air bags has been proven in various tests, and through actual use (e.g., more than 20,000 Mercedes-Benz cars). Although air bags would cost $300 to $1,000 per car, depending on sales volume, insurance experts forecast that an average motorist would save $660 in premiums over a 10-year period. Critics of a passive restraint system argue that air bags are complex and relatively untested, can go off when they should not, do not work in all situations, must be used in conjunction with seat belts, can injure riders not sitting normally, and are too expensive. In early 1984, the U.S. government agreed to buy 5,000 autos equipped with air bags as part of a "nationwide program designed to evaluate safety-device technology and economic viability."[23]

---

[23] John Holusha, "What Deregulation Means for G. M." *New York Times* (November 1, 1981), Section 3, pp. 1, 26; Albert R. Karr, "Air Bags Could Save Motorists About $660 Over 10 Years, State Insurance Aide Says," *Wall Street Journal* (September 14, 1983), p. 60; Albert R. Karr, "Auto Air Bags: U. S. Resumes Debate on Use," *Wall Street Journal* (November 29, 1983), pp. 35, 40; and Christopher Conte, "U. S. to Buy 5,000 Cars Equipped with Air Bags," *Wall Street Journal* (February 23, 1984), p. 6.

Consumerism

Whereas social responsibility involves the interface of marketing with all of its publics, consumerism is limited to the relationship of marketing with its consumers. *Consumerism* can be defined as

a social force within the environment designed to aid and protect the consumer by exerting legal, moral, and economic pressure on business.[24]

and

the widening range of activities of government, business, and independent organizations that are designed to protect individuals from practices that infringe upon their rights as consumers.[25]

Consumerism protects consumers by placing legal, moral, and economic pressure on business.

Consumerism has evolved through three distinct eras. The first era occurred in the early 1900s and concentrated on the need for a banking system, product purity, postal rates, antitrust, and product shortages. Emphasis was on business protection against unfair practices.

The second era lasted from the 1930s to the 1950s. Important issues were product safety, bank failures, labeling, misrepresentation, performance standards, stock manipulation, deceptive advertising, credit, and consumer refunds. Consumer groups, such as Consumers Union and Consumers' Research, and government legislation grew. Issues were initiated but seldom resolved.

There have been three distinct eras of consumerism. The most recent era began in the early 1960s.

The third era began in the early 1960s and continues. It deals with all areas of marketing and has had a great impact on business. Two major events dominated the beginning of this era: President John Kennedy's announcement of a *consumer bill of rights* and publication of Ralph Nader's *Unsafe at Any Speed*. President Kennedy said that all consumers had four basic rights: information, safety, choice in product selection, and a voice in decision making. See Figure 23-7. *Unsafe at Any Speed,* released in 1965, was a detailed examination and critique of the automobile industry.

President Kennedy stated a *consumer bill of rights:* information, safety, choice, and a voice in decision making.

Several other factors also contributed to the growth of the modern era. Birth defects related to the use of thalidomide by pregnant females occurred in the 1960s. A number of books, including the *Hidden Persuaders* by Vance Packard (about marketing's ability to influence people), *Silent Spring* by Rachel Carson (about marketing's contribution to a deteriorating environment), and *American Way of Death* by Jessica Mitford (about practices in the funeral industry) were published. Consumers became increasingly dissatisfied with product performance, marketer handling of complaints, and deceptive or unsafe business practices. In addition, consumers became more sophisticated and skeptical, and they set higher, and perhaps unrealistic, expectations. Product scarcity occurred for some items. Self-service retailing and complex products caused uncertainty for

[24] David W. Cravens and Gerald G. Hills, "Consumerism: A Perspective for Business," *Business Horizons,* Vol. 18 (August 1970), p. 21.
[25] George S. Day and David A. Aaker, "A Guide to Consumerism," *Journal of Marketing,* Vol. 34 (July 1970), p. 12.

Figure 23-7
Consumers' Basic Rights

- To be informed and protected against fraudulent, deceitful, and misleading statements, advertisements, labels, etc.; and to be educated as to how to use financial resources wisely.

- To be protected against dangerous and unsafe products.

- To be able to choose from among several available products and services.

- To be heard by government and business regarding unsatisfactory or disappointing practices.

some customers. The media began to publicize poor business practices more frequently. Government intervention heightened; in particular, the Federal Trade Commission expanded its activities in consumer issues.

During the 1980s, the modern era of consumerism has entered a mature phase, as a result of the increased emphasis on business deregulation (and self-regulation) and the rapid gains of the 1960s and 1970s. In addition, today, more companies take into account consumer issues when developing and implementing their marketing plans; far fewer firms ignore consumer input or publicly confront consumer groups. Cooperation between business and consumers is better, leading to a lower profile for consumerism.

In the following subsections, these key aspects of consumerism are examined: consumer information and education, consumer safety, consumer choice, consumers' right to be heard, responses of business to consumer issues, and the future of consumerism.

Consumer Information and Education

The right to be informed includes protection against fraudulent, deceitful, or grossly misleading information, advertising, labeling, pricing, packaging, or other practices. A number of federal and state laws have been enacted in this area.

One example on the federal level is the Magnuson-Moss Consumer Product Warranty Act regarding warranties. A *warranty* is an assurance given to consumers that a product will meet certain performance standards. An express

A *warranty* assures consumers that a product will meet performance standards.

(stated) warranty is one that is explicitly provided to the consumer, such as the accuracy of a watch. An implied (implicit) warranty does not have to be stated to be in effect; it stipulates that a product is fit for use, packaged and labeled properly, and conforms to promises made on the label. For the most part, the terms warranty and guarantee are synonomous. The major distinction is that the term guarantee is used more frequently in promotion, such as satisfaction guaranteed or money-back guarantee. Specific guarantee provisions are regulated by the same laws as warranties.

Magnuson-Mass ensures that warranties are properly stated and enforced through several provisions. Warranties must be made available prior to purchases, so that consumers may read them in advance. The FTC is empowered to require product-accompanying information regarding the identity and location of the warrantor, exceptions in warranty coverage, and how consumers may complain. A full warranty must cover all parts and labor for a specified period of time. A limited warranty may contain stipulations and exceptions as well as a provision for labor charges. Implied warranties may not be disclaimed. Figure 23-8 describes the limited warranty provided by Midas.

Individual states have regulations relating to information. As an illustration, cooling-off laws (allowing consumers to reconsider and, if they desire, cancel purchase commitments made in their homes with direct-to-home salespeople) are currently in force in about forty states. Unit-pricing legislation, aimed at enabling consumers to compare prices of products that come in many sizes (such as small, medium, large, family, and economy), is also on a state-by-state basis. Food stores are most affected by unit pricing and, in many cases, these stores must express price per unit of measure as well as total package price.

The existence of information does not mean that consumers will use it in their decision making. Studies have shown that consumer information is often ignored or misunderstood, especially by those who need it most (such as the poor). Accordingly, consumer education is necessary. **Consumer education** is defined as "a learning process whereby the consumer acquires the skills and knowledge to use his or her financial resources wisely in the marketplace."[26]

> Teaching consumers the wise use of financial resources in the marketplace is the goal of *consumer education*.

The great majority of state departments of education have consumer education staffs. Some states, such as Illinois, Oregon, Wisconsin, Florida, Kentucky, and Hawaii, require all students in public secondary schools to take a course in consumer education. Hundreds of consumer-education programs are conducted by federal, state, and local governments, as well as private profit and nonprofit institutions. These programs typically cover how to prudently purchase products and services, important features of credit agreements, contracts, and warranties, and consumer-protection laws.

Consumer Safety

In large part the concern over consumer product safety arises from the fact that annually more than 20 million people are hurt, 110,000 disabled, and 30,000 killed in incidents involving products other than automobiles. The yearly cost of product-related injuries is several billion dollars. It has been estimated that up to

> Yearly, there are over 20 million accidents involving nonautomobile products.

26 Paul N. Bloom and Mark J. Silver, "Consumer Education: Marketers Take Heed," *Harvard Business Review,* Vol. 54 (January–February 1976), p. 32.

Figure 23-8
The Midas Limited
Warranty

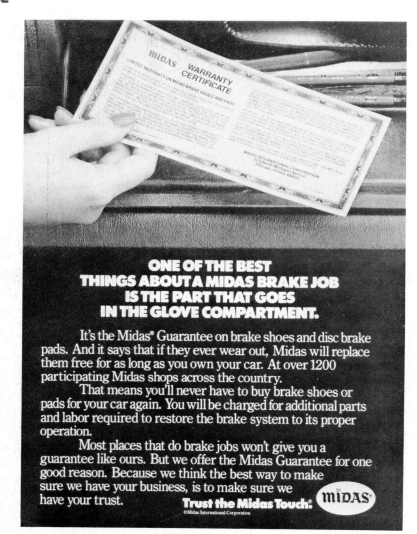

Reprinted by permission.

25 per cent of these injuries could be prevented if manufacturers produced safer, better-designed products. Table 23-3 contains a listing of the consumer products whose use results in the greatest number of injuries.

The ***Consumer Product Safety Commission (CPSC),*** established in 1972, is the federal agency with the major responsibility for product safety. It has jurisdiction over more than 11,000 products, such as aerosol spray cans, television sets, bicycles, lamps, ranges and ovens, ladders, carbonated beverages, bottles, aluminum wiring, and lawn mowers. The CPSC also regulates structural items in homes such as stairs, retaining walls, and electrical wiring.

The only products over which the CPSC does not have jurisdiction are food, drugs, cosmetics, tobacco, automobiles, tires, firearms, boats, pesticides, and aircraft. Each of these products is regulated by other agencies. For example, the Environmental Protection Agency has the authority to recall cars not meeting

The *Consumer Product Safety Commission (CPSC)* **has a number of enforcement tools at its disposal, including** *product recall.*

emission standards. The Food and Drug Administration regulates drugs, medical devices, radiation emissions, and food.

The CPSC has extensive powers. It can

1. Require products to be marked with clear and adequate warnings and instructions.
2. Issue mandatory standards pertaining to performance, construction, and packaging that may have the effect of forcing companies to redesign their products completely.
3. Require manufacturers, private labelers, distributors, and retailers to notify the agency immediately whenever they discover that a product manufactured or sold by them contains a defect that would create a substantial risk of injury. This covers defects in design, manufacture, or assembly.
4. Require manufacturers to conduct reasonable testing programs to make sure their products conform to established safety standards. After testing, manufacturers must supply distributors or retailers with certificates stating that all applicable consumer protection safety standards have been met.

If after investigation the CPSC determines a product hazard exists, it can issue orders compelling a manufacturer to bring the product into conformity with the provisions of the applicable safety rule or repair the defect in the product, exchange the product for a like or equivalent item that complies with safety requirements, or refund the purchase price of the product less a reasonable allowance for use.

Firms found in violation of safety standards can be fined from $2,000 to $500,000 per violation; top executives can be fined up to $50,000 and imprisoned for up to one year. However, the primary enforcement tool used by the CPSC is *product recall,* whereby the Commission orders companies to recall and modify (or discontinue) unsafe products.

The largest product recall involved 12.5 million hair dryers in 1979. The dryers were recalled because they contained asbestos. According to the CPSC, the

Product Group	Total Number of Injuries
1. Sports and recreational equipment	3,233,353
2. Home structures and construction materials	1,782,428
3. Home furnishings and fixtures	1,176,876
4. Housewares	385,483
5. Home workshop apparatus, tools, and attachments	271,678
6. Personal-use items	239,250
7. Packaging and containers for household products	216,648
8. Yard and garden equipment	214,139
9. Space heating, cooling, and ventilating appliances	116,997
10. Home and family maintenance products	108,684
11. General household appliances	82,071
12. Home communication, entertainment, and hobby equipment	59,039
13. Child nursery equipment and supplies	55,836
14. Toys	50,349

Table 23-3
Estimates of Hospital Emergency Room Treated Injuries Associated with the Use of Selected Consumer Products[a] (July 1, 1981 – June 30, 1982)

[a] A product was associated with an injury, but not necessarily caused the injury.
Source: United States Consumer Product Safety Commission—1982 Annual Report: Part Two (Washington, D.C., U.S. Government Printing Office, 1982).

Table 23-4
Selected Automobile Recalls in the U.S., 1983

240,000 1980 Buick Skylarks, Chevrolet Citations, Oldsmobile Omegas, and Pontiac Phoenixes—rear brake locking during braking could lead to spin outs

85,000 1980 Subaru—potential breaking of seatback could cause the driver to twist or fall backward while driving

160,000 1976–1978 Dodge Colts and Plymouth Arrows—exposure to road salt could cause mounting straps for fuel tanks to rust and break, leading to fuel tanks falling off

500,000 1980–1982 Chevrolet Chevettes and Pontiac T-1000s—a carburetor plug could dislodge, causing fuel to leak out (a fire hazard)

245,000 1981–1982 Ford Escort and Mercury Lynx station wagons—possible failure of front safety belts due to poor upper anchorages

100,000 1983 Ford Thunderbirds, Crown Victorias, LTDs, F-series trucks, and Econoline Club Wagons; Lincoln Town Cars, Mark VIs, and Continentals; and Mercury Grand Marquises, Marquises, and Cougars—"park" position may not have engaged properly, resulting in vehicles rolling as if in neutral

117,000 1978–1983 Audi 5000s—similarity in height of brake and accelerator pedals could lead to drivers inadvertantly stepping on both pedals at the same time

930,000 1976–1982 Volkswagen and Audi cars and trucks—electrical failure in fuel-pump circuit could cause stalling, an inability to start the engine, smoke, or a fire

Source: Consumer Reports, various issues.

dryers presented unreasonable cancer risks. The eleven affected manufacturers and retailers agreed to repair or replace the dryers or offer refunds if requested by consumers. These were some of the products that the CPSC ordered recalled between 1980 and 1984:[27]

- 30,000 children's play gyms—A child's head or neck could be trapped in ladder steps.
- 200,000 lawn rototillers—The operator's legs could be caught if the product locked in reverse.
- 16,000 attic ventilators—Miswiring could lead to a fire.
- 770,000 smoke detectors—A defective alarm may not have worked when smoke first started.
- 100,000 children's toothbrush trainers—A rubber piece could come loose and lodge in a child's throat.

In total, the CPSC has issued product recalls involving many millions of items (excluding automobiles). It has also banned products such as flammable contact adhesives, easily overturned refuse bins, certain asbestos-treated products, and Tris (a flame retardant used in children's clothing that was linked to cancer).

The automobile industry, under the jurisdiction of the National Highway Traffic Safety Admininstration, has had a number of motor vehicles recalled. During the period from 1975 to 1982, one third of all 1976 to 1980 model U.S. cars were recalled (some more than once), including 45 per cent of 1980 models. In comparison, 14 per cent of the Japanese cars sold in the U.S. were recalled.[28] Table 23-4 shows some of the major recalls during 1983.

[27] Consumer Reports, various issues.
[28] Associated Press, "So Far, Japanese Cars Are First in the Auto-Quality Race," Newsday (February 17, 1983), Part II, p. 7.

In addition to these government activities, consumers have the right to sue the manufacturer or seller of an injurious product. A suit filed on behalf of many affected consumers is known as a ***class-action suit.*** Consumers can sue on the basis of negligence, breach of warranty, strict liability, or misinterpretation or misrepresentation. With negligence, consumers must prove that carelessness on the part of the seller resulted in injury. With breach of warranty, the seller is responsible for failures to abide by expressed or implied warranties. The most common implied warranty is that the product is safe, usable, and fit for its reasonably intended purpose. Under strict liability, the manufacturer is liable when an article placed on the market is proven to have a defect that causes injury. Carelessness does not have to be proven. Under misrepresentation, the seller is liable for falsities leading to consumer misuse of products.

A company can minimize the effects of product recalls and reduce the possibility of expensive class-action suits by enacting a systematic communication program when it determines that a product is unsafe. This involves a broad announcement to affected consumers, identification of specific product models that are unsafe, a fair adjustment offer (repair, replacement, or refund), and prompt fulfillment of the adjustment offer.[29]

> A *class-action suit* can be based on a claim of negligence, breach of warranty, strict liability, or misrepresentation.

Consumer Choice

The right to choose means that consumers have available several products and brands from which to select. In this regard the government has taken various actions. Exclusive patent rights are limited to seventeen years. After this period, all firms can utilize the patents. Noncompetitive business practices such as unfair price cutting are restricted. Firms with trademarks, such as Borden's ReaLemon, are encouraged to license their products to competitors.

The government examines the potential impact of company mergers on consumer choice. In some cases, it has stopped proposed mergers or forced firms to divest themselves of certain subsidiaries if the product and service offerings in an industry would be lessened. Likewise, franchise restrictions requiring franchisees to purchase all goods and services from their franchisors have been reduced.

Retailers are encouraged to carry wide ranges of product categories and different brands within each category. The media are monitored to ensure that advertising space or time is made available to small as well as large firms. Imports are allowed to compete with American-made items. Information standards are enforced. A number of industries, such as banking, airline, and railroad, have been deregulated to foster price competition and encourage new firms to enter the market.

All of these activities are intended to increase competition and provide consumers with a number of alternatives when making purchases.

> When consumers have several alternatives available to them, they are given the right to choose.

Consumers' Right to Be Heard

The right to be heard means that consumers have input into decisions affecting them. As of this date, no overall federal consumer agency exists to represent consumer interests, although several federal agencies regulate various business

> Although there is no general federal consumer agency, there are federal, state, and local agencies involved with consumers.

---

[29] David L. Malickson, "Are You Ready for a Product Recall?" *Business Horizons*, Vol. 26 (January–February 1983), pp. 31–35.

practices pertaining to consumers. The addresses and phone numbers of these agencies, as well as those of trade associations, are listed in the *Consumer's Resource Handbook,* published by the Office of Consumer Affairs. Most states and municipalities have consumer affairs offices, as do many major corporations. Each encourages consumer input. During the last several years, these offices have been quite active.

In addition to government and industry consumer specialists, there are many consumer groups that have acted on behalf of the general public or specific consumer segments. These groups are quite motivated in their attempts to voice consumer complaints, represent consumers before government and industry hearings, and otherwise generate consumer input into the decision-making process of government and industry. Because a single consumer rarely has a significant impact, consumer groups frequently become the individual's voice.

Responses of Business to Consumer Issues

Business responses to consumerism range from illegal acts to supportive behavior, as shown in Table 23-5. The remedial alternatives for protecting consumers against unfair or deceptive practices are explained in Table 23-6.

Companies have become much more responsive to consumers; yet, questions remain about the effects of consumerism on firms.

Over the past two decades, great advances have been made in the reactions of business to consumerism; today many firms have formal programs and real commitments to resolve consumer issues. Nonetheless, a number of companies have raised legitimate questions about the impact of consumerism on their operations. Following are some of these questions:

Table 23-5
The Range of Business Responses to Consumer Issues

Response	Characteristics
Illegal behavior	Business practices that violate government statutes, such as price fixing, deceptive advertising, and price discrimination
Questionable behavior	Legal business practices that are highly criticized, such as advertising to children
Opportunistic behavior	Practices with which a firm capitalizes on the difficulties of a competitor, such as publicizing a product recall
Adaptive behavior (a) Cooperative (b) Noncooperative	Actions after new laws or court rulings (a) Complete compliance (b) Circumvention efforts, such as withdrawing rather than modifying popular, but dangerous, products
Defensive behavior (a) Cooperative (b) Noncooperative	Self-protective actions prior to government mandates (a) Voluntary improvements, such as unit pricing and nutritional labeling (b) Increased conflict with government, such as attacks on federal agencies and lobbying
Regulated behavior	Industries operating in heavily regulated environments, such as taxicabs, public utilities, and education
Supportive behavior	Voluntary efforts to improve practices taken at the initiative of business, such as labeling toys by the age of children

Source: Adapted from Paul N. Bloom and Nikhilesh Dholakia, "Marketer Behavior and Public Policy: Some Unexplored Territory," *Journal of Marketing,* Vol. 37 (October 1973), pp. 63–77.

Table 23-6
Remedial Alternatives for Consumer Protection

Alternative	Methods of implementation
Prevention	Consumer abuses prevented through 1. Voluntary codes of conduct by firms or trade associations. 2. Laws mandating information disclosure, such as truth-in-packaging, truth-in-lending, and unit pricing. 3. Substantiation of advertising claims.
Restitution	Compensation to consumers for product- or service-related losses, damages, or injuries through 1. Affirmative disclosure, requiring the firm to disclose both negative and positive points in its advertising. 2. Corrective advertising, requiring the firm to devote a proportion of future advertising to dispel past doubtful claims. 3. Refunds or replacement products. 4. Limitations on contracts, such as cooling-off laws, which give buyers the right to rescind certain door-to-door contracts (usually within a three-day period). 5. Arbitration.
Punishment	Future misconduct deterred by inflicting losses on wrongdoers through 1. Fines. 2. Loss of profits. 3. Class-action suits on behalf of many consumers.

Source: Dorothy Cohen, "Remedies for Consumer Protection: Prevention, Restitution, or Punishment," *Journal of Marketing,* Vol. 39 (October 1975), pp. 24–31.

1. Why do different states and municipalities have dissimilar laws regarding business practices? How can a national company be expected to comply with each of these regulations?
2. Do government rules cause unnecessary costs and time delays in the introduction of new products that outweigh the benefits of these rules?
3. Is it the responsibility of business to ensure that consumers obey laws (such as littering) and use products properly (such as seat belts)?
4. Is it the role of government or business to make sure that the marketplace is responsive to consumer needs? Is self-regulation preferred over government regulation?
5. Are multimillion dollar jury awards to injured consumers getting out of hand?

Selected responses to consumerism by manufacturers, retailers, and trade associations are discussed next.

MANUFACTURERS

A number of manufacturers have developed systematic programs to deal with consumer issues, as these examples show. In 1961, Maytag introduced Red Carpet Service to improve its appliance repair service. Zenith set up a customer relations department in 1968; Motorola created an Office of Consumer Affairs in 1970; and RCA implemented a consumer affairs office at the corporate level in 1972.

Today Whirlpool has more than 1,200 nationwide franchised repair and service outlets that employ only trained technicians. Frigidaire presents an Award of Merit for dealers and service units that meet rigid service standards. RCA trains

LIP SERVICE.

GE SERVICE.

Ever get the feeling when you buy an appliance that all the service you were promised was nothing more than lip service?

Well, at General Electric we've built an entire program around service. All *kinds* of service. To help you *before, during* and *after* you buy.

GE: OPEN FOR QUESTIONS 24 HOURS A DAY.

Imagine picking up your phone, day or night, and getting an answer to any question you have about a GE consumer product. That's The GE Answer Center.™ Call toll-free 800-626-2000. It's that easy.

STRONG PRODUCTS MEAN LONG WARRANTIES.

The longer the warranty, the better. That's why GE gives you a full 10-year warranty on the PermaTuf® tubs in our dishwashers. A full 2-year warranty on most GE telephones. An exclusive, full 2-year warranty on

® IS A TRADEMARK OF GENERAL ELECTRIC CO

electric skillets. And a limited 1-year warranty on GE Command Performance™ television products.

TWO KINDS OF HELP.

Should anything go wrong with a GE product, you'll have access to a nationwide network of factory-trained technicians.

Or if you'd rather fix it yourself, there's our Quick Fix™ system. Complete with repair manuals and easy-to-install parts.

GE GIVES YOU THE CREDIT YOU DESERVE.

We may even be able to help you finance your major appliance purchase. With fast, convenient credit at modest rates. So that buying a GE appliance will be a simple, easy experience.

NO ONE HELPS YOU LIKE GE.

You already know the frustration of lip service. Now try GE service. There's no other service like it.

WE BRING GOOD THINGS TO LIFE.

Figure 23-9
The General Electric Answer Center

Reprinted by permission.

thousands of service personnel annually; during one five-year period, 158,000 independent service people were trained.

General Electric processes complaints promptly through a well-defined system, and Motorola answers most complaints within twenty-four hours. Probably the best-known complaint-handling service is Whirlpool's Cool-Line, created in 1967. Cool-Line provides a national, toll-free telephone service. It is open twenty-four hours a day, seven days per week, and is staffed by consumer consultants. More than 90 per cent of the questions are answered over the telephone. Remaining problems are investigated and resolved by a field staff.[30] Figure 23-9 describes General Electric's answer center.

In the area of product recalls, manufacturers' actions have varied widely, as these two examples show:[31]

• When Rely-brand tampons were shown to have a possible link with toxic shock

[30] Kevin E. Dembinski, "Consumerism and the Appliance Industry," in Joel R. Evans (Editor), *Consumerism in the United States: An Inter-Industry Analysis* (New York: Praeger, 1980), pp. 29–32.

[31] Elizabeth Gatewood and Archie B. Carroll, "The Anatomy of Corporate Social Response: The Rely, Firestone 500, and Pinto Cases," *Business Horizons,* Vol. 24 (September–October 1981), pp. 9–16: Mark N. Dodosh, "Big Firestone Recall Changes Used Tires into Collector's Items," *Wall Street Journal* (October 30, 1978), pp. 1, 22: and "Firestone Recall," *New York Times* (November 25, 1979), p. 49.

syndrome, they were quickly and voluntarily removed from retailers' shelves by Procter & Gamble. The company halted all production and offered to buy back unused packages. Ads were placed warning women not to use Rely. Procter & Gamble's image was relatively unaffected, because of its prompt actions.

- Firestone Tire & Rubber Company agreed to recall its Firestone 500 tires only after heavy pressure from the National Highway Traffic Safety Commission and others. Information showed that 41 deaths and 65 injuries might have been caused by blowouts or other failures of the Firestone 500. To make matters worse, Firestone did not release test data that showed potential defects in the tires. By delaying the recall for so long, Firestone tarnished its image and ended up spending $135 million for the recall.

Now, more and more companies are employing voluntary recalls when they become aware of product defects or unsafe product features.

Despite manufacturers' greater interest in consumer issues, there are still situations in which they do battle with consumer organizations. For example, *Consumer Reports* provides monthly evaluations of a wide variety of products and services for its 1+ million readers. Since the magazine was first printed in 1936, its publisher (Consumers Union) has vigorously fought to keep its ratings from being quoted in advertisements and brochures. With rare exceptions, which Consumers Union successfully countered in court, firms honored this policy. Then, in 1983, Regina Power Team lightweight vacuum cleaner television ads quoted from *Consumer Reports* and Miller Beer cited its favorable rating in print ads. Consumers Union filed suit, but lost in the U.S. Court of Appeals.[32] In the meantime, *Consumer Reports* issued this statement in the February 1984 issue:

If you care about Miller's and Regina's conduct and the importance of CU's policy, you can help persuade them, and other potential abusers of *Consumer Reports,* that their reach for profits at our expense is bad business. How can you do that? You might weigh their violation of CU's policy in your decision about whether to buy their products. And you might also tell the individuals chiefly responsible for corporate conduct what you think of the conduct of their corporation. Here are the names and addresses.[33]

Later in 1984, *Consumer Reports* and Miller reached an out-of-court settlement. However, the dispute with Regina continued.

RETAILERS

Various retailers have expressed a concern for consumer issues, some for more than fifty years. For example, J.C. Penney adopted a consumer philosophy in 1913; Macy's established a Bureau of Standards to test merchandise in 1927; and Abraham & Straus recognized the need for merchandise labeling in 1937.

More recently, Sears developed an extensive education program and related literature; Hess Department Stores became heavily involved in community affairs and in 1977 introduced a "Consumer Expo," which demonstrates new products; and Giant Food, a large supermarket chain, developed its own consumer bill of rights about a decade ago:[34]

---

[32] Tamar Lewin, "When Ads Quote Ratings," *New York Times* (December 27, 1983), p. D2.

[33] "Help Keep *Consumer Reports* out of Ads," *Consumer Reports* (February 1984), p. 71.

[34] Esther Peterson, "Consumerism as a Retailer's Asset," *Harvard Business Review,* Vol. 52 (May–June 1974), pp. 91–92ff.

Figure 23-10
Giant Food's Consumer
Bill of Rights

Reprinted by permission.

1. Right to safety: no phosphates, removal of certain pesticides, age-labeling of toys.
2. Right to be informed: improved labeling, unit pricing, readable dating of perishable items, and nutritional labeling.
3. Right to choose: continued sale of cigarettes and food with additives.
4. Right to be heard: dialogue with reputable consumer groups, in-house consumer advocate.
5. Right to redress: money-back guarantee on all products.
6. Right to service: availability of store services.

See Figure 23-10.

An indication of the improved performance of retailers is the response of consumers to a 1982 survey by the Food Marketing Institute. According to that study, far fewer consumers indicated a willingness to write complaint letters to their congresspersons, get fellow consumers to sign petitions protesting high prices, or participate in boycotts of products than in 1974 (when a similar survey was conducted). In addition, one in four respondents believed an organized boycott was ineffective, illegal, or wrong.[35]

With *item price removal*, prices are only displayed on shelves or signs.

In one key area, retailers and consumer groups have opposing views. This involves ***item price removal,*** whereby prices are marked only on store shelves or aisle signs and not on individual items. See Figure 23-11. Many retailers, particu-

[35] Mary Johnson, "The New Consumer Advocate: Supermarkets," *Progressive Grocer* (January 1983), p. 83.

Figure 23-11
Item Price Removal

Item Pricing   Item Price Removal

Currently, most supermarkets place price tags on both the item itself and on the shelf in which it is stacked. Under item price removal, the price is shown only on the shelf. The store saves money by not affixing a price label on the item.

larly supermarkets, want to employ item price removal, since computerized checkouts allow them to ring up prices through premarked codes on packages. Retailers state that this practice reduces labor costs significantly and that these reductions can be passed on to consumers. Consumer groups believe the practice is deceptive and will make it difficult for them to guard against misrings. Item price removal is banned in a number of states and local communities. Giant Food is one of the major users of item price removal; it passes cost savings along to consumers.[36]

TRADE ASSOCIATIONS

Trade associations are organizations that represent groups of individual companies. The associations have been responsive to consumerism through a variety of activities, such as coordinating and distributing research findings, developing consumer and company education programs, developing product standards, and handling complaints.

The Major Appliance Consumer Action Panel (MACAP) is an effective educational and complaint-resolution program sponsored by the Association of Home Appliance Manufacturers, the Gas Appliance Manufacturers Association, and the American Retail Federation. The Bank Marketing Association stresses a Financial Advertising Code of Ethics (FACE) for member firms; the Direct Mail/Marketing

[36] Deborah A. Randolph. ''Giant Food Faces Fight on Two Fronts Over Cuts in Prices and Price Labeling,'' *Wall Street Journal* (April 14, 1981), p. 37. See also Michael K. Mills and Brian F. Harris, ''Public Policy and Shopping Effectiveness: The Case of Item-Price Removal,'' *Journal of Public Policy & Marketing*, Vol. 2 (1983), pp. 70–81.

Institute sets industry guidelines and operates a consumer action line; and the National Retail Merchants Association has a Consumer Affairs Committee and provides information to the public.

The Better Business Bureau (BBB) is the largest and broadest business-operated trade association involved with consumer issues. The BBB publishes educational pamphlets and books, investigates complaints, supervises arbitration panels, has available a Consumer Affairs Audit, outlines ethical behavior, presents symposiums, publicizes unsatisfactory practices and names the firms involved, and has local offices throughout the country. It emphasizes self-regulation as an alternative to government legislation. As an illustration, the Minnesota office of the BBB mediated 9,000 disputes in 1982 and resolved 81 per cent of them; an additional 2 per cent of disputes were settled through arbitration. Only 17 per cent of the complaints could not be handled amicably and resulted in court action or continuing disagreements.[37]

Sometimes, trade associations vigorously oppose potential government regulation. For example, the Consumer Product Safety Commission estimated that 123,000 injuries from chain saws required medical attention in 1981. As a result, the CPSC proposed mandatory safety standards for chain saws in 1982. However, the Chain Saw Manufacturers Association claimed that the accident figures were inflated and did not justify mandatory regulations. The Association published a 56-page report asserting, among other things, that a chair is more dangerous than a chain saw.[38]

Future of Consumerism

Throughout the 1980s, consumerism will consolidate previous gains.

Consumerism is now in a period of maturity, as pointed out earlier in the chapter. The decade of the 1980s has undergone and will continue to undergo much less activism than the 1960s and 1970s.[39] This is due to several factors: the current level and quality of self-regulation, the success of consumerism, the increased conservatism of Congress and the American people, and the importance of other issues.

As described throughout the text, and particularly in this chapter, organizations are much more responsive to consumer complaints and environmental conditions today. Because more firms have consumer affairs departments, employ voluntary product recalls, and conduct ongoing consumer surveys, there is less pressure for government agencies or consumer groups to intervene. Accordingly, there is a strong trend toward industry deregulation as a way of increasing competition, encouraging innovative marketing programs, and stimulating lower prices. Deregulation is resulting in greater flexibility for firms and a more uncertain environment for them.[40]

Future consumerism activity will be less necessary because of the successes of past actions. On the federal, state, and local levels, government protection for

---

[37] Sanford L. Jacobs, "Business Bureau Arbitration . . . Loan Sales . . . Harvard M.B.A.s," *Wall Street Journal* (January 17, 1983), p. 25.

[38] Ray Vicker, "Rise in Chain-Saw Injuries Spurs Demand for Safety Standards, But Industry Resists," *Wall Street Journal* (August 23, 1982), p. 17.

[39] See Paul N. Bloom and Stephen A. Greyser, "The Maturing of Consumerism," *Harvard Business Review*, Vol. 59 (November–December 1981), pp. 130–139.

[40] Paul N. Bloom, "Deregulation's Challenges for Marketers" in Bruce J. Walker, et al. (Editors), *An Assessment of Marketing Thought & Practice* (Chicago: American Marketing Association, 1982), pp. 337–340.

consumers has improved dramatically over the last twenty years. Class-action suits have won large settlements from firms, making it clear that unsafe practices will be financially costly. Consumer groups and independent media have publicized negative company practices, so that firms are aware that such activities will not go unnoticed. The major goal for consumerism during the 1980s will be to hold on to and consolidate the gains of the 1960s and 1970s.

Many members of Congress and sectors of the American public are now more conservative about the role of government in regulating business than in the 1960s and 1970s. They believe that government has become too big, impedes business practices, and causes unnecessary costs. As a result, government agency activities have been limited and their budgets closely monitored. Congress passed the FTC Improvement Act of 1980, which restricted the agency's powers. Under this act, Congress was given veto power over industrywide trade regulations approved by the FTC.[41] And, while total federal government expenditures rose by 25 per cent from fiscal 1981 to fiscal 1983, the budget of the FTC dropped by 5 per cent, the EPA by 15 per cent, the National Highway Traffic Safety Administration by 17 per cent, and the Civil Aeronautics Board by 45 per cent (the CAB was scheduled to go out of existence at the end of 1984).[42]

Finally, consumerism issues will not be as important to people as a number of other factors in the 1980s. These include unemployment, interest rates, industrial productivity, the rate of inflation, product and resource shortages, the federal budget deficit, and the negative international balance of trade.

The FTC Improvement Act of 1980 gave Congress the ability to veto FTC trade regulations.

Summary

Marketing interacts with the society it serves. It can have both positive and negative effects on such areas as the quality of life and consumer expectations.

Social responsibility involves business actions based on a sense of moral obligation. The socioecological view of marketing considers all stages of a product's life from raw materials to junkpile and includes the interests of consumers and nonconsumers.

To stem the depletion of natural resources, cooperative efforts among business, stockholders, government, employees, the general public, consumers, and others are needed. In response to excessive littering and abandoned cars, several states have enacted legislation. Various environmental pollutants such as fluorocarbon propellants and certain pesticides have also been removed from the market. Product obsolescence is a heavily criticized practice that encourages material wearout, style changes, and functional product changes.

Ethical behavior, based on honest and proper conduct, can be divided into two categories: process-related and product-related. Ethical considerations include the

[41] See Dorothy Cohen, "Unfairness in Advertising Revisited," *Journal of Marketing*, Vol. 46 (Winter 1982), pp. 73–80.
[42] Joann S. Lublin, "Federal Deregulation Runs into a Backlash, Even from Businesses," *Wall Street Journal* (December 14, 1983), p. 22; and "How Air Travelers' Rights Could Be Left Hanging," *Business Week* (April 2, 1984), p. 102.

consequences of actions, consumer happiness, honesty, fairness, concern for all people, and spin-off effects. Social responsibility has many benefits as well as a number of costs; the two need to be balanced.

Consumerism deals with the relationship of marketing and its consumers. It is defined as a social force within the environment designed to aid and protect the consumer by exerting legal, moral, and economic pressure on business. Consumerism has progressed through three eras: early 1900s, 1930s to 1950s, and 1960s to the present. The latter era has been the most important and began with President John Kennedy's announcement of a consumer bill of rights. The Federal Trade Commission is the major federal agency responsible for consumer protection.

The right to be informed includes protection against fraudulent, deceitful, or grossly misleading information, advertising, labeling, pricing, packaging, or other practices. Consumer education involves teaching consumers to use their financial resources wisely. The right to safety arises from the large numbers of people who are injured, disabled, or killed in accidents. The Consumer Product Safety Commission has the power to order product recalls or modifications. The right to choose stipulates that consumers have several products and brands from which to choose. The right to be heard is the consumer's right to a voice in business and government decision making. A number of consumer groups and government agencies provide this voice.

Many individual companies and trade associations are reacting positively to consumer issues. This group grows each year. A smaller number of organizations intentionally or unintentionally pursue unfair, misleading, or dangerous practices. There are remedies to correct these actions.

Consumerism is now in a period of maturity. The 1980s are witnessing less activism as a result of self-regulation, the past accomplishments of consumerism, the increased conservatism in the U.S., and the importance of other issues.

Questions for Discussion

1. Comment on the statement, "I look for opportunities that will help the community. In the end, that helps us too."
2. Why are people's perceptions of marketing mixed? What can be done to improve these perceptions?
3. Explain the responsibilities of the final consumer according to the socioecological view of marketing.
4. Now that petroleum shortages seem to have disappeared, consumers are returning to the purchase of larger, less fuel-efficient autos. Despite their best efforts, marketers have been unable to change this preference. Why?
5. Evaluate beverage container return laws from the perspective of the retailer. From the perspective of the consumer.
6. Evaluate the practice of planned obsolescence. Why is it so prevalent in the U.S.?
7. What is ethical behavior? Give examples of five unethical, but legal, activities.
8. Weigh the benefits and costs of social responsibility. How may a balance be struck between benefits and costs?

9. Explain the consumer bill of rights.
10. Do marketers do a good job of educating consumers? Explain your answer.
11. Evaluate the use of product recall as a tool for regulating product safety.
12. Do consumers in the U.S. have too many products and services from which to choose? Why or why not?
13. From a manufacturer's perspective, what would be the advantages and disadvantages of an overall federal agency representing consumer interests?
14. Why is item price removal a controversial practice? Under what circumstances should consumer groups support it?
15. Comment on the future of consumerism.

Case 1 Manville Corporation: A Profitable Firm Files for Bankruptcy to Stop Product Liability Lawsuits*

On August 26, 1982, Manville Corporation (a large construction and forest-products manufacturer) asked for court protection under Chapter 11 of the federal bankruptcy code, despite a net worth of $1.1 billion. Chapter 11 status allows companies to continue their operations and reorganize debt, without interference from creditors or other outside parties.

When Manville voluntarily filed for court protection, it was a very profitable firm that had no intention of going out of business or changing the way in which it operated. Rather, Manville sought to halt the lawsuits brought against it by people suffering health problems caused by exposure to asbestos and products made with asbestos that were produced by Manville. By gaining bankruptcy status, all pending lawsuits against the company would be ruled on by a bankruptcy judge (rather than state and federal courts), legal proceedings would be delayed, and new lawsuits could not be brought. Manville planned to remove itself from bankruptcy standing after its legal problems were resolved.

Manville defended its application for Chapter 11 protection in full-page newspaper ads appearing on August 27, 1982. Manville offered these reasons for its actions:

- 16,500 lawsuits were pending, with 500 new lawsuits being filed each month. It was estimated that 32,000 more lawsuits could be brought against the company. The total costs of settling these lawsuits at $40,000 per claim (Manville's average) would amount to more than $2 billion.
- Asbestos-related health problems were not discovered until 1964. Up to then existing medical knowledge showed that Manville operated properly. The largest group of plaintiffs against the company was shipyard workers using asbestos insulation on ships built or modified during World War II, when asbestos was viewed as safe.

---

* The data in this case are drawn from Neil Maxwell, "Manville Tries to Fight Wave of Problems, Including Costly Rise in Asbestos Lawsuits," *Wall Street Journal* (June 9, 1982), p. 31: Neil Maxwell, G. Christian Hill, and Raymond A. Joseph, "Radical Tactic," *Wall Street Journal* (August 27, 1982), pp. 1, 8; "Despite Strong Business, Litigation Forces Manville to File for Reorganization," *Wall Street Journal* (August 27, 1982), p. 29; Dean Rotbart, "Manville Unveils Backup Proposal of Restructuring," *Wall Street Journal* (May 13, 1983), p. 2; and Dean Rotbart, "Manville Corp. Faces Increasing Opposition to Bankruptcy Filing," *Wall Street Journal* (January 31, 1984), pp. 1, 20.

- The U.S. government should be responsible for a compensation program for asbestos-related injuries. Furthermore, it was virtually impossible for the company to defend itself in every state, under different statutes.

Manville's critics believed the firm was not acting in a socially responsible manner and was misusing bankruptcy protection (which was intended for companies with severe financial, not legal, problems). These critics asserted that

- Manville was trying to force the federal government to develop a bailout plan for the company.
- By cutting off lawsuits, Manville was not allowing plaintiffs to exercise their legal rights.
- Manville "fraudulently concealed" information about asbestos hazards. In 1980, the California Supreme Court ruled that plaintiffs were eligible for punitive damages because of this. These damages would not be covered by insurance, but by Manville itself.

In May 1983, Manville offered a reorganization plan which was not acceptable to critics; Manville asked litigants to negotiate or risk bankruptcy-court–imposed settlements. It revised the plan in November 1983. Both the original plan and the revision were rejected. And by early 1984, Manville was losing the backing of key commercial and trade creditors. Despite all the distractions, Manville reported a $100-million profit for the final quarter of 1983 (while remaining in bankruptcy).

QUESTIONS

1. Was Manville justified in applying for court protection? Explain your answer.
2. Should a company be liable for health hazards not discovered until years after a product is introduced? Why or why not?
3. How do you view the large settlements U.S. juries are awarding to plaintiffs in product liability trials? For example, a Texas woman was awarded $2 million by a jury ($1 million in punitive damages) for asbestos-related health problems of her deceased husband.
4. Will Manville's actions have a long-term impact on the company's image? Explain your answer from the perspective of both stockholders and consumers.

Case 2 Johnson & Johnson: Responding to the Tylenol Tragedy[†]

In September and October 1982, tragedy struck as seven Chicago people died from cyanide-laced Extra-Strength Tylenol capsules. Although the cyanide was placed in the capsules by a person or persons apparently in no way connected with the manufacture of the product, Johnson & Johnson (maker of Tylenol) was

[†] The data in this case are drawn from Nancy Giges, "J&J Begins Its Drive to Keep Tylenol Alive," *Advertising Age* (October 11, 1982), pp. 1, 78; Michael Waldholz, "Tylenol Maker Mounting Campaign to Restore Trust of Doctors, Buyers," *Wall Street Journal* (October 29, 1982), p. 33; Thomas Moore, "The Fight to Save Tylenol," *Fortune* (November 29, 1982), pp. 44–49; Dennis Kneale, "Sterling Drug Plans to Challenge Tylenol after Years of Caution, Misjudgment," *Wall Street Journal* (April 29, 1983), pp 35, 43; and Nancy Giges, "One Year Later, Tylenol Faces New Challenge," *Advertising Age* (September 26, 1983), pp. 3, 77.

confronted with a difficult situation that was unprecedented in U.S. business history.

Never before had a firm been in a position where the market's leading brand faced almost immediate extinction through no fault of its own. At the time of the tragedy, Tylenol held an overwhelming 40 per cent share of the nonprescription analgesic market. Said Jerry Della Femina, a prominent advertising executive:

I don't think they can ever sell another product under that name. There may be an advertising person who thinks he can solve this, and if they find him I want to hire him, because then I want him to turn our water cooler into a wine cooler.

Johnson and Johnson acted quickly and responsibly. All Tylenol capsules were withdrawn from retail shelves and the production of capsules was halted. The company announced a $100,000 reward for information leading to the arrest and conviction of the person(s) guilty of the poisonings. An extensive newspaper campaign offered to exchange Tylenol tablets for any Tylenol capsules consumers may have purchased. After a short moratorium on television advertising, Johnson & Johnson ran low-key institutional ads asking consumers "to continue to trust Tylenol." Two million pieces of literature were mailed to medical professionals. The company's chief executive appeared on the *Phil Donahue Show* and *Sixty Minutes.*

Next, Johnson & Johnson engaged in activities to restore Tylenol's sales, which had fallen to 6.5 per cent of industry sales the week after the poisonings (these sales were of tablets only). In November and December 1982, newspaper ads offered consumers $2.50 coupons toward the purchase of any Tylenol product, good through December 21, 1983. Totally new packaging for Tylenol capsules was developed and then introduced in December 1982, as production of the capsules resumed. The packaging featured a sealed cardboard box, a sealed plastic bottle top, and an inner seal covering the bottle. In addition, the label stated "Do not use if safety seals are broken." Product advertising resumed in January 1983.

Johnson & Johnson's rapid and conscientious actions had a positive impact on consumers. Within a month after the poisonings, Tylenol tablets had recaptured a 17.9 per cent market share of industry sales (the tablets had a 22.2 per cent share before the poisonings) and 77 per cent of regular Tylenol users stated that they would purchase the product in a tamper-resistant package. By nine weeks after the tragedy, Tylenol tablets had a market share of almost 30 per cent, nearly double the next brand. By the end of April 1983, Tylenol had a 35 per cent market share.

Tylenol's turnaround was very expensive for Johnson & Johnson. The cost of the product recall and lost profits were valued at $50 million. Repackaging was estimated to cost about $100 million; the company said this cost would be absorbed rather than passed along to consumers. In addition, $60 million was spent to advertise Tylenol in 1983 (about $20 million more than originally planned).

QUESTIONS

1. How was Johnson & Johnson able to overcome consumer fears so quickly?

2. Evaluate the current advertising for Tylenol.

3. Johnson & Johnson's chief executive made this statement regarding the Tylenol tragedy: "Every time business hires, builds, sells, or buys, it is acting for the people as well as for itself and it must be prepared to accept full responsibility." Assess this commentary.

4. In 1983, Johnson & Johnson had to recall Zomax, a prescription drug for arthritis sufferers and use after dental surgery. Inadequate labeling resulted in five reported deaths involving people who had allergic reactions to Zomax. The Food and Drug Administration stated that 1 in 15,000 consumers would have allergic reactions, ranging from a mild rash to shock. Compare the Zomax situation with that of Tylenol. Will Johnson & Johnson be able to re-establish Zomax? Explain your answer.

Part Seven Case Procter & Gamble: Opportunities and Pitfalls in International Marketing*

With annual sales of more than $13 billion, Procter & Gamble (P&G) ranks among the 25 largest U.S. industrial firms. It consistently ranks as the leading advertiser in the United States; 1982 expenditures were $726 million. P&G's well-known brands include Tide and Cheer detergents, Ivory soap, Crest toothpaste, Downy fabric softener, Duncan Hines food products, Orange Crush soda, Folger's coffee, Charmin bathroom tissues, Pampers and Luvs disposable diapers, and Head & Shoulders shampoo.

Despite its strength in many consumer products categories, P&G has encountered increasing pressure in the U.S. market over the past several years. There are resourceful competitors in almost every one of the company's product categories; and the relative stability of the U.S. population means that P&G and its competitors are battling it out for the sales of mature products. For example,

- Tide's market share fell from 27 per cent to 20 per cent between 1975 and 1983. In addition, Lever Brothers' Wisk detergent has moved to number two in the industry, ahead of Cheer.
- Ivory Soap is being challenged by Lever's Dove for industry leadership.
- The price of Downy fabric softener was dropped by 12 per cent in 1983, after Lever's Snuggle entered the market.
- P&G's market share for disposable diapers declined from 75 per cent in 1975 to 54 per cent in 1983, even though Luvs was added to complement Pampers. From 1982 to 1983, Kimberly-Clark's Huggies increased market share by 10 per cent (14 to 24). Disposable diapers represent an extremely important product category for P&G; in 1983, they accounted for 17 per cent of overall sales and 22 per cent of total profits.

P&G recognizes that international markets are prime targets for company growth, since many countries have not been exposed to some products that have saturated the U.S. (such as disposable diapers) and/or offer expanding populations. Therefore, it has been aggressively marketing products around the world. However, P&G has witnessed mixed results from its efforts; and, between 1980 and 1983, international profits declined by 41 per cent—even though P&G intensified its efforts.

The company must deal with a variety of environmental factors and competitive situations in each of its foreign markets. Described next are the opportunities and pitfalls facing P&G in three major international markets: Japan, Latin America, and Europe.

---

* The data in this case are drawn from ''Why Procter & Gamble Is Playing It Even Tougher,'' *Business Week* (July 18, 1983), pp. 176–186; Jack Burton and Dennis Chase, ''Sun Still Not Shining on P&G in Japan,'' *Advertising Age* (December 20, 1982), pp. 4, 36; Jack Burton, ''Japanese Diaper Marketers Challenge P&G—and Score,'' *Advertising Age* (December 12, 1983), pp. 40, 48; Laurel Wentz, ''P&G Targets Chile in Latin American Marketing Thrust,'' *Advertising Age* (November 28, 1983), p. 58; Laurel Wentz, ''P&G's 'Crush' on Latin America Rekindled,'' *Advertising Age* (January 16, 1984), pp. 4, 46–47; Howard Sharman, ''P&G on the Warpath Throughout Europe,'' *Advertising Age* (May 23, 1983), pp. 4, 54; Nancy Giges, ''P&G Struggles with Diaper Leak,'' *Advertising Age* (February 20, 1984), pp. 1, 68; and Faye Rice, ''Trouble at Procter & Gamble,'' *Fortune* (March 5, 1984), p. 70.

Japan

With a great deal of optimism, Procter & Gamble entered the Japanese market in 1973 with Cheer detergent. Shortly thereafter, it introduced Pampers disposable diapers. But despite an aggressive marketing effort, P&G lost $100 million in Japan between 1973 and 1979. Then, just when the company believed its products were ready to show sharp growth, the total Japanese detergent market dropped by 17 per cent and cultural factors caused Pampers sales to stagnate. From 1980 through 1984, P&G made no real progress. It is still losing money.

Procter & Gamble's failure to become profitable in Japan after a full decade of trying can be traced to several poor marketing practices and other factors. Specific problems with Cheer were that P&G could not effectively gain entry into the complex Japanese distribution system; it mistakenly purchased a declining Japanese soap company to promote Cheer. P&G priced it far below the level set by Japanese firms, who had been practicing nonprice competition; these firms started a costly price war. Commercials were too "hard sell" for Japanese consumers, who prefer more subtle "mood" ads; these commercials were on the most-hated list of Japanese viewers. P&G was told very late by the Japanese government that nonphosphate detergent rules would be enacted; Japanese competitors knew in advance and gained sales until Cheer could be modified.

Similar predicaments occurred with Pampers. First, the success of Pampers in the U.S. was based upon household laundry being done once or twice a week. In Japan, laundry is washed almost every day, limiting the uses of Pampers. Second, a Japanese firm developed a disposable diaper that fit babies better than Pampers. These diapers are more expensive than Pampers and marketed to occasional users; Pampers are sold to full-time users. Today, there are other Japanese competitors, with superior products. Pampers' market share fell from 90 per cent in 1981 to 45 per cent in early 1984.

As a result of these setbacks, P&G delayed the introduction of a line of skin-care products and other items. Said one Japanese competitor:

Here is an American powerhouse with plenty of money and muscle entering an Asian country, thinking they can dominate the market by using the sales techniques that proved successful in the U.S. and Europe. But they face an unmitigated disaster by breaking every rule in the book when it comes to Japanese market practices.

Latin America

Procter & Gamble has tried to market products in Latin American countries for a number of years. In some cases, it has done quite well; in others, it has fared very poorly, as these examples demonstrate:

- Argentina—P&G was forced to pull out of this market in 1982 as a result of an economic decline in the country (brought on by its Falkland Islands war with Great Britain) and an import ban on U.S.-made products that outlawed company products such as Pampers and Camay soap. A competitor, Johnson & Johnson, decided to manufacture Huggies in Argentina and now accounts for almost 60 per cent of disposable diaper sales there.
- Brazil—P&G has never been a major factor in Brazil, the largest country in Latin America; yet American and other foreign competitors have captured significant

market shares. In 1983, P&G based its first manager in Brazil and concentrated efforts on the sales of Orange Crush soda. But as one rival noted, "everyone's going to fight [P&G] and fight hard. They would have not only the cost of investing and setting up here, but also the cost of fighting with those already here—a very long-term investment."

- Chile—After generating high sales of Crest, Camay, Head & Shoulders, and Pampers, P&G left the Chilean market in 1982. Because it had imported products through local merchants, they were subject to a 20 per cent import tax and became 25 per cent more expensive than domestically manufactured brands. In 1983, P&G purchased a well-established Chilean manufacturer and re-entered the market, offering its own brands and those of the Chilean firm. Local production was planned for all brands.
- Mexico—P&G operates manufacturing facilities in Mexico, where several products are market leaders, including detergent and toilet soap products. Ads are tailored to Mexican life-styles. In 1984, it began test marketing shampoo and fabric softener, and developed plans for a powdered drink similar to General Foods' Tang. P&G has had problems with Crest toothpaste; it was incorrectly positioned as a "cavity-preventive" product in a market where "sexy smiles" are more important.
- Peru—P&G is very strong in Peru, where it introduced detergents and toilet soaps. Pampers is the market leader, even though a 55 per cent import tariff has been placed on it. Sales of domestically produced soda are growing rapidly. P&G has some manufacturing facilities in Peru.
- Venezuela—P&G's soaps and detergents are market leaders. It has manufacturing facilities there. Pert shampoo has not lived up to expectations.

In general, Procter & Gamble has succeeded in Latin American markets where it makes products locally, thoroughly researches cultural differences, and adapts its marketing approach to each country's conditions and needs. It has had less success when it manufactures products in the U.S. and ships them into Latin American countries, cultural differences are not studied, and a standardized marketing effort is utilized.

Europe

P&G has been active in Europe for decades. Of all the foreign markets in which its products are sold, European countries most closely resemble P&G's U.S. market. The populations are growing slowly; average education and income are relatively high; distribution and communication networks are in place; and several products are in the maturity phase of the product life cycle.

Europe is a crucial region for Procter & Gamble, since 20 per cent of overall profits are earned there (down from 25 per cent in past years). To maintain and improve its sales in Europe, P&G has expanded its marketing programs substantially since 1981. Commented one analyst, "They've taken the rubber band off the wallet." Added a competitor, "They've thrown the book at us."

P&G's strategy involves a high level of standardization, the influx of many new products, large advertising expenditures, and a willingness to sacrifice short-term profits for market-share growth. Standardization efforts include the use of the same brand names throughout Europe for a number of products (Pampers; Dash,

Ariel, Visir, and Bold detergents; Top Job cleaner; Head & Shoulders shampoo, etc.) and the utilization of popular advertising campaigns in several countries.

Procter & Gamble has introduced new products throughout Europe. In Great Britain alone, it has introduced Pampers, Bold, Ariel, Zest soap, Lenor concentrate, and Bounce fabric softener since 1981. In Germany, $142 million has been invested in manufacturing and distribution facilities. In Austria and France, Luv's elasticized diapers have been introduced. To get its products into the marketplace more quickly, P&G has greatly reduced the time new products spend in test marketing. For instance, Visir detergent was marketed nationally in France after only a 3-month test, while Unilever's Wisk was tested for a full year.

Advertising expenditures have risen sharply. For example, advertising expenses in Great Britain were $19 million in 1979 and rose to $80 million in 1982 (including $11 million just on Ariel detergent). The French advertising budget was doubled in 1982. The German budget increased by 50 per cent between 1980 and 1982.

P&G is stressing market share rather than immediate profits, as indicated by its willingness to invest heavily. The firm's aggressive strategy caused its British profits to fall from $24 million in 1978 to $1.25 million in 1982. In Germany, 1982 profits were only $105,000, on sales of $659 million. P&G's goal is to generate large profits by 1986.

Competitors are not sitting by idly, while P&G increases its marketing efforts. They are spending heavily in markets where P&G is expanding. Said one competitor, "We were surprised, but we came back with the heaviest advertising campaign ever in this country."

QUESTIONS

1. Compare P&G's marketing strategies in Japan, Latin America, and Europe.
2. Which represents better growth opportunities for P&G: Japan, Latin America, or Europe? Explain your answer.
3. Could P&G have avoided its problems in Japan? Why or why not?
4. How were the situations P&G encountered in marketing Cheer and Pampers in Japan different?
5. In several Latin American countries, P&G's approach was to first export "core" products (Crest, Pampers, Head & Shoulders) made in the U.S., then to build consumer demand, and finally to construct manufacturing facilities in those countries. Assess this approach.
6. Will P&G be able successfully to re-enter the Chilean market? Explain your answer.
7. Evaluate P&G's use of standardized brands and advertising campaigns in Europe.

Marketing
Management

In Part Eight the concepts introduced in Chapters 1 through 23 are tied together, and planning for the future is discussed. Chapter 24 explains how to integrate and analyze marketing plans. The elements leading to a well-integrated plan are examined: organizational mission, long-term competitive advantages, precisely defined target market, compatible subplans, coordination among SBUs, coordination of the marketing mix, and stability over time. The strategies of Kentucky Fried Chicken and Timex are contrasted. Next, marketing cost analysis, sales analysis, and the marketing audit are studied. These are important tools for evaluating the success or failure of marketing plans.

Chapter 25 demonstrates the importance of anticipating and planning for the future. Consumer demographic and life-style trends and their implications for marketers are studied. A number of environmental trends and their significance for marketers also are examined: competition, government, the economy, technology, resource shortages, media, and global events. The chapter concludes with a discussion of marketing strategies for the next decade. Emphasis is placed on evolving marketing techniques and responses to consumer and environmental trends. Marketing planning and research and product, distribution, promotion, and price planning over the decade are each examined.

Kentucky Fried Chicken is the leading fast-food chicken chain in the U.S., in large part due to its well-integrated marketing strategy. This strategy focuses on a unique product, strong customer loyalty, standardized operations, and consistency. Reprinted by permission.

Timex has recently encountered difficulties due to a poorly integrated strategy. Timex was too slow to implement new products and diverted resources to a computer line. Its future success will depend upon its renewed efforts in the watch market and consumer acceptance of its Healthcheck products. Reprinted by permission.

Part Eight   Integrating and Analyzing the Marketing Plan

Can American business survive on a diet of instant gratification?

Computers spew out production reports and sales figures hourly. And managers eat them up.

Investors hunger for bigger dividends and faster earnings growth.

The nightly news feeds us today's hot economic story complete with all the freshest buzzwords.

No matter what the economy, much of American business continues to feast on short-term results. Expecting profits to be served up like fast-food burgers. And economic solutions dished out like instant pudding.

To satisfy this appetite for short-term rewards, managers find it tempting to reduce investments for the future. Investments in new plant and equipment; in research and development.

We're W.R.Grace & Co. We've been doing business in all parts of the world, in all kinds of economies for 130 years. Short-term thinking has never been our way of doing business.

In the last 40 years, we've followed a strategy that has allowed us to diversify into growth industries. It's been a transition that has taken Grace from being primarily a Latin American trading and shipping concern to a

company with worldwide interests in chemicals, natural resources and specialized consumer services. A company with more than $6 billion in sales.

All that didn't just happen. It was planned that way—by people dedicated to the long-term point of view.

We've always believed in giving the future its fair

share of today's resources. Last year at Grace, investment in new plant and equipment was almost 5 times what it was 10 years ago. Research and development expenditures were nearly 3 times what they were a decade ago.

Right now we believe all of us must work to correct a fundamental flaw in the way American business is operating. Short-term results cannot be allowed to become our only criterion for success. Investors must be willing to relax some of the pressure on managers to produce immediate results. Managers must be given more security to make long-term investment decisions.

In turn, those in management must be prepared to make long-term commitments to invest in innovation—in new products and new technologies. And at the same time, to make long-range plans to restore our older industries to full strength.

American business cannot allow itself to over-indulge in short-term rewards. Long-lasting results will take time to develop. But that's what makes them so gratifying.

GRACE
One step ahead of a changing world.

W.R. Grace & Co., 1114 Avenue of the Americas, New York, N.Y. 10036

As W.R. Grace notes in this advertisement, it is imperative that firms be guided by long-run objectives when enacting integrated marketing plans. Short-run profits should not be sought at the expense of long-run innovations and expenditures. Reprinted by permission.

Every software ad you read seems to be talking about 'integrated software'. But it was 1-2-3™ from Lotus® that actually gave the phrase real meaning, because we combined spreadsheet, information management, and graphic functions in one simple, powerful program.

A program that is faster and easier to use than any other software available today.

In short, the tasks it can perform are really impressive, but why it can perform them is even more important.

Because we feel the real criterion for any management tool is its ability to let the human mind flourish and accomplish more than it ever has before.

That's why with 1-2-3 the thought process is not interrupted, so your mind no longer has to wait for your hands. To the novice, it makes everything plausible. To the expert, it makes anything possible.

The results: Business decisions come faster and easier.

1-2-3 from Lotus is truly compatible with the most important personal computer of all—the human mind.

And isn't that what integration really should mean?

Call 1-800-343-5414 (In Massachusetts call 617-492-7870) and find out more about 1-2-3 from Lotus.

Throughout the 1980s, the blurring of gender roles will continue as more women enter the labor force and progress in their careers. Lotus Development Corporation (a computer software firm) is appealing to blurring gender roles in these ads; one ad shows a man's head, the other a woman's head—but both use the same advertising message content, as shown above. Reprinted by permission.

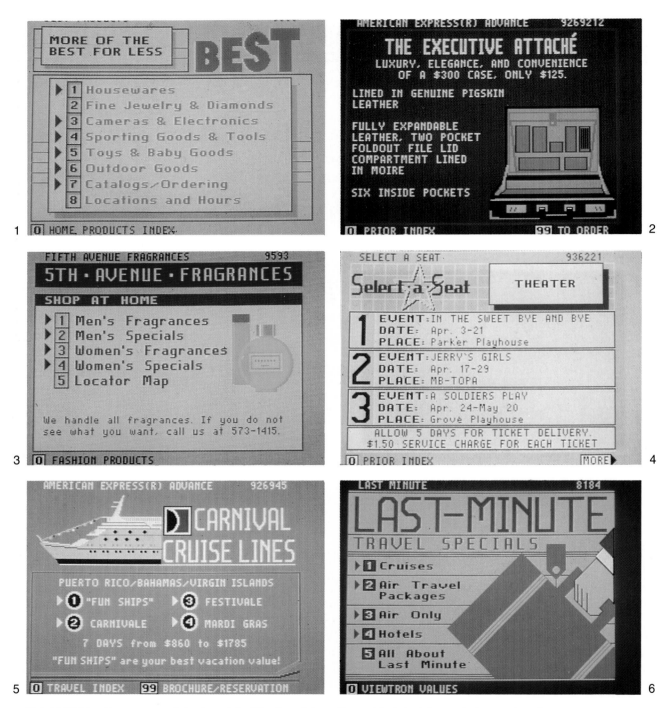

1

MORE OF THE BEST FOR LESS **BEST**

▶ 1 Housewares
2 Fine Jewelry & Diamonds
▶ 3 Cameras & Electronics
▶ 4 Sporting Goods & Tools
▶ 5 Toys & Baby Goods
▶ 6 Outdoor Goods
▶ 7 Catalogs/Ordering
8 Locations and Hours

0 HOME PRODUCTS INDEX

2

AMERICAN EXPRESS(R) ADVANCE   9269212

THE EXECUTIVE ATTACHÉ
LUXURY, ELEGANCE, AND CONVENIENCE OF A $300 CASE, ONLY $125.

LINED IN GENUINE PIGSKIN LEATHER

FULLY EXPANDABLE LEATHER, TWO POCKET FOLDOUT FILE LID COMPARTMENT LINED IN MOIRE

SIX INSIDE POCKETS

0 PRIOR INDEX   99 TO ORDER

3

FIFTH AVENUE FRAGRANCES   9593

5TH · AVENUE · FRAGRANCES

SHOP AT HOME

▶ 1 Men's Fragrances
▶ 2 Men's Specials
▶ 3 Women's Fragrances
▶ 4 Women's Specials
5 Locator Map

We handle all fragrances. If you do not see what you want, call us at 573-1415.

0 FASHION PRODUCTS

4

SELECT A SEAT   936221

Select a Seat   THEATER

1 EVENT: IN THE SWEET BYE AND BYE
DATE: Apr. 3-21
PLACE: Parker Playhouse

2 EVENT: JERRY'S GIRLS
DATE: Apr. 17-29
PLACE: MB-TOPA

3 EVENT: A SOLDIERS PLAY
DATE: Apr. 24-May 20
PLACE: Grove Playhouse

ALLOW 5 DAYS FOR TICKET DELIVERY.
$1.50 SERVICE CHARGE FOR EACH TICKET

0 PRIOR INDEX   MORE▶

5

AMERICAN EXPRESS(R) ADVANCE   926945

CARNIVAL CRUISE LINES

PUERTO RICO/BAHAMAS/VIRGIN ISLANDS

▶ 1 "FUN SHIPS"   ▶ 3 FESTIVALE
▶ 2 CARNIVALE   ▶ 4 MARDI GRAS

7 DAYS from $860 to $1785
"FUN SHIPS" are your best vacation value!

0 TRAVEL INDEX   99 BROCHURE/RESERVATION

6

LAST MINUTE   8184

LAST-MINUTE TRAVEL SPECIALS

▶ 1 Cruises
▶ 2 Air Travel Packages
▶ 3 Air Only
▶ 4 Hotels
5 All About Last Minute

0 VIEWTRON VALUES

Knight-Ridder Newspapers introduced its Viewtron interactive cable television ordering system in South Florida in 1983. The frames shown above are as they would actually appear on a subscriber's television screen. Frame 1 depicts one index of information; frames 2 to 6 show several goods and services that can be purchased at home. Reprinted by permission.

Part Eight   Marketing in the Future

Integrating and Analyzing the Marketing Plan

CHAPTER OBJECTIVES

1. To show the importance of integrated marketing plans
2. To study the elements that determine how well a marketing plan is integrated
3. To compare two actual marketing plans in terms of their level of integration
4. To examine marketing cost analysis, sales analysis, and the marketing audit as tools for analyzing a firm's marketing performance

CHAPTER OBJECTIVES

In 1983, *Fortune* magazine conducted its second annual survey to determine the most and least admired corporations in the U.S. About 3,500 corporate executives, outside directors, and financial analysts participated in the study. The largest ten firms in each of twenty-five industries (a total of 250 companies) were rated. Respondents were asked to rate only the ten biggest firms in their own industry on the basis of eight key attributes: quality of management; quality of products or services; innovativeness; long-run investment value; financial soundness; ability to attract, develop, and keep talented people; community and environmental responsibility; and the use of corporate assets. Companies were rated on a scale of 0 (poor) to 10 (excellent) for each attribute.

The ten most admired companies (based upon average ratings for the eight attributes) were IBM, Dow Jones, Hewlett-Packard, Merck, Johnson & Johnson, Time, General Electric, Anheuser-Busch, Coca-Cola, and Boeing. The ten least admired companies were International Harvester, Eastern Air Lines, Manville, Pan Am, American Motors, Republic Steel, Pabst Brewing, Trans World, Warner Communications, and U.S. Steel.

On an individual attribute basis, these were the most and least admired corporations:

Attribute	Most Admired	Least Admired
Quality of management	IBM	Warner Communications
Quality of products/services	Dow Jones	Eastern Air Lines
Innovativeness	Citicorp	International Harvester
Investment value	IBM	Eastern Air Lines
Financial soundness	IBM	International Harvester
Personnel management	Hewlett-Packard	International Harvester
Social responsibility	Johnson & Johnson	Manville
Use of assets	IBM	International Harvester

IBM was the most admired corporation for the second year in a row, rating among the best three firms for 6 of the 8 attributes (all but quality of products or services and innovativeness). IBM's chief executive cited the firm's commitments to excellence and customer service as its major strengths.

As Anheuser-Busch's chairman concluded, "Consumers trust certain companies. Consumers trust IBM. Consumers trust an Anheuser-Busch product. They trust a Boeing airplane."[1] Each of these firms places quality, integrity, and respect for customers alongside profits. Their strategies are well integrated and regularly analyzed.

Overview

Chapters 1 and 2 in the text introduced basic marketing concepts and described the marketing environment. Chapter 3 presented the strategic planning process in marketing. Chapters 4 through 20 centered on the specific aspects of planning in marketing: marketing research and information systems, describing and selecting target markets, and the four basic aspects of the marketing mix (product, distribution, promotion, and pricing). Chapters 21 through 23 broadened the scope of marketing to include international marketing, service and nonprofit marketing, and the societal elements of marketing.

This chapter describes how a marketing plan can be integrated and evaluated. An integrated marketing effort is imperative if the individual components of marketing (in particular, product, distribution, promotion, and pricing factors) are to be synchronized. Marketing analysis is necessary if the organization wants to appraise performance, capitalize on strengths, minimize weaknesses, and plan for the future.

[1] Nancy J. Perry, "America's Most Admired Corporations," *Fortune* (January 9, 1984), pp. 50–62.

Integrating the Marketing Plan

An integrated marketing plan is one in which all of the various parts of the plan are unified, consistent, and coordinated. While this appears to be a simple task, it is important to recall that a firm may have long-run, moderate-length, and short-run plans; the different strategic business units in an organization may require separate marketing plans; and each aspect of the marketing mix requires planning. For example,

The many parts of a marketing plan should be unified, consistent, and coordinated.

- An overall plan would be poorly integrated if short-run profits are made at the expense of moderate- or long-term profits. This could occur if marketing research or new-product planning expenditures are reduced to temporarily raise profits. A firm could also encounter difficulties if plans are changed too frequently, leading to a blurred image for consumers and a lack of focus for executives.
- Resources need to be allocated among SBUs, so that funds are given to those with high potential. The target markets, product images, price levels, etc. of each SBU must be distinctive, yet not in conflict with one another. Physical distribution efforts and channel-member arrangements need to be timed so that the system is not strained by two or more SBUs making costly demands simultaneously.
- Although a promotion plan primarily deals with one strategic element, it must also be integrated with product, distribution, and pricing plans. It must reflect the proper image for the company's products, encourage channel cooperation, and demonstrate that the products are worth the prices set.

In the following subsections, the elements of a well-integrated marketing plan are described, and the marketing plans of Kentucky Fried Chicken and Timex Corporation are examined and contrasted in terms of their level of integration.

Elements of a Well-Integrated Marketing Plan

A well-integrated marketing plan incorporates a clear organizational mission; long-term competitive advantages; a precisely defined target market; compatible long-, moderate-, and short-term subplans; coordination among SBUs; coordination of the marketing mix; and stability over time. These elements are shown in Figure 24-1 and explained in this subsection.

A well-integrated plan is based on seven key elements.

A clear organizational mission outlines a firm's commitment to a type of business and a place in the market. Organizational mission is involved each time a company adds or deletes products or services, seeks new customer groups or abandons existing ones, or acquires other firms or sells part of its own business (as detailed in Chapter 3). Both top management and marketers must be committed to an organizational mission for it to be achieved; and the mission has to be communicated to all company employees. For example, at First Chicago Bank, an organizational mission was enacted in order to "develop a standard of shared values, of how to behave to customers and to each other." This mission encour-

Organizational mission should be clear and understandable.

Figure 24-1
Elements Leading to a Well-Integrated Marketing Plan

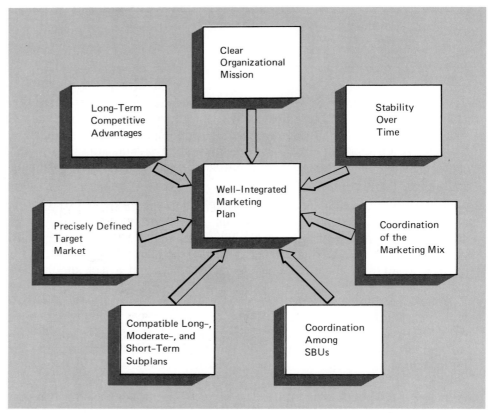

aged First Chicago to improve its consumer orientation, increase its willingness to take risks, become more entrepreneurial, and achieve employee teamwork.[2] See Figure 24-2.

Many experts believe organizational mission should be reappraised if[3]

1. The company has values that do not fit a changing environment.
2. The industry undergoes rapid changes.
3. The firm's performance is mediocre or worse.
4. The company is changing size (small to large or large to small).
5. Opportunities unrelated to the original mission arise.

Competitive advantages should center on company (product/ service) attributes that have long-range distinctiveness and appeal.

Long-term competitive advantages are company and product/service attributes whose distinctiveness and appeal to consumers can be maintained over an extended period of time. A firm must capitalize on the product/service attributes that are most important to consumers, and develop competitive advantages accordingly. For example, soap products emphasize brand image (recognition) and availability (distribution); physical product quality and servicing are relatively less important. Machine tools stress product quality and servicing; brand image and availability are of less interest.[4]

---

[2] Bro Uttal, "The Corporate Culture Vultures," *Fortune* (October 17, 1983), p. 71.

[3] Ibid., p. 70, For items 1 to 4.

[4] Robert E. MacAvoy, "Corporate Strategy and the Power of Competitive Analysis," *Management Review* (July 1983), pp. 12–13.

Figure 24-2
The Organizational
Mission of First Chicago
Bank

FIRST CHICAGO
The First National Bank of Chicago

MISSION AND COMMITMENT

MISSION

The Mission of First Chicago Corporation is to be the premier bank in the Midwest with a reputation for excellence in serving customers nationwide and throughout the world.

COMMITMENT

The customer is First Chicago's highest priority.	We are committed to providing our customers high quality and innovative services, thereby realizing long-term profitability from our relationships. We will enter into each relationship in the spirit of long-term partnership, aimed at making our customers' interests our interests.
We are strategically driven as an institution.	We will constantly seek better ways to achieve competitive advantage. Our strategies will be consistent over time, yet flexible enough to anticipate and take advantage of environmental changes. Effectively implementing our strategies will be essential to successful performance.
We are committed to a standard of excellence in all we do.	To attain the consistent superior performance to which we are committed, we must all hold ourselves individually responsible for performing our duties and fulfilling our responsibilities to the best of our abilities.
Teamwork is the way First Chicago works.	We serve our customers through people of different skills working together in teams. All of us must be willing and able to work together as leaders, participants and supporters of our various teams.
Our people are the key to our success.	We must attract, develop and retain highly principled and able people who are dedicated to personal accomplishment and the attainment of First Chicago's goals and objectives. To do this, we will demonstrate our concern for our people and motivate them to sustain the required excellence in all they do.

Reprinted by permission.

Since smaller firms usually cannot compete on the basis of low prices, they concentrate on other competitive advantages, such as[5]

- Providing unique offerings through specialization. Companies can design innovative products, handle customized orders, or otherwise tailor items for individual customers.
- Stressing product quality and reliability. ''The more crucial the performance of the product to the customers' needs, the lower will be their concern with pricing.''
- Making extra efforts to gain customer loyalty. These include easing the purchase process, giving personal attention, and promising long-term product and service availability. ''We know our . . . products are reliable and do not require visits. But when our clients see us physically inspecting our machines, sometimes merely dusting them off, they derive a sense of security and comfort.''

When implementing a marketing strategy, a firm should note that its competitive advantages may diminish if it expands too broadly, as this illustration demonstrates. Garland Corporation began as a maker of a limited line of women's sweaters. But, by 1980, Garland was making 103 different women's sweaters and 220 varieties of coordinated blouses and pants. During 1980, the firm lost several million dollars. Then, Garland brought in a new management team, which slashed the product line to just 20 styles of sweaters. Garland had learned that ''We're good at sweaters but not at anything else.'' Within one year, the firm

[5] Peter Wright, ''Competitive Strategies for Small Business,'' *Collegiate Forum* (Spring 1983), pp. 3–4.

Figure 24-3
Limited Express stores, owned by Limited Inc., offer a broad assortment of popular-priced sportswear and accessories for women 15 to 25 years of age. These stores feature innovative interior designs and the latest fashions.

Reprinted by permission.

returned to profitability. In 1982, it earned a net profit of $4.1 million on sales of $15.9 million.[6]

The target market should be identified precisely.

A precisely defined target market identifies the specific consumers the firm addresses in a marketing plan. It guides the company's marketing efforts and future direction. With multiple segmentation, a firm appeals to two or more distinct segments; it is essential that each be described precisely. For example, Limited Inc. has enacted separate strategies for each of its three major market segments: young women, full-size women, and upper-income women. The Limited stores carry trendy apparel for fashion-conscious young single women (ages 20 to 40) who work or attend college; Limited Express stores offer clothing for 15 to 25 year-old women. Lane Bryant and Roaman's stores cater to full-size women. Victoria's Secret is a mail-order retailer of high-priced lingerie.[7] Figure 24-3 shows an interior from a Limited Express store.

As Atari discovered when it introduced its first personal computers (which

[6] Steven Mintz, "Sales and Marketing to the Rescue," *Sales & Marketing Management* (April 4, 1983), pp. 35–36.
[7] "Limited Inc.: Expanding Its Position to Serve the Rubenesque Woman," *Business Week* (November 22, 1982), pp. 56, 58.

had very weak sales), a strategy that relies on an imprecise definition of the target market can go astray. As one analyst commented,

Top executives at Atari used to brag that they didn't know the first thing about using a computer. It was absentee management. They lost respect for their customers and didn't listen to what their customers were telling them.[8]

The long-, moderate-, and short-term marketing subplans of the company need to be compatible with one another. Long-term plans are the most general and set a broad framework for moderate-term plans. Short-term plans are the most specific; but, they should be derived from both moderate-and long-term plans, as the following Dayton Hudson example shows.

Long-, moderate-, and short-term subplans should be compatible.

Dayton Hudson is a national retailer that operates Target, an upscale discount store chain; Mervyn's, a discount department store chain; Dayton's, Hudson's, Diamond's, and John A. Brown, department store chains; B. Dalton Bookseller, a bookstore chain; Lechmere, a home and leisure products store chain; and Dayton Hudson Jewelers, a jewelry store chain. In all Dayton Hudson operates 1,000 stores throughout the U.S. and has annual sales exceeding $6.5 billion. Dayton Hudson's marketing strategy is based on a compatible combination of long-, moderate-, and short-term plans:[9]

- One day a month, executives meet to discuss long-range plans. The annual long-term return on investment goal is 15 to 16 per cent. A decentralized management structure places great control in the hands of the managers of each of its nine store chains. Marketing research studies are conducted regularly.
- Moderate-term plans focus on changes in target customers, service level requirements and projections, resource allocation, merchandise trends, and expansion. Between 1983 and 1986, Dayton Hudson planned to nearly double the number of Target stores, Mervyn's stores, and B. Dalton Bookseller outlets. The expansion would cost $2.5 billion.
- Short-term plans are geared to achieving and maintaining dominance (having the best possible assortment of the merchandise categories carried), quality (merchandise, management, service, and shopping environment), fashion (timeliness for wearing apparel, books, kitchen utensils, home furnishings, etc.), convenience (respect for consumer's time), and price (competitive and fair value).

Coordination among SBUs is enhanced when the functions, strategies, and resources allocated to each are described in long-term, moderate-term, and short-term plans. For instance, at Borg-Warner (a large conglomerate), there are about 100 SBUs, all of which submit annual plans. Each year, corporate planners identify 20 to 30 "crucial" SBUs. These SBUs have a strong positive or negative impact on company performance; or, their proposed strategies are questionable. 10 to 12 of the "crucial" SBUs are singled out for the special attention of top management, which coordinates the plans and allocates resources. Borg-Warner

SBUs should be coordinated.

---

[8] Leslie Wayne, "The Battle for Survival at Warner," *New York Times* (January 8, 1984), Section 3, p. 29.
[9] Kenneth A. Macke, "Managing Change: How Dayton Hudson Meets the Challenge," *Journal of Business Strategy*, Vol. 4 (Summer 1983), pp. 78–81; and Frank James, "Dayton Hudson Will End Test in Discounting," *Wall Street Journal* (February 22, 1984), p. 4.

management monitors strategy implementation to be sure of conformity with company policy.[10]

Sometimes, acquisitions make the coordination of SBUs especially difficult, as these illustrations demonstrate. Coca-Cola was unable to make the wine division that it established in 1977, after acquiring Taylor Wine, profitable and therefore sold it in 1983. It did not realize how different it was to market wine from soda. Wine marketing was affected by state and federal regulations, comparative advertising created ill will, getting on restaurant wine lists was difficult, and profit margins were extremely low.[11] Esmark (maker of Swift Foods products and Playtex personal-care items and a wide range of other products) acquired Norton Simon (maker of Max Factor cosmetics and Hunt-Wesson Foods, operator of Avis car rental, etc.) in 1983. Coordinating its new SBUs and integrating them into overall company marketing plans was not easy for Esmark.[12] In mid-1984, Esmark itself was acquired by Beatrice.

The marketing mix within each SBU should be coordinated.

The components of the marketing mix (product, distribution, promotion, and price) need to be coordinated within each SBU. For example, Thermos, an SBU of Household International, has this well-conceived marketing mix for its recently restyled line of outdoor living products:[13]

- Product—There are eight personal-size food (beverage) coolers and four larger cooler chests in the line. These products feature product information labels on all four sides, trays that do not accumulate frost, bright colors, and a company logo. A three-year warranty is provided. See Figure 24-4.
- Distribution—Mass merchandisers, drugstores, hardware stores, and sporting goods stores are among the retailers carrying the line. Thermos is very aggressive in obtaining and keeping shelf space.
- Promotion—A large sales force calls on retailers; and print ads and promotions are also directed at channel members. Television commercials (on shows such as *Good Morning America* and *The Price Is Right* and magazine ads (in *People* and other magazines) are aimed at final consumers.
- Price—Prices are competitive with Coleman and Igloo, the other leading firms in the product category. Rebates have been offered to both retailers and final consumers.

The stability of the plan should be maintained over time.

A marketing plan must have a certain degree of stability over time in order for it to be implemented and evaluated properly. This does not mean that a marketing plan should be inflexible, and therefore unable to adjust to a dynamic environment. Rather, it means that a broad marketing plan, consistent with the firm's organizational mission, should guide long-term efforts and be fine-tuned regularly; the basic plan should remain in effect for a number of years. Short-run marketing plans can be much more flexible, as long as they conform to long-term goals and the organizational mission. For example, low prices might be part of a

---

[10] Don Collier, ''How to Implement Strategic Plans,'' *Journal of Business Strategy*, Vol. 4 (Winter 1984), p. 95.

[11] ''Why Coca-Cola and Wine Didn't Mix,'' *Business Week* (October 10, 1983), p. 30.

[12] Betsy Morris, ''Esmark Facing Huge Challenge in Melding Norton Simon's Units, People with Its Own,'' *Wall Street Journal* (July 27, 1983), pp. 25, 30. See also Betsy Morris, ''Esmark May Be Poised for Change after a Decade of Major Acquisitions,'' *Wall Street Journal* (March 1, 1984), pp. 31, 53.

[13] ''Thermos Hopes to Cool Competition with a Revamped Marketing Strategy,'' *Marketing News* (December 23, 1983), pp. 1, 12.

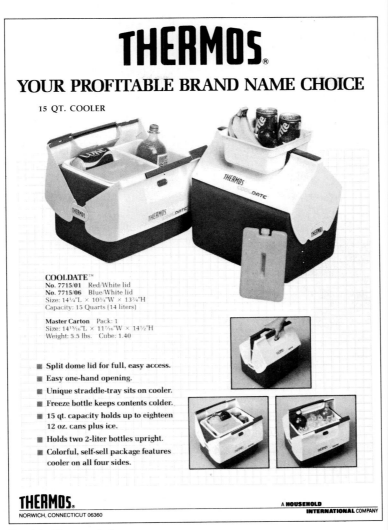

Figure 24-4
Outdoor Living Products from Thermos
This ad regarding one of the Thermos personal-size coolers is oriented toward retailers, and details the sales features of the product.

long-term marketing plan. However, in any particular year, prices might have to be raised in response to environmental forces.

An unstable marketing plan can result in a firm's customers, channel members, outside publics, and even employees being confused about the plan and the tactics used to carry it out. This confusion happened to Sears during the 1970s and early 1980s. Over a fairly short period, Sears tried several plans to improve sales. It went upscale, turned to sales promotions, switched to discounting, entered a period of retrenchment, and finally settled on its current strategy stressing moderate-priced, moderate-fashion clothing as well as a full range of financial services. The constant changes in strategy made it hard for customers to know what to expect when visiting a Sears store. As a result, some loyal customers were lost and many potential customers did not patronize Sears because they were unsure of its image. Sears' sales growth and profits only began to rise again when its present middle-road strategy was adopted; this is really a return to the organizational mission the company has had for most of its history, a mass-marketing strategy ("Sears, Where America Shops"). It is essential that Sears maintain an enduring image in the future.[14]

Next, the marketing plans of Kentucky Fried Chicken and Timex Corporation are analyzed. The two plans are then contrasted, using the elements that were identified in Figure 24-1.

Kentucky Fried Chicken: Turning to a Well-Integrated Marketing Strategy[15]

Between 1976 and 1978, Kentucky Fried Chicken (KFC), now a division of R. J. Reynolds, performed poorly. Sales declined at a level of 3 per cent per year, while pretax profits dropped at an annual rate of 26 per cent. As a result, "franchisees who were out-performing company operations were openly dissatisfied and hostile, and customers were going to competitors."

In some ways, the company was its own worst enemy. Many restaurants were sloppy, and their food was unappetizing. Even founder Colonel Harland Sanders publicly complained that the chain served "the worst fried chicken I've ever seen," and that the gravy "resembled wallpaper paste." Initially, rather than studying why business was poor and correcting existing problems, KFC tried to improve sales through a series of new product introductions and pricing tactics (such as discounting). These approaches were not successful.

Then, the chain turned its deteriorating situation around by developing a thorough, systematic, and integrated marketing plan—based on sound research and analysis. KFC set a goal of becoming the strongest, most profitable, and fastest growing chain in the fast-food service industry. It has accomplished this.

After some problems, Kentucky Fried Chicken devised and implemented a well-integrated marketing plan.

Research was conducted on the firm's environment, competition, and available resources. Several company strengths were revealed: positioning in an attractive industry segment, a strong distribution network of 6,000 restaurants worldwide (more than 4,400 in the U.S.), a 50 per cent market share in the fast-food chicken industry, and high potential consumer loyalty for a properly prepared product line.

Analysis of the findings by KFC management led to a marketing plan featuring these concepts:

- The firm would concentrate on fried chicken and severely cut back on its portfolio of businesses (such as a seafood chain, a Mexican food chain, and related equipment and supply companies). The wide portfolio had been developed when KFC was viewed as a food-service conglomerate.
- Menus and prices were evaluated on the basis of long-term instead of short-term implications.

[14] Ann Morrison, "Sears' Overdue Retailing Revival," *Fortune* (April 4, 1983), pp. 133–134; "Sears Opens Its First 'Store of the Future' in Philadelphia Area," *Marketing News* (August 19, 1983), p. 8; and Isadore Barmash, "Shaping a Sears Financial Empire," *New York Times* (February 12, 1984), Section 3, pp. 1, 6.

[15] David P. Garino, "Fried Chicken Competition Is Heating Up," *Wall Street Journal* (December 21, 1982), p. 1; David P. Garino, "At Kentucky Fried Chicken, It's Time to Set Itself Apart," *Wall Street Journal* (March 19, 1981), p. 29; Richard Kreisman, "Heublein Invests Heavily in KFC Stores," *Advertising Age* (June 7, 1982), p. 10; Richard P. Mayer, "Chain's Fortunes Improved When It Rearticulated Its Mission and Strategic Plan," *Marketing News* (July 9, 1982), p. 14; Scott Hume, "KFC to Stick with What It's Finally Doing Right," *Advertising Age* (June 27, 1983), pp. 4, 74; and Pamela G. Hollie, "Fast-Food Rivalry," *New York Times* (April 17, 1984), pp. D1, D2.

- The nutritional value of chicken was stressed. Advertising themes turned to "It's so nice to feel so good about a meal" and "we do chicken right." See Figure 24-5. The television advertising budget was expanded to $42 million annually by 1982.
- Chicken recipes and cooking procedures were standardized. Product quality was evaluated using "mystery shoppers." A systematic training program was instituted.
- Priority was given to new store development and remodeling. Forty new stores were opened in 1982; and a number of franchised units were bought back by KFC. New store openings in Japan, Australia, West Germany, Mexico, Brazil, Venezuela, etc. were also slated. Two thirds of company-owned outlets and one third of franchised stores were remodeled.

As a result of the proper integration of its marketing strategy, KFC was able to generate several years of real sales gains (after adjusting for price increases) at a time when the overall fast-food industry was experiencing sluggish growth. Total systemwide sales rose from $1.1 billion in 1977 to $2.6 billion in 1983. Average yearly sales per store grew from less than $300,000 in 1979 to about $525,000 during 1983. KFC had a 72 per cent share of fast-food chicken restaurant sales in 1983.

Even Colonel Sanders was impressed. At his 90th birthday party, not long before his death, he thanked the company for repairing his creation.

Figure 24-5
The Well-Known Slogan of Kentucky Fried Chicken

Photograph courtesy of Kentucky Fried Chicken.

Timex Corporation: A Dis-Integrating Marketing Strategy[16]

The Timex Corporation is in the midst of troubled times. Operating losses in 1982 totaled about $130 million on sales of $500 million. By 1983, the firm was approximately $100 million in debt. Its Dundee, Scotland plant, once the largest watch factory in the world, now does subcontracting work for other manufacturers. These problems are all relatively recent; as of the mid-1970s, Timex had annual pretax profits of around $40 million.

Timex's original marketing strategy was well-conceived and integrated. It produced low-cost watches by employing mass-production technology and hard-alloy bearings (which were inexpensive, yet durable). Timex offered jewelers a 30 per cent markup on its watches; but when the jewelers insisted on a 50 per cent markup, Timex decided to bypass them. It built up an impressive distribution network of drugstores, hardware stores, discount stores, variety stores, and even cigar stands. Television advertising showed that Timex watches strapped to boat propellers and other objects could "take a licking and keep on ticking." Production was limited to about 85 per cent of consumer demand in order to keep actual selling prices at or near suggested retail price levels. In the late 1960s, Timex had a 50 per cent market share of all watches sold in the U.S.

Then, substantial problems began to emerge in the early 1970s:

After a period of success, the management of Timex became complacent and allowed the marketing plan to become disjointed.

- Timex management was very slow to react to market trends. Despite competitors' success with digital watches and then quartz analog watches, Timex stayed with mechanical watches. By the end of 1981, 60 per cent of the watches produced by Timex were still mechanical. Timex also paid inadequate attention to watch fashion; it became known for "plain-Jane" watches.
- When Timex finally introduced its quartz watches, they were priced 50 per cent higher than competitors' brands. In addition, the watches were so heavy that employees nicknamed them "quarter-pounders."
- Instead of increasing customer demand through advertising, Timex kept reducing production and capacity to keep it below demand (which kept falling). Timex continued to keep high prices on mechanical watches and cut back on marketing support. According to a 1981 internal memo, Timex "started treating the mechanical watch as if it had only hours to live." Mechanical watch profits were channeled to new ventures. Distribution outlets fell from 250,000 to 100,000.
- Although watches still account for 90 per cent of its sales, Timex has not developed "wrist instruments," watches that can take a person's pulse and blood pressure or perform a variety of other functions. However, Seiko has a watch that takes a person's pulse, a Citizen Watch model takes a person's temperature, and Casio has a watch that translates 36 phrases into foreign languages.
- After 500,000 inexpensive Timex-Sinclair home computers were sold during

[16] Myron Magnet, "Timex Takes the Torture Test," *Fortune* (June 27, 1983), pp. 112–115 ff; Jeffrey H. Birnbaum, "Falling Profit Prompts Timex to Shed Its Utilitarian Image," *Wall Street Journal* (September 17, 1981), p. 29; and David E. Sanger, "Computers Dropped by Timex," *New York Times* (February 22, 1984), pp. D1, D3.

the last three months of 1982, extensive price competition by Commodore and others all but wiped out the demand for the overly simplistic Timex-Sinclair model. Said Casio's president, ''They've gotten themselves into another business that is on a toboggan as far as price goes.'' In early 1984, Timex announced that it was dropping computers.

- In 1983, Timex entered the home health-care market with a $49.95 digital scale, a $24.95 digital thermometer, and an easy-to-use $69.95 blood pressure cuff. See Figure 24-6. These products fit well with Timex's distribution system of 45,000 drugstores carrying Timex watches, and can capitalize on the Timex name. However, critics believe that Timex does not have an organizational mission and is merely ''clutching haphazardly at knicknacks and trifles that bear its name and can be pushed through its distribution network.''

To turn around its watch business, Timex is now marketing the world's thinnest quartz watch (priced at $100+), producing more fashionable watches, increasing television advertising, dropping prices (its cheapest digital watch is $7.95), and cutting back on mechanical watches. Nonetheless, many observers are skeptical about the company's ability to emerge from its difficulties, particularly in the face of a stagnant and highly competitive worldwide watch market and Timex's fragmented strategy.

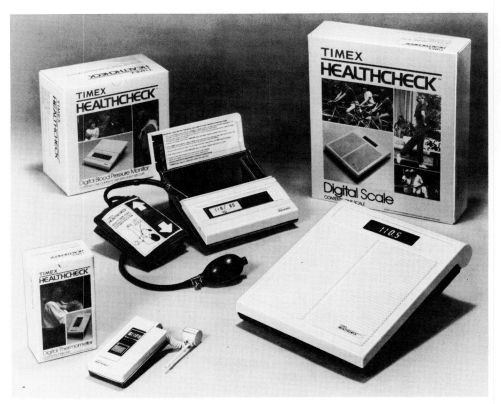

Figure 24-6
Timex Healthcheck Products
Timex has introduced a number of health-related products to complement its watch lines. These products are being carried by a number of drugstores and utilize Timex's strong brand awareness with consumers.

Reprinted by permission.

Contrasting the Marketing Plans of Kentucky Fried Chicken and Timex

The performance of Kentucky Fried Chicken and Timex is directly related to their marketing plans.

Table 24-1 contrasts the marketing plans of Kentucky Fried Chicken and Timex on the basis of the plans' level of integration. The table demonstrates the well-integrated nature of Kentucky Fried Chicken's plan and Timex's disjointed approach to marketing. The present status of these companies is in large part due to their ability and willingness (or the lack of them) to integrate their marketing efforts and carry out marketing plans in a systematic manner. Kentucky Fried Chicken overcame its problems by constructing and implementing a stable long-term marketing plan. Timex fell from a leadership position because it engaged in marketing myopia and did not plan for the future.

**Table 24-1
Kentucky Fried Chicken Versus Timex: Comparing the Level of Integration of Two Marketing Plans**

Element	Kentucky Fried Chicken	Timex
Clarity of organizational mission	Concentrates on fried chicken, incompatible businesses sold off	Involved with health-care products, yet watches account for 90 per cent of sales
Long-term competitive advantages	High market share, high store loyalty and name recognition, distribution strength	High brand recognition, distribution strength
Precision with which target market is defined	Specific: Family-oriented, largely take-out, nutritional appeal	Dispersed: watches priced from $7.95 to $100+, new products appealing to different customers
Compatibility of long-, moderate-, and short-term subplans	Menu, pricing, and expansion proposals based on long-term objectives; long-term gains no longer sacrificed for short-term profits	Management too slow to recognize long-term trends, excessive short-term orientation, overreliance on mechanical watches
Coordination among SBUs	KFC a self-contained unit of R. J. Reynolds with adequate resources and no conflicts with other SBUs	Computers were inappropriate through existing distribution network; home health-care items need physician endorsement; ad budget to be divided among watches and health-care items
Coordination across functional marketing areas	Standardization of recipes and cooking procedures, new locations carefully determined, "We do chicken right" theme, store remodeling, training programs, moderate prices	Poor product planning (heavy quartz watch, lack of fashion); reduced advertising for many years; high prices on noninnovative products, $100+ watches in drugstores
Stability of strategy over time	One, consistent strategy in effect since 1978; all future plans keyed to it	Strategy changes as recently as 1984, uncertainty about future direction and emphasis (watches? medical products?)

Analyzing the Marketing Plan

Marketing plan analysis involves the comparison of actual performance with planned performance for a specified period of time. If actual performance is unsatisfactory, corrective action may be necessary. Sometimes, plans have to be revised because of the impact of uncontrollable variables.[17]

Three techniques used to analyze marketing plans are discussed in the following subsections: marketing cost analysis, sales analysis, and the marketing audit. While the discussion of these techniques is restricted to their utility in evaluating marketing plans, they can also be employed in the development and modification of these plans.

Marketing plan analysis compares actual and planned achievements.

Marketing Cost Analysis

Marketing cost analysis evaluates the cost effectiveness of various marketing factors, such as different product lines, distribution methods, sales territories, channel members, salespersons, advertising media, and customer types. Through marketing cost analysis, a firm can determine which classifications are cost efficient and which are cost inefficient, and make appropriate adjustments in the future. While a company may be profitable, not all of its products, distribution methods, etc. are equally cost effective (or profitable). Marketing cost analysis can also provide information that may be needed to substantiate price compliance with the Robinson-Patman Act. In order for marketing cost analysis to work properly, the firm needs continuous and accurate accounting data. Table 24-2 presents several examples of marketing cost analysis.

Cost effectiveness is measured through *marketing cost analysis.*

The application of marketing cost analysis varies widely. One study of 146 industrial firms (with average annual sales of almost $155 million) found that 73 per cent of the companies engaged in marketing cost analysis by product, 33 per cent by customer group, 30 per cent by individual salesperson, 19 per cent by geographic area, and 11 per cent by order size.[18]

The procedure for utilizing marketing cost analysis consists of three stages: studying natural account expenses, reclassifying natural accounts into functional accounts, and allocating functional accounts by marketing classification.

STUDYING NATURAL ACCOUNT EXPENSES

The first step in marketing cost analysis is to determine the level of ***natural account expenses,*** which are reported by the names of the expenses and not by the expenditures' purposes. Natural expenses include salaries, rent, advertising, supplies, insurance, and interest. These expenses are the cost categories normally contained in ledger accounts. Table 24-3 shows a natural-account expense classification.

Natural account expenses include salaries, rent, and insurance.

[17] See Connie A. Cox, ''Gap Analysis: A New Business Planning Essential,'' *Business Marketing* (May 1983), pp. 71–74.

[18] Donald W. Jackson, Jr., Lonnie L. Ostrom, and Kenneth R. Evans, ''Measures Used to Evaluate Industrial Marketing Activities,'' *Industrial Marketing Management*, Vol. 11 (October 1982), pp. 269–274.

Table 24-2 Examples of Marketing Cost Analysis

Marketing Factor	Strategy/Tactics Studied	Problem/Opportunity Discovered	Action Applied
Product	Should a manufacturer accept a retailer's proposal that the firm make 700,000 private-label sneakers?	Substantial excess capacity exists; the private label would require no additional fixed costs.	A contract is signed. Different features for private and manu-facturer labels are planned.
Order size	What is the minimum order size a hardware manufacturer should accept?	Orders below $30 do not have positive profit margins; they are too costly to process.	Small orders are discouraged through surcharges and minimum order size.
Distribution	Should a men's suit manufac-turer sell direct to consumers as well as through normal channels?	Start-up and personal selling costs would be high. Addi-tional sales would be minimal.	Direct sales are not undertaken.
Personal selling	What are the costs of making a sale?	15 per cent of sales covers compensation and selling expenses, 2 per cent above the industry average.	Sales personnel are encouraged to phone customers before visiting them, to confirm appointments.
Advertising media	Which is more effective, televi-sion or magazine advertising?	Television advertising costs $.05 for every potential customer reached; magazine advertising costs $.07.	Television advertising is increased.
Customer type	What are the relative costs of selling X rays to dentists, physicians, and hospitals?	Per-unit costs of hospital sales are lowest (as are prices); per-unit costs of dentist and physician sales are highest (as are prices).	Current efforts are maintained. Each customer is serviced.

RECLASSIFYING NATURAL ACCOUNTS INTO FUNCTIONAL ACCOUNTS

Functional accounts denote the purpose or activity of expenditures.

Natural accounts are then reclassified into *functional accounts,* which indi-cate the purpose or activity for which expenditures have been made. Included as functional expenses are marketing administration, personal selling, advertising, transportation, warehousing, marketing research, and general administration. Table 24-4 reclassifies the natural accounts of Table 24-3 into functional ac-counts.

**Table 24-3
A Natural Account
Expense Classification**

Net sales (after returns and discounts)	$1,000,000	
Less: Cost of goods sold	450,000	
Gross profit		$550,000
Less: Operating expenses (natural account expenses)		
Salaries and fringe benefits	220,000	
Rent	40,000	
Advertising	30,000	
Supplies	6,100	
Insurance	2,500	
Interest expense	1,400	
Total operating expenses		300,000
Net profit before taxes		$250,000

Table 24-4 Reclassifying Natural Accounts into Functional Accounts

Natural Accounts	Total	Functional Accounts						
		Marketing Administration	Personal Selling	Advertising	Transportation	Warehousing	Marketing Research	General Administration
Salaries and fringe benefits	$220,000	$30,000	$50,000	$15,000	$10,000	$20,000	$30,000	$65,000
Rent	40,000	3,000	7,000	3,000	2,000	10,000	5,000	10,000
Advertising	30,000			30,000				
Supplies	6,100	500	1,000	500			1,100	3,000
Insurance	2,500		1,000			1,200		300
Interest expense	1,400							1,400
Total	$300,000	$33,500	$59,000	$48,500	$12,000	$31,200	$36,100	$79,700

Once functional accounts are established, cost analysis becomes clearer. For instance, if salaries and fringe benefits increase by $25,000 over the prior year, natural-account analysis would be unable to allocate the rise to a functional area. Functional-account analysis would be able to pinpoint the areas of marketing requiring higher personnel costs.

ALLOCATING FUNCTIONAL ACCOUNTS BY MARKETING CLASSIFICATION

The third step in marketing cost analysis assigns functional costs by product, distribution method, sales territory, channel member, salesperson, customer, or other classification. This develops each classification as a profit center. Table 24-5 illustrates how costs can be distributed among different products, using the data from Tables 24-3 and 24-4. From Table 24-5, it can be determined that product A has the highest sales and highest total profit. However, product C has the greatest profit as a per cent of sales.

Functional costs are assigned with each marketing classification as a profit center.

Table 24-5 Allocating Functional Expenses by Product

	Total	Product A	Product B	Product C
Net sales	$1,000,000	$500,000	$300,000	$200,000
Less: Cost of goods sold	450,000	250,000	120,000	80,000
Gross profit	$550,000	$250,000	$180,000	$120,000
Less: Operating expenses (functional account expenses)				
Marketing administration	33,500	16,000	10,000	7,500
Personal selling	59,000	30,000	17,100	11,900
Advertising	48,500	20,000	18,000	10,500
Transportation	12,000	5,000	5,000	2,000
Warehousing	31,200	20,000	7,000	4,200
Marketing research	36,100	18,000	11,000	7,100
General administration	79,700	40,000	23,000	16,700
Total operating expenses	300,000	149,000	91,100	59,900
Net profit before taxes	$250,000	$101,000	$ 88,900	$ 60,100
Profit as per cent of sales	25.0	20.2	29.6	30.1

When allocating functional costs, these points should be remembered. One, the assignment of some costs, such as marketing administration, among different products, customers, or other classifications is usually somewhat arbitrary. Two, the elimination of a poorly performing classification will shift overhead costs, such as general administration, among the remaining product or customer categories. This may diminish overall total profit. Three, the company should distinguish between separable expenses that are directly associated with a given classification category and can be eliminated if the category is discontinued and common expenses that are shared by various categories and cannot be eliminated if one is discontinued.

The company should also distinguish between order-generating and order-processing costs (described in Chapter 3) before making any strategic changes suggested by marketing cost analysis. The managers of Munsingwear learned that lesson the hard way:

> [They] set out to increase profits by cutting expenses. To do that, they changed the labels on the underwear boxes, making it difficult for retailers to find in their storerooms. . . . Even worse, they removed the distinctive waistbands encircled with Munsingwear's name. That saved a few cents in weaving costs for each brief, but neither shoppers nor retailers liked the blank waistbands.

These managers were soon replaced, and the product design of Munsingwear underwear was changed back to its former state.[19]

Sales Analysis

With *sales analysis*, data are evaluated to determine the correctness of a marketing strategy.

Sales analysis is the detailed study of sales data for the purpose of appraising the appropriateness of a marketing strategy. Without adequate sales analysis, the importance of certain market segments and territories may be overlooked, sales effort may be poorly matched with market potential, fashion trends may be overlooked, or assistance for sales personnel may not be forthcoming. Sales analysis enables plans to be set in terms of sales by product, product line, salesperson, region, customer type, time period, price line, or method of sale. It also compares actual sales against planned sales.

More companies engage in sales analysis than in marketing cost analysis. For example, the study of industrial firms cited in the previous subsection found that 89 per cent of the companies conduct sales analysis by product, 80 per cent by individual salesperson, 72 per cent by customer group, 69 per cent by geographic area, and 20 per cent by order size.[20]

The *sales invoice* and *control units* are essential aspects of sales analysis.

The main source of sales analysis data is the *sales invoice.* It contains information on customer name, quantity ordered, price paid, purchase terms, geographic location of purchaser, all different items bought at the same time, order date, shipping arrangements, and salesperson. Summary data can be generated by adding invoices. The use of computerized marking and inventory systems speeds the recording and improves the accuracy of sales data.

In conducting a sales analysis, proper control units must be selected. *Control units* are sales categories for which data are gathered, such as boys', men's,

[19] Frank E. James, ''Munsingwear Regains Order and Discipline But Faces a Tough Battle to Restore Profits,'' *Wall Street Journal* (September 6, 1983), p. 37.
[20] Jackson, Ostrom, and Evans, ''Measures Used to Evaluate Industrial Marketing Activities.''

girls', and women's clothing. Although a marketer can broaden a control system by summarizing several sales categories, wide categories cannot be broken down into components. Therefore, a narrow sales category is preferable to one that is too wide. It is also helpful to select control units that are consistent with other company, trade association, and government data. A stable classification system is necessary to compare data from different time periods.

7-Eleven and Levi Strauss are examples of companies that use sales analysis. 7-Eleven knows that its best-selling products are gasoline, fast-food sandwiches, disposable diapers, and *Playboy* magazine. 7-Eleven sells far more *Playboy* magazines, candy bars, and canned beer than any other U.S. retailer. Over half of its goods are consumed within thirty minutes after purchase. The typical customer is young, male, and spends about $2.25 per visit.[21]

Levi Strauss has a shipment analysis system that organizes invoices, customer credit approval information, and product descriptions into monthly sales summary profiles. These show specific product sales by units and dollars within each sales region. This information allows Levi Strauss to establish sales goals by garment and customer type and evaluate progress toward goals.[22]

A key principle in sales analysis is that summary data such as overall current sales or market share are usually insufficient to diagnose a firm's areas of strength and weakness. More intensive investigation is necessary. Two sales analysis techniques that offer in-depth probing are the 80–20 principle and sales exception reporting.

The **80–20 principle** states that in many organizations a large proportion of total sales (profit) comes from a small proportion of customers, products, or territories.[23] In order to function efficiently, firms should determine sales and profit by customer, product, or territory. Then marketing efforts would be allocated accordingly. Companies err when they examine only total sales (profit) rather than isolate and categorize data. Through faulty reasoning, they would place equal effort into each sale instead of concentrating on larger accounts. These errors are due to a related concept known as the **iceberg principle,** which states that superficial data are insufficient to make sound evaluations.

Through in-depth analysis, the Firestone Tire & Rubber Company discovered that it was operating under the 80–20 principle and responded appropriately. Of the 7,289 different tire types it produced (counting all widths, styles, sizes, and in-house and private brands), the Firestone brand represented 65 per cent of sales but only 25 per cent of all items. The frequent changeovers in the factory caused by product proliferation led to higher down time, higher costs, and lower quality standards. Firestone eliminated 2,400 items while retaining those with the highest profit margins.[24]

Simple sales analysis also can be enhanced by using **sales exception reporting,** which lists situations where sales goals are not met or sales opportunities are present. A slow-selling item report lists items whose sales are below those forecasted. It suggests corrective actions such as price reductions, promotions, and

> The *80–20 principle* notes that a large part of total sales (profits) often comes from few customers, products, or territories. Analysis errors may be due to the *iceberg principle*.

> *Sales exception reporting* centers on unmet goals or special opportunities.

[21] *1982 Major Market Study* (Dallas: 7-Eleven Research Department, 1982); and Shawn Tully, "Look Who's Champ of Gasoline Marketing," *Fortune* (November 1, 1982), p. 150.

[22] "Levi Strauss Computers Find Consumer Preferences," *Marketing News* (September 5, 1980), p. 8.

[23] See Alan J. Dubinsky and Richard W. Hansen, "Improving Marketing Productivity: The 80/20 Principle Revisited," *California Management Review,* Vol. 25 (Fall 1982), pp. 96–105.

[24] Thomas O'Hanlon, "Less Means More at Firestone," *Fortune* (October 20, 1980), p. 119.

sales incentives to increase unit sales. A fast-selling item report lists items whose sales exceed those forecasted. It points out sales opportunities and items that need more inventory on hand to prevent stockouts. Finally, sales exception reporting enables a firm to evaluate the validity of sales forecasts and make the proper modifications in them. Figure 24-7 presents examples of the 80–20 principle, the iceberg principle, and sales exception reporting.

Organizations also may use sales analysis to identify and monitor consumer buying patterns by answering the questions: who purchases, what is purchased, how are items purchased, when are purchases made, how much is purchased, and where are purchases made? Table 24-6 lists a number of consumer buying patterns that can be monitored through sales analysis.

A *marketing audit* examines a firm in a systematic, critical, and unbiased manner.

Marketing Audit

The ***marketing audit*** is defined as

a systematic, critical, and unbiased review and appraisal of the basic objectives and policies of the marketing function, and of the organization, methods, procedures, and

80–20 Principle

	Annual Sales		Marketing Expenditures	
	$	%	$	%
Product A	1,000,000	50.0	200,000	44.4
Product B	750,000	37.5	150,000	33.3
Product C	250,000	12.5	100,000	22.2
Total	$2,000,000	100.0	$450,000	100.0*

*Rounding error.

Although a company gets only 12.5 per cent of total sales from Product C, it spends 22.2 per cent of its marketing budget on that product.

Iceberg Principle

Only the tip of the iceberg is seen with superfical analysis (aggregate data).

The entire iceberg is seen only with in-depth analysis (detailed, categorized data).

Sales Exception Reporting

	Expected Sales	Actual Sales
Product 1	$50,000	$100,000
Product 2	$50,000	$ 50,000
Product 3	$75,000	$ 75,000
Product 4	$75,000	$ 50,000

Sales report

A review of the sales report indicates that Product 1 has done much better than expected, while Product 4 has done much worse.

Figure 24-7
Sales Analysis Concepts

Questions	Information from Sales Classified by
1. Who purchases?	Organizational vs. final consumer, geographic region, end use, purchase history, customer size, customer demographics
2. What is purchased?	Product line, price category, brand, country of origin, package size, options purchased
3. How are items purchased?	Form of payment, billing terms, delivery form, wrapping technique
4. When are purchases made?	Season, financial time period, day of week, time of day
5. How much is purchased?	Unit sales volume, dollar sales volume, profit margin
6. Where are purchases made?	Place of customer contact, purchase location, warehouse location

**Table 24-6
Consumer Buying
Patterns Uncovered by
Sales Analysis**

personnel employed to implement those policies and to achieve those objectives. Clearly, not every evaluation of marketing personnel, organizations, or methods is a marketing audit; at best, most such evaluations can be regarded as parts of the audit.[25]

The purpose of an audit is to generate topics of discussion for future planning and to identify the areas in which an organization needs to correct deficiencies. It includes an investigation of the firm's marketing objectives, strategy, implementation, and organization. An effective audit is conducted on a regular basis, comprehensive, systematic, and carried out in an independent manner.[26]

The marketing audit process consists of six steps, shown in Figure 26-8:

1. Determination of who does the audit. An audit may be conducted by company specialists, company division or department managers, or outside specialists.
2. Determination of when and how often the audit is conducted. An audit may be undertaken at the end of a calendar year, at the end of a company's annual reporting year, or when undertaking a physical inventory. An audit should be performed at least annually, although some companies prefer more frequent analysis. The audit should be completed during the same time period each year to allow comparisons. In some cases, unannounced audits are useful to keep employees alert and ensure spontaneity of answers.
3. Determination of areas to be audited. A **horizontal audit** (often referred to as a marketing-mix audit) studies the overall marketing performance of the company with particular emphasis on the interrelationship of variables and their relative importance. A **vertical audit** is an in-depth analysis of one aspect of the firm's marketing strategy, such as product planning. The two audits should be used in conjunction with one another because the horizontal audit often reveals areas that need further investigation.
4. Developing audit forms. Audit forms list the areas to be examined and the exact information required to evaluate each area. The forms usually resemble

A *horizontal audit* studies overall marketing; a *vertical audit* analyzes one aspect of marketing.

---

[25] Adapted from Abraham Schuchman, "The Marketing Audit: Its Nature, Purpose, and Problems," *Analyzing and Improving Marketing Performance*, Report No. 32 (New York: American Management Association, 1959), p. 13; and Alfred R. Oxenfeldt, *Executive Action in Marketing* (Belmont, Calif.: Wadsworth Publishing, 1966), p. 746.

[26] Hal W. Goetsch, "Conduct a Comprehensive Marketing Audit to Improve Marketing Planning," *Marketing News* (March 18, 1983), Section 2, p. 14; and Philip Kotler, *Marketing Management: Analysis, Planning, and Control*, Fifth Edition (Englewood Cliffs, N.J.: Prentice-Hall, 1984), p. 765.

Figure 24-8
The Marketing Audit
Process

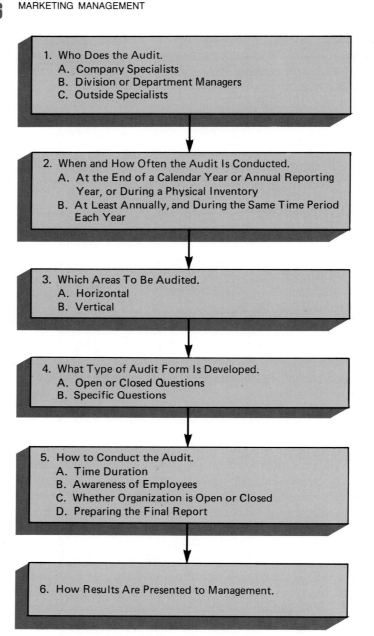

1. Who Does the Audit.
   A. Company Specialists
   B. Division or Department Managers
   C. Outside Specialists

2. When and How Often the Audit Is Conducted.
   A. At the End of a Calendar Year or Annual Reporting Year, or During a Physical Inventory
   B. At Least Annually, and During the Same Time Period Each Year

3. Which Areas To Be Audited.
   A. Horizontal
   B. Vertical

4. What Type of Audit Form Is Developed.
   A. Open or Closed Questions
   B. Specific Questions

5. How to Conduct the Audit.
   A. Time Duration
   B. Awareness of Employees
   C. Whether Organization is Open or Closed
   D. Preparing the Final Report

6. How Results Are Presented to Management.

questionnaires, and they are completed by the auditor. An illustration of a horizontal audit form is contained in Figure 24-9 on pages 738–739.[27]

5. Implementing the audit. The decisions to be made at this stage involve the

---

[27] For other examples of audit forms, see Goetsch, "Conduct a Comprehensive Marketing Audit to Improve Marketing Planning"; Barry Berman and Joel R. Evans, "The Marketing Audit: A New Tool for Public Libraries," *LJ Special Report 18* (New York: *Library Journal,* 1981), pp. 18–19; Edward G. Michaels, "Marketing Muscle," *Business Horizons,* Vol. 25 (May–June, 1982), p. 64; Thomas C. Tahi, "Do You Have an Advanced Marketing/Sales Operation?" *Marketing News* (September 16, 1983), Section 2, p. 4; and Alan J. Dubinsky and Richard W. Hansen, "The Sales Force Management Audit," *California Management Review,* Vol. 24 (Winter 1981), pp. 86–95.

time duration of the audit, whether employees are to be aware of the audit, whether the audit is performed while the organization is open or closed, and how the final report is to be prepared.

6. Presenting the results to management. The last step in an audit is to present the findings and recommendations to management. However, the auditing process is complete only after appropriate responses are taken by management. It is the responsibility of management, not the auditor, to determine these responses.

The idea of using independent evaluation to review performance is not new. For example, the accounting profession audits financial records for accuracy and honesty; inventory levels are frequently audited; many firms analyze their organizational structures on a periodic basis; long-term manpower needs and resources are regularly audited; and recently, firms have begun to evaluate their social responsibility performance.

Despite the long-standing application of audits, many firms have not adopted a formal marketing audit. Three factors account for this. One, success or failure is difficult to establish in marketing. An organization may have poor performance despite the best planning if environmental factors intervene. On the other hand, good results may be based on the firm's being at the right place at the right time. Two, when marketing audits are completed by company personnel, they may not be comprehensive enough to be considered audits. Three, the pressures of other activities often mean that only a small part of the firm is audited or that the audit is done on a nonregular basis.

Summary

An integrated marketing plan is one in which all of the various parts of the plan are unified, consistent, and coordinated. A clear organizational mission outlines a firm's commitment to a type of business and a place in the market. Long-term competitive advantages are company and product/service attributes whose distinctiveness and appeal to consumers can be maintained over an extended period of time. A precisely defined target market identifies the specific consumers a firm addresses in its marketing plan. The long-, moderate-, and short-term marketing subplans of the company need to be compatible with one another. Coordination among SBUs is enhanced when the functions, strategies, and resources of each are described and monitored by top management. The components of the marketing mix need to be coordinated within each SBU. The plan must have a certain degree of stability over time.

Kentucky Fried Chicken has a well-integrated marketing plan and is prospering. Timex has a poorly integrated marketing plan and is facing uncertainty about its future.

Marketing plan analysis involves the comparison of actual performance with planned performance for a specified period of time. If actual performance is

DOES YOUR DEPARTMENT, DIVISION, OR FIRM . . .

PLANNING, ORGANIZATION, AND CONTROL

1. Have specific objectives? _____
2. Devise objectives to meet changing conditions? _____
3. Study customer needs, attitudes, and behavior? _____
4. Organize marketing efforts in a systematic way? _____
5. Have a market planning process? _____
6. Engage in comprehensive sales forecasting? _____
7. Integrate buyer behavior research in market planning? _____
8. Have strategy and tactics within the marketing plan? _____
9. Have clearly stated contingency plans? _____
10. Monitor environmental changes? _____
11. Incorporate social responsibility as a criterion for decision making? _____
12. Control activities through marketing cost analysis, sales analysis, and the marketing audit? _____

MARKETING RESEARCH

13. Utilize marketing research for planning as well as problem solving? _____
14. Have a marketing information system? _____
15. Give enough support to marketing research? _____
16. Have adequate communication between marketing research and line executives? _____

PRODUCT

17. Utilize a systematic product planning process? _____
18. Plan product policy relative to the product life-cycle concept? _____
19. Have a procedure for developing new products? _____
20. Periodically review all products? _____
21. Monitor competitive developments in product planning? _____
22. Revise mature products? _____
23. Phase out weak products? _____

DISTRIBUTION

24. Motivate channel members? _____
25. Have sufficient market coverage? _____
26. Periodically evaluate channel members? _____
27. Evaluate alternative shipping arrangements? _____
28. Study warehouse and facility locations? _____
29. Compute economic order quantities? _____
30. Modify channel decisions as conditions warrant? _____

Figure 24-9
**A Horizontal Marketing
Audit Form**

DOES YOUR DEPARTMENT, DIVISION, OR FIRM . . .

Answer Yes or No to
Each Question

PROMOTION

31. Have an overall promotion plan? _____
32. Balance promotion components within the plan? _____
33. Measure the effectiveness of advertising? _____
34. Seek out favorable publicity? _____
35. Have a procedure for recruiting and retaining sales personnel? _____
36. Analyze the sales force organization periodically? _____
37. Moderate the use of sales promotions? _____

PRICE

38. Have a pricing strategy that is in compliance with government regulations? _____
39. Have a pricing strategy that satisfies channel members? _____
40. Estimate demand and cost factors before setting prices? _____
41. Plan for competitive developments? _____
42. Set prices that are consistent with image? _____
43. Seek to maximize total profits? _____

Figure 24-9
A Horizontal Marketing
Audit Forum (Continued)

unsatisfactory, corrective action may be necessary. Plans may have to be revised because of the impact of uncontrollable variables.

Marketing cost analysis evaluates the cost effectiveness of various marketing factors, such as different product lines, distribution methods, sales territories, channel members, salespersons, advertising media, and customer types. Continuous and accurate accounting data are needed. Marketing cost analysis involves studying natural account expenses, reclassifying natural accounts into functional accounts, and allocating accounts by marketing classification.

Sales analysis is the detailed study of sales data for the purpose of appraising the appropriateness of a marketing strategy. Sales analysis enables plans to be set in terms of sales by product, product line, salesperson, region, customer type, time period, price line, or method of sale. It also monitors actual sales against planned sales. More companies use sales analysis than marketing cost analysis. The main source of sales data is the sales invoice; control units must be specified. Sales analysis should take the 80–20 principle and sales exception reporting into account.

The marketing audit is a systematic, critical, and unbiased review and appraisal of the firm's marketing objectives, strategy, implementation, and organization. It contains six steps: determining who does the audit, establishing when and how often the audit is conducted, deciding what the audit covers, developing audit forms, implementing the audit, and presenting the results. A horizontal audit studies the overall marketing performance of a company. A vertical audit is an in-depth analysis of one aspect of marketing strategy.

Questions for Discussion

1. Should a firm ever focus on short-run profits rather than long-term profits? Why or why not?
2. Describe five potential conflicts among an organization's SBUs. How may these conflicts be reduced?
3. Explain how a pricing strategy for a felt-tip pen aimed at the office market would be integrated and coordinated with other functional marketing elements.
4. Evaluate the level of integration of your college or university's marketing plan using the elements outlined in Figure 24-1.
5. Develop a five-year marketing plan for Kentucky Fried Chicken. Include marketing objectives, the target market, and product, distribution, promotion, and price factors. Should Kentucky Fried Chicken add hamburgers? Explain your answer.
6. What must Timex do to improve its prospects for long-run success?
7. Explain how marketing cost analysis can substantiate price compliance with the Robinson-Patman Act.
8. Why is functional account cost analysis more useful than natural account analysis?
9. What factors must be considered when allocating functional accounts by marketing classification?
10. Distinguish between marketing cost analysis and sales analysis. Why do you think more firms use sales analysis?
11. When conducting sales analysis, why is it necessary that control units not be too wide?
12. Explain the 80–20 principle. Does it apply for all sales situations?
13. What information could a manufacturer obtain from a monthly analysis of its sales to wholesalers? How could this information improve marketing plans?
14. How could resistance to the marketing audit be overcome?
15. Develop a vertical audit for Avon to assess the performance of its direct-to-home sales force.

Case 1 Black & Decker: Integrating Strategy After a Major Acquisition*

Until recently, Black & Decker concentrated its efforts on consumer power tools, such as electric drills, lawn trimmers, and snow throwers. Then, Black & Decker began adding household products, such as the Dustbuster portable vacuum cleaner, rechargeable flashlights, and rechargeable scrub brushes. During 1983, Black & Decker's total sales reached $1.2 billion.

---

* The data in this case are drawn from "Black & Decker Buys a Place on the Kitchen Counter," *Business Week* (January 9, 1984), pp. 29–30; Paul A. Engelmayer, "Black & Decker Agrees to Acquire a GE Operation," *Wall Street Journal* (December 19, 1983), p. 15; Lisa Miller Mesdag, "The Appliance Boom Begins," *Fortune* (July 25, 1983), pp. 52–57; and "Black & Decker Agrees Net Should Jump 50% for Fiscal 1st Quarter," *Wall Street Journal* (January 30, 1984), p. 5.

In December 1983, Black & Decker agreed to purchase the small-appliances division of General Electric (GE) for about $300 million. Black & Decker acquired GE coffee makers, food processors, juicers, electric can openers, irons, and hair dryers. General Electric retained its audio electronics, major appliances, and video and lighting products.

According to Black & Decker's chief executive, "The home is really our [emerging] marketplace." The Dustbuster and related items moved Black & Decker out of the garage and backyard and into the house; the GE appliances will aid the process: "We're now in the basement; we see ourselves moving into the kitchen."

Black & Decker believes the GE small-appliance acquisition offers it several significant opportunities:

- The GE brand name can be used on existing small appliances for a three-year period (Black & Decker must honor all warranties). GE has strong customer awareness and a good reputation in the small-appliance field. GE ranked first or second in market share for all of its small appliances (except hair dryers).
- The distribution channels for power tools and small appliances are very similar. Stated Black & Decker's chief executive, "A good share of household appliances are sold in hardware stores, and *we're* very big there."
- Overseas markets have considerable sales potential for small appliances. These markets were not exploited by GE. In contrast, over half of Black & Decker's sales come from Europe. GE appliances sold in Europe would immediately carry the Black & Decker name.
- The acquisition enables the company to continue its diversification efforts and lessen its emphasis on power tools. Black & Decker may also expand into other related areas, such as locks, alarms, and energy-saving devices.

From GE's perspective, the sale of its small-appliance business enabled it to exit a relatively unprofitable product category (GE earned a profit of 3 per cent of sales; in contrast, Black & Decker earns a 10 per cent profit on household products) and focus more on large appliances, including refrigerators and washing machines. GE's chief executive commented that the large appliance division represented "the image of GE more than any other product GE has. It impacts everything from our stock price to employee recruiting on college campuses."

QUESTIONS
1. Evaluate Black & Decker's decision to purchase General Electric's small-appliance division.
2. Do you agree with Black & Decker's conclusions about the compatability of distribution channels for power tools and small appliances? Explain your answer.
3. Develop a procedure for Black & Decker to integrate GE appliances into the company's overall marketing strategy.
4. Should Black & Decker add locks, alarms, and energy-saving devices to its product line? Why or why not?

Case 2 Cedardale: Sales Analysis for a Health Club[†]

Cedardale is a multipurpose health club located in Haverhill, Massachusetts (about 35 miles from Boston). It offers tennis, volleyball, aerobics, Nautilis-equipment training, suntanning facilities, other activities, and even a bar. Cedardale occupies 130,000 square feet of space and has approximately 7,500 members. One of its owners describes Cedardale as a sports mall.

Like many other multipurpose clubs, Cedardale has organized its sales records by activity or facility. For example, the indoor tennis courts generate revenue of about $9 per square foot annually, while suntanning facilities have sales of $200 per square foot. The average revenue for the entire complex is $26 per square foot.

To increase sales, two of Cedardale's fourteen tennis courts were converted into aerobics dance studios and a Nautilis fitness center. One hundred paying customers can now use a space that at one point handled only 8. As a result, Cedardale's yearly revenues have risen to $3.5 million; and profits are 20 per cent of sales (the industry average is 3.4 per cent).

Table 1 shows the results of a survey of 175 multipurpose health clubs throughout the U.S. The table presents information by classification for average and superior clubs. Both total club revenue and the club revenue generated by each member (customer) are detailed.

Table 1

Revenue Data Based on a Survey of 175 Multipurpose Health Clubs, 1982

Classification	Total Revenue per Club		Club Revenue per Member	
	Industry Average	Top Five[a]	Industry Average	Top Five[a]
Membership dues	$321,244	$ 796,019	$219.13	$385.86
Court time	120,446	134,065	82.16	64.99
Lessons	33,006	56,428	22.51	27.35
Pro shop	48,565	147,202	33.13	71.35
Food & beverages	73,247	111,551	49.96	54.07
Other	122,375	229,209	83.48	111.11
Total revenue	$718,883	$1,474,474	$490.37	$714.73
Pretax earnings	$ 24,442	$ 334,949	$ 16.67	$162.36
Sales per square foot	$ 13.10	$ 21.34		
Number of members	1,466	2,063		

[a] Composite of the five clubs with the highest profit margins.
Source: International Racquet Sports Association. Reprinted by permission of the *New York Times.*

QUESTIONS

1. Analyze the data in Table 1.
2. Evaluate Cedardale on the basis of Table 1.
3. What other data would be useful in examining the performance of Cedardale that has not been presented in the case?

[†] The data in this case are drawn from R. B. Lynch, "The New Wave in Health Clubs," *New York Times* (November 13, 1983), Section 3, p. 4.

Marketing
in the Future

CHAPTER OBJECTIVES

1. To demonstrate the importance of anticipating and planning for the future
2. To study consumer trends and their marketing implications
3. To examine environmental trends and their marketing implications
4. To consider marketing strategies with emphasis on marketing planning and research, and product, distribution, promotion, and price planning over the next decade

*I*n 1982, two extremely influential business books were published: *Megatrends: Ten New Directions Transforming Our Lives* and *In Search of Excellence: Lessons from America's Best-Run Companies*. These books attained unprecedented popularity and quickly appeared on national best-seller lists, where they remained for well over a year; each achieved status as the number one best-seller in the U.S. for several weeks. From a marketing perspective, these books are valuable because they present important information about planning for the future in an interesting and readable format.

Megatrends by John Naisbitt is based upon the findings of the Naisbitt Group, which gathers information about emerging trends through content analysis. This analysis consists of reading daily newspapers in all U.S. cities with populations of 100,000 or more and classifying data into 13 broad categories and 200 specific subcategories. The Naisbitt Group

743

publishes reports three times per year, and sells them to companies for an annual fee of $15,000. In *Megatrends* (priced at $17.50 in hardcover), Naisbitt identifies the ten most influential trends occurring in the U.S.:

- The U.S. is shifting from an industrial to an information-based society.
- New technology will succeed only when people are ready for it.
- The U.S. is becoming more a part of a global structure and less of a dominant force.
- U.S. managers are beginning to plan for longer periods.
- Decentralization is increasing.
- Self-reliance is becoming more important to people.
- Citizens, workers, and consumers want a greater voice in government, business, and the marketplace.
- Hierarchal pyramids are disappearing in organizations.
- The Northeast declines, as the West and Southwest rise.
- People are demanding and receiving a greater variety of goods, services, life-styles, etc.

As one reviewer noted, "You can't stop these trends, but you can think about them and apply what you learn—perhaps—to help you reconceptualize your business in anticipation of change."[1]

In Search of Excellence by Thomas J. Peters and Robert H. Waterman, Jr. is based on in-depth research of 62 successful large American companies, conducted while the authors were senior executives at the management consulting firm of McKinsey & Co. Research focused on "innovative firms [who] are especially adroit at continually responding to change of any sort in their environments." The highest-rated firms included Bechtel, Boeing, Caterpillar Tractor, Dana, Delta Airlines, Digital Equipment, Emerson Electric, Fluor, Hewlett-Packard, IBM, Johnson & Johnson, McDonald's, Procter & Gamble, and 3M. The authors conclude that excellent companies share eight key characteristics. They

- Have a bias or predisposition for action.
- Are close to customers and possess a marketing orientation.
- Encourage employee autonomy and entrepreneurship.
- Believe productivity is gained through employee participation and an absence of a "we/they" philosophy.
- Have top executives who are regularly involved with operations ("hands on") and communicate organizational mission ("value driven").
- Do not lose sight of their field of expertise and competitive advantages ("stick to the knitting").
- Have simple organization charts and relatively few executives (less than 100) at company headquarters.
- Are simultaneously loose (lots of autonomy) and tight (strict adherence to a few core values).

---

[1] John Naisbitt, *Megatrends: Ten Directions Transforming Our Lives* (New York: Warner Books, 1982); and Tom Richman, "Peering into Tomorrow," *Inc.* (October 1982), pp. 45–48.

Peters and Waterman point out that managers must not lose sight of the basics in planning for the future: "quick action, service to customers, practical innovation, and the fact that you can't get any of these without virtually everyone's commitment."[2]

Anticipating and Planning for the Future

The next decade promises to be a significant one for U.S. marketers as they try to anticipate trends and plan long-run strategies. On the positive side, the decade ahead should see increasing consumer affluence, improvements in technological capabilities, expanding worldwide markets, greater deregulation of industry, and other opportunities. On the negative side, the decade will probably witness some resource shortages, greater competition from foreign companies, a relatively stagnant domestic market, and an uncertain economy among the potential problems.

There will be many opportunities and risks. External factors must be considered in long-range planning.

Long-range plans must take into account both the external variables facing the firm and its capacity for change. Specifically, what variables will affect the firm? What trends are forecast for them? Is the firm able to respond to these trends (for example, does it have the necessary resources and lead time)? A company that does not anticipate and respond to future trends has a good possibility of falling into Levitt's marketing myopia trap and losing ground to more far-sighted competitors.[3]

Said three important analysts:

American management, especially in the two decades after World War II, was universally admired for its strikingly effective performance. But times change. An approach shaped and refined during stable decades may be ill suited to a world characterized by rapid and unpredictable change, scarce energy, global competition for markets, and a constant need for innovation. This is the world of the 1980s and, probably, the rest of this century.[4]

A major distinction between the last decade and the next decade is marketing's new and rapidly expanding and demanding strategic role. . . . To meet this responsibility, marketing executives must quickly develop their capabilities in strategic analysis and planning, financial analysis, and strategic marketing. The requirements of this role are much greater than they were in the past. The chief marketing executive will be a major participant in strategic planning for the enterprise. In an increasing number of firms, this executive is directing the strategic planning for the firm because of the strong market-centered focus of strategic planning.[5]

---

[2] Thomas J. Peters and Robert H. Waterman, Jr., *In Search of Excellence: Lessons From America's Best-Run Companies* (New York: Harper & Row, 1982). See also, Susan Benner, "Peters' Principles: Secrets of Growth," *Inc.* (July 1983), pp. 34–39.

[3] Theodore Levitt, "Marketing Myopia," *Harvard Business Review,* Vol. 53 (September–October 1975), pp. 26–44, 173–181.

[4] Robert H. Hayes and William J. Abernathy, "Managing Our Way to Economic Decline," *Harvard Business Review,* Vol. 58 (July–August 1980), p. 68.

[5] David W. Cravens, "Strategic Marketing's New Challenge," *Business Horizons,* Vol. 26 (March–April 1983), p. 24.

Figure 25-1
The Factors Affecting Future Marketing Performance

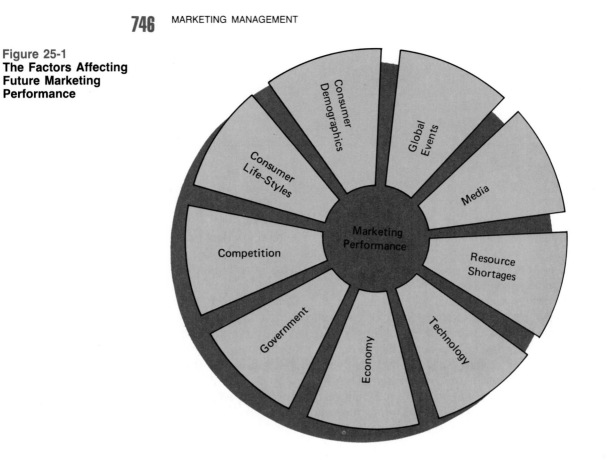

This chapter focuses on marketing over the next decade. First, consumers and environmental factors are analyzed. See Figure 25-1. Then each of the basic elements of marketing is examined.

Consumer Trends

In the coming decade, there will be continuing shifts in both the demographics and life-styles of consumers. These shifts will have a large impact on long-run marketing plans.

Although some population segments and characteristics will remain constant, others will change substantially.

Demographics

The decade will be marked by many of the demographic trends described in Chapter 5.[6] The total population of the United States will grow by a small percentage each year. The proportion of middle-aged and retired persons will

[6] For a look further into the future, see Gregory Spencer and John F. Long, "The New Census Bureau Projections," *American Demographics* (April 1983), pp. 24–31. This article reports on census projections extending to the year 2050.

increase greatly. Geographically, the most growth in U.S. population will occur in the Southeast and Southwest regions. Home ownership will stay strong; and most mobility will involve regional relocations. Real income will increase, although not as rapidly as in the past. The number of working women will continue to rise substantially, as will families with two working members. There will also be increases in the proportion of college-educated adults, those involved in white-collar jobs, and single-person households. Although families will be smaller than in the 1970s, two thirds of adults will continue to be married.

These demographic trends will greatly influence marketing strategies. For example, the rise in incomes will result in greater demand from some consumers for luxuries and high-quality, high-priced goods; and small households will demand individual servings of food. Table 25-1 shows selected implications of demographic trends for marketers. Following are two specific illustrations:

- Spiegel is orienting its mail-order catalogs to career women who are 21 to 54 years-old and have household incomes of $25,000+. This growing market represents about 30 per cent of all U.S. households. To reach these women,

Trends	Implications
Stable U.S. population	Many domestic markets are saturated. Foreign markets may hold greater opportunities for growth.
Increase in middle-aged and retired persons	There is potential for multiple-segmentation strategies. Wilson Sporting Goods markets golf clubs that assist golfers in getting the ball in flight more quickly. Levi Strauss has designed fuller-cut jeans. Procter & Gamble is marketing disposable diapers for incontinent adults. Universities are expanding their programs for adults.
Shift to Southeast and Southwest regions	The Northeast faces continued out-migration of population and industry. Brands distributed nationally will prosper as consumers move about.
Strong home market	There will be demand for home-oriented goods and services. Luxury townhouses will be popular, especially those with large master bedrooms that make it easier for two working people to dress in the morning.
Rise in real income	There will be opportunities for discretionary goods and services, such as home computers and vacation travel.
Increase in working women	These women have little time for shopping or preparation of foods. Faster checkouts, expanded evening hours, one-stop shopping, and convenience goods will be needed. Expenditures in business clothing, luggage, and airline travel will rise.
Increase in education	Consumers will be more discerning and critical.
Rise in white-collar jobs	Consumers will have more leisure time. There will be opportunities for entertainment forms.
Growth of single-person households	Smaller homes and condominiums will be demanded, as will single-serving products.
Stable percentage of married adults	For many, the traditional family life cycle will remain in effect. Joint decision making will be high.

Table 25-1
Selected Marketing Implications of Demographic Trends

Spiegel is adding expensive clothing and other products to its catalogs. It is turning away from its "blue-collar past."[7]

- Ford is placing greater emphasis on "yumps"—young, upwardly mobile professionals. Said a Ford executive, "These yumps are younger, better-educated, more affluent, and upscale. . . . Income is very important today. The car buyer's average income is between $30,000 and $35,000, and that is sharply different from five years ago."[8]

Life-Styles

Many distinct and emerging consumer life-styles are expected to continue over the next decade. Four of these are discussed in this subsection: voluntary simplicity, the me generation, the blurring of gender roles, and the poverty of time.

Voluntary simplicity is a life-style in which people seek material simplicity, have an ecological awareness, strive for self-determination, and purchase do-it-yourself products. It grew out of the 1960s and 1970s, when people first became aware that many natural resources were being depleted. This life-style will continue in the future. It will expand only if Americans are again faced with resource shortages and rising prices.

Voluntary simplicity is based on material simplicity and ecological awareness.

Consumers with a voluntary-simplicity life-style are more likely to seek a frugal, simple life. They are conservative, cautious, and thrifty shoppers. They do not buy expensive cars and fur coats, they make gifts instead of purchase them, they grow their own vegetables and make their own clothes, and they patronize garage sales and flea markets. These consumers are more concerned with a product's durability than its appearance and believe in conservation of scarce resources.[9] There is also more attraction to rational appeals and no-frills retailing.

The *me generation* stresses self-expression and self-improvement.

While voluntary simplicity and the conservation ethic will remain important to some consumers, there will also be advances in a more lavish life-style, that of the *me generation.* This life-style stresses "being good to myself," "improving myself," and "my life, my way."[10] Like voluntary simplicity, the me generation began in the 1960s and 1970s as free expression and self-expression became more acceptable.

The me-generation life-style places less emphasis on obligations, responsibilities, and loyalties. It involves less pressure to conform, as well as greater acceptance of diversity. Consumers with this life-style are particularly interested in staying young and taking care of themselves. They stress nutrition, exercise, weight control, and grooming.[11] Expensive cars and fur coats are bought; gifts are purchased, not made; and full-service retailers are patronized. These consumers are more concerned with a product's appearance than its durability and place limited importance on conservation, especially if it will have a negative effect on their life-style.

[7] Frank E. James, "Spiegel Employs New Tactics to Fight Its Blue-Collar Past," *Wall Street Journal* (March 29, 1984), p. 31.

[8] Ralph Gray, "Ford Trying to Pick up 'Yumps'," *Advertising Age* (March 19, 1984), p. 31.

[9] See "Conspicuous Consumption Out, Voluntary Simplicity In;" and " 'Ecological & Socially Concerned' Consumers Profiled," *Marketing News* (February 8, 1980), p. 8.

[10] Roger D. Blackwell, "Successful Retailers of '80s Will Cater to Specific Lifestyle Segments," *Marketing News* (March 7, 1980), p. 3.

[11] William Lazer, "Lucrative Marketing Opportunities Will Abound in the 'Upbeat' 1980s," *Marketing News* (July 11, 1980), p. 14.

As greater numbers of women enter the labor force, more husbands will assume the traditional roles of their wives, thus **blurring gender roles**. These husbands will work in the home, and share the tasks of managing a household and feeding the family.[12] In 1967, 60 per cent of the adult women respondents to a survey agreed with the statement, "A woman's place is in the home." By 1975, only 26 per cent agreed with this statement and the majority favored a marriage in which the husband and wife shared homemaking and child-care responsibilities.[13] Today, even more women believe in their right to work and share responsibilities. Younger, better-educated, more-affluent women are most prone to favor sharing.

Blurring gender roles involves men and women undertaking nontraditional duties.

One survey of 617 men by the Benton & Bowles advertising agency found that 80 per cent take care of children in households with children under age twelve, 74 per cent take out the garbage, 53 per cent wash the dishes, 47 per cent cook for the family, 39 per cent vacuum the home, 32 per cent shop for food, 29 per cent do the laundry, and 28 per cent clean the bathroom.[14] These percentages are expected to rise during the next decade.

For many consumer households, the increase in working women, the long distances between home and work, and the rise in people working at second jobs contribute to less rather than more free time. The ***poverty-of-time*** concept states that for some consumers greater affluence will result in less free time because the alternatives competing for time will expand. As the prices of houses, automobiles, food, and other goods and services continue to go up in the future, more households will require two incomes and a second job for the main earner.

Poverty of time exists when greater affluence results in less free time.

The poverty of time will lead these consumers to increase their usage of time-saving goods and services such as convenience foods, disposable packages, microwave ovens, restaurants, and professional lawn and household care. Currently, Americans annually purchase more than three million microwave ovens (up from 300,000 in 1973) and two million food processors, and over 40 per cent eat out at least once a month.

The broad implications of these four life-style trends on marketing strategy are shown in Table 25-2. These are two illustrations of how the life-styles may be broken down into even smaller market segments:

- The me generation consists of consumers who can be divided into three food segments: naturalists, sophisticates, and dieters. Naturalists want food with no artificial ingredients; they stress fresh fruit, rice, natural cereal, bran bread, wheat germ, yogurt, chocolate chips, and Jell-O. Sophisticates are upscale urban dwellers who favor wine, mixed drinks, beer, butter, rye/pumpernickel bread, bagels, frozen dinners, and doughnuts and packaged cakes. Dieters are weight-conscious consumers who emphasize skim milk, diet margarine, salads, fresh fruit, coffee, and sugar substitutes.[15]
- Blurring gender roles have resulted in 40 per cent of all grocery shoppers being male. However, the behavior of males is quite different from that of females.

[12] See "More Working Wives Expose Their Husbands to the Joy of Cooking," *Wall Street Journal*, (October 16, 1980), pp. 1, 21; and Nancy Giges, "More Men Food Shopping," *Advertising Age* (February 6, 1984), p. 12.

[13] Fred D. Reynolds, Melvin R. Crask, and William D. Wells, "The Modern Feminine Life Style," *Journal of Marketing*, Vol. 41 (July 1977), p. 38.

[14] Theodore Dunn, "Large Numbers of Husbands Buy Household Products, Do Housework," *Marketing News* (October 3, 1980), p. 1.

[15] Betsy Morris, "Study to Detect True Eating Habits Finds Junk-Food Fans in the Health-Food Ranks," *Wall Street Journal* (February 3, 1984), p. 25.

**Table 25-2
Selected Marketing
Implications of
Life-Style Trends**

Trend	Implications
Voluntary simplicity	Expansion will occur for do-it-yourself projects such as repair kits and "knock-down" furniture.
	There will be consumer interest in quality, durability, and simplicity (rational goals).
	No-frills retailing will grow.
	Fuel-efficient cars, bicycles, and public transportation will be used more frequently.
	Ecologically benign products will be desired. These will include recycled paper, phosphate-free detergents, and biodegradable packages.
	Sales of insulation, solar energy, and energy-efficient products will grow rapidly.
Me generation	Individuality in purchase decisions will gain greater acceptance.
	Luxuries will be desired.
	Nutritional themes will be important in food purchases.
	The interest in physical fitness will expand sales for health spas, bicycles, and exercise equipment.
	Health and beauty-aid products and personal-care retailing will grow.
	The concern for self-improvement will lead to more continuing education programs and the enrollment of adults in colleges.
Blurring of gender roles	Unisex products, services, and stores will be popular.
	Shopping conditions will be favorable to joint husband and wife purchase behavior.
	Advertising will feature couples.
	There will be demand for products and services that can be used jointly.
	Male and female stereotypes will no longer be applicable.
Poverty of time	Catalog and mail-order sales will grow.
	Service retailers will need to make and keep more accurate customer appointments.
	The sales of labor-saving devices will rise.
	One-stop shopping will be more important.
	Wardrobe consultants will save customers time.
	Well-known brands will facilitate shopping.

Male shoppers go to the store more frequently, spend less time in the store, spend less money each week, are more impulsive, have a stronger preference for national brands, and are less willing to compromise on food quality than female grocery shoppers.[16]

Environmental Trends

During the next decade, a number of environmental factors will affect marketing. These include competition, government, the economy, technology, resource shortages, media, and global events. These factors are described in the following subsections.

[16] Lynn Langway, "Frozen Foods Get Hot Again," *Newsweek* (May 23, 1983), p. 42.

Competition

The competitive environment may be analyzed from various perspectives: domestic and foreign, small firm and large firm, generic, and channel.

Most American industries are mature; and in these industries, domestic competition will remain at approximately current levels, because the number of U.S. firms in them will be relatively stable. In some industries, competition will increase because of major innovations, such as personal computers. In other industries, competition will intensify as a result of government deregulation. For example, AT&T will face greater competition in the telecommunications industry from GTE, ITT, MCI, Rolm, Western Union, RCA, and other U.S. firms in addition to its former subsidiaries.[17] Merrill Lynch will compete with Sears, Citicorp, American Express, Bank of America, and other firms as well as traditional brokerage companies for financial services business.[18]

The impact of foreign competition will continue and grow. In the United States, foreign manufacturers are now capturing large market shares—about 26 per cent for automobiles, over 30 per cent for sporting goods and microwave ovens, 90 per cent for motorcycles, and almost 100 per cent for videocassette recorders. Also imported in large numbers are tires, calculators, televisions, watches, cameras, and a wide range of other products. Competition in overseas markets will also be more intense for U.S. firms in the future.

The success of foreign firms is based on their ability to capitalize on innovations, better quality control than U.S. firms, somewhat lower costs than U.S. firms, and good distribution and promotion. According to a major study conducted in 1981 and 1982 that compared American and Japanese manufacturers of room air conditioners, the American firms had 70 times more assembly-line defects and had to make 17 times more first-year service calls than the Japanese firms. As a result, American firms incurred warranty compliance costs of 1.8–5.2 per cent of sales while Japanese firms averaged 0.6 per cent of sales. However, this study also determined that product quality was related to systematic management planning, not national traits or cultural advantages.[19]

To regain their competitive advantages, in greater numbers, U.S. firms will be involved with innovations, reducing the time necessary to respond to market conditions, and upgrading product quality during the next decade:[20]

- Research and development expenditures will continue to rise; they now exceed $40 billion annually.
- The U.S. labor force will become more mature and experienced.
- Productivity is expected to go up by 26 per cent between 1984 and 1990.
- Many obsolete plants will be closed and new ones built.
- There will be greater cooperation between management and employees.
- Quality control will be a major priority.

For example, Ford's concentration on product quality and cost control has resulted in significant improvements for all of its cars and trucks.[21] See Figure 25-2.

> Competition will be stable in mature industries; growth industries and those with foreign competitors will see intense competition.

---

[17] "Telecommunications: The Global Battle," *Business Week* (October 24, 1983), pp. 126–130.

[18] "Merrill Lynch's Big Dilemma," *Business Week* (January 16, 1984), pp. 60–67.

[19] David A. Garvin, "Quality on the Line," *Harvard Business Review,* Vol. 61 (September–October 1983), pp. 65–75.

[20] "The Revival of Productivity," *Business Week* (February 13, 1984), pp. 92–100.

[21] Jeremy Main, "Ford's Drive for Quality," *Fortune* (April 18, 1983), pp. 62–70; and "Quality Assurance Program Enables Ford to Build the Type of Car Consumers Want," *Marketing News* (March 2, 1984), p. 24.

Figure 25-2
The Importance of
Product Quality at Ford

At Ford Motor Company, there are a lot of people whose work on your car you'll never see. Like Hattie White, who welds sub-assemblies, Larry Giacomo, who stamps the floorpans, and Mike Duncan who solders the roof joints, but they all know that to build a good car you have to do everything right.

There's a new spirit at Ford

Motor Company. And everyone is involved — from the man in the corner office to the people on the assembly line.

This dedication to quality is already paying off. Overall, a 25% improvement in quality since 1980, as reported by new car owners.

At Ford Motor Company, Quality is Job 1.

Ford
Mercury
Lincoln
Ford Trucks

Reprinted by permission.

Before aggressively wooing foreign markets, U.S. firms will have to re-establish themselves among American consumers:

On balance you might argue that American cars are now as good as the imports, but the public clearly doesn't think so. In a recent survey for the American Society for Quality Control, Americans panned U.S.-made autos. That judgment may be too harsh, or lag behind the facts, but perception can be as important as reality. It has the same effect in the marketplace.[22]

Large firms will often dominate.

Over the last several decades, there has been a trend toward larger firms. This trend should continue. From the perspective of the small business, personal service will be the major differential advantage. Cooperative arrangements and franchises should enable small companies to buy in quantity and operate more efficiently. From the perspective of the large business, widespread distribution, well-known brands, and reasonable prices will be competitive tactics. During the coming decade, large firms will continue to diversify in order to avoid excessive

[22] Jeremy Main, "The Battle for Quality Begins," *Fortune* (December 29, 1980), pp. 29–30.

concentration in any one industry. Larger firms will be better able to develop and apply the expensive new technology of the 1980s than their smaller counterparts.

Generic competition will increase as consumers consider more purchase alternatives and companies diversify. Consumers will view entertainment, transportation, clothing, recreation, personal grooming, housing, and other products and services more broadly, thus intensifying competition among companies in adjacent industries. For example, entertainment alternatives include television, radio, theater, movies, sporting events, social activities, and continuing education. Transportation alternatives for final consumers include automobile, mass transit, taxi, car pool, private bus, air, ferry, motorcycle, bicycle, and walking or jogging. The growth in generic competition will cause firms to define their competitors more broadly and expand into newer businesses (such as Kodak making video cameras).

Channel competition will also increase in the future. First, the expansion of private labels and the different objectives of manufacturers, wholesalers, and retailers will continue. Second, many channel members will engage in vertical integration in order to become more efficient and gain greater control. This will close off some independent channel members. Third, retailers will be reluctant to carry new items without extensive promotional support.

> **Generic and channel competition will rise.**

Government

The most relevant government actions facing marketers are likely to involve deregulation, antitrust, and consumer protection.

The trend toward deregulation, noted earlier in the text, will continue. For example, the Federal Communications Commission is in the process of deregulating FM radio stations. Banks will be fully deregulated by 1985; they will be able to provide a broader range of financial services and competitive rates for savings. Further deregulation is predicted for other industries. Overall, deregulation will induce greater price competition, encourage competitors to enter the marketplace, and offer consumers further choices. Success and failure will be more determined by marketing skills than government supports and restraints.[23]

During the 1980s, the U.S. government will be less likely to seek to break up large firms (such as IBM) and more likely to approve mergers between leading companies (such as Texaco and Getty). The government will also be more restrained in monitoring Robinson-Patman violations, full-line forcing, territorial restrictions, and dealer terminations.[24]

Restricted powers for consumer protection agencies, such as the FTC (Federal Trade Commission) and CPSC (Consumer Product Safety Commission), will continue. These agencies will have less authority to investigate industries and impose trade rules. For example, the FTC has already been forced to cut back on actions

> **There will be emphasis on deregulation, with less involvement with antitrust and consumer protection.**

---

[23] See Paul N. Bloom, ''Deregulation's Challenges for Marketers'' in Bruce J. Walker et al. (Editors), *An Assessment of Marketing Thought and Practice* (Chicago: American Marketing Association, 1982), pp. 337–340; Thomas S. Robertson, Scott Ward, and William M. Caldwell, IV, ''Deregulation: Surviving the Transition,'' *Harvard Business Review,* Vol. 60 (July–August 1982), pp. 20–24; and Jeanne Saddler, ''In Rush to Deregulate, FCC Outpaces Others, Pleasing the Industry,'' *Wall Street Journal* (December 7, 1983), pp. 1, 21.

[24] ''A Powerful Bid to Rewrite the Antitrust Rule Book,'' *Business Week* (October 10, 1983), pp. 84 ff; and ''FTC Antitrust Moves Have Fallen Sharply According to a Study,'' *Wall Street Journal* (January 20, 1984), p. 5.

directed at children's advertising, insurance, opticians, and other areas. Business self-regulation will gain in importance and companies will act more responsibly on their own initiative.[25]

The Economy

Although the U.S. economy should undergo moderate growth, the outlook is uncertain.

Forecasting the U.S. economy is difficult because of the uncertainty of many factors, particularly inflation, unemployment, and such outside factors as OPEC (Organization of Petroleum Exporting Countries) prices. To illustrate the complexity of predicting the economy, consider that during 1982 alone the inflation rate fell from 8.4 per cent to 4.0 per cent, the unemployment rate rose from 8.5 per cent to 10.8 per cent (it dropped to under 8 per cent by early 1984), and the price of a barrel of oil fell by $4.

According to forecasters, such as Wharton Econometrics and others, the best projection for real GNP growth in the United States over the next decade is about 3 to 4 per cent each year; but the rate could be lower if budget and trade deficits are not reduced.[26] This growth rate is a strong improvement over that of the early 1980s.

After going through a lengthy period of stagflation (stagnant economy and high inflation), the U.S. is now in a stable period with much lower inflation, coupled with a slow-growth economy. To achieve the strongest possible U.S. economy, industry will need to accomplish several tasks. First, productivity improvements must be sustained. Second, wages and profits should be tied to better productivity and quality control. Third, more companies should develop their own credit facilities to offer consumers reasonable terms for large-ticket purchases. Fourth, a high rate of employment must be maintained to assure consumer purchasing power. Fifth, nationalistic approaches ("Buy American") should receive more attention. Sixth, U.S. firms need to learn from the successes of their foreign competitors. Seventh, price stability should be maintained as much as possible.

Technology

Video-shopping services will include electronic catalogs, telephone-oriented cable ordering systems, and interactive cable ordering systems.

Advances in computerization will offer great opportunities for new marketing techniques such as video-shopping services, electronic banking, and electronic mail. They will also enable firms to be more efficient in operations.[27]

The *video-shopping services* that are emerging can be divided into three categories: merchandise catalogs on videodiscs or videocassettes, telephone-oriented cable television ordering systems, and interactive cable television ordering systems. Traditional merchandise catalogs are being placed on videodiscs or videocassettes by retailers such as Sears. These catalogs are then viewed in the store or in the consumer's home through a video player (an order would be placed by telephone). For example, Sears began experimenting in this area in 1981 when it

---

[25] "The FTC's Miller Puts His Faith in the Free Market," *Business Week* (June 27, 1983), p. 66 ff.

[26] "The Rebound Is Here, But It Looks Lopsided," *Business Week* (February 20, 1984), pp. 108–110. See also, "America Rushes to High Tech for Growth," *Business Week* (March 28, 1983), pp. 84–90.

[27] See "Special Issue on Technology for Marketing & Marketing Research," *Marketing News* (November 25, 1983).

Reprinted by permission.

Figure 25-3
An Interactive Cable Television Ordering System
The Viewtron interactive system was introduced in South Florida in late 1983. Through the system, subscribers can shop electronically, without leaving their homes.

placed its 18,000-item summer catalog on a videodisc and tested it in several markets.[28]

Telephone-oriented cable television ordering systems rely on specialized "video-shopping programming." Products are displayed on programs and consumers order through special toll-free 800 telephone numbers. For example, "Shopping Channel" has over 150,000 subscribers in cities such as Hartford, Conn.; Louisville, Ken.; Springfield, Ill.; Midland, Tex.; and Newark, Ohio. The programming is shown seven days per week, 16 hours each day, in half-hour segments. Each segment is repeated five times every month.[29]

Interactive cable television ordering systems also use specialized programming but they enable consumers to place orders directly through their home computers. The Comp-U-Star system, provided by Comp-U-Card, is the largest such service that is available throughout the U.S. With Comp-U-Star, the consumer views a video-shopping program and then feeds information into his or her home computer (which is hooked into Comp-U-Card's main computer); the order is placed, billing completed, and delivery processed via the system. About 150,000 consumers have access to Comp-U-Star, which handles about 50,000 discounted brand-name products.[30] A growing number of in-home banking services are available through other interactive systems. About 50 banks are now testing their systems; and this number is expected to rise rapidly.[31] Figure 25-3 shows

[28] "At Sears, 'Thumbs Up' to the Video Catalog," *Business Week* (May 11, 1981), pp. 33–34.
[29] John E. Cooney, "New Channels for Sales," *Wall Street Journal* (July 14, 1981), p. 52.
[30] Bill Abrams, "Electronic Shopping Awaiting Consumer, Corporate Support," *Wall Street Journal* (June 16, 1983), p. 33.
[31] Ruth Stroud, "Bankers Put Chips on Convenience," *Advertising Age* (January 9, 1984), pp. 3, 57.

Viewtron, an interactive ordering system developed by Knight-Ridder Newspapers, Inc.

As of now, the use of these video-shopping services is very limited. From a manufacturer's or retailer's perspective, the systems are expensive, reach a limited audience, and require advanced technology. From a consumer's perspective, the systems do not replace seeing products in person, are costly to employ, and easily result in errors. Expansion of video-shopping is forecast, as the problems noted are resolved and cable television is installed in more homes. By 1990, it is expected that 60 per cent of U.S. homes will have cable television, up from 35 per cent in 1983. A recent study predicted that video-shopping will reach $50 billion in annual sales by 1995.[32]

Electronic banking involves the utilization of automatic teller machines and instant processing of retail purchases. It provides centralized record keeping and enables customers to conduct transactions 24 hours a day, seven days a week at many bank and nonbank locations (such as supermarkets). Deposits, withdrawals, and other transactions can be completed.

In 1982, more than 26,000 automatic teller machines were operating in banks, shopping centers, airports, and other high-traffic sites. This figure is expected to triple by 1987, and continue growing for many years thereafter. To allow customers to make financial transactions over wider geographic areas, a number of banks have formed automatic teller machine networks. There are now about 175 to 200 local and regional networks and about half a dozen national systems. For example, the Cirrus System enables customers to make transactions at 3,400 machines in 30 states.[33]

As electronic banking spreads, more firms will employ a debit-only transfer system. In this arrangement, when a purchase is made, the amount is immediately charged against the buyer's account; no delayed billing is permitted without an interest charge. The debit-only plan is quite different from current credit-card policy whereby consumers are sent end-of-month bills and then remit payment. A debit card will receive wide acceptance as a substitute for checks. As of 1982, 4 million Visa and MasterCard debit cards and 50 million bank debit cards had been issued.[34]

GTE's Telenet Corporation introduced **electronic mail** in August 1980. Its system is able to transmit a letter by computers and telephone lines from New York to San Francisco in several seconds. MCI and other firms have since started offering electronic mail service. Although initial customer interest in electronic mail has not met expectations, it is projected to be a multibillion dollar business by the late 1980s.[35] Figure 25-4 shows an ad for GTE Telenet.

Computerization will enable *electronic banking* to offer a wide variety of financial services and convenience.

Electronic mail can transmit a letter coast-to-coast in less than one minute.

[32] Bill Abrams, "Electronic Shopping Is Called Imminent, But Doubts Persist," *Wall Street Journal* (June 23, 1983), p. 33.
[33] "Electronic Banking: Networks for Retail Banking Making Money from Transactions," *Business Week* (January 18, 1982), pp. 70–80; and Daniel Hertzberg, "Banks Linking Cash Machines Across the U.S.," *Wall Street Journal* (November 16, 1983), pp. 33, 38.
[34] Ibid.
[35] Peter J. Schuyten, "The Promise of Electronic Mail," *New York Times* (November 2, 1980), pp. F1, F22, F23; David Burnham, "Electronic Mail Controversy," *New York Times* (October 10, 1983), pp. D1, D4; Virginia Inman, "MCI Unveils Service Using Its Phone Lines for Electronic Mail," *Wall Street Journal* (September 28, 1983), p. 18; and Virginia Inman, "MCI Mail Falling Short of Expectations, Begins Campaign to Increase Service's Use," *Wall Street Journal* (March 16, 1984), p. 29.

Improved computer technology will also lead to greater efficiency by, for example,[36]

- Developing "smart cards", which can be used by customers to charge purchases, pay bills, keep records, and store important information (such as medical insurance). These cards will resemble credit cards and be operated through computer terminals.
- Increasing the use of self-service operations by firms marketing gasoline, airline tickets, and rental cars, and for hotel registrations and payment.
- Providing data banks for real estate brokers, who will be better able to match buyers and sellers and secure mortgage sources for buyers.

Resource Shortages

Despite efforts at conservation, many raw materials, processed materials, and component parts may remain or become scarce in the next decade. The effects of these shortages may be further aggravated by the political instability and/or rapid price increases of product-supplying countries. In recent years shortages have occurred for a variety of basic commodities such as home heating oil, other petroleum-based products, plastics, synthetic fibers, aluminum, chrome, silver, tungsten, nickel, steel, glass, grain, fertilizer, cotton, and wool.

Sustained shortages may result in three actions by companies. First, substitute materials will be used in constructing products. This will require intensified research and product testing. Second, prices will be raised for products that cannot incorporate substitute materials. Third, companies will abandon some products where resources are unavailable or used ineffectively and demarket others where demand is greater than it is able to supply. In general, firms will use existing resources much more efficiently in the 1980s.

For example, the U.S. chemical industry relied on the same strategy for fifty years, from the 1920s to the 1970s. This strategy treated chemicals as basic commodities (such as ammonia and sulfuric acid) and relied on expanding sales through competitive, market-driven prices. Energy and raw materials costs were low, and technological advances and rising buyer demand steadily occurred. Then, in the early and mid-1970s, energy and other raw materials costs soared as sources became inadequate; technology advances slowed; and inflation decreased buyer demand. As a result, prices rose 12 per cent a year; and unit sales dropped significantly. Today, many firms are turning to specialty chemicals; these are customized to buyer specifications and offer special features such as technical service and packaging. These chemicals have higher prices (and earn higher profits) and are also more resistant to the effects of resource shortages.[37]

After acquiring the popular Duraflame synthetic fireplace logs in 1978, Clorox Co. quickly ran into trouble with the brand. The logs were made from petro-

Continued shortages may result in substitute materials, higher prices, and abandonment of some items.

[36] Martin Mayer, "Here Comes the Smart Card," *Fortune* (August 8, 1983), pp. 74–82; Maryann Mrowca, "Automated Self-Service Machines Spread After Their Success in Banks," *Wall Street Journal* (July 21, 1983), p. 29; and Joanne Lipman, "Home-Buying Process Is Changing Rapidly Because of Technology," *Wall Street Journal* (January 25, 1984), pp. 1, 14.

[37] William Copulsky, "An Update on Chemical Industry Strategies," *Journal of Business Strategy*, Vol. 4 (Winter 1984), pp. 70–73.

Figure 25-4
Electronic Mail by GTE Telenet.

Reprinted by permission.

leum derivatives which were in limited supply. This meant costs (and prices) escalated rapidly from 1978 to 1982, when Clorox had to drop the logs.[38]

[38] Jennifer Pendleton, ''Clorox Hones Battle Plan,'' *Advertising Age* (June 18, 1982), p. 92.

Media

Over the next decade, there will be both positive and restrictive trends involving the media. The role of cable television, with its well-defined market segments and lower costs than network television, will continue to grow. Newspapers, magazines, and other print media will expand their use of local and regional editions, thus enabling smaller firms to tailor advertising to their specific geographic markets. Innovations such as word processing will enable the media to receive advertisements closer to their air or publication date and minimize errors. Deregulation of the media will enable companies to have more choices in placing messages. Between the new and established media, firms will have a greater degree of flexibility than ever before.

On the restrictive side, media costs will keep on rising. For example, a thirty-second television commercial during the 1984 Winter Olympics cost $225,000; and the actual viewing audience was well below forecasts (causing ABC to make some price adjustments). The media will also be more critical in their evaluation of business practices during newscasts and editorials. Finally, messages will be carefully checked for accuracy, honesty, and other aspects of content before they are accepted for publication or broadcast.

The media will be more flexible, but costs will rise substantially.

Global Events

Global events will offer many potential opportunities and risks. Population growth, rising worldwide per capita incomes, heightened literacy, and standardization in measures will all contribute to opportunities in foreign markets. Political disruptions, nationalism, improved capabilities of foreign companies, and countries' interest in self-sufficiency each pose risks for both domestic and multinational firms. They must plan accordingly.[39]

Examples of global events which should be monitored during the 1980s are

Worldwide events will have an impact on both domestic and multinational firms.

- OPEC actions.
- Policies of economic communities (such as the European Community).
- Political unrest throughout the world.
- The rate of industrialization in foreign countries.
- Worldwide economic conditions.

Figure 25-5 outlines selected marketing implications of the environmental trends discussed in the preceding subsections.

---

[39] See "Argentina's New Hope," *Business Week* (February 6, 1984), pp. 60–68; John Huey, "Executives Assess Europe's Technology Decline," *Wall Street Journal* (February 1, 1984), p. 28; Michael R. Sesit, Roger Ricklefs, and Lawrence Ingrassia, "Strong U.S. Currency Gives Companies Here Competitive Problems," *Wall Street Journal* (January 18, 1984), pp. 1, 18; Amal Nag and Steve Frazier, "Despite Ford Venture, Mexico Faces Struggle to Be Competitive," *Wall Street Journal* (January 11, 1984), pp. 1, 25; Steve Lohr, "U.S. Brokers Expand in Japan," *New York Times* (February 7, 1984), pp. D1, D19; Gilbert D. Harrell and Richard O. Kiefer, "Multinational Strategic Market Portfolios," *MSU Business Topics*, Vol. 29 (Winter 1981), pp. 5–15; and A. Coskun Samli and Erdener Kaynack, "Marketing Practices in Less-Developed Countries," *Journal of Business Research*, Vol. 12 (March 1984), pp. 5–18.

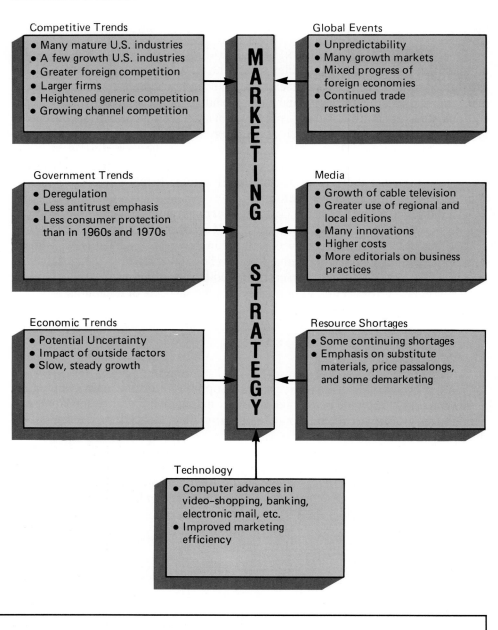

Marketing Trends

In order to succeed in the coming decade, marketers will need to enact strategies that are responsive to emerging consumer characteristics and needs and to the changes in the surrounding environment:

The word that best summarizes recommended marketing in the [future] is *precision*. Inflated costs will necessitate tighter budgets, lower inventories, and more efficient use of the sales force. Riskier markets stocked with shrewder customers will require more effective segmentation schemes and more caution in new product introduction. Marketers will have to approach the future with the flexibility to abandon traditionally successful techniques and the innovativeness to replace them.[40]

This section examines marketing planning and research, and product (service), distribution, promotion, and price strategies for the next decade.

Marketing Planning and Research

As a result of the increasing sophistication of marketing personnel and the tools available to them, the level of marketing planning and research will continue to improve. In applying strategic marketing, more firms will systematically define their target markets, offer clear differential advantages, and determine the timing of offerings. They will also consider risk much more carefully when establishing marketing plans.[41]

Strategic marketing planning and research will be used more frequently and consistently.

Following are several examples of expected trends in marketing planning and research:[42]

- Each year, a larger number of companies will be introducing the use of portfolio planning, whereby they carefully analyze each SBU and the interrelationships among them. One study found that most of the responding companies had introduced portfolio planning within the previous five years, and estimated that 25 to 30 major U.S. corporations add this planning tool every year.
- Companies will increasingly team up to develop or market new products. For instance, IBM and Rolm are working on communications technology; and DuPont and Storage Technology Corporation are cooperating on a project involving optical data storage media.
- Firms will place less emphasis on ''market-share madness'' and direct efforts toward profitable competitive advantages. Many firms, such as Miller Brewing, have spent considerable resources and stressed low prices to gain market leadership positions and discovered that such leadership is not necessarily profitable. Although Miller improved its market share from 4 per cent in the early 1970s to over 20 per cent in 1983, its profits were very low; and during 1983, its unit sales actually dropped. In fact, because of Miller's aggressiveness, total beer industry profits declined, while overall sales rose.
- There will be greater reliance on marketing research prior to new product introductions, as this Polaroid illustration indicates: ''There is a clear change since Dr. Land [the firm's founder] retired. Dr. Land went for what he felt were the big products, whether there was a market for them or not. Now Polaroid is marketing- versus product-directed. It is trying to find out what the consumer wants, to do market research as it never did before.''

[40] Alan J. Resnick, Harold E. Sand, and J. Barry Mason, ''Marketing Dilemma: Change in the '80s,'' *California Management Review,* Vol. 24 (Fall 1981), p. 57.

[41] Subhash Jain, ''The Evolution of Strategic Marketing,'' *Journal of Business Research,* Vol. 11 (December 1983), pp. 409–426; and Kiran K. Shah, ''Strategically Manage 6 Risk Areas,'' *Marketing News* (March 18, 1983), Section 2, pp. 1, 10.

[42] Phillippe Haspeslagh, ''Portfolio Planning: Uses and Limits,'' *Harvard Business Review,* Vol. 60 (January–February 1982), pp. 58–73; ''Suddenly U.S. Companies Are Teaming Up,'' *Business Week* (July 11, 1983), pp. 71–74; Henry Allessio, ''Market-Share Madness,'' *Journal of Business Strategy,* Vol. 3 (Fall 1982), pp. 76–79; and Gay Jervey, ''Polaroid Develops Marketing Orientation,'' *Advertising Age* (January 30, 1984), pp. 4, 77.

Product or Service Strategy

Personal computer, software, videocassette recorder, health food, and related service sales should grow substantially.

There will be further use of formal, systematic product and service strategies. Through comprehensive analysis, companies will be able to position each of their offerings against competition, maintain a balanced product or service mix, identify areas of strength and weakness, monitor items over the product life cycle, and develop long-run plans. Computers will ease this analysis.

During the coming decade, there will be product (service) categories in various phases of the product life cycle. Among the products (services) forecast to grow rapidly are home and small-business computers, computer software, videocassette recorders, health foods, and technology-related services:[43]

- As of early 1984, it was estimated that four million households owned home computers. By the end of 1985, the number is expected to reach 16 to 18 million; and the sales of home computers and small-business computers should continue to be very strong for many years thereafter (about $25 billion annually by 1989).
- With the computer boom, there will be a related growth in the sales of software. From $10 billion in sales during 1984, total annual software sales should reach about $40 billion by 1989 and maintain consistent sales thereafter.
- Between 1981 and 1982, annual sales of videocassette recorders rose from 1.3 to 2.0 million units. Currently, about 10 per cent of U.S. households own videocassette recorders. This figure should more than double by 1990. The sales of video tapes, movie rentals, and video cameras will rise accordingly.
- Health food sales were $3 billion during 1983. They are expected to rise to $16 billion per year by 1993. Frozen health food sales will be particularly strong, due to their convenience.
- Substantial education and servicing requirements will exist for the technological products growing over this decade. The number of vocational and executive training programs, learning centers, and repair and maintenance firms will rise to fill these needs.

While the sales of some mature products will be extended because of innovations, others will decline.

Some products will experience relatively little growth. For example, the markets for many household appliances are already saturated and leave little room for future growth. At present, virtually all U.S. households have refrigerators and gas or electric ranges, 77 per cent have clothes washers, and 98 per cent have televisions. Each of these products has a long life and is replaced infrequently. Of the categories mentioned, only television sales are expected to increase as the number of multiple television households expands. Of the 16 million televisions sold in the U.S. each year, just one third are replacement purchases. By the late 1980s there will be one television for every man, woman, and child in the United States.[44]

Many mature products will have extended life cycles because of new technology. For example, telephones will incorporate programmed numbers, bathroom scales will have electronic readouts, and postage scales will calculate costs. Seiko

---

[43] "Special Report: Personal Computer Marketing," *Advertising Age* (March 5, 1984), pp. M-11–M-62; "Software: The New Driving Force," *Business Week* (February 27, 1984), pp. 74–98; "10th Annual Consumer Survey," *Merchandising* (May 1982), pp. 17 ff; and "New Study Projects Health Food Sales Will Increase at Annual Rate of More Than 20%," *Marketing Review* (November–December 1983), p. 10.

[44] Walter Kiechel III, "Two-Income Families Will Reshape the Consumer Markets," *Fortune* (March 10, 1980), p. 117.

Reprinted by permission.

Figure 25-6
The Seiko TV-Watch
The Seiko TV-Watch has a watch with a digital readout and date, day, and alarm features. The high-resolution television screen measures 1.2 inches. The product weighs 2 ounces. When first marketed, it had a suggested retail list price of $495.

has combined television and watch technologies into its TV-Watch, shown in Figure 25-6. Other products will decline significantly, as newer items make them obsolete. These include regular movie cameras, pinball machines, traditional telegrams, mainframe computers, and videogame consoles.

Consumer interest in improved product quality will continue. Research shows that every year a higher proportion of those surveyed say they would be willing to pay more for better quality in merchandise. This trend can be attributed to better consumer education, increased product complexity, growing service requirements, and greater expectations. Accordingly, firms will need better quality-control techniques, heightened input from control personnel, modular parts to simplify repairs, large-scale service organizations, and expanded product testing.[45]

Product quality will have increased importance.

Distribution Strategy

Distribution strategy will take into account rising costs, advances in technology, and the evolving nature of retailing.

High energy and capital costs, along with the widespread adoption of vendor marking systems (such as UPC and OCR-A), will result in greater uses of computer-based inventory systems. The inventory systems will help control stock on hand and provide more frequent sales and cost analyses by product item. Computer models will also be used to route trucks and sales personnel.

[45] Bill Abrams, ''Research Suggests Consumers Will Increasingly Seek Quality,'' *Wall Street Journal* (October 15, 1981), p. 31; Frank Allen, ''Bosses Tout Quality of U.S. Goods, But Single Out Autos for Criticism,'' *Wall Street Journal* (October 12, 1981), pp. 29, 47; and ''Quality: The U.S. Drives to Catch Up,'' *Business Week* (November 1, 1982), pp. 66–80.

Product planning in the 1980s will respond to rising distribution costs.

Responses to rising distribution costs will frequently interrelate with product-planning decisions. For example, Sacramento Tomato Juice is now shipped as a concentrate to regional plants. At these plants, it is reconstituted by adding water and seasoning and canning operations are performed. As one brand manager noted:

> It costs about 18 cents to ship a 46-ounce can of juice across the country, and most of that weight is water. If we send the concentrate as a paste and it is reconstituted and shipped locally, that cost drops to 7 cents a can. . . . Any juice processor that does not go into concentrates will probably go out of business.[46]

Other products with high water contents that may require changed warehousing or product formulations to reduce transportation costs include soft drinks, beer, canned vegetables, canned food, and household bleach.

Three major trends in retailing will involve the continued expansion of discounting, nonstore retailing, and scrambled merchandising. Discount retailing will gain further because more manufacturers will seek alternative outlets through which to sell excess inventory, there is an increasing gap between high-end and low-end retailers, there is a sizable market segment of price-conscious consumers, and discounting is gaining greater consumer acceptance (particularly for brand-name merchandise). As noted in Chapter 14, emerging discount retailers include flea markets, factory outlet stores, off-price chains, and warehouse stores.

Discount malls **will be built in greater numbers, further enhancing off-price retailing.**

The newest development in discounting is the **discount mall,** in which a variety of low-price retailers are located together. The mall arrangement saves gasoline, encourages one-stop shopping, and expands the trading area of each retailer. Among the sites of discount malls are Macon, Ga.; Utica, N.Y.; and Lakeland, Tenn. Off-Center Chicago is a six-level, 63,000-square-foot mall that specializes in discount merchandise. Willow Chase Center is a 360,000 square-foot off-price mall with 24 stores in Houston. Figure 25-7 shows the Belz Factory Outlet Mall in Orlando, Florida, one of the largest outlet malls in the U.S.

Nonstore retailing and scrambled merchandising will continue to grow.

A second retailing trend will be the continued growth of nonstore retailing. This growth will result from the high cost of transportation, working women being unable to shop during conventional hours, the desire for leisure time, the popularity of national brands, and the size of the senior citizen market. Technology will also contribute to nonstore sales: toll-free 800 numbers can be called at any time, catalogs are pinpointed at specific markets, and home video-shopping is emerging.

A third trend centers on the perpetuation of scrambled merchandising, as stores seek to provide better product/service assortments and encourage one-stop shopping. More department stores will offer beauty parlors, travel agencies, restaurants, computerized ticket agencies, and financial services. More supermarkets/superstores will carry flowers, small appliances, toys, automatic teller machines, and stationery. More toy stores will stock home computers, adult games, furniture, gift items, and sporting goods.

---

[46] Mimi Sheraton, "To Retailers' Dismay, A Supermarket Classic Changes," *New York Times* (January 3, 1981), p. L44.

Figure 25-7
The Belz Factory Outlet
Mall in Orlando, Florida

Reprinted by permission of Belz Enterprises of Memphis, Tennessee.

Promotion Strategy

The advertising and personal selling aspects of promotion will undergo significant changes. Advertising will be influenced by new video tools and higher television rates. Personal selling will be affected by rising costs and computerization.

The largest shift in advertising strategy will be the result of the greater reliance on cable television, two-way interactive television, videocassettes, and videodiscs. For example, in 1983, cable advertising revenues were about $350 million; by 1990, these revenues are expected to near $2 billion. A recent study showed that cable customers will accept further advertising if it is between programs and helps keep subscription costs down.[47]

A major attraction of the new video tools is their ability to **narrowcast,** which is to present special programming to specific audiences. Narrowcasting makes cable television a natural for the advertising of local firms. It may also lead to coupons, premiums, and refund offers being presented on cable television. Specialty magazines and mail-order companies may be adversely affected if cable television provides better results.[48]

A *narrowcast* is video programming for specific audiences.

---

[47] Joanne Cleaver, "The Medium Is Potent If the Message Is Clear," *Advertising Age* (June 13, 1983), pp. M-28 ff.

[48] Hal Katz, "The Advantages of Narrowcasting," *Marketing & Media Decisions* (January 1984), pp. 74, 76.

Many advertisers are now experimenting with cable television. For example, Campbell produces ''Woman Watch'' and Mazda produces ''Sports Look,'' weekly cable programs. General Foods, Anheuser-Busch, and Procter & Gamble are among the leading advertisers on cable television.

More firms will use *multiunit advertising*, in which two or more products are placed in a single ad.

Advertising strategy will be responsive to higher commercial television rates. These rates increased at nearly double the inflation rate during the 1970s and this is expected to continue in the future. It is forecast that ***multiunit advertising,*** whereby two or more products are included in a single ad, will rise substantially. In addition, more companies will advertise on late-night television, when rates are much lower (not only are actual costs reduced, but costs per viewer can be as little as one sixth of those during prime time).[49] Finally, some firms will be turning away from television to other media.

Efforts will be made to make selling more efficient.

Personal selling costs such as transportation, hotel, and compensation will rise throughout the next decade. This will result in greater emphasis on effective routing of sales personnel to minimize travel time and expenses. Reduced attention will be given to small customers and orders by some firms (creating opportunities for others). Telephone selling will be more frequently used, especially for smaller accounts. Some firms may specify minimum order sizes and require surcharges for lesser orders.

Computerization will improve the efficiency of the sales force by providing information and fast service, coordinating orders, and identifying the most lucrative prospects.

Price Strategy

Doubts about costs will focus greater attention on cost-based pricing strategies.

The uncertainty with regard to future material, labor, and capital costs will focus further attention on cost-based pricing strategies. These include delay-quotation pricing in which prices are not confirmed until production is completed, raising across-the-board prices based on a firm's average costs, and reliance on escalator clauses. Higher costs and product shortages may also result in greater reliance on skimming prices for new products and salespeople having less flexibility to negotiate price.

High interest rates affect the credit policies of manufacturers and retailers. To complete sales they may have to arrange credit for customers, particularly when large-volume purchases are involved. For example, Xerox loans money to customers at low rates to encourage sales. XEEP (Xerox Equipment Equity Program) finances about half of the company's U.S. sales with corporate funds. Xerox could earn higher rates on its loans, but it believes that sales volume more than offsets the low interest charges.

Consumer reactions to prices will take various forms. They may hoard or stockpile goods whose prices they feel will increase or postpone purchases until they feel financially better prepared to buy. Marketers will respond by trying to maintain stable prices, explaining the relationship of costs to prices, expanding the use of coupons and specials, and concentrating on sales to less price-sensitive market segments.

Marketers will also react by offering more price alternatives, such as dis-

---

[49] Diane Mermigas, ''NBC Opens Piggyback Gate,'' *Advertising Age* (April 11, 1983), pp. 1, 68; and John Koten, ''Big Advertisers Are Waking to Benefits of Late-Night TV,'' *Wall Street Journal* (February 9, 1984), p. 29.

Figure 25-8
**Price Bundling For a
Bookcase**

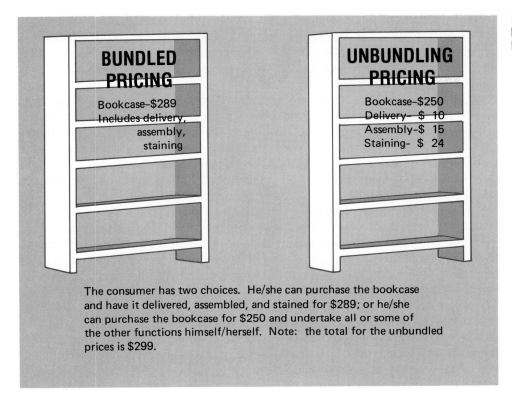

BUNDLED PRICING

Bookcase–$289
Includes delivery,
assembly,
staining

UNBUNDLING PRICING

Bookcase–$250
Delivery– $ 10
Assembly–$ 15
Staining– $ 24

The consumer has two choices. He/she can purchase the bookcase
and have it delivered, assembled, and stained for $289; or he/she
can purchase the bookcase for $250 and undertake all or some of
the other functions himself/herself. Note: the total for the unbundled
prices is $299.

counts for cash as well as extended payment plans. In particular, marketers will
use price bundling as a competitive tool. With **bundled pricing,** a firm offers a
basic product, options, and service for one total price. For example, the Coleco
Adam home computer has a price of $700; included in the price are the computer,
a disc drive, a printer, software, accessories, and an extended warranty. Individual items, such as the computer, cannot be purchased separately. With **unbundled
pricing,** a firm breaks down prices by individual components and allows the
consumer to decide what to purchase. For example, a discount department store
may have separate prices for a refrigerator, its delivery, its installation, and a
service contract. Some companies may offer consumers both pricing options, and
allow a slight discount for bundled pricing. See Figure 25-8.

Alternatives offered to
consumers will include
bundled pricing and
unbundled pricing.

Summary

The next ten years promise to be significant ones for U.S. marketers as they try to
anticipate trends and plan long-run strategies. During the coming decade, there
will be consumer affluence, technological advances, worldwide markets, and
deregulation, as well as energy and material shortages, foreign competition, a
stable U.S. market, and an uncertain economy.

There will be many demographic trends, including low population growth, an older society, movement to Southeast and Southwest regions, continued home ownership, regional mobility, higher real income, more working women, and increases in education, white-collar jobs, and single-person households. Two thirds of adults will be married.

Four newer life-style trends will continue. Voluntary simplicity is a life-style in which people seek material simplicity, have ecological awareness, strive for self-determination, and purchase do-it-yourself products. The me generation stresses being good to oneself. There is less emphasis on obligations and conformity. Blurring gender roles occurs when husbands work in the house, share the tasks of managing a household, and feed the family. The poverty-of-time concept states that for some consumers greater affluence will result in less free time because the alternatives competing for time will expand.

During the decade, a number of environmental factors will affect marketing. The future competitive environment may be analyzed from domestic/foreign, small firm/large firm, generic, and channel perspectives. Government actions will be involved with deregulation, less antitrust involvement, and a lower level of consumer protection than in the 1960s and 1970s. The economy will be difficult to predict and will be influenced by outside factors. The major technological breakthroughs will center on computerization and the resulting changes in consumer behavior and company strategies. Resource shortages may hamper marketing and lead to research efforts aimed at finding acceptable substitutes. The media will offer a variety of positive and restrictive trends. Global events will strongly influence company opportunities and risks.

In order to succeed, marketers must develop strategies that are responsive to consumer trends and the changes in the surrounding environment. The level of marketing planning and research will continue to improve as newer tools, such as portfolio planning, are used more frequently. Formal, systematic product and service strategies will be enacted with greater emphasis on comprehensive analysis. Companies need to identify growing and mature products and react accordingly. Distribution strategy will take into account rising costs, advances in technology, and the evolving nature of retailing. Advertising strategy will be influenced by new video tools and higher television rates. Personal selling strategy will be affected by rising costs and computerization. Price planning will carefully consider costs and offer consumers more alternatives, with greater interest in price bundling.

Questions for Discussion

1. Why is the role of marketing in a company's strategic planning process expected to increase in importance over the next decade?
2. How should each of these respond to the demographic trends in the U.S.?
   a. Candy manufacturer.

   b. *Sesame Street* television program.

   c. Expensive restaurant.

3. Contrast the voluntary-simplicity life-style with the me-generation life-style. What conclusions should marketers draw about these life-styles?

4. Discuss the implications of blurring gender roles for an appliance manufacturer and a department store.

5. Comment on the statement, ''On balance you might argue that American cars are now as good as imports, but the public clearly doesn't think so.''

6. Why is generic competition expected to increase? How should firms react to this?

7. What do you think will be the long-run effect of government deregulation? Explain your answer.

8. Determine the current inflation and employment rates, and the annual growth in GNP. Compare these figures with 1982 and 1983.

   a. What are the short-run marketing implications?

   b. What are the long-run marketing implications?

9. Apply the diffusion process (described in Chapter 10) to electronic banking services. Do you believe a large number of consumers will be attracted to these services within the next five years? Why or why not?

10. Evaluate the future of electronic mail.

11. Name five specific global events that could affect marketing in a positive way.

12. The sales of videocassette recorders have increased dramatically ever since they were introduced. What marketing actions will be necessary to sustain this sales growth over the next decade?

13. Do you think video-shopping will replace traditional mail-order catalog sales? Explain your answer.

14. Some experts believe the advertising potential of cable television is vastly overstated. Why do you think they feel this way? Do you agree? Why or why not?

15. Under what circumstances should a firm stress bundled prices? Unbundled prices? Explain your answer.

Case 1 Apple Computer: Will Its Future Be as Bright as Its Past?[*]

Steven Jobs and Stephen Wozniack, then in their very early 20s, founded the Apple Computer company in 1977. By 1983, the company had annual sales of about $1 billion; and over one and a half million Apple computers had been sold between 1977 and the end of 1983.

   Apple's success was due to several factors:

- It defined and developed the market for personal computers.
- It reduced the mystery of computers to consumers.
- Prices were relatively low.
- A solid distribution network was established.

[*] The data in this case are drawn from Peter Nulty, ''Apple's Bid to Stay in the Big Time,'' *Fortune* (February 7, 1983), pp. 36–41; Ann M. Morrison, ''Apple Bites Back,'' *Fortune* (February 20, 1984), pp. 86–100; Dennis Kneale, ''Apple Pins Macintosh Future on 'User Friendliness' of Lisa,'' *Wall Street Journal* (January 27, 1984), p. 33; and ''Apple Takes on Its Biggest Test Yet,'' *Business Week* (January 31, 1983), pp. 70–79.

- Independent programmers were encouraged to develop software. This led to a 16,000-program library.
- Young product designers were attracted to work for the company.

Despite its rapid growth, Apple has not been without its problems. The Apple II was its only major commercial success from 1977 through 1983. The widely promoted Apple III had design problems, which caused it to be recalled shortly after introduction in 1981. An improved Apple III has not met company expectations.

In 1983, Apple introduced Lisa, a "revolutionary" new computer that was very easy to learn and use. As a result of a poor marketing strategy, Lisa sales were quite poor (20,000 units in 1983). Among the errors Apple made with Lisa were these: the computer was not ready for distribution until several months after it was formally introduced; the $10,000 price was much too high in an intensely competitive environment; the computer operated relatively slowly; traditional dealers were bypassed as Apple created its own sales force for Lisa; and not enough software was available. During 1983, IBM's dollar sales of personal computers surpassed those of Apple for the first time; and Apple's profits fell 75 per cent for the fourth quarter of 1983 (compared with 1982).

To regain its momentum, Apple has engaged in a multifaceted strategy. Its new president was previously a senior-level marketing executive at PepsiCo. The product line has been broadened and better integrated. Current products include the Apple II, Macintosh, Apple III, and Lisa; each of these has a distinct market niche. Prices are more competitive (for example, the three new Lisa models range from $3,500 to $5,500). Dealer relations are improved. Advertising has been increased to $50 million per year.

Many analysts believe Apple's ability to maintain a strong market position in the future will be closely linked to the sales of its innovative Macintosh computer, introduced in January 1984. In marketing the Macintosh, Apple has avoided the errors it committed with Lisa. Macintosh was ready for distribution at the time it was formally announced. The $2,500 price was less than that of a comparably equipped IBM PC. Macintosh operates quite quickly. Traditional dealers are used. To ensure the availability of adequate software, about 100 independent programming firms were provided with Macintoshes prior to introduction. Apple hoped to sell 250,000 to 500,000 Macintosh computers during 1984.

QUESTIONS

1. In evaluating the potential sales of Macintosh, one dealer stated, "I think it's going to be impressive, but it's still going to be a tougher sales job than selling an IBM. I don't need salesmen to sell IBMs. I can have a 16-year-old kid sit there and take orders all day." Comment on this statement.
2. Unlike most other computer firms, Apple has decided that its models will *not* be "IBM-compatible"; Apple computers will be unable to run IBM software. Analyze this strategy.
3. A number of Apple's competitors are rooting for its Macintosh model to be a big seller. Why do you think these firms feel that way?
4. Read the articles cited in the case, and then assess Apple Computer in terms of the eight key characteristics of corporate excellence cited by Peters and Waterman in *In Search of Excellence* (identified in the opening vignette of this chapter).

Case 2 MTV: When Do The Profits Start?[†]

MTV is a twenty-four hour a day music-video cable television channel. It offers rock music to a primary audience of 12- to 34-year-olds. During a typical hour, viewers see about 11 music videotapes (supplied free to MTV by recording companies), "video jockey" reports on music and concert news, and up to 8 minutes of commercials.

MTV reaches viewers in 14 million homes. About 7 million households watch MTV at least once a week; at any one time, about 850,000 households (with an average of 2.6 viewers) are tuned to the channel. MTV is considered the most frequently watched and most popular channel on cable television. Table 1 shows the results of several surveys regarding viewer characteristics and behavior.

Although MTV has been able to attract a large, loyal audience, it has not attracted enough advertisers to be profitable. Said one advertising agency executive,

From the advertiser's standpoint, cable services like MTV are still the last thing they turn to. MTV and others are still viewed as just icing on the cake.

Thus far, MTV has obtained a lot of videogame, automobile, beer, and soft drink advertising. It has received little advertising from consumer-products firms such as Procter & Gamble and General Foods, despite relatively low advertising rates ($1,500 to $6,000 for a thirty-second commercial). In summing up his company's attitude toward MTV, one General Foods executive stated that more research on viewers' habits was needed: "Is it just something the teenagers in a

[†] The data in this case are drawn from Laura Landro, "MTV Music Channel Rocks Teen-Agers, But Big Advertisers Haven't Tuned In," *Wall Street Journal* (August 24, 1983), p. 8; and Kevin Higgins, "MTV Is a Cable TV Hit but Remains Unprofitable," *Marketing News* (September 2, 1983), p. 4.

**Table 1
MTV's Audience**

Characteristics

Males represent 56 per cent of the audience.

The median age of viewers is 23. Only 15 per cent of the audience is 35 or older.

The median household income of viewers is $30,600.

The average viewer watches MTV 4.4 days per week, about 62 minutes a day on weekdays and 87 minutes a day on weekends.

Behavior

MTV households are 36 per cent more likely to own two or more cars than average television households.

63 per cent of the audience has bought or planned to purchase a recording by a performer seen on MTV.

68 per cent of viewers rate MTV as very important or important in a record album purchase decision (compared with 62 per cent for radio and 45 per cent for television).

household turn to when commercials come on the networks?" MTV also has to overcome a "culture gap" between its viewing audience and the "more conservative" advertisers it seeks. This gap will be particularly hard to close, because MTV (like other cable channels) presents programs that are uncensored and uncut.

MTV's ability to generate a sizable audience has led to competitive programs on both commercial and cable television. This will make it even more difficult for MTV to increase advertising revenues—and earn profits.

QUESTIONS

1. Analyze the audience data in Table 1.
2. Since MTV draws such a large audience and has low rates, why is it having so much difficulty in drawing advertisers? Why is this a problem for all types of cable television programs?
3. MTV is discovering that narrowcasting has disadvantages as well as advantages. Explain this.
4. In comparing MTV to its leading competitors, a spokesperson said, "[MTV] is a 24-hour a day service, and because of the way it is formated, it sells a lot of records. I don't know whether a one-hour program airing once a week will sell records." Comment on this statement.
5. What other factors described in this chapter must MTV consider in planning its future strategy?

Part Eight Case General Motors: Reorganizing The World's Largest Auto Maker[*]

In 1921, Alfred P. Sloan, Jr., the chairman of the General Motors Corporation (GM), devised a company organization structure that would last for more than 60 years and enable GM to become the largest automobile manufacturer in the world. Before Sloan took control, General Motors was unable to match Ford, the industry leader, in producing small, economical cars. According to many automobile industry analysts, GM cars were of poor quality and a number of models were too similar (consumers had difficulty distinguishing among them). Under Sloan's direction, GM was organized into several distinct divisions in order to produce "a line of cars in each price area, from the lowest price up to one for a strictly high-grade" market.

Sloan decreed that there would be "no duplication by the corporation" in appealing to each price and size segment of the automobile market. Younger customers would be attracted to the inexpensive, small cars made by the Chevrolet division. As these customers grew older and became more affluent, they would upgrade the price and size of their car by moving to a Pontiac, then to an Oldsmobile, next to a Buick, and finally to a Cadillac. The largest and most expensive cars were offered by the Cadillac division.

Sloan's divisional structure remained in effect until 1984. Then, after months of rumors, GM executives announced plans to restructure the company into two automotive groups, one for large cars and one for small cars. The new organization would be phased in over a 3- to 5-year period. The announcement culminated three years of intensive analysis and review that involved more than 500 managers. The analysis began in 1980, when GM suffered a loss of $763 million—its only loss since the depression. Said GM's chairman, "Because of the crunch in our industry, we looked at every single thing we could do" to upgrade performance. A number of factors led to the firm's decision to reorganize.

Why GM Decided to Reorganize

While overall profits and sales revenue reached all-time company highs in 1983 (profits were $4 billion), unit car sales did not approach record levels. 4 million cars were sold in 1983, compared with 5 million cars per year and more in the late 1970s; and this followed greatly depressed sales from 1980 to 1982.

---

[*] The data in this case are drawn from ''Can GM Solve Its Identity Crisis?'' *Business Week* (January 23, 1984), pp. 32–33; ''GM Plans a Great Divide,'' *Newsweek* (January 9, 1984), pp. 68–69; John Holusha, ''GM's Overhaul: A Return to Basics,'' *New York Times* (January 15, 1984), pp. F1, F12; John Koten, ''GM Decision to Reorganize Starts Race for President Between Stempel, Reuss,'' *Wall Street Journal* (January 11, 1984), p. 24; Urban C. Lehner and Robert L. Simison, ''GM Unveils Plan for Realigning Auto Making,'' *Wall Street Journal* (January 11, 1984), p. 3; ''Many GM Dealers Fear Auto Maker's Plan to Reorganize May Hurt Their Businesses,'' *Wall Street Journal* (January 10, 1984), p. 35; Ralph Gray and Jesse Snyder, ''Marketing the New GM Looms as the Next Task,'' *Advertising Age* (January 9, 1984), pp. 1, 55; Ralph Gray and Jesse Snyder, ''Two Top GM Execs Expound on Changes,'' *Advertising Age* (January 30, 1984), p. 37; Ralph Gray and Jesse Snyder, ''Cadillac Seen as Third GM Unit,'' *Advertising Age* (February 6, 1984), pp. 3, 61; Anne B. Fisher, ''GM's Unlikely Revolutionist,'' *Fortune* (March 19, 1984), pp. 106–112; and ''The All-American Small Car Is Fading,'' *Business Week* (March 12, 1984), pp. 88–95.

GM's 1983 profitability was due to cost economies implemented during the industry's recession; high dollar sales were due to elevated prices.

The market share of key divisions was slipping. The Chevrolet division's share of the U.S. car market fell from 20.8 per cent in 1978 to 14.8 per cent in 1983. The Pontiac division's share of the U.S. car market dropped from 7.9 per cent in 1978 to 6.0 per cent in 1983.

The car models offered by the different divisions were no longer distinctive. This resulted in almost identical body styles and "look-alike" models, causing customer confusion and blurred images for the divisions. For example, the Chevrolet Cavalier and Cadillac Cimmaron looked quite similar, although the Cimmaron was priced about $6,000 higher. Also, the divisions had become virtually self-contained, full-line automobile companies with no size distinctions. Chevrolet produced cars as big as the largest Buicks; and Cadillac made a subcompact. Because of these overlaps, production costs were high—each division marketed its own version of similar products. Observed one auto industry analyst, "They lost the advantage of differentiation, and they still had poor costs."

GM was slow in reacting to market and technological/engineering changes. There were too many disjointed operations for executives to communicate satisfactorily and respond quickly enough to opportunities and problems. The process was also hindered by having two somewhat autonomous manufacturing facilities, Fisher Body and GM Assembly. Accordingly, GM faced delays in developing front-wheel drive for larger car models; and it received adverse publicity when faulty brakes and diesel engines were discovered in new cars.

GM's small cars were losing sales and money. From 1975 to 1983, its share of the U.S. small-car market declined from 25 per cent to 19 per cent. The Japanese could build a car comparable to GM's Chevrolet Chevette for $2,000 less than the Chevette. One university research study indicated that General Motors lost money on all car models smaller than the mid-size Chevrolet Celebrity and Pontiac 6000 in 1983. As one GM executive acknowledged, "Obviously our major thrust has got to be to pick up penetration in the younger market."

There was a growing lack of performance accountability for executives and other GM employees. This led to "second-best" decisions. Engineering was spread among the GM car divisions (e.g., Pontiac specialized in rear suspension, Buick in brakes), assembly operations were completed by GM Assembly, and Fisher Body designed car bodies and produced body panels. Total costs on each car model could not be controlled, because no single executive or group of them had authority for overall operations. "Too many people had a say about the product, but nobody had responsibility," remarked an auto analyst.

The Reorganization Plan

Under GM's reorganization plan, shown in Figure 1, there are small-car and large-car groups. Each group will be responsible for engineering and manufacturing all cars within its size designation. The existing car divisions will remain, but they will be involved only with marketing activities (not engineering and production) and be part of one of the two car groups. The small-car group will consist of Chevrolet and Pontiac, as well as GM of Canada. The large-car group will contain Buick, Oldsmobile, and Cadillac. The reorganization will eventually eliminate Fisher Body and GM Assembly.

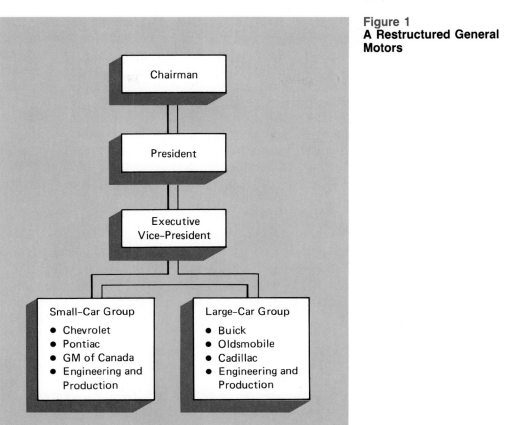

Figure 1
A Restructured General Motors

The divisions will continue to share basic car body models; but, greater effort will be given to distinguishing one line from another: "Instead of three presses punching out the same fender, they'll be punching out three different fenders." The new groups will not design and make cars outside their size designations. This means several models will be phased out: Chevrolet's Malibu, Monte Carlo, and Caprice; Pontiac's Bonneville, Grand Prix, Parisienne; Oldsmobile's Firenza and Omega; Buick's Skyhawk and Skylark; and Cadillac's Cimmaron.

To speed reaction time and coordinate activities better, design, engineering, production, and marketing functions are to be handled by complete staffs at each car group. The separation of manufacturing and marketing tasks is intended to make GM more consumer-oriented. Said an industry observer, "The key to the whole thing is the importance placed on the marketing function, and I know at the top they want more emphasis on marketing." Oldsmobile's group manager explained GM's philosophy:

The point of the whole exercise is that Oldsmobile will sell what the market wants and not try to sell what we're making, and that makes us more responsive to the market. Olds will have responsibility for marketing and product planning, not making diesels or V-8 engines.

The small-car, large-car organization also demonstrates that GM is preparing to compete effectively in the small-car field. While 40 per cent of the cars sold in the U.S. are in the small-car category, General Motors is relatively weak in this market. Its 1983 market share of 19 per cent for small cars was less than one third its large-car market share of 60 per cent. The new small-car group is headed by Lloyd Reuss, former general manager of Buick; Robert Stempel, the former general manager of Chevrolet, heads the large-car group. Both Reuss and Stempel were chosen to lead car groups that did not include their former divisions, in order to ensure that no favoritism would occur.

Unlike in the past, managers will have total responsibility "from bumper to bumper," with emphasis on the 3Rs (risk, responsibility, and reward). GM senior executives will be able to talk to the manager in charge and ask, "You designed 'em, you built 'em, and you priced 'em. What went wrong?" Reuss and Stempel will be completely accountable for their groups' sales and profits.

Potential Problems of Reorganization

General Motors' reorganization plan does have some potential problems. Dealers were not told about the plan in advance and many are worried that it will hurt their businesses. Some dealers are concerned that they will lose half their sales (e.g., Chevrolet dealers not being able to offer large cars) or be forced to become dual dealerships (e.g., offering Pontiacs and Buicks). They believe there will be disruptions and that a number of dealers may go out of business.

There will be a period of consumer confusion, since they must learn which car divisions will market which car sizes. Commented one analyst, "They've already done an outstanding job of confusing the consumer. Now they could confuse them even further."

Finally, about a month after the reorganization plan was announced, reports surfaced that GM was already considering the establishment of Cadillac as a third car group. According to Cadillac executives,

I really see ourselves moving in that direction. Not only do we have the best capability to work independently, but we are the only ones with an absolute need. We want to re-establish the degree of exclusivity the Cadillac nameplate has always stood for.

We have a lot of our people who don't think they work for General Motors—they think they work for Cadillac. You're not going to get much cooperation if you put a big 'Buick-Olds-Cadillac' sign over the door. Some of these people are third and fourth generation Cadillac workers.

QUESTIONS

1. Contrast GM's reorganization plan with Alfred Sloan's original plan from the 1920s.
2. Do you think GM could have overcome the problems cited in the case without such a drastic reorganization? Explain your answer.
3. Evaluate GM's new organization in terms of clarity of mission, long-term competitive advantages, precisely defined target markets, compatible subplans, coordination among SBUs, coordination of the marketing mix, and stability over time.
4. Develop a marketing-audit form that could be used to assess GM's new organization structure.
5. Comment on GM's separation of marketing and manufacturing activities.
6. Evaluate GM's use of small- and large-car groups, and the restrictions that will be imposed on each marketing division. Will the company be able to re-establish itself in the small-car market? Why or why not?
7. What must GM do to reduce the concerns of its dealers?
8. Should Cadillac be established as a third car group? Explain your answer.

Careers in Marketing

Career opportunities in marketing are quite extensive and diversified. Many marketing positions give a considerable amount of discretion to people early in their careers. For example, within six months to one year of being hired, assistant retail buyers are usually given budget authority for purchases involving hundreds of thousands of dollars. Beginning salespeople typically start to call on accounts within several weeks of being hired. Marketing research personnel actually develop preliminary questionnaires, determine sampling procedures, and interpret study results within a short time after initial employment. A marketing career is excellent preparation for a path to top management positions in all types of organizations.

A number of marketing positions are highly visible. These include sales personnel, sales managers, retail buyers, brand managers, industrial traffic managers, credit managers, and advertising and public relations personnel. This allows effective persons to be recognized, promoted, and properly compensated. In fact, the compensation in sales positions is usually based on sales volume and/or profitability and is directly linked to the individual's own performance.

Marketing offers career opportunities for people with varying educational backgrounds. An associate's or a bachelor's degree is generally required for most management training positions in retailing, inventory management, sales, public relations, and advertising. A master of business administration degree is increasingly necessary for marketing research, marketing consulting, brand management, senior management, and industrial sales positions. Frequently, marketing consultants, marketing research directors, and marketing professors have earned Ph.D. degrees in marketing or related subjects.

A marketing background can also train a person to operate his or her own business. Among the entrepreneurial opportunities available are careers as retail store owners, manufacturers' agents, wholesalers, insurance and real estate brokers, marketing consultants, marketing researchers, and free-lance advertising illustrators or copy writers.

Table 1 contains a detailed, but not exhaustive, listing of job titles in marketing. Table 2 shows the types of firms that employ people in marketing positions. Table 3 outlines selected marketing career opportunities for the 1980s.

Table 1   Selected Job Titles in Marketing

Job Title	Description
Account executive	Liaison person between an advertising agency and its clients. The individual is employed by the agency to study the clients' promotional objectives and create promotional programs (including message, layout, media, and timing).
Advertising copywriter	Creator of headlines and content for advertisements.
Advertising layout person	Producer of illustrations or one who uses other artists' illustrations to formulate advertisements.
Advertising manager	Director of a firm's advertising program. He or she determines media, copy, size of budget, advertising frequency, and the choice of an advertising agency.
Advertising production manager	Person who arranges to have an advertisement filmed (for television), recorded (for radio), or printed (for newspaper, magazines, etc.).
Advertising research director	Person who researches markets, evaluates alternative advertisements, assesses media, and tests advertisements.
Agent (broker)	Wholesaler who works for a commission or fee.
Commercial artist	Creator of advertisements for television, print media, and product packaging. This artist selects photographs and drawings and determines the layout and type of print to be used in newspaper and magazine advertisements. Sample scenes of television commercials are sketched for clients.
Consumer affairs specialist (customer relations specialist)	Company contact with consumers. This person handles consumer complaints and attempts to change the firm's policies to reflect customer needs. Community programs, such as lectures on product safety, arise from the consumer affairs specialist.
Credit manager	Supervisor of the firm's credit process, including eligibility for credit, terms, late payments, consumer complaints, and control.
Direct-to-home salesperson	Person who sells products and services to consumers by personal contact at the consumer's homes.
Display worker	Person who designs and sets up retail store displays.
Fashion designer	Designer of apparel, such as beachwear, hats, dresses, scarves, and shoes.
Franchisee	Person who leases or buys a business that has many outlets and a well-known name. The franchisee normally operates one outlet and participates in cooperative planning and advertising. The franchisor sets rules for operating all outlets.
Franchisor	Person who develops a company name and reputation and then leases or sells parts of the firm to independent businesspeople. The franchisor oversees the company, sets policy, and usually trains franchisees.
Freight forwarder	Wholesaler who consolidates small shipments from many companies.
Industrial designer	Designer who improves the appearance and function of machine-made products.
Industrial traffic manager	Arranger of transportation to and from firms and customers for raw materials, fabricated parts, finished goods, and equipment.
International marketer	Person who works overseas or in the international department of a domestic company and is involved with some aspect of marketing. International marketing positions are available in all areas of marketing.

Table 1 Selected Job Titles in Marketing (Continued)

Job Title	Description
Inventory manager	Person who controls the level and allocation of merchandise throughout the year. This manager evaluates and balances inventory amounts against the costs of holding merchandise.
Life insurance agent (broker)	Person who advises clients on life insurance policy types available relative to their needs. Policies provide life insurance and/or retirement income.
Manufacturers' representative (agent)	Salesperson who represents several, usually small, manufacturers that cannot afford their own sales force. The representative normally deals with wholesalers and retailers. He or she determines needs and then displays, demonstrates, and describes products and services, often at the customer's place of business.
Marketing manager (vice-president of marketing)	Executive who plans, directs, and controls the entire marketing functions of the company. The manager (vice-president) oversees all marketing decisions and personnel.
Marketing research project supervisor	Person who develops the research methodology, evaluates the accuracy of different sample sizes, analyzes data, and assesses statistical errors.
Media analyst	Person who evaluates the characteristics and costs of available media. The analyst examines audience size and traits, legal restrictions, types of messages used, and so on. The effectiveness of company messages is also measured.
Media director (space or time buyer)	Person who determine the day, time (for radio and television), media, location, and size of advertisements. The goal is to reach the largest desirable audience at the most efficient cost. The director (buyer) negotiates contracts for advertising space or air time.
Missionary salesperson	Support salesperson who provides information about new and existing products.
Packaging specialist	Person responsible for package design, durability, safety, appeal, size, and cost. This specialist must be familiar with all related legislation.
Pricing economist	Specialist who studies sources of supply, consumer demand, government restrictions, competition, and costs and then offers short-run and long-run pricing recommendations.
Product manager (brand manager)	Person who supervises the marketing of a product or brand category. In some firms there are product (brand) managers for existing items and new-product (brand) managers for new introductions. For a one-brand or one-product company, the product (brand) manager is actually the marketing manager.
Property and casualty insurance agent (broker)	Person who evaluates client risks from such perils as fire, burglary, and accidents, assesses coverage needs, and sells policies to indemnify losses.
Public relations director	Manager of a company's efforts to keep the public aware of its accomplishments and benefits to society and minimize negative reactions to company policies and activities. The director constantly measures public attitudes and seeks to maintain a favorable public opinion of the firm.
Purchasing agent	Buyer for a manufacturer, wholesaler, or retailer. The agent purchases items necessary for the operation of the firm and usually buys in bulk, seeks reliable suppliers, and sets precise specifications.
Real estate agent (broker)	Liaison who brings together a buyer and seller, lessor and lessee, or landlord and tenant. This salesperson receives a commission.
Retail buyer	Person responsible for purchasing items for resale. The buyer generally concentrates on a product area and develops a plan for proper styles, assortments, sizes, and amounts of the product. The buyer analyzes vendors on the basis of quality, style, availability, fit, flexibility, reliability, and price.
Retail department manager	Supervisor of one retail department, often at a branch store. The manager usually works with the buyer and is responsible for displaying merchandise, counting it, and reordering it. Department manager is often the first position a college graduate assumes after the initial training program.

Table 1 Selected Job Titles in Marketing (Continued)

Job Title	Description
Retail merchandise manager	Supervisor of several buyers. This manager sets the retailer's direction in terms of styles, product lines, image, pricing, and so on and allocates budgets among buyers.
Retail salesperson	Salesperson for a retailer who deals with final consumers.
Retail store manager	Supervisor of the day-to-day activities of a store. All in-store personnel report to this manager.
Sales engineer	Support salesperson involved with technical products or services.
Sales manager	Supervisor of the sales force, responsible for recruitment, selection, training, motivation, evaluation, compensation, and control.
Sales promotion director	Person involved with supplementary promotional activities, such as trading stamps, coupons, contests, giveaways, and free samples.
Salesperson	Company representative who interacts with consumers. A salesperson may require limited or extensive skills, deal with final or intermediate customers, work from an office or go out in the field, and be a career salesperson or progress in management.
Securities salesperson	Salesperson involved with the buying and selling of stocks, bonds, government securities, mutual funds, and other securities.
Traffic manager	Supervisor of the purchase and use of alternate methods of transportation. This manager routes shipments and monitors performance.
Warehouser	Person responsible for storage and movement of goods within a company's warehouse facilities. The warehouser maintains inventory records and makes sure older items are shipped out before newer ones (rotating stock).
Wholesale salesperson	Salesperson representing a wholesaler to retailers and other firms.

In the last century, jobs in marketing grew at a much more rapid rate than those in production. For example, from 1870 to 1950, the number of people employed in retailing and wholesaling activities increased more than 1200 per cent. In the same period, the number of production workers increased by 300 per cent.[1] The growth of marketing jobs has continued strongly since 1950. Today,

[1] Harold Barger, *Distribution's Place in the American Economy Since 1869* (Princeton, N.J.: Princeton University Press, 1955), pp. 4–5.

**Table 2
Selected Employers of
Marketing Personnel**

Advertising agencies	Marketing research firms
Agents and brokers	Marketing specialists
Common carriers	Media
Computer service bureaus	Nonprofit institutions
Consulting firms	Product-testing laboratories
Credit bureaus	Public relations firms
Delivery firms	Raw material extractors
Entertainment firms	Real estate firms
Exporters	Retailers
Financial institutions	Self-employed
Franchisees	Service firms
Franchisors	Shopping centers
Government	Sports teams
Industrial firms	Transportation firms
International firms	Warehousers
Manufacturers	Wholesalers

Job Classification	Employment Outlook
Advertising worker	Average
Credit manager	Slower than average
Display worker	Average
Industrial designer	Slower than average
Insurance agent (broker)	Average
Manufacturers' representative (agent)	Average
Manufacturer's salesperson	Average
Marketing research worker	Faster than average
Public relations specialist	Faster than average
Purchasing agent	Average
Real estate agent (broker)	Faster than average
Retail buyer	Average
Retail salesperson	Average
Securities salesperson	Faster than average
Wholesale salesperson	Average

Table 3
Outlook for Selected Marketing Careers During the 1980s

Source: Occupational Outlook Handbook, 1982–1983 Edition (Washington, D.C.: U.S. Government Printing Office, Bureau of Labor Statistics, April 1982); and Daniel E. Hecker, "A Fresh Look at Job Openings," *Occupational Outlook Quarterly* (Spring 1983), p. 29.

there are over twenty million people working in retailing and wholesaling activities, representing one fifth of all nonagricultural workers in the U.S. This does not include self-employed persons, those involved in services and transportation, or unpaid family workers.[2]

The strong demand for marketing personnel is based upon several factors. More service firms, nonprofit institutions, political candidates, and others are applying marketing principles. The deregulation of several major industries (such as banking, communication, and transportation) has encouraged companies in these industries to increase their marketing efforts. While production can be mechanized and automated, many marketing activities require personal contact. The rise in foreign competition and the maturity of several market segments are causing U.S. firms to expand and upgrade their marketing programs. The changes in U.S. society (such as blurring gender roles, recreational activities, and the rise in single-person households) need to be monitored through marketing research and marketing information systems, and adapted to via careful marketing planning. As the marketing vice-president at U.S. Steel noted, "Now the customer is the most important product . . . because if he doesn't like what we've got, he can go elsewhere."[3]

These are several indications of the opportunities available to people pursuing careers in marketing:[4]

● According to the Arthur Young Executive Demand Index, which evaluates job opportunities for executives, the demand for sales and marketing executives reached a five-year high point in 1983.

[2] *Statistical Abstract of the United States: 1982–1983* (Washington, D.C.: U.S. Bureau of the Census, 1982).

[3] Kim Foltz, Richard Manning, Michael Reese, and Nadine Joseph, "To Market, to Market," *Newsweek* (January 9, 1984), p. 71.

[4] Mark N. Vamos, "Marketers Beating 'Paper Entrepreneurs' in Career Wars," *Marketing News* (March 16, 1984), Section 1, pp. 1, 20; Pamela G. Hollie, "Market Is Wide Open for Marketing Executives," *New York Times* (Careers '84/October 16, 1983), p. 19; Elizabeth M. Fowler, "A Need for Strategic Planners," *New York Times* (October 12, 1983), p. D25; and "Marketing: The New Priority," *Business Week* (November 21, 1983), p. 96.

- In 1983, a major executive recruiting firm reported that one quarter of all positions it listed were in marketing, up from 8 per cent in 1979.
- 28 per cent of the 1983 MBA graduates from the Stanford Business School accepted marketing positions, compared with 15 per cent in 1978. 22 per cent of the 1983 MBA graduates from the Harvard Business School accepted marketing jobs, compared with 18 per cent in 1979.
- A Northwest Airlines spokesperson commented that "the marketing function has become more directly channeled to the corporate hierarchy. There are more people involved, and they communicate more to top management."
- During 1983, several computer companies hired outside senior marketing executives to lead them. For example, John P. Scully (former president of the beverage unit of PepsiCo) was named president of Apple Computer.
- General Motors and Ford have each added marketing executives as outside directors on their corporate boards. A Procter & Gamble executive sits on the General Motors board, while a Coca-Cola executive sits on the Ford board. Both auto makers hope to gain greater marketing insights from these directors.
- Stated the chairman of a large executive recruiting firm, "Nobody wants bean counters now. Everybody wants a president with marketing experience—someone who knows about product life cycles and developing product strategies."
- An important finding of a 1983 study by Coopers & Lybrand (a "Big 8" accounting firm) and Yankelovich, Skelly & White (a leading marketing research firm) is that one half of the executives surveyed believe that marketing will be the most important strategic area of the 1980s.

The 1983 starting salaries for marketing personnel typically ranged from $8,000 to $14,000 for those with an associate's degree, $12,000 to $23,000 for those with a bachelor's degree, and $17,000 to $40,000+ for those with a master of business administration degree. In addition to salary, many marketing positions provide a company car, bonus, and/or expense account that are not common to other professions. By 1990, entry-level marketing compensation is expected to rise significantly, much higher than the rate of inflation.

Table 4 outlines the compensation ranges for established personnel in selected marketing positions. Many of the positions have open-ended ranges, because

**Table 4
Annual Compensation for Personnel in Selected Marketing Positions[a]**

Advertising Positions	Compensation
Media Planner	$12,000–$ 30,000+
Assistant account executive	$14,000–$ 29,000+
Account executive	$25,000–$ 40,000+
Art director	$30,000–$ 65,000+
Vice-president/account supervisor	$45,000–$ 70,000+

Marketing Research Positions	Compensation
Full-time interviewer	$10,000–$ 16,000+
Field work director	$10,000–$ 35,000+
Junior analyst	$13,000–$ 18,000+
Analyst	$15,000–$ 27,000+
Senior analyst	$22,000–$ 37,000+
Assistant director	$22,000–$ 65,000+
Director	$28,000–$100,000+

Table 4
(Continued)

Product Management Positions	Compensation
Assistant product manager	$25,000–$ 45,000+
Product manager	$45,000–$ 65,000+
Group product manager	$50,000–$ 80,000+

Retailing Positions	Compensation
Executive trainee	$12,000–$ 18,000+
Downtown store manager	$17,000–$ 50,000+
Buyer	$23,000–$ 50,000+
Divisional merchandise manager	$23,000–$ 80,000+
Supermarket store manager	$25,000–$ 40,000+
General merchandise manager	$30,000–$100,000+

Sales Positions	Compensation
Real estate agent (broker)	$12,000–$100,000+
Insurance agent (broker)	$15,000–$100,000+
Manufacturers' representative (agent)	$16,000–$ 60,000+
Field sales trainee	$17,000–$ 25,000+
Field salesperson	$20,000–$ 32,000+
Senior field salesperson	$27,000–$ 45,000+
Securities salesperson	$29,000–$100,000+
Sales manager	$31,000–$ 55,000+

Miscellaneous Marketing Positions	Compensation
Display worker	$15,000–$ 30,000+
Industrial designer	$15,000–$ 30,000+
Public relations specialist	$22,000–$ 36,000+
Sales promotion director	$35,000–$ 50,000+
Distribution executive	$40,000–$ 60,000+
International general sales executive	$40,000–$ 75,000+

Top Marketing Positions	Compensation
Senior public relations executive	$40,000–$ 60,000+
Senior international executive	$50,000–$100,000+
Senior sales executive	$50,000–$100,000+
Vice-president/management supervisor–advertising agency	$60,000–$ 80,000+
Senior vice-president/management supervisor–advertising agency	$65,000–$115,000+
Marketing director	$70,000–$110,000+
Vice-president of marketing	$70,000–$700,000+

ᵃ Includes bonus.

Sources: Occupational Outlook Handbook, 1982–83 Edition (Washington, D.C.: U.S. Government Printing Office, Bureau of Labor Statistics, April 1982); "Salaries, Bonuses Rising at Ad Agencies," *Wall Street Journal* (August 18, 1983), p. 25; "Compensation," *Sales & Marketing Management* (February 20, 1984), pp. 62, 65; "Up and Down the Ladder," *Advertising Age* (January 2, 1984), p. M-17; "Marketing Briefs," *Marketing News* (March 16, 1984), Section 1, p. 20; Elizabeth M. Fowler, "Grocery Managers Wanted," *New York Times* (October 5, 1983), p. D23; Al Urbanski, "S&MM's Annual Survey of Executive Compensation," *Sales & Marketing Management* (August 15, 1983), pp. 41–46ff; and Dik Warren Twedt, *1983 Survey of Marketing Research* (Chicago: American Marketing Association, 1983), pp. 61, 63, 65.

commissions or bonuses depend on performance. The figures in Table 4 do not include expense accounts.

Figure 1 shows potential career paths for four selected areas of marketing. These career paths are general ones and are intended to give you a perspective

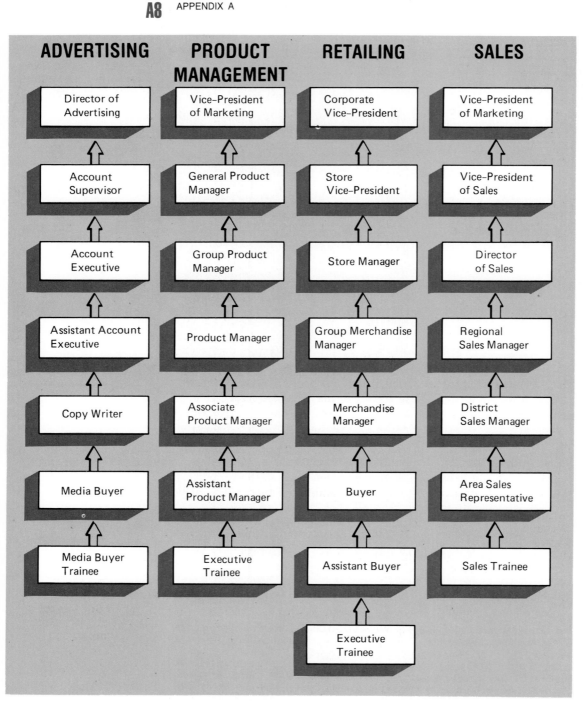

Figure 1
Selected Marketing
Career Paths

about "moving up the ladder." Individual firms have their own variations of the career paths. Also note that specialized career opportunities exist in each of the areas shown (such as sales training, support sales, final consumer versus organizational consumer sales, etc. in the sales area); and these are not revealed in Figure 1.

In the United States marketing executives are frequently chosen as the chief

American Brands	Deere	Monsanto
American Home Products	Walt Disney	National Can
American Motors	Dun & Bradstreet	NCR
American Stores	Federated Department Stores	North American Phillips
Apple Computer	Firestone	Owens Corning Fiberglas
Associated Dry Goods	General Foods	PepsiCo
Automatic Data Processing	General Mills	Philip Morris
Avco	Goodyear	Quaker Oats
Avnet	Hammermill Paper	Ralston Purina
Avon Products	Honeywell	R. J. Reynolds Industries
Black & Decker	George A. Hormel	Richardson-Vicks
Brown Forman Distillers	IBM	Sears Roebuck
Brunswick	K mart	J. P. Stevens
Burlington Industries	Kellogg	Textron
Campbell Soup	Kroger	Uniroyal
Caterpillar Tractor	Eli Lilly	U.S. Gypsum
CBS	LTV	U.S. Life
Cheesebrough-Ponds	Martin Marietta	Warner Lambert
Colgate-Palmolive	McDonald's	Xerox
Continental Group	MCI Communications	Zayre
Dayton Hudson	Metromedia	

Table 5
Selected Companies Whose Chief Executive Officers Had Marketing Backgrounds, 1983

Source: "Who Gets the Most Pay: Chief Executive Earnings," *Forbes* (June 6, 1983), pp. 126–127 ff.

executive officers of major industrial and nonindustrial corporations. Table 5 shows some of the U.S. companies that had chief executives with marketing backgrounds during 1983. The executives listed in this table each earn at least several hundred thousand dollars per year plus bonuses. According to a recent study of corporate chief executive officers, about one seventh have had a career emphasis in some functional area of marketing.[5] In addition, the senior marketing executive is included in the top management teams (five to nine managers) of 50 per cent of all major U.S. companies.[6]

Table 6 cites sources that may be contacted for additional marketing career information.

[5] James E. Piercy and J. Benjamin Forbes, "Industry Differences in Chief Executive Officers," *MSU Business Topics,* Vol. 29 (Winter 1981), p. 25.
[6] *Who Is Top Management?* (New York: Conference Board, 1982).

Career opportunity	Sources
Advertising	American Advertising Federation 1225 Connecticut Avenue, NW Washington, D.C. 20036
	American Association of Advertising Agencies 666 Third Avenue, 13th Floor New York, NY 10017
	Business Professional Advertising Association 205 East 42nd Street New York, NY 10017
Buying	Association of Buying Offices 100 West 31st Street New York, NY 10001

Table 6
Selected Sources of Additional Marketing Career Information

**Table 6
(Continued)**

Career opportunity	Sources
Commercial art	National Association of Schools of Art and Design 11250 Roger Bacon Dr., No. 5 Reston, VA 22090
Direct selling	Direct Selling Association 1730 M Street, NW, Suite 610 Washington, D.C. 20036
Industrial design	Industrial Designers Society of America 6802 Poplar Place McLean, VA 22101
Life insurance sales	American Council of Life Insurance 1850 K Street NW Washington, D.C. 20006
	National Association of Life Underwriters 1922 F Street, NW Washington, D.C. 20006
Manufacturers' representation	Sales & Marketing Executives International 330 West 42nd Street New York, NY 10036
Marketing	American Marketing Association 250 S. Wacker Drive, Suite 200 Chicago, IL 60606
	College Placement Annual 62 Highland Avenue Bethlehem, PA 18017
Marketing research	Chemical Marketing Research Association 139 Chestnut Avenue Staten Island, NY 10305
Physical distribution	National Council of Physical Distribution Management 2803 Butterfield Road, Suite 380 Oak Brook, IL 60521
Property and casualty insurance	Insurance Information Institute 110 William Street New York, NY 10038
	Independent Insurance Agents of America 100 Church Street, 19th Floor New York, NY 10007
	Professional Insurance Agents 400 N. Washington Street Alexandria, VA 22314
Public relations	Public Relations Society of America Inc. 845 Third Avenue New York, NY 10022
Real estate sales	National Association of Realtors 430 N. Michigan Avenue Chicago, IL 60611

Table 6
(Continued)

Career opportunity	Sources
Retailing	National Retail Merchants Association 100 West 31st Street New York, NY 10001
Securities sales	Securities Industry Association 120 Broadway New York, NY 10271
Supermarket industry	Food Marketing Institute 1750 K Street, NW, Suite 700 Washington, D.C. 20006
	National Association of Retail Grocers of the U.S. 1825 Samuel Morse Drive Reston, VA 22090
Traffic management	American Society of Traffic and Transportation P.O. Box 33095 Louisville, KY 40232
Wholesaling	National Association of Wholesaler-Distributors 1725 K Street, NW Washington, D.C. 20006

Marketing Mathematics

In order to properly design, implement, and review marketing programs, it is necessary to understand basic business mathematics from a marketing perspective. Accordingly, this appendix describes and illustrates the types of business mathematics with which marketers should be most familiar.

The appendix is divided into three areas: the profit-and-loss statement, marketing performance ratios, and pricing.

The Profit-and-Loss Statement

The *profit-and-loss (income) statement* presents a summary of the revenues and costs for an organization over a specific period of time. Such a statement is generally developed on a monthly, quarterly, and yearly basis. The profit-and-loss statement enables a marketer to examine overall and specific revenues and costs over similar time periods (for example, January 1, 1984 to December 31, 1984 versus January 1, 1983 to December 31, 1983), and analyze the organization's profitability. Monthly and quarterly statements enable the firm to monitor progress toward goals and revise performance estimates.

The profit-and-loss statement consists of these major components:

- *Gross sales*—The total revenues generated by the firm's products and services.
- *Net sales*—The revenues received by the firm after subtracting returns and discounts (such as trade, quantity, cash, and special promotional allowances).
- *Cost of goods sold*—The cost of merchandise sold by the manufacturer, wholesaler, or retailer.
- *Gross margin (profit)*—The difference between sales and the cost of goods sold; consists of operating expenses plus net profit.

A12

- *Operating expenses*—The cost of running a business, including marketing.
- *Net profit before taxes*—The profit earned after all costs have been deducted.

When examining a profit-and-loss statement, it is important to recognize one difference between manufacturers and retailers. For manufacturers, the cost of goods sold involves the cost of manufacturing products (raw materials, labor, and overhead). For retailers, the cost of goods sold involves the cost of merchandise purchased for resale (purchase price plus freight charges).

Table 1 shows an annual profit-and-loss statement for a manufacturer, the General Toy Company. From this table, these observations can be made:

- Total company sales for 1984 were $1,000,000. However, the firm gave refunds worth $20,000 for returned merchandise and allowances. In addition, discounts of $50,000 were provided. This left the company with actual (net) sales of $930,000.
- As a manufacturer, General Toy computed its cost of goods sold by adding the cost value of the beginning inventory on hand (items left in stock from the previous period) and the merchandise manufactured during the time period (costs included raw materials, labor, and overhead), and then subtracting the cost value of the inventory remaining at the end of the period. For General Toy this was $450,000 ($100,000 + $400,000 − $50,000).
- The gross margin was $480,000, calculated by subtracting the cost of goods sold from net sales. This sum was used for operating expenses, with the remainder accounting for net profit.
- Operating expenses involve all costs not considered in the cost of goods sold. Operating expenses for General Toy included sales force compensation, advertising, administration, rent, office supplies, and miscellaneous costs, a total of

Gross sales		$1,000,000
Less: Returns and allowances	$ 20,000	
Discounts	50,000	
Total sales deductions		70,000
Net sales		$ 930,000
Less cost of goods sold:		
Beginning inventory (at cost)	$100,000	
New merchandise (at cost)[a]	400,000	
Merchandise available for sale	$500,000	
Ending inventory (at cost)	50,000	
Total cost of goods sold		450,000
Gross margin		$ 480,000
Less operating expenses:		
Sales force compensation	$150,000	
Advertising	75,000	
Administration	75,000	
Rent	30,000	
Office supplies	20,000	
Miscellaneous	20,000	
Total operating expenses		370,000
Net profit before taxes		$ 110,000

Table 1
General Toy Company, Profit-and-Loss Statement for the Year January 1, 1984 Through December 31, 1984

[a] For a manufacturer, new merchandise costs refer to the raw materials, labor, and overhead costs incurred in the production of items for resale. For a retailer, new merchandise costs refer to the purchase costs of items (including freight) bought for resale.

$370,000. Of this amount, $225,000 was directly allocated for marketing costs (advertising, sales force).

- General Toy's net profit before taxes was $110,000, computed by deducting operating expenses from gross margin. This amount would be used to cover federal and state taxes as well as owner profits.

Performance Ratios

Performance ratios are used to measure the actual performance of a firm against company goals or industry standards. Comparative data can be obtained from trade associations, Dun & Bradstreet, Robert Morris Associates, and other sources. Among the most valuable performance ratios for marketers are the following:

$$(1) \text{ Sales efficiency ratio (percentage)} = \frac{\text{Net sales}}{\text{Gross sales}}$$

The *sales efficiency ratio (percentage)* compares net sales against gross sales. The highest level of efficiency is 1.00; in that case, there would be no returns, allowances, or discounts. General Toy had a sales efficiency ratio of 93 per cent ($930,000/$1,000,000) in 1984. This is a very good ratio; anything less would mean General Toy was too conservative in making sales.

$$(2) \text{ Cost-of-goods-sold ratio (percentage)} = \frac{\text{Cost of goods sold}}{\text{Net sales}}$$

The *cost-of-goods-sold ratio (percentage)* indicates the portion of net sales that is used to manufacture or purchase the goods sold. When the ratio is high, the firm has little revenue left to use for operating expenses and net profit. This could mean costs are too high or selling price is too low. In 1984, General Toy had a cost-of-goods-sold ratio of 48 per cent ($450,000/$930,000), a satisfactory figure.

$$(3) \text{ Gross margin ratio (percentage)} = \frac{\text{Gross margin}}{\text{Net sales}}$$

The *gross margin ratio (percentage)* shows the proportion of net sales that are allocated to operating expenses and net profit. When the ratio is high, the company has substantial revenue left for these items. During 1984, General Toy had a gross margin ratio of 52 per cent ($480,000/$930,000), a satisfactory figure.

$$(4) \text{ Operating expense ratio (percentage)} = \frac{\text{Operating expenses}}{\text{Net sales}}$$

The *operating expense ratio (percentage)* expresses these expenses in terms of net sales. When the ratio is high, the firm is spending a large amount on marketing and other operating costs. General Toy had an operating expense ratio of 40 per cent in 1984, which meant that forty cents of every sales dollar went for operations, a moderate amount.

$$(5) \text{ Net profit ratio (percentage)} = \frac{\text{Net profit before taxes}}{\text{Net sales}}$$

The *net profit ratio (percentage)* indicates the portion of each sales dollar that goes for profits (after all costs have been deducted). The net profit ratio varies drastically by industry. For example, in the supermarket industry, net profits are about 1 per cent of net sales; in the industrial chemical industry, net profits are about 6.5 per cent of net sales. The 1984 net profit for General Toy was 12 per cent of net sales ($110,000/$930,000), well above the industry average of 2.2 per cent.

$$(6) \text{ Stock turnover ratio} = \frac{\text{Net sales (in units)}}{\text{Average inventory (in units)}}$$

or

$$\frac{\text{Net sales (in sales dollars)}}{\text{Average inventory (in sales dollars)}}$$

or

$$\frac{\text{Cost of goods sold}}{\text{Average inventory (at cost)}}$$

The *stock turnover ratio* shows the number of times during a specified period, usually one year, that the average inventory on hand is sold. It can be calculated on the basis of units or dollars (in selling price or at cost). In the case of General Toy, the 1984 stock turnover ratio can be calculated on a cost basis. The cost of goods sold during 1984 was $450,000. Average inventory at cost = (Beginning inventory at cost + Ending inventory at cost)/2 = ($100,000 + $50,000)/2 = $75,000. The stock turnover ratio was ($450,000/75,000) = 6. This compared favorably with an industry average of 2.6 times. This meant General Toy sold its merchandise more than twice as quickly as competitors.

$$(7) \text{ Return on investment} = \frac{\text{Net sales}}{\text{Investment}} \times \frac{\text{Net profit}}{\text{Net sales}} = \frac{\text{Net profit}}{\text{Investment}}$$

The *return on investment (ROI)* compares profitability with the investment necessary to manufacture or distribute merchandise. For a manufacturer, this investment includes land, plant, equipment, and inventory costs. For a retailer, it involves inventory, the costs of land, the store and its fixtures, and equipment. To determine the return on investment for General Toy, total investment costs would be determined from its *balance sheet,* which lists the assets and liabilities of a firm at a particular time. The management at General Toy calculated that an overall investment of $550,000 was necessary to yield 1984 net sales of $930,000. Therefore, the firm's return on investment before taxes was 20 per cent ($110,000/$550,000). This was a little above the industry norm.

Pricing _____

The material in this section expands upon the discussion in Chapters 18 through 20. Four specific aspects of pricing are examined: price elasticity, fixed versus variable costs, markup, and markdown.

Price Elasticity

As defined in Chapter 18, *price elasticity* refers to the sensitivity of buyers to price changes in terms of the quantities they will purchase. Elasticity is based on availability of substitutes and urgency of need. It is expressed as the percentage change in quantity sold divided by the percentage change in price:

$$\text{Price elasticity} = \cfrac{\cfrac{\text{Quantity } 1 - \text{Quantity } 2}{\text{Quantity } 1 + \text{Quantity } 2}}{\cfrac{\text{Price } 1 - \text{Price } 2}{\text{Price } 1 + \text{Price } 2}}$$

For purposes of simplicity, price elasticity is often expressed as a positive number (as it will be here).

Table 2 shows a demand schedule for women's blouses at several different prices. When selling price is reduced by a small percentage from $40 to $35, the percentage change in quantity demanded rises significantly from 120 to 150 units. Maxine's blouses gain a strong competitive advantage. Demand is highly elastic (very price sensitive):

$$\text{Price elasticity} = \cfrac{\cfrac{120 - 150}{120 + 150}}{\cfrac{\$40 - \$35}{\$40 + \ 35}} = 1.7 \ \text{(expressed as a positive number)}$$

As price is reduced, total revenues go up.

At a price of $25, the market becomes more saturated: the percentage change in price from $25 to $20 is directly offset by the percentage change in quantity demanded from 240 to 300 units:

$$\text{Price elasticity} = \cfrac{\cfrac{240 - 300}{240 + 300}}{\cfrac{\$25 - \$20}{\$25 + \ 20}} = 1.0 \ \text{(expressed as a positive number)}$$

Total revenues remain the same at a price of $25 or $20. This is known as unitary demand, whereby total revenues stay constant as price changes.

At a price of $20, the market becomes extremely saturated, and further price reductions have little impact on demand. A large percentage change in price from $20 to $15 results in a small percentage change in quantity demanded, from 300

Selling Price	Quantity Demanded	Elasticity[a]	Total Revenue[b]
$40	120		$4,800
		] 1.7	
35	150		5,250
		] 1.5	
30	190		5,700
		] 1.3	
25	240		6,000 ← Maximum
		] 1.0	total
20	300		6,000 ← revenue
		] 0.5	
15	350		5,250
		] 0.3	
10	390		3,900

[a] Expressed as positive numbers.
[b] Total revenue = Selling price × Quantity demanded.

to 350 units. Maxine is able to sell relatively few additional blouses. Demand is inelastic (insensitive to price changes):

$$\text{Price elasticity} = \frac{\dfrac{300 - 350}{300 + 350}}{\dfrac{\$20 - \$15}{\$20 + \ 15}} = 0.5 \ \text{(expressed as a positive number)}$$

Notice that total revenue falls as demand changes from elastic to inelastic or inelastic to elastic.

Total revenue is maximized at the price levels where price and demand changes directly offset each other (in this example, $25 and $20). How does a firm choose between those prices? It depends on marketing philosophy. At a price of $25, profit will probably be higher because the firm needs to produce and sell fewer products, thus reducing costs. At a price of $20, more units are sold; this may increase the customer base for other products the firm offers and thereby raise overall company sales and profits.

Figure 1 graphically shows the demand elasticity for Maxine's Blouses. This figure illustrates that a demand curve is not necessarily straight and that a single demand schedule has elastic, unitary, and inelastic ranges.

It is important to remember that price elasticity refers to percentage changes, not to absolute changes. For example, a demand change from 120 to 150 units involves a greater percentage change than a demand change from 300 to 350 units. Furthermore, each product or brand would face a different demand schedule. Milk and magazines would have dissimilar demand schedules, despite similar price ranges, because of the different availability of substitutes and urgency of need.

Fixed Versus Variable Costs

When making pricing decisions, it is essential to distinguish between fixed and variable costs. *Fixed costs* are ongoing costs that are unrelated to production or sales volume; they are generally constant over a given range of output for a

Figure 1
Maxine's Blouses,
Demand Elasticity

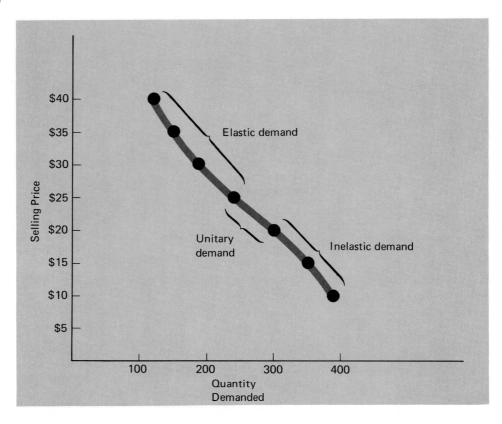

specific time period. In the short run, fixed costs cannot usually be changed. Examples of fixed costs are rent, full-time employee salaries, plant, equipment, real estate taxes, and insurance.

Variable costs are directly related to production or sales volume. As volume increases, total variable costs increase; as volume declines, total variable costs decline. Per-unit variable costs frequently remain constant over a given range of volume (e.g., total sales commission goes up as sales rise, while sales commission as a per cent of sales remains constant). Examples of variable costs are raw materials, sales commissions, parts, salaries of hourly employees, and product advertising.

Figure 2 graphically shows how fixed, variable, and total costs vary with production or sales volume for Eleanor's Cosmetics, a leased-department operator selling popular-priced cosmetics in a department store. In this figure, total fixed costs are $10,000. Variable costs are $5.00 per unit. Figure 2A depicts total costs: as volume increases, total fixed costs stay constant at $10,000, while total variable costs and total costs rise by $5.00 per unit. At 1,000 units, total fixed costs are $10,000, total variable costs are $5,000, and total costs are $15,000. At 5,000 units, total fixed costs are $10,000, total variable costs are $25,000, and total costs are $35,000.

Figure 2B depicts average costs: as volume increases, average fixed costs and average total costs decline (since fixed costs are spread over more units), while average variable costs remain the same. At 1,000 units, average fixed costs are

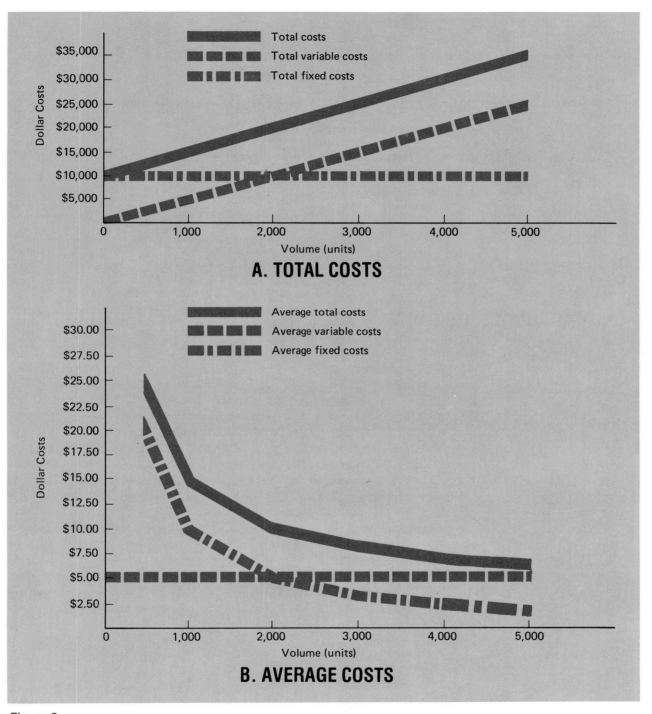

Figure 2
Fixed and Variable Costs for Eleanor's Cosmetics

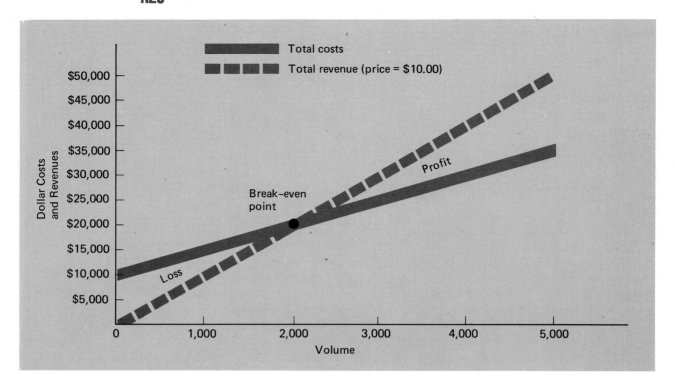

Figure 3
Break-Even Analysis for
Eleanor's Cosmetics

$10.00, average variable costs are $5.00, and average total costs are $15.00. At 5,000 units, average fixed costs are $2.00 ($10,000/5,000 units), average variable costs are $5.00, and average total costs are $7.00.

By knowing the relationship between fixed and variable costs, marketers are better able to set prices. They recognize that average total costs usually decline as sale volume expands, which allows them to set skimming prices when volume is low and penetration prices when volume is high. They also realize that the firm can reduce its losses with a selling price that is lower than average total costs; as long as the price is above average variable costs, a transaction will contribute toward the payment of fixed costs. Finally, the break-even point can be shown on a total-cost curve graph. See Figure 3.

With a selling price of $10.00 per unit, Eleanor's Cosmetics would lose money unless 2,000 units could be sold. At that amount, the firm breaks even. For all sales volumes above 2,000 units, the company would earn a profit of $5.00 per unit, an amount equal to the difference between selling price and average variable costs (fixed costs are assumed to be "paid off" when sales reach 2,000 units). A sales volume of 5,000 units would return a profit of $15,000 (total revenues of $50,000—total costs of $35,000).

Markup

Markup is the difference between merchandise cost and selling price for each channel member. Markup is usually expressed as a percentage:

$$\text{Markup percentage (on selling price)} = \frac{\text{Selling price} - \text{Merchandise cost}}{\text{Selling price}}$$

$$\text{Markup percentage (at cost)} = \frac{\text{Selling price} - \text{Merchandise cost}}{\text{Merchandise cost}}$$

Table 3 shows markup percentages on selling price and at cost for an item selling for $10.00 under varying costs. Since companies often consider markup percentage as the equivalent of the gross margin percentage discussed earlier in this appendix, they use the markup percentage on selling price in their planning. As with gross margin, markup is used to cover operating expenses and net profit.

It is necessary for channel members to understand the discounts provided to them by vendors (suppliers). In addition to the markups they receive for providing regular marketing functions, they may also obtain quantity, cash, seasonal, and/or promotional discounts. Transportation costs are added to the final purchase price; they are not discounted.

Table 4 shows the calculation of a purchase price by a television retailer, based on a functional markup of 40 per cent and individual discounts of 10 (quantity), 2 (cash), 5 (seasonal), and 5 (promotional) per cent. The discounts do not total 62 per cent off final selling price. They total 52.2 per cent, because the discounts are computed upon successive balances. For example, the 10 per cent quantity discount is computed on $165, which is the purchase price after deducting the markup allowed by the vendor.

Markdown

One of the major price adjustments made by most firms is the **markdown**, which is a reduction in the original selling price of an item in order to sell it. Markdowns are caused by slow sales, model changes, and other factors.

Markdown percentages can be computed in either of two ways:

$$\text{Markdown percentage (off-retail)} = \frac{\text{Original selling price} - \text{Reduced selling price}}{\text{Original selling price}}$$

$$\text{Markdown percentage (off-sale)} = \frac{\text{Original selling price} - \text{Reduced selling price}}{\text{Reduced selling price}}$$

Table 3
Markups on Selling Price and at Cost

Selling Price	Merchandise Cost	Markup (on Selling Price)	Markup (at Cost)
$10.00	$9.00	10%	11%
10.00	8.00	20	25
10.00	7.00	30	43
10.00	6.00	40	67
10.00	5.00	50	100
10.00	4.00	60	150
10.00	3.00	70	233
10.00	2.00	80	400
10.00	1.00	90	900

Formulas to convert markup percentages:

$$\text{Markup percentage (on selling price)} = \frac{\text{Markup percentage (at cost)}}{100\% + \text{Markup percentage (at cost)}}$$

$$\text{Markup percentage (at cost)} = \frac{\text{Markup percentage (on selling price)}}{100\% - \text{Markup percentage (on selling price)}}$$

Table 4
A Television Retailer's Final Purchase Price, After Deducting All Discounts—Model 123

Discounts Offered by Manufacturer (in %)

Markup	40
Quantity	10
Cash	2
Seasonal	5
Promotional	5

Suggested Final Selling Price $275.00

Shipping Charges $ 15.30

Computation of Purchase Price Paid by Retailer

List price	$275.00
Less functional markup ($275.00 × .40)	110.00
Balance	$165.00
Less quantity discount ($165.00 × .10)	16.50
Balance	$148.50
Less cash discount ($148.50 × .02)	2.97
Balance	$145.53
Less seasonal discount ($145.53 × .05)	7.28
Balance	$138.25
Less promotional discount ($138.25 × .05)	6.91
Balance after all discounts	$131.34
Plus shipping charges	15.30
Price to channel member	$146.64

Total of Discounts $143.66

Total Discount % ($143.66/$275)   52.2

For example, the off-retail markdown percentage for an item that originally sold for $20 and has been marked down to $15 is ($20 − $15)/$20 = 25. The off-sale markdown percentage is ($20 − $15)/$15 = 33. While the off-retail percentage is more accurate for price planning, the off-sale percentage indicates a larger price reduction to consumers and may generate increased volume.

Questions

1. What information can a marketer obtain from a profit-and-loss statement?
2. Develop a profit-and-loss statement for The Deluxe Phone Center, a retail store, based on the following:

Beginning inventory (at cost)	$ 300,000
New merchandise (at cost)	600,000
Ending inventory (at cost)	150,000
Gross sales	1,500,000
Returns and allowances	150,000
Marketing expenses	300,000
Administration, rent, supplies	225,000

3. Using the profit-and-loss statement from Question 2, calculate:
   a. Return on investment.
   b. Stock turnover ratio.
   c. Net profit ratio (percentage).
   d. Operating expense ratio (percentage).
   e. Gross margin ratio (percentage).
   f. Cost-of-goods-sold ratio (percentage).
   g. Sales efficiency ratio (percentage).
4. How would The Deluxe Phone Center determine whether or not its performance ratios are satisfactory?
5. A newspaper publisher has conducted research concerning its readers' sensitivity to price. These are the results:

Price	Estimate of Readership
$ .10	2,000,000
.25	1,000,000
.35	400,000

   a. Calculate price elasticity as price goes from $ .10 to $ .25 and from $ .25 to $ .35.
   b. At what price is total revenue maximized?
   c. What price should be set? Why?
6. A tire manufacturer has fixed costs of $1,000,000 and variable costs of $35.00 per tire.
   a. Calculate total costs for volumes of 10,000, 25,000, and 50,000 tires.
   b. Calculate average total, fixed, and variable costs for the same volumes.
   c. At a volume of 25,000 tires, would the firm make a profit or loss with a selling price of $85.00? What is the total profit or loss?
7. A supermarket retailer sells medium-size shaving cream containers for $.99; they are purchased for $.59. Large-size containers sell for $1.99; they are purchased for $.99.
   a. For each size container, determine the markup percentage on selling price and at cost.
   b. Why would the company use a different markup percentage for medium containers from that for large containers?
   c. If a shaving cream manufacturer offers the supermarket a 30 per cent markup on selling price for medium-size containers as well as a cash discount of 8 per cent and a quantity discount of 5 per cent, what is the purchase price to the supermarket? What is the overall discount? There are no transportation costs.
8. A glove manufacturer originally sold suede gloves for $30 per pair. An end-of-season sale has reduced the price of these gloves to $10.
   a. Compute the off-retail and off-sale markdown percentages.
   b. Why is there a difference in these calculations?

Glossary

Absolute Product Failure Occurs when a company is unable to regain its production and marketing costs. The firm incurs a financial loss.

Accelerator Principle Final consumer demand affects several layers of organizational consumers.

Accessory Equipment Industrial capital items, which require a moderate amount of decision making, are less expensive than installations, last a number of years, and do not change in form or become part of the final product.

Adaptation Responses to the surrounding environment, including both opportunities and threats.

Additional Markup Used to raise regular retail prices because demand is unexpectedly high or costs are rising.

Administered Channel One in which the dominant firm in the distribution process plans the marketing program and itemizes responsibilities.

Adoption Process The procedure an individual goes through when learning about and purchasing a new product. The adoption process consists of six stages: awareness, interest, evaluation, trial, adoption, and confirmation.

Advertising Any paid form of nonpersonal presentation and promotion of ideas, goods, and services by an identified sponsor.

Advertising Agency An outside company that usually works with a firm in the development of its advertising plan including themes, media selection, copywriting, and other tasks.

Advertising Costs Can be measured in terms of total media costs or per reader or viewer. Costs are expressed on a per-thousand audience basis, except newspapers which use a cost-per-million base.

Advertising Themes The overall appeals for a campaign. Themes can be product or service, consumer, or nonconsumer and nonproduct/service-related.

Agent A wholesaler that does not take title to goods and is compensated through payment of a commission or a fee. It may be a manufacturers' agent, selling agent, or commission (factor) merchant.

Airway The fastest, most expensive form of transportation.

All-You-Can-Afford Technique A means of developing a promotional budget in which the firm first allocates funds for every element of marketing except promotion. Whatever funds are left over are placed in a promotion budget.

Approaching Customers The stage in the selling process that consists of the preapproach and greeting.

Atmosphere The sum total of the physical characteristics of a retail store that are used to develop an image and draw customers.

Attitude (Opinion) A person's positive, neutral, or negative feelings about products, services, companies, issues, and institutions.

Attribute-Based Shopping Goods Products/services for which consumers seek information about and then evaluate product features, warranty, performance, options, and other factors.

Audience   The object of the message in a channel of communication.

Backward Invention   An international product strategy in which a firm appeals to developing countries by making products that are less complex than the ones it sells in its domestic market.

Bait-and-Switch Advertising   An illegal procedure whereby a retailer lures customers into a store by advertising items at exceptionally low prices and then telling customers that the items are out of stock or are of inferior quality. The retailer has no intention of selling the advertised items.

Balanced Product Portfolio   A strategy by which a firm maintains a combination of new, growing, and mature products.

Balanced Tenancy   Relates the type and number of stores within any planned center to the overall needs of the surrounding population. To ensure balance a shopping center may limit the merchandise lines any store carries.

Base-Point Pricing   A form of geographic pricing in which firms in an industry establish basing points from which costs of shipping are computed. The delivered price to a buyer reflects the cost of transporting goods from the basing point nearest to the buyer, regardless of the actual site of supply.

Battle of the Brands   Manufacturer, dealer, and generic brands each attempting to increase their market share at the expense of the other. In particular, this is a battle between manufacturers and retailers.

Benefit Segmentation   Uses the benefits people seek in consuming a given product as the means of segmenting markets.

Blanket Branding   *See* Family Branding.

Blurring Gender Roles   Occurs when husbands (wives) assume a greater share of the traditional role of their wives (husbands).

Bonded Warehouse   A public storage facility used to store imported or taxable merchandise, wherein goods are released only after appropriate taxes are paid. Allows firms to postpone tax payments until goods are ready to be shipped to customers.

Boston Consulting Group Matrix   A framework which enables a company to classify each of its strategic business units (SBUs) in terms of its market share relative to major competitors and the annual growth rate of the industry. The matrix identifies four types of products: star, cash cow, problem child (question mark), and dog, and suggests appropriate strategies for each.

Brand   A name, design, or symbol (or combination of these) that identifies the products and services of a seller or group of sellers.

Brand Decision Process   Consists of nonrecognition, recognition, preference, and insistence stages that consumers pass through.

Brand Extension   A strategy of applying an established brand name to new products.

Brand Loyalty   The consistent repurchase of and preference for a brand. The consumer attempts to minimize risk, time, and thought.

Brand Mark   A symbol, design, or distinctive coloring or lettering.

Brand Name   A word, letter, or group of words or letters that can be spoken.

Break-Even Analysis   *See* Traditional Break-Even Analysis *and* Modified Break-Even Analysis.

Broad Price Policy   Coordinates pricing decisions with the firm's target market, image, and marketing mix. It generates a coordinated series of actions, a consistent image, and a strategy that incorporates short- and long-term goals.

Broker   A temporary wholesaler, paid by a commission or fee. The most common is a food broker, who introduces buyers and sellers and helps complete transactions.

Bundled Pricing   An offering of a basic product, options, and service for one total price.

Business Advisory Services   Industrial services that include management consulting, advertising agency services, accounting services, and legal services.

Business Analysis   The stage in the new-product planning process which projects demand, costs, competition, investment requirements, and profits for new products.

Buyer-Seller Dyad   Two-way flow of communication between buyer and seller.

Buying Specialists   Employees of organizational consumers who have technical backgrounds and are trained in supplier analysis and negotiation.

Buying Structure of an Organization   Refers to the level of formality and specialization used in the purchase process. It depends on an organization's size, resources, diversity, and level of specialization.

Canned Sales Presentation   A memorized, repetitive sales presentation given to all customers interested in a particular item. This approach does not adapt to customer needs or traits but presumes that a general presentation will appeal to all customers.

Cash-and-Carry Wholesaling   A limited-service merchant wholesaler which enables a small businessperson to drive to a wholesaler, order products, and take them back to his/her store or business. No credit, delivery, merchandise, and promotional assistance are provided.

Cash Cow A category in the Boston Consulting Group matrix which describes a leading strategic business unit (high market share) in a relatively mature or declining industry (low growth). Cash cows generate more cash than is required to retain their market share.

Cease-and-Desist Order A form of consumer protection which legally requires a firm to discontinue deceptive practices or modify its promotion messages.

Chain-Markup Pricing A form of demand-based pricing in which final selling price is first determined, then markups for each channel member are examined, and the maximum acceptable costs to each member are computed. Chain-markup pricing extends demand-minus calculations from the retailer all the way back to the manufacturer.

Chain-Ratio Method A sales forecasting technique in which the firm starts with general information and then computes a series of more specific market information. These combined data yield a sales forecast.

Chain Retailer Involves common ownership of multiple retailing units.

Channel Functions The functions completed by some member of the channel: marketing research, buying, promotion, customer services, product planning, pricing, and distribution.

Channel Length Refers to the number of independent members along the channel.

Channel Member (Middleman) An organization or person in the distribution process.

Channel of Communication (Communication Process) The mechanism through which a source sends a message to its audience. It consists of source, encoding, message, medium, decoding, audience, feedback, and noise.

Channel of Distribution All the organizations or people involved with the movement and exchange of products or services.

Channel Width Refers to the number of independent members at any stage of the distribution process.

Class-Action Suit A suit filed on behalf of many affected consumers.

Class Consciousness The extent to which social status is desired and pursued by a person.

Client The constituency for which a nonprofit organization offers membership, elected officials, locations, ideas, products, and services.

Closing the Sale The stage in the sales process that involves getting the customer to agree to a purchase. The salesperson must be sure that no major questions remain before attempting to close a sale.

Clutter Involves the number of advertisements that are contained in a single program, issue, etc. of a medium.

CMSA *See* Consolidated Metropolitan Statistical Area.

Cognitive Dissonance Doubt that the correct purchase decision has been made. To overcome cognitive dissonance and dissatisfaction, the firm must realize that the purchase process does not end with the purchase.

Combination Compensation Plan A sales compensation plan that combines salary and commission plans to provide control, flexibility, and employee incentives.

Commercialization The final stage in the new-product planning process. The firm introduces the product to its full target market. This corresponds to the introductory stage of the product life cycle.

Commission (Factor) Merchant An agent who receives goods on consignment, accumulates them from local markets, and arranges for their sale in a central market location.

Common Carrier A company that must transport the goods of any firm interested in its services; it cannot refuse any shipments unless its rules are broken. Common carriers provide service on a fixed and publicized schedule between designated points. A regular fee schedule is published.

Common Market *See* European Community (EC).

Communication Process *See* Channel of Communication.

Company-Controlled Price Environment Characterized by a moderate level of competition, well-differentiated products and services, and strong control over price by individual firms.

Company-Specific Buying Factors Company-based variables which lead to either autonomous (independent) or joint decision making by organizational consumers. These variables include the degree of technology or production orientation, company size, and degree of centralization.

Comparative Advantage Concept in international marketing which states that countries have different rates of productivity for different products. Countries can benefit by exchanging goods in which they have relative production advantages for those in which they have relative disadvantages.

Comparative Message A promotion form that contrasts the firm's offerings with those of competitors.

Competition-Based Price Strategy Prices set in accordance with competitors. Prices may be below the market, at the market, or above the market.

Competitive Bidding Sellers asked to independently submit price bids for specific products, projects, and/or services.

Competitive Parity Technique A method in which the company's promotional budget is raised or lowered according to the actions of competitors.

Component Material Semimanufactured industrial good that undergoes further changes in form. A component material is considered as an expense rather than a capital item.

Concept Testing Stage in the new-product planning process in which potential consumers are asked to respond to a picture, written statement, or oral description of a new product, thus enabling the firm to determine attitudes prior to expensive, time-consuming prototype development.

Conclusive Research Structured data collection and analysis for the solution of a specific problem or objective.

Conflict Resolution Procedure in organizational buying for resolving disagreements in joint-decision-making situations. The alternatives are problem solving, persuasion, bargaining, and politicking.

Consistency of Product Mix The relationship among product lines in terms of their sharing a common end use, distribution outlets, consumer group(s), and price range.

Consolidated Metropolitan Statistical Area (CMSA) A Bureau of Census designation which contains several overlapping and interlocking Primary Metropolitan Statistical Areas (PMSAs).

Consumer Bill of Rights Stated by President Kennedy in 1962: information, safety, choice in product selection, and a voice in decision making.

Consumer Cooperative A form of retailer owned and operated by consumer members.

Consumer Demand Refers to the characteristics and needs of final consumers, industrial consumers, channel members, government institutions, international markets, and nonprofit institutions.

Consumer Demographics Easily identifiable and measurable statistics that are used to describe the population.

Consumer Education A learning process whereby the consumer acquires the skills and knowledge to use his or her financial resources wisely in the marketplace.

Consumer Price Index A federal government measure of the cost of living. Measures the monthly and yearly changes in the prices of selected consumer items in different product categories, expressing the changes in terms of a base year.

Consumer Product A good or service destined for the ultimate consumer's personal, family, or household use.

Consumer Product Safety Commission (CPSC) The major federal agency responsible for product safety. It has jurisdiction over more than 11,000 products.

Consumer Survey A method of sales forecasting that obtains information about purchase intentions, future expectations, rate of consumption, brand switching, time between purchases, and reasons for purchases.

Consumerism A social force within the environment designed to aid and protect the consumer by exerting legal, moral, and economic pressure on business.

Consumer's Decision Process Involves the steps a consumer goes through in purchasing a product or service: stimulus, problem awareness, information search, evaluation of alternatives, purchase, and postpurchase behavior. Demographics, social factors, and psychological factors affect the consumer's decision process.

Containerization A coordinated transportation practice that allows goods to be placed in sturdy containers, which serve as mobile warehouses. Containers can be placed on trains, trucks, ships, and planes.

Continuous Monitoring The stage in a marketing information system during which a changing environment is regularly viewed.

Contract Carrier A company that provides one or a few shippers with transportation services based on individual agreements. Contract carriers are not required to maintain rules or schedules and rates may be negotiated.

Contractual Channel Arrangement Specifies in writing all the terms regarding distribution functions, prices, and other factors for each channel member in an indirect channel.

Control The monitoring and reviewing of overall and specific performance.

Control Units Sales categories for which data are gathered, such as boys', men's, girls', and women's clothing.

Controllable Factors Decision elements that are directed by the organization and its marketers. Some of these are under the direction of top management; others by marketers.

Convenience Good An item purchased with a minimum of effort, where the buyer has knowledge of product characteristics prior to shopping. Types are staples, impulse, and emergency goods.

Convenience Store A retail store featuring food items that is open long hours and carries a limited number of items. Consumers typically use a convenience store for fill-in merchandise, often at off hours.

Cooperative Advertising Allows expenses to be shared by channel members. It can be vertical or horizontal.

Corporate Symbols Firm's name, logo, and trade characters that play a significant role in the creation of an overall company image.

Corrective Advertising A form of consumer protection which legally requires a firm to run new advertisements to correct the false impressions made by previous ones.

Cost-Based Price Strategy Sets prices by computing merchandise, service, and overhead costs and then adding the desired profit to these figures. Demand is not analyzed.

Cost-Plus Pricing   Form of cost-based pricing in which prices are computed by adding a predetermined profit to costs. It is the simplest form of cost-based pricing:

$$\text{Price} = \frac{\text{Total costs} + \text{Projected profit}}{\text{Units produced}}.$$

CPSC   *See* Consumer Product Safety Commission.

Culture   A group of people sharing a distinctive heritage.

Currency Stability   An economic factor that could affect sales and profits if a foreign country revalues its currency in relation to the company's home currency.

Customary Pricing   Occurs when a channel member sets product or service prices and seeks to maintain them for an extended period of time.

Data Analysis   The coding, tabulation, and analysis of marketing research data.

Data Storage   The stage in a marketing information system involving the retention of all types of relevant company records (such as sales, costs, personnel performance) as well as the information collected through marketing research and continuous monitoring.

Dealer (Private) Brand   An item that contains the name of the wholesaler or retailer. Dealers secure exclusive rights for their brands and are responsible for their distribution.

Decline Stage of the Product Life Cycle   Period during which industry sales decline and many firms leave the market because customers are fewer and they have less income to spend.

Decoding   The process in a channel of communication whereby the message sent by the source is interpreted by the audience.

Demand-Based Price Strategy   Prices set after researching consumer desires and ascertaining the ranges of prices acceptable to the target market.

Demand-Minus (Demand-Backward) Pricing   Form of demand-based pricing whereby the firm ascertains the appropriate final selling price and works backward to compute costs. The formula used in demand-minus pricing is

Maximum merchandise cost
= Price [(100 − Markup per cent)/100].

Department Store   A large retailer, employing 25+ people and usually selling a general line of apparel for the family, household linens and dry goods, and furniture, home furnishings, appliances, radios, and televisions. It is organized into separate departments for purposes of buying, promotion, service, and control.

Depth of Product Mix   The number of product items within each product line.

Derived Demand   Bases organizational consumers' purchases on the demand of final consumers. Manufacturers must be aware that they are selling through wholesalers and retailers and not to them.

Desk Jobber   *See* Drop Shipper.

Developing Country   Has rising education level and technology, but a per capita income of about $1,500.

Differential Advantage   The set of unique features in a company's marketing program that causes consumers to patronize the company and not its competitors.

Diffusion Process   Describes the manner in which different members of the target market often accept and purchase a product. The process spans the time from product introduction until market saturation.

Diminishing Returns   Reduced productivity possible if a firm attempts to attract nonconsumers when its market is relatively saturated. In some cases, the costs of attracting additional consumers may outweigh the revenues.

Direct Channel of Distribution   Involves the movement of goods and services from manufacturer to consumer without the use of independent middlemen.

Direct Ownership   A form of international marketing company organization that involves the full undertaking and control of all international operations.

Direct-to-Home Retailer   A nonstore retail operation which sells directly to consumers in their homes.

Discount   A reduction from final selling price that is available to channel members and final consumers for performing certain functions, paying in cash, buying large quantities, purchasing in off seasons, or enhancing promotions.

Discount Mall   A shopping location in which a variety of low-price retailers are situated together.

Discretionary Income   Earnings remaining for luxuries after necessities are bought.

Disposable Income   Aftertax income to be used for spending and/or savings.

Distributed Promotion   Communication efforts spread throughout the year.

Distribution Planning   The systematic decision making regarding the physical movement and transfer of ownership of a product or service from producer to consumer. It includes transportation, storage, and customer transactions.

Distribution Standards   Clear and measurable goals regarding customer service levels in physical distribution.

Diversification   A product/market opportunity matrix strategy in which a firm markets new products aimed at new markets.

Dog   A category in the Boston Consulting Group matrix which describes a low market-share strategic business unit (SBU) in a mature or declining industry. A dog usually has cost disadvantages and few growth opportunities.

Donor The constituency from which a nonprofit organization receives resources.

Drop Shipper (Desk Jobber) A form of limited-service merchant wholesaler that purchases goods from manufacturers/suppliers and arranges for their shipment to retailers or industrial users.

Dual Channel of Distribution A strategy whereby the firm appeals to different market segments or diversifies its business by selling through two or more different channels.

Dumping Selling a product in a foreign country at a price lower than that prevailing in the exporter's home market, below the cost of production, or both.

EC *See* Economic Community.

Economic Order Quantity (EOQ) The order volume corresponding to the lowest sum of order processing and holding costs.

80–20 Principle States that in many organizations a large proportion of total sales (profit) comes from a small proportion of customers, products, or territories.

Elastic Demand Occurs if relatively small changes in price result in large changes in quantity demanded.

Elasticity of Demand Defines the sensitivity of buyers to price changes in terms of the quantities they will purchase. Price elasticity is computed by dividing the percentage change in quantity demanded by the percentage change in price charged.

Electronic Banking Provides centralized record keeping and enables customers to conduct transactions 24 hours a day, seven days a week (at many bank and nonbank locations) through the use of automatic teller machines and instant processing of retail purchases.

Electronic Mail Enables letters to be transmitted by computers and telephone lines.

Embargo A form of trade restriction that prohibits specified products from entering a country.

Emergency Goods Convenience goods purchased out of urgent need.

Encoding The procedure in a channel of communication whereby a thought or idea is translated into a message by the source.

End-Use Analysis A process by which a seller determines the proportion of its sales that are made to organizational consumers in different industries.

EOQ *See* Economic Order Quantity.

Escalator Clause A form of price adjustment that allows a firm to contractually raise the price of an item to reflect higher costs in the item's essential ingredients without changing printed list prices.

Ethical Behavior Based on honest and proper conduct.

European Community (EC) Also known as the Common Market. The EC calls for no tariffs among members and a uniform tariff with nonmember nations. In addition, the agreement encourages common standards for food additives, labeling requirements, and package sizes, and a free flow of labor and capital.

Evaluation of Alternatives Stage in the consumer's decision process in which criteria for a decision are set and alternatives ranked.

Exchange The process by which consumers and publics give money, a promise to pay, or support for the offering of a firm, institution, person, place, or idea.

Exclusive Distribution A policy in which a firm severely limits the wholesalers and retailers it utilizes in a geographic area, perhaps employing only one or two retailers within a specific shopping district.

Exempt Carrier A transporter that is excused from legal regulations and must only comply with safety requirements. Exempt carriers are specified by law.

Expected Profit Concept A mathematical calculation applied to competitive bidding which states that as the bid price increases the profit to a firm increases but the probability of its winning the contract decreases. The long-run average expected profit at each bid amount equals the company's profit times its probability of obtaining the contract at this bid amount.

Experiment A type of research whereby one or more factors are manipulated under controlled conditions. Experiments are able to show cause and effect.

Exploratory Research Used when the researcher is uncertain about the precise topic to be investigated. This technique develops a clear definition of the research problem by utilizing informal analysis.

Exporting A form of international marketing company organization when a firm reaches international markets by selling directly through its own sales force or indirectly through foreign merchants or agents. An exporting structure requires minimal investment in foreign facilities.

Extended Consumer Decision Making Occurs when considerable time is spent on information search and the evaluation of alternatives before a purchase is made. Expensive, complex products or services with which the consumer has had little or no experience require this form of decision making.

Extended Product Includes not only the tangible elements of a product, service, or idea, but also the accompanying cluster of image and service features.

Fabricated Part Used in industrial goods without further changes in form. A fabricated part is considered as an expense rather than a capital item.

Factor Merchant *See* Commission Merchant.

Factory Pricing *See* FOB Mill Pricing.

Family A group of two or more persons residing together who are related by blood, marriage, or adoption.

Family (Blanket) Branding A strategy in which one name is used for several products. It may be applied to manufacturer and dealer brands.

Family Life Cycle Describes how a typical family evolves from bachelorhood to marriage to children to solitary retirement. At each stage in the cycle, needs, experience, income, and family composition change.

Federal Trade Commission (FTC) The major federal agency that monitors restraint of trade and enforces rules against unfair methods of competition.

Feedback Information about the uncontrollable environment, the organization's performance, and how well the marketing plan is received. Also, the audience's response to a message in a channel of communication.

Field Warehouse A public warehouse which issues a receipt for goods stored in a private warehouse or in transit to consumers. The field warehouse receipt can serve as collateral for a loan.

Final Consumer Purchases a product and or service for personal, family, or household use.

Fine A legal concept in consumer protection that levies a dollar penalty on a firm for a deceptive promotion or other illegal practices.

Flexible Pricing Allows the marketer to adjust prices based on the consumer's ability to negotiate or the buying power of a large customer.

FOB Mill (Factory) Pricing A form of geographic pricing in which the buyer selects the transportation form and pays all freight charges. The delivered price to the buyer depends on the freight charges.

Food Broker A middleman involved with food and related general merchandise items who introduces buyers and sellers to one another and brings them together to complete a sale.

Forward Invention An international product strategy in which a company develops new products for its international markets.

Franchise Wholesaling A full-service merchant-wholesaling format whereby independent retailers affiliate with an existing wholesaler in order to use a standardized storefront design, business plan, name, and purchase system.

Franchising A contractual arrangement between a franchisor who may be a manufacturer, wholesaler, or service sponsor and a retail franchisee, which allows the franchisee to conduct a certain form of business under an established name and according to a specific set of rules.

Freight Forwarder A transportation service firm which consolidates small shipments (usually less than 500 pounds each) from several companies, picks up merchandise at the shipper's place of business, and arranges for delivery at the buyer's door.

Frequency How often a medium can be used.

FTC *See* Federal Trade Commission.

Full Disclosure A consumer protection legal concept requiring that all data necessary for a consumer to make a safe and informed decision be provided.

Full-Line Discount Store A retailer characterized by low prices, a broad merchandise assortment, low-rent location, self-service, brand-name merchandise, wide aisles, use of shopping carts, and most merchandise displayed on the selling floor.

Full-Line Wholesaler *See* General-Merchandise Wholesaler.

Full-Service Merchant Wholesaler Assembles products, provides trade credit, stores and delivers merchandise, offers merchandise and promotion assistance, provides a personal sales force, offers research and planning support, makes information available, provides installation and repair services, and acts as the sales arm for its manufacturer.

Functional Accounts Occur when natural account expenses are reclassified by function. These accounts indicate the purpose or activity for which expenditures have been made. Examples of functional accounts are marketing administration, transportation, and marketing research.

GATT *See* General Agreement on Tariffs and Trade.

General Agreement on Tariffs and Trade (GATT) A multilateral agreement that allows every nation covered to obtain the best contract terms received by a single nation. GATT members agree to meet every two years and to negotiate for tariff reductions.

General-Merchandise (Full-Line) Wholesaler A full-service merchant wholesaler which carries a wide assortment of products, nearly all the items needed by the retailers to which it caters.

Generic Brand An item that contains the name of the product itself and does not emphasize the manufacturer's or dealer's name.

Generic Product The broadest definition of a product which centers on customer need fulfillment. It focuses on what a product means to the customer, not the seller.

Geographic Demographics The basic identifiable characteristics of towns, cities, states, and regions.

Geographic Pricing Outlines the responsibility for transportation charges. The basic forms of geographic pricing are FOB (free on board), uniform delivered price, zone pricing, and base-point pricing.

GNP *See* Gross National Product.

Government Consumer Uses products and services in

the performance of its duties and responsibilities. There are 1 federal, 50 state, and 80,000 local governmental groups.

Government-Controlled Price Environment Characterized by prices set or directed by the government.

Government Stability Refers to the consistency of political policies and the orderliness in installing leaders.

Gross National Product (GNP) The total value of goods and services produced in a country each year.

Growth Stage of the Product Life Cycle Period during which industry sales expand rapidly as a few more firms enter a highly profitable market that has substantial potential.

Hard Technology The way some services are industrialized by substituting machinery for people.

Heavy-Half A market segmentation concept stating that for a wide variety of products a small proportion of total consumers may account for a large percentage of a product or service's total sales.

Hidden Service Sector Causes service data to be underestimated because many firms that perform services are classified as manufacturers.

Hierarchy-of-Effects Model Outlines the intermediate and long-term promotional objectives the firm should pursue: awareness, knowledge, liking, preference, conviction, and purchase.

Horizontal Audit Studies the overall marketing performance of the company with particular emphasis on the interrelationship of variables and their relative importance.

Horizontal Integration The practice of a firm acquiring other businesses like itself.

Horizontal Price Fixing Agreements among manufacturers, among wholesalers, or among retailers to set prices. Such agreements are illegal according to the Sherman Antitrust Act and the Federal Trade Commission Act, regardless of how ''reasonable'' the prices are.

Household A person or group of persons occupying a housing unit, whether related or unrelated.

Hybrid Technology A technique for industrializing services that combines hard and soft technologies such as computer-based truck routing and specialized low-priced auto repair facilities.

Iceberg Principle States that superficial data are insufficient to make sound marketing evaluations.

Idea Generation The stage in the new-product planning process which involves the continuous, systematic search for opportunities. It involves a delineation of the sources of new ideas and methods for generating them.

Ideal Point A product-positioning concept that represents the combination of attributes consumers would like to see a product possess.

Importance of a Purchase Related to the degree of decision making, level of perceived risk, and amount of money to be spent/invested. The level of importance of a purchase has a major impact on the time and effort a consumer will spend shopping for a product or service and on the amount of money allocated.

Impulse Goods Convenience goods that the consumer did not plan to buy on a specific trip to a store.

Incremental Technique A promotional budget method in which the company bases its new budget on previous expenditures. A percentage is either added to or subtracted from this year's budget in order to determine next year's.

Independent Media Those not controlled by the firm; they can influence the government's, consumers', and public's perceptions of a company's products and overall image.

Independent Retailer A retailer operating only one outlet.

Indirect Channel of Distribution Involves the movement of goods and services from manufacturer to independent channel member to consumer.

Individual Branding *See* Multiple Branding.

Industrial Marketing Occurs when a firm deals with organizational consumers.

Industrial Product A good or service purchased for use in the production of other goods or services, in the operation of a business, or for resale to other consumers.

Industrial Services Include maintenance and repair, and business advisory services.

Industrial Supplies Convenience goods that are necessary for the daily operation of the firm.

Industrialization of Services Improves service efficiency by applying hard, soft, and hybrid technologies.

Industrialized Country Has high literacy, modern technology, and high per capita income.

Inelastic Demand Occurs when price changes have little impact on quantity demanded.

Information Search Stage in consumer's decision process that requires the assembly of a list of alternative products or services that will solve the problem at hand and a determination of the characteristics of each alternative. Information search may be either internal or external.

Inner-Directed Person One who is interested in pleasing him- or herself.

Innovativeness The willingness to try a new product or service that others perceive as having a high degree of risk.

Inseparability of Services Inability of many services to be separated from the service provider. Customer contact is considered an integral part of the service experience.

Installation An industrial good capital item used in the production process that does not become part of the final product.

Institutional Advertising Used to improve corporate image and not to sell products or services.

Intangibility of Services Inability of many services to be displayed, transported, stored, packaged, or inspected before buying.

Intensive Distribution A policy in which a firm uses a large number of wholesalers and retailers in order to obtain widespread market coverage, channel acceptance, and high-volume sales.

International Marketing Involves the marketing of goods and services outside the organization's home country.

Introduction Stage of the Product Life Cycle Period during which only one firm has entered the market and competition is limited. A consumer market must be developed.

Inventory Management Concerned with ensuring a continuous flow of goods and matching the quantity of goods in inventory with sales demand.

Isolated Store A free-standing retail outlet located on either a highway or side street.

Item Price Removal Practice whereby prices are marked only on store shelves or aisle signs and not on individual items.

JIT *See* Just-in-Time Inventory System.

Joint Decision Making The process by which two or more consumers have input into purchases.

Joint Venture A form of international marketing company organization in which a firm combines some aspect of its manufacturing or marketing efforts with those of a foreign company in order to share expertise, costs, and connections with important persons.

Jury of Executive or Expert Opinion A sales forecasting method by which the management of a company or other well-informed persons meet, discuss the future, and set sales estimates based on experience and intuition.

Just-in-Time (JIT) Inventory System A procedure by which the purchasing firm reduces the amount of inventory it keeps on hand by ordering more frequently and in greater quantity.

Law of Demand A theory stating that consumers usually purchase more units at a low price than at a high price.

Lead Time The time required by a medium for placing an advertisement.

Leader Pricing Advertising and selling key items in the product assortment at less than their usual profit margins. The objective of leader pricing is to increase store traffic or to gain greater consumer interest in an overall product line.

Leased Department A department in a retail store (usually a department, discount, or specialty store) that is rented to an outside party.

Less-Developed Country Has low literacy, limited technology, and per capita income generally less than $500.

Licensing Agreement Permits a company to use another firm's trademark by paying a fee.

Life-Style The pattern in which a person lives and spends time and money. The combination of personality and social values that has been internalized by an individual.

Limited Consumer Decision Making Occurs when a consumer uses each of the steps in the purchase process but does not need to spend a great deal of time in each of them. The consumer has some past experience with the product or service under consideration.

Limited-Line Wholesaler *See* Specialty-Merchandise Wholesaler.

Limited-Service Merchant Wholesaler Buys and takes title to merchandise, but does not perform all of the functions of a full-service merchant wholesaler. May not provide credit, merchandise assistance, or market research data.

List Price A regularly quoted price provided to customers. It is preprinted on price tags, in catalogs, and in dealer purchase orders.

Local Content Law Requires foreign-based manufacturers to establish local plants and to use locally produced components. The goal of these laws is to promote domestic employment.

Loss Leader An item priced below cost that is restricted by unfair-sales acts in many states. Retailers use loss leaders, typically well-known and heavily advertised brands, to draw customer traffic into a store.

Mail Order Retailing A nonstore retail operation which seeks customers through television, radio, print media, or the mail, receives orders through the mail or telephone, and ships merchandise to the customer's home.

Mail Order Wholesaler A limited-service merchant wholesaler that uses catalogs instead of a personal sales force to promote products and communicate with customers.

Maintenance and Repair Services Those industrial services that include painting, machinery repair, and janitorial services.

Major Innovation A new product that has not been previously sold by the company or any other firm.

Majority Fallacy Concept stating that companies sometimes fail when they go after the largest market segment because competition is intense. A potentially profitable market segment may be the one that is ignored by other firms.

Manufacturer A firm that produces products for resale to other consumers.

Manufacturer (National) Brand An item that contains the name of the manufacturer. The major marketing focus for manufacturer brands is to attract and retain consumers who are loyal to a firm's offering and to control the marketing effort for the brands.

Manufacturer/Channel Member Contract A written agreement that focuses on price policy, conditions of sale, territorial rights, services/responsibility mix, and contract duration and conditions of termination.

Manufacturer Wholesaling Occurs when the producer undertakes all wholesaling functions itself. Includes manufacturer's sales offices and manufacturer's branch offices.

Manufacturers' Agent An agent who works for several manufacturers and carries noncompetitive, complementary products in exclusive territories. A manufacturer may employ many agents, each with a unique product-territorial mix.

Manufacturer's Branch Office A form of manufacturer wholesaling that assigns warehousing and selling tasks to a branch office.

Manufacturer's Sales Office A form of manufacturer wholesaling that assigns selling tasks to a sales office, but maintains inventory only at production facilities.

Marginal Return of Promotion The amount of sales each additional increment of promotion will generate.

Markdown Reduction from the original retail price of an item to meet lower prices of competitors, counteract overstocking of merchandise, delete an assortment of odds and ends, and increase customer traffic.

Market Buildup Method A sales forecasting technique in which the firm gathers data from small, separate market segments and aggregates them.

Market-Controlled Price Environment Characterized by a high level of competition, similar products and services, and little control over price by individual companies.

Market Development A product/market opportunity matrix strategy in which a firm seeks greater sales of present products from new markets or new product uses.

Market Penetration A product/market opportunity matrix strategy in which a firm seeks to expand the sales of its present products through more intensive distribution, aggressive promotion efforts, and highly competitive prices.

Market Segmentation An appeal to one, well-defined consumer group through one marketing plan.

Market Share Analysis A method of sales forecasting that is similar to simple trend analysis, except that the company bases its forecast on the assumption that its share of industry sales will remain constant.

Marketing The anticipation, management, and satisfaction of demand through the exchange process.

Marketing Audit A systematic, critical, and unbiased review and appraisal of the basic objectives of the marketing function and of the organization, methods, procedures, and personnel employed to implement these policies and to achieve these objectives.

Marketing Company Era Recognition of the central role of marketing. The marketing department becomes the equal of others in the company. Company efforts are integrated and frequently re-evaluated.

Marketing Concept A consumer-oriented, integrated, goal-oriented philosophy for a firm, institution, or person.

Marketing Cost Analysis Evaluates the cost effectiveness of various marketing factors, such as different product lines, distribution methods, sales territories, channel members, salespersons, advertising media, and customer types.

Marketing Department Era Stage during which the marketing department participates in company decisions but remains in a subordinate or conflicting position to the production, engineering, and sales departments.

Marketing Environment Consists of controllable and uncontrollable factors, the organization's level of success or failure in reaching objectives, feedback, and adaptation.

Marketing Functions Include environmental analysis and marketing research, consumer analysis, product (service) planning, distribution planning, promotion planning, price planning, social responsibility, and marketing management.

Marketing Information System (MIS) A set of procedures and methods designed to generate, store, analyze, and disseminate anticipated marketing decision information on a regular, continuous basis.

Marketing Intelligence Network The part of a marketing information system that consists of marketing research, continuous monitoring, and data storage.

Marketing-Manager System A product management organizational format under which all the functional areas of marketing report to one manager. These areas include sales, advertising, sales promotion, and product planning.

Marketing Mix Describes the specific combination of marketing elements used to achieve objectives and satisfy the target market. The marketing mix consists of four major factors: product or service, distribution, promotion, and price.

Marketing Myopia A short-sighted, narrow-minded view of marketing and its environment.

Marketing Objectives More customer-oriented than the overall goals set by top management.

Marketing Organization The structural arrangement for directing marketing functions. The organization outlines authority, responsibility, and the tasks to be performed.

Marketing Performers Include manufacturers and service providers, wholesalers, retailers, marketing specialists, and organizational and final consumers.

Marketing Research The systematic gathering, recording, and analyzing of data about problems relating to the marketing of goods and services. It is used to obtain precise information to solve research problems.

Marketing Research Process Consists of a series of activities: definition of the problem or issue to be resolved, examination of secondary data, generation of primary data (if necessary), analysis of information, recommendations, and implementation of findings.

Marketing Strategy Outlines the manner in which marketing is used to accomplish an organization's objectives.

Markup Pricing A form of cost-based pricing in which prices are set by calculating per unit merchandise costs and then determining the markup percentages that are needed to cover selling costs and profit. The formula for markup pricing is

$$\text{Price} = \frac{\text{Merchandise costs}}{(100 - \text{Markup per cent})/100}.$$

Mass Marketing An appeal to a broad range of consumers by utilizing a single basic marketing program.

Massed Promotion Communication concentrated in peak periods, like holidays.

Maturity Stage of the Product Life Cycle Period during which industry sales stabilize as the market becomes saturated and many firms enter to capitalize on the still sizable demand.

Me Generation A consumer life-style that stresses "being good to myself," "improving myself," and "my life, my way."

Medium The personal or nonpersonal channel in a channel of communication used to convey a message.

Merchant Wholesaler Buys, takes title, and takes possession of products for its own accounts. Merchant wholesalers may be full-service or limited-service.

Message The combination of words and symbols transmitted to the audience through a channel of communication.

Message Permanence Refers to the number of exposures one advertisement generates and how long it remains with the audience.

Metropolitan Statistical Area (MSA) A Bureau of Census designation which contains either a city of at least a 50,000 population or an urbanized area of 50,000 population (with a total population of at least 100,000).

Middleman *See* Channel Member.

Minimum Price Laws *See* Unfair-Sales Acts.

Minor Innovation A new product that has not been previously sold by the firm but has been sold by others.

MIS *See* Marketing Information System.

Missionary Salesperson Type of sales support person used to distribute information about new products or services. This person does not sell, but describes the attributes of the new item, answers questions, and leaves written data.

Mixed Approach to International Marketing An international marketing strategy which combines standardized and nonstandardized efforts to enable a company to maximize production efficiencies, maintain a consistent image, exercise home-office control, and yet be sensitive and responsive to local needs.

Mixed-Brand Strategy Occurs when a combination of manufacturer and dealer brands (and sometimes generic brands) are sold by manufacturers and retailers.

Modification A new product involving an alteration in a company's existing product. It can be a new model, style, color, product improvement, or new brand.

Modified Break-Even Analysis Combines traditional break-even analysis with an evaluation of demand at various levels of price. Determines the price-quantity mix that maximizes profits.

Modified Rebuy Purchase Process A moderate amount of decision making undertaken by organizational consumers in the purchase of medium-priced products that have been bought infrequently before.

Monitoring Results Involves the comparison of planned performance against actual performance for a specified period of time.

Monopolistic Competition A situation in which there are several competing firms, each trying to offer a unique marketing mix.

Monopoly A situation in which only one firm sells a particular product or service.

Most-Favored Nation Principle Allows every nation covered by the General Agreement on Tariffs and Trade to obtain the best contract terms received by any single nation.

Motivation The driving force within individuals that impels them to act.

Motive A reason for behavior.

Motor Truck A transportation form that predominately transports small shipments over short distances.

MSA *See* Metropolitan Statistical Area.

Multidimensional Scaling A survey research tool in which respondents' attitudes are ascertained for many product and company attributes. Then computer analysis enables the firm to develop a single product or company rating, rather than a profile of several individual characteristics.

Multinational Marketing A complex form of international marketing that involves an organization engaged in marketing operations in many foreign countries.

Multiple (Individual) Branding Separate brands used for each item or product category sold by the firm.

Multiple-Buying Responsibility Two or more employees participating in joint decision making for complex or expensive purchases of organizational consumers.

Multiple Segmentation An appeal to two or more well-defined consumer groups through different marketing plans.

Multiple-Unit Pricing A practice by which a company offers final consumers discounts for buying in quantity in order to increase sales volume.

Multistage Approach to Pricing A popular technique for developing a broad price policy. Divides price planning into six successive steps, with each placing constraints on the next step.

Multistep Flow of Communication The communication theory which suggests that opinion leaders not only influence but are influenced by the general public (opinion receivers).

Multiunit Advertising The practice of including two or more products in a single ad to reduce media costs.

Narrowcast The presentation of specialized programming to a specific audience.

National Brand *See* Manufacturer Brand.

Nationalism Refers to a country's efforts to become self-reliant and raise its status in the eyes of the world community. Frequently, nationalism leads to tight restrictions for foreign companies and fosters the development of domestic industry at their expense.

Natural Account Expenses Costs which are reported by the names of the expenses and not the expenditures' purposes. Examples of natural account expenses are salaries, rent, and advertising.

Need-Satisfaction Approach A sales presentation method based on the principle that each customer has different characteristics and wants. The sales presentation is adapted to each customer.

Negotiation Situation in which the buyer uses bargaining ability and order size to influence prices.

New Product A modification of an existing product or an innovation that the consumer perceives as meaningful.

New-Product Manager System A product management organization form which utilizes a product manager for existing products and a new-product manager for new products. After a new product is introduced, it is managed by the product manager.

New-Product Planning Process Consists of seven basic steps: idea generation, product screening, concept testing, business analysis, product development, test marketing, and commercialization.

New-Task Purchase Process A large amount of decision making undertaken by organizational consumers in the purchase of expensive products that have not been bought before.

Noise Interference at any stage along the channel of communication.

Nongoods Service Provides personal service on the part of the seller. It does not involve a product.

Nonprice Competition Reduces the role of price as a factor in consumer demand. This is accomplished by the creation of a distinctive product or service as expressed through promotion, packaging, delivery, customer service, availability, and other factors.

Nonprofit Institution Involved with nonprofit marketing.

Nonprofit Marketing Conducted by organizations that operate in the public interest or to foster a cause and do not seek financial profits. Nonprofit marketing may involve organizations, people, places, and ideas as well as products and services.

Nonstore Retailing Retail form which does not utilize conventional store facilities. Includes vending machines, direct-to-home sales, and mail order.

Objective-and-Task Technique A promotional budget method in which the firm clearly outlines its promotional objectives and then establishes the appropriate budget.

Observation A research technique by which present behavior or the results of past behavior are observed and recorded. People are not questioned, and their cooperation is not necessary.

OCR-A *See* Optical Character Recognition.

Odd-Pricing Strategy Used when final selling prices are set at levels below even-dollar values such as 49¢, $4.95, and $199.

Oligopoly Situation in which there are few firms, generally large, that comprise most of an industry's sales.

One-Price Policy The same price charged to all customers who seek to purchase a product or service under similar conditions.

One-Sided Message A message in which the firm mentions only the benefits of its product or service.

Open Credit Account A credit purchase in which a buyer receives a monthly bill for goods bought during the preceding month. The account must be paid in full each month.

Opinion *See* Attitude.

Opinion Leader Person who influences the purchase behavior of other consumers through face-to-face interaction. An opinion leader normally has an impact over a narrow range of products.

Optical Character Recognition (OCR-A) Department store system for electronically coding information onto merchandise. OCR-A is readable by both machines and humans and can handle more information than the Universal Product Code (UPC).

Order Cycle The period of time from when the customer places an order until it is received.

Order-Generating Costs Costs that are revenue producing, such as advertising and personal selling.

Order Getter Type of salesperson who is involved with generating customer leads, providing information, persuading customers, and closing sales.

Order-Processing Costs Costs associated with filling out and handling order forms, computer time, and merchandise handling. Order-processing costs per unit usually drop as order size increases.

Order Size The appropriate amount of merchandise, parts, etc. to purchase at one time. Depends on the availability of quantity discounts, the resources of the firm, inventory turnover, the costs of processing each order, and the costs of maintaining goods in inventory.

Order Taker Type of salesperson who processes routine orders and reorders. The order taker usually handles products or services that are presold.

Organizational Buying Objectives Include the availability of items, reliability of sellers, consistency of quality, delivery, and price.

Organizational Consumer Purchases products and services for further production, usage in operating the organization, or resale to other consumers.

Organizational Consumer Expectations The perceived potential of alternative suppliers and brands to satisfy a number of explicit and implicit objectives.

Organizational Consumer's Decision Process Consists of expectations, the buying process, conflict resolution, and situational factors.

Organizational Mission A firm's long-term commitment to a type of business and a place in the market. Mission can be defined in terms of customer groups served, customer functions, and technologies utilized.

Outer-Directed Person One who is interested in pleasing the people around him or her.

Owned-Goods Service Involves an alteration or repair of a product owned by the consumer.

Package Includes a product's physical container, label, and inserts.

Packaging Functions Consist of containment and protection, usage, communication, market segmentation, channel cooperation, and new-product planning.

Patent Awards exclusive selling rights for 17 years to the inventor of a useful product or process.

Penetration Price A low price intended to capture the mass market for a product or service.

Perceived Risk The level of risk a consumer believes exists regarding the outcome of a purchase decision; this belief may or may not be correct. Perceived risk can be divided into five major types: functional, physical, financial, social, and psychological.

Percentage-of-Sales Technique A promotional budget technique in which a company ties the promotion budget to sales revenue.

Peripheral Service A complementary service needed to supplement the basic service offering.

Perishability of Services Occurs because unused capacity cannot be stored for future use or shifted from one time period to another for many services.

Personal Demographics The basic identifiable characteristics of individual people.

Personal Selling An oral presentation in a conversation with one or more prospective buyers for the purpose of making sales.

Personality The sum total of an individual's traits that make the individual unique.

Persuasive Impact The ability of a medium to stimulate consumers.

Physical Distribution The broad range of activities concerned with the efficient movement of finished goods from the end of the production line to the consumer. In some cases it includes the movement of raw materials from the source of supply to the beginning of the production line.

Physical Distribution Strategy Includes the transportation form or forms to be used, inventory levels and warehouse form(s), and the number and locations of plants, warehouses, and retail locations.

Physical Distribution System The coordination of a firm's transportation and inventory management strategies.

PIMS *See* Profit Impact of Market Strategy.

Pipeline A transportation form that involves continuous movement, with no interruptions, inventories, or intermediate storage locations.

Planned Obsolescence A practice that encourages short-run material wearout, style changes, and functional product changes.

Planned Shopping Center A retail location that is centrally owned or managed, planned, and operated as an entity, surrounded by parking, and based on balanced tenancy. The types are regional, community, and neighborhood.

PMSA *See* Primary Metropolitan Statistical Area.

Porter Generic Strategy Model A model that examines two major marketing-planning concepts and the alternatives available with each: selection of a target market (industrywide or segmented) and strategic advantage (uniqueness or price). These basic strategies are identified: overall cost leadership, differentiation, and focus.

Portfolio Analysis A technique by which an organization individually assesses and positions each of its opportunities, products, and/or businesses. Company efforts and resources are allocated and appropriate strategies are developed on the basis of these assessments.

Postpurchase Behavior Stage in the consumer's decision process when further purchases or re-evaluation of the purchase are undertaken.

Poverty of Time A consumer life-style where greater affluence results in less free time because the alternatives competing for time expand.

Predatory Pricing An illegal practice in which large companies cut prices on products in selected geographic areas below their cost with the intention of eliminating small, local competitors.

Prestige Pricing Assumes that consumers do not buy products or services at prices that are considered too low.

Price Represents the value of a product or service for both the seller and the buyer.

Price-Based Shopping Goods Products/services for which consumers judge product attributes to be similar and look around for the least expensive item/store.

Price Ceiling The maximum amount customers will pay for a given product or service.

Price Competition Demand influenced primarily through changes in price levels.

Price Discrimination A form of demand-based pricing in which the firm sets two or more distinct prices for a product or service in order to appeal to different final consumer or organizational consumer market segments. Price discrimination may be customer-, product version-, time-, or place-based.

Price Elasticity of Demand *See* Elasticity of Demand.

Price Floor The lowest acceptable price the firm can charge and attain its profit goal.

Price Guarantee A manufacturer's assurance to wholesalers or retailers that the prices they pay are the lowest available. Any discount given to competitors will also be given to the original purchaser.

Price Leadership A form of competition-based pricing in which one firm is usually the first to announce price changes and the other companies in the industry follow.

Price Lining Involves the sale of merchandise at a range of prices, with each individual price representing a distinct level of quality.

Price Planning The systematic decision making pertaining to all aspects of pricing by the organization.

Price-Quality Association Concept stating that consumers believe high prices mean high quality and low prices mean low quality.

Price War Situation in which various firms continually try to undercut each other's prices.

Primary Data Collected to solve the specific problem or issue under investigation.

Primary Demand Consumer demand for a product category. Important when the product or service is little known.

Primary Metropolitan Statistical Area (PMSA) A Bureau of Census designation which consists of at least 1 million people and includes a large urbanized county or a cluster of counties that have strong economic and social links as well as ties to neighboring communities.

Private Brand *See* Dealer Brand.

Private Carrier A shipper possessing its own transportation facilities.

Problem Awareness A stage in the consumer's decision-making process during which the consumer recognizes that the product or service under consideration may solve a problem of shortage or unfulfilled desire.

Problem Child A category in the Boston Consulting Group matrix which describes a low market-share strategic business unit (SBU) in a high-growth industry. A problem child requires substantial cash to maintain or increase market share in the face of strong competition.

Problem Definition A statement of the topic to be investigated in marketing research. It directs the research process toward the collection and analysis of specific information for the purpose of decision making.

Process-Related Ethical Issue Involves the unethical use of a marketing strategy or tactic.

Product A basic offering that is accompanied by a set of image features that seeks to satisfy consumers' needs.

Product-Adaptation Strategy An international product-planning strategy in which domestic products are modified to meet foreign conditions, taste preferences, electrical requirements, water conditions, or legal requirements.

Product Development A product/market opportunity matrix strategy in which a firm develops new or modified products to appeal to present markets.

Product Development Stage of New-Product Planning Converts a product idea into a physical form and identifies a basic marketing strategy.

Product Item A specific model, brand, or size of a product that the company sells.

Product Life Cycle A concept that attempts to describe a product's sales, profits, customers, competitors, and marketing emphasis from its inception until it is removed from the market. It is divided into introduction, growth, maturity, and decline stages.

Product Line A group of closely related items.

Product (Brand)-Manager System A product management organization format under which a middle manager focuses on a single product or a small group of products. This manager handles new and existing products and is involved with everything from marketing research to package design to advertising.

Product/Market Opportunity Matrix A broad method for strategy planning that suggests four alternative strategies for maintaining and/or increasing sales: market penetration, market development, product development, and diversification.

Product Mix Consists of all the different product lines that a firm offers. *See also* Consistency of Product Mix; Depth of Product Mix; *and* Width of Product Mix.

Product Planning The systematic decision making pertaining to all aspects of the development and management of a firm's products, including branding and packaging.

Product-Planning Committee A product management organization staffed by executives from functional areas including marketing, production, engineering, finance, and research and development. It handles product approval, evaluation, and development on a part-time basis.

Product Positioning Enables the firm to map its offerings in terms of consumer perceptions and desires, competition, other company products, and environmental changes.

Product Recall The primary enforcement tool of the Consumer Product Safety Commission.

Product-Related Ethical Issue Involves the ethical appropriateness of marketing a certain product.

Product Screening Stage in the new-product planning process when poor, unsuitable, or otherwise unattractive ideas are weeded out from further consideration.

Product-Specific Buying Factors Product-based variables which lead to either autonomous (independent) or joint decision making by organizational consumers. These variables include the degree of perceived risk, routineness of decision, and degree of time pressure.

Product Specifications The minimum specifications set by organizational consumers. They deal with engineer-

ing and architectural guidelines, purity and grade standards, horsepower, voltage, type of construction, and materials employed in construction.

Production Era Devotion to the physical distribution of goods and services due to high demand and low competition. Consumer research, product modifications, and adapting to consumer needs are unnecessary.

Profit-Based Objective A pricing objective which orients a firm's pricing strategy toward some type of profit goal: profit maximization, return on investment, and/or early recovery of cash.

Profit Impact of Market Strategy (PIMS) A program which gathers data from a number of corporations in order to establish relationships between a variety of business factors and two measures of organizational performance: return on investment and cash flow.

Promotion Any form of communication used by a firm to inform, persuade, or remind people about its products, services, image, ideas, community involvement, or impact on society.

Promotion Mix The overall and specific communication program of an organization consisting of a combination of advertising, publicity, personal selling, and/or sales promotion.

Promotion Planning Systematic decision making pertaining to all aspects of the development and management of a firm's promotional effort.

Prospecting The stage in a selling process which generates a list of customer leads. It is common with outside selling. Prospecting can be blind or lead in orientation.

Psychographics A technique with which life-styles can be measured. An AIO (activities, interests, and opinions) inventory is used in psychographic research to determine consumer life-styles.

Psychological Pricing Assumes consumers are perceptually sensitive to certain prices. Departures from these prices in either direction result in decreases in demand. Customary, odd, and prestige pricing are all forms of psychological pricing.

Public Relations Mass and personal communications that are image-directed.

Publicity Nonpersonal stimulation of demand for a product, service, or business by placing commercially significant news about it in a published medium or obtaining favorable presentation upon radio, television, or stage that is not paid for by an identified sponsor.

Publicity Types Consist of news publicity, business feature articles, service feature articles, finance releases, product releases, pictorial releases, background editorial material, and emergency publicity.

Publics' Demand Refers to the characteristics and needs of employees, unions, stockholders, consumer groups, the general public, government agencies, and other internal and external forces that affect company operations.

Pulling Strategy Demand first generated through direct advertising to customers; then dealer support is obtained.

Purchase Act An exchange of money or a promise to pay for the acquisition of a product or service.

Pure Competition Situation with many firms selling identical products or services.

Pure Nonstandardized Approach An international marketing strategy that assumes each market (country) is different and requires a distinct marketing plan.

Pure Standardized Approach An international marketing strategy in which a common marketing plan is used for all countries in which a firm operates.

Pushing Strategy Dealer support and cooperation first attained; then advertising is addressed to customers.

Question Mark *See* Problem Child.

Rack Jobber A full-service merchant wholesaler that furnishes the racks or shelves on which merchandise is displayed. The rack jobber owns the merchandise on its racks, selling the items on a consignment basis.

Railroad A transportation form that usually carries heavy, bulky items that are low in value (relative to their weight) over long distances.

Raw Material An unprocessed primary industrial material from extractive and agricultural industries. Raw material is considered as an expense rather than a capital item.

Reach Refers to the number of viewers or readers in the audience. For television and radio, reach is the total number of people viewing or listening to a program. For print media, reach equals circulation plus passalong rate.

Real Income Income adjusted for inflation.

Rebate A form of price adjustment in which a cash refund is given directly from the manufacturer to the consumer in order to stimulate consumption.

Reciprocity A procedure by which organizational consumers select suppliers who agree to purchase goods and services as well as sell them.

Reference Group A group that influences a person's thoughts or actions.

Relative Product Failure Occurs when the company is able to make a profit on an item but the product does not reach profit objectives and/or adversely affects image.

Rented-Goods Service Involves the leasing of a product for a specified period of time.

Reorder Point Establishes an inventory level at which new orders must be placed. The reorder point depends on order lead time, usage rate, and safety stock. The reorder point formula is

$$\text{Reorder point} = (\text{Order lead time} \times \text{Usage rate}) + (\text{Safety stock}).$$

Research Design The framework for a study used as a guide in collecting and analyzing data. A research design includes decisions relating to the person collecting data, data to be collected, group of people or objects studied, data-collection techniques employed, study costs, method of data collection, length of study period and time, and location of data collection.

Retail Catalog Showroom A warehouse-type outlet at which consumers select merchandise from a catalog. Customers frequently write up their own orders, products are usually stored in a back room, and there are limited displays.

Retail Cooperative A format that allows independent retailers to share purchases, storage and shipping facilities, advertising, planning, and other functions.

Retail Franchising *See* Franchising.

Retail Strategy Mix The combination of prices, products, sales personnel, hours, and other factors that a retailer employs.

Retailer An organization or individual that handles merchandise and services for sale to the ultimate (final) consumer.

Retailing Encompasses those business activities that involve the sale of goods and services to the ultimate (final) consumer for personal, family, or household use. Retailing is the final stage in the channel of distribution.

Revolving Credit Account A credit purchase in which the buyer agrees to make minimum payments during an extended period of time and pays interest on outstanding purchases.

Robinson-Patman Act Prohibits manufacturers and wholesalers from price discrimination in dealing with different channel members purchasing products of ''like quality,'' if the effect of such discrimination is to injure competition.

Routine Consumer Decision Making Occurs when the consumer buys out of habit and skips steps in the decision process. In this category are items that are purchased regularly.

S-Curve Effect Occurs if the sales of a product rise sharply after it is introduced because of a heavy initial promotion effort (ads, coupons, samples, etc.), drop slightly as promotional support is reduced, and then rise again as positive word-of-mouth communication takes place.

Sales Analysis The detailed study of sales data for the purpose of appraising the appropriateness of a marketing strategy.

Sales-Based Objective A pricing objective that orients a firm's pricing strategy toward high sales volume or expanding sales relative to competitors.

Sales Engineer Accompanies an order getter when a highly technical or complex item is being sold. This salesperson explains product specifications, alternatives, and long-range uses.

Sales Era Involves hiring a sales force and conducting advertising to sell merchandise, after production is maximized. The goal is to fit consumer desires to the attributes of the products being manufactured.

Sales Exception Reporting Lists situations where sales goals are not met or sales opportunities are present.

Sales-Expense Budget Allocates expenditures among salespeople, products, customers, and geographic areas for a given period of time.

Sales Force Survey A method of sales forecasting that enables sales personnel to pinpoint coming trends, strengths and weaknesses in the company's offering, competitive strategies, customer resistance, and the traits of heavy users.

Sales Forecast Projects expected company sales for a specific product or service to a specific consumer group over a specific period of time under a well-defined marketing program.

Sales Invoice The main source of sales analysis data. It contains information on customer name, quantity ordered, price paid, purchase terms, geographic location of purchaser, all different items bought at the same time, order date, shipping arrangements, and salesperson.

Sales Management The planning, analysis, and control of the personal sales function. It covers employee selection, training, territory allocation, compensation, and supervision.

Sales Penetration The degree to which a company achieves its sales potential:

Sales penetration = Actual sales ÷ Sales potential.

Sales Presentation Stage in the selling process that includes a description of the product or service, its benefits, available options and models, price, associated services (such as delivery and warranty), and a demonstration (if necessary).

Sales Promotion Involves marketing activities, other than advertising, publicity, or personal selling, that stimulate consumer purchases and dealer effectiveness. Included are shows, demonstrations, and various nonrecurrent selling efforts not in the ordinary routine.

Sales Promotion Conditions The requirements channel members or final consumers must meet to be eligible for a sales promotion.

Sales Promotion Orientation Refers to the focus of sales promotion toward channel members or final consumers.

Sampling Requires the analysis of selected people or objects in the specified population, rather than all of them.

SBU *See* Strategic Business Unit.

Scientific Method A philosophy for marketing research based on objectivity, accuracy, and thoroughness.

Scrambled Merchandising Occurs when a retailer adds products or product lines that are unrelated to each other and the retailer's original business.

Secondary Data Those data that have been previously gathered for purposes other than solving the current problem under investigation. The two types of secondary data are internal and external.

Segmentation Strategy Consists of determining consumer needs and characteristics, analyzing consumer similarities and differences, developing consumer group profiles, selecting consumer segment(s), positioning the offering, and establishing a marketing plan.

Selective Demand Consumer demand for a particular brand of a product.

Selective Distribution A policy by which the firm employs a moderate number of wholesalers and retailers.

Self-Fulfilling Prophecy A situation in which a company predicts that sales will decline and ensures this by removing marketing support.

Selling Against the Brand Retailers stocking manufacturers' brands and placing high prices on them in order to aid in selling private-label goods.

Selling Agent An agent that assumes responsibility for marketing the entire output of a manufacturer under a contractual agreement. It performs all wholesale functions except taking title to merchandise.

Selling Process Involves prospecting for customer leads, approaching customers, determining customer wants, giving a sales presentation, answering questions, closing the sale, and following up.

Semantic Differential A survey technique that uses rating scales of bipolar (opposite) adjectives. An overall company or product profile is then developed.

Service Marketing Encompasses the rental of products, the alteration or repair of products owned by consumers, and personal services.

Service Salesperson Usually interacts with customers after sales are completed. Delivery, installation, or other follow-up tasks are undertaken.

Shopping Good An item for which consumers lack sufficient information about product alternatives and their attributes prior to making a purchase decision. The two major kinds of shopping goods are attribute-based and price-based.

SIC *See* Standard Industrial Classification.

Simple Trend Analysis A method of sales forecasting by which the firm forecasts future sales on the basis of recent or current performance.

Simulation A computer-based marketing research tool that recreates the use of various marketing factors on paper rather than in a real setting.

Situation Analysis The identification of marketing opportunities and potential problems facing the company. Situation analysis seeks answers to two general questions: Where is the firm now? In what direction is the firm headed?

Situational Factors Those that can interrupt the organizational consumer's decision process and the actual selection of a supplier or brand. They can include strikes, machine breakdowns, organizational changes, and so on.

Skimming Price A high price intended to attract the market segment that is more concerned with product quality, uniqueness, or status than price.

Social Class The ranking of people within a culture. Social classes are based on income, occupation, education, and type of dwelling.

Social Marketing The use of marketing to increase the acceptability of social ideas.

Social Performance How a person carries out his or her roles as a worker, family member, citizen, and friend.

Social Responsibility The possession of a corporate conscience or a response to social problems based on a sense of moral obligation.

Socioecological View of Marketing Examines all the stages of a product's life span from raw materials to junkpile. The socioecological view incorporates the interests of all consumers who are influenced by the use of a product or service.

Soft Technology A way to industrialize services by substituting preplanned systems such as prepackaged vacation tours for individual services.

Sorting Process The distribution activities of accumulation, allocation, sorting, and assorting necessary to resolve the differences in the goals of manufacturers and final consumers.

Source of Communication The company, independent institution, or opinion leader that seeks to present a message to an audience. Part of the channel of communication.

Specialty Good An item to which consumers are brand loyal. They are fully aware of product attributes prior to making a purchase decision and are willing to make a significant purchase effort to acquire the brand desired.

Specialty-Merchandise (Limited-Line) Wholesaler A full-service merchant wholesaler that concentrates its efforts on a relatively narrow range of products and has an extensive assortment within that range.

Specialty Store A retailer that concentrates on the sale of one merchandise line.

Standard Industrial Classification (SIC) A coding system compiled by the U.S. Office of Management and Budget for which much data has been assembled. Manufacturers, wholesalers, and retailers are assigned SIC codes.

Standard of Living The average quantity and quality of goods and services consumed in a country.

Staples Low-priced convenience goods that are routinely purchased.

Star A category in the Boston Consulting Group matrix that describes a high market-share strategic business unit (SBU) in a high-growth industry. A star generates substantial profits but requires large amounts of resources to finance continued growth.

Status Quo-Based Objective A pricing objective which orients a firm's pricing strategy toward stability or continuing a favorable climate for operations.

Stimulus A cue (social, commercial, or noncommercial) or a drive (physical) meant to motivate or arouse a person to act.

Stock Turnover Represents the number of times during a specified period (usually one year) that the average inventory on hand is sold. Stock turnover is calculated in units or dollars:

$$\text{Annual rate of stock turnover (units)} = \frac{\text{Number of units sold during year}}{\text{Average inventory on hand (in units)}}$$

$$\text{Annual rate of stock turnover (dollars)} = \frac{\text{Net yearly sales (in retail dollars)}}{\text{Average inventory on hand (in retail dollars)}}.$$

Straight-Commission Plan A sales compensation plan that ties a salesperson's earnings directly to sales or profits.

Straight Extension Strategy An international product-planning strategy in which a company manufactures the same products for domestic and foreign sales.

Straight Rebuy Purchase Process Routine reordering by organizational consumers for the purchase of inexpensive items bought on a regular basis.

Straight-Salary Plan A sales compensation plan that pays a salesperson a flat fee per week, month, or year.

Strategic Business Unit (SBU) A distinct part of the overall organization with a specific market focus and a manager with complete responsibility for integrating all functions into a strategy. SBUs are the basic building blocks of a strategic marketing plan.

Strategic Plan Outlines what marketing actions a firm should undertake, why these actions are necessary, who is responsible for carrying them out, where they will be accomplished, and how they will be completed.

Strategic Planning Process Consists of seven interrelated steps: defining organizational mission, establishing strategic business units, setting marketing objectives, situation analysis, developing marketing strategy, implementing tactics, and monitoring results.

Strategy *See* Marketing Strategy.

Subjective Price The consumer's perception of a price as high or low.

Subliminal Advertising A controversial type of promotion that does not enable a consumer to consciously decode a message.

Substantiation A consumer protection legal concept which requires that a firm be able to prove all promotion claims it makes. This means thorough testing and evidence of performance are needed prior to making claims.

Supermarket A departmentalized food store with minimum annual sales of $2 million.

Superstore A large food-based retailer that is much more diversified than a supermarket.

Surcharges A form of price adjustment in which across-the-board price increases are published to supplement list prices. Frequently used with catalogs because of their simplicity; an insert is distributed with the catalog.

Survey The systematic gathering of information from respondents by communicating with them in person, over the telephone, or by mail.

Systems Selling A combination of goods and services sold by a single source. This enables the buyer to have single-source accountability, one firm with which to negotiate, and assurance of the compatibility of various parts and components.

Tactic Specific action undertaken to implement a given strategy.

Tangible Product The basic physical entity, service, or idea which has precise specifications and is offered under a given description or model number.

Target Market The defined customer group to which a firm appeals.

Target Pricing A form of cost-based pricing in which prices are set to provide a specified rate of return on investment for a standard volume of production. Mathematically it is

Target price = [(Investment costs × Target return on investment %)/Standard volume] + (Average total costs at standard volume).

Tariff The most common form of trade restriction in which a tax is placed on imported goods by a foreign government.

Technology Refers to the development and use of machinery, products, and processes.

Terms The provisions of price agreements, including discounts, timing of payments, and credit arrangements.

Test Marketing The stage in a new-product planning process in which a product is placed for sale in one or more selected areas and its actual sales performance under the proposed marketing plan is observed.

Time Expenditures Involve the types of activities in which a person participates and the amount of time allocated to them.

Total-Cost Approach Determines the distribution service level with the lowest total costs, including freight, warehousing, and the cost of lost business. The ideal system seeks a balance between low distribution costs and high opportunities for sales.

Trade Character A brand mark that is personified.

Trade Deficit Occurs when the value of imports exceeds the value of exports for a country.

Trade Quota A form of trade restriction in which limits are set on the amount of goods that may be imported into a country.

Trademark A brand name, brand mark, trade character, or combination thereof that is legally protected.

Traditional Break-Even Analysis Determines the sales quantity (in units or dollars) at which total costs equal total revenues at a given price:

$$\text{Break-even point (units)} = \frac{\text{Total fixed costs}}{\text{Price} - \text{Variable costs (per unit)}}$$

$$\text{Break-even point (sales dollars)} = \frac{\text{Total fixed costs}}{1 - \dfrac{\text{Variable costs (per unit)}}{\text{Price}}}.$$

Transportation Service Company Handles the shipments of moderate-sized packages. The three kinds of companies are government parcel post, private parcel service, and express service.

Truck/Wagon Wholesaler A limited-service merchant wholesaler which has a regular sales route, offers items from a truck or wagon, and delivers goods as they are sold.

Two-Sided Message A message in which a firm mentions both benefits and limitations of its product or service.

Two-Step Flow of Communication Theory stating that a message goes from the company to opinion leaders and then to the target market.

Unbundled Pricing A strategy that breaks down prices by individual components. This allows customers to purchase services on an optional basis.

Uncontrollable Factors Those elements affecting an organization's performance that cannot be directed by the organization and its marketers. These include consumers, competition, government, the economy, technology, and independent media.

Unfair-Sales Acts Legislation in several states preventing retailers from selling merchandise for less than the cost of the product plus a fixed percentage that covers overhead and profit.

Uniform Delivered Pricing A form of geographic pricing in which all buyers pay the same delivered price for the same quantity of goods, regardless of their location. The seller pays for shipping.

Unit Pricing Prices expressed per unit of measure as well as by total value. Enables consumers to compare price per quantity for competing brands and for various sizes of the same brand.

Unitary Demand Exists if changes in price are exactly offset by changes in quantity demanded so that total sales revenue remains constant.

Universal Product Code (UPC) Industrywide electronic system for coding information onto food and related merchandise. The UPC requires manufacturers to premark items with a series of thick and thin vertical lines; price and inventory data are contained but are not readable by employees and customers.

Unplanned Business District A retail location form in which a group of stores are located close to one another and the combination of stores is not based on prior planning. There are four types of unplanned business districts: central business district, secondary business district, neighborhood business district, and string.

UPC *See* Universal Product Code.

VALS (Values and Life-Styles) Program A classification system for segmenting consumers in terms of a broad range of demographic and life-style factors. The VALS program, developed by the Stanford Research Institute, divides American life-styles into 9 major categories.

Value Analysis A comparison of the benefits of different materials, components, and manufacturing processes in order to improve products, lower costs, or both.

Variability of Service Quality Due to the difficulty of diagnosing a problem (for repairs), the inability of the customer to verbalize his or her service needs, and the lack of standardization and mass production for most services.

Variable Markup Policy A form of cost-based markup pricing whereby separate categories of goods and ser-

vices receive different percentage markups. Variable markups recognize differences in personal selling efforts, customer service, alterations, and end-of-season markdown requirements.

Variable Pricing Prices modified to coincide with fluctuations in costs or consumer demand. The same product or service may be priced at two or more levels based on the customer's ability to pay, service location, or time.

Variety Store A retailer which sells a wide assortment of low-and-popularly priced merchandise.

Vending Machine A nonstore retail operation which involves coin-operated machinery, eliminates the use of sales personnel, allows around-the-clock sales, and can be placed outside rather than inside a store.

Vendor Analysis The rating of specific suppliers in terms of quality (such as the per cent of defective merchandise), service (such as delivery speed and reliability), and price (such as credit and transportation terms).

Venture Team A product management organization form in which a small, independent department consisting of a broad range of specialists manages a new product's entire development process from idea generation to market introduction. Team members work on a full-time basis and function as a separate unit within the company.

Vertical Audit An in-depth analysis of one aspect of the firm's marketing strategy.

Vertical Integration When a firm shortens its channel by acquiring a company at another stage in the channel.

Vertical Price Fixing Occurs when manufacturers or wholesalers control the retail prices of their products or services. This practice is sometimes illegal.

Video-Shopping Services Can take one of three forms: electronic catalog shown on a video player, cable television system with telephone ordering, or cable television system with ordering through a personal computer.

Voluntary Simplicity A consumer life-style in which people seek material simplicity, have an ecological awareness, strive for self-determination, and purchase do-it-yourself products.

Warehouse Receives, identifies, and sorts merchandise. It stores goods, implements product-recall programs, selects goods for shipment, coordinates shipments, and dispatches orders.

Warranty An assurance given to consumers that a product will meet certain performance standards.

Waste The portion of a medium's audience that is not in the firm's target market.

Waterway A transportation form that involves the movement of goods on barges via inland rivers and on tankers and general merchandise freighters through the Great

Lakes, incoastal shipping, and the St. Lawrence Seaway.

Wearout Rate The period of time it takes for a message to lose its effectiveness.

Wheel of Retailing A concept describing how low-end (discount) strategies can turn into high-end (high price) strategies, thus providing opportunities for new firms to enter as discounters.

Wholesale Cooperative A full-service merchant wholesaler owned by member firms which seeks to economize functions and offer broad support. There are producer-owned and retailer-owned wholesale cooperatives.

Wholesaler An organization or individual involved with wholesaling.

Wholesaling Involves the buying and handling of merchandise and its resale to retailers, organizational users, and/or other wholesalers but not the sale of significant volume to final consumers.

Width of Product Mix The number of different product lines a company has.

Word-of-Mouth Communication The process by which people express their opinions and product-related experiences to one another.

Zone Pricing A form of geographic pricing which provides for a uniform delivered price to all buyers within a geographic zone. In a multiple-zone system, delivered prices vary by zone.

Company Index

Name Index

Subject Index

*denotes listing of term in Glossary

The Growth of Modern Marketing Practices: From 1670 to the Present (Cont.)

1950
- Allied Stores builds the first regional shopping center in Seattle.

1952
- General Electric's annual report recognizes the importance of marketing.

1958
- The European Community (EC) is formed.

1960
- Kennedy and Nixon have the first televised presidential debate.

1960s
- Fast-food restaurants, home-improvement centers, furniture warehouses, and catalog showrooms are introduced.
- Consumerism expands significantly and has a major impact on firms.

1968
- The Boston Consulting Group develops the business portfolio analysis model.

Early 1970s
- The Universal Product Code (UPC) is established.

1971
- Federal Express launches the air-express delivery industry.
- McKinsey & Company develops the strategic business unit (SBU) concept for General Electric, which devises its business screen.

1973
- Resource shortages begin with the oil embargo.

1975
- The Strategic Planning Institute is formed to manage the PIMS project.